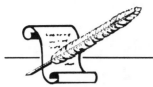

HISTORIC

DOCUMENTS

1973

Cumulative Index 1972-73

Congressional Quarterly, Inc.

Ref.

_1973_

Library of Congress Catalog Card Number: 72-97888
International Standard Book Number: 0-87187-043-6

Copyright 1974 by Congressional Quarterly, Inc.
1414 22nd Street, N.W., Washington, D.C. 20037

Printed in the United States of America

FOREWORD

Publication of *Historic Documents 1973* carries through a second year the project launched by Congressional Quarterly Service and Editorial Research Reports with *Historic Documents 1972*. The purpose of this continuing series of volumes is to give students, scholars, librarians, journalists and citizens convenient access to documents of basic importance in the broad range of public affairs.

To put the documents in perspective, each entry is preceded by a brief introduction containing background material, in some cases a short summary of the document itself and, where possible, pertinent subsequent developments. We believe this editorial input will prove increasingly useful in future years when the events and questions now covered are less fresh in one's memory and the documents may be hard to find or unobtainable.

The year 1973 presented a sharp contrast to 1972. In 1972, the new turn in American foreign policy highlighted by the President's journeys to Peking and to Moscow was followed by preoccupation at home with the political conventions and the presidential election. In 1973, after conclusion of the Vietnam cease-fire accord and return of the prisoners of war, the Watergate affair dominated public attention for months on end. Watergate and its multiple ramifications led to a dramatic decline in President Nixon's credibility, serious consideration of his impeachment, intensification of a smoldering conflict between the Congress and the White House and resignations galore among federal officials. Later, a drastic energy crisis emerged.

All these events added substantially to the usual outpouring of presidential statements, court decisions, commission reports, special studies, and speeches of national or international importance. We have selected for inclusion in this book as many as possible of the documents that in our judgment will be of more than transitory interest. Where space limitations prevented reproduction of the full texts, the excerpts used were chosen to set forth the essentials and, at the same time, preserve the flavor of the materials.

The talents of numerous CQ staffers went into preparation of the book. Robert Diamond and Buel W. Patch shared the tasks of supervision and copy editing. Diantha Johnson assembled the documents and wrote most of the introductions to the entries. Alice Mitchell prepared the cumulative index, which will facilitate use of both the 1972 and the 1973 volumes. Richard Young handled the production. Howard Chapman designed the cover.

BUEL W. PATCH
EDITOR

WASHINGTON, D.C.
January 1974

How to Use This Book

The documents are arranged in chronological order. If you know the approximate date of the report, speech, statement, court decision or other document you are looking for, glance through the titles for that month in the Summary of the Table of Contents below. For more detailed information on an entry in which you are interested, see the comprehensive Table of Contents that follows.

If the Table of Contents does not lead you directly to the document you want, make a double check by turning to the subject Index at the end of the book. There you may find references not only to the particular document you seek but also to other entries on the same or a related subject. The Index in this volume is the second of a projected **five-year cumulative index** of Historic Documents.

The introduction to each document is printed in italic type. The document itself, printed in roman type, follows the capitalization and punctuation of the original or official copy. Where the full text is not given, omissions of material are indicated by the customary series of dots.

Summary of Table of Contents

FEBRUARY

MARCH

AUGUST

SEPTEMBER

OCTOBER

NOVEMBER

DECEMBER

TABLE OF CONTENTS

January

February

March

April

May

State of the World

Surrender at Wounded Knee

Pentagon Papers Trial

Watergate Hearings

Brezhnev in West Germany

Nixon's Statement on Watergate

June

July

August

September

October

November

December

January

CONGRESS VS. THE PRESIDENT

January 2-8, 1973

Members of the 93rd Congress arrived in Washington at the beginning of January in a defiant mood—accusing President Nixon of trespassing on their legislative powers, and themselves threatening drastic measures to recapture those powers. This spirit of rebellion, developing during the 92nd Congress, was brought to a head by the December bombing in Vietnam and by the President's decision to impose a $250-billion ceiling on federal expenditures in fiscal 1973 by impounding some of the funds already appropriated by Congress. In addition, the legislators had been displeased by Nixon's refusal to allow several of his aides to testify before congressional committees.

Many members questioned whether Congress any longer had the power or the capacity to deal with the executive branch on equal terms. Sen. Thomas F. Eagleton (D Mo.) had spoken, not only for himself, when he said in December 1972 that there could be "little doubt that the executive branch has enroached widely on the constitutionally defined territory of Congress." He asserted that "We must now ask ourselves if Congress as a body is willing and able to provide a commensurate defense to resist this dangerous attack."

House and Senate Caucus Action

Rhetoric soon turned to action. House Democrats, meeting in caucus on Jan. 2, a day before the 93rd Congress convened, adopted a resolution calling for an end to all appropriations for American military activity in Vietnam once the prisoners of war had been returned. Speaker Carl Albert (D Okla.), addressing the caucus, promised a re-assertion of congressional power. He called it a matter of the highest priority and said he would work as hard at it as he had at anything in his life. Albert reportedly assured the caucus in its closed session that "if the President does not end this war, Congress will."

The House Democrats' resolution on Vietnam was endorsed at a Sen-ate Democratic conference on Jan. 4. A day earlier, the Senate Demo-crats had unanimously approved a lengthy policy statement prepared by Majority Leader Mike Mansfield (Mont.). In that statement Mans-field said: "There is no greater national need than the termination, forthwith, of our involvement in the war.... I do not know whether there is a legislative route to the end of this bloody travesty. I do know that the time is long since past when we can take shelter in a claim of legislative impotence. It remains for the Congress to bring about a com-plete disinvolvement."

The White House reacted promptly to the action of the Democrats. Presidential Press Secretary Ronald Ziegler protested, Jan. 3, that they might have "possibly prolonged the negotiations" in Paris. The enemy might be wondering, he said, what it could get out of Congress that it could not get from the President. The President himself reit-erated at a White House breakfast for congressional leaders, Jan. 5, that he was "determined to pursue a course that would lead to the proper kind of settlement."

Concern Over Impounding of Funds

As for erosion of the powers of Congress by White House impounding of appropriated funds, Mansfield had pointed out that Congress did not have the means to review over-all government expenditures and that, in consequence, the Senate and House had abdicated their "constitutional responsibility" for federal spending. Some critics never-theless sought to get a legal ruling on the impounding of appropriated funds. In one of several suits filed in federal courts for that pur-pose, 14 of the Senate's 17 committee chairmen intervened as friends of the court, challenging the administration's refusal to make avail-able funds appropriated by Congress. Sen. Sam J. Ervin Jr. (D N.C.), speaking for the 14 chairmen, said: "This practice of impoundment is contemptuous of the role of Congress in our tripartite system. The power of the purse belongs exclusively to Congress under the Consti-tution." Ervin added that, regardless of how the courts ruled, Congress should enact legislation making impoundment illegal.

The congressional majority's attitude toward the administration was aggravated, Jan. 5, when the President announced that three members of his cabinet—the Secretaries of Agriculture, of Health, Education and Welfare, and of Housing and Urban Development— would be given by executive order the additional duties of White House counselors. This action constituted a move toward carrying out many of the organizational changes embodied in an executive reorganization plan which had failed to gain the approval of the 92nd Congress.

As concern over relations between the executive and legislative branches of government mounted in Congress, Senate Democrats unanimously resolved that President Nixon's nominees pledge themselves, as a prerequisite to confirmation, to testify before Senate committees whenever asked to do so. The resolution was adopted Jan. 11 after an even more strongly worded proposal by Senate Armed Services Committee Chairman John C. Stennis (D Miss.) had been narrowly defeated. The resolution that was approved applied immediately to 37 Nixon nominees whose appointments had not been confirmed up to that time.

Six-Point Reform Program

The National Committee for an Effective Congress, a nonpartisan group founded in 1947 which has been active in promoting reform of the legislative branch, sent a letter to all members of the House and Senate on Jan. 8. The letter laid before them a six-point program which, in the committee's opinion, would enable the Congress "to recover its influence and reverse the President's rush to 'pharaohistic government.'" In submitting the six-point program for inclusion in the Congressional Record, Sen. Frank Church (D Idaho) warned of an "approaching constitutional crisis between Congress and an ever-more-powerful Executive."

Excerpts from Sen. Mansfield's statement to the Senate Democratic conference on Jan. 3, and full text of the Jan. 8 letter of the National Committee for an Effective Congress:

Mansfield's Statement

We meet, today, with a new majority. We meet with new responsibilities and a new mandate.

The same electorate that endorsed the President increased the Democratic majority in the Senate by two votes....

The recent election tells us something of what the people of the nation expect of the Senate. If there is one mandate to us above all others, it is to exercise our separate and distinct constitutional role in the operation of the Federal government. The people have not chosen to be governed by one branch of government alone. They have not asked for government by a single party. Rather, they have called for a reinforcement of the Constitution's checks and balances. This Democratic Conference must strive to provide that reinforcement. The people have asked of us an independent contribution to the nation's policies. To make that contribution is more than our prerogative, it is our obligation.

An independent Senate does not equate with an obstructionist Senate. Insofar as the Leadership is concerned, the Senate will not be at loggerheads with the President, personally, with his party or his Administration. The Senate will give most respectful attention to the President's words, his program and his appointments. Every President deserves that courtesy. During the period in which you have entrusted me with the leadership, every President has had that courtesy.

In a similar vein, the rights of the Republican Minority in the Senate will be fully sustained by the Majority Leadership and I anticipate the cooperation of the minority leadership in the operation of the Senate. I would say to the Minority, however, no less than to the Majority, that the Senate must be prepared to proceed in its own way. When conscience so dictates, we must seek to initiate and advance public programs from the Senate and, as indicated, to revise proposals of the Executive Branch.

It is my expectation that the House of Representatives will join in this approach. To that end, the Senate Leadership will seek to establish close and continuing liaison with that of the House. Looking to the needs of the entire nation, moreover, the Leadership will put out new lines of communication to the Governors Conference, notably to its Democratic Members, as well as to the National Democratic Party. We have much to learn from these sources about conditions in the nation. Their contribution can help to improve the design of federal activity to meet more effectively the needs of all states.

Vietnam

There is no greater national need than the termination, forthwith, of our involvement in the war in Viet Nam. This Conference has been in the vanguard in seeking a legislative contribution to rapid withdrawal from that ill-starred, misbegotten conflict. The Majority Conference has resolved overwhelmingly to that effect. Members have voted on the Senate floor, preponderantly, to that effect.

Nevertheless, the war is still with us. Notwithstanding intermittent lulls and negotiations, the prisoners of war remain prisoners and their numbers grow with each renewal of the bombing. The fact is that not a single prisoner has been released to date by our policies; the handful who have come home have done so in consequence of gestures from

Hanoi. The recoverable missing in action have yet to be recovered and their numbers grow. Americans still die in twos and threes and planeloads. Asians die by the hundreds and thousands. The fires of an enduring hostility are fed by unending conflict. We are in the process of leaving a heritage of hate in Southeast Asia to our children and our children's children. And for what?

With the election behind us, I most respectfully request every Member of the Conference to examine his position and his conscience once again on the question of Viet Nam. I do not know whether there is a legislative route to the end of this bloody travesty. I do know that the time is long since past when we can take shelter in a claim of legislative impotence. We cannot dismiss our own responsibility by deference to the President's. It is true that the President can still the guns of the nation in Viet Nam and bring about the complete withdrawal of our forces by a stroke of the pen. It is equally true that the Congress cannot do so. Nevertheless, Congress does have a responsibility. We are supplying the funds. We are supplying the men. So until the war ends, the effort must be made and made again and again. The Executive Branch has failed to make peace by negotiation. It has failed to make peace by elaborating the war first into Cambodia, then into Laos and, this year, with blockade and renewed bombing, into North Viet Nam. The effort to salvage a shred of face from a senseless war has succeeded only in spreading further devastation and clouding this nation's reputation.

It remains for the Congress to seek to bring about complete disinvolvement. We have no choice but to pursue this course. I urge every Member of this caucus to act in concert with Republican Senators, by resolution or any other legislative means to close out the military involvement in Viet Nam. If there is one area where Senate responsibility profoundly supersedes party responsibility, it is in ending the involvement in Viet Nam.

In view of the tendency of this war to flare unexpectedly, the Leadership now questions the desirability of the Congress ever again to be in *sine die* adjournment as we have been since October 18, 1972. In that Constitutional state the Congress is unable to be reassembled on an urgent basis except by call of the President. It is the Leadership's intention, therefore, to discuss this gap in Congressional continuity with the House leaders. It may well be desirable to provide, at all times, for recall of the Congress by the Congress itself. There is ample precedent for providing standby authority of this kind to the combined Leaderships.

Spending

If Indochina continues to preoccupy us abroad, the Senate is confronted, similarly, with an overriding domestic issue. The issue is control of the expenditures of the Federal government. We must try to move to meet it, squarely, at the outset of the 93rd Congress.

In the closing days of the last session, the President asked of Congress unilateral authority to readjust downward expenditures approved by the Congress within an overall limit of $250 billion. The President's objectives were meritorious but his concern at the imbalance in expenditures and revenues might better have been directed to the federal budget which is now a tool—not of the Congress, but of the Executive Branch. It is there that the origins of the great federal deficits of the past few years are to be found. The fact is that Congress has not increased but reduced the Administration's budget request, overall, by $20.2 billion in the last four years.

As the Conference knows, the House did yield to the President's request for temporary authority to readjust downward, arbitrarily, Congressional appropriations. The Senate did not do so. The Senate did not do so for good and proper reasons. The power of the purse rests with Congress under the Constitution and the usurpation or transfer of this fundamental power to the Executive Branch will take the nation a good part of the last mile down the road to government by Executive fiat. That is not what the last election tells us to do. That is not what the Constitution requires us to do.

I say that not in criticism of the President. The fault lies not in the Executive Branch but in ourselves, in the Congress. We cannot insist upon the power to control expenditures and then fail to do so. If we do not do the job, if we continue to abdicate our Constitutional responsibility the powers of the federal government will have to be recast so that it can be done elsewhere.

We must face the fact that as an institution, Congress is not readily equipped to carry out this complex responsibility. By tradition and practice, for example, each Senate committee proceeds largely in its own way in the matter of authorizing expenditures. There is no standing Senate mechanism for reviewing expenditures to determine where they may fit into an overall program of government. A similar situation exists in our dealings with the House. So, if we mean to face this problem squarely, it is essential for us to recognize that the problem is two-fold. It involves: (1) coordination of expenditures within the Senate and; (2) coordination with the House.

In the closing hours of the 92nd Congress, Congress created a Joint Committee to recommend procedures for improving Congressional control over the budget. While this committee cannot be expected to conclude its work by February 15, as the statute directs, it would be my expectation that by that date an interim report will have been submitted to the Congress. Thereafter, it is the Leadership's intention to seek the extension of the Joint Committee in the hope that a definitive answer can be found to the problem.

In the meantime, what of the coming session? Unless the Congress acts now to strengthen coordinated control of expenditures, it is predictable that the Executive Branch will press again for temporary authority to do so. It is predictable, too, that sooner or later a Congressional inertia will underwrite the transfer of this authority on a permament basis.

That is the reality and it ought to be faced squarely here in this caucus and on the floor of the Senate. Unless and until specific means are recommended by the Joint Committee, I would hope that the Conference will give the Leadership some guidance on how an overall expenditures ceiling may be set as a goal for the first session of the 93rd Congress. Shall we attempt to do it here in the Caucus? Shall we take a figure by suggestion from the President? Thereafter, how will we divide an overall figure among the various major priorities and programs? How much for defense? For welfare? For labor and so forth?

Who will exercise a degree of control over expenditures proposed in legislation? Can it be done by a committee of committee chairmen? The Appropriations Committee? Should the Majority Policy Committee monitor expenditure legislation before it reaches the Senate floor to determine compatibility with an overall limitation? In any case, where will the necessary budgeting technicians and skilled fiscal officers be obtained? From the General Accounting Office? The Congressional Research Service? By an expanded Senate staff?

I would note in this connection the provisions of the Reorganization Act of 1970 which called for a unified computerized system for the federal government. The system was to permit classifying various programs and expenditures of the government so that we might know, among other things, how much was being spent for each particular purpose. This knowledge is essential for effective control of expenditures on the basis of a program of priorities.

The computer project is being undertaken jointly by the Treasury and the Office of Management and Budget, in cooperation with the General Accounting Office. It is my understanding that the project has concentrated, to date, on the needs of the Executive Branch while those of the Congress are being overlooked. If that is so, this project had better be put back on the right track. If it is necessary, the Congress should alter the enabling legislation to make certain that we get the information that is needed to control expenditures. It would be my hope that the appropriate committees would move without delay to look into this situation.

Cooperation—A Two-Way Street

If the President seeks the cooperation of the Senate in negotiating an immediate end to the involvement in the Vietnamese war, in the control of expenditures or, in any other matter of national interest, he will have that cooperation. Cooperation depends, however, on a realistic give and take at both ends of Pennsylvania Avenue. In the name of cooperation, we cannot merely acquiesce in unilateral actions of

the Executive where the Constitutional powers of Congress are involved as they are in Viet Nam and in the control of expenditures. I
would also note in this connection the proclivity of the Executive
Branch to impound funds from time to time for activities approved by
the Congress. This dubious Constitutional practice denies and frustrates the explicit intention of the Legislative Branch.

There are some areas in which, clearly, we can work cooperatively
with the President. Defense expenditures, for example, can continue to
be reduced to a more realistic level. I am glad to note that the Armed
Services Committee and the Appropriations Committee both have been
moving to bring about a general reduction of requests of the Executive
Branch for these purposes....

In the civilian sector, the President has indicated that the Federal
bureaucracy is too large. There would certainly be grounds for close
cooperation with the Senate in this sphere. The misuse and underuse
of civil servants is a scandalous waste of public funds which is felt
especially at a time of rising federal salary scales. To overload the
agencies and departments with personnel is also demeaning and dead-
ening to the dedicated men and women in the federal service.

If the President will work with the Congress on this matter, I am
persuaded that the Civil Service can be reduced substantially from its
present 2.8 million employees. The reduction can be without personal
hardships, but a carefully developed program which would permit
greater flexibility in transfers among agencies and incentive retire-
ments. Such a program coupled with the natural attrition of death and
resignations and with accompanying limits on new hirings could do much
to improve the tone of government service and curb the payroll costs
which now stand at $32 billion a year.

The President has expressed an interest in proceeding with his
earlier proposed plans for reorganizing the Federal governmnent. Clearly, there is a need for reorganization of sprawling, over-extended, overlapping Executive departments, agencies and commissions. It must
be faced as a realistic matter, however, that any basic reorganization
in government is a difficult undertaking at best. In my judgment, a
wholesale approach is not likely to achieve anything more concrete
now than when it was first advanced two years ago. It would only be
a charade. It is my hope, therefore, that the President would concentrate on areas of maximum need. It seems to me that Members of
the Senate who have shown a deep interest in this problem can be very
helpful in working with the Administration to define those areas.

I would like to suggest...that attention be given to the appearance
in the Courts and Executive Agencies of what may be a tendency to
cloud by disconcerting interpretations the safeguards of the First
Amendment as they apply to practitioners in the press and other media
of communications. If this tendency does exist, the Congress has a
responsibility to try to check it. The press, radio and TV are prime

sources of light in the otherwise hidden recesses of our government and society. They are as essential to the fulfillment of our legislative responsibilities as they are to the general enlightenment of the public. At the very least, therefore, it seems, too, that a Senate inquiry is called for into the implications of recent court decisions and such official pronouncements as that of the Director of the Office of Telecommunications Policy regarding the "Fairness Doctrine." We share with the President and the Courts a Constitutional responsibility to protect the freedom of the press to operate as a free press....

The People's Mandate

I will close these remarks with a final reference to the last election. I suppose each of us interprets the national sentiment which is reflected in the outcome in terms of his own predilections. Certainly, I have done so. Therefore, "the state of the Senate," as seen from the viewpoint of the Democratic Majority might not necessarily dovetail with the mandate which the Administration delineates from President Nixon's re-election or that which is seen by the Republican Minority in the Congress.

Nevertheless, it does seem that the election tells all of us—President, Democratic Majority and Republican Minority—what the people of the nation do not want.

1. They do not want one party or one branch government during the next two years.

2. They do not want to turn back the clock on the national effort to improve the human climate and the physical environment in which the people of this nation must live.

3. They do not want a rate of change which whether too slow or too rapid produces major internal chaos and disruption.

4. Most of all, they do not want the President to persist nor the Congress to acquiesce in the indefinite continuance of the senseless bloodshed in Viet Nam and, with it, accept the indefinite postponement of the return of the POW's and the recoverable MIA's.

These negatives point the way to the positive path which the Senate Majority Leadership intends to pursue during the next two years. We will not abandon the effort to end the U.S. involvement in Viet Nam and to bring back the POW's and the recoverable MIA's, period. We will work to preserve and to enhance the faithfulness of this nation to its Constitutional principles and its highest ideals and, in so doing, we will not shut the door on essential changes....

Text of the letter of the National Committee for an Effective Congress, Jan. 8, 1973, follows on next page:

11

National Committee For An Effective Congress,

Washington, D.C., January 8, 1972.

DEAR MEMBER OF CONGRESS: It is with the greatest urgency that we write this letter to all members of the Senate and the House of Representatives, of both parties, with whom the NCEC has worked in the past.

The President's shocking resort to all-out bombing in Vietnam has finally forced the question of who in our government has the authority to make war. It has also focused attention on other developments which, in combination, constitute a grave assault on our entire system of government.

We are witnessing a dangerous trend toward an authoritarian Executive regime which, if continued, could destroy effective governmental checks and balances. It is obvious that Congressional compliance in past years has emboldened President Nixon in his thrust toward Constitutional-system busting. A Constitutional crisis is not threatened—it is here.

Patterns with wide-ranging implications are unfolding on four fronts:

(1) War-making and military operations continue in various parts of the world without reference to the Congress. Although declaration of war and governance of the military are powers specifically reserved to the legislative branch, this Administration proceeds alone and in secret, as if the illegal precedent of previous Administrations justified an even more blatant disregard for the Constitution.

The recent assertion by Congress of its prime responsibilities in this crucial area has been met with disdain by the executive. Following a Congressional proscription on funds for para-military ventures in Laos, for example, the Administration defiantly proceeded to spend money for precisely that purpose. In a further display of his contempt for Congress, the President declared when signing P.L. 92-156, the Military Procurement Appropriation, that he would not be bound by Title VI of that law calling for termination of the Vietnam War. It is important to note that the terms of the October 26 Kissinger-Le Duc Tho agreement fell well within the provisions of Title VI, the so-called Mansfield Amendment.

While the President has arrogated the power to make war, Congress remains the sole source of funds for waging war. Now, after assuring the country that "peace is at hand," that disarmament is progressing and armed conflict with China and Russia is improbable, the Administration seeks even larger military appropriations. For the 93rd Congress to appropriate increased monies without first reestablishing its war and military powers would show a reckless disregard for all recent experience and constitute another abdication of both Constitutional and moral responsiblity.

(2) The President's planned restructuring of the executive branch, down-grading the Cabinet and sequestering power inside the White House, would dramatically diminish Congressional controls on the Federal administration. A plan aimed in the same direction was rejected by Congress last year. Under the President's present reorganization, those vital areas where Congress has always shared policy-making with the Executive Branch would be placed beyond Congressional reach. Key officials in most cases would no longer be subject to confirmation, nor would they be accessible for consultation or questioning or their performance subject to legislative oversight. While cabinet officers would retain their limousines, authentic policy-making power would be put in the hands of the President's personal staff, sheltered by "executive immunity."

All this is being done in the name of greater efficiency. In fact, the design reproduces that of the Nixon foreign policy apparatus, where the untouchable Dr. Kissinger commands a personal foreign ministry while the accountable Secretary of State is a ceremonial figure, able to share very little with Congress except frustration. Similar atrophy awaits departments with jurisdiction over natural resources, urban matters, transportation, commerce, health, education and welfare. Broad domestic and economic policy will be directed by a small group of managers, under the dual command of John Ehrlichman and George Shultz who will operate behind the shield of "Special Presidential Assistant." The chain of command will flow through an inner network of assistant secretaries and bureau chiefs picked from the inner circle of White House loyalists. Cabinet officers will have nothing to do with their selection nor exercise any real authority over them. Thus, instead of the accountable "open government" Mr. Nixon promised the American people, the cabinet system will fade and control will be concentrated in an authoritarian President.

(3) The withholding and impounding of Congressionally appropriated funds represents a studied attempt by the Nixon Administration to kill by attrition what it failed to stop legislatively. Funds for education, environmental programs, agricultural relief, transportation, housing, to cite just a few examples, have been frozen. At the same time, funds for the Vietnam War and for military procurement flow freely. The executive has arbitrarily ignored the decisions of Congress.

A most glaring example is that of the water pollution control program passed late in 1972. The President lost two rounds on Capitol Hill, first when Congress voted the funds and again when it overrode his veto. His response then was to ignore the Congressional dictum and to mousetrap the money. Faced by continuing usurpation on the part of the Administration, Congress may be driven to use similar pressure tactics, holding back funds that the President seeks, or refusing to vote further borrowing authority to the Treasury. This is the ultimate fiscal weapon, only reluctantly employed. Against a President who wants

13

to kill off the major social programs developed over the past 40 years, however, Congress can play its trump card.

(4) The Administration is engaged in a heightened campaign to curb information and the communications media and to stifle individual dissent. The issue is fundamental. As James Madison said, "Public opinion sets bounds to every government and is the real sovereign in every free one." There is no surer or subtler way to coerce a Congressman than to manage the information available to his constituents and control the political climate. The President commands full and immediate access to information and can tell as little or as much as he likes, while the individual member of Congress must largely rely on the uninhibited, informed reporting of a free press.

The Administration has recently stepped up its attack on those publications which look too closely into its closets; it browbeats the offending media, prosecutes reporters, threatens broadcasters who must renew licenses.

Moreover, the flow of official information is more and more restricted and managed. The Public Broadcasting System's public affairs coverage is to be drastically reduced and, at the same time, subjected to greater political influence. The growing mass of communiques provide less and less enlightenment. Under the system envisaged, high policy-makers will sit behind the closed doors of executive privilege, just as inaccessible to the press as to the Congress. The President himself has studiously avoided confronting the press, speaking, when he does, from "the top of the mountain" with no question, no dialogue, no discussion allowed.

Along with the intimidation of the media and the restricting of news sources, there is increased invasion of individual citizens' lives with political harassment and trials, wire tapping, electronic surveillance, computerized dossiers, all arrayed against personal privacy and the exercise of civil liberties.

More ominous are recent court decisions limiting the protection of confidential news sources. This shows the Nixon philosophy penetrating the judiciary, historically the champion of the First Amendment. Only Congress is left to wage battle with the Nixon Administration to protect the freedoms of speech, press and information. In this vital area the Congress has as great a stake as in the confrontation over war-making, government spending, and the accountability of the federal establishment.

THE SLIPPAGE OF POWER

The executive's simultaneous advance on four fronts suggests that Mr. Nixon and his technocrats of power are not unmindful of grand designing. But like any expansionist drive, it follows the lines of least resistance, invading Congressional domain and moving into vacuums wherever Congress has failed to exercise its prerogatives. The process started long ago when Congress ceded its shared role in foreign affairs by accepting such devices as the "executive agreement" and acquiescing on any issue where the flag of "national security" was hoisted. This situation deteriorated with Congress' acceptance of expanding executive privilege and other assumed powers which now penetrate all phases of governmental operations.

There have been attempts to explain what motivates legislators to first seek the responsibility of office and then spend much of their official lives trying to escape these responsibilities. Congress' lemming-like behavior reached a new high last October when the House voted to surrender to the President all discretion over spending and budget cuts. It was a shocking display by a body which has spent so much time proclaiming its power over fiscal matters and fighting with the Senate to protect its supremacy. Although the measure was finally rejected, the incident revealed how deeply Congress is infected with a feeling of incapacity, and how strong is the urge to pass the burden of difficult decision to the President. Members feel relieved of personal responsibility, losing themselves in the mass of 435 Representatives and 100 Senators. If there are no funds for schools, housing, transportation, the President can be blamed, and if funds are forthcoming, the Member can always point to a speech, a last minute vote, or his name on an early bill cosponsoring the project. It is a riskless game that frustrates Constitutional intent.

We recognize the need for strong leadership, effective internal organization, and committee specialization in a legislative body. But ultimately the legislator must be held individually responsible and accountable. He cannot fade into the structure.

The reluctance of Members to vote their conscience and to accept personal responsibility has weakened the Congressional system and left a homogenized and docile body. We have seen how so grave an issue as the Vietnam War was obscured and papered over. Votes were taken on isolated, peripheral issues, while a confrontation on the overall policy was avoided. Members have repeatedly approved authorizations and appropriations for Vietnam, claiming they were voting not for the war but for "support of our troops."

No more evasive sophistry can be found than the declaration of a powerful House chairman that a vote for a supplemental military appropriations bill "does not involve a test as to one's basic views as to the war in Vietnam. The question here is that the soldiers are entitled to our support as long as they are there, regardless of our views otherwise." It is upon such tissue of rationalization that Congress has sustained the longest war in our history, underwritten an expeditionary force of over half a million men and spent billions of dollars, without ever approving the underlying policy.

If Congress is passive, failing to exercise its Constitutional prerogatives, refusing to deal with basic issues and making up false ones, it will fall far short of what its responsibility demands, and far short of what the public expects judging from the last election. In such a situation decisions are made by the Executive and his bureaucrats, without public accountability, constitutional restraint, and Congressional deliberation. We have come to this point.

MANDATE TO CONGRESS

The results of the 1972 election show that Congress has the strength, if it has the will, to recover its own influence and reverse the President's rush toward "pharaohistic government." The Congressional potential was greatly reinforced by the unprecedented independence shown by the voters. This was the meaning of the ticket splitting, voter selectivity, absence of coattails, obliterating of party and regional patterns.

If this election has a single message, it is that the American people voted against monolithic government. The voters decisively affirmed the system of checks and balances, exhibiting an intuitive desire to assure restraints on executive power. The mandate to Congress is at least equal to the President's.

This is illustrated by the outcome of the Senate races. Candidates who conducted shoe-string campaigns, who walked their districts and listened, defeated candidates who saturated the media with expensive prepackaged campaigns. Of the 17 Senate candidates backed by the NCEC, 13 won. The four Republicans—Senators Brooke, Case, Pearson, and Percy—piled up huge majorities, running ahead of the President and far in front of the orthodox party conservatives in their states. Winning Democrats endorsed by the NCEC include incumbents Metcalf, Mondale and Pell, and a total of six challenger candidates who surprised the pundits with the vitality and momentum of their campaigns—Abourezk, Biden, Clark, Haskell, Hathaway and Huddleston. In the House, the arithmetic is not so dramatic but the same evidence of public discernment prevailed.

AN ACTION PROGRAM

Congress has the tools to implement its mandate and restore constitutional balance:

(1) *The power of the purse* is the traditional and clearly the most formidable weapon. It can and should be effectively utilized not only to pursue positive goals and to assure that the letter and spirit of Congressional actions are carried out, but also to prevent or restrain executive actions deemed harmful by Congress.

The Vietnam War is the most striking example of how Congress' powers of restraint can be exercised. It remains the over-riding national issue, distorting and obscuring all others. It is now the immediate responsibility of Congress to end our involvement in Southeast Asia. Congress can do so by cutting off funds for Vietnam and future military ventures, by rescinding money obligated for war purposes, by further limiting the Treasury's borrowing authority, and by reducing or suspending other funds requested by the executive branch until Congress' injunctions are heeded. By reasserting its Constitutional controls over government spending and over the use of the armed forces, Congress can begin to challenge the self-generating machinery of war and the military determinism which has so engulfed this period of our national life. These same methods are available to Congress in the fight over impounded funds and to otherwise induce the President to implement positive programs enacted by Congress.

(2) *Congress must begin to restructure its own machinery if it is to effectively exercise its responsibility over taxing and spending in the future.* Members must have knowledge and understanding of the national budget and be able to communicate this to their own constituencies. A beginning was made with the creation last year of a Joint Committee [Joint Committee to Review the Operation of the Budget Ceiling and to Recommend Procedures for Insuring Congressional Control over Budgetary Outlay and Receipt Totals] to review the operation of the budget and recommend means of Congressional control. However, in its deliberations Congress must face certain questions:

(a) The False Bottom Budget—Since the Second World War, the executive has prided itself on hiding from Congress and the people funds for covert intelligence programs of the CIA and other agencies, secret military operations and military assistance programs, and overseas and domestic political activities. The budget has become less an explanation than a diversionary tactic. It is time that Congress demanded a full and intelligible public accounting so that it might judge programs and make future decisions undistorted by executive secrecy. More than one Congressman has thought he was voting for social welfare when he was in fact providing funds for a CIA program.

(b) Responsible spending—Congress now approaches the national budget on a piecemeal basis. To make possible rational evaluation of the executive budget, Congress must develop its own basic budget predicated on its assessment of national priorities and the needs of the people. A Congressional Budget Office, or its equivalent, staffed by experts and provided with modern computer equipment, should be established to assist in the preparation of such an annual legislative budget and to provide Congress expert evaluation of the President's budget in its entirety.

In addition, Congressional reluctance to adequately staff and equip existing committees is nowhere so evident as in this key area. This must be remedied. Such ill-considered economy has crippled legislators' ability to make informed decisions on complex questions requiring detailed technical knowledge. For example, to handle more than $250 billion of Federal expenditures the staff of the Senate Appropriations Committee numbers 37, and the House 29, including clerical personnel. Meanwhile, the President's Office of Management and Budget numbers 700, supported by battalions of departmental budget officers and banks of computers. It is neither necessary nor possible to match the executive branch staff in numbers, but it is essential that Congress be able to make its own evaluation and develop alternatives.

(c) Just as it should require an end to subterfuge by the Executive, Congress in turn must lift the veil of secrecy which has surrounded its own actions and open the appropriations process to press and public view.

(3) *The Senate's power to confirm or deny Presidential appointments,* with rare exceptions, has come to be treated more as a rubber stamp for executive decisions than as a vital Constitutional responsibility. Greater attention must be given this function both as a means to check unwarranted executive actions and as a forum for the clear expression of the will of Congress. Confirmation proceedings should include an examination of how the nominee views his or her prospective job, its powers and duties, and, in particular, if and how he intends to fulfill the statutory intent of Congress in administering programs and expending funds approved by Congress. In addition, Congress will have to decide what important offices, not now covered, should be subject to Senate confirmation. The NCEC recommends that the Director of the OMB, in particular, should be subject to such review.

In the case of foreign policy, military and national security positions, the Senate should require a clear demonstration that Presidential nominees fully recognize and understand all provisions of international law, United Nations directives, and matters relating to aggressive war and war crimes which may affect or govern any of their activities. Further the NCEC recommends that Congress now begin to consider the development of a code of personal responsibility and legal standards of accountability for executive officials acting in the above areas.

(4) *The Congressional oversight and investigatory powers should be vigorously employed* to determine if and how legislative intent is being carried out in the administration of programs and the expenditure of funds approved by the Congress, and to expose incidents of malfeasance. To this end, Congress can and should make greater use of the professional investigators, auditing expertise and technical capabilities of the General Accounting Office. Above all, Congress must remove a roadblock, increasingly employed by the Executive, by legislation clearly spelling out the proper limits to "executive privilege."

(5) *Congress should appoint a Joint Committee of the House and Senate to undertake a full review of emergency war powers* which Con-

gress itself has conferred by law onto the President—over 275 statutes in the last generation, ranging from controls over peanut acreage to the confiscation of national transportation systems. Many are outdated or potentially dangerous. We have seen, for example, how unpopular, controversial or covert operations have been shrouded from public view under the guise of "national security" or "national emergency." More important, these laws, coupled with the discretionary powers granted the President in numerous other statutes, amount to virtually unlimited power in the hands of an Executive who chooses to abuse them.

(6) Lastly, *Congress must address itself to its own reform.* While the Senate and House may take different approaches to the seniority question, anti-secrecy measures and streamlining of rules both must take affirmative action to make the process more flexible, more open, more democratic, more responsible. This will greatly help restore public confidence in Congress' ability to cope with its staggering responsibilities.

All of the suggestions we offer deal with the posture and functioning of Congress as a whole. They are not issues of party or personality—Democratic legislators versus a Republican Administration—but go to the heart of the American system. The problems are institutional, and the actions should be bipartisan.

Congress has a mandate from the people, and has the tools to deal with the present crisis. The only question is whether Congress has the necessary will. A failure to act with determination at this time will cause irreparable damage to our Constitutional democracy. Not by revolution, not by usurpation, but by acquiescence. This must not happen.

Sincerely,
Sidney H. Scheuer,
Chairman
Russell D. Hemenway,
National Director

NADER ON NATIONAL FORESTS

January 2, 1973

A Ralph Nader study group gave warning, at the start of 1973, of ruinous results if the U.S. Forest Service in the Department of Agriculture should proceed with a tentative plan to increase by 50 per cent the annual harvest of construction lumber from the national forests. The result, the group said, would be "the destruction of millions of acres of wilderness and recreation areas." The plan had been temporarily suspended because of budget limitations, but the Forest Service was reported to believe that it could be carried out under stringent qualifying conditions. Pressure for the plan was said to have been exerted by the logging industry to help it meet expected market needs.

Seventeen per cent of the country's wood supply was drawn from the national forests in 1972. Conservationists contended that too much lumber was already coming from those areas, thereby reducing their recreational value. They pointed to a Forest Service stipulation that land under its jurisdiction was to be used for grazing and wildlife and watershed protection as well as lumbering. The 13-member Nader team, headed by Daniel R. Barney, concurred with the conservationists. It asserted in a 300-page report, entitled "The Last Stand," that recreational and wildlife functions of the forests had been "shortchanged" by the emphasis on timber production. Fifty-four recommendations for legislative and administrative changes to establish a balance among the functions of the national forests were set forth in the report. (See excerpts from report of the Conservation Foundation on future of the National Park System, Historic Documents, 1972, p. 795.)

Ralph Nader vigorously condemned federal logging proposals in his introduction to the report: "Coached by the Nixon White House's heavy courtship of the timber industry," he wrote, "the Forest Service had collaborated increasingly with industry schemes to convert much of the national forests to timber factories, permanently damaging their recreational value." Nader challenged the economic rationale of the plan, that more lumber would lead to lower wood prices and more housing starts. This reasoning, he said, was "seriously flawed," for "the cost of lumber makes up only 9 per cent of the fully financed cost of the average single-family dwelling, and housing starts historically have not increased as lumber prices declined." He added that "The Office of Management and Budget had consistently stymied efforts by the Forest Service to devote more resources to recreation development, wildlife habitat and wilderness protection."

Nader's investigative team urged amendment of the Multiple Use-Sustained Yield Act of 1960, which set forth guidelines for administration of the forests, so that it would "direct that the national forests be managed chiefly for their long-run preservation as public forests and secondarily for the use of their material resources." An administration bill to put the national forests, together with other federal lands, into a new Department of Natural Resources was criticized by the report. It called instead for a Department of Conservation that would include the Forest Service, the Bureau of Outdoor Recreation and the Bureau of Sport Fisheries and Wildlife. The group reasoned that the administration's plan would lead to emphasis on "resource consumption over resource conservation, ecosystem protection and outdoor recreation." It said that "to transfer the Forest Service to such a department would be to destroy whatever remains of the agency's revered doctrine of multiple-use management."

The report urged a two-year suspension of clear-cutting, or stripping, of tracts of more than 40 acres, so as to enable the Forest Service to catch up with a five-year backlog of reforestation schedules. A 10 per cent, instead of the feared 50 per cent, increase in timber sales from national forests in 1973 and 1974 was announced in Washington May 29.

Text of introduction by Ralph Nader to The Last Stand, a 300-page report by a Nader study group on the National Forests and the U.S. Forest Service:

The National Forests, covering ten percent of the nation's land area, are America's last natural frontier. Like other frontiers of the American past, the Forests, if managed prudently, could contribute greatly to the quality as well as the quantity of American life. Already, for a public weary of the frustrations and ugliness of urban life, they offer a primeval haven of open space. As a corrective for polluted air, lakes and streams, the Forests serve as critical nourishment and filters. For grizzlies, the American bald eagle and other endangered species, they are in many areas the last refuge from encroaching development. And for the $43-billion wood products industry, which leveled most of the valuable timber once standing on private lands, they are the last reservoir of timber resources left to be drained.

In recognition of the conflicting values involved in these alternative uses of National Forests, Congress in 1960 enacted guidelines for their management which established the principles of multiple use and sustained yield. "Multiple use" demanded the general balancing of timber production with use of the forests for recreation, watershed, wildlife protection, and other non-logging activities. The "sustained yield" objective was to ensure that the timber harvest from National Forests did not exceed the renewal capacity of the forests, and thus to prevent a net depletion of the nation's forest resources.

The U.S. Forest Service, perhaps the most independent and discretionary agency in Washington, presides over the National Forests. Although many of its officials model themselves after Gifford Pinchot, the Service's progressive and legendary founder, the Service as a whole has come to observe only rhetorically the principles of multiple use and sustained yield. Coached by the Nixon White House's heavy courtship of the timber industry, the Forest Service has collaborated increasingly with industry schemes to convert much of the National Forests to timber factories, permanently damaging their recreation potential. The Forest Service, pressured by the Agriculture, Housing and Interior Secretaries of the Nixon Cabinet, has adopted a plan to increase timber production from the National Forests by fifty percent in the next ten years. The Service also plans nearly to double the 198,000 miles of permanent roads in the Forests and to permit cutting of the last substantial unlogged old-growth forests in the United States. Much of the increased logging will be accomplished through "clearcutting"— the Forest Service version of General Sherman's "scorched earth" warfare. Large tracts will be completely stripped of trees, then set afire to destroy logging debris, and finally "scarified"—the earth scraped bare with bulldozers—to prepare it for planting....

The economic rationale for this plan—more National Forest timber equals lower lumber prices equals more housing starts—is seriously flawed. The cost of lumber makes up only nine percent of the fully financed cost of the average single-family dwelling, and housing starts historically have not increased as lumber prices declined. The economic alternatives to increased logging of the National Forests are discussed in detail in this report.

The proposals to increase so drastically the logging of National Forests come at a time when Americans are clamoring for more open space and recreation facilities. Camp grounds in state and federal parks are jammed and the most popular parks, like Yellowstone, may soon be restricted to visits "by reservation." According to the National Park Service, visits to National Parks will increase over fifty percent in the next ten years. The National Park System is too small to absorb this human tide without drastic alterations in its character (witness recent proposals to build more roads and paved parking areas in Yellowstone where automobile visits are often little more than a bucolic version of the commuter's freeway crawl, with a few panhandling bears to break the monotony).

Last Undeveloped Refuge

The National Forests are the last undeveloped refuge for Americans' wanderlust. An increasing population, rising disposable income and leisure, and a growing interest in the natural environment are accelerating demands for new recreation areas. The National Forests will be the focus of this pressure for recreation expansion. Already vacationers spend more days at National Forests than at the National Parks and most other public recreation areas combined. The National Forests are ideally suited for these recreation activities where public participation is increasing the fastest—walking for pleasure, swimming, sightseeing, boating, camping, hiking, and bird-watching.

Despite the good intentions of many top administrators and agency foresters, the Forest Service has failed to manage the National Forests so as to satisfy America's spiraling recreation needs. Its eagerness to accelerate timber production and its stubborn devotion to clearcutting mock the principle of multiple-use management, intended to keep timber production in harmony with recreation and other non-timber uses of National Forests. Moreover, as this study convincingly shows, the Forest Service has persistently dragged its feet in preserving additional wild lands as "Wilderness Areas." In some cases, the agency has actually engaged in wilderness prevention, by building roads and logging to disqualify areas slated for wilderness designation.

The National Forests, like the nation's lakes, rivers, and oceans, are vulnerable to corporate interest groups eager to exploit them for short-term economic gain. Just as labor unions and local governments nation-wide resist pollution control because of their economic bondage to one dominant industry, many residents of southern and western states resist cutbacks in National Forest logging because they make their living in timber-related industries increasingly dependent on National Forest timber. The protection of National Forests, like that of lakes and rivers, suffers from the lack of indices to measure ecological, aesthetic and recreational values anywhere near as precise as the indices used to measure the economic benefits of pollution and clearcutting. How does one value the crucial ecological life-saving of these Forests for Americans? How does one quantify the city-dweller's delight in a forest of stately old trees, the sense of historical continuity and mystery that emanates from a centuries-old forest, the preservation of habitat for endangered species, or the camper's thrill at the silence and freshness of the deep woods? Not surprisingly, Congress favors timber production over these other values because it yields dollars for the federal treasury and votes and campaign contributions for its members. The sale of National Forest timber returns over $350 million a year to the U.S. Treasury. Recreation fees by contrast return less than $20 million. Incentives to treat National Forests as timber factories have been institutionalized in the fiscal planning of local governments as well. For example, to compensate counties which cannot tax National Forest land within their boundaries, the federal government pays them twenty-five percent of receipts from National Forest timber sales to support construction of public schools and roads.

Vulnerability of National Forests

The National Forests are uniquely vulnerable in other ways. A polluted river is a very public disgrace, but destroyed forests are often hidden away in our wilderness areas, undiscovered until the rising tide of recreationists spills over into their blasted acres—after it's too late for remedies. While rivers and lakes now have a federal agency—the Environmental Protection Agency—whose primary mission is to protect them, National Forests are "protected" by the Forest Service whose primary mission is presently to increase timber production. Similarly the Congressional committees who approve budgets and pass legislation for the National Forests are ruled by the same bias. Almost every Forest Service decision resolves for better or worse a value conflict. When abuses occur, as in West Virginia's Monongahela National Forest in 1964, their consequences endure for generations. A river, once the sources of pollution have been cut off, begins cleansing itself immediately. A forest, once it has been clearcut and reseeded, is lost as a recreational resource for decades. If the forest is primeval, with stately trees centuries old, it is likely to be lost forever.

The bureaucracy entrusted with management of our National Forests has clearly benefited from the consciousness-raising of environmental groups, notably the Sierra Club, in the last three years. But its efforts to keep recreation and wildlife uses of the forests in harmony with timber production, as tardy and tentative as they have been, have been crippled further by pressure from the White House on behalf of logging interests. No agribusiness interest group has found the doors to the White House more open than the timber industry. In 1969, when a coalition of environmental groups defeated the National Timber Supply Act with its goal of increasing the timber harvest from public lands by fifty percent, the logging and forest products industry lobbyists went to Presidential assistant Charles Colson, and had the same purpose achieved through executive action.

The Office of Management and Budget has consistently stymied efforts by the Forest Service to devote more resources to recreation development, wildlife habitat, and wilderness protection. As this report points out, a quick review of the Forest Service Budget gives one the impression of examining a major logging company's financial statement. The Forest Service-as-timber-company devotes over two-thirds of its $500 million annual budget to activities promoting timber production. When the Forest Service has attempted to remedy this imbalance, it has been silenced by the OMB. In the FY 1970 budget, for example, the OMB eliminated the Forest Service's planned increase of $3.6 million for "reforestation and stand improvement"; cut its requested increase of $8.7 million for "recreation-public use" to a mere $300,000; and refused major increases for improvement of wildlife habitat. When it came to budget items which benefited the timber industry, however, the OMB suddenly became a free spender. A Forest Service requested increase of $2.5 million for "timber sales administration and management" was more than doubled by OMB to $5.8 million, and a FS increase of $9.4 million for "forest roads and trails"—a key timber production item—was given a whopping boost to $17.5 million. It is no surprise then that recreational facilities and acquisition of new wilderness areas are lagging and that there is a backlog of 4.8 million acres of clearcut land awaiting reforestation.

The Last Stand is a disturbing case study of Congressional default and Presidential gamesmanship with special interests; it also suggests that the Forest Service's leadership, if its conservationist impulses were given more public support, would work to reduce the dominance of the loggers in the management of National Forests. The public forests are a great but fragile national treasure. If their fate is left to the forestry experts and timber interests by an uninformed public, then citizens concerned with the nation's ecological health, campers, hikers, wildlife enthusiasts, and sportsmen have only themselves to blame, for *The Last Stand* gives them a stern projection of what is to come.

PUNISHMENT OF DRUG PUSHERS

January 3, 1973

Governor Nelson A. Rockefeller set off a highly controversial debate when he told the New York legislature, in his 15th annual State of the State address, that he would seek its approval of rigorous new drug legislation. The Governor's program called for mandatory life sentences for adult hard-drug dealers and for addicts who had committed violent crimes. Rockefeller specified that defendants in such cases should have no opportunity for plea bargaining and no possibility of parole. For dealers and addicts between the ages of 16 and 19 years, he recommended life imprisonment, but with a possibility of parole after 15 years. Bounties of $1,000 would be paid to persons giving information leading to the conviction of pushers. Under the plan, life sentences would be the penalty—again with no plea bargaining and no chance of parole—for "conspiracy to sell or possess any quantity of a dangerous drug," and the state would confiscate all money "used in or derived from the drug traffic." Hard drugs would be defined as heroin, cocaine, morphine, opium, hashish, LSD and amphetamines. Marijuana was not included.

The number of heroin addicts in the United States in 1972 was estimated at around 600,000; nearly one-half of the addicts were believed to reside in New York City, where drug-related deaths in 1972 approached 1,500. Many more thousands were thought to use other drugs and narcotics. Of those addicted to heroin, three-fourths were believed to sell the drug at one time or another as a means of supporting their habit. Such estimates placed several hundred thousand New Yorkers among potential candidates for life imprisonment under the Governor's drug proposals. Rates of arrest and indictment in New York, at the time Rockefeller made his proposal, indicated that in the first year of operation the program would increase the total of all court-tried felony cases from 900 a year to nearly 10,000. Henry Ruth, director of the Criminal Justice Coordinating Council, estimated that in the new group—dealers and individuals who had committed violent crimes under the influence of drugs—6,500 would be found guilty and sentenced to life imprisonment.

Plea bargaining had been a means of reducing the number of cases brought to trial in the state of New York. But the Governor's call for an end to that practice could, according to some persons, result in an overburdened court system. Mayor John V. Lindsay reported Jan. 9 that New York City officials had told him that the program would require 270 additional state supreme court justices, new court and prison facilities, and other outlays—all mounting up to more than $5-billion in the first year.

Criticism and Support of Rockefeller Plan

Although in agreement with the Governor's intent to crack down on the drug pushers, the State Commission to Evaluate Drug Laws took issue with specifics of Rockefeller's plan. The Governor's legal counsel had sought independent and outside advice and had petitioned the State Commission to examine the proposals. The commission concluded that parts of the proposed legislation were unworkable and unconstitutional. But Rockefeller held firm to his plan, declaring: "I am totally intolerant of the position that we should not protect the people because it won't work in our system, because we need plea bargaining to clear our [court] calendars.... From a judge's point of view that's a big deal. He clears his calendar, he goes home and everything looks fine. I am concerned about society, about protecting the people, and therefore I think we've got to conform our courts to the needs of society, not society's protection to the needs of the courts."

The proposed legislation, stricter than any then existing in New York State, even for most murders, brought immediate and mixed response. In suburban communities, where the problem of drugs had not yet reached as great proportions as in the city, the Governor's program met with a generally sympathetic reaction. Black leaders in the city showed some concern lest the plan might be applied more strictly to blacks than to whites, but the black community welcomed it in much the same way as Harlem municipal worker Jocelyn Cooper: "I'm very much a liberal and a militant most of the time, but in terms of what he's advocating I'd like to see it happen."

Many persons, however, were concerned by the failure of the Governor's proposals to differentiate between the small-time pusher of hashish and the large-scale wholesaler of heroin. Others argued that rehabilitation was a viable approach to the drug problem that had shown some signs of succeeding. They criticized the Governor's plan because it ruled out almost all access to rehabilitation. Former Attorney General Ramsey Clark branded the proposals "utter madness." Said Clark: "It's not going to be the club, the gun, the iron bar and stone walls that solve this problem.... It will be character." Mayor Lindsay called the plan "merely a deceptive gesture offering nothing beyond momentary satisfaction and inevitable disillusionment." Lindsay agreed with Rockefeller on the need for an outright battle against large-scale drug dealers "who sit behind the scenes, supplying the ingredients of destruction." He advocated an intensified attack on illicit drug dealers through appointment of 48 narcotics judges, the tightening of plea bargaining and paroles, and the unification of federal, state and local narcotics enforcement.

Despite the bitter debate over his drug proposals, Rockefeller followed through by submitting to the legislature on Jan. 10 a bill to carry out what he had proposed in his message a week earlier. Hearings were scheduled promptly by chairmen whose committees had jurisdiction over the stringent new legislation, but some problems were anticipated in working out measures acceptable to legislators as well as to the Governor. However, by April 9, under continual attack by opponents of his proposals, Rockefeller had modified his position, dropping his call for mandatory life imprisonment, but proposing instead mandatory prison terms for a specified time and probation or supervision for the rest of a person's life after release from prison. He signed into law May 8 a version of his latter proposals.

> *Excerpts from New York Governor Nelson A. Rockefeller's State of the State message, Jan. 3, proposing mandatory life imprisonment for traffickers in narcotic drugs:*

...Virtually every poll of public concerns documents that the number one, growing concern of the American people is crime and drugs—coupled with an all-pervasive fear for the safety of their person and their property.

This reign of fear cannot be tolerated.

The law-abiding people of this State have the right to expect tougher and more effective action from their elected leaders to protect them from lawlessness and crime.

People are terrorized by the continued prevalence of narcotic addiction and the crime and human destruction it breeds.

People are outraged by the existence of corruption within the very law enforcement system itself.

People have lost patience with courts that dally and delay in bringing criminal elements to justice.

People are baffled and disheartened by revolving-door criminal justice and a correctional system that doesn't seem to correct.

I will now deal with each of these areas separately.

1. Narcotics

This is a time for brutal honesty regarding narcotics addiction.

In this State, we have tried every possible approach to stop addiction and save the addict through education and treatment—hoping that we could rid society of this disease and drastically reduce mugging on the streets and robbing in the homes.

We have allocated over $1 billion to every form of education against drugs and treatment of the addict through commitment, therapy, and rehabilitation.

But let's be frank—let's "tell it like it is":

We have achieved very little permanent rehabilitation—and have found no cure.

a. Need for Effective Deterrence to the Pushing of Hard Drugs

Lots of wonderful young people have died—and hundreds of thousands more have been and are being crippled for life.

Addiction has kept on growing.

A rising percentage of our high school and college students, from every background and economic level, have become involved, whether as victims or pushers or both.

The crime, the muggings, the robberies, the murders associated with addiction continue to spread a reign of terror.

Whole neighborhoods have been as effectively destroyed by addicts as by an invading army.

We face the risk of undermining our will as a people—and the ultimate destruction of our society as a whole.

This has to stop.

This is going to stop.

Frankly, all the laws we now have on the books won't work to deter the pusher of drugs.

The police are frustrated by suspended sentences and plea bargaining in the courts for those they have arrested—and therefore are discouraged from effectively enforcing the law.

The prosecutors are overwhelmed by the backlog of cases and settle for pleas of guilty on reduced charges—rather than press for a conviction on more serious charges that would have a real deterrent effect —because the latter would result in long drawn-out jury trials.

And the judges, weighed down by calendars running months and years behind, hand out suspended sentences or go along with pleas of guilty to minor offenses that result in sentences of only six months to a year.

We have this choice:

—Either we can go on as we have been, with little real hope of changing the present trend;

—Or we must take those stern measures that, I have become convinced, common sense demands.

We must create an effective deterrent to the pushing of the broad spectrum of hard drugs.

In my opinion, society has no alternatives.

I therefore am proposing the following program for dealing with the illegal pushers of drugs including heroin, amphetamines, LSD, hashish and other dangerous drugs.

(1) Life Prison Sentences for All Pushers

The hard drug pusher destroys lives just as surely as and far more cruelly than a cold-blooded killer.

He threatens our society as a whole, whether he engages in large scale trafficking or small-time operations.

—*Recommended Action:*

I, therefore, will ask for legislation making the penalty for *all* illegal trafficking in hard drugs a life sentence in prison.

To close all avenues for escaping the full force of this sentence, the law would forbid acceptance of a plea to a lesser charge, forbid probation, forbid parole and forbid suspension of sentence.

(2) Life Sentence for Violent Crimes by Addicts

In order to deter effectively the violent crimes committed by the addicted, I will in addition:

—*Recommended Action:*

Propose that crimes of violence committed by persons under the influence of hard drugs be punished by life imprisonment. The avenues of escape would similarly be closed.

(3) Removal of Youthful Offender Protections

It is just as important to have maximum deterrents effective against pushers in their late 'teens as against adult pushers, since both destroy youth and corrupt society.

—*Recommended Action:*

Therefore, I will submit legislation removing persons charged with illegal trafficking in hard drugs from the protections of the youthful offender law, except that they will be eligible for parole consideration after 15 years' imprisonment.

(4) Payment for Information on Hard Drug Pushers

If these deterrents are to be effective, there is need to create incentives to support the law, in order to counteract the incentives which already exist to subvert the law—particularly in the field of drugs.

—*Recommended Action:*

Therefore, I will propose the payment of a $1,000 State cash reward for the person or persons providing information leading to the apprehension and conviction of each hard drug pusher.

For the first time, there would thus be a statewide cash incentive to work for society instead of against it. This reward also could wreak havoc within the ranks of pushers—for they will live in constant fear from never knowing who is buying drugs for evidence to turn them in.

(5) 100 Percent Tax on Drug Pusher Assets

The most difficult elements to catch in the whole chain of illegal drug traffic operations are the so-called "masterminds"—the big profiteers of human misery.

—*Recommended Action:*

To assist in this effort, I will recommend a 100 percent State tax on all monies used in or derived from the illegal traffic in narcotics as an additional legal device for prosecuting hard drug pushers.

Further, I will ask for an escheat provision under which any property acquired wholly or in part from illegal trafficking in hard drugs will be subject to seizure by the State.

This deterrent will include swift confiscation of pushers' automobiles as well.

(6) Expanded Narcotics Courts

This program must not be held up or made ineffective by delayed action in overcrowded courts.

—*Recommended Action:*

Appropriate special State funds to expand the special Narcotics Court structure we set up in New York City with the help of Federal funds, and create wherever necessary similar special Narcotics Courts in the rest of the state.

These are tough laws.

These are drastic measures.

But I am thoroughly convinced, after trying everything else, that nothing less will do.

b. Need for Changes in the Narcotics Addiction Control Laws

The New York State Narcotics Addiction Control Commission, under the able direction of Chairman Howard Jones, is doing an outstanding job of caring for the growing number of those who have been crippled, mentally and physically, through drug addiction.

This is especially true considering the enormity of the drug problem.

These programs will continue, and I am proposing additional needed legislation as follows:

—*Recommended Action:*

—Extend the Commission's authority to make a civil commitment of an addict to include habitual use of amphetamines, barbiturates, LSD, hashish and other dangerous drugs not now within the Commission's scope.

—Give the court the choice of sending an addict convicted of a misdemeanor to jail or to the Narcotics Addiction Control Commission. The court can now only send such persons to the Commission, though many of them have no rehabilitation interest or potential and should instead be imprisoned.

—Give the court the option of placing an addict on probation, with treatment by the Narcotics Addiction Control Commission as a condition of probation.

—Hold in abeyance any indictment for a felony for persons committed to the Narcotics Addiction Control Commission.

—Provide funds for strengthening security in certain of the facilities of the Narcotics Addiction Control Commission.

—Provide funds for expanding drug rehabilitation programs for inmates in state correctional institutions....

[Ed. note: For proposals advocated by President Nixon to curb the U.S. drug problem and related crime, see p. 321.]

YOUTH VOTE TURNOUT

January 4, 1973

Few groups had gained potential political power as easily as the 11 million young people 18-20 years old who were made eligible to vote by the ratification in 1971 of the 26th Amendment to the Constitution. For more than a year they were courted by political candidates and parties and by assorted civic leaders who thought the new voters, including those 21-24 years old voting for President for the first time, might hold the balance of power in a close contest. The election was far from close, but even if it had been otherwise, there was question whether the ballots of the young voters would have had a decisive effect on the final result.

Pre-election polls had indicated that around 65 per cent of the 25 million men and women making up the whole 18-24 age group would register before November 1972. A special Census Bureau survey made public Jan. 4 ("Voter Participation in November 1972") showed that some 6.4 million, or only 58.1 per cent of the 11 million young Americans 18-20 years old, registered to vote and that only 48 per cent of the 11 million actually voted. For the entire 18-24 age group, 58.9 per cent registered and 49.6 per cent voted. By contrast, 75.3 per cent of those 25 years old and older registered and 65.9 per cent voted.

The survey findings dismayed leaders of young-voter organizations but confirmed the expectations of several voting analysts. "I said in 1970 that few groups are as electorally weak as young people," commented Richard Scammon of the Elections Research Center of the Governmental Affairs Institute. "And that was at a time when the conventional wisdom writers thought young people would revolutionize the vote. The cold fact is that young people eligible to vote are far less likely to participate than their elders."

Efforts to Get Out Youth Vote

Such prognostications had not deterred candidates and civic groups from striving to get young people to the polls on election day. Presidential aspirant George McGovern, buoyed up by polls indicating that he had received 62 per cent of the votes of 18 to 25-year-olds in the Democratic primaries, decided to make a major investment in wooing the youth vote. The Democratic National Committee's National Action Council, under the direction of Philip M. Seib, worked to register as many young people as possible, in the belief that the party would pick up about two-thirds of their votes. The national committee's priorities were on campuses, in ghettos and among blue-collar workers.

Republican Party workers also were active in the registration of young people, despite early predictions that the effort would work against them. A volunteer group called Young Voters for the President established headquarters in 35 states with more than 125,000 volunteers. Republicans were encouraged late in July by a Gallup poll indicating that, although McGovern was far ahead of President Nixon among already registered young voters, the President led among the unregistered young.

Nonpartisan youth registration organizations also attempted to rally the young American voters. The Movement for the Student Vote, headed by Ridley Whitaker, was active on 305 college campuses covering institutions with 80 per cent of the nation's college population. During the summer of 1972, Student Vote launched a drive called "First Vote," aimed at minority and working-class youths in inner cities. The Youth Citizenship Fund, financed, like Student Vote, largely through foundations, concentrated on non-student youths—the estimated 17 million of the 25 million young people who were workers, housewives, soldiers or job-seekers. Another group involved in the registration of non-student youths was Frontlash, which was supported by the AFL-CIO. Penn Kemble, head of Frontlash, estimated that about 40 per cent of non-student youths were registered by the summer of 1972. A Gallup poll in late spring 1972 indicated that 66 per cent of the student population was registered.

Opportunities for student voting increased steadily in 1972 as federal courts and many state legislatures sanctioned voting by students in their campus communities instead of by absentee ballot in their home communities. Marshall Lichtenstein of Student Vote reported that 43 states allowed students to register and vote in campus communities.

Forty-two per cent of registered students responding to a Gallup poll early in 1972 called themselves Democrats, 19 per cent Republicans, and

37 per cent independents. Those classifying themselves as left-of-center outnumbered by three to one those professing to be right-of-center. An Oct. 21, 1972, Gallup poll indicated that preferences of college students 21, 1972, Gallup poll indicated that preferences of college students were almost evenly divided between McGovern and Nixon. McGovern's share of the college vote had dropped sharply from the 26-per cent edge he had held over Nixon in a similar poll published July 22, 1972.

Text of "Voter Participation in November 1972" (three tables omitted) issued by the Bureau of the Census, Jan. 4:

Young adults who were eligible to vote for the first time in 1972 did not exercise their franchise as many had expected in the election of November 1972. Among the 11.0 million persons 18 to 20 years old who were old enough to vote for President for the first time, only some 48 percent reported that they voted. Among those 21 to 24 years old, 51 percent reported that they voted. In contrast, among those 25 years of age or over, 66 percent cast their ballots in the election. The highest voter participation rate was reported by persons 45 to 64 years old, as 71 percent of the persons in this age group reported that they voted. These estimates are advance figures for the civilian noninstitutional population from the November 1972 Current Population Survey conducted by the Bureau of the Census.

Participation in the election varied not only by age, but also by sex and race. A smaller proportion of women than of men were reported as having voted—62 percent for women versus 64 percent for men. The proportion of voters was higher for the white population of voting age than for the Negro population of voting age. About 65 percent of the whites, and 52 percent of Negroes, reported that they voted in the November 1972 election. About 38 percent of persons of Spanish origin reported that they voted. Overall voter participation rates in the election of November 1972 were about 5 percentage points lower than in the November 1968 Presidential election.

The survey results show that 98.5 million persons, or 72 percent of those eligible on the basis of age, were reported as registered to vote. Of those registered, 87 percent reported that they voted. The proportion of persons of voting age who were not registered was highest for persons in the youngest age groups, those 18 to 24 years old. Among persons of this age, 41 percent reported that they were not registered.

Approximately 73 percent of the white population of voting age reported that they registered, as compared with 66 percent of the Negro population and 44 percent of the persons of Spanish origin. Of these registered persons, about 88 percent of the whites and 80 percent of the Negroes reported that they voted. The percent of registered persons of Spanish origin who voted is estimated at around 84 percent. Because of small sample size, the estimates of voting rates among registered persons of Spanish origin may vary by plus or minus 5 percentage points and, therefore, may not differ from the rates for the other groups.

Among persons 18 to 24 years old in November 1972, 52 percent of whites and 35 percent of Negroes, reported that they voted; also 61 percent of whites and 48 percent of Negroes reported that they were registered.

Reported Registration and Voter Participation Rates, by Age and Race: November 1972

(Civilian noninstitutional population)

Age and race	Percent reported registered	Percent reported voted
All races	72.3	63.0
18 to 24 years old	58.9	49.6
25 years old and over	75.3	65.9
White	73.4	64.5
18 to 24 years old	60.6	51.9
25 years old and over	76.1	67.2
Negro	65.5	52.1
18 to 24 years old	47.7	34.7
25 years old and over	70.5	57.1

Statistics presented in this report are based on answers to a series of questions asked of a sample of persons of voting age 2 weeks after the elections of November 7. The questions were designed to provide information on voting behavior of the various segments of the population of voting age.

Official counts of the number of votes cast in the 1972 elections are not yet available for comparison with the figures from the Current Population Survey. However, previous Current Population Survey estimates of the number of persons voting have been somewhat higher than the official counts. This type of difference has also been noted in other surveys of voting behavior in which people are asked to report on whether they had voted. Despite this limitation, which may introduce some unknown biases in the results, the data presented in this report can be regarded as providing useful measures of differences in voting behavior among classes of the population....

Since the data are based on a sample of the population, they are, of course, also subject to sampling errors. Confidence limits of 95 percent probability were applied to all statements of this report. This means that the chances are at least 19 in 20 that a difference identified in the text indicates a true difference in the population rather than the chance variations arising from the use of samples....

A PATIENT'S BILL OF RIGHTS

January 8, 1973

A patient's right to refuse life-sustaining treatment, where state law permits, was among 12 points reaffirmed in a "Patient's Bill of Rights" issued Jan. 8 by the American Hospital Association. Believed to be the first generally available public policy statement from a national health organization outlining patients' privileges, the Bill emerged after a three-year study by hospital administrators, physicians and four consumer representatives.

Although the statement carried no force of law, the AHA said it expected most of its 700 member hospitals to make it available to their patients. John Alexander McMahon, president of the association, said in making the announcement: "I am sure that the majority of our hospitals have been practicing the contents of the Bill to the best of their ability. The twelve points are subject areas that have always needed to be spelled out to the patient so that he would know what his rights are in the hospital setting. This document covers the most commonly questioned situations that patients encounter in a hospital."

The Bill reflected the surge of consumer interest in health and medical care that had challenged traditional medical paternalism. A sophisticated public, more educated on medical affairs, had demanded increased information and inclusion in discussions leading to treatment decisions. Courts had told doctors they must clearly state therapy choices and any risks that might be involved in the available treatment. If a patient did not wish to submit to treatment that might temporarily prolong, but not save, his life, or if a patient had religious objections to a certain therapy, there might be a legal predicament. Doctors and legal advisers had sought to reconcile the Hippocratic Oath with a person's right to refuse medical treatment. The Patient's Bill of Rights tried to set guidelines for such situations.

The American Medical Association's legal department said in 1961 that "a patient has the right to withhold his consent to life-saving treatment" and to impose conditions on his therapy. The courts had not been as clear. Court decisions strictly differentiated between children, adults with terminal disorders, and adults with religious objections to treatment. They clearly held that a parent had no right, based on religious beliefs or any other grounds, to deny medical therapy to a child in immediate and present danger. Such denial was deemed sufficient to constitute "neglect" and, under the doctrine of "parens patriae," the state could assume guardianship of neglected children. Cases of competent adults frequently involved religious objection to blood transfusion. Where a situational basis to order treatment could be cited, such as dependent children, the courts tended to negate the right of an individual to refuse necessary medical care. Where the patient's life could not be saved, but only prolonged, the legal situation was cloudy. Attorney Angela Roddey Holder, writing in the Journal of the American Medical Association, *July 17, 1972, pointed out: "The paucity of decisions on this subject apparently indicates that in most cases physicians and patient reach an accord in their decision on this subject. One recent trial court decision [Fla Cir Ct, Dade Co., Docket 71-12687, 1971,* The Citation, No. 23, p. 12], *however, does indicate that the patient does have the right to refuse further treatment."*

The study group report said that a doctor must inform the individual of his medical condition in terms he could reasonably be expected to understand. This point was aimed at eliminating situations where physicians, too busy to provide their patients with a thorough understanding, veiled their explanations in scientific terms. The Bill also affirmed a patient's right to respectful care and to confidentiality of his medical records.

Charity hospitals were once almost the only hospitals where young doctors could gain practical experience. Now many private hospitals are affiliated with medical schools and offer opportunities for training not only to young doctors but also to medical students under the guidance of their professors. In the latter instance, patients become teaching cases for the students. The Patient's Bill of Rights stipulated that patients must be told when students are aiding in their care. It also said patients must give "informed consent" prior to any experimental treatment.

Text of "Patient's Bill of Rights" issued Jan. 8 by the American Hospital Association:

The American Hospital Association presents a Patient's Bill of Rights with the expectation that observance of these rights will contribute to more effective patient care and greater satisfaction for the patient, his physician, and the hospital organization. Further, the Association presents these rights in the expectation that they will be supported by the hospital on behalf of its patients, as an integral part of the healing process. It is recognized that a personal relationship between the physician and the patient is essential for the provision of proper medical care. The traditional physician-patient relationship takes on a new dimension when care is rendered within an organizational structure. Legal precedent has established that the institution itself also has a responsibility to the patient. It is in recognition of these factors that these rights are affirmed.

1. The patient has the right to considerate and respectful care.

2. The patient has the right to obtain from his physician complete current information concerning his diagnosis, treatment, and prognosis in terms the patient can be reasonably expected to understand. When it is not medically advisable to give such information to the patient, the information should be made available to an appropriate person in his behalf. He has the right to know by name the physician responsible for coordinating his care.

3. The patient has the right to receive from his physician information necessary to give informed consent prior to the start of any procedure and/or treatment. Except in emergencies, such information for informed consent should include but not necessarily be limited to the specific procedure and/or treatment, the medically significant risks involved, and the probable duration of incapacitation. Where medically significant alternatives for care or treatment exist, or when the patient requests information concerning medical alternatives, the patient has the right to such information. The patient also has the right to know the name of the person responsible for the procedures and/or treatment.

4. The patient has the right to refuse treatment to the extent permitted by law, and to be informed of the medical consequences of his action.

5. The patient has the right to every consideration of his privacy concerning his own medical care program. Case discussion, consultation, examination, and treatment are confidential and should be conducted discreetly. Those not directly involved in his care must have the permission of the patient to be present.

6. The patient has the right to expect that all communications and records pertaining to his care should be treated as confidential.

41

7. The patient has the right to expect that within its capacity a hospital must make reasonable response to the request of a patient for services. The hospital must provide evaluation, service, and/or referral as indicated by the urgency of the case. When medically permissible a patient may be transferred to another facility only after he has received complete information and explanation concerning the needs for and alternatives to such a transfer. The institution to which the patient is to be transferred must first have accepted the patient for transfer.

8. The patient has the right to obtain information as to any relationship of his hospital to other health care and educational institutions insofar as his care is concerned. The patient has the right to obtain information as to the existence of any professional relationships among individuals, by name, who are treating him.

9. The patient has the right to be advised if the hospital proposes to engage in or perform human experimentation affecting his care or treatment. The patient has the right to refuse to participate in such research projects.

10. The patient has the right to expect reasonable continuity of care. He has the right to know in advance what appointment times and physicians are available and where. The patient has the right to expect that the hospital will provide a mechanism whereby he is informed by his physician or a delegate of the physician of the patient's continuing health care requirements following discharge.

11. The patient has the right to examine and receive an explanation of his bill regardless of source of payment.

12. The patient has the right to know what hospital rules and regulations apply to his conduct as a patient.

No catalogue of rights can guarantee for the patient the kind of treatment he has a right to expect. A hospital has many functions to perform, including the prevention and treatment of disease, the education of both health professionals and patients, and the conduct of clinical research. All these activities must be conducted with an overriding concern for the patient, and, above all, the recognition of his dignity as a human being. Success in achieving this recognition assures success in the defense of the rights of the patient.

PHASE III ECONOMIC CONTROLS

January 11, 1973

President Nixon on Jan. 11 terminated mandatory wage and price controls over most of the U.S. economy, leaving fiscal and monetary policies as the principal weapons to continue the nation's fight against inflation. In an announcement nearly as unexpected as hig Aug. 15, 1971, order putting the economy under a wage-price freeze, the President freed most businesses and unions from mandatory restraints. He left controls in force in three "particularly trouble-some" areas: food prices, health costs and the construction industry.

For the rest of the economy, the President set up a system of voluntary guidelines backed by the threat that the government would intervene to roll back wage and price increases it considered inflationary. While he revamped the economic stabilization program by executive order, Nixon formally asked Congress to extend his authority to impose economic controls for one year past the April 30, 1973, expiration date of the Economic Stabilization Act of 1971. Setting as his goal an overall rate of inflation of 2.5 per cent by the end of 1973, the President made clear his belief that its attainment would depend on federal budgetary restraint. He called on Congress to cooperate in holding federal spending down to avoid the inflationary impetus of a large government deficit. (See excerpts from address by Federal Reserve Board Chairman Arthur F. Burns, Historic Documents, 1972, p. 961.)

Under the voluntary restraints set up by Phase III, businesses, unions and individuals were free to make their own decisions on wages and prices—at the risk of government action establishing manda-

tory standards if the Cost of Living Council (CLC) determined that private decisions were inconsistent with the national goal of reducing inflation to 2.5 per cent. An informed Price Commission source told Congressional Quarterly that although the controls were voluntary, "We still keep a club in the closet.... One of the things we could do would be to ask a company to make a report every day if we felt they were exceeding the price limitations. Not that this is the only thing we can do. In fact, we don't know now what we can do."

Under the Phase III apparatus, the CLC and the Internal Revenue Service monitored wage and price performance by reviewing reports filed by companies, auditing records and analyzing government and trade data. If the CLC determined that an action that had been or was about to be taken violated the stabilization program's goals, it could issue a temporary order setting interim price and wage levels or an order setting a legally binding level.

Structural Changes in Control Program

The President made a number of structural changes in the stabilization program, abolishing the Pay Board and Price Commission and transferring their functions to the Cost of Living Council. John T. Dunlop, dean of the faculty of arts and sciences at Harvard University, was appointed to succeed Donald Rumsfeld as director of the Cost of Living Council. Dunlop had been chairman of the Construction Industry Stabilization Committee, which supervised wage and price decisions in the construction industry.

As a general rule for Phase III, the White House said, price increases above levels authorized in Phase II were not to exceed cost increases. As under Price Commission regulations for Phase II, price increases were subjected to a profit-margin limit. In another Phase III change, a company was allowed to make price increases regardless of its profit margin if the average increase on all products did not exceed 1.5 per cent in one year.

For Phase III, the President retained at least temporarily the Pay Board's Phase II general standard limiting wage increases to 5.5 per cent a year. The Labor-Management Advisory Committee was created to advise the Cost of Living Council on whether existing wage standards should be modified.

In his message to Congress, Nixon promised "special efforts...to combat inflation in areas where rising prices have been particularly troublesome, especially in fighting rising food prices." Because of continuing food price increases, he said, existing controls would be continued "with special vigor for firms involved in food processing and food retailing." As under Phase II, raw agricultural product prices were left exempt from controls.

In continuing mandatory controls on health costs, the President appointed another CLC committee to review the impact of government programs on health services. He appointed also a committee of private individuals to advise the CLC on health costs. The President left intact the existing Construction Industry Stabilization Committee of Phase II. The construction industry had been under controls since March 29, 1971. The executive order putting Phase II into effect continued the existing voluntary program of restraints on interest and dividend increases administered by the Committee on Interest and Dividends.

Reaction to Phase III among members of Congress varied widely. Republicans who opposed controls in the first place praised the President's Phase III plans. Democrats who had urged imposition of controls in 1971 said they feared controls were being lifted too early. Chairman Wright Patman (D Texas) of the House Banking and Currency Committee, whose panel was scheduled to consider controls legislation, promised that Congress would "make its own independent judgment on the extension of wage and price controls." Areas where Congress could make such judgments were: the President's termination of controls on rents and lumber, continued reliance on voluntary interest and dividend restraints, and the relative impact of Phase III on wages and prices. Sen. William Proxmire (D Wis.), chairman of the Joint Economic Committee, predicted strong opposition if the Cost of Living Council reduced the existing 5.5 per cent wage increase standard without comparable action against prices.

Economist Walter Heller, who headed the Council of Economic Advisers under Presidents Kennedy and Johnson, commented: "Mr. Nixon is running some very substantial risks. A great deal depends on how much they use the club they kept in the closet." Paul Samuelson, a Nobel Prize-winning economist, predicted inflation would exceed 4 per cent in 1973. "The logic of the 1973 economic situation called for a continuation of price and wage controls, but I'm not sure logic applies to Nixonomics."

Labor's Attitude

Many labor union leaders welcomed the removal of most compulsory wage and price controls. AFL-CIO President George Meany, who stormed off the Phase II Pay Board in 1972 in protest against the stabilization program, termed the President's Jan. 11 action "a step in the right direction." Meany and four other labor leaders agreed to serve on a 10-member committee created to advise on revision of the wage increase standard. Some leaders expressed concern, however, that prices would soar under President Nixon's new program while a "tight lid" would still be kept on wages.

45

Arch Booth, executive vice president of the Chamber of Commerce of the United States, signaled business approval of Phase III in a statement that commended the President "for taking this first step toward orderly withdrawal of controls." He said that Phase III offered the hope that the entire apparatus of controls can be removed from the economy, instead of being permanently retained. Stock-market investors clearly were happy about Phase III. The Dow-Jones industrial average zoomed from a one-point gain earlier in the day to a 15-point gain shortly after the announcement. It eventually settled back to a gain for the day of slightly under six points.

President Nixon's message to Congress, Jan. 11, on Phase III of the wage-price control program:

To the Congress of the United States:

During 1969, the annual rate of inflation in the United States was about six percent. During my first term in office, that rate has been cut nearly in half and today the United States has the lowest rate of inflation of any industrial country in the free world.

In the last year and a half, this decline in inflation has been accompanied by a rapid economic expansion. Civilian employment rose more rapidly during the past year than ever before in our history and unemployment substantially declined. We now have one of the highest economic growth rates in the developed world.

In short, 1972 was a very good year for the American economy. I expect 1973 and 1974 to be even better. They can, in fact, be the best years our economy has ever experienced—provided we have the will and wisdom, in both the public and private sectors, to follow appropriate economic policies.

For the past several weeks, members of my Administration have been reviewing our economic policies in an effort to keep them up to date. I deeply appreciate the generous advice and excellent suggestions we have in our consultations with the Congress. We are also grateful for the enormous assistance we have received from hundreds of leaders representing business, labor, farm and consumer groups, and the general public. These discussions have been extremely helpful to us in reaching several central conclusions about our economic future.

One major point which emerges as we look both at the record of the past and the prospects for the future is the central role of our Federal monetary and fiscal policies. We cannot keep inflation in check unless we keep Government spending in check. This is why I have insisted that our spending for fiscal year 1973 not exceed $250 billion and that our proposed budget for fiscal year 1974 not exceed the revenues which the existing tax system would produce at full employment. I hope and expect that the Congress will receive this budget with a similar sense of fiscal discipline. The stability of our prices depends on the restraint of the Congress.

As we move into a new year, and into a new term for this Administration, we are also moving to a new phase of our economic stabilization program. I believe the system of controls which has been in effect since 1971 has helped considerably in improving the health of our economy. I am today submitting to the Congress legislation which would extend for another year—until April 30 of 1974—the basic legislation on which that system is based, the Economic Stabilization Act.

But even while we recognize the need for continued Government restraints on prices and wages, we also look to the day when we can enjoy the advantages of price stability without the disadvantages of such restraints. I believe we can prepare for that day, and hasten its coming, by modifying the present system so that it relies to a greater extent on the voluntary cooperation of the private sector in making reasonable price and wage decisions.

Under Phase III, prior approval by the Federal Government will not be required for changes in wages and prices, except in special problem areas. The Federal Government, with the advice of management and labor, will develop standards to guide private conduct which will be self-administering. This means that businesses and workers will be able to determine for themselves the conduct that conforms to the standards. Initially and generally we shall rely upon the voluntary cooperation of the private sector for reasonable observance of the standards. However, the Federal Government will retain the power—and the responsibility— to step in and stop action that would be inconsistent with our anti-inflation goals. I have established as the overall goal of this program a further reduction in the inflation rate to 2 1/2 percent or less by the end of 1973.

Under this program, much of the Federal machinery which worked so well during Phase I and Phase II can be eliminated, including the Price Commission, the Pay Board, the Committee on the Health Services Industry, the Committee on State and Local Government Cooperation, and the Rent Advisory Board. Those who served so ably as members of these panels and their staffs—especially Judge George H. Boldt, Chairman of the Pay Board, and C. Jackson Grayson, Jr., Chairman of the Price Commission—have my deep appreciation and that of their countrymen for their devoted and effective contributions.

This new program will be administered by the Cost of Living Council. The Council's new Director will be John T. Dunlop. Dr. Dunlop succeeds Donald Rumsfeld who leaves this post with the Nation's deepest gratitude for a job well done.

Under our new program, special efforts will be made to combat inflation in areas where rising prices have been particularly troublesome, especially in fighting rising food prices. Our anti-inflation program will not be fully successful until its impact is felt at the local supermarket or corner grocery store.

I am therefore directing that our current mandatory wage and price control system be continued with special vigor for firms involved in food processing and food retailing. I am also establishing a new committee to review Government policies which affect food prices and a non-Government advisory group to examine other ways of achieving price stability in food markets. I will ask this advisory group to give special attention to new ways of cutting costs and improving productivity at all points along the food production, processing and distribution chain. In addition, the Department of Agriculture and the Cost of Living Council yesterday and today announced a number of important steps to hold down food prices in the best possible way—by increasing food supply. I believe all these efforts will enable us to check effectively the rising cost of food without damaging the growing prosperity of American farmers. Other special actions which will be taken to fight inflation include continuing the present mandatory controls over the health and construction industries and continuing the present successful program for interest and dividends.

The new policies I am announcing today can mean even greater price stability with less restrictive bureaucracy. Their success, however, will now depend on a firm spirit of self-restraint both within the Federal Government and among the general public. If the Congress will receive our new budget with a high sense of responsibility and if the public will continue to demonstrate the same spirit of voluntary cooperation which was so important during Phase I and Phase II, then we can bring the inflation rate below 2 1/2 percent and usher in an unprecedented era of full and stable prosperity.

Richard Nixon

The White House,
   January 11, 1973.

Text of Executive Order 11695 issued Jan. 11 by President Nixon to provide further for stabilization of the economy:

On August 15, 1971, I issued Executive Order 11615 establishing a freeze on prices, rents, wages and salaries for a period of 90 days from the date of that order and establishing the Cost of Living Council as the agency with primary responsibility for administering the Economic Stabilization Program.

Subsequently, I issued Executive Order 11627 which continued the Cost of Living Council and established a Pay Board and a Price Commission. Under the terms of that order, the Cost of Living Council established broad stabilization goals for the Nation and the Pay Board and Price Commission, acting through their respective Chairmen, prescribed specific standards, criteria and regulations and made rulings and decisions aimed at carrying out goals of the Economic Stabilization Program.

On December 22, 1971, I signed into law amendments to the Economic Stabilization Act of 1970. To reflect changes made by these amendments and to reaffirm the existing delegation of authority to the Cost of Living Council, I substituted Executive Order 11640.

As the result of efforts under the Economic Stabilization Program, by public officials and private citizens alike, the rate of inflation has been significantly reduced. However, in furtherance of the goals and for the reasons set forth in my message to the Congress of this date, I have determined that to continue to stabilize the economy, reduce inflation, minimize unemployment, improve the Nation's competitive position in world trade, and protect the purchasing power of the dollar, all in the context of sound fiscal management and effective monetary policies, the Economic Stabilization Program should be continued, building upon the solid foundation of achievement accomplished in the past and redirecting our efforts to respond to the needs of the current year.

Now, THEREFORE, by virtue of the authority vested in me by the Constitution and statutes of the United States, particularly the Economic Stabilization Act of 1970, as amended, it is hereby ordered as follows:

SECTION 1. (a) The Cost of Living Council (hereinafter referred to as the "Council"), established by section 2 of the Executive Order 11615 of August 15, 1971, is hereby continued.

(b) The Council shall be composed of the following members: The Secretary of the Treasury, the Secretary of Agriculture, the Secretary of Commerce, the Secretary of Labor, the Secretary of Health, Education, and Welfare, the Secretary of Housing and Urban Development, the Director of the Office of Management and Budget, the Chairman of the Council of Economic Advisers, the Director of the Office of Emergency Preparedness, the Special Assistant to the President for Consumer Affairs and such others as the President may, from time to time, designate. The Secretary of the Treasury shall serve as Chairman of the Council and the Chairman of the Council of Economic Advisers shall serve as Vice Chairman. The Chairman of the Board of Governors of the Federal Reserve System shall serve as adviser to the Council.

(c) There shall be a Director of the Cost of Living Council who shall be appointed by the President, be a member of the Council, be a full-time official of the United States, be the Council's Chief Executive Officer, and be compensated at the rate prescribed for Level III of the Executive Schedule by section 5314 of Title 5 of the United States Code.

SEC. 2. (a) Except as otherwise provided in subsection (b) of this section, all the powers and duties conferred upon the President by the Economic Stabilization Act of 1970, as amended, are hereby delegated to the Chairman of the Council, including, without limitation, the power and duty to make the determinations and take the actions required or permitted by the act.

(b) The authority conferred by or pursuant to this order shall not extend to the prices charged for raw agricultural products until after the first sale thereof.

(c) The Council shall develop and recommend to the President policies, mechanisms and procedures to achieve and maintain stability of prices and costs in a growing economy. To this end it shall consult with representatives of agriculture, industry, labor, State and local governments, consumers and the public, including the National Commission on Productivity.

(d) In all of its actions the Council shall be guided by the need to maintain consistency of price and wage policies with fiscal, monetary, international and other economic policies of the United States.

(e) The Council shall inform the public, agriculture, industry, and labor concerning the need for controlling inflation and shall encourage and promote voluntary action to that end.

SEC. 3. (a) All orders, regulations, circulars, rulings, notices or other directives issued and all other actions taken by any agency pursuant to Executive Order 11588, as amended, Executive Order 11615, as amended, Executive Order 11627, as amended, and Executive Order 11640, as amended, and in effect on the date of this order are hereby confirmed and ratified, and shall remain in full force and effect as if issued under this order, unless or until altered, amended, or revoked by the Chairman or by such competent authority as the Chairman may specify, and shall be administered by the Chairman or by such competent authority as the Chairman may specify.

(b) The Chairman shall take such steps as are necessary to make appropriate disposition of actions in process under the Economic Stabilization Program and to effect an orderly transfer of stabilization functions pursuant to this order.

(c) This order shall not operate to defeat any suit, action, prosecution, or administrative proceeding, whether heretofore or hereafter commenced, with respect to any right possessed, liability incurred, or offense committed prior to this date.

(d) Renegotiation provisions in price, rent, wage or salary contracts which are dependent for their operation on modification or termination of the Economic Stabilization Program are hereby declared inoperative as unreasonably inconsistent with the goals of the Economic Stabilization Program. Except to the extent permitted pursuant to the provisions of section 4(a), this order shall not operate to permit:

(i) A retroactive increase in prices, rents, wages or salaries for goods or services sold or leased or work performed while the prices, rents, wages or salaries were subject to the rules of the Price Commission or the Pay Board, or

(ii) A prospective increase in prices, rents, wages or salaries under the terms of a contract subject to a Price Commission or Pay Board decision and order, except to the extent consistent with such decision and order.

SEC. 4. (a) The Chairman, in carrying out the provisions of this order, may continue to (i) prescribe definitions for any terms used herein, (ii) make exceptions or grant exemptions, (iii) issue regulations and orders, (iv) provide for the establishment of committees and other comparable groups, and (v) take such other actions as he determines to be necessary or appropriate to carry out the purposes of this order.

(b) The Chairman may redelegate to any agency, instrumentality, or official of the United States any authority under this order, and may, in administering this order, utilize the services of any other agency, Federal or State, as may be available or appropriate.

(c) On request of the Chairman, each executive department or agency is authorized and directed, consistent with law, to furnish the Council with any available information which the Council may require in the performance of its functions, and shall provide such other assistance in carrying out the provisions of this order as is permitted by law.

SEC. 5. (a) The Construction Industry Stabilization Committee (hereinafter referred to as the CISC) established by section 2 of Executive Order 11588 of March 29, 1971, is hereby continued and shall continue to act as an agency of the United States. The CISC shall perform such functions with respect to the stabilization of wages and salaries in the construction industry as the Chairman of the Council may delegate to it.

(b) The CISC shall be composed of twelve members. The CISC shall include four members representative of labor organizations in the construction industry, four members representative of employers in the construction industry, and four members representative of the public. The CISC shall conduct its proceedings in such manner as will be conducive to the proper dispatch of its business and to the ends of justice.

(c) The craft dispute boards (hereinafter referred to as "boards") established by associations of contractors and national and international unions under section 2 of Executive Order 11588 are hereby continued. Each board shall be composed of appropriate labor and management representatives. The boards shall perform such functions with respect to the stabilization of wages and salaries in the construction industry as the Chairman of the Council may prescribe.

(d) Upon a determination by a board or the CISC that a proposed wage or salary increase is not acceptable and certification of that determination by the Chairman of the Cost of Living Council the following actions shall be taken.

(i) In implementing the provisions of the Davis-Bacon Act of March 3, 1931 (46 Stat. 1494, as amended) and related statutes the provisions of which are dependent upon determinations by the Secretary of Labor under the Davis-Bacon Act, and including State statutes or laws requiring similar wage standards, the Secretary of Labor and all States shall not take into consideration any wage or salary increases in excess of that found to be acceptable in making determinations under that act and related statutes.

(ii) In order to assure that unacceptable wage rates shall not be utilized in Federal or federally related construction, the heads of all Federal departments and agencies, subject to the direction and coordination of the Chairman of the Cost of Living Council:

(1) shall review all plans for construction and financial assistance for construction in localities in which wage or salary increases have been certified by the Chairman of the Cost of Living Council to be unacceptable and shall, on the basis of that review, determine whether such plans can be approved or continued; and

(2) shall review current and prospective construction contracts for Federal construction and for construction on projects receiving Federal financial assistance in the area affected by a certification by the Chairman of the Cost of Living Council and shall, on the basis of such review, determine whether such contracts can be awarded or continued.

SEC. 6. (a) There is hereby established the Cost of Living Council Committee on Health to be composed of the Director of the Council, who shall be its Chairman, the Vice Chairman of the Council, the Secretary of the Treasury, the Secretary of Health, Education, and Welfare, the Director of the Office of Management and Budget, and such others as the President may, from time to time, designate. The Committee shall review Government activities significantly influencing health care expenses and make recommendations to the Chairman of the Council concerning these matters.

(b) There is hereby established a Health Industry Advisory Committee. This Committee shall be composed of such members as the President may, from time to time, appoint. The President shall designate the Chairman of the Committee. The Committee shall provide advice to the Council on the operation of the Economic Stabilization Program in the health industry and other matters related to health care expenses.

SEC. 7. (a) There is hereby established the Cost of Living Council Committee on Food which shall be composed of the Chairman of the Council, who shall be its Chairman, the Vice Chairman of the Council, the Director of the Council, the Secretary of Agriculture, the Director of the Office of Management and Budget and such others as the President may, from time to time, designate. The Committee shall review Government activities significantly affecting food costs and prices and make recommendations to the Chairman of the Council concerning these matters.

(b) There is hereby established a Food Industry Advisory Committee. This Committee shall be composed of such members as the President may, from time to time, appoint. The President shall designate the Chairman of the Committee. The Committee shall provide advice to the Council on the operation of the Economic Stabilization Program in the food industry and other matters related to food costs and prices.

SEC. 8. There is hereby established a Labor-Management Advisory Committee. This Committee shall be composed of such members as the President may, from time to time, appoint. The Committee shall provide advice to the Chairman of the Council on methods for improving the collective bargaining process and for assuring wage and salary settlements consistent with gains in productivity and the goal of stemming the rate of inflation.

SEC. 9. The Committee on Interest and Dividends established by section 9 of Executive Order 11627 is hereby continued. The Committee shall be composed of the Chairman of the Board of Governors of the Federal Reserve System, the Secretary of the Treasury, the Secretary of Commerce, the Secretary of Housing and Urban Development, the Chairman of the Federal Deposit Insurance Corporation, the Chairman of the Federal Home Loan Bank Board, and such others as the President may, from time to time, designate. The Chairman of the Board of Governors of the Federal Reserve System shall serve as Chairman of the Committee. This Committee shall, subject to review by the Council, formulate and execute a program for obtaining voluntary restraints on interest rates and dividends.

SEC. 10. (a) The Pay Board and Price Commission established by sections 7 and 8 of Executive Order 11627 are hereby abolished effective not more than 90 days from the date of this order or such earlier date as the Chairman of the Cost of Living Council may designate. The Board and the Commission during this transition period shall provide for winding up any outstanding matter involving them subject to the direction of the Chairman of the Council.

(b) The Committee on the Health Services Industry established by section 10 of Executive Order 11627 is hereby abolished.

(c) The Committee on State and Local Government Cooperation established by section 11 of Executive Order 11627 is hereby abolished.

(d) The Rent Advisory Board established by section 11A of Executive Order 11627, as amended, is hereby abolished.

(e) The Chairman of the Council shall make appropriate provision for the disposition of the records, property, personnel, and funds relating to the agencies and committees abolished by this section.

(f) In order that the confidential status of any records affected by this order shall be fully protected and maintained, the use of any confidential records transferred pursuant to this section shall be so restricted by the Chairman of the Council as to prevent the disclosure of information concerning individual persons or firms to persons who are not engaged in functions or activities to which such records are directly related, except as provided for by law or as required in the final disposition thereof pursuant to law.

SEC. 11. (a) Whoever willfully violates this order or any order or regulation continued or issued under authority of this order shall be subject to a fine of not more than $5,000 for each such violation. Whoever violates this order or any order or regulation continued or issued under authority of this order shall be subject to a civil penalty of not more than $2,500 for each such violation.

(b) The Chairman of the Council may in his discretion request the Department of Justice to bring actions for injunctions authorized under section 209 of the Economic Stabilization Act of 1970, as amended, whenever it appears to him that any person has engaged, is engaged, or is about to engage in any acts or practices constituting a violation of any regulation or order continued or issued pursuant to this order. The relief sought may include a mandatory injunction commanding any person to comply with any such order or regulation and restitution of monies received in violation of any such order or regulation.

(c) The Chairman of the Cost of Living Council, or his duly authorized agent, shall have authority for any purpose related to the Economic Stabilization Act of 1970, as amended, to sign and issue subpoenas for the attendance and testimony of witnesses and the production of relevant books, papers, and other documents, and to administer oaths, all in accordance with the provisions of section 206 of the Economic Stabilization Act of 1970, as amended.

SEC. 12. Executive Order 11588 of March 29, 1971, Executive Order 11640 of January 26, 1972, Executive Order 11660 of March 25, 1972, and Executive Order 11674 of June 29, 1972, are hereby superseded.

Richard Nixon

The White House
  January 11, 1973.

(Ed. Note: For subsequent developments, see the President's Annual Economic Report, p. 185; the State of the Union message on the economy, p. 219; the discussion of the international monetary crisis, p. 343.)

TELEVISION IN TURMOIL

January 11, 1973

The director of the White House Office of Telecommunications Policy, Dr. Clay T. Whitehead, further disturbed the television news community, Jan. 11, when he reiterated an earlier statement that the administration intended to push through changes in the laws regulating broadcasting. The proposed changes affecting renewal of station licenses "would restore equilibrium to the broadcasting system," Whitehead told a largely hostile audience of New York City members of the National Academy of Television Arts and Sciences. Although the 34-year-old telecommunications chief had warned that his speech would be "dull," a group of more than 500 chapter members crowded the Americana Hotel's Imperial Ballroom to hear the man whose address of Dec. 18, 1972, had prompted an outpouring of critical response.

Whitehead's Indianapolis Speech

Whitehead on that occasion had told the Indiana professional chapter of Sigma Delta Chi, journalistic society, that network news programs were marked by "elitist gossip," "ideological plugola" and "biased" news reporting. He announced that the administration would ask Congress to approve legislation that would hold local affiliates of television networks accountable for the content of all news, entertainment and commercials they broadcast—including the network programs. "Where there are only a few sources of national news on television...editorial responsibility must be exercised more effectively by local broadcasters and by network managers," Whitehead had said. "Station managers and network officials who fail to act to correct

55

imbalance or consistent bias from the networks—or who acquiesce by silence—can only be considered willing participants, to be held fully accountable at license renewal time."

The legislative proposals, Whitehead said, would amend the Communications Act of 1934 to establish two criteria which broadcasters would have to meet before the Federal Communications Commission (FCC) granted a license renewal: (1) "The broadcaster must demonstrate he had been substantially attuned to the needs and interests of the community he services...irrespective of whether...programs are created by the station, purchased from program suppliers or obtained from a network," and (2) "The broadcaster must show that he had afforded reasonable, realistic and practical opportunities for the presentation of conflicting views on controversial issues." The criteria would strengthen the FCC's fairness doctrine, which now requires broadcasters only to provide "reasonable opportunity for discussion of contrasting views on public issues."

Although Whitehead asserted that "everyone agrees fairness-doctrine enforcement is a mess," he said "three harsh realities" made it impossible to do away with the doctrine and remove broadcasters from "government intrusion": "First there is a scarcity of broadcasting outlets.... Second there is a substantial concentration of economic and social power in the networks and their affiliated stations. Third, there is a tendency for broadcasters and networks to be self-indulgent and myopic in viewing the First Amendment as protecting only their rights as speakers. They forget that its primary purpose is to assure a free flow and wide range of information to the public."

The proposed new license renewal legislation would contain two additional sections: the term of a broadcast license would be increased from three years to five years, and the FCC would be authorized to reject any challenge to an existing license, without holding a hearing, if it believed the holder of the license had met programing standards. Under the new proposals, Whitehead said broadcasters "can no longer accept network standards of taste, violence and decency in programing."

Reaction to Whitehead Criticism

The initial response to the Whitehead proposals came from the National Broadcasting Company (NBC). A spokesman said the "plan... seems to be an attempt to drive a wedge between television stations and networks." Later, NBC president Julian Goodman said: "Some federal government officials are waging a continuing campaign aimed at intimidating and discrediting the news media, and the public has expressed very little concern." Federal Communications Commissioner Nicholas Johnson asserted that Whitehead's criticism of "ideological bias" on television and radio was an attempt to purge from the air-

waves any news unfavorable to the White House. Johnson noted the "carrot and stick" give-and-take which, he said, would extend the length of time between license renewals from three to five years in exchange for a "crackdown on the news and public affairs materials being broadcast over their stations from the networks, especially if it came from CBS." Robert G. Fichtenberg, chairman of the freedom of information committee of the American Society of Newspaper Editors, characterized the proposal for new licensing standards as "one of the most ominous attacks yet on the people's right to a free flow of information and views."

Confronted with the criticism spurred by his speech, Whitehead wrote to a National Association of Broadcasters task force: "I grant you that the language I used in the Dec. 18 speech was strong.... But those who have twisted an appeal for the voluntary exercise of private responsibility into a call for government censorship—that they can denounce— have abandoned reasoned debate in favor of polemics." He asserted that neither his office "nor the White House has any power to effect the grant or denial of any broadcast license. And we have no intent or desire to influence in any way the grants or denials of licenses by the FCC."

Media Self-Criticism

The fourth annual Alfred I. duPont-Columbia University Survey of Broadcast Journalism, released Feb. 13, concluded that broadcast journalism was seriously threatened—more so than at any time in the 50 years of its existence—by "the adversary in Washington who often seemed more intent upon emasculating than reforming the broadcaster's vast enterprise." Citing a decline in news programing, the survey laid the blame on management: "Network television looked as though it were trying to lose its documentarians [by] refusing them the opportunity to do their best, cutting off their time and money, keeping them from prime spots on the schedules." Sponsors and the public must share the blame, the report added, for they "prefer fantasy to reality." The survey pointed out that "many administration spokesmen and friends" had begun a concentrated attack on broadcast journalism. "The negative vibrations...emanated in most part from one source, the White House, where staff members concerned with communications matters were particularly active.... Most visible was Clay T. Whitehead."

Discussion of the proposed license renewal legislation fitted into the news community's concern over other threats to the media. In 1972, four journalists had been jailed for refusing to disclose confidential sources of information. (See Historic Documents, 1972, p. 507.) Renewal of the licenses of two Florida television stations owned by a subsidiary of The Washington Post *had been challenged by persons with ties to*

the Nixon administration. Senior correspondent Robert MacNeil of the
National Public Affairs Center for Television on Jan. 26 accused the
Nixon administration of attempting to turn public television into "a
domestic Voice of America" which would broadcast "nothing but the
administration line." He pointed to two Nixon-appointed public television officials who had announced plans to de-emphasize public affairs
programing by canceling two national news programs. Fred Friendly,
Edward R. Murrow professor of journalism at the Columbia University
School of Journalism and a former president of CBS News, suggested
that "Nixon is creating...an 'open season' on journalism."

In his speech Jan. 11 in New York, Whitehead explained that the
administration's proposed television licensing renewal changes would
improve FCC procedures in that quarter. The FCC has been required to
grant applications "if the public interest, convenience, and necessity
will be served thereby," Whitehead pointed out. "This necessarily
means that the government will be involved, to some extent, in passing judgment on...the broadcaster's programing." But he also noted
that the Communications Act of 1934 "specifically denies the FCC the
'power of censorship' and the power to 'interfere with the right of free
speech of the broadcaster.' " As a result, Whitehead said, "The implementation of these two statutory goals requires a difficult balancing
act." The administration had chosen an approach to the dilemma that,
he contended, would "balance the competing goals of the Communications Act."

> Text of speech by Clay T. Whitehead, director of the
> White House Office of Telecommunications Policy, before
> the National Academy of Television Arts and Sciences in
> New York, Jan. 11, 1973:

A few weeks ago in Indianapolis, I delivered a speech which some
people misinterpreted and, even worse, quite a few people misunderstood. The speech was about the responsibilities of broadcasting licensees and about the Administration's proposal to change the license
renewal process. Most of that speech dealt with the first issue—the
licensee's responsibilities—and today I want to focus on the second
issue, and give you the facts about our license renewal bill.

Our system of broadcasting presents this country with a unique
dilemma which goes back to the basic policy embodied in the Communications Act of 1934. Section 309(a) of that Act requires the Federal
Communications Commission (FCC) to grant applications for broadcast
licenses if "the public interest, convenience, and necessity will be
served thereby." This necessarily means that the government will be
involved, to some extent, in passing judgment on the heart of the broadcast service—the broadcaster's programming. But then section 326 of
that same Act specifically denies the FCC the "power of censorship"

and the power to "interfere with the right of free speech" of the broadcaster.

The implementation of these two statutory goals requires a difficult balancing act. On the one hand, the broadcasting industry must be responsible to the public through the legal processes of the Communications Act that the public has recourse to see that this responsibility is being exercised. On the other hand, the Government can't use the Act to be too active an intermediary between the public and the industry —even with the best of intentions—because the net effect would be to make Government agents out of broadcasting licensees, rather than establish them as independent voices and sources of information in our marketplace of ideas.

The place in the federal licensing system where these competing statutory goals are most clearly evident is the license renewal process. The burden of balancing these interests is thrust squarely on the FCC's shoulders by the Communications Act, and the Act contemplates that they will be maintained in a state of equilibrium. But recently instability and uncertainty have developed in the broadcast licensing process. And when something as sensitive as licensing a medium of expression is involved, this instability and uncertainty give rise to the threat of arbitrary and subjective determinations that promote the Government's own view of what programming is good for the public to see and hear. In this unstable environment, the broadcaster will seek the shelter of whatever safe harbor is available. To ensure that his license is renewed, he will operate his station in a manner that pleases the government, and not one that best serves his local audiences.

To evaluate our proposal for restoring balance and stability to the license renewal process, it's important to know what our bill does do, and what it doesn't do. That is what has been most misunderstood and what I want to clear up for you today.

What our bill *does not* do is change the broadcaster's present obligations to be responsive to his community and to be even-handed in covering important public issues. These long-standing obligations of the broadcaster constitute the two principal criteria for license renewal in our bill: (1) the broadcaster must be substantially attuned to community needs and interests, and respond to those needs and interests in his programming—this is known as the ascertainment obligation; and (2) the broadcaster must provide reasonable opportunity for discussion of conflicting views on public issues—this is known as the fairness obligation. These criteria represent a distillation of what the public interest standard means in the context of license renewals, as stated by the Congress and the FCC.

These obligations bear repetition and emphasis, and serve as ideal criteria for license renewal because they require the broadcaster to turn toward his local audiences. He must serve *their* needs and see that *they* are adequately informed on public issues. If the broadcaster can render satisfactory service to his communities, based on these two criteria, then his license should be renewed.

Now for what our bill *does do*. It improves the license renewal process by making four changes in the present practices: (1) it extends the term of broadcast licenses from three to five years; (2) it eliminates the requirement for a comparative hearing whenever a competing application is filed for the same broadcast service; (3) it prohibits any restructuring of the broadcasting industry through the license renewal process; and (4) it prohibits the FCC from considering its own predetermined program criteria in applying the ascertainment and fairness standards of the bill.

Details of Bill's Provisions

In the interests of clarity, if not scintillating style, I'd like to bore you with the details of these provisions of our renewal bill.

The first change would be to extend broadcast license terms from three to five years. When the Communications Act was passed in 1934, the short three year license term was a reasonable precaution in dealing with a new and untried industry. A five year period, however, seems to be a more reasonable period at this stage in broadcasting history. It would inject more stability into the license renewal process and allow the broadcaster more time to determine the needs and interests of his local community and plan long-range programs of community service.

A longer renewal period would also go a long way toward lightening the serious burden that processing applications for renewal places on the FCC's resources and reducing the paperwork backlogs that cause delays in re-licensing stations. For example, as of this week, the trade press reports that 143 television and radio licenses are in limbo awaiting renewal.

Moreover, an extension to five years of the broadcaster's license does not mean he will be put out of the reach of the FCC or that he may ignore his public interest responsibilities for five years at a time. The bill would not affect the powers of the FCC to deal with complaints raised by the public. The licensee would continue to be answerable to his community at any time during the five year period.

The second change the bill would make in the renewal process would be to eliminate the requirement for a comparative hearing whenever a competing application is filed for the same broadcast service. Presently, when a broadcaster's license comes up for renewal and it is challenged by a competing application, the FCC *must* set a comparative hearing in which the competing applicant and the performance of the present applicant are evaluated together.

The FCC, under current procedures, is forbidden from exercising its independent judgment as to whether a comparative hearing is even necessary. Without initially assessing the past performance of the incumbent licensee, the FCC must throw him into a comparative hearing, which usually involves substantial expenditures of time, money and manpower. The comparative hearing is not unlike the medieval trials by battle, and the winner of this trial is not necessarily the person who will best serve the interests of the local community but rather the one who can afford to stay in the heat of battle the longest—the one with the most time, the deepest pocket, and the best lawyer. Certainly, in this day and age, we can devise more rational and equitable procedures especially when, in all cases, a substantial public interest is at stake.

Our license renewal bill would revise these procedures so that a hearing would be required only if the competing applicant has raised a substantial question regarding the present licensee's performance under the criteria set out in the bill. If the FCC determines there is no question, then the license would be renewed. Only if the Commission is unable to conclude that the licensee's performance warrants renewal would a hearing be required.

The third change in the bill would preclude the FCC from restructuring the broadcasting industry through license renewal hearings. Presently, the Commission can implement policy relating to industry structure—such as a policy restricting the types of companies that can own TV stations—through the criteria it uses to decide renewal hearings. This means the policy could be applied in a highly subjective and inconsistent manner. Restructuring of the broadcasting industry in this manner should not be allowed. Rather, if industry-wide policies are to be changed, they should be changed through the general rule-making procedures of the FCC, with full opportunities provided to the entire broadcast industry and all members of the public to participate in the proceeding.

The fourth and last change our license renewal bill would make in the renewal process would be to forbid the FCC use of predetermined performance criteria for the evaluation of renewal applications.

The Communications Act of 1934 does not anywhere define what constitutes the "public interest, convenience and necessity." And so, the responsibility for doing so has fallen on the FCC and the courts. As a result the "public interest" has come to mean no more than what the FCC and the courts want it to mean.

Presently, an important factor in determining the licensee's public interest performance is the extent to which he has programmed in 14 specific program categories predetermined by the FCC. And the trend is toward more detailed program categories, more program quotas and more percentages. The Administration's bill is designed to halt this trend toward quantification of the public interest. Confining the FCC's evaluation of the licensee's performance to the bill's ascertainment and fairness criteria makes the local community the touchstone of the concept of public service embodied in the Communications Act. Serving the local community's needs and interests instead of the desires of the Washington bureaucrats would become the broadcaster's number one priority.

You will recall my description of the dilemma that the Government faces in regard to the regulation of broadcasting. A lot of criticism that is being levelled at our license renewal bill seems to be coming from those who are unaware of this dilemma or misunderstand the present nature and extent of broadcast regulation.

The critics seem to want it both ways. They say they want to preserve absolutely the broadcaster's First Amendment rights. But they are uncomfortable about leaving such a powerful medium of expression unchecked by Government supervision. So they also feel that the public should have unrestricted rights to bring Government power to bear on the licensee at renewal time.

There is legitimate room for disagreement about how this balancing process can be best achieved. But the dilemma will not go away and those who criticize our bill can't have it both ways. Don't you want limits on Government power such as those in our bill? Or do you prefer the current scheme, with its burgeoning program categories, percentages, and renewals every three years? Do you want the Government to exercise *more* control over broadcasting? Or should the Government withdraw completely from broadcasting regulation and tell minority groups they have no recourse against the licensee?

When I say critics of our bill can't have it both ways, I mean they can't answer yes to all of these questions. There are a number of quite different, and mutually exclusive, approaches to broadcast regulation. Under one approach, we could expand the present trend of Government control and have the Government take over the broadcaster's responsibility to his local community. Under another approach, the Government could withdraw completely from regulation of broadcasting. This Administration has chosen a third approach, one that would restore equilibrium to the broadcasting system and balance the competing goals of the Communications Act. This approach relies on the exercise of more private responsibility and voluntary action by broadcast licensees who truly dedicate themselves to the communities they are licensed to serve. Which approach will you choose?

1973 REPORT ON SMOKING

January 16, 1973

Pregnant women who smoke are more likely than non-smokers to have underweight children, and the evidence is substantial that smoking increases risks of infant mortality. "Little cigars" may be as hazardous to health as cigarettes. These and other warnings were sounded by the U.S. Public Health Service in its seventh report on the health consequences of smoking. The 1973 report contained the strongest statement yet made on smoking by pregnant women. Hazards associated with smoking of little cigars were examined for the first time.

In its assessment of the risks to yet unborn children, the study estimated that 4,600 stillbirths a year in the United States could be tied to the smoking habits of the mothers. Two-thirds as many children died soon after birth as a result of the mother's smoking as died from accidents, the leading cause of death in children aged one to 14, according to the pediatrician who wrote that section of the report. However, the woman who quits smoking by the fourth month of pregnancy was found to face no greater risk of infant mortality than the non-smoking mother.

The report gave official sanction to studies which had shown that mothers who smoke bear children of lower average weight and of poorer survival prospects than do women who do not smoke. The Public Health Service said all medical studies had confirmed that mothers who smoke tend to give birth to smaller babies, but not all surveys had shown higher infant mortality. The latest report ex-

plained the reasons for differences in earlier findings and affirmed that a higher infant mortality rate could be attributable to smoking.

In a special section of the 381-page study, smokers were alerted to the dangers of little cigars. The manufacturing and packaging of this tobacco product had been similar to that of cigarettes. But "little cigars" fell under the definition of "cigar" and continued to be advertised on television after cigarette commercials were banned Jan. 2, 1971. The Federal Trade Commission urged Congress Jan. 23 to revise the Cigarette Advertising and Labeling Act of 1970 to re-define cigars weighing less than three pounds per thousand as cigarettes. The purpose of the proposed change was accomplished on Sept. 22 when President Nixon signed into law a bill adding little cigars to tobacco products that cannot be advertised on television or radio.

An adequate evaluation of the health effects of smoking the cigarette-sized cigars might take 10 to 15 years, according to the Public Health Service, but it nonetheless categorized the product as potentially dangerous. Of 25 brands tested, 22 were found to contain concentrations of carbon monoxide, hydrogencyanide, acetaldehyde, and other components in amounts comparable to those found in cigarettes. Research showed that smokers of little cigars, as of cigarettes, frequently inhaled, thus increasing the risks of lung and heart problems.

The report also raised doubts about the health consequences of smoking pipes and ordinary cigars. Such smokers were found to have mortality rates "slightly higher" than those of non-smokers, but "substantially lower" than those of cigarette smokers.

The first report concerning the health hazards of smoking was issued by the U.S. Surgeon General on Jan. 11, 1964. It found cigarette smoking a major cause of lung cancer and some other diseases. A higher incidence of coronary heart disease and pulmonary diseases among smokers was noted in the 1972 report. That study also disclosed that smoking in enclosed areas might be injurious to non-smokers in the areas as well as to the smokers themselves. (See Historic Documents, 1972, p. 45.)

The 1973 smoking report was signed by the assistant secretary for health in the Department of Health, Education and Welfare, Dr. Merlin K. DuVal. The six previous reports had been signed by the Surgeon General of the Public Health Service.

Excerpts from sections of "The Health Consequences of Smoking: January 1973" relating to smoking and pregnancy, pipe and cigar smoking, and little cigars follow:

Preface

This report is the seventh in a series issued by the Public Health Service reviewing and assessing the scientific evidence linking cigarette smoking to disease and premature death. The current report reiterates, strengthens, and extends the findings in earlier reports that cigarette smoking is a major health problem in the United States.

The evidence has broadened dramatically in recent years. A Public Health Service assessment of evidence available in 1959 was largely focused on the relationship of cigarette smoking and lung cancer. The first formal report on this subject in 1964 found that cigarette smoking was not only a major cause of lung cancer and chronic bronchitis, but was associated with illness and death from chronic bronchopulmonary disease, cardiovascular disease, and other diseases.

The 1973 report confirms all these relationships and adds new evidence in other areas as well. The evidence in the chapter on pregnancy strongly indicates a causal relationship between cigarette smoking during pregnancy and lower infant birth weight and a strong, probably causal, association between cigarette smoking and higher late fetal and neonatal mortality. Also reported is the convergence of other evidence which suggests that cigarette smoking during pregnancy interacts with other risk factors to increase the risk of an unfavorable outcome of pregnancy for certain women more than others.

For the first time in this series of reports, a separate chapter is devoted to pipe and cigar smoking and the health hazards involved. Included is an assessment of the health implications of the new small cigars which look like cigarettes.

A final chapter, new to the reports, concerns cigarette amoking and exercise performance. A review of a number of fitness tests comparing smokers to nonsmokers indicates that cigarette smoking impairs exercise performance for many types of athletic events and activities involving maximal work capacity.

The interrelationships of smoking and health are no less complex today than they were reported to be in the 1964 report. But since that time we have greatly broadened our knowledge and understanding of the problem. The current report symbolizes this progress.

Merlin K. DuVal, M.D.
Assistant Secretary for Health

PREGNANCY

Introduction

Cigarette smoking is a common habit among women of child-bearing age in the United States. In 1970, approximately one-third of American women of child-bearing age were cigarette smokers. The percentage of U.S. women who smoked throughout pregnancy is not definitely known, but is presumably lower, probably in the neighborhood of 20 to 25 percent. With a large fetal population at potential, but preventable, risk, the relationship between cigarette smoking and the outcome of pregnancy has been the focus of considerable and continuing research.

Every investigator who has examined the relationship has confirmed that the infants of women who smoke during pregnancy have a lower average birth weight than the infants of women who do not smoke during pregnancy. Much evidence indicates that cigarette smoking during pregnancy causes this reduction in infant birth weight. Several investigators have demonstrated that the fetal and neonatal mortality rate is significantly higher for the infants of smokers than for the infants of nonsmokers; other investigators have not found higher mortality for smokers' infants. Studies of the association between maternal cigarette smoking and congenital malformations have produced conflicting results....

Among all women in the United States, cigarette smokers are nearly twice as likely to deliver low birth weight infants as are nonsmokers. Assuming that 20 percent of pregnant women in the United States smoked cigarettes through the entire pregnancy (extrapolated from data on changes in smoking behavior during pregnancy collected for the British Perinatal Mortality Study), taking into account the apparently different risks of delivering a small-for-dates infant for Caucasian and non-Caucasian women who smoke during pregnancy, and considering the number of infants with a birth weight less than 2,500 grams born to Caucasian and non-Caucasian women, an excess of nearly 43,000 occurred in the 286,000 low birth weight infants among the 3,500,000 infants born in the United States in 1968, because of the increased risk among women who smoke of having small-for-dates infants.

Since neonatal mortality is higher for low birth weight infants, with gestational age held constant, the excess of small-for-dates infants among smoking mothers would imply a significant excess mortality risk as well.

Summary

1. The results of all 42 studies in which the relationship between smoking and birth weight was examined have demonstrated a strong

association between cigarette smoking and delivery of small-for-dates infants. On the average, the smoker has nearly twice the risk of delivering a low birth weight infant as that of a nonsmoker.

2. This association has been confirmed by both retrospective and prospective study designs.

3. A strong dose-response relationship has been established between cigarette smoking and the incidence of low birth weight infants. Available evidence suggests that the effect of smoking upon fetal growth reflects the number of cigarettes smoked daily during a pregnancy, and not the cumulative effect of cigarette smoking which occurred before the pregnancy began.

4. When a variety of known or suspected factors which also exert an influence upon birth weight have been controlled for, cigarette smoking has consistently been shown to be independently related to low birth weight.

5. The association has been found in many different countries, among different populations, and in a variety of geographical settings.

6. New evidence suggests that if a woman gives up smoking by the fourth month of pregnancy, her risk of delivering a low birth weight infant is similar to that of a nonsmoker.

7. The infants of smokers experience a transient acceleration of growth rate during the first six months after delivery, compared to infants of nonsmokers. This finding is compatible with viewing birth as the removal of the smoker's infant from a toxic influence.

8. The results of experiments in animals have shown that exposure to tobacco smoke or some of its ingredients results in the delivery of low birth weight offspring. New evidence demonstrates that chronic exposure of rabbits to carbon monoxide during gestation results in a dose-related reduction in the birth rate of their offspring.

9. Data from studies in humans have demonstrated that smokers' fetuses are exposed directly to agents within tobacco smoke, such as carbon monoxide, at levels comparable to those which have been shown to produce low birth weight offspring in animals.

CIGARETTE SMOKING AND FETAL AND INFANT MORTALITY

Introduction

Several previous studies of the relationship between cigarette smoking and higher fetal and infant mortality among the infants of smokers have been reviewed in the 1971 and 1972 reports on the health consequences of smoking. In many of these studies, the authors combined two or more categories of fetal and infant mortality. Different mortality outcomes, such as spontaneous abortion, stillbirth, and neonatal death, are influenced by different sets of factors. Among other factors, the frequency of abortion is influenced by congenital infections, hormonal deficiencies, and cervical incompetency. In addition to other factors, the frequency of stillbirth is influenced by premature separation of the placenta, uterine inertia, and dystocia. Along with other factors, the frequency of neonatal death is influenced by gestational maturity, birth injuries, and delivery room and nursery care. Separate analysis of the relationship of cigarette smoking to each different mortality outcome, with control of the unique set of factors which influence it, may facilitate understanding of the relationship.

Spontaneous Abortion

Previous epidemiological and experimental studies of the relationship between spontaneous abortion and cigarette smoking reviewed in the 1971 and 1972 reports on the health consequences of smoking form the basis of the following statements:

The results of several studies, both retrospective and prospective, have demonstrated a statistically significant association between maternal cigarette smoking and spontaneous abortion. Data from other studies have documented a strong dose-response relationship between the number of cigarettes smoked and the incidence of spontaneous abortions. In general, variables other than cigarette smoking (e.g., maternal age, parity, health, desire for the pregnancy, and use of medication), which may influence the incidence of spontaneous abortions, have not been controlled. The results of the one study, in which adjustment for the woman's desire for the pregnancy was performed, indicated that after such adjustment cigarette smoking during the pregnancy retained an association with spontaneous abortion of borderline significance. The time period during which cigarette smoking might exert an influence on the incidence of spontaneous abortions has not been determined. Abortions have been produced in animals only with large doses of nicotine; the relevance of these studies for humans is uncertain.

Summary

Although several investigators have found a significantly higher, dose-related incidence of spontaneous abortion among cigarette smokers as compared to nonsmokers, the lack of control of significant variables other than cigarette smoking does not permit a firm conclusion to be drawn about the nature of the relationship.

Stillbirth

Epidemiological studies of the association between cigarette smoking and stillbirth previously reviewed in the 1971 and 1972 reports on the health consequences of smoking form the basis for the following statements:

In one group of retrospective and prospective studies, a higher stillbirth rate was found for the infants of smokers as compared to those of nonsmokers. In another group of retrospective and prospective studies, no significant difference was detected in the stillbirth rate among the infants of smokers and nonsmokers. Differences in study size, numbers of cigarettes smoked, or the presence or absence of control of variables, such as age and parity, which may influence stillbirth rates, were probably not sufficient to explain the differences in results obtained.

Several recent epidemiological studies have added to our understanding of the relationship between cigarette smoking and stillbirth. Niswander and Gordon have reported data from 39,215 pregnancies followed prospectively and collected between 1959 and 1966 at 12 university hospitals in the United States. A random sample of women who presented to hospital prenatal clinics were enrolled in the study. The authors reported no increase in stillbirths among white smokers as compared with white nonsmokers. A higher incidence of stillbirths was found among black women who smoked than among nonsmoking black women, and a dose-response relationship with cigarettes smoked was suggested, although the findings did not attain statistical significance. The results were not adjusted for other variables. Rush and Kass found, in a prospective study of 3,296 pregnancies at Boston City Hospital, a nonsignificant increase in stillbirths among white women who smoked, but a statistically significant increase in stillbirths among black women who smoked. These findings are consistent with those previously outlined by Frazier, et al. and Underwood.

Rumeau-Roquette, in a prospective study of 4,824 pregnancies in Paris, demonstrated that the risk of stillbirth was significantly higher for cigarette smokers than for nonsmokers. The authors also presented evidence that a woman with either a previous stillbirth or at least one prior infant weighing less than 2,500 grams at birth was significantly more likely to have a future stillbirth infant than a woman without such an obstetrical history. After previous obstetrical history was controlled, smokers still retained a statistically significant increased risk of subsequent stillbirth as compared to nonsmokers. Of further interest was the finding that among women who previously had delivered only living infants, weighing over 2,500 grams, cigarette smoking had no influence on the stillbirth rate.

Previous experimental studies were reviewed in the 1971 and 1972 reports on the health consequences of smoking. The authors demonstrated that exposure of pregnant rabbits to tobacco smoke and pregnant rats to large doses of injected nicotine resulted in a significant increase in stillbirths.

Summary

1. The results of recent studies suggest that cigarette smoking is most strongly associated with a higher stillbirth rate among women who possess less favorable socioeconomic surroundings or an unfavorable previous obstetrical history. In the United States, black women have higher stillbirth rates than white women. The finding that cigarette smoking is associated with an even greater difference between the stillbirth rates of the two groups merits special attention. These findings may provide at least a partial explanation for the lack of a significant difference in stillbirth rates between smokers and non-smokers, which some investigators have found.

2. The results of experiments in animals demonstrate that exposure to tobacco smoke and some of its ingredients, such as nicotine, can result in a significant increase in stillbirth rate.

Late Fetal and Neonatal Deaths

Considerable variation has occurred in the definition of the study population among the studies in which the relationship of cigarette smoking to fetal mortality (other than abortion) and early infant mortality was examined. The most commonly identified study populations have been perinatal deaths, neonatal deaths, and late fetal plus neonatal deaths. Perinatal deaths are a combination of late fetal deaths (i.e., stillborn infants) and deaths occurring within the first week of life. Neonatal deaths include all deaths of liveborn infants within the first 28 days of life....

Summary

A strong, probably causal association between cigarette smoking and higher late fetal and infant mortality among smokers' infants is supported by the following evidence:

1. Twelve retrospective and prospective studies have revealed a statistically significant relationship between cigarette smoking and an elevated mortality risk among the infants of smokers. In three of these studies, of sufficient size to permit adjustment for other risk factors, a highly significant independent association between smoking and mortality was established. Part of the discrepancy in results between these studies and those in which a significant association between smoking and infant mortality was not demonstrated may be explained by a lack of adjustment for risk factors other than smoking.

2. Evidence is converging to suggest that cigarette smoking may be more harmful to the infants of some women than others; this may also, in part, explain the discrepancies between the results of the

studies in which a significantly higher mortality risk was shown for the infants of smokers compared to those of nonsmokers and the results of those studies in which significant differences in mortality risk were not found.

3. Within groups of similar birth weight, the infants of nonsmokers appear to have a higher mortality risk than do the infants of cigarette smokers. This results from the fact that the infants of nonsmokers within such similar birth weight groups are on the average gestationally less mature than the infants of cigarette smokers. Available evidence indicates that within groups of similar gestational age, infants of lower birth weight experience a higher mortality risk. Since the infants of cigarette smokers are small-for-gestational age, one should expect that if the infants of cigarette smokers and nonsmokers are compared within similar gestational age classes, the infants of cigarette smokers would have the higher mortality rate.

4. The results of recent studies have documented a statistically significant dose-response relationship between the number or amount of cigarettes smoked and late fetal and neonatal mortality.

5. New data suggest that if a woman gives up smoking by the fourth month of pregnancy, she will have the same risk of incurring a fetal or neonatal loss as a nonsmoker.

6. Available evidence strongly supports cigarette smoking as one cause of fetal growth retardation. The causes of excess deaths among the infants of smokers are those associated with small-for-dates babies.

7. Data from experiments in animals have demonstrated that exposure to tobacco smoke or some of its ingredients, such as nicotine or carbon monoxide, results in a significant increase in late fetal and/or neonatal deaths.

8. The results of studies in humans have shown that the fetus of a smoking mother may be directly exposed to agents such as carbon monoxide within tobacco smoke, at levels comparable to those which have been shown to produce stillbirth in experimental animals....

PIPES AND CIGARS

Introduction

This chapter is a review of the epidemiological, pathological and experimental data on the health consequences of smoking cigars and pipes, alone, together, and in various combinations with cigarettes. Previous reviews on the health consequences of smoking have dealt primarily with cigarette smoking. Although some of the material on pipes and cigars presented in this chapter has been presented in previous reports of the Surgeon General, this is the first attempt to summarize what is known about the health effects of pipe and cigar smoking. Since the use of pipes and cigars is limited almost exclusively to men in the United States, only data on men are included in this review.

The influence of pipe and cigar smoking on health is determined by examining the overall and specific mortality and morbidity experienced by users of these forms of tobacco compared to nonsmokers. Epidemiological evidence suggests that individuals who limit their smoking to only pipes or cigars have overall mortality rates that are slightly higher than nonsmokers. For certain specific causes of death, however, pipe and cigar smokers experience mortality rates that are as great as or exceed those experienced by cigarette smokers. This analysis becomes more complex when combinations of smoking forms are examined. The overall mortality rates of those who smoke pipes, cigars, or both in combination with cigarettes appear to be intermediate between the high mortality rates of cigarette smokers and the lower rates of those who smoke only pipes or cigars. This might seem to suggest that smoking pipes or cigars in combination with cigarettes diminishes the harmful effects of cigarette smoking. However, an analysis of mortality associated with smoking combinations of cigarettes, pipes, and cigars should be standardized for the level of consumption of each of the products smoked in terms of the amount smoked, duration of smoking, and the depth and degree of inhalation. For example, cigar smokers who also smoke a pack of cigarettes a day might be expected to have mortality rates somewhat higher than those who smoke only cigarettes at the level of a pack a day, assuming that both groups smoke their cigarettes in the same way. Mixed smokers who inhale pipe or cigar smoke in a manner similar to the way they smoke cigarettes might be expected to have higher mortality rates than mixed smokers who do not inhale their cigars and pipes and also resist inhaling their cigarettes. Unfortunately, little of the published material on mixed cigarette, pipe, and cigar smoking contains these types of analyses or controls.

A paradox seems to exist between the mortality rates of ex-smokers of pipes and cigars and ex-smokers of cigarettes. Ex-cigarette smokers experience a relative decline in overall and certain specific causes of mortality following cessation. This decline is important but indirect evidence that cigarette smoking is a major cause of the elevated mortality rates experienced by current cigarette smokers. In contrast to this finding, several prospective epidemiological investigations...have reported higher death rates for ex-pipe and ex-cigar smokers than for current pipe and cigar smokers. This phenomenon was analyzed by Hammond and Garfinkel. The development of ill health often results in a cigarette smoker giving up the habit, reducing his daily tobacco consumption, switching to pipes or cigars, or choosing a cigarette low in "tar" and nicotine. In many instances, a smoking-related disease is the cause of ill health. Thus, the group of ex-smokers includes some people who are ill from smoking-related diseases, and death rates are high among persons in ill health.

As a result, ex-cigarette smokers initially have higher overall and specific mortality rates than continuing cigarette smokers, but because of the relative decrease in mortality that occurs in those who quit smoking for reasons other than ill health, and because of the dwindling number of ill ex-smokers, a relative decrease in mortality is observed (within a few years) following cessation of cigarette smoking. The beneficial effects of cessation would be obvious sooner were it not for the high mortality rates of those who quit smoking for reasons of illness. A similar principle operates for ex-pipe and ex-cigar smokers, but because of the lower initial risk of smoking these forms and therefore the smaller margin of benefit following cessation, the effect produced by the ill ex-smokers creates a larger and more persistent impact on the mortality rates than is seen in cigarette smoking.

For the above reasons a bias is introduced into the mortality rates of current smokers and ex-smokers of pipes and cigars, so that a more accurate picture of mortality might be obtained by combining the ex-smokers with the current smokers and looking at the resultant mortality experience.

Because of a lack of data that would allow a precise analysis of mortality among ex-pipe and ex-cigar smokers, a detailed analysis of these groups could not be undertaken in this review....

LITTLE CIGARS

In the past year, several new brands of little cigars (weighing three pounds or less per 1,000) have appeared on the national market. These cigarette-sized products are manufactured, packaged, advertised, and sold in a manner similar to cigarettes. Little cigars enjoy several legal advantages over cigarettes: They have access to television advertising; they are taxed by the Federal Government and by most states, at much lower rates than cigarettes, resulting in a significant price advantage; and they do not carry the warning label required on cigarette packages and in cigarette advertising. A market appears to be developing for these products, as there has recently been a sharp increase in the shipment of little cigars destined for domestic consumption.

It is important to estimate the potential public health impact of these little cigars. An adequate epidemiological evaluation of the effect of little cigar smoking on health could take 10 to 15 years and is probably an impractical consideration; however, a review of the epidemiological, autopsy, and experimental data concerning the health consequences of cigarette, pipe, and cigar smoking summarized in this and previous reports is helpful in considering the potential impact on health of smoking little cigars. An analysis of the chemical constituents suggests that both cigarettes and cigars contain similar compounds in similar concentrations. Two exceptions are reducing sugars, which are not found in quantity in the fermented tobacco commonly used in cigars, and the pH of the inhaled smoke. The pH[hydrogen concentration factor]of the smoke from U.S. commercial cigarettes is below 6.2 from the first to the last puff, whereas the smoke from the last half of a cigar may reach as high as pH 8 to 9. With increasing pH, nicotine is increasingly present in the smoke as the free base. Skin painting experiments in mice indicate that tumor yields with cigar or pipe "tars" are nearly identical with those obtained with cigarette "tars." In addition, the epidemiological data suggest that depth of inhalation probably accounts for the fact that cigarettes are so much more harmful than cigars and pipes in contributing to the development of lung cancer, coronary heart disease, and non-neoplastic respiratory disease. For such diseases as cancer of the oral cavity, larynx, and esophagus, where smoke from cigars, pipes, and cigarettes is available to the target organ at comparable levels, the mortality ratios are very similar for all three forms of tobacco use. Several factors, including "tar," nicotine and the pH of the smoke, probably operate to influence inhalation patterns of smokers. The relative contribution of individual factors to the inhalability of a tobacco product has not been determined.

Smoking those brands of little cigars which can be inhaled by a significant portion of the population in a manner similar to the present use of cigarettes would probably result in an increased risk of developing those pulmonary and cardiovascular diseases which have been associated with cigarette smoking. On the other hand, smoking those little cigars which are used like most large cigars whereby the smoke is rarely inhaled would probably result in lower rates of those pulmonary and cardiovascular diseases than would be found among cigarette smokers.

Only a limited analysis is available comparing the chemical compounds found in little cigars, cigarettes, and large cigars. The FTC [Federal Trade Commission] analyzed the "tar" and nicotine content of all the little cigars and cigarettes currently available on the market. Little cigars have generally a higher "tar" and nicotine level than cigarettes, although considerable overlap results in some little cigar brands having "tar" and nicotine levels comparable to those of some brands of cigarettes. Hoffmann and Wynder recently compared three brands of little cigars with an unfiltered cigarette, a filtered cigarette, and a large cigar. They measured a number of smoke constituents, including: "tar," nicotine, carbon monoxide, carbon dioxide, reducing sugars, hydrogen cyanide, acetaldehyde, acrolein, pyridines, phenols, benz(a)anthracene, and benzo(a)pyrene. Cigarette A was the Kentucky reference cigarette, cigarette B was a popular brand of filter cigarette. Cigar A was an 85 mm. little cigar, cigar B was an 85 mm. little cigar, cigar C was a 95 mm. small cigar, and cigar D was a 112 mm. popular brand of medium sized cigar.

The smoke pH was analyzed puff by puff. Cigarette smoke was found to be acidic (pH less than 7) for the entire cigarette. The smoke from little cigars became alkaline only in the last puff or two, whereas about the last 40 percent of the puffs from the larger cigar were alkaline. Although the pH of the total condensate obtained from cigarettes is usually acidic and the total condensate obtained from cigars is usually alkaline, the above data indicate that smoke pH of tobacco products changes during the combustion process. Smoke from large cigars may be acidic during the first portion of the smoke and not become alkaline until the last half of the cigar is smoked.

Brunneman and Hoffmann, using the same techniques described above, examined the effect of 60 leaf constituents on smoke pH. For several varieties of cigarette tobacco, they found a high correlation between the total alkaloid and nitrogen content and smoke pH. Stalk position also affected smoke pH. Tobacco leaves near the top of the plant, which contain high levels of "tar" and nicotine, yielded a smoke with a much higher pH than leaves lower on the plant. At present it is not known to what extent these factors influence the pH of the smoke of tobaccos commonly used in cigars or how these kinds of pH changes influence the inhalability of tobacco smoke.

The inhalation of smoke, however, appears to be the most important factor determining the impact a cigar will have on overall health. Those physical and chemical characteristics of a tobacco product which most influence inhalation of tobacco smoke have not been accurately determined. Nevertheless, it appears likely that the smoke of some brands of cigars may be compatible with inhalation by a significant portion of the smoking population, since (a) little cigars have "tar" and nicotine levels which, in some brands, are similar to the levels found in cigarettes, and (b) the pH of the smoke of some little cigar brands is acidic for the major portion of the little cigar and becomes alkaline only in the last puff or two.

It is reasonable to conclude that smoking little cigars may result in health effects similar to those associated with smoking cigarettes if little cigars are smoked in amounts and with patterns of inhalation similar to those used by cigarette smokers, for the reasons cited above, and these additional reasons: (a) In those little cigars for which preliminary data are available, the concentrations of carbon monoxide, hydrogen cyanide, acetaldehyde, acrolein, pyridine, phenol, and polycyclic hydrocarbon levels are comparable to those found in cigarettes; (b) cigarette smokers who switch to cigars appear to be more likely to inhale cigar smoke than cigar smokers who have always smoked cigars; and (c) cigarette smokers who switch to little cigars may be inclined to use them as they did cigarettes because of the physical similarities between the little cigars and cigarettes, including their size and shape, the number in a package, the burning rate, and the time it takes to smoke them....

Conclusions

Pipe and cigar smokers in the United States as a group experience overall mortality rates that are slightly higher than those of non-smokers, but these rates are substantially lower than those of cigarette smokers. This appears to be due to the fact that the total exposure to smoke that a pipe or cigar smoker receives from these products is relatively low. The typical cigar smoker smokes fewer than five cigars a day and the typical pipe smoker smokes less than 20 pipefuls a day. Most pipe and cigar smokers report that they do not inhale the smoke. Those who do inhale, inhale infrequently and only slightly. As a result, the harmful effects of cigar and pipe smoking appear to be largely limited to increased death rates from cancer at those sites which are exposed to the smoke of these products. Mortality rates from cancer of the oral cavity, intrinsic and extrinsic larynx, pharynx, and esophagus are approximately equal in users of cigars, pipes, and cigarettes. Inhalation is evidently not necessary to expose these sites to tobacco smoke. Although these are serious forms of cancer, they account for only about 5 percent of the cancer mortality among men.

Coronary heart disease, lung cancer, emphysema, chronic bronchitis, cancer of the pancreas, and cancer of the urinary bladder are diseases which are clearly associated with cigarette smoking, but for cigar and pipe smokers death rates from these diseases are not greatly elevated above the rates of nonsmokers. These diseases seem to depend on moderate to deep inhalation to bring the smoke into direct contact with the tissue at risk or to allow certain constituents, such as carbon monoxide, to be systematically absorbed through the lungs or to affect the temporal patterns of absorption of other constituents such as nicotine that can be absorbed either through the oral mucosa or through the lungs. Evidence from countries where smokers tend to consume more cigars and inhale them to a greater degree than in the United States indicates that rates of lung cancer become elevated to levels approaching those of cigarette smokers.

Available data on the chemical constituents of cigar, pipe, and cigarette smoke suggest that there are marked similarities in the composition of these products. Pipe and cigar smoke, however, tends to be more alkaline than cigarette smoke, and fermented tobaccos commonly used in pipes and cigars contain less reducing sugars than the rapidly dried varieties commonly used in cigarettes.

Experimental evidence suggests that little difference exists between the tumorigenic activities of "tars" obtained from cigar or cigarette tobaccos. Malignant skin tumors appear somewhat more rapidly and in larger numbers in animals whose skin has been painted with cigar "tars" than in those animals painted with cigarette "tars."

One must conclude that some risk exists from smoking cigars and pipes as they are currently used in the United States, but for most diseases this is small compared to the risk of smoking cigarettes as they are commonly used. Nevertheless, changes in patterns of usage that would bring about increased exposure either through increased individual use of cigars and pipes or increased inhalation of pipe and cigar smoke have the potential of producing risks not unlike those now incurred by cigarette smokers. Mechanical or chemical modifications of pipe tobacco and cigars that would result in a smoke more compatible with inhalation could have this effect.

NIXON'S SECOND INAUGURAL

January 20, 1973

Richard Milhous Nixon, 37th President of the United States, was sworn in for his second term a few seconds after the stroke of noon Jan. 20. Chief Justice Warren E. Burger administered the oath of office at the East Front of the Capitol in the nation's 47th inaugural ceremony. The occasion was marked by traditional military pomp, prayers for peace, and boycotting of the ceremony by a number of members of Congress disturbed by the President's alleged usurpation of congressional authority. A group of anti-war demonstrators was gathered several blocks away.

Mr. Nixon stood bareheaded and without an overcoat despite the 40-degree temperature and a chill wind gusting up to 30 miles an hour. Midway through his 1,700-word second inaugural address, he sounded its main theme: "Abroad and at home, the time has come to turn away from the condescending policies of paternalism—of 'Washington knows best.' Let us encourage individuals at home and nations abroad to do more for themselves and decide more for themselves."

The first half of the address applied this philosophy in terms of foreign relations. The United States would honor its treaties and other international obligations and do its share in defending freedom around the world, but others would have to do their share too. "The time has passed when America will make every other nation's conflict our own, or make every other nation's future our responsibility, or presume to tell the people of other nations how to manage their own affairs."

This observation bore special significance in view of the turmoil in the United States during the Vietnam War years and the widespread belief that American involvement in the war had stemmed from a post-World War II policy of intervening anywhere communism threatened. Only 12 years before, President John F. Kennedy had said in his inaugural address: "Let every nation know, whether it wishes us well or ill, that we shall pay any price, bear any burden, meet any hardship, support any friend, oppose any foe to assure the survival and success of liberty." Although Nixon made no specific mention of Vietnam or Indochina, he assured his listeners more than once that "we stand on the threshold of a new era of peace." Three days later, he announced that an agreement had been reached to end the war.

Distrust of Social Programs

The President received the biggest applause from the 50,000 persons packed into temporary bleachers and standing sections when he signaled his distrust of multitudinous government social programs: "Government must learn to take less from people so that people can do more for themselves." Just as he appeared anxious to reverse America's cold-war policies, so did he seem determined to reverse the trend of federal problem-solving that began in New Deal days: "I offer no promise of a purely governmental solution for every problem. We have lived too long with that false promise. In trusting too much to government, we have asked of it more than it can deliver. This leads only to inflated expectations, to reduced individual effort and to a disappointment and frustration that erode confidence both in what government can do and in what people can do." A striking point in the address was an adaptation of John F. Kennedy's inaugural rhetoric by which Nixon called on Americans to "ask...not just what will government do for me, but what can I do for myself?"

Nixon's second inaugural was, as are most such addresses, the product of its times. In 1969, the President had squeaked to a narrow victory, a war was raging on the other side of the world, the cities were plagued by riots, and the college campuses were torn by student unrest. Four years later, Nixon had won a smashing re-election victory, the war was drawing to a close, and the cities and campuses were quiet.

National unity was the theme of the first inaugural. (See Historic Documents, 1972, p. 73.) In 1969, Nixon had reached out to the youth, the blacks and other minorities with promises that they would be given better housing, education and an enhanced quality of life: "Those who have been left out, we will try to bring in," the President had said. "Those left behind we will help catch up." In 1973, he said: "Let us remember that America was not built by government but by people—

not by welfare, but by work—not by shirking responsibility, but by seeking responsibility."

There were similarities, also, between the two speeches. In 1969, mindful of dissension caused by the war, Nixon admonished Americans that "We cannot learn from one another until we stop shouting at one another." In 1973, with peace near, he asked the people to debate their differences "with civility and decency." Something of 1973's emphasis on less reliance on Washington had been forecast in 1969 when the President had said: "We are approaching the limits of what government alone can do."

Congress divided along party lines in its reaction to the 1973 address. Republicans generally praised it as inspiring, but Democrats thought it lacked specifics, especially on Vietnam. The President had refused to discuss the war prior to announcement of the cease-fire agreement. Senate Minority Leader Hugh Scott (Pa.) said the speech "set the tone Americans are looking for to bring a lasting peace." Rep. Thomas P. O'Neill Jr. (D Mass.), the new House Majority Leader, described the address as "a couple of platitudes and promises." California Gov. Ronald Reagan expressed pleasure at the President's call for less government, but Sen. Walter F. Mondale (D Minn.) feared the consequences of a resultant trimming of the domestic budget.

While the inaugural parade from the Capitol to the White House was in progress, anti-war demonstrators, estimated to number anywhere from 25,000 to 100,000, marched from the Lincoln Memorial to the Washington Monument. There they were addressed by several members of Congress, including Rep. Bella S. Abzug (D N.Y.) and Sen. Philip A. Hart (D Mich.). Thirty-two House members had endorsed the rally.

Text of President Nixon's second inaugural address, Jan. 20, 1973:

Mr. Vice President, Mr. Speaker, Mr. Chief Justice, Senator Cook, Mrs. Eisenhower, and my fellow citizens of this great and good country we share together:

When we met here 4 years ago, America was bleak in spirit, depressed by the prospect of seemingly endless war abroad and of destructive conflict at home.

As we meet here today, we stand on the threshold of a new era of peace in the world.

The central question before us is: How shall we use that peace?

Let us resolve that this era we are about to enter will not be what other postwar periods have so often been: a time of retreat and isolation that leads to stagnation at home and invites new danger abroad.

81

Let us resolve that this will be what it can become: a time of great responsibilities greatly borne, in which we renew the spirit and the promise of America as we enter our third century as a Nation.

This past year saw far-reaching results from our new policies for peace. By continuing to revitalize our traditional friendships, and by our missions to Peking and to Moscow, we were able to establish the base for a new and more durable pattern of relationships among the nations of the world. Because of America's bold initiatives, 1972 will be long remembered as the year of the greatest progress since the end of World War II toward a lasting peace in the world.

The peace we seek in the world is not the flimsy peace which is merely an interlude between wars, but a peace which can endure for generations to come.

It is important that we understand both the necessity and the limitations of America's role in maintaining that peace.

Unless we in America work to preserve the peace, there will be no peace.

Unless we in America work to preserve freedom, there will be no freedom.

But let us clearly understand the new nature of America's role, as a result of the new policies we have adopted over these past 4 years.

We shall respect our treaty commitments.

We shall support vigorously the principle that no country has the right to impose its will or rule on another by force.

We shall continue, in this era of negotiation, to work for the limitation of nuclear arms and to reduce the danger of confrontation between the great powers.

We shall do our share in defending peace and freedom in the world. But we shall expect others to do their share.

The time has passed when America will make every other nation's conflict our own, or make every other nation's future our responsibility, or presume to tell the people of other nations how to manage their own affairs.

Just as we respect the right of each nation to determine its own future, we also recognize the responsibility of each nation to secure its own future.

Just as America's role is indispensable in preserving the world's peace, so is each nation's role indispensable in preserving its own peace.

Together with the rest of the world, let us resolve to move forward from the beginnings we have made. Let us continue to bring down the walls of hostility which have divided the world for too long, and to build in their place bridges of understanding—so that despite profound differences between systems of government, the people of the world can be friends.

Let us build a structure of peace in the world in which the weak are as safe as the strong, in which each respects the right of the other to live by a different system, in which those who would influence others will do so by the strength of their ideas and not by the force of their arms.

Let us accept that high responsibility not as a burden, but gladly—gladly because the chance to build such a peace is the noblest endeavor in which a nation can engage; gladly also because only if we act greatly in meeting our responsibilities abroad will we remain a great Nation, and only if we remain a great Nation will we act greatly in meeting our challenges at home.

We have the chance today to do more than ever before in our history to make life better in America—to ensure better education, better health, better housing, better transportation, a cleaner environment—to restore respect for law, to make our communities more livable—and to ensure the God-given right of every American to full and equal opportunity.

Because the range of our needs is so great, because the reach of our opportunities is so great, let us be bold in our determination to meet those needs in new ways.

Just as building a structure of peace abroad has required turning away from old policies that have failed, so building a new era of progress at home requires turning away from old policies that have failed.

Abroad, the shift from old policies to new has not been a retreat from our responsibilities, but a better way to peace.

And at home, the shift from old policies to new will not be a retreat from our responsibilities, but a better way to progress.

Abroad and at home, the key to those new responsibilities lies in the placing and the division of responsibility. We have lived too long with the consequences of attempting to gather all power and responsibility in Washington.

Abroad and at home, the time has come to turn away from the condescending policies of paternalism—of "Washington knows best."

A person can be expected to act responsibly only if he has responsibility. This is human nature. So let us encourage individuals at home and nations abroad to do more for themselves, to decide more for themselves. Let us locate responsibility in more places. And let us measure what we will do for others by what they will do for themselves.

That is why today I offer no promise of a purely governmental solution for every problem. We have lived too long with that false promise. In trusting too much in government, we have asked of it more than it can deliver. This leads only to inflated expectations, to reduced individual effort, and to a disappointment and frustration that erode confidence both in what government can do and in what people can do.

Government must learn to take less from people so that people can do more for themselves.

Let us remember that America was built not by government, but by people—not by welfare, but by work—not by shirking responsibility, but by seeking responsibility.

In our own lives, let each of us ask—not just what will government do for me, but what can I do for myself?

In the challenges we face together, let each of us ask—not just how can government help, but how can I help?

Your National Government has a great and vital role to play. And I pledge to you that where this Government should act, we will act boldly and we will lead boldly. But just as important is the role that each and every one of us must play, as an individual and as a member of his own community.

From this day forward, let each of us make a solemn commitment in his own heart: to bear his responsibility, to do his part, to live his ideals—so that together, we can see the dawn of a new age of progress for America, and together, as we celebrate our 200th anniversary as a nation, we can do so proud in the fulfillment of our promise to ourselves and to the world.

As America's longest and most difficult war comes to an end, let us again learn to debate our differences with civility and decency. And let each of us reach out for that one precious quality government cannot provide—a new level of respect for the rights and feelings of one another, a new level of respect for the individual human dignity which is the cherished birthright of every American.

Above all else, the time has come for us to renew our faith in ourselves and in America.

In recent years, that faith has been challenged.

Our children have been taught to be ashamed of their country, ashamed of their parents, ashamed of America's record at home and its role in the world.

At every turn we have been beset by those who find everything wrong with America and little that is right. But I am confident that this will not be the judgment of history on these remarkable times in which we are privileged to live.

America's record in this century has been unparalleled in the world's history for its responsibility, for its generosity, for its creativity, and for its progress.

Let us be proud that our system has produced and provided more freedom and more abundance, more widely shared, than any system in the history of the world.

Let us be proud that in each of the four wars in which we have been engaged in this century, including the one we are now bringing to an end, we have fought not for our selfish advantage, but to help others resist aggression.

And let us be proud that by our bold, new initiatives, by our steadfastness for peace with honor, we have made a breakthrough toward creating in the world what the world has not known before—a structure of peace that can last, not merely for our time, but for generations to come.

We are embarking here today on an era that presents challenges as great as those any nation, or any generation, has ever faced.

We shall answer to God, to history, and to our conscience for the way in which we use these years.

As I stand in this place, so hallowed by history, I think of others who have stood here before me. I think of the dreams they had for America and I think of how each recognized that he needed help far beyond himself in order to make those dreams come true.

Today I ask your prayers that in the years ahead I may have God's help in making decisions that are right for America and I pray for your help so that together we may be worthy of our challenge.

Let us pledge together to make these next 4 years the best 4 years in America's history, so that on its 200th birthday America will be as young and as vital as when it began, and as bright a beacon of hope for all the world.

Let us go forward from here confident in hope, strong in our faith in one another, sustained by our faith in God who created us, and striving always to serve His purpose.

▼▼▼

MCGOVERN AT OXFORD

January 21, 1973

Sen. George McGovern took a discouraging view of the American condition in a speech on Jan. 21 at St. Catherine's College, Oxford University, England. The defeated Democratic nominee for President deplored the "exhaustion" and "dispirit" of the Congress, the political parties, the liberal tradition and the press. The American people, he said, had been wearied by a succession of disappointments and frustrations and had been "oversold" on social programs to the point that "now they are wary of buying even sensible and essential social progress from any political leader." He believed that "this mood was central to the outcome of the 1972 election."

The senator's speech aroused indignant comment at home. Sen. Barry Goldwater (R Ariz.) said in the Senate, Jan. 23, that he was "astounded" by what he called "one of the major examples of bad taste that I have ever seen in American politics." A Washington Post *editorial asserted that McGovern had "indulged his penchant for casual and damaging overstatement" and termed the speech "a model of what a Democratic Party leader should not be thinking or saying at the moment."*

Yet there were positive aspects to the speech. The senator, looking to Congress for revitalization of the American political process, summoned the House and the Senate to "exercise positive leadership" in order to turn the United States away from the path to presidential "one-man rule." And he made specific recommendations designed to strengthen the legislative branch. (See p. 12 for text of plan to revitalize Congress submitted by the National Committee for an Effective Congress.)

Appealing to American liberals to "reverse the 40-year trend toward a stronger President and return to the 200-year-old tradition of shared power," McGovern said he was "convinced still that the society to which America should aspire is a liberal one." He voiced the belief that "an institutional revival of the Congress not only can lead America in a new direction; it can also spark a similar institutional revival outside government."

Excerpts from speech of Sen. George McGovern (D S.D.), Jan. 21, 1973, at St. Catherine's College, Oxford University:

I am grateful for your generous invitation to discuss the future of American politics. Let me begin with the past in order to explain the present, and then explore the possibilities of the future.

Just why the American electorate gave the present administration such an overwhelming mandate in November remains something of a mystery to me. I do not expect ever to find a fully satisfactory answer. I firmly believed throughout 1971 that the major hurdle to winning the Presidency was winning the Democratic nomination. I believed that any reasonable Democrat could defeat President Nixon. I now think that no one could have defeated him in 1972. And I am not certain that the Democratic Congress will hold him in check for the next four years. I am convinced that the United States is closer to one-man rule than at any time in our history—and this paradoxically by a President who is not popular.

Fundamentally, we have experienced an exhaustion of important institutions in America. Today only the Presidency is activist and strong, while other traditional centers of power are timid and depleted. This is why one man in the White House was able for so long to continue a conflict hated by so many of his countrymen.

The institution of Congress has been exhausted by Executive encroachment and legislative paralysis. For a decade, a war was waged without Congressional approval; for years, that war raged on in part due to Congressional inaction. The representatives of the people proved unwilling to end a policy opposed by the people.

But the impotence of Congress and the omnipotence of the Presidency have deeper roots and a longer history. In 1933, the Senate and the House passed Administration bills almost before they were printed or read. It was a time of crisis. But in the years since then, the Congress has acted as though the crisis were permanent. We now appear to accept the curious notion that the legislative initiative rests with the Executive branch. Indeed, students of American government are themselves surprised at the startling fact that nearly 90% of the legislation the Congress considers originates with the Administration.

And in the last generation, Presidential activism and Congressional passivity have been even more pronounced in the field of foreign policy. Congress was not asked for approval in the 1950s before the American troops were dispatched to Korea and Lebanon. The chairman of the Senate Foreign Relations Committee, who advised against the Bay of Pigs invasion, was ignored, while other members of Congress were not even consulted. The Senate was assured that the Gulf of Tonkin Resolution was no writ for a wider war; it was then used as an excuse for the widest war since 1945.

Now this tide—which has ebbed and flowed for four decades—has crested at a new high. Just before Christmas, the President, in the flush of his electoral landslide, unleashed the most barbarous bombing of the war without even forewarning the Congress. He then refused to explain it or to permit any of his subordinates to explain it.... The President's defense for his silence was that he was invoking the American doctrine of executive privilege, which is supposed to protect certain limited types of communication within the executive branch. The truth is that he was abusing executive privilege, which is not supposed to prevent review and the exercise of responsibility by the legislative branch.

Constitutional Rights of Congress

Our Constitution, like yours, is an organic document. Although the first Americans sketched the essential outlines of government, they wisely left the embellishment of the relationship among its three branches to experience. Thus, the assignment of specific authority is only in a few instances explicit. But among the rights clearly assigned to the Congress are the powers of war and peace and the power of the purse. The power to make or unmake war, as I have already suggested, has been stripped almost completely from the Senate and the House. And now, for the first time, the Executive has mounted a serious challenge to the Congressional control of appropriations. Perhaps the Congress invited this attack by a complacent acquiescence in the Vietnam disaster; in any case, the battle is on, and the Congress is losing.

Last fall, we submitted to the President a bill to clean up our nation's waterways. He vetoed the bill, and we passed it again over his veto. He then simply refused to spend the money as Congress directed. The success of this tactic was followed by the impoundment of funds for other domestic programs. Most incredibly, at the end of the last legislative session the President demanded that the Congress rubber-stamp such impoundments in advance. He asked us to agree to set a budgetary ceiling within which the sole power of appropriation was reserved to the executive branch. Even more incredible was the speed with which the House of Representatives approved this request, and its relatively narrow defeat in the Senate. And after Congress refused the President this authority, he just took it. One wonders why he even bothered to ask.

This is not the way of a government of laws or even of men, but of one man. Today the United States is moving dangerously in that direction. The Congress seems incapable of stopping what it opposes or securing what it seeks. It has been described by a Republican Senator as a "third or fourth-rate power" in Washington. And it may be fairly asked whether the Congress of the United States in the seventh decade of this century is in peril of going the way of the House of Lords in the first decade. The difference is that the diminution of the Lords made English government more democratic, while the diminution of the Congress makes American government more dictatorial.

And the exhaustion of the Congress is matched by the exhaustion of the political parties. The Republican Party, reduced to utter vassalage by the White House, offers little more than an administrative program. They offer the politics of efficiency—but to what end and impact?.... At the same time, the loyal opposition is neither loyal to a specific set of ideas nor effective in its opposition. The Democratic Party is in peril of becoming a party of incumbency out of power, much like the Whigs of the 19th Century—a party with no principles, no programs, living only from day to day, caring only for the perquisites of office, doing nothing, and worse, not caring that nothing is done. Though important and, I believe, enduring reforms have opened the Democratic Party to broader citizen participation, the purposes for which it stands remain disputed and undefined. For twenty-eight of the last forty years, those purposes were set by Democratic Presidents in the White House. Today, the party consists largely of fragments and factions, often still divided along the same lines as in 1968, when pro-administration and anti-war forces contended for its soul....

Exhaustion of the Press

But perhaps the most discouraging development of recent years is the exhaustion of the institution of the press. Under constant pressure from an administration that appears to believe that the right of a free press is the right to print or say what they agree with, the media have yielded subtly but substantially. During the campaign, I was subject to the close, critical reporting that is a tradition in American politics. It was not always comfortable, but it is always necessary. Yet Mr. Nixon escaped a similar scrutiny. The press never really laid a glove on him, and they seldom told the people that he was hiding or that his plans for the next four years were hidden. Six days after the Watergate gang was run to the ground, Mr. Nixon invited reporters into his office, and submitted to the only interrogation his managers allowed during the fall campaign. Not a single reporter could gather the courage to ask a question about the bugging and burglary of the Democratic National Committee....

And the exhaustion of American institutions is matched by an exhaustion of the American spirit. This even touches some liberal intellectuals, traditionally the most tireless group in America. Today you can hear such liberals saying that government cannot make any real difference for good in the lives of people—that whatever it touches will turn to failure.... The same dispirit envelops millions of other Americans.... They were oversold on the social experiments of the 1960s; now they are wary of buying even sensible and essential social progress from any political leader.... To my mind, this mood was central to the outcome of the 1972 election....

An Elective Dictatorship

Only a few years ago, liberal scholarship still celebrated the strong executive and sought to strengthen it even more. Now we have learned that the Presidency, too, is a neutral instrument, that power in the White House can be abused as well as used—that a reactionary or a warmaker can also read Richard Neustadt and James McGregor Burns.

Twice now our answer has been attempts to change the person in the Presidency. Both times we have ended in at least as much difficulty as we were before. It is now almost four years until the next national election. It is also time to ask whether American progressives should continue to rely on a quadrennial chance to capture what is becoming an elective dictatorship. We may lose again as we have before. And liberty is the real loser when so much authority is vested in a single office. There will be plenty of time to prepare for the next campaign. But now is the time for a determined effort to change, not the person in the White House, but the power of the Presidency. American liberals must reverse the forty-year trend toward a stronger President and return to the two-hundred-year-old tradition of shared power.

The Supreme Court is subject to fate and executive appointment, with only the Senate standing between the court and an ideological coup. So the true priority is to protect the place of the Congress in the Federal system. We must seek a pluralism of power, where Congress and the President guard and prod each other.

Some political scientists claim that this is the wrong aim. They say: Only the President can lead because only the President has a mandate. But Congress has a constructive mandate, made by a blend and balance of the regional interests reflected in each member's election. And that constructive mandate can be as effective as the President's universal mandate. The Congress can work to check the Executive and to move the country. It can seek cooperation with the President; it can also shape a kind of cooperative tension with him that can make change happen. In the words of an ancient philosopher: "That which is in opposition is in concert, and from things that differ comes... harmony."

In pursuit of a pluralism of power, the Congress has powerful weapons at its disposal. And after executive provocation without peer or precedent, the legislative branch at long last seems ready to act. Now the Congress must exert its authority to achieve a full measure of influence. For example, when the legislation that allows the President to control wages and prices comes up for renewal, the Senate and the House should not issue another blank check. We should include safeguards to assure that profits, dividends and interest rates are never again permitted a special break while the wages of workers bear the full burden. But the Congress should not wait for such opportunities. It should mount a consistent and coherent effort, founded on its foremost power—control over appropriations. James Madison wrote in *The Federalist Papers,* number 58:

> "The power over the purse may, in fact, be regarded as the most complete and effectual weapon with which any constitution can arm the immediate representatives of the people, for obtaining a redress of every grievance, and for carrying into effect every just and salutary measure."

This insight is borne out in the history of your own land. For five centuries, from Edward I to George III, English liberty was purchased piece by piece by the Parliamentary power of the purse. And in 1973, the Congressional power of the purse can sustain American liberty. It can be used to stop the abuse of executive privilege. Part or perhaps all of an appropriation could be conditioned on the Administration's consent for the appropriate officials to testify before House and Senate Committees.

It can be used to stop executive wars by whim. The Congress must refuse to fund conflicts it has not declared or even decided to fight. From the tragedy and travail of Vietnam, the Congress at least must learn the truth of Edmund Burke's warning: "The thing you fight for is not the thing which you recover; but depreciated, sunk, wasted and consumed in the contest." American ideals have been depreciated. American wealth has been sunk. Human lives have been wasted, and Indochina itself has been consumed in the contest. The United States must fight when the course is right. But never again should the Congress allow young American lives to be lost for the defense of a corrupt dictator anywhere in the world.

Recommendations to Congress

And these steps are only a beginning. For if the Congress is to assume a role of leadership, it must have not only the negative power to review and reverse policy, but also the positive power to make policy in the first place. It must know enough—so it will not hear the reply that the President always knows best. It must be structured for integrated decision-making—so it will not hear the reply that only the President can pull all the pieces together.

First, the Congress should establish a unified budget assessment mechanism. The Senate and House should establish a committee to estimate revenues, set a general level of expenditures, and establish priorities to relate specific appropriation decisions to that general level. This committee should have sufficient resources of expertise and information. There is no reason to let the President control the budget because he has the only Office of Management and Budget.

Second, the Congress should establish a similar mechanism for national security policy. With members drawn from the Appropriations, Foreign Relations and Armed Services Committees, such a unified committee could offer a thoughtful and sensible alternative to executive proposals. This committee, too, should have the necessary resources. If the President can have two State Departments, the Congress can have at least one agency to provide information and recommendations about foreign affairs and defense policy.

Third, the Congress should adjust the seniority system. No other legislative body in the Western World uses length of service as the sole standard for place and power in its committees. If the Congress is to carry out its constructive mandate, it must do what the mandate means, not what a few individuals from safe districts want. An activist, effective Congress must reflect the popular will. It cannot do so unless the members freely elect committee chairmen.

Finally, the Congress should defend its powers as it extends them. It must consider and choose from a number of alternatives to cancel or control the impoundment of its appropriations. Only then can the Congress assure the execution of the policies it has enacted.

So if the Congress has the will, there is a way to exercise positive leadership. For the long term, the question is—in what direction? I am convinced still that the society to which America should aspire is a liberal one. To those who charge that liberalism has been tried and found wanting, I answer that the failure is not in the idea, but in the course of recent history. The New Deal was ended by World War II. The New Frontier was closed by Berlin and Cuba almost before it was opened. And the Great Society lost its greatness in the jungles of Indochina.

Of course, liberal programs will sometimes fail anyway, for human decisions are frail always. Government is the creation of men and encompasses the weaknesses of men. Plans can be poorly conceived or poorly executed—though a Congress with sense and a bit of intelligence can work to prevent that. But that government is best, I believe, that best serves the demands of justice. So what Americans should seek is a system in which the principles of civil equality and individual liberty have the highest claim on statesmanship. We must strive to provide a decent standard of life for all citizens and to redistribute wealth and power so each citizen has a fair share. And along with this must come a foreign policy which puts humanity and morality ahead of Cold War myths and the prestige of leaders who would rather compound error than face reality.

Institutional Revival

And an institutional revival of the Congress not only can lead America in a new direction; it can also spark a similar institutional revival outside government.

Where power is pluralistic rather than presidential, the press will not have so much to fear from the executive branch. It could institute reforms such as the rotation of correspondents at the White House and among candidates in a national election, and the assignment of political reporters and not just "regulars" to the President during a campaign.

There are also hopeful signs of a reawakening in the Democratic Party. The party is scheduled to hold biennial conferences to set national policy, with the first one next year.

And as Democrats look ahead to 1976, they can be encouraged by the enduring gains of 1972. For I believe my campaign set the manner in which future candidates must seek the Democratic nomination— openly, candidly, not with the traditional strategy of saying as little as possible, but with a pledge to seek and speak the truth. I believe we also set a standard for the conduct of future campaigns—which will have to reveal their contributors and represent the people rather than the politicians. And never again will Americans accept wiretapping, Watergates, and the spectacle of a candidate hiding in the White House. Instead, they will expect at least a commitment to correct wrongs rather than committing them. Finally, I believe our campaign set forth the great issues that will dominate the debate of the 1970s, ranging from tax reform to a rational military budget.

And millions of Democrats, whether they are ordinary citizens or Senators, are anxious to carry the banner. I have faith that their energy and efforts can end the exhaustion of the electorate, enlist the country in a coalition of conscience as well as self interest, and expand the 28 million votes the national ticket won in 1972 into a majority that is right as well as new.

But as I have noted, the next election is four years away. For the immediate future, the key is the Congress. It must take the initiative and provide the inspiration. It must cure the paralysis and procrastination that have earned it the doubt, the disrespect and the cynicism of the American people. The *New York Times* recently described the

President as a leader who "behaves with the aloofness of a Roman emperor." It is useful to remember that no Roman emperor was crowned until the Roman Senate abdicated....

Throughout our history, America's greatest offering—as I said in accepting the Democratic presidential nomination—has been as "a witness to the world for what is noble and just in human affairs." This is what summoned the dock workers of Manchester to support Abraham Lincoln and the cause of liberty during our Civil War. And this is what America must restore. If we fail, other generations who are not free will look back and say that things cannot be any other way.

So in my mind, the challenge of the American future is to revive our institutions and resume our progress at home, while we act abroad with "a decent respect for the opinions of mankind."

SEVAREID ON "L.B.J."

January 22, 1973

Lyndon Baines Johnson, 36th President of the United States, died Jan. 22 after suffering a heart attack at his ranch near Johnson City, Texas. The 64-year-old former Chief Executive had been flown to Brooke Army Medical Center in San Antonio after aides found him stricken on his bedroom floor. He was pronounced dead on arrival.

As President, Mr. Johnson had called for a "Great Society" and had pushed through Congress the most comprehensive domestic program since the New Deal. Bills setting up the "War on Poverty," Medicare, Medicaid, the Department of Housing and Urban Development, and the Model Cities program were among 60 pieces of major legislation proposed and signed into law by Johnson.

The native Texan had become President upon the assassination of John F. Kennedy on Nov. 22, 1963. He had gone on in 1964 to win a full term in office by the largest popular vote ever cast for a presidential nominee. In a nationally televised address on March 31, 1968, Johnson had told of new efforts for peace in Vietnam and made the surprise announcement that he would not seek re-election. Ironically, death came to him 13 hours before the war settlement he had sought as President was initialed in Paris by Henry A. Kissinger and Le Duc Tho. However, it was learned later that President Nixon had informed him in advance that an agreement had been reached.

When Johnson died, the country was still in mourning for Harry S Truman, who had died Dec. 26, 1972. For the first time since the brief period between the death of Calvin Coolidge on Jan. 5, 1933, and the expiration of Herbert Hoover's term on March 4, 1933, the nation was without a living former President. Johnson's body was flown to Washington Jan. 24 to lie in state in the Rotunda of the Capitol where he had spent 24 years as congressman, senator, and then Majority Leader. Immediately after the death announcement, CBS commentator Eric Sevareid had summed up concisely on television the virtues and faults of "L.B.J."

Remarks by Eric Sevareid in commemoration of Lyndon B. Johnson on the CBS Evening News program, Jan. 22, 1973:

He was a great man with great flaws in his nature. He might have gone down in the books as one of America's greatest humanitarian Presidents. He was successful in passing more liberal high-minded legislation than any President before him, his mentor Roosevelt included. But the Vietnam failure branded him forever. The giant failure did not lie in not winning the war, but in enlarging it.

He was thought of as a master politician. It was only half true. He was a master indoor politician; he knew how to push and persuade cloakroom style. His training was Texas Democratic politics, which was club politics then. He was poor at outdoor politics, persuasion of the public at large. His charm and charisma, and he had them, were for private consumption. His sense of fun and humor was known only to his friends. He froze in front of the public cameras, became mannered, sententious, unreal.

As a President, he remained a Senator. He was a total product of the Congress. For him legislation was the beginning and end. He constantly carried a card in his pocket to whip out for visitors—a list of bills pending or passed. He acted as if these laws were self-enforcing. He seemed unaware that the great crisis of liberal government had already set in. It was breaking down at the functioning level. And successful functioning, as with civil rights, was releasing its inevitable tensions in the society.

He followed the only road he knew, the only road the country has ever discovered to improve the quality of its life. He had gargantuan appetites, never assuaged. He wanted all the power, all the money, all the love. He could do few things quietly and humbly. Even the many kindnesses he showed to others, many never reported, were done with a certain sweep. He would even buy dresses for staff wives in wholesale lots.

He believed he could do anything, and he believed the country could do anything, so he piled immense social programs on top of the great leap into space, on top of vast new weapons systems, on top of a major war. America's red ink flowed all over the world until the nation became technically bankrupt.

He could hate, but unlike some Presidents, he could forgive. He could occasionally admit he was wrong, in private. Truman could do that in public; so could Kennedy. Johnson could blast you in private—I knew that experience, too—but somehow he remained your friend. You never had to feel he would plant a dagger in your back.

He could look you in the eye, utter the most outrageous nonsense, and never blink. "Mrs. Johnson makes the business deals for the Johnson family," he said to Reston of *The Times* in explaining his fortune. "The President has no credibility problem; the press has it," he said to Walter Cronkite. "You fellows ought to have an ethics committee with Bobby Baker as chairman," he said to this reporter, among others. Baker had worked for him, not any of us.

His brown eyes had, surprisingly, a woman's softness. Indeed, there was a certain feminine, almost feline side to his nature. He could play people against one another, slyly observe the result, and tell the story to others with relish. So he spent half a day once trapping Congressmen, including Wilbur Mills, into believing, and telling others, that he would appoint so-and-so as Treasury Secretary, when he had already notified Henry Fowler that he was the man.

The loyalty he demanded of his staff was loyalty to Lyndon B. Johnson. If they quit him, even over an issue of principle, or criticized him later, even dispassionately, they went into his black book, and he would denounce them privately to others. Those who did neither, like Dean Rusk, he defended to his death.

He possessed enormous energy, a very keen intellect, immense force of will, and an unmeasurable advantage in his remarkable First Lady. But somewhere down deep was an insecurity. His origins were rough, his formal learning sketchy. He was overimpressed by those Eastern intellectuals and experts he purported to disdain. This and his overdone respect for the professional military with medals on their chests was part of his undoing.

The student rebellion against the war in '68, the McCarthy and Robert Kennedy campaigns, had much to do with his retirement from office. But the Tet offensive in Vietnam had more. It was a military defeat for the enemy, but a psychological defeat for the United States. And what really counted was that it was a psychological defeat for Lyndon Johnson, because he had been misinformed in advance of this offensive, and when the Commander in Chief can no longer believe in the information and advice of his generals, he is helpless. He was defeated inside his own regime, not on the battlefield.

He was one of the most powerful personalities I have known. He would fix you with those brown eyes for twenty minutes, never blinking. A gentleman ought to blink once in a while. He was not a gentleman, but he was a man.

SUPREME COURT ON ABORTION

January 22, 1973

Aware that it was dealing with one of the most emotional and sensitive issues of the 1970s, the Supreme Court on Jan. 22 laid down constitutional guidelines strictly limiting the power of the states to regulate abortion. In two separate 7-2 decisions, the Court held that the states **could not place any restrictions on a woman's decision to procure an abortion by a licensed physician in the first three months of pregnancy.**

However, the Court said the right to an abortion was not absolute. At certain points in time a state's interest in preserving the health of the mother or the potential life of the unborn infant becomes sufficient to justify some degree of regulation of abortion. In the second three months of pregnancy, a state's duty to protect its citizens entitles it to specify conditions under which an abortion may be performed. Only in the final 10 weeks of pregnancy, when the fetus is judged to be capable of surviving if born then, does a state have a constitutional right to **ban abortions other than those performed to save the life of the mother.**

The unusually detailed timetable of constitutional rights was set out in the Court's opinions sustaining two lower-court rulings—one invalidating a Texas law which made abortion a crime unless performed to **save a woman's life (Roe v. Wade) and another invalidating a 1968** *Georgia law strictly limiting the circumstances under which abortions could be legally performed (Doe v. Bolton). Anti-abortion laws in 30 states were affected by the Court's ruling on the Texas case. More lenient laws in 15 additional states were affected by the decision on the Georgia statute.*

The Court's pronouncement climaxed a movement to liberalize abortion laws. The Texas statute had been typical of those passed by most states in the late 1960s. *The latter group of statutes had legalized* had followed the pattern of the more liberal laws enacted by a dozen states in the late 1960s. The latter group of statutes had legalized abortions not only to preserve a woman's life or health, but also to terminate a pregnancy which was likely to result in the birth of a defective child or which was the result of rape. Hawaii, Alaska and Washington had removed almost all restrictions on abortions except residence requirements. New York allowed any woman attesting to be at least 18 years of age to have an abortion for any reason in the first 24 weeks of pregnancy.

The Court's medical law specialist, Associate Justice Harry A. Blackmun, delivered the opinion of the majority. It based its decision on the 14th Amendment's protection of the right to personal liberty, including the right to privacy. The majority found that the right to privacy was broad enough to encompass a woman's decision whether or not to bear a child. "The detriment that the state would impose upon the pregnant woman by denying this choice altogether is apparent," wrote Blackmun.

The Court held that the Georgia law, although more liberal than the Texas law, still infringed on a woman's rights. The decision struck down a requirement that an abortion be performed only in certain hospitals and after approval by the hospital's abortion committee and agreement by three doctors that the abortion should be performed. The decision also invalidated the Georgia law's requirement that abortions be performed only on residents of the state.

The majority in the abortion rulings included Nixon appointees Chief Justice Warren E. Burger and Associate Justices Blackmun and Lewis F. Powell Jr. Associate Justices William O. Douglas, Potter Stewart, Thurgood Marshall and the Court's only Catholic, William J. Brennan Jr., also sided with the majority. Associate Justices Byron White and William H. Rehnquist, the latter a Nixon appointee, filed dissenting opinions. Justice White took angry exception to a ruling that "values the convenience, whim or caprice of the putative mother more than the life or potential life of the fetus." Rehnquist questioned the breadth of the decisions and disagreed with the majority opinion that the right to privacy was involved in a decision to have an abortion.

Roman Catholic Cardinal Cooke of New York issued a statement calling the decision "shocking" and "horrifying." Cardinal Krol of Philadelphia termed the ruling "an unspeakable tragedy for this nation." The Rev. Dr. Howard E. Spragg, executive vice president of the Board of Homeland Ministries of the United Church of Christ, said:

"The decision is historic not only in terms of women's individual rights, but also in terms of the relationships of church and state."

Excerpts from the Supreme Court decisions on the Texas abortion law and on the Georgia abortion law, handed down Jan. 22, 1973:

Jane Roe et al., Appellants,	On Appeal from the United States
v.	District Court for the Northern
Henry Wade.	District of Texas.

[January 22, 1973]

MR. JUSTICE BLACKMUN delivered the opinion of the Court.

This Texas federal appeal and its Georgia companion, *Doe* v. *Bolton, post* ——, present constitutional challenges to state criminal abortion legislation. The Texas statutes under attack here are typical of those that have been in effect in many States for approximately a century. The Georgia statutes, in contrast, have a modern cast and are a legislative product that, to an extent at least, obviously reflects the influences of recent attitudinal change, of advancing medical knowledge and techniques, and of new thinking about an old issue.

We forthwith acknowledge our awareness of the sensitive and emotional nature of the abortion controversy, of the vigorous opposing views, even among physicians, and of the deep and seemingly absolute convictions that the subject inspires. One's philosophy, one's experiences, one's exposure to the raw edges of human existence, one's religious training, one's attitudes toward life and family and their values, and the moral standards one establishes and seeks to observe, are all likely to influence and to color one's thinking and conclusions about abortion.

In addition, population growth, pollution, poverty, and racial overtones tend to complicate and not to simplify the problem.

Our task, of course, is to resolve the issue by constitutional measurement free of emotion and of predilection. We seek earnestly to do this, and, because we do, we have inquired into, and in this opinion place some emphasis upon, medical and medical-legal history and what that history reveals about man's attitudes toward the abortive procedure over the centuries....

I

The Texas statutes...make it a crime to "procure an abortion," as therein defined, or to attempt one, except with respect to "an abortion procured or attempted by medical advice for the purpose of saving the life of the mother." Similar statutes are in existence in a majority of the States.

Texas first enacted a criminal abortion statute in 1854.... This was soon modified into language that has remained substantially unchanged to the present time....

II

Jane Roe, a single woman who was residing in Dallas County, Texas, instituted this federal action in March 1970 against the District Attorney of the county. She sought a declaratory judgment that the Texas criminal abortion statutes were unconstitutional on their face, and an injunction restraining the defendant from enforcing the statutes.

Roe alleged that she was unmarried and pregnant; that she wished to terminate her pregnancy by an abortion "performed by a competent, licensed physician, under safe, clinical conditions"; that she was unable to get a "legal" abortion in Texas because her life did not appear to be threatened by the continuation of her pregnancy; and that she could not afford to travel to another jurisdiction in order to secure a legal abortion under safe conditions. She claimed that the Texas statutes were unconstitutionally vague and that they abridged her right of personal privacy, protected by the First, Fourth, Fifth, Ninth, and Fourteenth Amendments. By an amendment to her complaint Roe purported to sue "on behalf of herself and all other women" similarly situated....

On the merits, the District Court held that the "fundamental right of single women and married persons to choose whether to have children is protected by the Ninth Amendment, through the Fourteenth Amendment," and that the Texas criminal abortion statutes were void on their face because they were both unconstitutionally vague and constituted an overbroad infringement of the plaintiffs' Ninth Amendment rights....

The appellee...suggests that Roe's case must now be moot because she and all other members of her class are no longer subject to any 1970 pregnancy.

The usual rule in federal cases is that an actual controversy must exist at stages of appellate or certiorari review, and not simply at the date the action is initiated....

But when, as here, pregnancy is a significant fact in the litigation, the normal 266-day human gestation period is so short that the pregnancy will come to term before the usual appellate process is complete. If that termination makes a case moot, pregnancy litigation seldom will survive much beyond the trial stage, and appellate review will be effectively denied. Our law should not be that rigid....

VI

It perhaps is not generally appreciated that the restrictive criminal abortion laws in effect in a majority of States today are of relatively recent vintage. Those laws, generally proscribing abortion or its attempt at any time during pregnancy except when necessary to preserve the pregnant woman's life, are not of ancient or even of common law origin. Instead, they derive from statutory changes effected, for the most part, in the latter half of the 19th century....

The American law.... By 1840,...only eight American States had statutes dealing with abortion. It was not until after the War Between the States that legislation began generally to replace the common law. Most of these initial statutes dealt severely with abortion after quickening but were lenient with it before quickening. Most punished attempts equally with completed abortions....

Gradually, in the middle and late 19th century the quickening distinction disappeared.... By the end of the 1950s, a large majority of the States banned abortion, however and whenever performed, unless done to save or preserve the life of the mother.... In the past several years, however, a trend toward liberalization of abortion statutes has resulted in adoption, by about one-third of the States, of less stringent laws....

It is thus apparent that at common law, at the time of the adoption of our Constitution, and throughout the major portion of the 19th century, abortion was viewed with less disfavor than under most American statutes currently in effect. Phrasing it another way, a woman enjoyed a substantially broader right to terminate a pregnancy than she does in most States today. At least with respect to the early stage of pregnancy, and very possibly without such a limitation, the opportunity to make this choice was present in this country well into the 19th century. Even later, the law continued for some time to treat less punitively an abortion procured in early pregnancy.

The position of the American Medical Association. The anti-abortion mood prevalent in this country in the late 19th century was shared by the medical profession. Indeed, the attitude of the profession may have played a significant role in the enactment of stringent criminal abortion legislation during that period.... On June 25, 1970, the House of Delegates adopted preambles [which] emphasized "the best interests of the patient," "sound clinical judgment," and "informed patient consent," in contrast to "mere acquiescence to the patient's demand." The resolutions asserted that abortion is a medical procedure that should be performed by a licensed physician in an accredited hospital only after consultation with two other physicians and in conformity with state law, and that no party to the procedure should be required to violate personally held moral principles....

VII

Three reasons have been advanced to explain historically the enactment of criminal abortion laws in the 19th century and to justify their continued existence....

It has been argued occasionally that these laws were the product of a Victorian social concern to discourage illicit sexual conduct. Texas, however, does not advance this justification in the present case, and it appears that no court or commentator has taken the argument seriously....

A second reason is concerned with abortion as a medical procedure. When most criminal abortion laws were first enacted, the procedure was a hazardous one for the woman. This was particularly true prior to the development of antisepsis.... Abortion mortality was high.... Thus it has been argued that a State's real concern in enacting a criminal abortion law was to protect the pregnant woman, that is, to restrain her from submitting to a procedure that placed her life in serious jeopardy.

Modern medical techniques have altered this situation.... Mortality rates for women undergoing early abortions, where the procedure is legal, appear to be as low as or lower than the rates for normal child-birth. Consequently, any interest of the State in protecting the woman from an inherently hazardous procedure, except when it would be equally dangerous for her to forgo it, has largely disappeared. Of course, important state interests in the area of health and medical standards do remain. The State has a legitimate interest in seeing to it that abortion, like any other medical procedure, is performed under circumstances that insure maximum safety for the patient....

The third reason is the State's interest—some phrase it in terms of duty—in protecting prenatal life....

(A)s long as at least *potential* life is involved, the State may assert interests beyond the protection of the pregnant woman alone....

It is with these interests, and the weight to be attached to them, that this case is concerned.

VIII

The Constitution does not explicitly mention any right of privacy. In a line of decisions, however, going back perhaps as far as...[1891], the Court has recognized that a right of personal privacy, or a guarantee of certain areas or zones of privacy, does exist under the Constitution....

This right of privacy, whether it be founded in the Fourteenth Amendment's concept of personal liberty and restrictions upon state action, as we feel it is, or, as the District Court determined, in the Ninth Amendment's reservation of rights to the people, is broad enough to encompass a woman's decision whether or not to terminate her pregnancy. The detriment that the State would impose upon the pregnant woman by denying this choice altogether is apparent. Specific and direct harm medically diagnosable even in early pregnancy may be involved. Maternity, or additional offspring, may force upon the woman a distressful life and future. Psychological harm may be imminent. Mental and physical health may be taxed by child care. There is also the distress, for all concerned, associated with the unwanted child, and there is the problem of bringing a child into a family already unable, psychologically and otherwise, to care for it. In other cases, as in this one, the additional difficulties and continuing stigma of unwed motherhood may be involved....

On the basis of elements such as these, appellants and some *amici* argue that the woman's right is absolute and that she is entitled to terminate her pregnancy at whatever time, in whatever way, and for whatever reason she alone chooses. With this we do not agree.... (A) state may properly assert important interests in safeguarding health, in maintaining medical standards, and in protecting potential life. At some point in pregnancy, these respective interests become sufficiently compelling to sustain regulation of the factors that govern the abortion decision. The privacy right involved, therefore, cannot be said to be absolute....

We therefore conclude that the right of personal privacy includes the abortion decision, but that this right is not unqualified and must be considered against important state interests in regulation....

Where certain "fundamental rights" are involved, the Court has held that regulation limiting these rights may be justified only by a "compelling state interest,"...and that legislative enactments must be narrowly drawn to express only the legitimate state interests at stake....

IX

The District Court held that the appellee failed to meet his burden of demonstrating that the Texas statute's infringement upon Roe's rights was necessary to support a compelling state interest.... Appellant and appellee both contest that holding. Appellant, as has been indicated, claims an absolute right that bars any state imposition of criminal penalties in the area. Appellee argues that the State's determination to recognize and protect prenatal life from and after conception constitutes a compelling state interest. As noted above, we do not agree fully with either formulation.

A. The appellee and certain *amici* argue that the fetus is a "person" within the language and meaning of the Fourteenth Amendment....

The Constitution does not define "person" in so many words.... All this, together with our observation,...that throughout the major portion of the 19th century prevailing legal abortion practices were far freer than they are today, persuades us that the word "person," as used in the Fourteenth Amendment, does not include the unborn....

Texas urges that, apart from the Fourteenth Amendment, life begins at conception and is present throughout pregnancy, and that, therefore, the State has a compelling interest in protecting that life from and after conception. We need not resolve the difficult question of when life begins. When those trained in the respective disciplines of medicine, philosophy, and theology are unable to arrive at any consensus, the judiciary, at this point in the development of man's knowledge, is not in a position to speculate as to the answer.

It should be sufficient to note briefly the wide divergence of thinking on this most sensitive and difficult question....

In areas other than criminal abortion the law has been reluctant to endorse any theory that life, as we recognize it, begins before live birth or to accord legal rights to the unborn except in narrowly defined situations and except when the rights are contingent upon live birth.... (T)he unborn have never been recognized in the law as persons in the whole sense.

X

...(T)he State does have an important and legitimate interest in preserving and protecting the health of the pregnant woman, whether she be a resident of the State or a nonresident who seeks medical consultation and treatment there, and that it has still *another* important and legitimate interest in protecting the potentiality of human life. These interests are separate and distinct. Each grows in substantiality as the woman approaches term and, at a point during pregnancy, each becomes "compelling."

With respect to the State's important and legitimate interest in the health of the mother, the "compelling" point, in the light of present medical knowledge, is at approximately the end of the first trimester. This is so because of the now established medical fact, referred to above, that until the end of the first trimester mortality in abortion is less than mortality in normal childbirth. It follows that, from and after this point, a State may regulate the abortion procedure to the extent that the regulation reasonably relates to the preservation and protection of maternal health. Examples of permissible state regulation in this area are requirements as to the qualifications of the person who is to perform the abortion; as to the licensure of that person; as to the facility in which the procedure is to be performed, that is, whether it must be a hospital or may be a clinic or some other place of less-than-hospital status; as to the licensing of the facility; and the like.

This means, on the other hand, that, for the period of pregnancy prior to this "compelling" point, the attending physician, in consultation with his patient, is free to determine, without regulation by the State, that in his medical judgment the patient's pregnancy should be terminated. If that decision is reached, the judgment may be effectuated by an abortion free of interference by the State.

With respect to the State's important and legitimate interest in potential life, the "compelling" point is at viability. This is so because the fetus then presumably has the capability of meaningful life outside the mother's womb. State regulation protective of fetal life after viability thus has both logical and biological justifications. If the State is interested in protecting fetal life after viability, it may go so far as to proscribe abortion during that period except when it is necessary to preserve the life or health of the mother.

Measured against these standards, Art. 1196 of the Texas Penal Code, in restricting legal abortions to those "procured or attempted by medical advice for the purpose of saving the life of the mother," sweeps too broadly....

XI

To summarize and to repeat:

1. A state criminal abortion statute of the current Texas type, that excepts from criminality only a *life saving* procedure on behalf of the mother, without regard to pregnancy stage and without recognition of the other interests involved, is violative of the Due Process Clause of the Fourteenth Amendment.

(a) For the stage prior to approximately the end of the first trimester, the abortion decision and its effectuation must be left to the medical judgment of the pregnant woman's attending physician.

(b) For the stage subsequent to approximately the end of the first trimester, the State, in promoting its interest in the health of the mother, may, if it chooses, regulate the abortion procedure in ways that are reasonably related to maternal health.

(c) For the stage subsequent to viability the State, in promoting its interest in the potentiality of human life, may, if it chooses, regulate, and even proscribe, abortion except where it is necessary, in appropriate medical judgment, for the preservation of the life or health of the mother.

2. The State may define the term "physician,"...to mean only a physician currently licensed by the State, and may proscribe any abortion by a person who is not a physician as so defined....

This holding, we feel, is consistent with the relative weights of the respective interests involved, with the lessons and example of medical and legal history, with the lenity of the common law, and with the demands of the profound problems of the present day. The decision leaves the State free to place increasing restrictions on abortion as the period of pregnancy lengthens, so long as those restrictions are tailored to the recognized state interests. The decision vindicates the right of the physician to administer medical treatment according to his professional judgment up to the points where important state interests provide compelling justifications for intervention. Up to those points the abortion decision in all its aspects is inherently, and primarily, a medical decision, and basic responsibility for it must rest with the physician. If an individual practitioner abuses the privilege of exercising proper medical judgment, the usual remedies, judicial and intraprofessional, are available....

It is so ordered.

MR. JUSTICE REHNQUIST, dissenting.

I

The Court's opinion decides that a State may impose virtually no restriction on the performance of abortions during the first trimester of pregnancy. Our previous decisions indicate that a necessary predicate for such an opinion is a plaintiff who was in her first trimester of pregnancy at some time during the pendency of her law suit.... The Court's statement of facts in this case makes clear, however, that the record in no way indicates the presence of such a plaintiff. We know only that plaintiff Roe at the time of filing her complaint was a pregnant woman; for aught that appears in this record, she may have been in her *last* trimester of pregnancy as of the date the complaint was filed.... In deciding such a hypothetical lawsuit the Court departs from the long-standing admonition that it should never "formulate a rule of constitutional law broader than is required by the precise facts to which it is to be applied."...

II

Even if there were a plaintiff in this case capable of litigating the issue which the Court decides, I would reach a conclusion opposite to that reached by the Court. I have difficulty in concluding, as the Court does, that the right of "privacy" is involved in this case.... (T)he Court's sweeping invalidation of any restrictions on abortion during the first trimester is impossible to justify...and the conscious weighing of competing factors which the Court's opinion apparently substitutes for the established test is far more appropriate to a legislative judgment than to a judicial one....

(T)he Court's opinion will accomplish the seemingly impossible feat of leaving this area of the law more confused than it found it.... The decision here to break the term of pregnancy into three distinct terms and to outline the permissible restrictions the State may impose in each one, for example, partakes more of judicial legislation than it does of a determination of the intent of the drafters of the Fourteenth Amendment.

The fact that a majority of the States, reflecting after all the majority sentiment in those States, have had restrictions on abortions for at least a century seems to me as strong an indication there is that the asserted right to an abortion is not "so rooted in the traditions and conscience of our people as to be ranked as fundamental...."

To reach its result the Court necessarily has had to find within the scope of the Fourteenth Amendment a right that was apparently completely unknown to the drafters of the Amendment....

There apparently was no question concerning the validity of this provision or of any of the other state statutes when the Fourteenth

Amendment was adopted. The only conclusion possible from this history is that the drafters did not intend to have the Fourteenth Amendment withdraw from the States the power to legislate with respect to this matter....

For all of the foregoing reasons, I respectfully dissent.

Mary Doe et al., Appellants, *v.* Arthur K. Bolton, as Attorney General of the State of Georgia, et al.	On Appeal from the United States District Court for the Northern District of Georgia

[January 22, 1973]

MR. JUSTICE BLACKMUN delivered the opinion of the Court.

In this appeal the criminal abortion statutes recently enacted in Georgia are challenged on constitutional grounds....

I

(T)he 1968 statutes are patterned upon the American Law Institute's Model Penal Code.... The ALI proposal has served as the model for recent legislation in approximately one-fourth of our States. The new Georgia provisions replaced statutory law that had been in effect for more than 90 years.... The predecessor statute paralleled the Texas legislation considered in *Roe* v. *Wade, ante,* and made all abortions criminal except those necessary "to preserve the life" of the pregnant woman....

Section 26-1201, with a referenced exception, makes abortion a crime, and Section 26-1203 provides that a person convicted of that crime shall be punished by imprisonment for not less than one nor more than 10 years. Section 26-1202(a) states the exception and removes from Section 1201's definition of criminal abortion, and thus makes non-criminal, an abortion "performed by a physician duly licensed" in Georgia when, "based upon his best clinical judgment...an abortion is necessary because

"(1) A continuation of the pregnancy would endanger the life of the pregnant woman or would seriously and permanently injure her health, or

"(2) The fetus would very likely be born with a grave, permanent, and irremediable mental or physical defect, or

"(3) The pregnancy resulted from forcible or statutory rape."

Section 26-1202 also requires, by numbered subdivisions of its subsection (b), that, for an abortion to be authorized or performed as a non-criminal procedure, additional conditions must be fulfilled. These are (1) and (2) residence of the woman in Georgia; (3) reduction to writing of the performing physician's medical judgment that an abortion is

justified for one or more of the reasons specified by Section 26-1202(a),
with written concurrence in that judgment by at least two other
Georgia-licensed physicians, based upon their separate personal medical examinations of the woman; (4) performance of the abortion in a
hospital licensed by the State Board of Health and also accredited by
the Joint Commission on Accreditation of Hospitals; (5) advance approval by an abortion committee of not less than three members of
the hospital's staff....

II

On April 16, 1970, Mary Doe, 23 other individuals...and two nonprofit
Georgia corporations that advocate abortion reform, instituted this
federal action in the Northern District of Georgia against the State's
attorney general.... The plaintiffs sought a declaratory judgment that
the Georgia abortion statutes were unconstitutional in their entirety....
Mary Doe alleged:

"(1) She was a 22-year-old Georgia citizen, married, and nine
weeks pregnant. She had three living children. The two older ones
had been placed in a foster home because of Doe's poverty and inability to care for them. The youngest, born July 19, 1969, had been
placed for adoption. Her husband had recently abandoned her and
she was forced to live with her indigent parents and their eight children. She and her husband, however, had become reconciled. He
was a construction worker employed only sporadically. She had been
a mental patient at the State Hospital. She had been advised that
an abortion could be performed on her with less danger to her health
than if she gave birth to the child she was carrying. She would be
unable to care for or support the new child.

"(2) On March 25, 1970, she applied to the Abortion Committee
of Grady Memorial Hospital, Atlanta, for a therapeutic abortion
under Section 26-1202. Her application was denied....

"(3) Because her application was denied, she was forced either to
relinquish 'her right to decide when and how many children she will
bear' or to seek an abortion that was illegal under the Georgia
statutes. This invaded her rights of privacy and liberty in matters
related to family, marriage, and sex, and deprived her of the right to
choose whether to bear children. This was a violation of rights guaranteed her by the First, Fourth, Fifth, Ninth, and Fourteenth Amendments....

On the merits, the court concluded that the limitation in the Georgia
statute of the "number of reasons for which an abortion may be
sought,"...improperly restricted Doe's rights of privacy...and of "personal liberty," both of which it thought "broad enough to include the
decision to abort a pregnancy,".... As a consequence, the court held
invalid those portions...limiting legal abortions to the three situations
specified;... The court, however, held that Georgia's interest in protec-

tion of health, and the existence of a "*potential* of independent human existence" (emphasis in original),...justified state regulation of "the manner of performance as well as the quality of the final decision to abort,"...and it refused to strike down the other provisions of the statutes....

IV

The net result of the District Court's decision is that the abortion determination, so far as the physician is concerned, is made in the exercise of his professional, that is, his "best clinical" judgment in the light of *all* the attendant circumstances. He is not now restricted to the three situations originally specified. Instead, he may range farther afield wherever his medical judgment, properly and professionally exercised, so dictates and directs him....

The appellants next argue that the District Court should have declared unconstitutional three procedural demands of the Georgia statute: (1) that the abortion be performed in a hospital accredited by the Joint Commission on Accreditation of Hospitals; (2) that the procedure be approved by the hospital staff abortion committee; and (3) that the performing physician's judgment be confirmed by the independent examinations of the patient by two other licensed physicians.... In Georgia there is no restriction of the performance of non-abortion surgery in a hospital not yet accredited by the JCAH so long as other requirements imposed by the State, such as licensing of the hospital and of the operating surgeon, are met....

This is not to say that Georgia may not or should not, from and after the end of the first trimester, adopt standards for licensing all facilities where abortions may be performed so long as those standards are legitimately related to the objective the State seeks to accomplish.... We hold that the hospital requirement of the Georgia law, because it fails to exclude the first trimester of pregnancy, see *Roe* v. *Wade, ante*, is also invalid....

Committee Approval. The second aspect of the appellants' procedural attack relates to the hospital abortion committee and to the pregnant woman's asserted lack of access to that committee.... (W)e see no constitutionally justifiable pertinence in the structure for the advance approval by the abortion committee. With regard to the protection of potential life, the medical judgment is already completed prior to the committee stage, and review by a committee once removed from diagnosis is basically redundant. We are not cited to any other surgical procedure made subject to committee approval as a matter of state criminal law....

Two-Doctor Concurrence. ...Required acquiescence by co-practitioners has no rational connection with a patient's needs and unduly infringes on the physician's right to practice.

The appellants attack the residency requirement of the Georgia law....

(W)e do not uphold the constitutionality of the residence requirement.... A contrary holding would mean that a State could limit to its own residents the general medical care available within its borders. This we could not approve....

The judgment of the District Court is modified accordingly and, as so modified, is affirmed.

MR. JUSTICE WHITE, with whom MR. JUSTICE REHNQUIST joins, dissenting.

At the heart of the controversy in these cases are those recurring pregnancies that pose no danger whatsoever to the life or health of the mother but are nevertheless unwanted for any one or more of a variety of reasons—convenience, family planning, economics, dislike of children, the embarrassment of illegitimacy, etc.... During the period prior to the time the fetus becomes viable, the Constitution of the United States values the convenience, whim or caprice of the putative mother more than the life or potential life of the fetus; the Constitution, therefore, guarantees the right to an abortion as against any state law or policy seeking to protect the fetus from an abortion not prompted by more compelling reasons of the mother.

With all due respect, I dissent. I find nothing in the language or history of the Constitution to support the Court's judgment. The Court simply fashions and announces a new constitutional right for pregnant mothers and, with scarcely any reason or authority for its action, invests that right with sufficient substance to override most existing state abortion statutes. The upshot is that the people and the legislatures of the 50 States are constitutionally disentitled to weigh the relative importance of the continued existence and development of the fetus on the one hand against a spectrum of possible impacts on the mother on the other hand. As an exercise of raw judicial power, the Court perhaps has authority to do what it does today; but in my view its judgment is an improvident and extravagant exercise of the power of judicial review which the Constitution extends to this Court.

The Court apparently values the convenience of the pregnant mother more than the continued existence and development of the life or potential life which she carries. Whether or not I might agree with that marshalling of values, I can in no event join the Court's judgment because I find no constitutional warrant for imposing such an order of priorities on the people and legislatures of the States. In a sensitive area such as this, involving as it does issues over which reasonable men may easily and heatedly differ, I cannot accept the Court's exercise of its clear power of choice by interposing a constitutional barrier to state efforts to protect human life and by investing mothers and doctors with the constitutionally protected right to exterminate it. This issue, for the most part, should be left with the people and to the political processes the people have devised to govern their affairs.

VIETNAM WAR SETTLEMENT
January 23-27, 1973

American military involvement in Vietnam was brought officially to an end upon the signing of a cease-fire agreement in Paris, Jan. 27, by representatives of the United States, South Vietnam, North Vietnam and the Viet Cong's provisional revolutionary government. Signing of the agreement climaxed a final spurt of intensive negotiations between Henry A. Kissinger, President Nixon's National Security Adviser, and Le Duc Tho of North Vietnam. The President had announced in a nationally televised address, Jan. 23, that an agreement to "end the war and bring peace with honor in Vietnam and Southeast Asia" had been concluded. He reported that the agreement had been initialed that day in Paris by Kissinger and Tho, and that an internationally supervised cease-fire would go into effect a few hours after the Jan. 27 signing ceremony.

Nixon told the national television audience that all American prisoners of war "throughout Indochina" would be returned to the United States within 60 days from the start of the cease-fire and that, in the same period, the 25,000 American troops still in Vietnam would be withdrawn. Defense Department lists showed 587 known prisoners of war and 1,335 missing servicemen. The President promised "the fullest possible accounting of those missing in action." He said that the Paris agreement, in accordance with conditions he had laid down, would guarantee the people of South Vietnam "the right to determine their own future without outside interference." It was his belief that the settlement "meets the goals and has the full support of President Thieu and the

*government of the Republic of Vietnam as well as that of our other
allies who are affected."*

Four Years of Negotiation

The peace negotiations that brought to a close the longest war in
American history had themselves been the most protracted in the
country's history. Talks between representatives of the United States
and North Vietnam had been initiated in Paris in mid-May 1968, during
the Johnson administration. A few days before President Nixon's first
inauguration in January 1969, the talks had been expanded to include
representatives of South Vietnam and of the National Liberation Front
(Viet Cong). The official negotiations were suspended three times,
and the private negotiations between Kissinger and Tho, which had begun Aug. 4, 1969, and which had been unknown to the public until disclosed by President Nixon on Jan. 25, 1972, were held only sporadically
at first. But some two months after the President on May 8, 1972, ordered the mining of North Vietnamese ports and a general blockade of
war supplies destined for North Vietnam, Kissinger and Le Duc Tho
entered into a series of meetings in Paris that lasted from July 19 to
Oct. 11, 1972.

Speculation that a settlement was at last in the offing arose when
Kissinger returned to Washington on Oct. 12, consulted with President
Nixon, and then flew on to Saigon to see President Thieu. On Oct. 26
a surprise Hanoi broadcast disclosed, in summary, the terms of a nine-
point peace settlement. Later that day, Kissinger, now back in Washington, held a White House news conference at which he announced
that the United States and North Vietnam had reached substantial
agreement on a plan for a cease-fire "in place," withdrawal of all American forces from Vietnam within 60 days, and establishment of a three-
part commission to supervise elections in South Vietnam. Denying
Hanoi's contention that Washington had agreed to sign the pact on Oct.
31, Kissinger nonetheless declared that "We believe peace is at hand."
Certain unresolved details, he said, could be worked out in a brief final
negotiating session. (See Historic Documents, 1972, p. 867.)

Negotiations were resumed in Paris Nov. 20, but they remained dead-
locked when Kissinger flew back to Washington on Dec. 13. (See Historic
Documents, 1972, p. 941.) Five days later, on Dec. 18, President Nixon
ordered bombing of the Hanoi-Haiphong region of North Vietnam. Intensive B-52 raids, which aroused considerable criticism in the United
States as well as in many other countries, continued until Dec. 30 when
renewal of the Paris negotiations was announced. Kissinger met with
Tho from Jan. 8 to Jan. 13 and then returned to Washington amid speculation that a settlement was imminent. Finally, on Jan. 22, two days
after Nixon's second inauguration, Kissinger again traveled to Paris
where he and Tho initialed the accord on Jan. 23. The President, in

his television address the same day, announced that Secretary of State William P. Rogers would fly to Paris for the official signing on Jan. 27.

Response to Peace Agreement

Members of Congress in this country and political leaders in South and North Vietnam responded to completion of the cease-fire agreement with expressions of relief, tempered in some cases by skepticism about the durability of the peace it was intended to bring. Both Le Duc Tho and President Thieu claimed victory for, respectively, North Vietnam and South Vietnam. "It is a moment of joy, a joy that is shared," said Tho. His country's victory, he declared, "crowned a valiant combat conducted in unity by the army and the people of Vietnam on all fronts at the cost of innumerable sacrifices and privations." Thieu was more circumspect. He said: "The signing of the agreement means the beginning of peace. But it does not mean peace. It is not that we are overly suspicious. It is because we have had plenty of experience with the Communists in this regard, and we don't place too much trust in their signature."

Americans, said Senate Minority Leader Hugh Scott (R Pa.), "should take pride in what has been accomplished: The fact that we have a peace. The fact that potentially it can become a lasting peace. The fact that we have a peace that guarantees return of our prisoners and accountability for our missing." Sen. Frank Church (D Idaho) announced, on the other hand, that he would sponsor a bill to prevent American forces from re-entering the war in Southeast Asia. The cease-fire, he thought, was "no more than a truce." He said that "A renewal of the fighting among the Vietnamese is probable, if not predictable, since none of the issues are resolved over which they have fought for the past 25 years."

At a White House news conference Jan. 24, the day the agreement was made public, Kissinger discussed the details of the document's 23 articles and four protocols. The transcript of Kissinger's opening statement at that conference follows the text of President Nixon's address announcing conclusion of the Vietnam settlement. The full text of the agreement itself concludes this three-part entry.

> *Text of address of President Nixon as delivered on live radio and television from the Oval Office of the White House, Jan. 23, 1973:*

Good evening. I have asked for this radio and television time tonight for the purpose of announcing that we today have concluded an agreement to end the war and bring peace with honor in Vietnam and in Southeast Asia.

The following statement is being issued at this moment in Washington and Hanoi:

At 12:30 Paris time today, January 23, 1973, the agreement on ending the war and restoring peace in Vietnam was initialed by Dr. Henry Kissinger on behalf of the United States, and Special Advisor Le Duc Tho on behalf of the Democratic Republic of Vietnam.

The agreement will be formally signed by the parties participating in the Paris Conference on Vietnam on January 27, 1973, at the International Conference Center in Paris.

The cease-fire will take effect at 2400 Greenwich Mean Time, January 27, 1973. The United States and the Democratic Republic of Vietnam express the hope that this agreement will insure stable peace in Vietnam and contribute to the preservation of lasting peace in Indochina and Southeast Asia.

That concludes the formal statement.

Peace with Honor

Throughout the years of negotiations, we have insisted on peace with honor. In my addresses to the nation from this room of January 25th and May 8th, I set forth the goals that we considered essential for peace with honor.

In the settlement that has now been agreed to, all the conditions that I laid down then have been met. A cease-fire, internationally supervised, will begin at 7 p.m. this Saturday, January 27th, Washington time. Within 60 days from this Saturday, all Americans held prisoners of war throughout Indochina will be released. There will be the fullest possible accounting for all of those who are missing in action.

During the same 60-day period, all American forces will be withdrawn from South Vietnam.

The people of South Vietnam have been guaranteed the right to determine their own future, without outside interference.

By joint agreement, the full text of the agreement and the protocols to carry it out, will be issued tomorrow.

Throughout these negotiations we have been in the closest consultation with President Thieu and other representatives of the Republic of Vietnam. This settlement meets the goals and has the full support of President Thieu and the Government of the Republic of Vietnam, as well as that of our other allies who are affected.

The United States will continue to recognize the Government of the Republic of Vietnam as the sole legitimate government of South Vietnam.

We shall continue to aid South Vietnam within the terms of the agreement and we shall support efforts by the people of South Vietnam to settle their problems peacefully among themselves.

We must recognize that ending the war is only the first step toward building the peace. All parties must now see to it that this is a peace that lasts, and also a peace that heals, and a peace that not only ends the war in Southeast Asia, but contributes to the prospects of peace in the whole world.

This will mean that the terms of the agreement must be scrupulously agreed to. We shall do everything the agreement requires of us and we shall expect the other parties to do everything it requires of them. We shall also expect other interested nations to help insure that the agreement is carried out and peace is maintained.

To the Parties in the Conflict

As this long and very difficult war ends, I would like to address a few special words to each of those who have been parties in the conflict.

First, to the people and Government of South Vietnam: By your courage, by your sacrifice, you have won the precious right to determine your own future and you have developed the strength to defend that right. We look forward to working with you in the future, friends in peace as we have been allies in war.

To the leaders of North Vietnam: As we have ended the war through negotiations, let us now build a peace of reconciliation. For our part, we are prepared to make a major effort to help achieve that goal; but just as reciprocity was needed to end the war, so, too, will it be needed to build and strengthen the peace.

To the other major powers that have been involved even indirectly: Now is the time for mutual restraint so that the peace we have achieved can last.

And finally, to all of you who are listening, the American people: Your steadfastness in supporting our insistence on peace with honor has made peace with honor possible. I know that you would not have wanted that peace jeopardized. With our secret negotiations at the sensitive stage they were in during this recent period, for me to have discussed publicly our efforts to secure peace would not only have violated our understanding with North Vietnam; it would have seriously harmed and possibly destroyed the chances for peace. Therefore, I know that you now can understand why, during these past several weeks, I have not made any public statements about those efforts.

The important thing was not to talk about peace; but to get peace and to get the right kind of peace. This we have done.

Now that we have achieved an honorable agreement, let us be proud that America did not settle for a peace that would have betrayed our allies, that would have abandoned our prisoners of war, or that would have ended the war for us but would have continued the war for the 50 million people of Indochina. Let us be proud of the 2-1/2 million young Americans who served in Vietnam, who served with honor and distinction in one of the most selfless enterprises in the history of nations. And let us be proud of those who have sacrificed, who gave their lives so that the people of South Vietnam might live in freedom and so that the world might live in peace.

In particular, I would like to say a word to some of the bravest people I have ever met—the wives, the children, the families of our prisoners of war and the missing in action. When others called on us to settle on any terms, you had the courage to stand for the right kind of peace so that those who died and those who suffered would not have died and suffered in vain, and so that where this generation knew war, the next generation would know peace. Nothing means more to me at this moment than the fact that your long vigil is coming to an end.

Just yesterday, a great American, who once occupied this office, died. In his life President Johnson endured the vilification of those who sought to portray him as a man of war. But there was nothing he cared about more deeply than achieving a lasting peace in the world.

I remember the last time I talked with him. It was just the day after New Year's. He spoke then of his concern with bringing peace, with making it the right kind of peace, and I was grateful that he once again expressed his support for my efforts to gain such a peace. No one would have welcomed this peace more than he.

And I know he would join me in asking for those who died and for those who live, let us consecrate this moment by resolving together to make the peace we have achieved a peace that will last.

Thank you and good evening.

Transcript of statement by Dr. Henry A. Kissinger, Assistant to the President for National Security Affairs, at White House press conference, Jan. 24, 1973 (subsequent questions and answers omitted):

Dr. Kissinger: The President last evening presented the outlines of the agreement and by common agreement between us and the North Vietnamese we have today released the text and I am here to explain, to go over briefly what these texts contain, and how we got there, what we have tried to achieve in recent months and where we expect to go from here.

Let me begin by going through the agreement which you have read.

The agreement, as you know, is in nine chapters. The first affirms the independence, sovereignty, unity and territorial integrity, as recognized by the 1954 Geneva Agreements on Vietnam, agreements which established two zones, divided by a military demarcation line.

Chapter II deals with a cease-fire. The cease-fire will go into effect at seven o'clock Washington time on Saturday night. The principal provisions of Chapter II deal with permitted acts during the cease-fire and with what the obligations of the various parties are with respect to the cease-fire.

Chapter II also deals with the withdrawal of American and all other foreign forces from Vietnam within a period of 60 days and it specifies the forces that have to be withdrawn. These are in effect all military personnel and all civilian personnel dealing with combat operations. We are permitted to retain economic advisors, and civilian technicians, serving in certain of the military branches.

Chapter II further deals with the provisions for re-supply and the introduction of outside forces. There is a flat prohibition against the introduction of any military force into South Vietnam from outside of South Vietnam, which is to say that whatever forces may be in South Vietnam from outside South Vietnam, specifically North Vietnamese forces, cannot receive reinforcements, replacements, or any other form of augmentation by any means whatsoever. With respect to military equipment, both sides are permitted to replace all existing military equipment on a one-to-one basis under international supervision and control.

There will be established, as I will explain when I discuss the protocols, for each side, three legitimate points of entry through which all replacement equipment has to move. These legitimate points of entry will be under international supervision.

Return of Prisoners

Chapter III deals with the return of captured military personnel and foreign civilians, as well as with the question of civilian detainees within South Vietnam.

This, as you know, throughout the negotiations, presented enormous difficulties for us. We insisted throughout that the question of American prisoners of war and of American civilians captured throughout Indochina should be separate from the issue of Vietnamese civilian personnel detained, partly because of the enormous difficulty of classifying the Vietnamese civilian personnel by categories of who was detained for reasons of the civil war and who was detained for criminal activities.

And secondly, because it was foreseeable that negotiations about the release of civilian detainees would be complex and difficult and because we did not want to have the issue of American personnel mixed up with the issues of civilian personnel in South Vietnam.

This turned out to be one of the thorniest issues, that was settled at some point and kept reappearing throughout the negotiations. It was one of the difficulties we had during the December negotiations.

As you can see from the agreement, the return of American military personnel and captured civilians is separate in terms of obligation, and in terms of the time frame from the return of Vietnamese civilian personnel.

The return of American personnel and the accounting of missing in action is unconditional and will take place within the same time frame as the American withdrawal.

The issue of Vietnamese civilian personnel will be negotiated between the two Vietnamese parties over a period of three months, and as the agreement says, they will do their utmost to resolve this question within the three month period.

So I repeat, the issue is separated, both in terms of obligation and in terms of the relevant time frame from the return of American prisoners which is unconditional.

We expect that American prisoners will be released at the intervals of two weeks or fifteen days in roughly equal installments. We have been told that no American prisoners are held in Cambodia. American prisoners held in Laos and North Vietnam will be returned to us in Hanoi. They will be received by American medical evacuation teams and flown on American airplanes from Hanoi to places of our own choice, probably Vientiane.

There will be international supervision of both this provision and of the provision for the missing in action. And all American prisoners will, of course, be released, within 60 days of the signing of the agreement. The signing will take place on January 27, in two installments, the significance of which I will explain to you when I have run through the provisions of the agreement and the associated protocol.

Self-Determination for South Vietnamese

Chapter IV of the agreement deals with the right of the South Vietnamese people to self-determination. Its first provision contains a joint statement by the United States and North Vietnam in which those two countries jointly recognize the South Vietnamese people's right to self-determination, in which those two countries jointly affirm that the South Vietnamese people shall decide for themselves the political system that they shall choose and jointly affirm that no foreign country shall impose any political conditions on the South Vietnamese people.

The other principal provision of the agreement that it implemented is the South Vietnamese people's right to self-determination. The two South Vietnamese parties will decide, will agree among each other, on free elections for offices to be decided by the two parties at a time to be decided by the two parties. These elections will be supervised and organized first by an institution which has the title of National Council for National Reconciliation and Concord, whose members will be equally appointed by the two sides which will operate on the principle of unanimity, and which will come into being after negotiation between the two parties who are obligated by this agreement to do their utmost to bring this institution into being within 90 days.

Leaving aside the technical jargon, the significance of this agreement, of this part of the agreement, is that the United States has consistently maintained that we would not impose any political solution on the people of South Vietnam. The United States has consistently maintained that we would not impose a coalition government or a disguised coalition government on the people of South Vietnam.

If you examine the provisions of this chapter, you will see, first, that the existing government in Saigon can remain in office; second, that the political future of South Vietnam depends on agreement between the South Vietnamese parties and not on an agreement that the United States has imposed on these parties; thirdly, that the nature of this political evolution, the timing of this political evolution, is left to the South Vietnamese parties, and that the organ that is created to see to it that the elections that are organized will be conducted properly, is one in which each of the South Vietnamese parties has a veto.

The other significant provision of this agreement is the requirement that the South Vietnamese parties will bring about a reduction of their armed forces, and that the forces being reduced will be demobilized.

Reunification of North and South

The next chapter deals with the reunification of Vietnam and the relationship between North and South Vietnam. In the many negotiations that I have conducted over recent weeks, not the least arduous was the negotiation conducted with the ladies and gentlemen of the press, who constantly raised issues with respect to sovereignty, the existence of South Vietnam as a political entity, and other matters of this kind. I will return to this issue at the end when I sum up the agreement, but it is obvious that there is no dispute in the agreement between the parties that there is an entity called South Vietnam, and that the future unity of Vietnam, as it comes about, will be decided by negotiation between North and South Vietnam; that it will not be achieved by military force; indeed, that the use of military force, with respect to bringing about unification, or any other form of coercion is impermissible according to the terms of this agreement.

Secondly, there are specific provisions in this chapter with respect to the Demilitarized Zone. There is a repetition of the agreement of 1954 which makes the demarcation line along the 17th Parallel provisional, which means pending reunification. There is a specific provision that both North and South Vietnam shall respect the Demilitarized Zone on either side of the provisional military demarcation line, and there is another provision that indicates that among the subjects that can be negotiated will be modalities of civilian movement across the demarcation line, which makes it clear that military movement across the Demilitarized Zone is in all circumstances prohibited.

Now, this may be an appropriate point to explain what our position has been with respect to the DMZ. There has been a great deal of discussion about the issue of sovereignty and about the issue of legitimacy, which is to say which government is in control of South Vietnam.

And finally, about why we laid such great stress on the issue of the
Demilitarized Zone. We had to place stress on the issue of the Demilitarized Zone because the provisions of the agreement with respect to
infiltration, with respect to replacement, with respect to any of the
military provisions, would have made no sense whatsoever if there was
not some demarcation line that defined where South Vietnam began. If
we had accepted the proposition that would have in effect eroded the
Demilitarized Zone, then the provisions of the agreement with respect
to restrictions about the introduction of men and material into South
Vietnam would have been unilateral restrictions applying only to the
United States and only to our allies. Therefore, if there was to be any
meaning to the separation of military and political issues, if there was
to be any permanence to the military provisions that had been negotiated, then it was essential that there was a definition of where the
obligations of this agreement began. As you can see from the text of the
agreement, the principles that we defended were essentially achieved.

Chapter VI deals with the international machinery, and we will discuss that when I talk about the associated protocols of the agreement.

Chapter VII deals with Laos and Cambodia. Now, the problem of
Laos and Cambodia has two parts. One part concerns those obligations
which can be undertaken by the parties signing the agreement—that is
to say, the three Vietnamese parties and the United States—those measures they can take which affect the situation in Laos and Cambodia.

A second part of the situation in Laos has to concern the nature of the
civil conflict that is taking place within Laos and Cambodia and the solution of which, of course, must involve as well the two Laotian parties
and the innumerable Cambodian factions.

Laos and Cambodia

Let me talk about the provisions of the agreement with respect to
Laos and Cambodia and our firm expectations as to the future in Laos
and Cambodia.

The provisions of the agreement with respect to Laos and Cambodia
reaffirm, as an obligation to all the parties, the provisions of the 1954
agreement on Cambodia and of the 1962 agreement on Laos, which
affirm the neutrality and right to self-determination of those two countries. They are, therefore, consistent with our basic position with respect
also to South Vietnam.

In terms of the immediate conflict, the provisions of the agreement
specifically prohibit the use of Laos and Cambodia for military and any
other operation against any of the signatories of the Paris Agreement
or against any other country. In other words, there is a flat prohibition
against the use of base areas in Laos and Cambodia.

There is a flat prohibition against the use of Laos and Cambodia for
infiltration into Vietnam or, for that matter, into any other country.

Finally, there is a requirement that all foreign troops be withdrawn from Laos and Cambodia, and it is clearly understood that North Vietnamese troops are considered foreign with respect to Laos and Cambodia.

Now, as to the conflict within these countries which could not be formally settled in an agreement which was not signed by the parties of that country, let me make this statement, without elaborating: It is our firm expectation that within a short period of time there will be a formal cease-fire in Laos which, in turn, will lead to a withdrawal of all foreign forces from Laos and, of course, to the end of the use of Laos as a corridor of infiltration.

Secondly, the situation in Cambodia, as those of you who have studied it will know, is somewhat more complex because there are several parties headquartered in different countries. Therefore, we can say about Cambodia that it is our expectation that a de facto cease-fire will come into being over a period of time relevant to the execution of this agreement.

Our side will take the appropriate measures to indicate that it will not attempt to change the situation by force. We have reason to believe that our position is clearly understood by all concerned parties, and I will not go beyond this in my statement.

Chapter VIII deals with the relationship between the United States and the Democratic Republic of Vietnam.

As I have said in my briefings on October 26th and on December 16th, and as the President affirmed on many occasions, the last time in his speech last evening, the United States is seeking a peace that heals. We have had many armistices in Indochina. We want a peace that will last.

And, therefore, it is our firm intention in our relationship to the Democratic Republic of Vietnam to move from hostility to normalization and from normalization to conciliation and cooperation, and we believe that under conditions of peace we can contribute throughout Indochina to a realization of the human aspirations of all the people of Indochina and we will, in that spirit, perform our traditional role of helping people realize these aspirations in peace.

Chapter IX of the agreement is the usual implementing provision.

So much for the agreement.

The Four Protocols

Now, let me say a word about the protocols. There are four protocols or implementing instruments to the agreement: On the return of American prisoners, on the implementation and institution of an international control commission, on the regulations with respect to the cease-fire and the implementation and institution of a joint military commission among the concerned parties, and a protocol about the deactivation and removal of mines.

I have given you the relevant provisions of the protocol concerning the return of prisoners. They will be returned at periodic intervals in Hanoi to American authorities and not to American private groups. They will be picked up by American airplanes, except for prisoners held in the southern part of South Vietnam, which will be released at designated points in the south, again, to American authorities.

We will receive on Saturday, the day of the signing of the agreement, a list of all American prisoners held throughout Indochina and both parties, that is to say, all parties have an obligation to assist each other in obtaining information about the prisoners, missing in action, and about the location of graves of American personnel throughout Indochina.

The International Commission has the right to visit the last place of detention of the prisoners, as well as the place from which they are released.

Now, to the International Control Commission. You may remember one of the reasons for the impasse in December was the difficulty of agreeing with the North Vietnamese about the size of the International Commission, its function, or the location of its teams.

On this occasion, there is no point in rehashing all the differences. It is, however, useful to point out that at that time the proposal of the North Vietnamese was that the International Control Commission have a membership of 250, no organic logistics or communication, dependent entirely on its authority to move on the party it was supposed to be investigating and over half of its personnel were supposed to be located in Saigon, which is not the place where most of the infiltration that we were concerned with was likely to take place.

We have distributed to you an outline of the basic structure of this Commission. Briefly stated, its total number is 1,160 drawn from Canada, Hungary, Indonesia, and Poland. It has headquarters in Saigon. It has seven regional teams, 26 teams based in localities throughout Vietnam which were chosen either because forces were in contact there or because we estimated that these were the areas where the violations of the cease-fire were most probable.

There are 12 teams at border crossing points. There are seven teams that are set aside for points of entry, which have yet to be chosen, for the replacement of military equipment. That is for Article 7 of the agreement. There will be three on each side and there will be no legitimate point of entry into South Vietnam other than those three points. The other border and coastal teams are there simply to make certain that no other entry occurs and any other entry is by definition illegal. There has to be no other demonstration except the fact that it occurred.

This leaves one team free for use, in particular, at the discretion of the Commission and of course the seven teams that are being used for the return of the prisoners can be used at the discretion of the Commission after the prisoners are returned.

There is one reenforced team located at the Demilitarized Zone and its responsibility extends along the entire Demilitarized Zone. It is in fact a team and a half. It is 50 percent larger than a normal border team and it represents one of the many compromises that were made between our insistence on two teams, their insistence on one team and by a brilliant stroke, we settled on a team and a half. (Laughter)

With respect to the operation of the International Commission, it is supposed to operate on the principle of unanimity, which is to say that its reports, if they are Commission reports, have to have the approval of all four members. However, each member is permitted to submit his own opinion so that as a practical matter, any member of the Commission can make a finding of a violation and submit a report at the first instance to the party.

The International Commission will report for the time being to the four parties to the agreement. We expect an international conference will take place at the Foreign Ministers' level.

Within a month of the signing of the agreement, that international conference will establish a relationship between the International Commission and itself, or any other international body that is mutually agreed upon, so that the International Commission is not only reporting to the parties that it is investigating, but for the time being, until the international conference has met, there was no other practical group to which the International Commission could report.

Joint Military Commissions

In addition to this international group, there are two other institutions that are supposed to supervise the cease-fire. There is first of all, an institution called the Four-Party Joint Military Commission, which is composed of ourselves and the three Vietnamese parties, which is located in the same place as the International Commission, charged with roughly the same functions, but as a practical matter, it is supposed to conduct the preliminary investigations. Its disagreements are automatically referred to the International Commission, and moreover, any party can request the International Commission to conduct an investigation regardless of what the Four-Party Commission does, and regardless of whether the Four-Party Commission has completed its investigation or not.

After the United States has completed its withdrawal, the Four-Party Military Commission will be transformed into a Two-Party Commission composed of the two South Vietnamese parties. The total number of supervisory personnel, therefore, will be in the neighborhood of 4,500 during the period that the Four-Party Commission is in existence, and in the neighborhood of about 3,000 after the Four-Party Commission ceases operating and the Two-Party Commission comes into being.

Finally, there is a protocol concerning the removal and deactivation of mines which is self-explanatory, and discusses the relationship between our efforts and the efforts of the DRV concerning the removal and deactivation of mines, which is one of the obligations we have undertaken in the agreement.

Signing of the Agreement

Now, let me point out one other problem. On Saturday, January 27th, the Secretary of State on behalf of the United States, will sign the agreement bringing the cease-fire and all the other provisions of the agreement and protocols into force. He will sign in the morning a document involving four parties, and in the afternoon a document between us and the Democratic Republic of Vietnam. These documents are identical, except that the preamble differs in both cases.

The reason for this somewhat convoluted procedure is that, while the agreement provides that the two South Vietnamese parties should settle their disputes in an atmosphere of national reconciliation and concord, I think it is safe to say that they have not yet quite reached that point; indeed, that they have not yet been prepared to recognize each other's existence.

This being the case, it was necessary to devise one document in which neither of the South Vietnamese parties was mentioned by name and, therefore, no other party could be mentioned by name on the principle of equality. So the four-party document, the document that will have four signatures, can be read with great care and you will not know until you get to the signature page whom, exactly, it applies to. It refers only to the parties participating in the Paris Conference, which are, of course, well known to the parties participating in the Paris Conference. (Laughter)

It will be signed on two separate pages. The United States and the GVN are signing on one page, and the Democratic Republic of Vietnam and its ally are signing on a separate page, and this procedure has aged us all by several years. (Laughter)

Then there is another document which will be signed by the Secretary of State and the Foreign Minister of the Democratic Republic of Vietnam in the afternoon. That document, in its operative provisions, is word for word the same as the document which will be signed in the morning, and which contains the obligations to which the two South Vietnamese parties are obligated.

It differs from that document only in the preamble and in its concluding paragraph. In the preamble it says the United States, with the concurrence of the Government of the Republic of Vietnam, and the DRV, with the concurrence of the Provisional Revolutionary Government, and the rest is the same, and then the concluding paragraph has the same adaptation. That document, of course, is not signed by either

Saigon or its opponent and, therefore, their obligations are derived from the four-party document.

I do not want to take any time in going into the abstruse legalism. I simply wanted to explain to you why there were two different signature ceremonies, and why, when we handed out the text of the Agreement, we appended to the document which contains the legal obligations which apply to everybody—namely, the four parties—we appended another section that contained a different preamble and a different implementing paragraph which is going to be signed by the Secretary of State and the Foreign Minister of the Democratic Republic of Vietnam.

This will be true with respect to the agreement and three of the protocols. The fourth protocol regarding the removal of mines applies only to the United States and the Democratic Republic of Vietnam and, therefore, we are in the happy position of having to sign only one document.

Summary of Final Negotiations

Now, then, let me summarize for you how we got to this point, and some of the aspects of the agreement that we consider significant, and then I will answer your questions.

As you know, when I met with this group on December 16th, we had to report that the negotiations in Paris seemed to have reached a stalemate. We had not agreed at that time, although we didn't say so. We could not find a formula to take into account the conflicting views with respect to signing. There were disagreements with respect to the DMZ and with the associated aspects of what identity South Vietnam was to have in the agreement.

There was a total deadlock with respect to the protocols, which I summed up in the December 16th press conference. The North Vietnamese approach to international control and ours were so totally at variance that it seemed impossible at that point to come to any satisfactory conclusion, and there began to be even some concern that the separation which we thought we had achieved in October between the release of our prisoners and the question of civilian prisoners in South Vietnam was breaking down.

When we reassembled on January 8th, we did not do so in the most cordial atmosphere that I remember. However, by the morning of January 9th it became apparent that both sides were determined to make a serious effort to break the deadlock in negotiations, and we adopted a mode of procedure by which issues in the agreement and issues of principle with respect to the protocols were discussed at meetings between Special Advisor Le Duc Tho and myself, while concurrently an American team headed by Ambassador Sullivan and a Vietnamese team headed by Vice Minister Thach would work on implementation of the principles as they applied to the protocols.

For example, the Special Advisor and I might agree on the principle of broader control posts and their number, but then the problem of how to locate, according to what criteria, and with what mode of operation presented enormous difficulty.

Let me on this occasion also point out that these negotiations required the closest cooperation throughout our government, between the White House and the State Department, between all the elements of our team, and that, therefore, the usual speculation of who did what to whom is really extraordinarily misplaced.

Without a cooperative effort by everybody, we could not have achieved what we have presented last night and this morning.

The Special Advisor and I then spent the week, first on working out the unresolved issues with respect to the protocols, and finally, the surrounding circumstances of schedules and procedures.

Ambassador Sullivan remained behind to draft the implementing provisions of the agreements that had been achieved during the week. The Special Advisor and I remained in close contact.

So by the time we met again yesterday, the issues that remained were very few, indeed, and while we settled relatively rapidly, I may on this occasion also point out that the North Vietnamese are the most difficult people to negotiate with that I have ever encountered when they do not want to settle. They are also the most effective that I have dealt with when they finally decide to settle. That is why we have gone through peaks and valleys in these negotiations of extraordinary intensity.

Situation on October 26

Now then, let me sum up where this agreement has left us. First with respect to what we said we would try to achieve, and then with respect to some of its significance and, finally, with respect to the future.

First, when I met this group on October 26th and delivered myself of some epigrammatic phrases, we obviously did not want to give a complete check list, and we did not want to release the agreement as it then stood, because it did not seem to us desirable to provide a check list against which both sides would then have to measure success and failure in terms of their prestige.

At that time, too, we did not say—it had always been foreseen that there would be another three or four days of negotiations after this tentative agreement had been reached. The reason why we asked for another negotiation was because it seemed to us at that point that for a variety of reasons, which I explained then and again on December 16th, those issues could not be settled within the time frame that the North Vietnamese expected.

It is now a matter of history, and it is, therefore, not essential to go into a debate of on what we based this judgment. But that was the reason why the agreement was not signed on October 31, and not any of the speculations that have been so much in print and on television.

Now, what did we say on October 26th we wanted to achieve? We said, first of all, that we wanted to make sure that the control machinery would be in place at the time of the cease-fire. We did this because we had information that there were plans by the other side to mount a major offensive to coincide with the signing of the cease-fire agreement.

This objective has been achieved by the fact that the protocols will be signed on the same day as the agreement, by the fact that the International Control Commission and the four-party military commission will meet within 24 hours of the agreement going into effect or no later than Monday morning, Saigon time; that the regional teams of the International Control Commission will be in place 48 hours thereafter, and that all other teams will be in place within 15 and a maximum of 30 days after that.

Second, we said that we wanted to compress the time interval between the cease-fire we expected in Laos and Cambodia and the cease-fire in Vietnam.

For reasons which I have explained to you, we cannot be as specific about the cease-fires in Laos and Cambodia as we can about the agreements that are being signed on Saturday, but we can say with confidence that the formal cease-fire in Laos will go into effect in a considerably shorter period of time than was envisaged in October, and since the cease-fire in Cambodia depends to some extent on developments in Laos, we expect the same to be true there.

We said that certain linguistic ambiguities should be removed. The linguistic ambiguities were produced by the somewhat extraordinary negotiating procedure whereby a change in the English text did not always produce a correlative change in the Vietnamese text. The linguistic ambiguities to which we referred in October have, in fact, been removed. At that time I mentioned only one, and therefore I am free to recall it.

I pointed out that the United States position had consistently been a rejection of the imposition of a coalition government on the people of South Vietnam. I said then that the National Council of Reconciliation was not a coalition government, nor was it conceived as a coalition government.

The Vietnamese language text, however, permitted an interpretation of the words "administrative structure" as applied to the National Council of Reconciliation which would have lent itself to the interpretation that it came close or was identical with a coalition government.

You will find that in the text of this agreement the words "administrative structure" no longer exist and therefore this particular, shall we say, ambiguity has been removed.

I pointed out in October that we had to find a procedure for signing which would be acceptable to all the parties for whom obligations were involved. This has been achieved.

I pointed out on October 26th that we would seek greater precision with respect to certain obligations particularly, without spelling them out, as they applied to the Demilitarized Zone and to the obligations with respect to Laos and Cambodia. That, too, has been achieved.

And I pointed out in December that we were looking for some means, some expression, which would make clear that the two parts of Vietnam would live in peace with each other, and that neither side would impose its solution on the other by force.

This is now explicitly provided, and we have achieved formulations in which in a number of the paragraphs, such as Article 14, 18(e) and 20, there is specific reference to the sovereignty of South Vietnam.

There are specific references, moreover, to the same thing in Article 6 and Article 11 of the ICCS protocol. There are specific references to the right of the South Vietnamese people to self-determination.

Adaptations Achieved

And therefore, we believe that we have achieved the substantial adaptations that we asked for on October 26th. We did not increase our demands after October 26th and we substantially achieved the clarifications which we sought.

Now then, it is obvious that a war that has lasted for 10 years will have many elements that cannot be completely satisfactory to all the parties concerned. And in the two periods where the North Vietnamese were working with dedication and seriousness on a conclusion, the period in October and the period after we resumed talks on January 8th, it was always clear that a lasting peace could come about only if neither side sought to achieve everything that it had wanted; indeed, that stability depended on the relative satisfaction and therefore on the relative dissatisfaction of all of the parties concerned. And therefore, it is also clear that whether this agreement brings a lasting peace or not depends not only on its provisions, but also on the spirit in which it is implemented.

It will be our challenge in the future to move the controversies that could not be stilled by any one document from the level of military conflict to the level of positive human aspirations and to absorb the enormous talents and dedication of the people of Indochina in tasks of construction, rather than in tasks of destruction.

We will make a major effort to move to create a framework where we hope in a short time the animosities and the hatred and the suffering of this period will be seen as aspects of the past, and where the debates concern differences of opinion as to how to achieve positive growth.

Of course, the hatred will not rapidly disappear, and, of course, people who have fought for 25 years will not easily give up their objectives, but also people who have suffered for 25 years may at least come to know that they can achieve their realization by other and less brutal means.

The President said yesterday that we have to remain vigilant, and so we shall, but we shall also dedicate ourselves to positive efforts. And for us at home, it should be clear by now that no one in this war has had a monopoly of anguish and that no one in these debates has had a monopoly of moral insight, and now that at last we have achieved an agreement in which the United States did not prescribe the political future to its allies; an agreement which should preserve the dignity and the self-respect of all of the parties that together with healing the wounds in Indochina we can begin to heal the wounds in America.

Text of Agreement on Ending the War and Restoring Peace in Vietnam, *signed in Paris, Jan. 27, 1973:*

The Parties participating in the Paris Conference on Vietnam.

With a view to ending the war and restoring peace in Vietnam on the basis of respect for the Vietnamese people's fundamental national rights and the South Vietnamese people's right to self-determination, and to contributing to the consolidation of peace in Asia and the world,

Have agreed on the following provisions and undertake to respect and to implement them:

Chapter I

THE VIETNAMESE PEOPLE'S FUNDAMENTAL NATIONAL RIGHTS

Article 1

The United States and all other countries respect the independence, sovereignty, unity, and territorial integrity of Vietnam as recognized by the 1954 Geneva Agreements on Vietnam.

Chapter II

CESSATION OF HOSTILITIES - WITHDRAWAL OF TROOPS

Article 2

A cease-fire shall be observed throughout South Vietnam as of 2400 hours G.M.T., on January 27, 1973.

At the same hour, the United States will stop all its military activities against the territory of the Democratic Republic of Vietnam by ground, air and naval forces, wherever they may be based, and end the mining of the territorial waters, ports, harbors, and waterways of the Democratic Republic of Vietnam. The United States will remove, permanently deactivate or destroy all the mines in the territorial waters, ports, harbors, and waterways of North Vietnam as soon as this Agreement goes into effect.

The complete cessation of hostilities mentioned in this Article shall be durable and without limit of time.

Article 3

The parties undertake to maintain the cease-fire and to ensure a lasting and stable peace.

As soon as the cease-fire goes into effect:

(a) The United States forces and those of the other foreign countries allied with the United States and the Republic of Vietnam shall remain in-place pending the implementation of the plan of troop withdrawal. The Four-Party Joint Military Commission described in Article 16 shall determine the modalities.

(b) The armed forces of the two South Vietnamese parties shall remain in-place. The Two-Party Joint Military Commission described in Article 17 shall determine the areas controlled by each party and the modalities of stationing.

(c) The regular forces of all services and arms and the irregular forces of the parties in South Vietnam shall stop all offensive activities against each other and shall strictly abide by the following stipulations:

—All acts of force on the ground, in the air, and on the sea shall be prohibited;

—All hostile acts, terrorism and reprisals by both sides will be banned.

Article 4

The United States will not continue its military involvement or intervene in the internal affairs of South Vietnam.

Article 5

Within sixty days of the signing of this Agreement, there will be a total withdrawal from South Vietnam of troops, military advisers, and military personnel, including technical military personnel and military personnel associated with the pacification program, armaments, munitions, and war material of the United States and those of the other foreign countries mentioned in Article 3 (a). Advisers from the above-mentioned countries to all paramilitary organizations and the police force will also be withdrawn within the same period of time.

Article 6

The dismantlement of all military bases in South Vietnam of the United States and of the other foreign countries mentioned in Article 3(a) shall be completed within sixty days of the signing of this Agreement.

Article 7

From the enforcement of the cease-fire to the formation of the government provided for in Articles 9 (b) and 14 of this Agreement, the two South Vietnamese parties shall not accept the introduction of troops, military advisers, and military personnel including technical military personnel, armaments, munitions, and war material into South Vietnam.

The two South Vietnamese parties shall be permitted to make periodic replacement of armaments, munitions and war material which have been destroyed, damaged, worn out or used up after the cease-fire, on the basis of piece-for-piece, of the same characteristics and properties, under the supervision of the Joint Military Commission of the two South Vietnamese parties and of the International Commission of Control and Supervision.

Chapter III

THE RETURN OF CAPTURED MILITARY PERSONNEL AND FOREIGN CIVILIANS, AND CAPTURED AND DETAINED VIETNAMESE CIVILIAN PERSONNEL

Article 8

(a) The return of captured military personnel and foreign civilians of the parties shall be carried out simultaneously with and completed not later than the same day as the troop withdrawal mentioned in Article 5. The parties shall exchange complete lists of the above-mentioned captured military personnel and foreign civilians on the day of the signing of this Agreement.

(b) The parties shall help each other to get information about those military personnel and foreign civilians of the parties missing in action, to determine the location and take care of the graves of the dead so as to facilitate the exhumation and repatriation of the remains, and to take any such other measures as may be required to get information about those still considered missing in action.

(c) The question of the return of Vietnamese civilian personnel captured and detained in South Vietnam will be resolved by the two South Vietnamese parties on the basis of the principles of Article 21 (b) of the Agreement on the Cessation of Hostilities in Vietnam of July 20, 1954. The two South Vietnamese parties will do so in a spirit of national reconciliation and concord, with a view to ending hatred and enmity, in order to ease suffering and to reunite families. The two South Vietnamese parties will do their utmost to resolve this question within ninety days after the cease-fire comes into effect.

Chapter IV

THE EXERCISE OF THE SOUTH VIETNAMESE PEOPLE'S RIGHT TO SELF-DETERMINATION

Article 9

The Government of the United States of America and the Government of the Democratic Republic of Vietnam undertake to respect the following principles for the exercise of the South Vietnamese people's right to self-determination:

(a) The South Vietnamese people's right to self-determination is sacred, inalienable, and shall be respected by all countries.

(b) The South Vietnamese people shall decide themselves the political future of South Vietnam through genuinely free and democratic general elections under international supervision.

(c) Foreign countries shall not impose any political tendency or personality on the South Vietnamese people.

Article 10

The two South Vietnamese parties undertake to respect the cease-fire and maintain peace in South Vietnam, settle all matters of contention through negotiations, and avoid all armed conflict.

Article 11

Immediately after the cease-fire, the two South Vietnamese parties will:

—achieve national reconciliation and concord, end hatred and enmity, prohibit all acts of reprisal and discrimination against individuals or organizations that have collaborated with one side or the other;

—ensure the democratic liberties of the people: personal freedom, freedom of speech, freedom of the press, freedom of meeting, freedom of organization, freedom of political activities, freedom of belief, freedom of movement, freedom of residence, freedom of work, right to property ownership, and right to free enterprise.

Article 12

(a) Immediately after the cease-fire, the two South Vietnamese parties shall hold consultations in a spirit of national reconciliation and concord, mutual respect, and mutual non-elimination to set up a National Council of National Reconciliation and Concord of three equal segments. The Council shall operate on the principle of unanimity. After the National Council of National Reconciliation and Concord has assumed its functions, the two South Vietnamese parties will consult about the formation of councils at lower levels. The two South Vietnamese parties shall sign an agreement on the internal matters of South Vietnam as soon as possible and do their utmost to accomplish this within ninety days after the cease-fire comes into effect, in keeping with the South Vietnamese people's aspirations for peace, independence and democracy.

(b) The National Council of National Reconciliation and Concord shall have the task of promoting the two South Vietnamese parties' implementation of this Agreement, achievement of national reconciliation and concord and ensurance of democratic liberties. The National Council of National Reconciliation and Concord will organize the free and democratic general elections provided for in Article 9 (b) and decide the procedures and modalities of these general elections. The institutions for which the general elections are to be held will be agreed upon through consultations between the two South Vietnamese parties. The National Council of National Reconciliation and Concord will also decide the procedures and modalities of such local elections as the two South Vietnamese parties agree upon.

Article 13

The question of Vietnamese armed forces in South Vietnam shall be settled by the two South Vietnamese parties in a spirit of national reconciliation and concord, equality and mutual respect, without foreign interference, in accordance with the postwar situation. Among the questions to be discussed by the two South Vietnamese parties are steps to reduce their military effectives and to demobilize the troops being reduced. The two South Vietnamese parties will accomplish this as soon as possible.

Article 14

South Vietnam will pursue a foreign policy of peace and independence. It will be prepared to establish relations with all countries irrespective of their political and social systems on the basis of mutual respect for independence and sovereignty and accept economic and technical aid from any country with no political conditions attached. The acceptance of military aid by South Vietnam in the future shall come under the authority of the government set up after the general elections in South Vietnam provided for in Article 9 (b).

Chapter V

THE REUNIFICATION OF VIETNAM AND THE RELATIONSHIP BETWEEN NORTH AND SOUTH VIETNAM

Article 15

The reunification of Vietnam shall be carried out step by step through peaceful means on the basis of discussions and agreements between North and South Vietnam, without coercion or annexation by either party, and without foreign interference. The time for reunification will be agreed upon by North and South Vietnam.

Pending reunification:

(a) The military demarcation line between the two zones at the 17th parallel is only provisional and not a political or territorial boundary, as provided for in paragraph 6 of the Final Declaration of the 1954 Geneva Conference.

(b) North and South Vietnam shall respect the Demilitarized Zone on either side of the Provisional Military Demarcation Line.

(c) North and South Vietnam shall promptly start negotiations with a view to reestablishing normal relations in various fields. Among the questions to be negotiated are the modalities of civilian movement across the Provisional Military Demarcation Line.

(d) North and South Vietnam shall not join any military alliance or military bloc and shall not allow foreign powers to maintain military bases, troops, military advisers, and military personnel on their respective territories, as stipulated in the 1954 Geneva Agreements on Vietnam.

Chapter VI

THE JOINT MILITARY COMMISSIONS, THE INTERNATIONAL COMMISSION OF CONTROL AND SUPERVISION, THE INTERNATIONAL CONFERENCE

Article 16

(a) The Parties participating in the Paris Conference on Vietnam shall immediately designate representatives to form a Four-Party

Joint Military Commission with the task of ensuring joint action by the parties in implementing the following provisions of this Agreement:

—The first paragraph of Article 2, regarding the enforcement of the cease-fire throughout South Vietnam;

—Article 3 (a), regarding the cease-fire by U.S. forces and those of the other foreign countries referred to in that Article;

—Article 3 (c), regarding the cease-fire between all parties in South Vietnam;

—Article 5, regarding the withdrawal from South Vietnam of U.S. troops and those of the other foreign countries mentioned in Article 3 (a);

—Article 6, regarding the dismantlement of military bases in South Vietnam of the United States and those of the other foreign countries mentioned in Article 3 (a);

—Article 8 (a), regarding the return of captured military personnel and foreign civilians of the parties;

—Article 8 (b), regarding the mutual assistance of the parties in getting information about those military personnel and foreign civilians of the parties missing in action.

(b) The Four-Party Joint Military Commission shall operate in accordance with the principle of consultations and unanimity. Disagreements shall be referred to the International Commission of Control and Supervision.

(c) The Four-Party Joint Military Commission shall begin operating immediately after the signing of this Agreement and end its activities in sixty days, after the completion of the withdrawal of U.S. troops and those of the other foreign countries mentioned in Article 3 (a) and the completion of the return of captured military personnel and foreign civilians of the parties.

(d) The four parties shall agree immediately on the organization, the working procedure, means of activity, and expenditures of the Four-Party Joint Military Commission.

Article 17

(a) The two South Vietnamese parties shall immediately designate representatives to form a Two-Party Joint Military Commission with the task of ensuring joint action by the two South Vietnamese parties in implementing the following provisions of this Agreement:

—The first paragraph of Article 2, regarding the enforcement of the cease-fire throughout South Vietnam, when the Four-Party Joint Military Commission has ended its activities;

—Article 3 (b), regarding the cease-fire between the two South Vietnamese parties;

—Article 3 (c), regarding the cease-fire between all parties in South Vietnam, when the Four-Party Joint Military Commission has ended its activities;

—Article 7, regarding the prohibition of the introduction of troops into South Vietnam and all other provisions of this article;

—Article 8 (c), regarding the question of the return of Vietnamese civilian personnel captured and detained in South Vietnam;

—Article 13, regarding the reduction of the military effectives of the two South Vietnamese parties and the demobilization of the troops being reduced.

(b) Disagreements shall be referred to the International Commission of Control and Supervision.

(c) After the signing of this Agreement, the Two-Party Joint Military Commission shall agree immediately on the measures and organization aimed at enforcing the cease-fire and preserving peace in South Vietnam.

Article 18

(a) After the signing of this Agreement, an International Commission of Control and Supervision shall be established immediately.

(b) Until the International Conference provided for in Article 19 makes definitive arrangements, the International Commission of Control and Supervision will report to the four parties on matters concerning the control and supervision of the implementation of the following provisions of this Agreement:

—The first paragraph of Article 2, regarding the enforcement of the cease-fire throughout South Vietnam;

—Article 3 (a), regarding the cease-fire by U.S. forces and those of the other foreign countries referred to in that Article;

—Article 3 (c) regarding the cease-fire between all the parties in South Vietnam;

—Article 5, regarding the withdrawal from South Vietnam of U.S. troops and those of the other foreign countries mentioned in Article 3 (a);

—Article 6, regarding the dismantlement of military bases in South Vietnam of the United States and those of the other foreign countries mentioned in Article 3 (a);

—Article 8 (a), regarding the return of captured military personnel and foreign civilians of the parties.

The International Commission of Control and Supervision shall form control teams for carrying out its tasks. The four parties shall agree immediately on the location and operation of these teams. The parties will facilitate their operation.

(c) Until the International Conference makes definitive arrangements, the International Commission of Control and Supervision will report to the two South Vietnamese parties on matters concerning the control and supervision of the implementation of the following provisions of this Agreement:

—The first paragraph of Article 2, regarding the enforcement of the cease-fire throughout South Vietnam, when the Four-Party Joint Military Commission has ended its activities;

—Article 3 (b), regarding the cease-fire between the two South Vietnamese parties;

—Article 3 (c), regarding the cease-fire between all parties in South Vietnam, when the Four-Party Joint Military Commission has ended its activities;

—Article 7, regarding the prohibition of the introduction of troops into South Vietnam and all other provisions of this Article;

—Article 8 (c), regarding the question of the return of Vietnamese civilian personnel captured and detained in South Vietnam;

—Article 9 (b), regarding the free and democratic general elections in South Vietnam;

—Article 13, regarding the reduction of the military effectives of the two South Vietnamese parties and the demobilization of the troops being reduced.

The International Commission of Control and Supervision shall form control teams for carrying out its tasks. The two South Vietnamese parties shall agree immediately on the location and operation of these teams. The two South Vietnamese parties will facilitate their operation.

(d) The International Commission of Control and Supervision shall be composed of representatives of four countries: Canada, Hungary, Indonesia and Poland. The chairmanship of this Commission will rotate among the members for specific periods to be determined by the Commission.

(e) The International Commission of Control and Supervision shall carry out its tasks in accordance with the principle of respect for the sovereignty of South Vietnam.

(f) The International Commission of Control and Supervision shall operate in accordance with the principle of consultations and unanimity.

(g) The International Commission of Control and Supervision shall begin operating when a cease-fire comes into force in Vietnam. As regards the provisions in Article 18 (b) concerning the four parties, the International Commission of Control and Supervision shall end its activities when the Commission's tasks of control and supervision regarding these provisions have been fulfilled. As regards the provisions in Article 18 (c) concerning the two South Vietnamese parties, the International Commission of Control and Supervision shall end its activities on the request of the government formed after the general elections in South Vietnam provided for in Article 9 (b).

(h) The four parties shall agree immediately on the organization, means of activity, and expenditures of the International Commission of Control and Supervision. The relationship between the International Commission and the International Conference will be agreed upon by the International Commission and the International Conference.

Article 19

The parties agree on the convening of an International Conference within thirty days of the signing of this Agreement to acknowledge the signed agreements; to guarantee the ending of the war, the maintenance of peace in Vietnam, the respect of the Vietnamese people's fundamental national rights, and the South Vietnamese people's right to self-determination; and to contribute to and guarantee peace in Indochina.

The United States and the Democratic Republic of Vietnam, on behalf of the parties participating in the Paris Conference on Vietnam, will propose to the following parties that they participate in this International Conference: the People's Republic of China, the Republic of France, the Union of Soviet Socialist Republics, the United Kingdom, the four countries of the International Commission of Control and Supervision, and the Secretary General of the United Nations, together with the parties participating in the Paris Conference on Vietnam.

Chapter VII

REGARDING CAMBODIA AND LAOS

Article 20

(a) The parties participating in the Paris Conference on Vietnam shall strictly respect the 1954 Geneva Agreements on Cambodia and the 1962 Geneva Agreements on Laos, which recognized the Cambodian and the Lao peoples' fundamental national rights, i. e., the independence, sovereignty, unity, and territorial integrity of these countries. The parties shall respect the neutrality of Cambodia and Laos.

The parties participating in the Paris Conference on Vietnam undertake to refrain from using the territory of Cambodia and the territory of Laos to encroach on the sovereignty and security of one another and of other countries.

(b) Foreign countries shall put an end to all military activities in Cambodia and Laos, totally withdraw from and refrain from reintroducing into these two countries troops, military advisers and military personnel, armaments, munitions and war material.

(c) The internal affairs of Cambodia and Laos shall be settled by the people of each of these countries without foreign interference.

(d) The problems existing between the Indochinese countries shall be settled by the Indochinese parties on the basis of respect for each other's independence, sovereignty, and territorial integrity, and non-interference in each other's internal affairs.

Chapter VIII

THE RELATIONSHIP BETWEEN THE UNITED STATES AND THE DEMOCRATIC REPUBLIC OF VIETNAM

Article 21

The United States anticipates that this Agreement will usher in an era of reconciliation with the Democratic Republic of Vietnam as with all the peoples of Indochina. In pursuance of its traditional policy, the United States will contribute to healing the wounds of war and to post-war reconstruction of the Democratic Republic of Vietnam and throughout Indochina.

Article 22

The ending of the war, the restoration of peace in Vietnam, and the strict implementation of this Agreement will create conditions for establishing a new, equal and mutually beneficial relationship between the United States and the Democratic Republic of Vietnam on the basis of respect for each other's independence and sovereignty, and non-interference in each other's internal affairs. At the same time this will ensure stable peace in Vietnam and contribute to the preservation of lasting peace in Indochina and Southeast Asia.

Chapter IX

OTHER PROVISIONS

Article 23

This Agreement shall enter into force upon signature by plenipotentiary representatives of the parties participating in the Paris Conference on Vietnam. All the parties concerned shall strictly implement this Agreement and its Protocols.

Done in Paris this twenty-seventh day of January, One Thousand Nine Hundred and Seventy-Three, in Vietnamese and English. The Vietnamese and English texts are official and equally authentic.

[Separate Numbered Page]

For the Government of the
United States of America

For the Government of the
Republic of Vietnam

_____

_____

William P. Rogers
Secretary of State

Tran Van Lam
Minister for Foreign Affairs

[Separate Numbered Page]

For the Government of the
Democratic Republic of Vietnam

For the Provisional Revolutionary
Government of the Republic of
South Vietnam

_____

_____

Nguyen Duy Trinh
Minister for Foreign Affairs

Nguyen Thi Binh
Minister for Foreign Affairs

PROTOCOL

to the Agreement on Ending the War and Restoring Peace in Vietnam

Concerning

the Removal, Permanent Deactivation, or Destruction of Mines in the Territorial Waters, Ports, Harbors, and Waterways of the Democratic Republic of Vietnam

The Government of the United States of America, the Government of the Democratic Republic of Vietnam, in implementation of the second paragraph of Article 2 of the Agreement on Ending the War and Restoring Peace in Vietnam signed on this date, have agreed as follows:

Article 1. The United States shall clear all the mines it has placed in the territorial waters, ports, harbors, and waterways of the Democratic Republic of Vietnam. This mine clearing operation shall be accomplished by rendering the mines harmless through removal, permanent deactivation, or destruction.

Article 2. With a view to ensuring lasting safety for the movement of people and watercraft and the protection of important installations, mines shall, on the request of the Democratic Republic of Vietnam, be removed or destroyed in the indicated areas; and whenever their removal or destruction is impossible, mines shall be permanently deactivated and their emplacement clearly marked.

Article 3. The mine clearing operation shall begin at twenty-four hundred (2400) hours G.M.T. on January 27, 1973. The representatives of the two parties shall consult immediately on relevant factors and agree upon the earliest possible target date for the completion of the work.

Article 4. The mine clearing operation shall be conducted in accordance with priorities and timing agreed upon by the two parties. For this purpose, representatives of the two parties shall meet at an early date to reach agreement on a program and a plan of implementation. To this end:

(a) The United States shall provide its plan for mine clearing operations, including maps of the minefields and information concerning the types, numbers and properties of the mines;

(b) The Democratic Republic of Vietnam shall provide all available maps and hydrographic charts and indicate the mined places and all other potential hazards to the mine clearing operations that the Democratic Republic of Vietnam is aware of;

(c) The two parties shall agree on the timing of implementation of each segment of the plan and provide timely notice to the public at least forty-eight hours in advance of the beginning of mine clearing operations for that segment.

Article 5. The United States shall be responsible for the mine clearance on inland waterways of the Democratic Republic of Vietnam. The Democratic Republic of Vietnam shall, to the full extent of its capabilities, actively participate in the mine clearance with the means of surveying, removal and destruction and technical advice supplied by the United States.

Article 6. With a view to ensuring the safe movement of people and watercraft on waterways and at sea, the United States shall in the mine clearing process supply timely information about the progress of mine clearing in each area, and about the remaining mines to be destroyed. The United States shall issue a communique when the operations have been concluded.

Article 7. In conducting mine clearing operations, the U.S. personnel engaged in these operations shall respect the sovereignty of the Democratic Republic of Vietnam and shall engage in no activities inconsistent with the Agreement on Ending the War and Restoring Peace in Vietnam and this protocol. The U.S. personnel engaged in the mine clearing operations shall be immune from the jurisdiction of the Democratic Republic of Vietnam for the duration of the mine clearing operations.

The Democratic Republic of Vietnam shall ensure the safety of the U.S. personnel for the duration of their mine clearing activities on the territory of the Democratic Republic of Vietnam, and shall provide this personnel with all possible assistance and the means needed in the Democratic Republic of Vietnam that have been agreed upon by the two parties.

Article 8. This protocol to the Paris Agreement on Ending the War and Restoring Peace in Vietnam shall enter into force upon signature by the Secretary of State of the Government of the United States of America and the Minister for Foreign Affairs of the Government of the Democratic Republic of Vietnam. It shall be strictly implemented by the two parties.

Done in Paris this twenty-seventh day of January, One Thousand Nine Hundred and Seventy-Three, in Vietnamese and English. The Vietnamese and English texts are official and equally authentic.

For the Government of the United States of America	For the Government of the Democratic Republic of Vietnam
William P. Rogers Secretary of State	Nguyen Duy Trinh Minister for Foreign Affairs

PROTOCOL

to the Agreement on Ending the War and Restoring Peace in Vietnam

Concerning

the Cease-fire in South Vietnam and the Joint Military Commissions

The parties participating in the Paris Conference on Vietnam, in implementation of the first paragraph of Article 2, Article 3, Article 5, Article 6, Article 16 and Article 17 of the Agreement on Ending the War and Restoring Peace in Vietnam signed on this date which provide for the cease-fire in South Vietnam and the establishment of a Four-Party Joint Military Commission, have agreed as follows:

Cease-fire in South Vietnam

Article 1. The high commands of the parties in South Vietnam shall issue prompt and timely orders to all regular and irregular armed forces and the armed police under their command to completely end hostilities throughout South Vietnam, at the exact time stipulated in Article 2 of the Agreement and ensure that these armed forces and armed police comply with these orders and respect the cease-fire.

Article 2. (a) As soon as the cease-fire comes into force and until regulations are issued by the Joint Military Commissions, all ground, river, sea and air combat forces of the parties in South Vietnam shall remain in place; that is, in order to ensure a stable cease-fire, there shall be no major redeployments or movements that would extend each party's area of control or would result in contact between opposing armed forces and clashes which might take place.

(b) All regular and irregular armed forces and the armed police of the parties in South Vietnam shall observe the prohibition of the following acts:

(1) Armed patrols into areas controlled by opposing forces and flights by bomber and fighter aircraft of all types, except for unarmed flights for proficiency training and maintenance.

(2) Armed attacks against any person, either military or civilian, by any means whatsoever, including the use of small arms, mortars, artillery, bombing and strafing by airplanes and any other type of weapon or explosive device.

(3) All combat operations on the ground, on rivers, on the sea and in the air.

(4) All hostile acts, terrorism or reprisals; and

(5) All acts endangering lives or public or private property.

Article 3. (a) The above-mentioned prohibitions shall not hamper or restrict:

(1) Civilian supply, freedom of movement, freedom to work, and freedom of the people to engage in trade, and civilian communication and transportation between and among all areas in South Vietnam;

(2) The use by each party in areas under its control of military support elements, such as engineer and transportation units, in repair and construction of public facilities and the transportation and supplying of the population;

(3) Normal military proficiency training conducted by the parties in the areas under their respective control with due regard for public safety.

(b) The Joint Military Commissions shall immediately agree on corridors, routes, and other regulations governing the movement of military transport aircraft, military transport vehicles, and military transport vessels of all types of one party going through areas under the control of other parties.

Article 4. In order to avert conflict and ensure normal conditions for those armed forces which are in direct contact, and pending regulation by the Joint Military Commissions, the commanders of the opposing armed forces at those places of direct contact shall meet as soon as the cease-fire comes into force with a view to reaching an agreement on temporary measures to avert conflict and to ensure supply and medical care for these armed forces.

Article 5. (a) Within fifteen days after the cease-fire comes into effect, each party shall do its utmost to complete the removal or de-activation of all demolition objects, minefields, traps, obstacles or other dangerous objects placed previously, so as not to hamper the pop-ulation's movement and work, in the first place on waterways, roads and railroads in South Vietnam. Those mines which cannot be removed or deactivated within that time shall be clearly marked and must be removed or deactivated as soon as possible.

(b) Emplacement of mines is prohibited, except as a defensive mea-sure around the edges of military installations in places where they do not hamper the population's movement and work, and movement on waterways, roads and railroads. Mines and other obstacles already in place at the edges of military installations may remain in place if they are in places where they do not hamper the population's movement and work, and movement on waterways, roads and railroads.

Article 6. Civilian police and civilian security personnel of the parties in South Vietnam who are responsible for the maintenance of law and order, shall strictly respect the prohibitions set forth in Article 2 of this protocol. As required by their responsibilities, normally they shall be authorized to carry pistols, but when required by unusual cir-cumstances, they shall be allowed to carry other small individual arms.

Article 7. (a) The entry into South Vietnam of replacement arma-ments, munitions, and war material permitted under Article 7 of the agreement shall take place under the supervision and control of the Two-Party Joint Military Commission and of the International Commis-sion of Control and Supervision and through such points of entry only as are designated by the two South Vietnamese parties. The two South Vietnamese parties shall agree on these points of entry within fifteen days after the entry into force of the cease-fire. The two South Viet-namese parties may select as many as six points of entry which are not included in the list of places where teams of the International Com-mission of Control and Supervision are to be based contained in Article 4(d) of the protocol concerning the International Commission. At the same time, the two South Vietnamese parties may also select points of entry from the list of places set forth in Article 4 (d) of that protocol.

(b) Each of the designated points of entry shall be available only for that South Vietnamese party which is in control of that point. The two South Vietnamese parties shall have an equal number of points of entry.

Article 8. (a) In implementation of Article 5 of the agreement, the United States and the other foreign countries referred to in Article 5 of the agreement shall take with them all their armaments, muni-tions, and war material. Transfers of such items which would leave them in South Vietnam shall not be made subsequent to the entry into force of the agreement except for transfers of communications, transport, and other non-combat material to the Four-Party Joint Military Commission or the International Commission of Control and Supervision.

(b) Within five days after the entry into force of the cease-fire, the United States shall inform the Four-Party Joint Military Commission and the International Commission of Control and Supervision of the general plans for timing of complete troop withdrawals which shall take place in four phases of fifteen days each. It is anticipated that the numbers of troops withdrawn in each phase are not likely to be widely different, although it is not feasible to ensure equal numbers. The approximate numbers to be withdrawn in each phase shall be given to the Four-Party Joint Military Commission and the International Commission of Control and Supervision sufficiently in advance of actual withdrawals so that they can properly carry out their tasks in relation thereto.

Article 9. (a) In implementation of Article 6 of the agreement, the United States and the other foreign countries referred to in that article shall dismantle and remove from South Vietnam or destroy all military bases in South Vietnam of the United States and of the other foreign countries referred to in that article, including weapons, mines, and other military equipment at these bases, for the purposes of making them unusable for military purposes.

(b) The United States shall supply the Four-Party Joint Military Commission and the International Commission of Control and Supervision with necessary information on plans for base dismantlement so that those Commissions can properly carry out their tasks in relation thereto.

The Joint Military Commissions

Article 10. (a) The implementation of the agreement is the responsibility of the parties signatory to the agreement.

The Four-Party Joint Military Commission has the task of ensuring joint action by the parties in implementing the agreement by serving as a channel of communication among the parties, by drawing up plans and fixing the modalities to carry out, coordinate, follow and inspect the implementation of the provisions mentioned in Article 16 of the agreement, and by negotiating and settling all matters concerning the implementation of those provisions.

(b) The concrete tasks of the Four-Party Joint Military Commission are:

(1) To coordinate, follow and inspect the implementation of the above-mentioned provisions of the agreement by the four parties.

(2) To deter and detect violations, to deal with cases of violation, and to settle conflicts and matters of contention between the parties relating to the above-mentioned provisions.

(3) To dispatch without delay one or more joint teams, as required by specific cases, to any part of South Vietnam, to investigate alleged

violations of the agreement and to assist the parties in finding measures to prevent recurrence of similar cases.

(4) To engage in observation at the places where this is necessary in the exercise of its functions.

(5) To perform such additional tasks as it may, by unanimous decision, determine.

Article 11. (a) There shall be a Central Joint Military Commission located in Saigon. Each party shall designate immediately a military delegation of fifty-nine persons to represent it on the central commission. The senior officer designated by each party shall be a general officer, or equivalent.

(b) There shall be seven Regional Joint Military Commissions located in the regions shown on the annexed map and based at the following places:

Regions	Places
I	Hue
II	Danang
III	Pleiku
IV	Phan Thiet
V	Bien Hoa
VI	My Tho
VII	Can Tho

Each party shall designate a military delegation of sixteen persons to represent it on each regional commission. The senior officer designated by each party shall be an officer from the rank of lieutenant colonel, or equivalent.

(c) There shall be a joint military team operating in each of the areas shown on the annexed map and based at each of the following places in South Vietnam:

Region I
Quang Tri
Phu Bai

Region II
Hoi An
Tam Ky
Chu Lai

Region III
Kontum
Hau Bon
Phu Cat
Tuy An
Ninh Hoa
Ban Me Thuot

Region IV
Da Lat

Bao Loc
Phan Rang
Region V
An Loc
Xuan Loc
Ben Cat
Cu Chi
Tan An
Region VI
Moc Hoa
Giong Trom
Region VII
Tri Ton
Vinh Long
Vi Thanh
Khanh Hung
Quan Long

Each party shall provide four qualified persons for each joint military team. The senior person designated by each party shall be an officer from the rank of major to lieutenant colonel or equivalent.

(d) The Regional Joint Military Commissions shall assist the Central Joint Military Commission in performing its tasks and shall supervise the operations of the joint military teams. The region of Saigon-Gia Dinh is placed under the responsibility of the central commission which shall designate joint military teams to operate in this region.

(e) Each party shall be authorized to provide support and guard personnel for its delegations to the Central Joint Military Commission and Regional Joint Military Commissions, and for its members of the joint military teams. The total number of support and guard personnel for each party shall not exceed five hundred and fifty.

(f) The Central Joint Military Commission may establish such joint subcommissions, joint staffs and joint military teams as circumstances may require. The central commission shall determine the numbers of personnel required for any additional sub-commissions, staffs or teams it establishes, provided that each party shall designate one-fourth of the number of personnel required and that the total number of personnel for the Four-Party Joint Military Commission, to include its staffs, teams, and support personnel, shall not exceed three thousand three hundred.

(g) The delegations of the two South Vietnamese parties may, by agreement, establish provisional sub-commissions and joint military teams to carry out the tasks specifically assigned to them by Article 17 of the agreement. With respect to Article 7 of the agreement, the two South Vietnamese parties' delegations to the Four-Party Joint Military Commission shall establish joint military teams at the points of entry into South Vietnam used for replacement of armaments, munitions and war material which are designated in accordance with Article 7 of this protocol. From the time the cease-fire comes into force to the time when the Two-Party Joint Military Commission becomes operational, the two South Vietnamese parties' delegations to the Four-Party Joint Military Commission shall form a provisional sub-commission and provisional joint military teams to carry out its tasks concerning captured and detained Vietnamese civilian personnel. Where necessary for the above purposes, the two parties may agree to assign personnel additional to those assigned to the two South Vietnamese delegations to the Four-Party Joint Military Commission.

Article 12. (a) In accordance with Article 17 of the agreement which stipulates that the two South Vietnamese parties shall immediately designate their respective representatives to form the Two-Party Joint Military Commission, twenty-four hours after the cease-fire comes into force, the two designated South Vietnamese parties' delegations to the Two-Party Joint Military Commission shall meet in Saigon so as to reach an agreement as soon as possible on organization and operation of the Two-Party Joint Military Commission, as well as the measures and organization aimed at enforcing the cease-fire and preserving peace in South Vietnam.

(b) From the time the cease-fire comes into force to the time when the Two-Party Joint Military Commission becomes operational, the two South Vietnamese parties' delegations to the Four-Party Joint Military Commission at all levels shall simultaneously assume the tasks of the Two-Party Joint Military Commission at all levels, in addition to their functions as delegations to the Four-Party Joint Military Commission.

(c) If, at the time the Four-Party Joint Military Commission ceases its operation in accordance with Article 16 of the agreement, agreement has not been reached on organization of the Two-Party Joint Military Commission, the delegations of the two South Vietnamese parties serving with the Four-Party Joint Military Commission at all levels shall continue temporarily to work together as a provisional Two-Party Joint Military Commission and to assume the tasks of the Two-Party Joint Military Commission at all levels until the Two-Party Joint Military Commission becomes operational.

Article 13. In application of the principle of unanimity, the Joint Military Commissions shall have no chairmen, and meetings shall be convened at the request of any representative. The Joint Military Commissions shall adopt working procedures appropriate for the effective discharge of their functions and responsibilities.

Article 14. The Joint Military Commissions and the International Commission of Control and Supervision shall closely cooperate with and assist each other in carrying out their respective functions. Each Joint Military Commission shall inform the International Commission about the implementation of those provisions of the agreement for which that Joint Military Commission has responsibility and which are within the competence of the International Commission. Each Joint Military Commission shall inform the International Commission about the implementation of those provisions of the agreement for which that Joint Military Commission has responsibility and which are within the competence of the International Commission. Each Joint Military Commission may request the International Commission to carry out specific observation activities.

Article 15. The central Four-Party Joint Military Commission shall begin operating twenty-four hours after the cease-fire comes into force. The regional Four-Party Joint Military Commissions shall begin operating forty-eight hours after the cease-fire comes into force. The joint military teams based at the places listed in Article 11 (c) of this protocol shall begin operating no later than fifteen days after the cease-fire comes into force. The delegations of the two South Vietnamese parties shall simultaneously begin to assume the tasks of the Two-Party Joint Military Commission as provided in Article 12 of this protocol.

Article 16. (a) The parties shall provide full protection and all necessary assistance and cooperation to the Joint Military Commissions at all levels, in the discharge of their tasks.

(b) The Joint Military Commissions and their personnel, while carrying out their tasks, shall enjoy privileges and immunities equivalent to those accorded diplomatic missions and diplomatic agents.

(c) The personnel of the Joint Military Commissions may carry pistols and wear special insignia decided upon by each Central Joint Military Commission. The personnel of each party while guarding commission installations or equipment may be authorized to carry other individual small arms, as determined by each Central Joint Military Commission.

Article 17. (a) The delegation of each party to the Four-Party Joint Military Commission and the Two-Party Joint Military Commission shall have its own offices, communication, logistics and transportation means, including aircraft when necessary.

(b) Each party, in its areas of control shall provide appropriate office and accommodation facilities to the Four-Party Joint Military Commission and the Two-Party Joint Military Commission at all levels.

(c) The parties shall endeavor to provide to the Four-Party Military Commission and the Two-Party Joint Military Commission, by means of loans, lease, or gift, the common means of operation, including equipment for communication, supply, and transport, including aircraft when necessary. The Joint Military Commissions may purchase from any source necessary facilities, equipment, and services which are not supplied by the parties. The Joint Military Commissions shall possess and use these facilities and this equipment.

(d) The facilities and the equipment for common use mentioned above shall be returned to the parties when the Joint Military Commissions have ended their activities.

Article 18. The common expenses of the Four-Party Joint Military Commission shall be borne equally by the four parties, and the common expenses of the Two-Party Joint Military Commission in South Vietnam shall be borne equally by these two parties.

Article 19. This protocol shall enter into force upon signature by plenipotentiary representatives of all the parties participating in the Paris Conference on Vietnam. It shall be strictly implemented by all the parties concerned.

Done in Paris this twenty-seventh day of January, One Thousand Nine Hundred and Seventy-Three, in Vietnamese and English. The Vietnamese and English texts are official and equally authentic.

For the Government of the
United States of America

For the Government of the
Republic of Vietnam

William P. Rogers
Secretary of State

Tran Van Lam
Minister for Foreign Affairs

For the Government of the Democratic Republic of Vietnam	For the Provisional Revolutionary Government of the Republic of South Vietnam

Nguyen Duy Trinh
Minister for Foreign Affairs

Nguyen Thi Binh
Minister for Foreign Affairs

To be signed at the International
Conference Center, Paris
Saturday afternoon, Paris time,
January 27, 1973

PROTOCOL

to the Agreement on Ending the War and Restoring Peace in Vietnam

Concerning

the Cease-fire in South Vietnam and the Joint Military Commissions

The Government of the United States of America, with the concurrence of the Government of the Republic of Vietnam, the Government of the Democratic Republic of Vietnam, with the concurrence of the Provisional Revolutionary Government of the Republic of South Vietnam, in implementation of the first paragraph of Article 2, Article 5, Article 6, Article 16 and Article 17 of the Agreement on Ending the War and Restoring Peace in Vietnam signed on this date which provide for the cease-fire in South Vietnam and the establishment of a Four-Party Joint Military Commission and a Two-Party Joint Military Commission, have agreed as follows:

(Text of Protocol Articles 1-18 same as above)

Article 19. The protocol to the Paris Agreement on Ending the War and Restoring Peace in Vietnam concerning the cease-fire in South Vietnam and the Joint Military Commissions shall enter into force upon signature of this document by the Secretary of State of the Government of the United States of America and the Minister for Foreign Affairs of the Government of the Democratic Republic of Vietnam, and upon signature of a document in the same terms by the Secretary of State of the Government of the United States of America, the Minister for Foreign Affairs of the Government of the Republic of Vietnam, the Minister for Foreign Affairs of the Provisional Revolutionary Government of the Republic of South Vietnam. The protocol shall be strictly implemented by all the parties concerned.

Done in Paris this twenty-seventh day of January, One Thousand Nine Hundred and Seventy-Three, in Vietnamese and English. The Vietnamese and English texts are official and equally authentic.

For the Government of the
United States of America

For the Government of the
Democratic Republic of
Vietnam

William P. Rogers
Secretary of State

Nguyen Duy Trinh
Minister for Foreign Affairs

PROTOCOL

to the Agreement on Ending the War
and Restoring Peace in Vietnam

Concerning

the Return of Captured Military Personnel
and Foreign Civilians and Captured and Detained
Vietnamese Civilian Personnel

The parties participating in the Paris conference on Vietnam, in implementation of Article 8 of the Agreement on Ending the War and Restoring Peace in Vietnam signed on this date providing for the return of captured military personnel and foreign civilians, and captured and detained Vietnamese civilian personnel, have agreed as follows:

The Return of Captured Military Personnel
and Foreign Civilians

Article 1. The parties signatory to the agreement shall return the captured military personnel of the parties mentioned in Article 8(a) of the agreement as follows:

● All captured military personnel of the United States and those of the other foreign countries mentioned in Article 3 (a) of the agreement shall be returned to United States authorities;

● All captured Vietnamese military personnel, whether belonging to regular or irregular armed forces, shall be returned to the two South Vietnamese parties; they shall be returned to that South Vietnamese party under whose command they served.

Article 2. All captured civilians who are nationals of the United States or of any other foreign countries mentioned in Article 3 (a) of the agreement shall be returned to United States authorities. All other

155

captured foreign civilians shall be returned to the authorities of their country of nationality by any one of the parties willing and able to do so.

Article 3. The parties shall today exchange complete lists of captured persons mentioned in Articles 1 and 2 of this protocol.

Article 4. (a) The return of all captured persons mentioned in Articles 1 and 2 of this protocol shall be completed within sixty days of the signing of the agreement at a rate no slower than the rate of withdrawal from South Vietnam of United States forces and those of the other foreign countries mentioned in Article 5 of the agreement.

(b) Persons who are seriously ill, wounded or maimed, old persons and women shall be returned first. The remainder shall be returned either by returning all from one detention place after another or in order of their dates of capture, beginning with those who have been held the longest.

Article 5. The return and reception of the persons mentioned in Articles 1 and 2 of this protocol shall be carried out at places convenient to the concerned parties. Places of return shall be agreed upon by the Four-Party Joint Military Commission. The parties shall ensure the safety of personnel engaged in the return and reception of those persons.

Article 6. Each party shall return all captured persons mentioned in Articles 1 and 2 of this protocol without delay and shall facilitate their return and reception. The detaining parties shall not deny or delay their return for any reason, including the fact that captured persons may, on any grounds, have been prosecuted or sentenced.

The Return of Captured and
Detained Vietnamese Civilian Personnal

Article 7. (a) The question of the return of Vietnamese civilian personnel captured and detained in South Vietnam will be resolved by the two South Vietnamese parties on the basis of the principles of Article 21 (b) of the Agreement on the Cessation of Hostilities in Vietnam of July 20, 1954, which reads as follows:

> "The term 'civilian internees' is understood to mean all persons who, having in any way contributed to the political and armed struggle between the two parties, have been arrested for that reason and have been kept in detention by either party during the period of hostilities."

(b) The two South Vietnamese parties will do so in a spirit of national reconciliation and concord with a view to ending hatred and enmity in order to ease suffering and to reunite families. The two South Vietnamese parties will do their utmost to resolve this question within ninety days after the cease-fire comes into effect.

(c) Within fifteen days after the cease-fire comes into effect, the two South Vietnamese parties shall exchange lists of the Vietnamese civilian personnel captured and detained by each party and lists of the places at which they are held.

Treatment of Captured Persons During Detention

Article 8. (a) All captured military personnel of the parties and captured foreign civilians of the parties shall be treated humanely at all times, and in accordance with international practice.

They shall be protected against all violence to life and person, in particular against murder in any form, mutilation, torture and cruel treatment, and outrages upon personal dignity. These persons shall not be forced to join the armed forces of the detaining party.

They shall be given adequate food, clothing, shelter and the medical attention required for their state of health. They shall be allowed to exchange post cards and letters with their families and receive parcels.

(b) All Vietnamese civilian personnel captured and detained in Souᵗʰ Vietnam shall be treated humanely at all times, and in accordance with international practice.

They shall be protected against all violence to life and person, in particular against murder in any form, mutilation, torture and cruel treatment, and outrages against personal dignity. The detaining parties shall not deny or delay their return for any reason, including the fact that captured persons may, on any grounds, have been prosecuted or sentenced. These persons shall not be forced to join the armed forces of the detaining party.

They shall be given adequate food, clothing, shelter, and the medical attention required for their state of health. They shall be allowed to exchange post cards and letters with their families and receive parcels.

Article 9. (a) To contribute to improving the living conditions of the captured military personnel of the parties and foreign civilians of the parties, the parties shall, within fifteen days after the cease-fire comes into effect, agree upon the designation of two or more national Red Cross societies to visit all places where captured military personnel and foreign civilians are held.

(b) To contribute to improving the living conditions of the captured and detained Vietnamese civilian personnel, the two South Vietnamese parties shall, within fifteen days after the cease-fire comes into effect, agree upon the designation of two or more national Red Cross societies to visit all places where the captured and detained Vietnamese civilian personnel are held.

With Regard to Dead and Missing Persons

Article 10. (a) The Four-Party Joint Military Commission shall ensure joint action by the parties in implementing Article 8 (b) of the

157

agreement. When the Four-Party Joint Military Commission has ended its activities, a four-part joint military team shall be maintained to carry on this task.

(b) With regard to Vietnamese civilian personnel dead or missing in South Vietnam, the two South Vietnamese parties shall help each other to obtain information about missing persons, determine the location and take care of the graves of the dead, in a spirit of national reconciliation and concord, in keeping with the people's aspirations.

Other Provisions

Article 11. (a) The Four-Party and Two-Party Joint Military Commissions will have the responsibility of determining immediately the modalities of implementing the provisions of this protocol consistent with their respective responsibilities under Articles 16 (a) and 17 (a) of the agreement. In case the Joint Military Commissions, when carrying out their tasks, cannot reach agreement on a matter pertaining to the return of captured personnel they shall refer to the International Commission for its assistance.

(b) The Four-Party Joint Military Commission shall form, in addition to the teams established by the protocol concerning the cease-fire in South Vietnam and the Joint Military Commissions, a sub-commission on captured persons and, as required, joint military teams on captured persons to assist the commission in its tasks.

(c) From the time the cease-fire comes into force to the time when the Two-Party Joint Military Commission becomes operational, the two South Vietnamese parties' delegations to the Four-Party Joint Military Commission shall form a provisional sub-commission and provisional joint military teams to carry out its tasks concerning captured and detained Vietnamese civilian personnel.

(d) The Four-Party Joint Military Commission shall send joint military teams to observe the return of the persons mentioned in Articles 1 and 2 of this protocol at each place in Vietnam where such persons are being returned, and at the last detention places from which these persons will be taken to the places of return. The Two-Party Joint Military Commission shall send joint military teams to observe the return of Vietnamese civilian personnel captured and detained at each place in South Vietnam where such persons are being returned, and at last detention places from which these persons will be taken to the places of return.

Article 12. In implementation of Articles 18 (b) and 18 (c) of the agreement, the International Commission of Control and Supervision shall have the responsibility to control and supervise the observance of Articles 1 through 7 of this protocol through observation of the return of captured military personnel, foreign civilians and captured and detained Vietnamese civilian personnel at each place in Vietnam where these persons are being returned, and at the last detention places from which these persons will be taken to the places of return, the examination of lists, and the investigation of violations of the provisions of the above-mentioned articles.

Article 13. Within five days after signature of this protocol, each party shall publish the text of the protocol and communicate it to all the captured persons covered by the protocol and being detained by that party.

Article 14. This protocol shall come into force upon signature by plenipotentiary representatives of all the parties participating in the Paris Conference on Vietnam. It shall be strictly implemented by all the parties concerned.

Done in Paris this twenty-seventh day of January, One Thousand Nine Hundred and Seventy-Three, in Vietnamese and English. The Vietnamese and English texts are official and equally authentic.

For the Government of the
United States of America

William P. Rogers
Secretary of State

For the Government of the
Democratic Republic of
Vietnam

Nguyen Duy Trinh
Minister for Foreign Affairs

For the Government of the
Republic of Vietnam

Tran Van Lam
Minister for Foreign Affairs

For the Provisional
Revolutionary Government of
the Republic of South Vietnam

Nguyen Thi Binh
Minister for Foreign Affairs

To be signed at the International
Conference Center, Paris, Saturday
afternoon, Paris time, January 27, 1973:

PROTOCOL

to the Agreement on Ending the War
and Restoring Peace in Vietnam

Concerning

the Return of Captured Military Personnel
and Foreign Civil. ins and Captured and Detained
Vietnamese Civilian Personnel

The Government of the United States of America, with the concurrence of the Government of the Republic of Vietnam, the Government of the Democratic Republic of Vietnam, with the concurrence of the Provisional Revolutionary Government of the Republic of South Vietnam, in implementation of Article 8 of the Agreement on Ending the War and Restoring Peace in Vietnam signed on this date providing for the return of captured military personnel and foreign civilians, and captured and detained Vietnamese civilian personnel, have agreed as follows:

(Text of Protocol Articles 1-13 same as above)

Article 14. The protocol to the Paris Agreement on Ending the War and Restoring Peace in Vietnam concerning the return of captured military personnel and foreign civilians and captured and detailed Vietnamese civilian personnel shall enter into force upon signature of this document by the Secretary of State of the Government of the United States of America and the Minister for Foreign Affairs of the Government of the Democratic Republic of Vietnam, and upon signature of a document in the same terms by the Secretary of State of the Government of the United States of America, the Minister for Foreign Affairs of the Government of the Republic of Vietnam, the Minister for Foreign Affairs of the Government of the Democratic Republic of Vietnam, and the Minister for Foreign Affairs of the Provisional Revolutionary Government of the Republic of South Vietnam. The protocol shall be strictly implemented by all the parties concerned.

Done in Paris this twenty-seventh day of January, One Thousand Nine Hundred and Seventy-Three, in Vietnamese and English. The Vietnamese and English texts are official and equally authentic.

For the Government of the
United States of America

For the Government of the
Democratic Republic of Vietnam

William P. Rogers
Secretary of State

Nguyen Duy Trinh
Minister for Foreign Affairs

PROTOCOL

to the Agreement on Ending the War
and Restoring Peace in Vietnam

Concerning

the International Commission
of Control and Supervision

The parties participating in the Paris conference on Vietnam, in implementation of Article 18 of the Agreement on Ending the War and

Restoring Peace in Vietnam signed on this date providing for the formation of the International Commission of Control and Supervision, have agreed as follows:

Article 1. The implementation of the agreement is the responsibility of the parties signatory to the agreement.

The functions of the International Commission are to control and supervise the implementation of the provisions mentioned in Article 18 of the agreement. In carrying out these functions, the International Commission shall:

(a) Follow the implementation of the above-mentioned provisions of the agreement through communication with the parties and on-the-spot observation at the places where this is required.

(b) Investigate violations of the provisions which fall under the control and supervision of the Commission.

(c) When necessary, cooperate with the Joint Military Commissions in deterring and detecting violations of the above-mentioned provisions.

Article 2. The International Commission shall investigate violations of the provisions described in Article 18 of the agreement on the request of the Four-Party Joint Military Commission, or of the Two-Party Joint Military Commission, or of any party, or, with respect to Article 9 (b) of the agreement on general elections, of the National Council of National Reconciliation and Concord, or in any case where the International Commission has other adequate grounds for considering that there has been a violation of those provisions. It is understood that, in carrying out this task, the International Commission shall function with the concerned parties' assistance and cooperation as required.

Article 3. (a) When the International Commission finds that there is a serious violation in the implementation of the agreement or a threat to peace against which the Commission can find no appropriate measure, the Commission shall report this to the four parties to the agreement so that they can hold consultations to find a solution.

(b) In accordance with Article 18 (f) of the agreement, the International Commission's reports shall be made with the unanimous agreement of the representatives of all the four members. In case no unanimity is reached, the Commission shall forward the different views to the four parties in accordance with Article 18 (b) of the agreement, or to the two South Vietnamese parties in accordance with Article 18 (c) of the agreement, but these shall not be considered as reports of the Commission.

Article 4. (a) The headquarters of the International Commission shall be at Saigon.

(b) There shall be seven regional teams located in the regions shown on the annexed map and based at the following places:

Regions	Places
I	Hue
II	Danang
III	Pleiku
IV	Phan Thiet
V	Bien Hoa
VI	My Tho
VII	Can Tho

The International Commission shall designate three teams for the region of Saigon-Gia Dinh.

(c) There shall be twenty-six teams operating in the areas shown on the annexed map and based at the following places in South Vietnam:

Region I	Region V
Quang Tri	An Loc
Phu Bai	Xuan Loc
Region II	Ben Cat
Hoi An	Cu Chi
Tam Ky	Tan An
Chu Lai	**Region VI**
Region III	Moc Hoa
Kontum	Giong Trom
Hau Bon	**Region VII**
Phu Cat	Tri Ton
Tuy An	Vinh Long
Ninh Hoa	Vi Thanh
Ban Me Thuot	Khanh Hung
Region IV	Quan Long
Da Lat	
Bao Loc	
Phan Rang	

(d) There shall be twelve teams located as shown on the annexed map and based at the following places:

Gio Linh (to cover the area south of the provisional military demarcation line)

Lao Bao	
Ben Het	Vung Tau
Duc Co	Xa Mat
Chu Lai	Bien Hoa Airfield
Qui Nhon	Hong Ngu
Nha Trang	Can Tho

(e) There shall be seven teams, six of which shall be available for assignment to the points of entry which are not listed in paragraph

(d) above and which the two South Vietnamese parties choose as points for legitimate entry to South Vietnam for replacement of armaments, munitions, and war material permitted by Article 7 of the agreement. Any team or teams not needed for the above-mentioned assignment shall be available for other tasks, in keeping with the Commission's responsibility for control and supervision.

(f) There shall be seven teams to control and supervise the return of captured and detained personnel of the parties.

Article 5. (a) To carry out its tasks concerning the return of the captured military personnel and foreign civilians of the parties as stipulated by Article 8 (a) of the agreement, the International Commission shall, during the time of such return, send one control and supervision team to each place in Vietnam where the captured persons are being returned, and to the last detention places from which these persons will be taken to the places of return.

(b) To carry out its tasks concerning the return of the Vietnamese civilian personnel captured and detained in South Vietnam mentioned in Article 8 (c) of the agreement, the International Commission shall, during the time of such return, send one control and supervision team to each place in South Vietnam where the above-mentioned captured and detained persons are being returned, and to the last detention places from which these persons shall be taken to the places of return.

Article 6. To carry out its tasks regarding Article 9 (b) of the agreement on the free and democratic general elections in South Vietnam, the International Commission shall organize additional teams, when necessary. The International Commission shall discuss this question in advance with the National Council of National Reconciliation and Concord. If additional teams are necessary for this purpose, they shall be formed thirty days before the general elections.

Article 7. The International Commission shall continually keep under review its size, and shall reduce the number of its teams, its representatives or other personnel, or both, when those teams, representatives or personnel have accomplished the tasks assigned to them and are not required for other tasks. At the same time, the expenditures of the International Commission shall be reduced correspondingly.

Article 8. Each member of the International Commission shall make available at all times the following numbers of qualified personnel:

(a) One senior representative and twenty-six others for the headquarters staff.

(b) Five for each of the seven regional teams.

(c) Two for each of the other international control teams, except for the teams at Gio Linh and Vung Tau, each of which shall have three.

(d) One hundred sixteen for the purpose of providing support to the Commission Headquarters and its teams.

Article 9. (a) The International Commission, and each of its teams, shall act as a single body comprising representatives of all four members.

(b) Each member has the responsibility to ensure the presence of its representatives at all levels of the International Commission. In case a representative is absent, the member concerned shall immediately designate a replacement.

Article 10. (a) The parties shall afford full cooperation, assistance, and protection to the International Commission.

(b) The parties shall at all times maintain regular and continuous liaison with the International Commission. During the existence of the Four-Party Joint Military Commission, the delegations of the parties to that commission shall also perform liaison functions with the International Commission. After the Four-Party Joint Military Commission has ended its activities, such liaison shall be maintained through the Two-Party Joint Military Commission, liaison missions, or other adequate means.

(c) The International Commission and the Joint Military Commissions shall closely cooperate with and assist each other in carrying out their respective functions.

(d) Wherever a team is stationed or operating, the concerned party shall designate a liaison officer to the team to cooperate with and assist it in carrying out without hindrance its task of control and supervision. When a team is carrying out an investigation, a liaison officer from each concerned party shall have the opportunity to accompany it, provided the investigation is not thereby delayed.

(e) Each party shall give the International Commission reasonable advance notice of all proposed actions concerning those provisions of the agreement that are to be controlled and supervised by the International Commission.

(f) The International Commission, including its teams, is allowed such movement for observation as is reasonably required for the proper exercise of its functions as stipulated in the agreement. In carrying out these functions, the International Commission, including its teams, shall enjoy all necessary assistance and cooperation from the parties concerned.

Article 11. In supervising the holding of the free and democratic general elections described in Articles 9 (b) and 12 (b) of the agreement in accordance with modalities to be agreed upon between the National Council of National Reconciliation and Concord and the International Commission, the latter shall receive full cooperation and assistance from the National Council.

Article 12. The International Commission and its personnel who have the nationality of a member state shall, while carrying out their tasks, enjoy privileges and immunities equivalent to those accorded diplomatic missions and diplomatic agents.

Article 13. The International Commission may use the means of communication and transport necessary to perform its functions. Each South Vietnamese party shall make available for rent to the International Commission appropriate office and accommodation facilities and shall assist it in obtaining such facilities. The International Commission may receive from the parties, on mutually agreeable terms, the necessary means of communication and transport and may purchase from any source necessary equipment and services not obtained from the parties. The International Commission shall possess these means.

Article 14. The expenses for the activities of the International Commission shall be borne by the parties and the members of the International Commission in accordance with the provisions of this article:

(a) Each member country of the International Commission shall pay the salaries and allowances of its personnel.

(b) All other expenses incurred by the International Commission shall be met from a fund to which each of the four parties shall contribute twenty-three percent (23%) and to which each member of the International Commission shall contribute two percent (2%).

(c) Within thirty days of the date of entry into force of this protocol, each of the four parties shall provide the International Commission with an initial sum equivalent to four million, five hundred thousand (4,500,000) French francs in convertible currency, which sum shall be credited against the amounts due from that party under the first budget.

(d) The International Commission shall prepare its own budgets. After the International Commission approves a budget, it shall transmit it to all parties signatory to the agreement for their approval. Only after the budgets have been approved by the four parties to the agreement shall they be obliged to make their contributions. However, in case the parties to the agreement do not agree on a new budget, the International Commission shall temporarily base its expenditures on the previous budget, except for the extraordinary, one-time expenditures for installation or for the acquisition of equipment, and the parties shall continue to make their contributions on that basis until a new budget is approved.

Article 15. (a) The headquarters shall be operational and in place within 24 hours after the cease-fire.

(b) The regional teams shall be operational and in place, and three teams for supervision and control of the return of the captured and detained personnel shall be operational and ready for dispatch within 48 hours after the cease-fire.

(c) Other teams shall be operational and in place within fifteen to thirty days after the cease-fire.

Article 16. Meetings shall be convened at the call of the chairman. The International Commission shall adopt other working procedures appropriate for the effective discharge of its functions and consistent with respect for the sovereignty of South Vietnam.

Article 17. The members of the International Commission may accept the obligations of this protocol by sending notes of acceptance to the four parties signatory to the agreement. Should a member of the International Commission decide to withdraw from the International Commission, it may do so by giving three months notice by means of notes to the four parties to the agreement, in which case those four parties shall consult among themselves for the purpose of agreeing upon a replacement member.

Article 18. This protocol shall enter into force upon signature by plenipotentiary representatives of all the parties participating in the Paris Conference on Vietnam. It shall be strictly implemented by all the parties concerned.

Done in Paris this twenty-seventh day of January, One Thousand Nine Hundred and Seventy-Three, in Vietnamese and English. The Vietnamese and English texts are officially and equally authentic.

For the Government of the United States of America	For the Government of the Republic of Vietnam
William P. Rogers Secretary of State	Tran Van Lam Minister for Foreign Affairs
For the Government of the Democratic Republic of Vietnam	For the Provisional Revolutionary Government of the Republic of South Vietnam
Nguyen Duy Trinh Minister for Foreign Affairs	Nguyen Thi Binh Minister for Foreign Affairs

To be signed at the International Conference Center, Paris, Saturday afternoon, Paris time, January 27, 1973:

PROTOCOL

to the Agreement on Ending the War and Restoring Peace in Vietnam

Concerning

the International Commission of Control and Supervision

The Government of the United States of America, with the concurrence of the Government of the Republic of Vietnam, the Government of the Democratic Republic of Vietnam, with the concurrence of the

Provisional Revolutionary Government of the Republic of South Vietnam, in implementation of Article 18 of the Agreement on Ending the War and Restoring Peace in Vietnam signed on this date providing for the formation of the International Commission of Control and Supervision, have agreed as follows:

(Text of Protocol Articles 1-17 same as above.)

Article 18. The protocol to the Paris Agreement on Ending the War and Restoring Peace in Vietnam concerning the International Commission of Control and Supervision shall enter into force upon signature of this document by the Secretary of State of the Government of the United States of America and the Minister for Foreign Affairs of the Government of the Democratic Republic of Vietnam, and upon signature of a document in the same terms by the Secretary of State of the Government of the United States of America, the Minister for Foreign Affairs of the Government of the Republic of Vietnam, the Minister for Foreign Affairs of the Government of the Republic of Vietnam, and the Minister for Foreign Affairs of the Provisional Revolutionary Government of the Republic of South Vietnam. The protocol shall be strictly implemented by all the parties concerned.

Done in Paris this twenty-seventh day of January, One Thousand Nine Hundred and Seventy-Three, in Vietnamese and English. The Vietnamese and English texts are official and equally authentic.

For the Government of the
United States of America

_____

William P. Rogers
Secretary of State

For the Government of the
Democratic Republic of
Vietnam

_____

Nguyen Duy Trinh
Minister for Foreign Affairs

PRESIDENT'S BUDGET MESSAGE

January 28-29, 1973

A sharp cutback in federal spending on social programs was the main feature of the $268.7-billion budget for the fiscal year 1974 which President Nixon sent to Congress on Jan. 29. In a message accompanying the budget, and in a radio speech the preceding evening, the President laid strong emphasis on the necessity of combating inflation. Nixon's proposal to cut back social programs as a means of achieving budget goals was in line also with his advocacy of a "new federalism." Under the latter concept, some of the responsibilities that have been increasingly concentrated in Washington would be dispersed among state and local governments—through discontinuance or restriction of the federal programs and through allocation of special revenue-sharing funds to be used for the same or other purposes as states and localities saw fit.

To replace "70 outmoded narrower categorical grant programs," four special revenue-sharing plans were proposed—for education, law enforcement, manpower training, and urban community development. Funds to finance those plans, when in full operation, would amount to an estimated total of $6.9-billion. Dismantling or reduction of some of the major social programs, together with tight curbs on new federal outlays, the President said, provided the only responsible course to follow in order to ward off a tax increase. "I do not believe the American people want higher taxes any more than they want inflation," he added. "I am proposing to avoid both."

Budget Goals

The Nixon budget set $249.8-billion as the limit for spending in the fiscal year (FY) 1973 and $268.7-billion as the limit for FY 1974, beginning July 1, 1973. Revenues were expected to rise by $31-billion in FY 1974, reflecting an upward surge in the economy and a consequent rise in federal tax collections. An $18.9-billion increase in outlays in FY 1974 would leave a $12.7-billion deficit that year, down from an estimated $24.8-billion deficit in FY 1973. It was noted that on the full-employment budget basis the $12.7-billion deficit would be equivalent to a $300-million surplus. In his 1971 budget message, Nixon had explained that under a full-employment budget "spending does not exceed the revenues the economy could generate under the existing tax system at the time of full employment." The country is considered to have full employment when the jobless rate averages no more than 4 per cent.

Administration efforts to hold down spending were reflected in the proposed budget by a projected overall increase in 1974 outlays amounting to only $18.9-billion, or 8 per cent, over total 1973 outlays. Most of the increase would be caused by a $4.7-billion rise in defense spending, a $9.1-billion rise in Social Security, Medicare and Medicaid payments, and a $1.9-billion payment on the national debt. The President made it clear that, with an expected $31-billion increase in revenues in FY 1974, no tax increase would be necessary if Congress did not force spending beyond the limits set by the budget.

A Budget Innovation

A major innovation in the 1974 budget was a detailed projection of the budget figures for an additional year. Spending prospects for fiscal 1975, as well as 1974, were included. Nixon said the projection for FY 1975 left "very little room for the creation of new programs and no room for the postponement of the reductions and terminations proposed in this [1974] budget." On a full-employment basis, outlays in 1975 would rise to $288-billion and receipts to $290-billion, resulting in a full-employment surplus of $2-billion. A substantial approach to full employment thus could produce an actual budget balance in FY 1975, the first since FY 1969.

"Holding 1973 spending to $250-billion and achieving full-employment balance in 1974 and 1975 will be difficult," the President admitted. But he warned that if the projected spending levels for 1973 were exceeded, "the ballooning effect of one year's expenditures on the next would in turn have meant that 1974's expenditures would be about $288-billion, far beyond full-employment revenues, and 1975's expenditures would be approximately $312-billion, leading to a huge, inflationary deficit." The President offered his budget as "clear evidence of the kind of change in direction demanded by the great majority of the American people," and he urged Congress to "join me in a concerted effort to control federal spending" by enacting a rigid $268.7-billion ceiling on fiscal 1974 outlays.

Democratic Protest

The response from Democrats in Congress who did not share the President's view of his re-election mandate was immediate and negative. House Speaker Carl Albert (D Okla.) vowed that Congress "will not permit the President to lay waste the great programs...inaugurated by Franklin D. Roosevelt and advanced and enlarged by every Democratic President since then." Senate Labor and Public Welfare Committee Chairman Harrison A. Williams Jr. (D N.J.) termed the President's budget "contemptuous of the real needs of the American people." Republicans praised it as bold and responsible.

The budget focused attention once again on the continuing question of federal spending. Sen. Hubert H. Humphrey (D Minn.) in an article in The New York Times of Feb. 14 challenged the $268.7-billion ceiling set by the President: "The point is that the budget ceiling ought to be set, not by executive edict, but by Congress working together with the President on a ceiling that both meets the needs of our nation and is fiscally prudent." In the fall of 1972, many members of Congress had warned of an impending constitutional crisis when Nixon had urged that body to set a $250-billion ceiling on federal spending.

Submission of the budget also fueled the ongoing controversy over impoundment. The administration had let it be known that appropriation of funds for programs it opposed would lead to additional impounding. Congress in February began work on measures to require the President to spend funds previously held up for the Rural Environmental Assistance Program (REAP) and for federal airport grants. There was no precedent to indicate what could be done if Nixon vetoed the measures, Congress overrode the vetoes, and the President still refused to spend the money. Although previous Presidents had impounded funds, Nixon's use of the practice as a budget-cutting device stirred Sen. Sam J. Ervin Jr. (D N.C.), chairman of the Government Operations Committee and also of the Judiciary Subcommittee on the Separation of Powers, to introduce a bill setting up a procedure under which Congress might get the last word on impoundment of appropriated funds. When hearings on the bill began Jan. 30, some observers were hopeful that a showdown might be in sight on the cloudy constitutional question of which branch of government really controls the nation's purse strings.

Text of the President's nationwide radio address Jan. 28, 1973, on the budget for fiscal year 1974, and excerpts from his message to Congress on the same subject the following day:

The President's Radio Address

The New Budget: Charting a New Era of Progress

Good evening

At noon tomorrow, I will send to the Congress one of the most important documents I will sign as President—my budget proposals for the coming fiscal year.

This budget will not require higher taxes. It will not drive prices higher. And it will give us the chance I spoke of in my Inaugural Address—to make our new era of peace a new era of progress.

In the last few decades, the cost of government has skyrocketed. For every one dollar we were spending in 1952, we are spending nearly four dollars today. If the budget continues to double every 10 years, it will be over a trillion dollars by the 1990's—20 years from now—or as big as our entire economy is now.

We must resist this trend, for several reasons. The first involves your taxes.

Since 1950, the share of personal income taken for taxes by all levels of government has doubled—to more than 20 percent of your family budget. This growing burden works to dull individual incentive and discourage individual responsibility. As government takes more from people, people can do less for themselves. The only way to restrain taxes is to restrain spending.

In the campaign last fall, I promised I would not propose any new tax increases. By keeping a tight lid on spending, my new budget keeps that promise.

The second reason for resisting bigger government is its impact on our economy. We saw in the 1960's what happens when government spends beyond its means. The result is runaway inflation, the most insidious of all taxes, which begins by picking your pockets, goes on to threaten your very jobs. Not only the size of your tax bill but also the size of your grocery bill and the security of your job itself—all of these are at stake when we draw up the Federal budget.

In the past 4 years, we have put our economy back on course again. Since 1969, inflation has been cut nearly in half. Jobs increased more rapidly last year than at any time since 1947—25 years ago. Real spendable weekly earnings—that is what you have left to spend after paying your taxes and after allowing for inflation—showed their greatest improvement since 1955.

Best of all, the prospects for the coming year are very bright. 1973 could be our best year ever, ushering in a new era of prolonged and growing prosperity.

The greatest threat to our new prosperity is excessive government spending. My budget calls for spending $250 billion in the current fiscal year, $269 billion next year, and $288 billion in fiscal year 1975. These are large amounts but they would be $20 billion higher for each of the next 2 years if we had just gone about spending as usual. That, in turn, would have meant either an annual budget deficit of $30 billion a year, which would have led to higher prices, or a 15 percent increase in your income taxes.

To keep the totals even this low required a rigorous effort within the executive branch. But we cannot do the job alone.

If we are going to keep taxes and prices down, the Congress must keep spending down. That is why it is so important for the Congress to set a firm ceiling on its overall expenditures—so that the Congress will consider not only the particular merits of individual programs but also what happens to taxes and prices when you add them all together.

The third reason my new budget tries to curb the growth of government is that relying on bigger government is the wrong way to meet our Nation's needs. Government has grown by leaps and bounds since the 1930's, but so have problems—problems like crime and blight and inflation and pollution. The bigger government became, the more clumsy it became, until its attempts to help often proved a hindrance.

The time has come to get rid of old programs that have outlived their time or that have failed. Whenever the return on our tax dollars is not worth the expenditure, we must either change that program or end it.

In the next few days, you will hear about some very sharp reductions in some very familiar programs. Some have been regarded as sacred cows in the past. No matter what their real value, no one dared to touch them. Let me give you just a few examples.

Last year we spent nearly $200 million on the Hill-Burton program to help build more hospitals, but today the shortage of hospital beds which existed through the fifties and the sixties has been more than met. And yet, the Hill-Burton program continues to pour out funds, regardless of need.

Or take some of our urban renewal programs. They have cost us billions of dollars, with very disappointing results. And little wonder. How can a committee of Federal bureaucrats, hundreds or thousands of miles away, decide intelligently where building should take place? That is a job for people you elect at the local level, people whom you know, people you can talk to.

And then there is our aid to schools near Federal facilities. There was a time when this program made sense, when Federal workers were a drain on local resources. Now most Federal workers pay full local taxes. Yet we still have been paying out more than $500 million a year in compensation to these communities, many of which are among the richest in the country. And so I propose we change that program. Let us spend our education dollars where they are really needed.

Our search for waste has led us into every nook and cranny of the bureaucracy. And because economy must begin right at home, we are cutting the number of people who work in the President's own Executive Office from 4,200 to 1,700. That is a 60 percent reduction.

We also found we could save $2.7-billion in the projected defense budget for 1974 and $2.1 billion in the projected agricultural budget.

But after talking about these cuts, let's get one thing straight. Cutting back on Federal programs does not mean cutting back on progress. In fact, it means a better way to progress. When we cut a million dollars from a Federal program, that money is not lost and its power to do good things eliminated; rather, that money is transferred to other budgets where its power to do good things is multiplied. Some of it will stay in family budgets where people can use it as they, themselves, see fit.

Much will go back to State and county and municipal governments, back to the scene of the action, where needs are best understood, where public officials are most accessible and, therefore, most accountable.

And finally, some of the money we save will be shifted to other Federal programs—where it can do the most good with least waste for the most people.

I am proposing, for example, to double spending for major pollution control programs. I am asking for an 8 percent increase to fight crime and drug abuse, for a 20 percent increase in research to meet the energy crisis, for a 21 percent increase to fight cancer and heart disease.

In fact, overall spending for human resource programs will be increased to a level almost twice what it was when I first came to office. Instead of spending one-third of our budget on human resources and nearly half of our budget on defense—as we were doing in 1969—we have exactly reversed those priorities.

We can be thankful that with the war in Vietnam now ended, this is a true peacetime budget in every sense of the word.

In the days and weeks ahead, I shall be spelling out my recommendations in much greater detail. My budget will go to the Congress tomorrow; my Economic Report on Wednesday. And instead of delivering just one State of the Union Address, covering a laundry list of programs, I shall present my State of the Union report this year in a series of detailed messages on specific subjects. Together, these statements will chart a new course for America—a course that will bring more progress by putting more responsibility and money in more places.

In holding down spending, what is at stake is not just a big, impersonal Federal budget. What is at stake is your job, your taxes, the prices you pay, and whether the money you earn by your work is spent by you for what you want or by Government for what someone else wants.

It is important that the struggle to hold the line against bigger government not become a contest which pits one branch of government against another, but one which joins the President and the Congress in meeting a common challenge. And those in the Congress who enlist in this struggle need your support.

Every Member of the Congress gets enormous pressure from special interests to spend your money for what they want. And so I ask you to back up those Congressmen and those Senators, whether Democrats or Republicans, who have the courage to vote against higher spending. They hear from the special interests; let them hear from you.

It is time to get big government off your back and out of your pocket. I ask your support to hold government spending down, so that we can keep your taxes and your prices from going up.

Thank you and good evening.

Excerpts from Budget Message, Jan. 29

To the Congress of the United States:

The 1974 budget fulfills my pledge to hold down Federal spending so that there will be no need for a tax increase.

This is a budget that will continue to move the Nation's economy toward a goal it has not achieved in nearly two decades: a high employment prosperity for America's citizens without inflation and without war.... The 1974 budget proposes a leaner Federal bureaucracy, increased reliance on State and local governments to carry out what are primarily State and local responsibilities, and greater freedom for the American people to make for themselves fundamental choices about what is best for them.

This budget concerns itself not only with the needs of all the people, but with an idea that is central to the preservation of democracy: the "consent of the governed."

The American people as a whole—the "governed"—will give their consent to the spending of their dollars if they can be provided a greater say in how the money is spent and a greater assurance that their money is used wisely and efficiently by government. They will consent to the expenditure of their tax dollars as long as individual incentive is not sapped by an ever-increasing percentage of earnings taken for taxes.

Since the mid-1950's, the share of the Nation's output taken by all governments in the United States—Federal, State, and local—has increased from a quarter to a third. It need not and should not go higher.

The increase in government claims on taxpayers was not for defense programs. In fact, the defense share of the gross national product declined by one-quarter while the share for civilian activities of all governments grew by three-fourths, rising from 14% of the gross national product in 1955 to about 25% in 1972.

In no sense have Federal civilian programs been starved; their share of the gross national product will increase from 6 1/2% in 1955 to 14% in 1972. Nor will they be starved by the budget that I am proposing. A generous increase in outlays is provided each year by the normal growth in revenues. Higher Federal tax rates are not needed now or in the years ahead to assure adequate resources for properly responsive government—*if* the business of government is managed well. And revenue sharing will help State and local governments avoid higher taxes.

During the past 2 years, with the economy operating below capacity and the threat of inflation receding, the Federal budget provided fiscal stimulus that moved the economy toward full employment. The 1974 budget recognizes the Federal Government's continuing obligation to help create and maintain—through sound monetary and fiscal policies—the conditions in which the national economy will prosper and new job opportunities will be developed. However, instead of operating primarily as a stimulus, the budget must now guard against inflation.

The surest way to avoid inflation or higher taxes or both is for the Congress to join me in a concerted effort to control Federal spending. I therefore propose that before the Congress approves *any* spending bill, it establish a rigid ceiling on spending, limiting total 1974 outlays to the $268.7 billion recommended in this budget.

I do not believe the American people want higher taxes any more than they want inflation. I am proposing to avoid both higher taxes and inflation by holding spending in 1974 and 1975 to no more than revenues would be at full employment.

1975 Projections in the 1974 Budget

This year's budget presents, for the first time, a detailed preview of next year's. I have taken this step to demonstrate that if we stay within the 1974 and 1975 estimated outlays presented in this budget, we will prevent a tax increase—and that the 1974 budget is a sound program for the longer range future, not simply for today. This innovation in budget presentation is a blueprint for avoiding inflation and tax increases, while framing more responsive instruments of government and maintaining prosperity.

Our ability to carry out sound fiscal policy and to provide the resources needed to meet emerging problems has been limited by past decisions. In 1974, $202 billion in outlays, or 75% of the budget, is *virtually uncontrollable* due to existing law and prior-year commitments. But just as every budget is heavily influenced by those that have preceded it, so it strongly influences those that follow.

Control over the budget can be improved by projecting future available resources and the known claims on them, and then making current decisions within the constraints they impose. That is why, in my first budget, I began the practice of showing projections of future *total* revenues and outlays under current and proposed legislation. In the 1973 budget, 5-year projections of the cost of legislative proposals for major new and expanded programs were added.

This budget presents an even closer look at the implications of the 1974 proposals for the 1975 budget. It projects, in agency and functional detail, the outlays in 1975 that will result from the major program proposals in the 1974 budget, including the outlay savings that can be realized from program reductions in 1973 and 1974. In so doing, it takes into consideration the longer range effect of each of our fiscal actions.

Most importantly, this budget shows the narrow margin between projected outlays and full-employment revenues in 1975, despite the economy measures that are recommended. Program reductions and terminations of the scale proposed are clearly necessary if we are to keep control of fiscal policy in the future.

The 1974 budget program implies 1975 full-employment outlays of about $288 billion, $19 billion (7%) more than in 1974. This is within our estimate of full-employment revenues of $290 billion for 1975. There is, however, very little room for the creation of new programs requiring additional outlays in 1975 and *no room for the postponement of the reductions and terminations proposed in this budget.*

The program reductions and terminations I have proposed will result in more significant savings in 1975 and later years than in 1973 and 1974. It is for this reason, too, that I have included the 1975 projections in my budget this year. The Federal spending pipeline is a very long one in most cases, and the sooner we start reducing costs the better for the Nation.

The estimated 1975 outlays for the various Federal agencies are, of course, tentative. The outlay total, however, is the approximate amount that will represent appropriate Federal spending in 1975 if we are to avoid new taxes and inflation. As program priorities change and require increases in some areas, offsetting decreases must be found in others. As the projections indicate, this is necessary for both 1974 and 1975.

Fiscal Policy and the Budget Process

FISCAL POLICY.—In July 1970, I adopted the full-employment budget principle in order to make the budget a tool to promote orderly economic expansion.

Consistent with this principle, the budget that I submitted to the Congress last January proposed fiscal stimulus as part of a balanced economic program that included sound monetary policy and the new economic policy that I launched on August 15, 1971. My confidence that the American economy would respond to sensible stimulus in this context has been fully justified. During 1972, employment increased by 2.3 million persons, real output rose by 7½%, business fixed investment was 14% higher, and the rate of increase in consumer prices declined.

From 1971 through 1973, the full-employment budget principle permitted and called for substantial actual budget deficits. For this reason, some people have forgotten the crucial point that the full-employment principle requires that deficits be reduced as the economy approaches full employment—and that it establishes the essential discipline of an upper limit on spending at all times.

The full-employment budget principle permits fiscal stimulation when stimulation is appropriate and calls for restraint when restraint is appropriate. But it is not self-enforcing. It signals us what course to steer, but requires us to take the actions necessary to keep on course. These steps are not taken for us, and they are rarely easy.

As we look ahead, with the economy on the upswing, the full-employment budget principle—and common sense—prescribe a shift away from fiscal stimulus and toward smaller budget deficits. We *must* do what is necessary to make this shift.

Holding 1973 spending to $250 billion and achieving full-employment balance in 1974 and 1975 will be difficult. Reduction of some activities and termination of others are necessary and are proposed in this budget. Nonetheless, the budget provides significant increases for many important programs.

If we did not budget with firm restraint, our expenditures in 1973 would be over $260 billion. The ballooning effect of one year's expenditures on the next would in turn have meant that 1974's expenditures would be about $288 billion, far beyond full-employment revenues, and 1975's expenditures would be approximately $312 billion, leading to a huge, inflationary deficit.

If spending is to be controlled, the Congress must establish a spending ceiling promptly. Otherwise, the seeds sown in individual authorization and appropriation actions will produce ever-growing Federal spending not only in the coming fiscal year but in the years beyond.

Should the Congress cause the total budgeted outlays to be exceeded, it would inescapably face the alternatives of higher taxes, higher interest rates, renewed inflation, or all three. I oppose these alternatives; with a firm rein on spending, none of them is necessary.

REFORMING CONGRESSIONAL BUDGET PROCEDURES.—Delay in congressional consideration of the budget is a major problem. Each time I have submitted a budget, the Congress has failed to enact major portions of it before the next budget was prepared. Instead, it has resorted to the device of continuing resolutions to carry on the activities for which it has not made appropriations. Such delay needlessly compounds the complexities of budget preparation, and frustrates the potential of the budget as an effective management and fiscal tool.

The complexity of the budgeting process is another problem. Because of modifications made to reflect the desires of the more than 300 congressional committees and subcommittees that influence it, the process has become more complicated and less comprehensible.

The fragmented nature of congressional action results in a still more serious problem. Rarely does the Congress concern itself with the budget totals or with the effect of its individual actions on those totals. Appropriations are enacted in at least 15 separate bills. In addition, "backdoor financing" in other bills provides permanent appropriations, authority to contract in advance of appropriations, authority to borrow and spend without an appropriation, and program authorizations that require mandatory spending whether or not it is desirable in the light of current priorities.

At the same time, a momentum of extravagance is speeded by requirements created initially by legislative committees sympathetic to particular and narrow causes. These committees are encouraged by special interest groups and by some executive branch officials who are more concerned with expansion of their own programs than with total Federal spending and the taxes required to support that spending. Since most programs have some attractive features, it is easy for the committees and the Congress itself to authorize large sums for them. These authorizations, however, create pressure on the appropriations committees to appropriate higher amounts than the Nation's fiscal situation permits.

Last October, the Congress enacted legislation establishing a joint committee to consider a spending ceiling and to recommend procedures for improving congressional control over budgetary outlay and receipt totals.

I welcome this effort and pledge the full cooperation of my Administration in working closely with the committee and in other efforts of the Congress toward this end.

Specific changes in congressional procedures are, of course, the business of the Congress. However, the manner in which the Congress reviews and modifies the budget impinges so heavily on the management of the executive branch that I am impelled to suggest a few subjects that deserve high priority in the committee's deliberations, including:

—adoption of a *rigid* spending ceiling to create restraint on the total at the beginning of each annual review;

—avoidance of new "backdoor financing" and review of existing legislation of this type;

—elimination of annual authorizations, especially annual authorizations in specific amounts; and

—prompt enactment of all necessary appropriation bills before the beginning of the fiscal year.

The Congress must accept responsibility for the budget *totals* and must develop a systematic procedure for maintaining fiscal discipline. To do otherwise in the light of the budget outlook is to accept the responsibility for increased taxes, higher interest rates, higher inflation, or all three. In practice, this means that should the Congress pass any legislation increasing outlays beyond the recommended total, it must find financing for the additional amount. Otherwise, such legislation will inevitably contribute to undue inflationary pressures and thus will not be in the public interest. And it will be subject to veto.

I will do everything in my power to avert the need for a tax increase, but I cannot do it alone. The cooperation of the Congress in controlling total spending is absolutely essential.

Summary of the 1974 Budget

The 1974 budget proposes an approximate balance in full-employment terms and an actual deficit that is about one-half the 1973 deficit. The 1975 budget totals I propose here would also yield a balance in full-employment terms....

The full-employment budget balance in 1974 assures support for continuation of the economy's upward momentum without rekindling inflation. Greater stimulus in 1974 would be dangerous, and would put an unsupportable burden on future budgets.

Budget receipts in 1974 are estimated to be $256 billion. This is an increase of $31 billion over 1973, reflecting growing prosperity, higher personal income, and rising corporate profits. The receipts estimates also reflect the impact of tax cuts resulting from the Tax Reform Act of 1969, the new economic policy and the Revenue Act of 1971, as well as the payroll tax increases enacted to finance higher social security benefits.

Budget outlays in 1974 are expected to be $268.7 billion....

Even so, this budget necessarily proposes an increase in outlays of $19 billion, or nearly 8% over the previous year. It provides amply for America's security and well-being in the year ahead.

The 1974 budget program projects full-employment outlays of $288 billion in 1975, which, together with the revenues that would be produced under existing law, will mean full-employment balance in that year.

About $288 billion of *budget authority*—the new authority to make commitments to spend—is requested for 1974. Of the total, about $173 billion will require new action by the Congress....

A RESTRUCTURED FEDERAL GOVERNMENT.—A thorough overhaul of the Federal bureaucracy is long overdue, and I am determined to accomplish it.

As the role of government has grown over the years, so has the number of departments and agencies which carry out its functions. Unfortunately, very little attention has been given to the ways in which each new unit would fit in with all the old units. The consequence has been a hodgepodge of independent, organizationally unrelated offices that pursue interrelated goals. As a result, able officials at all levels have been frustrated, public accountability has been obscured, and decentralization and coordination of Federal operations have been impeded. This overlapping of responsibilities has increased the costs of government. It has generated interagency conflict and rivalry and, most importantly, it has imposed inexcusable inconvenience on the public that is supposed to be served.

To help remedy this situation, I proposed to the Congress in 1971 that the executive branch be restructured by consolidating many functions now scattered among several departments and agencies into four new departments. These new departments would be organized around four major domestic purposes of government: community development, human resources, natural resources, and economic affairs—thus consolidating in a single chain of command programs that contribute to the achievement of a clearly stated mission.... I plan now to streamline the executive branch along these lines as much as possible within existing law, and to propose similar legislation on departmental reorganization to the 93rd Congress....

Reorganization of the executive branch is a necessary beginning but reorganization alone is not enough.

Increased emphasis will also be placed on program performance. Programs will be evaluated to identify those that must be redirected, reduced, or eliminated because they do not justify the taxes required to pay for them. Federal programs must meet their objectives and costs must be related to achievements....

A REVITALIZED FEDERAL SYSTEM—Restructuring of the Federal Government is only one step in revitalizing our overall federal system. We must also make certain that State and local governments can fulfill their role as partners with the Federal Government....

On October 20, 1972, I signed a program of General Revenue Sharing into law. This program provides State and local governments with more than $30 billion over a 5-year period ' ginning January 1, 1972. This historic shift of power away from Washington will help strengthen

State and local governments and permit more local decision making about local needs....

I remain convinced that the principle of special revenue sharing is essential to continued revitalization of the federal system. I am, therefore, proposing the creation of special revenue sharing programs in the 1974 budget.

These four programs consist of broad-purpose grants, which will provide State and local governments with $6.9 billion to use with considerable discretion in the areas of education, law enforcement and criminal justice, manpower training, and urban community development. They will replace 70 outmoded, narrower categorical grant programs and will, in most cases, eliminate matching requirements.

The funds for special revenue sharing will be disbursed according to formulas appropriate to each area. In the case of manpower revenue sharing, an extension of existing law will be proposed. Current administrative requirements will be removed so that State and local governments can group manpower services in ways that best meet their own local needs.

The inefficiency of the present grant systems makes favorable action on special revenue sharing by the Congress an urgent priority....

Building A Lasting Structure of Peace

Building a lasting peace requires much more than wishful thinking. It can be achieved and preserved only through patient diplomacy and negotiation supported by military strength....

The 1974 budget supports America's efforts to establish such a peace in two important ways. First, it maintains the military strength we will need to support our negotiations and diplomacy. Second, it proposes a sound fiscal policy that, supported by a complementary monetary policy, will contribute to prosperity and economic stability here and abroad....

One of the results of our negotiations, taken together with the success of the Nixon Doctrine, our substantial disengagement from Vietnam, and the increased effectiveness of newer weapons systems, has been a significant but prudent reduction in our military forces. Total manpower has been reduced by about one-third since 1968, and will be further reduced as we end the draft and achieve an All-Volunteer Force. At the same time, our allies are assuming an increasing share of the burden of providing for their defense.

As a result, defense outlays have been kept in line. In 1974, they will be substantially the same as in 1968. During the same period, the total budget has grown by 50%, and nondefense outlays have grown by 91%, or $90 billion. When adjusted for pay and price increses, defense spending in 1974 will be about the same as in 1973 and about one-third *below* 1968....

Conclusion

The respect given to the common sense of the common man is what has made America the most uncommon of nations.

Common sense tells us that government cannot make a habit of living beyond its means. If we are not willing to make some sacrifices in holding down spending, we will be forced to make a much greater sacrifice in higher taxes or renewed inflation.

Common sense tells us that a family budget cannot succeed if every member of the family plans his own spending individually—which is how the Congress operates today. We must set an overall ceiling and affix the responsibility for staying within that ceiling.

Common sense tells us that we must not abuse an economic system that already provides more income for more people than any other system by suffocating the productive members of the society with excessive tax rates.

Common sense tells us that it is more important to save tax dollars than to save bureaucratic reputations. By abandoning programs that have failed, we do not close our eyes to problems that exist; we shift resources to more productive use.

It is hard to argue with these common sense judgments; surprisingly, it is just as hard to put them into action. Lethargy, habit, pride, and politics combine to resist the necessary process of change, but I am confident that the expressed will of the people will not be denied.

Two years ago, I spoke of the need for a new American Revolution to return power to people and put the individual *self* back in the idea of *self-government*. The 1974 budget moves us firmly toward that goal.

RICHARD NIXON

January 29, 1973.

ANNUAL ECONOMIC REPORT

January 30, 1973

President Nixon told Congress at the end of January that 1972 was "a very good year for the American economy" and that 1973 could be a "great" one if steps were taken to guard against a renewed inflationary spiral. In a message accompanying the annual report of the Council of Economic Advisers, the President recounted the economic successes of 1972 that led to one of the largest one-year growth increases in 25 years, but he cautioned that the main economic problem of 1973 would be "to prevent this expansion from becoming an inflationary boom." The report of the economic advisers echoed the warning that the economy's rapid growth must be braked by midyear to avoid renewed inflation, and it pointed to the necessity of bringing the federal budget into full-employment balance in order to meet that goal.

The council predicted a 10 per cent rise in gross national product during 1973 to top 1972's 9.7 per cent increase. Output, after adjusting for price increases, was expected to rise by 6.75 per cent as compared to 6.5 per cent in 1972; the rate of inflation for the year as a whole, as measured with respect to GNP, was projected to remain at about 3 per cent, the same as in 1972; and unemployment was predicted to drop to the "neighborhood" of 4.5 per cent. These figures differed from those of private forecasters, the GNP projection being higher and the inflation rate being somewhat lower. The council reasoned that three factors would bear out its predictions: federal expenditures would be limited to $268.7-billion as proposed by the President in his budget *message (see p. 43), food prices would rise less than in 1972, and Phase III would be successful in curbing wage and price increases.*

In his economic message, the President reiterated his hard line on federal spending and again called on Congress to curb the spending: "Nothing is easier or more pleasant...than to spend money," Nixon said. "But beyond some point, which our budget plans already reach, everything that the government gives out with one hand it must take back with the other, in higher taxes, or more inflation or both. Spending proposals must be looked at in this way, by asking whether they are worth either of these costs. Much government spending fails this test."

As to controls, the President said the government would "maintain the legal authority, the practical capacity and the will" to enforce its anti-inflation wage and price guidelines as set forth in Phase III. (See p. 43.) He noted his request to Congress to renew for another year the President's authority to check excessive wage and price increases. He made it clear, however, that he did not wish to have controls become a permanent economic device: "We must prepare for the end of wage and price controls and be willing to show the same courage in taking them off as was shown in imposing them." The council's report said wage and price controls probably reduced the rate of inflation in 1972 but to what extent was uncertain. The council advocated retaining the controls in 1973 to avoid the risk of disruption by "unrestrained behavior by particular sectors of the price-wage spectrum." However, it said the Phase III controls, coupled with federal monetary and fiscal policy, should be sufficient to reduce the rate of inflation to 2.5 per cent by the end of 1973. (See speech by Federal Reserve Board Chairman Arthur F. Burns, Historic Documents, 1972, p. 961.)

The council's report met head-on a contention of liberal Democrats that the President was working to curb inflation at the expense of continued unemployment. The report concurred with earlier White House statements that an unemployment figure of 4 per cent could not be met without a high rate of inflation. The CEA pointed to a changing work-force composition and said the traditional 4 per cent unemployment rate might not be a practical bottom figure when such temporary workers as women and teen-agers were being increasingly counted as unemployed. The optimal employment rate, said the council, should be "a condition in which persons who want work and seek it realistically on reasonable grounds can find employment."

The council noted some disappointment in the continued trade deficit, which it attributed to U.S. expansion in a period of sub-normal expansion in other countries. Economic conditions abroad kept down foreign demand for American goods. Also, fuel imports necessitated by a domestic fuel shortage increased the deficit even though offset by U.S. grain sales to the Soviet Union in the summer of 1972.

For the first time, the Council of Economic Advisers devoted a special section of its report to the economic role of women in the United States. It found that job integration of men and women had increased only slightly in recent years, that the earnings gap between the sexes was as wide as when first surveyed in 1956, and that job discrimination continued despite the increased number of women in the work force. Without making any legislative suggestions, the report said: "Women have gained much more access to market employment than they used to have, but they have not gained full equality within the market in the choice of jobs, opportunities for ᵤdvancement, and other matters related to employment and compensation."

Text of President Nixon's Annual Economic Report to the Congress, released on Jan. 30:

THE ECONOMIC REPORT FOR 1973

To the Congress of the United States:

As predicted, 1972 was a very good year for the American economy.

From the end of 1971 to the end of 1972, total output rose by about 7½ percent. This is one of the largest 1-year increases in the past 25 years. This growth took place in a largely peacetime economy; it was not achieved by a war-fed, inflationary boom. In fact, real defense spending declined 5 percent during the year. More important is the fact that the big increase of production in the year just ended was accompanied by a reduced rate of inflation. Consumer prices increased a little more than 3 percent from 1971 to 1972—a far cry from the runaway inflation rate of 6 percent that confronted us in 1969.

A year ago, looking ahead to 1972, I said that the great problem was to get the unemployment rate down from the 6-percent level where it was in 1971. During 1972 the rate was reduced to a little over 5 percent. We should get this down further, and expect to do so, but what was accomplished was gratifying. It is especially significant that the total number of people at work rose by 2.3 million from 1971 to 1972, the largest 1-year increase in 25 years.

Everything was not ideal in 1972—in the economy any more than in other aspects of our national life. Rising food prices were a major concern. The U.S. balance of trade with other countries did not improve as we had hoped. But all-in-all it was a very good year.

The economic performance of 1972 owed much to sound and forceful Government policy. The history of this policy goes back before 1972, and back before the dramatic moves taken on August 15, 1971. It goes back to the decision made in 1969 to bring to an end the dangerous inflation that had started in the mid-sixties. The decision was carried out by slowing down the rise of Federal spending and continuing the temporary tax increase that had been enacted in 1968 and by tightening monetary conditions. As a result, much of the cause of the inflation was removed and the rise in the cost of living was moderated. Without these steps, the subsequent success of price and wage controls would have been impossible.

Curbing inflation and cutting back on defense production necessarily involved a downturn in the economy and a rise of unemployment. To keep this from going too far, fiscal and monetary policy shifted in an expansive direction in 1970. And to speed up both the decline of inflation and the recovery of the economy, I announced the New Economic Policy on August 15, 1971. Temporary controls were imposed on prices, rents, and wages. Taxes were reduced. A little later we moved to stimulate the economy further by boosting Government expenditures in the first half of 1972, mainly by bringing forward expenditures that would have been made later.

The policies that began in 1969 contributed to the economic progress so visible in 1972. But Government policies alone did not do the job. Credit goes largely to a strong private economy and to the private citizens who cooperated in raising productivity, maintaining industrial peace, and conforming to the standards of the control system. The Government helped to create conditions in which private people could adapt to a growing economy that was far less defense-oriented and much less inflationary. But it was the individual American who made the adaptations.

The immediate economic goals for the domestic economy in 1973 are clear. Output and incomes should expand. Both the unemployment rate and the rate of inflation should be reduced further, and realistic confidence must be created that neither need rise again.

Vigorous Economic Expansion Underway

The prospects for achieving these goals in 1973 are bright—if we behave with reasonable prudence and foresight. By all signs a vigorous economic expansion is underway and will continue during the year. This will raise output and employment and reduce unemployment. The problem, as far as can now be foreseen, will be to prevent this expansion from becoming an inflationary boom.

That is why I put restraining Federal expenditures at the top of the list of economic policies for 1973. Nothing is easier or more pleasant, at least for a bureaucracy, than to spend money. But beyond some point, which our budget plans already reach, everything that the Government gives out with one hand it must take back with the other, in higher taxes or more inflation or both. Spending proposals must be looked at in this way, by asking whether they are worth either of these costs. Much Government spending fails this test.

I am proposing a budget with expenditures of $250 billion in the current fiscal year—an increase of $18 billion from last year. I am proposing a $19 billion increase for next year, to $269 billion. Although those are large totals and large increases, they reflect a sense of responsibility and discipline. I urgently seek the cooperation of the country and the Congress in staying within my budget proposals.

Only by holding the line on Federal spending will we be able to reduce the inflation rate further in 1973. Productivity should still be rising strongly. Inflationary expectations have been subdued. Workers have been experiencing large gains in their real incomes and so the pressure to catch up will be less than it was earlier. Anti-inflationary forces are at work, but it will be necessary to keep our healthy expansion from becoming an overheated boom.

The system of wage and price controls in effect during 1972 helped bring about a combination of less inflation and more production. But it is not the best system for 1973. After intensive consultation with all parts of the American society we have concluded that controls should be substantially modified. There are several problem areas—food, construction, and medical care costs—where special efforts at restraint are needed, in some cases more intense than last year.

In the economy at large there is need to establish more firmly a pattern of behavior consistent with reasonable price stability. At the same time our own experience and the experience of other countries demonstrate that as controls continue, unless they are suitably modified, red tape multiplies, inequities increase, interferences with production and productivity become more severe, and the possibility is enhanced that prices will explode when controls are lifted. Therefore, we are modifying the control system in several ways.

We are setting forth standards of reasonable price and wage behavior to which we ask business and labor to conform. Private economic units will be able to determine by themselves whether price or wage increases are within the standards or not. They will not require advance approval from the Government. However, the Government will maintain the legal authority, the practical capacity, and the will to intervene where necessary to stop action that is unreasonably inconsistent with the standards. I am asking Congress to extend the Economic Stabilization Act for 1 year, to April 30, 1974, to continue the authority. There should be no doubt about the fact that the authority will be used where needed.

An essential part of our anti-inflation program must be an increase of food supplies to restrain increases of food prices and bring about reductions where possible. The combination of natural occurrences holding down food production in the United States and abroad with rising consumers' incomes at home caused a sharp increase in food prices last year. These same forces will be at work in the early part of this year. But we have taken steps to increase food supplies. Quotas which previously limited the import of meat have been suspended. Restrictions on the acreage planted to major field crops have been relaxed. An increased amount of dried milk is being allowed into the country. Subsidies on agricultural exports have been eliminated. Grazing of cattle is being permitted on acreage diverted from crop production. We have established new machinery in the Federal Government to assure that high priority is given to holding down food prices.

Decline of Inflation and Unemployment in 1973

Restraint in budget policy, the new system of cooperative price and wage controls and special efforts to increase food supplies, coupled with the productivity and vigor of the private economy, should make 1973 another year in which inflation and unemployment decline and output rises. But what is at stake in the policies of 1973 is more than economic performance in 1973. What is at stake is whether we can make 1973 the prelude to a sustained period of growth and stability in a free economy. Since 1968 the Government and the economy have been largely absorbed in the negative task of correcting the destabilizing consequences of the financing of the Vietnam war. That period is almost over. Now we can stop putting out fires and turn to building a better economic order.

We must develop more reliable and responsible attitudes and methods for dealing with the Federal budget, so that it is not perpetually on the margin of an inflationary explosion. We must prepare for the end of wage and price controls, and be willing to show the same courage in taking them off as was shown in imposing them. We must weed out the restrictive effects of the large number of other economic controls exercised by the Federal Government, most of them having their origins decades ago, and many of them interfering with productivity and production. And we must strengthen the forces of competition in a vigorous free-enterprise economy.

Nowhere is the need to make 1973 a year of economic reform more apparent than in our international relations. Our actions of August 15, 1971, put the world on the path of negotiation for improvement of the international economy. Last year we made proposals for the reform of the international financial system, and these proposals are now the subject of discussion by high-level officials of the member countries of the International Monetary Fund. This year we expect to enter negotiations on the subject of trade.

We want the American people to be able to buy those foreign goods and services that are better, cheaper, or more interesting than our own. That raises the American standard of living. We want our people to be able to invest abroad when that is the most profitable thing to do. But we also want the American people to be able to pay for these purchases and investments in the way that is best for us. That means, first, that we must be able to pay by selling abroad the things that we produce best, and selling them on the best terms that we can freely obtain. Second, it means that we must be able to pay in a way that is sustainable so that we are not confronted with the need for sudden and possibly painful adjustments.

Export Expansion

Existing arrangements are not favorable to us in either respect. We have been buying from abroad in rapidly increasing amounts, and that has helped the American people. But our exports, with which we seek to pay for these imports, have been subject to high barriers, particularly in the case of our agricultural products. We have not been able to sell enough to pay for our overseas expenditures, and so we have had to pay by incurring more and more short-term debts abroad. This is not a situation that can go on indefinitely; its sudden ending could be disruptive. Therefore we want to bring about those reforms that will permit us to earn our way.

Our proposals have been, and will be, put forth in the U.S. national interest. But this is not contrary to the interest of other countries. International competition is shifting from the military and political arenas to the economic. This is a great advantage, because in economic competition every participant can win—there need be no losers. The effort of each nation to produce and sell what it can do most efficiently will benefit others. This is the fundamental belief underlying our proposals for reform and the fundamental reason for thinking that a satisfactory agreement will be reached.

The general prediction is that 1973 will be another very good year for the American economy. I believe that it *can* be a great year. It can be a year in which we reduce unemployment and inflation further and enter into a sustained period of strong growth, full employment, and price stability. But 1973 will be a great year only if we manage our fiscal affairs prudently and do not exceed the increases in Federal expenditures that I have proposed. This is the practical lesson of the experience from 1965 to 1968, when loose fiscal policy turned a healthy expansion into a feverish boom followed by a recession. I am determined to live by this lesson. And I urgently appeal to the Congress to join me in doing so.

RICHARD NIXON

JANUARY 31, 1973.

NIXON NEWS CONFERENCE
January 31, 1973

At the first news conference of his second term, President Nixon spoke out boldly on Vietnam, emphasized his opposition to amnesty for draft dodgers or deserters, and insisted on his right to impound funds appropriated by Congress. The conference, his first with reporters since Oct. 5, 1972, was announced only moments before the President arrived in the briefing room where the 30-minute question and answer session took place.

Many of the reporters' questions focused on Vietnam, in light of the cease-fire agreement signed in Paris on Jan. 27. Nixon announced that National Security Adviser Henry A. Kissinger would go to Hanoi early in February to discuss implementation of the peace accord and plans for post-war reconstruction. It was also disclosed that South Vietnamese President Thieu would meet with Mr. Nixon in the spring at San Clemente, Calif. Very much in control of the political give-and-take, the President confidently asserted that his administration had indeed won "peace with honor" in Vietnam: "I know it gags some of you to write that phrase, but it is true, and most Americans realize it is true...."

Nixon reiterated his opposition to amnesty for men who had refused to serve in the military during the Vietnam war: "Now amnesty means forgiveness. We cannot provide forgiveness for them. Those who served paid their price. Those who deserted must pay their price, and the price is not a junket in the Peace Corps, or something like that, as some have suggested. The price is a criminal penalty for disobeying the laws of the United States." During the 1972 presidential campaign, Nixon had told the parents of a Mantua, Ohio, serviceman killed in the war that "the draft dodgers are never going to get amnesty when boys like yours died, never." (See Historic Documents, 1972, p. 3.)

Either Congress or the President can grant amnesty and steps to that end had already been initiated in Congress. However, Rep. Edward I. Koch (D N.Y.), sponsor of one of three amnesty proposals introduced in the House, was doubtful of passage without presidential support. "I know this bill cannot be passed over his opposition," said Koch. "I hope his objective will be reconciliation." The Department of Defense had records of 6,000 draft evaders and of 32,000 deserters from the armed forces living abroad who would be affected by such legislation, but leaders of the anti-war movement placed the figure at between 60,000 and 100,000.

The President's press conference was marked by an unusual number of controversial statements. The Peace Corps took issue with the characterization of service in that volunteer organization as a "junket." Peace Corps Director Dan Hess said he regretted the statement but conceded that it probably had not been intended as an insult. However, a request for "clarification" was made to the White House by Hess. Nixon also disclosed for the first time that John T. Downey, who had been held by the Communist Chinese since 1952 when his military aircraft was forced down over their territory, was a C.I.A. agent.

But the most backlash came from a statement by the President concerning the firing of a top Pentagon contracts expert. Nixon said he had personally approved the decision that A. Ernest Fitzgerald "be fired or discharged or asked to resign." Fitzgerald had brought a suit before the Civil Service Commission on the ground that he had been fired, not because of economy cutbacks as the Air Force contended, but because he had given unfavorable testimony before the Joint Economic Committee about multi-billion dollar Air Force cost overruns. On Jan. 30, Secretary of the Air Force Robert C. Seamans Jr. had invoked executive privilege at a Civil Service hearing rather than discuss the role of the White House in the case. Fitzgerald, who had once been nominated for the Air Force's top civilian award, had been transferred from the office of the assistant secretary for financial matters following his testimony before the congressional committee; shortly thereafter he was notified that his job would be eliminated. Fitzgerald's attorney commented that the President's news conference statement reinforced the defense's contention that Fitzgerald's dismissal constituted punishment for his testimony and was therefore in violation of Civil Service regulations.

White House Press Secretary Ronald Ziegler issued a statement the day following the news conference to the effect that the President, after reading the transcript of the session, realized that he "misspoke."

Ziegler said that the President "was mistaken in his reference to Mr. Fitzgerald" and that he did not know what case, if any, Nixon had had in mind.

Transcript of President Nixon's news conference at the White House on Jan. 31:

THE PRESIDENT. I think Miss Thomas has the first question.

Meeting With President Thieu

Q. Can you tell us whether you are going to meet with President Thieu some time this spring and also give us a better feel on Dr. Kissinger's trip, the purpose and so forth?

THE PRESIDENT. At some time this spring I do plan to meet with President Thieu. I have discussed the matter with him in correspondence and I also discussed it yesterday in my meeting with the Foreign Minister. It will be at a time mutually convenient.

The UPI story, incidentally, was on the mark except for the location. The location we have agreed on will be the Western White House this spring.

Dr. Kissinger's Trip to Hanoi

As far as Dr. Kissinger's trip is concerned, this is a matter that we feel is very important in terms of developing the postwar relationship with North Vietnam. When we look at this very intricate agreement, which Dr. Kissinger so brilliantly briefed for the members of the press, and if you have read it, you will see why I use the word intricate, we can see that insofar as its terms are concerned, if the agreement is kept, there is no question about the fact that we will have peace in not only Vietnam but in Indochina for a very long period of time. But the question is whether both parties, in fact, all parties involved, have a will to peace, if they have incentives to peace, if they have desire to peace.

Now, on this particular point, it is necessary, of course, for us to talk to the South Vietnamese, as we are. It is also vitally important that we have a direct communication with the North Vietnamese. And Dr. Kissinger will be going to Hanoi to meet with the top leaders of the Government of the DRV. There he will discuss the postwar relationship. He will, of course, discuss the current status of compliance with the peace agreements which we have made and he will also discuss, in terms of postwar relationships, the matter of the reconstruction program for all of Indochina.

As the leaders probably reported after my meeting with them, the day after I announced the cease-fire agreement, I raised with the leaders the point that the United States would consider for both North Vietnam and South Vietnam and the other countries in the area a reconstruction program.

I, of course, recognized in raising this with the leaders that there would have to be Congressional consultation and Congressional support. In terms of this particular matter at this time, Dr. Kissinger will be having an initial conversation with the North Vietnamese with regard to this whole reconstruction program.

I should also say that I have noted that many Congressmen and Senators and many of the American people are not keen on helping any of the countries in that area, just as they are not keen on foreign aid generally. But as far as I am concerned, whether it is with the North or the South or the other countries in the area, I look upon this as a potential investment in peace. To the extent that the North Vietnamese, for example, participate with us and with other interested countries in reconstruction of North Vietnam, they will have a tendency to turn inward to the works of peace rather than turning outward to the works of war.

This, at least, is our motive, and we will know more about it after Dr. Kissinger completes his talks with them, which we think will be quite extensive and very frank since he has already, obviously, paved the way for it.

Welcoming of Prisoners of War

Q. Mr. President, Dr. Kissinger is going to Vietnam and is due there in Hanoi on February 10. Is this related in any way with the first prisoners of war to come out of Hanoi?

THE PRESIDENT. Not at all.

Q. I mean, is the date a coincidence?

THE PRESIDENT. The date is a pure coincidence, and Dr. Kissinger will not be meeting with the prisoners of war. Incidentally, speaking of the POW question, I have noted some speculation in the press, and it isn't—I should say—it's speculation that is justified, because I understand there was a Defense Department report to this effect, that I was going to go out to Travis Air Force Base to meet the first POW's when they came in.

I do not intend to do so. I have the greatest admiration for the prisoners of war, for their stamina and their courage and the rest, and also for their wives and their parents and their children who have been so strong during this long period of their vigil.

This is a time that we should not grandstand it; we should not exploit it. We should remember that it is not like astronauts coming back from the moon after what is, of course, a very, shall we say, spectacular and dangerous journey, but these are men who have been away sometimes for years. They have a right to have privacy, they have a right to be home with their families just as quickly as they possibly can, and I am going to respect that right, of course, to the extent that any of them or their families desiring to visit the White House can be sure that they will be very high on the list.

Domestic Divisions and Amnesty

Q. Mr. President, do you have anything specifically in mind to help heal the wounds in this country, the divisions over the war, and, specifically, anything down the road much farther in terms of amnesty?

THE PRESIDENT. Well, it takes two to heal wounds, and I must say that when I see that the most vigorous criticism or, shall we say, the least pleasure out of the peace agreements comes from those that were the most outspoken advocates of peace at any price, it makes one realize whether some want the wounds healed. We do.

We think we have taken a big step toward ending a long and difficult war which was not begun while we were here, and I am not casting any aspersions on those Presidents who were in office who can no longer be here to speak for themselves, for the causes of the war. I am simply saying this: that as far as this Administration is concerned, we have done the very best that we can against very great obstacles, and we finally have achieved a peace with honor.

I know it gags some of you to write that phrase, but it is true, and most Americans realize it is true, because it would be peace with dishonor had we—what some have used, the vernacular—"bugged out" and allowed what the North Vietnamese wanted: the imposition of a Communist government or a coalition Communist government on the South Vietnamese. That goal they have failed to achieve. Consequently, we can speak of peace with honor and with some pride that it has been achieved.

Now, I suppose, Mr. Sheldon, that your question with regard to amnesty may deal with the problems of healing the wounds. Certainly I have sympathy for any individual who has made a mistake. We have all made mistakes. But also, it is a rule of life, we all have to pay for our mistakes.

One of the most moving wires I received, of the many thousands that have come in to the White House since the peace announcement, was from a man who was in prison in Michigan, I believe it is, and he spoke about a group of his fellow inmates. They are in a work camp, so I suppose they are being rehabilitated to come out.

He wrote very emotionally about what we had done and he felt it was an achievement they were very proud of. I feel sorry for that man; on the other hand, it is not my right, and I should not exercise such a right, because he so wrote to me, to say "Now you are forgiven for what you did."

Now, as far as amnesty is concerned, I have stated my views, and those views remain exactly the same. The war is over. Many Americans paid a very high price to serve their country, some with their lives, some as prisoners of war for as long as 6 to 7 years, and, of course, 2½ million, 2 to 3 years out of their lives, serving in a country far away in a war that they realize had very little support among the so-called better people, in the media and the intellectual circles and the rest, which had very little support, certainly, among some elements of the Congress, particularly the United States Senate, but which fortunately did have support among a majority of the American people, who some way, despite the fact that they were hammered night after night and day after day with the fact that this was an immoral war, that America should not be there, that they should not serve their country, that morally what they should do was desert their country.

Certainly as we look at all of that, there might be a tendency to say now, to those few hundreds who went to Canada or Sweden or someplace else, and chose to desert their country that because they had a higher morality, we should now give them amnesty.

Now, amnesty means forgiveness. We cannot provide forgiveness for them. Those who served paid their price. Those who deserted must pay their price, and the price is not a junket in the Peace Corps, or something like that, as some have suggested. The price is a criminal penalty for disobeying the laws of the United States. If they want to return to the United States they must pay the penalty. If they don't want to return, they are certainly welcome to stay in any country that welcomes them.

Mr. Theis.

Postwar Reconstruction in Indochina

Q. Do you have any floor or ceiling dollar figure in mind for the rehabilitation of North Vietnam or the rest of Indochina?

THE PRESIDENT. Mr. Theis, that is a matter that the Members of the Congress raised with me, as you might imagine, and they raised it not only with regard to North Vietnam but with regard to South Vietnam and Cambodia and Laos in this period as we move into the cease-fire and, we hope, peacetime reconstruction.

I cannot give you that figure now, because it is a matter that has to be negotiated and it must be all part of one pattern. The figure, of course, will come out. The figures will come out, but they must first be discussed with the bipartisan leadership because, with all of this talk about the powers of the Presidency, let me say I am keenly aware of the fact that even though I might believe that a program of reconstruction for North Vietnam, as well as South Vietnam, is an investment in peace, the Congress has to believe it. The Congress has to support it. And this is going to be one of the more difficult assignments I have had as President, but I think we can make it if the Congress sees what the stakes are.

Interest Rates on Agricultural Loans

Q. Mr. President, sir, Senator Hollings says on a recent trip to South-east Asia, he discovered that we are letting some countries, including Japan, have 2 percent money, yet we have denied our own farmers in rural co-operatives 2 percent money. We are telling them they have to have their loans at 5 percent. Would you comment on this and how this might relate to your upcoming program of aid to Southeast Asia?

THE PRESIDENT. Well, as far as the program of aid is concerned and the percentage of interest that is paid, we will, of course, have in mind the interest of the American people. We want to be fair, of course, to those who have been our allies and in the great tradition of America when it fights wars, to those who have been our enemies, like Germany and Japan, who, with America's help now have become our two greatest competitors in the free world.

Now, when you get down to whether the percentage will be 2 percent or 5 percent or 3 percent, that is a matter to be negotiated, but we will be fair and we will see that our farmers also are treated fairly.

Let me say, if I could, with regard to REA—and Miss McClendon, because you are somewhat of an expert on this—I have always supported REA because I used to represent the old 12th District. When I lived there and represented it, it was primarily agricultural, orange groves; now it is primarily people, subdivided. But as one who came from that area, I naturally had a great interest in this matter of REA and the rest, and supported it.

But what I have found is that when I first voted for REA, 80 percent of the loans went for the purpose of rural development and getting electricity to farms. Now 80 percent of this 2 percent money goes for country clubs and dilettantes, for example, and others who can afford living in the country. I am not for 2 percent money for people who can afford 5 percent or 7.

Relations With Europe

Q. Mr. President, you and people in your Administration have been quoted as calling 1973 the year of Europe. Could you tell us exactly what that means to you and, specifically, will you be making a trip to Europe in the next month or so?

THE PRESIDENT. I will not be making any trips to Europe certainly in the first half of this year. Whether I can make any trips later on re-mains to be seen. As a matter of fact, so that all of you can plan not to take shots, I plan no trips whatever in the first half of this year outside the United States. The meeting with President Thieu, if it does work out, at a time mutually convenient, will take place some time in the spring.

Now, the fact that I don't take a trip to Europe does not mean that this will not be a period when there will be great attention paid to

Europe, because it just happens as we complete the long and difficult war in Vietnam, we now must turn to the problems of Europe. We have been to the People's Republic of China. We have been to the Soviet Union. We have been paying attention to the problems of Europe, but now those problems will be put on the front burner.

There is the problem of trade, for example. There is the problem of the European Security Conference which we must discuss. There is the problem of mutual balanced force reduction. All of this will require consultation with our European allies. And in that connection, that is one of the reasons that the Heath visit is so enormously important. I am spending more time with Mr. Heath than I have with some other visitors. I mean by that not that time proves everything, but not only will we have the usual dinners and luncheons and so forth, but I am spending a full day with him at Camp David because I want to get his thoughts about what the position of the United States and our European friends should be with regard to the European Security Conference, with regard to the MBFR, and, of course, what the position of the United States should be and the new, broader European Community should be in this period when we can either become competitors in a constructive way or where we can engage in economic confrontation that could lead to bitterness and which would hurt us both.

We want to avoid that, even though it has been predicted by some in this country who really fear the new Europe. I do not fear it if we talk to them and consult at this time.

Governor Connally and the 1976 Election

Q. Mr. President.

THE PRESIDENT. Mr. Deakin.

Q. You are quoted as telling a recent visitor that you believe that Governor Connally will be the Republican nominee of 1976. Is that correct?

THE PRESIDENT. Well I had thought we had just completed an election. [Laughter]

Q. Just a little foresight there.

THE PRESIDENT. Having just completed one, let me give some advice, if I can, to all of those who may be thinking of becoming candidates in 1976.

I have a considerable amount of experience in getting nominations and winning elections and also losing them. So, consequently, I would suggest that as far as the Presidential candidate is concerned, he is out of his mind if he allows any activity in his behalf or participates in any activity in his behalf, running for the nomination before the elections of 1974 are concluded.

If I were advising people who are interested in becoming and running for President, for the nomination in either party, I would say the best way to get the nomination now is not to be out seeking it. The best way to get it is to work as hard as you can for the success of the candidates of your party, be they for the House or the Senate or Governor, and do it in a selfless way until after 1974 and immediately after 1974 take off and run as fast as you can. And I have always done that and with mixed results. [*Laughter*]

But as far as Governor Connally is concerned, you all know my very high respect for him. I have stated my belief that he could handle any job that I can think of in this country or in the world for that matter, but I would be out of my mind if I were to be endorsing anybody for the Presidency at the present time when there are a number of people who have indicated—or whose friends have indicated—that they might have an interest in the position and that is just fine.

If Governor Connally—and, of course, many have suggested that the Vice President would be interested—I assume that several Governors might be interested. In fact, one of these days, perhaps right after the '74 elections, I will give you my list and it will be quite a long one because I am not going to make my choice until after they have been through a few primaries.

Shooting of Senator Stennis

Q. Can you give us your reaction to the shooting of Senator Stennis?

THE PRESIDENT. Well, I called Mrs. Stennis last night, as I am sure many others of his friends did, and it is just one of those senseless things that happens, apparently. When she told me that all they got was his billfold, she said it didn't have much in it, and his Phi Beta Kappa key and also his watch, apparently. So, it's one of those things that happens in our cities today—fortunately not happening as much as it did previously.

The point that I would make with regard to Senator Stennis, and this is what I told her, is that I just hope that the doctors did the most superb job they have ever done. I hope that his spirit would see him through this physically and in every other way, because of all the Senators in the United States Senate, Democrat or Republican, in terms of our being able to achieve the honorable peace we have achieved, John Stennis was the most indispensable.

Gun Control

Q. Mr. President, I would like to ask you, along those lines, you said it was such a senseless thing. The White House, this Administration, has not spoken out very strongly against gun controls, particularly handguns. I would like to know perhaps if maybe you are going to have second thoughts about that now?

THE PRESIDENT. Well, as you know, the problem with that is not so much the White House speaking out on handguns and Saturday night specials, which I think this may have been. I haven't seen the latest reports, but the doctor last night told me it was a .22 caliber cheap gun kind of a thing and Mrs. Stennis said it sounded like firecrackers. Obviously if they had had a .45, he would be dead.

We have, and I have, as you know, advocated legislation to deal with what we call the Saturday night specials which can be acquired by anybody, including juveniles, and apparently there are some suggestions that juveniles were those involved in this case. I am not charging that, incidentally. I am saying what I read in the papers, most of which, as you know, is true.

So, under the circumstances, I feel that Senator Hruska, who introduced the bill before and then it came a cropper in the Senate Judiciary Committee, will now work with the Judiciary Committee in attempting to find the formula which will get the support necessary to deal with this specific problem, without, at the same time, running afoul of the rights of those who believe that they need guns for hunting and all that sort of thing.

Let me say, personally, I have never hunted in my life. I have no interest in guns and so forth. I am not interested in the National Rifle Association or anything from a personal standpoint. But I do know that in terms of the United States Congress, what we need is a precise definition which will keep the guns out of the hands of the criminals and not one that will impinge on the rights of others to have them for their own purposes in a legitimate way.

Incidentally, the legislation that we originally suggested or that we discussed with Senator Hruska, I thought precisely dealt with the problem, but it did not get through the Senate. My guess is that Senator Stennis—everything perhaps has a down side and an up side; I guess everything really does. But the very fact that Senator Stennis was the victim of one of these things—we thought this was the case when Governor Wallace was—but in this instance, it was apparently one of these small hand guns that most people, most reasonable people, except for the all-out opponents of any kind of legislation in this field—most reasonable people believe it should be controlled. Perhaps we can get some action. I hope the Senate does act.

I have asked the Attorney General—had asked incidentally before this happened—as one of his projects for this year to give us a legislative formula, not one that would simply speak to the country, and not get through, but one that can get through the Congress. That is the problem.

Executive Privilege

Q. Mr. President.

THE PRESIDENT. Mr. Mollenhoff.

Q. Did you approve of the use of executive privilege by Air Force Secretary Seamans in refusing to disclose the White House role in the firing of air cost analyst Fitzgerald?

It came up yesterday in the Civil Service hearings. He used executive privilege. You had stated earlier that you would approve all of these uses of executive privilege, as I understood it, and I wondered whether your view still prevails in this area or whether others are now entitled to use executive privilege on their own in this type of case?

THE PRESIDENT. Mr. Mollenhoff, your first assumption is correct. In my dealings with the Congress—I say mine, let me put it in a broader sense—in the dealings of the Executive with the Congress, I do not want to abuse the executive privilege proposition where the matter does not involve a direct conference with or discussion within the Administration, particularly where the President is involved. And where it is an extraneous matter as far as the White House is concerned, as was the case when we waived executive privilege for Mr. Flanigan last year, as you will recall, we are not going to assert it.

In this case, as I understand it—and I did not approve this directly, but it was approved at my direction by those who have the responsibility within the White House—in this case it was a proper area in which the executive privilege should have been used.

On the other hand, I can assure you that all of these cases will be handled on a case-by-case basis and we are not going to be in a position where an individual, when he gets under heat from a Congressional committee, can say, "Look, I am going to assert executive privilege."

He will call down here, and Mr. Dean, the White House Counsel, will then advise him as to whether or not we approve it.

Q. I want to follow one question on this.

THE PRESIDENT. Sure.

Q. This seems to be an expansion of what executive privilege was in the past and you were quite critical of executive privilege in 1948 when you were in the Congress——

THE PRESIDENT. I certainly was.

Q. You seem to have expanded it from conversation with the President himself to conversation with anyone in the executive branch of the Government and I wonder, can you cite any law or decision of the courts that supports that view?

THE PRESIDENT. Well, Mr. Mollenhoff, I don't want to leave the impression that I am expanding it beyond that. I perhaps have not been as precise as I should have been. And I think yours is a very legitimate question because you have been one who has not had a double standard on this. You have always felt that executive privilege, whether I was complaining about its use when I was an investigator or whether I am now defending its use when others are doing the investigating—I understand that position.

Let me suggest that I would like to have a precise statement prepared which I will personally approve so that you will know exactly what it is. I discussed this with the leaders and we have talked, for example—the Republicans, like Senator Javits and Senator Percy, are very interested in it, not just the Democrats, and I understand that. But I would rather, at this point, not like to have just an off the top of my head press conference statement delineate what executive privilege will be.

I will simply say the general attitude I have is to be as liberal as possible in terms of making people available to testify before the Congress, and we are not going to use executive privilege as a shield for conversations that might be just embarrassing to us, but that really don't deserve executive privilege.

A. Ernest Fitzgerald

Q. The specific situation with regard to Fitzgerald, I would like to explore that. That dealt with a conversation Seamans had with someone in the White House relative to the firing of Fitzgerald and justification or explanations. I wonder if you feel that that is covered and did you have this explained to you in detail before you made the decision?

THE PRESIDENT. Let me explain. I was totally aware that Mr. Fitzgerald would be fired or discharged or asked to resign. I approved it and Mr. Seamans must have been talking to someone who had discussed the matter with me.

No, this was not a case of some person down the line deciding he should go. It was a decision that was submitted to me. I made it and I stick by it.

Impoundment of Funds

Q. Mr. President, how do you respond to criticism that your impoundment of funds abrogates power or authority that the Constitution gave to Congress?

THE PRESIDENT. The same way that Jefferson did, and Jackson did, and Truman did.

When I came in on this, Mr. Mollenhoff—he is one of the few old timers around here who will remember it—you remember when Senator Symington, who has now turned the other way on this, but you remember when we were talking about the 70 group air force. You remember that on that case I voted as a Congressman to override President Truman's veto. I think it was 70 wing or 70 group air force, where we insisted on a 70 group air force and he said the budget would only provide for 48.

Despite the fact that the Congress spoke not just as the Leaders spoke to me the other day, but by veto, overwhelming in both Houses, President Truman impounded the money. He did not spend it. And he had a right to. The constitutional right for the President of the United States to impound funds and that is not to spend money, when the spending of money would mean either increasing prices or increasing taxes for all the people, that right is absolutely clear.

The problem we have here is basically that the Congress wants responsibility, they want to share responsibility. Believe me, it would be pleasant to have more sharing of responsibility by the Congress. But if you are going to have responsibility, you have to be responsible, and this Congress—and some of the more thoughtful Members of Congress and that includes most of the Leadership, in the very good give-and-take we had the other day—this Congress has not been responsible on money. We simply had this.

There is a clear choice. We either cut spending or raise taxes and I made a little check before the leaders' meeting. I checked on the campaigns of everybody who had run for office across this country, Democrat and Republican. I didn't find one Member of Congress, liberal or conservative, who had campaigned on the platform of raising taxes in order that we could spend more.

Now the point is that the Congress has to decide, does it want to raise taxes in order to spend more or does it want to cut, as the President is trying to cut. The difficulty, of course, and I have been a Member of Congress, is that the Congress represents special interests.

The Interior Committee wants to have more parks and the Agriculture Committee wants cheap REA loans and the HEW Committee or the Education and Labor Committee wants more for education and the rest, and each of these wants we all sympathize with, but there is only one place in this Government where somebody has got to speak not for the special interests which the Congress represents but for the general interest.

The general interest of this country, the general interest whether it be rich or poor or old, is don't break the family budget by raising the taxes or raising prices, and I am going to stand for that general interest. Therefore, I will not spend money if the Congress overspends, and I will not be for programs that will raise the taxes and put a bigger burden on the already overburdened American taxpayer.

American Prisoners in China

Q. Mr. President, there are two American fliers still being held prisoner in China, and they are sort of in limbo—well, three Americans but two fliers. I wonder if you could give us their status, and do you expect them to be returned with the other prisoners?

THE PRESIDENT. This matter we discussed when we were in the People's Republic of China, and we have every reason to believe that these fliers will be released on the initiative of the People's Republic of China as the POW situation is worked out in Vietnam.

I won't go beyond that because this is a matter that should be left to the People's Republic of China, but we have, we believe, every assurance that will happen.

Q. Downey, also?

THE PRESIDENT. Downey is a different case, as you know. Downey involves a CIA agent. His sentence of 30 years has been, I think, commuted to 5 years, and we have also discussed that with Premier Chou

En-lai. I would have to be quite candid. We have no assurance that any change of action, other than the commutation of the sentence, will take place, but we have, of course, informed the People's Republic through our private channels that we feel that would be a very salutary action on his part.

But that is a matter where they must act on their own initiative, and it is not one where any public pressures or bellicose statements from here will be helpful in getting his release.

Reporter. Thank you, Mr. President.

Ed. note: For subsequent developments, see Nixon's meeting in April with Thieu, p. 447; the return of the POW's p. 245; executive privilege, p. 337.

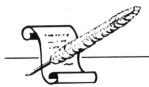

February

THE STATE OF THE UNION

February 2, 1973

President Nixon, never a man to be bound by tradition, found a new way to deliver his State of the Union message in 1973. A year earlier, he had experimented with a dual State of the Union message—a relatively brief and generalized address delivered to Congress in person and a long and detailed written message covering a wide range of current problems (see Historic Documents, 1972, p. 73).

The approach in 1973 was not dual but multiple. Six written messages were sent to Congress over a period of six weeks, and each of the five messages supplementing the initial "overview" was preceded by a presidential radio speech covering roughly the same ground. Mr. Nixon thus went beyond the constitutional provision that the President "shall from time to time give to the Congress information of the State of the Union, and recommend to their consideration such measures as he shall judge necessary and expedient." Through his radio speeches, less formal than the usual televised address to a joint session of Congress, President Nixon gave "information of the State of the Union" directly to the public and thereby no doubt sought to generate popular support for his recommendations to the Congress.

In the initial written message to Congress, Feb. 2, the President said that "with so many changes in government programs under consideration—and with our very philosophy about the relationship between the individual and the state at an historic crossroads—a single, all-embracing State of the Union message would not appear to be adequate." The subsequent messages on "specific areas of policy" would outline

Chronology of State of the Union Messages, 1973

Subject	Date of radio speech	Date sent to Congress
1. General overview	. . .	Feb. 2
2. Natural resources and the environment	Feb. 14	Feb. 15
3. Economic affairs	Feb. 21	Feb. 22
4. Human resources	Feb. 24	Mar. 1
5. Community development	Mar. 4	Mar. 8
6. Law enforcement and drug abuse	Mar. 10	Mar. 14

"a fresh approach to government"—an approach intended to "aid and encourage people, communities and institutions to deal with as many of the difficulties and challenges facing them as possible." Emphasizing the need to hold the line in federal spending, Nixon declared that it was "vital at this time to restore a greater sense of responsibility at the state and local level, and among individual Americans." (See p. 213.)

The President announced that the series of detailed messages to follow would cover natural resources, economic affairs, human resources, community development, and foreign and defense policy. In the end, a message on law enforcement and drug abuse replaced foreign policy. "Considered as a whole," Nixon said in his Feb. 2 overview, "this series of messages will be a blueprint for modernizing the concept and the functions of American government to meet the needs of our people. Converting it into reality will require a spirit of cooperation and shared commitment on the part of all branches of the government, for the goals we seek are not those of any single party or faction; they are goals for the betterment of all Americans."

Following are the full text of President Nixon's lead-off State of the Union message of Feb. 2 and excerpts from the first two of the written messages on particular subjects (see p. 303 for excerpts from the later messages):

THE STATE OF THE UNION

To the Congress of the United States:

The traditional form of the President's annual report giving "to the Congress Information of the State of the Union" is a single message or address. As the affairs and concerns of our Union have multiplied over the years, however, so too have the subjects that require discussion in State of the Union Messages.

This year in particular, with so many changes in Government programs under consideration—and with our very philosophy about the relationship between the individual and the State at an historic crossroads—a single, all-embracing State of the Union Message would not appear to be adequate.

I have therefore decided to present my 1973 State of the Union report in the form of a series of messages during these early weeks of the 93rd Congress. The purpose of this first message in the series is to give a concise overview of where we stand as a people today, and to outline some of the general goals that I believe we should pursue over the next year and beyond. In coming weeks, I will send to the Congress further State of the Union reports on specific areas of policy including economic affairs, natural resources, human resources, community development and foreign and defense policy.

The new course these messages will outline represents a fresh approach to Government: an approach that addresses the realities of the 1970s, not those of the 1930s or of the 1960s. The role of the Federal Government as we approach our third century of independence should not be to dominate any facet of American life, but rather to aid and encourage people, communities and institutions to deal with as many of the difficulties and challenges facing them as possible, and to help see to it that every American has a full and equal opportunity to realize his or her potential.

If we were to continue to expand the Federal Government at the rate of the past several decades, it soon would consume us entirely. The time has come when we must make clear choices—choices between old programs that set worthy goals but failed to reach them and new programs that provide a better way to realize those goals; and choices, too, between competing programs—*all* of which may be desirable in themselves but only *some* of which we can afford with the finite resources at our command.

Because our resources are not infinite, we also face a critical choice in 1973 between holding the line in Government spending and adopting expensive programs which will surely force up taxes and refuel inflation.

211

Finally, it is vital at this time that we restore a greater sense of responsibility at the State and local level, and among individual Americans.

Where We Stand

The basic state of our Union today is sound, and full of promise.

We enter 1973 economically strong, militarily secure and, most important of all, at peace after a long and trying war.

America continues to provide a better and more abundant life for more of its people than any other nation in the world.

We have passed through one of the most difficult periods in our history without surrendering to despair and without dishonoring our ideas as a people.

Looking back, there is a lesson in all this for all of us. The lesson is one that we sometimes had to learn the hard way over the past few years. But we did learn it. That lesson is that even potentially destructive forces can be converted into positive forces when we know how to channel them, and when we use common sense and common decency to create a climate of mutual respect and goodwill.

By working together and harnessing the forces of nature, Americans have unlocked some of the great mysteries of the universe.

Men have walked the surface of the moon and soared to new heights of discovery.

This same spirit of discovery is helping us to conquer disease and suffering that have plagued our own planet since the dawn of time.

By working together with the leaders of other nations, we have been able to build a new hope for lasting peace—for a structure of world order in which common interest outweighs old animosities, and in which a new generation of the human family can grow up at peace in a changing world.

At home, we have learned that by working together we can create prosperity without fanning inflation; we can restore order without weakening freedom.

The Challenges We Face

These first years of the 1970s have been good years for America.

Our job—all of us together—is to make 1973 and the years to come even better ones. I believe that we can. I believe that we can make the years leading to our Bicentennial the best four years in American history.

But we must never forget that nothing worthwhile can be achieved without the will to succeed and the strength to sacrifice.

Hard decisions must be made, and we must stick by them.

In the field of foreign policy, we must remember that a strong America—an America whose word is believed and whose strength is respected—is essential to continued peace and understanding in the world. The peace with honor we have achieved in Vietnam has strengthened this basic American credibility. We must act in such a way in coming years that this credibility will remain intact, and with it, the world stability of which it is so indispensable a part.

At home, we must reject the mistaken notion—a notion that has dominated too much of the public dialogue for too long—that ever bigger Government is the answer to every problem.

We have learned only too well that heavy taxation and excessive Government spending are not a cure-all. In too many cases, instead of solving the problems they were aimed at, they have merely placed an ever heavier burden on the shoulders of the American taxpayer, in the form of higher taxes and a higher cost of living. At the same time they have deceived our people because many of the intended beneficiaries received far less than was promised, thus undermining public faith in the effectiveness of Government as a whole.

The time has come for us to draw the line. The time has come for the responsible leaders of both political parties to take a stand *against* overgrown Government and *for* the American taxpayer. We are not spending the Federal Government's money, we are spending the taxpayer's money, and it must be spent in a way which guarantees his money's worth and yields the fullest possible benefit to the people being helped.

The answer to many of the domestic problems we face is not higher taxes and more spending. It is less waste, more results and greater freedom for the individual American to earn a rightful place in his own community—and for States and localities to address their own needs in their own ways, in the light of their own priorities.

By giving the people and their locally elected leaders a greater voice through changes such as revenue sharing, and by saying "no" to excessive Federal spending and higher taxes, we can help achieve this goal.

Coming Messages

The policies which I will outline to the Congress in the weeks ahead represent a reaffirmation, not an abdication, of Federal responsibility. They represent a pragmatic rededication to social compassion and national excellence, in place of the combination of good intentions and fuzzy follow-through which too often in the past was thought sufficient.

In the field of economic affairs, our objectives will be to hold down taxes, to continue controlling inflation, to promote economic growth, to increase productivity, to encourage foreign trade, to keep farm income high, to bolster small business, and to promote better labor-management relations.

In the area of natural resources, my recommendations will include programs to preserve and enhance the environment, to advance science and technology, and to assure balanced use of our irreplaceable natural resources.

In developing human resources, I will have recommendations to advance the Nation's health and education, to improve conditions of people in need, to carry forward our increasingly successful attacks on crime, drug abuse and injustice, and to deal with such important areas of special concern as consumer affairs. We will continue and improve our Nation's efforts to assist those who have served in the Armed Services in Viet-Nam through better job and training opportunities.

We must do a better job in community development—in creating more livable communities, in which all of our children can grow up with fuller access to opportunity and greater immunity to the social evils and blights which now plague so many of our towns and cities. I shall have proposals to help us achieve this.

I shall also deal with our defense and foreign policies, and with our new approaches to the role and structure of Government itself.

Considered as a whole, this series of messages will be a blueprint for modernizing the concept and the functions of American Government to meet the needs of our people.

Converting it into reality will require a spirit of cooperation and shared commitment on the part of all branches of the Government, for the goals we seek are not those of any single party or faction, they are goals for the betterment of all Americans. As President, I recognize that I cannot do this job alone. The Congress must help, and I pledge to do my part to achieve a constructive working relationship with the Congress. My sincere hope is that the executive and legislative branches can work together in this great undertaking in a positive spirit of mutual respect and cooperation.

Working together—the Congress, the President and the people—I am confident that we can translate these proposals into an action program that can reform and revitalize American Government and, even more important, build a better life for all Americans.

RICHARD NIXON

Excerpts from the President's State of the Union message on Natural Resources and the Environment, Feb. 15, 1973:

NATURAL RESOURCES AND THE ENVIRONMENT

...Today I wish to report to the Congress on the state of our natural resources and environment. It is appropriate that this topic be first of our substantive policy discussions in the State of the Union presentation, since nowhere in our national affairs do we have more gratifying progress—nor more urgent, remaining problems....

When we came to office in 1969, we tackled this problem with all the power at our command. Now there is encouraging evidence that the United States has moved away from the environmental crisis that could have been and toward a new era of restoration and renewal. Today, in 1973, I can report to the Congress that we are well on the way to winning the war against environmental degradation—well on the way to making our peace with nature.

While I am disappointed that the 92nd Congress failed to act upon 19 of my key natural resources and environment proposals, I am pleased to have signed many of the proposals I supported into law during the past four years. They have included air quality legislation, strengthened water quality and pesticide control legislation, new authorities to control noise and ocean dumping, regulations to prevent oil and other spills in our ports and waterways, and legislation establishing major national recreation areas at America's Atlantic and Pacific gateways, New York and San Francisco.

On the organizational front, the National Environmental Policy Act of 1969 has reformed programs and decision-making processes in our Federal agencies and has given citizens a greater opportunity to contribute as decisions are made. In 1970 I appointed the first Council on Environmental Quality—a group which has provided active leadership in environmental policies. In the same year, I established the Environmental Protection Agency and the National Oceanic and Atmospheric Administration to provide more coordinated and vigorous environmental management. Our natural resource programs still need to be consolidated, however, and I will again submit legislation to the Congress to meet this need.

The results of these efforts are tangible and measurable. Day by day, our air is getting cleaner; in virtually every one of our major cities the levels of air pollution are declining. Month by month, our water pollution problems are also being conquered, our noise and pesticide problems are coming under control, our parklands and protected wilderness areas are increasing.

Year by year, our commitment of public funds for environmental programs continues to grow; it has increased four-fold in the last four years.... In addition to what Government is doing in the battle against pollution, our private industries are assuming a steadily growing share of responsibility in this field. Last year industrial spending for pollution control jumped by 50 percent, and this year it could reach as much as $5 billion....

Some 92 nations have concluded an international convention to control the ocean dumping of wastes. An agreement is now being forged in the Intergovernmental Maritime Consultative Organization to end the intentional discharge of oil from ships into the ocean.... Representatives of almost 70 countries are meeting in Washington this week at our initiative to draft a treaty to protect endangered species of plant and animal wildlife. The U.S.-USSR environmental cooperation agreement which I signed in Moscow last year makes two of the world's greatest industrial powers allies against pollution. Another agreement which we concluded last year with Canada will help to clean up the Great Lakes....

Principles To Guide Us

A record is not something to stand on; it is something to build on. And in this field of natural resources and the environment, we intend to build diligently and well. As we strive to transform our concern into action, our efforts will be guided by five basic principles:

The first principle is that we must strike a balance so that the protection of our irreplaceable heritage becomes as important as its use. The price of economic growth need not and will not be deterioration in the quality of our lives and our surroundings.

Second, because there are no local or State boundaries to the problems of our environment, the Federal Government must play an active, positive role. We can and will set standards and exercise leadership. We are providing necessary funding support. And we will provide encouragement and incentive for others to help with the job. But Washington must not displace State and local initiative, and we shall expect the State and local governments—along with the private sector—to play the central role in making the difficult, particular decisions which lie ahead.

Third, the costs of pollution should be more fully met in the free marketplace, not in the Federal budget. For example, the price of pollution control devices for automobiles should be borne by the owner and the user and not by the general taxpayer. The costs of eliminating pollution should be reflected in the costs of goods and services.

Fourth, we must realize that each individual must take the responsibility for looking after his own home and workplace....

Finally, we must remain confident that America's technological and economic ingenuity will be equal to our environmental challenges. We will not look upon these challenges as insurmountable obstacles. Instead, we shall convert the so-called crisis of the environment into an opportunity for unprecedented progress....

Controlling Pollution

I was keenly disappointed when the last Congress failed to take action on many of my legislative requests related to our natural resources and environment.... Among these 19 proposals are eight whose passage would give us much greater control over...pollution:

—*Toxic Substances.* Many new chemicals can pose hazards to humans and the environment and are not well regulated. Authority is now needed to provide adequate testing standards for chemical substances and to restrict or prevent their distribution if testing confirms a hazard.

—*Hazardous Wastes.* Land disposal of hazardous wastes has always been widely practiced but is now becoming more prevalent because of strict air and water pollution control programs. The disposal of the extremely hazardous wastes which endanger the health of humans and other organisms is a problem requiring direct Federal regulation. For other hazardous wastes, Federal standards should be established with guidelines for State regulatory programs to carry them out.

—*Safe Drinking Water.* Federal action is also needed to stimulate greater State and local action to ensure high standards for our drinking water. We should establish national drinking water standards, with primary enforcement and monitoring powers retained by the State and local agencies, as well as a Federal requirement that suppliers notify their customers of the quality of their water.

—*Sulfur Oxides Emissions Charge.* We now have national standards to help curtail sulfur emitted into the atmosphere from combustion, refining, smelting and other processes, but sulfur oxides continue to be among our most harmful air pollutants. For that reason, I favor legislation which would allow the Federal Government to impose a special financial charge on those who produce sulfur oxide emissions. This legislation would also help to ensure that low-sulfur fuels are allocated to areas where they are most urgently needed to protect the public health.

—*Sediment Control.* Sediment from soil erosion and runoff continues to be a pervasive pollutant of our waters. Legislation is needed to ensure that the States make the control of sediment from new construction a vital part of their water quality programs.

—*Controlling Environmental Impacts of Transportation.* As we have learned in recent years, we urgently need a mass transportation system not only to relieve urban congestion but also to reduce the concentrations of pollution that are too often the result of our present methods of transportation. Thus I will continue to place high priority upon my request to permit use of the Highway Trust Fund for mass transit purposes and to help State and local governments achieve air quality, conserve energy, and meet other environmental objectives.

—*United Nations Environmental Fund.* Last year the United Nations adopted my proposal to establish a fund to coordinate and support international environmental programs. My 1974 budget includes a request for $10 million as our initial contribution toward the Fund's five-year goal of $100 million, and I recommend authorizing legislation for this purpose.

—*Ocean Dumping Convention.* Along with 91 other nations, the United States recently concluded an international convention calling for regulation of ocean dumping. I am most anxious to obtain the advice and consent of the Senate for this convention as soon as possible.

Congressional action is also needed on several other international conventions and amendments to control oil pollution from ships in the oceans....

Protecting Our Natural Heritage

An important measure of our true commitment to environmental quality is our dedication to protecting the wilderness and its inhabitants. We must recognize their ecological significance and preserve them as sources of inspiration and education. And we need them as places of quiet refuge and reflection.

Important progress has been made in recent years, but still further action is needed in the Congress. Specifically, I will ask the 93rd Congress to direct its attention to the following areas of concern:

—*Endangered Species.* The limited scope of existing laws requires new authority to identify and protect endangered species before they are so depleted that it is too late. New legislation must also make the taking of an endangered animal a Federal offense.

—*Predator Control.* The widespread use of highly toxic poisons to kill coyotes and other predatory animals has spread persistent poisons to range and forest lands, without adequate foresight of environmental effects. I believe Federal assistance is now required so that we can find better means of controlling predators without endangering other wildlife.

—*Wilderness Areas.* Historically, Americans have always looked westward to enjoy wilderness areas. Today we realize that we must also preserve the remaining areas of wilderness in the East, if the majority of our people are to have the full benefit of our natural glories. Therefore I will ask the Congress to amend the legislation that established the Wilderness Preservation System so that more of our Eastern lands can be included.

—*Wild and Scenic Rivers.* New legislation is also needed to continue our expansion of the national system of wild and scenic rivers. Funding authorization must be increased by $20 million to complete acquisitions in seven areas, and we must extend the moratorium on Federal licensing for water resource projects on those rivers being considered for inclusion in the system.

—*Big Cypress National Fresh Water Preserve.* It is our great hope that we can create a reserve of Florida's Big Cypress Swamp in order to protect the outstanding wildlife in that area, preserve the water supply of Everglades National Park and provide the Nation with an outstanding recreation area. Prompt passage of Federal legislation would allow the Interior Department to forestall private or commercial development and inflationary pressures that will build if we delay.

—*Protecting Marine Fisheries.* Current regulation of fisheries off U.S. coasts is inadequate to conserve and manage these resources. Legislation is needed to authorize U.S. regulation of foreign fishing off U.S. coasts to the fullest extent authorized by international agreements. In addition, domestic fishing should be regulated in the U.S. fisheries zone and in the high seas beyond that zone.

—*World Heritage Trust.* The United States has endorsed an international convention for a World Heritage Trust embodying our proposals to accord special recognition and protection to areas of the world which are of such unique natural, historical, or cultural value that they are a part of the heritage of all mankind. I am hopeful that this convention will be ratified early in 1973.

—*Weather Modification.* Our capacity to affect the weather has grown considerably in sophistication and predictability, but with this advancement has also come a new potential for endangering lives and property and causing adverse environmental effects. With additional Federal regulations, I believe that we can minimize these dangers....

The environmental awakening of recent years has triggered substantial progress in the fight to preserve and renew the great legacies of nature. Unfortunately, it has also triggered a certain tendency to despair. Some people have moved from complacency to the opposite extreme of alarmism, suggesting that our pollution problems were hopeless and predicting impending ecological disaster. Some have suggested that we could never reconcile environmental protection with continued economic growth.

I reject this doomsday mentality—and I hope the Congress will also reject it. I believe that we can meet our environmental challenges without turning our back on progress. What we must do is to stop the hand-wringing, roll up our sleeves and get on with the job.

Excerpts from the President's State of the Union message on The American Economy, Feb. 22, 1973:

THE AMERICAN ECONOMY

...The state of our Union depends fundamentally on the state of our economy. I am pleased to report that our economic prospects are very bright. For the first time in nearly 20 years, we can look forward to a period of genuine prosperity in a time of peace. We can, in fact, achieve the most bountiful prosperity that this Nation has ever known.

That goal can only be attained, however, if we discipline ourselves and unite on certain basic policies:

—We must be restrained in Federal spending.

—We must show reasonableness in labor-management relations.

—We must comply fully with the new Phase III requirements of our economic stabilization program.

—We must continue our battle to hold down the price of food.

—And we must vigorously meet the challenge of foreign trading competition....

Basically, the economy affects people in three ways.

First, it affects their jobs—how plentiful they are, how secure they are, how good they are.

Second, it affects what people are paid on their jobs—and how much they can buy with that income.

Finally, it affects how much people have to pay back to the Government in taxes.

Job Picture Encouraging

To begin with, the job picture today is very encouraging.

The number of people at work in this country rose by 2.3 million during 1972—the largest increase in 25 years. Unemployment fell from the 6 percent level in 1971 to 5 percent last month.... Five percent unemployment is too high. Nevertheless, it is instructive to examine that 5 percent figure more closely.

For example:

—Only 40 percent of those now counted as unemployed are in that status because they lost their last job. The rate of layoffs at the end of last year was lower than it has been since the Korean War.

—The other 60 percent either left their last job voluntarily, are seeking jobs for the first time or are re-entering the labor force after being out of it for a period of time.

—About 45 percent of the unemployed have been unemployed for less than five weeks.

—As compared with earlier periods when the overall unemployment rate was about what it is now, the unemployment rate is significantly lower for adult males, household heads and married men. Among married men it is only 2.4 percent. Unemployment among these groups should decline even further during 1973.

This employment gain is even more remarkable since so many more people have been seeking jobs than usual. For example, nearly three million Americans have been released from defense-related jobs since 1969—including over one million veterans.

The unemployment rate for veterans of the Vietnam War now stands at 5.9 percent, above the general rate of unemployment but slightly below the rate for other males in the 20-to-29-year-old age bracket. While much better than the 8.5 percent of a year ago, this 5.9 percent rate is still too high. The employment problems of veterans, who have given so much for their country, will remain high on my list of concerns for the coming year.

Women and young people have also been seeking work in record numbers. Yet, as in the case of veterans, jobs for these groups have been increasing even faster. Unemployment among women and young people has thus declined—but it is also much too high and constitutes a great waste for our Nation....

Pay and Purchasing Power

The second great question is what people are paid on their jobs and how much it will buy for them.

Here the news is also good. Not only are more people working, but they are getting more for their work. Average per capita income rose by 7.7 percent during 1972, well above the average gain during the previous ten years.

The most important thing, however, is that these gains were not wiped out by rising prices—as they often were in the 1960's. The Federal Government spent too much, too fast in that period and the result was runaway inflation.

While wages may have climbed very rapidly during those years, purchasing power did not. Instead, purchasing power stalled or even moved backward. Inflation created an economic treadmill that sometimes required a person to achieve a 6 percent salary increase every year just to stay even.

Now that has changed. The inflation rate last year was cut nearly in half from what it was four years ago. The purchasing power of the average worker's take-home pay rose more last year than in any year since 1955; it went up by 4.3 percent—the equivalent of two extra weekly paychecks.

We expect inflation to be reduced even further in 1973—for several reasons.

A fundamental reason is the Nation's growing opposition to runaway Federal spending. The public increasingly perceives what such spending does to prices and taxes. As a result, we have a good chance now, the best in years, to curb the growth of the Federal budget. That will do more than anything else to protect the family budget.

Other forces are working for us too.

Productivity increased sharply last year—which means the average worker is producing more and can therefore earn more without driving prices higher. In addition, the fact that real spendable earnings rose so substantially last year will encourage reasonable wage demands this year. Workers will not have to catch up from an earlier slump in earnings.

Finally, we now have a new system of wage and price controls—one that is the right kind of system for 1973.

Firm Controls In Force; Food Prices Fought

Any idea that controls have virtually been ended is totally wrong. We still have firm controls. We are still enforcing them firmly. All that has changed is our method of enforcing them.

The old system depended on a Washington bureaucracy to approve major wage and price increases in advance. Although it was effective while it lasted, this sytem was beginning to produce inequities and to get tangled in red tape. The new system will avoid these dangers. Like most of our laws, it relies largely on self-administration, on the voluntary cooperation of the American people.

But if some people should fail to cooperate, we still have the will and the means to crack down on them.

To any economic interests which might feel that the new system will permit them, openly or covertly, to achieve gains beyond the safety limits we shall prescribe, let me deliver this message in clear and unmistakable terms:

We will regard any flouting of our anti-inflationary rules and standards as nothing less than attempted economic arson threatening our national economic stability—and we shall act accordingly.

We would like Phase III to be as voluntary as possible. But we will make it as mandatory as necessary.

Our new system of controls has broad support from business and labor—the keystone for any successful program. It will prepare us for the day when we no longer need controls. It will allow us to concentrate on those areas where inflation has been most troublesome— construction, health care and especially food prices.

We are focusing particular attention and action on the tough problem of food prices. These prices have risen sharply at the wholesale level in recent months, so that figures for retail prices in January and February will inevitably show sharp increases. In fact, we will probably see increases in food prices for some months to come.

The underlying cause of this problem is that food supplies have not risen fast enough to keep up with the rapidly rising demand.

But we must not accept rising prices as a permanent feature of American life. We must halt this inflationary spiral by attacking the causes of rising food prices on all fronts. Our first priority must be to increase supplies of food to meet the increasing demand.

We are moving vigorously to expand our food supplies:

—We are encouraging farmers to put more acreage into production of both crops and livestock.

—We are allowing more meat and dried milk to come in from abroad.

—We have ended subsidies for agricultural exports.

—And we are reducing the Government's agricultural stockpiles and encouraging farmers to sell the stock they own.

Measures such as these will stop the rise of wholesale food prices and will slow the rise of retail food prices. Unfortunately, nothing we can do will have a decisive effect in the next few months. But the steps I have taken will have a powerful effect in the second half of the year....

Holding the Line on Taxes

The third important economic question concerns how much money people pay out in taxes and how much they have left to control themselves.... The only way to hold the line on taxes is to hold the line on Federal spending. This is why we are cutting back, eliminating or reforming Federal programs that waste the taxpayers' money.

My Administration has now had four years of experience with all of our Federal programs. We have conducted detailed studies comparing their costs and results. On the basis of that experience I am convinced that the cost of many Federal programs can no longer be justified.... Such programs may have appealing names; they may sound like good causes. But behind a fancy label can lie a dismal failure. And unless we cut back now on the programs that have failed, we will soon run out of money for the programs that succeed....

To hold the line on Federal spending, it is absolutely vital that we have the full cooperation of the Congress. I urge the Congress, as one of its most pressing responsibilities, to adopt an overall spending ceiling for each fiscal year. I also ask that it establish a regular procedure for ensuring that the ceiling is maintained....

Economic Proposals to Congress

America is assuredly on the road to a new era of prosperity. The roadsigns are clear, and we are gathering more momentum with each passing month. But we can easily lose our way unless the Congress is on board, helping to steer the course.

As we face 1973, in fact, we may be sure that the state of our economy in the future will very much depend upon the decisions made this year on Capitol Hill.

Over the course of the next few months, I will urge prompt Congressional action on a variety of economic proposals. Together, these proposals will constitute one of the most important packages of economic initiatives ever considered by any Congress in our history. I hope—as do all of our people—that the Congress will act with both discipline and dispatch.

Among the items included in my 1973 economic package are:

—*Extension of the Economic Stablization Program.* Present authority will soon expire, and I have asked the Congress to extend the law for one year to April 30, 1974. I hope this will be done without adding general mandatory standards or prescribing rigid advance decisions— steps that would only hamper sound administration of the program. A highly complex economy simply cannot be regulated effectively for extended periods in that way.

—*Tax Program.* I shall recommend a tax program that builds further reforms on those we achieved in 1969 and 1971.

—*Property Tax Relief.* I shall also submit recommendations for alleviating the crushing burdens which property taxes now create for older Americans.

—*Tax Credit for Nonpublic Schools.* I shall propose legislation which would provide for income tax credit for tuition paid to nonpublic elementary and secondary schools. These institutions are a valuable national resource relieving the public school system of enrollment pressures, injecting a welcome variety into our educational process, and expanding the options of millions of parents.

—*Trade Legislation.* Another item high on our agenda will be new trade proposals which I will soon send to the Congress. They would make it easier for us not only to lower our trade barriers when other countries lower theirs but also to raise our barriers when that is necessary to keep things fair.

—*Other Reforms.* To modernize and make them more equitable and beneficial, I shall also later submit recommendations for improving the performance of our private pension system, our unemployment compensation program, our minimum wage laws and the manner in which we deal with our transportation systems.

—*Spending Limits.* Finally, but most importantly, I ask the Congress to act this year to impose strict limits on Federal spending....

We must...recognize that no one in the Congress is now charged with adding all of our Federal expenditures together—and considering their total impact on taxes and prices. It is as if each member of a family went shopping on his own, without knowing how much money was available in the overall family budget or how much other members of the family were spending or charging on various credit accounts.

To overcome these problems, I urge prompt adoption by the Congress of an overall spending ceiling for each fiscal year. This action would allow the Congress to work jointly with me in holding spending to $250 billion in the current fiscal year, $269 billion next year, and $288 billion in fiscal year 1975. Beyond the adoption of an annual ceiling, I also recommend that the Congress consider internal reforms which would establish a regular mechanism for deciding how to maintain the ceiling.

I have no economic recommendation to make to the Congress which is more important to the economic well-being of our people....

Making A Choice

We stand on the threshold of a new era of prolonged and growing prosperity for the United States.

Unlike past booms, this new prosperity will not depend on the stimulus of war.

It will not be eaten away by the blight of inflation.

It will be solid; it will be steady; and it will be sustainable.

If we act responsibly, this new prosperity can be ours for many years to come. If we don't, then, as Franklin Roosevelt once warned, we could be "wrecked on (the) rocks of loose fiscal policy."

The choice is ours. Let us choose responsible prosperity.

REPORT ON CIVIL RIGHTS

February 9, 1973

The U.S. Commission on Civil Rights, for the fourth time in three years, sharply criticized the Nixon administration's efforts to enforce laws aimed at eliminating discrimination against, and protecting the rights of, minority groups. In a 427-page study based on surveys extending to all federal agencies dealing with domestic affairs, the commission concluded that "the government's civil rights program is not adequate or even close to it." Blame for inadequate enforcement was laid to failures of leadership at almost every level of every agency, with President Nixon bearing the ultimate responsibility.

"Presidential leadership has brought us far along the road toward the accomplishment of international understanding, cooperation and friendships with many of our hitherto implacable enemies. For this the nation should be grateful," the commission said. "Presidential leadership has not brought equality to bear on the creation of a similar situation within the nation. Without the leadership of the President, this job not only becomes infinitely more difficult, but a steady erosion of the progress toward equal rights, equal justice and equal protection under the Constitution will occur." The report described administration efforts in the civil rights field as lacking in "creativity, resources, a sense of urgency, a firmness in dealing with violators, and most important—a sense of commitment."

In October 1970, in its first report on federal efforts to enforce civil rights laws, the commission had said that "executive branch enforcement of civil rights mandates was so inadequate as to render the laws meaningless." It added that "this deplorable situation did not develop accidentally." In its third follow-up report, issued Feb. 9, 1973, the commission said it had "found that the inertia of agencies in the area of civil rights has persisted." Several examples of innovative efforts "here and there" were cited, but "no government-wide plan for civil rights enforcement" was found. "There is not even effective coordination between agencies with similar responsibilities," the commission concluded.

The civil rights enforcement study, though not released until February, had actually been completed in September 1972. It was the last report prepared during the chairmanship of the Rev. Theodore M. Hesburgh, president of the University of Notre Dame, who resigned in November 1972 after 16 years at the head of the Civil Rights Commission. Hesburgh had been sharply critical of the Nixon administration's civil rights record—a circumstance thought to have been responsible for acceptance of his resignation.

Excerpt from the U.S. Civil Rights Commission's report of Feb. 9, 1973:

STATEMENT OF THE UNITED STATES COMMISSION ON CIVIL RIGHTS ON "THE FEDERAL CIVIL RIGHTS ENFORCEMENT EFFORT—TWO YEARS LATER"

More than two years ago this Commission issued the first in a series of reports evaluating the structure and mechanisms of the Federal civil rights enforcement effort. We undertook these studies because while there was an impressive array of Federal civil rights laws, Executive orders, and policies, the promise of equal justice for all Americans had not approached reality. We felt that the Federal Government was the single institution in our society possessing the legal authority, the resources, and—potentially, at least—the will for attacking social and economic injustice on a comprehensive scale.

In that report, the Commission identified weaknesses in civil rights enforcement which continue to permit such grievous wrongs as segregation in our schools, discriminatory housing and employment, disproportionate hardship to minorities in urban development and highway construction, and inequitable distribution of health services and other Federal benefits.

Today we are releasing a third follow-up report, which was submitted last September to the Office of Management and Budget for its use in reviewing budget submissions of the Federal agencies. Our basic conclusion is that the Federal effort is highly inadequate; that it has not improved as much as we would have expected since our last report in November 1971; and that strong leadership and direction are absolutely necessary to prevent a continuation of the ineffective enforcement program developed over the last nine years. We issue this report in the hope that our findings will be studied by the President, his agency heads, the Congress, and the American people and that strong remedial action will be promptly undertaken.

Our findings are dismayingly similar to those in our earlier reports. The basic finding of our initial report, issued in October 1970, was that executive branch enforcement of civil rights mandates was so inadequate as to render the laws practically meaningless. Many deficiencies ran throughout the overall effort. We found, for example, that the size of the staff with full-time equal opportunity responsibilities was insufficient. At the same time, because of their low position in their organizational hierarchy, civil rights officials lacked authority to bring about change in the substantive programs conducted by their agencies. Moreover, it became abundantly clear that agency civil rights enforcement efforts typically were disjointed and marked by a lack of comprehensive planning and goals. Agencies failed to search out patterns of bias, preferring instead to respond to individual complaints. Even where noncompliance was plainly substantiated, protracted negotiations were commonplace and sanctions were rare. Finally, we found a lack of Government-wide coordination of civil rights efforts.

Bureaucrats' Resistance to Enforcement

This deplorable situation did not develop accidentally. Nor were the commission's findings a surprise to those knowledgeable about civil rights and the role of the Federal Government. The enforcement failure was the result, to a large extent, of placing the responsibility for ensuring racial and ethnic justice upon a massive Federal bureaucracy which for years had been an integral part of a discriminatory system. Not only did the bureaucrats resist civil rights goals; they often viewed any meaningful effort to pursue them to be against their particular program's self-interest.

Many agency officials genuinely believed they would incur the wrath of powerful members of Congress or lobbyists—and thereby jeopardize their other programs—if they actively attended to civil rights concerns. Moreover, since nonenforcement was an accepted mode of behavior, any official who sought to enforce civil rights laws with the same zeal applied to other statutes ran the risk of being branded as an activist, a visionary, or a troublemaker. Regrettably, there were few countervailing pressures. Minorities still lacked the economic and political power to influence or motivate a reticent officialdom.

In spite of these inherent difficulties, we knew that Government employees respond to direct orders. We were convinced that if our Presidents and their agency head and subcabinet level appointees had persisted in making clear that the civil rights laws were to be strictly enforced, and had disciplined those who did not follow directives and praised those who did, racial and ethnic inequality would not have been as prevalent as it was in 1970. Leadership—presidential, political, and administrative—and the development of realistic management processes are the keystones to a vigorous and effective Federal enforcement effort. Our study concluded that this leadership unfortunately was lacking. Despite certain halting steps forward and a few promising public pronouncements, Presidents and their appointees seldom assumed their potential role as directors of the Government's efforts to protect the rights of minority Americans.

The Commission's two followup reports, issued in May and November 1971, found that some agencies had made some progress in improving their civil rights structures and mechanisms. Important action had been taken by such agencies as the Office of Management and Budget and the Department of Housing and Urban Development. But other agencies—such as the Federal Power Commission, the Department of the Interior, and the Law Enforcement Assistance Administration of the Department of Justice—had made almost no headway in developing the tools necessary to combat discrimination.

In this, our most recent assessment, we have found that the inertia of agencies in the area of civil rights has persisted. In no agency did we find enforcement being accorded the priority and high-level commitment that is essential if civil rights programs are to become fully effective. Significant agency actions frequently are accompanied by extensive delays—in the issuance of regulations, in the implementation of regulations, and, greatest of all, in the use of sanctions when discrimination is found. Innovative steps occur here and there, but they are uncoordinated with those of other agencies. For example, the Department of Housing and Urban Development and the General Services Administration have issued regulations implementing their 1971 agreement to assure availability of housing for lower-income families, open without discrimination, in any area in which a Federal installation is to be located. Neither agency, however, has undertaken the responsibility of devising an overall plan to see that every Federal agency assigns a high priority to this effort.

There is no Government-wide plan for civil rights enforcement. There is not even effective coordination between agencies with similar responsibilities in, for example, the employment area, where the Civil Service Commission, the Equal Employment Opportunity Commission, and the Office of Federal Contract Compliance share enforcement duties. The Equal Employment Opportunity Coordinating Council, created by Congress in March 1972 for this precise purpose, had not addressed any substantive issues in the first six months of its existence.

There have been some noteworthy actions, and the agencies which have instituted new and more effective compliance procedures should be duly recognized. For example, the Department of Housing and Urban Development has issued regulations requiring builders and developers, prior to the approval of HUD assistance, to demonstrate that they have undertaken positive actions to sell or rent to minorities. The Department of Health, Education, and Welfare performs special studies in the health and social services area, apart from its normal program of onsite civil rights reviews. These studies have examined such issues as language barriers to the delivery of services to non-English speaking minorities. The Department of Agriculture's Office of Equal Opportunity has been involved in extensive upgrading of its enforcement mechanism. This includes a system whereby the Department's constituent agencies are required to set goals for minority participation in their programs. The Environmental Protection Agency, although a relatively new agency, has demonstrated energy and creativity in its efforts to enforce the provisions of Title VI of the Civil Rights Act of 1964 prohibiting discrimination in the distribution of Federal assistance. The Civil Service Commission, working with the language of an Executive order which Congress now has enacted into law, has begun to enlarge its equal opportunity staff and change its procedures.

Cases of Inaction

For every step forward, however, numerous cases of inaction can be cited. The Department of the Interior has begun to conduct onsite reviews of the State and local park systems it funds, but it has not yet developed a comprehensive compliance program. It has not, for example, provided adequate guidance to these park systems concerning actions prohibited by Title VI. The Federal Power Commission still refuses to assume jurisdiction over the employment practices of its regulatees, despite a Justice Department opinion that it has authority to do so. The Interstate Commerce Commission has delayed a decision on the very same point for over 18 months.

The Federal financial regulatory agencies have not begun to collect racial and ethnic data. Neither have they made the necessary effort to use the traditional examination process to detect discriminatory lending practices barred by Title VIII of the Civil Rights Act of 1968. The Office of Federal Contract Compliance has been downgraded within the Department of Labor and its effectiveness has commensurately diminished. The Internal Revenue Service continues to construe in an unjustifiably narrow manner its duty to keep discriminatorily operated private schools from receiving tax-exempt status. Its school reviews have been perfunctory and its cooperation with the Department of Health, Education, and Welfare is almost nonexistent.

A year ago we noted some encouraging signs in the Department of Justice's coordination of the Title VI programs of the various Federal agencies. Now the Department's activities again have become lethargic. Evidence of this is the fact that proposed uniform amendments to agency Title VI regulations have not been issued more than five years after the need was recognized by Department officials.

Even among those agencies where we found improvements, serious problems persist. Some agencies still do not adequately review the recipients of their assistance. The Department of Housing and Urban Development, for example, conducted only 186 reviews of the 12,000 agencies it funded during Fiscal Year 1972. HUD has yet to set priorities for scheduling reviews. Even when reviews are conducted, there is reason to believe that they are often superficial. The Department of Agriculture reports that it reviewed more than 24,000 of its recipients last year. Yet only one instance of noncompliance was discovered—a remarkable, if not unbelievable record, considering the extensive discrimination which pervades federally funded agriculture programs.

Other agencies continue to utilize low standards. The Civil Service Commission refuses to validate its tests according to the standard used by the Equal Employment Opportunity Commission, the Office of Federal Contract Compliance, and the Department of Justice and approved by the Supreme Court of the United States.

In one of the most important areas of national life—the provision of equal educational opportunities for our children, we now find lowered compliance standards for elementary and secondary schools and what appears to be the elimination of the threat of fund termination which has rendered the Department of Health, Education, and Welfare's enforcement program ineffective.

In the face of this dismaying picture, the Office of Management and Budget, the one Federal entity with authority over all agencies, has maintained its interest, but has not accelerated its civil rights efforts in keeping with the demonstrated need. Execution of OMB's civil rights responsibilities is left largely to the discretion of individual staff members. OMB has not established a full-time and adequately staffed civil rights unit with responsibility for interagency policymaking and monitoring. No one has been charged by the Director of OMB with the specific duty of holding the staff accountable for identifying and fulfilling the civil rights aspects of their assignments. The total potential of the budget and management review process for civil rights evaluation thus has not been realized.

A Matter of Critical Importance

This latest Commission study has reinforced the findings of the three preceding reports that the Government's civil rights program is not adequate or even close to it. This matter is of critical importance to the Nation's well-being, for we are not dealing with abstract rights, but with the fundamental rights of all people—a decent job, an adequate place to live, and a suitable education. Everyone must have the opportunity to share fully in the bounty of our society—not as stepchildren or wards of the Government but as dignified citizens of this, the greatest Nation on earth.

The Federal Government's constitutional and moral obligations are clear. The long-term stability of this Nation demands an end to discrimination, in its institutional forms as well as in its overt individual manifestations. Yet large-scale discrimination continues.

Our faith in the ability of even our imperfect democratic society to live up to its commitments when challenged to do so gives us hope that the future will be less bleak than are the past and present.

That challenge can only come from the aggressive leadership by those in government at all levels who have taken a solemn vow to uphold the Constitution. Historically, the Presidency has been a major focal point through which the power of the Nation as well as its conscience has been expressed.

If our hope for lasting peace among the Nations of the world requires a rapprochement with those Nations from which we have been estranged, then our hope for domestic tranquility between our diverse population requires no less. Presidential leadership has brought us far along the road toward the accomplishment of international understanding, cooperation and friendship with many of our hitherto implacable enemies. For this the Nation should be grateful. Presidential leadership has not yet been brought equally to bear on the creation of a similar situation within the Nation. Without the leadership of the President, this job not only becomes infinitely more difficult, but a steady erosion of the progress toward equal rights, equal justice and equal protection under the Constitution will occur. History suggests that so long as one man is not free the freedom of all is in jeopardy.

The first requirement of any such effort on the part of the Chief Executive and his appointees is that of an unequivocal, forceful implementation of all the civil rights laws now on the books.

In the past, the Government's vast resources frequently have been effectively marshaled to cope with natural disasters, economic instability, and outbreaks of crime. Can we afford to do less when dealing with this country's greatest malignancy—racial and ethnic injustice?

The answer is clearly "no." But days pass into weeks, then into months, and finally into years, and Federal civil rights enforcement proceeds at a snail's pace. It lacks creativity, resources, a sense of urgency, a firmness in dealing with violators, and—most important—a sense of commitment. Time is running out on the dream of our forebears.

While we do not feel that our efforts have thus far produced significant results, this Commission remains committed to reviewing periodically the civil rights enforcement activities of the Federal agencies. We are aware that there now are a number of new agency heads and that some steps have been taken in the six-month period since we completed this review. We intend, therefore, to complete another evaluation of the Government's efforts in six months.

But our activities in this field cannot begin to meet the need. Private groups and individuals must become more involved in monitoring the Federal Government's activities. This involvement may well lead, as it has in the past, to judicial and administrative proceedings seeking relief where Federal activities have been weak or ineffective. Such involvement most certainly leads to a more informed citizenry and a more responsive bureaucracy.

Every citizen has a right to expect that his or her Government will rededicate itself to the principle of equality and an effective program of enforcement to support that commitment. Without that commitment, this Nation will not keep faith with the clear mandate of the Constitution.

▼▼▼

ENVIRONMENTAL RISKS OF SST

February 12, 1973

An ad hoc committee of the National Academy of Sciences-National Academy of Engineering issued a report Feb. 12 calling for extensive research into environmental risks in the development and wide use of supersonic aircraft. The panel of scientists recommended a broad range of studies to determine, so far as possible, the changes in the atmosphere that might be brought about by SST emissions and the derivative effects on life on earth. Their primary concern was whether the thin layer of ozone in the upper atmosphere, which partially screens out biologically harmful solar ultraviolet radiation, might be reduced by chemical reaction to the jet emissions. As little as a 5 per cent decrease in the amount of ozone could be expected to cause a 26 per cent increase in the intensity of ultraviolet radiation reaching the earth, the scientists said. They warned that this probably would lead to a minimum of 8,000 additional cases of skin cancer and 300 more deaths each year in the United States.

Admitting that all the facts were not yet in and that predictions were difficult, the scientists nonetheless cited results other than those affecting man that could have even greater long-range significance. They pointed out that increases in the amount of solar ultraviolet radiation could diminish the biological productivity of the ocean, interfere with mating and other behavioral patterns of insects and other lower animals, and damage plants, especially agricultural products that constitute the world's foodstuffs. The panel emphasized the importance of ozone by observing that most forms of life prob-

ably developed in prehistoric times after formation of the ozone shield—presumably because that layer in the atmosphere was a prerequisite for the evolution and maintenance of terrestrial life.

Human and plant cells sensitive to light would also be affected by increased ultraviolet radiation, the scientists said. DNA, the cell that carries an organism's genetic blueprint, might react to overexposure to light in a way that would cause mutation of the organism or even death. Plankton, the basis of the ocean's food chain, also are highly sensitive to light and might be adversely affected by increases in the amount of ultraviolet radiation.

The special NAS-NAE panel was headed by Kendric C. Smith of the Stanford University School of Medicine. It had been convened by the Academies' Environmental Studies Board in 1971 as a result of controversy over the impact on the environment of the SST. Congress, on the prompting of environmentalists and budget-cutters, had denied funding of the SST in 1971. At that time warnings had been sounded that the supersonic aircraft would create unbearable sonic booms and might alter the earth's atmosphere and change the average temperatures of the earth. Because of the penetrating sonic boom, the Federal Aviation Administration imposed "an almost complete ban" on supersonic flights over the continental United States by civilian aircraft. The rule, which took effect April 27, 1973, would allow exceptions only when it was shown that the sonic booms would not reach ground level.

NASA geophysicist Richard J. Allenby asserted that "scientists cannot be sure if a large fleet of supersonic aircraft would warm up the earth or not." He noted that some subscribe to a "greenhouse" theory that the earth would be warmed by the penetration of ultraviolet light that could not escape, but that others believed that the earth would be cooled because of a reduction of heat-retaining elements in the atmosphere.

Issuance of the panel's report entitled "Biological Impacts of Increased Intensities of Solar Ultraviolet Radiation" coincided with renewed discussion of the SST. President Nixon in his fiscal 1974 budget had proposed to more than double federal spending for research on the SST, from $11-million in 1973 to $28-million in 1974. The increased funding, he said, would give the United States "the option to initiate development of an advanced supersonic transport" later in the decade.

Text of the Introduction, Conclusions and Recommendations of the report issued Feb. 12 by the National Academy of Sciences-National Academy of Engineering follows:

I. Introduction

Solar radiation is a very important element in our environment, yet, perhaps because of its ubiquity, the wide scope of its chemical and biological effects is often not fully appreciated. The sun is necessary for life: We are warmed by its rays, and we are able to see because our eyes respond to that portion of the solar spectrum known as visible light. More important, visible light is required for photosynthesis—the process by which plants obtain the energy needed for their growth and for man's sustenance.

Nevertheless, many of the effects of solar radiation are detrimental. Most people are aware that a painful sunburn can be caused by excessive exposure to the sun and that sunlight causes colors to fade and materials to age. Skin cancer is also produced by excessive exposure to sunlight. There are many other effects of solar radiation on cells, including the production of chemical changes (mutations) in their hereditary (genetic) material. Recent study has shown that plant and animal cells are able, to varying extents, to repair radiation-induced genetic damage. Evidently, plants and animals have evolved such repair systems in order to help protect themselves from the detrimental radiations of the sun and thereby allow themselves to receive the benefit of other wavelengths of solar radiation. The situation is one of balance: Sunlight is necessary for life, yet in excess it can be harmful.

It is the ultraviolet (UV) portion of sunlight that is most detrimental to plant and animal cells. The small amount of ozone in the earth's stratosphere filters out these harmful wavelengths of ultraviolet light and thus prevents most such radiation from reaching the surface of the earth. The formation of this protective shield of ozone in prehistoric time was most likely a prerequisite for the evolution of terrestrial life. Even in the presence of this ozone layer, however, a significant amount of biologically inactivating ultraviolet radiation does reach the surface of the earth.

Recent testimony in the *Congressional Record* and an article in *Science* suggest that water and especially the oxides of nitrogen emitted as combustion products in the operation of numerous commercial supersonic transport (SST) aircraft may partially destroy the protective shield of stratospheric ozone. This would allow an increased amount of ultraviolet radiation to reach the surface of the earth. Other human activities that lead to the large scale emission of particulate matter into the atmosphere may decrease the amount of solar radiation reaching the earth. It is important, therefore, to explore the consequences to man and his environment of changes in both the intensity and character of the solar UV radiation reaching the earth's surface.

The goals of this report are:

1. To review some of the known effects of ultraviolet radiation on man and other living organisms;

2. To assess, as far as possible, the consequences to man and other living organisms should the amount of solar ultraviolet radiation reaching the surface of the earth increase;

3. To identify those areas where knowledge is inadequate and where further research is urgently needed.

II. Conclusions

The Committee's review and discussion of the currently available information concerning the effects of ultraviolet radiation on man and other living organisms have led to the following conclusions:

• Knowledge of the wavelength distribution and intensity of the solar radiation that reaches the surface of the earth is important for understanding the biological effects of sunlight. It is the ultraviolet portion of sunlight that, in excess, is most harmful to plants and animals. A small amount of ozone in the earth's atmosphere filters out most of the ultraviolet radiation from sunlight. The concentration of ozone in the stratosphere is lowest at the equator and increases toward the higher latitudes. There are also daily and seasonal fluctuations in the ozone concentration, but, on an annual basis, the amount of ozone is rather constant for a given location. Thus, any change in the average ozone concentration will probably be of biological significance even though such a change might be less than present daily or seasonal fluctuations.

Because of the radiation-absorbing properties of ozone, a small decrease in ozone concentration will result in a much larger increase in ultraviolet radiation reaching the earth. For example, it has been estimated that a 5 percent decrease in average ozone concentration over the midlatitude of the United States would cause a 26 percent increase in ultraviolet radiation at 297.5 nanometer [(nm) equals 10 meter]; a 50 percent decrease in ozone would yield a 10-fold increase in radiation at this wavelength (one of the most biologically detrimental wavelengths of solar radiation). The question then arises as to whether man and other living organisms could sustain such increases in exposure to solar ultraviolet radiation.

• The biological effects of light are the consequence of the absorption of specific wavelengths of light by specific chemical molecules and their resultant photochemical alteration. Deoxyribonucleic acid (DNA) is the most important molecule in a cell since it carries the genetic information of that cell. DNA is easily modified by exposure to ultraviolet radiation, and this is the principal reason why ultraviolet radiation is detrimental to living organisms.

Most living cells have a significant enzymatic capacity for repairing ultraviolet radiation damage to their DNA; however, living things are in a delicate balance between the continual photochemical destruction of cellular components by solar radiation and their biochemical repair. If this balance is upset by exposure to increased amounts of ultraviolet radiation or by interference with repair, the organism will be injured and may die, or mutations may appear in offspring.

●In addition to biochemical repair mechanisms, organisms employ a number of other means to resist the damaging effects of sunlight. These are mainly (1) avoiding exposure to sunlight by appropriate behavioral responses to environmental cues (e.g., heat, visible light, etc.) and (2) preventing sunlight from reaching the sensitive tissues and cells by development of light-absorbing and light-scattering coats of hair, feathers, shells, or superficial pigment.

●A significant amount of ultraviolet radiation is transmitted through the skin of man and causes various degrees of damage to living cells absorbing it. Melanin, a dark pigment, is the main absorber of ultraviolet radiation in human skin and is highly efficient in protecting deeper structures from exposure to ultraviolet radiation. Too little is known about the relative penetration of various wavelengths of solar radiation deeper than the skin, even though important body functions (e.g., sexual maturation, biological time clocks) are known to be light-dependent.

●The induction of the three most common malignant tumors of human skin—basal cell and squamous cell carcinomas and malignant melanomas—is correlated with exposure to sunlight. The incidence of each shows a marked increase with the lack of skin pigmentation, with the inability to tan, with increasing time spent out-of-doors, and with decreasing latitudes of residence. (The ozone layer becomes thinner, and the average intensity of ultraviolet radiation increases with decreasing latitudes.)

From the relationship between the concentration of ozone in the upper atmosphere, its transmission of ultraviolet radiation, and the relationship between current levels of solar ultraviolet radiation and neoplastic changes in human skin, it has been calculated that a 5 percent decline in ozone would produce at least 8,000 extra cases of skin carcinomas and melanomas per year in a population the size of the white population of the United States.

●Sunlight produces a variety of detrimental effects in man, of which sunburn is the most common. In addition, chronic skin changes leading to wrinkling, discoloration, and thinning of the skin, which the white population interpret as aging, are primarily the result of exposure to ultraviolet radiation and are slowed by the presence of melanin in the skin. Tanning, the production of new melanin, is a protective response to the radiation injury of skin. However, many

239

light-skinned people, genetically incapable of tanning adequately, are liable to repeated injury and consequent premature development of skin changes. While some features of the processes leading to skin damage by ultraviolet radiation are reasonably well understood, the molecular bases for these effects are not adequately known.

- A variety of chemicals, some used in medicine and some found in the environment, sensitize human skin and increase the effectiveness of solar radiation in producing phototoxic and photoallergic reactions. As more and more chemical agents are introduced into our environment, either deliberately or accidentally, the number of patients with such disorders will continue to increase, particularly if solar ultraviolet radiation intensities also increase.

- Sunlight has long been believed to have prophylactic and healing powers for the promotion of health. This accounts for the behavior of millions of people who annually flock to beaches. Although the physiological, biochemical, and psychological mechanisms remain largely unstudied and unknown, there is evidence for two beneficial effects. First, ultraviolet radiation kills bacteria, of which some are beneficial to man and some are harmful. Prior to the discovery of antibiotics, ultraviolet radiation was used for the treatment of skin infected with tubercle bacilli and streptococci. Second, in man and all other animals with calcified internal skeletons, ultraviolet radiation converts provitamin D in the skin to vitamin D. A deficiency in vitamin D leads to rickets; an excessive amount of vitamin D, however, can be toxic. Whether man and other animals would benefit or be harmed by an increased production of vitamin D from an increased amount of solar ultraviolet radiation cannot be predicted from available information.

- Solar ultraviolet radiation of the wavelengths reaching the surface of the earth is transmitted through pure water. Because of the great amount of life in the world's oceans and its importance to man, any deleterious effects of increased ultraviolet radiation in this environment could have serious ecological consequences. Present information on the depth to which ultraviolet radiation penetrates natural bodies of water, as well as the effect it has on the organisms therein, is fragmentary.

- Unlike man and other vertebrates, most insects see in a portion of the ultraviolet (near ultraviolet, at wavelengths from 300 to 400 nm), as well as in the portion of the solar spectrum that is visible to man. Moreover, near ultraviolet light is a distinct color for many species of insects and has special significance in influencing the behavior of members of this large and ecologically important group of animals. For example, because near ultraviolet light is the most effective light in attracting insects, insect traps are fitted with ultraviolet lamps. Conversely, because lamps that are poor in blue and ultraviolet light offer much less stimulation to insects, yellow bulbs are frequently used to illuminate porches and patios. There are other examples, less obvious but vastly more important ecologically: celestial navigation by insects using the blue and ultraviolet polarization pattern of skylight, recognition of flowers by their distinct colors and patterns of color generated by ultraviolet reflectance, and sex recognition in butterflies based on ultraviolet reflectance patterns from wings.

An increase in the intensity of ultraviolet radiation, at wavelengths shorter than 320 nm, would increase the relative brightness of objects reflecting in this spectral region. However, neither the effects on insect behavior nor possible deleterious consequences of increased chronic exposure of the receptor cells can be accurately predicted from available data.

●Under laboratory conditions, ultraviolet radiation is clearly detrimental to a wide variety of plant species ranging from bacteria to higher plants. Agricultural species are among the plants most sensitive to ultraviolet radiation. Although it is not possible to predict the exact biological consequences of increased ultraviolet radiation at the earth's surface, sensitive plant species may well be endangered. Natural defenses against ultraviolet radiation and efficient repair systems exist in plants, but these may not be sufficient to cope with higher intensities of ultraviolet radiation.

III. Recommendations

Sufficient knowledge is at hand to warrant utmost concern over the possible detrimental effects on our environment by the operation of large numbers of supersonic aircraft. In order to better analyze and predict the consequences to man and other living organisms of a significant reduction in the stratospheric ozone concentration by these aircraft, this Committee recommends that the following research be carried out in the very near future.

Monitoring the Quality and Quantity of Solar Radiation

A network of monitoring stations should be established to determine the spectral distribution and intensity of natural ultraviolet radiation reaching the surface of the earth. These stations should be located at various latitudes and altitudes and be capable of extended operation so that short-term and long-term changes in the intensity and spectral quality of solar ultraviolet radiation can be adequately recorded. This information is needed not only as a base line for monitoring possible environmental changes (e.g., from SST's) but is also critically necessary in order to evaluate numerous biological effects of sunlight (e.g., the regional incidence of skin cancer) that now are only correlated with changes in latitude (i.e., changes in ozone concentration) or altitude.

It is important that these measurements provide narrow-band spectral data rather than mean values of intensity for wide wavelength intervals.

Laboratory Use of Wavelengths of Light Found in Sunlight

Most of our information on the chemical and biological effects of ultraviolet radiation comes from experiments using so-called germicidal lamps that emit radiation at a wavelength (254 nm) not normally found in sunlight reaching the earth's surface. Several published studies on bacteria, plant viruses, and man show that the biological damage produced at 254 nm is different from that produced with ultraviolet radiation at wavelengths found in sunlight. Therefore, the chemical and biological effects of the wavelengths of ultraviolet radiation found in sunlight should be studied. This may require the development of lamps that match the output of the sun in the ultraviolet region measured at the surface of the earth.

The biological effects of ultraviolet radiation have usually been studied in the laboratory in the absence of visible radiation. There is growing evidence that visible light can, under different conditions, either help cells to repair ultraviolet-radiation-induced damage or can potentiate the detrimental biological effects of ultraviolet radiation. Thus, to better understand the effects of sunlight on man and his environment, experiments should be performed using natural sunlight or artificial lamps whose spectral output closely approximates that of sunlight.

Skin Cancer in Man

Studies are needed to describe and quantify the interactions between environment, behavior, and genetic background that lead to the development of the malignant skin tumors in man induced by ultraviolet radiation. Such studies should contribute to methods for the early recognition of individuals with a high risk of developing skin cancer, so that they can receive specific advice.

Studies in laboratory animals are urgently needed to establish the basic mechanisms for the induction, by ultraviolet radiation, of the various types of malignant skin tumors.

Phototoxicity and Photoallergy

Too little is known about the mechanism of photosensitization and photoallergy in animals and man. The rapid and unselective introduction of many potentially photoactive agents into our environment necessitates development of methods to predict the extent and type of photoinjury by such agents. A national registry of cases of phototoxicity would speed the removal of such agents from commerce.

Beneficial Effects of Ultraviolet Radiation

Claims made in earlier literature, supported by few data, of beneficial effects of ultraviolet radiation on man, such as the lowering of blood pressure and blood cholesterol, the relief of asthma, and improvements in cardiovascular functions should be reinvestigated under carefully controlled conditions.

Photobiological Resistance of Plants and Animals

Do plants and animals have sufficient reserve capacity (natural defense shields plus repair capacity) to endure an intensity of ultraviolet radiation greater than that now reaching the earth? The sensitivity to natural ultraviolet radiation and the damage repair capacity of both animals and plants should be studied in order to answer this question. In addition to laboratory studies, it is imperative to carry out field experiments in which normal solar irradiation is supplemented with UV radiation at those wavelengths (i.e., 280-320 nm) where an increase in intensity is expected if there is a decrease in the concentration of stratospheric ozone.

Although artificial sources of ultraviolet radiation, particularly those emitting at 254 nm, are quite effective in producing mutations, too little is known about the effectiveness of natural sunlight in producing mutations. It is important that further research be directed toward the assessment of the mutagenic capacity of natural sunlight (with and without supplementation by artifical UV radiation) in a wide variety of plants and animals.

Effects of Ultraviolet Radiation on the Behavior of Insects

Since insects are so necessary to our ecology, and since their vision extends into the ultraviolet portion of sunlight, information is needed on the behavioral effects of different amounts and wavelengths of ultraviolet light on insects and other animals under realistic ecological conditions. Studies of behavioral ecology and sensory physiology on a much wider sample of animal species in both tropical and temperate environments are necessary.

Effects of Ultraviolet Radiation on Ecosystems

Environmental changes can have profound effects on ecosystems as well as individual organisms. Effects that are not immediately lethal to individuals may nevertheless endanger reproductive capacity and thus the future of whole species. (The possible deleterious effects of DDT on several species of birds provide a recent example.) The study of the biological effects of ultraviolet radiation should therefore include experiments on real and model ecosystems.

Education

This Committee was convened in response to a specific issue—the possibility that SST's will damage the earth's ozone shield, and its charge was correspondingly limited—to assess the effects of increased ultraviolet radiation on living organisms. We have nevertheless been unable to avoid the following observation:

In society where political decisions are influenced by the way people vote, it is imperative that both the public at large and their political leaders be sensitive to issues and arguments based on scientific criteria, in addition to more traditional political and economic concerns. Therefore, if the general public is to understand the profound importance of sunlight in our daily life, beyond the obvious of warmth and vision, photochemists and photobiologists should concern themselves with demonstrating the relevance of their expertise to national problems. The most important conceptual roadblocks that need to be overcome are: (1) the lack of respect for the importance of the biological effects of sunlight simply because sunlight is ubiquitous and (2) the concept that if something is natural it must be totally beneficial and safe. It must be made clear that life on earth is in a delicate balance between the beneficial and detrimental effects of sunlight.

Priorities

Of the recommended projects listed in this section, the following are the ones that the Committee feels are the most critical for an early assessment of the biological impact of a possible increase in solar ultraviolet radiation.

1. Ground-level stations should be established at various latitudes to monitor the intensity and wavelength distribution of solar ultraviolet radiation. This information is needed not only as a base line for monitoring possible environmental changes but also to properly evaluate data that are currently available on the latitudinal variations in the incidence of skin cancer in man.

2. The ability of important agricultural plants to grow and produce when exposed to additional amounts of ultraviolet radiation over the region of 280-320 mn (those wavelengths expected to be most affected by changes in stratospheric ozone concentration) should be determined. These experiments should include both laboratory and field studies.

3. Because of the unique importance of plankton in the ecological food chain, their sensitivity to solar ultraviolet radiation should be studied systematically, including both laboratory and field studies. An important adjunct to these studies would be the accurate measurement of the depth of penetration into natural waters of the various wavelengths of solar ultraviolet radiation.

4. Laboratory experiments using animals are urgently needed to gain more insight into the molecular bases and dose response characteristics of ultraviolet-radiation-induced skin cancer.

5. The public should be informed that, even today, excessive exposure to solar radiation should be avoided.

RETURN OF THE POW'S

February 12, 1973

The first 116 American prisoners of war to be released by the North Vietnamese under the Jan. 27 Paris peace agreement touched down at Clark Air Force Base in the Philippines on Feb. 12, completing the first leg of their journey home. Their return from Vietnam constituted the initial phase of prisoner repatriation. It was to be followed by the release, within 60 days of the signing of the peace agreement, of the rest of the total of 587 men who had been held by the North Vietnamese and the Viet Cong.

Navy Captain Jeremiah Denton, a captive for eight years, was the first POW to disembark from one of the three military evacuation jets that had flown the first contingent from Hanoi to Clark. As the highest ranking officer on the plane, the 48-year-old captain spoke for himself and for the other returning prisoners when he said: "We are honored to have had the opportunity to serve our country under these difficult circumstances. We are profoundly grateful to our Commander in Chief and to our nation for this day." After a second's pause, Denton exclaimed, "God bless America!"

The Pentagon had planned a low-key reception for the POW's; there were only military personnel and newsmen to welcome them at Clark. The former prisoners were individually escorted to medical quarters and shielded from press inquiries. Although President Nixon had decided to take no part in the welcoming ceremonies, Air Force Col. Robinson Risner telephoned the White House, shortly after arriving in the Philippines, to personally thank Nixon for his part in bringing the prisoners home. "Mr.

President," Risner said, "all of the men would like to meet you personally to express their gratitude for what you have done. You will have our support for as long as we live." The President told Risner, who had been captured in 1966, that the sacrifices of American prisoners of war and their families had made possible "an honorable peace" in Vietnam. "Your sacrifice has not been in vain," Nixon assured him.

For some, the return of the prisoners symbolized an American victory in Vietnam. For others, it marked an end only to U.S. involvement in the Indochina conflict. Still others looked to the release of the men to give America a new sense of hope and to aid in reuniting a society divided by a controversial war. "We want very much to get on with the business of peace and reconstruction here," said Secretary of State William P. Rogers in Washington. A teary-eyed Rogers declared: "I can't think of anything that gets us off to a better start than to watch these returning POW's. If that doesn't make America proud, then I don't know what will."

From Clark, the ex-prisoners flew to Travis Air Force Base in California and then to air bases near their homes. The military had devised an "Operation Homecoming" aimed to ease the returning men into a society in some respects markedly changed from the one they left long before. News accounts of events of the years they had sat out in prison camps were provided at the military hospitals where they were confined for physical examinations. A dictionary of current American slang was prepared by the Air Force to update the men's knowledge of words and phrases currently in vogue. Brochures were sent to POW families suggesting means of adjusting to the arrival of a long-absent husband or son. But the acculturation shock was still apparent: "I find it a little disconcerting to find women wearing pants and men wearing women's hairstyles," remarked Navy Captain Harry T. Jenkins Jr. Other ex-prisoners smiled at being told of "hot pants." "I told one guy that Miami won the Super Bowl," said a pilot, "and he said 'What's the Super Bowl?'" But the main concern of the former prisoners appeared to be their families. Navy Capt. Howard E. Rutledge, who became a grandfather while in captivity, said: "We want to catch up with our families. They've all outgrown us. They're kind of new to us, and we're kind of new to them."

Condition of Returning POW's

Despite long years of captivity, most of the men appeared to be in remarkably good physical condition, especially those who had been held in the North rather than in the jungles of South Vietnam. Some told of contracting malaria, beri beri and other diseases, but few appeared undernourished and most had maintained or regained their weight. They told newsmen that they had had adequate, although limited, food and quarters. "A lot depended on the camp commanders," said Douglas K.

Ramsey, a 38-year-old Foreign Service officer who spent seven years in Vietcong captivity. "In seven years there, I ran into dogs and real jewels. Some people I would invite today into my home for a drink; others I'd invite behind a woodshed and only one of us would return."

The former prisoners talked also about activities that had occupied them during their confinement. One group pieced together the Bible, with each prisoner contributing what he remembered of the scriptures. A mathematically minded soldier spent hours multiplying three-digit numbers in his head. During five years at the prison camp near Hanoi facetiously tagged the "Hanoi Hilton," Air Force Capt. Barry Bridger of Bladensboro, N.C., practiced gymnastics. Although he had never participated in such activities in high school or college, Bridger worked up to a point where he could do 49 consecutive handstand push-ups.

When repatriation was virtually completed, the POW's no longer felt bound to heed the Pentagon's advice to avoid disclosures about another side of prison life lest they endanger the release of prisoners not yet freed. It was then that accounts of torture and gross mistreatment by the Viet Cong and the North Vietnamese began to come out. Former captives recounted instances of being mercilessly beaten and of being contorted into horribly painful positions by mouth bits and ropes and held there for long periods of time. As the number of these accounts increased and public revulsion grew, prospects waned for congressional fulfillment of President Nixon's promise of reconstruction aid to North Vietnam.

Snags in Release Schedule

After the first contingent of POW's was released, subsequent releases were temporarily delayed by disagreements over interpretation of the peace agreement. American officials had expected the second major release to take place about Feb. 27, even though the Paris agreement had not specified a particular date. It was assumed that the releases would keep pace with the timetable for withdrawal of troops still stationed in South Vietnam: four phases of 15 days each. North Vietnamese stalling on the release of American prisoners evoked an angry response from the White House on Feb. 27 and threatened to disrupt the international conference on Vietnam that had convened the day before in Paris. But after high-level meetings in Paris and Saigon, the Communists agreed on March 1 to release 136 additional POW's. The third installment, numbering 108, took off for the Philippines March 14, one day after the United States officially expressed concern over reported infiltration of arms and men into South Vietnam from the North in violation of the cease-fire agreement. Withdrawal of the last group of troops was delayed while the United States insisted that nine men held in Laos were covered by the terms of prisoner repatriation. The final group of POW's left Hanoi on March 29 as the last 2,500 American troops were pulling out of South Vietnam.

Excerpts from the Air Force dictionary of slang, issued for use by POW's:

TO OUR RETURNED PRISONERS OF WAR:

This pamphlet was put together in an effort to give you a head start, and perhaps bring you up to date, on the current slang expressions being used by the young people of America. During your long absence the language of the youth has changed in somewhat the same way as the language you used differed from that of your parents during your younger years.... This is a part of the language and the slang being used by the youth of today - your sons and your daughters.

As a matter of fact, we contacted various young people to provide us these words and went so far as to ask your sons, daughters and your wives what slang expressions were being used in their community - their home. It may not be complete, but at least it's a start.

The main purpose of putting this together is perhaps to get you and your offspring off to somewhat of an equal start. So Big Daddy, when your young son or daughter comes to you and says, "Do you dig?" You can say, "Lay it on me, dude and right on?" We hope it helps.

ACID	Refers to the hallucinogenic drug, Lysergic Acid Diethylamide, (LSD)
ACTION	Activity or excitement of any kind; usually refers to parties or informal entertainment
AFRO	Natural Black hair style; hair not straightened, but left in its natural curly state and styled. Also prefix denoting Black (Ex: Afro-American)
BAD NEWS	Any unpleasant situation or event. Also, a depressing or undesirable person
BAD SCENE	Unpleasant experience, place or event; a disappointment
BAG	Person's way of life, now generally replaced by the term "trip". Ex: "He's into a jazz trip."
BEAR	Teen-agers' definition of "Mother"
BE DOWN ON	Dislike or disapprove of something or someone, usually intensely. Ex: "He's down on pollution."
BEAUTIFUL	Expression of approval; usually exclamatory
BLACK PANTHERS	Militant organization of Blacks who are engaged in promoting the welfare of Black people. The organization is now downplaying armed confrontation and encouraging community self-help and building popular support in the Black Community.

BLOW YOUR COOL	Loss of control of temper or emotions. The term still used, though far less frequently
BLOW YOUR MIND	Be totally overcome by an idea, place, thing, or person
BLUES	Feeling of depression. Among Whites the term "down" as in "I'm really down" is much more common
BOPPER	Hip, aware young person in tune with the modern scene. Usually short for teeny bopper
BROTHER	Term mostly used by a Black man or woman to identify a Black male, and as a term of address. Also being used by Chicanos and American Indians
BROWN	Mexican-Americans, Mexicans, Chicanos
BROWN BERETS	Pro-Mexican-American militant organization, similar to the Black Panther organization
BUMMER	Unpleasant experience, especially with drugs. It is also an exclamation of disgust or sympathy for another's bad experience
BURN	Hurt emotionally, being taken
BUST, BUSTED	Arrested, arrest
COOL	Self-assured, knowledgeable. One who is aware of the times
COP OUT	Refuse to face issue or responsibility, usually a social one
COUNTERCULTURE	A style of living. Values are different to current society. Usually associated with hippies and communes
CRACKER	White person, usually Southern-racists is connotated (usually, but not always)
CRASH	Go to sleep, usually quickly. Also, to come down from drugs
CUT OUT	Leave, split, truck on out
DINGBAT	Same as ding-a-ling. Someone goofing off. Scatterbrained
DO YOUR OWN THING	Follow your own interest and activities. Usage has decreased in frequency
DOPE	Any drug; though most frequently in reference to marijuana
DOWN	1) Unhappy, depressed. 2) No longer under the influence of a drug
DUDE	Any male
EGO TRIP	An achievement or success

EXPERIENCE | An unusual occurrence or event that is out of the ordinary. Always interesting, but not necessarily a positive reaction

FLARES | Pants which widen as they get to the ankle. Almost like the Navy Bell Bottoms

FOXY | Reference to neat or cool girls

FREAK | May mean anybody who is identified by looks or behavior as "counterculture" type. Usually indicates drug usage, especially marijuana

FUNKY | Earthy, homey, simple. An event or behavior associated with country, bluegrass and soul music. Usually a positive expression, but may be negative depending on context and tone

GAS, IT'S A | Cool, great. Refers to an event. Ex: A favorite TV program might be referred to as "It's a gas."

GAY | Homosexual. Accepted term by homosexuals

GAY LIB | Gay Liberation. An activist movement of homosexuals seeking public acceptance of their life style

GET INTO | Become absorbed or involved in something intensely, usually with a positive attitude

GET IT TOGETHER | To get organized

GOING DOWN | The truth and details of what is occurring in a situation. Ex: "Hey, man, what's going down in Nam now?" Also means, what's happening?

GOOD PEOPLE | Generous and kind humanistic people who are either a part of or sympathetic to the "counterculture"

GRASS | Marijuana; dope, pot, reefer, weed

HALLUCINOGEN | Drug that produces visual hallucinations similar to those experienced by psychotic patients

HANG IN THERE | To continue pursuing a course of action, usually in the face of adversity. Keep charging

HANG IT UP | Forget it; give up something, stop

HANG LOOSE | 1) To relax or remain calm. 2) Wait. 3) Take things as they come

HANG UP | 1) Dislike, a mental block. 2) Reoccurring problem, source of irritation or disappointment with no apparent solution

HASSLE | 1) Problem; troublesome or irritating situation or event, conflict situation. 2) To disagree, argue or bother

HEAD	Drug user; freak
HEAD SHOP	Small store where records, incense, hash pipes, underground comics, and other items used by heads can be bought. Generally connotates a store catering to freaks.
HEAVY	Deep, complicated, meaningful. Bad or disgusting
HIPPY	Predominantly middle-class white youth, ranging in age from 12 to 25; some drop out of society, do not work, take drugs, have long hair. Anybody with long hair is considered a hippy.
HONKY, HONKIE	Any white person, connotates racist
HOODED	Addicted, specifically to a drug, but generally the habitual consuming of anything
HUNG UP ON	To be very attached to someone or something in a positive way or to be disturbed or annoyed
IN	Socially acceptable within a group, usually a subculture, now used sarcastically to indicate disgust with attention to conforming
INTO	Involved, interested, engrossed in, pursuing the study of. Ex: "She's into astrology."
JESUS FREAK	Someone who has turned to Jesus. In modern youth, someone who was on drugs but turned to Jesus and is no longer using drugs
JOINT	Marijuana cigarette, joint reefer
LAY IT ON	To give information about something
MAXI	Meaning larger. Ex: "maxicoat", a long coat of ankle length
MESSED UP	Mentally disturbed and often physically ill or exhausted, specifically from a drug or traumatic experience. Describes any negative condition of a person or situation
MIDI	Meaning middle size. Usually refers to female coat, dress or skirt of length to the middle of the calf
MINI	Meaning short or small. Ex: "miniskirt", A short skirt to mid thigh
MS	Women's Lib term which is an abbreviation meaning either "Miss" or "Mrs"
NATURAL FOODS	Mostly used by counterculture people. Includes food which is free of any chemicals used in growing such as fertilizers, spray, etc.
NO WAY	Impossible

OUT OF IT	To be out of touch with reality when under the influence of a drug, especially hallucinogens. To lack understanding and awareness, especially in a subculture
PLASTIC	Phony, unreal, dehumanized, superficial, valueless. Very important concept used in reference to both people and objects, especially an environment or situation
POT	Marijuana
PSYCH OUT	To confuse or to become confused or disturbed
PSYCHED UP	Excited, prepared mentally
PSYCHEDELIC	Refers to a new social movement including the change in moral structure, music, dress and the arts
PUT ON	Phony behavior
RAP	Conversation, usually about a "meaningful" subject. A sort of lecture or specific approach to a subject. Ex: "He gave a rap on the elections."
RIGHT ON!	Exclamation of agreement with importance or truth of a statement. Means the same as "perfect"
RIP OFF	Steal and/or cheat. Mislead in order to gain the upper hand
SCENE	Place of action. An experience
SHADES	Eye glasses - usually sun glasses
SHAG	Haircut
SOUL	An inherent quality Black people feel they have and Whites rarely do. It implies an awareness and understanding of life and a naturalness of expression
STRAIGHT	1) Off drugs either at the time or permanently 2) Not homosexual
TRIP	1) Noun: Experience, especially drug experience 2) Verb: To use a drug, especially hallucinogens
TRUCKING	Walking—using legs to get somewhere
TUNE IN	Become aware of or involved in something. Focus attention on something
TURN ON	Get high on drugs. Arouse sexually
TURN OFF	Disgust or repulse someone
TURN ON TO	Become interested or begin to like
UNDERGROUND	Unsanctioned by prevailing social attitudes; anti-establishment
UP TIGHT	In a state of tension. Worried, upset, or inhibited

VIBES	Vibrations. Nonverbal expressions of thoughts or feelings
WHATEVER	Equivalent to "that's what I meant". Usually implies boredom with topic or lack of concern for a precise definition of meaning
WHERE'S IT AT WITH YOU?	"How do you feel?"
WOMEN'S LIB	Women's Liberation activist movement to secure equal rights for women
YIPPIE	Person associated with the Youth International Party, an eccentric group of hippies

Excerpts from Information Pamphlet provided by the Department of Defense to the families of U.S. servicemen who were prisoners of war or were missing in action in Southeast Asia:

THE SECRETARY OF DEFENSE
Washington, D.C. 20301

22 September 1972

To The Families of Our Men Who Are Missing or Captured
in Southeast Asia:

Your men - our missing or captured servicemen - have made sacrifices that few Americans are called upon to make. As the family member of one of these men you have had to bear uncertainty, sorrow and many very difficult problems.

From my personal involvement I can assure you that our Government has made and continues to make every possible effort to improve the welfare of our men held captive and secure their release, to gain information on all of our men about whom we believe the enemy has knowledge, and to assist you through this difficult period of your lives. I believe you know the unalterable commitment made by our President that our men will not be abandoned. This commitment is shared throughout our Government and I know by our fellow Americans.

As the Secretary of Defense I have special responsibilities to these men and to you, their families. One responsibility, which requires very careful and detailed planning, involves the actions that will be required when our men are repatriated. I have directed that our procedures be designed to provide careful and considerate attention to the needs of our returned men so that they may resume normal, healthy lives with their families. Our principal consideration will be their medical well-being—both physical and psychological. While it would be impractical to provide you with the minute details of the planning by all echelons of the Defense establishment, this pamphlet has been prepared for your use in understanding our preparations for the return of our men, the care they will receive and what assistance and information you will be provided. We will continue in every possible channel to obtain information about our missing men who may not return.

It is my intention that all Defense Department actions concerned with the repatriation and rehabilitation of our men returning from captivity be accomplished with careful attention to detail and with primary consideration for the returnees. My firm goal is a smooth transition back into the environment here at home. My earnest hope is that we will be implementing our repatriation plans in the near future.

(signed)   MELVIN P. LAIRD

RETURN TO US CONTROL

...When our men return to US control, they will be immediately placed under medical auspices. Families of both PW and MIA personnel will be notified of the repatriation as rapidly as possible through official Service casualty assistance channels. The men will be moved quickly from the point of release to an overseas central processing site.

OVERSEAS CENTRAL PROCESSING

At the overseas central processing site hospital facility, a thorough medical assessment of the physical condition of the returnees will be made. This examination will indicate any medical attention which may be necessary prior to the flight home and identify any conditions which may require further treatment. The physician-in-charge will determine when each individual is ready for aero-medical evacuation to the United States.

In addition to the medical processing, the returnees will also receive initial debriefings. These interviews by experienced personnel will be for the specific purpose of obtaining information about other men still missing or detained in Southeast Asia. Because the enemy has provided little information concerning our men, it is extremely important that these debriefings take place as soon as medical authorities think appropriate. This vital information is necessary to assist us in our continuing efforts to determine the fate of our missing men and those who have not returned from captivity.

The men will receive pay in amounts sufficient for their immediate needs and will be fitted with uniforms (complete uniforms in individual sizes for all our captured and missing men are currently stored in the Pacific area). They will receive current information about their families, including any messages and photographs their families may have provided for them. Each man may make a telephone call at Government expense to his family. Ample background information will be available to the men concerning significant historical events that have transpired during their period of captivity.

Throughout this processing period, each man will be given careful individual attention with primary regard for his health and welfare. Since it can be expected that the medical condition of the returnees will vary, the time to complete overseas medical processing will be a matter of individual medical determination. For some, this period could be as long as ten days to two weeks.

The families of returned men will be kept advised of the progress of their men and the expected time of their arrival at the processing locations in the United States. In addition, Service casualty officers will maintain contact with the families of men who do not return and will pass to them any information received concerning their loved ones....

ENROUTE

In the United States, the men will be transported in most instances to Service hospitals near the homes of their primary next of kin. Exceptions will be made in those instances where the medical needs of the returnees require specialized facilities or treatment. Families will be advised as soon as possible after the decision on hospital assignment has been made.

To prevent personal inconvenience and a chance of missing the returnee, family members should not travel to any military facility overseas or in the United States unless specifically recommended and authorized by the returnee's Service.

SERVICE HOSPITAL TREATMENT AND PROCESSING IN THE UNITED STATES

Family reunions will occur as soon as possible after the returnees arrive at the Service hospitals in the United States. The precise manner and timing of the reunion and those in attendance will be determined by medical advice and the desires of the returnee and his family.

Family members will be given all possible assistance regarding arrangements for their travel to and from the returnee's assigned hospital. The Service of which the returnee is a member will provide the next of kin with all pertinent information concerning the various available modes of transportation which would best serve the area of the assigned hospital. This information will be passed to the families through normal Service casualty assistance channels.

The Services will arrange for family lodging on or near the processing installation. Families will be given all possible assistance in the use of base facilities including area orientation, continuing explanation of individual processing sequence, and transportation on the installation. Additionally, a Service representative will be provided to serve as an escort for each family during their visit.

The medical evaluation and treatment of each returnee will continue for as long and in as much detail as is clinically indicated by the physician-in-charge. Concurrently, when permitted by medical considerations, the returnee will complete personnel processing and detailed debriefing on experiences while in captivity. Career, financial, and legal assistance will be provided to both the returnee and his family in as much detail as is required to thoroughly meet rehabilitation and re-adjustment needs. In addition, the historical background information which was available at the overseas processing site will be duplicated here for convenience of the men.

The processing sequence will be thorough, but planned and organized so that it will not be hurried or tiring to the returnee. Ample periods will be left for rest, exercise, and association with family members. Where possible, the intent and purpose of processing actions - medical, administrative, and debriefing - will be explained to the returnee and his family.

The length of time a man will be assigned to the hospital will depend on his individual medical needs. As a general policy, each man will be granted a generous period of convalescent leave when medically appropriate. This leave period may be given prior to or in conjunction with his transfer to another military installation.

FURTHER ASSIGNMENT

Each man's career will depend upon a variety of considerations, including his own desires regarding continued military services. If he desires to remain on active duty, he will be given special training to bring him up to date with his contemporaries. If he elects to pursue a civilian career, he will be provided all possible assistance by his Service in counseling and preparation for his chosen field of endeavor. Regardless of his choice, his medical condition will be monitored at various intervals to ensure that required medical assistance is provided for as long as medical authorities deem necessary. Returnees will be provided careful, considerate counseling and will not be pressed to make decisions on future assignments.

PUBLIC AFFAIRS

Because of the deep-seated national and international interest in any event connected with our men who are prisoners of war or missing in action, the news media will display intense interest in the repatriation process. Public Affairs officers of the Services and the Defense Department will ensure that official releases of information to the media will be made with specific regard for the well-being of the men, their families, and our national interests. The Services will ensure that the returnees have the assistance of public affairs briefings and that the families are provided public affairs guidance and assistance as desired.

After the serviceman has arrived at the US Service hospital and has had the opportunity to visit with his family, press interviews may be conducted in accordance with his individual desires when debriefing requirements have been met and such interviews will not inhibit progress of his medical treatment.

FAMILY ASSISTANCE

A special Defense Department study panel has considered in detail the various facets of the rehabilitation and readjustment process. Lessons learned from previous repatriations have been examined, as well as direct inputs received from former prisoners of war. Additionally, many family members and consultants have contributed valuable information. The panel studied the entire rehabilitation process for ways in which the Defense Department and the Military Services can provide the best possible support and assistance. Findings of the panel have been approved and have been distributed to the appropriate departments and agencies for implementation.

One of the most significant aspects of the rehabilitation and readjustment process is that of family counseling. A program is being coordinated with the Military Departments which will provide all possible counseling services to the families of our missing and captured men. Every effort will be employed to meet the needs of the returnees, their families, and the families of the men who do not return. As information is received concerning missing servicemen, it will be provided to the families through official Service casualty channels. The Service will provide all possible assistance to family needs.

The determination of the fate of some of our missing men may require additional initiatives following the detailed analysis of information provided us by the returnees. Every possible avenue will be sought through negotiation, impartial inspection, site investigation, graves registration team employment and any other initiative which shows promise of results. The status of our men who do not return will be resolved at the earliest possible time.

The Services will continue to provide families with more detailed information regarding initial notification methods, planned destination hospitals in the United States, family travel procedures, information regarding quarters at or near the hospital and other matters of personal interest.

Finally, attached is a list of the most frequently asked questions concerning our repatriation planning and procedures. While this is by no means an attempt to answer all possible queries, it should serve to provide information regarding some significant aspects of the repatriation process.

REPRESENTATIVE QUESTIONS WITH ANSWERS REGARDING SUBJECTS RELATIVE TO OUR MISSING AND CAPTURED MEN AND THEIR FAMILIES

1. Question:

Will I be able to join my husband/son at the overseas processing base? If not, why?

Answer:

Present plans do not include provisions for next of kin visits at the overseas processing facilities. Lodging suitable for visiting family members is practically nonexistent. Emphasis at the overseas processing site will be placed on a thorough medical assessment of the returnee's physical condition and the preparations necessary for his trip home. If his overseas medical processing time is extended, provisions will be made for a family visit to take place at the overseas processing site. This decision would be made by the Service Secretary concerned based on recommendations of appropriate medical authorities. No attempt to travel overseas should be made by family members without or against Service advice. Such family travel could result in arrival overseas after the returnee has departed for the United States.

2. Question:

What will you tell the returnee about his family?

Answer:

He will be given pertinent information about his family to include their current location and telephone number. He will also be given any messages or photographs which you have requested be available for him upon his return. News of serious illnesses or deaths in his family will be given him by Service officials when deemed appropriate by medical authorities. Authority for release of this information to the returnee will be obtained from the family.

3. Question:

Is it necessary that my husband/son be treated at a hospital of his own Service?

Answer:

He will be returning to the familiar environment of his own Service. Additionally, his personnel, financial, and medical records will be more efficiently maintained and administered by personnel who are expert in the procedures of his Service.

4. Question:

Will I get to the processing base in the United States before my husband/son?

Answer:

We plan to have you there ahead of time so that you can meet him as soon as possible after his arrival.

5. Question:

I am apprehensive about my first meeting with my husband. How should I behave? What topics should I discuss or avoid? Should I appear cheerful or sympathetic?

Answer:

As much assistance as possible will be provided to both the returnee and his family regarding the reunion. Family members will have been given information about their relative after he has returned. The returnee will have been provided whatever current information is available about his family. Additional advice from appropriate Service medical and casualty officers will be available upon request. Act natural, relax, and be yourself.

6. Question:

Should I bring the children?

Answer:

Your children are entitled to travel with you to the medical facility in the United States at Government expense. Service casualty officers will keep you advised of the time when he is expected to arrive and other particulars concerning your travel and visit. The decision to bring the children is a personal one and should be made individually on the part of each family.

7. Question:

Should I bring some of his clothes?

Answer:

His Service will have furnished him a tailored uniform and he will have a comfort kit containing toilet articles and other basic needs which was provided for him at the overseas central processing site. He might appreciate your bringing a favorite bathrobe, pair of slippers or his favorite shaving lotion when you come for the reunion.

8. Question:

How much time will I be able to spend with him in the hospital? Will we have time alone?

Answer:

The length and frequency of family visits in the hospital will depend on the medical needs of the returnee. As soon as possible after his arrival, a daily routine will be established which will allow planning by family members and an orderly schedule for his medical treatment. Provisions will be in effect for private visits with his next of kin.

9. Question:

How long can I stay at the processing location in the United States?

Answer:

The length of time family members will remain at the Service hospitals in the United States will be a matter to be determined following the arrival of the returnees. The period of time our men will be assigned to these hospitals will undoubtedly vary among individuals. In any case, if the man's hospital assignment is to be prolonged, the returnee's dependents are entitled to move to that hospital location at Government expense.

10. Question:

Will he need a special diet when he comes home?

Answer:

In most cases, a special diet will not be necessary during the period of convalescent leave. In those instances where a special diet has been prescribed, families will be provided appropriate information by the attending physician.

11. Question:

How much time does he have to make a decision on a permanent assignment?

Answer:

The returnee's career decision must be made on an individual basis. All possible assistance and counseling will be available to him in making his determination. He will not be rushed into this decision. Once his goal is established, he will be provided further specialized guidance and assistance whether his choice is to remain in the Service or to pursue a civilian career. He may make this decision when he is ready, at the hospital, during or following convalescent leave.

12. Question:

How long do you think it will be after the end of our involvement in Vietnam before the status of the missing men is resolved?

Answer:

The period of time involved in the resolution of status of our missing men will depend upon the availability of substantive information relative to these cases. When our men held prisoner are returned to us, we will obtain some information about other men still missing or detained. Analysis of this information may in itself allow resolution of some of the MIA cases and will assuredly be of assistance to us in our continuing efforts to determine the fate of those men who have not returned. These efforts will include negotiation, impartial inspections, site investigation, graves registration team employment and any other initiative which shows promise of results. In any event, each MIA case will be a matter of careful individual determination and every effort will be made to resolve them as soon as possible.

13. Question:

What evidence is required before a death finding can be made?

Answer:

Under law, determinations of death are made by the Secretary of each Service by one of two methods: (1) Determination based upon conclusive evidence of death, or (2) Determination based upon a presumption of death.

In the former category, the specific evidence required is not outlined in the law. Title 37, United States Code provides that this determination is made by the Service Secretary only when he is satisfied that all available evidence clearly established that the Service member is deceased.

Presumptive findings of death, on the other hand, are made by the same authority when the Service Secretary decides after evaluation of all available information, that the Service member can no longer be reasonably presumed to be living.

14. Question:

What are my benefits and entitlements should a determination of death be made?

Answer:

SERVICE BENEFITS - Determination of Death

Allotment - If an allotment was being paid to dependents, it is stopped. Dependents may retain allotment monies received prior to determination of death regardless of the time interval between the date on which death actually occurred and the date the determination is made.

Six Months Death Gratuity - Paid based upon member's rank at the time the determination is made - $3,000 maximum.

Unpaid Pay and Allowances - Paid up to date the determination is made to the person designated by the member.

Use of Base Facilities - Continues until widow remarries, and for dependent children, up to an age where they would no longer normally be dependent upon the member.

Transportation of Dependents and Household Goods - Up to one year from date determination is made but can be extended by Service Secretary on an individual basis.

OTHER BENEFITS - Determination of Death

Servicemens Group Life Insurance (SGLI) - Paid on amount in effect at established date of death.

National Service Life Insurance (NSLI) - Paid on face amount of policy plus refund of all premiums paid for policy years subsequent to established date of death.

Dependency and Indemnity Compensation (DIC) - Starts from date of death or last month for which full pay and allowance is received, whichever is later.

Social Security - Paid in a lump sum retroactive to established date of death, then continue monthly from date determination is made.

Transcript of an interview with the wife of Senior M. Sgt. Arthur Cormier, USAF (seven years a POW in North Vietnam) on NBC's "First Tuesday" program, Feb. 6, 1973, as reprinted by The Washington Post, *Feb. 11, 1973:*

MRS. CORMIER: I am not the feminine woman that I was seven years ago if one defines feminity as sort of passivity and concerned more with home and the running of the home and motherhood. Those were my limits, really, seven years ago. I was terribly interested in—in raising my children and—and running my home. Those are still my primary interests. However I have been forced by circumstances to become quite aggressive, sort of terribly cold. Do you know how long it's been since I kissed a man? It's been a long time. I don't even know if I remember how anymore, and that scares me.

Q. Do you love him?

A. Oh, yes. Very much. In fact, I guess I realize now how much I do....

On the one hand, I--I cannot wait for him to get home. My life is kind of held in abeyance until he arrives, because I want so much to continue it with him. On the other hand, I do feel that this will be a time when a person will come into my life who will pass judgment, and it's kind of scary and I'm kind of nervous about it.

It's just kind of a very scary feeling to think that—let me—let me put it this way. Someone has—has said to me. "Oh, well," you know, "you have a second chance, a second marriage." And I don't really, because if this were a second marriage the two of us would be sort of starting out from equal footing and we would both have made a decision to—to stick with one another or whatever it may be.

This time I have a man coming into my house, and it is very much my house, I shopped for it and paid for it and fixed it up, took care of the storms and the screens, and it's very much mine; I'll have a man coming in who is very much a stranger, who is biologically the father of my children, but they are my children, I have raised them, I've walked the floor at night with them; he's really not had much of an influence in their lives at all. And now he's kind of coming back in from the assumption he has a place here, but we're going to have to make a place for him is really the problem....

And he's bound to come in here and—and realize that we have survived pretty well without him. And I'm sure that he's going to wonder what is his—his role and his place in this family.

Q. What about getting together when he gets out? I understand that the—the government has all sorts of plans made which you feel don't include the family much. Is that it?

A. Well, there are—their plan calls for having the men returned to specified centers in the United States and then ship the families into these centers at government expense to spend the time there, at least the initial rehabilitation period there with the man, which does not allow very much in terms of thinking about a second honeymoon. My husband has mentioned a sec—the possibility of a second honeymoon in his letters, and I'm wondering how he's going to feel about a second honeymoon in the base hospital at Andrews Air Force Base. I—well, the —the idea of the antiseptic and sterility of the place kind of turns me off; and I'm sure it will him.

Q. Your children have grown up in very crucial years without their father. Do you think that can ever be made up, that time lost?

A. No. No, I—I really don't think it can. I think what also cannot be made up is the fact that they have grown up without him. Their thinking and their actions and the—their value system is all kind of mine. And while I believe very much in my value system, it's—it's not been sort of tempered by another person. And I don't think that that's very good. It's not the way I pictured it when I went down the aisle as a bride; definitely not what I had in mind....

You're talking with a wife who is able to say these things because I have some security that I have a person coming home. But so many of these wives do not have that—that security. And it's so very difficult for them to be able to—to think about this sort of coldly. I guess that some of us are—are able to; we've been able to—to put our feelings aside and sort of talk about it. An awful lot of families are not able to.

Also, you must remember that I'm seven years into this. If you had—if you were in Washington last October to the league meeting, you would have seen all the brand-new families, families whose relative had been shot down in '70 or '71 or '72. It seems incredible that people are still being shot down, but they are. And so really I'm sort of an old China hand at this. There are so many wives who are not....

Q. When your husband comes back are you afraid that he's going to be treated as the POW freak, with his mother crying every time she looks at him and—and your saying, you know, "We've got our life to continue, and our life to start"?

A. Well, this is one of—of my fears. I am sort of concerned about my role. No matter which way I play it, I am bound to come out as kind of being the heavy. And if I appear to have managed with a reasonable degree of success, then I will appear to have gone on without him. If I did not manage at all, then it—I will not have risen to the occasion. If the children are well-behaved and present relatively few problems, then I will be the—the sole parent; he will really have not had any involvement. If the children had a tremendous amount of problems, then it would be because I haven't taken care of them. There's this tremendous possibility that I can lose. I can lose on so many counts. He could fall in love with the stewardess on the way back in the plane, because it may be the first round-eyed American girl that he's met.

He's coming back to a situation which is already set. The schedules are there; the lifestyle is there. I'm much older than I was, although he is also, but I'm much more set in my ways. The children are older. And we all have our—our schedules and our routine. And I see that I could lose, and it kind of not only worries me but it kind of angers me too.

One of the previous returnees came home and divorced his wife because she was too liberal. So that's pretty scary. Am I going to be too liberal? Well. Am I going to be too aggressive, too self-possessed, too cold? I don't know.

Q. Do you worry that perhaps he won't measure up to your standards anymore?

A. No I guess I'm more concerned about my measuring up to his. It—it just sounds so very trite, but I—I keep thinking of how am I going to share anything with him. How is it going to be to have him sharing my life; to have him checking the checkbook and the bank balances? How is it going to be to feel that he's listening in on phone conversations that I have? How will I ever share my closet, my bathroom with him? How—how do I—I share my life with a man who to all intents and purposes at this point is a total stranger and yet is the father of my children and the man with whom I want very much to share? But I don't know about my ability to share anymore. I don't know how I'm going to feel if I am awakened in the middle of some night when he's had a bad dream and decides that I am a Vietcong intruder. I don't know how it will be when—when he comes back and says, "What was it all for?" and I don't know what it was for.

ANTI-HIJACKING PACT WITH CUBA

February 15, 1973

A five-year agreement was entered into by the United States and Cuba in mid-February to put a stop to, or at least to reduce to a minimum, the hijacking of American airplanes to Havana. The agreement, entitled "Memorandum of understanding on hijacking of aircraft and vessels and other offenses," took effect immediately after it was signed simultaneously by Secretary of State William P. Rogers in Washington and by Cuban Foreign Minister Raul Roa Garcia in Havana.

Each of the parties agreed to return to the country of origin or to bring to trial in its own courts any person who had diverted an airplane or ship from its normal route and brought it to the territory of the other party. A hijacker was to be tried "for the offense punishable by the most severe penalty according to the circumstances and the seriousness of the act." Return of the hijacked aircraft or vessel and its crew and passengers to the country of origin was to be facilitated, as was return of "any funds obtained by extortion or other illegal means."

The agreement included similar provisions applicable to any person promoting, directing or forming part of "an expedition which from its territory...carries out acts of violence or depredation against aircraft or vessels...coming from or going to the territory of the other party or who...carries out such acts or other similar unlawful acts in the territory of the other party." A saving clause for political refugees provided that the party in whose territory any perpetrators of acts for-

bidden by the agreement "first arrive may take into consideration any extenuating or mitigating circumstances in those cases in which the persons responsible for the acts were being sought for strictly political reasons and were in real and imminent danger of death without a viable alternative for leaving the country...."

Secretary Rogers announced the agreement with Cuba at a news conference at the State Department less than half an hour after it had been signed. On that occasion he ventured the opinion that conclusion of the pact meant that "there will be no safe haven for hijackers in Cuba or the United States." At the same time, he said that the agreement, while a "good sign," was "not enough to change American policy" toward Cuba. The United States would not ease its diplomatic and trade boycott of Cuba until noticeable changes were made in the "policies and attitudes of the Cuban government." President Nixon also was on record as saying that Cuba would have to alter its policies before there could be a change in American policy toward that country. (See Historic Documents, 1972, p. 882.)

Washington had severed ties with Cuba in 1961 when Fidel Castro, who had then been in power for two years, announced that he was a Marxist and intended to nationalize all Cuban industries. Since that time, 101 hijackings of American aircraft to Cuba had been attempted and 84 had succeeded. Meanwhile, thousands of Cubans had fled in stolen boats to Florida and other points in this country. Rogers said the anti-hijacking agreement was "an attempt to deal with a very difficult problem in a practical way." He stressed the point that "nothing in the agreement is inconsistent with the traditional and strongly felt American view of the right to emigrate freely."

The agreement had been arrived at after three months of negotiations carried on, in the absence of U.S.-Cuban diplomatic relations, through the good offices of the Swiss ambassador acting for the United States in Havana and of the Czechoslovak charge d'affaires acting for Cuba in Washington. The biggest stumbling block was the problem of reconciling the right of political asylum with the need to penalize hijackers. The objective of the United States was to gain Cuba's commitment to punish American hijackers without jeopardizing this country's right to welcome Cuban refugees. Cuba was said to have been adamant at first in insisting upon punishment of refugees as well as hijackers. The final agreement effected a delicate balance between the opposing points of view.

First Case Under New Agreement

The delicacy of the balance was demonstrated a month after the agreement was signed. Two members of a Cuban fishing boat's crew, who had botched an attempt to hijack the boat to Mexico, jumped *overboard on March 18 as the vessel was starting back to Cuba after refueling at Key West. Although the State Department acknowledged the next day that the new anti-hijacking agreement did not exactly fit this case, it concluded that the two crewmen, who had been picked up by anti-Castro exiles, had violated the spirit of the agreement and therefore could not be granted asylum by the United States. The men then surrendered to immigration authorities and made formal application for asylum. Assuming that rejection of the application would be followed by an appeal, a final test of the anti-hijacking agreement's effect on prospective Cuban refugees was expected to be long in coming.*

Text of anti-hijacking agreement signed by the United States and Cuba on Feb. 15, 1973:

MEMORANDUM OF UNDERSTANDING ON

HIJACKING OF AIRCRAFT AND VESSELS

AND OTHER OFFENSES

The Government of the United States of America and the Government of the Republic of Cuba, on the bases of equality and strict reciprocity, agree:

First: Any person who hereafter seizes, removes, appropriates or diverts from its normal route or activities an aircraft or vessel registered under the laws of one of the parties and brings it to the territory of the other party shall be considered to have committed an offense and therefore shall either be returned to the party of registry of the aircraft or vessel to be tried by the courts of that party in conformity with its laws or be brought before the courts of the party whose territory he reached for trial in conformity with its laws for the offense punishable by the most severe penalty according to the circumstances and the seriousness of the acts to which this Article refers. In addition, the party whose territory is reached by the aircraft or vessel shall take all necessary steps to facilitate without delay the continuation of the journey of the passengers and crew innocent of the hijacking of the aircraft or vessel in question, with their belongings, as well as the journey of the aircraft or vessel itself, with all goods carried with it, including any funds obtained by extortion or other illegal means, or the return of the foregoing to the territory of the first party; likewise, it shall take all steps to protect the physical integrity of the aircraft or vessel and all goods, carried with it, including any funds obtained by extortion or other illegal means, and the physical integrity of the passengers and crew innocent of the hijacking, and their belongings, while they are in its territory as a consequence of or in connection with the acts to which this Article refers.

In the event that the offenses referred to above are not punishable under the laws existing in the country to which the persons committing them arrived, the party in question shall be obligated, except in the case of minor offenses, to return the persons who have committed such acts, in accordance with the applicable procedures, to the territory of the other party to be tried by its courts in conformity with its laws.

SECOND: Each party shall try with a view to severe punishment in accordance with its laws any person who, within its territory, hereafter conspires to promote, or promotes, or prepares, or directs, or forms part of an expedition which from its territory or any other place carries out acts of violence or depredation against aircraft or vessels of any kind or registration coming from or going to the territory of the other party or who, within its territory, hereafter conspires to promote, or promotes, or prepares, or directs, or forms part of an expedition which from its territory or any other place carries out such acts or other similar unlawful acts in the territory of the other party.

THIRD: Each party shall apply strictly its own laws to any national of the other party who, coming from the territory of the other party, enters its territory, violating its laws as well as national and international requirements pertaining to immigration, health, customs and the like.

FOURTH: The party in whose territory the perpetrators of the acts described in Article FIRST arrive may take into consideration any extenuating or mitigating circumstances in those cases in which the persons responsible for the acts were being sought for strictly political reasons and were in real and imminent danger of death without a viable alternative for leaving the country, provided there was no financial extortion or physical injury to the members of the crew, passengers, or other persons in connection with the hijacking.

FINAL PROVISIONS:

This Agreement may be amended or expanded by decision of the parties.

This Agreement shall be in force for five years and may be renewed for an equal term by express decision of the parties.

Either party may inform the other of its decision to terminate this Agreement at any time while it is in force by written denunciation submitted six months in advance.

This Agreement shall enter into force on the date agreed by the parties.

Done in English and Spanish texts which are equally authentic.

NIXON IN SOUTH CAROLINA

February 20, 1973

President Nixon, returning from a sojourn at Key Biscayne, stopped off in South Carolina on Feb. 20 to address a joint session of that state's legislature. Speaking without a text, the President discussed the agreement ending the Vietnam War and explained what the United States hoped to gain by it in terms of both immediate and long-term results. It was the first speech the President had made to a legislative body since the Vietnam agreement was signed on Jan. 27, and it was generally believed that he chose to speak to the South Carolina legislature because it had been the first of several state legislatures to give formal endorsement to the Vietnam accord.

In his 25-minute speech at Columbia, S.C., Nixon asserted that a "peace with honor" had been attained. The United States had achieved its goal of preventing the "imposition by force of a Communist government" on South Vietnam. "We can be proud," he observed, "that we stuck it out until we did reach that goal." A more far-reaching outcome of the agreement ending the longest war in American history would be not only peace in South Vietnam but also the ability of the United States to "exercise more effective leadership in the cause of world peace." The President believed that "the chances for us to build a peace that will last are better than they have been at any time since the end of World War II."

Nixon drew perhaps the loudest applause when he declared that the United States must remain strong militarily and "be sure that the President never goes to the negotiating table representing the second

269

strongest nation in the world." He pointed out that the settlement of the war in Vietnam, when added to the "opening" with the Soviet Union and with China, might encourage "a tendency for us to sit back and assume that we are going to have peace, instant peace." On the contrary, peace could not be maintained unless the United States assumed the strong military posture that would assure "the trust of our allies and the respect of our potential adversaries in the world."

The President explained the administration's insistence on a full-fledged peace agreement by saying: "Had we taken another course— had we, for example, followed the advice of some of the well-intentioned people who said 'Peace at any price. Get our prisoners of war back in exchange for withdrawing'—had we taken that course, then respect for America not only among our allies but particularly among those who might be our potential adversaries would have been eroded, perhaps fatally." He emphasized that the men who had been casualties of war "did not die in vain" and that those who had served in Vietnam and had been prisoners of war "did not make the sacrifices they made in vain." To honor those who had served, the American people should "work together to build a lasting peace in the world, a peace that can last not only in Southeast Asia, but a peace that the United States can help to build for this whole world in which we live."

Not only foreign but also domestic policy was touched on by the President in South Carolina. Apropos of his interest in a "new federalism," Nixon said: "For much too long, power has been flowing from the people, from the cities, from the counties, from the states, to Washington, D.C." He wanted to reverse that flow and noted that, through revenue-sharing and in other ways, "power should flow...back to the states and the people." Some observers interpreted the President's appearance before the South Carolina legislature as a bid for support of decentralization in government as well as a gesture of appreciation for southern political support. Others wondered if it might have been intended as a rebuff to members of Congress who had complained of the President's refusal to consult with them on Vietnam policy or had severely criticized that policy.

Text of President Nixon's address before the South Carolina legislature, Feb. 20, 1973:

Governor West, Mr. Speaker, Mr. President, Senator Thurmond, Senator Hollings, my colleagues from the House of Representatives in Washington, D.C., all of the distinguished members of the Senate and the House of Representatives of the State of South Carolina:

I had not realized until the Governor had introduced me so eloquently that this is the first time that a President of the United States has stood in this place. I am honored to be here for that reason, and I am also honored to be here because this is the first State Legislature in the Nation which passed a resolution supporting the peace settlement in Vietnam.

Before speaking of that settlement, I would like to refer briefly to some of the distinguished people who are here in this chamber today, and first, to one of the truly great First Ladies of America, Mrs. James Byrnes.

All of you know of the friendship that I was privileged to have with Governor Byrnes. You will remember that I mentioned the fact on his death that no man in the whole history of this country had held more offices and more high offices at both the State and Federal level than he had held during his long and distinguished career. He was also a very wise and farsighted man who was willing to give good counsel on occasion when he was asked.

I remember when I was defeated when I ran for President in 1960, I asked Governor Byrnes whether I should run for Governor of California. He thought a moment and said, "Yes, you should." I ran for Governor. I lost, but the advice was very farsighted because if I had not run for Governor and had not lost, I wouldn't be standing here today.

I also want to pay tribute on this occasion to Speaker Blatt. It was interesting for me to note, and I note it now for the whole Nation, that he has been Speaker in this House longer than any man has held that position in the whole history of America, and I pay a tribute to him for having that high position today.

I am also very proud today that Secretary Dent, Secretary of Commerce, is present with us. He is the first man from South Carolina to serve in a President's Cabinet since James Byrnes was Secretary of State.

And then, too, I wish to pay my respects on this occasion to the delegation from Washington, D.C. I could say much about them in terms of their very strong support of policies that we believe are best for America. I will simply say that on this occasion, under the very strong leadership of Senator Strom Thurmond, there is no delegation from any State in the Union that has given more firm support to the policies that made the achievement of a peace settlement possible.

It is interesting to note that the delegation in the Senate is half and half, Republican and Democratic. The delegation in the House of Representatives is about half and half, Republican and Democratic. But as the late Mendel Rivers used to say, when the defense of America and the honor of America is involved, we are not Republicans, we are not Democrats, we are Americans, and that is the spirit which has motivated the delegation from South Carolina always in the House of Representatives and the United States Senate.

Now I would like to turn to the settlement which has been discussed at considerable length, probably, on the floor of this chamber when the resolution was passed, and also throughout the country since that settlement was announced. I should like to speak to you quite candidly about the settlement in terms of what it really means—what it means to America, what it means to the people of South Vietnam, and what it means to the world.

In referring to that settlement, I think it is important for us to note that I have often used the term "peace with honor." What does peace with honor mean? And here we go back into the long history of this terribly difficult war, the longest in this Nation's history.

Because the war has been so long, and because it has been so difficult, there is a tendency for us to forget how the United States became involved, and why. It would be very easy now, looking back, to point out the mistakes that were made in the conduct of the war, to even question whether or not the United States should have become involved in the first place. But let us get one thing very clear: When, during the course of President Kennedy's Administration, the first men were sent to Vietnam for combat, when, during the course of President Johnson's Administration others were sent there to continue the activities in the military area, they were sent there for the most selfless purpose that any nation has ever fought a war.

We did not go to South Vietnam, and our men did not go there, for the purpose of conquering North Vietnam. Our men did not go to South Vietnam for the purpose of getting bases in South Vietnam or acquiring territory or domination over that part of the world. They went for a very high purpose, and that purpose can never be taken away from them or this country. It was, very simply, to prevent the imposition by force of a Communist government on the 17 million people of South Vietnam. That was our goal, and we achieved that goal, and we can be proud that we stuck it out until we did reach that goal.

Now the question, of course, will be raised by historians—the instant historians of the present and those who look at it in the future and attempt to evaluate this long and difficult war—was the purpose worth it? Was the sacrifice worth it?

Only historians in the future, perhaps, will be able to judge that accurately, but we, at this time, and, I know, you, as you passed your resolution, must have considered the alternatives.

We had alternatives. I recall when I first became President there were those of my own party who suggested that after all, I had not made the decision that involved the United States with combat troops in Vietnam in the first place and, therefore, from a political and partisan standpoint, the better course of action and the easy course of action was to get out of Vietnam, to bring our men home, and to bring them home and to get our prisoners of war back regardless of what happened to South Vietnam.

That would have been a rather easy position, politically, to take. On the other hand, when we examine it for what it really meant and could have meant to the United States, we can see why I had to reject it and why the people of the United States have supported that rejection during the 4 years which finally ended with the peace settlement.

If, for example, the North Vietnamese would have accepted the proposition of returning our prisoners of war simply for our getting out our own troops from Vietnam, and that is a highly doubtful proposition, but if they had, let us see what it would have meant.

We would have fought a long war. We would have lost tens of thousands of Americans who were killed in action and we would have fought it for what purpose? Only to get our prisoners of war back. If you wonder whether or not that purpose would have been adequate, let me say that a letter that I received from a mother in California perhaps will answer the question.

"As a mother of a young man who gave his life in this war, I felt very strongly about wanting an honorable peace agreement. Had you agreed to anything less, you would have let down not only the boys remaining in Vietnam, but also those who died in this war. It was difficult enough to accept our son's death, but to know it was all in vain would have been even more a tragedy. We feel that our son James would have felt as we do, and would have supported your policy."

I say to the members of this Assembly gathered here that James did not die in vain, that the men who went to Vietnam and have served there with honor did not serve in vain, and that our POW's, as they return, did not make the sacrifices that they made in vain, and I say it because of what we did in Vietnam.

Where Honor Is Due

It is my firm conviction that the United States can now exercise more effective leadership in the cause of world peace which the Governor has so eloquently described a moment ago. On this occasion, I think it is well for us to think of a number of people whom we should honor today. We, of course, should honor our prisoners of war who have come back after their great ordeal standing tall, proud of their country, proud of their service.

We should honor also those who have died, and in honoring them, let's honor some of the bravest women this Nation has ever seen, the wives, the mothers, not only of the POW's, but of those who died, the mother of a boy like James.

And finally, let us honor the 2½ million men who served, who did not desert America, but who served, served in a difficult war, came back, often not with honor in terms of what they found from their neighbors and friends, but came back to what could have been a rather discouraging reception.

Now that we have brought an end to the war, let us honor them all, and the way to honor them, I say, is for us to work together to build a lasting peace in the world, a peace that can last not only in Southeast

Asia, but a peace that the United States can help to build for this whole world in which we live.

Ending a war is not unusual for the United States. After all, in this century we ended World War I, we ended World War II, we ended Korea, and now we have ended the American involvement in Vietnam. The critical question is: How do we end a war and then go from there to build a peace? And I address that question in relationship to this war for just a moment.

The year 1972 saw some historic breakthroughs in terms of America's search for peace, along with other nations: the opening of the dialogue with the People's Republic of China, with leaders who represent one-fourth of all the people who live on the face of the globe; the discussions that took place in Moscow last May and early June, discussions which led to a number of agreements, but particularly an agreement between the two superpowers to limit nuclear arms, the first step toward arms limitation, and, of course, more talks will take place this year with the leaders of the Soviet Union.

Now, when we consider those great events, the opening to China, which we are already beginning to develop, as you have noted in your papers recently, the opening with the Soviet Union of the discussions that can lead eventually, we trust, to arms control and perhaps further down the line to reduction of the nuclear arms that burdens us, burdens them, and threatens the whole world with destruction—as we look at those great events, combined with the end of the war in Vietnam, there could be a tendency for us to sit back and assume that we are going to have peace, instant peace, because of these new developments.

What we must recognize is that we would not have had the kind of fruitful and constructive discussions that we have had with the Soviet Union, and in my view we would not have had the opening of the dialogue with the People's Republic of China unless the United States had been strong—strong not only in its arms, but also unless the United States had been strong in terms of its will, its determination.

A nation which is strong militarily and yet is not respected is not a nation that is worth talking to. America is strong militarily, and America has demonstrated by its willingness to stand by a small, weak country, until we achieved an honorable peace, that we deserve, first the trust of our allies and the respect of our potential adversaries in the world. And that, again, gives us a reason why we can look back on this long and difficult war and say that American men sacrificed—some their lives, some long imprisonment, and some away from home in a land which most of them did not know—that Americans have made that sacrifice in a cause that was important not just for Vietnam, but for America's position of leadership in the whole world because America comes out of this long and difficult struggle strong militarily and respected in the world.

Had we taken another course, had we, for example, followed the advice of some of the well intentioned people who said, "Peace at any price. Get our prisoners of war back in exchange for withdrawing," had we taken that course, then respect for America, not only among our allies but particularly among those who might be our potential adversaries, would have been eroded, perhaps fatally.

And so I say to you here today as we look to the future, the chances for us to build a peace that will last are better than they have been at any time since the end of World War II. We will continue the dialogue with the Soviet leaders. We will continue the dialogue with the People's Republic of China. And, in this year ahead, we will renew discussions that we have been having in the past with our friends in Europe and in other parts of the world, because as we talk to those who have been our adversaries in the past, we must not overlook the vital necessity of strengthening the bonds we have with our allies and our friends around the world.

Never the Second Strongest

But as we conduct those discussions, I would urge upon this legislative body what I have often urged upon the Congress of the United States: Let us be sure that as the President of the United States and his representatives negotiate with great powers in the world, let us be sure that he never goes to the negotiating table representing the second strongest nation in the world.

Because America is strong and has been strong, we have been able to negotiate successfully. We must maintain our strength and, of course, we will reduce it, but it must be on a mutual basis and not on a unilateral basis, because reducing unilaterally would remove any incentive for others in the world to reduce their strength at the same time.

Having spoken of military strength, let me also speak briefly of other kinds of strength that we need if we are going to build a world of peace and if America is going to continue the great role that we are destined to play as we near our 200th birthday as a nation.

It is essential that government—and here in this legislative chamber all of us are participants in the role of government—it is essential that government in America be strengthened in terms of being more responsive to the people.

By that I mean that government must get closer to the grass roots, and by getting closer to the grass roots, what I am very simply suggesting is this: For much too long, power has been flowing from the people, from the cities, from the counties, from the States, to Washington, D.C. And that is why, beginning with an historic move on revenue-sharing, and in other areas, I feel firmly we must turn it around, and that power should flow away from the concentration in Washington back to the States and the people. That is where it belongs and that is where it is staying.

Let us also remember that if America is to play the kind of a role that it must play and we want it to play, we need to be a united country. By being a united country, that doesn't mean that we agree on everything. It means that we have disagreements between parties, disagreements on a number of issues. That is the very essence of a free society.

But let the time be gone when this country is divided region against region, North versus South, race against race, black versus white, one economic group against another, labor versus management, simply because they are members of different groups. Let the time be gone when we divide Americans by age, the old against the young, in terms of what they produce, the city against the farm.

It does not mean that we all have the same interest. It does not mean that we do not have areas where we disagree. But what it does mean is that this nation, when the great issues are involved—the security of America, the honor of America—let us speak of those issues and speak to those issues as one united people.

In that connection, as I speak for the first time as President of the United States to a legislature in the South, one of the things I am most proud of during the time I have served as President, and during the three times I have had the great honor to run for President, is that I have never divided this country North against South, East against West, one region against the other.

I believe this is one country, and let us all work to make it one country, because it is one United States of America that can lead the world to peace, the kind of peace that all of us want in the years ahead.

Finally, today, if we are to play the role that we are destined to play, we need faith. I think that the faith of all Americans was restored by what we have seen in the past few days as our prisoners of war came down the ramp of those planes and set foot for the first time on American soil, some of them after 6, 7 years of imprisonment.

You wonder how this nation, or any nation, could have brought into life men who would be so strong, men who could endure so much. And the important thing is, as we saw them come down those stairs, they came down with their heads high, proud of their country, proud of what they had done, and that is another reason why peace with honor was so vitally important. Because if this war, long and difficult as it was, had been ended solely for the basis of obtaining their release, you can see that for them it would have been the greatest disappointment.

I close with a message from one of them. When he sent this cable to me a few days ago, he did not know, and could not have known, that I would be addressing the South Carolina State Legislature today. The cable was to me, but as you can see as I read it, it is to all of you as well.

It is from Robert N. Daughtrey, Major, United States Air Force.

"My faith in our fellow Americans never faltered. Thank you for returning us with honor. I assure you we returned filled with pride and faith in the future.

"God bless you. God bless America."

SUPREME COURT ON APPORTIONMENT IN STATE LEGISLATURES

February 21, 1973

The Supreme Court, in a 5-3 decision handed down Feb. 21, relaxed its standards for application of the one-man, one-vote rule so far as it concerned the apportionment of seats in state legislatures. The Court held that the one-man, one-vote principle, established by the Warren Court (see Historic Documents, 1972, p. 935), need not be applied as strictly with respect to state legislatures as to the national House of Representatives. Reversing a federal district court decision, the Supreme Court upheld the constitutionality of a 1971 Virginia state legislative reapportionment plan that allowed a variation of as much as 16.4 per cent between the population of the largest and the population of the smallest of the state's 52 House of Delegates districts.

The ruling was the first in which the Supreme Court made a distinction between state legislative and congressional district lines in determining an allowable variation in population. It was thought that the decision would result in the reopening of a half-dozen cases involving legislative reapportionment plans which lower courts had invalidated because of smaller variations in population. In 1969 the Supreme Court had invalidated a Missouri reapportionment plan for congressional districts with a maximum variation of only 5.9 per cent, and a New York plan for congressional districts with a variation of 13.1 per cent.

In the Virginia case, the majority opinion of the Court, delivered by Associate Justice William H. Rehnquist, called for reinstatement of the legislature's reapportionment plan, saying that such a plan could include a certain amount of arithmetical discrepancy if it was deliberately drawn to conform with the boundaries of political subdivisions. "The State can scarcely be condemned for simultaneously attempting to move toward smaller districts and to maintain the integrity of its political subdivision lines," Rehnquist wrote. He added: "Virginia was free as a matter of federal constitutional law to construe the mandate of its Constitution more liberally in the case of legislative redistricting than in the case of congressional redistricting, and the plan adopted by the legislature indicates that she has done so."

The one-man, one-vote principle for congressional districting was laid down in a 6-3 Supreme Court decision (Wesberry v. Sanders) in February 1964. The Court sought in that case to make certain that the vote of any one citizen would have, as nearly as possible, the same political strength as that of every other citizen. When there is a marked variation in the population of electoral districts, voters in smaller districts acquire disproportionate political influence. The 1964 and several subsequent Court opinions attempted to define the degree of variation that could exist without seriously jeopardizing the ideal of equal representation.

Addressing this point, Rehnquist wrote in the 1973 opinion: "Neither courts nor legislatures are furnished any specialized calipers which enable them to extract from the general language of the Equal Protection Clause of the Fourteenth Amendment the mathematical formula which establishes what range of percentage deviations are permissible and what are not." He pointed out that the 16.4 per cent discrepancy was "substantially less than the percentage deviations [in legislative, not congressional, reapportionment] which have been found invalid in the previous decisions of this Court." Rehnquist noted at the same time: "While this percentage may well approach tolerable limits, we do not believe it exceeds them. Virginia has not sacrificed substantial equality to justifiable deviations."

Chief Justice Warren E. Burger and Associate Justices Potter Stewart, Byron R. White, and Harry A. Blackmun, with Rehnquist, comprised the majority in the Virginia case. Associate Justice Lewis F. Powell Jr., a resident of Virginia, did not participate in the deliberation.

In a dissenting opinion, which concurred in part with the majority opinion, Associate Justice William J. Brennan Jr. wrote for himself and Associate Justices William O. Douglas and Thurgood Marshall: "While the legislature's plan does not disregard constitutional requirements to the flagrant extent of many earlier cases, it does nevertheless demonstrate a systematic pattern of substantial deviation from the constitutional ideal." Brennan added that "the Commonwealth failed to prove that the variations were justified by need to insure representation of political subdivisions or a need to respect county boundaries in the drawing of district lines." The minority maintained that political subdivisions such as villages and towns need not be contained wholly within a single legislative district because the state legislature seldom dealt with issues which would require special representation of those areas.

A month later, on March 20, the Supreme Court seemed to retreat considerably further from the one-man, one-vote principle when it sustained election of the Tulare (Calif.) Water District's board of directors solely by the landowners of the district. Each landowner, moreover, had one vote for each $100 of property value, and the largest corporate landowner was entitled to cast 37,800 votes. The Court majority, composed of the same justices as in the Virginia case, plus Associate Justice Powell, said the Tulare Water District could be exempted from the one-man, one-vote rule "by reason of its special limited purpose and of the disproportionate effect of its activities on landowners as a group."

Associate Justice Douglas, speaking for the three dissenting justices, contended that the small landowners and tenant farmers, sharecroppers and land renters "all should have a say [because] irrigation, water storage, the building of levees, flood control implicate the entire community." Douglas pointed out that under a system of weighted voting "the corporate voter is put in the saddle." The New York Times reported March 22 that officials in the New York metropolitan area, where there were thousands of special-purpose governmental districts for water supply, fire protection, sewage disposal, etc., were confused by the Supreme Court's decision in the California case and wondering if it might exempt those districts also from the one-man, one-vote rule.

Excerpts from the Supreme Court's decision of Feb. 21, 1973, on reapportionment of Virginia's state legislative districts:

John S. Mahan, Secretary,
State Board of Elections,
    et al., Appellants,
71-364   v
Henry E. Howell, Jr., et al.

City of Virginia Beach,
    Appellant,
71-373   v.
Henry E. Howell, Jr., et al.

Robert L. Weinberg,
    Appellant,
71-444   v.
Edgar A. Prichard et al.

On Appeals from the United States District Court for the Eastern District of Virginia.

MR. JUSTICE REHNQUIST delivered the opinion of the Court.

Acting pursuant to the mandate of its newly revised state constitution, the Virginia General Assembly enacted statutes apportioning the State for the election of members of its House of Delegates and Senate. Two suits were brought challenging the constitutionality of the House redistricting statute on the grounds that there were impermissible population variances in the districts, that the multimember districts diluted representation, and that the use of multimember districts constituted racial gerrymandering. The Senate redistricting statute was attacked in a separate suit which alleged that the city of Norfolk was unconstitutionally split into three districts, allocating Navy personnel "homeported" in Norfolk to one district and isolating Negro voters in one district....

The consolidated District Court entered an interlocutory order which ...declared the legislative reapportionment statutes unconstitutional and enjoined the holding of elections in electoral districts other than those established by the court's opinion.... Appellants, the Secretary of the State Board of Elections and its members and the City of Virginia Beach, have appealed directly to this Court....

I

The statute apportioning the House provided for a combination of 52 single-member, multimember and floater delegate districts from which 100 delegates would be elected. As found by the lower court, the ideal district in Virginia consisted of 46,485 persons per delegate, and the maximum percentage variation from that ideal under the Act was 16.4%—the 12th district being over-represented by 6.8% and the 16th district being under-represented by 9.6%.... Of the 52 districts, 35 were within 4% of perfection and nine exceeded a 6% variance from the ideal. With one exception the delegate districts followed political jurisdictional lines of the counties and cities. That exception, Fairfax County, was allotted 10 delegates but was divided into two five-member districts.

The District Court concluded that the 16.4% variation was sufficient to condemn the House statute under the "one person, one vote" doctrine. While it noted that the variances were traceable to the desire of the General Assembly to maintain the integrity of traditional county and city boundaries, and that it was impossible to draft district lines to overcome unconstitutional disparities and still maintain such integrity, it held that the State proved no governmental necessity for strictly adhering to political subdivision lines. Accordingly, it undertook its own redistricting and devised a plan having a percentage variation of slightly over 10% from the ideal district, a percentage it believed came "within the passable constitutional limits as 'a good-faith effort to achieve absolute equality'...."

Appellants contend that...striking down the General Assembly's re-apportionment plan was erroneous, and that proper application of the standards enunciated in *Reynolds* v. *Sims*... would have resulted in a finding that the statute was constitutional.

In *Kirkpatrick* v. *Preisler* and *Wells* v. *Rockefeller*, this Court in-validated state reapportionment statutes for federal congressional districts having maximum percentage deviations of 5.97% and 13.1% respectively. The express purpose of these cases was to elucidate the standard first announced in the holding of *Wesberry* v. *Sanders*.... that "the command of Art. I, Sec. 2, that Representatives be chosen 'by the People of the several States' means that as nearly as is prac-ticable one man's vote in a congressional election is to be worth as much as another's".... The principal question thus presented for review is whether or not the Equal Protection Clause of the Fourteenth Amendment likewise permits only "the limited population variances which are unavoidable despite a good-faith effort to achieve absolute equality" in the context of state legislative reapportionment.

This Court first recognized that the Equal Protection Clause of the Fourteenth Amendment requires both houses of a bicameral state leg-islature to be apportioned substantially on a population basis in *Rey-nolds* v. *Sims, supra*. In so doing, it suggested that in the implemen-tation of the basic constitutional principle—equality of population among the districts—more flexibility was constitutionally permissible with respect to state legislative reapportionment than in congressional redistricting.... Consideration was given to the fact that, almost in-variably, there is a significantly larger number of seats in state legis-lative bodies to be distributed within a State than congressional seats, and that therefore it may be feasible for a State to use political sub-division lines to a greater extent in establishing state legislative dis-tricts than congressional districts while still affording adequate state-wide representation.... The Court reiterated that the overriding ob-jective in reapportionment must be "substantial equality of popula-tion among the various districts, so that the vote of any citizen is ap-proximately equal in weight to that of any other citizen in the State...."

By contrast, the Court in *Wesberry* v. *Sanders, supra*, recognized no excuse for the failure to meet the objective of equal representation for equal numbers of people in congressional districting other than the practical impossibility of drawing equal districts with mathematical precision. Thus, whereas population alone has been the sole criterion of constitutionality in congressional redistricting under Art. I, Sec. 2, broader latitude has been afforded the States under the Equal Pro-tection Clause in state legislative redistricting because of the consider-ations enumerated in *Reynolds* v. *Sims*.... The dichotomy between the two lines of cases has consistently been maintained.... For example, one asserted justification for population variances was that they were necessarily a result of the State's attempt to avoid fragmenting political subdivisions by drawing congressional district lines along existing political subdivision boundaries. This argument was rejected in the congressional context. But...an apportionment for a county legislature having a maximum deviation from equality of 11.9% was upheld in the face of an equal protection challenge, in part because New York had a long history of maintaining the integrity of existing local government units within the county.

Application of the "absolute equality" test of *Kirkpatrick* and *Wells* to state legislative redistricting may impair the normal functioning of state and local governments. Such an effect is readily apparent from an analysis of the District Court's plan in this case.

We conclude therefore that the constitutionality of Virginia's legislative redistricting plan was not to be judged by the more stringent standards that *Kirkpatrick* and *Wells* make applicable to congressional reapportionment, but instead by the equal protection test enunciated in *Reynolds v. Sims*.... We reaffirm its holding that "the Equal Protection Clause requires that a State make an honest and good faith effort to construct districts, in both houses of its legislature, as nearly of equal population as is practicable." We likewise reaffirm its conclusion that "[s]o long as the divergences from a strict population standard are based on legitimate considerations incident to the effectuation of a rational state policy, some deviations from the equal-population principle are constitutionally permissible with respect to the apportionment of seats in either or both of the two houses of a bicameral state legislature." ...

The asserted justification for the divergences in this case—the State's policy of maintaining the integrity of political subdivision lines—is not a new one to this Court....

[But] a State's policy urged in justification of disparity in district population, however rational, cannot constitutionally be permitted to emasculate the goal of substantial equality.

There was uncontradicted evidence offered in the District Court to the effect that the legislature's plan, subject to minor qualifications, "produces the minimum deviation above and below the norm, keeping intact political boundaries...." That court itself recognized that equality was impossible if political boundaries were to kept intact in the process of districting. But it went on to hold that since the State "proved no governmental necessity for strictly adhering to political subdivision lines," the legislative plan was constitutionally invalid.... The State can scarcely be condemned for simultaneously attempting to move toward smaller districts and to maintain the integrity of its political subdivision lines.... Virginia was free as a matter of federal constitutional law to construe the mandate of its Constitution more liberally in the case of legislative redistricting than in the case of congressional redistricting, and the plan adopted by the legislature indicates that she has done so.... Nothing in the fact that Virginia has followed the constitutional mandate of this Court in the case of congressional redistricting, or that it has chosen in some instances to ignore political subdivision lines in the case of the State Senate, detracts from the validity of its consistently applied policy to have at least one house of its bicameral legislature responsive to voters of political subdivisions as such....

We hold that the legislature's plan for apportionment of the House of Delegates may reasonably be said to advance the rational state policy of respecting the boundaries of political subdivisions. The remaining inquiry is whether the population disparities among the districts which have resulted from the pursuit of this plan exceed constitutional limits. We conclude that they do not....

Neither courts nor legislatures are furnished any specialized calipers which enable them to extract from the general language of the Equal Protection Clause of the Fourteenth Amendment the mathematical formula which establishes what range of percentage deviations are permissible, and what are not. The 16-odd percent maximum deviation which the District Court found to exist in the legislative plan for the reapportionment of the House is substantially less than the percentage deviations which have been found invalid in the previous decisions of this Court. While this percentage may well approach tolerable limits, we do not believe it exceeds them. Virginia has not sacrificed substantial equality to justifiable deviations....

II

The General Assembly divided the State into 40 single-member senatorial districts. Under the plan, the City of Virginia Beach was added to the City of Norfolk and the entire area was divided into three single-member districts which the court below found conformed almost ideally, numerically, to the "one person, one vote" principle. But all naval personnel "homeported" at the U. S. Naval Station, Norfolk, about 36,700 persons, were assigned to the Fifth District because that is where they were counted on official census tracts. It was undisputed that only about 8,100 of such personnel lived aboard vessels assigned to the census tract within the Fifth District....

Appellants charge that the District Court was not justified in overturning the districts established by the General Assembly since the Assembly validly used census tracts in apportioning the area and that the imposition by the court of a multimember district contravened the valid legislative policy in favor of single-member districts. We conclude that under the unusual, if not unique, circumstances in this case the District Court did not err in declining to accord conclusive weight to the legislative reliance on census figures. That court justifiably found that with respect to the three single-member districts in question, the legislative plan resulted in both significant population disparities and the assignment of military personnel to vote in districts in which they admittedly did not reside. Since discriminatory treatment of military personnel in legislative reapportionment is constitutionally impermissible, *Davis v. Mann,...* we hold that the interim relief granted by the District Court as to the State Senate was within the bounds of the discretion confided to it.

Application of interim remedial techniques in voting rights cases has largely been left to the district courts....

The court below was faced with severe time pressures.... The cases were finally heard on June 16, and the court's interlocutory order was entered on July 2, just two weeks prior to the revised July 16th filing deadline for primary candidates.

Prior to the time the court acted, this Court had handed down *Whitcomb* v. *Chavis...*recognizing that multimember districts were not *per se* violative of the Equal Protection Clause. The court conscientiously considered both the legislative policy and this Court's admonition in *Connor* v. *Johnson...*that in fashioning apportionment remedies, the use of single-member districts is preferred. But it was confronted with plausible evidence of substantial malapportionment with respect to military personnel, the mandate of this Court that voting discrimination against military personnel is constitutionally impermissible,... and the fear that too much delay would have seriously disrupted the Fall 1971 elections. Facing as it did this singular combination of unique factors we cannot say that the District Court abused its discretion in fashioning the interim remedy of combining the three districts into one multimember district. We therefore affirm the order of that Court insofar as it dealt with the State Senate.

Affirmed in part, reversed in part.

MR. JUSTICE POWELL took no part in the consideration or decision in these cases.

———

MR. JUSTICE BRENNAN, with whom MR. JUSTICE DOUGLAS and MR. JUSTICE MARSHALL join, concurring in part and dissenting in part.

I agree with the Court in...*City of Virginia Beach* v. *Howell,* that the joinder by the District Court of three senatorial districts in the Norfolk-Virginia Beach area to create one multimember senatorial district for the 1971 election was permissible under the special circumstances of this case.... I dissent, however, in...*Mahan* v. *Howell,* from the Court's action in setting aside the District Court's finding that the apportionment of the State House of Delegates violated the Equal Protection Clause of the Fourteenth Amendment.

The Court approves a legislative apportionment plan that is conceded to produce a total deviation of *at least* 16.4% from the constitutional ideal. Of course, "the fact that a 10% or 15% variation from the norm is approved in one State has little bearing on the validity of a similar variation in another State." *Swann* v. *Adams*.... "What is marginally permissible in one State may be unsatisfactory in another, depending on the particular circumstances of the case." *Reynolds* v. *Sims*.... Since every reapportionment case presents as its factual predicate a unique combination of circumstances, decisions upholding or invalidating a legislative plan cannot normally have great precedential significance.... But language in the Court's opinion today suggests that more may be at stake than the application of well-established principles to a novel set of facts. In my view, the problem in the case before us is in no sense one of first impression, but is squarely controlled by our prior decisions.... It is appropriate, therefore, to call to mind again the controlling principles and to show that, properly applied to the facts of the case before us, they preclude a reversal of the District Court's decision.

I

...the General Assembly in 1971 divided the Commonwealth into 52 legislative districts from which the 100 members of the House of Delegates were to be elected.... While the legislature's plan does not disregard constitutional requirements to the flagrant extent of many earlier cases, it does nevertheless demonstrate a systematic pattern of substantial deviation from the constitutional ideal. Under the 1971 plan more than 25% of the delegates would be elected from districts in which the population deviates from the ideal by more than 5%. Almost 60% of the delegates would represent districts which deviate by more than 3%. Four legislators would be elected from districts which are over- or under-represented by more than 8%. And the maximum deviation—the spread between the most over-represented and the most under-represented districts—would be at least 16.4%, and might be as high as 23.6%, depending on the method of calculation.

Assuming a maximum deviation of 16.4%, the legislature's plan is still significantly less representative than many plans previously struck down by state and lower federal courts. Appellees maintain, however, that the total deviation, properly computed, is in fact 23.6%—a figure closely approximating the 25.65% deviation which led us to invalidate the Senate plan in *Swann* v. *Adams*,.... the 26.48% deviation which led us to invalidate the House plan in *Kilgarlin* v. *Hill*...and the 24.78% deviation which led us to invalidate the House plan in *Whitcomb* v. *Chavis*....

The District Court pointed out that the "range of deviation may exceed 16.4%,"...but it had no occasion to consider whether 23.6% was the more accurate figure because of its finding that "[u]nder either mode of calculation...the statewide range of deviation will not pass constitutional muster...." But if the legislature's plan does, in fact, "pass constitutional muster" on the assumption of a 16.4% deviation, then it is surely fair to ask whether the plan would still be valid assuming a total deviation of 23.6%. The Court refuses either to confront the question directly or to render it moot by determining that the figure of 23.6% is irrelevant because improperly derived. Instead, it attempts to obscure the issue by contending that the Commonwealth and the City of Virginia Beach disputed appellees' assertion of a 23.6% total deviation. That contention is wholly incorrect. Neither in the answers filed in the District Court, nor in the briefs, nor at oral argument did the Commonwealth or the City of Virginia Beach quarrel with appellees' method of calculating the deviation in floterial districts.... The Court's refusal to consider the question can only mean that appellees have the option of reopening this litigation in the District Court in an attempt to persuade that court that the true measure of the deviation is 23.6% and that a deviation on this order is fatal to the Commonwealth's plan.

In my view, there is no need to prolong this litigation by resolution in the court below of an issue which this Court should, but inexplicably does not decide.... The State has proved no governmental necessity for strictly adhering to political subdivision lines.... Accordingly, the District Court promulgated its own apportionment plan which significantly reduced the extent of deviation.

Under the District Court's plan the maximum deviation would be 7.2%, excluding one district which is geographically isolated from the mainland of the Commonwealth.... In short, while the District Court did not achieve its stated goal of "perfect mathematical division" because of the "multiplicity of delegates, the geography of the State and the diversity of population concentrations,"...its plan would still produce measurably greater equality of representation.

Appellants...maintain that the legislature's plan achieved the highest degree of equality possible without fragmenting political subdivisions. The principal question presented for our decision is whether on the facts of this case an asserted state interest in preserving the integrity of county lines can justify the resulting substantial deviations from population equality.

II

The holdings of our prior decisions can be restated in two unequivocal propositions. First, the paramount goal of reapportionment must be the drawing of district lines so as to achieve precise equality in the population of each district. "[T]he Equal Protection Clause requires that a State make an honest and good faith effort to construct districts, in both houses of its legislature, as nearly of equal population as is practicable...." The Constitution does not permit a State to relegate considerations of equality to secondary status and reserve as the primary goal of apportionment the service of some other state interest.

Second, it is open to the State, in the event that it should fail to achieve the goal of population equality, to attempt to justify its failure by demonstrating that precise equality could not be achieved without jeopardizing some critical governmental interest. The Equal Protection Clause does not exalt the principle of equal representation to the point of nullifying every competing interst of the State. But we have held firmly to the view that variations in weight accorded each vote can be approved only where the State meets its burden of presenting cogent reasons in explanation of the variations, and even then only where the variations are small....

The validity of these propositions and their applicability to the case before us are not at all diminished by the fact that...two of the many cases in which the propositions were refined and applied—concerned the division of States into federal congressional districts rather than legislative reapportionment. Prior to today's decision we have never held that different constitutional *standards* are applicable to the two situations. True, there are significant differences between congressional districting and legislative apportionment, and we have repeatedly recognized those differences.... But the recognition of these differences is hardly tantamount to the establishment of two distinct controlling standards. What our decisions have made clear is that certain state interests which are pertinent to legislative reapportionment can have no possible relevance to congressional districting. Thus, the need to preserve the integrity of political subdivisions as political subdivisions may in some instances justify small variations in the population of districts from which state legislators are elected. But that interest can hardly be asserted in justification of malapportioned congressional districts. *Kirkpatrick* v. *Preisler, supra.* While the State may have a broader range of interests to which it can point in attempting to justify a failure to achieve precise equality in the context of legislative apportionment, it by no means follows that the State is subject to a lighter burden of proof or that the controlling constitutional standard is in any sense distinguishable....

The opinion in *Kirkpatrick* does not suggest that a different standard might be applicable to congressional districting. On the contrary, the "as nearly as is practicable" standard with which we were concerned is identical to the standard that *Reynolds* v. *Sims* specifically made applicable to controversies over state legislative apportionment....

III

I would affirm the District Court's decision because on this record the Commonwealth of Virginia failed—just as the State of Florida failed in *Swann* v. *Adams* and the State of Texas failed in *Kilgarlin* v. *Hill*—to justify substantial variations in the population of the districts from which members of the House of Delegates are elected. The panel which heard the case below consisted of four judges, all from Virginia, and I share their unanimous view that the Commonwealth failed to prove that the variations were justified by a need to insure representation of political subdivisions or a need to respect county boundaries in the drawing of district lines.

If variations in the population of legislative districts are to be upheld, the Court must determine, before turning to the justifications which are asserted in defense of the variations, that they are "free from any taint of arbitrariness or discrimination.".... The District Court found as a fact that the 1971 plan did include a "built-in bias tending to favor [a] particular geographic area."...

But even assuming that the Commonwealth's plan can be considered free of any "taint of arbitrariness or discrimination," appellants have failed to meet their burden of justifying the inequalities. They insist that the legislature has followed a consistent practice of drawing district lines in conformity with county boundaries. But a showing that a State has followed such a practice is still a long step from the necessary showing that the State *must* follow that practice. Neither in the State Constitution nor in any Act of the Assembly has Virginia explicitly indicated any interest in preserving the integrity of county lines or in providing representation of political subdivisions as political subdivisions.... On the contrary, the Virginia Constitution establishes a single standard for both legislative apportionment and congressional districting, and that standard requires only that lines be drawn so as to insure, "as nearly as is practicable," representation in proportion to population. And the origins of the constitutional provision make clear that equality in district population, not the representation of political subdivisions is the Commonwealth's pre-eminent goal.

In short, the best that can be said of appellants' efforts to secure county representation is that the plan can be effective only with respect to some unspecified but in all likelihood small number of issues which affect a single county and which are overwhelmingly important to the voters of that county; and even then it provides effective representation only where the affected county represents a large enough percentage of the voters in the district to have a significant impact on the election of the delegate.... Thus, even making each of the logical and empirical assumptions implicit in the view that violating county lines would effectively disenfranchise certain persons on certain local issues, the number of persons affected would still be less than 1-1/2% of the total state population.

IV

On this record—without showing of the specific need for county representation or a showing of how such representation can be meaningfully provided to small counties whose votes would be submerged in a multicounty district—I see no basis whatsoever for upholding the Assembly's 1971 plan and the resulting substantial variations in district population. Accordingly, I would affirm the judgment of the District Court holding the plan invalid under the Equal Protection Clause of the Fourteenth Amendment.

CHINA-U.S. LIAISON OFFICES

February 22, 1973

The United States and the People's Republic of China announced in a joint communique, shortly after National Security Adviser Henry A. Kissinger had returned from a visit to Peking, that so-called liaison offices would be established in the capital of each country. The announcement of this step toward normalization of Sino-American relations was made exactly a year and a day after President Nixon's historic arrival in the People's Republic to meet with Chinese officials. (See Historic Documents, 1972, p. 183.) The decision to open liaison offices brought the two nations to the brink of formal diplomatic relations after two decades of almost total isolation from each other.

Although Washington asserted that the new relationship with the People's Republic of China would not directly affect American ties with the Republic of China on Taiwan, the Nationalist government there said it would consider the Washington-Peking agreement null and void because it contravened "the wishes of the Chinese people." Neither Peking nor Taipei had exchanged ambassadors with any country maintaining diplomatic relations with the other. Technically, the liaison offices would not be called embassies and their chief officials would not have the title of ambassador or minister, but they would be accorded full diplomatic immunity and privileges, including the right to dispatch coded messages to their governments. At a Washington news conference on Feb. 22, following issuance of the joint communique that day, Kissinger scarcely veiled the fact that the offices would be embassies in all but name. They would handle "trade as well

as other matters," he said, and would "cover the whole gamut of relationships."

Other questions taken up during Kissinger's visit to Peking, Feb. 15-
19, included plans for settling long-standing claims on American
property seized by the Communists when they gained full control of
mainland China in 1949, and claims on Chinese assets that had been
frozen in this country; the release of three Americans held by the
Chinese Communists; and expansion of cultural, medical and athletic
exchanges. At the 12-nation conference on Vietnam that opened in
Paris Feb. 26, Secretary of State William P. Rogers and Chinese
Foreign Minister Chi Peng-fei initiated talks on the claims question.
The Defense Department had estimated that assets in the United
States of mainland China claimants amounted to $76.5-million; the
assets had been frozen since Dec. 17, 1950. Private claims by American
citizens and corporations on property nationalized by the People's
Republic were estimated at $198.8-million.

Kissinger announced at his news conference that, as a "sign of
goodwill," Peking would release two American airmen captured in
China during the Vietnam War and another American, who had been
sentenced to life imprisonment after his plane was shot down over
Manchuria in 1952 during the Korean War. Air Force Major
Philip E. Smith and Navy Commander Robert J. Flynn had been held
by the Chinese since Sept. 20, 1965, and Aug. 21, 1967, respectively.
John Thomas Downey, hitherto referred to as a private American citizen, was identified as a C.I.A. agent by President Nixon at a press
conference on Jan. 31, 1973 (see p. 193). Release of the three men—
Downey on March 12 and Smith and Flynn on March 15—came much
more quickly than originally expected.

Among the cultural exchanges agreed to at Peking were plans to
send the Philadelphia Symphony Orchestra to Peking and a reciprocal
agreement to bring an archaeological exhibit from Peking's Forbidden
City to the United States in 1974. Other exchanges would include
Chinese nuclear physicists, water conservation experts, and gymnasts
and American medical, scientific, basketball, swimming, and teacher
delegations.

Significance of New Move

The move toward full-blown diplomatic relations between the United
States and China seemed to negate the repeated rejection by Chinese
Premier Chou En-lai of any "two-China policy, a one-China, one
Taiwan policy, or any similar policy." However, the problem of recon-
ciling U.S. relations with both Chinese governments persisted. At the
conclusion of President Nixon's trip to China in February 1972, Peking

had stated in a joint communique that "the Taiwan question is the crucial question obstructing the normalization of relations between China and the United States; the government of the People's Republic of China is the sole legal government of China; Taiwan is a province of China...." In the same communique, the United States said it supported "a peaceful settlement of the Taiwan question by the Chinese themselves" and noted that it planned to "progressively reduce its forces and military installations on Taiwan as the tension in the area diminishes." Asked about the apparent modification of American policy on Taiwan, Kissinger said at his news conference that the 1973 U.S.-China communique "reaffirmed" what had been stated the year before, that both countries continued to hold their own "perspective" on the issue of Taiwan, and "We, of course, continue to maintain our diplomatic relations with Taiwan."

For the most part, congressional reaction to the establishment of liaison offices was favorable. Approval was forthcoming from academic communities as well. Professor John K. Fairbank of Harvard said: "This goes farther than many people had expected. Peking is acquiescing to the American military forces not being withdrawn from Taiwan. This indicates that they are not concerned about the American military continuing for some time. This suggests that they have some concern of their own about security vis-a-vis the Soviet Union."

Appointment of Bruce

President Nixon announced later (at a March 15 news conference) that David K.E. Bruce, a 75-year-old career diplomat who had served as ambassador to Great Britain, to West Germany, and to France, would come out of retirement to accept appointment as this country's chief envoy to Peking. The President said he had selected Bruce "because I thought it was very important to appoint a man of great stature to this position." He added that "the Chinese accepted that view themselves and we expect soon to hear from them as to the appointment of the man they will have as his opposite number here in Washington." That decision came on March 30 when the New China News Agency announced that veteran Chinese diplomat Huang Chen would be arriving in Washington to head the Chinese liaison office there. Huang left a post in Paris where he had served since 1964 as the People's Republic's first ambassador to France. He had played a major role in opening up the avenues to improved Sino-American relations, initiating talks with the U.S. ambassador to France, Arthur K. Watson, after President Nixon's visit to Peking in 1972.

The date for opening the U.S. liaison office in Peking was set for approximately May 1. Nixon said the office would be staffed by 20

Americans, 10 of whom would be at the expert level. The two top deputies named to serve under Bruce were Alfred le Sesne Jenkins, director of the State Department's Office of the People's Republic of China and Mongolian Affairs, and John H. Holdridge, chief expert on China for the White House National Security Council.

Text of U.S.-China joint communique on establishment of liaison offices in Washington and Peking, Feb. 22, 1973:

Dr. Henry A. Kissinger, Assistant to the U.S. President for National Security Affairs, visited the People's Republic of China from February 15 to February 19, 1973. He was accompanied by Herbert G. Klein, Alfred Le S. Jenkins, Richard T. Kennedy, John H. Holdridge, Winston Lord, Jonathan T. Howe, Richard Solomon, and Peter W. Rodman.

Chairman Mao Tse-tung received Dr. Kissinger. Dr. Kissinger (and) members of his party held wide-range conversations with Premier Chou En-lai, Foreign Minister Chi Peng-fei, Vice Foreign Minister Chiao Kuan-hua, and other Chinese officials. Mr. Jenkins held parallel talks on technical subjects with Assistant Foreign Minister Chang Wen-chin. All these talks were conducted in an unconstrained atmosphere and were earnest, frank and constructive.

The two sides reviewed the development of relations between the two countries in the year that has passed since President Nixon's visit to the People's Republic of China and other issues of mutual concern. They reaffirmed the principles of the Joint Communique issued at Shanghai in February 1972 and their joint commitment to bring about a normalization of relations. They held that the progress that has been made during this period is beneficial to the people of their two countries.

The two sides agreed that the time was appropriate for accelerating the normalization of relations. To this end, they undertook to broaden their contacts in all fields. They agreed on a concrete program of expanding trade as well as scientific, cultural and other exchanges.

To facilitate this process and to improve communications, it was agreed that in the near future each side will establish a liaison office in the capital of the other. Details will be worked out through existing channels.

The two sides agreed that normalization of relations between the United States and the People's Republic of China will contribute to the relaxation of tension in Asia and in the world.

Dr. Kissinger and his party expressed their deep appreciation for the warm hospitality extended to them.

Excerpts from news conference of Dr. Henry A. Kissinger, Assistant to the President for National Security Affairs, Feb. 22, 1973:

...Ladies and gentlemen, I thought I would begin by making some remarks about my trip to the People's Republic of China, then take some questions on that, including the communique, and then perhaps a few additional comments to the briefing that Ron has already given you on the Hanoi communique.

To put this communique into perspective and to elaborate on it for a bit, one should review the evolution of our China policy. When we first began our contacts with the People's Republic of China in 1969 through third parties, and in 1971 directly, the United States had not had any contact with the People's Republic in nearly 20 years, that is, no contact on a really substantial level.

Our early conversations were concerned primarily with building confidence, with explaining each other's position, with establishing channels of communication. Last year our achievements consisted of setting out directions and indicating the roads that might be traveled. After the end of the war in Vietnam, and in these discussions in Peking, we were able to begin to travel some of these roads and to move from the attempt to eliminate the obstructions and the mistrust to some more concrete and positive achievements.

What happened in these meetings was really a continuation of possibilities that had been outlined during the President's visit and during the conversations between the President and Chairman Mao and Prime Minister Chou En-lai, except that now they took some more concrete form. As the communique points out, we reviewed the progress in Sino-American relations in great detail, and we reviewed the international situation in great detail.

We discussed the principles of the Shanghai communique, particularly those that dealt with the desirability of normalization of relations, the desirability of reducing the danger of military conflict, the affirmation by both sides that neither would seek hegemony in the Pacific area, and each of them opposed the attempt of anyone else to achieve it, and that the relations between China and the United States would never be directed against any third country.

In that spirit, it was decided to accelerate the normalization of relations, to broaden contacts in all fields, and an initial concrete program for extending these contacts was developed.

Given this new range of contacts, it was decided that the existing channel in Paris was inadequate and that, therefore, each side would establish a liaison office in the capital of the other. This liaison office would handle trade as well as all other matters, except the strictly formal diplomatic aspects of the relationship, but it would cover the whole gamut of relationships. This liaison office will be established in the nearest future. Both sides will make proposals within the next few weeks to the other about their technical requirements, and henceforth it will be possible for the United States and the People's Republic of China to deal with each other in the capital of the other.

Now, in order to give some concrete expression to this desire for the normalization of relationships, it was agreed that a number of steps be taken.

First of all, the Chinese, as a sign of good will, have informed us that they would release, within the same time period as our withdrawal from Vietnam, the two military prisoners that they hold in China, Lieutenant Commander (Robert J.) Flynn and Major Philip (E.) Smith. They have been held in China since 1967 and 1965, respectively. They will be released within the next few weeks.

Prime Minister Chou En-lai also asked me to inform the President that the Chinese penal code provided for the periodic review of the sentences of prisoners and that this provision would be applied in the case of John Downey.

The Chinese penal code provides for commutation of sentences on the basis of good behavior. We have been told that the behavior of Mr. Downey has been exemplary and that his case would be reviewed in the second half of this year.

With respect to outstanding issues that have been discussed in other channels, it was agreed that the linked issue of United States private claims against the People's Republic of China and PRC blocked assets in the United States would be negotiated on a global basis in the immediate future. Discussions will begin on this subject between Secretary of State Rogers and the Chinese Foreign Minister next week when both are attending the International Conference on Vietnam in Paris, and we expect these negotiations to be concluded rapidly and in a comprehensive way, and we are certain that both sides are approaching them in a constructive spirit and in an attitude consistent with our intention to accelerate the improvement of our relations.

With respect to increased exchanges between the two countries, the Chinese have agreed to invite, during this year, the Philadelphia Symphony by the fall of 1973, a medical group during the spring, a scientific group during the summer, a group of elementary and high school teachers, again during the summer, and increased visits by Congressmen and Senators, as well as athletic teams, an amateur basketball team, and swimming and diving teams.

The People's Republic has agreed to send to the United States the archaeological exhibit from the Forbidden City, which will probably come here in 1974, a group of water conservation experts, insect hormone specialists, high energy physicists, and a gymnastic team.

When the liaison offices are established, possibility will exist for developing further contacts and accelerating this entire process.

The major point we want to make is this: Our contacts with the People's Republic of China have moved from hostility towards normalization. We both believe that it is essential for the peace of the world that the United States and the People's Republic of China act with a sense of responsibility in world affairs, that we are part of an international community in which all nations have a stake in preserving the peace, and that, therefore, as the Shanghai communique has already said and as was reaffirmed once again, the normalization of relations between the United States and the People's Republic is not directed against any other nation, but is part of a pattern that the President has pursued of building a structure of peace in which all nations can participate and in which all nations have a stake.

It remains for me only to say that we were received with extraordinary courtesy and that the discussions were conducted in what was always described as an unconstrained atmosphere.

Now I will take your questions on China and after that a few comments on North Vietnam.

U.S. TROOPS ON TAIWAN

Q. Dr. Kissinger, did you come to any agreement with regard to Taiwan and U.S. troops there?

DR. KISSINGER. Inevitably the issue of Taiwan is one in which the People's Republic and we do not have the same perspective. The leaders of the People's Republic stated their view and we expressed our general commitments.

We, of course, continue to maintain diplomatic relations with Taiwan. The level of our troops on Taiwan is not the subject of negotiation, but will be governed by the general considerations of the Nixon Doctrine with respect to danger in the area. There exists no immediate plan for any withdrawal, but there will be a periodic review.

LIAISON OFFICES

Q. Doctor, what will be the rank of the liaison office heads? Will they be ambassadors?

DR. KISSINGER. Mr. Lisagor has addressed me by my academic title, which is very impressive to me.

We are not giving any formal diplomatic rank on either side. As soon as the person is selected, which should be within a month, I think his statute will then determine it, but there will be no formal title other than the one I have given.

Q. To what do you attribute the Chinese decision to send a permanent representative here in view of their previous refusal to have a permanent person any place where Taiwan is recognized?

DR. KISSINGER. The liaison office is, of course, not a formal diplomatic office, but I don't want to speculate on the motive for the Chinese decision.

Our policy had always been clear from our first contact. Certainly from the time that the President visited the People's Republic, he pointed out to Prime Minister Chou En-lai the types of American representation that would be available for establishment in Peking, which ranged from trade missions through various other possibilities to the idea of a liaison office.

Why the Chinese leaders have decided at this particular moment to accept this and to establish an office of their own in Washington, I would not want to speculate on, except that it is certainly consistent with speeding up the process of normalization.

Q. Was there any restriction or understanding on the size of the respective delegations?

DR. KISSINGER. No, but we expect it to be of moderate size at the beginning.

EXCHANGE OF JOURNALISTS

Q. Dr. Kissinger, how about the exchange of journalists and opening of permanent bureaus in both countries?

DR. KISSINGER. This is one of the topics that will be discussed through the existing channel and then through the liaison office. The Chinese side has indicated that it would be willing to send some journalists over here and it is, of course, clearly understood that we want to increase our journalistic contacts in the People's Republic.

I think there is some understanding in principle with respect to that, the details of which have to be worked out.

TRADE PROGRAM

Q. What is the concrete program of expanding trade that the communique refers to?

DR. KISSINGER. The initial step in a further expansion has to be the discussion of the two issues that I have mentioned, namely the blocked assets and the private claims. When these two issues are resolved, which we expect to be fairly soon, then further steps can be taken.

Up to now, the trade has been essentially in private channels on the United States side and has proceeded more rapidly than anybody projected 2 or 3 years ago.

FUTURE REPRESENTATION

Q. Dr. Kissinger, do you see the liaison office as something, as far as you can go, in terms of permanent representation, short of diplomatic relations, or do you see something further down the road?

DR. KISSINGER. We have no further steps in mind. This is as far as we can go for the moment.

MILITARY EQUIPMENT TO INDOCHINA

Q. Dr. Kissinger, did you have a chance to discuss with the Chinese leaders the possibility of mutual restraint in sending military equipment to Vietnam?

DR. KISSINGER. Our view on the question of military equipment to Indochina is clear and we have made clear to all the countries with which we have talked the importance of tranquility in Indochina to the peace of the world, and Indochina was one of the subjects that was discussed in Peking.

MEETING WITH CHAIRMAN MAO

Q. Dr. Kissinger, could you tell us something of the nature and the detail of your discussions with Chairman Mao?

DR. KISSINGER. I am debating whether to spend 10 minutes saying "No," or just to say "No." [*Laughter.*]

I will say one or two general things. One, I obviously cannot go into the details of the discussion. The atmosphere was cordial. Chairman Mao was in apparently good health and spoke with great animation for about 2 hours, and conveyed an extended personal message to the President, as the Chinese announcement made clear....

FLOW OF ARMS INTO INDOCHINA

Q. How do you assess the possibility of some kind of mutual arrangement with the Chinese to cut off the flow of arms into Indochina?

DR. KISSINGER. The problem isn't whether any formal arrangements can be made or should be made. The problem is whether the major countries now recognize that the agreement in Vietnam gives everybody an opportunity to return that area for the first time in a generation to a period of tranquility and to permit the peoples of Indochina an opportunity to work out their own fate without force and without outside pressure. And, if this is understood by all the major countries, then they can draw their own conclusions and act on the basis of their own considerations, rather than to attempt to codify this in a formal agreement.

Q. To follow that up, do you think that the Chinese do, then, understand this as we do?

DR. KISSINGER. I don't want to speculate on the Chinese intentions, but I have the impression that the participants in this conference next week all have to recognize an obligation to make whatever contribution they can to peace in Indochina.

PRIVATE CLAIMS AND BLOCKED ASSETS

Q. Could you give an idea of the amounts of the private claims and the blocked assets?

DR. KISSINGER. The private claims are in the neighborhood of $250 million. The blocked assets are in the neighborhood of $78 million. But this may vary slightly because we are not sure that we know either all the claims or all the blocked assets. But it is roughly correct....

TRADE INTERESTS

Q. Did the Chinese, at the working level, indicate any specific interest in either what they wanted to buy from the United States or what they thought they could sell to the United States?

DR. KISSINGER. I would be the most unlikely subject for such a conversation, because I couldn't respond in any intelligible way. But we will set up procedures for them to express such an interest to more qualified personnel....

DIPLOMATIC PRIVILEGES FOR LIAISON OFFICE PERSONNEL

Q. Can we clear up whether the people in the liaison offices will have diplomatic privileges or not?

DR. KISSINGER. The people in the liaison offices will have diplomatic privileges and will have opportunity to communicate with their own governments by code.

CHINESE MOVEMENT IN THE UNITED STATES

Q. Will the Chinese be allowed freedom of movement in the United States?

DR. KISSINGER. All of this will be worked out....

March

MORE STATE OF THE UNION MESSAGES
March 1-14, 1973

President Nixon dispatched to Congress in March three more installments of his annual State of the Union message. The new installments raised to a total of six the number of sections into which the report for 1973 was divided. The first section, termed by the President an "overview" of the State of the Union, had been forwarded to the legislative branch on Feb. 2. Nixon explained then that "with so many changes in government programs under consideration," the usual "single, all-embracing State of the Union message would not appear to be adequate." Consequently, he would send additional messages to Congress on "specific areas of policy." A few days earlier, in a Jan. 28 radio speech on his budget proposals, he had referred to the "detailed messages" on the State of the Union and declared: "Together, these statements will chart a new course for America—a course that will bring more progress by putting more responsibility and money in more places."

Two of the detailed messages, one on Natural Resources and the Environment and another on the American Economy, reached Capitol Hill on Feb. 15 and 22, respectively. The next three messages were devoted to Human Resources (March 1), Community Development (March 8), and Law Enforcement and Drug Abuse Prevention (March 14). Foreign policy, originally to be covered in this series, was eventually left to the annual State of the World message (see p. 515). Each of the detailed State of the Union messages was preceded by a presidential radio speech on the same subject. (See p. 209 for text of the overview message and excerpts from the first two detailed messages.)

Human Resources

Nixon asserted in his Human Resources message on March 1 that the results of numerous federal programs instituted in the 1960s to help meet human needs had "in case after case amounted to dismal failure." The American people, he said, deserved "compassion that works—not simply compassion that means well." The President laid down four basic principles to govern human resources policy in the 1970s: (1) Removal of "barriers which might impede an individual's opportunity to realize his or her full potential"; (2) concentration by the federal government "more on providing incentives and opening opportunities, and less on delivering direct services"; (3) federal encouragement of state and local governments to supply needed services and of the private sector to address social problems; and (4) avoidance of "ballooning deficits" incurred in the name of social welfare.

The President restated his goal of developing an insurance system to guarantee adequate financing of health care for every family. He said he would "again ask Congress to establish a new program of Education Revenue Sharing," and he repeated a proposal to give a tax credit to parents of children attending parochial and other non-public elementary and secondary schools. Administrative measures to institute a reform of manpower training through a revenue-sharing program were promised. Because "the welfare mess cannot be permitted to continue," and Congress was not disposed to pass "an overall structural reform bill," Nixon said vigorous steps would be taken to strengthen the management of the major existing program of Aid to Families with Dependent Children (AFDC). Other problems touched upon in the Human Resources message included property tax relief for older Americans, transfer of most anti-poverty activities from the Office of Economic Opportunity (OEO) to Cabinet departments, and Indian and veterans' affairs.

Community Development

Highlight of the Community Development message on March 8 was a proposal to replace existing grant-in-aid programs for community development by a special revenue-sharing program to be set up under a "Better Communities Act." One of the purposes of the new legislation would be to "reduce the excessive federal control that has been so frustrating to local governments." Present activities could be continued, but decisions on the use of available funds would be up to local leaders. The President in his message gave assurance that no city would receive

304

"less money for community development than it has received under the categorical grant programs." But the system of averaging prescribed for distribution of revenue-sharing funds in the "Better Communities Act," as submitted to Congress on April 19, raised sharp complaints because it would give many large cities substantially smaller amounts than they had received most recently under the categorical grant programs.

The message repeated a two-year-old proposal for creation in the federal government of a Department of Community Development "to pull under one roof various programs now in the Departments of Housing and Urban Development, Transportation, Agriculture, and other agencies." The President called also for enactment of a "Responsive Governments Act" to assist state and local governments in strengthening their planning and management of community development projects financed by special revenue-sharing funds. "Thus the Responsive Government Act," he pointed out, "is a vitally necessary companion piece to the Better Communities Act."

Nixon recommended that Congress authorize expenditure, out of the Highway Trust Fund, of $3.65-billion over the next three years to help finance capital improvements for mass transit systems—a recommendation that was approved by the Senate but rejected, April 19, by a vote of 215 to 190 in the House of Representatives. A final proposal was to centralize federal disaster assistance in the new Department of Community Development.

Law Enforcement and Drug Abuse

In his message on Law Enforcement and Drug Abuse Prevention, March 14, President Nixon detailed the stepping-up of federal efforts, and of federal assistance to state and local efforts, to reduce crime. As in the case of various other federal-state-local endeavors, he proposed the combination of separate forms of federal assistance into a special revenue-sharing fund to be distributed to states and local governments on a formula basis. In that way, he asserted, the states and localities would gain "both the flexibility and the clear authority they need to meet their law enforcement challenges."

The President announced also his intention to submit to Congress a "Criminal Code Reform Act" aimed at "a comprehensive revision of existing federal criminal laws." Such a revision would require long and careful consideration by Congress, Nixon acknowledged, but he asked for immediate enactment of separate bills to effect proposed changes in the Criminal Code relating to (1) the death penalty and (2) heroin trafficking.

Restoration of the death penalty, struck down by the Supreme Court to all intents and purposes in a 1972 decision (see Historic Documents,

1972, p. 499), *was recommended for "war-related treason, sabotage, and espionage, and for all specifically enumerated crimes under federal jurisdiction from which death results." The "Heroin Trafficking Act" proposed by the President would provide mandatory sentences of from 10 years to life for first offenders trafficking in more than four ounces of heroin, and a mandatory life sentence without parole for second offenders trafficking in more than four ounces.* (For penalties proposed by New York Gov. Nelson D. Rockefeller, see p. 27.)

Excerpts from the President's State of the Union message on Human Resources, March 1, 1973:

HUMAN RESOURCES

...As we consider the subject of human resources in this fourth section of my 1973 State of the Union Message, we must not confine ourselves solely to a discussion of the year past and the year ahead. Nor can we be content to frame the choices we face in strictly governmental and programmatic terms—as though Federal money and programs were the only variables that mattered in meeting human needs....

Let us begin then, by recognizing that by almost any measure, life is better for Americans in 1973 than ever before in our history, and better than in any other society of the world in this or any earlier age....

Secondly, let us recognize that the American system which has brought us so far so fast is not simply a system of Government helping people. *Rather it is a system under which Government helps people to help themselves and one another.*

The real miracles in raising millions out of poverty, for example, have been performed by the free-enterprise economy, not by Government anti-poverty programs.... Even where the public sector has played a major role, as in education, the great strength of the system has derived from State and local governments' primacy and from the diverse mixture of private and public institutions in the educational process—both factors which have facilitated grassroots influence and popular participation.

We should not tamper lightly, then, with the delicately balanced social, economic, and political system which has been responsible for making this country the best place on earth to live—and which has tremendous potential to rectify whatever shortcomings may still persist.

But we Americans—to our great credit—are a restless and impatient people, a nation of idealists. We dream not simply of alleviating poverty, hunger, discrimination, ignorance, disease, and fear, but of eradicating them altogether—and we would like to do it all today.

During the middle and late 1960's, under the pressure of this impatient idealism, Federal intervention to help meet human needs increased sharply. Provision of services from Federal programs directly to individuals began to be regarded as the rule in human resources policy, rather than the rare exception it had been in the past.... Well-intentioned as this effort may have been, the results in case after case amounted to dismal failure....

The American people deserve better than this. They deserve compassion that works—not simply compassion that means well. They deserve programs that say yes to human needs by saying no to paternalism, social exploitation and waste....

Principles for the 1970's

Consistently since 1969, this Administration has worked to establish a new human resources policy, based on a healthy skepticism about Federal Government omniscience and omnicompetence, and on a strong reaffirmation of the right and the capacity of individuals to chart their own lives and solve their own problems through State and local government and private endeavor. We have achieved a wide variety of significant reforms.

Now the progress made and the experience gained over the past four years, together with the results of careful program reviews which were conducted over this period, have prepared us to seek broader reforms in 1973 than any we have requested before.

In the time since the outlines of these proposals emerged in the new budget, intense controversy and considerable misunderstanding about both their purposes and their effects have understandably arisen among persons of goodwill on all sides.

To provide a more rational, less emotional basis for the national debate which will—and properly should—surround my recommendations, I would invite the Congress to consider four basic principles which I believe should govern our human resources policy in the 1970's:

- —Government at all levels should seek to support and nurture, rather than limit, the diversity and freedom of choice which are hallmarks of the American system. The Federal Government in particular must work to guarantee an equal chance at the starting line by removing barriers which might impede an individual's opportunity to realize his or her full potential.
- —The Federal Government should concentrate more on providing incentives and opening opportunities, and less on delivering direct services. Such programs of direct assistance to individuals as the Federal Government does conduct must provide even-handed treatment for all, and must be carefully designed to ensure that the benefits are actually received by those who are intended to receive them.
- —Rather than stifling initiative by trying to direct everything from Washington, Federal efforts should encourage State and local governments to make those decisions and supply those services for which their closeness to the people best qualifies them. In

addition, the Federal Government should seek means of encouraging the private sector to address social problems, thereby utilizing the market mechanism to marshal resources behind clearly stated national objectives.

—Finally, all Federal policy must adhere to a strict standard of fiscal responsibility. Ballooning deficits which spent our economy into a new inflationary spiral or a recessionary tailspin in the name of social welfare would punish most cruelly the very people whom they seek to help. On the other hand, continued additions to a personal tax burden which has already doubled since 1950 would reduce incentives for excellence and would conflict directly with the goal of allowing each individual to keep as much as possible of what he or she earns to permit maximum personal freedom of choice.

The new post of Counsellor to the President for Human Resources, which I have recently created within the Executive Office of the President, will provide a much-needed focal point for our efforts to see that these principles are carried out in all Federal activities aimed at meeting human needs, as well as in the Federal Government's complex relationships with State and local governments in this field. The coordinating function to be performed by this Counsellor should materially increase the unity, coherence, and effectiveness of our policies.

The following sections present a review of the progress we have made over the past four years in bringing each of the various human resources activities into line with these principles, and they outline our agenda for the years ahead.

Health

I am committed to removing financial barriers that would limit access to quality medical care for all American families. To that end, we have nearly doubled Federal outlays for health since the beginning of this Administration. Next year, they will exceed $30 billion.

Nearly 60 percent of these funds will go to finance health care for older Americans, the disabled, and the poor, through Medicare and Medicaid....

A major goal of this Administration has been to develop an insurance system which can guarantee adequate financing of health care for every American family. The 92nd Congress failed to act upon my 1971 proposal to accomplish this goal, and now the need for legislation has grown still more pressing. *I shall once again submit to the Congress legislation to help meet the Nation's health insurance needs.*

Federal health policy should seek to safeguard this country's pluralistic health care system and to build on its strengths, minimizing reliance on Government-run arrangements. We must recognize appropriate limits to the Federal role, and we must see that every health care dollar is spent as effectively as possible.

This means discontinuing federally funded health programs which have served their purpose, or which have proved ineffective, or which involve functions more suitably performed by State and local government or the private sector.

The Hill-Burton hospital grants program, for example, can no longer be justified on the basis of the shortage of hospital facilities which prompted its creation in 1946. That shortage has given way to a surplus— so that to continue this program would only add to the Nation's excess of hospital beds and lead to higher charges to patients. It should be terminated.

We are also proposing to phase out the community mental health center demonstration program while providing funding for commitments to existing arrangements extending up to eight years. This program has helped to build and establish some 500 such centers, which have demonstrated new ways to deliver mental health services at the community level....

Education

1973 must be a year of decisive action to restructure Federal aid programs for education. Our goal is to provide continued Federal financial support for our schools while expanding State and local control over basic educational decisions.

I shall again ask the Congress to establish a new program of Education Revenue Sharing. This program would replace the complex and inefficient tangle of approximately 30 separate programs for elementary and secondary education with a single flexible authority for use in a few broad areas such as compensatory education for the disadvantaged, education for the handicapped, vocational education, needed assistance in federally affected areas, and supporting services.

Education Revenue Sharing would enlarge the opportunities for State and local decision-makers to tailor programs and resources to meet the specific educational needs of their own localities. It would mean less red tape, less paper work, and greater freeedom for those at the local level to do what they think is best for their schools—not what someone in Washington tells them is best....

The time has also come to redefine the Federal role in higher education, by replacing categorical support programs for institutions with substantially increased funds for student assistance. *My budget proposals have already outlined a plan to channel much more of our higher education support through students themselves, including a new grant program which would increase funds provided to $948 million and the number assisted to over 1,500,000 people—almost a five-fold increase over the current academic year....*

Finally, in order to enhance the diversity provided by our mixed educational system of public and private schools, I will propose to the

Congress legislation to provide a tax credit for tuition payments made by parents of children who attend non-public elementary and secondary schools.

Manpower

The Federal manpower program is a vital part of our total effort to conserve and develop our human resources. Up to the present time, however, the "manpower program" has been not a unified effort, but a collection of separate categorical activities, many of them overlapping.... While many well-run local programs are more than worth what they cost, many other individual projects are largely ineffective—and their failure wastes money which could be used to bolster the solid accomplishments of the rest....

I believe that the answer to much of this problem lies in our program of Manpower Revenue Sharing—uniting several previously fragmented manpower activities under a single umbrella and then giving most of the responsibility for running this effort to those governments which are closest to the working men and women who need assistance. *In the next 16 months, administrative measures will be taken to institute this needed reform of the manpower system within the present legal framework....*

Welfare

With the failure of the past two Congresses to enact my proposals for fundamental reform of the Nation's public assistance system, that system remains as I described it in a message last year—"a crazy quilt of injustice and contradiction that has developed in bits and pieces over the years."

The major existing program, Aid to Families with Dependent Children (AFDC), is as inequitable, inefficient, and inadequate as ever.

> —The administration of this program is unacceptably loose. The latest national data indicate that in round numbers, one of every 20 persons on the AFDC rolls is totally ineligible for welfare; 3 more are paid more benefits than they are entitled to; and another is underpaid. About one-quarter of AFDC recipients, in other words, are receiving improper payments.

> —Complex program requirements and administrative red tape at the Federal and State levels have created bureaucracies that are difficult to manage.

> —Inconsistent and unclear definitions of need have diluted resources that should be targeted on those who need help most.

> —Misguided incentives have discouraged employable persons from work and induced fathers to leave home so their families can qualify for welfare.

After several years of skyrocketing increases, however, outlays for this program have begun to level off. This results from the strong resurgence of our economy and expansion of the job market, along with some management improvements in the AFDC program and strengthened work requirements which were introduced into the program last year.

Since the legislative outlook seems to preclude passage of an overall structural reform bill in the immediate future, I have directed that vigorous steps be taken to strengthen the management of AFDC through administrative measures and legislative proposals....

One thing is certain: the welfare mess cannot be permitted to continue. A system which penalizes a person for going to work and rewards a person for going on welfare is totally alien to the American tradition of self-reliance and self-respect. That is why welfare reform has been and will continue to be one of our major goals; and we will work diligently with the Congress in developing ways to achieve it....

Older Americans

One measure of the Nation's devotion to our older citizens is the fact that programs benefitting them—including Social Security and a wide range of other activities—now account for nearly one-fourth of the entire Federal budget.

Social Security benefits levels have been increased 51 percent in the last four years—the most rapid increase in history. Under new legislation which I initially proposed, benefits have also become inflation-proof, increasing automatically as the cost of living increases.

Over 1 1/2 million older Americans or their dependents can now receive higher Social Security benefits while continuing to work. Nearly 4 million widows and widowers are also starting to receive larger benefits—$1 billion in additional income in the next fiscal year. And millions of older Americans will be helped by the new Supplemental Security Income program which establishes a Federal income floor for the aging, blind, and disabled poor.

Nevertheless, we are confronted with a major item of unfinished business. Approximately two-thirds of the twenty million persons who are 65 and over own their own homes. A disproportionate amount of their fixed income must now be used for property taxes. *I will submit to the Congress recommendations for alleviating the often crushing burdens which property taxes place upon many older Americans.*

Economic Opportunity

No one who started life in a family at the bottom of the income scale, as I did and as many Members of the Congress did, can ever forget how that condition felt, or ever turn his back on an opportunity to help alleviate it in the lives of others.

We in the Federal Government have such an opportunity to help combat poverty. Our commitment to this fight has grown steadily during the past decade, without regard to which party happened to be in power, from under $8 billion in total Federal anti-poverty expenditures in 1964 to more than $30 billion in my proposed budget for 1974....

At the beginning of this period, when Government found itself unprepared to respond to the sharp new national awareness of the plight of the disadvantaged, creation of an institutional structure separate from the regular machinery of Government and specifically charged with helping the poor seemed a wise first step to take. Thus the Office of Economic Opportunity was brought into being in 1964.

A wide range of useful anti-poverty programs has been conceived and put into operation over the years by the Office of Economic Opportunity. Some programs which got their start within OEO have been moved out into the operating departments and agencies of the Government when they matured, and they are thriving there. VISTA, for example, became part of ACTION in 1971, and Head Start was integrated with other activities focused on the first five years of life under HEW's Office of Child Development. OEO's other programs have now developed to a point where they can be similarly integrated.

Accordingly, in keeping with my determination to make every dollar devoted to human resources programs return 100 cents worth of real benefits to the people who most need those benefits, I have decided that most of the anti-poverty activities now conducted by the Office of Economic Opportunity should be delegated or transferred into the Cabinet departments relating to their respective fields of activity. Adhering strictly to statutory procedures, and requesting Congressional approval whenever necessary, I shall take action to effect this change....

Funding for the transferred activities will stay level, or in many cases will even increase. The only major OEO program for which termination of Federal funding is recommended in my budget is Community Action. New funding for Community Action activities in fiscal year 1974 will be at the discretion of local communities.

After more than 7 years of existence, Community Action has had an adequate opportunity to demonstrate its value within the communities it serves, and to build locally based agencies.... Further Federal spending on behalf of this concept, beyond the $2.8 billion which has been spent on it since 1965, no longer seems necessary or desirable.

Legal Services

One other economic opportunity effort deserving special mention is the Legal Services Program. Notwithstanding some abuses, legal services has done much in its seven-year history to breathe new life into the cherished concept of equal justice for all by providing access to quality legal representation for millions of Americans who would otherwise have been denied it for want of funds.

The time has now come to institutionalize legal services as a permanent, responsible, and responsive component of the American system of justice.

I shall soon propose legislation to the Congress to form a legal services corporation so constituted as to permit its attorneys to practice according to the highest professional standards, provided with safeguards against politicization of its activities, and held accountable to the people through appropriate monitoring and evaluation procedures....

The American Indian

For Indian people the policy of this Administration will continue to be one of advancing their opportunities for self-determination, without termination of the special Federal relationship with recognized Indian tribes.

Just as it is essential to put more decision-making in the hands of State and local governments, I continue to believe that Indian tribal governments should assume greater responsibility for programs of the Bureau of Indian Affairs and the Department of Health, Education and Welfare which operate on their reservations. *As I first proposed in 1970, I recommend that the Congress enact the necessary legislation to facilitate this take-over of responsibility. Also, I recommend that the 1953 termination resolution be repealed....*

I shall also propose new legislation to foster local Indian self-determination by developing an Interior Department program of bloc grants to Federally recognized tribes as a replacement for a number of existing economic and resource development programs....

Because Indian rights to natural resources need better protection, I am again urging the Congress to create an Indian Trust Counsel Authority to guarantee that protection....

To accelerate organizational reform, I have directed the Secretary of the Interior to transfer day to day operational activities of the Bureau of Indian Affairs out of Washington to its field offices. *And I am again asking the Congress to create a new Assistant Secretary position within the Interior Department to deal with Indian matters....*

Budget for Human Resources

After more than a decade of war, we have successfully completed one of the most unselfish missions ever undertaken by one nation in the defense of another. Now the coming of peace permits us to turn our attention more fully to the works of compassion, concern, and social betterment here at home.

The seriousness of my commitment to make the most of this opportunity is demonstrated by the record level of funding for human resource programs proposed in our new budget—$125 billion in all—

nearly twice the amount that was being spent on such programs when I
took office in 1969.

This is both a generous budget and a reform budget. The reforms
it proposes will put muscle behind the generosity it intends. The overall
effect of these reforms will be the elimination of programs that are
wasteful so that we can concentrate on programs that work. They will
make possible the continued growth of Federal efforts to meet human
needs—while at the same time helping to prevent a runaway deficit
that could lead to higher taxes, higher prices, and higher interest rates
for all Americans....

RICHARD NIXON

The White House,
March 1, 1973.

*Excerpts from the President's State of the Union message
on Community Development, March 8, 1973:*

COMMUNITY DEVELOPMENT

Today, in this fifth report to the Congress on the State of the Union,
I want to discuss the quality of life in our cities and towns and set forth
new directions for community development in America.... The time has
come to recognize the errors of past Federal efforts to support community development and to move swiftly to correct them.

The results of past errors form a disturbing catalogue:

—They have distorted local priorities.

—They have spawned a massive glut of red tape.

—They have created an adversary climate between local communities and Washington which has often led to waste, delay and mutual
frustration.

—They have contributed to a lack of confidence among our people
in the ability of both local and national governments to solve problems
and get results.

—They have led to the creation of too many complex and often
competing Federal programs.

—Perhaps worst of all, they have undercut the will and the ability
of local and State governments to take the initiative to mobilize their
own energies and those of their citizens.

The Federal policy that will work best in the last third of this century
is not one that tries to force all of our communities into a single
restrictive mold. The Federal policy that will work best is one that helps
people and their leaders in each community meet their own needs in
the way they think best.

It is this policy which binds together the many aspects of our community development programs.

The Better Communities Act

In the near future, I will submit to the Congress the Better Communities Act to provide revenue sharing for community development. Beginning July 1, 1974, this act would provide $2.3 billion a year to communities to be spent as they desire to meet their community development needs. In the interim period before the legislation becomes effective, funds already available to the Department of Housing and Urban Development will be used to maintain and support community development.

The Better Communities Act is intended to replace inflexible and fragmented categorical grant-in-aid programs, and to reduce the excessive Federal control that has been so frustrating to local governments.

Rather than focusing and concentrating resources in a coordinated assault on a set of problems, the categorical system scatters these resources, and diminishes their impact upon the most needy. Excessive Federal influence also limits the variety and diversity of development programs. Local officials should be able to focus their time, their resources and their talents on meeting local needs and producing results, instead of trying to please Washington with an endless torrent of paperwork.

I first proposed such legislation in 1971, and although the Congress failed to enact it, significant support was expressed in both the Senate and the House. Since that time, members of my Administration have been consulting with Congressional leaders, mayors, Governors, other local officials and their representatives. Many constructive suggestions have been received and will be incorporated in my new legislative proposal. As a result, I believe the Better Communities Act will represent our best hope for the future of community development and will deserve rapid approval by the Congress.

Among the most significant features of the Better Communities Act are these:

—*Hold-Harmless Provision:* The flow of money to cities and urban counties is to be based on a formula reflecting community needs, as determined by objective standards. In the years immediately following enactment, funds would be used to assure that no city receives less money for community development than it has received under the categorical grant programs.

—*Assistance for Smaller Communities:* Funding is also to be provided for our smaller communities, recognizing the vital importance of small towns and rural communities to the future of the Nation.

—*The Role of State Government:* State governments have always played an important part in meeting the community development needs of their communities. The Act will recognize this role.

—*Local Decision Making:* While each of the activities now supported by categorical grants may be continued, it would be up to local leaders to determine how that money will be spent.

—*Minimizing Red Tape:* Recipients would be required to show the Federal Government only that they are complying with Federal statutes in the way they are spending their revenue sharing money.

—*Elimination of Matching:* Shared revenues would not have to be matched by local funds.

—*Protection for Minorities:* Under no circumstances could funds provided under the Better Communities Act be used for purposes that would violate the civil rights of any person.

A Department of Community Development

One of the most serious deficiencies in the effort of the Federal Government to assist in community development has been the fragmentation and scattering of Federal programs among a variety of departments and agencies. All too often State or local officials seeking help for a particular project must shuttle back and forth from one Federal office to another, wasting precious time and resources in a bureaucratic wild goose chase.

In order to coordinate our community development activities more effectively, I proposed nearly two years ago that we create a Department of Community Development which would pull under one roof various programs now in the Departments of Housing and Urban Development, Transportation, Agriculture, and other agencies.

After extensive hearings on this proposal, the Committee on Government Operations of the House of Representatives reached this conclusion:

"The Department of Community Development will be a constructive center in the Federal Government for assistance to communities, large and small. It will facilitate rational planning, orderly growth, and the effective employment of resources to build viable communities throughout the United States. It will help to strengthen the physical and institutional bases for cooperative action by Federal, State and local governments."

This Administration fully agrees, of course, and will continue to work with the Congress for the prompt creation of a Department of Community Development.

In the interim, I recently appointed a Presidential Counsellor on Community Development who will coordinate community development programs and policies in the executive branch. But only when the Congress approves the basic departmental reorganization proposed by the

Administration can our efforts to eliminate waste, confusion and duplication, and to promote community betterment more efficiently, be fully effective.

The Responsive Governments Act

For nearly 20 years, the Federal Government has provided assistance to State and local governments in order to strengthen their planning and management capabilities.

This aid, provided under the Comprehensive Planning Assistance Program, has always been helpful, but the program itself has several major flaws. It has tended, for instance, to stress one aspect of public administration—planning—without adequately recognizing other essential features such as budgeting, management, personnel administration, and information-gathering....

This Administration proposed new planning and management legislation to the 92nd Congress, but it was not approved. In the meantime, we took what steps we could to improve the existing program. Some progress has been made, but corrective legislation is still needed.

I shall therefore propose that the 93rd Congress enact a new Responsive Governments Act. I shall also propose that we provide $110 million for this act in fiscal year 1974—almost one-fifth of the entire amount that has been spent under the present law in the last two decades.

This Responsive Governments Act would assist State and local governments in meeting several important goals:

—Developing reliable information on their problems and opportunities;

—Developing and analyzing alternative policies and programs;

—Managing the programs;

—And evaluating the results, so that appropriate adjustments can be made.

The ability to plan and manage is vital to effective government. It will be even more important to State and local governments as they are freed from the restraints of narrow categorical Federal programs and must decide how to spend revenue sharing funds. Thus the Responsive Governments Act is a vitally necessary companion piece to the Better Communities Act.

Housing

...During the past four years, the Federal Government has provided housing assistance to an additional 1.5 million American families of low and moderate income. This represents more housing assistance than the total provided by the Federal Government during the entire 34-year history of our national housing program preceding this Administration.

In addition, a healthy, vigorous, private housing industry has provided 6 million new unsubsidized units of housing for Americans in the last four years. Housing starts for each of the last three years have reached record high levels—levels, in fact, that are more than double the average for the preceding 21 years.

Most importantly, the percentage of Americans living in substandard housing has dropped dramatically from 46 percent in 1940 to 37 percent in 1950 to 18 percent in 1960 to 8 percent in 1970. Americans today are better housed than ever before in our history.

At the same time, however, there has been mounting evidence of basic defects in some of our housing programs. It is now clear that all too frequently the needy have not been the primary beneficiaries of these programs; that the programs have been riddled with inequities; and that the cost for each unit of subsidized housing produced under these programs has been too high. In short, we shall be making far more progress than we have been and we should now move to place our housing policies on a much firmer foundation....

In pursuing our goal of decent homes for all Americans, we know that better means are needed—that the old and wasteful programs, programs which have already obligated the taxpayer to payments of *between $63 billion and $95 billion* during the next 40 years, are not the answer.

One of my highest domestic priorities this year will be the development of new policies that will provide aid to genuinely needy families and eliminate waste.

A major housing study is now underway within the Government, under the direction of my Counsellor for Community Development. Within the next six months, I intend to submit to the Congress my policy recommendations in this field, based upon the results of that study.

Transportation

To thrive, a community must provide for the efficient movement of its people and its products. Yet in recent years, the growing separation of the city from its suburbs and changing employment patterns have made transportation more of a community problem than a community asset. To improve community development we must meet the challenge of transportation planning and provide more flexible means for communities to meet their transportation needs....

Nothing can do more to lift the face of our cities, and the spirit of our city dwellers, than truly adequate systems of modern transportation. With the best highway system in the world, and with 75 percent of our people owning and operating automobiles, we have more transportation assets per capita than any other people on earth. Yet the commuter who uses a two-ton vehicle to transport only himself to and from work each day is not making the most efficient use of our transportation system and is himself contributing to our transportation and environmental problems.

Good public transportation is essential not only to assure adequate transportation for all citizens, but to forward the common goal of less congested, cleaner and safer communities. As I pointed out a few weeks ago in my message on the environment and natural resources, effective mass transit systems that relieve urban congestion will also reduce pollution and the waste of our limited energy resources.

As we build such systems, we must be aware of the two special challenges in coordinating the needs of the inner city and the suburb and in alleviating potential disruptions which new transportation systems can bring to neighborhood life.

To further these efforts I again continue to urge Congress to permit a portion of the Highway Trust Fund to be used in a more flexible fashion, thus allowing mass transit capital investments where communities so desire.

I recommend that the Congress authorize the expenditure by State and local governments of $3.65 billion over the next three years from the Highway Trust Fund for urban transportation needs, including capital improvements for bus and rapid rail systems. I also recommend continuing the rural highway program at the $1 billion a year level, and providing ample resources to advance the Interstate system as it approaches its 1980 funding completion date. This legislation can meet old needs while at the same time addressing new ones....

It is very important to recognize that this proposal does not represent an arbitrary Federal shift of funds from highways to transit. What it does stress is the right of local governments to choose the best solutions for their urban transportation problems....

Rural Development

...Twice in the last two years, I have recommended legislation which would provide new revenues for rural development. Under my latest proposal, loans and guarantees would have been made for projects selected and prepared by the States.

While the 92nd Congress did not enact either of these proposals, it did enact the Rural Development Act of 1972, establishing additional lending authority for rural needs. Like the Administration's proposals, this lending authority provides for insured loans and guaranteed loans which allow maximum participation of the private sector....

This Administration will implement the Rural Development Act in a manner consistent with the revenue sharing concept, allowing major project selections and priority decisions to be made by the State and local governments whenever possible. It is our intent, after fully evaluating the effectiveness of this approach, to seek whatever additional legislation may be needed.

319

Disaster Assistance

To a community suffering the ravages of a natural disaster, nothing is more important than prompt and effective relief assistance. As our population grows and spreads, each storm, earthquake, drought or freeze affects larger numbers of people....

Until now, disaster relief efforts have involved a number of different agencies and have been coordinated by the Executive Office of the President. The experience of the past few years has demonstrated that:

—We are not doing nearly enough to prepare in advance for disasters.

—States, local governments and private individuals should assume a larger role in preparing for disasters, and in relieving the damage after they have occurred.

—Responsibility for relief is presently too fragmented among too many authorities.

—At the Federal level, disaster relief should be managed by a single agency.

I intend to make 1973 a turning point in the quality of governmental response to natural disasters.

To achieve this goal, I have already proposed Reorganization Plan Number 1 of 1973, which is now before the Congress. It calls for the delegation of all responsibility for coordinating disaster relief to the Secretary of Housing and Urban Development, who is also my Counsellor for Community Development. This transfer of operations would take place at the beginning of the new fiscal year and would be carried out in such a way that the effective relations which now exist with State disaster officials would in no way be harmed, while a new sense of unity and mobility at the Federal level would be fostered.

If the Congress enacts my proposal for a new Department of Community Development, that new department would be responsible for directing *all* Federal disaster activities, including those of several other agencies which perform disaster roles.

In addition to the improvements I have proposed in Reorganization Plan Number 1, I will shortly submit a new Disaster Assistance Act to the Congress. This new act is designed to improve the delivery of Federal assistance, to provide a more equitable basis for financing individual property losses, and to forge a more balanced partnership for meeting disasters head-on—a partnership not only among governments at all levels but also between governments and private citizens.

Under these proposals, each level of government would accept responsibility for those things it can do best. While the Federal Government would continue to assist with financing, State and local governments would have far more latitude and responsibility in the use of those funds. They would also be encouraged to assert stronger leadership in efforts to minimize the damage of future disasters.

For homeowners, farmers and businessmen who have suffered disaster losses, the Federal Government would continue to provide direct assistance.

I will also recommend to the Congress an expansion of the national flood insurance program to allow participation by more communities in flood-prone areas and to increase the limits of coverage....

RICHARD NIXON

The White House,
March 8, 1973.

Excerpts from the President's State of the Union message on Law Enforcement and Drug Abuse Prevention, March 14, 1973:

LAW ENFORCEMENT AND DRUG ABUSE PREVENTION

This sixth message to the Congress on the State of the Union concerns our Federal system of criminal justice. It discusses both the progress we have made in improving that system and the additional steps we must take to consolidate our accomplishments and to further our efforts to achieve a safe, just, and law-abiding society.

In the period from 1960 to 1968 serious crime in the United States increased by 122 percent according to the FBI's Uniform Crime Index. The rate of increase accelerated each year until it reached a peak of 17 percent in 1968....

The decade of the 1960s was characterized in many quarters by a growing sense of permissiveness in America—as well intentioned as it was poorly reasoned—in which many people were reluctant to take the steps necessary to control crime. It is no coincidence that within a few years' time, America experienced a crime wave that threatened to become uncontrollable.

This Administration came to office in 1969 with the conviction that the integrity of our free institutions demanded stronger and firmer crime control. I promised that the wave of crime would not be the wave of the future. An all-out attack was mounted against crime in the United States.

—The manpower of Federal enforcement and prosecution agencies was increased.

—New legislation was proposed and passed by the Congress to put teeth into Federal enforcement efforts against organized crime, drug trafficking, and crime in the District of Columbia.

—Federal financial aid to State and local criminal justice systems— a forerunner of revenue sharing—was greatly expanded through Administration budgeting and Congressional appropriations, reaching a total of $1.5 billion in the three fiscal years from 1970 through 1972.

These steps marked a clear departure from the philosophy which had come to dominate Federal crime fighting efforts, and which had brought America to record-breaking levels of lawlessness. Slowly, we began to bring America back. The effort has been long, slow, and difficult. In spite of the difficulties, we have made dramatic progress.

In the last four years the Department of Justice has obtained convictions against more than 2500 organized crime figures, including a number of bosses and under-bosses in major cities across the country. The pressure on the underworld is building constantly.

Today, the capital of the United States no longer bears the stigma of also being the Nation's crime capital. As a result of decisive reforms in the criminal justice system the serious crime rate has been cut in half in Washington, D.C..... Because of the combined efforts of Federal, State, and local agencies, the wave of serious crime in the United States is being brought under control. Latest figures from the FBI's Uniform Crime Index show that serious crime is increasing at the rate of only one percent a year—the lowest recorded rate since 1960. A majority of cities with over 100,000 population have an actual reduction in crime.

These statistics and these indices suggest that our anti-crime program is on the right track. They suggest that we are taking the right measures. They prove that the only way to attack crime in America is the way crime attacks our people—without pity. Our program is based on this philosophy, and it is working.

Now we intend to maintain the momentum we have developed by taking additional steps to further improve law enforcement and to further protect the people of the United States.

Law Enforcement: Special Revenue Sharing

...While the Federal Government does not have full jurisdiction in the field of criminal law enforcement, it does have a broad, constitutional responsibility to insure domestic tranquility. I intend to meet that responsibility.

At my direction, the Law Enforcement Assistance Administration (LEAA) has greatly expanded its efforts to aid in the improvement of State and local criminal justice systems. In the last three years of the previous administration, Federal grants to State and local law enforcement authorities amounted to only $22 million. In the first three years of my Administration, this same assistance totaled more than $1.5 billion—more than 67 times as much. I consider this money to be an investment in justice and safety on our streets, an investment which has been yielding encouraging dividends.

But the job has not been completed. We must now act further to improve the Federal role in the granting of aid for criminal justice. Such improvement can come with the adoption of Special Revenue Sharing for law enforcement.

I believe the transition to Special Revenue Sharing for law enforcement will be a relatively easy one. Since its inception, the LEAA has given block grants which allow State and local authorities somewhat greater discretion than does the old-fashioned categorical grant system. But States and localities still lack both the flexibility and the clear authority they need in spending Federal monies to meet their law enforcement challenges.

Under my proposed legislation, block grants, technical assistance grants, manpower development grants, and aid for correctional institutions would be combined into one $680 million Special Revenue Sharing fund which would be distributed to States and local governments on a formula basis. This money could be used for improving any area of State and local criminal justice systems....

The Criminal Code Reform Act

The Federal criminal laws of the United States date back to 1790 and are based on statutes then pertinent to effective law enforcement. With the passage of new criminal laws, with the unfolding of new court decisions interpreting those laws, and with the development and growth of our Nation, many of the concepts still reflected in our criminal laws have become inadequate, clumsy, or outmoded.

In 1966, the Congress established the National Commission on Reform of the Federal Criminal Laws to analyze and evaluate the criminal Code. The Commission's final report of January 7, 1971, has been studied and further refined by the Departments of Justice, working with the Congress. In some areas, this Administration has substantial disagreements with the Commission's recommendations. But we agree fully with the almost universal recognition that modification of the Code is not merely desirable but absolutely imperative.

Accordingly, I will soon submit to the Congress the Criminal Code Reform Act aimed at a comprehensive revision of existing Federal criminal laws. This act will provide a rational, integrated code of Federal criminal law that is workable and responsive to the demands of a modern Nation....

The most significant feature of this chapter [Part One of the Code] is a codification of the "insanity" defense. At present the test is determined by the courts and varies across the country. The standard has become so vague in some instances that it has led to unconscionable abuse by defendants.

My proposed new formulation would provide an insanity defense only if the defendant did not know what he was doing. Under this formulation, which has considerable support in psychiatric and legal circles, the only question considered germane in a murder case, for example, would be whether the defendant knew that he was pulling the trigger of a gun. Questions such as the existence of a mental disease or defect and whether the defendant requires treatment or deserves imprisonment would be reserved for consideration at the time of sentencing....

The reforms set forth in Parts One and Two of the Code would be of little practical consequence without a more realistic approach to those problems which arise in the post-conviction phase of dealing with Federal offenses.

For example, the penalty structure prescribed in the present criminal Code is riddled with inconsistencies and inadequacies.... Part Three of the new Code classifies offenses into 8 categories for purposes of assessing and levying imprisonment and fines.... To reduce the possibility of unwarranted disparities in sentencing, the Code establishes criteria for the imposition of sentence. At the same time, it provides for parole supervision after all prison sentences, so that even hardened criminals who serve their full prison terms will receive supervision following their release.

There are certain crimes reflecting such a degree of hostility to society that a decent regard for the common welfare requires that a defendant convicted of those crimes be removed from free society. For this reason my proposed new Code provides mandatory minimum prison terms for trafficking in hard narcotics; it provides mandatory minimum prison terms for persons using dangerous weapons in the execution of a crime; and it provides mandatory minimum prison sentences for those convicted as leaders of organized crime.

The magnitude of the proposed revision of the Federal Criminal Code will require careful detailed consideration by the Congress. I have no doubt this will be time-consuming. There are, however, two provisions in the Code which I feel require immediate enactment. I have thus directed that provisions relating to the death penalty and to heroin trafficking also be transmitted as separate bills in order that the Congress may act more rapidly on these two measures.

Death Penalty

The sharp reduction in the application of the death penalty was a component of the more permissive attitude toward crime in the last decade.

I do not contend that the death penalty is a panacea that will cure crime. Crime is the product of a variety of different circumstances— sometimes social, sometimes psychological—but it is committed by human beings, and at the point of commission it is the product of that individual's motivation. If the incentive not to commit crime is stronger than the incentive *to* commit it, then logic suggests that crime will be reduced. It is in part the entirely justified feeling of the prospective criminal that he will not suffer for his deed which, in the present circumstances, helps allow those deeds to take place.

Federal crimes are rarely "crimes of passion." Airplane hi-jacking is not done in a blind rage; it has to be carefully planned. The use of incendiary devices and bombs is not a crime of passion, nor is kidnapping; all these must be thought out in advance. At present those who plan these crimes do not have to include in their deliberations the possibility that they will be put to death for their deeds. I believe that in making their plans, they should have to consider the fact that if a death results from their crime, they too may die.

Under those conditions, I am confident that the death penalty can be a valuable deterrent. By making the death penalty available, we will provide Federal enforcement authorities with additional leverage to dissuade those individuals who may commit a Federal crime from taking the lives of others in the course of committing that crime.

Hard experience has taught us that with due regard for the rights of all—including the right to life itself—we must return to a greater concern with protecting those who might otherwise be the innocent victims of violent crime than with protecting those who have committed those crimes. The society which fails to recognize this as a reasonable ordering of its priorities must inevitably find itself, in time, at the mercy of criminals.

America was heading in that direction in the last decade, and I believe that we must not risk returning to it again. Accordingly, I am proposing the re-institution of the death penalty for war-related treason, sabotage, and espionage, and for all specifically enumerated crimes under Federal jurisdiction from which death results.

The Department of Justice has examined the constitutionality of the death penalty in the light of the Supreme Court's recent decision in *Furman v. Georgia.* It is the Department's opinion that *Furman* holds unconstitutional the imposition of the death penalty only insofar as it is applied arbitrarily and capriciously. I believe the best way to accommodate the reservations of the Court is to authorize the automatic imposition of the death penalty where it is warranted.

Under the proposal drafted by the Department of Justice, a hearing would be required after the trial for the purpose of determining the existence or nonexistence of certain rational standards which delineate aggravating factors or mitigating factors.

Among those mitigating factors which would preclude the imposition of a death sentence are the youth of the defendant, his or her mental capacity, or the fact that the crime was committed under duress. Aggravating factors include the creation of a grave risk of danger to the national security, or to the life of another person, or the killing of another person during the commission of one of a circumscribed list of serious offenses, such as treason, kidnapping, or aircraft piracy.

The hearing would be held before the judge who presided at the trial and before either the same jury or, if circumstances require, a jury specially impaneled. Imposition of the death penalty by the judge would be mandatory if the jury returns a special verdict finding the existence of one or more aggravating factors and the absence of any mitigating factor. The death sentence is *prohibited* if the jury finds the existence of one or more mitigating factors.

Current statutes containing the death penalty would be amended to eliminate the requirement for jury recommendation, thus limiting the imposition of the death penalty to cases in which the legislative guidelines for its imposition clearly require it, and eliminating arbitrary and capricious application of the death penalty which the Supreme Court has condemned in the *Furman* case.

Drug Abuse

No single law enforcement problem has occupied more time, effort and money in the past four years than that of drug abuse and drug addiction. We have regarded drugs as "public enemy number one," destroying the most precious resource we have—our young people—and breeding lawlessness, violence and death.

When this Administration assumed office in 1969, only $82 million was budgeted by the Federal Government for law enforcement, prevention, and rehabilitation in the field of drug abuse.

Today that figure has been increased to $785 million for 1974—nearly 10 times as much. Narcotics production has been disrupted, more traffickers and distributors have been put out of business, and addicts and abusers have been treated and started on the road to rehabilitation....

In January of 1972, a new agency, the Office of Drug Abuse Law Enforcement (DALE), was created within the Department of Justice. Task forces composed of investigators, attorneys, and special prosecuting attorneys have been assigned to more than forty cities with heroin problems. DALE now arrests pushers at the rate of 550 a month and has obtained 750 convictions.

At my direction, the Internal Revenue Service (IRS) established a special unit to make intensive tax investigations of suspected domestic traffickers. To date, IRS has collected $18 million in currency and property, assessed tax penalties of more than $100 million, and obtained 25 convictions. This effort can be particularly effective in reaching the high level traffickers and financiers who never actually touch the heroin, but who profit from the misery of those who do.

The problem of drug abuse in America is not a law enforcement problem alone. Under my Administration, the Federal Government has pursued a balanced, comprehensive approach to ending this problem. Increased law enforcement efforts have been coupled with expanded treatment programs.

The Special Action Office for Drug Abuse Prevention was created to aid in preventing drug abuse before it begins and in rehabilitating those who have fallen victim to it.... The Special Action Office for Drug Abuse Prevention is currently developing a special program of Treatment Alternatives to Street Crime (TASC) to break the vicious cycle of addiction, crime, arrest, bail, and more crime. Under the TASC program, arrestees who are scientifically identified as heroin-dependent may be assigned by judges to treatment programs as a condition for release on bail, or as a possible alternative to prosecution....

Nationwide, in the last two years, the rate of new addiction to heroin registered its first decline since 1964. This is a particularly important trend because it is estimated that one addict "infects" six of his peers.

The trend in narcotic-related deaths is also clearly on its way down. My advisers report to me that virtually complete statistics show such fatalities declined approximately 6 percent in 1972 compared to 1971.

In spite of these accomplishments, however, it is still estimated that one-third to one-half of all individuals arrested for street crimes continue to be narcotics abusers and addicts. What this suggests is that in the area of enforcement we are still only holding our own, and we must increase the tools available to do the job.

The work of the Special Action Office for Drug Abuse Prevention has aided in smoothing the large expansion of Federal effort in the area of drug treatment and prevention. Now we must move to improve Federal action in the area of law enforcement....

One area where I am convinced of the need for immediate action is that of jailing heroin pushers. Under the Bail Reform Act of 1966, a Federal judge is precluded from considering the danger to the community when setting bail for suspects arrested for selling heroin. The effect of this restriction is that many accused pushers are immediately released on bail and are thus given the opportunity to go out and create more misery, generate more violence, and commit more crimes while they are waiting to be tried for these same activities....

Sentencing practices have also been found to be inadequate in many cases. In a study of 955 narcotics drug violators who were arrested by the Bureau of Narcotics and Dangerous Drugs and convicted in the courts, a total of 27 percent received sentences other than imprisonment. Most of these individuals were placed on probation.

This situation is intolerable. I am therefore calling upon the Congress to promptly enact a new Heroin Trafficking Act.

The first part of my proposed legislation would increase the sentences for *heroin* and *morphine* offenses.

For a first offense of *trafficking* in less than four ounces of a mixture or substance containing heroin or morphine, it provides a mandatory sentence of not less than five years nor more than fifteen years. For a first offense of trafficking in four or more ounces, it provides a mandatory sentence of not less than ten years or for life.

For those with a prior felony narcotic conviction who are convicted of trafficking in less than four ounces, my proposed legislation provides a mandatory prison term of ten years to life imprisonment. For second offenders who are convicted of trafficking in *more* than four ounces, I am proposing a mandatory sentence of life imprisonment without parole.

While four ounces of a heroin mixture may seem a very small amount to use as the criterion for major penalties, that amount is actually worth 12-15,000 dollars and would supply about 180 addicts for a day. Anyone selling four or more ounces cannot be considered a small time operator.

For those who are convicted of *possessing* large amounts of heroin but cannot be convicted of trafficking, I am proposing a series of lesser penalties.

To be sure that judges actually apply these tough sentences, my legislation would provide that the mandatory minimum sentences cannot be suspended, nor probation granted.

The second portion of my proposed legislation would deny pre-trial release to those charged with trafficking in heroin or morphine unless the judicial officer finds that release will not pose a danger to the persons or property of others. It would also prohibit the release of anyone convicted of one of the above felonies who is awaiting sentencing or the results of an appeal.

These are very harsh measures, to be applied within very rigid guidelines and providing only a minimum of sentencing discretion to judges. But circumstances warrant such provisions. All the evidence shows that we are now doing a more effective job in the areas of enforcement and rehabilitation. In spite of this progress, however, we find an intolerably high level of street crime being committed by addicts. Part of the reason, I believe, lies in the court system which takes over after drug pushers have been apprehended. The courts are frequently little more than an escape hatch for those who are responsible for the menace of drugs.

Sometimes it seems that as fast as we bail water out of the boat through law enforcement and rehabilitation, it runs right back in through the holes in our judicial system. I intend to plug those holes. Until then, all the money we spend, all the enforcement we provide, and all the rehabilitation services we offer are not going to solve the drug problem in America.

Finally, I want to emphasize my continued opposition to legalizing the possession, sale or use of marijuana. There is no question about whether marijuana is dangerous, the only question is how dangerous. While the matter is still in dispute, the only responsible governmental approach is to prevent marijuana from being legalized. I intend, as I have said before, to do just that....

"Saturday Night Specials"

In the coming months, I will propose legislation aimed at curbing the manufacture and sale of cheap handguns commonly known as "Saturday night specials." I will propose reforms of the Federal criminal system to provide speedier and more rational criminal trial procedures, and I will continue to press for innovation and improvement in our correctional systems.... This is sound, responsible legislation. I am confident that the approval of the American people for measures of the sort that I have suggested will be reflected in the actions of the Congress.

RICHARD NIXON

The White House,
March 14, 1973.

12-NATION VIETNAM CONFERENCE

March 2, 1973

Stalling by North Vietnam at the end of February on the release of American prisoners of war evoked an angry response from the White House. It also threatened to disrupt the 12-nation International Conference on Vietnam that had convened in Paris on Feb. 26. The conference had hardly got under way when Secretary of State William P. Rogers was ordered by President Nixon to stay away from the proceedings until the POW question had been resolved. After high-level meetings in Paris and Saigon, the Communists on March 1 promised to proceed with release of the prisoners. The Pentagon announced simultaneously that U.S. troop withdrawals from South Vietnam and minesweeping operations in the North, suspended because of the POW foul-up, would go forward again. Sessions of the Paris conference were thereupon resumed.

Foreign ministers of the 12 nations represented at the conference signed an agreement on March 2 affirming the terms of the Vietnam cease-fire accord concluded a month earlier in the same room of the Hotel Majestic. The Act of Paris, as the 12-nation document was called, was regarded as an instrument for bringing pressure on the opposing sides in Vietnam to live up to the provisions of the cease-fire agreement of Jan. 27. That agreement had called for the convening of an international conference on Vietnam within 30 days "to acknowledge the signed agreements; to guarantee the ending of the war, the maintenance of peace in Vietnam, the respect of the Vietnamese people's fundamental national rights, and the South Vietnamese people's right to self-determination; and to contribute to and guarantee peace in Indochina. " (See p. 115.)

The underlying purpose was believed to be to put China and the Soviet Union, the principal suppliers of war materials to North Vietnam, on record in support of the cease-fire agreement. Although the Act set up no special machinery for dealing with breaches of the cease-fire, it noted that the parties to the cease-fire agreement could, individually or jointly, keep signatories of the Act informed about implementation of the cease-fire. Likewise, the parties to the cease-fire were made responsible for forwarding to other signatories of the Act of Paris reports made by the International Commission of Control and Supervision (ICCS)—the body composed of Canada, Indonesia, Hungary and Poland, which had been created to monitor observance of the cease-fire.

The Act of Paris made provision for consultation among its signatories on remedial measures that might be taken in event of violations of the cease-fire threatening the peace or territorial integrity of Vietnam or the right of the South Vietnamese people to self-determination. The Act provided also for reconvening of the international conference upon a joint request of the United States and North Vietnam or a request by any six or more parties to the Act. Although cease-fire violations by North Vietnam and by South Vietnam continued to be reported in large numbers, no move was made to reconvene the conference. On April 16, Hanoi in a note to the signatories of the Act of Paris accused South Vietnam, "with the backing of the United States," of carrying out "tens of thousands of operations" in violation of the cease-fire, whereas it pictured North Vietnam and the Vietcong as having "strictly respected and scrupulously implemented" the cease-fire. The United States, in a note of reply directed to the conference nations a week later, rejected Hanoi's accusations as "utterly groundless" and proceeded to detail a long list of alleged violations on the part of the Vietnamese Communists.

Five days before the American note was made public on April 24, the United States had reinforced previous warnings to Hanoi by suspending minesweeping operations in North Vietnamese waters and by recalling its chief negotiator from talks in Paris on reconstruction aid to North Vietnam. Secretary Rogers declared on April 19 that "We're going to use every possible method, every diplomatic device possible," to bring about adherence to the cease-fire accord. That was the purpose of a new meeting between Henry A. Kissinger and Le Duc Tho, arranged after some delay to take place in Paris in mid-May.

Text of the Act of the International Conference on Vietnam, signed at Paris on March 2, 1973:

ACT

Of The International Conference on Viet-Nam

The Government of the United States of America;

The Government of the French Republic;

The Provisional Revolutionary Government of the Republic of South Viet-Nam;

The Government of the Hungarian People's Republic;

The Government of the Republic of Indonesia;

The Government of the Polish People's Republic;

The Government of the Democratic Republic of Viet-Nam;

The Government of the United Kingdom of Great Britain and Northern Ireland;

The Government of the Republic of Viet-Nam;

The Government of the Union of Soviet Socialist Republics;

The Government of Canada; and

The Government of the People's Republic of China;

In the presence of the Secretary-General of the United Nations;

With a view to acknowledging the signed Agreements; guaranteeing the ending of the war, the maintenance of peace in Viet-Nam, the respect of the Vietnamese people's fundamental national rights, and the South Vietnamese people's right to self-determination; and contributing to and guaranteeing peace in Indochina;

Have agreed on the following provisions, and undertake to respect and implement them;

Article 1

The Parties to this Act solemnly acknowledge, express their approval of, and support the Paris Agreement on Ending the War and Restoring Peace in Viet-Nam signed in Paris on January 27, 1973, and the four Protocols to the Agreement signed on the same date (hereinafter referred to respectively as the Agreement and the Protocols).

Article 2

The Agreement responds to the aspirations and fundamental national rights of the Vietnamese people, *i.e.*, the independence, sovereignty, unity, and territorial integrity of Viet-Nam, to the right of the South Vietnamese people to self-determination, and to the earnest desire for peace shared by all countries in the world. The Agreement constitutes

333

a major contribution to peace, self-determination, national independence, and the improvement of relations among countries. The Agreement and the Protocols should be strictly respected and scrupulously implemented.

Article 3

The Parties to this Act solemnly acknowledge the commitments by the parties to the Agreement and the Protocols to strictly respect and scrupulously implement the Agreement and the Protocols.

Article 4

The Parties to this Act solemnly recognize and strictly respect the fundamental national rights of the Vietnamese people, *i.e.,* the independence, sovereignty, unity, and territorial integrity of Viet-Nam, as well as the right of the South Vietnamese people to self-determination. The Parties to this Act shall strictly respect the Agreement and the Protocols by refraining from any action at variance with their provisions.

Article 5

For the sake of a durable peace in Viet-Nam, the Parties to this Act call on all countries to strictly respect the fundamental national rights of the Vietnamese people, *i.e.,* the independence, sovereignty, unity, and territorial integrity of Viet-Nam and the right of the South Vietnamese people to self-determination and to strictly respect the Agreement and the Protocols by refraining from any action at variance with their provisions.

Article 6

(a) The four parties to the Agreement or the two South Vietnamese parties may, either individually or through joint action, inform the other Parties to this Act about the implementation of the Agreement and the Protocols. Since the reports and views submitted by the International Commission of Control and Supervision concerning the control and supervision of the implementation of those provisions of the Agreement and the Protocols which are within the tasks of the Commission will be sent to either the four parties signatory to the Agreement or to the two South Vietnamese parties, those parties shall be responsible, either individually or through joint action, for forwarding them promptly to the other Parties to this Act.

(b) The four parties to the Agreement or the two South Vietnamese parties shall also, either individually or through joint action, forward this information and these reports and views to the other participant in the International Conference on Viet-Nam for his information.

Article 7

(a) In the event of a violation of the Agreement or the Protocols which threatens the peace, the independence, sovereignty, unity, or territorial integrity of Viet-Nam, or the right of the South Vietnamese people to self-determination, the parties signatory to the Agreement and the Protocols shall, either individually or jointly, consult with the other Parties to this Act with a view to determining necessary remedial measures.

(b) The International Conference on Viet-Nam shall be reconvened upon a joint request by the Government of the United States of America and the Government of the Democratic Republic of Viet-Nam on behalf of the parties signatory to the Agreement or upon a request by six or more of the Parties to this Act.

Article 8

With a view to contributing to and guaranteeing peace in Indochina, the Parties to this Act acknowledge the commitment of the parties to the Agreement to respect the independence, sovereignty, unity, territorial integrity, and neutrality of Cambodia and Laos as stipulated in the Agreement, agree also to respect them and to refrain from any action at variance with them, and call on other countries to do the same.

Article 9

This Act shall enter into force upon signature by plenipotentiary representatives of all twelve Parties and shall be strictly implemented by all the Parties. Signature of this Act does not constitute recognition of any Party in any case in which it has not previously been accorded.

DONE in twelve copies in Paris this second day of March, One Thousand Nine Hundred and Seventy-Three, in English, French, Russian, Vietnamese, and Chinese. All texts are equally authentic.

For the Government of the United States of America
 The Secretary of State   William P. Rogers

For the Government of the French Republic
 The Minister for   Maurice Schumann
 Foreign Affairs

For the Provisional Revolutionary Government of the Republic of
South Viet-Nam
The Minister for   Nguyen Thi Binh
Foreign Affairs

For the Government of the Hungarian People's Republic
The Minister for   Janos Peter
Foreign Affairs

For the Government of the Republic of Indonesia
The Minister for   Adam Malik
Foreign Affairs

For the Government of the Polish People's Republic
The Minister for   Stefan Olszowski
Foreign Affairs

For the Government of the Democratic Republic of Viet-Nam
The Minister for   Nguyen Duy Trinh
Foreign Affairs

For the Government of the United Kingdom of Great Britain and
Northern Ireland
The Secretary of State   Alec Douglas-Home
for Foreign and
Commonwealth Affairs

For the Government of the Republic of Viet-Nam
The Minister for   Tran Van Lam
Foreign Affairs

For the Government of the Union of Soviet Socialist Republics
The Minister for   Andrei A. Gromyko
Foreign Affairs

For the Government of Canada
The Secretary of State   Mitchell Sharp
for External Affairs

For the Government of the People's Republic of China
The Minister for   Chi Peng-Fei
Foreign Affairs

▼▼▼

EXECUTIVE PRIVILEGE

March 12, 1973

President Nixon in a statement on March 12 declared that it was his privilege, under the constitutional doctrine of separation of powers, to forbid members of his staff, past as well as present, to submit to questioning by committees of the Congress. Extension of executive privilege to White House aides, he asserted, was a "practical necessity," for "in the performance of their duties for the President those staff members must not be inhibited by the possibility that their advice and assistance will ever become a matter of public debate, either during their tenure in government or at a later date." While repeating that it would be normal practice for a member or former member of his personal staff to decline a request for a formal appearance before a congressional committee, he said it would be his policy "to provide all necessary and relevant information through informal contacts between my present staff and committees of the Congress in ways which preserve intact the constitutional separation of the branches."

An explanation of his position on the controversial question of executive privilege had been promised by the President at news conferences on Jan. 31 and March 2. The statement was finally issued when questions about the FBI investigation of the Watergate bugging incident came up during Senate Judiciary Committee confirmation hearings on the appointment of L. Patrick Gray III as permanent FBI director. The committee indicated that it wanted presidential counsel John W. Dean III to appear before it to answer accusations that he had compromised the investigation of Watergate by sitting in on FBI interviews with White House aides and insisting on obtaining copies of those inter-

views. Nixon had said at his March 2 news conference that he would not let Dean testify. On March 13, a day after the formal statement on executive privilege had been issued, the Senate Judiciary Committee voted 16-0 to "invite" the presidential counselor to testify at the Gray hearings, an invitation which was promptly declined.

The President had noted in his March 12 statement that hundreds of officials of federal departments and agencies had testified at congressional hearings during his first term. But he pointed out that "requests for congressional appearances by members of the President's personal staff present a different situation and raise different considerations." Under the doctrine of the separation of powers, Nixon maintained, "the manner in which the President personally exercises his assigned executive powers is not subject to questioning by another branch of government," and "if the President is not subject to such questioning, it is equally appropriate that members of his staff not be so questioned, for their roles are in effect an extension of the Presidency." This differentiation between members of the White House staff and other government officials was explained in some detail in the guidelines which the March statement set forth for the appearance of executive branch officials before Congress.

Although the statement said that executive privilege had been invoked only three times during Nixon's first term, a Library of Congress study, requested by Rep. William S. Moorhead (D Pa.) and released March 27, indicated that the privilege had been invoked 19 times in that period—more often than in any previous administration. However, the discrepancy in numbers seemed to be a matter of semantics; White House Press Secretary Ronald L. Ziegler said, for example, that National Security Adviser Henry A. Kissinger's repeated refusals to testify on Capitol Hill were mere statements rather than formal invocations of the doctrine of executive privilege.

An increase in the exercise of executive privilege in Nixon's second term would not be surprising in view of the growing centralization of power in the White House. Three Cabinet members—Secretary of Agriculture Earl L. Butz, Secretary of Health, Education and Welfare Caspar W. Weinberger, and Secretary of Housing and Urban Development James T. Lynn—were named presidential counselors in the respective fields of natural resources, human resources, and community development. One of the guidelines on executive privilege provided that a Cabinet member or other government official who served also on the President's personal staff should "comply with any reasonable request to testify [before Congress] in his non-White House capacity"; but he would be expected to decline to testify in his White House capacity.

The Senate Judiciary Committee's quarrel with the White House was soon superseded by a threatened confrontation between the President and Sen. Sam J. Ervin (D N.C.), chairman of a select Senate com-

mittee set up to conduct a broad investigation of the Watergate affair and related incidents. Ervin was determined that White House aides appear before the committee and testify under oath. On March 18, on the CBS "Face the Nation" program, he declared that he would order the Senate sergeant at arms to arrest any White House aide who refused to testify.

Ervin's stand led to protracted negotiations with the White House, and on April 17 President Nixon announced that "an agreement has been reached which is satisfactory to both sides." "All members of the White House staff," he said, "will appear voluntarily when requested by the committee. They will testify under oath and they will answer fully all proper questions." But the President added that "executive privilege is expressly reserved and may be asserted during the course of the questioning as to any questions."

Nixon's announcement was to some extent a dramatic reversal of his March 12 statement. However, the announcement contained the following caveat: "This arrangement is one that covers this hearing only, in which wrongdoing has been charged. This kind of arrangement, of course, would not apply to other hearings. Each of them will be considered on its merits." It remained to be seen whether in the long run the new arrangement would have set a precedent or would remain an exception.

Text of President Nixon's statement of March 12, 1973, on executive privilege and of a related memorandum of March 24, 1969:

Executive Privilege

Statement by the President, March 12, 1973

During my press conference of January 31, 1973, I stated that I would issue a statement outlining my views on executive privilege.

The doctrine of executive privilege is well established. It was first invoked by President Washington, and it has been recognized and utilized by our Presidents for almost 200 years since that time. The doctrine is rooted in the Constitution, which vests "the Executive Power" solely in the President, and it is designed to protect communications within the executive branch in a variety of circumstances in time of both war and peace. Without such protection, our military security, our relations with other countries, our law enforcement procedures, and many other aspects of the national interest could be significantly damaged and the decision making process of the executive branch could be impaired.

The general policy of this Administration regarding the use of executive privilege during the next 4 years will be the same as the one we have followed during the past 4 years and which I outlined in my press conference: Executive privilege will not be used as a shield to prevent embarrassing information from being made available but will be exercised only in those particular instances in which disclosure would harm the public interest.

I first enunciated this policy in a memorandum of March 24, 1969, which I sent to Cabinet officers and heads of agencies. The memorandum read in part:

"The policy of this Administration is to comply to the fullest extent possible with Congressional requests for information. While the Executive branch has the responsibility of withholding certain information the disclosure of which would be incompatible with the public interest, this Administration will invoke this authority only in the most compelling circumstances and after a rigorous inquiry into the actual need for its exercise. For those reasons Executive privilege will not be used without specific Presidential approval."

In recent weeks, questions have been raised about the availability of officials in the executive branch to present testimony before committees of the Congress. As my 1969 memorandum dealt primarily with guidelines for providing information to the Congress and did not focus specifically on appearances of officers of the executive branch and members of the President's personal staff, it would be useful to outline my policies concerning the latter question.

During the first 4 years of my Presidency, hundreds of administration officials spent thousands of hours freely testifying before committees of the Congress. Secretary of Defense Laird, for instance, made 86 separate appearances before Congressional committees, engaging in over 327 hours of testimony. By contrast, there were only three occasions during the first term of my Administration when executive privilege was invoked anywhere in the executive branch in response to a Congressional request for information. These facts speak not of a closed Administration but of one that is pledged to openness and is proud to stand on its record.

Requests for Congressional appearances by members of the President's personal staff present a different situation and raise different considerations. Such requests have been relatively infrequent through the years, and in past administrations they have been routinely declined. I have followed that same tradition in my Administration, and I intend to continue it during the remainder of my term.

Under the doctrine of separation of powers, the manner in which the President personally exercises his assigned executive powers is not subject to questioning by another branch of Government. If the President is not subject to such questioning, it is equally appropriate that members of his staff not be so questioned, for their roles are in effect an extension of the Presidency.

This tradition rests on more than Constitutional doctrine: It is also a practical necessity. To insure the effective discharge of the executive responsibility, a President must be able to place absolute confidence in the advice and assistance offered by the members of his staff. And in the performance of their duties for the President, those staff members must not be inhibited by the possibility that their advice and assistance will ever become a matter of public debate, either during their tenure in Government or at a later date. Otherwise, the candor with which advice is rendered and the quality of such assistance will inevitably be compromised and weakened. What is at stake, therefore, is not simply a question of confidentiality but the integrity of the decisionmaking process at the very highest levels of our Government.

The considerations I have just outlined have been and must be recognized in other fields, in and out of government. A law clerk, for instance, is not subject to interrogation about the factors or discussions that preceded a decision of the judge.

For these reasons, just as I shall not invoke executive privilege lightly, I shall also look to the Congress to continue this proper tradition in asking for executive branch testimony only from the officers properly constituted to provide the information sought, and only when the eliciting of such testimony will serve a genuine legislative purpose.

As I stated in my press conference on January 31, the question of whether circumstances warrant the exercise of executive privilege should be determined on a case-by-case basis. In making such decisions, I shall rely on the following guidelines:

1. In the case of a department or agency, every official shall comply with a reasonable request for an appearance before the Congress, provided that the performance of the duties of his office will not be seriously impaired thereby. If the official believes that a Congressional request for a particular document or for testimony on a particular point raises a substantial question as to the need for invoking executive privilege, he shall comply with the procedures set forth in my memorandum of March 24, 1969. Thus, executive privilege will not be invoked until the compelling need for its exercise has been clearly demonstrated and the request has been approved first by the Attorney General and then by the President.

2. A Cabinet officer or any other Government official who also holds a position as a member of the President's personal staff shall comply with any reasonable request to testify in his non-White House capacity, provided that the performance of his duties will not be seriously impaired thereby. If the official believes that the request raises a substantial question as to the need for invoking executive privilege, he shall comply with the procedures set forth in my memorandum of March 24, 1969.

3. A member or former member of the President's personal staff normally shall follow the well-established precedent and decline a request for a formal appearance before a committee of the Congress.

At the same time, it will continue to be my policy to provide all necessary and relevant information through informal contacts between my present staff and committees of the Congress in ways which preserve intact the Constitutional separation of the branches.

MEMORANDUM OF March 24, 1969, FOR THE HEADS OF EXECUTIVE DEPARTMENTS AND AGENCIES

SUBJECT: ESTABLISHING A PROCEDURE TO GOVERN COMPLIANCE WITH CONGRESSIONAL DEMANDS FOR INFORMATION

The policy of this Administration is to comply to the fullest extent possible with Congressional requests for information. While the Executive branch has the responsibility of withholding certain information the disclosure of which would be incompatible with the public interest, this Administration will invoke this authority only in the most compelling circumstances and after a rigorous inquiry into the actual need for its exercise. For those reasons Executive privilege will not be used without specific Presidential approval. The following procedural steps will govern the invocation of Executive privilege:

1. If the head of an Executive department or agency (hereafter referred to as "department head") believes that compliance with a request for information from a Congressional agency addressed to his department or agency raises a substantial question as to the need for invoking Executive privilege, he should consult the Attorney General through the Office of Legal Counsel of the Department of Justice.

2. If the department head and the Attorney General agree, in accordance with the policy set forth above, that Executive privilege shall not be invoked in the circumstances, the information shall be released to the inquiring Congressional agency.

3. If the department head and the Attorney General agree that the circumstances justify the invocation of Executive privilege, or if either of them believes that the issue should be submitted to the President, the matter shall be transmitted to the Counsel to the President, who will advise the department head of the President's decision.

4. In the event of a Presidential decision to invoke Executive privilege, the department head should advise the Congressional agency that the claim of Executive privilege is being made with the specific approval of the President.

5. Pending a final determination of the matter, the department head should request the Congressional agency to hold its demand for the information in abeyance until such determination can be made. Care shall be taken to indicate that the purpose of this request is to protect the privilege pending the determination, and that the request does not constitute a claim of privilege.

RICHARD NIXON

INTERNATIONAL MONETARY CRISES AND DOLLAR DEVALUATION

March 16, 1973

A series of international monetary crises early in 1973 jolted the financial world, forced the United States to devalue the dollar, sent the price of gold skyrocketing in European markets, and culminated in a 14-nation agreement which it was hoped would bring the situation under control. The monetary accord, signed in Paris March 16 at the conclusion of a meeting attended by officials of the United States, Canada, the nine European Economic Community (Common Market) countries, Sweden, Switzerland and Japan, was designed to assure the reopening of official currency dealings March 19 under "orderly conditions." Representatives of the 14 nations agreed to measures aimed at easing problems created by an excess of dollars abroad. For the United States, the agreement meant imposing more controls on short-term capital flows, initiating more action to bring dollars back to the United States, and possibly government intervention in support of currency exchange rates.

It was thought that the most important clause of the accord was a stipulation that "Each nation...will be prepared to intervene at its initiative in its own market, when necessary and desirable, acting in a flexible manner" to support the value of its currency and to establish greater international monetary stability. The statement bore out an earlier indication that the United States, if necessary, would depart from its long-held policy of refusing to buy and sell other currencies to support the dollar. The "hands-off" American approach had flourished in what was termed the "period of benign neglect." But European buying and selling of currencies, while having the effect of supporting

*the dollar, had fostered inflationary conditions in Europe and threat-
ened to cause a full-scale monetary and trade war with the United
States. The Paris agreement, although not binding, indicated a desire
on Washington's part to call a truce and work toward reconstructing
the monetary situation in a spirit of cooperation.*

*Treasury Secretary George P. Shultz, representing the United States
at the Paris meeting, left open the American options. The major target
of the monetary officials would be bankers, Arab sheiks, multinational
corporations and others trying to manipulate the currency exchanges
for their own ends. The 14-nation agreement was in part an indication
that the governments would try to convince these groups that they
could not force the markets up and down at will. But French Finance
Minister Valery Giscard d'Estaing let it be known that the tactics employed by the various governments would not be publicized or even
hinted at, because, he said, "We would be organizing the speculation
we are trying to avoid."*

Factors Underlying Dollar Devaluation

*International monetary difficulties had been touched off in Janu-
ary when Italy, bothered by a weakening lira, had established a two-
tier lira exchange. This action sent dollars streaming out of Italy into
Switzerland where Swiss authorities were prompted to float their
franc, a move which redirected the dollar flow into West Germany. It
became known at about that time that West Germany had shown a $6-
billion trade surplus in 1972 while the United States had registered a
record trade deficit of $6.5-billion. Ensuing frantic dealings flooded
Europe and Japan with $6-billion in unwanted dollars. After some
hectic international consultations, the United States announced that it
was devaluing the dollar against nearly all major world currencies.*

*Secretary Shultz made the announcement Feb. 12 at a late evening
news conference in Washington. The action was the second such move
in 14 months. Reduction of the par value of the dollar by 11 per cent
was effected by raising the official price of gold to $42.22 an ounce
from the $38 an ounce price set in December 1971 by the Smithsonian
Agreement. That agreement had effected a general currency exchange
rate realignment, including devaluation of the dollar by 8.57 per cent
(price change rate realignment, raised from $35 to $38 an ounce).*

*The February 1973 devaluation ended, for the time being, the wave
of currency speculation which had created pressure to change the exchange rates put into effect by the Smithsonian Agreement. The immediate cause of the February crisis had been the speculative selling
of dollars for West German marks and Japanese yen by individuals,
bankers, Middle Eastern nations and large corporations in expectation*

of an upward revaluation of those currencies against the dollar. The underlying cause was the overvaluation of the dollar, meaning that the dollar's par value as set by the Smithsonian Agreement was greater than its actual worth in relation to the strength of the U.S. economy as judged in international markets. Conversely, the mark and the yen were undervalued. At the root of the lack of confidence in the dollar's strength were continuing deficits in the U.S. trade balance and in the country's overall balance of international payments. Although the Smithsonian Agreement of December 1971 had been expected to improve the U.S. balance, the trade deficit continued to rise in 1972. Another factor—although disputed by the Nixon administration —was doubt overseas about the effectiveness of the Phase III voluntary wage and price controls (announced early in January 1973) as a curb on U.S. inflation.

New Monetary Crisis

Despite the devaluation on Feb. 12, confidence in the dollar weakened considerably and the price of gold in open European markets soared momentarily, reaching $90 an ounce on Feb. 20. The United States stood firm by its decision not to devalue again; President Nixon stressed that point at a news conference March 2. But another monetary crisis swept across Europe early in March with dollar prices continuing to plummet. Authorities ordered European and Japanese foreign exchange markets closed. On March 12, six of the nine EEC countries announced a joint float whereby their currencies were pegged with respect to one another and floated as a package. Britain, Italy and Ireland announced that they would maintain separate floats. On March 15, Sweden and Norway announced their adherence to the joint float. It was this financial turbulence that led the finance ministers of the 14 nations to proclaim the March 16 agreement.

Reaction to the pact was largely favorable, but market specialists considered the relief no more than temporary. They expected international speculators to test out soon the defenses which the 14 nations had sought to set up. That time was not long in coming. By early May, with disclosures about the Watergate scandal throwing into doubt the capacity of the U.S. government to take firm action, confidence in the dollar once again fell and the price of gold in European markets climbed to record highs.

> *Text of statement by Secretary of the Treasury George P. Shultz, Feb. 12, 1973, announcing devaluation of the dollar, followed by text of the March 16 accord:*

The United States, as do other nations, recognizes the need to reform and strengthen the framework for international trade and investment. That framework must support our basic objective of enhancing the living standards of all nations. It must encourage the peaceful competition that underlies economic progress and efficiency. It must provide scope for each nation—while sharing in the mutual benefits of trade—to respect its own institutions and its own particular needs. It must incorporate the fundamental truth that prosperity of one nation should not be sought at the expense of another.

This great task of reform is not for one country alone, nor can it be achieved in a single step. We can take satisfaction in what has been accomplished on a cooperative basis since the actions announced on August 15, 1971 [suspension of dollar convertibility] clearly signaled our recognition of the need for decisive change.

• Intense negotiations established an important fact in December 1971: mutual agreement can be reached on changes in the parity of the United States dollar, in order to promote the agreed goal of a better balance in international trade and payments.

• Monetary negotiations have been started by the "Committee of Twenty" on the premise that better ways must be found to prevent large payments imbalances which distort national economies, disturb financial markets, and threaten the free flow of trade. The United States has made practical and specific proposals for international monetary reform.

• The groundwork is being laid for comprehensive trade negotiations. Those negotiations should look beyond industrial tarrifs to encompass also other barriers to the free flow of goods. They should assure fair competitive treatment of the products of all countries. They should also seek agreed ways of avoiding abrupt dislocations of workers and businesses.

In September 1972 the President told the financial leaders of the world that "The time has come for action across the entire front of international economic problems. Recurring monetary crises, such as we have experienced all too often in the past decade; unfair currency alignments and trading arrangements, which put the workers of one nation at a disadvantage with workers of another nation; great disparities in development that breed resentment; a monetary system that makes no provision for the realities of the present and the needs of the future—all these not only injure our economies, they also create political tensions that subvert the cause of peace."

At the same meeting [International Monetary Fund. *See Historic Documents*, 1972, p. 815] I outlined the principles of a monetary system that would enable all nations, including the United States, to achieve and maintain overall balance in their international payments. Those principles would promote prompt adjustment and would provide equitable treatment for all nations—large and small, rich and poor.

Yet, in recent months we have seen disquieting signs. Our own trade has continued in serious deficit, weakening our external financial position. Other nations have been slow in eliminating their excessive surpluses, thereby contributing to uncertainty and instability. In recent days, currency disturbances have rocked world exchange markets. Under the pressure of events, some countries have responded with added restrictions, dangerously moving away from the basic objectives we seek.

Progress in the work of the Committee of Twenty has been too slow and should move with a greater sense of urgency. The time has come to give renewed impetus to our efforts in behalf of a stronger international economic order.

To that end, in consultation with our trading partners and in keeping with the basic principles of our proposals for monetary reform, we are taking a series of actions designed to achieve three interrelated purposes:

(a) to speed improvement of our trade and payments position in a manner that will support our effort to achieve constructive reform of the monetary system;

(b) to lay the legislative groundwork for broad and outward-looking trade negotiations, paralleling our efforts to strengthen the monetary system; and

(c) to assure that American workers and American businessmen are treated equitably in our trading relationships.

For these purposes:

First, the President is requesting that the Congress authorize a further realignment of exchange rates. This objective will be sought by a formal 10 per cent reduction in the par value of the dollar....

Although this action will, under the existing Articles of Agreement of the International Monetary Fund, result in a change in the official relationship of the dollar to gold, I should like to stress that this technical change has no practical significance. The market price of gold in recent years has diverged widely from the official price, and under these conditions gold has not been transferred to any significant degree among international monetary authorities. We remain strongly of the opinion that orderly arrangements must be negotiated to facilitate the continuing reduction of the role of gold in international monetary affairs.

Consultations with our leading trading partners in Europe assure me that the proposd change in the par value of the dollar is acceptable to them, and will therefore be effective immediately in exchange rates for the dollar in international markets. The dollar will decline in value by about 10 per cent in terms of those currencies for which there is an effective par value, for example the Deutsche mark and the French franc.

Japanese authorities have indicated that the yen will be permitted to float. Our firm expectation is that the yen will float into a relationship vis-a-vis other currencies consistent with achieving a balance of payments equilibrium not dependent upon significant government intervention.

These changes are intended to supplement and work in the same direction as the changes accomplished in the Smithsonian Agreement of December 1971. They take into account recent developments and are designed to speed improvement in our trade and payments position. In particular, they are designed, together with appropriate trade liberalization, to correct the major payments imbalance between Japan and the United States which has persisted in the past year.

Other countries may also propose changes in their par values or central rates to the International Monetary Fund. We will support all changes that seem warranted on the basis of current and prospective payments imbalances, but plan to vote against any changes that are inappropriate.

We have learned that time must pass before new exchange relationships modify established patterns of trade and capital flows. However, there can be no doubt we have achieved a major improvement in the competitive position of American workers and American business.

The new exchange rates being established at this time represent a reasonable estimate of the relationships which—taken together with appropriate measures for the removal of existing trade and investment restraints—will in time move international economic relationships into sustainable equilibrium. We have, however, undertaken no obligations for the U.S. Government to intervene in foreign exchange markets.

Second, the President has decided to send shortly to the Congress proposals for comprehensive trade legislation. Prior to submitting that legislation, intensive consultations will be held with Members of Congress, labor, agriculture, and business to assure that the legislation reflects our needs as fully as possible.

This legislation, among other things, should furnish the tools we need to:

(i) provide for lowering tariff and non-tariff barriers to trade, assuming our trading partners are willing to participate fully with us in that process;

(ii) provide for raising tariffs when such action would contribute to arrangements assuring that American exports have fair access to foreign markets;

(iii) provide safeguards against the disruption of particular markets and production from rapid changes in foreign trade; and

(iv) protect our external position from large and persistent deficits.

In preparing this legislation, the President is particularly concerned that, however efficient our workers and businesses, and however exchange rates might be altered, American producers be treated fairly and that they have equitable access to foreign markets. Too often, we have been shut out by a web of administrative barriers and controls. Moreover, the rules governing trading relationships have, in many instances, become obsolete and, like our international monetary rules, need extensive reform.

We cannot be faced with insuperable barriers to our exports and yet simultaneously be expected to end our deficit.

At the same time, we must recognize that in some areas the United States, too, can be cited for its barriers to trade. The best way to deal with these barriers on both sides is to remove them. We shall bargain hard to that end. I am convinced the American workers and the American consumer will be the beneficiaries.

In proposing this legislation, the President recognizes that the choice we face will not lie between greater freedom and the status quo. Our trade position must be improved. If we cannot accomplish that objective in a framework of freer and fairer trade, the pressures to retreat inward will be intense.

We must avoid that risk, for it is the road to international recrimination, isolation, and autarky.

Third, in coordination with the Secretary of Commerce, we shall phase out the Interest Equalization Tax and the controls of the Office of Foreign Direct Investment. Both controls will be terminated at the latest by December 31, 1974.

I am advised that the Federal Reserve Board will consider comparable steps for their Voluntary Foreign Credit Restraint Program.

The phasing out of these restraints is appropriate in view of the improvement which will be brought to our underlying payments position by the cumulative effect of the exchange rate changes, by continued success in curbing inflationary tendencies, and by the attractiveness of the U.S. economy for investors from abroad. The termination of the restraints on capital flows is appropriate in the light of our broad objective of reducing governmental controls on private transactions.

The measures I have announced today—the realignment of currency values, the proposed new trade legislation, and the termination of U.S. controls on capital movements—will serve to move our economy and the world economy closer to conditions of international equilibrium in a context of competitive freedom. They will accelerate the pace of successful monetary and trade reform.

They are not intended to, and cannot, substitute for effective management of our domestic economy. The discipline of budgetary and monetary restraint and effective wage-price stabilization must and will be pursued with full vigor. We have proposed a budget which will avoid a revival of inflationary pressure in the United States. We again call upon the Congress, because of our international financial requirement as well as for the sake of economic stability at home, to assist in keeping Federal expenditures within the limits of the President's budget. We are continuing a strong system of price and wage controls. Recent international economic developments reemphasize the need to administer these controls in a way that will further reduce the rate of inflation. We are determined to do that.

The cooperation of our principal trading and financial partners in developing a joint solution to the acute difficulties of the last few days has been heartening. We now call upon them to join with us in moving more rapidly to a more efficient international monetary system and to a more equitable and freer world trading system so that we can make adjustments in the future without crises and so that all of our people can enjoy the maximum benefits of exchange among us.

Text of 14-nation monetary accord signed in Paris March 16, 1973:

[1]

The ministers and central bank governors of the 10 countries participating in the general arrangements to borrow and the member countries of the European Economic Community met in Paris on March 16, 1973, under the chairmanship of Valery Giscard d'Estaing, Minister of the Economy and of Finance of France. P. P. Schweitzer, managing director of the International Monetary Fund, took part in the meeting, which was also attended by Nello Celio, head of the Federal Department of Finance of the Swiss Confederation; E. Stopper, president of the Swiss National Bank, W. Haferkamp, vice president of the Commission of the European Economic Community; E. Van Lennep, secretary general of the Organization for Economic Co-operation and Development; Rene Larre, general manager of the Bank for International Settlements, and Jeremy Morse, chairman of the deputies of the Committee of 20 of the I.M.F.

[2]

The ministers and governors heard a report by the chairman of their deputies, Rinaldo Ossola, on the results of the technical study which the deputies have carried out in accordance with the instructions given to them.

[3]

The ministers and governors took note of the decisions of the members of the E.E.C. announced on Monday. Six members of the E.E.C. and certain other European countries, including Sweden, will maintain 2 1/4 per cent margins between their currencies. The currencies of certain countries, such as Italy, the United Kingdom, Ireland, Japan and Canada, remain for the time being, floating. However, Italy, the United Kingdom and Ireland have expressed the intention of associating themselves as soon as possible with the decision to maintain E.E.C. exchange rates within margins of 2 1/4 per cent and meanwhile of remaining in consultation with their E.E.C. partners.

[4]

The ministers and governors reiterated their determination to ensure jointly an orderly exchange-rate system. To this end, they agreed on the basis for an operational approach toward the exchange markets in the near future and on certain further studies to be completed as a matter of urgency.

[5]

They agreed in principle that official intervention in exchange markets may be useful at appropriate times to facilitate the maintenance of orderly conditions, keeping in mind also the desirability of encouraging reflows of speculative movements of funds. Each nation stated that it will be prepared to intervene at its initiative in its own market, when necessary and desirable, acting in a flexible manner in the light of market conditions and in close consultation with the authorities of the nation whose currency may be bought or sold. The countries which have decided to maintain 2 1/4 per cent margins between their currencies have made known their intention of concerting among themselves the application of these provisions. Such intervention will be financed when necessary through use of mutual credit facilities. To ensure adequate resources for such operations, it is envisaged that some of the existing "swap" facilities will be enlarged.

[6]

Some countries have announced additional measures to restrain capital inflows. The United States authorities emphasized that the phasing out of their controls of longer-term capital outflows by the end of 1974 was intended to coincide with strong improvement in the United States balance-of-payments position. Any step taken during the interim period toward the elimination of these controls would take due account of exchange-market conditions and the balance-of-payments trends. The United States authorities are also reviewing actions that may be appropriate to remove inhibitions on the inflow of capital into the United States. Countries in a strong payments position will review the possibility of removing or relaxing any restrictions on capital outflows, particularly long-term.

[7]

Ministers and governors noted the importance of dampening speculative capital movements. They stated their intentions to seek more complete understanding of the sources and nature of the large capital flows which have recently taken place. With respect to Eurocurrency markets, they agreed that methods of reducing the volatility of these markets will be studied intensively, taking into account the implications for the longer-run operation of the international monetary system. These studies will address themselves, among other factors, to limitations on placement of official reserves in that market by member nations of the I.M.F. and to the possible need for reserve requirements comparable to those in national banking markets. With respect to the former, the ministers and governors confirmed that their authorities would be prepared to take the lead by implementing certain undertakings that their own placements would be gradually and prudently withdrawn. The United States will review possible action to encourage a flow of Eurocurrency funds to the United States as market conditions permit.

[8]

In the context of discussions of monetary reform, the ministers and governors agreed that proposals for funding or consolidation of official currency balances deserved thorough and urgent attention. This matter is already on the agenda of the Committee of 20 of the I.M.F.

[9]

Ministers and governors reaffirmed their attachment to the basic principles which have governed international economic relations since the last war—the greatest possible freedom for international trade and investment and the avoidance of competitive changes of exchange rates. They stated their determination to continue to use the existing organizations of international economic cooperation to maintain these principles for the benefit of all their members.

[10]

Ministers and governors expressed their unanimous conviction that international monetary stability rests, in the last analysis, on the success of national efforts to contain inflation. They are resolved to pursue fully appropriate policies to this end.

[11]

Ministers and governors are confident that, taken together, these moves will launch an internationally responsible program for dealing with the speculative pressures that have recently emerged and for maintaining orderly international monetary arrangements while the work of reform of the international monetary system is pressed ahead. They reiterated their concern that this work be expedited and brought to an early conclusion in the framework of the Committee of 20 of the I.M.F.

PLAN FOR NORTHERN IRELAND

March 20, 1973

The British government made public on March 20 long-awaited proposals whereby the Roman Catholic minority in Northern Ireland would gain a share of the political power held for 50 years exclusively by the Protestant Unionist party. Announcement of a plan for dealing with the Protestant-Catholic conflict in Ulster had been expected since March 1972, when the British suspended the government and parliament of Northern Ireland, imposed direct rule from London, and indicated that it would devise means to assure Catholics greater participation in the political affairs of that province. The new plan was the most far-reaching of British suggestions for putting an end to the persistent contention between the two opposing factions in Northern Ireland.

Bitter antagonism between the Protestant majority and the Catholic minority had led in recent years to frequent outbreaks of bombing and killing. The New York Times *reported on March 14 that the number of fatalities had mounted to 748 since the civil unrest became acute in 1969; and the death toll continued to rise. Northern Ireland's million or so Protestants always adamantly opposed union with the Republic of Ireland, where Catholics constitute more than 90 per cent of the population. The Unionist party, representing Northern Ireland's Protestants, had regularly monopolized elective offices. Catholics, numbering only some 500,000, complained of discrimination in housing and jobs, of disproportionate representation in the province's parliament and in local councils, and of rough handling by the Protestant-dominated police during demonstrations.*

Units of the British army had been called in to handle the clashes between Catholic and Protestant factions. Meanwhile, members of the outlawed Irish Republican Army (IRA) became active against the Protestants. While more fragmented and less precise in its goals than the Protestants, the Catholic leadership sought a guarantee of power sharing, an assurance of equal rights and equal protection of the law, and, eventually, the reunification of all of Ireland. Protestant leaders, on the other hand, wanted a return to rule by the majority, whereby they could again exercise full control over parliament and the police force.

The British proposals announced in March attempted to forge a compromise between these conflicting aspirations and to reshape the political structure of Northern Ireland. The proposals, embodied in a White Paper entitled "Northern Ireland Constitutional Proposals," called for replacement of the suspended parliament by a newly created 80-member assembly. The assembly would be elected under a system of proportional representation that would give Ulster's Catholics a fair voice in the affairs of the province. The chairmen of the assembly's committees, to include some Catholics, would comprise the executive body, and the chairmen would head the government departments. Defense, foreign policy, and policing decisions would remain in the hands of British officials. "The executive itself can no longer be solely based upon any single party, if that party draws its support and its elected representation virtually entirely from only one section of a divided community," the White Paper said.

Few of Northern Ireland's Protestants or Catholics initially applauded the British proposals. Moderates on both sides found some aspects of the plan worthwhile, but hard-liners took a guarded, if not hostile, position. "We knew we couldn't please everyone. But it is a reasonable deal for reasonable people," said William Whitelaw, British Secretary of State for Northern Ireland Affairs. "The unreasonable will always find reasons why it will fail. They will say that the power sharing won't work. I say it must work."

Only three days after the British government made the plan known, the militant Provisional wing of the IRA announced that it would keep on fighting. Meanwhile, indications of cautious support for the proposals among moderate Catholic groups led some to speculate that the IRA decision, if made good, might drastically reduce the influence of the Provisionals whose tactics were not acceptable to all Catholics.

Protestant groups divided over acceptance of the plan. Brian Faulkner, the Unionist party leader and former prime minister of Northern Ireland, gave cautious approval although calling for modifications. But in late April, the Grand Orange Lodge, a powerful order to which nearly all Protestant leaders belonged, rejected the proposed sharing of power with the Catholics. This action, which put the Orange order in direct opposition to the Unionist party for the first time in the province's 50-year history, was thought to strike a sharp blow to the prospects for acceptance of the proposals. They had already been denounced by several militant Protestant organizations, including the Rev. Ian Paisley's Democratic Unionist party.

An overwhelmingly favorable initial vote on the proposals in the House of Commons in March paved the way for the election of the Northern Ireland assembly on June 28. Even though the plan gave Protestants assurance that Ulster would not be swallowed up by the predominantly Catholic Republic of Ireland, and guaranteed Catholics a share of political power in the province and in the new assembly, there was concern lest some factions, holding out for further concessions, might boycott the assembly elections and make it impossible to give the plan a fair trial.

Text of the Summary and Conclusion of the British Government's report on its plan for reinstitution of self-government in Northern Ireland:

SUMMARY AND CONCLUSION

Summary of Proposals

There follows a broad summary of the detailed proposals made in this White Paper:

(i) A comprehensive constitutional Bill will be presented to Parliament with the objective of bringing new permanent arrangements for the government of Northern Ireland into effect within the second year of the direct rule provisions of the Northern Ireland (Temporary Provisions) Act (para. 30).

(ii) The Bill will declare that Northern Ireland will remain part of the United Kingdom for as long as that is the wish of a majority of its people (para. 32).

(iii) As part of the United Kingdom, Northern Ireland will maintain its existing representation of twelve Members in the United Kingdom Parliament (para. 33).

(iv) There will be a Northern Ireland Assembly of about 80 members elected on this occasion by the single transferable vote method of proportional representation applied to the twelve Westminster Constituencies (para. 39).

(v) Elections to the Assembly will be held as soon as possible (para. 40).

(vi) The Assembly will have a fixed term of four years (para. 41).

(vii) The Assembly itself will elect its presiding officer and work out its own detailed methods and procedures (paras. 42 and 43).

(viii) There will be committees of the Assembly, whose members will reflect the balance of parties, associated with each Northern Ireland Department. The Chairmen of these committees who collectively will form the Executive will be the political Heads of the Departments and the committees will be associated with the development of new law and policy (para. 44).

(ix) Between the election of the Assembly and a devolution of powers the advisory functions of the Northern Ireland Commission will be undertaken by a committee composed of members of the Assembly (para. 47).

(x) There will continue to be a Secretary of State for Northern Ireland who will be a member of the United Kingdom Cabinet. He will undertake the necessary consultation leading to the devolution of powers, administer certain services reserved to the United Kingdom Government and be responsible for United Kingdom interests in Northern Ireland (paras. 48-50).

(xi) The purpose of the Secretary of State's consultations with parties in the Assembly will be to find an acceptable basis for the devolution of powers which will meet prescribed conditions, in particular as to the formation of an Executive which can no longer be solely based upon any single party, if that party draws its support and its elected representation virtually entirely from only one section of a divided community. Members of the Executive will be required to take an appropriate official oath or make an affirmation (paras. 51-53).

(xii) The United Kingdom Parliament will continue to have the power to legislate in respect of any matter whatever in Northern Ireland (para. 54).

(xiii) The Assembly, after a devolution of powers, will be able to legislate in respect of most matters affecting Northern Ireland. There will, however, be a limited range of matters on which it may legislate only with agreement and certain others which, because of their national importance, will be excluded from its legislative competence. Where agreement is required, a measure, having been passed by the Assembly, will be laid before the United Kingdom Parliament (paras. 56 and 57).

(xiv) Measures of the Northern Ireland Assembly will have the force of law when approved by the Queen in Council (para. 57).

(xv) Since the Government has no higher priority than to defeat terrorism and end violence, Parliament will be asked to approve specific emergency legislation for the more effective combatting of terrorism, including giving effect to the recommendations of the Report of the Diplock Commission. This will make possible the repeal of the Special Powers Act and the re-enactment by the United Kingdom Parliament of those provisions which are regarded as essential (paras. 58-62).

(xvi) The constitutional Bill will debar the Assembly from passing legislation of a discriminatory nature and from legislating to require an oath or declaration as a qualification for employment, office, etc., where this is not required in comparable circumstances in the rest of the United Kingdom. An Order-in-Council will shortly be brought forward to remove existing obligations which conflict with this principle (e.g. in relation to the requirement for a statutory declaration of allegiance by local government councillors) (paras 63 and 64).

(**xvii**) The Bill will provide for the discharge of executive functions in Northern Ireland on the following broad basis:

(a) in general United Kingdom Ministers other than the Secretary of State will retain their existing responsibilities in relation to Northern Ireland (para. 66);

(b) certain matters previously the responsibility of the Northern Ireland Government will be permanently reserved to the United Kingdom Government (that is, the appointment of certain judges, magistrates, etc.; the conduct of public prosecutions; elections and the franchise; and exceptional measures in the law and order field to cope with emergency situations) (para. 67);

(c) certain other matters, notably in the "law and order" field, will be reserved to the United Kingdom Government because of the current security situation. Arrangements will, however, be made to secure the effective representation of local interests in relation to such matters, including a general advisory role for the Northern Ireland Executive itself, the addition of elected representatives to the Police Authority and the creation of links between District Councils and the police in their areas (paras. 68-70); and

(d) responsibility for all other matters will rest with the Northern Ireland Executive (para. 71).

(**xviii**) The Executive of Northern Ireland will consist of the political Heads of Northern Ireland Departments (including a central secretariat whose Head will preside over the Executive). Their formal appointment will be effected by the Secretary of State in accordance with any agreed understanding as to the formation of the Executive (paras. 72 and 73).

(**xix**) The Northern Ireland Civil Service will remain a distinct service under the Crown (para. 76).

(**xx**) The constitutional Bill will forbid executive action of a discriminatory nature by central and local government and other public bodies (para. 77).

(**xxi**) There will be no weakening whatever in Northern Ireland's links with the Crown. Where executive power is not devolved to the Northern Ireland Executive, it will be exercised either by The Queen in Council or by Her Majesty's Government. There will cease to be an office of Governor of Northern Ireland (para. 81).

(**xxii**) No further appointments will be made to the Privy Council of Northern Ireland (para. 82).

(**xxiii**) The Bill will include financial provisions of a straightforward character designed to accomplish as rapidly as possible the task of physical reconstruction, to create a sound base for the economy and to help Northern Ireland achieve those standards of living, employment and social conditions which prevail in Great Brtain (paras. 83-86).

(xxiv) The Government will discuss with the Northern Ireland institutions what arrangements can be made to provide them with a large measure of freedom to determine expenditure priorities (paras. 88 and 89).

(xxv) The Bill will include proposals to provide the individual with the safeguards and protections of a charter of human rights. The statutory safeguards against abuse of legislative and executive powers have already been described (para. 95).

(xxvi) Appropriate arrangements will be made for *ex post facto* reviews of the handling of complaints against the police, with an independent element, to conform with those which the Government is planning to introduce in Great Brtain (para. 97).

(xxvii) The Government will present to Parliament proposals to deal with job discrimination in the private sector (paras. 100-103).

(xxviii) The Bill will provide for the appointment by the Secretary of State of a Standing Advisory Commission on Human Rights (para. 104).

(xxix) In the context of the provisions constituting a charter of human rights, society is entitled to expect an acceptance by individual citizens of their obligations to the community as a whole (para. 105).

(xxx) The Government favours, and is prepared to facilitate, the establishment of institutional arrangements for consultation and co-operation between Northern Ireland and the Republic of Ireland (para. 110).

(xxxi) Progress towards setting up such institutions can best be made through discussion between the interested parties. Accordingly, following the Northern Ireland elections, the Government will invite representatives of Northern Ireland and of the Republic of Ireland to take part in a conference to discuss how best to pursue three interrelated objectives. These are the acceptance of the present status of Northern Ireland, and of the possibility—which would have to be compatible with the principle of consent—of subsequent change in that status; effective consultation and co-operation in Ireland for the benefit of North and South alike; and the provision of a firm basis for concerted governmental and community action against terrorist organisations (para. 112).

(xxxii) The United Kingdom Government must be associated with discussion of subjects touching upon its interests (para. 114).

Conclusion

117. Under the proposed settlement, Northern Ireland will continue to have a greater degree of self-government than any other part of the United Kingdom. While benefitting in full measure from all the practical advantages of the British connection—for the proposals embody political, financial and economic arrangements which are in general both flexible and generous—Northern Ireland will continue, to a very large extent, to make its own laws and administer its own services,

particularly in relation to such crucial issues as employment, housing, development of the regional infrastructure and education.

118. These proposals are designed to benefit the law-abiding majority in both communities, who may have conflicting views on the ultimate constitutional destiny of Northern Ireland, but who seek to advance those views by peaceful democratic means alone, and have strong mutual interests in making social and economic progress. The proposals provide an opportunity for all such people to stand together against those small but dangerous minorities which would seek to impose their views by violence and coercion, and which cannot, therefore, be allowed to participate in working institutions they wish to destroy.

119. To all those who support the continued union with Great Britain, the proposals offer firm assurances that this union will endure and be defended, for as long as that is the wish of a majority of the people of Northern Ireland. They seek to strengthen the democratic institutions of Northern Ireland by winning for them that wide-ranging consent upon which the government of a free country must rest. They commit the whole United Kingdom to a major effort to narrow the gap in standards of living, employment and social conditions between Northern Ireland and Great Britain.

120. To all those who seek the unification of Ireland by consent, but are genuinely prepared to work for the welfare of Northern Ireland, the proposals offer the opportunity to play no less a part in the life and public affairs of Northern Ireland than is open to their fellow citizens.

121. To all, whatever their religion or their political beliefs, the proposals extend effective protection against any arbitrary or discriminatory use of power.

122. These, then, are the Government's proposals to Parliament, to the country, and above all to the people of Northern Ireland themselves, for a way forward out of the present violence and instability. At every point, they require the co-operation of those people themselves if they are to have any prospect of success. They can be frustrated if interests in Northern Ireland refuse to allow them to be tried or if any section of the community is determined to impose its will on another. It should now be perfectly clear that these are prescriptions for disaster. The Government believes, however, that the majority of the people of Northern Ireland have an overwhelming desire for peace and that they will accept the opportunity which these proposals offer.

COURT ON PUBLIC SCHOOL FINANCING
March 21, 1973

The Supreme Court ruled in effect, March 21, that education is not a fundamental right protected by the Constitution. Its 5-4 decision reversed the determination of a lower court that the Texas system of financing public schools amounted to "discrimination on the basis of wealth" in violation of the equal protection clause of the Fourteenth Amendment. By reversing the lower tribunal the Supreme Court let stand a financing system which, it conceded, resulted in wide disparities in per-pupil funding "largely attributable to differences in the amounts of money collected through local property taxation." The Court noted that the Texas system nevertheless provided "at least a minimum foundation education" for each pupil through $1-billion in funds from general state revenues distributed to the counties in proportion to property valuations. State funds were supplemented by local property tax revenues. (See Historic Documents, 1972, p. 221.)

The case had been brought by 15 Mexican-American families residing in a poor school district of San Antonio where a relatively high property tax rate had raised total per-pupil expenditures in 1967-68 to only $356. In Alamo Heights, the wealthiest district in the metropolitan area, per-pupil expenditures the same year were $594 although the tax rate there was lower.

Justice Lewis F. Powell Jr., delivering the opinion of the Court, said that the Justices comprising the majority were "unable to agree" that there was "a fundamental right to education," but he asserted that "nothing this Court holds today in any way detracts from our historic dedication to public education." He contended that the "importance of a service performed by the state does not determine whether it must be regarded as fundamental..." It is not within the province of this Court, he said, "to create substantive constitutional rights in the name of guaranteeing equal protection of the laws." The lawyers for the Mexican-American families, basing their case on the equal protection clause of the Fourteenth Amendment, had contended that the First Amendment rights of free speech and assembly were impaired for persons disadvantaged by lack of adequate educational opportunities.

To this the Court countered: "We have never presumed to possess either the ability or the authority to guarantee to the citizenry the most effective speech or the most informed electoral choice.... These may be desirable goals...but they are not values to be implemented by judicial intrusion into otherwise legitimate state activities." The decision called the complaint of the Mexican-American families an "inappropriate case in which to subject state action to strict judicial scrutiny." Powell concluded that the Justices "lack both the expertise and the familiarity with local problems so necessary to the making of wise decisions with respect to the raising and disposition of public revenues. Yet we are urged to direct the states either to alter drastically the present system or to throw out the property tax altogether in favor of some other form of taxation."

Justice Thurgood Marshall, in a dissenting opinion in which Justice William O. Douglas concurred, said "the majority's holding can only be seen as a retreat from our historic commitment to equality of educational opportunity and as unsupportable acquiescence in a system which deprives children in their earliest years of the chance to reach their full potentials as citizens." Marshall observed that education was "far too vital to permit state discrimination on grounds as tenuous as those presented by this record." Nor was it acceptable, he added "to remit these appellees to the vagaries of the political system which, contrary to the majority's suggestion, has proved singularly unsuited to the task of providing a remedy for this discrimination."

Reminding the Court of a previous decision which acknowledged that "inequality in the educational facilities provided to students may make for discriminatory state action as comtemplated by the equal protection clause," Marshall asserted that that clause "is not addressed to the minimal sufficiency but rather to the unjustifiable inequalities of state action. It mandates nothing less than that persons similarly circumstanced shall be treated alike." He compared discrimination on the basis of group wealth to classifications based on race or alienage, over which, he said, "the disadvantaged individual *has no significant control." The Justice pointed out that the poorer districts in Texas cannot opt to have the best education in the state by imposing the highest tax rate. Rather the quality of education is largely determined by the amount of taxable property in the district—a factor over which local voters can exercise no control.*

Brief dissenting opinions were filed also by Justice William J. Brennan Jr. and Justice Byron R. White. Justice Potter Stewart delivered a separate concurring opinion.

Excerpts from the opinion of the Court in the case of San Antonio Independent School District et al., Appellants v. Demetrio P. Rodriguez et al., March 21, 1973:

MR. JUSTICE POWELL delivered the opinion of the Court.

This suit attacking the Texas system of financing public education was initiated by Mexican-American parents whose children attend the elementary and secondary schools in the Edgewood Independent School District, an urban school district in San Antonio, Texas. They brought a class action on behalf of school children throughout the State who are members of minority groups or who are poor and reside in school districts having a low property tax base.... The complaint was filed in the summer of 1968 and a three-judge court was impaneled in January 1969. In December 1971 the panel rendered its judgment in a *per curiam* opinion holding the Texas school finance system unconstitutional under the Equal Protection Clause of the Fourteenth Amendment. The State appealed.... We reverse the decision of the District Court.

I

...Recognizing the need for increased state funding to help offset disparities in local spending and to meet Texas' changing educational requirements, the state legislature in the late 1940's undertook a thorough evaluation of public education with an eye toward major reform. In 1947 an 18-member committee, composed of educators and legislators, was appointed to explore alternative systems in other States and to propose a funding scheme that would guarantee a minimum or basic educational offering to each child and that would help overcome interdistrict disparities in taxable resources. The Committee's efforts led to the passage of the Gilmer-Aiken bills, named for the Committee's co-chairmen, establishing the Texas Minimum Foundation School Program....

The Program calls for state and local contributions to a fund earmarked specifically for teacher salaries, operating expenses, and transportation costs. The State, supplying funds from its general revenues, finances approximately 80% of the Program, and the school districts are responsible—as a unit—for providing the remaining 20%. The districts' share, known as the Local Fund Assignment, is apportioned among the school districts under a formula designed to reflect each district's relative taxpaying ability....

The school district in which appellees reside, the Edgewood Independent School District, has been compared throughout this litigation with the Alamo Heights Independent School District. This comparison between the least and most affluent districts in the San Antonio area serves to illustrate the manner in which the dual system of finance operates and to indicate the extent to which substantial disparities exist despite the State's impressive progress in recent years. Edgewood is one of seven public school districts in the metropolitan area. Approximately 22,000 students are enrolled in its 25 elementary and secondary schools. The district is situated in the core-city sector of San Antonio in a residential neighborhood that has little commercial or industrial property. The residents are predominantly of Mexican-American descent: approximately 90% of the student population is Mexican-American and over 6% is Negro. The average assessed property value per pupil is $5,960—the lowest in the metropolitan area—and the median family income ($4,686) is also the lowest. At an equalized tax rate of $1.05 per $100 of assessed property—the highest in the metropolitan area—the district contributed $26 to the education of each child for the 1967-1968 school year above its Local Fund Assignment for the Minimum Foundation Program. The Foundation Program contributed $222 per pupil for a state-local total of $248. Federal funds added another $108 for a total of $356 per pupil.

Alamo Heights is the most affluent school district in San Antonio. Its six schools, housing approximately 5,000 students, are situated in a residential community quite unlike the Edgewood District. The school population is predominantly Anglo, having only 18% Mexican-Americans and less than 1% Negroes. The assessed property value per pupil exceeds $49,000 and the median family income is $8,001. In 1967-1968 the local tax rate of $.85 per $100 of valuation yielded $333 per pupil over and above its contribution to the Foundation Program. Coupled with the $225 provided from that Program, the district was able to supply $558 per student. Supplemented by a $36 per pupil grant from federal sources, Alamo Heights spent $594 per pupil....

It was these disparities, largely attributable to differences in the amounts of money collected through local property taxation, that led the District Court to conclude that Texas' dual system of public school finance violated the Equal Protection Clause. The District Court held that the Texas system discriminates on the basis of wealth in the manner in which education is provided for its people.... Finding that wealth is a "suspect" classification and that the Texas system could be sustained only if the State could show that it was premised upon some compelling state interest. On this issue the court concluded that "[n]ot only are defendants unable to demonstrate compelling interests...they fail even to establish a reasonable basis for these classifications."

Texas virtually concedes that its historically rooted dual system of financing education could not withstand the strict judicial scrutiny that this Court has found appropriate in reviewing legislative judgments that interfere with fundamental constitutional rights or that involve suspect classifications. If, as previous decisions have indicated, strict scrutiny means that the State's system is not entitled to the usual presumption of validity, that the State rather than the complainants must carry a "heavy burden of justification," that the State must demonstrate that its educational system has been structured with "precision" and is "tailored" narrowly to serve legitimate objectives and that it has selected the "least drastic means" for effectuating its objectives, the Texas financing system and its counterpart in virtually every other State will not pass muster....

This, then, establishes the framework for our analysis. We must decide, first, whether the Texas system of financing public education operates to the disadvantage of some suspect class or impinges upon a fundamental right explicitly or implicitly protected by the Constitution, thereby requiring strict judicial scrutiny. If so, the judgment of the District Court should be affirmed. If not, the Texas scheme must still be examined to determine whether it rationally furthers some legitimate, articulated state purpose and therefore does not constitute an invidious discrimination in violation of the Equal Protection Clause of the Fourteenth Amendment.

II

The District Court's opinion does not reflect the novelty and complexity of the constitutional questions posed by appellees' challenge to Texas' system of school finance. In concluding that strict judicial scrutiny was required, that court relied on decisions dealing with the rights of indigents to equal treatment in the criminal trial and appellate processes, and on cases disapproving wealth restrictions on the right to vote. Those cases, the District Court concluded, established wealth as a suspect classification. Finding that the local property tax system discriminated on the basis of wealth, it regarded those precedents as controlling. It then reasoned, based on decisions of this Court affirming the undeniable importance of education, that there is a fundamental right to education and that, absent some compelling state justification, the Texas system could not stand.

We are unable to agree....

A

The wealth discrimination discovered by the District Court in this case, and by several other courts that have recently struck down school financing laws in other States, is quite unlike any of the forms of wealth discrimination heretofore reviewed by this Court. Rather than focusing on the unique features of the alleged discrimination, the courts in these cases have virtually assumed their findings of a suspect classification through a simplistic process of analysis: since, under the traditional systems of financing public schools, some poorer people receive less expensive educations than other more affluent people, these systems discriminate on the basis of wealth. This approach largely ignores the hard threshold questions, including whether it makes a difference for purposes of consideration under the Constitution that the class of disadvantaged "poor" cannot be identified or defined in customary equal protection terms, and whether the relative—rather than absolute—nature of the asserted deprivation is of significant consequence....

However described, it is clear that appellees' suit asks this Court to extend its most exacting scrutiny to review a system that allegedly discriminates against a large, diverse, and amorphous class, unified only by the common factor of residence in districts that happen to have less taxable wealth than other districts. The system of alleged discrimination and the class it defines have none of the traditional indicia of suspectness: the class is not saddled with such disabilities, or subjected to such a history of purposeful unequal treatment, or relegated to such a position of political powerlessness as to command extraordinary protection from the majoritarian political process.

We thus conclude that the Texas system does not operate to the peculiar disadvantage of any suspect class.... Appellees also assert that the State's system impermissibly interferes with the exercise of a "fundamental" right and that accordingly the prior decisions of this Court require the application of the strict standard of judicial review.... It is this question—whether education is a fundamental right, in the sense that it is among the rights and liberties protected by the Constitution—which has so consumed the attention of courts and commentators in recent years.

B

Nothing this Court holds today in any way detracts from our historic dedication to public education. We are in complete agreement with the conclusion of the three-judge panel below that "the grave significance of education both to the individual and to our society" cannot be doubted. But the importance of a service performed by the State does not determine whether it must be regarded as fundamental for purposes of examination under the Equal Protection Clause....

It is not the province of this Court to create substantive constitutional rights in the name of guaranteeing equal protection of the laws. Thus the key to discovering whether education is "fundamental" is not to be found in comparisons of the relative societal significance of education as opposed to subsistence or housing. Nor is it to be found by weighing whether education is as important as the right to travel. Rather, the answer lies in assessing whether there is a right to education explicitly or implicitly guaranteed by the Constitution....

Education, of course, is not among the rights afforded explicit protection under our Federal Constitution. Nor do we find any basis for saying it is implicitly so protected. As we have said, the undisputed importance of education will not alone cause this Court to depart from the usual standard for reviewing a State's social and economic legislation. It is appellees' contention, however, that education is distinguishable from other services and benefits provided by the State because it bears a peculiarly close relationship to other rights and liberties accorded protection under the Constitution. Specifically, they insist that education is itself a fundamental personal right because it is essential to the effective exercise of First Amendment freedoms and to intelligent utilization of the right to vote. In asserting a nexus between speech and education, appellees urge that the right to speak is meaningless unless the speaker is capable of articulating his thoughts intelligently and persuasively. The "marketplace of ideas" is an empty forum for those lacking basic communicative tools. Likewise, they argue that the corollary right to receive information becomes little more than a hollow privilege when the recipient has not been taught to read, assimilate, and utilize available knowledge.

A similar line of reasoning is pursued with respect to the right to vote. Exercise of the franchise, it is contended, cannot be divorced from the educational foundation of the voter. The electoral process, if reality is to conform to the democratic ideal, depends on an informed electorate: a voter cannot cast his ballot intelligently unless his reading skills and thought processes have been adequately developed.

We need not dispute any of these propositions. The Court has long afforded zealous protection against unjustifiable governmental interference with the individual's rights to speak and to vote. Yet we have never presumed to possess either the ability or the authority to guarantee to the citizenry the most *effective* speech or the most *informed* electoral choice. That these may be desirable goals of a system of freedom of expression and of a representative form of government is not to be doubted. These are indeed goals to be pursued by a people whose thoughts and beliefs are freed from governmental interference. But they are not values to be implemented by judicial intrusion into otherwise legitimate state activities.

Even if it were conceded that some identifiable quantum of education is a constitutionally protected prerequisite to the meaningful exercise of either right, we have no indication that the present levels of educational expenditure in Texas provide an education that falls short. Whatever merit appellees' argument might have if a State's financing system occasioned an absolute denial of educational opportunities to any of its children, that argument provides no basis for finding an interference with fundamental rights where only relative differences in spending levels are involved and where—as is true in the present case—no charge fairly could be made that the system fails to provide each child with an opportunity to acquire the basic minimal skills necessary for the enjoyment of the rights of speech and of full participation in the political process....

We have carefully considered each of the arguments supportive of the District Court's finding that education is a fundamental right or liberty and have found those arguments unpersuasive. In one further respect we find this a particularly inappropriate case in which to subject state action to strict judicial scrutiny. The present case, in another basic sense, is significantly different from any of the cases in which the Court has applied strict scrutiny to state or federal legislation touching upon constitutionally protected rights. Each of our prior cases involved legislation which "deprived," "infringed," or "interfered" with the free exercise of some such fundamental personal right or liberty....

Every step leading to the establishment of the system Texas utilizes today—including the decisions permitting localities to tax and expend locally, and creating and continuously expanding state aid—was implemented in an effort to *extend* public education and to improve its quality. Of course, every reform that benefits some more than others may be criticized for what it fails to accomplish. But we think it plain that, in substance, the thrust of the Texas system is affirmative and reformatory and, therefore, should be scrutinized under judicial principles sensitive to the nature of the State's efforts and to the rights reserved to the States under the Constitution.

C

It should be clear, for the reasons stated above and in accord with the prior decisions of this Court, that this is not a case in which the challenged state action must be subjected to the searching judicial scrutiny reserved for laws that create suspect classifications or impinge upon constitutionally protected rights.

We need not rest our decision, however, solely on the inappropriateness of the strict scrutiny test. A century of Supreme Court adjudication under the Equal Protection Clause affirmatively supports the application of the traditional standard of review, which requires only that the State's system be shown to bear some rational relationship to legitimate state purposes. This case represents far more than a challenge to the manner in which Texas provides for the education of its children. We have here nothing less than a direct attack on the way in which Texas has chosen to raise and disburse state and local tax revenues. We are asked to condemn the State's judgment in conferring on political subdivisions the power to tax local property to supply revenues for local interests. In so doing, appellees would have the Court intrude in an area in which it has traditionally deferred to state legislatures. This Court has often admonished against such interferences with the State's fiscal policies....

Thus we stand on familiar ground when we continue to acknowledge that the Justices of this Court lack both the expertise and the familiarity with local problems so necessary to the making of wise decisions with respect to the raising and disposition of public revenues. Yet we are urged to direct the States either to alter drastically the present system or to throw out the property tax altogether in favor of some other form of taxation. No scheme of taxation, whether the tax is imposed on property, income or purchases of goods and services, has yet been devised which is free of all discriminatory impact. In such a complex arena in which no perfect alternatives exist, the Court does well not to impose too rigorous a standard of scrutiny lest all local fiscal schemes become subjects of criticism under the Equal Protection Clause.

In addition to matters of fiscal policy, this case also involves the most persistent and difficult questions of educational policy, another area in which this Court's lack of specialized knowledge and experience counsels against premature interference with the informed judgments made at the state and local levels. Education, perhaps even more than welfare assistance, presents a myriad of "intractable economic, social, and even philosophical problems".... The very complexity of the problems of financing and managing a statewide public school system suggest that "there will be more than one constitutionally permissible method of solving them," and that, within the limits of rationality, "the legislature's efforts to tackle the problems" should be entitled to respect.... On even the most basic questions in this area the scholars and educational experts are divided. Indeed, one of the hottest sources of controversy concerns the extent to which there is a demonstrable correlation between educational expenditures and the quality of education—an assumed correlation underlying virtually every legal conclusion drawn by the District Court in this case. Related to the questioned relationship between cost and quality is the equally unsettled controversy as to the proper goals of a system of education....

III

...Appellees do not question the propriety of Texas' dedication to local control of education. To the contrary, they attack the school finance system precisely because, in their view, it does not provide the same level of local control and fiscal flexibility in all districts. Appellees suggest that local control could be preserved and promoted under other financing systems that resulted in more equality in educational expenditures. While it is no doubt true that reliance on local property taxation for school revenues provides less freedom of choice with respect to expenditures for some districts than for others, the existence of "some inequality" in the manner in which the State's rationale is achieved is not alone a sufficient basis for striking down the entire system.... It may not be condemned simply because it imperfectly effectuates the State's goals.... Nor must the financing system fail because, as appellees suggest, other methods of satisfying the State's interest, which occasion "less drastic" disparities in expenditures, might be conceived. Only where state action impinges on the exercise of fundamental constitutional rights or liberties must it be found to have chosen the least restrictive alternative.... It is also well to remember that even those districts that have reduced ability to make free decisions with respect to how much they spend on education still retain under the present system a large measure of authority as to how available funds will be allocated. They further enjoy the power to make numerous other decisions with respect to the operation of the schools....

Appellees further urge that the Texas system is unconstitutionally arbitrary because it allows the availability of local taxable resources to turn on "happenstance." They see no justification for a system that allows, as they contend, the quality of education to fluctuate on the basis of the fortuitous positioning of the boundary lines of political subdivisions and the location of valuable commercial and industrial property. But any scheme of local taxation—indeed the very existence of identifiable local governmental units—requires the establishment of jurisdictional boundaries that are inevitably arbitrary. It is equally inevitable that some localities are going to be blessed with more taxable assets than others. Nor is local wealth a static quantity. Changes in the level of taxable wealth within any district may result from any number of events, some of which local residents can and do influence. For instance, commercial and industrial enterprises may be encouraged to locate within a district by various actions—public and private.

Moreover, if local taxation for local expenditure is an unconstitutional method of providing for education then it may be an equally impermissible means of providing other necessary services customarily financed largely from local property taxes, including local police and fire protection, public health and hospitals, and public utility facilities of various kinds. We perceive no justification for such a severe denigration of local property taxation and control as would follow from appellees' contentions. It has simply never been within the constitutional prerogatives of this Court to nullify statewide measures for financing

public services merely because the burdens or benefits thereof fall unevenly depending upon the relative wealth of the political subdivisions in which citizens live.

In sum, to the extent that the Texas system of school finance results
in unequal expenditures between children who happen to reside in different districts, we cannot say that such disparities are the product
of a system that is so irrational as to be invidiously discriminatory.
Texas has acknowledged its shortcomings and has persistently endeavored—not without some success—to ameliorate the differences
in levels of expenditures without sacrificing the benefits of local participation. The Texas plan is not the result of hurried, ill-conceived legislation. It certainly is not the product of purposeful discrimination
against any group or class. On the contrary, it is rooted in decades of
experience in Texas and elsewhere, and in major part is the product
of responsible studies by qualified people. In giving substance to the
presumption of validity to which the Texas system is entitled....it is
important to remember that at every stage of its development it has
constituted a "rough accommodation" of interests in an effort to arrive at practical and workable solutions.... One also must remember
that the system here challenged is not peculiar to Texas or to any
other State. In its essential characteristics the Texas plan for financing public education reflects what many educators for a half century
have thought was an enlightened approach to a problem for which
there is no perfect solution. We are unwilling to assume for ourselves
a level of wisdom superior to that of legislators, scholars, and educational authorities in 49 States, especially where the alternatives proposed are only recently conceived and nowhere yet tested. The constitutional standard under the Equal Protection Clause is whether the
challenged state action rationally furthers a legitimate state purpose
or interest.... We hold that the Texas plan abundantly satisfies this
standard.

IV

In light of the considerable attention that has focused on the District Court opinion in this case and on its California predecessor,
Serrano v. *Priest*,...a cautionary postscript seems appropriate. It cannot be questioned that the constitutional judgment reached by the
District Court and approved by our dissenting brothers today would
occasion in Texas and elsewhere an unprecedented upheaval in public
education. Some commentators have concluded that, whatever the
contours of the alternative financing programs that might be devised
and approved, the result could not avoid being a beneficial one. But,
just as there is nothing simple about the constitutional issues involved
in these cases, there is nothing simple or certain about predicting the
consequences of massive change in the financing and control of public

education. Those who have devoted the most thoughtful attention to the practical ramifications of these cases have found no clear or dependable answers and their scholarship reflects no such unqualified confidence in the desirabilty of completely uprooting the existing system.

The complexity of these problems is demonstrated by the lack of consensus with respect to whether it may be said with any assurance that the poor, the racial minorities, or the children in overburdened core-city school districts would be benefitted by abrogation of traditional modes of financing education....

These practical considerations, of course, play no role in the adjudication of the constitutional issues presented here. But they serve to highlight the wisdom of the traditional limitations on this Court's function. The consideration and initiation of fundamental reforms with respect to state taxation and education are matters reserved for the legislative processes of the various States, and we do no violence to the values of federalism and separation of powers by staying our hand. We hardly need add that this Court's action today is not to be viewed as placing its judicial imprimatur on the status quo. The need is apparent for reform in tax systems which may well have relied too long and too heavily on the local property tax. And certainly innovative new thinking as to public education, its methods and its funding, is necessary to assure both a higher level of quality and greater uniformity of opportunity. These matters merit the continued attention of the scholars who already have contributed much by their challenges. But the ultimate solutions must come from the lawmakers and from the democratic pressures of those who elect them.

Reversed.

Excerpts from the dissenting opinion of Justice Marshall in which Justice Douglas concurred:

The Court today decides, in effect, that a State may constitutionally vary the quality of education which it offers its children in accordance with the amount of taxable wealth located in the school districts within which they reside. The majority's decision represents an abrupt departure from the mainstream of recent state and federal court decisions concerning the unconstitutionality of state educational financing schemes dependent upon taxable local wealth. More unfortunately, though, the majority's holding can only be seen as a retreat from our historic commitment to equality of educational opportunity and as unsupportable acquiescence in a system which deprives children in their earliest years of the chance to reach their full potential as citizens. The Court does this despite the absencce of any substantial justification for a sceme which arbitrarily channels educational resources in accordance with the fortuity of the amount of taxable wealth within each district.

In my judgment, the right of every American to an equal start in life, so far as the provision of a state service as important as education is concerned, is far too vital to permit state discrimination on grounds as tenuous as those presented by this record. Nor can I accept the notion that it is sufficient to remit these appellees to the vagaries of the political process which, contrary to the majority's suggestion, has proven singularly unsuited to the task of providing a remedy for this discrimination. I, for one, am unsatisfied with the hope of an ultimate "political solution sometime in the indefinite future while, in the meantime, countless children unjustifiably receive inferior educations that "may affect their hearts and minds in a way unlikely ever to be undone."

I

...However praiseworthy Texas' equalizing efforts, the issue in this case is not whether Texas is doing its best to ameliorate the worst features of a discriminatory scheme, but rather whether the scheme itself is in fact unconstitutionally discriminatory in the face of the Fourteenth Amendment's guarantee of equal protection of the laws....

Authorities concerned with educational quality no doubt disagree as to the significance of variations in per pupil spending.... We sit, however, not to resolve disputes over educational theory but to enforce our Constitution. It is an inescapable fact that if one district has more funds available per pupil than another district, the former will have greater choice in educational planning than will the latter. In this regard, I believe the question of discrimination in educational quality must be deemed to be an objective one that looks to what the State provides its children, not to what the children are able to do with what they receive. That a child forced to attend an underfunded school with poorer physical facilities, less experienced teachers, larger classes, and a narrower range of courses than a school with substantially more funds—and thus with greater choice in educational planning— may nevertheless excel is to·the credit of the child, not the State.... Indeed, who can ever measure for such a child the opportunities lost and the talents wasted for want of a broader, more enriched education? Discrimination in the opportunity to learn that is afforded a child must be our standard.

Hence, even before this Court recognized its duty to tear down the barriers of state enforced racial segregation in public education, it acknowledged that inequality in the educational facilities provided to students may make for discriminatory state action as contemplated by the Equal Protection Clause....

Alternatively, the appellants and the majority may believe that the Equal Protection Clause cannot be offended by substantially unequal state treatment of persons who are similarly situated so long as the State provides everyone with some unspecified amount of education which evidently is "enough." The basis for such a novel view is far from clear. It is, of course, true that the Constitution does not require precise equality in the treatment of all persons.... But this Court has never suggested that because some "adequate" level of benefits is provided to all, discrimination in the provision of services is therefore constitutionally excusable. The Equal Protection Clause is not addressed to the minimal sufficiency but rather to the unjustifiable inequalities of state action. It mandates nothing less than that "all persons similarly circumstanced shall be treated alike."

In my view, then, it is inequality—not some notion of gross inadequacy—of educational opportunity that raises a question of denial of equal protection of the laws.... Here appellees have made a substantial showing of wide variations in educational funding and the resulting educational opportunities afforded to the school children of Texas. This discrimination is, in large measure, attributable to significant disparities in the taxable wealth of local Texas school districts. This is a sufficient showing to raise a substantial question of discriminatory state action in violation of the Equal Protection Clause.

Despite the evident discriminatory effect of the Texas financing scheme, both the appellants and the majority raise substantial questions concerning the precise character of the disadvantaged class in this case.... Texas has chosen to provide free public education for all its citizens, and it has embodied that decision in its constitution. Yet, having established public education for its citizens, the State, as a direct consequence of the variations in local property wealth endemic to Texas' financing scheme, has provided some Texas school children with substantially less resources for their education than others. Thus, while on its face the Texas scheme may merely discriminate between local districts, the impact of that discrimination falls directly upon the children whose educational opportunity is dependent upon where they happen to live. Consequently, the District Court correctly concluded that the Texas financing scheme discriminates, from a constitutional perspective, between school age children on the basis of the amount of taxable property located within their local districts....

I believe it is sufficient that the overarching form of discrimination in this case is between the school children of Texas on the basis of the taxable property wealth of the districts in which they happen to live.... And I do not believe that a clearer definition of either the disadvantaged class of Texas school children or the allegedly unconstitutional discrimination suffered by the members of that class under the present Texas financing scheme could be asked for, much less needed....

II

I therefore cannot accept the majority's labored efforts to demonstrate that fundamental interests, which call for strict scrutiny of the challenged classification, encompass only established rights which we are somehow bound to recognize from the text of the Constitution itself....

The majority is, of course, correct when it suggests that the process of determining which interests are fundamental is a difficult one. But I do not think the problem is insurmountable.... Although not all fundamental interests are constitutionally guaranteed, the determination of which interests are fundamental should be firmly rooted in the text of the Constitution. The task in every case should be to determine the extent to which constitutionally guaranteed rights are dependent on interests not mentioned in the Constitution.... Only if we closely protect the related interests from state discrimination do we ultimately ensure the integrity of the constitutional guarantee itself. This is the real lesson that must be taken from our previous decisions involving interests deemed to be fundamental....

In summary, it seems to me inescapably clear that this Court has consistently adjusted the care with which it will review state discrimination in light of the constitutional significance of the interests affected and the invidiousness of the particular classification. In the context of economic interests, we find that discriminatory state action is almost always sustained for such interests are generally far removed from constitutional guarantees.... But the situation differs markedly when discrimination against important individual interests with constitutional implications and against particularly disadvantaged or powerless classes is involved. The majority suggests, however, that a variable standard of review would give this Court the appearance of a "superlegislature." I cannot agree. Such an approach seems to be a part of the guarantees of our Constitution and of the historic experiences with oppression of and discrimination against discrete, powerless minorities which underlie that Document....

Since the Court now suggests that only interests guaranteed by the Constitution are fundamental for purposes of equal protection analysis and since it rejects the contention that public education is fundamental, it follows that the Court concludes that public education is not constitutionally guaranteed. It is true that this Court has never deemed the provision of free public education to be required by the Constitution. Indeed, it has on occasion suggested that state supported education is a privilege bestowed by a State on its citizens.... Nevertheless, the fundamental importance of education is amply indicated by the prior decisions of this Court, by the unique status accorded public education by our society, and by the close relationship between education and some of our most basic constitutional values.

The special concern of this Court with the educational process of our country is a matter of common knowledge.... Education directly affects the ability of a child to exercise his First Amendment interests both as a source and as a receiver of information and ideas, whatever interests he may pursue in life.... Of particular importance is the relationship between education and the political process....

The factors just considered, including the relationship between education and the social and political interests enshrined within the Constitution, compel us to recognize the fundamentality of education and to scrutinize with appropriate care the bases for state discrimination affecting equality of educational opportunity in Texas' school districts....

As the Court points out, no previous decision has deemed the presence of just a wealth classification to be sufficient basis to call forth "rigorous judicial scrutiny" of allegedly discriminatory state action.... The means for financing public education in Texas are selected and specified by the State. It is the State that has created local school districts, and tied educational funding to the local property tax and thereby to local district wealth. At the same time, governmentally imposed land use controls have undoubtedly encouraged and rigidified natural trends in the allocation of particular areas for residential or commercial use, and thus determined each district's amount of taxable property wealth. In short, this case, in contrast to the Court's previous wealth discrimination decisions can only be seen as "unusual in the extent to which governmental action *is* the cause of the wealth classifications...."

The only justification offered by appellants to sustain the discrimination in educational opportunity caused by the Texas financing scheme is local educational control.... At the outset, I do not question that local control of public education, as an abstract matter, constitutes a very substantial state interest.... [But] on this record, it is apparent that the State's purported concern with local control is offered primarily as an excuse rather than as a justification for interdistrict inequality.... Local school districts cannot choose to have the best education in the State by imposing the highest tax rate. Instead, the quality of the educational opportunity offered by any particular district is largely determined by the amount of taxable property located in the district—a factor over which local voters can exercise no control....

In my judgment, any substantial degree of scrutiny of the operation of the Texas financing scheme reveals that the State has selected means wholly inappropriate to secure its purported interest in assuring its school districts local fiscal control.... If, for the sake of local education control, this Court is to sustain interdistrict discrimination in the educational opportunity afforded Texas school children, it should require that the State present something more than the mere sham now before us.

III

In conclusion it is essential to recognize that an end to the wide variations in taxable district property wealth inherent in the Texas financing scheme would entail none of the untoward consequences suggested by the Court or by the appellants.

First, affirmance of the District Court's decisions would hardly sound the death knell for local control of education. It would mean neither centralized decisionmaking nor federal court intervention in the operation of public schools....

Nor does the District Court's decision even necessarily eliminate local control of educational funding. The District Court struck down nothing more than the continued interdistrict wealth discrimination inherent in the present property tax. Both centralized and decentralized plans for educational funding not involving such interdistrict discrimination have been put forward. The choice among these or other alternatives remains with the State, not with the federal courts.... Yet no one in the course of this entire litigation has ever questioned the constitutionality of the local property tax as a device for raising educational funds. The District Court's decision, at most, restricts the power of the State to make educational funding dependent exclusively upon local property taxation so long as there exist interdistrict disparities in taxable property wealth. But it hardly eliminates the local property tax as a source of educational funding or as a means of providing local fiscal control.

The Court seeks solace for its action today in the possibility of legislative reform.... The possibility of legislative action is, in all events, no answer to this Court's duty under the Constitution to eliminate unjustified state discrimination. In this case we have been presented with an instance of such discrimination, in a particularly invidious form, against an individual interest of large constitutional and practical importance. To support the demonstrated discrimination in the provision of educational opportunity the State has offered a justification which, on analysis, takes on at best an ephemeral character. Thus, I believe that the wide disparities in taxable district property wealth inherent in the local property tax element of the Texas financing scheme render that scheme violative of the Equal Protection Clause. I would therefore affirm the judgment of the District Court.

FOREIGN ECONOMIC POLICY REPORT

March 22, 1973

President Nixon, transmitting to Congress the first annual report of the White House Council on International Economic Policy, challenged American business to meet head-on the competition posed by foreign enterprises. He urged Americans not to "shrink" from such competition but rather to "face up to more intense long-term competition in the world's markets." Parts of the report outlined the economic reasoning underlying a subsequent White House request for delegation to the President of broader tariff-making authority than Congress had hitherto granted.

The "Trade Reform Act of 1973," proposed by Nixon in a message to Congress on April 10, would renew and broaden the power of the President to negotiate foreign trade agreements—a power that had lapsed in 1967 shortly after completion of a 53-nation agreement under the so-called Kennedy round of tariff negotiations. The legislation proposed in April was designed to put the United States in a strong bargaining position for the new round of GATT (General Agreement on Tariffs and Trade) negotiations scheduled to get under way early in 1974. The bill sent to Capitol Hill would authorize the President for a period of five years to "eliminate, reduce or increase customs duties" through multilateral trade agreements not subject to ratification by Congress. It would empower the President also to negotiate reductions of certain nontariff barriers under agreements which would go into effect if not disapproved within 90 days by the House or the Senate.

In his message transmitting the Economic Policy report to Congress, Nixon underscored his rejection of the protectionist views of organized labor. The AFL-CIO had advocated passage of the Burke-Hartke bill to limit foreign imports and to reduce incentives for American foreign investment. But the President, summoning American business to compete in foreign markets, said: "Those who would have us turn inward, hiding behind a shield of import restrictions of indefinite duration, might achieve short-term gains and benefit certain groups, but they would exact a high cost from the economy as a whole." The result, Nixon warned, would be higher prices and lower real income for everyone.

The report itself was especially critical of European Economic Community (EEC) and Japanese trade restrictions. It declared that "successful trade negotiations are...essential if we are to resist the growing demands...for more protection and if we are to improve our own trade balance." The United States, it added, would "seek an international agereement providing for temporary import 'safeguards' " and it would "also seek legislation to give the President authority to ensure that, regardless of the outcome of the upcoming multilateral trade negotiations, American goods will have fair and equitable access to foreign markets."

In a later section, the report laid particular emphasis on opening foreign markets to American exports of farm products. It went so far as to say that "if there is no commitment to meaningful and realistic negotiations in the agricultural sector, it would be difficult for the United States to proceed with multilateral trade negotiations in other sectors." Its trade proposals, the report concluded, were "needed to achieve a more balanced and freer international economic system and to reduce our current trade deficts."

Referring to "the special category of East-West trade," the Council on International Economic Policy said that "we intend to move forward in promoting economic normalization with the Communist countries" and "seek from Congress the authority to extend most-favored-nation status to Communist countries with which we negotiate satisfactory trade agreements." Most Communist countries are not affiliated with GATT. The United States in October 1972 concluded a trade agreement with the Soviet Union (see Historic Documents 1972, p. 845), but its implementation depended on granting of most-favored-nation status to that country. Such action requires the assent of Congress, which has been delayed by objections to Moscow's restrictions on emigration of Russian Jews. The proposed "Trade Reform Act of 1973" would authorize the President to extend most-favored-nation treatment to any country when he deemed it in the national interest, but such action could be vetoed by either House or Senate within a three-month period.

Chairman Wilbur D. Mills (D Ark.) of the House Ways and Means Committee, which handles tariff legislation, said after the trade reform bill was introduced that Nixon was "asking for more of a grant of authority than we have given any other President," but he agreed that it was "essential if we are to move forward."

Text of President Nixon's International Economic Report, March 22, 1973, and excerpts from the First Annual Report of the Council on International Economic Policy.

INTERNATIONAL ECONOMIC REPORT
OF THE PRESIDENT

To the Congress of the United States:

The Nation is again at peace. We also are firmly on the course of strong economic growth at home. Now we must turn more of our attention to the urgent problems we face in our economic dealings with other nations. International problems may seem to some of us to be far away, but they have a very direct impact on the jobs, the incomes and the living standards of our people. Neither the peace we have achieved nor the economic growth essential to our national welfare will last if we leave such matters unattended, for they can diminish our prosperity at home and at the same time provoke harmful friction abroad.

Our major difficulties stem from relying too long upon outdated economic arrangements and institutions despite the rapid changes which have taken place in the world. Many countries we helped to rebuild after World War II are now our strong economic competitors. Americans can no longer act as if these historic developments had not taken place. We must do a better job of preparing ourselves—both in the private sector and in the Government—to compete more effectively in world markets, so that expanding trade can bring greater benefits to our people.

In the summer of 1971, this Administration initiated fundamental changes in American foreign economic policy. We have also introduced proposals for the reform of the international monetary and trading systems which have lost their ability to deal with current problems. The turmoil in world monetary affairs has demonstrated clearly that greater urgency must now be attached to constructive reform.

At home, we have continued our fight to maintain price stability and to improve our productivity—objectives which are as important to our international economic position as to our domestic welfare.

What is our next step?

In my State of the Union message on the economy last month, I outlined certain measures to strengthen both our domestic and international economic position. One of the most important is trade reform.

In choosing an international trade policy which will benefit all Americans, I have concluded that we must face up to more intense long-term competition in the world's markets rather than shrink from it. Those who would have us turn inward, hiding behind a shield of import restrictions of indefinite duration, might achieve short-term gains and benefit certain groups, but they would exact a high cost from the economy as a whole. Those costs would be borne by all of us in the form of higher prices and lower real income. Only in response to unfair competition, or the closing of markets abroad to our goods, or to provide time for adjustment, would such restrictive measures be called for.

My approach is based both on my strong faith in the ability of Americans to compete, and on my confidence that all nations will recognize their own vital interest in lowering economic barriers and applying fairer and more effective trading rules.

The fact that most of these comments are addressed to the role of our Government should not divert attention from the vital role which private economic activity will play in resolving our current problems. The cooperation and the initiative of all sectors of our economy are needed to increase our productivity and to keep our prices competitive. This is essential to our international trading position. Yet there are certain necessary steps which only the Government can take, given the worldwide scope of trading activity and the need for broad international agreement to expand trade fairly and effectively. I am determined that we shall take those steps.

I know that the American people and their representatives in the Congress can be counted on to rise to the challenge of the changing world economy. Together we must do what is needed to further the prosperity of our country, and of the world in which we live.

RICHARD NIXON

The White House,
   March 22, 1973.

Excerpts from Chapter I, "An Overview," of the First Annual Report of the Council on International Economic Policy:

With the bold initiatives announced by President Nixon on the evening of 15 August 1971, the postwar economic era came to a close, and a new age began. It is an age in which the United States no longer holds overwhelming dominance in the world economy, and in which the growing interdependence of nations can produce both increasing friction and unprecedented potential for abundance.

That age is still only beginning. As a start toward realizing its full promise, the United States in 1972 and early 1973 made clear its determination to bring about basic reforms in the world's monetary and trading patterns to fit the realities of our time. Further major initiatives will be taken in 1973, both in international negotiations and in seeking legislation to make those negotiations more fruitful.

New policies and proposals have been developed. Their central purpose is to provide a framework for economic activity that will contribute most to our national and international well-being. This report outlines the events that led to those policies and offers a rationale for cooperative action in a world economy that grows ever more closely bound together.

A Quarter Century of Progress

By any quantitative measure the post-World War II era has been the most successful in international economic history. For more than a quarter of a century the world has enjoyed economic growth uninterrupted by either global war or global depression. Rising incomes have created mass markets, and the rapid pace of technological development has led to more efficient production of countless products. Most developed countries now have standards of living which offer much more than simple survival to most of the population. And many less developed countries, after centuries of stagnation, have begun to make impressive economic progress.

Peaceful cooperation and growing prosperity were the essential ingredients in the acceleration of world economic interdependence during the last 25 years. For a century prior to World War II, international commerce had grown at the rate of about 4% a year. Since 1945, foreign trade has expanded by more than 7% a year. Vastly improved transport and communications have provided for swift and efficient exchange of goods. The rise of the multinational corporation and the emergence of international capital and money markets have facilitated international transactions and the flow of investment.

Emerging Problems

While closer economic ties have benefited the world, they also created new possibilities for discord among nations. Governments around the world are facing new difficulties because of the problems created by the large and rapid movement of goods and capital. Most major countries now export a greater proportion of their production of goods...and import a larger share of their consumption than ten years ago, so that foreign trade has an increasingly pronounced effect on jobs and income. Countries with limited trade barriers are finding that sudden import surges seriously disrupt their domestic markets for some products, leaving workers and businesses insufficient time to adjust to the rapid changes in competitive conditions.

At the same time, with growing world economic interdependence, each nation's domestic economic policies are having an increasingly greater impact on other countries. Efforts to solve unemployment problems in one country can cause workers to lose jobs somewhere else. Attempts to ease inflationary pressures by tightening the money supply in one country can be severely hampered by a large influx of interest-sensitive foreign capital. Thus is is no longer possible for a country to assert absolute sovereignty over its own domestic economic policies without affecting the welfare of other nations....

Current international economic institutions...fail to reflect fully the intricate relationship between trade, monetary, and investment matters. Breakdowns in the monetary system can make trade and investment transactions more difficult and costly. Trade barriers, in turn, have vitiated the effectiveness of currency adjustments. Various government investment practices have produced distortions in trade patterns. Despite these interconnections, international rules and procedures have generally treated each type of transaction separately. The International Monetary fund oversees international monetary movements, the General Agreement on Tariffs and Trade is responsible for trade regulations, while investment procedures are unattended or scattered throughout several other international institutions.

The Changing US Role

Through most of the post-World War II years, the formulation of US international economic policy has been largely subordinated to international political objectives. We wished to promote political stability and close mutual ties in the Free World to lessen the risk of Communist encroachment. The United States believed that economic well-being would contribute to political stability; that, with most developed nations highly dependent on foreign trade, a lowering of barriers to commerce would stimulate economic growth; and that the development of trade and other economic ties would promote Free World unity. To this end we have pursued liberal trade and payments policies for more than 25 years. These policies have been successful; they contributed greatly both to rapid economic growth at home and abroad and to the achievement of our political objectives.

The United States then could easily afford these policies. This nation emerged from World War II as the only major power not devastated by the war. Although our position of economic dominance naturally declined as other countries rebuilt, we fared well in the competition for world markets well into the 1960s. A decade ago our trade surplus was averaging more than $5 billion annually, an amount sufficiently large so that we could spend substantial amounts abroad to meet our political and military objectives without undermining our balance of payments position. We could also run a balance-of-payments deficit of several billion dollars a year without serious problems because the world economy needed the dollars to handle the rapidly increasing volume of international economic transactions. In addition, because of our strong international economic position and because the economic recovery of Western Europe and Japan were key components in our foreign policy, we tolerated certain foreign practices which restricted our ability to export.

Now many of the conditions underlying this policy have changed. Given the renewed strength of Western Europe and Japan, the political rationale for tolerating practices that unfairly impair our competitive position no longer exists. The United States has lost much of its overwhelming economic predominance in the industrial Free World....

At the same time, our ability to spend the huge sums required to meet our international responsibilities and to incur persistent balance-of-payments deficits without adversely affecting international monetary stability has come to an end. The huge flow of dollars into the international monetary system in recent years has tended to undermine confidence in the dollar. Largely underlying this deteriorating foreign economic position is our worsening trade balance. Instead of trade surpluses, we now have sizable deficits.

The improved capabilities of our trading partners have given us new competition at home and abroad. Many countries have been proportionately outspending us in terms of new plant and equipment.... An important part of our capital and technological skills have been devoted to Free World defense.... The imposing technology lead which the United States had following World War II has been narrowing, as other countries have proved able to absorb or develop advanced technology.

Excess demand, causing the high inflation rate between 1964 and 1971, also slowed our exports and expanded our imports. Some nations had similar inflationary problems but remained competitive by devaluing their currencies. We were restrained from making such a move, however, because of the central role of the US dollar in the world's monetary system.

While imports of consumer goods rose, foreign trade barriers frequently frustrated our efforts to expand our exports of those products in which we enjoyed an advantage, such as advanced technology and, especially, agriculture.

As a result of our declining self-sufficiency in raw materials, the United States is also facing rapidly rising imports of mineral resources.

As we have depleted our high-quality domestic resources, we have been turning to foreign suppliers. Each year we increase our dependence on foreign sources of important minerals, such as crude oil and bauxite.

Toward a More Equitable System

President Nixon took the initiative on 15 August 1971 to overcome our immediate difficulties and to set the stage for fundamental reform of the world's economic system. International currency rate realignments reached in December 1971 and February and March 1973 have strengthened our competitive position..., as has the successful effort to reduce domestic inflation. In fact, the United States in the last 18 months has had the lowest consumer price increases among the major developed countries. As a result, the relationship of our manufacturing costs to those of the other developed countries is once again about what it was in the mid-1960s.

The second part of the President's program has now begun. Far-reaching US proposals to reform the international monetary system were made at the annual International Monetary Fund (IMF) meeting in September 1972 in Washington, and negotiations are proceeding in the Fund's Committee of Twenty; we are hopeful that a new agreement in principle can be reached at the IMF meeting this September in Nairobi. The United States has also obtained commitments to begin broad, multinational trade negotiations late in 1973.

A wide range of choices confronts us as we seek to develop a new international economic policy. It is quite clear that we cannot afford simply to revert to the international trade and financial practices of the period before 15 August 1971. The record of the last two or three years tells the story: Whatever other advantages might accrue, the risks, in terms of the future viability of the international economic system, would simply be too high. It is equally clear that it would be unacceptable for the United States to retreat from its international responsibilities....

US self-interest and that of the world community would be best served by an international economic course which facilitates as much as possible the highly beneficial, market-directed flow of goods and capital but avoids inflicting undue hardships that can result when the flow becomes an unexpected flood. Achieving this balance will require painstaking bargaining among nations because of growing public sensitivity to international economic issues.

Devising effective economic policies in today's world involves much more than a simple choice between "protectionism" and "free trade." Long-term protection against foreign competition results in a lower living standard, in lower overall production, and fewer jobs in the very economy it seeks to assist, while unrestricted free trade can impose intolerable burdens on some economic sectors in an era of fast-changing patterns of production and commerce.

386

The responsibility for creating a viable international economic system rests with all nations. The United States and many other countries have consistently supported policies to encourage world economic integration. We continue to seek international agreements ensuring a freer and more open world economy—one in which each nation has a fair share of both the benefits and the burdens of making the system work. The alternative is an uninviting prospect—fragmentation of the world into self-seeking, inward-looking blocs and national economies, bringing mutually damaging trade wars and sharpened political rivalries....

For our part, we must be prepared to face intense competition in the changing and growing world market. We must continue the battle for price stability and greater productivity. We must be willing to adapt some parts of our economy to changes abroad. We must not shrink from the adjustments needed to compete more effectively in the world's markets. Out potential gains—in terms of jobs and income, in the enhanced prospects of a peaceful world—mean too much.

Policy Proposals

Monetary

Our most pressing need is to reform the international monetary system. The increasing frequency of currency crises and the erection of capital controls during the last few years are symptomatic of the inadequacy of present arrangements. The exchange market disruptions in February and March 1973 emphasize the need to establish new monetary rules and procedures.

In our view, the Bretton Woods system's greatest weakness lies in the adjustment process. The US proposals introduced in September 1972 provide for strengthening pressures on deficit and surplus countries to adjust their imbalances. The choice of policies to achieve this result however, as between exchange rate adjustments and other measures, is left to the countries concerned. Our plan calls for currency margins around the central rates in the range of those permitted by the Smithsonian Conference. The dollar should also be allowed the same degree of flexibility around its par value as other currencies. Countries would also be permitted to float their currencies under agreed international guidelines.

Trade

Along with monetary reform, we must also establish new international arrangements for the conduct of trade. These new arrangements could provide a badly needed alternative to payments adjustment, and also prevent trade barriers from frustrating the impact of necessary currency realignments. Since exchange-rate adjustments benefit some sectors of any economy but hurt others, governments frequently face pressures to counteract their effects through trade barriers. There also exist long-standing practices explicitly designed to insulate certain segments of an economy from international price competition. For example, the European Community and Japan have devices for the protection of their agricultural products which fully offset the effect of any currency depreciation, at a cost to their consumers and to our farmers. We must also recognize that our own system is not entirely free of these devices.

Successful trade negotiations are also essential if we are to resist the growing demands, both at home and abroad, for more protection and if we are to improve our own trade balance. In recent years the principle of nondiscrimination among trading partners has been badly undermined by the increasing use of bilateral preferential agreements, tending to move the world toward economic blocs. Painstakingly negotiated tariff reductions have in part been impaired by discrimination and other trade-distorting measures. Trade frictions have increased because many nations now enjoying excellent trade positions have failed to remove import barriers imposed under earlier adverse conditions.

While our aim is to try to obtain the benefits of expanding trade for all, we recognize that abrupt shifts in trading patterns can bring hardship. We have seen how our own rapidly increasing imports of some manufactured goods cause disruption and make orderly adjustment to new competitive conditions difficult. Other countries have had similar problems.

We realize that a country's production pattern is not static and that, in order to remain competitive and meet the needs of its people, change is both desirable and inevitable. However, failure to allow the industrial structure sufficient time to shift into more competitive products or to become more competitive in the lines currently produced, can result in undesirable strains on the efficiency of the economy as a whole. Therefore, while we believe permanent import restrictions are counterproductive, we do see a need for a temporary "safeguards" system which allows the natural upgrading process to take place more efficiently and with a minimum of dislocation in labor markets.

We look to the upcoming negotiations to go beyond tariff cutting and to eliminate or lower other and sometimes more significant barriers to the exchange of goods among nations. While most developed countries reduced their *tariff* rates during the 1960s by about one-third, *nontariff* barriers have increased in relative importance. In negotiating reductions in barriers of all types, we will seek as liberal a worldwide trade posture as our major trading partners are willing to accept for themselves.

In the negotiations for which we are now seeking legislative authority, we will specifically propose that tariffs be substantially reduced in phases, and that nontariff barriers be harmonized. We will also seek an international agreement providing for temporary import "safeguards." Reduction of agricultural barriers must accompany liberalization on industrial products.

We also support the concept of generalized preferences for the products of the less developed countries, but we cannot extend preferential access to this market to countries that will continue to discriminate in their markets against our exports in favor of those of other developed countries. In the special category of East-West trade, we intend to move forward in promoting economic normalization with the Communist countries. In this connection, we will seek from Congress the authority to extend most-favored-nation status to Communist countries with which we negotiate satisfactory trade agreements.

We also seek legislation to give the President authority to ensure that, regardless of the outcome of the upcoming multilateral trade negotiations, American goods will have fair and equitable access to foreign markets. Under these proposals the President would be able to lower or raise tariff and other barriers as appropriate and to provide incentives to other countries to lower highly restrictive trade barriers. Broader discretion would also be available to deal with persistent balance of payments problems and to remove certain import restrictions as an anti-inflationary measure. These actions are needed to achieve a more balanced and freer international economic system and to reduce our current trade deficits.

Other Major International Issues

International Investment

The impact of US private foreign investment abroad on jobs at home and our balance of payments has been a topic of much recent discussion. Some argue that such investment has, on balance, cost us jobs at home while others argue just the opposite. Available statistics indicate that the net effect of foreign investment on US jobs has been positive, and more extensive statistics are being gathered.

Nearly all US firms that have invested abroad have done so to compete more effectively in foreign markets. Foregoing such investment would mean that US companies would lose out to foreign competition. Government studies indicate that this would have adverse consequences for their domestic operations and for their domestic employment. They would no longer benefit from the parent firm's direct exports to its subsidiary abroad and from the investment income earned.

Although few products of US-owned firms overseas are sold in the United States, direct investment for sales to this market has become a target of complaint because such products do, of course, compete with those of domestic American firms. But this criticism ignores an important additional source of competition: companies undertaking such investments have principally done so to remain competitive with foreign producers in the US market. In any case, it should be recognized that our most sensitive import problems stem not from US-owned plants abroad but rather, as in the cases of textiles, shoes, and steel, from foreign-owned companies.

We are also becoming increasingly aware of the deficiencies in current international principles or understandings concerning direct investment. In many cases, US investors face restrictions in establishing and operating foreign businesses, while companies from these same countries have little trouble making similar investments here.

We continue to encourage investment in developing countries. In some less developed countries, such investment is not welcome. While we question the wisdom of that policy, we recognize the right of each country to determine its own priorities and development goals. When properties of US citizens are expropriated, however, the United States will insist, in accordance with President Nixon's statement of January 1972, that such action be carried out in accordance with international law, and with provision for prompt, adequate, and effective compensation.

Assistance to Less Developed Countries

Foreign aid continues to be essential to the economic growth of most of the developing world. Our reasons for continuing to provide such assistance range far beyond the humanitarian, encompassing mutual benefits—both economic and political—to these countries and to ourselves. We and other industrial nations are increasingly linked to the less developed countries by trade and investment.

Our long experience in assisting less developed countries to achieve economic progress has taught us valuable lessons, among them the recognition that there is no "typical" less developed country. While they all suffer from some degree of poverty, there is a wide range between the poorest and the ones closest to "developed" status. Some are much better equipped with the human resources crucially needed to achieve sustained economic progress, while others have been favored by largescale mineral deposits which, when developed, provide considerable amounts of needed foreign exchange. Still others unfortunately have neither. While economic assistance contributes significantly to economic growth, there is a limit to the degree which it can accelerate the development process, given the time required to upgrade local human and institutional resources....

Official foreign aid is only one ingredient of a less developed country's ability to progress. The capital and technical know-how that our businessmen have provided, stimulating local industry, have complemented what our government programs have done for the improvement of educational facilities, roads, agriculture and other needed infrastructure.

Energy

US energy consumption has been growing at an exceptionally high rate for the past ten years, spurred by the rapid expansion of the economy. At the same time, US production of fossil fuels—oil, natural gas, and coal—has remained relatively constant for several years.

The only fuel available to fill the near-term gap between decreasing domestic supplies and increasing demand is imported petroleum. In 1972, the United States was one of the world's two largest importers of petroleum, our purchases almost equaling those of Japan. Imports totaled 4.7 million barrels per day. The landed costs of these imports reached about $5 billion last year. All indications for the 1970s point to growing demands and decreasing domestic supplies of energy in the United States.

We have for some time been studying these energy-related problems, which defy any simple solution. Besides consideration of national security, production costs, and balance of payments, we must also take into account the environmental requirements—the need to minimize both the pollution of our air and the scarring of our landscape. This report presents some of the many factors being considered in developing the President's policy proposals for meeting our future energy needs.

ROOTS OF THE DRUG PROBLEM

March 22, 1973

The National Commission on Marihuana and Drug Abuse, in its second and final report to the President and Congress, recommended a new approach to narcotics addiction of all kinds with the emphasis on treatment rather than punishment. The 13-member panel concluded that the long-run solution to the nation's drug problems lay in far-reaching revision of American attitudes toward drug use which, it had become convinced, were "inconsistent and founded on many misconceptions." The commission members, critical of federal efforts to curb drug abuse, asserted that the drug programs were "ill-defined," "lavishly funded," and tended to "perpetuate the problem." It proposed the creation of a single federal agency to deal with all aspects of drug abuse from prevention to enforcement of the law.

In a letter accompanying the report, Raymond P. Shafer, chairman of the National Commission, said the commission had sought "to examine the roots of the drug problem in the United States, to analyze the assumptions upon which present policy is based, and to recommend policy directions for both the public and private sectors." It had come to the conclusion that "policy should be focused on the behavioral concomitants of drug use rather than on the drugs themselves." By adopting that approach, "policy makers can refine national objectives and devise more effective strategies for reducing the social costs of drug misuse." Acceptance of the resultant low-key analysis of "drug abuse"—a term that the commission said should be stricken from the official vocabulary of government—would be of even more lasting value, several experts believed, than the commission's lengthy recommendations.

The commission, made up of nine presidential appointees and four members of Congress, urged the following actions: new efforts to control the availability of alcohol, the most abused drug; a moratorium on distribution of drug information, because the commission members had found most of it inaccurate; creation of super-agencies in individual states comparable to the one recommended at the federal level; lowering of penalties for drug possession; and suspension of efforts to effect mandatory minimum jail sentences for drug pushers, because they might lead juries to acquit drug traffickers so as to avoid imposing very harsh penalties.

Throughout the 481-page report, the commission stressed that social and heavy drinking posed a problem similar to the one caused by recreational and habitual use of heroin, amphetamines, barbiturates, LSD, and other drugs. "Instead of assuming that mood alteration through some drugs is inherently objectionable, while similar use of others is not," the report said, "the public and its leaders must focus directly on the appropriate role of drug-induced mood alteration." Dr. Shafer told a news conference that "The enemy is not drugs or drug use, but the behavioral conduct of certain types of drug users." He said that the commission's study had indicated that people did not turn to drugs and alcohol when "a satisfactory alternative was available to them." As examples of such alternatives, Shafer cited the "chance to work" for the poor and "purposeful political and environmental activity" for the middle class.

White House reaction to the Shafer commission's report was frosty. In making its recommendations, the commission had run counter to several White House policies. The panel's position on mandatory minimum jail sentences for drug traffickers was in direct opposition to that of the President (See p. 326) and of New York Gov. Nelson A. Rockefeller (See p. 27). On the day the commission presented its report, the White House announced that the President planned to combine all federal drug law enforcement agencies within a new single office in the Justice Department, a move that fell short of one of the major recommendations of the commission's report.

The commission, headed by Shafer, included Dr. Dana L. Farnsworth, vice chairman, Dr. Henry Brill, Rep. Tim Lee Carter (R Ky.), Mrs. Joan Ganz Cooney, Dr. Charles O. Galvin, John A. Howard, Sen. Harold E. Hughes (D Iowa), Sen. Jacob K. Javits (R N.Y.), Rep. Paul G. Rogers (D Fla.), Dr. Maurice H. Seevers, Dr. J. Thomas Ungerleider and Mitchell Ware.

> Excerpts from Chapter One, "Defining the Issues," of the final report of the National Commission on Marihuana and Drug Abuse, March 22, 1973, follow:

CHAPTER ONE

DEFINING THE ISSUES

The need to solve the "drug problem" has been a recurrent theme of political and social commentary in the United States for most of the past decade. The apparent increase in drug use—itself defined as the problem—has precipitated a serious inquiry into its causes, a massive investment of social efforts to contain it, and a mobilization of medical and para-medical resources to treat its victims.

The Commission does not deny that a "drug problem" exists. We share the public's concern that an apparent rise in crime and other anti-social behavior may be related in part to drug-using or drug-seeking behavior. Likewise, we share the public alarm over the attraction to drug use by large portions of this nation's youth, particularly when such use is indiscriminate and apparently oblivious to its risks. The lives and futures of our young can only be hurt by such behavior. We share, too, the frustration which comes from knowing that drug use spreads by example and that a continuing growth in the using population augurs no better for tomorrow.

While recognizing that a drug problem exists, we cannot allow our distress to interfere with the performance of our mandate. We were appointed not to fan public anxiety, but to convert it into meaningful activity with constructive proposals. This can be done only by refusing to accept at face value many of the common assumptions about drugs and the drug problem. We must examine the reasons behind the fears, conducting the inquiry without passion and with candor. Confident social action comes from an understanding of the problem and from an impartial assessment of the impact of alternative strategies. We have sought to define the problem and to provide at least an initial assessment of the possible responses to it.

The Commission has carefully surveyed the social response to the contemporary drug problem, and has been struck by a persisting uneasiness which seems to color the entire effort. On the street and in the councils of government, increasing numbers of drug abuse "experts" wonder whether their commitment and efforts have had any actual impact on the problem. Many of them assume optimistic positions in public while suspecting privately that no solution will be found. The Commission understands the reasons for this malaise. We are convinced that public policy, as presently designed, is premised on incorrect assumptions, is aimed at the wrong targets, and is too often unresponsive to human needs and aspirations....

DEFINITIONAL CONFUSION: WHAT IS DRUG ABUSE?

The use of psychoactive drugs is commonplace in American life. Distribution of these drugs is an integral part of the social and economic order. In 1970, 214 million prescriptions for psychoactive drugs were issued, representing annual retail sales of approximately $1 billion (Balter and Levine, 1971). The alcohol industry produced over one billion gallons of spirits, wine and beer for which 100 million consumers paid about $24 billion.

What is the pertinence of this information for a Commission mandated to report to the American people on drug abuse?"...

The Commission concluded early in its deliberations that the focus of inquiry should not be determined by general impressions or facile labels. Instead, formulation of a coherent social policy requires a consideration of the entire range of psychoactive drug consumption, and a determination as to whether and under what circumstances drug-using behavior becomes a matter of social concern....

"Drug"—The All-Purpose Concept

The meaning of the word drug often varies with the context in which it is used. From a strictly scientific point of view, a drug is any substance other than food which by its chemical nature affects the structure or function of the living organism.... However, when used in the context of drug "abuse" or the drug "problem," the meaning of "drug" becomes social rather than scientific.

In its social sense, drug is not a neutral term. This point is best illustrated by the fact that "drug problem" is frequently used not as a descriptive phrase, but a substitute for the word drug.... Local leaders often feel compelled to report not simply that drugs are available or that they are used, but that there is a "drug problem."...

The public tends uniformly to regard heroin as a drug, as well as other substances associated with the drug problem, such as marihuana, cocaine, the amphetamines and the barbiturates. Some psychoactive substances, such as alcohol and tobacco, are generally not regarded as drugs at all. In neither public law nor public discussion is alcohol regarded as a drug....

The imprecision of the term "drug" has had serious social consequences. Because alcohol is excluded, the public is conditioned to regard a martini as something fundamentally different from a marihuana cigarette, a barbiturate capsule or a bag of heroin. Similarly, because the referents of the word "drug" differ so widely in the therapeutic and social contexts, the public is conditioned to believe that "street" drugs act according to entirely different principles than "medical" drugs. The result is that the risks of the former are exaggerated and the risks of the latter are overlooked.

This confusion must be dispelled. Alcohol *is* a drug.... All drugs have multiple effects. The lower the dose, the more important non-drug factors become in determining drug effect. At high dose levels, and for some individuals at much lower dose levels, all drugs may be dangerous. The individual and social consequences of drug use escalate with frequency and duration of use. American drug policy will never be coherent until it is founded on uniform principles such as these, which apply to *all* drugs.

Drug Abuse: Synonym for Social Disapproval

Drug abuse is another way of saying drug problem. Now immortalized in the titles of federal and state governmental agencies (and we might add, in our own), this term has the virtue of rallying all parties to a common cause: no one could possibly be *for* abuse of drugs any more than they could be *for* abuse of minorities, power or children. By the same token, the term also obscures the fact that "abuse" is undefined where drugs are concerned. Neither the public, its policy makers nor the expert community share a common understanding of its meaning or of the nature of the phenomenon to which it refers.

The Commission has noted over the last two years that the public and press often employ drug *abuse* interchangeably with drug *use*.... The Commission was curious about whether the public had any more precise conception of the meaning of drug abuse than the experts. In our second National Survey, public attitudes on this issue were probed.... Roughly 30% of both youth and adult populations associate drug abuse with the use of drugs for other than medical purposes, including any use of those substances which have been prohibited because they have no medical uses. In contrast, large numbers of both adults and youth relate the term to the consequences of drug taking. Excessive doses (27% and 16%), dependence (17% and 15%) and danger to health (11% and 10%) are the most common examples. Also of interest were those respondents who indicated that they didn't know what drug abuse meant (13% and 20%)....

Drug abuse is an entirely subjective concept. It is any drug use the respondent frowns upon. Most respondents disapprove of the use of medically-distributed pills for other than medical purposes (those sanctioned by a physician), any use of heroin, and any use which suggests that the user is dependent or seeking pleasure. Significantly fewer respondents seem to disapprove of daily use of alcohol, weekly use of marihuana and experimentation with legitimate pills not obtained through a physician....

Drug abuse may refer to any type of drug or chemical without regard to its pharmacologic actions. It is an eclectic concept having only one uniform connotation: societal disapproval.

The Commission believes that the term drug abuse must be deleted from official pronouncements and public policy dialogue. The term has no functional utility and has become no more than an arbitrary codeword for that drug use which is presently considered wrong. Continued use of this term, with its emotional overtones, will serve only to perpetuate confused public attitudes about drug-using behavior....

The Roots of a "Problem"

We have focused our initial attention on vocabulary for an important reason. The linguistic symbols which our society attaches to certain drugs and drug-related conduct illustrate the extent to which present attitudes and social responses are rooted in the past. "Drug abuse" is only the most recent in a long line of such symbols which this society has applied to disapproved drug-taking behavior or to disapproved substances....

Current social policy is largely an accumulation of *ad hoc* policy responses to the use of particular substances. "Street" use of a previously unknown substance at a time of social tension tends to generate a set of untested assumptions about the drug, often including a presumed consequence of undesirable behavior, and to result in a restrictive legal policy, all of which become imbedded in public attitude.

Drug policy as we know it today is a creature of the 20th Century. Until the last third of the 19th Century, America's total legal policy regarding drugs was limited to regulation of alcohol distribution,... localized restrictions on tobacco smoking, and the laws of the various states regulating pharmacies and restricting the distribution of "poisons...."

A public response was triggered by use of...drugs and cocaine in a social context. Beginning with increased Chinese immigration after the Civil War, the practice of smoking opium took root on the West Coast and spread rapidly across the country to most urban areas. Although the practice was confined mainly to the Chinese, it also appeared to attract "sporty characters" and the underworld figures in the cities.

In 1875, San Francisco enacted an ordinance prohibiting the smoking or possession of opium, the possession of opium pipes and the maintenance of "opium dens." As the practice spread, it generated a succession of similar state laws and local ordinances. Despite a growing problem of opiate dependence arising from unrestrained distribution of these drugs within the medical system in the United States, it was the "street" use of the opiates and cocaine which accelerated professional and public interest in their habit-forming properties.

By the turn of the century, the nation had become aware of a large opiate-dependent population in its midst.... As a result of increased awareness, the medical profession and state legislatures intensified their efforts to control availability of these substances, primarily by tightening the restrictions on medical distribution and prohibiting non-medical distribution. In 1906, the Congress passed the Pure Food and Drug Act, the first major federal drug legislation, which required labelling of all preparations containing "habit-forming" drugs, and proprietaries containing significant quantities of opiates soon disappeared....

By 1910, the medical profession had become seriously concerned about the habit-forming characteristics of heroin. The publicity attending its pleas for legislative controls on the availability of this drug, together with a crusade being waged by law enforcement officials against the street use of opiates and cocaine, aroused public anxiety about a "narcotics problem" of major proportions. Although almost every state had regulatory laws of some kind, most observers contended that the states could not control the problem. Federal legislation was also said to be necessary to implement international treaties. In addition, the movement for national alcohol prohibition began gathering steam in 1913, sensitizing the public to the possibility of national drug prohibitions. All these factors culminated in passage of the Harrison Narcotic Act in 1914....

The Harrison Act crystallized a national policy of curtailing the availability of "habit-forming" substances. The previous failure to appreciate the habit-forming properties of new substances had now resulted in professional and legislative preoccupation with this issue. Whereas the term narcotics formerly referred to those substances which produced stupefaction and sleep ("narcosis"), including alcohol, the term... was not associated with any unfamiliar drug which appeared on the streets among those populations which were associated with the opiates and cocaine. The acute effects of the various specific drugs became blurred. Because physicians and policy makers had now become exceedingly cautious about the dependence issue, any new drug was carefully scrutinized for habit-forming properties; if the drug was used on the streets it was often presumed "habit-forming" and therefore classified as a "narcotic."

Within the next three decades, peyote and marihuana were inserted in the "narcotics" laws of many states; chloral hydrate, which had been covered by earlier drug laws, was also included in the definition of "narcotics" in the new legislation. It should be noted that legal classification of a drug as a "narcotic" tended to malign its therapeutic utility. For example, heroin, and later marihuana, were purged from the pharmacopoeia altogether. In sum, the word "narcotics" had been purged of its scientific meaning and became, instead, a symbol of socially disapproved drugs.

Other substances were introduced into the practice of medicine, notably the barbiturates and amphetamines, but they were regulated under general pharmacy laws rather than under the "narcotics" laws. Although amphetamines were introduced in 1929 and the short-acting barbiturates appeared a few years later, they did not enter the illicit marketplace on a massive scale in the United States until the 1960's and consequently were not associated with the narcotics until then.

During the last decade, succeeding waves of hallucinogens, amphetamines and barbiturates escaped from the laboratories, pharmacies and medicine chests and found their way into the streets. Together with marihuana, which moved from one socio-economic "street" to another, use of these drugs defined a new phenomenon and became associated with a new kind of drug user. To a substantial degree, the narcotics policy had from the beginning been identified with under-privileged minorities, criminals and social outsiders in general, although a common feature of each periodic drug scare, including cocaine at the turn of the century, heroin in the 1920s, marihuana in the 1930's and heroin again in the 1950's, was the fear that drug use would spread to youth. However, the drug problem of the 1960's was clearly identified with the children of the middle and upper classes. Drug use was now associated with unfamiliar life styles, youthful defiance of the established order, the emergence of a visible street culture, campus unrest, communal living, protest politics and even political radicalism.

The drug taking of this youth population coincided with pervasive social anxieties regarding social disorder in general and youthful behavior specifically. To many, youthful drug use offered a convenient explanation for these problems, and as the Commission noted in its first Report, marihuana in particular came to symbolize the entire spectrum of social concern. Existing legislative controls and vocabulary were closely tied to the old stereotypes and society responded to this new drug-using behavior through separate legislative action (the Drug Abuse Control Amendments of 1965) and a new linguistic symbol. "Dangerous drugs" emerged as the statutory label for the non-narcotic drugs, such as hallucinogens, amphetamines and barbiturates, whose non-medical use was socially disapproved.

The single-mindedness of American drug policy is illustrated clearly by the reorganization of the federal drug bureaucracy which took place in 1968. For technical reasons stemming from the revenue structure of the Harrison Act, narcotics enforcement had always been lodged in the Treasury Department. When the "dangerous drugs" were brought under regulatory control in 1965, enforcement responsibility was assigned to a new bureau in the Department of Health, Education, and Welfare. Then in 1968, the responsibilities of the two agencies were merged in a new agency established in the Department of Justice: the Bureau of Narcotics and Dangerous Drugs. Public policy had the appearance of coherence once again.

But this was not enough. Marihuana use continued to increase throughout the decade, and the public was caught up in a highly emotional debate. For the first time since the inception of the American "narcotics" policy, public opinion focused on some of the fundamental assumptions. Not surprisingly, debate on the marihuana issue was often couched in terms of the statutory vocabulary which has come to symbolize drug policy. For example, the scientifically indefensible classification of marihuana as a "narcotic" immediately provoked an erosion of the symbolic coherence which had previously characterized drug policy. Similarly, the inevitable comparison between alcohol and marihuana called into question the substantive separation between narcotics and dangerous drug policies on the one hand and alcohol policy on the other. After all, alcohol can legitimately be classified as a "narcotic" in a very specific sense of that term, and it is surely a "dangerous drug" as well.

Until the close of the 1960's, official defenses of marihuana policy continued to be premised on the implications of the statutory vocabulary. Although the narcotic ideology was quickly abandoned, many official pronouncements continued to link marihuana with the opiates because of their association in the law and to insist that marihuana was a "dangerous drug" even if it was not a "narcotic." An historical understanding apprises us that these classifications are reflections of, rather than reasons for, social disapproval.

It became clear by the end of the decade that "narcotics" and "dangerous drugs" were no longer adequate symbols of social policy; consequently "drug abuse" was adopted as a replacement symbol. However, the need to distinguish marihuana use from other forms of "drug abuse" resulted in yet another distinction: marihuana was classified as a "soft" drug as opposed to the "hard" drugs, suggesting the same kind of distinction drawn between "hard liquor" and other alcoholic beverages. But, as has been the case with all drug vocabulary, this distinction serves a social rather than a scientific purpose. This terminology generally indicates an attempt to distinguish marihuana from heroin and cocaine, the stereotypical "hard" drugs. However, there is no consensus whatsoever as to which other substances, if any, are considered to be "hard."...

Like "drug abuse," the hard-soft terminology reflects a nascent effort to reestablish a sphere of "bad" drug use. Within the official community as well as the general public, attempts are being made to grade drugs according to their potential hazards, particularly their capacity for inducing physical dependence. To the extent that this is true, the new linguistic symbols suggest that public concern has in some ways returned full circle to where it began almost a century ago.

THE SOCIAL RESPONSE: FALSE PREMISES AND THE

PERPETUATION OF A PROBLEM

As this brief historial summary illustrates, American drug policy is almost seven decades old, and not once during this period have the underlying assumptions been systematically evaluated and a broad, coherent foundation for policy making established. As a result, each new occurrence in drug development and each new use pattern have been viewed as unfamiliar, with the unfamiliarity breeding a sense of crisis, and the crisis precipitating *ad hoc* policy responses.

The Commission feels strongly that the present institutional response, despite sincere efforts to move it in the right direction, continues to be rooted in the mistakes of the past, and, indirectly, tends to perpetuate the "problem." Accordingly, it is useful to scrutinize the goals toward which the policy is directed and the premises which support it, as well as to describe briefly some of the present governmental responses which are guided by these assumptions. Finally, as a prelude to the remainder of the Report, the concluding sections of this Chapter will attempt to "wipe the slate clean" and to sketch a general framework for defining the problem and formulating a coherent social policy.

The Assumptions and Premises of Present Policy

Elimination of Non-Medical Drug Use

American drug policy has been predicated on one fundamental notion: that the societal objective is to eliminate "non-medical" drug use. Inquiry has rarely been addressed to whether this goal is desirable or possible. Failure to address such questions is abetted by the exclusion of certain drugs and certain types of drug taking from the realm of social distress. For example, the non-medical use of alcohol and tobacco would be inconsistent with the declared goal; thus, statutory vocabulary and social folklore have established the fiction that they are not drugs at all. Although use of these substances may arouse concern, they are not viewed in the wider context of drug use.

Another area excluded from public discussion is drug use sanctioned by medical judgment.... Drug policy makers cannot truthfully assert that this society aims to eliminate non-medical drug use. No semantic fiction will alter the fundamental composition of alcohol and tobacco. Further, even if the objective is amended to exclude these drugs, human history discounts the notion that drug-using behavior can be so tightly confined as a medical system implies.... The medical/non-medical distinction has become increasingly blurred as emotional ailments increase....

Deferring for the moment our own view as to what society's objective in this area ought to be, we do know that it is not as clear cut as official pronouncements imply.... Policy makers must recognize the scope and complexity of drug-using behavior and develop rational distinctions between that which should be disapproved and that which should be tolerated, or even approved. Within the area of disapproval, policy makers should not consider all disapproved drug use to be of equal importance; priorities must be assigned on the basis of actual and potential social consequence, and not just on the basis of numbers of users.

Risk-Taking and Health

Often cited in support of societal disapproval of non-medical drug use is the proposition that individuals should not risk their health by using drugs. Without regard to the philosophical propriety of this premise as a guide for social policy, this view appears to be somewhat at odds with the facts about drug use and with prevailing social attitudes toward risk-taking in other areas....

The Commission believes that persons who take this approach have misconstrued the nature of the drug issue. The asumption that all psychoactive drug use is a high-risk behavior presumes a progression from irregular use of low doses to continuous use of high doses, thereby ignoring pharmacological variations among drugs and the importance of frequency of use, method of administration, dose, and non-drug factors as determinants of risk. In fact, injury to health is associated primarily with chronic heavy use and at times with the acute effects of high doses.

Further, there is no correlation whatsoever between the capacity of psychoactive drugs to induce behavioral disorders and their capacity to induce organic or somatic toxicity or pathology.... Nonetheless, the approach often applied to "drugs of abuse" is the same as that applied to non-psychoactive substances: risks to individual health will be tolerated only if the medical needs for the substance justify the risks.... Who is to weigh the perceived advantages of drug use against the risk, the individual or the society?....

Society has long been aware of the individual and social risks of alcohol use. Even with the effort now being made to inform the public of the risks of tobacco use, society still permits this drug to be widely available. In both cases, society clearly subordinates the risks inherent in such behavior, deferring instead to individual judgment.

The Commission is not suggesting that health risks are irrelevant to the formulation of drug policy. However, whatever appropriate weight is given to health considerations, it is a peripheral, rather than focal, concern. Drug policy must be based on the social consequences of drug use, and on the social impact of drug-induced behavior.

Motivation for Mood Alteration

Subsumed within the societal goal of eliminating non-medical drug use is the value judgment that use of drugs for the explicit purpose of mood alteration is *per se* undesirable. To harmonize this judgment with approved conduct, we avoid analyzing the motivations of similar behaviors.... Within the medical setting, the individual is increasingly making the decision to use medically approved drugs and selecting them according to their capacity to alter his mood.... Whatever the biological and psychological foundations for the common human desire to alter consciousness, policy makers must recognize that drugs have always been used for this purpose.... Instead of assuming that mood alteration through some drugs is inherently objectionable, while similar use of others is not, the public and its leaders must focus directly on the appropriate role of drug-induced mood alteration. It is no longer satisfactory to defend social disapproval of use of a particular drug on the ground that it is a "mind-altering drug" or a "means of escape." For so are they all.

Drugs and Individual Responsibility

Implicit in present policy is the concern that many individuals cannot be trusted to make prudent or responsible decisions regarding drug-taking.... A deep-seated popular belief that some drugs diminish or destroy the individual's capacity to control his behavior is reflected in hypotheses such as "drugs cause crime" or "drugs cause dropping out" or "drugs cause mental illness." Any perceived correlation between use of the drug and the unwanted consequence is attributed to the drug, removing the individual from any and all responsibility. Similarly, while it is true that certain drugs offer more intense psychological rewards than others, seduction characteristics are attributed to all psychoactive drugs, suggesting a chain of progression from light to heavy use, from weak to stronger drugs, all without the intervention of individual choice....

The effects of any drug, psychoactive drugs included, are mainly dose related. At low or moderate doses they are determined mainly by non-drug factors, such as the psychological characteristics of the individual, the reasons why he uses the drug, what he expects the effects will be, the physical and social setting in which he uses it, and how he perceives its use or non-use in relation to self-defined goals....

An Overview of the Present Response

Because of this confusion about objectives, the formal institutional response to the drug problem has been more reflexive than rational, more situation-oriented than strategic. The *ad hoc* responses to use of specific psychoactive drugs have interfered with examination of the fundamental questions relating to behavior patterns and the appropriate means of social control.... This procedure tends to perpetuate the public focus on the drugs rather than on the prevention of behavior about which society is concerned. When the drug appears in the streets, as it inevitably does, social institutions respond as if the behavior was unanticipated, and because they are ill-prepared to deal with the situation, an atmosphere of crisis is generated.

Because the focus has always been on the elimination of prohibited substances altogether and on the elimination of the street use of therapeutically useful drugs, social institutions have directed primary attention to the problem of *use* of *specific drugs*. Patterns of drug-using behavior have been ignored except as an afterthought of intervention. When increases in prohibited drug use continue to escalate, policy makers respond, not by reassessing the problem from different perspectives, but rather by pressing for ever-more costly mechanisms of control; costly both in terms of resources and important social values. Drug policy can be thus summed up: increased use of disapproved drugs precipitates more spending, more programs, more arrests and more penalties, all with little positive effect in reducing use of these drugs....

Risk-Education

An important operating assumption of the present response is that if people are educated about the risks of drug taking, they will not use drugs. It is presumed that presentation of information regarding dangers and risks can quiet curiosity and the desire for anticipated pleasant psychological sensations, the factors which account for most individual drug experiences....

Campaigns have been mounted in the past, both through the mass media and the schools, about the dangers of alcohol use and cigarette smoking.... Still the consumption of alcohol continues and the number of persons smoking cigarettes increases.

This same kind of educational effort has been directed at the illicit drugs with no apparent impact on behavior. Little insight has been gained as to why this approach has not worked with alcohol and cigarettes, or as to whether risk-oriented curricula may actually arouse interest rather than dampen it. Further, assuming that such programs might be useful, little thought has been given to how to transmit the information, the assumption again being that the facts speak for themselves....

Coercion

If information about risks and moral suasion is insufficient to convince many people not to use drugs, it is assumed that the threat of a criminal sanction will do so. While a criminal proscription does function as a deterrent to some degree for all behavior, the strength of this factor varies according to the nature of the offense, the characteristics of the actor, the probability of detection and the certainty of punishment. With regard to drug consumption, all of these factors diminish the utility of the criminal sanction. Drug consumption is an expressive conduct which normally occurrs in private among groups which are least influenced by legal condemnation. In addition, the consumption-related offenses are no longer supported by the strong social consensus which once existed, and the emerging ambivalence is reflected in the dispositional decisions of police, prosecutors and courts....

Sickness

Anyone choosing to use drugs, despite the enumerated risks, moral suasion and threat of criminalization, is often considered abnormal, emotionally ill and weak of character. The last decade has seen the pendulum of legislative opinion swing toward the belief that drug dependence and even drug *use* is a "medical" problem, that it can be "treated," and that the user can be "rehabilitated." Like many ideas which aim to correct those previously in vogue, the medical approach has itself become a runaway concept. Policy makers have adopted policy guidewords such as "treatment," "rehabilitation," "contagion," and "epidemic," without regard to their utility in the present context.

The "sickness" label has been attached to all uses of prohibited drugs without regard to their patterns of drug-taking behavior.... To label drug users in general as mentally ill is to place a large segment of American society in need of formal medical assistance.

With regard to drug dependence in particular, the public has been led to believe that the condition is as definable and treatable as ordinary illnesses of the body. In reality, there is not, at the present time, any generally applicable cure for drug-dependent persons let alone non-dependent users of drugs....

Public policy is committed to the treatment and rehabilitation of all drug-dependent persons. While thousands of persons have been aided by treatment efforts in recent years, social objectives continue to outstrip professional understanding of the condition and official capacity to deliver the necessary services.

Perpetuating the Problem

Because of the intensity of the public concern and the emotionalism surrounding the topic of drugs, all levels of government have been pressured into action with little time for planning. The political pressures involved in this governmental effort have resulted in a concentration of public energy on the most immediate aspects of drug use and a reaction along the paths of least political resistance. The recent result has been the creation of ever larger bureaucracies, ever increasing expenditures of monies, and an outpouring of publicity so that the public will know that "something" is being done. Perhaps the major consequence of this *ad hoc* policy planning has been the creation, at the federal, state and community levels, of a vested interest in the perpetuation of the problem among those dispensing and receiving funds....

All of these responses stem from one fundamental flaw in present drug policy: the problem is defined incorrectly. The uneasiness which the Commission has encountered among thoughtful observers and officials arises largely from their own perceptions that the present response, although massive, has so far been relatively ineffective. Yet, any challenge to the basic premises of policy may be viewed by some as a disavowal of the entire social response. The Commission does not believe the present policy should be abandoned out of hand. Instead, we hope that policy can be made more coherent and more flexible. In order to do so, we must put aside preconceived notions, setting out afresh to redefine the problem.

DEFINING THE PROBLEM

The Meaning of Drug Use

Throughout history man has used available psychoactive substances to seek relief from cold, hunger, deprivation, anxiety, pain and boredom. He also has used such substances to receive pleasure or to achieve new experiences.... Drugs have effects other than those which are sought; and all drug-effects vary with amount and frequency of use, the characteristics of the user, and the set and setting in which they are used.

Man does not ordinarily continue to do something that does not fulfill some real or imagined need.... Use of specific substances may determine group membership, or status within a group, or among groups. It may function as either a symbol or symptom of rebellion, alienation, independence or sophistication.

To better understand current self-defined drug use and to determine the scope of social concern,... the inquiry must shift from drugs to people, from pharmacological effects to the meaning and function of drug use....

407

Drug-Using Behavior

The initial step in understanding the meaning of drug use and its impact on the social order is to regard this phenomenon as we would any other human behavior.... Because drug-using behavior is not a unitary phenomenon, the social consequences of this behavior are tied directly to the individual's reason for the drug use and in turn to the frequency, duration, intensity, dose, set and setting of use. The Commission has divided the entire spectrum of drug-using behavior into five patterns reflecting essentially distinct meanings for the individual users.

The most common type of drug-using behavior can be classified as *experimental:* a short-term, non-patterned trial of one or more drugs, motivated primarily by curiosity or a desire to experience an altered mood state.... Most non-experimental drug-using behavior can be classified as *recreational,* which occurs in social settings among friends or acquaintances who desire to share an experience which they define as both acceptable and pleasurable. Generally, recreational use is both voluntary and patterned and tends not to escalate to more frequent or intense use patterns....

A pattern of drug-using behavior which has grown significantly during the last decade is *circumstantial* drug use. This behavior is generally motivated by the user's perceived need or desire to achieve a new and anticipated effect in order to cope with a specific problem, situation or condition of a personal or vocational nature.... A much smaller group of drug users may be regarded as having escalated from recreational or circumstantial use patterns into *intensified* drug-using behavior. Although this is the most amorphous of the behavioral categories, the Commission refers in general to drug use which occurs at least daily and is motivated by an individual's perceived need to achieve relief from a persistent problem or stressful situation, or his desire to maintain a certain self-prescribed level of performance....

The most disturbing pattern of drug-using behavior, encompassing the smallest number of drug users, is *compulsive* use which consists of a patterned behavior at a high frequency and high level of intensity, characterized by a high degree of psychological dependence and perhaps physical dependence as well. The distinguishing feature of this behavior is that drug use dominates the individual's existence, and preoccupation with drug taking precludes other social functioning....

Drug-Related Risk

An understanding of the different types of drug-using behavior is the starting point for problem definition. In these behavioral classifications, the key element is the meaning of drug use to the individual

The specific drug being used is subsumed within this framework. In reaching the next step in the problem definition process, we must focus on the individual and social risks attending drug use and those factors which distinguish drug-using behavior from other forms of experimental and recreational activities and other forms of coping behavior....

The above propositions apply to all drugs. However, an additional axiom is crucial to formulation of social policy: *specific drugs are qualitatively different in terms of individual and social risk.* Drug-using behavior is not a unitary phenomenon; nor are all drugs the same....

Risks to individual health

The health risks arising from the acute effects of a drug experience are related primarily to dose and the set and setting of use.... The major concern from the standpoint of individual health is the effect of repeated administration of the drug over a long term, rather than the acute effect of the drug experience. The possibilities of organ damage as well as impairment of psychological function increase with the frequency and intensity of use; also, chronic use of tolerance-producing drugs increases the risk of overdose as well as the likelihood of physical or psychological damage. Individual drugs vary widely in toxicity, in tolerance and in psychological effect.

Drug-Induced Behavior

Whether a person under the influence of a drug will become aggressive or passive, will have impaired psychomotor capacity or will exhibit otherwise disordered behavior depends on the entire range of variables determining drug effect. Set and setting play a most important role, particularly when low doses are consumed. However, drugs are qualitatively different in this connection and can be compared. A regular user of psychoactive substances is generally able to compensate for some of the acute behavioral effects. Over the long term, however, additional risks may be encountered; as a result of chronic use, a person may become significantly more aggressive or passive, may become significantly less adept at muscular control, or may deteriorate mentally, becoming incapable of engaging in voluntary learning efforts. Most important, the likelihood of adverse long-term effects on behavior is increased substantially if the person becomes dependent upon the substance. It is for this reason that we have isolated the dependence liability of various substances as a separate risk factor.

Dependence Liability

Whether a person who continues to use a psychoactive substance will become dependent on the substance, escalating from recreational or circumstantial patterns to intensified or compulsive patterns, is an issue where the characteristics of the drug and the individual play equally important roles.... The behavioral consequences of chronic use also differ among drugs, as does the potential for behavioral disruption when the dependent person's drug-taking is interrupted. From these perspectives, chronic use of dependence-producing doses of barbiturates poses significantly different problems from chronic use of cocaine.

Because the health and behavioral risks of drug use increase with frequency, intensity and duration of use, the likelihood of dependence is a crucial determinant of social concern.

Evaluating the Social Consequences of Drug Use

As we wrote in our first Report on marihuana, the social impact of the use of a particular drug or of a specific pattern of drug-using behavior involves three distinct considerations. First is the *impact on public safety* of drug-induced behavior or drug dependence.... The second general area of social consequence is the *impact on the public health and public welfare* arising from drug use....

When drug use is approached from the public health and welfare standpoint, it must be viewed as part of the larger health and welfare system which deals with many related problems.... In the drug area, health resources must be allocated and available to deal with acute reactions, overdoses and diseases, such as hepatitis, among predictable proportions of drug-using populations. This may require a shift of limited medical services from one health area to another. More important, medical and social services must be organized for delivery to persons whose intensified or compulsive drug use is correlated with impairment of social functioning (treatment and rehabilitation), as well as to populations who might develop these patterns of use (prevention).

Finally, an understanding of the social impact of drug use must also include the *impact on the normative social order*.... Only when the impact of drug use on the normative social order is placed in proper perspective can we hope to dispel the climate of crisis in which drug policy is now made.

Defining America's Drug Problem

Theoretically, social concern about use of a particular substance relative to another should correlate with the verified social costs attending the use of each drug in that society. As the incidence of intensified and compulsive use increases, so too should the public's concern with the problem. However, the current problem definition in the United States bears little relationship to actual social cost. The intense public concern regarding use of most drugs in large measure reflects anxiety for the future rather than empirical considerations rooted in the present. The result has been an overestimation of the nature of the problem attending use of some drugs, such as marihuana, and an underestimation of the problem attending use of other drugs, such as barbiturates and alcohol....

The Limits of Social Control

The Commission believes that the contemporary American drug problem has emerged in part from our institutional response to drug use.... We have failed to weave policy into the fabric of social institutions. Instead, policy has been imposed from the top, often without regard to possible impact on the institutional fabric itself, much less on drug use. It is worthwhile, then, to consider the general requirements of social control and the general guidelines upon which policy making should be based.... The policy maker's task in this area is not to choose between social control or social disinterest; rather, it is to determine if and when informal mechanisms of social control must be supplemented with formal ones....

In its most basic sense, drug taking is socially controlled when it is routinized, ritualized and structured in ways which reduce to a minimum the occurrence of drug-induced behavior which the culture considers undesirable.... In contemporary mass societies, however, responsibility for social control over increasing spheres of human conduct has tended to pass from the family and church to educational, economic and governmental institutions. This reliance on formal institutions, coupled with the impersonality and complexity of industrial and post-industrial societies, has made the task of social control of drug-taking behavior all the more difficult. For this reason, together with the proliferation of available substances, the problem appears far more pervasive in these societies, especially when they are heterogeneous and individualistic....

The success of social control through law is always difficult to measure. First, "tolerable limits" is a relative concept.... A second factor which complicates heavy reliance on social control through law are the values different societies place on the rights of individuals....

We must consider the current American response to its drug problem. First, reliance on law is unlikely to be effective in American society unless it is joined consciously and directly with use of other institutions of social control. Second, drug policy should not be made in a vacuum. A proposed policy must be analyzed both in terms of its likely impact on drug-taking behavior as well as its likely impact on other social values and institutions. Third, the problems to which the society directs its formal response must be those which exceed the level of socially tolerable limits. For example, most drug use, even of disapproved substances, is socially controlled to some degree by informal institutions such as peer groups and families. Formal social efforts should be directed to those behaviors which are not adequately controlled by informal mechanisms of social control, aiming primarily to support the informal control mechanisms and intervening directly only as a last resort....

THE COMMISSION'S ROLE

The Commission believes that the first step toward resolving the drug problem is to reconsider the present diagnosis of the ailment. The social response is presently a large part of the problem, one which is compounded with each unanticipated crisis. To break this cycle, it is necessary to refocus our attention on that behavior which carries the most serious social consequence. Preoccupation with the drugs themselves must be replaced by an understanding of the behavioral impact of drug use. We must deal directly with the ambivalence of our attitudes with respect to drugs, conforming our beliefs to reality and our conduct to our ideals. Only then will a coherent policy emerge, one which can withstand legitimate criticism, and one which will have a beneficial impact on the problem.

Promises which cannot be kept must not be made. The public must be apprised that disapproved drug use is part of a larger social pattern, and that all the money and effort that the American society can muster will never be able to deal effectively with this behavior if the problem continues to be defined as it is now. Drug policy making must take into account a wide range of social phenomena of which drug use is a small part, and institutional responses must be framed in the context of broader social roles. Unless present policy is redirected, we will perpetuate the same problems, tolerate the same social costs, and find ourselves as we do now, no further along the road to a more rational legal and social approach than we were in 1914.

The Commission has not attempted to devise utopian policy recommendations. Instead we have attempted primarily to formulate a policy-making process, one which includes all of the important variables and which separates various crucial issues. We have applied this process in order to provide a plan of action to be implemented *immediately*. But we would be remiss if we were only to propose recommendations for the present. The Commission feels that a coherent social policy requires a fundamental alteration of social attitudes toward drug use, and a willingness to embark on new courses when previous actions have failed.

▼▼▼

EMERGENCE OF WATERGATE SCANDAL

March 23, 1973

A break-in at an office building in Washington, D.C., early in the morning of June 17, 1972, developed in the spring of 1973 into one of the most publicized pieces of political skulduggery in American history. The name of the building in which five men were arrested at 2:30 a.m. that day became the word commonly used to describe not only the break-in itself, but also the widening circle of events surrounding it. The name was Watergate.

The five men were arrested at Democratic National Committee headquarters in the swank Watergate apartment-office-hotel-shopping complex. The men were wearing surgical gloves to avoid leaving fingerprints and were carrying electronic eavesdropping equipment. Incredulity, sometimes mixed with cynical laughter, typified the initial public reaction to the bungled break-in. But, as one disclosure followed another, the laughter faded and the Watergate incident was recognized for what it was: one segment of a much larger political puzzle involving espionage and sabotage, implicating White House officials and financed with hundreds of thousands of dollars in secret campaign funds.

In a little more than seven months, the five burglars and two of their accomplices had either pleaded guilty to or been convicted of felonies. But most of the puzzle remained unsolved by the early spring of 1973. A federal grand jury continued its investigations; three civil suits awaited trial in U.S. District Court in Washington; and a constitutional dispute over the President's right to refuse to permit his staff to testify before congressional committees to answer allegations of involvement in illegal operations cost a nominee the prestigious job of FBI director. All the unanswered questions created a growing uneasiness among Republican officials who feared damage to their party. An increasing number of Republicans were speaking out publicly against the administration's handling of the charges and were demanding candor and cooperation with investigators.

Secret Contributions and Secret Funds

After the initial reports on the June 17 break-in, the Watergate incident dropped temporarily from the headlines. But even during its absence from the news, a federal grand jury was conducting an investigation that led to the indictment of seven men. Many of the revelations that gradually came to light were the results of diligent digging by and occasional leaks to the press. As the grand jury was hearing witnesses throughout the summer of 1972 in connection with the Watergate bugging, reports began to emerge about enormous sums of money, obtained under unusual circumstances, for use in the Republicans' intelligence operations.

A report from the General Accounting Office released Aug. 26 cited five "apparent" and four "possible" violations of the Federal Election Campaign Act of 1971 by the Finance Committee to Re-elect the President. The report, and seven subsequent reports, charged that certain contributions not made public had been collected after April 7, 1972, when the act and its reporting requirements went into effect. One of the undisclosed contributions had turned up in the Florida bank account of convicted Watergate conspirator Bernard L. Barker. Investigations led to the indictment of the Re-election Finance Committee on eight counts of campaign violations. After submitting a plea of "no contest," the committee was fined $8,000.

Recurrent references had been made since the fall of 1972 to a secret fund, kept in a safe in the office of Maurice H. Stans, chairman of the Finance Committee to Re-elect the President, that was allegedly used to pay expenses of the Watergate bugging and other espionage and sabotage operations. Press reports said that high Republican officials including former Attorney General John N. Mitchell and White House chief of staff H. R. Haldeman had knowledge of the fund and were authorized to make payments from it, but Mitchell and Stans continually denied having any such knowledge. At an Aug. 29 news conference, President Nixon said that no one then employed in his administration had been involved in the Watergate bugging. He said a complete investigation of the incident by John W. Dean, counsel to the President, permitted him to declare "categorically that his investigation indicates that no one in the White House staff, no one in this administration, presently employed, was involved in this very bizarre incident." The President added: "What really hurts in matters of this sort is not the fact that they occur, because over-zealous people in campaigns do things that are wrong, what really hurts is if you try to cover it up."

The five men arrested by Washington police at the Democratic head-quarters June 17 were: Bernard L. Barker, a Miami, Fla., realtor and former employee of the Central Intelligence Agency (CIA), who re-portedly had played a role in the 1962 Bay of Pigs invasion of Cuba; Virgilio R. Gonzalez, a Cuban emigrant and locksmith; Eugenio R. Martinez, a member of Barker's real estate firm and an anti-Castro Cuban exile with CIA associations; James W. McCord Jr., security coordinator for the Republican National Committee and the Commit-tee for the Re-election of the President, a former FBI agent and CIA employee; and Frank A. Sturgis of Miami, an associate of Barker who had connections with the CIA and had participated in anti-Castro activities. These men were charged with attempted burglary and eavesdropping and were indicted Sept. 15 along with E. Howard Hunt Jr., a former White House consultant, writer of spy novels and former CIA employee; and G. Gordon Liddy, counsel to the Finance Commit-tee to Re-elect the President, a former FBI agent, a former Treasury Department official, and a former member of the White House staff.

Trial of Conspirators

At a trial in January 1973, Hunt, Barker, Sturgis, Gonzalez and Martinez pleaded guilty, while Liddy and McCord stood trial and were convicted. The case took a dramatic turn on March 23 when a letter from McCord to the trial judge, dated March 17, was read in court. McCord said in the letter to Chief U.S. District Court Judge John J. Sirica that he and other persons caught spying on the Democrats had been under "political pressure to plead guilty and remain silent." He asserted that "others" had been involved in the Watergate operation and that government witnesses had perjured themselves at his trial.

Breaking the nine-month silence maintained by the seven Watergate defendants, McCord asked for a private meeting with Judge Sirica because he would "not feel confident" talking to the FBI or to the prosecutors who "work for the Justice Department." He said he wanted to speak with the judge despite his belief that "retaliatory measures will be taken against me, my family, and my friends." The two-page letter was read in court on the day Judge Sirica sentenced the other Watergate defendants. Sentencing of McCord was postponed to allow him to testify before the grand jury and the special Senate committee investigating the case. The surprise letter followed months of efforts to wrench more information from the witnesses at the trial of the Water-gate defendants. Judge Sirica had openly expressed his skepticism that witnesses were telling all they knew of the clandestine operations.

Text of James W. McCord Jr.'s letter to U.S. District Judge John J. Sirica, read in court March 23, 1973:

Certain questions have been posed to me from your honor through the probation officer, dealing with details of the case, motivations, intent, mitigating circumstances.

In endeavoring to respond to these questions, I am whipsawed in a variety of legalities. First, I may be called before a Senate committee investigating this matter. Secondly, I may be involved in a civil suit, and thirdly there may be a new trial at some future date.

Fourthly, the probation officer may be called before the Senate committee to present testimony regarding what may otherwise be a privileged communication between defendant and judge.

As I answered certain questions to the probation officer, it is possible such answers could become a matter of record in the Senate and therefore available for use in the other proceedings just described.

My answers would, it would seem to me, violate my Fifth Amendment rights, and possibly my Sixth Amendment right to counsel and possibly other rights.

On the other hand, to fail to answer your questions may appear to be noncooperation, and I can therefore expect a much more severe sentence.

There are other considerations which are not to be lightly taken. Several members of my family have expressed fear for my life if I disclose knowledge of the facts in this matter, either publicly or to any government representative.

Whereas I do not share their concerns to the same degree, nevertheless, I do believe that retaliatory measures will be taken against me, my family, and my friends should I disclose such facts. Such retaliation could destroy careers, income, and reputations of persons who are innocent of any guilt whatever.

Be that as it may, in the interest of justice, and in the interest of restoring faith in the criminal justice system, which faith has been severely damaged in this case, I will state the following to you at this time which I hope may be of help to you in meting justice in this case:

1. There was political pressure applied to the defendants to plead guilty and remain silent.

2. Perjury occurred during the trial in matters highly material to the very structure, orientation and impact of the Government's case, and to the motivation and intent of the defendants.

3. Others involved in the Watergate operation were not identified during the trial, when they could have been those testifying.

4. The Watergate operation was not a C.I.A. operation. The Cubans may have been misled by others into believing that it was a C.I.A. operation. I know for a fact that it was not.

5. Some statements were unfortunately made by a witness which left the court with the impression that he was stating untruths, or with-

holding facts of his knowledge, when in fact only honest errors of memory were involved.

6. My motivations were different than those of the others involved, but were not limited to, or simply those offered in my defense during the trial. This is no fault of my attorneys, but of the circumstances under which we had to prepare my defense.

Following sentence, I would appreciate the opportunity to talk to you privately in chambers. Since I cannot feel confident in talking with an F.B.I. agent, in testifying before a grand jury whose U.S. attorneys work for the Department of Justice, or in talking with other Government representatives, such a discussion with you would be of assistance to me.

I have not discussed the above with my attorneys as a matter of protection for them.

I give this statement freely and voluntarily, fully realizing that I may be prosecuted for giving a false statement to a judicial official, if the statements herein are knowingly untrue. The statements are true and correct to the best of my knowledge and belief.

Text of statement by E. Howard Hunt Jr. in court March 23, 1973:

I stand before you, a man convicted first by the press, then by my own admissions, freely made even before the beginning of my trial. For 26 years I served my country honorably and with devotion: first as a naval officer on the wartime North Atlantic, then as an Air Force officer in China. And finally, as an officer of the Central Intelligence Agency combating our country's enemies abroad.

In my entire life I was never charged with a crime, much less convicted of one. Since the 17th of June 1972, I lost my employment, then my beloved wife, both in consequence of my involvement in the Watergate affair. Today I stand before the bar of justice alone, nearly friendless, ridiculed, disgraced, destroyed as a man.

These have been a few of the many tragic consequences of my participation in the Watergate affair, and they have been visited upon me in overwhelming measure.

What I did was wrong, unquestionably wrong in the eyes of the law, and I can accept that. For the last eight months I have suffered an ever-deepening consciousness of guilt, of responsibility for my acts, and of the drastic penalties they entail. I pray however that this court—and the American people—can accept my statement today that my motives were not evil.

The offenses I have freely admitted are the first in a life of blameless and honorable conduct. As a man already destroyed by the consequences of his acts I can represent no threat to our society, now or at any conceivable future time. And as to the factor of deterrence, your honor, the Watergate case has been so publicized that I believe it fair to say the American public knows that political offenses are not to be tolerated by our society within our democratic system.

The American public knows also that because of what I did, I have lost virtually everything that I cherished in life—my wife, my job, my reputation. Surely, these tragic consequences will serve as an effective deterrent to anyone else who might contemplate engaging in a similar activity.

The offenses to which I pleaded guilty even before trial began were not crimes of violence. To be sure, they were an affront to the state, but not to the body of a man or to his property. The real victims of the Watergate conspiracy, your honor, as it has turned out, are the conspirators themselves. But there are other prospective victims.

Your honor, I am the father of four children, the youngest a boy of 9. Had my wife and I not lost our employment because of Watergate involvement, she would not have sought investment security for our family in Chicago where she was killed last December. My children's knowledge of the reason for her death is ineradicable—as is mine. Four children without a mother. I ask they not lose their father, as well.

Your honor, I cannot believe the ends of justice would be well served by incarcerating me. To do so would add four more victims, to the disastrous train of events in which I was involved. I say to you, in all candor, that my family desperately needs me at this time. My problems are unique and real, and your honor knows what they are. My probation officer has discussed them with me at some length.

I have spent almost an entire lifetime helping and serving my country, in war and peace. I am the one who now needs help. Throughout the civilized world we are renowned for our American system of justice. Especially honored is our judicial concept of justice tempered with mercy. Mercy, your honor, not vengeance and reprisal, as in some lands. It is this revered tradition of mercy that I ask your honor to remember while you ponder my fate.

Text of statement by Judge Sirica on sentencing G. Gordon Liddy, March 23, 1973:

The court, at this time, wishes to briefly state some of the considerations which have contributed to its sentencing decisions in this case.

In the first instance, it seems clear that the defendants realized, at the time they acted, that their conduct violated the law. Now, it is true that "ignorance of the law is no excuse," and that one may be held accountable for a failure to obey the law whether he has read the statute books or not. Despite this fact, however, the court believes that the knowing and deliberate violation of laws deserves a greater condemnation than a simple, careless, or uncomprehending violation.

It is appropriate to consider, in addition, the nature of the misconduct, and the gravity of the offenses committed. The indictment contains two counts of burglary, a serious crime. Other counts refer to Title 18 United States Code Sec. 2511 concerning the privacy of oral and wire communications. The Senate report on the bill which included what is now Sec. 2511 contained the following statement:

The tremendous scientific and technological developments that have taken place in the last century have made possible today the widespread use and abuse of electronic surveillance techniques. As a result of these developments, privacy of communication is seriously jeopardized by these techniques of surveillance... no longer is it possible...for each man to retreat into his home and be left alone. Every spoken word relating to each man's personal, marital, religious, political, or commercial concerns can be intercepted by an unseen auditor and turned against the speaker to the auditor's advantage. (2 U.S. Code Congressional and Administrative News, 90th Congress, 2nd Session at 2154).

Sec. 2511 was designed to prevent this great evil. Obviously, however, it has not stopped these defendants from knowingly committing the acts of which they stand convicted. From the evidence presented in the course of these proceedings, the court has reached the opinion that the crimes committed by these defendants can only be described as sordid, despicable and thoroughly reprehensible.

The court has also considered the purposes to be served by imposing sentences in this case. In view of the foregoing, and taking into account the background of the defendants, it seems obvious to the court that rehabilitation is *not* the principal purpose to be served. Nor is it appropriate to impose sentence here with the intent of satisfying someone's desire for reprisal. In this matter, the sentences should be imposed with an eye toward a just punishment for the grave offenses committed and toward the deterrent effect the sentences might have on other potential offenders.

I shall not attempt to enumerate every item which the court has pondered. Numerous other considerations, both favorable and unfavorable to the defendants, have played a part in the court's decisions. Suffice it to say that the sentences which the court will now impose, are the result of careful thought extending over a period of several weeks. I think the sentences are appropriate and just.

Text of statement by Judge Sirica, March 23, 1973, on sentencing the five defendants who pleaded guilty:

With respect to the five defendants who have entered guilty pleas, Messrs. Hunt, Barker, Martinez, Sturgis, and Gonzalez, the court finds that it requires more detailed information before it can make a final determination of the sentences to be imposed. The court will therefore implement, at this time, the provisions of Title 18 United States Code Sec. 4208(b). That section reads as follows:

(b) If the court desires more detailed information as a basis for determining the sentence to be imposed, the court may commit the defendant to the custody of the Attorney General, which commitment shall be deemed to be for the maximum sentence of imprisonment prescribed by law, for a study as described in Subsection (c) hereof. The results of such study, together with any recommendations which the Director of the Bureau of Prisons believes would be helpful in determining the disposition of the case, shall be furnished to the court within three months unless the court grants time, not to exceed an additional three months, for further study. After receiving such reports and recommendations, the court may in its discretion: (1) place the prisoner on probation as authorized by Section 3651 of this title, or (2) affirm the sentence of imprisonment originally imposed, or reduce the sentence of imprisonment, and commit the offender under any applicable provision of law. The term of the sentence shall run from date of original commitment under this section.

The effect of the court's ruling, then, is this:

First: Each of you five defendants now before me are provisionally committed for the maximum sentence of imprisonment prescribed by law for your offenses.

Second: A study will be conducted under the direction of the Bureau of Prisons. Within three months, the court will be furnished with the results of this study together with any recommendations made by the Director of the Bureau of Prisons. Should more than three months be required, the court may grant time for further study up to an additional three months.

Third: Once the studies with respect to each defendant are completed and the court has analyzed the information contained therein, the court will make a final disposition of your cases. The court will have basically three alternatives: (1) to affirm the sentence of imprisonment originally imposed, that is, the maximum sentence, (2) to reduce the sentence of imprisonment as the court deems appropriate, or (3) to place the defendant on probation. In any case, the terms of sentence will begin to run from the date of original commitment.

The fact that I am submitting the matter for further study does not mean that I have given little or no thought to a sentencing decision. The court has already given a great deal of consideration to sentencing in each of your cases. I have carefully studied the presentence reports and the trial transcripts. Among other things, I have taken into consideration, and will keep in mind, the fact that each of you voluntarily entered pleas of guilty. On the other side of the scale, however, is the fact that none of you have been willing to give the government or other appropriate authorities any substantial help in trying this case or in investigating the activities which were the subject of this case. I think, under the case law, the court is entitled to consider this fact in determining sentences. For the record, I will cite two cases which discuss this aspect of sentencing: UNITED STATES v. SWEIG, 454 F.2d 181 (2nd Cir. 1972) and UNITED STATES v. VERMEULIN, 436 F2nd 72 (2nd Cir. 1970) cert. denied 402 U.S. 911. I believe I may also properly suggest to you that in the interval between now and when the Bureau of Prisons' studies are completed you give serious consideration to lending your full cooperation to investigating authorities. Now I want to speak plainly about this matter. You will all no doubt be given an opportunity to provide information to the grand jury which has been, and still is, investigating the "Watergate affair" and to the Senate Select Committee on Presidential Campaign Activities. I sincerely hope that each of you will take full advantage of any such opportunity. My sentiments in this regard are identical to those expressed on February 28th of this year by Judge Warren J. Ferguson, a United States District Judge in Los Angeles, California, and a man for whom I have the highest admiration. Judge Ferguson has before him a matter which is, in many respects, analogous to this case. That proceeding grew out of certain unlawful transactions revealed a few years ago involving a one-time sergeant major of the Army. This man and others pleaded guilty before Judge Ferguson on the 28th to an information charging them with fraud and corruption in the operation of United States military clubs in parts of Europe, Vietnam and the United States. At the time of the plea, Judge Ferguson made a statement which I am going to read now. He has stated the matter exceptionally well.

There are various sentencing philosophies: To deter other people from committing crime, to deter the defendant himself from committing other crimes against the Government, to rehabilitate people and all of the other various philosophical reasons why judges sentence people.

In this case, for various reasons which are not necessary for the court to express from the bench, I am more concerned that the activities to which you have pled guilty will not occur in the future by any other sergeant of the Army, sergeant major of the Army, any master sergeant of the Army, or any staff sergeant of the Army or anybody else in the military system and I don't know whether or not the three of you are isolated incidents of the things to which you have pled guilty and whether or not it is the system which permitted this activity to take place.

The things we say here, if I can paraphrase a great President, will not be long remembered. You and I are individuals and life is pretty slender and what I do to you basically is not going to affect other sergeant majors in the Army and another war that comes along in our future, and they will come. But I want to do all I can to insure that in future wars or future military operations that the system, the system itself, prohibits the conduct to which you have entered your guilty pleas. Because if that is accomplished then there has been a benefit to the Government, really.

I don't think the Government wants a pound of flesh out of you. That is very little benefit to the Government. That is very little benefit to society. That is very little benefit to anybody except an expression that society does not approve of the things you have entered your guilty pleas to. But you will pass on and there will be other people taking your place and Wooldridge will be forgotten about and Higdon will be forgotten about and nobody will remember Bass as individuals. There will be a flurry of publicity as a result of your guilty pleas, naturally, but in a week or so it will be forgotten about.

But you see, I don't want it forgotten. So I have told your attorneys that the sentence that I will impose upon you—and I am making no promise of leniency; I want that clearly and positively understood; I am making no promise of leniency—but the sentence I will impose will depend primarily on whether or not you cooperate with the Permanent Subcommittee on Investigation of the United States Senate and if you are asked to testify and give evidence before that Permanent Subcommittee and if you testify openly and completely, regardless of what the implications are to yourself or to anyone else or to the system so that the branch of the Government which can take corrective action of the system is able to take action on the system so that this activity simply does not occur again, then I will take that into consideration because I want to see something beneficial to the Government come out of these proceedings.

Now, I don't know what the subcommittee will do but I fully expect you to cooperate absolutely, completely and entirely with whoever from that subcommittee, whether it is a senator or whether it is a staff investigator. Whoever it is who interrogates you, you will openly and honestly testify.

Now I believe that the "Watergate affair," the subject of this trial, should not be forgotten. Some good can and should come from a revelation of sinister conduct whenever and wherever such conduct exists. I am convinced that the greatest benefit that can come from this prosecution will be its impact as a spur to corrective action so that the type of activities revealed by the evidence at trial will not be repeated in our nation. For these reasons, I recommend your full cooperation with the grand jury and the Senate Select Committee. You must understand that I hold out no promises or hopes of any kind to you in this matter, but I do say that should you decide to speak freely, I would have to weigh that factor in appraising what sentence will be finally imposed in each case. Other factors will, of course, be considered, but I mention this one because it is one over which you have control.

In conclusion, the court's aim is to acquire a thorough acquaintance with the character and history of the defendants so as to be able to impose that sentence which most fully comports with justice in each individual case.

The court's order of commitment is as follows:

In the case of the United States of America v. George Gordon Liddy, et al., Defendant No. 2, Everette Howard Hunt, Jr.,

Defendant No. 4, Bernard L. Barker,

Defendant No. 5, Eugenio Rolando Martinez,

Defendant No. 6, Frank A. Sturgis,

Defendant No. 7, Virgilio R. Gonzalez,

The court having decided that it would like further detailed information as a basis for determining the sentence to be imposed in this case, the court hereby commits the defendants to the custody of the attorney general pursuant to 18 United States Code Sec. 4208(b) for a complete study. This commitment is deemed to be for the maximum sentence of imprisonment prescribed by law. However, it is not a final disposition. The statute provides that the results of such study shall be furnished to the court within three months unless the court grants time, not to exceed an additional three months, for further study. The statute further provides that the term of whatever sentence the court finally imposes on the defendants shall run from the date of commitment under this section which is, of course, today's date.

The court recommends to the Director of the Bureau of Prisons that he study these cases from the standpoint of a suitable place of confinement in a federal institution.

CHRONOLOGY OF WATERGATE EVENTS

June 17, 1972-March 23, 1973

1972

June 17—Barker, McCord, Sturgis, Martinez and Gonzalez arrested at headquarters of the Democratic National Committee and charged with burglary.

June 18—Former Attorney General and Nixon campaign manager John N. Mitchell denies any connection with incident. Democratic Chairman Lawrence F. O'Brien calls for FBI investigation.

June 22—President Nixon, at press conference, claims "no involvement whatever" in bugging incident.

June 28—G. Gordon Liddy, counsel to Finance Committee to Reelect the President fired by Mitchell for refusing to answer FBI questions.

July 1—Mitchell resigns as Nixon's campaign manager; Clark MacGregor named successor.

July 14—Hugh W. Sloan Jr. resigns as treasurer of Finance Committee.

Aug. 4—U.S. District Judge Charles R. Richey rules Justice Department cannot represent White House aide Charles Colson in charges concerning Watergate.

Aug. 14—Justice Department to appeal Richey ruling that it cannot represent Colson.

Aug. 15—O'Brien announces new evidence that Democratic headquarters bugged before June 17.

Aug. 19—Wright Patman, chairman of House Banking and Currency Committee, orders staff investigation of Watergate.

Aug. 26—General Accounting Office (GAO) reports "apparent" and "possible" violations of Federal Election Campaign Act by Finance Committee to Re-elect the President.

Aug. 28—Attorney General Richard G. Kleindienst promises that Justice Department's investigation of Watergate will be "the most extensive, thorough and comprehensive investigation since the assassination of President Kennedy."

Aug. 29—President Nixon says at news conference that "no one in the White House staff, no one in this administration, presently employed, was involved...."

Sept. 2—Mitchell, testifying in Democrats' suit against the Committee for the Re-election of the President, says he had no advance knowledge of bugging incident.

Sept. 6—Common Cause sues the Finance Committee to Re-elect the President to force disclosure of names of persons contributing total of more than $10-million to Nixon campaign before April 7.

Sept. 11—Democrats file amended complaint accusing Maurice Stans, Liddy, Sloan and Hunt of political espionage, in addition to the original five defendants.

Sept. 12—Barker admits his part in break-in operations but says "Just because I get in trouble, I don't want nobody else to get in trouble."

Sept. 15—Federal grand jury returns eight-count indictment against the five men arrested at Watergate and Liddy and Hunt. Charges include tapping telephones, planting electronic eavesdropping devices and stealing documents.

Sept. 20—New articles report that two Re-election Committee officials, Robert C. Mardian and Frederick La Rue, destroyed financial records of the group after the bugging incident.

Oct. 5—News articles report that Alfred C. Baldwin 3d, a former F.B.I. agent, delivered sets of eavesdropping logs to the Re-election Committee before June 17 incident.

Oct. 10—News articles report massive campaign of sabotage and intelligence directed by officials of the White House and the Re-election Committee.

Oct. 22—News reports say Justice Department files show that Jeb Stuart Magruder, a Re-election Committee official, authorized expenditures for Watergate bugging.

Oct. 25—News stories, citing federal investigators, say that H. R. Haldeman, the President's chief of staff, was one of officials authorized to approve payments from secret campaign fund for espionage and sabotage.

Oct. 26—Clark MacGregor acknowledges that officials of Re-election Committee controlled special cash fund, but denies that fund was used to sabotage the Democrats' campaign.

1973

Jan. 8—Criminal trial opens.

Jan. 10—Hunt pleads guilty.

Jan. 11—Sen. Sam Ervin (D N.C.) agrees to head Senate investigation of Watergate case.

Jan. 15—Barker, Sturgis, Martinez and Gonzalez plead guilty.

Jan. 30—Liddy and McCord convicted of all charges.

Feb. 7—Senate votes to set up special committee to investigate Watergate case.

March 23—Judge Sirica discloses letter from McCord charging that higher-ups were involved, that there was perjury in the trial and that the defendants were pressured to plead guilty. Judge Sirica postpones sentencing for McCord, sentences Liddy to six years, eight months to 20 years, and the four other defendants to indeterminate sentences.

MEAT PRICE CEILINGS

March 29, 1973

In an abrupt reversal of policy, President Nixon at the end of March ordered the imposition of price ceilings on beef, lamb and pork for "as long as it is necessary to do the job." The President told the nation in a televised speech: "Meat prices must not go higher. And with the help of the housewife and the farmer, they can and they should go down." The action was aimed not only at preventing further increases in meat prices but also at encouraging a drop in prices. The ceilings applied to whole-sale and retail prices but not to live animals.

Barely two weeks earlier, the President had stated his opposition to food price ceilings. "The difficulty with offering rigid price controls on meat prices and food prices is that it would not stop...the rise in prices," Nixon had said at a March 15 news conference. "The point is that every bit of evidence that has been presented shows that it would discourage supply, it would lead to black markets, and we would eventually have to come to rigid price controls, wage controls, and rationing." As recently as March 20, Secretary of Agriculture Earl L. Butz had said that persons who wanted meat price ceilings were "damn fools." But pressure had mounted for some action to curb the skyrocketing prices of meat. Meat boycotts by shoppers and criticism from Congress and labor became more widespread as meat prices rose to record highs.

Nixon's announcement of meat price ceilings surprised television viewers who had tuned in to hear a speech which they expected would deal only with the withdrawal of the last American troops from Vietnam and the return of the last group of prisoners of war. But the President touched on various other matters in addition to the war, and in addition to meat prices.

In referring to the war, he noted that "for the first time in 12 years, no American military forces are in Vietnam." And despite the difficulties encountered in negotiating with Hanoi, "we can be proud...of the fact that we have achieved our goal of obtaining an agreement which provides peace with honor in Vietnam." The President called on Americans to honor those who had served in Vietnam and those who had sacrificed their lives there. He also mentioned the distress he had felt in ordering renewal of intensive bombing over the North in December 1972, and he extended his appreciation to the "great majority of Americans...who, despite an unprecedented barrage of criticism from a small but vocal minority, stood firm for peace with honor."

Turning to domestic affairs, Nixon spoke of his administration's success in curbing inflation, citing meat prices as "the major weak spot" in that fight. He emphasized the need to hold down the federal budget (see p. 169), but he cautioned against further cuts in defense spending. "I ask for your support tonight for keeping the strength which enabled us to make such great progress toward world peace in this past year and which is indispensable as we continue our bold new initiatives for peace in the years ahead."

Sen. Edmund S. Muskie (D Maine) was selected by the Democratic leadership in Congress to make the party's response to the President's televised address. Although the three major television networks declined to carry the Democrat's speech, portions of his April 2 remarks were televised on network news broadcasts. Congress did not dispute the need to keep down federal spending, Muskie said, "but we disagree on what our spending priorities should be.... The President chooses to put the emphasis on military spending. Congress will shift that emphasis to domestic problems." He criticized "the President's attempt to blame the Congress for inflation" as "unfair and untrue" and asserted that his response to soaring prices—imposition of a meat price ceiling— "does too little and comes too late."

At a White House briefing just prior to the President's speech, Treasury Secretary George P. Shultz had explained that the meat price ceiling would not apply directly to farmers, but he conceded that it would affect them ultimately if it resulted in lower prices. Shultz also said the President would ask Congress for discretionary power to suspend tariffs and quotas on imported foods when demand exceeded supply. Quotas on food products had already been lifted, but the discretionary authority would allow the President to suspend tariffs on meat, which still remained at 3.5 per cent on beef and 2.5 per cent on lamb.

*Text of the President's televised speech of March 29 and
the statement, the same day, by George P. Shultz, Secretary
of the Treasury and chairman of the Cost of Living Council,
on meat price ceilings:*

Good evening.

Four years and two months ago, when I first came into this office as
President, by far the most difficult problem confronting the Nation was
the seemingly endless war in Vietnam. 550,000 Americans were in Vietnam. As many as 300 a week were being killed in action. Hundreds were
held as prisoners of war in North Vietnam. No progress was being made
at the peace negotiations.

I immediately initiated a program to end the war and win an honorable
peace.

Eleven times over the past 4 years I have reported to the Nation from
this room on the progress we have made toward that goal. Tonight, the
day we have all worked and prayed for has finally come.

For the first time in 12 years, no American military forces are in Vietnam. All of our American POW's are on their way home. The 17 million
people of South Vietnam have the right to choose their own government
without outside interference, and because of our program of Vietnamization, they have the strength to defend that right. We have prevented
the imposition of a Communist government by force on South Vietnam.

There are still some problem areas. The provisions of the agreement
requiring an accounting for all missing in action in Indochina, the provisions with regard to Laos and Cambodia, the provisions prohibiting
infiltration from North Vietnam into South Vietnam have not been
complied with. We have and will continue to comply with the agreement.
We shall insist that North Vietnam comply with the agreement. And the
leaders of North Vietnam should have no doubt as to the consequences
if they fail to comply with the agreement.

But despite these difficulties, we can be proud tonight of the fact
that we have achieved our goal of obtaining an agreement which provides
peace with honor in Vietnam.

On this day, let us honor those who made this achievement possible:
those who sacrificed their lives, those who were disabled, those who
made every one of us proud to be an American as they returned from
years of Communist imprisonment, and every one of the 2½ million
Americans who served honorably in our Nation's longest war. Never
have men served with greater devotion abroad with less apparent support at home.

Let us provide these men with the veterans benefits and the job opportunities they have earned. Let us honor them with the respect they
deserve. And I say again tonight, let us not dishonor those who served
their country by granting amnesty to those who deserted America.

Tonight I want to express the appreciation of the Nation to others who helped make this day possible. I refer to you, the great majority of Americans listening to me tonight, who, despite an unprecedented barrage of criticism from a small but vocal minority, stood firm for peace with honor. I know it was not easy for you to do so.

We have been through some difficult times together. I recall the time in November 1969 when hundreds of thousands of demonstrators marched on the White House, the time in April 1970 when I found it necessary to order attacks on Communist bases in Cambodia, the time in May 1972 when I ordered the mining of Haiphong and air strikes on military targets in North Vietnam in order to stop a massive Communist offensive in South Vietnam, and then—and this was perhaps the hardest decision I have made as President—on December 18, 1972, when our hopes for peace were so high and when the North Vietnamese stone-walled us at the conference table, I found it necessary to order more air strikes on military targets in North Vietnam in order to break the deadlock.

On each of these occasions, the voices of opposition we heard in Washington were so loud they at times seemed to be the majority. But across America, the overwhelming majority stood firm against those who advocated peace at any price—even if the price would have been defeat and humiliation for the United States.

Because you stood firm—stood firm for doing what was right, [Air Force Lt.] Colonel [George G.] McKnight was able to say for his fellow POW's, when he returned home a few days ago, "Thank you for bringing us home on our feet instead of on our knees."

Let us turn now to some of our problems at home. Tonight I ask your support in another battle. But we can be thankful this is not a battle in war abroad, but a battle we must win if we are to build a new prosperity without war and without inflation at home.

What I refer to is the battle of the budget—not just the battle over the Federal budget, but even more important, the battle of your budget, the family budget of every home in America.

One of the most terrible costs of war is inflation. The cost of living has skyrocketed during and after every war America has been engaged in. We recognized this danger 4 years ago. We have taken strong action to deal with it. As a result of our policies, we have cut the rate of inflation in half from the high point it reached in 1969 and 1970. And today, our rate of inflation in the United States is the lowest of that of any industrial nation in the world.

Meat Prices

But these positive statistics are small comfort to a family trying to make both ends meet. And they are no comfort at all to the housewife who sees meat prices soaring every time she goes to the market. The major weak spot in our fight against inflation is in the area of meat prices. I have taken action to increase imports from abroad and production at home. This will increase the supply of meat, and it will help bring prices down later this year.

But what we need is action that will stop the rise in meat prices now. And that is why I have today ordered the Cost of Living Council to impose a ceiling on prices of beef, pork and lamb. The ceiling will remain in effect as long as it is necessary to do the job.

Meat prices must not go higher. And with the help of the housewife and the farmer they can and they should go down.

This ceiling will help in our battle against inflation. But it is not a permanent solution. We must act on all fronts, and here is where the Federal budget comes in.

I have submitted to Congress for the next fiscal year the largest budget in our history—$268 billion.

The amount I have requested in this budget for domestic programs in such fields as health, housing, education, aid to the elderly, the handicapped, the poor, is twice as big as the amount I asked for for these items 4 years ago. However, some Members of Congress believe the budget in these areas should be even higher.

Now, if I were to approve the increases in my budget that have been proposed in the Congress, it would mean a 15 percent increase in your taxes, or an increase in prices for every American. And that is why I shall veto the bills which would break the Federal budget which I have submitted. If I do not veto these bills, increased prices or taxes would break the family budget of millions of Americans—including, possibly, your own.

This is not a battle between Congress and the President. It is your battle. It is your money, your prices, your taxes I am trying to save.

Twenty-five years ago, as a freshman Congressman, I first came into this office. I met Harry Truman, who was then President of the United States. I remember he had a sign on the desk. It read, "The buck stops here." Now that meant, of course, that a President can't pass the buck to anyone else when a tough decision has to be made. It also means that your buck stops here. If I do not act to stop the spending increases which Congress sends to this desk, you will have to pay the bill.

Now I admit there is an honest difference of opinion on the matter of the Federal budget. If you are willing to pay the higher taxes or prices that will result if we increase Federal spending over my budget, as some in Congress have proposed, you should ask your Senators and your Congressmen to override my vetoes, but if you want to stop the rise in taxes and prices, I have a suggestion to make. I remember when I was a Congressman and a Senator, I always seemed to hear from those who wanted government to spend more; I seldom heard from the people who have to pay the bill—the taxpayer. And if your Congressman or Senator has the courage to vote against more government spending, so that you won't have to pay higher prices or taxes, let him know that you support him.

Winning the battle to hold down the Federal budget is essential if we are to achieve our goal of a new prosperity—prosperity without war and without inflation. I ask you tonight for your support in helping to win this vitally important battle.

Defense Budget

Let me turn, finally, tonight to another great challenge we face.

As we end America's longest war, let us resolve that we shall not lose the peace. During the past year we have made great progress toward our goal of a generation of peace for America and the world. The war in Vietnam has been ended. After 20 years of hostility and confrontation we have opened a constructive new relationship with the People's Republic of China where one-fourth of all the people in the world live. We negotiated last year with the Soviet Union a number of important agreements, including an agreement which takes a major step in limiting nuclear arms.

Now there are some who say that in view of all this progress toward peace, why not cut our defense budget?

Well, let's look at the facts. Our defense budget today takes the lowest percentage of our gross national product that it has in 20 years. There is nothing I would like better than to be able to reduce it further. But we must never forget that we would not have made the progress toward lasting peace that we have made in this past year unless we had had the military strength that commanded respect.

This year we have begun new negotiations with the Soviet Union for further limitations on nuclear arms. And we shall be participating later in the year in negotiations for mutual reduction of forces in Europe.

If prior to these negotiations we in the United States unilaterally reduce our defense budget, or reduce our forces in Europe, any chance for successful negotiations for mutual reduction of forces or limitation of arms will be destroyed.

There is one unbreakable rule of international diplomacy. You can't get something in a negotiation unless you have something to give. If we cut our defenses before negotiations begin, any incentive for other nations to cut theirs will go right out the window.

If the United States reduces its defenses and others do not, it will increase the danger of war. It is only a mutual reduction of forces which will reduce the danger of war. And that is why we must maintain our strength until we get agreements under which other nations will join us in reducing the burden of armaments.

What is at stake is whether the United States shall become the second strongest nation in the world. If that day ever comes, the chance for building a new structure of peace in the world would be irreparably damaged, and free nations everywhere would be living in mortal danger.

A strong Unites States is not a threat to peace. It is the free world's indispensable guardian of peace and freedom.

I ask for your support tonight, for keeping the strength—the strength which enabled us to make such great progress toward world peace in the past year and which is indispensable as we continue our bold new initiatives for peace in the years ahead.

As we consider some of our problems tonight, let us never forget how fortunate we are to live in America at this time in our history. We have ended the longest and most difficult war in our history in a way that maintains the trust of our allies and the respect of our adversaries. We are the strongest and most prosperous nation in the world. Because of our strength, America has the magnificent opportunity to play the leading role of bringing down the walls of hostility which divide the people of the world, in reducing the burden of armaments in the world, of building a structure of lasting peace in the world. And because of our wealth, we have the means to move forward at home on exciting new programs— programs for progress which will provide better environment, education, housing, and health care for all Americans and which will enable us to be more generous to the poor, the elderly, the disabled and the disadvantaged than any nation in the history of the world.

These are goals worthy of a great people. Let us, therefore, put aside those honest differences about war which have divided us and dedicate ourselves to meet the great challenges of peace which can unite us. As we do, let us not overlook a third element, an element more important even than military might or economic power, because it is essential for greatness in a nation.

The pages of history are strewn with the wreckage of nations which fell by the wayside at the height of their strength and wealth because their people became weak, soft, and self-indulgent and lost the character and the spirit which had led to their greatness.

As I speak to you tonight, I am confident that will not happen to America. And my confidence has been increased by the fact that a war which cost America so much in lives and money and division at home has, as it ended, provided an opportunity for millions of Americans to see again the character and the spirit which made America a great nation.

A few days ago in this room, I talked to a man who had spent almost 8 years in a Communist prison camp in North Vietnam. For over 4 years he was in solitary confinement. In that 4-year period he never saw and never talked to another human being except his Communist captors. He lived on two meals a day, usually just a piece of bread, a bowl of soup. All he was given to read was Communist propaganda. All he could listen to was the Communist propaganda on radio.

I asked him how he was able to survive it and come home, standing tall and proud, saluting the American flag. He paused a long time before he answered. And then he said, "It is difficult for me to answer. I am not very good at words. All I can say is that it was faith—faith in God and faith in my country."

If men who suffered so much for America can have such faith, let us who have received so much from America renew our faith—our faith in God, our faith in our country, and our faith in ourselves.

If we meet the great challenges of peace that lie ahead with this kind of faith, then one day it will be written: This was America's finest hour. Thank you and good evening.

Statement by George P. Shultz, Secretary of the Treasury and Chairman of the Cost of Living Council, March 29, 1973:

By direction of President Nixon the Cost of Living Council is today implementing a series of new mandatory controls designed to restrain the rising prices of meat.

These anti-inflation actions feature:

—A ceiling on prices of beef, lamb, and pork effective today, which will remain in force for as long as necessary to do the job. The ceiling affects meat processors, meat wholesalers, and meat retailers. It sets ceiling prices on all levels of transaction for meat items, both on the buyer and seller in each sale.

—Prenotification to and approval by the Cost of Living Council of all pay adjustments affecting employees in the food industry.

—A ceiling price posting requirement for all meat retailers, which calls for prominent public display at all meat counters no later than April 9.

—Establishment of a nationwide enforcement network operated by Economic Stabilization Program officers of the Internal Revenue Service to assure compliance with new ceiling prices.

As an important step to restrain inflation and to aid the American consumer, the President is seeking authority from the Congress to suspend tariffs and quotas on imports of food. This authority would be used when the President determines that supply is inadequate to meet domestic demand at reasonable prices. Coupled with the actions that have been taken to increase food supplies, this will further help to moderate food price increases.

The President has also emphasized it is imperative that the Economic Stabilization Program and the Department of Agriculture continue to monitor and encourage food production at the farm level, and assure that steps already taken will result in increased protein supplies.

The Cost of Living Council Committee on Food, after taking a hard look at all aspects of the food situation, issued a report on the problem on March 20. The report pointed out that a shortage of protein food supplies in the United States and abroad had pushed the prices of food up to record high levels. It also spelled out a number of steps taken by the Government to restrain food price increases by moving to expand food supplies, reducing impediments to imports, and maintaining mandatory Phase III controls on the food industry. The report predicted that the effect of these supply actions will moderate food price increases in the second half of 1973. We firmly believe they will.

However, the report also made clear that continued escalation of food prices posed a serious threat to our stabilization program goal of reducing the rate of inflation to 2.5 percent by the end of this year.

Here are some of the hard facts. During Phase II, food prices at the grocery store increased by 5.2 percent, and red meat, beef, and pork went up by 11.8 percent. Food at retail, excluding meat, increased at a much more moderate rate of 2.9 percent. This was well within the Phase II goal of the stabilization program. But the core of the present problem is the rise in the price of red meat, which has soared 10 to 15 percent at wholesale in the past 3 months.

Waiting until the end of 1973 for food prices to level off is not good enough. Rising prices are threatening to erode the gains recorded by wage earners in Phase II when real spendable earnings increased substantially.

To those groups of Americans affected by this decision, I would say this: The housewife, who wields the most powerful anti-inflation weapon through her buying decisions, can bring about stabilization by refusing to pay high meat prices. The housewife can help bring about an end to rising meat prices by resisting high prices and by shopping wisely.

To the American farmer, who has an unmatched ability to produce more food at less cost than any nation in the world, we look for every effort that will encourage bountiful crops and animal production. We encourage farmers to continue to expand their production of crops and marketings of beef and pork during the ceiling period to insure that shortages do not develop.

To all consumers, we ask for cooperation. A united effort is needed now: prudent food buying decisions, an understanding that we face a temporary supply problem, and the confidence that we will defeat food inflation and attain the goals of the Economic Stabilization Program in 1973.

NEW LABOR-MANAGEMENT PACT

March 29, 1973

An unprecedented agreement, virtually guaranteeing uninterrupted American steel production through July 1977, was announced March 29 in Pittsburgh by I. W. Abel, president of the United Steelworkers of America, and R. Heath Larry, vice chairman of the U.S. Steel Corporation and chairman of the negotiating committee for 10 of the country's major steel producing companies. The agreement, heralded as ushering in a new era of labor-management relations, committed the unions and the companies to submit to "final and binding arbitration" any issues not resolved in the 1974 contract negotiations. Furthermore, the unions agreed not to call general strikes and the steel companies agreed not to resort to lockouts in support of their respective bargaining positions. Strikes or lockouts would be permitted only in cases of failure to resolve a local collective bargaining issue and only at the plant where the issue arose.

This "Experimental Negotiating Agreement," resulting from years of talks, launched a new approach to settling labor-management differences in a basic industry that had suffered severe economic losses from strikes. In a joint statement accompanying announcement of the pact, Abel and Larry said "the periodic potentiality of a shutdown of steel operations" had been largely responsible for attracting large volumes of foreign steel, which had had "a serious adverse effect on the U.S. balance of payments as well as on the employees and the domestic steel industry." Imports of steel had been blamed for eliminating 150,000 steelworkers' jobs and for the laying-off of 100,000 workers after the 1971 contract was signed. The new agreement was expected not only to check a further rise in steel imports but also, Larry said, to "help us recapture part of the market we have lost."

The agreement, covering 350,000 workers in the steel industry, provided for an annual 3 per cent wage increase for workers and retained the cost-of-living adjustments and incentive wages instituted under the current three-year contract due to expire on Aug. 1, 1974. Negotiations on other terms of the next contract were to begin no later than Feb. 1, 1974. After April 15, 1974, any unresolved contract issues were to be submitted to an arbitration panel of five members for decision on or before July 10, 1974. Abel said, "We have wide-open negotiations coming up in 1974 with no holds barred." He also expressed hope that the agreement would "modernize and provide new jobs" and he suggested that the nation's railroads and railway unions give it consideration.

Companies signing the pact with the United Steelworkers of America were Allegheny Ludlum Industries, Inc., Armco Steel Corporation, Bethlehem Steel, Inland Steel, Jones & Laughlin Steel, National Steel, Republic Steel, United States Steel, Wheeling Pittsburgh Steel, and the Youngstown Sheet & Tube Company.

Excerpts from the labor-management agreement in the steel industry, signed March 29, 1973, in Pittsburgh, Pa.:

This Experimental Negotiating Agreement, dated March 29, 1973, is between United Steelworkers of America (hereinafter referred to as the "Union") and the Coordinating Committee Steel Companies (hereinafter referred to as the "Companies") and is applicable to Union-represented employees in the plants listed in Appendix A (hereinafter referred to as "employees").

It is highly desirable to provide stability of steel operations, production and employment for the benefit of the employees, customers, suppliers and stockholders of the Companies, and the public. To attain this objective requires that the Union and the Companies settle issues which arise in collective bargaining in such a way as to avoid industry-wide strikes or lockouts or government intervention. The parties are confident that they possess the requisite ability and skills to resolve whatever differences may exist between them in future negotiations through the process of free collective bargaining.

The parties believe that this Agreement will enhance the success of the 1974 negotiations, will avert a strike-hedge steel inventory buildup and will reduce foreign steel imports into the United States.

In view of the foregoing, it is agreed by the Union and the Companies that they will make every effort to resolve through negotiations any differences which may arise in bargaining. After thorough bargaining in good faith the parties may submit any unresolved issue (which is not excluded from arbitration by this Agreement or any subsequent agreement between the parties) to final and binding arbitration by an

438

Impartial Arbitration Panel in accordance with the provisions hereinafter set forth. The submission of any issue to final and binding arbitration shall not preclude the parties from continuing to bargain on such issue prior to the issuance of a decision by the Impartial Arbitration Panel.

A. Strikes and Lockouts:

Except as otherwise provided in Paragraph 5 of Section D of this Agreement, the Union on behalf of the employees agrees not to engage in strikes, work stoppages or concerted refusals to work in support of its bargaining demands, and the Companies agree not ·to resort to lockouts of employees to support their bargaining positions.

B. Wage Increases:

1. Effective August 1, 1974, the rates in effect July 31, 1974, shall be increased as follows:
   a. Each standard hourly job class rate for nonincentive jobs shall be increased by 3% of such rate.
   b. Each hourly job class rate for incentive jobs shall be increased by the same cents per hour as the corresponding standard hourly job class rate for nonincentive jobs with no increase in the hourly additive.
   c. Each standard salary rate shall be increased by 3%.
2. Effective Augsut 1, 1975, the rates established by B-1 above shall be increased as [in the preceding year].
3. Effective August 1, 1976, the rates established by B-2 above shall be increased as [in the preceding year].
4. For hourly paid employees...and for salaried employees covered by basic labor agreements containing base rates differing from the scale of rates in Appendix A of the basic labor agreement between United States Steel Corporation and the Union..., the base rates shall be increased each August 1 by the same percentage as set forth above.

C. Bonus:

In consideration of the contribution made by employees to stability of steel operations, each employee as of August 1, 1974, shall receive $150.00 in the pay period next closed and calculated after September 30, 1974....

D. The Negotiations and Arbitration:

1. It is the intention of the parties hereto that all issues, except as otherwise provided herein, which arise in collective bargaining between the parties shall be either resolved by them or decided by the Impartial Arbitration Panel. In order to achieve this objective:

a. The negotiating teams representing the Union and the Companies will begin negotiations not later than February 1, 1974, for new agreements applicable to employees....

b. Not later than April 15, 1974, the parties shall:

(1) reach a full settlement agreement on all issues; or

(2) agree that certain specified issues are settled (through collective bargaining or special procedures) and certain other issues will be submitted to the Impartial Arbitration Panel (established in accordance with the provisions of Section E of this Agreement) for final and binding decision; or

(3) withdraw all offers and counter-offers and, except as otherwise provided herein, submit to the Impartial Arbitration Panel for final and binding decision such issues as the parties respectively may urge upon the Panel.

2. If arbitration is required, the parties shall not later than April 20, 1974, submit to the Impartial Arbitration Panel an agreed upon list of issues to be submitted to the Panel or, if no agreement has been reached on such a list, their respective lists or formulations of such issues. Within twenty days thereafter each party shall submit to the Panel and to each other a detailed written statement supporting its position on the issues before the Panel for determination. Within ten days subsequent to the filing of written statements of position with the Panel, the parties may file with the Panel and exchange written replies to each other's statements, which shall be restricted to responses to the other party's written statement. Subsequent to the receipt of the written statements of position and replies, the Panel shall conduct hearings and shall render its decisions in accordance with Paragraphs 4, 5 and 6 of Section E of this Agreement.

3. Prior to the commencement of hearings by the Panel, representatives of the parties shall meet with the Chairman of the Panel and establish procedures to be followed at the hearings....

4. The Panel's decision shall be rendered not later than midnight, July 10, 1974. Subsequent to the issuance of the Panel's decision, the parties shall have until midnight, July 20, 1974, to reach agreement as to any contract language and any other steps required to implement the Panel's decision. Absent final agreement by the parties by July 20, 1974, as to such language or other implementing steps, either party may immediately refer any such unresolved questions to the Panel which shall make a final and binding determination on such questions on or before midnight, July 31, 1974.

5. Local collective bargaining issues:

a. Definition

A local collective bargaining issue is an issue entered at plant level, proposing establishment of or change in a condition of employment at that particular plant which:

(1) would not, if adopted, be inconsistent with any provision of a company agreement (as defined below) or involve any addition to or modification of any such provision or agreement;

(2) would not be an arbitrable grievance as defined in the applicable basic labor agreement; and

(3) does not relate to a grievance settlement or an arbitration award; provided, however, this subparagraph (3) does not apply to nonarbitrable grievances....

b. Procedure for disposition

The Parties shall make every effort to settle local collective bargaining issues and in order to achieve this objective shall proceed as follows:

(1) Discussions with respect to these issues shall commence at plant level at such time as the parties locally shall deem necessary but in no event later than April 1, 1974....

(2) Any local issue not disposed of by May 1, 1974, shall be referred to and dealt with by the respective Chairmen of the Union-Company negotiating committee.

(3) Should any such issue or issues initiated by the Union remain unresolved as of June 10, 1974, the Union Co-Chairman shall decide whether the issue or issues shall be withdrawn or put to a secret ballot vote available to all employees at that plant... who worked or were on vacation in the last pay period closed on or before June 10, 1974. Such election, to be valid, must take place no later than June 30, 1974.... If a majority of those voting vote in favor of a strike, and if the matter is not otherwise resolved, the matter shall no later than July 8, 1974 be referred by the Union Co-Chairman to the President of the International Union along with a request for permission to strike the plant in which the issue or issues originated. His decision on the request for permission to strike shall be forwarded in writing to the Union Co-Chairman with a copy to the Company Co-Chairman not later than July 15, 1974. Should permission to strike be granted by the President of the International Union, he shall at the same time specify the date on which the strike, if it is to occur, must commence, which shall not be earlier than the first scheduled turn of August 1, 1974, and such strike shall be confined to the plant where the issue or issues originated....

Should any local collective bargaining issue or issues initiated by a Company remain unresolved as of June 10, 1974, the Company shall decide whether the issue or issues shall be withdrawn or become the basis for a lockout at the plant involved.... The Company's decision shall be forwarded in writing to the Union Co-Chairman not later than July 15, 1974. Should the Company decide to lockout at a plant in support of a local collective bargaining issue or issues, the notice shall specify the date on which the lockout, if it is to occur, must commence, which shall not be earlier than the first scheduled turn of August 1,

1974, and such lockout shall be confined to the plant where the issue or issues originated....

Any such strike or lockout shall cease upon the resolution of the local collective bargaining issue or issues because of which such strike or lockout commenced.

6. Issues excluded from arbitration

The Impartial Arbitration Panel shall not have jurisdiction of, and the parties shall not present to the Panel, any issue affecting or relating to:

a. The Section 2-B Local Working Conditions provisions of the basic labor agreements between the United States Steel Corporation and the Union and counterpart provisons in the agreements of the other Companies.

b. The Union Membership and Checkoff provisions of any such agreements.

c. The Cost-of Living Adjustment provisions of any such agreements, but the Panel shall consider the cost of such item in rendering its decisions on wages and other issues presented to it.

d. The uniformity (or current relationship of parity, in the event that uniformity does not prevail) of wages and benefits between and among the various units, plants or operations covered by this Agreement. Nor shall the Panel make any determination which would result in a different application, than has historically prevailed, of the wage or benefit features of its award as among such units, plants or operations.

e. The wage increases and bonus granted under Sections B and C of this Agreement, but the Panel shall consider the cost of such items in rendering its decisions on wages and other issues presented to it.

f. The no-strike and no-lockout provisions of any such agreements.

g. The management rights provisions of any such agreements.

E. The Impartial Arbitration Panel:

1. Appointment.

The Impartial Arbitration Panel shall consist of five members, one appointed by the Union, one appointed by the Companies and three impartial members appointed by agreement of the parties. Two of the three impartial members shall be persons who are thoroughly familiar with collective bargaining agreements in the steel industry. The Union and the Companies will inform each other as to the identity of their respective members on or before February 1, 1974, and also on or before such date agree upon the three impartial members of the Panel and designate a Chairman.

2. Successorship.

In the event of refusal to serve, death, incapacity or resignation of any member of the Panel, a successor having essentially the same qualifications as his predecessor on the Panel shall be immediately appointed to fill such vacancy in the manner provided for the appointment of members in E-1 above.

3. Method of voting.

All matters presented to the Panel for its determination shall be decided by a majority vote of the impartial members of the Panel. The members representing the Union and the Companies shall not have a vote. The Panel, prior to a vote on any issue in dispute before it, shall, upon the joint request of the Union's and Companies' members of the Panel, refer the issue back to the parties for further negotiations, provided that such a request is made not later than June 30, 1974.

4. Time and place of hearing.

The Panel shall hold hearings at such times and places as agreed to by the parties for the purpose of developing those facts and additional arguments which the parties may desire to present or which the Panel may require.... The hearings shall begin not later than June 1, 1974.

5. Conduct of the hearing.

a. The record of the hearings shall include all documents, written statements and exhibits which may be submitted, together with a stenographic record. The Panel shall, in the absence of agreement of the parties, have authority to make whatever reasonable rules are necessary for the conduct of an orderly hearing....

b. The Panel or any of its members may, at the hearing, call as witnesses such members, employees and representatives of the parties as may be necessary, and may participate in the examination of witnesses for the purpose of expediting the hearings or eliciting material facts....

c. The hearings may be conducted informally. The receipt of evidence at the hearing need not be governed by statutory or common law rules of evidence.

d. In order to encourage frank discussions between the parties during negotiations, those conversations which occurred and proposals made during such negotiations shall not be referred to in connection with the presentation of any issue to the Panel, except as the parties agree otherwise.

443

6. Decisions of the Panel.

a. All decisions of the Panel shall be in writing and shall set forth the facts and reasons for the Panel's conclusions with sufficient specificity to enable the parties to understand and implement the Panel's decisions.

b. Decisions of the Panel shall be effective as of August 1, 1974, and specific provisions of the award shall become applicable as of dates provided in the award.

c. Decisions of the Panel shall be final and binding on the parties.

7. Duration of the Panel.

The members of the Panel shall continue to serve until August 1, 1974, to assist the parties in the interpretation and implementation of the Panel's decisions.

8. Compensation and Costs of the Panel.

The Union's member of the Panel shall be paid by the Union and the Companies' member of the Panel shall be paid by the Companies. The compensation and expenses of the impartial members of the Panel, as well as the costs incurred by the Panel in conducting the hearings, shall be borne equally by the Union and the Companies.

F. Term of the New Agreements:

The term of the new agreements shall be three years.

G. Continuation of Existing Agreement Terms:

Except as contained in or required by the award of the Panel or as agreed to by the parties, the provisions of the existing agreements...will be carried forward in the new agreements. Should it become desirable to revise the cost-of-living formula...the parties will negotiate in an attempt to reach agreement on such revision and, failing such agreement, either party may submit the issue of such revision to arbitration.

H. Term of Experimental Negotiating Agreement:

This Agreement shall become effective upon execution by the officers of the International Union and an authorized official of each of the Companies and shall terminate August 1, 1974, except to the extent that its continuation beyond that date is deemed necessary by the parties to achieve the objectives of this Agreement.

April

NIXON-THIEU SUMMIT
April 2-3, 1973

South Vietnamese President Nguyen Van Thieu paid a six-day visit to the United States in April and obtained from President Nixon a pledge of substantial economic assistance to his country through 1973, and a promise "to seek congressional authority for a level of funding for the next year sufficient to assure economic stability and rehabilitation." In a joint communique issued April 3 at the conclusion of two days of talks at the Western White House in San Clemente, Calif., the two presidents announced that a "full consensus" had been reached between them in "a very cordial atmosphere." What it all meant was less clear. The White House admitted that the language of the document was "purposely indefinite."

Among other things, the two presidents reaffirmed their suppport of the Agreement on Ending the War and Restoring Peace in Vietnam and of the International Conference on Vietnam. (See p. 115 and p. 331.) In non-specific terms, they promised to "scrupulously" observe the cease-fire agreement and affirmed their "strong expectations" that other signatories would similarly abide by the agreement in order to "permit normalization of relations with all countries of Southeast Asia." Nixon and Thieu endorsed efforts to arrange a political reconciliation between Saigon and the Viet Cong, and voiced their concern over the continued fighting in Laos and Cambodia. Acknowledging that a lasting peace in Vietnam was dependent on "peace in neighboring countries," they called for implementation of the provisions of the truce agreement that provided for the withdrawal of all foreign troops from those two countries.

447

Earlier news reports had depicted Thieu as anxious to gain the assurance of American air support should the Communists mount another large-scale offensive. But the Nixon administration reportedly had kept him at arm's length, fearing that a state visit would be politically embarrassing. Then, with the cease-fire agreement signed and the last POW's and American troops brought home, President Nixon had extended an official invitation to the South Vietnamese president.

After leaving California, Thieu flew to Washington to address a luncheon at the National Press Club. He vowed there that he would "never, never...again ask American troops to come back to Vietnam." He was confident that his government could defend itself even without American air support if the Communists launched another invasion. Thieu expressed his gratitude to the United States for coming "to help us in time of danger; you kept your word to a small nation even when the going was rough and you kept it till the day an acceptable arrangement could be found to terminate the war." While in Washington, he met with congressional leaders and also with John B. Connally and George Meany, persons he had indicated were important acquaintances.

On his way back to Saigon, South Vietnam's president stopped over in several European capitals and was confronted with protest demonstrations. In Rome, April 8, police battled demonstrators near St. Peter's Square while Thieu was being received by Pope Paul VI. In Bonn two days later, thousands of German youths fought police and stormed city hall during a meeting of Thieu with West German President Gustav Heinemann. North Vietnam had called the trip to this country a scheme by the United States "to maintain its involvement and continue its intervention in the internal affairs of our country."

> *Text of the joint communique issued April 3, 1973, at San Clemente, Calif., following formal talks of President Nixon and South Vietnamese President Nguyen Van Thieu:*

The President of the United States, Richard M. Nixon, and the President of the Republic of Vietnam, Nguyen Van Thieu, met for two days of discussions in San Clemente at the outset of President Thieu's official visit to the United States. Taking part in these discussions on the United States side were the Secretary of State, William P. Rogers; the Assistant to the President for National Security Affairs, Henry A. Kissinger; the Ambassador of the United States to the Republic of Vietnam, Ellsworth Bunker; the Ambassador-designate of the United States to the Republic of Vietnam, Graham Martin; and other officials. On the side of the Republic of Vietnam the Minister for Foreign Affairs, Tran Van Lam; the Minister of Economy, Pham Kim Ngoc; the Minister of Finance, Ha Xuan Trung; the Special Assistant to the President for Foreign Affairs, Nguyen Phu Duc; the Vietnamese Ambassador to the United States, Tran Kim Phuong, and other officials also participated in the discussions.

The discussions were held in a very cordial atmosphere appropriate to the enduring relationship of friendship which exists between the governments of the Republic of Vietnam and the United States. The two Presidents discussed the course of U.S.-Vietnamese relations since their meeting at Midway Island on June 8, 1969 and the postwar relationship between the two countries. They reached full consensus in their views.

President Nixon and President Thieu reviewed the progress that has been made in economic, political and defense affairs in Vietnam since the Midway meeting. President Nixon expressed gratification with the proficiency of South Vietnam's armed forces and noted their effective and courageous performance in halting the invasion launched by North Vietnam on March 30, 1972. The President also expressed satisfaction with the development of political institutions and noted the political stability that has prevailed in South Vietnam in recent years. President Thieu reaffirmed his determination to assure social and political justice for the people of South Vietnam.

The two Presidents expressed their satisfaction at the conclusion of the Agreement on Ending the War and Restoring Peace in Vietnam, as well as the Act of the International Conference on Vietnam which endorsed this Agreement. They asserted the determination of their two governments to implement the provisions of the Agreement scrupulously. They also affirmed their strong expectation that the other parties signatory to the Agreement would do the same in order to establish a lasting peace in Vietnam. The two Presidents expressed their appreciation to the other members of the international community who helped in achieving the Agreement and particularly to the four member governments of the International Commission of Control and Supervision whose representatives are observing its implementation. They consider that the International Commission, acting in cooperation with the Four Parties to the Agreement, is an essential element in the structure of restoring peace to Vietnam and expressed their determination to further encourage the most effective and objective possible supervision of the Agreement.

President Nixon informed President Thieu of his great interest in the meetings between representatives of the two South Vietnamese parties which are currently taking place in France in an effort to achieve an internal political settlement in South Vietnam. President Thieu said that his government is resolved at these meetings to achieve a settlement which will fully insure the right of self-determination by the South Vietnamese people in accordance with the Agreement on Ending the War. President Thieu expressed his earnest desire for a reconciliation among the South Vietnamese parties which will fulfill the hopes of the South Vietnamese people for peace, independence, and democracy.

Both Presidents, while acknowledging that progress was being made toward military and political settlements in South Vietnam, nevertheless viewed with great concern infiltrations of men and weapons in sizeable numbers from North Vietnam into South Vietnam in violation of the Agreement on Ending the War, and considered that actions which would threaten the basis of the Agreement would call for appropriately vigorous reactions. They expressed their conviction that all the provisions of the Agreement, including in particular those concerning military forces and military supplies, must be faithfully implemented if the cease-fire is to be preserved and the prospects for a peaceful settlement are to be assured. President Nixon stated in this connection that the United States views violations of any provision of the Agreement with great and continuing concern.

Both Presidents also agreed that there could be lasting peace in Vietnam only if there is peace in the neighboring countries. Accordingly they expressed their earnest interest in the achievement of a satisfactory implementation of the cease-fire agreement reached in Laos on February 21. They expressed their grave concern at the fact that Article 20 of the Agreement which calls for the unconditional withdrawal of all foreign forces from Laos and Cambodia has not been carried out. They agreed that this Article should be quickly implemented.

In assessing the prospects for peace throughout Indochina the two Presidents stressed the need for vigilance on the part of the governments in the Indochinese states against the possibility of renewed Communist aggression after the departure of United States ground forces from South Vietnam. They stressed the fact that this vigilance will require the continued political, economic, and military strength of the governments and nations menaced by any renewal of this aggressive threat. Because of their limited resources, the nations of the region will require external assistance to preserve the necessary social and economic stability for peaceful development.

In this context, President Thieu affirmed the determination of the Vietnamese people and the Government to forge ahead with the task of providing adequate and timely relief to war victims, reconstructing damaged social and economic infrastructures, and building a strong and viable economy so that the Vietnamese nation can gradually shoulder a greater burden in the maintenance of peace and the achievement of economic progress for its people. The two Presidents agreed that in order to attain the stated economic goals as quickly as possible, the Republic of Vietnam will need greater external economic assistance in the initial years of the postwar era. President Nixon reaffirmed his wholehearted support for the endeavors of postwar rehabilitation, reconstruction and development of the Republic of Vietnam. He informed President Thieu of the United States intention to provide adequate and substantial economic assistance for the Republic of Vietnam during the remainder of this year and to seek Congressional authority for a level of funding for the next year sufficient to assure essential economic stability and rehabilitation for that country as it now moves from war to peace. He recognized that the economic development and self-sufficiency of South Vietnam depend to a significant extent on its ability to promote and attract foreign investment. He also expressed his intention to seek Congressional support for a longer-range program for the economic development of South Vietnam now that the war has ended.

The two Presidents expressed their earnest hope that other nations as well as international institutions will act promptly on a positive and concerted program of international assistance to the Republic of Vietnam. They also agreed that consultations should soon be held in this regard with all interested parties.

The two Presidents expressed hope that the implementation of the Agreement on Vietnam would permit a normalization of relations with all countries of Southeast Asia. They agreed that this step and a regional reconstruction program will increase the prospects of a lasting peace in the area.

President Nixon discussed the future security of South Vietnam in the context of the Nixon Doctrine. The President noted that the assumption by the Republic of Vietnam of the full manpower requirements for its own defense was fully in keeping with his doctrine. He affirmed that the United States for its part, expected to continue in accordance with its Constitutional processes, to supply the Republic of Vietnam with the material means for its defense consistent with the Agreement on Ending the War.

President Thieu asked President Nixon to convey to the American people and particularly to families bereaved by the loss of loved ones, the deep and abiding appreciation of the people of South Vietnam for the sacrifices made on their behalf and the assistance given to the Republic of Vietnam in its long struggle to maintain its freedom and preserve its right of self-determination.

Prior to the departure of President Thieu for Washington to continue his official visit to the United States, both Presidents agreed that through the harsh experience of a tragic war and the sacrifices of their two peoples a close and constructive relationship between the American and the South Vietnamese people has been developed and strengthened. They affirmed their full confidence that this association would be preserved as the foundation of an honorable and lasting peace in Southeast Asia.

President Thieu expressed his gratitude for the warm hospitality extended to him and his party by President Nixon.

ATTEMPT TO DISMANTLE OEO

April 11, 1973

The Office of Economic Opportunity (OEO), doomed to starvation by omission from President Nixon's fiscal 1974 budget, was rescued from extinction—at least temporarily—by the decision of a federal judge in mid-April. In a classic illustration of the system of checks and balances, U.S. District Judge William B. Jones ordered the administration to halt action already under way to dismantle an agency created and funded by Congress to aid the poor. Ruling in three consolidated suits brought by OEO community action agencies and by labor unions representing OEO employees, Jones ordered Howard Phillips, acting director of OEO, to desist from steps being taken to terminate the agency's programs. He also declared null and void all orders issued for that purpose.

"An administrator's responsibility to carry out the congressional objectives of a program," the judge held, "does not give him the power to discontinue that program.... When Congress orders that a program go forth,....it is for the Congress in the responsible exercise of its legislative power to make provisions for termination. Until those provisions are made, the function of the executive is to administer the program in accord with the legislated purposes."

Phillips subsequently commented that he did not think the court's decision would prevent him from completing on schedule his mission to disassemble OEO. "We have to recognize," he said, "that the President had not proposed any money for OEO in the fiscal 1974 budget. I don't foresee anything that would change that." Since as-

453

suming office, Phillips had been critical of various OEO activities. He had charged repeatedly that lawyers in the legal services program were using federal funds for political purposes and that much of their effort was directed toward embarrassing the government.

While no funds had been requested for OEO in the fiscal 1974 budget submitted to Congress in January (see p. 169), some OEO programs had been parceled out to other departments. No program transfer or budget request had been made for the most controversial OEO project, the Community Action Program (CAP); CAP was a loosely organized project involving nearly 1,000 local agencies that focused on employment, health and other antipoverty efforts. However, the 1974 budget requests included an appropriation of $36.5-million to the Department of Health, Education and Welfare to finance an independent legal services corporation.

The plans to phase out major OEO programs and the agency itself had generated strong opposition. Senators Jacob K. Javits (R N.Y.) and Gaylord Nelson (D Wis.) introduced with 34 co-sponsors a resolution calling on the President to continue OEO through 1974 and to submit a revised budget for its programs and activities. The U.S. Conference of Mayors and the National League of Cities jointly issued a 79-page analysis sharply criticizing the budget cuts affecting the cities. But the President in his State of the Union radio speech on human resources, Feb. 24, insisted that distribution of OEO's functions among other departments would make the programs "more efficient by linking them with other related federal activities."

The rationale for scuttling OEO was shaken March 21 by a 62-page report of the General Accounting Office that seemed to refute arguments that the legal services program had been oriented toward law reform to the neglect of specific needs of poor people. The report concluded that poverty lawyers rarely had time to work for reform of laws that disadvantaged the poor. It added that the lawyers had no time to help the poor organize to improve their situation through legal action.

Bickering between the White House and Congress ended abruptly when Judge Jones ruled the OEO dismantlement illegal. Still in question was whether Congress would appropriate funds to fulfill its previous authorization of funding through June 1974. The judge on June 11 struck another blow at attempts to dismantle OEO. In a suit brought by four senators, he ruled that OEO acting director Howard Phillips was serving illegally and enjoined him from taking further action as head of the agency. Sen. Harrison A. Williams Jr. (D N.J.), chairman of the Senate Labor and Public Welfare Committee which handled OEO legislation, and Senators Claiborne Pell (D R.I.), Walter F. Mondale (D Minn.) and William D. Hathaway (D Maine) had filed suit March 14 seeking removal of Phillips on the ground that he was serving unlawfully in the absence of confirmation by the Senate. President Nixon had appointed Phillips acting director Jan. 30 but had never submitted his name to the Senate for confirmation.

Excerpts from the opinion of U.S. District Judge William B. Jones, April 11, 1973, ruling illegal the action taken to dismantle the Office of Economic Opportunity:

UNITED STATES DISTRICT COURT
FOR THE DISTRICT OF COLUMBIA

OPINION

These three consolidated actions have been brought to declare unlawful and enjoin what the plaintiffs allege to be the unlawful dismantlement of the Office of Economic Opportunity (OEO) by the defendant, Howard J. Phillips, Acting Director of OEO. The plaintiffs in *Local 2677, American Federation of Government Employees, et al.* v. *Phillips,* Civil Action No. 371-73 (hereinafter *Local 2677*), by an amended complaint, are the labor organization-bargaining agent for the Washington, D.C. headquarters employees of OEO, and two individual OEO headquarters employees. Suit is brought on behalf of all OEO employees throughout the country who have been or are about to be adversely affected by the alleged unlawful acts of the defendant. The plaintiffs in *West Central Missouri Rural Development Corp., et al.* v. *Phillips,* Civil Action No. 375-73 (hereinafter *West Central*), are four Community Action Agencies (CAAs)...which bring their suit on behalf of all 930 CAAs receiving funds from OEO under section 221 of the Economic Opportunity Act of 1964, as amended.... In the third suit, *National Council of O.E.O. Locals, A.F.G.E., AFL-CIO, et al.* v. *Phillips, et al.,* Civil Action No. 379-73 (hereinafter *National Council*), the plaintiffs are the exclusive agency-wide representative for all nonsupervisory OEO employees, an association of CAA executive directors, three CAAs, two headquarters employees of OEO, several CAA employees, and several beneficiaries of programs funded by OEO through CAAs. *National Council* is likewise brought as a class action on behalf of all OEO employees, all CAAs and their employees, and all beneficiaries of CAA programs.... [T]he Court finds that there are no material facts in dispute and the case is ripe for summary judgment...

Statement of the Case

The plaintiffs assert that the defendant has been acting illegally for several reasons. It is sufficient for the disposition of these cases to consider only three of their contentions. First, the plaintiffs claim that the Economic Opportunity Amendments of 1972 (hereinafter 1972

Amendments),...in particular sections 2(a), 3(c) (2), and 28, forbid the defendant from taking the actions he has to terminate OEO funding of CAAs. Second, the claim is made that the activities of the defendant regarding the alleged termination of CAA functions is an illegal reorganization because the terms of the Reorganization Act...have not been complied with. Finally, the plaintiffs contend that the defendant's directives are illegal and of no effect because he failed to publish them in the Federal Register as required by section 22 of the 1972 Amendments.... The defendant has raised several technical defenses in addition to his defenses on the merits. The Court finds against the defendant on these points for reasons set forth below.

The Court finds for the plaintiffs on all three of these basic substantive theories.

Case or Controversy

The defendant argues that these cases are brought prematurely and thus fail to present a justiciable case or controversy. An examination of the uncontroverted facts reveals that this contention is totally unfounded and that the present cases present a justiciable case or controversy....

The defendant asserts that the complaint of the plaintiffs is premature because the defendant's compliance with his statutory duties regarding CAAs cannot be determined until June 30, 1973. The basic theory underlying this assertion is that until that time the defendant will be in compliance with all applicable statutes because the OEO's CAA function will not cease before that date and because he will reserve and make available for obligation to CAAs in fiscal year 1973 the $328,900,000 mandated by section 3(c) (2) of the 1972 Amendments....

Surely it cannot be maintained that the plaintiffs must wait until the CAAs have gone out of existence before they may challenge acts of the defendant which they claim are illegal. Courts do not require that an injury be complete before they will adjudicate the issues....

In rebuttal the defendant argues that no case or controversy can exist until Congress appropriates money for OEO to operate in fiscal 1974. The plaintiffs, however, do not argue that OEO must spend new funds in fiscal year 1974 which have not been appropriated. Rather they challenge as unlawful the current and announced practices of the defendant as they affect the plaintiffs today, even though those practices will affect them as well after June 30, 1973. In that context, this case is justiciable.

Political Question

The defendant contends further that this case is not justiciable because it involves a political question. That theory is bottomed on the assumption that what the plaintiffs really ask of this Court is for it to interject itself between the Executive and Legislative branches of the federal government regarding the Executive budget proposals for OEO for fiscal year 1974. If that were the circumstance, the defendant would clearly be correct. But the Court holds that not to be the circumstance and that this case does not present a nonjusticiable political question.

...[T]he plaintiffs are challenging the defendant's exercise of his statutory powers as Acting Director of OEO as unlawful and in direct violation of certain statutory obligations.... It is their [the plaintiffs'] contention that Congress has already spoken through law on the manner in which the OEO, and in particular the CAA program of OEO, must be operated and that the defendant is acting contrary to that mandate.

Therefore this dispute is one which readily is within the judicial power.... [T]he Court must determine whether an executive official is following the explicit mandates of the Congress and the Constitution, which is the judicial function in our tripartite government....

Sovereign Immunity

The defendant argues that in reality these are unconsented suits against the United States which must be dismissed because of sovereign immunity. In support of this theory, it is contended that enjoining the defendant would be a judgment which would draw upon the Treasury because it would require the expenditure of funds not yet appropriated, and further that it would interfere with the public administration of the laws.... But this argument proceeds on a fundamentally incorrect premise. The relief which the plaintiffs seek would not be a drain on the public purse. No injunction to spend unappropriated funds is sought. What the plaintiffs do demand is that the defendant be enjoined from acting in a manner which violates his statutory duties under the Economic Opportunity Act or that he be declared to be acting unconstitutionally. Thus this suit clearly falls within the exception to the doctrine of sovereign immunity which allows suits against federal officials who have allegedly acted beyond their statutory powers or have exercised their statutory powers in a constitutionally void manner....

Having rejected the defenses to jurisdiction of the defendant as inapplicable to the present proceeding, the Court now turns to the substantive consideration of the plaintiffs' claims.

Termination of CAA Funding as Violative of the Economic Opportunity Act of 1964, as Amended

As set forth earlier, on January 29, 1973, President Nixon submitted his 1974 Budget Message to Congress. The budget message requests that no funds be appropriated OEO in fiscal year 1974. CAA functions are to be transferred to local agencies through the use of special revenue sharing. The existence of OEO as a federal agency is to cease. On the same date, the defendant issued a memorandum to all OEO regional offices, regarding the "termination of section 221...funding." Before discussing this termination program in more detail, a brief outline of the CAA function of OEO will help place this controversy in the proper perspective.

A CAA [Community Action Agency] is a state, a political subdivision of a state, a combination of political subdivisions, or a public or private nonprofit agency formally designated as a CAA by a state or appropriate political subdivision. The CAA designation is official for purposes of receiving funds and administering programs upon ratification by the Director of OEO....

After official designation, a CAA is the local apparatus for citizen participation in the policy planning and implementation of the community action programs (CAP).... In addition, a CAA must carry out the purposes of the Act in conformity with criteria prescribed by the OEO Director.

...[A]ny individual CAA may decide to use its funds for locally determined priorities, such as health care or manpower training. CAAs typically administer their programs through a network of neighborhood centers that provide the opportunity for close contact with, and participation by, the intended beneficiaries of the program. OEO grants to CAAs are on a yearly basis, with provisions for termination, suspension, or certain reductions in fundings to any individual CAA....

In addition, CAAs are eligible to apply for grants from OEO...to fund specific antipoverty programs, such as legal services, comprehensive health services, and alcoholic counseling and recovery. Section 222 also enables CAAs to receive funds to administer programs under the Act funded by other federal agencies, such as Headstart preschool and elementary funds from the Department of Health, Education and Welfare, and several work training and employment programs funded by the Department of Labor. Official designation as a CAA entitles it to receive funding from different federal departments for certain programs under the Act on a priority basis. If funds are available for the program in the area served by the CAA, the CAA receives the funds automatically in preference to other potential recipients. Section 221 funds typically pay the overhead on facilities that are used to dispense those other services for which CAAs may obtain OEO and other federal funds.

In September 1972, the Congress passed the Economic Opportunity Amendments of 1972,...and that Act was signed into law by the President. Section 2(a) of the Amendments authorized and directed the continuance of the CAP [Community Action] program, as administered by CAAs, through the end of fiscal year 1975.... Section 3(c) (2) of the Amendments,...authorized and earmarked certain funding levels for section 221 programs through June 30, 1974. Finally, section 28 of the Amendments provided [that]... "the Director of the Office of

Economic Opportunity shall not delegate his functions under section 221 and title VII of such Act to any other agency."

The January 29, 1973, memorandum of the defendant Phillips instructed all grantees of funds under section 221 that they must begin phasing out their programs because the fiscal year 1974 budget does not provide any funds for section 221 grants.... Under this state of facts, the Court is compelled to find that the defendant is terminating the CAA function of OEO and that CAAs are being required to use their funds to phase out their programs rather than carry out their purposes under section 221 of the Act.

The plaintiffs claim that the defendant's program to terminate OEO's CAA function now is unlawful because the Congress last fall in section 2(a) of the 1972 Amendments,...provided that the Director of OEO "shall" carry out section 221 programs through June 30, 1975. The plaintiffs acknowledge that if Congress fails to provide funds for OEO to operate after June 30, 1973, either by continuing resolution or an appropriation, the defendant has no obligation to spend any money. But they argue that until funds do expire on June 30, 1973, the defendant is bound to operate OEO as before January 29, 1973, through the duty imposed upon the President...to "take Care that the Laws be faithfully executed." The plaintiffs construe the defendant's obligation ...to continue to operate section 221 programs to be to carry out section 221 functions until either no funds are left or Congress terminates the program. This would entail the continued refunding of CAAs as before, contingent upon funds being appropriated for actual expenditure. In other words, CAAs would operate as before, including the reprocessing of grants, and cease operation only if funds actually do not become available.

The defendant contends that because the budget message of the President, as the latest assessment of national needs and priorities, requests no funds for OEO to operate after June 30, 1973, the fiscally responsible course for the defendant to undertake is to phase out the CAA program that will be out of existence on July 1, 1973. In support of this theory, the defendant cites the general proposition of the law with which the plaintiffs are in total agreement—that the defendant cannot be forced to spend any funds which have not yet been appropriated. The defendant, however, goes on to argue that once the President has submitted his budget to the Congress, a program administrator must look to that message. If no funds are proposed for his agency, it is his duty to terminate that agency's functions to effect the least "waste" of funds. Because the Court can find no support for this position in the budget act, the OEO act, the history of OEO appropriations, or the Constitution itself, the Court finds for the plaintiffs on this count.

The Budget and Accounting Act of 1921...was the original legislation which required that the President submit a proposed budget at the beginning of each session of Congress. The pertinent section of that Act, as amended, requires that

(a) The President shall transmit to Congress during the first fifteen days of each regular session, the Budget,...

...(5) estimated expenditures and *proposed appropriations* necessary in his judgment for the support of the Government for the ensuing fiscal year....(emphasis added).

There is no question both from the text of the Act and the legislative history that the budget is nothing more than a proposal to the Congress for the Congress to act upon as it may please. No citation of authority is required to show that the Congress not infrequently acts contrary to its requests.

...Termination of the CAA function because no appropriation bill had yet been passed and no funds were requested in the budget would not be in keeping with the obligations to maintain fiscal responsibility as those obligations are defined by the Act itself. Those obligations are clearly intended to insure the fiscal responsibility of an ongoing program.

Moreover, if the defendant were correct in his argument, it would have been the responsibility of every OEO Director to terminate the section 221 program before the end of the fiscal year. Since its inception in 1964, Congress has never funded OEO prior to the end of the fiscal year.

...That construction would in effect give the President a veto power through the use of his budget message, a veto power not granted him by Article I, section 7, of the Constitution....

Congress, by its use of a multiple year authorization, has indicated its intent that the CAA function of OEO continue for at least that period of time. Moreover, in passing the 1972 Amendments which contained that multiple year authorization, the Congress found that the CAA program in particular should continue. The House Committee on Education and Labor, in reporting out the bill which was enacted as the 1972 Amendments..."intend[ed] that...there be no diminution in program levels for local initiative...." The Senate Committee on Labor and Public Welfare was equally impressed with the CAA program: "The committee was especially impressed in the hearings at the demonstration of maturity, sophistication, and competence by community action agencies and their spokesmen...."

...The clear Congressional intent of the multiple year authorization was that the program continue, especially in the light of the late appropriations process that has been detailed earlier. The multiple year authorization enables the Congress to evidence its intent to continue to fund a program (with the option to terminate it if it so pleases) without being forced to make that intent known by appropriating funds before the end of the fiscal year.

In effect the defendant argues that by use of the budget message the Executive can force the Congress to legislate to keep an authorized program from terminating. The defendant contends further that he can use the funds appropriated by Congress to run section 221 programs to terminate them and force the Congress to act before the time that it has set for itself (June 30, 1973) to act on appropriating the funds as allowed by the authorization. Thus the Executive would effectively legislate the termination of section 221 programs before Congress has declared that they shall end. Article I, section 1, of the Constitution vests "[a]ll legislative powers" in the Congress. No budget message of the President can alter that power and force the Congress to act to preserve legislative programs from extinction prior to the time Congress has declared that they shall terminate, either by its action or inaction.

The defendant concedes at pages 22-23, note 5, of his original memorandum that the OEO Director is under an obligation to carry on programs in any year in which funds are appropriated. That is all the plaintiffs seek here—that the defendant carry on section 221 programs through fiscal 1973, and not terminate them, as this Court has found that the defendant is doing.

An authorization does not necessarily mean that a program will continue. Congress, of course, may itself decide to terminate a program before its authorization has expired, either indirectly by failing to supply funds through a continuing resolution or appropriation, or by explicitly forbidding the further use of funds for the programs, as it did in the case of the supersonic transport. But Congress has not chosen either of these courses, although it may in the future. Until that time, historical precedent, logic, and the text of the Constitution itself obligate the defendant to continue to operate the section 221 programs as was intended by the Congress, and not terminate them.

The conclusion that the Executive must continue to operate an authorized program until the funds expire or Congress declares otherwise is supported, although not conclusively, by the sparse case law which relates even tangentially to the problem....

...Mr. Justice Black [in *Youngstown Sheet and Tube Co.* v. *Sawyer*, (1952)] wrote for the majority that authorization for the President's actions "must stem either from an act of Congress or from the Constitution itself." ...The Court held:

...In the framework of our Constitution, the President's power to see that the laws are faithfully executed refutes the idea that he is to be a lawmaker. The Constitution limits his functions to the recommending of laws he thinks wise and the vetoing of laws he thinks bad. And the Constitution is neither silent nor equivocal about who shall make laws which the President is to execute.

...The Constitution does not subject this lawmaking power of Congress to presidential...supervision or control....

The Founders of this Nation entrusted the lawmaking power to the Congress alone in both good and bad times.

...As the Court has found earlier, if the power sought here were found valid, no barrier would remain to the executive ignoring any and all Congressional authorizations if he deemed them, no matter how conscientiously, to be contrary to the needs of the nation. Historical precedent provides evidence that multiple year authorizations indicate Congressional intent that a program continue....

The defendant really argues that the Constitution confers the discretionary power upon the President to refuse to execute laws passed by Congress with which he disagrees. In *Kendall* v. *United States,...* the Supreme Court held that the Postmaster General could not refuse to pay a contractor for services rendered once Congress has specifically directed payment.... The Court held that that "principle, which if carried out in its results, to all cases falling within it, would be clothing the President with a power entirely to control the legislation of Congress, and paralyze the administration of justice."...

In the present case, the Congress has not directed that funds be granted to any particular CAA. The OEO Director has been granted discretion in the disbursing of funds so as to effectuate the goals of the program.... But discretion in the implementation of a program is not the freedom to ignore the standards for its implementation.... An administrator's responsibility to carry out the Congressional objectives of a program does not give him the power to discontinue that program, especially in the face of a Congressional mandate that it shall go on....

Counsel for the defendant urged at oral argument that unless the defendant ignored that Congressional command and terminated section 221 programs, financial chaos would result on July 1, 1973, if the Congress failed to include OEO in a continuing resolution or pass an appropriation bill.... But Congress has shown how the problem posed by counsel for the defendant would be solved in its past action terminating funding for the SST program.... Thus when Congress orders that a program go forth and later changes its mind, it is for the Congress in the responsible exercise of its legislative power to make provisions for termination. Until those provisions are made, the function of the Executive is to administer the program in accord with the legislated purposes.

Termination of CAA Funding as Violative of the Reorganization Act

Another theory argued by the plaintiffs in support of their complaints is that the actions of the defendant Phillips in terminating section 221 funding are violative of the Reorganization Act,....The Court finds for the plaintiffs on this count, for reasons set forth below. This finding is independent of that regarding the defendant's duty not to terminate section 221 funding under his responsibility to administer the program, and constitutes a separate ground for this Court's decision.

As has been discussed in detail,... the defendant has announced plans to terminate section 221 funding and the OEO as a separate federal agency. Steps have already been taken to implement that plan, and as the extensive affidavits filed by the plaintiffs in *West Central* demonstrate, that termination effect is already being felt by CAAs. The Court repeats its earlier finding that the defendant is terminating or abolishing the section 221 function of OEO.

The Reorganization Act of 1949, as amended...is a broad delegation of authority by Congress to the President to initiate and propose changes in the organization and functions of the Executive branch. The Act is in part a Congressional recognition that an essential element of any legislative program is the organization and characteristics of the executive agencies that administer that program....

The purposes of a reorganization as set forth in section 901(a) of the Act are generally to promote the more efficient management of executive branch functions, *economy,* or the elimination of duplication of effort. Sections 903(a) (2) and (6) go on to provide that

(a) When the President, after investigation, finds that—

...(2) the abolition of all or a part of the functions of an agency; [or]

...(6) the abolition of the whole or a part of an agency which agency or part does not have, or on the taking effect of the reorganization plan will not have, any functions;

is necessary to accomplish one or more of the purposes of section 901(a)..., he shall prepare a reorganization plan for making of the reorganizations as to which he has made findings and which he includes in the plan, and transmit the plan...to Congress....

This Court has found that the defendant's directives require the use of section 221 funds for phase-out purposes and forbid their use for any other purposes, including the implementation of section 221 programs. Thus the section 221 function has already been abolished. The defendant has stated unequivocally that the CAA function and OEO itself will cease on or before June 30, 1973, and that his plans are to reach that goal by April 28, 1973. Moreover the defendant has evidenced clear reliance on the budget message of the President as justification for that plan. The budget message...states that the President proposes that the CAA function and OEO shall cease to exist. As found earlier, the Court must conclude that the program of the defendant is terminating or abolishing the CAA function and OEO itself. Section 903(a) of the Reorganization Act requires that a reorganization plan be submitted to the Congress before the abolition of that function or the agency itself can take place. Thus in the absence of any contrary legislation, the defendant's plans to terminate the CAA function and the OEO itself are unlawful as beyond his statutory authority.

The defendant argues that section 602(d) of the Economic Opportunity Act,... provides the defendant with the statutory authority to transfer many OEO functions to other agencies. Although this is correct, the defendant himself concedes that Section 602(d) provides no basis for the transfer not only of section 221 and CED [Community Economic Development] functions by reason of section 28 of the 1972 Amendments to the Act, but also of the legal services program,... because of a 1969 amendment to the Act.... Moreover, the legislative history of the 1972 Amendments demonstrates the Congressional intent that neither section 221 nor CED functions can be transferred without using the Reorganization Act procedures.

The defendant nevertheless argues that he has not proposed that section 221 funding be delegated to any other agency but rather that it be terminated and that the prohibition of section 28 does not apply. Even if that argument were valid, section 602(d) would still provide no basis for bypassing the Reorganization Act because it allows only the delegation of a function, not its abolition....

The defendant plans to abolish OEO as an agency because it will no longer have any functions to carry out. Assuming for the moment that the defendant were to accomplish this by delegating all OEO functions but legal services and CED...as he plans, and to transfer those to other agencies through substantive legislation, as he plans, the defendant would still be in violation of the Economic Opportunity Act. Section 602(d),...requires that programs may be delegated "subject to provisions to assure the maximum possible liaison" between OEO and the other agency. No such liaison could be maintained if OEO were no longer in existence....

Therefore the Court finds that the termination of section 221 funding by the defendant is violative of the provisions of the Reorganization Act and beyond his statutory power and will be enjoined as unlawful.

The plaintiffs rely on an additional theory for declaring the actions of the defendant in terminating section 221 funding to be unlawful. Section 22 of the 1972 Amendments to the Economic Opportunity Act... provides:

> All rules, regulations, guidelines, instructions, and application forms published or promulgated pursuant to this chapter [the OEO Act] shall be published in the Federal Register at least thirty days prior to their effective date.

It is conceded by the defendant that the January 29, 1973, and March 15, 1973, directives on the termination of section 221 funding... have never been published in the Federal Register, although the defendant claims that the latter has been prepared for publication. The Court holds that until section 2971b has been complied with, the directives of the defendant are illegal as issued beyond the defendant's statutory authority....

...Defendant Phillips' motion to dismiss or for summary judgment is denied.

Date: April 11, 1973   Wm. B. Jones, Judge

ENERGY: CHALLENGE OR CRISIS?

April 18, 1973

Millions of Americans felt the crunch of the energy shortage for the first time during the winter of 1972-73. Accustomed to plentiful and relatively low-cost supplies of oil, gas and coal, some people suddenly found themselves without enough fuel to heat their houses adequately or to keep factories running full blast. During bitter January cold spells, schools shut down in Denver. Idling of factories in Alabama and Louisiana deprived thousands of workers of their jobs. A major oil company announced that it would have to ration heating oil in four eastern states. Even when temperatures warmed as winter turned to spring, oil shortages remained a problem. Three major suppliers announced in May that they would ration the gasoline delivered to filling stations. Former Commerce Secretary Peter G. Peterson was blunt: "Popeye is running out of cheap spinach."

President Nixon transmitted to Congress April 18 a long-awaited message on the steps he had taken and would take to deal with the growing energy shortage. Terming the situation a challenge rather than a crisis, he set forth a comprehensive program ranging from short-run measures to cope with immediate energy deficits to long-run plans for stimulating domestic production to meet future needs. Among the chief actions taken or proposed by the President were termination of the 14-year-old oil import quota system, a partial decontrolling of natural gas prices, intensive offshore exploration for oil and gas deposits, construction of deepwater ports capable of handling the largest oil tankers, and a $130-million increase in funds for research and development of future energy resources of all kinds.

465

Confronted with a situation where the United States, with 6 per cent of the world's population, uses more than one-third of the world's energy supplies, the President opted to increase the amounts of energy available domestically rather than to place controls on skyrocketing American demands for fuel. He emphasized that steps must be taken to augment domestic production by providing incentives for exploration and development of the country's energy resources. Incentives would be accompanied by some unavoidable price rises, Nixon admitted, but the price rises would be less than if no steps were taken to increase production. By removing impediments to importation of low-cost fuel from abroad, prices would be kept down by expanding the supply. However, the message warned of the danger of continuing to rely heavily on foreign energy sources.

Initial congressional reaction to the President's message was largely partisan. Sen. Henry M. Jackson (D Wash.), who had introduced a bill to establish a 10-year, $20-billion program of energy research and development, said: "While the President's message is long on pages, it can be summed up in one word: inadequate." A different assessment was given by Sen. Paul J. Fannin of Arizona, ranking Republican on the Interior Committee, which handles some phases of energy legislation. Fannin called the message "one of the most comprehensive and most important messages which will be delivered to Congress this year." Sen. Ernest F. Hollings (D S.C.), a member of the Commerce Committee, which deals with legislation on regulation of natural gas, said of the President's proposal to move toward decontrol of natural gas prices: "Such a step can only result in billions of dollars of extra cost to consumers without any assurance that more gas would be committed than is now planned."

Postscript to the April Message

On June 29, two months after the energy message had been sent to Congress, Nixon announced the appointment of John A. Love, Republican governor of Colorado, to head an Energy Policy Office in the Executive Office of the President. The new office was to absorb and expand the activities of a Special Energy Committee and a National Energy Office created by the President at the end of April. In his June statement, Nixon also made known his intention to ask Congress to establish a cabinet-level Department of Energy and Natural Resources, to be "responsible for the balanced utilization and conservation of America's energy and natural resources."

In addition, the President announced that he was setting up an Energy Research and Development Administration to plan, manage and conduct the government's energy research and development and to work with industry to implement promising technological advances. He proposed a $10-billion funding level for a five-year period beginning *in fiscal 1975 and, in the meantime, the expenditure of $100-million in fiscal 1974 on existing and new projects.*

The President said also that he was directing the Atomic Energy Commission to undertake, under the direction of the Energy Policy Office, an immediate review of federal and private energy research and development activities. The review was to be followed by recommendations for an "integrated energy research and development program for the nation." Finally, the President announced the creation of an Energy Research and Development Advisory Council, composed of experts from outside the government, to report to the Energy Policy Office.

Text of President Nixon's message to Congress on energy policy, April 18, 1973:

To the Congress of the United States:

At home and abroad, America is in a time of transition. Old problems are yielding to new initiatives, but in their place new problems are arising which once again challenge our ingenuity and require vigorous action. Nowhere is this more clearly true than in the field of energy.

As America has become more prosperous and more heavily industrialized, our demands for energy have soared. Today, with 6 percent of the world's population, we consume almost a third of all the energy used in the world. Our energy demands have grown so rapidly that they now outstrip our available supplies, and at our present rate of growth, our energy needs a dozen years from now will be nearly double what they were in 1970.

In the years immediately ahead, we must face up to the possibility of occasional energy shortages and some increase in energy prices.

Clearly, we are facing a vitally important energy challenge. If present trends continue unchecked, we could face a genuine energy crisis. But that crisis can and should be averted, for we have the capacity and the resources to meet our energy needs if only we take the proper steps—and take them now.

More than half the world's total reserves of coal are located within the United States. This resource alone would be enough to provide for our energy needs for well over a century. We have potential resources of billions of barrels of recoverable oil, similar quantities of shale oil and more than 2,000 trillion cubic feet of natural gas. Properly managed, and with more attention on the part of consumers to the conservation of energy, these supplies can last for as long as our economy depends on conventional fuels.

In addition to natural fuels, we can draw upon hydroelectric plants and increasing numbers of nuclear powered facilities. Moreover, long before our present energy sources are exhausted, America's vast capabilities in research and development can provide us with new, clean and virtually unlimited sources of power.

Thus we should not be misled into pessimistic predictions of an energy disaster. But neither should we be lulled into a false sense of security. We must examine our circumstances realistically, carefully weigh the alternatives—and then move forward decisively.

Weighing the Alternatives

Over 90 percent of the energy we consume today in the United States comes from three sources: natural gas, coal and petroleum. Each source presents us with a different set of problems.

Natural gas is our cleanest fuel and is most preferred in order to protect our environment, but ill-considered regulations of natural gas prices by the Federal Government have produced a serious and increasing scarcity of this fuel.

We have vast quantities of coal, but the extraction and use of coal have presented such persistent environmental problems that, today, less than 20 percent of our energy needs are met by coal and the health of the entire coal industry is seriously threatened.

Our third conventional resource is oil, but domestic production of available oil is no longer able to keep pace with demands.

In determining how we should expand and develop these resources, along with others such as nuclear power, we must take into account not only our economic goals, but also our environmental goals and our national security goals. Each of these areas is profoundly affected by our decisions concerning energy.

If we are to maintain the vigor of our economy, the health of our environment, and the security of our energy resources, it is essential that we strike the right balance among these priorities.

The choices are difficult, but we cannot refuse to act because of this. We cannot stand still simply because it is difficult to go forward. That is the one choice Americans must never take.

The energy challenge is one of the great opportunities of our time. We have already begun to meet that challenge, and realize its opportunities.

National Energy Policy

In 1971, I sent to the Congress the first message on energy policies ever submitted by an American President. In that message I proposed a number of specific steps to meet our projected needs by increasing our supply of clean energy in America.

Those steps included expanded research and development to obtain more clean energy, increased availability of energy sources located on Federal lands, increased efforts in the development of nuclear power, and a new Federal organization to plan and manage our energy programs.

In the twenty-two months since I submitted that message, America's energy research and development efforts have been expanded by 50 percent.

In order to increase domestic production of conventional fuels, sales of oil and gas leases on the Outer Continental Shelf have been increased. Federal and State standards to protect the marine environment in which these leases are located are being tightened. We have developed a more rigorous surveillance capability and an improved ability to prevent and clean up oil spills.

We are planning to proceed with the development of oil shale and geothermal energy sources on Federal lands, so long as an evaluation now underway shows that our environment can be adequately protected.

We have also taken new steps to expand our uranium enrichment capacity for the production of fuels for nuclear power plants, to standardize nuclear power plant designs, and to ensure the continuation of an already enviable safety record.

We have issued new standards and guidelines, and have taken other actions to increase and encourage better conservation of energy.

In short, we have made a strong beginning in our effort to ensure that America will always have the power needed to fuel its prosperity. But what we have accomplished is only a beginning.

Now we must build on our increased knowledge, and on the accomplishments of the past twenty-two months, to develop a more comprehensive, integrated national energy policy. To carry out this policy we must:

—increase domestic production of all forms of energy;

—act to conserve energy more effectively;

—strive to meet our energy needs at the lowest cost consistent with the protection of both our national security and our natural environment;

—reduce excessive regulatory and administrative impediments which have delayed or prevented construction of energy-producing facilities;

—act in concert with other nations to conduct research in the energy field and to find ways to prevent serious shortages; and

—apply our vast scientific and technological capacities—both public and private—so we can utilize our current energy resources more wisely and develop new sources and new forms of energy.

The actions I am announcing today and the proposals I am submitting to the Congress are designed to achieve these objectives. They reflect the fact that we are in a period of transition, in which we must work to avoid or at least minimize short-term supply shortages, while we act to expand and develop our domestic supplies in order to meet long-term energy needs.

We should not suppose this transition period will be easy. The task ahead will require the concerted and cooperative efforts of consumers, industry, and government.

Developing Our Domestic Energy Resources

The effort to increase domestic energy production in a manner consistent with our economic environmental and security interests should focus on the following areas:

Natural Gas

Natural gas is America's premium fuel. It is clean-burning and thus has the least detrimental effect on our environment.

Since 1966, our consumption of natural gas has increased by over one-third, so that today natural gas comprises 32 percent of the total energy we consume from all sources. During this same period, our proven and available reserves of natural gas have decreased by a fifth. Unless we act responsibly, we will soon encounter increasing shortages of this vital fuel.

Yet the problem of shortages results less from inadequate resources than from ill-conceived regulation. Natural gas is the fuel most heavily regulated by the Federal Government—through the Federal Power Commission. Not only are the operations of interstate natural gas pipelines regulated, as was originally and properly intended by the Congress, but the price of the natural gas supplied to these pipelines by thousands of independent producers has also been regulated.

For more than a decade the prices of natural gas supplied to pipelines under this extended regulation have been kept artificially low. As a result, demand has been artificially stimulated, but the exploration and development required to provide new supplies to satisfy this increasing demand have been allowed to wither. This form of government regulation has contributed heavily to the shortages we have experienced, and to the greater scarcity we now anticipate.

As a result of its low regulated price, more than 50 percent of our natural gas is consumed by industrial users and utilities, many of which might otherwise be using coal or oil. While homeowners are being forced to turn away from natural gas and toward more expensive fuels, unnecessarily large quantities of natural gas are being used by industry.

Furthermore, because prices within producing States are often higher than the interstate prices established by the Federal Power Commission, most newly discovered and newly produced natural gas does not enter interstate pipelines. Potential consumers in non-producing States thus suffer the worst shortages. While the Federal Power Commission has tried to alleviate these problems, the regulatory framework and attendant judicial constraints inhibit the ability of the Commission to respond adequately.

It is clear that the price paid to producers for natural gas in interstate trade must increase if there is to be the needed incentive for increasing supply and reducing inefficient usage. Some have suggested additional regulation to provide new incentives, but we have already seen the pitfalls in this approach. We must regulate less, not more. At the same time, we cannot remove all natural gas regulations without greatly inflating the price of gas currently in production and generating windfall profits.

To resolve this issue, I am proposing that gas from new wells, gas newly-dedicated to interstate markets, and the continuing production of natural gas from expired contracts should no longer be subject to price regulation at the wellhead. Enactment of this legislation should stimulate new exploration and development. At the same time, because increased prices on new unregulated gas would be averaged in with the prices for gas that is still regulated, the consumer should be protected against precipitous cost increases.

To add further consumer protection against unjustified price increases, I propose that the Secretary of the Interior be given authority to impose a ceiling on the price of new natural gas when circumstances warrant. Before exercising this power, the Secretary would consider the cost of alternative domestic fuels, taking into account the superiority of natural gas from an environmental standpoint. He would also consider the importance of encouraging production and more efficient use of natural gas.

Outer Continental Shelf

Approximately half of the oil and gas resources in this country are located on public lands, primarily on the Outer Continental Shelf (OCS). The speed at which we can increase our domestic energy production will depend in large measure on how rapidly these resources can be developed.

Since 1954, the Department of the Interior has leased to private developers almost 8 million acres on the Outer Continental Shelf. But this is only a small percentage of these potentially productive areas. At a time when we are being forced to obtain almost 30 percent of our oil from foreign sources, this level of development is not adequate.

I am therefore directing the Secretary of the Interior to take steps which would triple the annual acreage leased on the Outer Continental Shelf by 1979, beginning with expanded sales in 1974 in the Gulf of Mexico and including areas beyond 200 meters in depth under conditions consistent with my oceans policy statement of May, 1970. By 1985, this accelerated leasing rate could increase annual energy production by an estimated 1.5 billion barrels of oil (approximately 16 percent of our projected oil requirements in that year), and 5 trillion cubic feet of natural gas (approximately 20 percent of expected demand for natural gas that year).

In the past, a central concern in bringing these particular resources into production has been the threat of environmental damage. Today, new techniques, new regulations and standards, and new surveillance capabilities enable us to reduce and control environmental dangers substantially. We should now take advantage of this progress. The resources under the Shelf, and on all our public lands, belong to all Americans, and the critical needs of all Americans for new energy supplies require that we develop them.

If at any time it is determined that exploration and development of a specific shelf area can only proceed with inadequate protection of the environment, we will not commence or continue operations. This policy was reflected in the suspension of 35 leases in the Santa Barbara Channel in 1971. We are continuing the Santa Barbara suspensions, and I again request that the Congress pass legislation that would provide for appropriate settlement for those who are forced to relinquish their leases in the area.

At the same time, I am directing the Secretary of the Interior to proceed with leasing the Outer Continental Shelf beyond the Channel Islands of California if the reviews now underway show that the environmental risks are acceptable.

I am also asking the Chairman of the Council on Environmental Quality to work with the Environmental Protection Agency, in consultation with the National Academy of Sciences and appropriate Federal agencies, to study the environmental impact of oil and gas production on the Atlantic Outer Continental Shelf and in the Gulf of Alaska. No drilling will be undertaken in these areas until its environmental impact is determined. Governors, legislators and citizens of these areas will be consulted in this process.

Finally, I am asking the Secretary of the Interior to develop a long-term leasing program for *all* energy resources on public lands, based on a thorough analysis of the Nation's energy, environmental, and economic objectives.

Alaskan Pipeline

Another important source of domestic oil exists on the North Slope of Alaska. Although private industry stands ready to develop these reserves and the Federal Government has spent large sums on environmental analyses, this project is still being delayed. This delay is not related to any adverse judicial findings concerning environmental impact, but rather to an outmoded legal restriction regarding the width of the right of way for the proposed pipeline.

At a time when we are importing growing quantities of oil at great detriment to our balance of payments, and at a time when we are also experiencing significant oil shortages, we clearly need the two million barrels a day which the North Slope could provide—a supply equal to fully one-third of our present import levels.

In recent weeks I have proposed legislation to the Congress which would remove the present restriction on the pipeline. I appeal to the Congress to act swiftly on this matter so that we can begin construction of the pipeline with all possible speed.

I oppose any further delay in order to restudy the advisability of building the pipeline through Canada. Our interest in rapidly increasing our supply of oil is best served by an Alaskan pipeline. It could be completed much more quickly than a Canadian pipeline; its entire capacity would be used to carry domestically owned oil to American markets where it is needed; and construction of an Alaskan pipeline would create a significant number of American jobs both in Alaska and in the maritime industry.

Shale Oil

Recoverable deposits of shale oil in the continental United States are estimated at some 600 billion barrels, 80 billion of which are considered easily accessible.

At the time of my Energy Message of 1971, I requested the Secretary of the Interior to develop an oil shale leasing program on a pilot basis and to provide me with a thorough evaluation of the environmental impact of such a program. The Secretary has prepared this pilot project and expects to have a final environmental impact statement soon. If the environmental risks are acceptable, we will proceed with the program.

To date there has been no commercial production of shale oil in the United States. Our pilot program will provide us with valuable experience in using various operational techniques and acting under various environmental conditions. Under the proposed program, the costs both of development and environmental protection would be borne by the private lessee.

Geothermal Leases

At the time of my earlier Energy Message, I also directed the Department of the Interior to prepare a leasing program for the development of geothermal energy on Federal lands. The regulations and final environmental analysis for such a program should be completed by late spring of this year.

If the analysis indicates that we can proceed in an environmentally acceptable manner, I expect leasing of geothermal fields on Federal lands to begin soon thereafter.

The use of geothermal energy could be of significant importance to many of our western areas, and by supplying a part of the western energy demand, could release other energy resources that would otherwise have to be used. Today, for instance, power from the Geysers geothermal field in California furnishes about one-third of the electric power of the city of San Francisco.

New technologies in locating and producing geothermal energy are now under development. During the coming fiscal year, the National Science Foundation and the Geological Survey will intensify their research and development efforts in this field.

Coal

Coal is our most abundant and least costly domestic source of energy. Nevertheless, at a time when energy shortages loom on the horizon, coal provides less than 20 percent of our energy demands, and there is serious danger that its use will be reduced even further. If this reduction occurs, we would have to increase our oil imports rapidly, with all the trade and security problems this would entail.

Production of coal has been limited not only by competition from natural gas—a competition which has been artifically induced by Federal price regulation—but also by emerging environmental concerns and mine health and safety requirements. In order to meet environmental standards, utilities have shifted to natural gas and imported low-sulphur fuel oil. The problem is compounded by the fact that some low-sulphur coal resources are not being developed because of uncertainty about Federal and State mining regulations.

I urge that highest national priority be given to expanded development and utilization of our coal resources. Present and potential users who are able to choose among energy sources should consider the national interest as they make their choice. Each decision against coal increases petroleum or gas consumption, compromising our national self-sufficiency and raising the cost of meeting our energy needs.

In my State of the Union Message on Natural Resources and the Environment earlier this year, I called for strong legislation to protect the environment from abuse caused by mining. I now repeat that call. Until the coal industry knows the mining rules under which it will have to operate, our vast reserves of low-sulphur coal will not be developed as rapidly as they should be and the under-utilization of such coal will persist.

The Clean Air Act of 1970, as amended, requires that primary air quality standards—those related to health—must be met by 1975, while more stringent secondary standards—those related to the "general welfare"—must be met within a reasonable period. The States are moving very effectively to meet primary standards established by the Clean Air Act, and I am encouraged by their efforts.

At the same time, our concern for the "general welfare" or national interest should take into account considerations of national security and economic prosperity, as well as our environment.

If we insisted upon meeting both primary and secondary clean air standards by 1975, we could prevent the use of up to 155 million tons of coal per year. This would force an increase in demand for oil of 1.6 million barrels per day. This oil would have to be imported, with an adverse effect on our balance of payments of some $1.5 billion or more a year. Such a development would also threaten the loss of an estimated 26,000 coal mining jobs.

If, on the other hand, we carry out the provisions of the Clean Air Act in a judicious manner, carefully meeting the primary, health-related standards, but not moving in a precipitous way toward meeting the secondary standards, then we should be able to use virtually all of that coal which would otherwise go unused.

The Environmental Protection Agency has indicated that the reasonable time allowed by the Clean Air Act for meeting secondary standards could extend beyond 1975. Last year, the Administrator of the Environmental Protection Agency sent to all State governors a letter explaining that during the current period of shortages in low-sulphur fuel, the States should not require the burning of such fuels except where necessary to meet the primary standards for the protection of health. This action by the States should permit the desirable substitution of coal for low-sulphur fuel in many instances. I strongly support this policy.

Many State regulatory commissions permit their State utilities to pass on increased fuel costs to the consumer in the form of higher rates, but there are sometimes lags in allowing the costs of environmental control equipment to be passed on in a similar way. Such lags discourage the use of environmental control technology and encourage the use of low-sulphur fuels, most of which are imported.

To increase the incentive for using new environmental technology, I urge all State utility commissions to ensure that utilities receive a rapid and fair return on pollution control equipment, including stack gas cleaning devices and coal gasification processes.

As an additional measure to increase the production and use of coal, I am directing that a new reporting system on national coal production be instituted within the Department of the Interior, and I am asking the Federal Power Commission for regular reports on the use of coal by utilities.

I am also stepping up our spending for research and development in coal, with special emphasis on technology for sulphur removal and the development of low-cost, clean-burning forms of coal.

Nuclear Energy

Although our greatest dependence for energy until now has been on fossil fuels such as coal and oil, we must not and we need not continue this heavy reliance in the future. The major alternative to fossil fuel energy for the remainder of this century is nuclear energy.

Our well-established nuclear technology already represents an indispensable source of energy for meeting present needs. At present there are 30 nuclear power plants in operation in the United States; of the new electrical generator capacity contracted for during 1972, 70 percent will be nuclear powered. By 1980, the amount of electricity generated by nuclear reactors will be equivalent to 1.25 billion barrels of oil, or 8 trillion cubic feet of gas. It is estimated that nuclear power will provide more than one-quarter of this country's electrical production by 1985, and over half by the year 2000.

Most nuclear power plants now in operation utilize light water reactors. In the near future, some will use high temperature gas-cooled reactors. These techniques will be supplemented during the next decade by the fast breeder reactor, which will bring about a 30-fold increase in the efficiency with which we utilize our domestic uranium resources. At present, development of the liquid metal fast breeder reactor is our highest priority target for nuclear research and development.

Nuclear power generation has an extraordinary safety record. There has never been a nuclear-related fatality in our civilian atomic energy program. We intend to maintain that record by increasing research and development in reactor safety.

The process of determining the safety and environmental acceptability of nuclear power plants is more vigorous and more open to public participation than for any comparable industrial enterprise. Every effort must be made by the Government and industry to protect public health and safety and to provide satisfactory answers to those with honest concerns about this source of power.

At the same time, we must seek to avoid unreasonable delays in developing nuclear power. They serve only to impose unnecessary costs and aggravate our energy shortages. It is discouraging to know that nuclear facilities capable of generating 27,000 megawatts of electric power which were expected to be operational by 1972 were not completed. To replace that generating capacity we would have to use the equivalent of one-third of the natural gas the country used for generating electricity in 1972. This situation must not continue.

In my first Energy Special Message in 1971, I proposed that utilities prepare and publish long-range plans for the siting of nuclear power plants and transmission lines. This legislation would provide a Federal-State framework for licensing individual plants on the basis of a full and balanced consideration of both environmental and energy needs. The Congress has not acted on that proposal. I am resubmitting that legislation this year with a number of new provisions to simplify licensing, including one to require that the Government act on all completed license applications within 18 months after they are received.

I would also emphasize that the private sector's role in future nuclear development must continue to grow. The Atomic Energy Commission is presently taking steps to provide greater amounts of enriched uranium fuel for the Nation's nuclear power plants. However, this expansion will not fully meet our needs in the 1980's; the Government now looks to private industry to provide the additional capacity that will be required.

Our nuclear technology is a national asset of inestimable value. It is essential that we press forward with its development.

The increasing occurrence of unnecessary delays in the development of energy facilities must be ended if we are to meet our energy needs. To be sure, reasonable safeguards must be vigorously maintained for protection of the public and of our environment. Full public participation and questioning must also be allowed as we decide where new energy facilities are to be built. We need to streamline our governmental procedures for licensing and inspections, reduce overlapping jurisdictions and eliminate confusion generated by the government.

To achieve these ends I am taking several steps. During the coming year we will examine various possibilities to assure that all public and private interests are impartially and expeditiously weighed in all government proceedings for permits, licensing and inspections.

I am again proposing siting legislation to the Congress for electric facilities and for the first time, for deepwater ports. All of my new siting legislation includes provision for simplified licensing at both Federal and State levels. It is vital that the Congress take prompt and favorable action on these proposals.

Encouraging Domestic Exploration

Our tax system now provides needed incentives for mineral exploration in the form of percentage depletion allowances and deductions for certain drilling expenses. These provisions do not, however, distinguish between exploration for new reserves and development of existing reserves.

In order to encourage increased exploration, I ask the Congress to extend the investment credit provisions of our present tax law so that a credit will be provided for all exploratory drilling for new oil and gas fields. Under this proposal, a somewhat higher credit would apply for successful exploratory wells than for unsuccessful ones, in order to put an additional premium on results.

The investment credit has proven itself a powerful stimulus to industrial activity. I expect it to be equally effective in the search for new reserves.

Importing To Meet Our Energy Needs

Oil Imports

In order to avert a short-term fuel shortage and to keep fuel costs as low as possible, it will be necessary for us to increase fuel imports. At the same time, in order to reduce our long-term reliance on imports, we must encourage the exploration and development of our domestic oil and the construction of refineries to process it.

The present quota system for oil imports—the Mandatory Oil Import Program—was established at a time when we could produce more oil at home than we were using. By imposing quantitative restrictions on imports, the quota system restricted imports of foreign oil. It also encouraged the development of our domestic petroleum industry in the interest of national security.

Today, however, we are not producing as much oil as we are using, and we must import ever larger amounts to meet our needs.

As a result, the current Mandatory Oil Import Program is of virtually no benefit any longer. Instead, it has the very real potential of aggravating our supply problems, and it denies us the flexibility we need to deal quickly and efficiently with our import requirements. General dissatisfaction with the program and the apparent need for change has led to uncertainty. Under these conditions, there can be little long-range investment planning for new drilling and refinery construction.

Effective today, I am removing by proclamation all existing tariffs on imported crude oil and products. Holders of import licenses will be able to import petroleum duty free. This action will help hold down the cost of energy to the American consumer.

Effective today, I am also suspending direct control over the quantity of crude oil and refined products which can be imported. In place of these controls, I am substituting a license-fee quota system.

Under the new system, present holders of import licenses may import petroleum exempt from fees up to the level of their 1973 quota allocations. For imports in excess of the 1973 level, a fee must be paid by the importer.

This system should achieve several objectives.

First, it should help to meet our immediate energy needs by encouraging importation of foreign oil at the lowest cost to consumers, while also providing incentives for exploration and development of our domestic resources to meet our long-term needs. There will be little paid in fees this year, although all exemptions from fees will be phased out over several years. By gradually increasing fees over the next two and one-half years to a maximum level of one-half cent per gallon for crude oil and one and one-half cents per gallon for all refined products, we should continue to meet our energy needs while encouraging industry to increase its domestic production.

Second, this system should encourage refinery construction in the United States, because the fees are higher for refined products than for crude oil. As an added incentive, crude oil in amounts up to three-fourths of new refining capacity may be imported without being subject to any fees. This special allowance will be available to an oil company during the first five years after it builds or expands its refining capacity.

Third, this system should provide the flexibility we must have to meet short and long-term needs efficiently. We will review the fee level periodically to ensure that we are imposing the lowest fees consistent with our intention to increase domestic production while keeping costs to the consumer at the lowest possible level. We will also make full use of the Oil Import Appeals Board to ensure that the needs of all elements of the petroleum industry are met, particularly those of independent operators who help to maintain market competition.

Fourth, the new system should contribute to our national security. Increased domestic production will leave us less dependent on foreign supplies. At the same time, we will adjust the fees in a manner designed to encourage, to the extent possible, the security of our foreign supplies. Finally, I am directing the Oil Policy Committee to examine incentives aimed at increasing our domestic storage capacity or shut-in production. In this way we will provide buffer stocks to insulate ourselves against a temporary loss of foreign supplies.

Deepwater Ports

It is clear that in the foreseeable future, we will have to import oil in large quantities. We should do this as cheaply as we can with minimal damage to the environment. Unfortunately, our present capabilities are inadequate for these purposes.

The answer to this problem lies in deepwater ports which can accommodate those larger ships, providing important economic advantages while reducing the risks of collision and grounding. Recent studies by the Council on Environmental Quality demonstrate that we can expect considerably less pollution if we use fewer but larger tankers and deep-water facilities, as opposed to the many small tankers and conventional facilities which we would otherwise need.

If we do not enlarge our deepwater port capacity it is clear that both American and foreign companies will expand oil transshipment terminals in the Bahamas and the Canadian Maritime Provinces. From these terminals, oil will be brought to our conventional ports by growing numbers of small and medium size transshipment vessels, thereby increasing the risks of pollution from shipping operations and accidents. At the same time, the United States will lose the jobs and capital that those foreign facilities provide.

Given these considerations, I believe we must move forward with an ambitious program to create new deepwater ports for receiving petroleum imports.

The development of ports has usually been a responsibility of State and local governments and the private sector. However, States cannot issue licenses beyond the three-mile limit. I am therefore proposing legislation to permit the Department of the Interior to issue such licenses. Licensing would be contingent upon full and proper evaluation of environmental impact, and would provide for strict navigation and safety, as well as proper land use requirements. The proposed legislation specifically provides for Federal cooperation with State and local authorities.

Conserving Energy

The abundance of America's natural resources has been one of our greatest advantages in the past. But if this abundance encourages us to take our resources for granted, then it may well be a detriment to our future.

Common sense clearly dictates that as we expand the types and sources of energy available to us for the future, we must direct equal attention to conserving the energy available to us today, and we must explore means to limit future growth in energy demand.

We as a nation must develop a national energy conservation ethic. Industry can help by designing products which conserve energy and by using energy more efficiently. All workers and consumers can help by continually saving energy in their day-to-day activities: by turning out lights, tuning up automobiles, reducing the use of air conditioning and heating, and purchasing products which use energy efficiently.

Government at all levels also has an important role to play, both by conserving energy directly, and by providing leadership in energy conservation efforts.

I am directing today that an Office of Energy Conservation be established in the Department of the Interior to coordinate the energy conservation programs which are presently scattered throughout the Federal establishment. This office will conduct research and work with consumer and environmental groups in their efforts to educate consumers on ways to get the greatest return on their energy dollar.

To provide consumers with further information, I am directing the Department of Commerce, working with the Council on Environmental Quality and the Environmental Protection Agency, to develop a voluntary system of energy efficiency labels for major home appliances. These labels should provide data on energy use as well as a rating comparing the product's efficiency to other similar products. In addition, the Environmental Protection Agency will soon release the results of its tests of fuel efficiency in automobiles.

There are other ways, too, in which government can exercise leadership in this field. I urge again, for example, that we allow local officials to use money from the Highway Trust Fund for mass transit purposes. Greater reliance on mass transit can do a great deal to help us conserve gasoline.

The Federal Government can also lead by example. The General Services Administration, for instance, is constructing a new Federal office building using advanced energy conservation techniques, with a goal of reducing energy use by 20 percent over typical buildings of the same size. At the same time, the National Bureau of Standards is evaluating energy use in a full-size house within its laboratories. When this evaluation is complete, analytical techniques will be available to help predict energy use for new dwellings. This information, together with the experience gained in the constructuion and operation of the demonstration Federal building, will assist architects and contractors to design and construct energy-efficient buildings.

Significant steps to upgrade insulation standards on single and multi-family dwellings were taken at my direction in 1971 and 1972, helping to reduce heat loss and otherwise conserve energy in the residential sector. As soon as the results of these important demonstration projects are available, I will direct the Federal Housing Administration to update its insulation standards in light of what we have learned and to consider their possible extension to mobile homes.

Finally, we should recognize that the single most effective means of encouraging energy conservation is to ensure that energy prices reflect their true costs. By eliminating regulations such as the current ceiling on natural gas prices and by ensuring that the costs of adequate environmental controls are equitably allocated, we can move toward more efficient distribution of our resources.

Energy conservation is a national necessity, but I believe that it can be undertaken most effectively on a voluntary basis. If the challenge is ignored, the result will be a danger of increased shortages, increased prices, damage to the environment and the increased possibility that conservation will have to be undertaken by compulsory means in the future. There should be no need for a nation which has always been rich in energy to have to turn to energy rationing. This is a part of the energy challenge which every American can help to meet, and I call upon every American to do his or her part.

Research And Development

If we are to be certain that the forward thrust of our economy will not be hampered by insufficient energy supplies or by energy supplies that are prohibitively expensive, then we must not continue to be dependent on conventional forms of energy. We must instead make every useful effort through research and development to provide both alternative sources of energy and new technologies for producing and utilizing this energy.

For the short-term future, our research and development strategy will provide technologies to extract and utilize our existing fossil fuels in a manner most compatible with a healthy environment.

In the long run, from 1985 to the beginning of the next century, we will have more sophisticated development of our fossil fuel resources and the full development of the Liquid Metal Fast Breeder Reactor. Our efforts for the distant future center on the development of technologies—such as nuclear fusion and solar power—that can provide us with a virtually limitless supply of clean energy.

In my 1971 Energy Special Message to the Congress I outlined a broadly based research and development program. I proposed the

481

expansion of cooperative Government-industry efforts to develop the Liquid Metal Fast Breeder Reactor, coal gasification, and stack gas cleaning systems at the demonstration level. These programs are all progressing well.

My budget for fiscal year 1974 provides for an increase in energy research and development funding of 20 percent over the level of 1973.

My 1974 budget provides for creation of a new central energy fund in the Interior Department to provide additional money for non-nuclear research and development, with the greatest part designated for coal research. This central fund is designed to give us the flexibility we need for rapid exploitation of new, especially promising energy technologies with near-term payoffs.

One of the most promising programs that will be receiving increased funding in fiscal year 1974 is the solvent refined coal process which will produce low-ash, low-sulphur fuels from coal. Altogether, coal research and development and proposed funding is increased by 27 percent.

In addition to increased funding for the Liquid Metal Fast Breeder Reactor, I am asking for greater research and development on reactor safety and radioactive waste disposal, and the production of nuclear fuel.

The waters of the world contain potential fuel—in the form of a special isotope of hydrogen—sufficient to power fusion reactors for thousands of years. Scientists at the Atomic Energy Commission now predict with increasing confidence that we can demonstrate laboratory feasibility of controlled thermonuclear fusion by magnetic confinement in the near future. We have also advanced to the point where some scientists believe the feasibility of laser fusion could be demonstrated within the next several years. I have proposed in my 1974 budget a 35 percent increase in funding for our total fusion research and development effort to accelerate experimental programs and to initiate preliminary reactor design studies.

While we look to breeder reactors to meet our mid-term energy needs, today's commercial power reactors will continue to provide most of our nuclear generating capacity for the balance of this century. Although nuclear reactors have had a remarkable safety record, my 1974 budget provides additional funds to assure that our rapidly growing reliance on nuclear power will not compromise public health and safety. This includes work on systems for safe storage of the radioactive waste which nuclear reactors produce. The Atomic Energy Commission is working on additional improvements in surface storage and will continue to explore the possibility of underground burial for long-term containment of these wastes.

Solar energy holds great promise as a potentially limitless source of clean energy. My new budget triples our solar energy research and development effort to a level of $12 million. A major portion of these funds would be devoted to accelerating the development of commercial systems for heating and cooling buildings.

Research and development funds relating to environmental control technologies would be increased 24 percent in my 1974 budget. This research includes a variety of projects related to stack gas cleaning and includes the construction of a demonstration sulphur dioxide removal plant. In addition, the Atomic Energy Commission and the Environmental Protection Agency will continue to conduct research on the thermal effects of power plants.

While the Federal Government is significantly increasing its commitment to energy reserach and development, a large share of such research is and should be conducted by the private sector.

I am especially pleased that the electric utilities have recognized the importance of research in meeting the rapidly escalating demand for electrical energy. The recent establishment of the Electric Power Research Institute, which will have a budget in 1974 in excess of $100 million, can help develop technology to meet both load demands and environmental regulations currently challenging the industry.

Historically the electric power industry has allocated a smaller portion of its revenues to research than have most other technology-dependent industries. This pattern has been partly attributable to the reluctance of some State utility commissions to include increased research and development expenditures in utility rate bases. Recently the Federal Power Commission instituted a national rule to allow the recovery of research and development expenditures in rates. State regulatory agencies have followed the FPC's lead and are liberalizing their treatment of research and development expenditures consistent with our changing national energy demands.

I am hopeful that this trend will continue and I urge all State utility commissions to review their regulations regarding research and development expenditures to ensure that the electric utility industry can fully cooperate in a national energy research and development effort.

It is foolish and self-defeating to allocate funds more rapidly than they can be effectively spent. At the same time, we must carefully monitor our progress and our needs to ensure that our funding is adequate. When additional funds are found to be essential, I shall do everything I can to see that they are provided.

International Cooperation

The energy challenge confronts every nation. Where there is such a community of interest, there is both a cause and a basis for cooperative action.

Today, the United States is involved in a number of cooperative, international efforts. We have joined with the other 22 member-nations of the Organization for Economic Cooperation and Development to produce a comprehensive report on long-term problems and to develop an agreement for sharing oil in times of acute shortages. The European

Economic Community has already discussed the need for cooperative efforts and is preparing recommendations for a Community energy policy. We have expressed a desire to work together with them in this effort.

We have also agreed with the Soviet Union to pursue joint research in magnetohydrodynamics (MHD), a highly efficient process for generating electricity, and to exchange information on fusion, fission, the generation of electricity, transmission and pollution control technology. These efforts should be a model for joint research effort with other countries. Additionally, American companies are looking into the possibility of joint projects with the Soviet Union to develop natural resources for the benefit of both nations.

I have also instructed the Department of State, in coordination with the Atomic Energy Commission, other appropriate Government agencies, and the Congress to move rapidly in developing a program of international cooperation in research and development on new forms of energy and in developing international mechanisms for dealing with energy questions in times of critical shortages.

I believe the energy challenge provides an important opportunity for nations to pursue vital objectives through peaceful cooperation. No chance should be lost to strengthen the structure of peace we are seeking to provide in the world, and few issues provide us with as good an opportunity to demonstrate that there is more to be gained in pursuing our national interests through mutual cooperation than through destructive competition or dangerous confrontation.

Federal Energy Organization

If we are to meet the energy challenge, the current fragmented organization of energy-related activities in the executive branch of the Government must be overhauled.

In 1971, I proposed legislation to consolidate Federal energy-related activities within a new Department of Natural Resources. The 92nd Congress did not act on this proposal. In the interim I have created a new post of Counsellor to the President on Natural Resources to assist in the policy coordination in the natural resources field.

Today I am taking executive action specifically to improve the Federal organization of energy activities.

I have directed the Secretary of the Interior to strengthen his Department's organization of energy activities in several ways.

—The reponsibilities of the new Assistant Secretary for Energy and Minerals will be expanded to incorporate all departmental energy activities;

—The Department is to develop a capacity for gathering and analysis of energy data;

—An Office of Energy Conservation is being created to seek means for reducing demands for energy;

—The Department of the Interior has also strengthened its capabilities for overseeing and coordinating a broader range of energy research and development.

By Executive order, I have placed authority in the Department of the Treasury for directing the Oil Policy Committee. That Committee coordinates the oil import program and makes recommendations to me for changes in that program. The Deputy Secretary of the Treasury has been designated Chairman of that Committee.

Through a second Executive order, effective today, I am strengthening the capabilities of the Executive Office of the President to deal with top level energy policy matters by establishing a special energy committee composed of three of my principal advisors. The order also reaffirms the appointment of a Special Consultant, who heads an energy staff in the Office of the President.

Additionally, a new division of Energy and Science is being established within the Office of Management and Budget.

While these executive actions will help, more fundamental reorganization is needed. To meet this need, I shall propose legislation to establish a Department of Energy and Natural Resources (DENR) building on the legislation I submitted in 1971, with heightened emphasis on energy programs.

This new Department would provide leadership across the entire range of national energy. It would, in short, be responsible for administering the national energy policy detailed in this message.

Conclusion

Nations succeed only as they are able to respond to challenge, and to change when circumstances and opportunities require change.

When the first settlers came to America, they found a land of untold natural wealth, and this became the cornerstone of the most prosperous nation in the world. As we have grown in population, in prosperity, in industrial capacity, in all those indices that reflect the constant upward thrust in the American standard of living, the demands on our natural resources have also grown.

Today, the energy resources which have fueled so much of our national growth are not sufficiently developed to meet the constantly increasing demands which have been placed upon them. The time has come to change the way we meet these demands. The challenge facing us represents one of the great opportunities of our time—an opportunity to create an even stronger domestic economy, a cleaner environment, and a better life for all our people.

The proposals I am submitting and the actions I will take can give us the tools to do this important job.

The need for action is urgent. I hope the Congress will act with dispatch on the proposals I am submitting. But in the final

analysis, the   ultimate responsibility does not rest merely with the
Congress or with this Administration. It rests with all of us—with
government, with industry and with the individual citizen.

Whenever we have been confronted with great national challenges
in the past, the American people have done their duty. I am confident we shall do so now.

NEW ATLANTIC CHARTER

April 23, 1973

Action to make clear and firm the mutual foreign policy objectives of the United States and its allies was outlined April 23 by Henry A. Kissinger, national security adviser to President Nixon. Kissinger, speaking at the annual luncheon of the Associated Press in New York, proposed a new Atlantic charter to reinvigorate "shared ideals and common purposes with our friends." He set the President's proposed trip to Europe late in 1973 as the target date for drafting a charter "setting the goals for the future." And he suggested that Japan be included as a "principal partner" with the Western European nations in order that the Atlantic community not become "an exclusive club."

"New realities" produced by the successes of the past, Kissinger explained, made necessary new approaches in the relations of the allies. The conditions he cited included Europe's increased strength as a result of economic unification, the growth of the European role in the East-West strategic military balance, the rise of Japan on the global scene necessitating its inclusion in "Atlantic solutions," the emergence of national identities and rivalries as international tensions relaxed, and the need for international efforts to solve such global problems as the energy shortage.

"To foster unity" among the Atlantic nations, Kissinger continued, the allied states must overcome a number of problems arising in part from the fact that the alliance had "organized itself in different ways in the many different dimensions of its common enterprise." As he pointed out: "We deal with each other regionally and even competitively in economic matters, on an integrated basis in defense, and

as nation-states in diplomacy. When various collective institutions were rudimentary, the potential inconsistency in their modes of operation was not a problem. But after a generation of evolution and with the new weight and strength of our allies, the various parts of the construction are not always in harmony and sometimes obstruct each other."

In Washington the day after Kissinger spoke, high-ranking administration officials said his call for the new Atlantic charter had been meant to signal Western European leaders that Nixon wanted to sign a major document of agreed principles during his visit to Europe later in 1973. These sources said the President envisioned the emergence of a document that would set forth the general lines to govern inter-allied relations in future years.

The proposal was received guardedly by Britain and West Germany, and France withheld comment. A month later, the diplomatic politeness had cooled. Initial French suspicion that the charter would become a device to insure American domination of Europe was matched by hesitation in London and Bonn. One British official told The New York Times May 21: "We think the phrase [Atlantic charter] itself has virtually passed from the vocabulary in European capitals. It looked too much like a gimmick and nobody really seemed to want to embrace it. We are not ready for a document of that kind. The problem now is how Europe will eventually respond to the speech."

A desire to keep the United States out of European affairs was voiced early in May by Italian journalist Oriana Fallaci. She told journalists attending the annual meeting of the American Society of Newspaper Editors to be watchful of U.S. relations with Europe and sensitive to a wave of creeping fascism. "The White House has said and repeated that 1973 will be the 'Year of Europe.' Bad news," said the writer who had gained prominence for her piercing interviews with Kissinger and South Vietnamese President Nguyen Van Thieu. "I would like to be religious, to pray to God to ask him to order the White House people to have 1973 as the year of someone else, possibly nobody else."

> Excerpts from speech by Henry A. Kissinger, national security adviser to President Nixon, at Associated Press luncheon, New York City, April 23, 1973:

This year has been called the Year of Europe, but not because Europe was less important in 1972 or in 1969. The alliance between the United States and Europe has been the cornerstone of all postwar foreign policy. It provided the political framework for American engagements in Europe and marked the definitive end of U.S. isolationism. It insured the sense of security that allowed Europe to recover from the devastation of the war. It reconciled former enemies. It was the stimulus for an unprecedented endeavor in European unity and the principal means to forge the common policies that safeguarded Western security in an era of prolonged tension and confrontation. Our values, our goals and our basic interests are most closely identified with those of Europe.

Nineteen Seventy Three is the Year of Europe because the era that was shaped by decisions of a generation ago is ending. The success of those policies has produced new realities that require new approaches:

● The revival of Western Europe is an established fact as is the historic success of its movement toward economic unification.

● The East-West strategic military balance has shifted from American preponderance to near equality, bringing with it the necessity for a new understanding of the requirements of our common security.

● Other areas of the world have grown in importance. Japan has emerged as a major power center. In many fields "Atlantic" solutions to be viable must include Japan.

● We are in a period of relaxation of tensions. But as the rigid divisions of the past two decades diminish, new assertions of national identity and national rivalry emerge.

● Problems have arisen, unforeseen a generation ago, which require new types of cooperative action. Insuring the supply of energy for industrialized nations is an example.

'Dramatic Transformation'

These factors have produced a dramatic transformation of the psychological climate in the West—a change which is the most profound current challenge to Western statesmanship. In Europe a new generation—to whom war and its dislocations are not personal experiences—takes stability for granted. But it is less committed to the unity that made peace possible and to the effort required to maintain it. In the United States decades of global burdens have fostered and the frustrations of the war in Southeast Asia have accentuated a reluctance to sustain global involvements on the basis of preponderant American responsibility.

Inevitably this period of transition will have its strains. There have been complaints in America that Europe ignores its wider responsibilities in pursuing economic self-interest too one-sidedly and that Europe is not carrying its fair share of the burden of the common defense. There have been complaints in Europe that America is out to divide Europe economically or to desert Europe militarily or to bypass Europe diplomatically. Europeans appeal to the United States to accept their independence and their occasionally severe criticism of us in the name of Atlantic unity, while at the same time they ask for a veto on our independent policies—also in the name of Atlantic unity.

Our challenge is whether a unit forged by a common perception of danger can draw new purpose from shared positive aspirations.

If we permit the Atlantic partnership to atrophy, or to erode through neglect, carelessness or mistrust, we risk what has been achieved, and we shall miss our historic opportunity for even greater achievement.

In the Forties and Fifties the task was economic reconstruction and security against the danger of attack. The West responded with courage and imagination. Today the need is to make the Atlantic relationship as dynamic a force in building a new structure of peace, less geared to crisis and more conscious of opportunities, drawing its inspirations from its goals rather than its fears. The Atlantic nations must join in a fresh act of creation, equal to that undertaken by the postwar generation of leaders of Europe and America.

'New Era of Creativity'

This is why the President is embarking on a personal and direct approach to the leaders of Western Europe. In his discussions with the heads of government of Britain, Italy,. the Federal Republic of Germany and France, the Secretary General of NATO and other European leaders, it is the President's purpose to lay the basis for a new era of creativity in the West.

His approach will be to deal with Atlantic problems comprehensively. The political, military and economic issues in Atlantic relations are linked by reality, not by our choice nor for the tactical purpose of trading one off against the other. The solutions will not be worthy of the opportunity if left to technicians. They must be addressed at the highest level.

In 1972 the President transformed relations with our adversaries to lighten the burdens of fear and suspicion.

In 1973 we can gain the same sense of historical achievement by reinvigorating shared ideals and common purposes with our friends.

The United States proposes to its Atlantic partners that, by the time the President travels to Europe toward the end of the year, we will have worked out a new Atlantic charter setting the goals for the future —a blueprint that:

- Builds on the past without becoming its prisoner.
- Deals with the problems our success has created.
- Creates for the Atlantic nations a new relationship in whose progress Japan can share.

We ask our friends in Europe, Canada and ultimately Japan to join us in this effort. This is what we mean by the Year of Europe.

Atlantic Relationships

The problems in Atlantic relationships are real. They have arisen in part because during the Fifties and Sixties the Atlantic community organized itself in different ways in the many different dimensions of its common enterprise.

- In economic relations, the European Community has increasingly stressed its regional personality; the United States, at the same time, must act as part of and be responsible for a wider international trade and monetary system. We must reconcile these two perspectives.
- In our collective defense, we are still organized on the principle of unity and integration, but in radically different strategic conditions. The full implications of this change have yet to be faced.
- Diplomacy is the subject of frequent consultations, but is essentially being conducted by traditional nation states. The U.S. has global interests and responsibilities. Our European allies have regional interests. These are not necessarily in conflict, but in the new era neither are they automatically identical.

In short, we deal with each other regionally and even competitively in economic matters, on an integrated basis in defense, and as nation-states in diplomacy. When the various collective institutions were rudimentary, the potential inconsistency in their modes of operation was not a problem. But after a generation of evolution and with the new weight and strength of our allies, the various parts of the construction are not always in harmony and sometimes obstruct each other.

If we want to foster unity, we can no longer ignore these problems. The Atlantic nations must find a solution for the management of their diversity, to serve the common objectives which underlie their unity. We can no longer afford to pursue national or regional self-interest without a unifying framework. We cannot hold together if each country or region asserts its autonomy whenever it is to its benefit and invokes unity to curtail the independence of others.

We must strike a new balance between self-interest and the common interest. We must identify interests and positive values beyond security in order to engage once again the commitment of peoples and parliaments. We need a shared view of the world we seek to build.

No element of American postwar policy has been more consistent than our support of European unity. We encouraged it at every turn. We knew that a united Europe would be a more independent partner. But we assumed, perhaps too uncritically, that our common interests would be assured by our long history of cooperation. We expected that political unity would follow economic integration, and that unified Europe working cooperatively with us in an Atlantic partnership would ease many of our international burdens.

It is clear that many of these expectations are not being fulfilled.

We and Europe have benefited from European economic integration. Increased trade within Europe has stimulated the growth of European economies and the expansion of trade in both directions across the Atlantic.

But we cannot ignore the fact that Europe's economic success and its transformation from recipient of our aid to a strong competitor has produced a certain amount of friction. There has been turbulence and a sense of rivalry in international monetary relations.

Fear of Trade Obstacles

In trade, the natural economic weight of a market of 250 million people has pressed other states to seek special arrangements to protect their access to it. The prospect of a closed trading system embracing the European Community and a growing number of other nations in Europe, the Mediterranean and Africa appears to be at the expense of the United States and other nations which are excluded. In agriculture, where the United States has a comparative advantage, we are particularly concerned that Community protective policies may restrict access for our products.

This divergence comes at a time when we are experiencing a chronic and growing deficit in our balance of payments and protectionist pressures of our own. Europeans in turn question our investment policies and doubt our continued commitment to their economic unity.

The gradual accumulation of sometimes petty, sometimes major economic disputes must be ended and be replaced by a determined commitment on both sides of the Atlantic to find cooperative solutions.

The United States will continue to support the unification of Europe. We have no intention of destroying what we worked so hard to help build. For us European unity is what it has always been—not an end in itself but a means to the strengthening of the West. We shall continue to support European unity as a component of a larger Atlantic partnership.

This year we begin comprehensive trade negotiations with Europe as well as with Japan. We shall also continue to press the effort to reform the monetary system so that it promotes stability rather than constant disruptions. A new equilibrium must be achieved in trade and monetary relations.

We see these negotiations as an historic opportunity for positive achievement....

The United States intends to adopt a broad political approach that does justice to our overriding political interest in an open and balanced trading order with both Europe and Japan. This is the spirit of the President's trade bill and of his speech to the International Monetary Fund last year. It will guide our strategy in the trade and monetary talks. We see these negotiations not as a test of strength, but as a test of joint statesmanship.

Atlantic unity has always come most naturally in the field of defense.... Today we remain united on the objective of collective defense, but we face the new challenge of maintaining it under radically changed strategic conditions and with the new opportunity of enhancing our security through negotiated reductions of forces.

The West no longer holds the nuclear predominance that permitted it in the fifties and sixties to rely almost solely on a strategy of massive nuclear retaliation.... The collective ability to resist attack in

Western Europe by means of flexible responses has become central to a rational strategy and crucial to the maintenance of peace....

While the Atlantic alliance is committed to a strategy of flexible response in principle, the requirements of flexibility are complex and expensive. Flexibility by its nature requires sensitivity to new conditions and continual consultation among the allies to respond to changing circumstances....

Much Still to Be Done

A great deal remains to be accomplished to give reality to the goal of flexible reponse:

• There are deficiencies in important areas of our conventional defense.

• There are still unresolved issues in our doctrine, for example, on the crucial question of the role of tactical nuclear weapons.

• There are anomalies in NATO deployments as well as in its logistics structure.

To maintain the military balance that has insured stability in Europe for 25 years, the alliance has no choice but to address these needs and to reach an agreement on our defense requirements....

The President has asked me to state that America remains committed to doing its fair share in Atlantic defense. He is adamantly opposed to unilateral withdrawals of U.S. forces from Europe. But we owe to our peoples a rational defense posture, at the safest minimum size and cost, with burdens equitably shared. This is what the President believes must result from the dialogue with our allies in 1973.

When this is achieved the necessary American forces will be maintained in Europe, not simply as a hostage to trigger our nuclear weapons but as an essential contribution to an agreed and intelligible structure of Western defense. This too will enable us to engage our adversaries intelligently in negotiations for mutual balanced reductions.

In the next few weeks, the United States will present to NATO the product of our own preparations for the negotiations on mutual balanced force reductions, which will begin this year....

Our objective in the dialogue on defense is a new consensus on security addressed to new conditions and to the hopeful new possibilities of effective arms limitations....

There is an increasing uneasiness—all the more insidious for rarely being made explicit—that superpower diplomacy might sacrifice the interests of traditional allies and other friends. Where our allies' interests have been affected by our bilateral negotiations, as in the talks on the limitation of strategic arms, we have been scrupulous in consulting them; where our allies are directly involved, as in the negotiations on Mutual Balanced Force Reductions, our approach is to proceed jointly on the basis of agreed positions. Yet some of our friends in Europe have seemed unwilling to accord America the same trust in our motives as they received from us or to grant us the same tactical flexibility that they employed in pursuit of their own policies. The United States is now often taken to task for flexibility where we used to be criticized for rigidity.

All of this underlines the necessity to articulate a clear set of common objectives together with our allies....

We do not agree on all policies. In many areas of the world our approaches will differ, especially outside of Europe. But we do require an understanding of what should be done jointly and of the limits we should impose on the scope of our autonomy.

Contribution by the United States

We have no intention of buying an illusory tranquillity at the expense of our friends. The United States will never knowingly sacrifice the interests of others. But the perception of common interests is not automatic; it requires constant redefinition. The relaxation of tensions to which we are committed makes allied cohesion indispensable, yet more difficult. We must insure that the momentum of detente is maintained by common objectives rather than by drift, escapism or complacency.

The agenda I have outlined here is not an American prescription but an appeal for a joint effort of creativity. The historic opportunity for this generation is to build a new structure of international relations for the decades ahead. A revitalized Atlantic partnership is indispensable for it.

The United States is prepared to make its contribution:

• We will continue to support European unity. Based on the principles of partnership, we will make concessions to its further growth. We will expect to be met in a spirit of reciprocity.

• We will not disengage from our solemn commitments to our allies. We will maintain our forces and not withdraw from Europe unilaterally. In turn, we expect from each ally a fair share of the common effort for the common defense.

• We shall continue to pursue the relaxation of tensions with our adversaries on the basis of concrete negotiations in the common interest. We welcome the participation of our friends in a constructive East-West dialogue.

• We will never consciously injure the interests of our friends in Europe or in Asia. We expect in return that their policies will take seriously our interests and our responsibilities.

• We are prepared to work cooperatively on new common problems we face. Energy, for example, raises the challenging issues of assurance of supply, impact of oil revenues on international currency stability, the nature of common political and strategic interests and long-range relations of oil-consuming to oil-producing countries. This could be an area of competition; it should be an area of collaboration.

● Just as Europe's autonomy is not an end in itself, so the Atlantic community cannot be an exclusive club. Japan must be a principal partner in our common enterprise.

We hope that our friends in Europe will meet us in this spirit. We have before us the example of the great accomplishments of the past decades—and the opportunity to match and dwarf them. This is the task ahead. This is how in the nineteen-seventies the Atlantic nations can truly serve our peoples and the cause of peace.

Excerpts from speech by Oriana Fallaci, Italian journalist, at annual meeting of the American Society of Newspaper Editors, May 4, 1973:

...I have been told that I could speak on any subject I wanted, that is, the subject that I was mostly interested in. Well, the subject I am mostly interested in, being obsessed by it—it is Fascism in all its forms and colors.... In America, you are living a very black moment indeed. The ministers and friends of Mr. Nixon who got involved in the Watergate scandal represent something that goes far beyond a single scandal. It represents something that hurts the trust of the people towards the institutions of democracy, of democracy itself.

But in Italy we are living a very black moment, too, maybe blacker than yours, because more than yours, possibly, it hurts the trust of the people towards the institutions of democracy. You certainly know that Fascism is raising its poisonous head again and not only with the Black Shirts—that is, in terms of bombs and killings and physical violence—but with apparently minor threats of a more subtle and less evident Fascism, like the telephone espionage which has been recently discovered, our Watergate.

As you certainly know since a couple of months, the magistrate at the bench is inquiring about the fact that the telephones of the most important and democratic politicians and newspapers, and newspaper men, have been bugged for years, So the telephones of a few offices of the President of the Republic—yes, a few offices of my dear President Leoni, whom I know well enough to love very much and to respect so much.

So, you see, the only advantage that our Watergate has in front of your Watergate is that, though indirectly, even our President was bugged, which means that our President is innocent.

But this concerns me very little because, I repeat, this one is the only advantage that we have on you. The rest is a terrible disadvantage.

After our Watergate, no minister in Italy has offered his resignation. Nobody in Italy has been fired by the government. The fishes in jail are small fishes, and it may seem hilarious but we don't know exactly who spied and for whom, though it is obvious those who spied were not democratic people acting for democratic forces.

Personally, I think that they were Fascists. In fact, the small fishes in jail are declared Fascists. I don't tell it to make you feel better. Journalists should never feel better, otherwise, they get lazy and they forget to be angry. Being angry is very good for a journalist.

I tell it because I want to point out that in different, yet similar, ways, according to our historical experiences and realities and temperaments, we are both living a period of tragic crisis, of hidden Fascism, a threat that can lead us anywhere, to the worst included.

Being a pessimist by nature, I am inclined to think that culture itself, our Western culture, is in danger, poisoned by the people that we put in power, or who are in power, anyhow. In such a moment, in such a mud, like the mud that we are sinking in, who else but the press can defend that culture and call the people of good will to save their rights, the rights of democracy? We are the first ones to know, and we must be the first ones who want to know more.

This is evident, and you have well demonstrated it while covering your Watergate story. We are the first ones to denounce and we must be the first ones who want to denounce more. This is evident, too.

But what is not evident always is that we are the first ones to exercise democracy and freedom, that is, truth and courage—the courage to tell the truth, to protest, to condemn, whatever the cost may be, because should things go worse, we could be the first ones to pay, the first ones to die. When Fascism rose up to win in the twenties in Italy, the first places to be burned, along with the political parties' headquarters, were the newspapers that denounced the Black Shirts. The first people to be killed, along with the democratic politicians, were the journalists who denounced the Black Shirts.

I always go back to the Black Shirts, I hate them so profoundly; but we all know that Fascism does not dress itself with black shirts only. Mr. Almeranti, that is the chief of the MSI, or neo-Fascist party in Italy, does not use a black shirt. I always see him with a white one, or a pale blue one, or a yellow one, like your various Messrs. Almeranti's. His voice does not roar when he talks. It is sweet and low and polite, especially when he talks about law and order.

The point is that like your various Messrs. Almeranti's, like every Mr. Almeranti, he speaks about law and order, and he only brings illegality and disorder, Watergates.

Then it is up to us journalists to take off their masks.... You are the most powerful press in the world. I often think that you are even too powerful, because you belong to such a powerful country, because you are so rich, and therefore, you can use all the tools that richness offers. But also because the English language is known more than the Italian language, or the French language, or the German language. When you are giving information, that one is the information. I can contest it a thousand times in my Italian newspaper, or my French or German one; my version will never go beyond my frontiers if it cannot be printed in English. I can tell a fact that you have ignored, and if this fact is not translated into English—and very often it is not—most of the world will go on ignoring it. Then your responsibility is double.

You have been very busy in the last eight years with writing about Vietnam, Indochina. Now that Indochina seems over, though it is far from being over, as we see in Cambodia, you are going to be very busy with another subject abroad. The White House has said and repeated that 1973 will be the "Year of Europe." Bad news.

After having seen how well all the White House people took care of Indochina, I shake at the idea that they prepare themselves to take care of Europe. I love Europe too much; I believe in Europe too much. I was educated in the idea of Europe, a united Europe since the days of the Italian Resistance against the Nazi Fascists. I used to say that, before being a Florentine—which I am, very much—I am a European. So, believe me, I would like to be religious, to pray to God to ask him to order the White House people to have 1973 as the year of someone else, possibly of nobody else.

But 1973 will be the Year of Europe, as I said, and since they said it, not even God could divert their choice. Besides, I am not used to praying God, anyway and instead of God I would like to pray to you, to ask you to keep your eyes open and your souls even more open when covering Europe from now on. Europe, and, for instance, Italy, where funny things have been happening around the Fascist threat in the last years.

Many foreign groups have been helping the Italian Fascists in the last years, Greeks, Spanish, Portuguese, and—I am sorry—Americans. It is no more a secret for anybody; our press has been giving various elements about that, none of those elements have been denied by anybody. Stories about CIA people having precise contacts with the MSI people; stories about financial helps coming to the MSI through the American banks; names of a diplomat here or an ex-diplomat there meeting the founders of the Aliguari Nazionale, that is, the paramilitary Fascist organization which is apt to be declared outlaw. Episodes, even, very embarrassing to tell, like the episodes of a certain Luigi Turchi, one of those MSI Congressmen, a Fascist who came to the United States to campaign for Mr. Nixon among the Italian emigres, and not for a capricious or generous impulse. Mr. Turchi is not capricious, and he is not generous. He is one of those who observe very strictly that old Neapolitan rule, you give something to me, I give something to you.

You would find it out easily, if you would meet him. He comes often to the United States. If I have been well informed, he should arrive today, again, accompanied by his wife. He apparently travels accompanied by his wife. So you cannot even hope that he comes because he is in love with a beautiful American girl, nor can I hope that he comes for business, in the good sense of the word. His only activity is politics, in the bad sense of the word.

He loves your President more than he love mine. After Mr. Nixon was helped by him in the campaign, he gave him a photo of his, with a nice dedicace, etc. Well, I know that during a campaign, it is so frequent to give a photo with a nice dedicace, even to people who should not have it. I am sure that Mr. Nixon despises Mr. Turchi as much as I do, but it would have been better for all if that damn photo had not been published by Mr. Turchi on his Fascist newspaper, La Piazza.

Please do not misunderstand me. I am not transferring to anybody the shameful guilt of being threatened again by the Fascists in my country. I am not blaming anybody but ourselves, our ruling class which is stupid and old and guilty of a thousand things, from the Christian Democrats who are in power to the Communists who are in opposition. Unfortunately, we do not need the help of anybody to have those despicable Turchis and Almerantis and company at work.

But just because of that, we do not either need the help of anybody wishful to transfer some hidden dreams of international Fascism to us....So when some episodes, even sporadic episodes, scattered episodes, casual episodes, demonstrate that the Greek and the Spanish and the Portuguese are not always alone, or have not always been alone in bothering our painfully and recently conquered democracy, you American press should intervene and tell it.

You have been great in covering the Watergate story; you have been great in covering Vietnam. Be great in covering the interests of Dr. Kissinger and Mr. Nixon for Europe, and when in Europe, please give a look to us Italians. Please dig into what I told you. You might get very excited....

And to you, free people of a free press, honest people of an honest press, what happens to us may happen to you. What is important for us is important for you.... And if other threats exist for us, apart from the threats of the Fascists, we want to take care of them by ourselves, without being bothered by certain helps.... This is good information to give....

WATERGATE: WHITE HOUSE SHAKE-UP
April 30, 1973

A seemingly never-ending avalanche of disclosures, charges and countercharges related to the Watergate scandal continued to dominate Washington's headlines and conversations during April. The Republican national chairman and other leaders voiced alarm at the potential damage to their party. Vice President Agnew rallied to his leader. There was concern lest the business of governing the nation be sidetracked by White House preoccupation with events that threatened the probity of the President and his ability to carry out his programs. During the last week of the month, the President himself publicly accepted responsibility for any wrongdoing in the affair. A cabinet officer and three top White House aides resigned. Allegations of corruption went beyond the capital city and reached into the Pentagon Papers trial in Los Angeles. (See p. 537.)

The President on April 30 announced the resignations of four men: H. R. Haldeman, White House chief of staff; John D. Ehrlichman, chief counselor for domestic affairs; John W. Dean III, presidential counsel; and Attorney General Richard Kleindienst. At the same time, Nixon announced the nomination of Defense Secretary Elliot L. Richardson as attorney general and the appointment of Leonard Garment as presidential counsel. Gen. Alexander M. Haig Jr., Army vice chief of staff and former chief deputy to Henry A. Kissinger, the President's national security adviser, was appointed interim White House chief of staff May 4. Addressing the nation on the evening of April 30, Nixon said he took full responsibility for any improper activities connected with his 1972 presidential campaign. He pledged that "justice will be pursued fairly, fully and impartially." Richardson would have full charge of the administration's Watergate investigations and would have authority to appoint a special prosecutor in the case.

Growing Republican dissatisfaction with the administration's Watergate investigation was credited with hastening the President's April 30 speech. At a cabinet meeting April 20, Nixon was quoted as having said in reference to the Watergate scandal, "We've had our Cambodias before"; in 1970, the President had been strongly criticized for his decision to invade Cambodia. George Bush, the Republican national chairman, told reporters after the April 20 cabinet meeting: "I came out of there with the conviction that he wants to get the truth, wants to see the criminal justice system work and work fully."

Throughout April, headlines on the Watergate scandal were topped daily by new disclosures. The first career casualty of the month was the withdrawal April 5 of the nomination of L. Patrick Gray as permanent director of the FBI. Gray had incurred difficulty from the outset of Senate hearings on his nomination. He had been accused of campaigning for the President while serving as acting director of the federal agency. He admitted turning over FBI files on the Watergate investigation to White House counsel John Dean, and he remarked that Dean "probably lied" to him when the latter said he did not know whether Watergate conspirator E. Howard Hunt had an office in the White House.

Meanwhile, the Watergate defendants, G. Gordon Liddy and the four Cuban nationals arrested at the Watergate complex, refused to answer grand jury questioning as to further illegal activities. Liddy repeatedly invoked the Fifth Amendment before the grand jury. U.S. Federal District Judge John J. Sirica sentenced him April 3 to an additional jail term for contempt of court. Sirica ordered the four Miamians to testify, indicating that their eventual sentencing would take into account their cooperation with investigators of the Watergate affair. On April 5 another convicted conspirator, James W. McCord Jr., whose letter to Judge Sirica (see p. 413) had broken open the Watergate investigation, was granted immunity from any further prosecution. McCord then started testifying before the grand jury.

Republican concern, added to Democratic outrage, mounted. The White House remained silent. The President had let it be known that his staff would not be permitted to testify before congressional committees looking into the case. Then, in a dramatic switch of policy April 17, the President announced that "all members of the White House staff will appear voluntarily when requested by the committee." The President told reporters at a brief press conference that "they will testify under oath and they will answer fully all proper questions." Nixon said he had begun "intensive new inquiries" into the Watergate affair on March 21 "as a result of serious charges which came to my attention." Without further elaboration, he said there had been "major new developments in the case." His reversal of position apparently averted a showdown with the chairman of the Senate select committee on the Watergate, Sam J. Ervin Jr. (D N.C.). Ervin had insisted that past and present members of the White House staff be made available to testify under oath before the committee.

An increasing number of White House personnel and others were implicated in the case during April. The Washington Post reported April 19 that Jeb Stuart Magruder, former deputy director of the Committee for the Re-election of the President, had accused former Attorney General John N. Mitchell and the President's counsel, John W. Dean III, of participating in planning prior to the bugging and break-in at the Democratic National Committee headquarters at the Watergate complex. Mitchell repeated his denials of prior knowledge of the bugging incident. But when asked if he had heard discussions of such plans, he replied, "I have heard discussions of such things. They've always been cut off at all times, and I would like to know who it was that kept bringing them back and back and back." Mitchell said he had not approved of any bugging operations "at any time or under any circumstances."

Other Watergate developments in April:

April 20—The New York Times *reported that Dean had supervised cash payments of $175,000 in Republican campaign funds to the seven Watergate defendants and their lawyers after the break-in. Dean's attorney said the report was "absolutely untrue."*

April 23—The Washington Star-News, *quoting unidentified sources, said there was a secret fund of up to $500,000. Part of the money was reportedly used to pay for Republican sabotage and espionage operations in the 1972 campaign. The President's personal lawyer, Herbert W. Kalmbach, was said to have controlled the fund.*

April 25—The President's re-election committee was reported by The Washington Post *to have spent at least $8,400 in May 1972 on a campaign to give a distorted view of public reaction to the President's decision to mine Haiphong Harbor. Jeb Stuart Magruder was said to have authorized the expenditures for telegrams to the White House in support of the mining and for a $4,400 advertisement in* The New York Times.

April 27—Following disclosures that he had destroyed records pertaining to the Watergate case, L. Patrick Gray resigned as acting director of the FBI. Within two hours the President appointed William D. Ruckelshaus, administrator of the Environmental Protection Agency, to succeed Gray.

April 27—The General Accounting Office (GAO) urged "in the strongest terms" that the Justice Department move quickly on GAO reports charging the Finance Committee to Re-elect the President with "apparent violations" of the Federal Elections Campaign Act. The GAO report included new charges that Hugh W. Sloan Jr., former treasurer of the finance committee, "knowingly and willfully" submitted false financial reports to the GAO Office of Federal Elections.

April 28—Nixon was reported to be in virtual seclusion at Camp David, Md. He was visited by Secretary of State William P. Rogers, Secretary of Defense Elliot L. Richardson, White House press secretary Ronald L. Ziegler, presidential consultant Leonard Garment, and by Haldeman, Ehrlichman and Kleindienst.

April 30—The President, in his television speech on the Watergate, announced the resignations of Haldeman, Ehrlichman, Dean and Kleindienst.

> *Documents below include the text of the President's television address to the nation on the Watergate, April 30; texts of letters of resignation of Richard G. Kleindienst, H. R. Haldeman and John D. Ehrlichman; announcement of withdrawal of the nomination of L. Patrick Gray III to serve as permanent director of the FBI, April 5; and text of Gray's letter of resignation, April 27:*

The President's Address to the Nation, April 30, 1973

Good evening:

I want to talk to you tonight from my heart on a subject of deep concern to every American.

In recent months, members of my Administration and officials of the Committee for the Re-election of the President—including some of my closest friends and most trusted aides—have been charged with involvement in what has come to be known as the Watergate affair. These include charges of illegal activity during and preceding the 1972 Presidential election and charges that responsible officials participated in efforts to cover up that illegal activity.

The inevitable result of these charges has been to raise serious questions about the integrity of the White House itself. Tonight I wish to address those questions.

Last June 17, while I was in Florida trying to get a few days rest after my visit to Moscow, I first learned from news reports of the Watergate break-in. I was appalled at this senseless, illegal action, and I was shocked to learn that employees of the Re-election Committee were apparently among those guilty. I immediately ordered an investigation by appropriate Government authorities. On September 15, as you will recall, indictments were brought against seven defendants in the case.

As the investigations went forward, I repeatedly asked those conducting the investigation whether there was any reason to believe that members of my Administration were in any way involved. I received repeated assurances that there were not. Because of these continuing reassurances, because I believed the reports I was getting, because I had faith in the persons from whom I was getting them, I discounted the stories in the press that appeared to implicate members of my Administration or other officials of the campaign committee.

Until March of this year, I remained convinced that the denials were true and that the charges of involvement by members of the White House Staff were false. The comments I made during this period, and the comments made by my Press Secretary in my behalf, were based on the information provided to us at the time we made those comments. However, new information then came to me which persuaded me that there was a real possibility that some of these charges were true, and suggesting further that there had been an effort to conceal the facts both from the public, from you, and from me.

As a result, on March 21, I personally assumed the responsibility for coordinating intensive new inquiries into the matter, and I personally ordered those conducting the investigations to get all the facts and to report them directly to me, right here in this office.

I again ordered that all persons in the Government or at the Re-election Committee should cooperate fully with the FBI, the prosecutors, and the grand jury. I also ordered that anyone who refused to cooperate in telling the truth would be asked to resign from government service. And, with ground rules adopted that would preserve the basic constitutional separation of powers between the Congress and the Presidency, I directed that members of the White House Staff should appear and testify voluntarily under oath before the Senate committee which was investigating Watergate.

I was determined that we should get to the bottom of the matter, and that the truth should be fully brought out—no matter who was involved.

At the same time, I was determined not to take precipitate action, and to avoid, if at all possible, any action that would appear to reflect on innocent people. I wanted to be fair. But I knew that in the final analysis, the integrity of this office—public faith in the integrity of this office—would have to take priority over all personal considerations.

Announcement of Resignations

Today, in one of the most difficult decisions of my Presidency, I accepted the resignations of two of my closest associates in the White House—Bob Haldeman, John Ehrlichman—two of the finest public servants it has been my privilege to know.

I want to stress that in accepting these resignations, I mean to leave no implication whatever of personal wrongdoing on their part, and I leave no implication tonight of implication on the part of others who have been charged in this matter. But in matters as sensitive as guarding the integrity of our democratic process, it is essential not only that rigorous legal and ethical standards be observed, but also that the public, you, have total confidence that they are both being observed and enforced by those in authority and particularly by the President of the United States. They agreed with me that this move was necessary in order to restore that confidence.

Because Attorney General Kleindienst—though a distinguished public servant, my personal friend for 20 years, with no personal involvement whatever in this matter—has been a close personal and professional associate of some of those who are involved in this case, he and I both felt that it was also necessary to name a new Attorney General.

The Counsel to the President, John Dean, has also resigned.

As the new Attorney General, I have today named Elliot Richardson, a man of unimpeachable integrity and rigorously high principle. I have directed him to do everything necessary to ensure that the Department of Justice has the confidence and the trust of every law abiding person in this country.

I have given him absolute authority to make all decisions bearing upon the prosecution of the Watergate case and related matters. I have instructed him that if he should consider it appropriate, he has the authority to name a special supervising prosecutor for matters arising out of the case.

Whatever may appear to have been the case before, whatever improper activities may yet be discovered in connection with this whole sordid affair, I want the American people, I want you to know beyond the shadow of a doubt that during my term as President, justice will be pursued fairly, fully, and impartially, no matter who is involved. This office is a sacred trust and I am determined to be worthy of that trust.

Looking back at the history of this case, two questions arise:

How could it have happened?

Who is to blame?

Political commentators have correctly observed that during my 27 years in politics I have always previously insisted on running my own campaigns for office.

But 1972 presented a very different situation. In both domestic and foreign policy, 1972 was a year of crucially important decisions, of intense negotiations, of vital new directions, particularly in working toward the goal which has been my overriding concern throughout my political career—the goal of bringing peace to America, peace to the world.

That is why I decided, as the 1972 campaign approached, that the Presidency should come first and politics second. To the maximum extent possible, therefore, I sought to delegate campaign operations, to remove the day-to-day campaign decisions from the President's office and from the White House. I also, as you recall, severely limited the number of my own campaign appearances.

Who Is To Blame?

Who, then, is to blame for what happened in this case?

For specific criminal actions by specific individuals, those who committed those actions must, of course, bear the liability and pay the penalty.

For the fact that alleged improper actions took place within the White House or within my campaign organization, the easiest course would be for me to blame those to whom I delegated the responsibility to run the campaign. But that would be a cowardly thing to do.

I will not place the blame on subordinates—on people whose zeal exceeded their judgment, and who may have done wrong in a cause they deeply believed to be right.

In any organization, the man at the top must bear the responsibility. That responsibility, therefore, belongs here, in this office. I accept it. And I pledge to you tonight, from this office, that I will do everything in my power to ensure that the guilty are brought to justice, and that such abuses are purged from our political processes in the years to come, long after I have left this office.

Some people, quite properly appalled at the abuses that occurred, will say that Watergate demonstrates the bankruptcy of the American political system. I believe precisely the opposite is true. Watergate represented a series of illegal acts and bad judgments by a number of individuals. It was the system that has brought the facts to light and that will bring those guilty to justice—a system that in this case has included a determined grand jury, honest prosecutors, a courageous judge, John Sirica, and a vigorous free press.

It is essential now that we place our faith in that system—and especially in the judicial system. It is essential that we let the judicial process go forward, respecting those safeguards that are established to protect the innocent as well as to convict the guilty. It is essential that in reacting to the excesses of others, we not fall into excesses ourselves.

It is also essential that we not be so distracted by events such as this that we neglect the vital work before us, before this Nation, before America, at a time of critical importance to America and the world.

Since March, when I first learned that the Watergate affair might, in fact, be far more serious than I had been led to believe, it has claimed far too much of my time and my attention.

Whatever may now transpire in the case, whatever the actions of the grand jury, whatever the outcome of any eventual trials, I must now turn my full attention—and I shall do so—once again to the larger duties of this office. I owe it to this great office that I hold, and I owe it to you—to my country.

I know that as Attorney General, Elliot Richardson will be both fair and he will be fearless in pursuing this case wherever it leads. I am confident that with him in charge, justice will be done.

There is vital work to be done toward our goal of a lasting structure of peace in the world—work that cannot wait, work that I must do.

Tomorrow, for example, Chancellor Brandt of West Germany will visit the White House for talks that are a vital element of "The Year of Europe," as 1973 has been called. We are already preparing for the next Soviet-American summit meeting later this year.

This is also a year in which we are seeking to negotiate a mutual and balanced reduction of armed forces in Europe, which will reduce our defense budget and allow us to have funds for other purposes at home so desperately needed. It is the year when the United States and Soviet negotiators will seek to work out the second and even more important round of our talks on limiting nuclear arms, and of reducing the danger of a nuclear war that would destroy civilization as we know it. It is a year in which we confront the difficult tasks of maintaining peace in Southeast Asia and in the potentially explosive Middle East.

There is also vital work to be done right here in America: to ensure prosperity, and that means a good job for everyone who wants to work; to control inflation, that I know worries every housewife, everyone who tries to balance a family budget in America; to set in motion new and better ways of ensuring progress toward a better life for all Americans.

When I think of this office—of what it means—I think of all the things that I want to accomplish for this Nation, of all the things I want to accomplish for you.

Second-Term Goals

On Christmas Eve, during my terrible personal ordeal of the renewed bombing of North Vietnam, which after 12 years of war, finally helped to bring America peace with honor, I sat down just before midnight. I wrote out some of my goals for my second term as President.

Let me read them to you.

"To make it possible for our children, and for our children's children, to live in a world of peace.

"To make this country be more than ever a land of opportunity—of equal opportunity, full opportunity for every American.

"To provide jobs for all who can work, and generous help for those who cannot work.

"To establish a climate of decency, and civility, in which each person respects the feelings and the dignity and the God-given rights of his neighbor.

"To make this a land in which each person can dare to dream, can live his dreams—not in fear, but in hope—proud of his community, proud of his country, proud of what America has meant to himself and to the world."

These are great goals. I believe we can, we must work for them. We can achieve them. But we cannot achieve these goals unless we dedicate ourselves to another goal.

We must maintain the integrity of the White House, and that integrity must be real, not transparent. There can be no whitewash at the White House.

We must reform our political process—ridding it not only of the violations of the law, but also of the ugly mob violence, and other inexcusable campaign tactics that have been too often practiced and too readily accepted in the past, including those that may have been a response by one side to the excesses or expected excesses of the other side. Two wrongs do not make a right.

I have been in public life for more than a quarter of a century. Like any other calling, politics has good people, and bad people. And let me tell you, the great majority in politics—in the Congress, in the Federal Government, in the State Government—are good people. I know that it can be very easy, under the intensive pressures of a campaign, for even well-intentioned people to fall into shady tactics—to rationalize this on the grounds that what is at stake is of such importance to the Nation that the end justifies the means. And both of our great parties have been guilty of such tactics in the past.

In recent years, however, the campaign excesses that have occurred on all sides have provided a sobering demonstration of how far this false doctrine can take us. The lesson is clear: America, in its political campaigns, must not again fall into the trap of letting the end, however great that end is, justify the means.

I urge the leaders of both political parties, I urge citizens, all of you, everywhere, to join in working toward a new set of standards, new rules and procedures to ensure that future elections will be as nearly free of such abuses as they possibly can be made. This is my goal. I ask you to join in making it America's goal.

When I was inaugurated for a second term this past January 20, I gave each member of my Cabinet and each member of my senior White House Staff a special 4-year calendar, with each day marked to show the number of days remaining to the Administration. In the inscription on each calendar, I wrote these words: "The Presidential term which begins today consists of 1,461 days—no more, no less. Each can be a day of strengthening and renewal for America; each can add depth and dimension to the American experience. If we strive together, if we make the most of the challenge and the opportunity that these days offer us, they can stand out as great days for America, and great moments in the history of the world."

I looked at my own calendar this morning up at Camp David as I was working on this speech. It showed exactly 1,361 days remaining in my term. I want these to be the best days in America's history, because I love America. I deeply believe that America is the hope of the world. And I know that in the quality and wisdom of the leadership America gives lies the only hope for millions of people all over the world, that they can live their lives in peace and freedom. We must be worthy of that hope, in every sense of the word. Tonight, I ask for your prayers to help me in everything that I do throughout the days of my Presidency to be worthy of their hopes and of yours.

God bless America and God bless each and every one of you.

Presidential statement read by press secretary Ronald L. Ziegler announcing resignations and appointments, together with assignment of responsibilities regarding the Watergate investigation, April 30, 1973:

I have today received and accepted the resignation of Richard G. Kleindienst as Attorney General of the United States. I am appointing Elliot L. Richardson to succeed him as Attorney General and will submit Mr. Richardson's name to the Senate for confirmation immediately.

Mr. Kleindienst asked to be relieved as Attorney General because he felt that he could not appropriately continue as head of the Justice Department now that it appears its investigation of the Watergate and related cases may implicate individuals with whom he has had a close personal and professional association. In making this decision, Mr. Kleindienst has acted in accordance with the highest standards of public service and legal ethics. I am accepting his resignation with regret and with deep appreciation for his dedicated service to this Administration.

Pending Secretary Richardson's confirmation as Attorney General, I have asked him to involve himself immediately in the investigative process surrounding the Watergate matter. As Attorney General, Mr. Richardson will assume full responsibility and authority for coordinating all Federal agencies in uncovering the whole truth about this matter and recommending appropriate changes in the law to prevent future campaign abuses of the sort recently uncovered. He will have total support from me in getting this job done.

In addition, I have today accepted the resignations of two of my closest friends and most trusted assistants in the White House, H. R. Haldeman and John D. Ehrlichman.

I know that their decision to resign was difficult; my decision to accept it was difficult; but I respect and appreciate the attitude that led them to it.

I emphasize that neither the submission nor the acceptance of their resignations at this time should be seen by anyone as evidence of any wrongdoing by either one. Such an assumption would be both unfair and unfounded.

Throughout our association, each of these men has demonstrated a spirit of selflessness and dedication that I have seldom seen equaled. Their contributions to the work of this Administration have been enormous. I greatly regret their departure.

Finally, I have today requested and accepted the resignation of John W. Dean III from his position on the White House Staff as Counsel.

Effectively immediately, Leonard Garment, Special Consultant to the President, will take on additional duties as Counsel to the President, and will continue acting in this capacity until a permanent successor to Mr. Dean is named. Mr. Garment will represent the White House in all matters relating to the Watergate investigation and will report directly to me.

Texts of letters of resignation from Attorney General Richard G. Kleindienst and assistants to the President H. R. Haldeman and John D. Ehrlichman, April 30, 1973:

Dear Mr. President:

It is with deep regret and after long and searching thought that I hereby submit my resignation as Attorney General, to take effect upon the appointment and qualification of my successor.

Even though, as you know, I had previously indicated a desire to leave the government this year for family and financial reasons, the circumstances surrounding the disclosures made to me on Sunday, April 15, 1973 by Assistant Attorney General Petersen, United States Attorney Titus, and Assistant United States Attorney Silbert, dictate this decision at this time. Those disclosures informed me, for the first time, that persons with whom I had had close personal and professional associations could be involved in conduct violative of the laws of the United States. Fair and impartial enforcement of the law requires that a person who has not had such intimate relationships be the Attorney General of the United States.

It is not for me to comment now on the tragedy that has occurred. However, I will always be mindful to your charge to me from the very beginning that the entire matter be fully investigated and that the full effect of the law be administered no matter who it might involve or affect. You can be proud of the Department of Justice for the manner in which it, from the beginning, has responded to that charge.

Finally, let me express my deep personal appreciation to you for having appointed me the 68th Attorney General of the United States. It is the greatest honor I shall ever have. I shall always be humbly proud to have been a part of the Department of Justice and to have had the opportunity to serve my country as a part of your Administration.

Sincerely,
RICHARD G. KLEINDIENST

Dear Mr. President:

As you know, I had hoped and expected to have had an earlier opportunity to clear up various allegations and innuendos that have been raised in connection with matters related to the Watergate case. It now appears that this process may consume considerable time. Meanwhile, there is apparently to be no interruption in the flood of stories arising every day from all sorts of sources.

I fully agree with the importance of a complete investigation by the appropriate authorities of all the factors that may be involved; but am deeply concerned that, in the process, it has become virtually impossible under these circumstances for me to carry on my regular responsibilities in the White House.

It is imperative that the work of the Office of the President not be impeded and your staff must be in a position to focus their attention on the vital areas of domestic and international concern that face you, rather than being diverted by the daily rumors and developments in the Watergate case. For these reasons, I submit my resignation as Assistant to the President.

I intend to cooperate fully with the investigation—and will at my request be meeting this week for that purpose with the U.S. Attorneys and with the counsel to the Senate Select Committee.

I am convinced that, in due course, I will have the opportunity not just to clear up any allegations or implications of impropriety but also to demonstrate that I have always met the high and exacting standards of integrity which you have so clearly and properly demanded of all who serve on the White House staff.

I have full confidence that when the truth is known the American people will be totally justified in their pride in the Office of the President and in the conduct of that office by President Nixon.

Respectfully,

H. R. HALDEMAN

Dear Mr. President:

For the past two weeks it has become increasingly evident that, regardless of the actual facts, I have been a target of public attack. The nature of my position on your staff has always demanded that my conduct be both apparently and actually beyond reproach. I have always felt that the appearance of honesty and integrity is every bit as important to such a position as the fact of one's honesty and integrity.

Unfortunately, such appearances are not always governed by facts. Realistically, they can be affected by repeated rumor, unfounded charges or implications and whatever else the media carries. For instance, this week totally unfounded stories appeared in the *Los Angeles Times* claiming I had asked our Embassy in Lebanon to help the Vesco group in a banking deal. I not only did not do so but, in actual fact, I caused the State Department to cable the Embassy that no one at the White House had any interest in the Vesco dealings. Since I have already reported to you many of the facts in the Gray case, I need only say that at no time did I directly or indirectly suggest that Mr. Gray should do other than keep the Hunt documents, although there have been reports to the contrary. Equally without merit are the source stories about some alleged involvement in the Watergate matter.

As I analyze my situation, I have to conclude that my present usefulness to you and ability to discharge my duties have been impaired by these attacks, perhaps beyond repair.

It is not fair to you and my staff colleagues for me to try to do my job under these circumstances. Too much of my time and attention is and will be consumed in concern for and straightening out such allegations. At my request, I am going to have separate interviews this week with the District Attorney and the Senate Committee Counsel. Thus, I am looking forward to an early review of the facts and evidence with the appropriate authorities, and I should spend the time necessary in relation thereto.

One of the toughest problems we have in this life is in seeing the difference between the apparent and the real, and in basing our actions only on that which is real. We all must do that more than we do. I have confidence in the ultimate prevalence of truth; I intend to do what I can to speed truth's discovery.

Therefore, Mr. President, I submit to you my resignation. There are on the Domestic Council staff so many good people of ability that I am confident a transition of my responsibilities can be affected without loss of progress. I will do all I can to assist in accomplishing the transition.

Yours sincerely,

JOHN D. EHRLICHMAN,
Assistant to the President.

Statement by the President on his intention to withdraw the nomination of L. Patrick Gray III, at Mr. Gray's request, April 5, 1973:

Pat Gray is an able, honest, and dedicated American.

Because I asked my counsel, John Dean, to conduct a thorough investigation of alleged involvement in the Watergate episode, Director Gray was asked to make FBI reports available to Mr. Dean. His compliance with this completely proper and necessary request exposed Mr. Gray to totally unfair innuendo and suspicion, and thereby seriously tarnished his fine record as Acting Director and promising future at the Bureau.

In view of the action of the Senate Judiciary Committee today, it is obvious that Mr. Gray's nomination will not be confirmed by the Senate. Mr. Gray has asked that I withdraw his nomination. In fairness to Mr. Gray, and out of my overriding concern for the effective conduct of the vitally important business of the FBI, I have regretfully agreed to withdraw Mr. Gray's nomination.

I have asked Mr. Gray to remain Acting Director until a new nominee is confirmed.

Text of a statement by L. Patrick Gray III announcing his resignation as acting director of the FBI, April 27:

Serious allegations concerning certain acts of my own during the ongoing Watergate investigation are now a matter of public record. As a consequence, I have today tendered my resignation as Acting Director of the Federal Bureau of Investigation, effective immediately.

This action is required to preserve in both image and fact the reputation, the integrity and the effectiveness of the F.B.I.

This superb investigative agency has been in no way involved in any of those personal acts or judgments that may now be called into question—and my own continued presence at the helm must not be permitted to create even the hint or implication of involvement, false though it is.

The F.B.I. deserves the full trust of the American people: That is bedrock and must always remain so.

I depart from the F.B.I. with a clear conscience, the knowledge that I have done my duty as best I have been able to see that duty and with an admiration and respect for the men and women of the F.B.I. that only one who has led them and served with them can ever fully understand.

May

STATE OF THE WORLD
May 3, 1973

Against a backdrop of detente with the Soviet Union and the People's Republic of China, and the conclusion of a shaky cease-fire agreement in Vietnam, the Nixon administration turned in 1973 to new challenges in the foreign field. Relations with traditional allies in Western Europe, Japan and Latin America were slated to have high priority, the President said in his annual State of the World message to Congress on May 3. The United States in 1973 would also give attention to easing tensions in the Middle East and promoting economic progress in Africa and Asia, national security adviser Henry A. Kissinger told reporters at a briefing on the message. In addition, the agenda included arms limitation and problems of security.

The message noted that the administration had brought about relaxation of tensions with the Soviet Union and with China in 1972. (See Historic Documents, 1972, p. 183-192, 431-463, 882, and 889-890.) The White House had concluded that peace could not be realized when it depended solely on an uneasy equilibrium between two nuclear giants. Nor could it be attained when a fourth of humanity—the People's Republic of China—was excluded from the international community. Furthermore, the Vietnam War had to be ended.

In setting forth new goals, Nixon's fourth annual message on foreign policy emphasized a revitalization of traditional alliances and the maintenance of military strength in conjunction with efforts to reach new arms control agreements. Nixon also emphasized the need for a "fresh dimension of international cooperation" and the responsible participation of all nations in "a structure of peace"—greater participation by other nations along with sustained participation by the United States. Themes of shared responsibilities and greater self-reliance on the part of allies of the United States were stressed throughout the message. They echoed remarks Nixon had made in January when he said, "The time has passed when America will make every other nation's conflict our own, or make every other nation's future our responsibility." (See p. 82.)

On the subject of Vietnam, the President said that the foundation for peace in Indochina had been laid, but that its achievement depended on the spirit in which the cease-fire agreement was implemented. He warned that Hanoi "would risk revived confrontation with us" if it continued to infiltrate men and materiel into South Vietnam in violation of the agreement. Concerning the Atlantic Alliance, the message envisioned a "more mature and viable partnership" which would provide equitable terms for U.S. products in world markets, a realistic defense strategy with an equitable sharing of burdens, and reconciliation of national interests with the requirement of unity on fundamental security issues. As for American relations with Japan, the President said, "In this year of new commitment to strengthening our ties with Western Europe, I am determined no less to strengthen our alliance with Japan," but he noted that there were going to be major hurdles to overcome, especially in the economic sphere.

Reaction to the message on Capitol Hill centered on the continued American bombing of Cambodia. The message had observed that in Cambodia "Communist military operations have reached new levels" and that the general situation there was "ominous." In his briefing on the message, Kissinger was no more hopeful, saying only that "we are not too pessimistic that over a period of weeks, maybe months, some cease-fire negotiations will start." Before the Senate Foreign Relations Committee, May 9, Secretary of State William P. Rogers contended that the bombing did not conflict with the Vietnam cease-fire agreement so long as a separate cease-fire had not been signed with Cambodia. This view was buttressed by reference to the President's constitutional powers as commander in chief.

Congressional pressure to put an immediate end to the bombing nevertheless mounted. A seemingly unbreakable deadlock between Congress and the President developed toward the close of the fiscal year when the legislators demonstrated their determination to add stop-the-bombing amendments to necessary appropriations bills and the President appeared equally determined to veto all such measures. The deadlock was finally broken July 1 when Nixon signed two funding bills, each of which carried a compromise amendment barring on and after Aug. 15, 1973, all "combat activities by United States military forces in or over or from off the shores of North Vietnam, South Vietnam, Laos or Cambodia."

Text of "Introduction" and "Conclusion" of President Nixon's message to Congress, May 3, 1973, on United States Foreign Policy for the 1970s: Shaping a Durable Peace:

INTRODUCTION

In January 1969, America needed to change the philosophy and practice of its foreign policy.

Whoever took office four years ago would have faced this challenge. After a generation, the postwar world had been transformed and demanded a fresh approach. It was not a question of our previous policies having failed; indeed, in many areas they had been very successful. It was rather that new conditions, many of them achievements of our policies, summoned new perspectives.

The World We Found

The international environment was dominated by seemingly intractable confrontation between the two major nuclear powers. Throughout the nuclear age both the fears of war and hopes for peace revolved around our relations with the Soviet Union. Our growing nuclear arsenals were largely directed at each other. We alone had the capacity to wreak catastrophic damage across the planet. Our ideologies clashed. We both had global interests, and this produced many friction points. We each led and dominated a coalition of opposing states.

As a result, our relationship was generally hostile. There were positive interludes, but these were often atmospheric and did not get at the roots of tension. Accords were reached on particular questions, but there was no broad momentum in our relationship. Improvements in the climate were quickly replaced by confrontation and, occasionally, crisis. The basic pattern was a tense jockeying for tactical advantage around the globe.

This was dangerous and unsatisfactory. The threat of a major conflict between us hung over the world. This in turn exacerbated local and regional tensions. And our two countries not only risked collision but were constrained from working positively on common problems.

The weight of China rested outside the international framework. This was due partly to its own attitude and its preoccupation with internal problems, and partly to the policies of the outside world, most importantly the United States. In any event, this Administration inherited two decades of mutual estrangement and hostility. Here the problem was not one of a fluctuating relationship but rather of having no relationship at all. The People's Republic of China was separated not only from us but essentially from the world as a whole.

China also exemplified the great changes that had occurred in the Communist world. For years our guiding principle was containment of what we considered a monolithic challenge. In the 1960's the forces of nationalism dissolved Communist unity into divergent centers of power and doctrine, and our foreign policy began to differentiate among the Communist capitals. But this process could not be truly effective so long as we were cut off from one-quarter of the globe's people. China in turn was emerging from its isolation and might be more receptive to overtures from foreign countries.

The gulf between China and the world distorted the international landscape. We could not effectively reduce tensions in Asia without talking to Peking. China's isolation compounded its own sense of insecurity. There could not be a stable world order with a major power remaining outside and hostile to it.

Our principal alliances with Western Europe and Japan needed adjustment. After the devastation of the Second World War we had helped allies and former adversaries alike. Fueled by our assistance and secure behind our military shield, they regained their economic vigor and political confidence.

Throughout the postwar period our bonds with Europe had rested on American prescriptions as well as resources. We provided much of the leadership and planning for common defense. We took the diplomatic lead. The dollar was unchallenged. But by the time this Administration took office, the tide was flowing toward greater economic and political assertiveness by our allies. European unity which we had always encouraged, was raising new issues in Atlantic relations. The economic revival of Europe was straining the Atlantic monetary and commercial framework. The relaxation of tensions with the Communist world was generating new doctrines of defense and diplomacy.

The imperatives of change were equally evident in our Pacific partnership with Japan. Its recovery of strength and self-assurance carried political and psychological implications for our relationship. Its spectacular economic growth had made it the world's third industrial power; our entire economic relationship was undergoing transformation. The earlier paternalism of U.S.-Japanese relations no longer suited either partner.

The Vietnam war dominated our attention and was sapping our self-confidence. Our role and our costs had steadily grown without decisive impact on the conflict. The outlook at the conference table was bleak. The war was inhibiting our policy abroad and fostering dissent and self-doubt at home. There was no prospect of either an end to the fighting or an end to our involvement.

Although the historical imperatives for a new international approach existed independently, the war made this challenge at once more urgent and more difficult. More than any other factor, it threatened to exhaust the American people's willingness to sustain a reliable foreign policy. As much as any other factor, the way we treated it would shape overseas attitudes and American psychology.

The context for our national security policy was fundamentally altered. From the mid-1940's to the late 1960's we had moved from America's nuclear monopoly to superiority to rough strategic balance with the Soviet Union. This created fresh challenges to our security and introduced new calculations in our diplomacy. The U.S. defense effort remained disproportionate to that of our allies who had grown much stronger. The threats from potential enemies were more varied and less blatant than during the more rigid bipolar era. These changes, combined with spiraling military costs and the demands of domestic programs, were prompting reexamination of our defense doctrines and posture. They were underlining the importance of arms control as an element in national security. They were also leading some in this country to call for policies that would seriously jeopardize our safety and world stability.

Around the world, friends were ready for a greater role in shaping their own security and well-being. In the 1950's and 1960's other nations had looked to America for ideas and resources, and they found us a willing provider of both. Our motives were sound, the needs were clear, and we had many successes. By 1969, scores of new nations, having emerged from colonial status or dependency on major powers, were asserting themselves with greater assurance and autonomy.

Four years ago this growing capacity of friends was not reflected in the balance of contributions to security and development. This meant that others could do more, and the United States need do proportionately less, in the provision of material resources. More fundamentally, it meant that increasingly the devising of plans belonged outside of Washington. The sweeping American presence was likely to strain our capabilities and to stifle the initiative of others.

There were new issues that called for global cooperation. These challenges were not susceptible to national solutions or relevant to national ideologies. The vast frontiers of space and the oceans beckoned international exploration for humanity's gain. Pollution of air, sea, and land could not be contained behind national frontiers. The brutal tools of assassination, kidnapping, and hijacking could be used to further any cause in any country. No nation's youth was immune from the scourge of international drug traffic. The immediate tragedies of national disasters and the longer-term threat of overpopulation were humanitarian, not political, concerns.

At home we faced pressures that threatened to swing America from over-extension in the world to heedless withdrawal from it. The American people had supported the burdens of global leadership with enthusiasm and generosity into the 1960's. But after almost three decades, our enthusiasm was waning and the results of our generosity were being questioned. Our policies needed change, not only to match new realities in the world but also to meet a new mood in America. Many Americans were no longer willing to support the sweeping range of our postwar role. It had drained our financial, and especially our psychological, reserves. Our friends clearly were able to do more. The Vietnam experience was hastening our awareness of change. Voices in this country were claiming that we had to jettison global concerns and turn inward in order to meet our domestic problems.

Therefore the whole underpinning of our foreign policy was in jeopardy. The bipartisan consensus that once existed for a vigorous American internationalism was now being torn apart. Some of the most active proponents of America's commitment in the world in previous decades were now pressing for indiscriminate disengagement. What was once seen as America's overseas obligation was now seen as our overseas preoccupation. What was once viewed as America's unselfishness was now viewed as our naivete. By 1969 we faced the danger that public backing for a continuing world role might be swept away by fatigue, frustration and over-reaction.

This Administration's Approach

We were determined to shape new policies to deal with each of these problems. But our first requirement was philosophic. We needed a fresh vision to inspire and to integrate our efforts.

We began with the conviction that a major American commitment to the world continued to be indispensable. The many changes in the postwar landscape did not alter this central fact. America's strength was so vast, our involvement so broad, and our concerns so deep, that to remove our influence would set off tremors around the globe. Friends would despair, adversaries would be tempted, and our own national security would soon be threatened. There was no escaping the reality of our enormous influence for peace.

But the new times demanded a new definition of our involvement. For more than a score of years our foreign policy had been driven by a global mission that only America could fulfill—to furnish political leadership, provide for the common defense, and promote economic development. Allies were weak and other nations were young, threats were palpable and American power was dominant.

By 1969, a mission of this scale was no longer valid abroad or supportable at home. Allies had grown stronger and young nations were maturing, threats were diversified and American power was offset. It was time to move from a paternal mission *for* others to a cooperative mission *with* others. Convinced as we were that a strong American role remained essential for world stability, we knew, too, that a peace that depends primarily on the exertions of one nation is inherently fragile.

So we saw the potential and the imperative of a pluralistic world. We believed we could move from an environment of emergencies to a more stable international system. We made our new purpose a global structure of peace—comprehensive because it would draw on the efforts of other countries; durable because if countries helped to build it, they would also help to maintain it.

To pursue this fundamental vision, we had to move across a wide and coordinated front, with mutually reinforcing policies for each challenge we faced.

Peace could not depend solely on the uneasy equilibrium between two nuclear giants. We had a responsibility to work for positive relations with the Soviet Union. But there was ample proof that assertions of good will or transitory changes in climate would not erase the hard realities of ideological opposition, geopolitical rivalry, competing alliances, or military competition. We were determined not to lurch along—with isolated agreements vulnerable to sudden shifts of course in political relations, with peaks and valleys based on atmosphere, with incessant tension and maneuvering. We saw as well that there were certain mutual interests that we could build upon. As the two powers capable of global destruction, we had a common stake in preserving peace.

Thus we decided to follow certain principles in our policy toward the Soviet Union. We would engage in concrete negotiations designed to produce specific agreements, both where differences existed and where cooperation was possible. We would work with Moscow across a broad front, believing that progress in one area would induce progress in others. Through the gathering momentum of individual accords we would seek to create vested interests on both sides in restraint and the strengthening of peace. But this process would require a reduction in tactical maneuvering at each other's expense in favor of our shared interest in avoiding calamitous collision, in profiting from cooperation, and in building a more stable world.

Peace could not exclude a fourth of humanity. The longer-term prospects for peace required a new relationship with the People's Republic of China. Only if China's weight was reflected in the international system would it have the incentive, and sense of shared responsibility, to maintain the peace. Furthermore, the time was past when one nation could claim to speak for a bloc of states; we would deal with countries on the basis of their actions, not abstract ideological formulas. Our own policies could be more flexible if we did not assume the permanent enmity of China. The United States had a traditional interest in an independent and peaceful China. We seemed to have no fundamental interests that need collide in the longer sweep of history. There was, indeed, rich potential benefit for our two peoples in a more normal relationship.

So we launched a careful process of private diplomacy and public steps to engage the People's Republic of China with us and involve it more fully in the world. We did so, confident that a strong, independent China was in our national interest; resolved that such a process need not—and would not—be aimed at any other country; and looking for a reciprocal attitude on the part of the Chinese.

Peace must draw upon the vitality of our friends. Our alliances with Western Europe and Japan would continue as major pillars of our foreign policy, but they had not kept pace with the changed international environment. We thus sought to forge more equal partnerships based on a more balanced contribution of both resources and plans.

America had been the automatic source of political leadership and economic power. Now we needed new modes of action that would accommodate our partners' new dynamism. The challenge was to reconcile traditional unity with new diversity. While complete integration of policy was impossible, pure unilateralism would be destructive.

Before, we were allied in containment of a unified Communist danger. Now Communism had taken various forms; our alliances had stabilized the European and Northeast Asian environments; and we had laid the foundations for negotiation. We had to decide together not only what we were against, but what we were for.

Peace required the ending of an ongoing war. Our approach to the Vietnam conflict and our shaping of a new foreign policy were inextricably linked. Naturally, our most urgent concern was to end the war. But we had to end it—or at least our involvement—in a way that would continue to make possible a responsible American role in the world.

We could not continue on the course we inherited, which promised neither an end to the conflict nor to our involvement. At the same time, we would not abandon our friends, for we wanted to shape a structure of peace based in large measure on American steadiness. So we sought peace with honor—through negotiation if possible, through Vietnamization if the enemy gave us no choice. The phased shifting of defense responsibilities to the South Vietnamese would give them the time and means to adjust. It would assure the American people that our own involvement was not open-ended. It would preserve our credibility abroad and our cohesion at home.

Given the enemy's attitude, peace was likely to take time, and other problems in the world could not wait. So we moved promptly to shape a new approach to allies and adversaries. And by painting on this larger canvas we sought both to put the Vietnam war in perspective and to speed its conclusion by demonstrating to Hanoi that continued conflict did not frustrate our global policies.

Peace needed America's strength. Modifications in our defense policy were required, but one central truth persisted—neither our nation nor peace in the world could be secure without our military power. If superiority was not longer practical, inferiority would be unthinkable.

We were determined to maintain a national defense second to none. This would be a force for stability in a world of evolving partnerships and changing doctrines. This was essential to maintain the confidence of our friends and the respect of our adversaries. At the same time, we would seek energetically to promote national and international security through arms control negotiations.

Peace involved a fresh dimension of international cooperation. A new form of multilateral diplomacy was prompted by a new set of issues. These challenges covered a wide range—the promise of exploration, the pollution of our planet, the perils of crime—but they were alike in going beyond the traditional considerations of doctrine and geography. They required cooperation that reached not only across boundaries but often around the globe. So we resolved to work both with friends and adversaries, in the United Nations and other forums, to practice partnership on a global scale.

Above all, peace demanded the responsible participation of all nations. With great efforts during the postwar period we had promoted the revitalization of former powers and the growing assurance of new states. For this changed world we needed a new philosophy that would reflect and reconcile two basic principles: *A structure of peace requires the greater participation of other nations, but it also requires the sustained participation of the United States.*

To these ends, we developed the Nixon Doctrine of shared responsibilities. This Doctrine was central to our approach to major allies in the Atlantic and Pacific. But it also shaped our attitude toward those in Latin America, Asia, and Africa with whom we were working in formal alliances or friendship.

Our primary purpose was to invoke greater efforts by others—not so much to lighten our burdens as to increase their commitment to a new and peaceful structure. This would mean that increasingly they would man their own defenses and furnish more of the funds for their security and economic development. The corollary would be the reduction of the American share of defense or financial contributions.

More fundamental than this material redistribution, however, was a psychological reorientation. Nations had habitually relied on us for political leadership. Much time and energy went into influencing decisions in Washington. Our objective now was to encourage them to play a greater role in formulating plans and programs. For when others design their security and their development, they make their destiny truly their own. And when plans are their plans, they are more motivated to make them realities.

The lowering of our profile was not an end in itself. Other countries needed to do more, but they could not do so without a concerned America. Their role had to be increased, but this would prove empty unless we did what we must. We could not go from overinvolvement to neglect. A changing world needed the continuity of America's strength.

Thus we made clear that the Nixon Doctrine represented a new definition of American leadership, not abandonment of that leadership. In my 1971 Report, I set forth the need for a responsible balance:

"The Nixon Doctrine recognizes that we cannot abandon friends, and must not transfer burdens too swiftly. We must strike a balance between doing too much and thus preventing self-reliance, and doing too little and thus undermining self-confidence.

"The balance we seek abroad is crucial. We only compound insecurity if we modify our protective or development responsibilities without giving our friends the time and the means to adjust, materially and psychologically, to a new form of American participation in the world.

"Precipitate shrinking of the American role would not bring peace. It would not reduce America's stake in a turbulent world. It would not solve our problems, either abroad or at home."

Peace had a domestic dimension. Steadiness abroad required steadiness at home. America could continue to make its vital contribution in the world only if Americans understood the need and supported the effort to do so. But understanding and support for a responsible foreign policy were in serious jeopardy in 1969. Years of burdens, Cold War tensions, and a difficult war threatened to undermine our constancy.

While new policies were required to meet transformed conditions abroad, they were equally imperative because of the changing climate at home. Americans needed a new positive vision of the world and our place in it. In order to continue to do what only America could, we had to demonstrate that our friends were doing more. While maintaining strong defenses, we also had to seek national security through negotiations with adversaries. And where American families were most directly affected, we had to gain a peace with honor to win domestic support for our new foreign policy as well as to make it credible abroad.

We have thus paid great attention, as in these Reports, to the articulation, as well as the implementation, of our new role in the world.

The Past Year

My previous Reports chronicled our progress during the first three years of this Administration. Despite shifting currents, and recognizing that the calendar cannot draw neat dividing lines, there has been a positive evolution.

In 1969, we defined our basic approach, drawing the blueprint of a new strategy for peace.

In 1970, we implemented new policies, building toward peace.

In 1971, we made essential breakthroughs, and a global structure of peace emerged.

This past year we realized major results from our previous efforts. Together they are shaping a durable peace.

—Three years of careful groundwork produced an historic turning point in our relations with the *People's Republic of China*. My conversations with Chinese leaders in February 1972 reestablished contact between the world's most powerful and the world's most populous countries, thereby transforming the postwar landscape. The journey to Peking launched a process with immense potential for the betterment of our peoples and the building of peace in Asia and the world. Since then we have moved to concrete measures which are improving relations and creating more positive conditions in the region. China is becoming fully engaged with us and the world. The process is not inexorable, however. Both countries will have to continue to exercise restraint and contribute to a more stable environment.

—The May 1972 summit meeting with the leadership of the *Soviet Union* achieved a broad range of significant agreements. Negotiations across a wide front, which set the stage for the meeting, were successfully concluded in Moscow. Progress in one area reinforced progress in others. For the first time two nations agreed to limit the strategic weapons that are the heart of their national survival. We launched cooperative ventures in several fields. We agreed on basic principles to govern our relations. Future areas of cooperation and negotiation were opened up. There has been, in sum, major movement toward a steadier and more constructive relationship. On the other hand, areas of tension and potential conflict remain, and certain patterns of Soviet behavior continue to cause concern.

—The attainment of an honorable settlement in *Vietnam* was the most satisfying development of this past year. Successful Vietnamization and intensive negotiations culminated in the Agreement signed on January 27, 1973. This was quickly followed by a settlement in neighboring Laos in February. The steady courage and patience of Americans who supported our policy through the years were echoed in the moving salutes of our returning men. But the coals of war still glow in Vietnam and Laos, and a ceasefire remains elusive altogether in Cambodia. Much work remains to consolidate peace in Indochina.

—In *Western Europe* the inevitable strains of readjustment persisted as we moved from American predominance to balanced partnerships. Generally these were healthy manifestations of the growing strength of countries who share common values and objectives. With less fanfare, but no less dedication, than in our negotiations with adversaries, we consulted closely with our friends. Such a process may not be as susceptible to dramatic advances, but we believe that we have paved the way for substantial progress in Atlantic relations in the coming months. Major political, security and economic negotiations are on the agenda. They will test the wisdom and adaptability of our Alliance.

—There was continued evolution toward a more mature and equitable partnership with *Japan*. Confidence in our shared purposes, which appeared shaken in 1971, has since been reaffirmed. Nevertheless we have not yet fully defined our new political relationship, and serious economic problems confront us. Our relations with Tokyo will be an area of prime attention during the coming year.

—In the past year we advanced toward major reform of the *international economic system*. With others we have launched proposals to create a more stable international monetary system, and a more open world trading order through new international trade negotiations. This process of readjustment is not without crises, however, and voices of narrow nationalism are heard on both sides of the ocean. We have a long and difficult way to go.

—The explosive *Middle East* continued in the twilight zone between peace and open conflict. The ceasefire arranged at our initiative lasted into its third year, but no genuine progress was made toward a permanent settlement. Some foreign military forces were withdrawn from the region, but the mix of local animosities and external power still makes the Middle East a most dangerous threat to world peace. Efforts to find political solutions are menaced by the upward spiral of terrorism and reprisal.

—For the *South Asian Subcontinent* it was a year of rebuilding and readjustment after the conflict in 1971. India, Pakistan, and the new nation of Bangladesh made tentative moves toward accommodation. But there is still a long road to the stability and reconciliation that are required if the massive human needs of one-fifth of mankind are to be met.

—In the *Western Hemisphere* the United States followed its deliberate policy of restraint, encouraging others to furnish concepts as well as resources for Hemispheric development. A healthy process of regional initiatives and self-definition is now underway, and the foundations have been established for a more mature partnership with our Latin American friends. The common task of redefining and imparting fresh purpose to our community, however, is far from completed.

—*Asia* has witnessed a settlement of the Vietnam war and major developments in relations among the principal powers. It is there that the Nixon Doctrine has been most extensively applied. There has been positive growth in self-help and regional cooperation. But these nations are entering a period of delicate readjustment and American steadiness will be crucial.

—In *Africa* our goals remained economic development, racial justice, and a stable peace resting on independent states. We continue to recognize, however, that these are largely the tasks of the African nations themselves—and there were both hopeful and discouraging events this past year. Our policies of political restraint and economic support are designed to help Africa realize its rich potential.

—We moved down the interrelated paths of *national security,* arms control, and a strong defense. The strategic arms limitation pacts with the Soviet Union were a milestone, but major tasks remain—the extension of limitations on strategic arms and then their reduction; the mutual and balanced reduction of conventional forces in Central Europe. In our defense posture we have maintained a clearly sufficient power, and we reached an all-volunteer army. But we are still searching for doctrines and deployments fully adequate to changing times and surging costs. Our fundamental principle remains keeping America strong enough to preserve our vital interests and promote the prospects of peace.

—We paid increasing attention to *global issues* that more and more demand international solutions. Progress was encouraging in some areas, such as reducing the flow of drugs. The world community still refused to grapple effectively, however, with other issues such as terrorism. The global dimension of diplomacy has been developing unevenly.

Since last year's Report, there has been historic progress. A changed world has moved closer to a lasting peace. Many events were colorful, but their true drama is that they can herald a new epoch, not fade as fleeting episodes.

As in any year, however, there were disappointments as well as successes. And wherever there is progress, new challenges are added to an always unfinished agenda.

Shaping a peaceful world requires, first of all, an America that stays strong, an America that stays involved.

But the United States alone cannot realize this goal. Our friends and adversaries alike must share in the enterprise of peace.

The President and the Administration alone cannot pursue this goal. We need the cooperation of the Congress and the support of the American people.

It is to these audiences at home and abroad that this Report is addressed.

CONCLUSION

In the past four years, there have been fundamental changes and signal successes. We have cleared away vestiges of the past. We have erased or moderated hostilities. And we are strengthening partnerships.

The specific events or policies, however important, reflect a more profound enterprise. We are seeking the philosophical, as well as the practical, reorientation of our foreign policy. This is the primary challenge of a radically different world. If America is to provide the leadership that only it can, Americans must identify with new visions and purposes.

As we look toward this nation's two hundredth birthday, we shall continue our efforts—with the people and the Congress—to create this new consensus.

In the transition from the bipolar world of American predominance to the multipolar world of shared responsibilities, certain themes need emphasis. They indicate not only what our approach is, but what it is not.

We seek a stable structure, not a classical balance of power. Undeniably, national security must rest upon a certain equilibrium between potential adversaries. The United States cannot entrust its destiny entirely, or even largely, to the goodwill of others. Neither can we expect other countries so to mortgage their future. Solid security involves external restraints on potential opponents as well as self-restraint.

Thus a certain balance of power is inherent in any international system and has its place in the one we envision. But it is not the over-riding concept of our foreign policy. First of all, our approach reflects the realities of the nuclear age. The classical concept of balance of power included continual maneuvering for marginal advantages over others. In the nuclear era this is both unrealistic and dangerous. It is unrealistic because when both sides possess such enormous power, small additional increments cannot be translated into tangible advantage or even usable political strength. And it is dangerous because attempts to seek tactical gains might lead to confrontation which could be catastrophic.

Secondly, our approach includes the element of consensus. All nations, adversaries and friends alike, must have a stake in preserving the international system. They must feel that their principles are being respected and their national interests secured. They must, in short, see positive incentive for keeping the peace, not just the dangers of breaking it. If countries believe global arrangements threaten their vital concern, they will challenge them. If the international environment meets their vital concerns, they will work to maintain it. Peace requires mutual accommodation as well as mutual restraint.

Negotiation with adversaries does not alter our more fundamental ties with friends. We have made a concerted effort to move from confrontation to negotiation. We have done well. At the same time, our determination to reduce divisions has not eroded distinctions between friends and adversaries. Our alliances remain the cornerstones of our foreign policy. They reflect shared values and purposes. They involve major economic interests. They provide the secure foundation on which to base negotiations.

Although their forms must be adapted to new conditions, these ties are enduring. We have no intention of sacrificing them in efforts to engage adversaries in the shaping of peace. Indeed such efforts cannot succeed, nor can they have lasting meaning, without the bonds of traditional friendships. There is no higher objective than the strengthening of our partnerships.

Detente does not mean the end of danger. Improvements in both the tone and substance of our relations have indeed reduced tensions and heightened the prospects for peace. But these processes are not automatic or easy. They require vigilance and firmness and exertion. Nothing would be more dangerous than to assume prematurely that dangers have disappeared.

Thus we maintain strong military power even as we seek mutual limitation and reduction of arms. We do not mistake climate for substance. We base our policies on the actions and capabilities of others, not just on estimates of their intentions.

Detente is not the same as lasting peace. And peace does not guarantee tranquility or mean the end of contention. The world will hold perils for as far ahead as we can see.

We intend to share responsibilities, not abdicate them. We have emphasized the need for other countries to take on more responsibilities for their security and development. The tangible result has often been a reduction in our overseas presence or our share of contributions. But our purpose is to continue our commitment to the world in ways we can sustain, not to camouflage a retreat. We took these steps only when our friends were prepared for them. They have been successfully carried out because American backing remained steady. They have helped to maintain support in this country for a responsible foreign policy.

I underlined the vital importance of the redefined American role two years ago:

"Our participation remains crucial. Because of the abundance of our resources and the stretch of our technology, America's impact on the world remains enormous, whether by our action or by our inaction. Our awareness of the world is too keen, and our concern for peace too deep, for us to remove the measure of stability which we have provided for the past 25 years."

Measured against the challenges we faced and the goals we set, we can take satisfaction in the record of the past four years. Our progress has been more marked in reducing tensions than in restructuring partnerships. We have negotiated an end to a war and made future wars less likely by improving relations with major adversaries. Our bonds with old friends have proved durable during these years of profound change. But we are still searching for more balanced relationships. This will be our most immediate concern, even as we pursue our other goals.

Where peace is newly planted, we shall work to make it thrive.

Where bridges have been built, we shall work to make them stronger.

Where friendships have endured, we shall work to make them grow.

During the next four years—with the help of others—we shall continue building an international structure which could silence the sounds of war for the remainder of this century.

SURRENDER AT WOUNDED KNEE

May 8, 1973

More than 100 last-ditch supporters of the American Indian Movement (AIM) surrendered their arms to federal marshals May 8, ending a 70-day occupation of the South Dakota hamlet of Wounded Knee. The Indian capitulation followed the signing of a final agreement May 5 after countless meetings between AIM representatives and federal officials. A previous agreement had collapsed in early April, but assurances from Leonard Garment, counsel to President Nixon, paved the way to a new accord. In a letter to government spokesmen at Wounded Knee, Garment reaffirmed an earlier pledge that at least five White House representatives would meet with the Oglala Sioux elders on their reservation the third week in May. The AIM supporters accepted the gesture and signed the pact.

More than 300 Indians had seized the South Dakota reservation town on Feb. 27, proclaiming demands running from action on ancient grievances to requests for new congressional action. Seizing 11 residents as hostages, the Indians took control of the community and barricaded themselves inside a hilltop church. They vowed to hold out until their demands were met. During the next two and one-half months, two Indians died from wounds sustained in gunfights with federal officials blockading the town, and one of the marshals, hit by a bullet, was paralyzed. Numerous other people were injured; estimates of material damage topped $240,000.

War paint, circling U.S. Air Force Phantom "reconnaissance" planes, "demilitarized zones," television crews, and dramatic cries such as "Massacre us or meet our human demands," gave the bizarre episode an air of self-conscious staging. Even the site seemed to reflect studied parallelism to the massacre by the 7th Cavalry of nearly 200 of Big Foot's Sioux on Dec. 29, 1890. AIM leader Russell Means had given major newspapers and the television networks advance notification that something important would occur at Wounded Knee on Feb. 27. Later, events were occasionally staged and re-staged for the benefit of camera crews. Means was succinct: "We want to see headlines that say 'U.S. surrenders to Indians.'"

If some people considered the Indians' tactics extreme, still others thought the government overreacted. War planes were sent to fly over the occupied village; state, local and federal patrols, outnumbering the Indians, encircled the town and set up roadblocks on roads leading into Wounded Knee. Government officials with field glasses watched movements within the occupied hamlet. "Cease-fire observers" monitored exchanges of gunfire.

AIM demands were varied. Representatives said they wanted to focus public attention on "the trail of broken treaties." AIM spokesman Carter Camp declared, "We're ready to stay and ready to die." The Indians demanded that the federal government remove from office the Pine Ridge Indian Reservation administration headed by Richard Wilson. Even though Wilson had been elected by the Indians themselves to govern the reservation in which Wounded Knee was situated, AIM supporters denounced his government as corrupt and dictatorial. They insisted that he extended federal assistance only to his friends and supporters. Besides seeking the overthrow of Wilson, AIM leaders demanded that Sen. Edward M. Kennedy (D Mass.) launch a full-scale Senate investigation into the government's treatment of all Indians, particularly the South Dakota Sioux. They wanted Senate Foreign Relations Committee Chairman J. William Fulbright (D Ark.) to look into the breaking of 371 treaties with the Indians.

The government countered by setting a deadline of 6 p.m. March 8 for evacuation of Wounded Knee. Federal officials rejected outright the demand to oust Wilson. Similarily, they dropped a previous offer of safe passage out of the village. As the deadline approached, no one seemed willing to bend. Finally, an hour before a threatened confrontation, Dennis Banks, an Indian leader, raced his Cadillac into the Wounded Knee occupation camp and announced to the painted warriors that both sides had agreed to a cease-fire proposed by the National Council of Churches of Christ. Subsequent negotiations between the government and the Indians were repeatedly interrupted. Meetings dragged through weeks with agreement continually eluding the two sides. Finally, Garment's letter, confirming White House recognition of the trouble, set in motion the final stages toward agreement. The surrender of arms actually was carried out a day earlier than the agreement specified.

In a Louis Harris survey of 1,472 households in mid-March, 51 per cent of those responding expressed sympathy for the Indians as opposed to the government. Asked their opinion of how American Indians had been treated in this country, 60 per cent said the treatment had been poor, 15 per cent only fair, 12 per cent pretty good, and 3 per cent excellent.

The Wounded Knee occupation resulted in indictments for many of the militant Indians. Although more than one-half of those who originally seized the hamlet left during a truce or disappeared under the cover of darkness, indictments exceeded 50. Russell Means, the chief AIM spokesman, was indicted May 2 along with four others on charges of conspiring to transport arms to Wounded Knee illegally and to cross state lines with intent to incite a riot.

Text of the agreement signed May 5 by federal officials and representatives of the American Indian Movement (AIM) to end the 70-day siege of **Wounded Knee,** *South Dakota:*

AGREEMENT

To effect the May 1973 meetings between White House representatives and headmen and chiefs of the Teton Sioux contemplated in the April 5, 1973 Agreement between the parties, it is agreed that both the dispossession of arms of the occupants of Wounded Knee and the end of the armed occupation of Wounded Knee will be accomplished in the following manner:

1. The details of this Agreement will be implemented starting at 7:00 A.M., Wednesday, May 9, 1973, and will proceed with expedition until the armed confrontation at Wounded Knee is ended.

2. At 7:00 A.M. the Government will remove all its APC's [armored personnel carriers] from the Wounded Knee perimeter and put one chief or headman in each Government bunker, and the occupants of Wounded Knee will, simultaneously, evacuate all their bunkers, roadblocks, other fortifications, and buildings and assemble at the Tipi Chapel.

3. Upon assembly, all weapons, ammunition, explosives, and explosive devices will be turned over to C.R.S. [Community Relations Service] by the occupants of Wounded Knee. C.R.S. will transport the weaponry to the old tipi site for examination by Government officials. Those weapons which are both legal, and tagged in a manner identifying the owners, will be returned to the owners

within 24 hours. All illegal weapons and untagged weapons will be seized. A list of all weapons shall be delivered through C.R.S. to the Government by 5:00 P.M., Sunday, May 6, 1973, so that the weapons turned over to the Government on May 9, 1973 can be checked against the May 6, 1973 list. 19 CRS personnel to be in Wounded Knee Tuesday and Wednesday.

4. After C.R.S. has turned all weapons over to Government officials at the old tipi site, the processing of the occupants of Wounded Knee will begin. C.R.S. will monitor the processing. The occupants of Wounded Knee will divide themselves into three groups:

    a. Those with outstanding arrest warrants against them;

    b. Resident occupants of Wounded Knee who resided there prior to February 26, 1973; and

    c. All others.

The occupants comprising each of these three groups will identify themselves with the aid of the agreed-upon form filled out in advance. These forms will be delivered by C.R.S. to Government officials by 5:00 P.M., Sunday, May 6, 1973.

5. The occupant group with outstanding warrants against them will proceed first to the old tipi site for processing. The Government will provide transportation to the old tipi site from the Tipi Chapel area.

6. When the warranted occupants have been processed, the resident occupant group whose presence in Wounded Knee predates February 26, 1973 will be processed in like manner.

7. Finally, the "all other" group will be processed in like manner.

8. Processing will be accomplished pursuant to the terms of paragraphs 2(a) and 2(b) of the April 5, 1973 Agreement. There may be a dozen or so people subject to arrest despite the absence of an outstanding arrest warrant. These people will be processed pursuant to Paragraph 2(a) of the April 5, 1973 Agreement.

9. After those occupants who have been arrested are en route to Rapid City, and the "all other" group is en route from the Pine Ridge reservation, the permanent residents of Wounded Knee will be escorted to their homes by Government officials pursuant to Paragraph 2(c) of the April 5, 1973 Agreement. The searches set forth in Paragraph 2(c) of the April 5, 1973 Agreement will then take place.

10. When the procedures required by Paragraph 9 above have been completed and the Government is satisfied that Wounded Knee is safe for occupancy, the following will take place:

a. Government bunkers will be evacuated and covered over;

b. Wounded Knee bunkers will be covered over by Government officials;

c. Government roadblocks will be eliminated;

d. A residual force of Marshals and other Government people will be established pursuant to Paragraph 2(d) of the April 5, 1973 Agreement. It is contemplated that the presence of a portion of this force will be required in Wounded Knee for a period of time subsequent to the end of the confrontation. Paragraph 2(f) of the April 5, 1973 Agreement will become operative.

11. The Government renews its commitment to perform on its obligations set forth in Paragraphs 3, 4 and 5 of the April 5, 1973 Agreement.

Signed:

Wayne B. Colburn
Director,
U.S. Marshals Service,
for the United States
Government

Kent Frizzell
Solicitor
U.S. Department of Interior,
for the United States
Government

Richard R. Hellstern
Dep. Asst. Attorney
General, U.S. Department
of Justice, for the United
States Government

And for the Oglala Sioux Residents and the American Indian Movement:

Frank Kills Enemy
Issaac Brave Eagle
Frank Fools Crow
Eugene White Hawk

Gladys Bissonette
Roger Iron Cloud...

and others

Dated: May 5, 1973

▼▼▼

PENTAGON PAPERS TRIAL

May 11, 1973

Publication by The New York Times *of a secret government study on the Vietnam War engulfed the government and the press in a battle over the extent of the people's right to know. Beginning June 13, 1971, the* Times *printed daily installments of a series of documents from a Pentagon study of policy decisions that had drawn the United States into military involvement in Indochina. The Justice Department on June 16, 1971, obtained a court injunction temporarily halting publication, but the Supreme Court ruled June 30 that publication could be resumed. The government subsequently brought various charges, including espionage and theft, against Dr. Daniel Ellsberg and Anthony J. Russo Jr. The two men were accused of taking the documents from files of the Rand Corporation in Santa Monica, Calif., where they had worked, and forwarding copies of parts of the study to the* Times *and other newspapers. The trial in Los Angeles of Ellsberg and Russo was expected to help define some of the complex constitutional questions raised by the case, but it was caught up in an unraveling web of government espionage and sabotage and came to an abrupt end on May 11, 1973.*

All charges against Ellsberg and Russo were dismissed by presiding U.S. District Judge W. Matthew Byrne Jr. Byrne read a statement which effectively precluded a retrial. He cited government misconduct as the main reason for his ruling. The decision followed the sensational disclosure that several of the convicted Watergate conspirators, with help from the Central Intelligence Agency (CIA), had participated in a burglary of the office of Ellsberg's psychiatrist in Los Angeles late in August 1971. E. Howard Hunt Jr. admitted to the Watergate grand jury in Washington, May 2, 1973, that he and G. Gordon Liddy had headed the operation on orders that he thought came from President Nixon. He said the orders had been relayed through former presidential assistant John D. Ehrlichman. The burglary was carried out by three Miami residents, two of whom were among the men apprehended in the Democratic National Committee headquarters at the Watergate complex June 17, 1972. Furthermore, it was disclosed that the government had used FBI wiretaps to pick up conversations held by Ellsberg in 1969 and 1970, but the FBI could not locate the records of the wiretaps.

Byrne declared in dismissing the case that it was perhaps impossible to determine the extent to which the rights of the defendants had been compromised by the government's actions, or the degree to which the government's case had been based on information obtained through the wiretaps. "The conduct of the government has placed the case in such a posture that it precludes the fair, dispassionate resolution of these issues by the jury." These actions, "shielded so long from public view," he said, "offend 'a sense of justice.'"

Background of the Case

The break-in at the office of the psychiatrist had come about as a result of an investigation ordered by the President into the "emotional and private" life of the defendant. The order was part of a broader directive to investigate news leaks that the President felt had jeopardized national security. CIA psychiatrists who had compiled a "personality" profile of Ellsberg for the White House later testified that it was the first such profile of an American citizen ever compiled by the CIA. CIA Director James R. Schlesinger admitted to a Senate subcommittee May 9 that the agency had been "insufficiently cautious" in providing materials to Hunt for the break-in at the psychiatrist's office.

In response to questions posed by Ellsberg's and Russo's attorneys, it was learned that Ehrlichman had offered Judge Byrne the post of director of the FBI at a meeting in April 1973 at the President's home in San Clemente, Calif. Nixon had walked in to greet Byrne at the conclusion of the session. The judge's reaction: "I could not and would not give consideration to any other position until this case is concluded." The defense attorneys accordingly asked for a dismissal of the case, stating, in part, "...we would, were we to use blunt language, characterize this as an attempt to offer a bribe to the court."

The dismissal of the case May 11 did not vindicate the defendants, nor did it contribute to resolution of the constitutional questions that had been raised. Rather, it chastised the government. The judge offered the defense two options: to dismiss the case, or to submit it to a jury. In the latter instance, some of the counts against the pair would have been dropped. Ellsberg, Russo and their attorneys elected dismissal.

Ellsberg's attorneys had argued that he and Russo made copies of the Pentagon study with the intention of giving them to Congress. They had hoped that pressure might thus be brought to bear on the administration to end the war. When Congress had not responded, the Pentagon Papers were taken to The New York Times. The defense reasoned that it had been necessary to break certain regulations pertaining to the "top secret" material in order to accomplish a greater good.

When the Times began publication of the secret study, the Justice Department, the White House and the Pentagon immediately protested. The concern of the Pentagon focused on the relation of the Pentagon Papers to national security. Although the study covered a period that ended in 1968, the Pentagon alerted the Justice Department to "this violation of security." After the June 30, 1971, ruling by the Supreme Court, many sections of the 40-volume study became part of the public record. Paperback versions were sold.

The government's attempt to halt publication was unique inasmuch as it amounted to prior censorship of the press. The charges of espionage leveled against Ellsberg and Russo were similarly unique because all agreed that Ellsberg had not been in collusion with a foreign government. Ellsberg himself said he believed the American public was entitled to know what prompted government decisions.

In the aftermath of the Byrne ruling, Ellsberg vowed to press charges against the government for invasion of privacy. Ironically, just an hour after the decision was made final, the FBI located the missing files on the wiretaps implicating Ellsberg. They had been cached in a safe in Ehrlichman's outer office at the White House.

Text of Judge Byrne's ruling in Ellsberg-Russo case, May 11, 1973:

This ruling is based upon the motion in that scope that Mr. (Leonard) Boudin has just stated. It is not based solely on the wiretap, nor is it based solely on the break-in and the information that has been presented over the last several days.

Commencing on April 26, the Government has made an extraordinary series of disclosures regarding the conduct of several governmental agencies regarding the defendants in this case. It is my responsibility to assess the effect of this conduct upon the rights of the defendants. My responsibility relates solely and only to this case, to

539

the rights of the defendants and their opportunities for a fair trial with due process of law.

As the record makes clear, I have attempted to require the government and to allow the defendants to develop all relevant information regarding these highly unusual disclosures. Much information has been developed, but new information has produced new questions, and there remain more questions than answers.

The disclosures made by the government demonstrate that governmental agencies have taken an unprecedented series of actions with respect to these defendants. After the original indictment, at a time when the government's rights to investigate the defendants are narrowly circumscribed, White House officials established a special unit to investigate one of the defendants in this case. The special unit apparently operated with the approval of the FBI, the agency officially charged with the investigation of this case.

We may have been given only a glimpse of what this special unit did regarding this case, but what we know is more than disquieting. The special unit came to Los Angeles and surveyed the vicinity of the offices of the psychiatrist of one of the defendants. After reporting to a White House assistant and apparently receiving specific authorization, the special unit then planned and executed the break-in of the psychiatrist's office in search of the records of one of the defendants.

From the information received, including the last document filed today, it is difficult to determine what, if anything, was obtained from the psychiatrist's office by way of photographs.

The Central Intelligence Agency, presumably acting beyond its statutory authority, and at the request of the White House, had provided disguises, photographic equipment and other paraphernalia for covert operations.

The government's disclosure also revealed that the special unit requested and obtained from the CIA two psychological profiles of one of the defendants.

Of more serious consequences is that the defendants and the court do not know the other activities in which the special unit may have been engaged and what has happened to the results of these endeavors. They do not know whether other material gathered by the special unit was destroyed, and though I have inquired of the government several times in this regard, no answer has been forthcoming....

These recent events compound the record already pervaded by incidents threatening the defendants' right to a speedy and fair trial. The government has time and again failed to make timely productions of exculpatory information in its possession requiring delays and disruptions in the trial.

Within the last forty-eight hours, after both sides had rested their case, the government revealed interception by electronic surveillance of one or more conversations of defendant Ellsberg. The government can only state and does only state that the interception or interceptions took place.

Indeed, the government frankly admits that it does not know how many such interceptions took place or when they took place or between whom they occurred or what was said. We only know that the conversation was overheard during a period of the conspiracy as charged in the indictment.

Of greatest significance is the fact that the government does not know what has happened to the authorizations for the surveillance, nor what has happened to the tapes nor to the logs nor any other records pertaining to the overheard conversations. This lack of records appears to be present not only in the Justice Department, but in the Federal Bureau of Investigation, from the response forwarded by Mr. Petersen yesterday that the records of both the FBI and the Justice Department appear to have been missing.

The matter is somewhat compounded also by the fact that the documents had been missing since the period of July to October of 1971.

The FBI reports that, while the files did once exist regarding this surveillance, they now apparently have been removed from both the Justice Department and the FBI. As I state it, it is reported by the FBI that the records have been missing since mid-1971.

There is no way the defendants or the court or, indeed, the government itself can test what effect these interceptions may have had on the government's case here against either or both of the defendants. A continuation of the government's investigation is no solution with reference to this case. The delays already encountered threaten to compromise the defendants' rights, and it is the defendants' rights and the effect on this case that is paramount, and each passing day indicates that the investigation is further from completion as the jury waits.

Moreover, no investigation is likely to provide satisfactory answers where improper government conduct has been shielded so long from public view and where the government advises the court that pertinent files and records are missing or destroyed.

My duties and obligations relate to this case and what must be done to protect the right to a fair trial.

The charges against these defendants raise serious factual and legal issues that I would certainly prefer to have litigated to completion.... However, while I would prefer to have them litigated, the conduct of the government has placed the case in such a posture that it precludes the fair dispassionate resolution of these issues by a jury.

In considering the alternatives before me, I have carefully weighed the granting of a mistrial, without taking any further action. The defendants have opposed such a course of action, asserting their rights, if the case is to proceed, to have the matter tried before this jury. I have concluded that a mistrial alone would not be fair.

Under all the circumstances, I believe that the defendants should not have to run the risk, present under existing authorities, that they might be tried again before a different jury.

The totality of the circumstances of this case which I have only briefly sketched offend "a sense of justice." The bizarre events have incurably infected the prosecution of this case. I believe the authority to dismiss this case in these circumstances is fully supported by pertinent case authorities....

I have decided to declare a mistrial and grant the motion to dismiss.

I am of the opinion, in the present status of the case...that the only remedy available that would assure due process and the fair administration of justice is that this trial be terminated and the defendants' motion for dismissal be granted and the jury discharged.

The order of dismissal will be entered; the jurors will be advised of the dismissal, and the case is terminated.

Texts of two memorandums handed over to the U.S. District Court in Los Angeles by the Justice Department and made public May 8, 1973:

Memorandum for the record (1)
Subject: Summary of contacts by Mr. [Blank] with Mr. E. Howard Hunt.

1. On 4 December 1972 Mr. [Blank 1] was interviewed for the purpose of obtaining full details on his contacts with "Edward" and an associate during the summer months of 1971. Mr. [Blank 1] has now identified "Edward" as being E. Howard Hunt.

2. Mr. [Blank 1] advised that in the summer of 1971 he and his section chief were called into the office of the deputy division chief, who briefed them to the effect that a disguise, documentation and other support were to be provided to an individual identified as "Edward."

[Blank 1] met with "Edward" the following day and made all the necessary arrangements to immediately provide him with a disguise and alias documentation. "Edward" was observed signing his name to those items which required a signature, and he tried a mouth device that was utilized in connection with the operations.

3. Approximately two weeks later, "Edward" called to indicate that he needed some help with the disguises glasses. [Blank 1] is not sure of timing, but he recalls that Mr. [Blank 2] accompanied him to the meeting because [Blank 2] had been asked to provide "Edward" with a tape recorder. [Blank 2] showed "Edward" how the tape recorder worked, and then departed from the house without waiting for [Blank 1].

The latter individual made some adjustment to the glasses. And it was probably at this meeting that "Edward" inquired about a backstopped telephone number and address in New York. [Blank 1] indicated that he would have to check with his superiors. Mr. [Blank 1] is not absolutely certain, but it is his best recollection that "Edward" also requested a disguise and alias documentation for an associate.

4. At the next meeting, "Edward" was accompanied by an unknown associate, who expressed a requirement for a disguise, alias documentation and a camera. [Blank 1] immediately made all the necessary arrangements for this support, and the associate was appropriately briefed on the use of the camera.

"Edward" and his unknown friend talked about having to stop by the Pentagon before going to the airport, and it was indicated that further assistance would be required immediately upon their return from the trip. "Edward" did not indicate where he was going, but he left the impression that it had something to do with the investigation of drugs.

5. In what was assumed to be a long-distance telephone call, Mr. [Blank 1] was contacted at his home in less than three weeks. At this time "Edward" asked that he be met at Dulles Airport at about 6:00 A.M. the following day. Mr. [Blank 1] met "Edward" and his associate at Dulles Airport early the following morning, when he was given some film and asked to have it developed later in the afternoon. Mr. [Blank 1] is certain that the pictures were developed and delivered to "Edward" in accordance with his priority request.

It was also at about this time that Mr. [Blank 1] was informed by his supervisor that additional operational support was to be curtailed because "Edward's" requests were beyond what was authorized. In this last meeting with "Edward," [Blank 1] delivered the photographs and indicated that additional operational support would not be forthcoming without specific authorization. However, "Edward" was obviously in a hurry, apparently having some type of appointment, and the meeting lasted less than 10 minutes.

6. Mr. [Blank 1] stated that he cannot be sure, but he estimates that he met with "Edward" on about five different occasions. In response to inquiry, Mr. [Blank 1] advised that he is now reasonably certain that "Edward" is E. Howard Hunt, based upon 1972 publicity relating to the Watergate incident. With respect to the second individual, "Edward's" associate, Mr. [Blank 1] stated that he was a "similar type" to Gordon Liddy. Mr. [Blank 1] does not recall the use of the name "Tom," and it is his best recollection that the second individual used the name "George."

Memorandum for the record (2)
Subject: Summary of Mr. [Blank] knowledge of C.I.A. assistance to Mr.
  E. Howard Hunt.

1. On 22 July 1971, Mr. E. Howard Hunt, known to be working at the White House, visited General Cushman. He stressed that he had been authorized to conduct a very sensitive operation by the White House and that it should be held as a very secret matter. Mr. Hunt stated that he had a requirement to elicit information and in order

to accomplish this he would like some false alias documentation and physical disguise. General Cushman responded that he would look into it and get in touch with Mr. Hunt at his White House office.

2. Pursuant to General Cushman's instructions, Mr. Hunt was met by technical personnel on 23 July and provided with a set of alias documents and a disguise (wig, glasses, and a speech alteration device).

3. Thereafter, Mr. Hunt requested certain additional support; on 20 August, Mr. Hunt was given a recorder and business cards. He arranged for an associate to be documented and disguised. He asked for a backstopped address and phone in New York, but they were not provided.

4. Mr. Hunt was later given a concealed camera. On 26 August Mr. Hunt telephoned a C.I.A. officer and asked to be met at the airport to pick up and develop certain film. This was done, and Mr. Hunt was met later in the day when the developed film was returned.

5. On 27 August Mr. [Blank] instructed the technical personnel to withhold further assistance to Mr. Hunt because his requests had gone beyond the original understandings. Furthermore, they appeared to involve the agency in domestic clandestine operation. Mr. [Blank] immediately reported these facts to General Cushman and sought guidance. General Cushman called the appropriate individual in the White House with these concerns and explained that the agency could not meet the kinds of requests Mr. Hunt was levying. The White House official stated he would restrain Mr. Hunt. Since 27 August, 1971, neither General Cushman nor Mr. [Blank] had any further contact with Mr. Hunt on this subject.

Texts of three documents made public by Judge Byrne, May 10, 1973: (1) a memorandum of Acting FBI Director William D. Ruckelshaus on electronic surveillance of Daniel Ellsberg; (2) an FBI report on interview with former White House counsel Charles W. Colson; and (3) a CIA report on dealings with Liddy and Hunt:

RUCKELSHAUS MEMO

Attached hereto is a brief memorandum concerning the ongoing investigation of alleged wiretaps possibly relevant to the Ellsberg case. My recommendation is that this memorandum be immediately filed with the court.

May 9, 1973
Preliminary Report Concerning Ongoing Investigation
of Possible Wiretaps of Newsmen and Others

Shortly after assuming office as Acting Director of the F.B.I., my attention was called to the newspaper allegation that F.B.I. personnel had been wiretapping unidentified newsmen. I was also informed that a search of the F.B.I. records had not disclosed the existence of any such wiretaps. Nevertheless, on May 4, 1973, I initiated an investigation to interview present and retired F.B.I. personnel for the purpose of determining, if possible, whether there had been any such taps.

A preliminary report which I received last night indicates that an F.B.I. employee recalls that in late 1969 and early 1970 Mr. Ellsberg had been overheard talking from an electronic surveillance of Dr. Morton Halperin's residence. It is this employee's recollection that the surveillance was of Dr. Halperin, and that Mr. Ellsberg was then a guest of Dr. Halperin.

I have no information concerning the substance of the conversation, nor has the investigation to date been able to find any record of such a conversation. The investigation, of course, is not complete, and further facts bearing upon the wiretaps may be uncovered.

Nevertheless, in view of the court's expressed desire for prompt information relating to this matter, I am at this time giving you this preliminary report which may be relevant to the trial now in progress.

COLSON INTERVIEW

Charles W. Colson, former special counsel to the President, was interviewed in the presence of his attorneys, David Shapiro and Judah Best, in their offices at 1735 New York Avenue, N.W., Washington, D.C.

Mr. Colson was advised he was being contacted at the request of the Department of Justice to determine if he could furnish information about an investigation conducted on behalf of the White House into the public disclosures of the Pentagon papers and specifically for information he may have about an alleged burglary of the office of Daniel Ellsberg's psychiatrist by E. Howard Hunt and G. Gordon Liddy during the course of that investigation.

Mr. Colson voluntarily signed a waiver of rights (FD 395) and advised as follows:

Mr. Colson recalled attending meetings in early July, 1971, at the White House concerning the disclosures of the Pentagon papers and described those meetings as "kind of panic sessions" to determine what was going on and trying to establish what was going to be published next by the newspapers and the accuracy of these publications.

Mr. Colson indicated he was not involved in the White House investigation into the Pentagon papers disclosures but was engaged in the Government's litigation to stop publication of the papers. He was engaged on an almost full-time basis at this time with the preparation of the President's Aug. 15 economics decision initiating Phase I of the price freeze.

When the Pentagon papers were first published in *The New York Times*, there was a need in the White House for someone to do research and coordinate assignments involving investigation into the leak.

Colson recalled he recommended Hunt, whom he had known for a period of years, and several other individuals for this assignment. Hunt was subsequently interviewed by John D. Ehrlichman, former assistant to the President.

Later, Mr. Colson received a telephone call from Mr. Ehrlichman, who was then in California with the President, asking whether Hunt could be brought in and directing that he should be put to work on the investigation.

Mr. Colson asked his staff secretary to process the necessary papers regarding the employment. Hunt was assigned to Colson's staff for internal budget processing only.

Mr. Colson knew that the "plumbers" [publicly identified as Egil Krogh Jr., David Young, Hunt and Liddy] were conducting a check for a personality profile of Daniel Ellsberg to determine what motivated him, what kind of "wild things" he might do. Mr. Colson said there was an enormous concern over leaks of sensitive information at the time.

No Advance Information

Mr. Colson had no discussion or advance information of the alleged burglary. He knew the plumbers were going to the West Coast but did not know which of them would actually make the trip.

He first heard about the alleged burglary sometime later at a meeting, and he could not recall the time of the meeting or who was present. He thought the meeting may have been a private one with Mr. Ehrlichman.

He believes Mr. Ehrlichman told him, he does not recall specifically, but he gained the impression from the conversation that "they" tried to get the records of Ellsberg's psychiatrist and did not get them. Ehrlichman told him this was a national security matter and not to be discussed with anyone. Mr. Colson never had any discussion of a burglary attempt on the home of Ellsberg's psychiatrist.

Mr. Colson was asked if he had any other discussions with White House staff members about the burglary. He recalled in connection with the Watergate investigation prior to the time when he was questioned by the Federal Bureau of Investigation and gave a deposition to Mr. Silbert of the United States Attorney's office. He asked John Dean, counsel to the President, what to do if the Pentagon papers question came up.

Dean told him that if asked he was not to discuss the matter, inasmuch as it was a national security matter of the highest classification, and that he [Dean] would interrupt such questions if present. He recalled receiving the same instructions from Mr. Ehrlichman in late March or April, 1973. He never discussed the burglary with Hunt or Liddy.

A Chance Meeting

Concerning a current newspaper story that Hunt reportedly tried to talk to Mr. Colson sometime later about the burglary, Colson recalled a chance meeting with Hunt one morning in his outer office. Hunt was waiting for him, but Mr. Colson could not recall when the meeting took place.

Hunt told him he was on his way to give a briefing on what "they" had learned about Ellsberg, and that he had about a half an hour before the briefing, and he wanted to talk to Colson about it. Colson told Hunt he did not have time to talk to him then, that he was in a hurry. Hunt did not try to broach the subject matter again.

Concerning the memorandum from Colson to Jon Huntsman dated Sept. 13, 1971, requesting in accordance with an earlier arrangement the reimbursement of Hunt for the following expenses: Air fares for two men from New York City to Washington, D.C., $63; dinner check, Miami—$35.85; hotel bill for three men, Los Angeles—$156.90, Colson advised as follows:

Colson furnished a copy of this memorandum from his own office files to the Federal Bureau of Investigation in the summer of 1972 when he was asked about Hunt's travel. This was the first occasion on which he had seen the memorandum, and he did not know to what the entries on the memorandum related or the identity of the three men referred to in the memo.

Colson never saw any of Hunt's vouchers or claims for reimbursement. These were initialed and submitted by Colson's secretary.

Concerning a recent newspaper story according to which Egil Krogh reportedly said he requested funds from Colson for implementing the effort to acquire information about Ellsberg, Colson could not recall Krogh asking him for money for the trip to California.

He has a vague recollection that at about that time Mr. Ehrlichman spoke to him about getting some funds, maybe for Krogh, but when he checked with Mr. Ehrlichman later, Ehrlichman could not recall the request.

From time to time Colson saw memorandums prepared for the White House group working on the Pentagon papers investigation, but he saw no reports prepared by that group. The memoranda which were shown to him by Hunt because of Colson's general interest in the issue of the Pentagon papers spoke of Hunt's frustrations trying to get things done in the plumbers' unit and Hunt's analysis of the investigation.

Colson saw nothing related to the psychological study of Ellsberg. The normal channel for papers generated by the plumbers was to Egil Krogh and David Young. Colson had no information about the whereabouts or results of investigation conducted by that group.

Colson had no knowledge of other illegal activities engaged in by the group conducting the Pentagon papers investigation on behalf of the White House.

C.I.A. REPORT

Question: Did we have any other dealings with Liddy while he was in the Treasury or the White House?

Response: We did not have any prior dealings with George Gordon Liddy in an operational sense. Our records do reflect, however, that in December, 1969, security action was initiated to grant Liddy a number of agency special clearances in connection with his employment by the Department of the Treasury. At that time, Liddy was listed as a member of the Presidential task force reporting on narcotics, marijuana, and dangerous drugs.

In August, 1971, Mr. George Gordon Liddy was briefed on several additional sensitive programs in connection with his assignment to the White House staff. Memos prepared in August and September, 1971, indicate that Liddy was working with Mr. David R. Young to investigate leaks of classified information to the news media. Liddy was debriefed of these special clearances on 22 February 1972. In effect, Mr. Liddy held agency clearances because of his White House duties, but he was not utilized by C.I.A.

Question: More details are desired about the tape recorder and the miniature camera which apparently Hunt had secured from the agency sometime in August, 1971.

Answer: All the details about the tape recorder are contained in Item G. On 25 August 1971 Mr. Hunt was furnished with a commercial Tessina camera disguised in a tobacco pouch. At Mr. Hunt's request, an unidentified associate was also given support material and documents. These items were provided to him on the understanding that they were required in connection with his official duties.

The agency is not aware of the purpose for which these items were intended or used. The agency refused a request to assist actively by providing a backstopped address and phone contact. On 27 August 1971 Mr. Hunt, on arrival from California, returned the concealed Tessina camera as unsuitable for his use. He requested that a roll of undeveloped film be developed for him immediately. He was met later the same day and given the developed prints and film.

At this point, the agency determined that Mr. Hunt's requests for agency support had escalated to an unacceptable level, and no further agency contact with or assistance to Mr. Hunt of any sort occurred after August, 1971.

WATERGATE HEARINGS

May 17, 1973

Exactly 11 months after the arrest of five intruders at Democratic national headquarters on June 17, 1972, a special Senate committee opened hearings on the ever-growing Watergate scandal. Sen. Sam J. Ervin Jr. (D N.C.), chairman of the seven-member Select Committee on Presidential Campaign Activities, brought down the gavel May 17 to begin the first phase of a three-pronged investigation. Ervin announced that the Senate panel would first probe the planning and execution of the wiretapping and break-in and the alleged cover-up of the Watergate incident. Then, he said, the senators planned to explore allegations of broader campaign espionage and sabotage. In a final segment, they would look into alleged violations of campaign spending laws. The resolution creating the committee gave the panel until Feb. 28, 1974, to submit a final report.

As testimony began in front of television floodlights that emblazoned the pillars, chandeliers and marble walls of the caucus room of the Russell Senate Office Building, Ervin declared: "If the allegations that have been made in the wake of the Watergate affair are substantiated, there has been a very serious subversion of the integrity of the electoral process and the committee will be obliged to consider the manner in which such a subversion affects the continued existence of this nation as a representative democracy, and how, if we are to survive, such subversions are to be prevented in the future."

The committee's vice chairman, Sen. Howard H. Baker Jr. (R Tenn.), noted that the Senate hearings could accomplish what "neither a grand jury investigation nor a judicial proceeding is equipped to serve, and that is to develop the facts in full view of all of the people of America." It is the American people, Baker stressed, "who must decide, based on the evidence spread before them, what Watergate means and how we all should conduct our public business in the future." He added that "If one of the effects of Watergate is public disillusionment with partisan politics, if people are turned off and drop out of the political system, this will be the greatest Watergate casualty of all."

Witnesses testified in the room that had been the site of the famed Teapot Dome hearings of 1923 and of the McCarthy hearings in 1953 and 1954. Ervin described the Watergate inquiry as "the most important investigation ever entrusted to the Congress." In the first phase of the hearings, testimony was taken morning and afternoon on 37 days. Thirty-three witnesses, from campaign workers to high government officials, appeared before the committee. Varying accounts of the incidents surrounding the Watergate affair were heard from the convicted Watergate conspirators James W. McCord Jr. and Bernard L. Barker right up to the former top administration officials H. R. Haldeman, John D. Ehrlichman, John W. Dean III, former Attorney General John N. Mitchell and former Commerce Secretary Maurice H. Stans. When the committee recessed for six weeks on Aug. 8, the official transcript filled 7,573 pages.

> *Texts of statements by Chairman Sam J. Ervin Jr. (D N.C.) and Vice Chairman Howard H. Baker Jr. (R Tenn.) at opening of the special Senate committee's Watergate hearings, May 17, 1973:*

Senator Ervin:

Today the Select Committee on Presidential Campaign Activities begins hearings into the extent to which illegal, improper or unethical activities were involved in the 1972 presidential election campaign.

S. Res. 60 which established the Select Committee was adopted unanimously by the Senate on February 7, 1973. Under its provisions every member of the Senate joined in giving the Committee a broad mandate to investigate, as fully as possible, all the ramifications of the Watergate break-in which occurred on Saturday, June 17, 1972. Under the terms of the authorizing resolution, the Committee must complete its study and render its report on or before February 28, 1974. Of necessity, that report will reflect the considered judgement of the Committee on whatever new legislation is needed to help safeguard the electoral process through which the President of the United States is chosen.

We are beginning these hearings today in an atmosphere of the utmost gravity, the questions that have been raised in the wake of the June 17 break-in strike at the very undergirding of our democracy. If the many allegations made to this date are true, then the burglars who broke into the headquarters of the Democratic National Committee at the Watergate were in effect breaking into the home of every citizen of the United States. And if these allegations prove to be true, what they were seeking to steal was not the jewels, money or other property of American citizens, but something much more valuable—their most precious heritage, the right to vote in a free election. Since that day, a mood of incredulity has prevailed among our populace, and it is the constitutional duty of this Committee to act expeditiously to allay the fears being expressed by the citizenry, and to establish the factual bases upon which these fears have been founded.

The first phase of the Committee's investigation will probe the planning and execution of the wiretapping and break-in of the Democratic National Committee's headquarters at the Watergate complex, and the alleged cover-up that followed. Subsequent phases will focus on allegations of campaign espionage and subversion and allegations of extensive violations of campaign financing laws. The clear mandate of the unanimous Senate Resolution provides for a bipartisan investigation of every phase of political espionage and illegal fund raising. Thus it is clear that we have the full responsibility to recommend any remedial legislation necessary.

In pursuing its task, it is clear that the Committee will be dealing with the workings of the democratic process under which we operate in a nation that still is the last, best hope of mankind in his eternal struggle to govern himself decently and effectively.

We will be concerned with the integrity of a governmental system designed by men who understood the lessons of the past and who, accordingly, established a framework of separated governmental powers in order to prevent any one branch of the government from becoming dominant over the others. The founding fathers, having participated in the struggle against arbitrary power, comprehended some eternal truths respecting men and government. They knew that those who are entrusted with power are susceptible to the disease of tyrants, which George Washington rightly described as "love of power and the proneness to abuse it." For that reason, they realized that the power of public officers should be defined by laws which they, as well as the people, are obligated to obey, a truth enunciated by Daniel Webster when he said that "Whatever government is not a government of laws is a despotism, let it be called what it may."

To the end of ensuring a society governed by laws, these men embodied in our Constitution the enduring principles in which they so firmly believed, establishing a legislature to make all laws, an executive to carry them out, and a judicial system to interpret them. Recently, we have been faced with massive challenges to the historical framework created in 1787, with the most recent fears having been focused upon assertions by Administrations of both parties of executive power over the Congress—for example, in the impoundment of appropriated funds and the abuse of executive privilege. Those challenges, however, can and are being dealt with by the working of the system itself—i.e., through the enactment of powerful statutes by the Congress, and the rendering of decisions by the courts upholding the law-making power of the Congress.

Difficulty of Committee's Task

In dealing with the challenges posed by the multitudinous allegations arising out of the Watergate affair, however, the Select Committee has a task much more difficult and complex than dealing with intrusions of one branch of the government upon the powers of the others. It must probe into assertions that the very system itself has been subverted and its foundations shaken.

To safeguard the structural scheme of our governmental system, the founding fathers provided for an electoral process by which the elected officials of this nation should be chosen. The Constitution, later-adopted amendments, and more specifically, statutory law, provide that the electoral processes shall be conducted by the people; outside the confines of the formal branches of the government, and through a political process that must operate under the strictures of law and ethical guidelines, but independent of the overwhelming power of the government itself. Only then can we be sure that each election truly reflects the will of the people, and that the electoral process cannot be made to serve as the mere handmaiden of a particular administration in power.

If the allegations that have been made in the wake of the Watergate affair are substantiated, there has been a very serious subversion of the integrity of the electoral process, and the Committee will be obliged to consider the manner in which such a subversion affects the continued existence of this nation as a representative democracy, and how, if we are to survive, such subversions may be prevented in the future.

It has been asserted that the 1972 campaign was influenced by a wide variety of illegal or unethical activities, including the widespread wiretapping of the telephones, political headquarters, and even the residences of candidates and their campaign staffs and of members of the press; by the publication of forged documents designed to defame certain candidates or enhance others through fraudulent means; the infiltration and disruption of opponents' political organizations and gatherings; the raising and handling of campaign contributions through means designed to circumvent, either in letter or in spirit, the provisions of campaign disclosure acts; and even the acceptance of campaign contributions based upon promises of illegal interference in governmental processes on behalf of the contributors. Finally, and perhaps most disturbingly, it has been alleged that, following the Watergate break-in, there has been a massive attempt to cover up all the improper activities, extending even so far as to pay off potential witnesses and in particular, the seven defendants in the Watergate trial in exchange for their promise to remain silent—activities which, if true, represent interference in the integrity of the prosecutorial and judicial processes of this nation. Moreover, there has been evidence of the use of governmental instrumentalities in efforts to exercise political surveillance over candidates in the 1972 campaign.

Let me emphasize at the outset that our judicial process thus far has convicted only the seven persons accused of burglarizing and wiretapping the Democratic National Committee Headquarters at the Watergate complex on June 17. The hearings which we initiate today are not designed to intensify or reiterate unfounded accusations or to poison further the political climate of our nation. On the contrary, it is my conviction and that of the other Committee members that the accusations that have been leveled and the evidence of wrongdoing that has surfaced has cast a black cloud of distrust over our entire society. Our citizens do not know whom to believe, and many of them have concluded that all the processes of government have become so compromised that honest governance has been rendered impossible.

Need for Candid Investigation

We believe that the health, if not the survival of our social structure and of our form of government requires the most candid and public investigation of all the evidence and of all the accusations that have been leveled at any persons, at whatever level, who were engaged in the 1972 campaign. My colleagues on the Committee and I are determined to uncover all the relevant facts surrounding these matters, and to spare no one, whatever his station in life may be, in our efforts to accomplish that goal. At the same time, I want to emphasize that the purpose of these hearings is not prosecutorial or judicial, but rather investigative and informative.

No one is more cognizant than I of the separation of powers issues that hover over these hearings. The Committee is fully aware of the ongoing grand jury proceedings that are taking place in several areas of the country, and of the fact that criminal indictments have been returned already by one of these grand juries. Like all Americans, the members of this Committee are vitally interested in seeing that the judicial processes operate effectively and fairly, and without interference from any other branch of government. The investigation of this Select Committee was born of crisis, unabated as of this very time, the crisis of a mounting loss of confidence by American citizens in the integrity of our electoral process which is the bedrock of our democracy. The American people are looking to this Committee, as the representative of all the Congress, for enlightenment and guidance regarding the details of the allegations regarding the subversion of our electoral and political processes. As the elected representatives of the people, we would be derelict in our duty to them if we failed to pursue our mission expeditiously, fully, and with the utmost fairness. The aim of the Committee is to provide full and open public testimony in order that the nation can proceed toward the healing of the wounds that now afflict the body politic. It is that aim that we are here to pursue today, within the terms of the mandate imposed upon us by our colleagues and in full compliance with all applicable rules of law. The nation and history itself are watching us. We cannot fail our mission.

Senator Baker:

I believe there is no need for me to further emphasize the gravity of the matters that we begin to explore publicly here this morning. Suffice it to say, there are most serious charges and allegations made against individuals and against institutions. The very integrity of our political process has been called into question.

Commensurate with the gravity of the subject matter under review and the responsibilities of this Committee and the witnesses who come before it, we have a great burden to discharge and carry. This Committee is not a court, nor is it a jury. We do not sit to pass judgment on the guilt or innocence of anyone. The greatest service that this Committee can perform for the Senate, for the Congress, and for the people of this nation is to achieve a full discovery of all the facts that bear on the subject of this inquiry. This Committee was created by the Senate to do exactly that: to find as many of the facts, circumstances, and relationships as we could, to assemble those facts into a coherent and intelligible presentation, and to make recommendations to the Congress for any changes in statute law or the basic charter document of the United States that may seem indicated.

But this Committee can serve another quite important function that neither a grand jury investigation nor a judicial proceeding is equipped to serve, and that is to develop the facts in full view of all of the people of America. Although juries will eventually determine the guilt or the innocence of persons who have been and may be indicted for specific violations of the law, it is the American people who must be the final judge of Watergate. It is the American people who must decide, based on the evidence spread before them, what Watergate means about how we all should conduct our public business in the future.

When the resolution which created this Committee was being debated on the floor of the Senate in February of this year, I and other Republican Senators expressed concern that the inquiry might become a partisan effort by one party to exploit the temporary vulnerability of another. Other congressional inquiries in the past had been conducted by committees made up of equal numbers of members from each party. I offered an amendment to the resolution which would have given the Republican members equal representation on this Committee. That amendment did not pass. But any doubts that I might have had about the fairness and impartiality of this investigation have been swept away during the last few weeks. Virtually every action taken by this Committee since its inception has been taken with complete unanimity of purpose and procedure. The integrity and fairness of each member of this Committee and of its fine professional staff have been made manifest to me, and I know they will be made manifest to the American people during the course of this proceeding. This is not in any way a partisan undertaking, but, rather it is a bipartisan search for the unvarnished truth.

Strength of the Republic's Institutions

I would like to close, Mr. Chairman, with a few thoughts on the political process in this country. There has been a great deal of discussion across the country in recent weeks about the impact that Watergate might have on the President, the office of the Presidency, the Congress, on our ability to carry on relations with other countries, and so on. The Constitutional institutions of this republic are so strong and so resilient that I have never doubted for a moment their ability to function without interruption. On the contrary, it seems clear to me the very fact that we are now involved in the public process of cleaning our own house, before the eyes of the world, is a mark of the greatest strength. I do not believe that any other political system could endure the thoroughness and the ferocity of the various inquiries now underway within the branches of government and in our courageous, tenacious free press.

No mention is made in our Constitution of political parties. But the two-party system, in my judgment, is as integral and as important to our form of government as the three formal branches of the central government themselves. Millions of Americans participated actively, on one level or another, and with great enthusiasm, in the presidential election of 1972. This involvement in the political process by citizens across the land is essential to participatory democracy. If one of the effects of Watergate is public disillusionment with partisan politics, if people are turned off and drop out of the political system, this will be the greatest Watergate casualty of all. If, on the other hand, this national catharsis in which we are now engaged should result in a new and better way of doing political business, if Watergate produces changes in laws and campaign procedures, then Watergate may prove to be a great national opportunity to revitalize the political process and to involve even more Americans in the day-to-day work of our two great political parties. I am deeply encouraged by the fact that I find no evidence at this point in time to indicate that either the Democratic National Committee or the Republican National Committee played any role in whatever may have gone wrong in 1972. The hundreds of seasoned political professionals across this country, and the millions of people who devoted their time and energies to the campaign, should not feel implicated or let down by what has taken place.

With these thoughts in mind, I intend to pursue, as I know each member of this Committee intends to pursue, an objective and even-handed but thorough, complete, and energetic inquiry into the facts. We will inquire into every fact and follow every lead, unrestrained by any fear of where that lead might ultimately take us.

Thank you, Mr. Chairman.

BREZHNEV IN WEST GERMANY

May 18-22, 1973

Results of the thaw in East-West relations were demonstrated in West Germany in May when Soviet Communist Party General Secretary Leonid I. Brezhnev paid an historic visit to the Federal Republic's capital. During his five-day stay, Brezhnev conferred with West German Chancellor Willy Brandt, signed three treaties, and delivered a television speech to the German people. As the first Soviet leader to visit Bonn, Brezhnev was greeted cordially by the public.

The three agreements signed May 19 were aimed at increasing economic and technical cooperation and cultural exchanges. The first agreement was a 10-year accord that could greatly expand the mutual trade of the two countries. Its provisions laid the basis for exchanges of Russian raw materials and energy for German technology, skills and industrial plants. The pact was in line with talks the Soviet party chief had held with German industrialists in an attempt to gain their assistance in building a $1-billion steel plant at Kursk, an administrative center 400 miles southwest of Moscow. The site held special significance because the Russians had defeated a Nazi army there in a crucial battle in the summer of 1943.

The second agreement provided for appointment of a mixed commission to handle the technical and financial details of German-Soviet exchanges in art, music, sports, education, tourism, journalism and science. It also covered arrangements for increasing the opportunities in each country for the study of the language and literature of the other. The third agreement concerned landing rights for

German and Russian airlines, enabling West German Lufthansa planes to fly to Japan via Moscow and Soviet Aeroflot planes to land in West Germany. Each of the three accords recognized the right of West Germany to represent West Berlin with respect to the terms of the agreement.

Brezhnev and Brandt conferred on the means for further implementation of a 1970 Moscow-Bonn treaty of friendship and, in a joint declaration, they promised "strict adherence" to the 1971 four-power accord on Berlin. Both the friendship treaty and the four-power accord had gone into effect on June 3, 1972. (See Historic Documents, 1972, p. 467.) The latter agreement had recognized certain ties between the Federal Republic and West Berlin, including the right of West Germany to represent the western sector of the divided city in "international organizations" but not its right to govern West Berlin. The Brezhnev-Brandt joint declaration left noticeably unmenioned the question of whether West Germany might represent West Berlin when West and East Germany became members of the United Nations.

The declaration pledged the two leaders to support efforts to achieve agreement on the mutual reduction of military forces in Europe. Consideration of that question by representatives of the North Atlantic Treaty Organization (NATO) and the Warsaw Pact had begun May 14 in Vienna. Brezhnev and Brandt also vowed to work for the success of the European security conference talks in Helsinki.

When Brezhnev spoke to the German people on television, he emphasized the historic significance of his talks with Brandt, saying: "It was not easy for the Soviet people and hence its leaders to open this new page in our relations. Memories of the past war, the tremendous sacrifices and destruction which Hitler's aggression brought us, are still raw in the minds of millions of Soviet people." Deploring the fact that Europe "has more than once been the hotbed of aggressive wars that have brought tremendous destruction and the death of millions of people," Brezhnev declared: "We want a new continent in its place—a continent of peace, mutual trust and reciprocally advantageous cooperation among all countries." Toward the end of his 19-minute speech, the Soviet leader noted that "many burning and explosive problems" were "awaiting solution," but he concluded that "on the whole, one can perhaps say that our planet today is closer to durable, lasting peace than ever before."

> Text of English translation, distributed by the Soviet Embassy in Washington, of speech by Soviet Communist Party General Secretary Leonid I. Brezhnev on West German television, May 21, 1973, follows on next page:

My arrival here at the invitation of Federal Chancellor Willy Brandt and our talks—all this in itself indicates that relations between our countries are developing successfully.

My first direct talks with Chancellor Brandt were associated with a great event in the history of relations between our countries and—it is safe to say—in the political development of Europe. We first met in Moscow in 1970 in connection with the signing of the treaty between the Union of Soviet Socialist Republics and the Federal Republic of Germany. By signing the document containing a realistic recognition of the present situation in Europe and by undertaking solemnly not to use force or threat of force against each other, the Soviet Union and the Federal Republic of Germany embarked on a new path in their relations.

To be frank, it was not easy for the Soviet people and hence its leaders to open this new page in our relations. Memories of the past war, the tremendous sacrifices and destruction which Hitler's aggression brought us, are still raw in the minds of millions of Soviet people. We were able to step over the past in our relations with your country because we do not want it to recur.

With the socialist German state, our ally, the German Democratic Republic, the Soviet Union has been linked for a long time with bonds of close, sincere and selfless friendship.

We approach our relations with the Federal Republic of Germany also from a position of good will and peace. We are sincerely prepared for cooperation, which, as we are convinced, can be very beneficial to both sides and to universal security. We want a lasting peace and we think that the Federal Republic of Germany is also interested in peace and needs it.

We know that it was not simple for the government of Chancellor Brandt either to come over to this treaty. The cold war has a force of inertia and it takes certain efforts to overcome it. The more so since supporters of dangerous confrontation between the two worlds have not yet disappeared from the political scene.

Therefore people in the Soviet Union appreciate the realism, will and farsightedness displayed by the leaders of the Federal Republic of Germany, above all, Federal Chancellor Willy Brandt, in the struggle for the conclusion and entry into force of the treaties with the Soviet Union and the Polish People's Republic, which laid the beginning for new relations between your country and the European socialist states.

In this content, I should like to pay tribute to all supporters of good-neighborly relations between the FRG and the Soviet Union. Many of them who have passed through the battle with fascism spared no effort in the struggle for peace and friendship between our peoples. The Soviet Union highly appreciates their contribution to this noble cause.

Development of Soviet-West German Relations

Our meeting with Chancellor Brandt in Oreanda in the autumn of 1971 was an important landmark in the successful development of our relations along the lines of the Moscow treaty. In a quiet, businesslike atmosphere, free from the tyranny of diplomatic protocol, we had an opportunity to outline further prospects of development of relations between the Soviet Union and the Federal Republic as well as certain areas of possible cooperation between our countries on an international plane.

The plans made are now being carried into life. We can already say with certainty today that the development of peaceful and mutually beneficial relations of cooperation between the Soviet Union and the Federal Republic is not an abstract hypothesis and not a theoretical plan or an emotional wish, as it seemed not so long ago—but quite a real thing which exists and keeps growing in scope and strength.

It goes without saying that opportunities for the development of such relations between our countries are far from being exhausted. We are at the beginning of this process, our talks with Chancellor Brandt confirm that there is a good outlook for the future, specifically in the field of economic relations. Apart from the expansion of ordinary trade, there is an opportunity to conclude long-term deals on a large-scale, deals based on economic cooperation between our countries and aimed at carrying out important joint projects.

These are not short-term, time-serving deals of a more or less chance character. But they open the way to joint actions in major economic sectors and are designed to bring guaranteed benefit to both sides for many years to come. This means specifically an opportunity for a more rational organization of production and naturally guaranteed employment for the workers of your country. What is particularly important is that such cooperation helps lay a sound foundation for good-neighborly relations between our countries.

Both the Soviet Union and the Federal Republic of Germany are countries with a high level of development of science, technology and culture. Our scientists have a great deal to tell and to show to their colleagues. People in both our countries will be interested, I am sure, to see and listen to the best works of literature, music, theater and fine arts of the other country. This is confirmed by the interest shown by your public in the current USSR days in Dortmund.

As you know, a number of concrete agreements on economic and cultural relations and air service have been signed in the past few days between our countries and they demonstrate mutual understanding and readiness for cooperation on both sides.

But however important good relations may be for both of our states and their peoples, it is no less important that their establishment and development in our days are part of a wider process of radical improvement of international life in Europe and elsewhere in the world.

The quarter century period of the cold war is now giving way to relations of peace, mutual respect and cooperation between the states of the East and the West.

This is precisely the aim of the policy of peaceful coexistence pursued by the Soviet Union in regard to states with the opposite social system. It has been expressed most completely today in the widely known peace program approved by the 24th Congress of the Communist Party of the Soviet Union, and in the materials of last April's plenum of the CPSU Central Committee. Inscribed there, among other things, is the goal set by our country of implementing a radical turn towards detente and peace on the European continent. I would like you to know that the Soviet Union, its Communist Party, all our people, will vigorously and consistently strive towards this goal.

The Europe that has more than once been the hotbed of aggressive wars that have brought tremendous destruction and the death of millions of people must become forever a thing of the past. We want a new continent in its place—a continent of peace, mutual trust and reciprocally advantageous cooperation among all states.

Among the positive elements of contemporary European development is also, undoubtedly, the gradual improvement in the relations of the Federal Republic of Germany with its Eastern neighbors—with Poland, the GDR, Czechoslovakia and other socialist countries of Europe.

We attach great importance to the businesslike, constructive cooperation that we have established with the Federal Republic of Germany, France, the United States and other countries in such an important matter as preparations for an all-European conference on security and cooperation.

There are still many burning and explosive problems awaiting solution in the world. For example, the conflict in the Middle East, where the Arab lands are still held by the occupationists and where, therefore, dangerous tension persists, has not been settled yet. There are opponents of relaxation and of ending the arms race in other areas too. However, mankind's horizons are, after all, growing brighter. The war in Vietnam has ended.

World Peace in Sight

The favorable development of Soviet-American relations goes on. On the whole, one can perhaps say that our planet today is closer to durable, lasting peace than ever before. And the Soviet Union is shifting all its weight to buttress this beneficial tendency.

Our peaceable foreign policy expresses the very essence of our society, expresses its profound inner needs. The 250 million Soviet people are engaged in the realization of grandiose projects of peaceful construction. In the North and in the South of our vast country, in Siberia and in Central Asia, we are building giant power stations, hundreds of plants and factories, creating irrigation systems on territories that in size could vie with many a European state.

Our goal is for the Soviet people to live better tomorrow than they live today. Soviet people are tangibly aware of the fruits of these collective efforts.

This, of course, does not mean that we in the Soviet Union have resolved all problems and face no difficulties. Problems that will take a lot of solving do exist, and apparently will always exist in all times. But a specific feature of the problems facing us is that they are associated with the confident growth of the country, of its economic and cultural potential, and we are seeking solutions exclusively on the roads of further peaceful construction, of raising the cultural and living standards of the people, of developing our socialist society.

I would like to add that our plans are by no means plans designed for autarky. Our course is not towards isolating our country from the outside world. On the contrary, we proceed from the fact that it will develop under conditions of growing all-round cooperation with the outside world, and not only with socialist countries at that, but in considerable measure with the states of the opposite social system as well.

Esteemed viewers, our stay in the Federal Republic is of necessity rather brief. But even the little that my comrades and I were, able to see on the soil of West Germany leaves a pleasant impression.

We were interested to see your dynamic and at the same time rich in tradition capital—the old Bonn, the birthplace of the brilliant Beethoven, whose university was attended by the great creator of the theory of scientific communism, Karl Marx.

We are very grateful to Federal Chancellor Willy Brandt, Federal President Gustav Heinemann, Foreign Minister Walter Scheel and all representatives of the FRG Government for their hospitality, for organizing our joint work so well.

In conclusion Leonid Brezhnev wished the people of the FRG a peaceful and happy life, fruitful endeavors and prosperity.

NIXON'S STATEMENT ON WATERGATE

May 22, 1973

Five days after the Senate Select Committee on Presidential Campaign Activities opened its hearings on the Watergate affair and all its ramifications, President Nixon issued a long statement to set the record straight from the viewpoint of the White House. In addition to denying any prior knowledge of the Watergate break-in, the President outlined in some detail operations initiated under his auspices in the name of national security—operations which he noted had become "entangled" in the Watergate case although "totally unrelated" to it. He admitted for the first time that some persons within the White House had apparently tried to cover up the Watergate incident. While conceding that some of his own directives might have led to the cover-up, he insisted that they had not had that purpose. Furthermore, he reiterated earlier statements that he would not resign as President.

Nixon declared that "allegations surrounding the Watergate affair have so escalated that I feel a further statement from the President is required at this time." He credited accounts of the scandal, presumably news media accounts, with having generated "a climate of sensationalism...in which second- or third-hand hearsay charges are headlined as fact and repeated as fact." Then he "categorically" denied any personal involvement in the long list of alleged misdeeds associated with the Watergate affair: "I had no prior knowledge of the Watergate operations. I took no part in, nor was I aware of, any subsequent efforts that may have been made to cover up Watergate." The President specifically noted three reasons for his new explanatory statement. Those three aims were to set forth the facts about his own relationship to the Watergate matter, to lend "some perspec-

tive" to the "sensational—and inaccurate" charges in the press, and to "draw the distinction between national security operations and the Watergate case."

Events relating to the inquiry had moved forward rapidly after the end of April, when President Nixon in a nationwide television broadcast announced the resignations of his two principal assistants, H. R. Haldeman and John D. Ehrlichman, and also of John W. Dean III, counsel to the President (see p. 499). Two former cabinet officers, Attorney General John N. Mitchell and Secretary of Commerce Maurice H. Stans, were indicted May 10 on charges of obstructing justice; they were accused of obtaining a $200,000 cash contribution to the Nixon campaign fund from financier Robert L. Vesco in return for promises to intercede on his behalf with the Securities and Exchange Commission (SEC) about an alleged mutual fund swindle. Other events subsequent to the April resignations included the dismissal by a federal judge of all charges against the defendants in the Pentagon Papers trial (see p. 537).

Before the Senate hearings started, White House Press Secretary Ronald L. Ziegler let it be known that the President would not be drawn into discussion of the daily testimony on Capitol Hill. At a Republican fund-raising dinner in Washington May 9, Nixon did seek to reassure party members about Watergate. "I didn't get where I am by ducking tough issues," he said. The President also pledged that Attorney General-designate Elliot L. Richardson and his special Watergate prosecutor would have "the total cooperation of the executive branch of this government" in investigating the scandal. "They will get to the bottom of this thing. They will see to it that all of those who are guilty are prosecuted and are brought to justice."

The public in general, however, seemed unconvinced. Forty-five per cent of the persons responding to a Harris Survey in May said they thought the President had known in advance about the Watergate break-in. By the first week of June, despite the President's statement of May 22, a Gallup Poll found that 67 per cent of the respondents believed that Nixon was involved either in the planning or the cover-up. The same poll showed that the proportion approving Nixon's handling of his job as President had dropped to 44 per cent from 68 per cent following signing of the Vietnam cease-fire agreement in January.

The 4,000-word May 22 statement was not delivered as a television speech or read at a news conference, but several members of the President's staff submitted to an intensive and occasionally acrimonious grilling by reporters. The statement failed to smooth many of the ruffled political feathers. Editorial reaction was largely critical. There were complaints that the President had not been totally candid and that he seemed to be taking refuge under the cloak of national security. On May 24 The Washington Post called the statement "pathetic, *unconvincing, confused." It accused the President of "invoking the sacred and serious national security claim frivolously and to ends for which it was never intended." The New York Times commented: "Even on the President's own intellectual premises, his statement raises serious doubts about his own conduct.... Mr. Nixon has reiterated several specific denials about the extent of his knowledge of and therefore his culpability for various misdeeds. Those denials have to stand the test of time. Meanwhile, it is abundantly clear that an inflated and erroneous conception of 'national security' led to criminal behavior which has brought the office of the President into grave dispute."*

Text of President Nixon's statement of May 22, 1973, on the Watergate affair:

Recent news accounts growing out of testimony in the Watergate investigations have given grossly misleading impressions of many of the facts, as they relate both to my own role and to certain unrelated activities involving national security.

Already, on the basis of second- and third-hand hearsay testimony by persons either convicted or themselves under investigation in the case, I have found myself accused of involvement in activities I never heard of until I read about them in news accounts.

These impressions could also lead to a serious misunderstanding of those national security activities which, though totally unrelated to Watergate, have become entangled in the case. They could lead to further compromise of sensitive national security information.

I will not abandon my responsibilities. I will continue to do the job I was elected to do.

In the accompanying statement, I have set forth the facts as I know them as they relate to my own role.

With regard to the specific allegations that have been made, I can and do state categorically:

1. I had no prior knowledge of the Watergate operation.

2. I took no part in, nor was I aware of, any subsequent efforts that may have been made to cover up Watergate.

3. At no time did I authorize any offer of executive clemency for the Watergate defendants, nor did I know of any such offer.

4. I did not know, until the time of my own investigation, of any effort to provide the Watergate defendants with funds.

5. At no time did I attempt, or did I authorize others to attempt, to implicate the CIA in the Watergate matter.

6. It was not until the time of my own investigation that I learned of the break-in at the office of Mr. Ellsberg's psychiatrist, and I specifically authorized the furnishing of this information to Judge Byrne.

7. I neither authorized nor encouraged subordinates to engage in illegal or improper campaign tactics.

In the accompanying statement, I have sought to provide the background that may place recent allegations in perspective. I have specifically stated that executive privilege will not be invoked as to any testimony concerning possible criminal conduct or discussions of possible criminal conduct, in the matters under investigation. I want the public to learn the truth about Watergate and those guilty of any illegal actions brought to justice.

Allegations surrounding the Watergate affair have so escalated that I feel a further statement from the President is required at this time.

A climate of sensationalism has developed in which even second- or third-hand hearsay charges are headlined as fact and repeated as fact.

Important national security operations which themselves had no connection with Watergate have become entangled in the case.

As a result, some national security information has already been made public through court orders, through the subpoenaing of documents, and through testimony witnesses have given in judicial and Congressional proceedings. Other sensitive documents are now threatened with disclosure. Continued silence about those operations would compromise rather than protect them, and would also serve to perpetuate a grossly distorted view—which recent partial disclosures have given—of the nature and purpose of those operations.

The purpose of this statement is threefold:

—First, to set forth the facts about my own relationship to the Watergate matter;

—Second, to place in some perspective some of the more sensational —and inaccurate—of the charges that have filled the headlines in recent days, and also some of the matters that are currently being discussed in Senate testimony and elsewhere;

—Third, to draw the distinction between national security operations and the Watergate case. To put the other matters in perspective, it will be necessary to describe the national security operations first.

In citing these national security matters, it is not my intention to place a national security "cover" on Watergate, but rather to separate them out from Watergate—and at the same time to explain the context in which certain actions took place that were later misconstrued or misused.

Long before the Watergate break-in, three important national security operations took place which have subsequently become entangled in the Watergate case.

—The first operation, begun in 1969, was a program of wiretaps. All were legal, under the authorities then existing. They were undertaken to find and stop serious national security leaks.

—The second operation was a reassessment, which I ordered in 1970, of the adequacy of internal security measures. This resulted in a plan and a directive to strengthen our intelligence operations. They were protested by Mr. Hoover, and as a result of his protest they were not put into effect.

—The third operation was the establishment, in 1971, of a Special Investigations Unit in the White House. Its primary mission was to plug leaks of vital security information. I also directed this group to prepare an accurate history of certain crucial national security matters which occurred under prior administrations, on which the Government's records were incomplete.

Here is the background of these three security operations initiated in my Administration.

1969 Wiretaps

By mid-1969, my Administration had begun a number of highly sensitive foreign policy initiatives. They were aimed at ending the war in Vietnam, achieving a settlement in the Middle East, limiting nuclear arms, and establishing new relationships among the great powers. These involved highly secret diplomacy. They were closely interrelated. Leaks of secret information about any one could endanger all.

Exactly that happened. News accounts appeared in 1969, which were obviously based on leaks—some of them extensive and detailed—by people having access to the most highly classified security materials.

There was no way to carry forward these diplomatic initiatives unless further leaks could be prevented. This required finding the source of the leaks.

In order to do this, a special program of wiretaps was instituted in mid-1969 and terminated in February 1971. Fewer than 20 taps, of varying duration, were involved. They produced important leads that made it possible to tighten the security of highly sensitive materials. I authorized this entire program. Each individual tap was undertaken in accordance with procedures legal at the time and in accord with longstanding precedent.

The persons who were subject to these wiretaps were determined through coordination among the Director of the FBI, my Assistant for National Security Affairs, and the Attorney General. Those wiretapped were selected on the basis of access to the information leaked, material in security files, and evidence that developed as the inquiry proceeded.

Information thus obtained was made available to senior officials responsible for national security matters in order to curtail further leaks.

The 1970 Intelligence Plan

In the spring and summer of 1970, another security problem reached critical proportions. In March a wave of bombings and explosions struck college campuses and cities. There were 400 bomb threats in one

24-hour period in New York City. Rioting and violence on college campuses reached a new peak after the Cambodian operation and the tragedies at Kent State and Jackson State. The 1969-70 school year brought nearly 1,800 campus demonstrations and nearly 250 cases of arson on campus. Many colleges closed. Gun battles between guerilla-style groups and police were taking place. Some of the disruptive activities were receiving foreign support.

Complicating the task of maintaining security was the fact that, in 1966, certain types of undercover FBI operations that had been conducted for many years had been suspended. This also had substantially impaired our ability to collect foreign intelligence information. At the same time, the relationships between the FBI and other intelligence agencies had been deteriorating. By May 1970, FBI Director Hoover shut off his agency's liaison with the CIA altogether.

On June 5, 1970, I met with the Director of the FBI (Mr. Hoover), the Director of the Central Intelligence Agency (Mr. Richard Helms), the Director of the Defense Intelligence Agency (Gen. Donald V. Bennett), and the Director of the National Security Agency (Adm. Noel Gayler). We discussed the urgent need for better intelligence operations. I appointed Director Hoover as chairman of an interagency committee to prepare recommendations.

On June 25, the committee submitted a report which included specific options for expanded intelligence operations, and on July 23 the agencies were notified by memorandum of the options approved. After reconsideration, however, prompted by the opposition of Director Hoover, the agencies were notified 5 days later, on July 28, that the approval had been rescinded. The options initially approved had included resumption of certain intelligence operations which had been suspended in 1966. These in turn had included authorization for surreptitious entry—breaking and entering, in effect—on specified categories of targets in specified situations related to national security.

Because the approval was withdrawn before it had been implemented, the net result was that the plan for expanded intelligence activities never went into effect.

The documents spelling out this 1970 plan are extremely sensitive. They include—and are based upon—assessments of certain foreign intelligence capabilities and procedures, which of course must remain secret. It was this unused plan and related documents that John Dean removed from the White House and placed in a safe deposit box, giving the keys to Judge Sirica. The same plan, still unused, is being headlined today.

Coordination among our intelligence agencies continued to fall short of our national security needs. In July 1970, having earlier discontinued the FBI's liaison with the CIA, Director Hoover ended the FBI's normal liaison with all other agencies except the White House. To help remedy this, an Intelligence Evaluation Committee was created in December

1970. Its members included representatives of the White House, CIA, FBI, NSA, the Departments of Justice, Treasury, and Defense, and the Secret Service.

The Intelligence Evaluation Committee and its staff were instructed to improve coordination among the intelligence community and to prepare evaluations and estimates of domestic intelligence. I understand that its activities are now under investigation. I did not authorize nor do I have any knowledge of any illegal activity by this Committee. If it went beyond its charter and did engage in any illegal activities, it was totally without my knowledge or authority.

The Special Investigations Unit

On Sunday, June 13, 1971, The New York Times published the first installment of what came to be known as "The Pentagon Papers." Not until a few hours before publication did any responsible Government official know that they had been stolen. Most officials did not know they existed. No senior official of the Government had read them or knew with certainty what they contained.

All the Government knew, at first, was that the papers comprised 47 volumes and some 7,000 pages, which had been taken from the most sensitive files of the Departments of State and Defense and the CIA, covering military and diplomatic moves in a war that was still going on.

Moreover, a majority of the documents published with the first three installments in The Times had not been included in the 47-volume study—raising serious questions about what and how much else might have been taken.

There was every reason to believe this was a security leak of unprecedented proportions.

It created a situation in which the ability of the Government to carry on foreign relations even in the best of circumstances could have been severely compromised. Other governments no longer knew whether they could deal with the United States in confidence. Against the background of the delicate negotiations the United States was then involved in on a number of fronts—with regard to Vietnam, China, the Middle East, nuclear arms limitations, U.S.-Soviet relations, and others—in which the utmost degree of confidentiality was vital, it posed a threat so grave as to require extraordinary actions.

Therefore during the week following the Pentagon Papers publicaion, I approved the creation of a Special Investigations Unit within the White House—which later came to be known as the "plumbers." This was a small group at the White House whose principal purpose was to stop security leaks and to investigate other sensitive security matters. I looked to John Ehrlichman for the supervision of this group.

Egil Krogh, Mr. Ehrlichman's assistant, was put in charge. David Young was added to this unit, as were E. Howard Hunt and G. Gordon Liddy.

The unit operated under extremely tight security rules. Its existence and functions were known only to a very few persons at the White House. These included Messrs. Haldeman, Ehrlichman and Dean.

At about the time the unit was created, Daniel Ellsberg was identified as the person who had given the Pentagon Papers to The New York Times. I told Mr. Krogh that as a matter of first priority, the unit should find out all it could about Mr. Ellsberg's associates and his motives. Because of the extreme gravity of the situation, and not then knowing what additio.al national secrets Mr. Ellsberg might disclose, I did impress upon Mr. Krogh the vital importance to the national security of his assignment. I did not authorize and had no knowledge of any illegal means to be used to achieve this goal.

However, because of the emphasis I put on the crucial importance of protecting the national security, I can understand how highly motivated individuals could have felt justified in engaging in specific activities that I would have disapproved had they been brought to my attention.

Consequently, as President, I must and do assume responsibility for such actions despite the fact that I at no time approved or had knowledge of them.

I also assigned the unit a number of other investigatory matters, dealing in part with compiling an accurate record of events related to the Vietnam war, on which the Government's records were inadequate (many previous records having been removed with the change of administrations) and which bore directly on the negotiations' then in progress. Additional assignments included tracing down other national security leaks, including one that seriously compromised the U.S. negotiating position in the SALT talks.

The work of the unit tapered off around the end of 1971. The nature of its work was such that it involved matters that, from a national security standpoint, were highly sensitive then and remain so today.

These intelligence activities had no connection with the break-in of the Democratic headquarters, or the aftermath.

I considered it my responsibility to see that the Watergate investigaion did not impinge adversely upon the national security area. For example, on April 18, 1973, when I learned that Mr. Hunt, a former member of the Special Investigations Unit at the White House, was to be questioned by the U.S. Attorney, I directed Assistant Attorney General Petersen to pursue every issue involving Watergate but to confine his investigation to Watergate and related matters and to stay out of national security matters. Subsequently, on April 25, 1973, Attorney General Kleindienst informed me that because the Government had clear evidence that Mr. Hunt was involved in the break-in of the office of the psychiatrist who had treated Mr. Ellsberg, he, the Attorney General, believed that despite the fact that no evidence had been obtained from Hunt's acts, a report should nevertheless be made to the court trying the Ellsberg case. I concurred, and directed that the information be transmitted to Judge Byrne immediately.

Watergate

The burglary and bugging of the Democratic National Committee headquarters came as a complete surprise to me. I had no inkling that any such illegal activities had been planned by persons associated with my campaign; if I had known, I would not have permitted it. My immediate reaction was that those guilty should be brought to justice, and, with the five burglars themselves already in custody, I assumed that they would be.

Within a few days, however, I was advised that there was a possibility of CIA involvement in some way.

It did seem to me possible that, because of the involvement of former CIA personnel, and because of some of their apparent associations, the investigation could lead to the uncovering of covert CIA operations totally unrelated to the Watergate break-in.

In addition, by this time, the name of Mr. Hunt had surfaced in connection with Watergate, and I was alerted to the fact that he had previously been a member of the Special Investigations Unit in the White House. Therefore, I was also concerned that the Watergate investigation might well lead to an inquiry into the activities of the Special Investigations Unit itself.

In this area, I felt it was important to avoid disclosure of the details of the national security matters with which the group was concerned. I knew that once the existence of the group became known, it would lead inexorably to a discussion of these matters, some of which remain, even today, highly sensitive.

I wanted justice done with regard to Watergate; but in the scale of national priorities with which I had to deal—and not at that time having any idea of the extent of political abuse which Watergate reflected—I also had to be deeply concerned with ensuring that neither the covert operations of the CIA nor the operations of the Special Investigations Unit should be compromised. Therefore, I instructed Mr. Haldeman and Mr. Ehrlichman to ensure that the investigation of the break-in not expose either an unrelated covert operation of the CIA or the activities of the White House investigations unit—and to see that this was personally coordinated between General Walters, the Deputy Director of the CIA, and Mr. Gray of the FBI. It was certainly not my intent, nor my wish, that the investigation of the Watergate break-in or of related acts be impeded in any way.

On July 6, 1972, I telephoned the Acting Director of the FBI, L. Patrick Gray, to congratulate him on his successful handling of the hijacking of a Pacific Southwest Airlines plane the previous day. During the conversation Mr. Gray discussed with me the progress of the Watergate investigation, and I asked him whether he had talked with General Walters. Mr. Gray said that he had, and that General Walters had assured him that the CIA was not involved. In the discussion, Mr.

Gray suggested that the matter of Watergate might lead higher. I told him to press ahead with his investigation.

It now seems that later, through whatever complex of individual motives and possible misunderstandings, there were apparently wide-ranging efforts to limit the investigation or to conceal the possible involvement of members of the Administration and the campaign committee.

I was not aware of any such efforts at the time. Neither, until after I began my own investigation, was I aware of any fundraising for defendants convicted of the break-in at Democratic headquarters, much less authorize any such fundraising. Nor did I authorize any offer of executive clemency for any of the defendants.

In the weeks and months that followed Watergate, I asked for, and received, repeated assurances that Mr. Dean's own investigation (which included reviewing files and sitting in on FBI interviews with White House personnel) had cleared everyone then employed by the White House of involvement.

In summary, then:

(1) I had no prior knowledge of the Watergate bugging operation, or of any illegal surveillance activities for political purposes.

(2) Long prior to the 1972 campaign, I did set in motion certain internal security measures, including legal wiretaps, which I felt were necessary from a national security standpoint and, in the climate then prevailing, also necessary from a domestic security standpoint.

(3) People who had been involved in the national security operations later, without my knowledge or approval, undertook illegal activities in the political campaign of 1972.

(4) Elements of the early post-Watergate reports led me to suspect, incorrectly, that the CIA had been in some way involved. They also led me to surmise, correctly, that since persons originally recruited for covert national security activities had participated in Watergate, an unrestricted investigation of Watergate might lead to and expose those covert national security operations.

(5) I sought to prevent the exposure of these covert national security activities, while encouraging those conducting the investigation to pursue their inquiry into the Watergate itself. I so instructed my staff, the Attorney General, and the Acting Director of the FBI.

(6) I also specifically instructed Mr. Haldeman and Mr. Ehrlichman to ensure that the FBI would not carry its investigation into areas that might compromise these covert national security activities, or those of the CIA.

(7) At no time did I authorize or know about any offer of executive clemency for the Watergate defendants. Neither did I know until the time of my own investigation of any efforts to provide them with funds.

Conclusion

With hindsight, it is apparent that I should have given more heed to the warning signals I received along the way about a Watergate cover-up and less to the reassurances.

With hindsight, several other things also become clear:

—With respect to campaign practices, and also with respect to campaign finances, it should now be obvious that no campaign in history has ever been subjected to the kind of intensive and searching inquiry that has been focused on the campaign waged in my behalf in 1972.

It is clear that unethical, as well as illegal, activities took place in the course of that campaign.

None of these took place with my specific approval or knowledge. To the extent that I may in any way have contributed to the climate in which they took place, I did not intend to; to the extent that I failed to prevent them, I should have been more vigilant.

It was to help ensure against any repetition of this in the future that last week I proposed the establishment of a top-level, bipartisan, independent commission to recommend a comprehensive reform of campaign laws and practices. Given the priority I believe it deserves, such reform should be possible before the next Congressional elections in 1974.

—It now appears that there were persons who may have gone beyond my directives, and sought to expand on my efforts to protect the national security operations in order to cover up any involvement they or certain others might have had in Watergate. The extent to which this is true, and who may have participated and to what degree, are questions that it would not be proper to address here. The proper forum for settling these matters is in the courts.

—To the extent that I have been able to determine what probably happened in the tangled course of this affair, on the basis of my own recollections and of the conflicting accounts and evidence that I have seen, it would appear that one factor at work was that at critical points various people, each with his own perspective and his own responsibilities, saw the same situation with different eyes and heard the same words with different ears. What might have seemed insignificant to one seemed significant to another; what one saw in terms of public responsibility, another saw in terms of political opportunity; and mixed through it all, I am sure, was a concern on the part of many that the Watergate scandal should not be allowed to get in the way of what the Administration sought to achieve.

The truth about Watergate should be brought out—in an orderly way, recognizing that the safeguards of judicial procedure are designed to find the truth, not to hide the truth.

With his selection of Archibald Cox—who served both President Kennedy and President Johnson as Solicitor General—as the special supervisory prosecutor for matters related to the case, Attorney General-designate Richardson has demonstrated his own determination to see the truth brought out. In this effort he has my full support.

Considering the number of persons involved in this case whose testimony might be subject to a claim of executive privilege, I recognize that a clear definition of that claim has become central to the effort to arrive at the truth.

Accordingly, executive privilege will not be invoked as to any testimony concerning possible criminal conduct or discussions of possible criminal conduct, in the matters presently under investigation, including the Watergate affair and the alleged cover-up.

I want to emphasize that this statement is limited to my own recollections of what I said and did relating to security and to the Watergate. I have specifically avoided any attempt to explain what other parties may have said and done. My own information on those other matters is fragmentary, and to some extent contradictory. Additional information may be forthcoming of which I am unaware. It is also my understanding that the information which has been conveyed to me has also become available to those prosecuting these matters. Under such circumstances, it would be prejudicial and unfair of me to render my opinions on the activities of others; those judgments must be left to the judicial process, our best hope for achieving the just result that we all seek.

As more information is developed, I have no doubt that more questions will be raised. To the extent that I am able, I shall also seek to set forth the facts as known to me with respect to those questions.

June

NEW PHASE OF PHASE III

June 13, 1973

In tacit admission of the failure of Phase III to hold down inflation, President Nixon on June 13 imposed a new 60-day price freeze on all goods except unprocessed food products at the farm level. In a televised address to the nation, the President announced the freezing of prices at levels in effect the week of June 1-8, thus requiring a rollback of prices increased since that week. By limiting the freeze to prices, Nixon left wages, interest rates and dividends under existing Phase III controls. Rents continued free of federal control. As a back-up weapon against rising food costs, Nixon asked Congress for more flexible authority to limit exports for the purpose of fighting inflation. If necessary, he pledged to use such authority to keep exports of animal feeds at levels that would not force higher domestic meat prices.

The President seemed to be heading away from the course he had advocated as recently as six weeks before. At that time he had said a freeze "would cause shortages" and that his administration would move toward a less regulated economy. But inflationary pressures were building and Phase III appeared unable to cope with them. Since Phase III was introduced in January 1973 (see p. 43), the economy had suffered through record price increases, particularly in food; a second devaluation of the dollar followed by continued international monetary turbulence; a shaky stock market; and fading public confidence in the federal government's ability to put a brake on inflation. Congress, skeptical about Phase III, stepped up pressure for tougher action by threatening to legislate a firmer controls system.

When the President finally took action on June 13, it was the second time in two years that he had clamped a lid on prices. As when he imposed Phase I on Aug. 15, 1971, he resorted to a freeze as shock treatment for an inflation-plagued economy. Under the Phase III controls, partially suspended by the new freeze, Nixon largely relied on voluntary compliance by business and labor to keep prices down. But Phase III was generally viewed as ineffective in dealing with the inflationary pressures generated by the boom in the economy during the first half of 1973. Indeed, many economists credited the lax standards with feeding the latest inflation spiral. Treasury Secretary George P. Shultz admitted at a White House press briefing before the announcement of the new freeze that "Everybody thinks that Phase III was a failure. We're not arguing about that."

In announcing the new two-month lid on prices, the President promised to devise in the interim "a new and more effective system of controls...to contain the forces that have sent prices so rapidly upward in the past few months." He bought time for the new Phase IV controls which, he asserted, would "involve tighter standards and more mandatory compliance procedures than under Phase III." (See p. 703.)

Text of President Nixon's address on June 13, 1973, announcing a series of anti-inflationary actions, including a 60-day freeze on prices:

Good evening.

I want to talk to you tonight about some strong actions that I have ordered today with regard to the American economy—actions which will be important to you in terms of the wages you earn and the prices you pay.

But first, since we have been hearing so much about what is wrong with our economy over the past few months, let us look at some of the things that are right about the American economy.

We can be proud that the American economy is by far the freest, the strongest, and the most productive economy in the world. It gives us the highest standard of living in the world. We are in the middle of one of the biggest, strongest booms in our history.

More Americans have jobs today than ever before.

The average worker is earning more today than ever before.

Your income buys more today than ever before.

In August 1971, I announced the New Economic Policy. Since then, the Nation's output has increased by a phenomenal 1 1/2 percent—a more rapid growth than in any comparable period in the last 21 years. Four and a half million new civilian jobs have been created—and that is more than in any comparable period in our whole history. At the same time, real per capita disposable income—that means what you have left to spend after taxes and after inflation—has risen by 7 1/2 percent in that period. This means that, in terms of what your money will actually buy, in the past year and a half your annual income has increased by the equivalent of 4-weeks' pay.

Now, when we consider these facts, we can see that in terms of jobs, of income, of growth, we are enjoying one of the best periods in our history.

We have every reason to be optimistic about the future.

But there is one great problem that rightly concerns every one of us, and that is, as you know, rising prices, and especially rising food prices.

By the end of last year, we had brought the rate of inflation in the United States down to 3.4 percent. That gave us the best record in 1972 of any industrial country in the world.

But now prices are going up at unacceptably high rates.

The greatest part of this increase is due to rising food prices. This has been caused in large measure by increased demand at home and abroad, by crop failure abroad, and, as many people in various areas of the country know, by some of the worst weather for crops and livestock that we have ever experienced.

But whatever the reasons, every American family is confronted with a real and pressing problem of higher prices. And I have decided that the time has come to take strong and effective action to deal with that problem.

Effective immediately, therefore, I am ordering a freeze on prices. This freeze will hold prices at levels no higher than those charged during the first 8 days of June. It will cover all prices paid by consumers. The only prices not covered will be those of unprocessed agricultural products at the farm levels, and rents.

Wages, interest, and dividends will remain under their present control systems during the freeze.

Now, the reason I decided not to freeze wages is that the wage settlements reached under the rules of Phase III have not been a significant cause of the increase in prices. And as long as wage settlments continue to be responsible and noninflationary, a wage freeze will not be imposed.

The freeze will last for a maximum of 60 days. This time will be used to develop and put into place a new and more effective system of controls which will follow the freeze.

This new Phase IV [set] of controls will be designed to contain the forces that have sent prices so rapidly upward in the past few months. It will involve tighter standards and more mandatory compliance procedures than under Phase III. It will recognize the need for wages and prices to be treated consistently with one another.

In addition to food prices, I have received reports from various parts of the country of many instances of sharp increases in the price of gasoline. And therefore, I have specifically directed the Cost of Living Council to develop new Phase IV measures that will stabilize both the prices at the retail level of food and the price of gasoline at your service station.

In announcing these actions, there is one point I want to emphasize to every one of you listening tonight. The Phase IV that follows the freeze will not be designed to get us permanently into a controlled economy. On the contrary, it will be designed as a better way to get us out of a controlled economy, to return as quickly as possible to the free market system.

We are not going to put the American economy into a straitjacket. We are not going to control the boom in a way that would lead to a bust. We are not going to follow the advice of those who have proposed actions that would lead inevitably to a permanent system of price and wage controls, and also rationing.

Such actions would bring good headlines tomorrow, and bad headaches 6 months from now for every American family in terms of rationing, black markets, and eventually a recession that would mean more unemployment.

It is your prosperity that is at stake. It is your job that is at stake.

The actions I have directed today are designed to deal with the rise in the cost of living without jeopardizing your prosperity or your job.

Because the key to curbing food prices lies in increasing supplies, I am not freezing the price of unprocessed agricultural products at the farm level. This would reduce supplies instead of increasing them. It would eventually result in even higher prices for the foods you buy at the supermarket.

Beginning in 1972, we embarked on a comprehensive new program for increasing food supplies. Among many other measures, this has included opening up 40 million more acres for crop production, In the months ahead, as these new crops are harvested, they will help hold prices down. But unfortunately, this is not yet helping in terms of the prices you pay at the supermarket today, or the prices you will be paying tomorrow.

A Major Reason For High Food Prices

One of the major reasons for the rise in food prices at home is that there is now an unprecedented demand abroad for the products of America's farms. Over the long run, increased food exports will be a vital factor in raising farm income, in improving our balance of payments in supporting America's position of leadership in the world. In the short term, however, when we have shortages and sharply rising prices of food here at home, I have made this basic decision: In allocating the products of America's farms between markets abroad and those in the United States, we must put the American consumer first.

Therefore, I have decided that a new system for export controls on food products is needed—a system designed to hold the price of animal feedstuffs and other grains in the American market to levels that will make it possible to produce meat and eggs and milk at prices you can afford.

I shall ask the Congress, on an urgent basis, to give me the new and more flexible authority needed to impose such a system. In exercising such authority, this will be my policy: We will keep the export commitments we have made as a nation. We shall also consult with other countries to seek their cooperation in resolving the worldwide problem of rising food prices. But we will not let foreign sales price meat and eggs off the American table.

I have also taken another action today to stop the rise in the cost of living. I have ordered the Internal Revenue Service to begin immediately a thoroughgoing audit of the books of companies which have raised their prices more than 1 1/2 percent above the January ceiling.

The purpose of the audit will be to find out whether these increases were justified by rising costs. If they were not, the prices will be rolled back.

The battle against inflation is everybody's business. I have told you what the Administration will do. There is also a vital role for the Congress, as I explained to the Congressional leaders just a few moments ago.

The most important single thing the Congress can do in holding down the cost of living is to hold down the cost of government. For my part, I shall continue to veto spending bills that we cannot afford, no matter how noble-sounding their names may be. If these budget-busters become law, the money would come out of your pocket—in higher prices, higher taxes, or both.

There are several specific recommendations I have already made to the Congress that will be important in holding down prices in the future. I again urge quick action on all of these proposals.

Congress should give the President authority to reduce tariffs in selected cases in order to increase supplies of scarce goods and thereby hold down their prices. This action will help on such scarce items as meat, plywood, and zinc. And in particular, the tariff we now have on imported meat should be removed.

Congress should provide authority to dispose of more surplus commodities now held in Government stockpiles.

Congress should let us go ahead quickly with the Alaska pipeline so that we can combat the shortage of oil and gasoline we otherwise will have. I will also soon send to the Congress a major new set of proposals on energy, spelling out new actions I believe are necessary to help us meet our energy needs and thereby lessen pressures on fuel prices.

In its consideration of new farm legislation, it is vital that the Congress put high production ahead of high prices, so that farm prosperity will not be at the cost of higher prices for the consumer. If the Congress sends me a farm bill, or any other bill, that I consider inflationary, I shall veto that bill.

How the Public Can Help

Beyond what the Administration can do, beyond what the Congress can do, there is a great deal you can do. The next 60 days can decide the question of whether we shall have a continuing inflation that leads to a recession or whether we deal responsibly with our present problems and so go forward with a vigorous prosperity and a swift return to a free market.

You can help, by giving your Senators and Congressmen your support when they make the difficult decisions to hold back on necessary Government spending.

You can help, by saying no to those who would impose a permanent system of controls on this great, productive economy of ours which is the wonder of the world.

Let there be no mistake: If our economy is to remain dynamic, we must never slip into the temptation of imagining that in the long run, controls can substitute for a free economy or permit us to escape the need for discipline in fiscal and monetary policy. We must not let controls become a narcotic; we must not become addicted.

There are all sorts of seemingly simple gimmicks that would give the appearance or offer the promise of controlling inflation, but that would carry a dangerous risk of bringing on a recession, and that would not be effective in controlling inflation. Rigid, permanent controls always look better on paper then they do in practice.

We must never go down that road, which would lead us to economic disaster.

We have a great deal to be thankful for as Americans tonight.

We are the best-clothed, best-fed, best-housed people in the world; we are the envy of every nation in that respect.

This year, for the first time in 12 years, we are at peace in Vietnam—and our courageous prisoners of war have returned to their homes.

This year, for the first time in a generation, no American is being drafted into the Armed Forces.

This year, we find our prospects brighter than at any time in the modern era for a lasting peace, and for the abundant prosperity such a peace can make possible.

Next Monday, I will meet at the summit here in Washington with General Secretary Brezhnev of the Soviet Union. Based on the months of preparatory work that has been done for this meeting, and based on the extensive consultation and correspondence we have had, much of it quite recently, I can confidently predict tonight that out of our meetings will come major new progress toward reducing both the burden of arms and the danger of war and toward a better and more rewarding relationship between the world's two most powerful nations.

Today, in America, we have a magnificent opportunity. We hold the future—our future—in our hands. By standing together, by working together, by joining in bold yet sensible policies to meet our temporary problems without sacrificing our lasting strengths, we can achieve what America has not had since President Eisenhower was in this office: full prosperity without war and without inflation. This is a great goal, and working together, we can and we will achieve that goal.

Thank you and good evening.

Executive Order 11723, issued June 13, 1973, FURTHER PROVIDING FOR THE STABILIZATION OF THE ECONOMY:

On January 11, 1973 I issued Executive Order 11695 which provided for establishment of Phase III of the Economic Stabilization Program. On April 30, 1973 the Congress enacted, and I signed into law, amendments to the Economic Stabilization Act of 1970 which extended for one year, until April 30, 1974, the legislative authority for carrying out the Economic Stabilization Program.

During Phase III, labor and management have contributed to our stabilization efforts through responsible collective bargaining. The American people look to labor and management to continue their constructive and cooperative contributions. Price behavior under Phase III has not been satisfactory, however. I have therefore determined to impose a comprehensive freeze for a maximum period of 60 days on the prices of all commodities and services offered for sale except the prices charged for raw agricultural products. I have determined that this action is necessary to stabilize the economy, reduce inflation, minimize unemployment, improve the Nation's competitive position in world trade and protect the purchasing power of the dollar, all in the context of sound fiscal management and effective monetary policies.

Now, THEREFORE, by virtue of the authority vested in me by the Constitution and statutes of the United States, particularly the Economic Stabilization Act of 1970, as amended, it is hereby ordered as follows:

SECTION 1. Effective 9:00 p.m., e.s.t., June 13, 1973, no seller may charge to any class of purchaser and no purchaser may pay a price for any commodity or service which exceeds the freeze price charged for the same or a similar commodity or service in transactions with the same class of purchaser during the freeze base period. This order shall be effective for a maximum period of 60 days from the date hereof, until 11:59 p.m., e.s.t., August 12, 1973. It is not unlawful to charge or pay a price less than the freeze price and lower prices are encouraged.

Sec. 2. Each seller shall prepare a list of freeze prices for all commodities and services which he sells and shall maintain a copy of that list available for public inspection, during normal business hours, at each place of business where such commodities or services are offered for sale. In addition, the calculations and supporting data upon which the list is based shall be maintained by the seller at the location where the pricing decisions reflected on the list are ordinarily made and shall be made available on request to representatives of the Economic Stabilization Program.

Sec. 3. The provisions of this order shall not extend to the prices charged for raw agricultural products. The prices of processed agricultural products, however, are subject to the provisions of this order. For those agricultural products which are sold for ultimate consumption in their original unprocessed form, this provision applies after the first sale.

Sec. 4. The provisions of this order do not extend to (a) wages and salaries, which continue to be subject to the program established pursuant to Executive Order 11695 (b) interest and dividends, which continue to be subject to the program established by the Committee on Interest and Dividends and (c) rents which continue to be subject to controls only to the limited extent provided in Executive Order 11695:

Sec. 5. The Cost of Living Council shall develop and recommend to the President policies, mechanisms and procedures to achieve and maintain stability of prices and costs in a growing economy after the expiration of this freeze. To this end, it shall consult with representatives of agriculture, industry, labor, consumers and the public.

Sec. 6 (a) Executive Order 11695 continues to remain in full force and effect and the authority conferred by and pursuant to this order shall be in addition to the authority conferred by or pursuant to Executive Order 11695 including authority to grant exceptions and exemptions under appropriate standards issued pursuant to regulations.

(b) All powers and duties delegated to the Chairman of the Cost of Living Council by Executive Order 11695 for the purpose of carrying out the provisions of that order are hereby delegated to the Chairman of the Cost of Living Council for the purpose of carrying out the provisions of this order.

Sec. 7. Whoever willfully violates this order or any order or regulation continued or issued under authority of this order shall be subject to a fine of not more than $5,000 for each such violation. Whoever violates this order or any order or regulation continued or issued under authority of this order shall be subject to a civil penalty of not more than $2,500 for each such violation.

SEC. 8. For purposes of this Executive Order, the following definitions apply:

"Freeze price" means the highest price at or above which at least 10 percent of the commodities or services concerned were priced by the seller in transactions with the class of purchaser concerned during the freeze base period. In computing the freeze price, a seller may not exclude any temporary special sale, deal or allowance in effect during the freeze base period.

"Class of purchaser" means all those purchasers to whom a seller has charged a comparable price for comparable commodities or services during the freeze base period pursuant to customary price differentials between those purchasers and other purchasers.

"Freeze base period" means

(a) the period June 1 to June 8, 1973; or

(b) in the case of a seller who had no transactions during that period the nearest preceding seven-day period in which he had a transaction.

"Transaction" means an arms length sale between unrelated persons and is considered to occur at the time of shipment in the case of commodities and the time of performance in the case of services.

RICHARD NIXON

The White House,
    June 13, 1973

BREZHNEV IN AMERICA

June 16-25, 1973

Soviet Communist Party General Secretary Leonid I. Brezhnev paid his first visit to the United States in late June, when he crossed the Atlantic for a 10-day summit in this country. In the course of his stay, Brezhnev conferred with President Nixon, congressional leaders and American businessmen and addressed the nation in a taped television speech that was aired June 24. Ten agreements and a joint communique came out of the Nixon-Brezhnev talks. The Soviet party chief departed June 25.

Brezhnev and his five-man entourage including Foreign Minister Andrei Gromyko and Foreign Trade Minister Nikolai S. Patolichev had landed June 16 at Andrews Air Force Base, where they were welcomed by Secretary of State William P. Rogers. The party was then whisked off to Camp David, Maryland, for two days of rest and preparation before Brezhnev was officially greeted by the President June 18. In welcoming ceremonies at the White House, the two leaders pledged to build on the successes of the 1972 Moscow summit (See Historic Documents, 1972, p. 431-463, 655, 657, 660) and to work together to assure lasting world peace.

The next day, during a luncheon with 25 congressional leaders, including the full Senate Foreign Relations Committee, Brezhnev attempted to persuade the senators and representatives that they should vote to grant the Soviet Union most-favored-nation tariff status. In that connection, he declared that 97 per cent of those Soviet Jews who had sought to emigrate had been issued visas. Russia's alleged restriction of Jewish emigration had stalled congressional action to bestow tariff benefits on the Soviet Union.

Brezhnev again stressed the Soviet desire for expanded trade with the United States when he met June 22 with 51 American businessmen. After a luncheon in honor of Foreign Trade Minister Patolichev the same day, the National Association of Manufacturers announced that it would seek approval by Congress of the sought-after most-favored-nation treatment for imports from the Soviet Union. Brezhnev left Washington June 22 to fly to California for further talks with Nixon at the Western White House. He was the first foreign dignitary to stay at the San Clemente compound.

Nixon and Brezhnev had sat in at signing ceremonies in Washington June 19 for four accords negotiated by government representatives and signed by heads of the respective government departments. Included among the treaties was a five-year oceanography pact that could lead to improved weather forecasting. It established a joint committee to exchange data and convene meetings and laid the groundwork for joint research on ocean currents, biological productivity, deep sea drilling and ocean-atmosphere interaction. A second five-year agreement concerned transportation. It authorized exchanges of personnel and information on efficiency, safety and noise problems in transportation. The third accord pertained to cultural exchanges, extending a previous two-year agreement to 1979. Over three years, the two leaders agreed to raise the minimum number of individuals and groups exchanged. A fourth pact called for the "regular exchange" of information on long-term agricultural supply and demand.

As a directive to Soviet and American negotiators at the ongoing strategic arms limitation talks (SALT) in Geneva, Brezhnev and Nixon on June 21 signed a declaration of principles aimed at speeding up the sessions and completing a new SALT treaty by the end of 1974. The declaration called for an agreement that would limit and eventually reduce the number and possibly the quality of offensive weapons. The new treaty would replace the interim five-year agreement signed in 1972 after Round One of the SALT talks. (See Historic Documents, 1972, p. 431.) Modernization and replacement of strategic weapons would be allowed under the permanent agreement. On the question of monitoring observance of treaty provisions, the United States apparently gave way to Soviet objections to on-site inspection. Instead, the leaders settled on "national technical means" of verifying implementation. Although the latest accord mentioned no specifics, it could lead to limitations on strategic bombers and multiple independently targeted re-entry vehicles (MIRV's)—limitations which were not included in the 1972 interim agreement.

To enhance cooperation in peaceful nuclear energy research and to increase the exchange of information and personnel, Brezhnev and Nixon signed another agreement June 21, calling for joint research facilities "at all stages up to industrial scale operations." Joint Soviet-American efforts in this respect would focus primarily on controlled thermonuclear fusion, fast breeder reactors, and the fundamental properties of matter.

Still another agreement, signed June 22, was aimed at cooperation to avoid future international crises or military confrontations. It sought to preclude nuclear war between the United States and the Soviet Union or between either one of the two countries and another nation. The leaders committed themselves to begin "urgent consultations" whenever relations between countries "appear to involve risk of nuclear conflict." Either power would be expected under the terms of the agreement to inform its allies, other countries and the United Nations. A clause was added stating that the pact was not to affect the right of either party to take action in self-defense or to fulfill its obligations to its allies.

Two accords dealing with trade and one with air passenger service were also signed during the Soviet-American summit. Secretary of the Treasury George P. Shultz and Soviet Foreign Trade Minister Patolichev signed two trade protocols June 20 eliminating double taxation of companies or individuals of one country living or working in the other country. On June 23, Soviet Civil Aviation Minister Boris P. Bugayev and U.S. Transportation Secretary Claude S. Brinegar signed a protocol intended to expand the number of flights between the two countries and the number of available landing sites.

The joint communique issued June 25 summarized in part the proceedings between the two leaders during the preceding week. The communique hailed as "a historic landmark" the June 22 agreement to reduce the risks of nuclear war. It expressed the optimism of the two leaders that a permanent agreement could be reached in 1974 to restrict offensive weapons. It also said that "at an appropriate time" a world disarmament conference, long backed by the Russians, could be convened. Turning to trade and economic relations, the communique set a goal for U.S.-U.S.S.R. trade at a total of $2- to $3-billion over the next three years. The statement conspicuously avoided mention of most-favored-nation status. As for the world situation, the leaders "expressed their deep concern" over events in the Middle East, but hailed the signing of the cease-fire agreement on Vietnam.

After days of talks with various American leaders, Brezhnev on June 24 made a speech directed to the general public. The 47-minute taped address stressed the "historic significance" of the agreements concluded during his visit. He pointed out that the United States and the Soviet Union had "special responsibilities for the destinies of universal peace and for preventing war," in part because of their "economic and military might." He expressed the hope that the Soviet-American ex-

ample of rapprochement would "help draw more and more nations into the process of detente throughout the world."

> *Following are the texts of four documents emerging from the Nixon-Brezhnev summit: the declaration of principles on the SALT talks, June 21; the agreement on prevention of nuclear war, June 22; Brezhnev's television and radio address, aired June 24; and the joint communique, issued June 25:*

Basic Principles of Negotiations on the Further Limitation of Strategic Offensive Arms, signed June 21

The President of the United States of America, Richard Nixon, and the General Secretary of the Central Committee of the CPSU, L.I. Brezhnev,

Having thoroughly considered the question of the further limitation of strategic arms, and the progress already achieved in the current negotiations,

Reaffirming their conviction that the earliest adoption of further limitations of strategic arms would be a major contribution in reducing the danger of an outbreak of nuclear war and in strengthening international peace and security,

Have agreed as follows:

First. The two Sides will continue active negotiations in order to work out a permanent agreement on more complete measures on the limitation of strategic offensive arms, as well as their subsequent reduction, proceeding from the Basic Principles of Relations between the United States of America and the Union of Soviet Socialist Republics signed in Moscow on May 29, 1972, and from the Interim Agreement between the United States of America and the Union of Soviet Socialist Republics of May 26, 1972, on Certain Measures with Respect to the Limitation of Strategic Offensive Arms.

Over the course of the next year the two Sides will make serious efforts to work out the provisions of the permanent agreement on more complete measures on the limitation of strategic offensive arms with the objective of signing it in 1974.

Second. New agreements on the limitation of strategic offensive armaments will be based on the principles of the American-Soviet documents adopted in Moscow in May 1972 and the agreements reached in Washington in June 1973; and in particular, both Sides will be guided by the recognition of each other's equal security interests and by the recognition that efforts to obtain unilateral advantage, directly or indirectly, would be inconsistent with the strengthening of peaceful relations between the United States of America and the Union of Soviet Socialist Republics.

Third. The limitations placed on strategic offensive weapons can apply both to their quantitative aspects as well as to their qualitative improvement.

Fourth. Limitations on strategic offensive arms must be subject to adequate verification by national technical means.

Fifth. The modernization and replacement of strategic offensive arms would be permitted under conditions which will be formulated in the agreements to be concluded.

Sixth. Pending the completion of a permanent agreement on more complete measures of strategic offensive arms limitation, both Sides are prepared to reach agreements on separate measures to supplement the existing Interim Agreement of May 26, 1972.

Seventh. Each Side will continue to take necessary organizational and technical measures for preventing accidental or unauthorized use of nuclear weapons under its control in accordance with the Agreement of September 30, 1971 between the United States of America and the Union of Soviet Socialist Republics.

Washington, June 21, 1973

For the United States
of America:
RICHARD NIXON
President of the United
States of America

For the Union of Soviet
Socialist Republics:
L. I. BREZHNEV
General Secretary of the
Central Committee,
CPSU

Agreement Between the United States of America and the Union
of Soviet Socialist Republics on the Prevention of Nuclear War,
signed June 22

The United States of America and the Union of Soviet Socialist Republics, hereinafter referred to as the Parties,

Guided by the objectives of strengthening world peace and international security,
Conscious that nuclear war would have devastating consequences for mankind,
Proceeding from the desire to bring about conditions in which the danger of an outbreak of nuclear war anywhere in the world would be reduced and ultimately eliminated,
Proceeding from their obligations under the Charter of the United Nations regarding the maintenance of peace, refraining from the threat or use of force, and the avoidance of war, and in conformity with the agreements to which either Party has subscribed,

Proceeding from the Basic Principles of Relations between the United States of America and the Union of Soviet Socialist Republics signed in Moscow on May 29, 1972,

Reaffirming that the development of relations between the United States of America and the Union of Soviet Socialist Republics is not directed against other countries and their interests,

Have agreed as follows:

ARTICLE I

The United States and the Soviet Union agree that an objective of their policies is to remove the danger of nuclear war and of the use of nuclear weapons.

Accordingly, the Parties agree that they will act in such a manner as to prevent the development of situations capable of causing a dangerous exacerbation of their relations, as to avoid military confrontations, and as to exclude the outbreak of nuclear war between them and between either of the Parties and other countries.

ARTICLE II

The Parties agree, in accordance with Article I and to realize the objective stated in that Article, to proceed from the premise that each Party will refrain from the threat or use of force against the other Party, against the allies of the other Party and against other countries, in circumstances which may endanger international peace and security. The Parties agree that they will be guided by these considerations in the formulation of their foreign policies and in their actions in the field of international relations.

ARTICLE III

The Parties undertake to develop their relations with each other and with other countries in a way consistent with the purposes of this Agreement.

ARTICLE IV

If at any time relations between the Parties or between either Party and other countries appear to involve the risk of a nuclear conflict, or if relations between countries not parties to this Agreement appear to involve the risk of nuclear war between the United States of America and the Union of Soviet Socialist Republics or between either Party and other countries, the United States and the Soviet Union, acting in accordance with the provisions of this Agreement, shall immediately enter into urgent consultations with each other and make every effort to avert this risk.

ARTICLE V

Each Party shall be free to inform the Security Council of the United Nations, the Secretary General of the United Nations and the Governments of allied or other countries of the progress and outcome of consultations initiated in accordance with Article IV of this agreement.

ARTICLE VI

Nothing in this Agreement shall affect or impair:

(a) the inherent right of individual or collective self-defense as envisaged by Article 51 of the Charter of the United Nations,

(b) the provisions of the Charter of the United Nations, including those relating to the maintenance or restoration of international peace and security, and

(c) the obligations undertaken by either Party towards its allies or other countries in treaties, agreements, and other appropriate documents.

ARTICLE VII

This Agreement shall be of unlimited duration.

ARTICLE VIII

This Agreement shall enter into force upon signature.

DONE at Washington on June 22, 1973, in two copies each in the English and Russian languages, both texts being equally authentic.

For the United Staes
of America:
RICHARD NIXON

President of the United
States of America

For the Union of Soviet
Socialist Republics:
L. I. BREZHNEV

General Secretary of the
Central Committee,
CPSU

General Secretary Brezhnev's TV and Radio Address, June 24

Dear Americans: I highly appreciate this opportunity of directly addressing the people of the United States on my visit to your country.

I would like first of all to convey to all of you the greetings and friendly feelings of millions of Soviet people who are following with great interest my visit to your country and our talks with President Nixon and who are looking forward to this new Soviet-American summit meeting making a fruitful contribution to better relations between our countries and stronger universal peace.

Our discussions with President Nixon and other U.S. Government officials have been going on for several days, and they have been very intensive indeed. We came to this country anticipating that these would be responsible negotiations devoted to major questions bearing on the development of Soviet-American relations and to a search for ways in which our two nations could promote the further invigoration of the entire international atmosphere. Today I have every reason to say that those hopes were justified. We are satisfied with the way the talks went and with the results already achieved. New agreements have been signed in Washington, and in many respects they broaden the sphere of peaceful and mutually advantageous cooperation between the United States of America and the Union of Soviet Socialist Republics. Another big step has been taken along the path that we jointly mapped out a year ago during our meeting in Moscow.

Let me say frankly that personally I am also pleased that this visit has given me an opportunity to gain some firsthand impressions of America, to see some aspects of the American way of life, to meet with prominent government and public leaders of your country, and to have some contact with the life of Americans.

You are well aware that, in the past, relations between our countries developed very unevenly. There were periods of stagnation; there were ups and downs. But I guess I would not be making a mistake if I said that the significance of good relations between the Soviet Union and the United States has always been quite clear to the more far-sighted statesmen. In this connection we have good reason to recall that this is the year of the 40th anniversary of the establishment of diplomatic relations between our countries on the initiative of President Franklin D. Roosevelt.

In World War II the Soviet Union and the United States became allies and fought side by side against nazism, which threatened the freedom of nations and civilization itself. The jubilant meeting of Soviet and American soldiers on the Elbe River at the hour of victory over Hitlerism is well remembered in our country.

The wartime alliance could have been expected to usher in a new era of broad peaceful cooperation between the Soviet Union and the United States. I can tell you with confidence that that is what our country wanted. We wanted to cement and develop the good relations whose foundations had been laid during the war.

Things went differently, however. What came was not peace, but the cold war, a poor substitute for genuine peace. For a long time it poisoned relations between our countries and international relations as a whole. Some of its dismal influence can unfortunately be felt in certain things to this day.

Under the circumstances, it was no easy task indeed to make a turn from mutual distrust to detente, normalization, and mutually advantageous cooperation. It took courage and political foresight; it took a lot of painstaking work. We appreciate the fact that President Nixon and his administration joined their efforts with ours to really put Soviet-American relations on a new track.

I have heard that the American political vocabulary includes the expression "to win the peace." The present moment in history is, I believe, perhaps the most suitable occasion to use that expression. We jointly won the war. Today our joint efforts must help mankind win a durable peace. The possibility of a new war must be eliminated.

The outcome of the two meetings between the leaders of the Soviet Union and the United States and the practical steps taken in the intervening year convincingly show that important results have already been attained. It transpired that a reasonable and mutually acceptable approach to many problems, which previously seemed insoluble, can in fact be found. Not so long ago I suppose it would have been hard even to imagine the possibility of such progress.

Last year's agreements are, on the whole, being successfully implemented. Tangible progress is being made in almost all spheres—and it is a progress secured through joint efforts. The inauguration of a regular passenger shipping line between Leningrad and New York, the establishment of consulates general in Leningrad and San Francisco, the initiation of friendly ties between Soviet and American cities, and livelier athletic exchanges are all becoming part of the daily lives of the peoples of our two countries today.

Agreement on Preventing Nuclear War

The best possible evidence that Soviet-American relations are moving ahead, and not marking time, is provided by the important document signed the other day by President Nixon and myself, the agreement between the Soviet Union and the United States on the prevention of nuclear war. I trust I will not be accused of making an overstatement if I say that this document is one of historic significance. The Union of Soviet Socialist Republics and the United States of America have concluded an agreement to prevent the outbreak of nuclear war between themselves and to do their utmost to prevent the outbreak of nuclear war generally. It is surely clear how important this is for the peace and tranquility of the peoples of our two countries and for the improvement of the prospects for a peaceful life for all mankind.

Even if our second meeting with the President of the United States yielded no other results, it could still be said with full grounds that it will take a fitting place in the annals of Soviet-American relations and in international affairs as a whole. The entire world can now see that, having signed last year the fundamental document entitled "Basic Principles of Relations Between the Union of Soviet Socialist Republics and the United States of America," our two nations regard it not as a mere declaration of good intent but as a program of vigorous and consistent action, a program they have already begun to implement, and one which they are determined to go on implementing.

It is also of no little significance that our countries have agreed on the main principles of further work to prepare a new agreement on strategic arms limitation, a broader one this time and of far longer duration. This means that the exceptionally important job begun in May 1972 in Moscow is continuing. It means that political detente is being backed up by military detente. And this is something from which all the peoples and the very cause of peace stand to gain.

The other day representatives of our two governments also signed new agreements on Soviet-American cooperation in several specific fields. Together with the earlier agreements concluded during the past year, they make up an impressive file of documents on cooperation between our two nations and our two great peoples in some widely ranging fields: from the peaceful uses of atomic energy to agriculture and from outer space to the ocean depths.

Of course, the Soviet Union and the United States are countries which are, so to speak, self-sufficient. Until recently that was, in fact, how things were in our relations. However, we, as well as many Americans, realize only too well that renunciation of cooperation in the economic, scientific, technological, and cultural fields is tantamount to both sides turning down substantial extra benefits and advantages. And most important, such a renunciation would be so pointless as to defy any reasonable argument. This is particularly true of economic ties. Today, I believe, both you and we would agree that in this area it is not enough simply to overcome such an anomaly generated by the cold war as the complete freezing of Soviet-American trade. Life poses questions of far greater importance. I have in mind, above all, such forms of economic relations as stable large-scale ties in several branches of the economy and long-term scientific and technological cooperation, and in our age this is very important. The contacts we have had with American officials and businessmen confirm that it is along these lines that the main prospects for further economic cooperation between our countries can be traced.

It is alleged at times that the development of such cooperation is one-sided and only benefits the Soviet Union. But those who say so are either completely ignorant to the real state of affairs or deliberately turn a blind eye to the truth.

Economic Cooperation

And the truth is that broader and deeper economic cooperation in general and the long-term and large-scale deals which are now either being negotiated or have already been successfully concluded by Soviet organizations and American firms are bound to yield real and tangible benefits to both sides. This is something that has been confirmed quite definitely by American businessmen whom I have had an opportunity to talk with both in this country and earlier in Moscow. It was in that context that we discussed the matter with President Nixon, too.

To this I would like to add that both the Soviet Leadership and, as I see it, the U.S. Government attach particular importance to the fact that the development of long-term economic cooperation will also have very beneficial political consequences. It will consolidate the present trend toward better Soviet-American relations generally.

Prospects for the broad development of Soviet-American exchanges in culture and the arts are, as we see it, also good. Both our countries have much to share in this field. To live at peace we must trust each other, and to trust each other we must know each other better. We, for our part, want Americans to visualize our way of life and our way of thinking as completely and correctly as possible.

By and large, we can say that quite a lot has already been done to develop Soviet-American relations. Yet we are still only at the beginning of a long road. Constant care is needed to preserve and develop the new shoots of good relationships. Tireless efforts are needed to define the most essential and most suitable forms of cooperation in various fields. Patience is needed to understand the various specific features of the other side and to learn to do business with each other.

I believe those who support a radical improvement in relations between the Soviet Union and the United States can look to the future with optimism, for this objective meets the vital interests of both our nations and the interests of peace-loving people all over the world.

The general atmosphere in the world depends to no small extent on the climate prevailing in relations between our two countries. Neither economic or military might nor international prestige give our countries any special privileges, but they do invest them with special responsibility for the destinies of universal peace and for preventing war. In its approach to ties and contacts with the United States, the Soviet Union is fully aware of that responsibility.

We regard the improvement of Soviet-American relations not as an isolated phenomenon, but as an integral and very important part of the wider process of radically improving the international atmosphere. Mankind has outgrown the rigid cold war armor which it was once forced to wear. It wants to breathe freely and peacefully. And we will be happy if our efforts to better Soviet-American relations help draw more and more nations into the process of detente—be it in Europe or Asia, in Africa or Latin America, in the Middle or the Far East.

We regard it as a very positive fact that the normalization of Soviet-American relations is contributing to the solution of the great and important problem of consolidating peace and security in Europe and of convening the all-European conference.

The improvement of Soviet-American relations undoubtedly played its useful role in promoting the termination of the long-drawnout war in

Viet-Nam. Now that the agreement ending the Viet-Nam war has come into effect and both our countries, together with other nations, are signatories to the document of the Paris Conference on Viet-Nam, it seems to us to be particularly important that the achieved success be consolidated and that all the peoples of Indochina be given the chance to live in peace.

There still exist hotbeds of dangerous tension in the world. In our discussions with President Nixon we touched upon the situation in the Middle East, which is still very acute. We believe that in that area justice should be assured as soon as possible and a stable peace settlement reached that would restore the legitimate rights of those who suffered from the war and insure the security of all peoples of that region. That is important for all the peoples of the Middle East, with no exception. It is also important for the maintenance of universal peace.

In short, the ending of conflicts and the prevention of new crisis-fraught situations is an essential condition for creating truly reliable guarantees of peace. And our two countries are called upon to make a worthy contribution to that cause. In our discussions President Nixon and I have devoted a great deal of attention to these matters.

I would like to emphasize at this point that in discussing questions of our bilateral relations and international problems of a general nature we invariably took into account the fact that both the Soviet Union and the United States have their own allies and their own obligations toward various other states. It should be stated quite definitely that our talks, both in their spirit and in the letter of the signed agreements, fully take that fact into consideration.

But the main purport of all that we discussed and agreed upon with President Nixon in the field of international affairs is the firm determination of both sides to make good relations between the U.S.S.R. and the U.S.A. a permanent factor of international peace.

In our time—and I am sure you know this—there are still too many people who would rather make noise about military preparations and the arms race than discuss problems of detente and peaceful cooperation in a constructive spirit.

What can be said on that account?

The Soviet people are perhaps second to none when it comes to knowing what war means. In World War II we won a victory of world-historic significance. But in that war over 20 million Soviet citizens died. Seventy thousand of our towns and villages were devastated, and one-third of our national wealth was destroyed.

Lessons of War

The war wounds have now been healed. Today the Soviet Union is a mightier and more prosperous country than ever before. But we remember the lessons of the war only too well, and that is why the peoples of the Soviet Union value peace so highly, that is why they strongly approve the peace policy of our party and government.

For us peace is the highest achievement to which all men should strive if they want to make their life a worthy one. We believe in reason, and we feel that this belief is shared also by the peoples of the United States and of other nations. If that belief were lost, or if it were obscured by a blind faith in strength alone, in the power of nuclear arms or some other kind of weapon, the fate of civilization—of humanity itself—would be miserable indeed.

Our path has not been an easy one. Our people are proud that in a historically short period of time, after the victory of the Socialist Revolution, backward Russia transformed itself into a major industrial power and achieved outstanding successes in science and culture. We take pride in having built a new society—a most stable and confidently developing society—which has assured all our citizens of social justice and has made the values of modern civilization the property of all the people. We are proud that dozens of previously oppressed nations and nationalities in our country have become genuinely equal and that in our close-knit family of nations they are developing their economy and culture.

We have great plans for the future. We want to raise considerably the living standards of the Soviet people. We want to make new advances in education and medicine. We want to make our villages and towns more comfortable to live in and more beautiful. We have drafted programs to develop the remote areas of Siberia, the North and the Far East, with their immense natural resources. And every Soviet individual is deeply conscious of the fact that the realization of those plans requires peace and peaceful cooperation with other nations.

Of course, like any other country, we have quite a few problems and quite a few shortcomings. But the solution to all the problems we face requires, as in the case of other nations, not war or an artificial fanning of tension, but peace and creative labor, which, we are convinced, are the only things that can guarantee well-being and abundance of material and spiritual benefits for all members of society.

I have attempted to give a brief account of the thoughts and plans of the Soviet people and to explain the nature of the Soviet Union's foreign policy. Its peaceful essence stems from the very core of our society. And it is by no mere chance that the very concept of peaceful coexistence, which today is turning more and more into a universally recognized basis for the development of relations between states with different social systems, was evolved by Vladimir Ilyich Lenin, the founder of the Soviet state.

You probably know that two years ago the 24th congress of our ruling party, the Communist Party of the Soviet Union, approved the Soviet peace program, which is a concrete embodiment of the policy of peaceful coexistence in modern conditions. It is a program of active contribution to international detente and to securing a truly lasting peace on earth for many generations to come. It expreses not only the convictions and intentions of our people but also, we are sure, the aspirations of millions and millions of peace-loving people all over the world. We are implementing this program, working hand in hand with our friends and allies, the Socialist countries. On the basis of this program we seek to build relations of good will and mutually beneficial cooperation with all countries that have a similar desire. And the improvement of Soviet-American relations occupies its rightful place in that program.

Dear viewers: The importance and complexity of the problems on the agenda of our talks with President Nixon, of our meeting and discussions with members of the Senate Foreign Relations Committee, headed by Senator Fulbright, and with prominent representatives of the American business community, called for a tight work schedule on this visit.

As I have already pointed out, these were fruitful discussions held in a good atmosphere. This gives us a feeling of satisfaction.

At the same time, I do personally regret that the extreme pressure of business has not given me and my colleagues who accompanied me and took part in our work a chance to see more of your country. While still in Moscow, and then here, in the United States, I received many warm letters from various American cities, organizations, companies, and private citizens kindly inviting me to visit this or that town, to see plants, farms, and universities, or to be a guest in the homes of Americans. I am taking this opportunity to express my sincere gratitude to all those who wrote such letters. I regret that, for the reasons I have just mentioned, I was unable to take up those invitations.

Of course, it would have been interesting to visit New York and Chicago and Detroit and Los Angeles, to see some of your industrial projects and farms, to talk to American working people, whose achievements are admired by Soviet people. Perhaps the future will offer such an opportunity, especially since President Nixon and I have definitely agreed that in the future our contacts will be placed on a regular footing. We are looking forward to President Nixon's visit to the Soviet Union next year.

But even though this brief visit did not give me a chance to see as much as I would like to in America, I nevertheless have every reason, when I return home, to tell my colleagues and all Soviet people both about the important political results of the visit and about the atmosphere of good will and the trend in favor of peace, of detente, and of improving relations between our two countries. It is a trend which we felt during our stay in the United States and during our contacts with government and public leaders of your country and with many American citizens. I can assure you that these feelings are fully shared by Soviet people.

I do not believe I will be divulging a major secret if I tell you that in my talks with President Nixon over the last few days we not only addressed ourselves to current political problems but also tried to look ahead and to take into account the future interests of the peoples of both our countries. In so doing we proceeded from the assumption that in politics those who do not look ahead will inevitably find themselves in the rear, among the stragglers. A year ago in Moscow we laid the foundation for improving Soviet-American relations. Now this great and important objective has been successfully brought closer. It is our hope that this trend will continue, for it meets the interests of our two great peoples and of all mankind.

In conclusion, I want to express my sincere gratitude to the American people, to the President and the Government of the United States for their hospitality, for their kindness and numerous expressions of warm feelings toward the Soviet people and us, their representatives.

Dear Americans, please accept my wishes for well-being and happiness to all of you.

Thank you.

Joint U.S.-U.S.S.R. Communique, June 25

At the invitation of the President of the United States, Richard Nixon, extended during his official visit to the USSR in May 1972, and in accordance with a subsequent agreement, General Secretary of the Central Committee of the Communist Party of the Soviet Union, Mr. Leonid I. Brezhnev, paid an official visit to the United States from June 18 to June 25. Mr. Brezhnev was accompanied by A. A. Gromyko, Minister of Foreign Affairs of the USSR, Member of the Politbureau of the Central Committee, CPSU; N. S. Patolichev, Minister of Foreign Trade; B. P. Bugayev, Minister of Civil Aviation; G. E. Tsukanov and A. M. Aleksandrov, Assistants to the General Secretary of the Central Committee, CPSU; L. I. Zamyatin, General Director of TASS; E. I. Chazov, Deputy Minister of Public Health of the USSR; G. M. Korniyenko, Member of the Collegium of the Ministry of Foreign Affairs of the USSR; G. A. Arbatov, Director of the USA Institute of the Academy of Sciences of the USSR.

President Nixon and General Secretary Brezhnev held thorough and constructive discussions on the progress achieved in the development of US-Soviet relations and on a number of major international problems of mutual interest.

Also taking part in the conversations held in Washington, Camp David, and San Clemente, were:

On the American side William P. Rogers, Secretary of State; George P. Shultz, Secretary of the Treasury; Dr. Henry A. Kissinger, Assistant to the President for National Security Affairs.

On the Soviet side A. A. Gromyko, Minister of Foreign Affairs of the USSR, Member of the Polibureau of the Central Committee, CPSU; A. F. Dobrynin, Soviet Ambassador to the USA; N.S. Patolichev, Minister of Foreign Trade; B. P. Bugayev, Minister of Civil Aviation; A. M. Aleksandrov and E. E. Tsukanov, Assistants to the General Secretary of the Central Committee, CPSU; G. M. Korniyenko, Member of the Collegium of the Ministry of Foreign Affairs of the USSR.

I. THE GENERAL STATE OF US-SOVIET RELATIONS

Both Sides expressed their mutual satisfaction with the fact that the American-Soviet summit meeting in Moscow in May 1972 and the joint decisions taken there have resulted in a substantial advance in the strengthening of peaceful relations between the USA and the USSR and have created the basis for the further development of broad and mutually beneficial cooperation in various fields of mutual interest to the peoples of both countries and in the interests of all mankind. They noted their satisfaction with the mutual effort to implement strictly and fully the treaties and agreements concluded between the USA and the USSR, and to expand areas of cooperation.

They agreed that the process of reshaping relations between the USA and the USSR on the basis of peaceful coexistence and equal security as set forth in the Basic Principles of Relations Between the USA and the USSR signed in Moscow on May 29, 1972, is progressing in an encouraging manner. They emphasized the great importance that each Side attaches to these Basic Principles. They reaffirmed their commitment to the continued scrupulous implementation and to the enhancement of the effectiveness of each of the provisions of that document.

Both Sides noted with satisfaction that the outcome of the US-Soviet meeting in Moscow in May 1972 was welcomed by other States and by world opinion as an important contribution to strengthening peace and international security, to curbing the arms race and to developing businesslike cooperation among States with different social systems.

Both Sides viewed the return visit to the USA of the General Secretary of the Central Committee of the CPSU, L. I. Brezhnev, and the talks held during the visit as an expression of their mutual determination to continue the course toward a major improvement in US-Soviet relations.

Both Sides are convinced that the discussions they have just held represent a further milestone in the constructive development of their relations.

Convinced that such a development of American-Soviet relations serves the interests of both of their peoples and all of mankind, it was decided to take further major steps to give these relations maximum stability and to turn the development of friendship and cooperation between their peoples into a permanent factor for worldwide peace.

II. THE PREVENTION OF NUCLEAR WAR AND THE LIMITATION OF STRATEGIC ARMAMENTS

Issues related to the maintenance and strengthening of international peace were a central point of the talks between President Nixon and General Secretary Brezhnev.

Conscious of the exceptional importance for all mankind of taking effective measures to that end, they discussed ways in which both Sides could work toward removing the danger of war, and especially nuclear war, between the USA and the USSR and between either party and other countries. Consequently, in accordance with the Charter of the United Nations and the Basic Principles of Relations of May 29, 1972, it was decided to conclude an Agreement Between the USA and the USSR on the Prevention of Nuclear War. That Agreement was signed by the President and the General Secretary on June 22, 1973. The text has been published separately.

The President and the General Secretary, in appraising this Agreement, believe that it constitutes a historical landmark in Soviet-American relations and substantially strengthens the foundations of international security as a whole. The United States and the Soviet Union state their readiness to consider additional ways of strengthening peace and removing forever the danger of war, and particularly nuclear war.

In the course of the meetings, intensive discussions were held on questions of strategic arms limitation. In this connection both Sides emphasized the fundamental importance of the Treaty on the Limitation of Anti-Ballistic Missile Systems and the Interim Agreement on Certain Measures with Respect to the Limitation of Strategic Offensive Arms signed between the USA and the USSR in May 1972 which, for the first time in history, place actual limits on the most modern and most formidable types of armaments.

Having exchanged views on the progress in the implementation of these agreements, both Sides reaffirmed their intention to carry them out and their readiness to move ahead jointly toward an agreement on the further limitation of strategic arms.

Both Sides noted that progress has been made in the negotiations that resumed in November 1972, and that the prospects for reaching a permanent agreement on more complete measures limiting strategic offensive armaments are favorable.

Both Sides agreed that the progress made in the limitation of strategic armaments is an exceedingly important contribution to the strengthening of US-Soviet relations and to world peace.

On the basis of their discussions, the President and the General Secretary signed on June 21, 1973, Basic Principles of Negotiations on the Further Limitation of Strategic Offensive Arms. The text has been published separately.

The USA and the USSR attach great importance to joining with all States in the cause of strengthening peace, reducing the burden of armaments, and reaching agreements on arms limitation and disarmament measures.

Considering the important role which an effective international agreement with respect to chemical weapons would play, the two Sides agreed to continue their efforts to conclude such an agreement in cooperation with other countries.

The two Sides agree to make every effort to facilitate the work of the Committee on Disarmament which has been meeting in Geneva. They will actively participate in negotiations aimed at working out new measures to curb and end the arms race. They reaffirm that the ultimate objective is general and complete disarmament, including nuclear disarmament, under strict international control. A world disarmament conference could play a role in this process at an appropriate time.

III. INTERNATIONAL QUESTIONS: THE REDUCTION OF TENSIONS AND STRENGTHENING OF INTERNATIONAL SECURITY

President Nixon and General Secretary Brezhnev reviewed major questions of the current international situation. They gave special attention to the developments which have occurred since the time of the US-Soviet summit meeting in Moscow. It was noted with satisfaction that positive trends are developing in international relations toward the further relaxation of tensions and the strengthening of cooperative relations in the interests of peace. In the opinion of both Sides, the current process of improvement in the international situation creates new and favorable opportunities for reducing tensions, settling outstanding international issues, and creating a permanent structure of peace.

Indochina

The two Sides expressed their deep satisfaction at the conclusion of the Agreement on Ending the War and Restoring Peace in Vietnam, and also at the results of the International Conference on Vietnam which approved and supported that Agreement.

The two Sides are convinced that the conclusion of the Agreement on Ending the War and Restoring Peace in Vietnam, and the subsequent signing of the Agreement on Restoring Peace and Achieving National Concord in Laos, meet the fundamental interests and aspirations of the people of Vietnam and Laos and open up a possibility for establishing a lasting peace in Indochina, based on respect for the independence, sovereignty, unity and territorial integrity of the countries of that area. Both Sides emphasized that these agreements must be strictly implemented.

They further stressed the need to bring an early end to the military conflict in Cambodia in order to bring peace to the entire area of Indochina. They also reaffirmed their stand that the political futures of Vietnam, Laos, and Cambodia should be left to the respective peoples to determine, free from outside interference.

Europe

In the course of the talks both Sides noted with satisfaction that in Europe the process of relaxing tensions and developing cooperation is actively continuing and thereby contributing to international stability.

The two Sides expressed satisfaction with the further normalization of relations among European countries resulting from treaties and agreements signed in recent years, particularly between the USSR and the FRG [Federal Republic of Germany]. They also welcome the coming into force of the Quadripartite Agreement of September 3, 1971. They share the conviction that strict observance of the treaties and agreements that have been concluded will contribute to the security and well-being of all parties concerned.

They also welcome the prospect of United Nations membership this year for the FRG and the GDR [German Democratic Republic] and recall, in this connection, that the USA, USSR, UK and France have signed the Quadripartite Declaration of November 9, 1972, on this subject.

The USA and the USSR reaffirm their desire, guided by the appropriate provisions of the Joint US-USSR Communique adopted in Moscow in May 1972, to continue their separate and joint contributions to strengthening peaceful relations in Europe. Both Sides affirm that ensuring a lasting peace in Europe is a paramount goal of their policies.

In this connection satisfaction was expressed with the fact that as a result of common efforts by many States, including the USA and the USSR, the preparatory work has been successfully completed for the Conference on Security and Cooperation in Europe which will be convened on July 3, 1973. The USA and the USSR hold the view that the Conference will enhance the possibilities for strengthening European security and developing cooperation among the participating States. The USA and the USSR will conduct their policies so as to realize the goals of the Conference and bring about a new era of good relations in this part of the world.

Reflecting their continued positive attitude toward the Conference, both Sides will make efforts to bring the Conference to a successful conclusion at the earliest possible time. Both Sides proceed from the assumption that progress in the work of the Conference will produce possibilities for completing it at the highest level.

The USA and the USSR believe that the goal of strengthening stability and security in Europe would be further advanced if the relaxation of political tensions were accompanied by a reduction of military tensions in Central Europe. In this respect they attach great importance to the negotiations on the mutual reduction of forces and armaments and associated measures in Central Europe which will begin on October 30, 1973. Both Sides state their readiness to make, along with other States, their contribution to the achievement of mutually acceptable decisions on the substance of this problem, based on the strict observance of the principle of the undiminished security of any of the parties.

Middle East

The parties expressed their deep concern with the situation in the Middle East and exchanged opinions regarding ways of reaching a Middle East settlement.

Each of the parties set forth its position on this problem.

Both parties agreed to continue to exert their efforts to promote the quickest possible settlement in the Middle East. This settlement should be in accordance with the interests of all states in the area, be consistent with their independence and sovereignty and should take into due account the legitimate interests of the Palestinian people.

IV COMMERCIAL AND ECONOMIC RELATIONS

The President and the General Secretary thoroughly reviewed the status of and prospects for commercial and economic ties between the USA and the USSR. Both Sides noted with satisfaction the progress achieved in the past year in the normalization and development of commercial and economic relations between them.

They agreed that mutually advantageous cooperation and peaceful relations would be strengthened by the creation of a permanent foundation of economic relationships.

They recall with satisfaction the various agreements on trade and commercial relations signed in the past year. Both Sides note that American-Soviet trade has shown a substantial increase, and that there are favorable prospects for a continued rise in the exchange of goods over the coming years.

They believe that the two countries should aim at a total of 2-3 billion dollars of trade over the next three years. The Joint US-USSR Commercial Commission continues to provide a valuable mechanism to promote the broad-scale growth of economic relations. The two Sides noted with satisfaction that contacts between American firms and their Soviet counterparts are continuing to expand.

Both Sides confirmed their firm intention to proceed from their earlier understanding on measures directed at creating more favorable conditions for expanding commercial and other economic ties between the USA and the USSR.

It was noted that as a result of the Agreement Regarding Certain Maritime Matters signed in October 1972, Soviet and American commercial ships have been calling more frequently at ports of the United States and the USSR, respectively, and since late May of this year a new regular passenger line has started operating between New York and Leningrad.

In the course of the current meeting, the two Sides signed a Protocol augmenting existing civil air relations between the USA and the USSR providing for direct air services between Washington and Moscow and New York and Leningrad, increasing the frequency of flights and resolving other questions in the field of civil aviation.

In the context of reviewing prospects for further and more permanent economic cooperation, both Sides expressed themselves in favor of mutually advantageous long term projects. They discussed a number of specific projects involving the participation of American companies, including the delivery of Siberian natural gas to the United States. The President indicated that the USA encourages American firms to work out concrete proposals on these projects and will give serious and sympathetic consideration to proposals that are in the interest of both Sides.

To contribute to expanded commercial, cultural and technical relations between the USA and the USSR, the two Sides signed a tax convention to avoid double taxation on income and eliminate, as much as possible, the need for citizens of one country to become involved in the tax system of the other.

A Protocol was also signed on the opening by the end of October 1973 of a Trade Representation of the USSR in Washington and a Commercial Office of the United States in Moscow. In addition a Protocol was signed on questions related to establishing a US-Soviet Chamber of Commerce. These agreements will facilitate the further development of commercial and economic ties between the USA and the USSR.

V. FURTHER PROGRESS IN OTHER FIELDS OF BILATERAL COOPERATION

The two Sides reviewed the areas of bilateral cooperation in such fields as environmental protection, public health and medicine, exploration of outer space, and science and technology, established by the agreements signed in May 1972 and subsequently. They noted that those agreements are being satisfactorily carried out in practice in accordance with the programs as adopted.

In particular, a joint effort is under way to develop effective means to combat those diseases which are most widespread and dangerous for mankind: cancer, cardiovascular or infectious diseases and arthritis. The medical aspects of the environmental problems are also subjects of cooperative research.

Preparations for the joint space flight of the Apollo and Soyuz spacecraft are proceeding according to an agreed timetable. The joint flight of these spaceships for a rendezvous and docking mission, and mutual visits of American and Soviet astronauts in each other's spacecraft, are scheduled for July 1975.

Building on the foundation created in previous agreements, and recognizing the potential of both the USA and the USSR to undertake cooperative measures in current scientific and technological areas, new projects for fruitful joint efforts were identified and appropriate agreements were concluded.

Peaceful Uses of Atomic Energy

Bearing in mind the great importance of satisfying the growing energy demands in both countries and throughout the world, and recognizing that the development of highly efficient energy sources could contribute to the solution of this problem, the President and General Secretary signed an agreement to expand and strengthen cooperation in the fields of controlled nuclear fusion, fast breeder reactors, and research on the fundamental properties of matter. A Joint Committee on Cooperation in the Peaceful Uses of Atomic Energy will be established to implement this agreement, which has a duration of ten years.

Agriculture

Recognizing the importance of agriculture in meeting mankind's requirement for food products and the role of science in modern agricultural production, the two Sides concluded an agreement providing for a broad exchange of scientific experience in agricultural research and development, and of information on agricultural economics. A US-USSR Joint Committee on Agricultural Cooperation will be established to oversee joint programs to be carried out under the Agreement.

World Ocean Studies

Considering the unique capabilities and the major interest of both nations in the field of world ocean studies, and noting the extensive experience of US-USSR oceanographic cooperation, the two Sides have agreed to broaden their cooperation and have signed an agreement to this effect. In so doing, they are convinced that the benefits from further development of cooperation in the field of oceanography will accrue not only bilaterally but also to all peoples of the world. A US-USSR Joint Committee on Cooperation in World Ocean Studies will be established to coordinate the implementation of cooperative programs.

Transportation

The two Sides agreed that there are opportunities for cooperation between the USA and the USSR in the solution of problems in the field of transportation. To permit expanded, mutually beneficial cooperation in this field, the two Sides concluded an agreement on this subject. The USA and the USSR further agreed that a Joint Committee on Cooperation in Transportation would be established.

Contacts, Exchanges and Cooperation

Recognizing the general expansion of US-USSR bilateral relations and, in particular, the growing number of exchanges in the fields of science, technology, education and culture, and in other fields of mutual interest, the two Sides agreed to broaden the scope of these activities under a new General Agreement on Contacts, Exchanges, and Cooperation, with a duration of six years. The two Sides agreed to this in the mutual belief that it will further promote better understanding between the peoples of the United States and the Soviet Union and will help to improve the general state of relations between the two countries.

Both Sides believe that the talks at the highest level, which were held in a frank and constructive spirit, were very valuable and made an important contribution to developing mutually advantageous relations between the USA and the USSR. In the view of both Sides, these talks will have a favorable impact on international relations.

They noted that the success of the discussions in the United States was facilitated by the continuing consultation and contacts as agreed in May 1972. They reaffirmed that the practice of consultation should continue. They agreed that further meetings at the highest level should be held regularly.

Having expressed his appreciation to President Nixon for the hospitality extended during the visit to the United States, General Secretary Brezhnev invited the President to visit the USSR in 1974. The invitation was accepted.

June 24, 1973

Richard Nixon

Leonid I. Brezhnev

NEW RULES ON OBSCENITY

June 21, 1973

The Supreme Court's conservative majority agreed June 21 to a new set of rules for determining what is or is not obscenity under the law. In a complex of five decisions, the four Nixon appointees and Justice Byron R. White moved to tighten the standards under which books, plays and movies may be banned. The Court ruling was one of several decisions since 1957 which sought to clarify the meaning of "offensive" or "pornographic" as a basis for legal action. The Court had ruled in 1957 that obscenity was not protected by the First Amendment ban on laws abridging freedom of speech. As a result, the Justices had struggled since that time to formulate a workable definition of the term "obscenity." The June 21 pronouncement ended the search, for the time being at least.

The Court's majority agreed to new "concrete guidelines" aimed at expediting the legal process of banning materials by defining more precisely what was offensive. The decision was expected to enable states henceforth to enact "carefully limited" laws banning books, films or plays that "appeal to the prurient interest in sex, which portray sexual conduct in a patently offensive way, and which, taken as a whole, do not have serious literary, artistic, political or scientific value." This latest rule replaced a three-pronged standard established by the Court in 1966 whereby the material in question had to be found to appeal primarily to a prurient interest, to be patently offensive when judged by community standards, and to be utterly without redeeming social value.

*In another break with former rulings, the Court held that the ques-
tion of what was offensive could be judged against local, not national,
standards. "Adult" books and films were included in the ruling even
though those materials were distributed or exhibited in bookstores and
theaters where juveniles were excluded and persons offended by such
material were warned. Furthermore, the majority found that Congress
had the power to ban importation of obscene books and films and to
prohibit them from being carried in interstate transportation—including items intended only for the personal use of the possessor.*

*Dissenting from the majority opinion, written in all five cases by Chief
Justice Warren E. Burger, were Justices William O. Douglas, William
J. Brennan Jr., Thurgood Marshall and Potter Stewart. Each of the
four dissenters feared that the majority decision would restrict legitimate freedom of expression. Justice Douglas said he would prefer
government censorship, accomplished by constitutional amendment,
to the vagaries and risks inherent in the new ruling. The other three
justices would limit obscenity only as it concerned young people and
persons who did not wish it forced upon them.*

*The obscenity decision drew cries of disapproval from publishers,
film distributors, writers, librarians and civil liberties lawyers around
the country. Some said the decision raised more questions than it
resolved. Further debate was expected on the meaning of "prurient,"
"patently offensive," and without "serious" value. These judgments
were to be left to individual juries. The Court reasoned that such a
procedure would allow different communities to ban different material
according to local attitudes. However, the Court failed to state whether
a "community" was a local precinct, a city or a state. Many attorneys
predicted another decision would be needed to resolve that ambiguity.
Ephraim London, a noted lawyer handling obscenity cases, pointed out
that films shown in Times Square movie houses were not shown in
Queens. He wondered whether the Queens community would set the
standards for movies featured there, or whether a larger community
would determine what films could be shown in all of New York. Frank
Kelley, attorney general of Michigan, observed: "This really sets us
back in the dark ages. Now prosecuting attorneys in every county and
state will be grandstanding and every jury in every little community
will have a crack at each new book, play and movie."*

*Most everyone seemed to agree that the new rules on obscenity
would lead to an increase in pornography prosecutions. Ross Sacket,
chairman of the Association of American Publishers, bemoaned the
prospect that "we now have 50 battles to fight." Bob Guccione, publisher of the "male" magazine [Penthouse], forecast: "The immediate effect of this decision will be to drive a multibillion-dollar
industry underground—and I mean strictly hard-core porno industry,
and that means graft and crime in the real sense. It's the same thing*

as a return to Prohibition." Robert L. Bernstein, head of Random House, denounced the decision as "a call to arms to every crazy vigilante group in this country." But he had a comforting word for the publishing business: "Remember when publishers could say 'banned in Boston' on their books? Perhaps they'll capitalize on the present situation by saying 'banned by Burger et al.'" Warren Weaver Jr., Supreme Court correspondent of The New York Times, *said the decision amounted to "a triumph for the President in his campaign against 'permissiveness.'"*

Excerpts from the opinion of the Court in two of the five obscenity cases (Miller v. California and Paris Adult Theatre I v. Slaton) and from the dissenting opinion of Justice Douglas in the Miller case and the dissenting opinion of Justices Brennan, Marshall and Stewart in the Paris Adult Theatre case:

No. 70-73

Marvin Miller, Appellant, *v.* State of California	On Appeal from the Appellate Department, Superior Court of California, County of Orange.

[June 21, 1973]

MR. CHIEF JUSTICE BURGER delivered the opinion of the Court in which White, Blackmun, Powell and Rehnquist, J.J., joined:

This is one of a group of "obscenity-pornography" cases being reviewed by the Court in a re-examination of standards enunciated in earlier cases involving what Mr. Justice Harlan called "the intractable obscenity problem."...

I

This case involves the application of a State's criminal obscenity statute to a situation in which sexually explicit materials have been thrust by aggressive sales action upon unwilling recipients who had in no way indicated any desire to receive such materials. This Court has recognized that the States have a legitimate interest in prohibiting dissemination or exhibition of obscene material when the mode of dissemination carries with it a significant danger of offending the sensibilities of unwilling recipients or of exposure to juveniles....

It is in this context that we are called on to define the standards which must be used to identify obscene material that a State may regulate without infringing the First Amendment as applicable to the States through the Fourteenth Amendment.

The dissent of MR. JUSTICE BRENNAN reviews the background of the obscenity problem, but since the Court now undertakes to formulate standards more concrete than those in the past, it is useful for us to focus on two of the landmark cases in the somewhat tortured history of the Court's obscenity decisions. In *Roth v. United States,* 354 U.S. 476 (1957), the Court sustained a conviction under a federal statute punishing the mailing of "obscene, lewd, lascivious or filthy..." materials. The key to that holding was the Court's rejection of the claim that obscene materials were protected by the First Amendment....

Nine years later in *Memoirs* v. *Massachusetts,* 383 U.S. 413 (1966), the Court veered sharply away from the *Roth* concept and, with only three Justices in the plurality opinion, articulated a new test of obscenity. The plurality held that under the *Roth* definition:

> "...as elaborated in subsequent cases, three elements must coalesce: it must be established that (a) the dominant theme of the material taken as a whole appeals to a prurient interest in sex; (b) the material is patently offensive because it affronts contemporary community standards relating to the description or representation of sexual matters; and (c) the material is utterly without redeeming social value."...

While *Roth* presumed "obscenity" to be "utterly without redeeming social value," *Memoirs* required that to prove obscenity it must be affirmatively established that the material is "*utterly* without redeeming social value." Thus, even as they repeated the words of *Roth,* the *Memoirs* plurality produced a drastically altered test that called on the prosecution to prove a negative, *i.e.*, that the material was "*utterly* without redeeming social value"—a burden virtually impossible to discharge under our criminal standards of proof. Such considerations caused Justice Harlan to wonder if the "*utterly* without redeeming social value" test had any meaning at all....

Apart from the initial formulation in the *Roth* case, no majority of the Court has at any given time been able to agree on a standard to determine what constitutes obscene, pornographic material subject to regulation under the State's police power.... This is not remarkable, for in the area of freedom of speech and press the courts must always remain sensitive to any infringement on genuinely serious literary, artistic, political, or scientific expression. This is an area in which there are few eternal verities.

The case we now review was tried on the theory that the California Penal Code Section 311 approximately incorporates the three-stage *Memoirs* test, *supra.* But now the *Memoirs* test has been abandoned as unworkable by its author and no member of the Court today supports the *Memoirs* formulation.

II

...We acknowledge...the inherent dangers of undertaking to regulate any form of expression. State statutes designed to regulate obscene materials must be carefully limited.... As a result, we now confine the permissible scope of such regulation to works which depict or describe sexual conduct. That conduct must be specifically defined by the applicable state law, as written or authoritatively construed. A state offense must also be limited to works which, taken as a whole, appeal to the prurient interest in sex, which portray sexual conduct in a patently offensive way, and which, taken as a whole, do not have serious literary, artistic, political, or scientific value.

The basic guidelines for the trier of fact must be: (a) whether "the average person, applying contemporary community standards" would find that the work, taken as a whole, appeals to the prurient interest.... (b) whether the work depicts or describes, in a patently offensive way, sexual conduct specifically defined by the applicable state law, and (c) whether the work, taken as a whole, lacks serious literary, artistic, political, or scientific value. We do not adopt as a constitutional standard the *"utterly* without redeeming social value" test of *Memoirs* v. *Massachusetts,...* (1966); that concept has never commanded the adherence of more than three Justices at one time.... If a state law that regulates obscene material is thus limited, as written or construed, the First Amendment values applicable to the States through the Fourteenth Amendment are adequately protected by the ultimate power of appellate courts to conduct an independent review of constitutional claims when necessary....

We emphasize that it is not our function to propose regulatory schemes for the States. That must await their concrete legislative efforts. It is possible, however, to give a few plain examples of what a state statute could define for regulation under the second part (b) of the standard announced in this opinion, *supra*:

(a) Patently offensive representations or descriptions of ultimate sexual acts, normal or perverted, actual or simulated.

(b) Patently offensive representations or descriptions of masturbation, excretory functions, and lewd exhibition of the genitals.

Sex and nudity may not be exploited without limit by films or pictures exhibited or sold in places of public accommodation any more than live sex and nudity can be exhibited or sold without limit in such public places. At a minimum, prurient, patently offensive depiction or description of sexual conduct must have serious literary, artistic, political, or scientific value to merit First Amendment protection.... For example, medical books for the education of physicians and related personnel necessarily use graphic illustrations and descriptions of human anatomy. In resolving the inevitably sensitive questions of fact and law, we must continue to rely on the jury system, accompanied by the safeguards that judges, rules of evidence, presumption of innocence and other protective features provide, as we do with rape, murder and a host of other offenses against society and its individual members.

MR. JUSTICE BRENNAN, author of the opinions of the Court, or the plurality opinions, in *Roth* v. *United States, Jacobellis* v. *Ohio, Ginzburg* v. *United States, Mishkin* v. *New York,* and *Memoirs* v. *Massa-*

chusetts, has abandoned his former positions and now maintains that no formulation of this Court, the Congress, or the States can adequately distinguish obscene material unprotected by the First Amendment from protected expression.... Paradoxically, MR. JUSTICE BRENNAN indicates that suppression of unprotected obscene material is permissible to avoid exposure to unconsenting adults, as in this case, and to juveniles, although he gives no indication of how the division between protected and nonprotected materials may be drawn with greater precision for these purposes than for regulation of commercial exposure to consenting adults only. Nor does he indicate where in the Constitution he finds the authority to distinguish between a willing "adult" one month past the state law age of majority and a willing "juvenile" one month younger.

Under the holdings announced today, no one will be subject to prosecution for the sale or exposure of obscene materials unless these materials depict or describe patently offensive "hard core" sexual conduct specifically defined by the regulating state law, as written or construed. We are satisfied that these specific prerequisites will provide fair notice to a dealer in such materials that his public and commercial activities may bring prosecution.... If the inability to define regulated materials with ultimate, god-like precision altogether removes the power of the States or the Congress to regulate, then "hard core" pornography may be exposed without limit to the juvenile, the passerby, and the consenting adult alike, as, indeed, MR. JUSTICE DOUGLAS contends.... In this belief, however, MR. JUSTICE DOUGLAS now stands alone.

It is certainly true that the absence, since *Roth*, of a single majority view of this Court as to proper standards for testing obscenity has placed a strain on both state and federal courts. But today, for the first time since *Roth* was decided in 1957, a majority of this Court has agreed on concrete guidelines to isolate "hard core" pornography from expression protected by the First Amendment. Now we may abandon the casual practice of *Redrup* v. *New York, supra,* and attempt to provide positive guidance to the federal and state courts alike.

This may not be an easy road, free from difficulty. But no amount of "fatigue" should lead us to adopt a convenient "institutional" rationale—an absolutist, "anything goes" view of the First Amendment—because it will lighten our burdens. "Such an abnegation of judicial supervision in this field would be inconsistent with our duty to uphold the constitutional guarantees."...

III

Under a national Constitution, fundamental First Amendment limitations on the powers of the States do not vary from community to community, but this does not mean that there are, or should or can be, fixed, uniform national standards of precisely what appeals to the "prurient interest" or is "patently offensive." These are essentially questions of fact, and our nation is simply too big and too diverse for this Court to reasonably expect that such standards could be articulated for all 50 States in a single formulation, even assuming the prerequisite consensus exists. When triers of fact are asked to decide whether "the average person, applying contemporary community standards" would consider certain materials "prurient," it would be unrealistic to require that the answer be based on some abstract formulation. The adversary system, with lay jurors as the usual ultimate factfinders in criminal prosecutions, has historically permitted triers-of-fact to draw on the standards of their community, guided always by limiting instructions on the law. To require a State to structure obscenity proceedings around evidence of a *national* "community standard" would be an exercise in futility.

As noted before, this case was tried on the theory that the California obscenity statute sought to incorporate the tripartite test of *Memoirs*. This, a "national" standard of First Amendment protection enumerated by a plurality of this Court, was correctly regarded at the time of trial as limiting state prosecution under the controlling case law. The jury, however, was explicitly instructed that, in determining whether the "dominant theme of the material as a whole...appeals to the prurient interest" and in determining whether the material "goes substantially beyond customary limits of candor and affronts contemporary community standards of decency," it was to apply "contemporary community standards of the State of California."

During the trial, both the prosecution and the defense assumed that the relevant "community standards" in making the factual determination of obscenity were those of the State of California, not some hypothetical standard of the entire United States of America. Defense counsel at trial never objected to the testimony of the State's expert on community standards or to the instructions of the trial judge on "state-wide" standards. On appeal to the Appellate Department, Superior Court of California, County of Orange, appellant for the first time contended that application of state, rather than national, standards violated the First and Fourteenth Amendments.

We conclude that neither the State's alleged failure to offer evidence of "national standards," nor the trial court's charge that the jury consider state community standards, were constitutional errors. Nothing in the First Amendment requires that a jury must consider hypothetical and unascertainable "national standards" when attempting to determine whether certain materials are obscene as a matter of fact....

It is neither realistic nor constitutionally sound to read the First Amendment as requiring that the people of Maine or Mississippi accept public depiction of conduct found tolerable in Las Vegas, or New York City.... People in different States vary in their tastes and attitudes, and this diversity is not to be strangled by the absolutism of imposed uniformity. As the Court made clear in *Mishkin* v. *New York,*...the primary concern with requiring a jury to apply the standard of "the average person, applying contemporary community standards" is to be certain that, so far as material is not aimed at a deviant group, it will be judged by its impact on an average person, rather than a particularly susceptible or sensitive person—or indeed a toally insensitive one....

IV

The dissenting Justices sound the alarm of repression. But, in our view, to equate the free and robust exchange of ideas and political debate with commercial exploitation of obscene material demeans the grand conception of the First Amendment and its high purposes in the historic struggle for freedom. It is a "misuse of the great guarantees of free speech and free press...." *Breard* v. *Alexandria....* The First Amendment protects works which, taken as a whole, have serious literary, artistic, political or scientific value, regardless of whether the government or a majority of the people approve of the ideas these works represent.... But the public portrayal of hard core sexual conduct for its own sake, and for the ensuing commercial gain, is a different matter.

MR. JUSTICE BRENNAN finds "it is hard to see how state-ordered regimentation of our minds can ever be forestalled."... These doleful anticipations assume that courts cannot distinguish commerce in ideas, protected by the First Amendment, from commercial exploitation of obscene material.... One can concede that the "sexual revolution" of recent years may have had useful byproducts in striking layers of prudery from a subject long irrationally kept from needed ventilation. But it does not follow that no regulation of patently offensive "hard core" materials is needed or permissible; civilized people do not allow unregulated access to heroin because it is a derivative of medicinal morphine.

In sum we (a) reaffirm the *Roth* holding that obscene material is not protected by the First Amendment, (b) hold that such material can be regulated by the States, subject to the specific safeguards enunciated above, without a showing that the material is "*utterly* without redeeming social value," and (c) hold that obscenity is to be determined by applying "contemporary community standards,"...not "national standards." The judgment of the Appellate Department of the Superior Court, Orange County, California, is vacated and the case remanded to that court for further proceedings not inconsistent with the First Amendment standards established by this opinion....

Vacated and remanded for further proceedings.

MR. JUSTICE DOUGLAS, dissenting.

I

Today we leave open the way for California to send a man to prison for distributing brochures that advertise books and a movie under freshly written standards defining obscenity which until today's decision were never the part of any law....

Those are the standards we ourselves have written into the Constitution. Yet how under these vague tests can we sustain convictions for the sale of an article prior to the time when some court has declared it to be obscene?

Today the Court retreats from the earlier formulations of the constitutional test and undertakes to make new definitions. This effort, like the earlier ones, is earnest and well-intentioned. The difficulty is that we do not deal with constitutional terms, since "obscenity" is not mentioned in the Constitution or Bill of Rights. And the First Amendment makes no such exception from "the press" which it undertakes to protect nor, as I have said on other occasions, is an exception necessarily implied, for there was no recognized exception to the free press at the time the Bill of Rights was adopted which treated "obscene" publications differently from other types of papers, magazines, and books. So there are no constitutional guidelines for deciding what is and what is not "obscene." The Court is at large because we deal with tastes and standards of literature. What shocks me may be sustenance for my neighbor. What causes one person to boil up in rage over one pamphlet or movie may reflect only his neurosis, not shared by others. We deal here with problems of censorship which, if adopted, should be done by constitutional amendment after full debate by the people.

Obscenity cases usually generate tremendous emotional outbursts. They have no business being in the courts. If a constitutional amendment authorized censorship, the censor would probably be an administrative agency. Then criminal prosecutions could follow as if and when publishers defied the censor and sold their literature. Under that regime a publisher would know when he was on dangerous ground. Under the present regime—whether the old standards or the new ones are used—the criminal law becomes a trap. A brand new test would put a publisher behind bars under a new law improvised by the courts after the publication. That was done in *Ginzburg* and has all the evils of an *ex post facto* law.

My contention is that until a civil proceeding has placed a tract beyond the pale, no criminal prosecution should be sustained....

In any case—certainly when constitutional rights are concerned—we should not allow men to go to prison or be fined when they had no "fair warning" that what they did was criminal conduct.

II

...Obscenity—which even we cannot define with precision—is a hodge-podge. To send men to jail for violating standards they cannot understand, construe, and apply is a monstrous thing to do in a Nation dedicated to fair trials and due process.

III

...There is no "captive audience" problem in these obscenity cases. No one is being compelled to look or to listen. Those who enter news stands or bookstalls may be offended by what they see. But they are not compelled by the State to frequent those places; and it is only state or governmental action against which the First Amendment, applicable to the States by virtue of the Fourteenth, raises a ban.

The idea that the First Amendment permits government to ban publications that are "offensive" to some people puts an ominous gloss on freedom of the press. That test would make it possible to ban any paper or any journal or magazine in some benighted place. The First Amendment was designed "to invite dispute," to induce "a condition of unrest," to "create dissatisfactions with conditions as they are," and even to stir "people to anger." ...The idea that the First Amendment permits punishment for ideas that are "offensive" to the particular judge or jury sitting in judgment is astounding. No greater leveler of speech or literature has ever been designed. To give the power to the censor, as we do today, is to make a sharp and radical break with the traditions of a free society. The First Amendment was not fashioned as a vehicle for dispensing tranquilizers to the people. Its prime function was to keep debate open to "offensive" as well as to "staid" people. The tendency throughout history has been to subdue the individual and to exalt the power of government. The use of the standard "offensive" gives authority to government that cuts the very vitals out of the First Amendment. As is intimated by the Court's opinion, the materials before us may be garbage. But so is much of what is said in political campaigns, in the daily press, on TV or over the radio. By reason of the First Amendment—and solely because of it—speakers and publishers have not been threatened or subdued because their thoughts and ideas may be "offensive" to some.

The standard "offensive" is unconstitutional in yet another way. In *Coates* v. *Cincinnati*, 402 U.S. 611, we had before us a municipal ordinance that made it a crime for three or more persons to assemble on a street and conduct themselves "in a manner annoying to persons passing by." We struck it down, saying "...In our opinion this ordinance is unconstitutionally vague because it subjects the exercise of the right of assembly to an unascertainable standard, and unconstitutionally broad because it authorizes the punishment of constitutionally protected conduct. Conduct that annoys some people does not annoy others. Thus, the ordinance is vague, not in the sense that it requires a person to conform his conduct to an imprecise but comprehensive normative standard, but rather in the sense that no standard of conduct is specified at all...."

How we can deny Ohio the convenience of punishing people who "annoy" others and allow California power to punish people who publish materials "offensive" to some people is difficult to square with constitutional requirements.

If there are to be restraints on what is obscene, then a constitutional amendment should be the way of achieving the end. There are societies where religion and mathematics are the only free segments. It would be a dark day for America if that were our destiny. But the people can make it such if they choose to write obscenity into the Constitution and define it.

We deal with highly emotional, not rational, questions. To many the Song of Solomon is obscene. I do not think we, the judges, were ever given the constitutional power to make definitions of obscenity. If it is to be defined, let the people debate and decide by a constitutional amendment what they want to ban as obscene and what standards they want the legislatures and the courts to apply. Perhaps the people will decide that the path towards a mature, integrated society requires that all ideas competing for acceptance must have no censor. Perhaps they will decide otherwise. Whatever the choice, the courts will have some guidelines. Now we have none except our own predilections.

No. 71-1051

Paris Adult Theatre I et al, Petitioners, v. Lewis R. Slaton, District Attorney, Atlanta Judicial Circuit, et al.	On Writ of Certiorari to the Supreme Court of Georgia.

...We have directed our holdings, not at thoughts or speech, but at depiction and description of specifically defined sexual conduct that States may regulate within limits designed to prevent infringement of First Amendment rights. We have also reaffirmed the holdings of *United States* v. *Reidel, supra,* and *United States* v. *Thirty-Seven Photographs, supra,* that commerce in obscene material is unprotected by any constitutional doctrine of privacy.... In this case we hold that the States have a legitimate interest in regulating commerce in obscene material and in regulating exhibition of obscene material in places of public accommodation, including so-called "adult" theaters from which minors are excluded. In light of these holdings, nothing precludes the State of Georgia from the regulation of the allegedly obscene materials exhibited in Paris Adult Theatre I or II, provided that the applicable Georgia law, as written or authoritatively interpreted by the Georgia courts, meets the First Amendment standards set forth in *Miller* v. *California,...*

Vacated and remanded for further proceedings.

MR. JUSTICE BRENNAN, with whom MR. JUSTICE STEWART and MR. JUSTICE MARSHALL join, dissenting.

This case requires the Court to confront once again the vexing problem of reconciling state efforts to suppress sexually oriented expression with the protections of the First Amendment, as applied to the States through the Fourteenth Amendment. No other aspect of the First Amendment has, in recent years, demanded so substantial a commitment of our time, generated such disharmony of views, and remained so resistant to the formulation of stable and manageable standards. I am convinced that the approach initiated 15 years ago in *Roth* v. *United States*, and culminating in the Court's decision today, cannot bring stability to this area of the law without jeopardizing fundamental First Amendment values, and I have concluded that the time has come to make a significant departure from that approach.

In this civil action in the Superior Court of Fulton County the State of Georgia sought to enjoin the showing of two motion pictures, It All Comes Out In The End, and Magic Mirror, at the Paris Adult Theatres (I and II) in Atlanta, Georgia. The State alleged that the films were obscene under the standards set forth in Georgia Code Section 26-2101. The trial court denied injunctive relief, holding that even though the films could be considered obscene, their commercial presentation could not constitutionally be barred in the absence of proof that they were shown to minors or unconsenting adults. Reversing, the Supreme Court of Georiga found the films obscene, and held that the care taken to avoid exposure to minors and unconsenting adults was without constitutional significance....

II

...Recognizing that "the freedoms of expression... are vulnerable to gravely damaging yet barely visible encroachments," *Bantam Books, Inc.* v. *Sullivan,...*we have demanded that "sensitive tools" be used to carry out the "separation of legitimate from illegitimate speech." *Speiser* v. *Randall,....* The essence of our problem in the obscenity area is that we have been unable to provide "sensitive tools" to separate obscenity from other sexually oriented but constitutionally protected speech, so that efforts to suppress the former do not spill over into the suppression of the latter. The attempt, as the late Mr. Justice Harlan observed, has only "produced a variety of views among the members of the Court unmatched in any other course of constitutional adjudication....

In the face of this divergence of opinion the Court began the practice in 1967 in *Redrup v. New York*... of *per curiam* reversals of convictions for the dissemination of materials that at least five members of the Court, applying their separate tests, deemed not to be obscene. This approach capped the attempt in *Roth* to separate all forms of sexually oriented expression into two categories—the one subject to full governmental suppression and the other beyond the reach of governmental regulation to the same extent as any other protected form of speech or press. Today a majority of the Court offers a slightly altered formulation of the basic *Roth* test, while leaving entirely unchanged the underlying approach.

III

Our experience with the *Roth* approach has certainly taught us that the outright suppression of obscenity cannot be reconciled with the fundamental principles of the First and Fourteenth Amendments. For we have failed to formulate a standard that sharply distinguishes protected from unprotected speech, and out of necessity, we have resorted to the *Redrup* approach, which resolves cases as between the parties, but offers only the most obscure guidance to legislation, adjudication by other courts, and primary conduct. By disposing of cases through summary reversal or denial of certiorari we have deliberately and effectively obscured the rationale underlying the decision. It comes as no surprise that judicial attempts to follow our lead conscientiously have often ended in hopeless confusion.

Of course, the vagueness problem would be largely of our own creation if it stemmed primarily from our failure to reach a consensus on any one standard. But after 15 years of experimentation and debate I am reluctantly forced to the conclusion that none of the available formulas, including the one announced today, can reduce the vagueness to a tolerable level while at the same time striking an acceptable balance between the protections of the First and Fourteenth Amendments, on the one hand, and on the other the asserted state interest in regulating the dissemination of certain sexually oriented materials. Any effort to draw a constitutionally acceptable boundary on state power must resort to such indefinite concepts as "prurient interest," "patent offensiveness," "serious literary value," and the like. The meaning of these concepts necessarily varies with the experience, outlook, and even idiosyncracies of the person defining them. Although we have assumed that obscenity does exist and that we "know it when [we] see it," *Jacobellis* v. *Ohio,...*, we are manifestly unable to describe it in advance except by reference to concepts so elusive that they fail to distinguish clearly between protected and unprotected speech.

We have more than once previously acknowledged that "constitutionally protected expression...is often separated from obscenity only by a dim and uncertain line.".... I need hardly point out that the factors which must be taken into account are judgmental and can only be applied on "a case-by-case, sight-by-sight" basis. *Mishkin* v. *New York*,... These considerations suggest that no one definition, no matter how precisely or narrowly drawn, can possibly suffice for all situations, or carve out fully suppressable expression from all media without also creating a substantial risk of encroachment upon the guarantees of the Due 'Process Clause and the First Amendment.

The vagueness of the standards in the obscenity area produces a number of separate problems, and any improvement must rest on an understanding that the problems are to some extent distinct. First, a vague statute fails to provide adequate notice to persons who are engaged in the type of conduct that the statute could be thought to proscribe. The Due Process Clause of the Fourteenth Amendment requires that all criminal laws provide fair notice of "what the State commands or forbids.".... In this context, even the most painstaking efforts to determine in advance whether certain sexually oriented expression is obscene must inevitably prove unavailing. For the insufficiency of the notice compels persons to guess not only whether their conduct is covered by a criminal statute, but also whether their conduct falls within the constitutionally permissible reach of the statute. The resulting level of uncertainty is utterly intolerable, not alone because it makes "[b]ookselling...a hazardous profession,"...but as well because it invites arbitrary and erratic enforcement of the law....

In addition to problems that arise when any criminal statute fails to afford fair notice of what it forbids, a vague statute in the areas of speech and press creates a second level of difficulty. We have indicated that "stricter standards of permissible statutory vagueness may be applied to a statute having a potentially inhibiting effect on speech; a man may the less be required to act at his peril here, because the free dissemination of ideas may be the loser."...[W]e have held that the definition of obscenity must be drawn as narrowly as possible so as to minimize the interference with protected expression....

Similarly, we have held that a State cannot impose criminal sanctions for the possession of obscene material absent proof that the possessor had knowledge of the contents of the material....

The problems of fair notice and chilling protected speech are very grave standing alone. But it does not detract from their importance to recognize that a vague statute in this area creates a third, although admittedly more subtle, set of problems. These problems concern the institutional stress that inevitably results where the line separating protected from unprotected speech is excessively vague. In *Roth* we conceded that "there may be marginal cases in which it is difficult to determine the side of the line on which a particular fact situation falls...." ... Our subsequent experience demonstrates that almost every case is "marginal." And since the "margin" marks the point of separation between protected and unprotected speech, we are left with a system in which almost every obscenity case presents a constitutional question of exceptional difficulty. "The suppression of a particular writing or other tangible form of expression is...an *individual* matter, and in the nature of things every such suppression raises an individual constitutional problem, in which a reviewing court must determine for *itself* whether the attacked expression is suppressable within constitutional standards....

As a result of our failure to define standards with predictable application to any given piece of material, there is no probability of regularity in obscenity decisions by state and lower federal courts. That is not to say that these courts have performed badly in this area or paid insufficient attention to the principles we have established. The problem is, rather, that one cannot say with certainty that material is obscene until at least five members of this Court, applying inevitably obscure standards, have pronounced it so. The number of obscenity cases on our docket gives ample testimony to the burden that has been placed upon this Court.

But the sheer number of the cases does not define the full extent of the institutional problem. For quite apart from the number of cases involved and the need to make a fresh constitutional determination in each case, we are tied to the "absurd business of perusing and viewing the miserable stuff that pours into the Court...." ...While the material may have varying degrees of social importance, it is hardly a source of edification to the members of this Court who are compelled to view it before passing on its obscenity....

The severe problems arising from the lack of fair notice, from the chill on protected expression, and from the stress imposed on the state and federal judicial machinery persuade me that a significant change in direction is urgently required. I turn, therefore, to the alternatives that are now open.

IV

1. The approach requiring the smallest deviation from our present course would be to draw a new line between protected and unprotected speech, still permitting the States to suppress all material on the unprotected side of the line. In my view, clarity cannot be obtained pursuant to this approach except by drawing a line that resolves all doubts in favor of state power and against the guarantees of the First Amendment. We could hold, for example, that any depicton or description of human sexual organs, irrespective of the manner or purpose of the portrayal, is outside the protection of the First Amendment and therefore open to suppression by the States. That formula would, no doubt, offer much fairer notice of the reach of any state statute drawn at the boundary of the State's constitutional power. And it would also,

in all likelihood, give rise to a substantial probability of regularity in most judicial determinations under the standard. But such a standard would be appallingly overbroad.... Yet short of that extreme it is hard to see how any choice of words could reduce the vagueness problem to tolerable proportions, so long as we remain committed to the view that some class of materials is subject to outright suppression by the State.

2. The alternative adopted by the Court today recognizes that a prohibition against any depiction or description of human sexual organs could not be reconciled with the guarantees of the First Amendment. But the Court does retain the view that certain sexually oriented material can be considered obscene and therefore unprotected by the First and Fourteenth Amendments....

The Court evidently recognizes that difficulties with the *Roth* approach necessitate a significant change of direction. But the Court does not describe its understanding of those difficulties, nor does it indicate how the restatement of the *Memoirs* test is in any way responsive to the problems that have arisen. In my view, the restatement leaves unresolved the very difficulties that compel our rejection of the underlying *Roth* approach, while at the same time contributing substantial difficulties of its own.... In *Roth* we held that certain expression is obscene, and thus outside the protection of the First Amendment, precisely *because* it lacks even the slightest redeeming social value.... The Court's approach necessarily assumes that some works will be deemed obscene—even though they clearly have *some* social value—because the State was able to prove that the value, measured by some unspecified standard, was not sufficiently "serious" to warrant constitutional protection. That result is not merely inconsistent with our holding in *Roth*; it is nothing less than a rejection of the fundamental First Amendment premises and rationale of the *Roth* opinion and an invitation to widespread suppression of sexually oriented speech. Before today, the protections of the First Amendment have never been thought limited to expressions of *serious* literary or political value....

...[I]t is beyond dispute that the approach can have no ameliorative impact on the cluster of problems that grow out of the vagueness of our current standards. Indeed, even the Court makes no argument that the reformulation will provide fairer notice to booksellers, theatre owners, and the reading and viewing public. Nor does the Court contend that the approach will provide clearer guidance to law enforcement officials or reduce the chill on protected expression. Nor, finally, does the Court suggest that the approach will mitigate to the slightest degree the institutional problems that have plagued this Court and the State and Federal Judiciary as a direct result of the uncertainty inherent in any definition of obscenity...

Ultimately, the reformulation must fail because it still leaves in this Court the responsibility of determining in each case whether the materials are protected by the First Amendment....

4. Finally, I have considered the view, urged so forcefully since 1957 by our Brothers BLACK and DOUGLAS, that the First Amendment bars the suppression of any sexually oriented expression. That position would effect a sharp reduction, although perhaps not a total elimination, of the uncertainty that surrounds our current approach. Nevertheless, I am convinced that it would achieve that desirable goal only by stripping the States of power to an extent that cannot be justified by the commands of the Constitution, at least so long as there is available an alternative approach that strikes a better balance between the guarantee of free expression and the States' legitimate interests.

V

Our experience since *Roth* requires us not only to abandon the effort to pick out obscene materials on a case-by-case basis, but also to reconsider a fundamental postulate of *Roth:* that there exists a definable class of sexually oriented expression that may be totally suppressed by the Federal and State Governments. Assuming that such a class of expression does in fact exist, I am forced to conclude that the concept of "obscenity" cannot be defined with sufficient specificity and clarity to provide fair notice to persons who create and distribute sexually oriented materials, to prevent substantial erosion of protected speech as a by-product of the attempt to suppress unprotected speech, and to avoid very costly institutional harms. Given these inevitable side-effects of state efforts to suppress what is assumed to be *unprotected* speech, we must scrutinize with care the state interest that is asserted to justify the suppression. For in the absence of some very substantial interest in suppressing such speech, we can hardly condone the ill-effects that seem to flow inevitably from the effort....

Like the proscription of abortions, the effort to suppress obscenity is predicated on unprovable, although strongly held, assumptions about human behavior, morality, sex, and religion. The existence of these assumptions cannot validate a statute that substantially undermines the guarantees of the First Amendment, any more than the existence of similar assumptions on the issue of abortion can validate a statute that infringes the constitutionally-protected privacy interests of a pregnant woman.

If, as the Court today assumes, "a state legislature may...act on the... assumption that...commerce in obscene books, or public exhibitions focused on obscene conduct, have a tendency to exert a corrupting and debasing impact leading to antisocial behavior," *Paris Adult Theatre* v. *Slaton,*...then it is hard to see how state-ordered regimentation of our minds can ever be forestalled. For if a State may, in an effort to maintain or create a particular moral tone, prescribe what its citizens cannot read or cannot see, then it would seem to follow that in pursuit of that same objective a State could decree that its citizens must read certain books or must view certain films.... However laudable its goal—and that is obviously a question on which reasonable minds may differ—the State cannot proceed by means that violate the Constitution....

In short, while I cannot say that the interests of the State—apart from the question of juveniles and unconsenting adults—are trivial or nonexistent, I am compelled to conclude that these interests cannot justify the substantial damage to constitutional rights and to this Nation's judicial machinery that inevitably results from state efforts to bar the distribution even of unprotected material to consenting adults.... I would hold, therefore, that at least in the absence of distribution to juveniles or obtrusive exposure to unconsenting adults, the First and Fourteenth Amendments prohibit the state and federal governments from attempting wholly to suppress sexually oriented materials on the basis of their allegedly "obscene" contents. Nothing in this approach precludes those governments from taking action to serve what may be strong and legitimate interests through regulation of the manner of distribution of sexually oriented material.

...Difficult questions must still be faced, notably in the areas of distribution to juveniles and offensive exposure to unconsenting adults. Whatever the extent of state power to regulate in those areas, it should be clear that the view I espouse today would introduce a large measure of clarity to this troubled area, would reduce the institutional pressure on this Court and the rest of the State and Federal judiciary, and would guarantee fuller freedom of expression while leaving room for the protection of legitimate governmental interests. Since the Supreme Court of Georgia erroneously concluded that the State has power to suppress sexually oriented material even in the absence of distribution to juveniles or exposure to unconsenting adults, I would reverse that judgment and remand the case to that court for further proceedings not inconsistent with this opinion.

THE PRESS AND THE GOVERNMENT

June 25, 1973

The Nixon administration's handling of press relations incurred the criticism of prominent representatives of the Washington press corps June 25. By a 7-to-4 vote, the board of governors of the National Press Club accepted and endorsed a wide-ranging and sometimes bitterly worded report on news media relations with the federal government. The club's Professional Relations Committee, which was responsible for the final chapter, concluded that President Nixon had achieved "the most 'closed' administration in recent decades." In his handling of information pertinent to the Watergate affair, White House Press Secretary Ronald L. Ziegler was accused of having "misled the public and affronted the professional standards of the Washington press corps." And the committee asserted that the White House "had engaged in an unprecedented, government-wide effort to control, restrict and conceal information to which the public is entitled."

The 116-page study was undertaken independently of the Watergate controversy, but the Press Club's Professional Relations Committee pointed out that "those scandals serve unexpectedly, and with dramatic intensity, to focus the diverse issues in the Nixon administration's relationship with the press." The committee went on to say: "The Watergate scandals grew and flourished in an unhealthy atmosphere of secrecy, official lies, and attempted manipulation of newspapers, radio and television. Moreover, only an administration so insulated from the press and so contemptuous of its reporting function could have ignored the press's disclosures of scandal over the last year and attempted the complex cover-up which is now breaking down."

629

When told of the gist of the report, one of the White House representatives who had cooperated with those who conducted the study told Congressional Quarterly he felt "kind of badly about it." Ken W. Clawson, deputy director of communications, said: "Maybe it hasn't been true [in other sections of the White House], but I know we've spent an awful lot of time" cooperating with reporters' requests for information. "We're only one division; maybe that hasn't been true otherwise; but I don't think you'll find a reporter in this town that will say he called here and at least an effort wasn't made on his behalf." Ziegler could not be reached for comment.

The report was the result of a June 26, 1972, meeting of the Press Club's board of governors at which the Professional Relations Committee was instructed to conduct an investigation of the administration's "relationship with and to the press" and to make a public report to the board. In the fall of 1972, the committee enlisted the help of Lewis W. Wolfson, Associate Professor of Communication at American University in Washington, D.C., and a team of 20 graduate students, former students, and members of the Press Club. The team worked from a standard set of questions covering a number of fields in which relations between the administration and the press had become strained during the Nixon years. The students fanned out to interview two dozen members of the Washington press corps, 15 White House officials, and one member of the Committee for the Re-election of the President.

Three of the Nixon men—Clawson, Director of Communications Herbert G. Klein (since resigned), and DeVan Shumway, press chief of the Committee for the Re-election of the President—were interviewed by students under Wolfson's direction. But further efforts to reach White House officials were blocked by Ziegler. He told the club there would be no White House cooperation and disassociated the administration from remarks by by Clawson, Klein and Shumway.

The text of the report endorsed and accepted by the board of governors was written by Wolfson on the basis of the information gathered. The final statement of conclusions and recommendations was drafted by William Shannon of The New York Times, a member of the Press Club's Professional Relations Committee. The full committee on professional relations approved the recommendations June 12.

> Text of Chapter One of "The Press Covers Government: The Nixon Years from 1969 to Watergate," a study conducted by the Department of Communication, American University, for the National Press Club; and text of Conclusions and Recommendations by the Professional Relations Committee of the National Press Club follow:

The Truth about Government:
The Nixon Administration vs. The Washington
Press Corps

"The First Amendment presupposes that right conclusions are more likely to be gathered out of a multitude of tongues than through any kind of authoritative selection. To many, this is—and always will be—folly. But we have staked upon it our all."

—*Learned Hand*

By Lewis W. Wolfson

We knew when we undertook this study that while both officials and journalists pledge to inform the public fully, they hardly see eye to eye on what is full information about government, even in the best of times.

Politicians want news people to be "constructive" on behalf of their programs and their view of the national interest, as former White House press secretary George Reedy has pointed out. And, though the President and other officials are given an expansive, uncontradicted forum for their pronouncements in much of America's news media every day, they still will not readily accept the fact that for news people that is not enough. No journalist can remain true to his trade if he simply reports what officials think is "constructive" news about government.

This debate over defining what should be reported became news itself in the last two presidential administrations, starting with the Johnson Administration's crisis of credibility, and continuing with Nixon officials' efforts to discount much of the press's reporting of Washington and so, many feel, to try to discredit its appraisal of their performance.

The public needs no coaching to mistrust the media. But there is much evidence that Americans do need to recognize that this clash over the openness of government is not simply a matter of journalists' peevishness, as officials might try to picture it; it is the public's battle as well. The truth of this finding was brought home with unexpected force even as we were completing the study, as the Watergate exposures unfolded.

Watergate already stands as a landmark in American journalism. It was the press, and essentially the press alone, that unearthed the most scandalous misuse of the powers of government in this century. Watergate showed again how all of us profit when a single news organization persists in a lonely crusade in the face of massive official pressure and public indifference. It demonstrates beyond words the press's responsible pursuit of its First Amendment charge to act as a free and independent check on government.

631

The exposures early in Nixon's second term seemed almost to be the fated result of the unprecedented official suspicion and dislike of the media that, we found, had grown up in Nixon's first term. The contempt that some members of this administration have shown for the role of a free press has, in good measure, visited this tragedy upon them, and upon the country. Had there been more access to officials, more frankness in government, more honest dialogue about the press's role instead of harangues on its failings, restraints might have been set on the secretive instinct of the officials who created a web of covert political operations that led to their downfall.

But, while government clearly has hampered the press in its reporting during the Nixon years, this was not meant to be a one-sided study. Another lession of the Watergate is that there are many in the media who did not try to search further when they might have, and many other stories of government that remain untold. Thus, before examining further the deterioration of press-official relations, it seems appropriate to first look generally at the state of reporting from Washington.

The Press's Failure to Keep Up

Changing public needs flash by the press with stunning rapidity these days. But, despite the new demands that this places on the federal government, America's news organizations rarely seem to pause to review their coverage to ensure that they are keeping up with government's changing responsibilities. Too often the news media seem to leave it to officials to "discover" problems and prescribe national priorities for dealing with them—frequently in terms of their own political fortunes rather than the public's interest.

We found no shortage of men and women in the national press corps who are clear-eyed about the press's failings. They know that it is not necessarily true to its independent role here, no matter how often editors and reporters may invoke the press's freedom to be independent under the First Amendment. Indeed, some felt that the news media should be held to account equally with public officials for any breakdown in 'the system' that can be attributed to the public's poor information about the state of government and the country's other political and social institutions.

But the 'press corps' that fans out in Washington each day is hardly monolithic either in the thoughtfulness of its members about the reporting of government, or their wherewithal to tell the story. One or two-man bureaus that must daily grind out items for strings of newspapers or broadcast outlets might as well be on another planet from the 41-man Washington staff of reporter-analysts for The New York Times, or the network newsmen whose names are household words for millions of Americans.

They do look alike in one respect: all often seem to be scrambling that could open up to public officials as cable television and other new technology generate a sudden pressure for more news of Washington.

The changes ahead obviously pose great opportunities for the news media. But they also will lay on them an even heavier responsibility to exercise independent judgment in newsgathering and reporting. If they fail to meet that challenge, it inevitably will mean that America's news media more than ever will be leaving it to the politicians to feed the public a steady diet of "constructive" news of government.

A Narrow View From The Top

Eight years ago, in a report to a group of leading House Republicans (called Operation Enlightenment), Bruce Ladd pointed out to the GOP that they have "no exclusive monopoly on truth." He said that even if a journalist may personally favor the Democratic Party, officials should recognize that "a newsman's personal political beliefs rarely have influence on his professional competence as a reporter." Newsmen, like politicians, "want superior performance in reporting," Ladd said. He called this "the mutual interest and mutual challenge" of both the press and Republicans.

Officials professed to pursue that interest in the first Republican Administration since Ladd wrote those words. But, as they seized upon the "bully pulpit" of the White House to discuss media responsibilities, Nixon Administration leaders showed little of this spirit of a shared search for better reporting of government. It seemed to be attack, not dialogue, that Vice President Agnew and others most had in mind.

There was no hint of an admission of their own frailties. No official critic would concede that his favored brand of "objective" reporting well might abet the Administration's purposes without really serving the public's interest in knowing what goes on in government. None showed much sympathy about the pressures on the news media.

In short, with their narrow-gauged approach, and statements salted by such oversimplifications as "Eastern establishment" and "ideological plugola," top Nixon officials debased a genuine opportunity to give the public a greater appreciation of the news media's problems in developing more thoughtful reporting of Washington. It is almost as if they were telling Americans that the more simplistic the reporting of government, the better off they would be.

The Deteriorating Adversary Relationship

In the end, the study's main concern was to go beyond the public exchanges and examine what had happened in day-to-day relations between Nixon officials and journalists, and how that affected the quality of reporting of government.

helter skelter in pursuit of the day's story. Washington press practices still develop nearly as "informally and haphazardly" as when Douglass Cater wrote that line about them more than a decade ago. Reporters still move in herds much of the time, writing the same stories and following formulas for coverage of Washington that may no longer be relevant to the reporting of complex issues.

The press thrusts itself compulsively into the task of chronicling all the 'breaking' news, often at the expense of providing explanation and analysis. Much federal decisionmaking remains a mystery to the public, making it hard for people to intelligently debate policy that may change their lives. The press explores government's mistakes only on a hit-or-miss basis, and it rarely alerts people to tomorrow's problems until they are upon us.

The press corps still can count some notable successes during the last four years. The Washington Post and others acted in true press tradition when they pursued the Watergate scandal undaunted by supposedly authoritative government denials and derision. The Pentagon Papers fight gave new heart to reporters to ferret out information that government tries to conceal. And aggressive probing produced many in-depth newspaper, magazine and television stories that showed how government aggravates social problems as much as it solves them.

But the wrenching experience of the Vietnam war, and other policy failures, have made many more journalists conscious of how often they have left it to high officials to make vital national decisions without the challenge of informed public debate. And some correspondents concede that there are whole areas of government—the Congress, for example—that the news media scarcely penetrate despite their enormous impact on people's lives.

The press has been looking at itself more in the last four years, at least in part because of the sudden spotlight of criticism from the White House and others. But even with advances in coverage, it cannot be said that news organizations are moving smartly to deploy their forces to give people a better picture of the workings of the system. While they fend off critiques by self-interested politicians, America's news executives have only timidly reached out for suggestions for improving reporting on government so that the public achieves a better grasp of what is going on in that "mystery off there" that so often decides their fate, as Walter Lippmann once described the federal government.

The need for such soul-searching seems particularly acute at a time when public confidence in both the press and government is perilously low. It also may be that America's journalists have less time than they think to stake out their role in government news reporting before others do it for them. Today's attempts to manipulate coverage may well seem tame by comparison with the apparatus for instant publicity

We found in the press corps an overwhelming feeling that Washington's traditional adversary jousting between journalists and officials had deepened into an attempted freeze by government on any but the most superficial "straight news" reporting of the Nixon presidency.

Even in the worst moments in previous Administrations, correspondents felt, most Washington-wise politicians seemed to adopt certain unwritten rules for their encounters with news people. The adversary battle was a love-hate relationship. You talked to the press, even if you wanted to say as little as possible. You were friendly when it served your purposes, suddenly unavailable when you didn't want to talk. You could play favorites. You could rage at the reporter who, you thought, had 'burned' you. You could even cut him off for a while, though rarely for good. After all, you did need the press.

And sometimes both of you could even let down your hair over a late-afternoon scotch, with the greater mutual understanding between the journalist and his sources that develops over a period of time. You gave a little to get a little, and everybody had a vague feeling that somehow good government was being served, even if journalists and politicians could never agree on exactly what the public should know about what went on in Washington.

In the first Nixon Administration it was different, the correspondents say. White House and other officials who came here with little previous experience in national politics were not used to having reporters hanging around outside the door while they were making decisions, and picking over policy after it had been set. They were not inclined to abide by the traditional adversary conventions. From there, it was only a small step to trying to put the press on the defensive by discrediting its reports about government.

Indeed, Nixon Administration officials reacted to the traditional give-and-take by framing a policy of massive official hostility to all but a few, selected portions of the news media—even while they argued that it was the press that was overreacting to *their* criticism.

The hard-nosed reporter who had gone through the minuets of the Eisenhower and Kennedy years, and the often unprecedented slugging matches in the Johnson Administration to get sound information on policy decisions, felt that there was now a calculated effort to make it difficult for him to report on anything other than the official view of what was going on in the federal government.

Was Richard Nixon's first Administration an 'open' one, as promised? we asked. Most said that, to the contrary, this was the most 'closed' Administration in memory, both in the access to information, and in access to the people who knew how the decisions had been made.

There was praise for communications director Hebert Klein's efforts to make agencies more responsive on routine requests for information and interviews. There was ready acknowledgement that some officials (most notably Henry Kissinger) did give out reliable information on policy on a regular basis, as had key officials in past administrations.

But the people interviewed felt that the whole approach of the White House on even minimally sensitive questions was to discourage such dialogue and to try to diminish whatever impact their reporting might have on the public's insight into his administration.

White House reporters, especially, felt that they were at the mercy of a very sophisticated presidential public relations apparatus that aggressively sought out television coverage in controlled settings, simultaneously downgrading the importance of in-depth questioning about policy, and trying to undermine the integrity of the national press corps in the public's eye. The Nixon people "tried to shift the credibility gap from the presidency to the press," as one person put it.

All the other moves of the last four years—the disdain for the tradition of periodic presidential press conferences, attempts to bypass the press corps to influence local editors, the 'suggestions' from Clay Whitehead about the content of network news, the subpoenaing of news people—were seen by correspondents as part of the pattern of throwing fences up around free and searching reporting of the federal government, and trying to keep the most influential—and most troublesome— news organizations on the defensive.

Some correspondents felt that the official freeze probably could not, and would not, be sustained in Nixon's second term. But most of the members of the press corps whom we interviewed felt that the basic Administration attitude toward the news media would not change, even if there were periods of more amicable relations.

The Urgent Need

It is hard to be certain at this point whether this burst of attention to Washington reporting will prompt a sharper awareness of the press's responsibilities, or whether the deepening resentments of the last four years have pushed further out of reach the ultimate objective of getting across to the American people the real news of Washington—what Cater has called the "essential truth" about government that makes democracy possible.

In the long run, debate of any kind seems a sign of health. Anything that is so important to good government as improved reporting should be a matter for national discussion, and the news media should welcome that. It is difficult to argue that their operations in Washington cannot stand more scrutiny and planning. Nor is it to be doubted that the local view of the federal government, which Nixon Administration officials have so passionately sought, must be heard out in the press and on television.

But national leaders don't enhance the debate if they play politics with journalism's shortcomings. A politician might decry "instant" analysis of government; a statesman will also call for fuller, more thoughtful analysis by America's news media. He will seek the common objective of full analysis by America's news media. He will seek the common objective of full reporting by all agents of a free press, no matter what risk that "multitude of tongues" might hold for his own public image.

We found in this study an urgent need for a will on the part of both officials and journalists to seek superior reporting of complex public issues and of the decisions being made by the most powerful government in the world. If 'the system' is in trouble, then it would seem to be in the interest of this (or any) administration and of the press— adversaries though they may be—to awaken to the fact that the American people need to know what's really going on at its center in Washington if they are to feel more a part of democratic government than they do now.

Conclusions and Recommendations by the Professional Relations Committee of the National Press Club

The following statement of conclusions and recommendations was approved by the Professional Relations Committee of the National Press Club on June 12, 1973:

It is a coincidence that work on this study parelleled in time the gradual unfolding of the Watergate scandals; the study had broader, independent origins. Yet, those scandals serve unexpectedly, and with dramatic intensity, to focus the diverse issues in the Nixon Administration's relationship with the press.

The Watergate scandals grew and flourished in an unhealthy atmosphere of secrecy, official lies, and attempted manipulation of newspapers, radio and television. Moreover, only an administration so insulated from the press and so contemptuous of its reporting function could have ignored the press's disclosures of scandal over the last year and attempted the complex cover-up which is now breaking down.

The Professional Relations Committee of the National Press Club on the basis of the facts set forth in this study, which are corroborated by our own daily experience as journalists, concludes that President Nixon has not only fallen short of his publicly-stated goal of achieving an "open administration," but has actually moved in the opposite direction. The Nixon Administration is the most "closed" administration in recent decades.

We find evidence of numerous and persistent attempts by the Administration to restrict the flow of legitimate public information necessary to the effective functioning of a responsible government in a self-governing society.

At the highest level, President Nixon has failed to hold regular and frequent press conferences, and has thereby deprived the press of the only forum in which it can question the President, and deprived the public of vital access to presidential thinking on public issues. By holding fewer news conferences in the last four years than any of his predecessors in the previous 36 years, Mr. Nixon has seriously weakened a well-established and essential American institution. To renew a regular and continuing dialogue with the public, we recommend that the President hold once-a-week press conferences announced in advance.

The White House press secretary has been reduced to a totally-programed spokesman without independent authority or comprehensive background knowledge of Administration policies. Rather than opening a window to the White House, the press secretary closes doors. Information about public business is supplied on a selective, self-serving basis. Legitimate questions about public affairs are not answered on a day-to-day basis; even worse, such questions are often not seriously considered.

Ronald Ziegler as White House press secretary, particularly during the Watergate disclosures of the past year, has misled the public and affronted the professional standards of the Washington press corps.

We believe there is need for a better public understanding concerning the function of a White House press secretary, or any other government information officer. They hold public offices paid for by public funds. The only justification for such an office is to improve the flow of information from the government to the public. There is no need, for example, for a White House press secretary in the name of "improved coordination" to control the access of working reporters to responsible Administration officials. Such contacts ought to be on a person-to-person basis. Officials entrusted with the conduct of important government business can be expected to be mature enough to manage their own relations with the press without arbitrary outside control. Ideally, the White House press secretary would intervene in these relations only to open up access for reporters with officials who proved unresponsive to press queries. If the post of White House press secretary is to serve a function for the press and public, it should be occupied by an individual—not necessarily with news experience—but of stature and broad background.

The Office of the Director of Communications has operated as a propaganda ministry. There is no place in our society for this kind of operation.

We commend the Administration for adopting a policy of on-the-record news conferences for Henry Kissinger, the President's national security adviser. As against that gain, however, we have to set the fact that Administration officials seriously abused the Washington institution of the "backgrounder" which, notwithstanding its inherent difficulties, has served a useful purpose. If abuses have been less frequent in the last two years, that is because the number of backgrounders has dwindled.

Despite Administration claims to the contrary, we conclude that the cause of freedom of information—public access to government reports and records—made no net progress in the first Nixon term, and was sometimes actively hindered. Many federal agencies dodged the spirit and intent of the Freedom of Information Act.

We note specific dangers in the Nixon Administration's aggressive attitude toward public and commercial television. It has sought to influence the news, commentary and documentary programs of public broadcasting stations. We strongly recommend that the institutional structure of public broadcasting be strengthened and its financing arranged in ways that will guarantee that the content of it programs is completely and unquestionably insulated from direct control by the White House or Congress.

The Office of Telecommunications Policy has raised the specter of government censorship of commercial television more seriously than at any time in history. The Administration appears to want a role in deciding what news should be reported about its own activities and how it should be reported. Nothing could be further from the spirit of the First Amendment to the Constitution.

Threats to the freedom of the press in the last four years have come from the courts as well as from the Administration, but in several cases the Administration has been behind these threats. Four reporters have gone to jail for protecting sources and the prospect is that more will go in the future, perhaps joined by editors and publishers. Although this issue spans Congress and the courts as well as the executive branch, it has to be noted that the record of the Justice Department under the Nixon Administration has been particularly hostile to adequate legal protection for newsmen in the practice of their profession.

In this context, the nation's press is not wholly without blame for the unfavorable drift of public policy. We deplore the failure of many publishers, network officials, radio and televison station owners, and editorial page editors to protest vigorously the Administration's incursions into press rights, the concealment of information, and the narrowing of news channels.

In summary, we conclude that the Nixon Administration has engaged in an unprecedented, government-wide effort to control, restrict and conceal information to which the public is entitled, and has conducted for its own political purposes a concerted campaign to discredit the press. The Administration appears unwilling to accept the traditional role of an independent press in a free society. It is to be hoped that this Administration attitude will change, but we see no strong likelihood of such change. We urge the nation's press to muster all of the resources at its command to resist any and all forms of intimidation and control, and to assert its legal rights and the proud traditions of its profession.

COURT BAN ON PUBLIC AID
TO NONPUBLIC SCHOOLS
June 25, 1973

Already boxed in by rising costs and changing social values, the na-
tion's private and parochial schools suffered yet another crippling
blow June 25—this time at the hands of the U.S. Supreme Court. On
the final day of its 1972-73 term, the Court rejected as unconstitu-
tional the state statutes of New York and Pennsylvania that sought to
provide public aid for nonpublic schools and thereby to offset the
expense of private education. In three sweeping decisions, the Court
reasserted its earlier holdings that state funding of religious schools
was not permissible under the First Amendment's Establishment Clause
that decrees separation of church and state. The June 25 rulings
similarly dealt a severe blow to the Nixon administration's proposals to
grant tax relief to parents of private school students.

In the first decision, the justices struck down by an 8-1 vote a New
York law that provided payments to nonpublic schools, based on the
number of pupils, to cover the costs of tests and examinations required
by the state. Chief Justice Warren E. Burger, who had written all of the
Court's religious liberty opinions in the past four years, delivered the
opinion of the Court. The New York statute was voided because "despite
the obviously integral role of testing in the total teaching process, no
attempt is made under the statute, and no means are available, to as-
sure that internally prepared tests are free of religious instruction." The
Court refused to accept the state's contention that it should be allowed
to pay for activities "mandated" by its own laws or regulations. It said
the task of protecting states against "excessive entanglement" in reli-
gious education "would be irreversibly frustrated if the Establishment

Clause were read as permitting a State to pay for whatever it requires a private school to do" (Levitt v. Committee for Public Education). Associate Justice Byron R. White dissented.

In a 6-3 decision, the Court also invalidated a three-pronged 1972 New York law that provided for (1) direct grants for maintenance and repair of nonpublic schools serving low-income families, (2) payments to reimburse low-income parents for private school tuition fees, and (3) tax credits for parents of nonpublic school students who did not qualify for reimbursement. Associate Justice Lewis F. Powell Jr., speaking for the majority, expanded upon a 1971 opinion delivered by Chief Justice Burger. A "now well defined three-part test," Powell said, had emerged from the Court's decisions on "the full sweep of the Establishment Clause cases." He pointed out that "taken together these decisions dictate that to pass muster under the Establishment Clause the law in question, first, must reflect a clearly secular legislative purpose,...second, must have a primary effect that neither advances nor inhibits religion,...and third, must avoid excessive government entanglement with religion...."

In the Court's view, the New York statute failed this test: "No attempt is made to restrict payments to those expenditures related to upkeep of facilities used exclusively for secular purposes," and "it simply cannot be denied that this section has a primary effect that advances religion in that it subsidizes directly the religious activities of sectarian elementary and secondary schools." In addition, "New York's tuition reimbursement program also fails the 'effect' test, for ...the effect of the aid is unmistakably to provide desired financial support for non-public, sectarian institutions." Similarly, the tax credit to parents who do not qualify for reimbursement is equally unconstitutional. "The qualifying parent under either program receives the same form of en-couragement and reward for sending his children to nonpublic schools" (Committee for Public Education v. Nyquist).

Separate Opinion in New York Case

Chief Justice Burger and Associate Justices White and William H. Rehnquist filed a separate opinion, concurring in part and dissenting in part, but stressing their belief in the constitutionality of state aid to parents that might ultimately be used by them to further religious education. They reasoned that "the Establishment Clause does not for-bid governments, state or federal, from enacting a program of general welfare under which benefits are distributed to private individuals, even though many of those individuals may elect to use those benefits in ways that 'aid' religious instruction or worship."

Justice Powell also delivered the opinion of the Court invalidating, by a 6-3 vote, a Pennsylvania program providing for reimbursement of a share of the tuition paid by all parents with children in private schools.

The Court found "no constitutionally significant distinctions between this law and the one declared invalid today in Nyquist." Pennsylvania had argued that, since partial reimbursements of tuition fees were made to all parents with children in nonpublic schools, no assumption could be made as to how individual parents would spend the money. But the Court said: "Whether that benefit be viewed as a simple tuition subsidy, as an incentive to parents to send their children to sectarian schools, or as a reward for having done so, at bottom its intended consequence is to preserve and support religion-oriented institutions" (Sloan v. Lemon).

Catholic schools, which accounted for 85 per cent of nonpublic enrollment, were thought to be hardest hit by the Supreme Court's action. Many people went so far as to say the Court's decisions had undermined the very existence of parochial schools. Father Joseph P. Bynon, superintendent of Roman Catholic diocesan schools in Brooklyn, N.Y., asserted that "It seems to be a biased, twisted interpretation of the First Amendment." But the implications of the rulings were unmistakable. Statutes in seven other states were effectively killed and hopes dimmed, at least temporarily, for the future of aid to the nation's 11,000 parochial elementary and secondary schools. The Catholic schools seemed the most hard pressed; 3,000 of them had shut their doors since 1965 and enrollment had dropped by 1.8 million students. Father Emmet Harrington of Portland, Ore., summed up the problem: "People have been expecting someone else to bail us out. Now we realize that we will have to do it on our own."

Mississippi and South Carolina Cases

The Court handed down on June 25 two other decisions bearing on state aid to private educational institutions. In Norwood v. Harrison, the Justices unanimously rejected as unconstitutional a Mississippi statute authorizing the state to purchase textbooks to be distributed free to private academies, many of which came into existence in apparent response to desegregation of public schools. Chief Justice Burger declared in the opinion that struck down the law as violative of the Fourteenth Amendment's Equal Protection Clause: "The constitutional infirmity of the Mississippi textbook program is that it significantly aids the organization and continuation of a separate system of private schools which, under the District Court holding, may discriminate if they so desire. A State's constitutional obligation requires it to steer clear not only of operating the old dual system of racially segregated schools but also of giving significant aid to institutions that practice racial or other invidious discrimination."

The other case (Hunt v. McNair) involved a South Carolina law under which bonds had been issued to provide funds for construction of a Baptist-controlled college. The Court let stand that statute by a 6-3 vote.

The majority found that the financing was permissible because the bonds, backed by the South Carolina Educational Facilities Authority, did not impose a direct or indirect obligation upon the state. Since the provisions of the law were available to all institutions of higher learning in South Carolina, the Court concluded that the primary purpose of the statute was not to advance or inhibit sectarian interests. The law did not "foreshadow excessive entanglement between the state and religion."

Excerpts from Supreme Court opinion delivered June 25, 1973, by Chief Justice Burger in the case of Arthur Levitt, as Comptroller of the State of New York and Ewald B. Nyquist, as Commissioner of Education of the State of New York, Appellants, v. Committee for Public Education and Religious Liberty et al:

In this case we are asked to decide whether Chapter 138 of New York State's Laws of 1970, under which the State reimburses private schools throughout the State for certain costs of testing and recordkeeping, violates the Establishment Clause of the First Amendment. A three-judge district court, with one judge dissenting, held the Act unconstitutional....

In April 1970, the New York Legislature appropriated $28,000,000 for the purpose of reimbursing nonpublic schools throughout the State.... [T]he State has in essence sought to reimburse private schools for performing various "services" which the state "mandates." Of these mandated services, by far the most expensive for nonpublic schools is the "administration, grading and the compiling and reporting of the results of tests and examinations." Such "tests and examinations" appear to be of two kinds: (a) state-prepared examinations, such as the "Regents examinations" and the "Pupil Evaluation Program Tests," and (b) traditional teacher-prepared tests, which are drafted by the non-public school teachers for the purpose of measuring the pupils' progress in subjects required to be taught under state law. The overwhelming majority of testing in nonpublic, as well as public, schools is of the latter variety.

Church-sponsored as well as secular nonpublic schools are eligible to receive payments under the Act. The District Court made findings that the Commissioner of Education had "construed and applied" the Act "to include as permissible beneficiaries schools which (a) impose religious restrictions on admissions; (b) require attendance of pupils at religious activities; (c) require obedience by students to the doctrines and dogmas of a particular faith; (d) require pupils to attend instruction in the theology or doctrine of a particular faith; (e) are an integral part of the religious mission of the church sponsoring it; (f) have as a substantial purpose the inculcation of religious values; (g) impose religious restrictions on faculty appointments; and (h) impose religious restrictions on what or how the faculty may teach."...

Section 8 of the Act states: "Nothing contained in this act shall be construed to authorize the making of any payment under this act for religious worship or instruction." However, the Act contains no provision authorizing state audits of school financial records to determine whether a school's actual costs in complying with the mandated services are less than the annual lump sum payment. Nor does the Act require a school to return to the State moneys received in excess of its actual expenses....

In *Committee for Public Education and Religious Liberty* v. *Nyquist*, the Court has today struck down a provision of New York law authorizing "direct money grants from the State to 'qualifying' non-public schools to be used for the 'maintenance and repair...of school facilities and equipment to ensure the health, welfare and safety of enrolled pupils.'" The infirmity of the statute in *Nyquist* lay in its undifferentiated treatment of the maintenance and repair of facilities devoted to religious and secular functions of recipient, sectarian schools. Since "[n]o attempt is made to restrict payments to those expenditures related to the upkeep of facilities used exclusively for secular purposes," the Court held that the statute has the primary effect of advancing religion and is, therefore, violative of the Establishment Clause....

The statute now before us, as written and as applied by the Commissioner of Education, contains some of the same constitutional flaws that led the Court to its decision in *Nyquist*.... Chapter 138 provides for a direct money grant to sectarian schools for performance of various "services." Among those services is the maintenance of a regular program of traditional internal testing designed to measure pupil achievement. Yet, despite the obviously integral role of testing in the total teaching process, no attempt is made under the statute, and no means are available, to assure that internally prepared tests are free of religious instruction.

We cannot ignore the substantial risk that these examinations, prepared by teachers under the authority of religious institutions, will be drafted with an eye, unconsciously or otherwise, to inculcate students in the religious precepts of the sponsoring church. We do not "assume that teachers in parochial schools will be guilty of bad faith or any conscious design to evade the limitations imposed by the statute and the First Amendment."... But the potential for conflict "inheres in the situation," and because of that the State is constitutionally compelled to assure that the state-supported activity is not being used for religious indoctrination.... Since the State has failed to do so here, we are left with no choice under *Nyquist* but to hold that Chapter 138 constitutes an impermissible aid to religion; this is so because the aid that will be devoted to secular fuctions is not identifiable and separable from aid to sectarian activities....

To the extent that appellants argue that the State should be permitted to pay for any activity "mandated" by state law or regulation, we must reject the contention. State or local law might, for example, "mandate" minimum lighting or sanitary facilities for all school buildings, but such commands would not authorize a State to provide support for those facilities in church-sponsored schools. The essential inquiry in each case, as expressed in our prior decisions, is whether the challenged state aid has the primary purpose or effect of advancing religion or religious education or whether it leads to excessive entanglement by the State in the affairs of the religious institution.... That inquiry would be irreversibly frustrated if the Establishment Clause were read as permitting a state to pay for whatever it requires a private school to do.

We hold that the lump sum payments under Chapter 138 violate the Establishment Clause. Since Chapter 138 provides only for a single per-pupil allotment for a variety of specified services, some secular and some potentially religious, neither this Court nor the District Court can properly reduce that allotment to an amount corresponding to the actual costs incurred in performing reimbursable secular services. That is a legislative, not a judicial function.

Accordingly, the judgment of the District Court is affirmed.

Mr. Justice Douglas, Mr. Justice Brennan, and Mr. Justice Marshall are of the view that affirmance is compelled by our decision today in *Committee for Public Education and Religious Liberty* v. *Nyquist.*

Mr. Justice White dissents.

> *Excerpts from Supreme Court opinion delivered June 25, 1973, by Associate Justice Lewis F. Powell Jr. in the case of Committee for Public Education and Religious Liberty v. Nyquist:*

This case raises a challenge under the Establishment Clause of the First Amendment to the constitutionality of a recently enacted New York law which provides financial assistance, in several ways, to non-public elementary and secondary schools in that State. The case involves an intertwining of societal and constitutional issues of the greatest importance.

James Madison, in his Memorial and Remonstrance Against Religious Assessments, admonished that a "prudent jealousy" for religious freedoms required that they never become "entangled...in precedents." His strongly held convictions, coupled with those of Thomas Jefferson and others among the Founders, are reflected in the first Clauses of the First Amendment of the Bill of Rights, which state that "Congress shall make no law respecting an establishment of religion, or prohibiting the free exercise thereof." Yet, despite Madison's admonition and the "sweep of the absolute prohibition" of the Clauses, this Nation's history has not been one of entirely sanitized separation between Church and State. It has never been thought either possible or desirable to enforce a regime of total separation, and as a consequence cases arising under these Clauses have presented some of the most perplexing questions to come before this Court. Those cases have occasioned thorough and thoughtful scholarship by several of this Court's most respected former Justices, including Justices Black, Frankfurter, Harlan, Jackson, Rutledge, and Chief Justice Warren.

As a result of these decisions and opinions, it may no longer be said that the Religion Clauses are free of "entangling" precedents. Neither, however, may it be said that Jefferson's metaphoric "wall of separation" between Church and State has become "as winding as the famous serpentine wall" he designed for the University of Virginia.... Indeed, the controlling constitutional standards have become firmly rooted and the broad contours of our inquiry are now well defined. Our task, therefore, is to assess New York's several forms of aid in the light of principles already delineated....

I

...The first section of the challenged enactment, entitled Health and Safety Grants for Nonpublic School Children," provides for direct money grants from the State to "qualifying" nonpublic schools to be used for the "maintenance and repair of...school facilities and equipment to ensure the health, welfare and safety of enrolled pupils." A "qualifying" school is any nonpublic, nonprofit elementary or secondary school which "has been designated during the [immediately preceding] year as serving a high concentration of pupils from low-income families for purposes of Title IV of the Federal Higher Education Act of 1965." Such schools are entitled to receive a grant of $30 per pupil per year, or $40 per pupil per year if the facilities are more than 25 years old. Each school is required to submit to the Commissioner of Education an audited statement of its expenditures for maintenance and repair during the preceding year, and its grant may not exceed the total of such expenses. The Commissioner is also required to ascertain the average per-pupil cost for equivalent maintenance and repair services in the public schools, and in no event may the grant to nonpublic qualifying schools exceed 50% of that figure.... This section is prefaced by a series of legislative findings which shed light on the State's purpose in enacting the law. These findings conclude that the State "has a primary responsibility to ensure the health, welfare and safety of children attending...nonpublic schools"; that the "fiscal crisis in nonpublic education...has caused a diminution of proper maintenance and repair programs, threatening the health, welfare and safety of nonpublic school children" in low-income urban areas; and that "a healthy and safe school environment" contributes "to the stability of urban neighborhoods." For these reasons, the statute declares that "the state has the right to make grants for maintenance and repair expenditures which are clearly secular, neutral and non-ideological in nature."

The remainder of the challenged legislation...is a single package captioned the "Elementary and Secondary Education Opportunity Program." It is composed, essentially, of two parts, a tuition grant program and a tax benefit program. Section 2 establishes a limited plan providing tuition reimbursements to parents of children attending elementary or secondary nonpublic schools. To qualify under this section the parent must have an annual taxable income of less than $5,000. The amount of reimbursement is limited to $50 for each grade school child and $100 for each high school child. Each parent is required, however, to submit to the Commissioner of Education a verified statement containing a receipted tuition bill, and the amount of state reimbursement may not exceed 50% of that figure. No restrictions are imposed on the use of the funds by the reimbursed parents.

This section, like Sec. 1, is prefaced by a series of legislative findings designed to explain the impetus for the State's action. Expressing a dedication to the "vitality of our pluralistic society," the findings state that a "healthy competitive and diverse alternative to public education is not only desirable but indeed vital to a state and nation that have continually reaffirmed the value of individual differences." The findings further emphasize that the right to select among alternative educational systems "is diminished or even denied to children of lower-income families, whose parents, of all groups, have the least options in determining where their children are to be educated." Turning to the public schools, the findings state that any "precipitous decline in the number of non-public school pupils would cause a massive increase in public school enrollment and costs," an increase that would "aggravate an already serious fiscal crisis in public education" and would "seriously jeopardize the quality education for all children." Based on these premises, the statute asserts the State's right to relieve the financial burden of parents who send their children to nonpublic schools through this tuition reimbursement program. Repeating the declaration contained in Sec. 1, the findings conclude that "such assistance is clearly secular, neutral and nonideological."

The remainder of the "Elementary and Secondary Education Opportunity Program," contained in Secs. 3, 4, and 5 of the challenged law, is designed to provide a form of tax relief to those who fail to qualify for tuition reimbursement. Under these sections parents may subtract from their adjusted gross income for state income tax purposes a designated amount for each dependent for whom they have paid at least $50 in nonpublic school tuition. If the taxpayer's adjusted gross income is less than $9,000 he may subtract $1,000 for each of as many as three dependents. As the taxpayer's income rises, the amount he may subtract diminishes. Thus, if a taxpayer has adjusted gross income of $15,000, he may subtract only $400 per dependent, and if his income is $25,000 or more, no deduction is allowed. The amount of the deduction is not dependent upon how much the taxpayer actually paid for nonpublic school tuition, and is given in addition to any deductions to which the taxpayer may be entitled for other religious or charitable contributions. As indicated in the memorandum from the Majority Leader and President pro tem of the Senate, submitted to each New York legislator during consideration of the bill, the actual tax benefits under these provisions were carefully calculated in advance. Thus, comparable tax benefits pick up at approximately the point at which tuition reimbursement benefits leave off....

The District Court, relying on findings in a similar case recently decided by the same court, adopted a profile of these sectarian, nonpublic schools similar to the one suggested in the plaintiffs' complaint. Qualifying institutions, under all three segments of the enactment, could be ones that:

> "(a) impose religious restrictions on admissions; (b) require attendance of pupils at religious activities; (c) require obedience by students to the doctrines and dogmas of a particular faith; (d) require pupils to attend instruction in the theology or doctrine of a particular faith; (e) are an integral part of the religious mission of the church sponsoring it; (f) have as a substantial purpose the inculcation of religious values; (g) impose religious restrictions on faculty appointments; and (h) impose religious restrictions on what or how the faculty may teach."

Of course, the characteristics of individual schools may vary widely from that profile. Some 700,000 to 800,000 students, constituting almost 20% of the State's entire elementary and secondary school population, attend over 2,000 nonpublic schools, approximately 85% of which are church-affiliated. And while "all or practically all" of the 280 schools entitled to receive "maintenance and repair" grants "are related to the Roman Catholic Church and teach Catholic religious doctrine to some degree," institutions qualifying under the remainder of the statute include a substantial number of Jewish, Lutheran, Episcopal, Seventh Day Adventist, and other church-affiliated schools.

Plaintiffs argued below that because of the substantially religious character of the intended beneficiaries, each of the State's three enactments offended the Establishment Clause. The District Court, in an opinion carefully canvassing this Court's recent precedents, held unanimously that...maintenance and repair grants and...tuition reimbursement grants were invalid. As to the income tax provisions,...however, a majority of the District Court, over the dissent of Circuit Judge Hays, held that the Establishment Clause had not been violated.... We affirm the District Court insofar as it struck down Secs. 1 and 2 and reverse its determination regarding Secs. 3, 4, and 5.

II

The history of the Establishment Clause has been recounted frequently and need not be repeated here.... It is enough to note that it is now firmly established that a law may be one "respecting the establishment of religion" even though its consequence is not to promote a "state religion,"...and even though it does not aid one religion more than another but merely benefits all religions alike.... It is equally well established, however, that not every law that confers an "indirect," "remote," or "incidental" benefit upon religious institutions is, for that reason alone, constitutionally invalid....

Most of the cases coming to this Court raising Establishment Clause questions have involved the relationship between religion and education. Among these religion-education precedents, two general categories of cases may be identified: those dealing with religious activities within the public schools, and those involving public aid in varying forms to sectarian educational institutions. While the New York legislation places this case in the latter category, its resolution requires consideration not only of the several aid-to-sectarian-education cases but also of our other education precedents and of several important non-education cases. For the now well defined three-part test that has emerged from our decisions is a product of considerations derived from the full sweep of the Establishment Clause cases. Taken together these decisions dictate that to pass muster under the Establishment Clause the law in question, first, must reflect a clearly secular legislative purpose,...second, must have a primary effect that neither advances nor inhibits religion,...and, third, must avoid excessive government entanglement with religion....

In applying these criteria to the three distinct forms of aid involved in this case, we need touch only briefly on the requirement of a "secular legislative purpose." As the recitation of legislative purposes appended to New York's law indicates, each measure is adequately supported by legitimate, nonsectarian state interests. We do not question the propriety, and fully secular content, of New York's interest in preserving a healthy and safe educational environment for all of its school children. And we do not doubt—indeed, we fully recognize—the validity of the State's interests in promoting pluralism and diversity among its public and nonpublic schools. Nor do we hesitate to acknowledge the reality of its concern for an already overburdened public school system that might suffer in the event that a significant percentage of children presently attending nonpublic schools should abandon those schools in favor of the public schools.

But the propriety of a legislature's purposes may not immunize from further scrutiny a law which either has a primary effect that advances religion, or which fosters excessive entanglements between Church and State. Accordingly, we must weigh each of the three aid provisions challenged here against these criteria of effect and entanglement.

A

The "maintenance and repair" provisions of Sec. 1 authorize direct payments to nonpublic schools, virtually all of which are Roman Catholic schools in low income areas.... No attempt is made to restrict payments to those expenditures related to the upkeep of facilities used exclusively for secular purposes, nor do we think it possible within the context of these religion-oriented institutions to impose such restrictions. Nothing in the statute, for instance, bars a qualifying school from paying out of state funds the salary of employees who maintain the school chapel, or the cost of renovating classrooms in which religion is taught, or the cost of heating and lighting those same facilities. Absent appropriate restrictions on expenditures for these and similar purposes, it simply cannot be denied that this section has a primary effect that advances religion in that it subsidizes directly the religious activities of sectarian elementary and secondary schools.

The state officials nevertheless argue that these expenditures for "maintenance and repair" are similar to other financial expenditures approved by this Court. Primarily they rely on *Everson* v. *Board of Education, Board of Education* v. *Allen*, and *Tilton* v. *Richardson*.... In *Everson*, the Court, in a five-to-four decision, approved a program of reimbursements to parents of public as well as parochial school children for bus fares paid in connection with transportation to and from school, a program which the Court characterized as approaching the "verge" of impermissible state aid. In *Allen*, decided some 20 years later, the Court upheld a New York law authorizing the provision of *secular* textbooks for all children in grades seven through 12 attending public and nonpublic schools. Finally, in *Tilton*, the Court upheld federal grants of funds for the construction of facilities to be used for clearly *secular* purposes by public and nonpublic institutions of higher learning.

These cases simply recognize that sectarian schools perform secular, educative functions as well as religious functions, and that some forms of aid may be channelled to the secular without providing direct aid to the sectarian. But the channel is a narrow one, as the above cases illustrate. Of course it is true in each case that the provision of such neutral, nonideological aid, assisting only the secular functions of sectarian schools, served indirectly and incidentally to promote the religious function by rendering it more likely that children would attend sectarian schools and by freeing the budgets of those schools for use in other nonsecular areas. But an indirect and incidental effect beneficial to religious institutions has never been thought a sufficient defect to warrant the invalidation of a state law....

What we have said demonstrates that New York's maintenance and repair provisions violate the Establishment Clause because their effect, inevitably, is to subsidize and advance the religious mission of sectarian schools. We have no occasion, therefore, to consider the further question whether those provisions as presently written would also fail to survive scrutiny under the administrative entanglement aspect of the three-part test because assuring the secular use of all funds requires too intrusive and continuing a relationship between Church and State....

B

New York's tuition reimbursement program also fails the "effect" test, for much the same reasons that govern its maintenance and repair grants....

There can be no question that these grants could not, consistently with the Establishment Clause, be given directly to sectarian schools, since they would suffer from the same deficiency that renders invalid the grants for maintenance and repair. In the absence of an effective means of guaranteeing that the state aid derived from public funds will be used exclusively for secular, neutral, and nonideological purposes, it is clear from our cases that direct aid in whatever form is invalid.... The controlling question here, then, is whether the fact that the grants are delivered to parents rather than schools is of such significance as to compel a contrary result. The State and intervenor-appellees rely on *Everson* and *Allen* for their claim that grants to parents, unlike grants to institutions, respect the "wall of separation" required by the Constitution....

The tuition grants here are subject to no such restrictions [as were found in *Everson* and *Allen*]. There has been no endeavor "to guarantee the separation between secular and religious educational functions and to ensure that State financial aid supports only the former."... Indeed, it is precisely the function of New York's law to provide assistance to private schools, the great majority of which are sectarian. By reimbursing parents for a portion of their tuition bill, the State seeks to relieve their financial burdens sufficiently to assure that they continue to have the option to send their children to religion-oriented schools. And while the other purposes for that aid—to perpetuate a pluralistic educational environment and to protect the fiscal integrity of over-burdened public schools—are certainly unexceptionable, the effect of the aid is unmistakably to provide desired financial support for nonpublic, sectarian institutions....

Although we think it clear, for the reasons above stated, that New York's tuition grant program fares no better under the "effect" test than its maintenance and repair program, in view of the novelty of the question we will address briefly the subsidiary arguments made by the state officials and intervenors in its defense.

First, it has been suggested that it is of controlling significance that New York's program calls for *reimbursement* for tuition already paid rather than for direct contributions which are merely routed through the parents to the schools, in advance of or in lieu of payment by the parents. The parent is not a mere conduit, we are told, but is absolutely free to spend the money he receives in any manner he wishes. There is no element of coercion attached to the reimbursement, and no assurance that the money will eventually end up in the hands of religious schools. The absence of any element of coercion, however, is irrelevant to questions arising under the Establishment Clause.... A similar inquiry governs here: if the grants are offered as an incentive to parents to send their children to sectarian schools by making unrestricted cash payments to them, the Establishment Clause is violated whether or not the actual dollars given eventually find their way into the sectarian institutions. Whether the grant is labeled a reimbursement, a reward or a subsidy, its substantive impact is still the same. In sum, we agree with the conclusion of the District Court that "[w]hether he gets it during the current year, or as reimbursement for the past year, is of no constitutional importance."...

Second, the Majority Leader and President pro tem of the State Senate argues that it is significant here that the tuition reimbursement grants pay only a portion of the tuition bill, and an even smaller portion of the religious school's total expenses. The New York state limits reimbursement to 50% of any parent's actual outlay. Additionally, intervenor estimates that only 30% of the total cost of nonpublic education is covered by tuition payments, with the remaining coming from "voluntary contributions, endowments and the like." On the basis of these two statistics, appellee reasons that the "maximum tuition reimbursement by the State is thus only 15% of the educational costs in the nonpublic schools." And, "since compulsory education laws of the State, by necessity require significantly more than 15% of school time to be devoted to teaching secular courses," the New York statute provides "a statistical guarantee of neutrality." It should readily be seen that this is simply another variant of the argument we have rejected as to maintenance and repair costs,...and it can fare no better here....

Finally, the State argues that its program of tuition grants should survive scrutiny because it is designed to promote the free exercise of religion. The State notes that only "low-income parents" are aided by this law, and without state assistance their right to have their children educated in a religious environment "is diminished or even denied." It is true, of course, that this Court has long recognized and maintained the right to choose nonpublic over public education.... It is also true that a state law interfering with a parent's right to have his child educated in a sectarian school would run afoul of the Free Exercise Clause. But this Court repeatedly has recognized that tension inevitably exists between the Free Exercise and the Establishment Clauses,...and that it may often not be possible to promote the former without offending the latter. As a result of this tension, our cases require the State to maintain an attitude of "neutrality," neither "advancing" nor "inhibiting" religion. In its attempt to enhance the opportunities of the poor to choose between public and nonpublic education, the State has taken a step which can only be regarded as one "advancing" religion. However great our sympathy, ...for the burdens experienced by those who must pay public school taxes at the same time that they support other schools because of the constraints of "conscience and discipline," and notwithstanding the "high social importance" of the State's purposes,... neither may justify an eroding of the limitations of the Establishment Clause now firmly emplanted.

C

Sections 3, 4, and 5 establish a system for providing income tax benefits to parents of children attending New York's nonpublic schools.

In practical terms there would appear to be little difference, for purposes of determining whether such aid has the effect of advancing religion, between the tax benefit allowed here and the tuition grant allowed under Sec. 2. The qualifying parent under either program receives the same form of encouragement and reward for sending his children to nonpublic schools. The only difference is that one parent receives an actual cash payment while the other is allowed to reduce by an arbitrary amount the sum he would otherwise be obliged to pay over to the State. We see no answer to Judge Hays' dissenting statement below that "[i]n both instances the money involved represents a charge made upon the state for the purpose of religious education."...

Appellees defend the tax portion of New York's legislative package on two grounds. First, they contend that it is of controlling significance that the grants or credits are directed to the parents rather than to the schools.... Our treatment of this issue in Part IIB is applicable here and requires rejection of this claim. Second, appellees place their strongest reliance on *Walz* v. *Tax Commission,* in which New York's property tax exemption for religious organizations was upheld. We think that *Walz* provides no support for appellees' position. Indeed, its rationale plainly compels the conclusion that New York's tax package violates the Establishment Clause....

...*Walz* is a product of the same dilemma and inherent tension found in most government-aid-to-religion controversies. To be sure, the exemption of church property from taxation conferred a benefit, albeit an indirect and incidental one. Yet that "aid" was a product not of any purpose to support or to subsidize, but of a fiscal relationship designed to minimize involvement and entanglement between Church and State. "The exemption," the Court emphasized, "tends to complement and reinforce the desired separation insulating each from the other." Furthermore, "[e]limination of the exemption would tend to expand the involvement of government by giving rise to tax valuation of church property, tax liens, tax foreclosures, and the direct confrontations and conflicts that follow in the train of those legal processes." The granting of the tax benefits under the New York statute, unlike the extension of an exemption, would tend to increase rather than limit the involvement between Church and State....

III

Because we have found that the challenged sections have the impermissible effect of advancing religion, we need not consider whether such aid would result in entanglement of the State with religion in the sense of "[a] comprehensive, discriminating, and continuing state surveillance." But the importance of the competing societal interests implicated in this case prompts us to make the further observation that, apart from any specific entanglement of the State in particular religious programs, assistance of the sort here involved carries grave potential for entanglement in the broader sense of continuing political strife over aid to religion.

Few would question most of the legislative findings supporting this statute. We recognized in *Board of Education* v. *Allen,* that "private education has played and is playing a significant and valuable role in raising levels of knowledge, competency, and experience," and certainly private parochial schools have contributed importantly to this role. Moreover, the tailoring of the New York statute to channel the aid provided primarily to afford low-income families the option of determining where their children are to be educated is most appealing. There is no doubt that the private schools are confronted with increasingly grave fiscal problems, that resolving these problems by increasing tuition charges forces parents to turn to the public schools, and that this in turn —as the present legislation recognizes—exacerbates the problems of public education at the same time that it weakens support for the parochial schools.

These, in briefest summary, are the underlying reasons for the New York legislation and for similar legislation in other States. They are substantial reasons. Yet they must be weighed against the relevant provisions and purposes of the First Amendment, which safeguard the separation of Church from State and which have been regarded from the beginning as among the most cherished features of our constitutional system.

One factor of recurring significance in this weighing process is the potentially divisive political effect of an aid program. As Mr. Justice Black's opinion in *Everson* v. *Board of Education* emphasizes, competition among religious sects for political and religious supremacy has occasioned considerable civil strife, "generated in large part" by competing efforts to gain or maintain the support of government.... [W]e know from long experience with both Federal and State Governments that aid programs of any kind tend to become entrenched, to escalate in cost, and to generate their own aggressive constituencies. And the larger the class of recipients, the greater the pressure for accelerated increases. Moreover, the State itself, concededly anxious to avoid assuming the burden of educating children now in private and parochial schools, has a strong motivation for increasing this aid as public school costs rise and population increases. In this situation, where the underlying issue is the deeply emotional one of Church-State relationships, the potential for serious divisive political consequences needs no elaboration. And while the prospect of such divisiveness may not alone warrant the invalidation of state laws that otherwise survive the careful scrutiny required by the decisions of this Court, it is certainly a "warning signal" not to be ignored.

Our examination of New York's aid provisions, in light of all relevant considerations, compels the judgment that each, as written, has a "primary effect that advances religion" and offends the constitutional prohibition against laws "respecting the establishment of religion." We therefore affirm the three-judge court's holding as to Sections 1 and 2 and reverse as to Sections 3, 4, and 5.

It is so ordered.

Excerpts from Supreme Court opinion delivered June 25, 1973, by Associate Justice Lewis F. Powell Jr. in the case of Grace Sloan, as State Treasurer of the Commonwealth of Pennsylvania, et al., Appellants, v. Alton J. Lemon et al:

On June 28, 1971, this Court handed down *Lemon* v. *Kurtzman,...* in which Pennsylvania's "Nonpublic Elementary and Secondary Education Act" was held unconstitutional as violative of the Establishment Clause of the First Amendment. That law authorized the State to reimburse nonpublic, sectarian schools for their expenditures on teachers' salaries, textbooks, and instructional materials used in specified "secular" courses....

On August 27, 1971, the Pennsylvania General Assembly promulgated a new aid law, entitled the "Parent Reimbursement Act for Nonpublic Education," providing funds to reimburse parents for a portion of tuition expenses incurred in sending their children to nonpublic schools. Shortly thereafter, this suit, challenging the enactment and seeking declaratory and injunctive relief, was filed in the United States District Court for the Eastern District of Pennsylvania....

I

Pennsylvania's "Parent Reimbursement Act for Nonpublic Education" provides for reimbursement to parents who pay tuition for their children to attend the State's nonpublic elementary and secondary schools. Qualifying parents are entitled to receive $75 for each dependent enrolled in an elementary school, and $150 for each dependent in a secondary school, unless that amount exceeds the amount of tuition actually paid. The money to fund this program is to be derived from a portion of the revenues from the State's tax on cigarette sales, and is to be administered by a five-member committee appointed by the Governor, known as the "Pennsylvania Parent Assistance Authority." In an effort to avoid the "entanglement" problem that flawed its prior aid statute, *Lemon* v. *Kurtzman,* the new legislation specifically precludes the administering authority from having any "direction, supervision or control over the policy determinations, personnel, curriculum, program of instruction or any other aspect of the administration or operation of any nonpublic school or schools." Similarly, the statute imposes no restrictions or limitations on the uses to which the reimbursement allotments can be put by the qualifying parents.

Like the New York tuition program, the Pennsylvania law is prefaced by "legislative findings," which emphasize its underlying secular purposes: parents who send their children to nonpublic schools reduce the total cost of public education; "inflation, plus the sharply rising costs of education, now combine to place in jeopardy the ability of such parents fully to carry this burden"; if the State's 500,000 nonpublic school children were to transfer to the public schools, the annual operating costs to the State would be $400 million, and the added capital costs would exceed $1 billion; therefore, "parents who maintain students in nonpublic schools provide a vital service" and deserve at least partial reimbursement for alleviating an otherwise "intolerable public burden." We certainly do not question now, any more than we did two Terms ago in *Lemon,* the reality and legitimacy of Pennsylvania's secular purposes....

For purposes of determining whether the Pennsylvania tuition reimbursement program has the impermissible effect of advancing religion, we find no constitutionally significant distinctions between this law and the one declared invalid today in *Nyquist.* Each authorizes the States to use tax-raised funds for tuition reimbursements payable to parents who send their children to nonpublic schools. Neither tells parents how they must spend the amount received.... Since Pennsylvania authorizes grants to all parents of children in nonpublic schools—regardless of income level—it is argued that no such assumption can be made as to how individual parents will spend their reimbursed amounts.

Our decision, however, is not dependent upon any such speculation. Instead we look to the substance of the program, and no matter how it is characterized its effect remains the same. The State has singled out a class of its citizens for a special economic benefit. Whether that benefit be viewed as a simple tuition subsidy, as an incentive to parents to send their children to sectarian schools, or as a reward for having done so, at bottom its intended consequence is to preserve and support religion-oriented institutions. We think it plain that this is quite unlike the sort of "indirect" and "incidental" benefits that flowed to sectarian schools from programs aiding *all* parents by supplying bus transportation and secular textbooks for their children.... Yet such aid approached the "verge" of the constitutionally impermissible.... Again today we decline to approach or overstep the "precipice" of establishment against which the Religion Clauses protect. We hold that Pennsylvania's tuition grant scheme violates the constitutional mandate against the "sponsorship" or "financial support" of religion or religious institutions....

II

Apart from the Establishment Clause issues central to this case, appellant-intervenors...make an equal protection claim that was not directly ruled on by the District Court. These intervenors are 12 parents whose children attend nonpublic schools. Two parents, the Watsons, send their child to a nonsectarian school while the remainder send their children to sectarian schools....

Appellants ask this Court to declare the provisions severable and thereby to allow tuition reimbursement for parents of children attending schools that are not church-related. If the parents of children who attend nonsectarian schools receive assistance, their argument continues, parents of children who attend sectarian schools are entitled to the same aid as a matter of equal protection. The argument is throughly spurious. In the first place, we have been shown no reason to upset the District Court's conclusion that aid to the non-sectarian could not be severed from aid to the sectarian. The statute nowhere sets up this suggested dichotomy between sectarian and nonsectarian schools, and to approve such a distinction here would be to create a program quite different from the one the legislature actually adopted....

III

In holding today that Pennsylvania's post-*Lemon* attempt to avoid the Establishment Clause's prohibition against government entanglements with religion has failed to satisfy the parallel bar against laws having a primary effect that advances religion, we are not unaware that appellants and those who have endeavored to formulate systems of state aid to nonpublic education may feel that the decisions of this Court have, indeed, presented them with the "insoluble paradox" to which Mr. Justice White referred in his dissent in *Lemon*. But if novel forms of aid have not readily been sustained by this Court, the "fault" lies not with the doctrines which are said to create a paradox but rather with the Establishment Clause itself: "Congress" and the States by virtue of the Fourteenth Amendment "shall make no law respecting the establishment of religion." With that judgment we are not free to tamper, and while there is "room for play in the joints,"...the Amendment's proscription clearly forecloses Pennsylvania's tuition reimbursement program.

Affirmed.

▼▼▼

DEAN'S WATERGATE TESTIMONY

June 25-29, 1973

John W. Dean III, fired as presidential counsel on April 30, made his long-awaited public appearance before the Senate Select Committee on Presidential Campaign Activities on June 25. He promptly became the first witness to implicate President Nixon directly in White House efforts to cover up the Watergate scandal. Testifying under a grant of limited immunity, Dean said he believed that the President was aware of the cover-up as early as September 1972. The 34-year-old lawyer told the committee that during a meeting with Nixon Sept. 15, 1972, the President congratulated him because disclosure of Watergate involvement had reached no higher than G. Gordon Liddy, former legal counsel to the Nixon re-election and finance committees. Dean said he "left the meeting with the impression that the President was well aware of what had been going on regarding the success of keeping the White House out of the Watergate scandal, and I also had expressed to him my concern that I was not confident that the cover-up could be maintained indefinitely."

It took Dean six hours to read the 245 pages of his carefully prepared opening statement. In that statement, he gave details of several conversations with the President which indicated to him that Nixon knew of the alleged cover-up. Following a brief preface in which he admitted his own role in obstructing justice, assisting in the commission of perjury and making unauthorized use of funds in his personal possession, Dean said: "It is my honest belief that while the President was involved, that he did not realize or appreciate at any time the implications of his involvement, and I think that when the facts come out, I hope the President is forgiven."

Dean's testimony differed from that given later by H. R. Haldeman and John D. Ehrlichman, the special White House advisers who had resigned April 30. Nixon had said in announcing their resignations (see p. 499) that it was *"one of the most difficult decisions of my Presidenty"* to let go *"two of the finest public servants it has been my privilege to know."* Of Dean, the only one actually fired, Nixon said tersely that he *"also resigned."*

Throughout the early spring of 1973, rumors prevalent in Washington suggested in-fighting at the White House where, apparently, two camps—with two different versions of the events surrounding Watergate—had emerged. Dean was said then to be allied with former Attorney General and former director of the Committee for the Re-election of the President John N. Mitchell. Mitchell was subsequently tagged as Dean's *"patron"* by J. Fred Buzhardt, special counsel to the President. It was understood that the other group, including Haldeman and Ehrlichman, held the support of the President. As a result, on April 19, 1973, Dean put out, without prior approval from the White House, a statement which asserted in part: *"Some may hope or think that I will become a scapegoat in the Watergate case. Anyone who believes this does not know me, know the true facts nor understand our system of justice."* Dean released another statement, through his attorney May 10, to the effect that he was *"of course aware of efforts to discredit me personally in the hope of discrediting my testimony."*

Buzhardt vs. Dean

Toward the end of the third of Dean's five days in the witness chair, he was confronted with a memorandum sent to the Senate investigating committee by Buzhardt. Read by Sen. Daniel K. Inouye (D Hawaii), who said he wanted to give the President *"his day in court,"* the memo said there was no reason to doubt that Dean was *"the principal actor in the Watergate cover-up."* Moreover, the document continued, Dean became *"the principal author of the political and constitutional crisis that Watergate now epitomizes."* Disclosure of the facts immediately after the break-in, Buzhardt asserted, would have produced the *"kind of embarrassment"* that *"an immensely popular President could easily have weathered."* But the problem of Watergate *"had been magnified 1,000-fold because the truth is coming to light so belatedly, because of insinuations that the White House was a party to the cover-up, and, above all, because the White House was led to say things about Watergate that have since been found to have been untrue. These added consequences were John Dean's doing."*

Dean was grilled exhaustively by the senators on the Watergate investigating committee, but he held fast to his story. The only time he appeared to slip up on a question of fact was in reference to a meeting he had had with Nixon's personal attorney, Herbert W. Kalmbach. Confronted with hotel records showing that Kalmbach had been staying at the Statler-Hilton Hotel in Washington, instead of the Mayflower Hotel as Dean had stated, Dean's attorney recouped by informing the committee that the Hilton's coffee shop, where the two men had met, was called the Mayflower. The audience burst into applause.

Knowing that other witnesses were expected to contradict his version of events, Dean asserted near the end of his 25 hours of testimony: "I am quite aware of the fact that in some circumstances it is going to be my word against two men, it is going to be my word against three men, and probably in some cases it is going to be my word against four men. But I am prepared to stand on my word and the truth and the knowledge and the facts I have. I know the truth is my ally in this, and I think, ultimately, the truth is going to come out."

Dean's prediction that his testimony would be contradicted was soon borne out. When Ehrlichman appeared before the Senate committee, July 24-27 and 30, he charged that Dean's statement that Watergate was the "major thing" occurring in the White House from June 17 to Sept. 15, 1972, was "falser than all the other falsehoods" in his testimony. From there on out, Ehrlichman's denials of Dean's accusations were abundant. To Dean's charge that orders to burglarize the office of Daniel Ellsberg's psychiatrist had come from the President's "oval office," Ehrlichman countered that he himself had approved a "covert operation" that resulted in the break-in, but he attributed the specific authorization to Egil Krogh Jr., a young presidential aide. He denied Dean's testimony that he had ordered Dean to try to get the Central Intelligence Agency to help out in the cover-up. Ehrlichman also denied that he had once ordered Dean to throw a briefcase into the Potomac River and to shred documents found in E. Howard Hunt's safe after the Watergate break-in. In his 30-page opening statement, Ehrlichman had implied that Dean misled Nixon and himself about White House involvement in the break-in and the cover-up.

Haldeman echoed Ehrlichman's sentiments when he took the witness chair July 30. He insisted that Dean was investigating the Watergate episode for the President and that Dean's assurances of no White House involvement in the affair formed the basis of Nixon's statement of Aug. 29, 1972, that the White House was not involved in Watergate. Haldeman, who had attended the Sept. 15, 1972, meeting with Nixon and Dean, and who admitted to listening to a tape of *that meeting, said he disagreed with Dean's conclusion that Nixon was aware of the cover-up and was congratulating Dean on his efforts. Haldeman also disputed Dean's account of an important March 13, 1973, meeting with Nixon at which, Dean alleged, Nixon said there would be no problem in raising $1-million for Watergate defendants and discussed executive clemency for E. Howard Hunt. In the two hours it took Haldeman to read his 89-page statement, he consistently contradicted Dean's testimony.*

One of the more sensational disclosures to come out of Dean's appearance was the existence of an "enemies list." In submitting documents about "dealing with our political enemies," Dean said that the techniques suggested and sometimes used included audits by the Internal Revenue Service, denial of federal grants, and prosecution and litigation.

> *Excerpts from the opening statement of John W. Dean III before the Senate Watergate committee, June 25, 1973; all excerpts relate to Dean's meetings with President Nixon in 1972 and 1973. Also included in the entry are the texts of two confidential memorandums submitted by Dean: one from Dean to John D. Ehrlichman, Aug. 16, 1971, on "dealing with our political enemies"; the other from former special White House counsel Charles W. Colson to Dean, Sept. 9, 1971, containing the names of 20 persons on the "priority list" of political enemies.*

Dean's testimony:

Meeting with the President, Sept. 15, 1972

...On Sept. 15 the Justice Department announced the handing down of the seven indictments by the federal grand jury. Late that afternoon I received a call requesting me to come to the President's oval office. When I arrived at the oval office I found Haldeman [H.R. Haldeman, then White House chief of staff] and the President. The President asked me to sit down. Both men appeared to be in very good spirits and my reception was very warm and cordial. The President then told me that Bob [Haldeman] had kept him posted on my handling of the Watergate case. The President told me I had done a good job and he appreciated how difficult a task it had been and the President was pleased that the case had stopped with Liddy [conspirator G. Gordon Liddy]. I responded that I could not take credit because others had done much more difficult things than I had done. As the President discussed the present status of the situation I told him that all that I had been able to do was to contain the case and assist in keeping it out of the White House. I also told him that I thought there was a long way to go before this matter would end and that I certainly could make no assurances that the day would not come when this matter would start to unravel.

Early in our conversation the President said to me that former FBI Director Hoover had told him shortly after he had assumed office in 1969 that his campaign had been bugged in 1968. The President said that at some point we should get the facts out on this and use this to counter the problems that we were encountering.

The President asked me when the criminal case would come to trial and would it start before the election. I told the President that I did not know. I said that the Justice Department had held off as long as possible the return of the indictments, but much would depend on which judge got the case. The President said that he certainly hoped that the case would not come to trial before the election.

The President then asked me about the civil cases that had been filed by the Democratic National Committee and Common Cause and about the counter-suits that we had filed. I told him that the lawyers at the re-election committee were handling these cases and that they did not see the Common Cause suit as any real problem before the election because they thought they could keep it tied up in discovery. I then told the President that the lawyers at the re-election committee were very hopeful of slowing down the civil suit filed by the Democratic National Committee because they had been making *ex parte* contacts with the judge handling the case and the judge was very understanding and trying to accommodate their problems. The President was pleased to hear this and responded to the effect that "well, that's helpful." I also recall explaining to the President about the suits that the re-election lawyers had filed against the Democrats as part of their counter offensive.

There was a brief discussion about the potential hearings before the Patman committee (the House Banking and Currency Committee). The President asked me what we were doing to deal with the hearings and I reported that Dick Cook, who had once worked on Patman's committee's staff, was working on the problem. The President indicated that Bill Timmons (White House congressional liaison chief) should stay on top of the hearings, that we did not need the hearings before the election.

The conversation then moved to the press coverage of the Watergate incident and how the press was really trying to make this into a major campaign issue. At one point in this conversation I recall the President telling me to keep a good list of the press people giving us trouble, because we will make life difficult for them after the election. The conversation then turned to the use of the Internal Revenue Service to attack our enemies. I recall telling the President that we had not made much use of this because the White House didn't have the clout to have it done, that the Internal Revenue Service was a rather Democratically oriented bureaucracy and it would be very dangerous to try any such activities. The President seemed somewhat annoyed and said that the Democratic administrations had used this tool well and after the election we would get people in these agencies who would be responsive to the White House requirements....

I left the meeting with the impression that the President was well aware of what had been going on regarding the success of keeping the White House out of the Watergate scandal, and I also had expressed to him my concern that I was not confident that the coverup could be maintained indefinitely.

Meeting Of Feb. 27, 1973

This was the first meeting I had had with the President since my Sept. 15, 1972, meeting which related to the Watergate. It was at this meeting that the President directed that I report directly to him regarding all Watergate matters. He told me that this matter was taking too much time from Haldeman's and Ehrlichman's [John D. Ehrlichman, then chief adviser on domestic affairs] normal duties, and he also told me that they were principals in the matter, and I, therefore, could be more objective than they. The President then told me of his meetings with Sen. Baker [Howard H. Baker (R Tenn.)] and the attorney general [Richard G. Kleindienst]. He told me that Sen. Baker had requested that the attorney general be his contact point and that I should keep in contact with the attorney general to make sure that the attorney general and Sen. Baker were working together.

He asked me to follow up immediately to determine if the attorney general and Baker had met. I informed him that I had earlier discussed this with the attorney general and that the attorney general was planning to meet with Sen. Baker and Sen. Ervin [Sen. Sam J. Ervin Jr., chairman of the investigating committee] to discuss turning over FBI data regarding the Watergate investigation. A brief discussion followed in which the President recounted what had already been reported to me by Haldeman, that he had told Sen. Baker that he would not permit White House staff to appear before the select committee, rather he would only permit the taking of written interrogatories. He asked me if I agreed with this and I said that written interrogatories were something that could be handled, whereas appearances might create serious problems. He told me he would never let Haldeman and Ehrlichman go to the Hill.

He also told me that Sen. Gurney [Edward J. Gurney (R Fla.), a member of the select committee] would be very friendly to the White House and that it would not be necessary to contact him, because the President said Sen. Gurney would know what to do on his own.

On the way out of his office, he told me I had done an excellent job of dealing with this matter during the campaign; that it had been the only issue that (George) McGovern had had and the Democrats had tried to make something out of it but to no avail. I told him as we were walking together out of the office that I had only managed to contain the matter during the campaign, but I was not sure it could be contained indefinitely. He told me that we would have to fight back and he was confident that I could do the job.

Meeting Of Feb. 28

I had received word before I arrived at my office that the President wanted to see me. He asked me if I had talked to the attorney general regarding Sen. Baker. I told him that the attorney general was seeking to meet with both Sen. Ervin and Sen. Baker, but that a meeting date had not yet been firmed up. I told him that I knew it was the attorney general's wish to turn over the FBI investigation, and the President said that he didn't think we should, but asked me what I thought of the idea. I told him that I did not think that there was much damaging information in the FBI investigation although there could be some bad public relations from it. He told me to think about this matter.

He also said that he had read in the morning paper about the Vesco case and asked me what part if any his brother Ed had had in the matter. I told him what I knew of his brother's involvement, which was that he was an innocent agent in the contribution transaction. We then discussed the leak to *Time* magazine of the fact that the White House had placed wiretaps on newsmen and White House staff people. The President asked me if I knew how this had leaked. I told him that I did not; that I knew several people were aware of it. But I didn't know any who had leaked it....

We...talked about the executive privilege statement, and the President expressed his desire to get the statement out well in advance of the Watergate hearings so that it did not appear to be in response to the Watergate hearings.... I told him that I thought he should know that I was also involved in the post-June 17 activities regarding Watergate. I briefly described to him why I thought I had legal problems in that I had been a conduit for many of the decisions that were made and therefore could be involved in an obstruction of justice. He would not accept my analysis and did not want me to get into it in any detail other than what I had just related. He reassured me not to worry, that I had no legal problems. (Note: I raised this on another occasion with the President, when Dick Moore [a White House aide] was present.)

Meeting Of March 1

The first meeting on this date and the afternoon meeting which occurred on March 1 related to preparing the President for his forthcoming press conference. The President asked me a number of questions about the Gray [L. Patrick Gray III, nominee for FBI director] nomination hearings and facts that had come out during these hearings. In particular I can recall him stating that there should be no problem with the fact that I had received the FBI reports. He said that I was conducting an investigation for him and that it would be perfectly proper for the counsel to the President to have looked at these reports. I did not tell the President that I had not conducted an investigation for him, because I assumed he was well aware of this fact and that the so-called Dean investigation was a public relations matter, and that frequently the President made reference in press conferences to things that never had, in fact, occurred.

I also was aware that often in answering Watergate questions that he had made reference to my report and I did not feel that I could tell the President that he could not use my name. There had been considerable adverse publicity stemming from the Gray hearings and the fact that Gray was turning over FBI information to the Senate Judiciary Committee which caused the President to tell me at this morning meeting that Gray must be "pulled up short"...

He...told me the FBI Watergate materials should not be turned over by Gray. I informed him that I had had a meeting several days prior with Mr. Sullivan [William C. Sullivan, former assistant FBI director] who had been at the FBI for many years, and Sullivan had alluded to the fact that the FBI had been used for political purposes by past administrations. I cited a few examples that Mr. Sullivan had given me. The President told me to get this information from Sullivan.... He also told me that I should gather any material I could gather regarding the uses and abuses of the FBI by past administrations so that we could show that we had not abused the FBI for political purposes. The President told me that he was convinced that he had been wiretapped in 1968 and the fact that DeLoach [Cartha DeLoach, assistant FBI director] had not been forthcoming indicated to the President that DeLoach was probably lying. He told me that I should call Don Kendall, DeLoach's employer, and tell him that DeLoach had better start telling the truth because "the boys are coming out of the woodwork." He said this ploy may smoke DeLoach out. He also asked me who else might know about the bugging of his 1968 campaign, and I suggested that Mr. [Clyde] Tolson, Hoover's former assistant, might have some knowledge of it. He told me that he probably ought to call Mr. Tolson and wish him happy birthday or good health and possibly get some information from him when he talked to him.

Meeting Of March 7

The President was very unhappy with Gray's performance before the Senate Judiciary Committee. In my meeting with him on this date, he made a reference to the fact that Gray's comment regarding my sitting in on the investigations by the FBI was absurd. He felt it was perfectly proper that I was present at those interviews and said that Gray's attitude that he "jolly well" went forward because he had no alternative was absurd.... At the end of the meeting, the President instructed me to tell the attorney general to cut off Gray from turning over any further Watergate reports to the Senate Judiciary Committee. He said this just had to cease.

Meeting Of March 13

This was a rather lengthy meeting, the bulk of which was taken up by a discussion about the Gray hearings and the fact that the Senate Judiciary Committee had voted to invite me to appear in connection with Gray's nomination. It was at this time we discussed the potential of litigating the matter of executive privilege and thereby preventing anybody from going before any Senate committee until that matter was resolved. The President liked the idea very much, particularly when I mentioned to him that it might be possible that he could also claim attorney/client privilege on me so that the strongest potential case on executive privilege would probably rest on the counsel to the President. I told him that obviously this area would have to be researched. He told me that he did not want Haldeman and Ehrlichman to go before the Ervin hearings and that if we were litigating the matter on Dean, that no one would have to appear.

Toward the end of the conversation, we got into a discussion of Watergate matters specifically. I told the President about the fact that there were money demands being made by the seven convicted defendants, and that the sentencing of these individuals was not far off. It was during this conversation that Haldeman came into the office. After this brief interruption by Haldeman's coming in, but while he was still there, I told the President about the fact that there was no money to pay these individuals to meet their demands. He asked me how much it would cost. I told him that I could only make an estimate that it might be as high as a million dollars or more. He told me that that was no problem, and he also looked over at Haldeman and repeated the same statement. He then asked me who was demanding this money and I told him it was principally coming from Hunt [defendant E. Howard Hunt Jr.] through his attorney.

The President then referred to the fact that Hunt had been promised executive clemency. He said that he had discussed this matter with Ehrlichman, and contrary to instructions that Ehrlichman had given Colson [Charles W. Colson, then a special counsel to the President] not to talk to the President about it, that Colson had also discussed it with him later. He expressed some annoyance at the fact that Colson had also discussed this matter with him. The conversation then turned back to a question from the President regarding the money that was paid to the defendants. He asked me how this was done. I told him I didn't know much about it other than the fact that the money was laundered so it could not be traced and then there were secret deliveries. I told him I was learning about things I had never known before, but the next time I would certainly be more knowledgeable. This comment got a laugh out of Haldeman....

Meetings Of March 14

The meetings which occurred on this day principally involved preparing the President for a forthcoming press conference. I recall talking about executive privilege and making Dean a test case in the courts on executive privilege. The President said that he would like very much to do this and if the opportunity came up in the press conference, he would probably so respond.

I also recall that during the meetings which occurred on this day that the President was going to try to find an answer that would get Ziegler [Ronald L. Ziegler, presidential press secretary] off the hook of the frequent questions he was asked regarding the Watergate. He said that he was going to say that he would take no further questions on the Watergate until the completion of the Ervin hearings and that Ziegler could in turn repeat the same statement and avoid future interrogation by the press on the subject.

Meeting Of March 15

It was late in the afternoon after the President's press conference that he asked Dick Moore and I to come over to visit with him. He was in a very relaxed mood and entered into a general discussion about the press conference. The President was amazed and distressed that the press had paid so little attention to the fact that he made an historic announcement about Ambassador [David K.E.] Bruce opening up the liaison office in Peking. He said he was amazed when the first question following that announcement was regarding whether or not Dean would appear before the Senate Judiciary Committee in connection with the Gray hearings....

Meeting Of March 17

This was St. Patrick's Day, and the President was in a very good mood and very relaxed, and we engaged in a rambling conversation with only some brief reference to the Gray hearings and the problems that were then confronting the White House regarding the President's statements on executive privilege and his willingness to go to court on the matter. He opined that he did not think that the Senate would be dumb enough to go for the bait he had given them but he was hopeful that they might.

Meeting Of March 20

It was during the afternoon of March 20 that I talked again with Dick Moore about this entire coverup matter. I told Moore that there were new and more threatening demands for support money. I told him that Hunt had sent a message to me—through Paul O'Brien [an attorney for the President's re-election committee]—that he wanted $72,000 for living expenses and $50,000 for attorney's fees, and if he did not receive it that week, he would reconsider his options and have a lot to say about the seamy things he had done for Ehrlichman while at the White House.

I told Moore that I had about reached the end of the line, and was now in a position to deal with the President to end the coverup. I did not discuss with Moore the fact that I had discussed money and clemency with the President earlier, but I told him that I really didn't think the President understood all of the facts involved in the Watergate and particularly the implications of those facts. I told him that the matter was continually compounding itself, and I felt that I had to lay the facts out for the President as well as the implication of those facts. Moore encouraged me to do so.

Meetings Of March 21

As I have indicated, my purpose in requesting this meeting particularly with the President was that I felt it necessary that I give him a full report of all the facts that I knew and explain to him what I believed to be the implication of those facts. It was my particular concern with the fact that the President did not seem to understand the implications of what was going on. For example, when I had earlier told him that I thought I was involved in an obstruction of justice situation he had argued with me to the contrary after I had explained it to him.

Also, when the matter of money demands had come up previously, he had very nonchalantly told me that that was no problem, and I did not know if he realized that he himself could be getting involved in an obstruction of justice situation by having promised clemency to Hunt. What I had hoped to do in this conversation was to have the President tell me that we had to end the matter—now. Accordingly, I gave considerable thought to how I would present this situation to the President and try to make as dramatic a presentation as I could

to tell him how serious I thought the situation was that the coverup
continue.

I began by telling the President that there was a cancer growing
on the Presidency and that if the cancer was not removed that the
President himself would be killed by it. I also told him that it was
important that this cancer be removed immediately because it was
growing more deadly every day. I then gave him what I told him would
be a broad overview of the situation and I would come back and fill
in the details and answer any questions he might have about the matter.

I proceeded to tell him how the matter had commenced in late
January and early February, but that I did not know how the plans
had finally been approved. I told him I had informed Haldeman what
was occurring, and Haldeman told me I should have nothing to do with
it. I told him that I had learned that there had been pressure from
Colson on Magruder, but I did not have all the facts as to the degree
of pressure. I told him I did not know if Mitchell had approved the
plans, but I had been told that Mitchell had been a recipient of the
wiretap information and that Haldeman had also received such information through Strachan [Gordon C. Strachan, a Haldeman aide].

I then proceeded to tell him some of the highlights that had occurred
during the coverup. I told him that Kalmbach [Herbert W. Kalmbach,
then Nixon's personal attorney] had been used to raise funds to pay
these seven individuals for their silence at the instructions of Ehrlichman, Haldeman and Mitchell and I had been the conveyor of this
instruction to Kalmbach. I told him that after the decision had been
made that Magruder (Jeb Stuart Magruder, deputy campaign director) was to remain at the re-election committee, I had assisted
Magruder in preparing his false story for presentation to the grand
jury. I told him that cash that had been at the White House had been
funneled back to the re-election committee for the purpose of paying
the seven individuals to remain silent.

I then proceeded to tell him that perjury had been committed, and
for this coverup to continue it would require more perjury and more
money. I told him that the demands of the convicted individuals
were continually increasing and that with sentencing imminent, the
demands had become specific. I told him that on Monday the 19th,
i had received a message from one of the re-election committee
lawyers who had spoken directly with Hunt and that Hunt had
sent a message to me demanding money. I then explained to him the
message that Hunt had told Paul O'Brien the preceding Friday to
be passed on to me. I told the President I'd asked O'Brien why to
Dean and O'Brien had asked Hunt the same question. But Hunt had
merely said you just pass this message on to Dean.

The message was that Hunt wanted $72,000 for living expenses and
$50,000 for attorneys' fees, and if he did not get the money and get

it quickly that he would have a lot of seamy things to say about what he had done for John Ehrlichman while he was at the White House. If he did not receive the money, he would have to reconsider his options. I informed the President that I had passed this message on to both Haldeman and Ehrlichman. Ehrlichman asked me if I had discussed the matter with Mitchell. I had told Ehrlichman that I had not done so, and Ehrlichman asked me to do so. I told the President I had called Mitchell pursuant to Ehrlichman's request but I had no idea of what was happening with regard to the request.

I then told the President that this was just typical of the type of blackmail that the White House would continue to be subjected to and that I didn't know how to deal with it. I also told the President that I thought that I would, as a result of my name coming out during the Gray hearings, be called before the grand jury and that if I was called to testify before the grand jury or the Senate committee, I would have to tell the facts the way I know them. I said I did not know if executive privilege would be applicable to any appearance I might have before the grand jury. I concluded by saying that it is going to take continued perjury and continued support of these individuals to perpetuate the coverup and that I did not believe it was possible to so continue it; rather I thought it was time for surgery on the cancer itself and that all those involved must stand up and account for themselves and that the President himself get out in front of this matter. I told the President that I did not believe that all of the seven defendants would maintain their silence forever. In fact, I thought that one or more would very likely break rank.

After I finished, I realized that I had not really made the President understand, because after he asked a few questions, he suggested that it would be an excellent idea if I gave some sort of briefing to the cabinet and that he was very impressed with my knowledge of the circumstances but he did not seem particularly concerned with their implications. It was after my presentation to the President and during our subsequent conversation that the President called Haldeman into the office and the President suggested that we have a meeting with Mitchell, Haldeman and Ehrlichman to discuss how to deal with this situation. What emerged from that discussion after Haldeman came into the office was that John Mitchell should account for himself for the pre-June-17 activities, and the President did not seem concerned about the activities which had occurred after June 17....

In the late afternoon of March 21, Haldeman and Ehrlichman and I had a second meeting with the President. Before entering this meeting I had a brief discussion in the President's outer office of the Executive Office Building suite with Haldeman in which I told him that we had two options: One is that this thing goes all the way and deals with both the pre-activities and the post-activities; or the second alternative, if the coverup was to proceed, we would have to draw the wagons in a circle around the White House and that the White House protect only itself. I told Haldeman that it had been the White House's assistance to the re-election committee that had gotten us into much of this problem and now the only hope would be to protect ourselves from further involvement.

The meeting with the President that afternoon with Haldeman, Ehrlichman and myself was a tremendous disappointment to me, because it was quite clear that the coverup as far as the White House was going to continue. I recall that while Haldeman, Ehrlichman and I were sitting at a small table in front of the President in his Executive Office Building suite, that I for the first time said in front of the President that I thought that Haldeman, Ehrlichman and Dean were all indictable for obstruction of justice and that was the reason I disagreed with all that was being discussed at that point in time.

I could tell that both Haldeman, and particularly Ehrlichman, were very unhappy with my comments. I had let them very clearly know that I was not going to participate in the matter any further and that I thought it was time that everybody start thinking about telling the truth. I again repeated to them I did not think it was possible to perpetuate further the coverup, and the important thing now was to get the President out in front of it.

Meeting Of March 22

The meeting with the President, Ehrlichman, Haldeman, Mitchell and me was again a general discussion of the Senate Watergate hearings situation and did not accomplish anything. Rather it was a further indication that there would be no effort to stop the coverup from continuing. I recall that Mitchell told the President that he felt that the only problem that he now had was the fact that he was taking a public beating on his posture on executive privilege; that the statement on executive privilege was too broad and that probably something should be done to change his posture on this matter. Mitchell was not suggesting that members of the White House go to the Hill to testify, rather that some more cooperative position be developed to avoid the adverse publicity.

It was at this time that the President said that Kleindienst [then Attorney General Richard G. Kleindienst] was supposed to be working these things out with Sen. Baker, and he apparently had not been doing so. The President said that Timmons had told him that a member of Sen. Baker's staff was very desirous of a meeting to get guidance. It was at this point that the President called the attorney general and told him that he should get up to meet with Baker as soon as possible and get some of these problems regarding executive privilege and the turning of documents over resolved with the committee immediately....

The President told me that the White House should start directly dealing with the committee and that I should go up and commence discussions with Sen. Ervin as to the parameters of executive privilege. I told the President that I did not think this would be wise because I was very much the party in issue with regard to the Judiciary Committee hearings and that it would be unwise for me to go to the Hill and negotiate my own situation. The President agreed and Ehrlichman said that he would commence discussions.

The meeting was almost exclusively on the subject of how the White House should posture itself vis-a-vis the Ervin committee hearings. There was absolutely no indication of any changed attitude, and it was like one of many meetings I had been in before, in which the talk was of strategies for dealing with the hearings rather than any effort to get the truth out as to what had happened both before June 17 and after June 17.

Following this meeting with the President, it was apparent to me that I had failed in turning the President around on this subject, but Ehrlichman and Haldeman began taking over with regard to dealing with a new problem, which had become John Dean, as they were aware that I was very unhappy about the situation.

Meeting Of April 15

The President was very cordial when we met. I was somewhat shaken when I went in to meet him, because I knew I had taken it upon myself to end the coverup, and what I had started was going to cause serious problems for the President. I shall attempt to recall the highlights of the conversation that transpired in the meeting which occurred about 9 p.m. on April 15.

I told the President that I had gone to the prosecutors, and that I did not believe that this was an act of disloyalty but rather, in the end, it would be an act of loyalty. I told him that I told the prosecutors of my own involvement and the involvement of others. At one point in the conversation, I recall the President asking me about Haldeman's knowledge of the Liddy plans. He asked me if I had told him earlier about the fact that I had met with Haldeman after the second meeting in Mitchell's office and told Haldeman what was going on and my reaction to what was going on. I told the President that I had reported this fact to him earlier.

The President then made some reference to Henry Petersen [assistant attorney general in charge of the Watergate investigation] asking about why Haldeman had not turned if off at that point and told me to testify that I had told Haldeman about the meeting in Mitchell's office. The President almost from the outset began asking me a number of leading questions, which made me think that the conversation was being taped and that a record was being made to protect himself. Although I became aware of this because of the nature of the conversation, I decided that I did not know it for a fact and that I had to believe that the President would not tape such a conversation. Some question came up, by the President, as to whether I had immunity. As best as I can recall, I told him my lawyers had discussed this with the prosecutors, but certainly I had no deal with the government. He told me that he did not want to do anything to hurt my negotiations with the government. I do not recall commenting on his remark.

I also recall that the conversation turned to the matter of Liddy not talking. He said something about Liddy was waiting for a signal and I told him that possibly he was waiting for a signal from the President. I discussed with him the fact that maybe if Liddy's lawyer met with him that Liddy would begin to open up, because I said that I thought that that would be very helpful if Liddy did talk. It was during this part of the conversation that the President picked up the telephone and called Henry Petersen and pretended with Petersen that I was not in the room but that the matter of Liddy's coming forward and talking had arisen during our conversation. The President relayed to Petersen that if Liddy's lawyer wanted to see him to get a signal, that the President was willing to do this. The President also asked me about Petersen, and I told him if anyone could give him good advice, Henry Petersen could.

The President also asked me if I remembered what day it was in March that I had reported to him on some of the details of the Watergate matter. He said that he thought it was the 21st but wasn't certain. I said that I could not recall for certain without checking. At another point in the conversation the matter of the degree of discussions that I had had with the prosecutors came up, and I informed the President that I had had no discussions with the prosecutors relating to conversations I had had with him or in anything in the area of national security. The President told me that I could not talk about national security areas and that I should not talk about conversations I had had with him, because they were privileged conversations.

Toward the end of the conversation, the President recalled the fact that at one point we had discussed the difficulty in raising money and that he had said that one million dollars was nothing to raise to pay to maintain the silence of the defendants. He said that he had, of course, only been joking when he made that comment.

As the conversation went on, and it is impossible for me to recall anything other than the high points of it, I became more convinced that the President was seeking to elicit testimony from me and put his perspective on the record and get me to agree to it. The most interesting thing that happened during the conversation was, very near the end, he got up out of his chair, went behind his chair to the corner of the Executive Office Building office and in a barely audible tone said to me, he was probably foolish to have discussed Hunt's clemency with Colson. I do not recall that I responded. The conversation ended shortly thereafter.

As I was on my way out of the office after exchanging parting pleasantries, I told the President that I hoped that my going to the prosecutors and telling the truth would not result in the impeachment of the President. He jokingly said, "I certainly hope so also," and he said that it would be handled properly.

Meeting Of April 16

I arrived at [Nixon's] office about 9:45, and rather than going to the reception entrance normally used by other members of the staff and me, I went into Mr. Steve Bull's office. Mr. Bull is the one who had informed me that the President wanted to see me, so I went to his office. Mr. Bull told me I would have to wait a few minutes because the President was in another meeting. A few minutes later, Haldeman and Ehrlichman emerged laughing from the President's office, and when they saw me in Mr. Bull's office, their faces dropped. They said hello, put on a serious look and departed. I went into the President's office.

The President told me that he had been thinking about this entire matter and thought it might be a good idea if he had in his drawer a letter from me requesting that he accept my resignation or in the alternative an indefinite leave of absence. He said that he had prepared two letters for my signature and he would not do anything with them at this time but thought it would be good if he had them. He then passed me a Manila file folder with two letters in it. The President said that he had prepared the letters himself and that no one would know I had signed them. I read the letters and was amazed at what I was being asked to sign. I have submitted to the committee copies of the letters, but since they are very brief I will read them.

● The first letter, dated April 16, 1973, read:
Dear Mr. President:
In view of my increasing involvement in the Watergate matter, my impending appearance before the grand jury and the probability of its action, I request an immediate and indefinite leave of absence from my position on your staff.

● The second letter, which was even more incriminating, read:
Dear Mr. President:
As a result of my involvement in the Watergate matter, which we discussed last night and today, I tender you my resignation effective at once.

After reading the letters, I looked the President squarely in the eyes and told him that I could not sign the letters. He was annoyed with me, and somewhat at a loss for words. He said that maybe I would like to draft my own letter. I told him that the letters that he had asked me to sign were virtual confessions of anything regarding the Watergate.

I also asked him if Ehrlichman and Haldeman had signed letters of resignation. I recall that he was somewhat surprised at my asking this and he said no, they had not, but they had given him a verbal assurance to the same effect. He then elaborated that Haldeman and Ehrlichman had said that if they were called before the grand jury they would seek an indefinite leave of absence. They had given him their verbal assurances. I then told him that he had my verbal assurance to the same effect.

It was a tense conversation, but I was not going to sign the letters under any circumstances. As I sat there talking with the President, I had very much on my mind the laughter in Ehrlichman's and Haldeman's voices when they walked out of the office before they realized that I was waiting outside to see the President. To break the impasse, the President said that he would like me to draft my own letter and report back to him later. He said that he was working on a statement regarding the Watergate and the recent developments that had come to his attention as a result of his meetings with Kleindienst and Petersen and would appreciate my thoughts. He said that he would also like a suggested draft letter for Haldeman and Ehrlichman or maybe a form letter that everyone could sign. I told him I would draft a letter and would report back to him.

The President called me to come to his EOB office about 4 that afternoon. He asked me if I had drafted a letter. I said that I had as well as I had prepared some thoughts for his statement. He asked to see the letter, a copy of which I have submitted to the committee, but again shall read it because it is very brief:

Dear Mr. President:

You have informed me that Bob Haldeman and John Ehrlichman have verbally tendered their requests to be given an immediate and indefinite leave of absence from your staff. By this letter I also wish to confirm my request that I be given such a leave of absence from your staff.

After the President read the letter, he handed it back to me and said it isn't what he wanted. I then told him that I would not resign unless Haldeman and Ehrlichman resigned. I told him that I was not willing to be the White House scapegoat for the Watergate. He said that he understood my position and he wasn't asking me to be a scapegoat. I then gave him my recommendations of the draft statement. Before he read the draft statement he said that he had checked his records and it had been on March 21 that I had met with him and given him the report on the problems of the Watergate and its coverup.

I have submitted to the committee a copy of the draft statement I prepared for the President. The gist of the statement was two-fold:

First, the President had learned of new facts in the case over the weekend, and as a result of this information had directed Henry Petersen to take charge and leave no stone unturned; secondly, that he had accepted requests from Haldeman, Ehrlichman and Dean to be placed on leave of absence. The President said virtually nothing about the statement, and after reading it told me to talk with Len Garment (a Nixon adviser), who he said was also preparing a draft.

MEMORANDUMS SUBMITTED BY DEAN

Dean to Ehrlichman on "Dealing With...Enemies":

This memorandum addresses the matter of how we can maximize the fact of our incumbency in dealing with persons known to be active in their opposition to our Administration. Stated a bit more bluntly— how we can use the available federal machinery to screw our political enemies.

After reviewing this matter with a number of persons possessed of expertise in the field, I have concluded that we *do not* need an elaborate mechanism or game plan, rather we need a good project coordinator and full support for the project. In brief, the system would work as follows:

● Key members of the staff [e.g., Colson, (Harry) Dent, (Peter) Flanigan, (Patrick) Buchanan] should be requested to inform us as to who they feel we should be giving a hard time.

● The project coordinator should then determine what sorts of dealings these individuals have with the federal government and how we can best screw them (e.g., grant availability, federal contracts, litigation, prosecution, etc.).

● The project coordinator then should have access to and the full support of the top officials of the agency or department in proceeding to deal with the individual.

I have learned that there have been many efforts in the past to take such actions, but they have ultimately failed—in most cases—because of lack of support at the top. Of all those I have discussed this matter with, Lyn Nofziger appears the most knowledgeable and most interested. If Lyn had support he would enjoy undertaking this activity as the project coordinator. You are aware of some of Lyn's successes in the field, but he feels that he can only employ limited efforts because there is a lack of support.

Colson to Dean on "The Priority List":

1. Picker, Arnold M., United Artists Corporation: Top Muskie fundraiser. Success here could be both debilitating and very embarrassing to the Muskie machine. If effort looks promising, both

Ruth and David Picker should be programmed and then a follow-through with United Artists.

2. Barkan, Alexander E., National Director of AFL-CIO's Committee on Political Education: Without a doubt the most powerful political force programmed against us in 1968. ($10 million dollars, 4.6 million votes, 115 million pamphlets, 176,000 workers—all programmed by Barkan's C.O.P.E.—So says Teddy White in The Making of the President '68.) We can expect the same effort this time.

3. Guthman, Ed, Managing Editor L. A. Times: Guthman, former Kennedy aide, was a highly sophisticated hatchetman against us in '68. It is obvious he is the prime mover behind the current Key Biscayne effort. It is time to give him the message.

4. Dane, Maxwell, Doyle, Dane and Bernbach: The top Democratic advertising firm—They destroyed Goldwater in '64. They should be hit hard starting with Dane.

5. Dyson, Charles, Dyson-Kissner Corporation: Dyson and Larry O'Brien were close business associates after '68. Dyson has huge business holdings and is presently deeply involved in the Businessmen's Educational Fund which bankrolls a national radio network of 5 minute programs—Anti-Nixon in character.

6. Stein, Howard, Dreyfus Corporation: Heaviest contributor to McCarthy in '68. If McCarthy goes, will do the same in '72. If not, Lindsay or McGovern will receive the funds.

7. Lowenstein, Allard: Guiding force behind the 18 year old "dump Nixon" vote drive.

8. Halperin, Morton, leading executive at Common Cause: A scandal would be most helpful here.

9. Woodcock, Leonard, UAW: No comments necessary.

10. S. Sterling Munro, Jr., Senator Jackson's AA: We should give him a try. Positive results would stick a pin in Jackson's white hat.

11. Feld, Bernard T., President, Council for Livable World: Heavy far left funding. They will program an "all court press" against us in '72.

12. Davidoff, Sidney: (Mayor) Lindsay's top personal aide: A first class S.O.B., wheeler-dealer and suspected bagman. Positive results would really shake the Lindsay camp and Lindsay's plans to capture youth vote. Davidoff in charge.

13. Conyers, John, Congressman, Detroit: Coming on fast. Emerging as a leading black anti-Nixon spokesman. Has known weakness for white females.

14. Lambert, Samuel M., President, National Education Association: Has taken us on vis-a-vis federal aid to parochial schools—a '72 issue.

15. Mott, Stewart Rawlings: Nothing but big money for radic-lib candidates.

16. **Dellums, Ronald,** Congressman, California: Had extensive EMK-Tunney support in his election bid. Success might help in California next year.

17. **Schorr, Daniel,** Columbia Broadcasting System: A real media enemy.

18. **S. Harrison Dogole:** President of Global Security Systems: Fourth largest private detective agency in U.S. Heavy Humphrey contributor. Could program his agency against us.

19. **Paul Newman:** Radic-Lib causes. Heavy McCarthy involvement '68. Used effectively in nationwide T.V. commercials. '72 involvement certain.

20. **McGrory, Mary,** Columnist: Daily hate Nixon articles.

July

OECD SURVEY OF U.S. ECONOMY

July 1, 1973

Fears that the American economy might slip before long into recession, if not depression, were given added credence July 1 by an international economic report. The Paris-based Organization for Economic Cooperation and Development noted in an annual survey that the United States risked undergoing a major recession if it did not take corrective economic action. Warning that policy decisions would be of crucial importance in the ensuing year and a half, the OECD urged Washington to consider adopting a more flexible fiscal course as a means of lending increased stability to the economic situation. The survey reflected the concern of the OECD's economists that continued inflation coupled with the boom in the United States, if left unchecked, might have disastrous results.

The 45-page report zeroed in on prospective problems that might develop from the consistently high demand pressures exerted by American consumers, businesses and government. For example, even with the reimposition of wage and price controls, it might become "virtually impossible" to maintain acceptable price levels in an economic environment of excessive demand, shortages and supply jam-ups. Furthermore, should the high domestic demand lead to an increase of imports, the gains netted from recent improvement in the American balance-of-payments outlook might be canceled out.

Indications that the U.S. economy would experience a slowdown later in 1973 and early in 1974 were a source of satisfaction. But while chances of avoiding excessive demand growth "would seem good," the economists pointed out that "many uncertainties" had to be considered. Two of the complicating factors were (1) the difficulty of interpreting economic indicators and (2) the undetermined level and scope of the federal budget in fiscal 1974.

Washington policymakers were cautioned against relying solely on monetary policy to slow down the boom. High interest rates produced by tightening the money supply might bring on a serious economic decline. The OECD's economists asserted that a tax increase might be advisable, especially if federal expenditures exceeded the totals recommended by President Nixon in his budget message in January. (See p. 169.) Because tax measures could not be expected to move swiftly through Congress, the OECD suggested that the President be given "limited standby authority, such as exists in a number of other countries, to vary tax rates and certain types of expenditures without prior legislative consent." That suggestion was based on the belief that "in a modern economy prompt action is sometimes needed to keep the economy on an even keel."

The Organization for Economic Cooperation and Development succeeded the postwar Organization for European Economic Cooperation (OEEC) in 1961, when the United States and Canada were added to its membership. Japan became a member in 1964. OECD seeks to promote the highest sustainable level of economic growth and a rising standard of living in member countries and to contribute to the expansion of world trade on a nondiscriminatory basis. Each year OECD specialists make individual surveys of the economies of the 24 member countries. In its review of the American economy, as in all of its other surveys, the OECD economists work with national authorities but arrive at policy recommendations independently.

Text of the Introduction and of Chapters II, IV and V of the OECD's 1973 economic survey of the United States:

INTRODUCTION

Aided by an expansionary policy stance, the United States economy achieved high real growth in recent quarters; all major demand components have performed strongly, with the exception of net exports and Federal purchases. Price performance has been mixed, with an overall deceleration in inflation last year but with some of the major price indices increasing more rapidly in early 1973, largely but not exclusively as a result of sharply higher food costs. Partly because the increase in the labour force has been exceptionally strong, the rate of unemployment has declined only gradually, still averaging 5.6 per cent in 1972 compared with 5.9 per cent in the previous year, but coming down to the 5 per cent level by early 1973.

Present policies and recent behaviour of the leading indicators point to a continuation of relatively strong growth into 1974, with growing pressure on resources. The authorities may therefore be faced in the near future with the task of slowing the expansion to a rate closer to the growth of capacity in order to avoid excessive demand pressures. Expected high productivity gains this year should continue to moderate the behaviour of unit labour costs in the face of somewhat stronger upward pressure on wages, thus aiding the Administration's anti-inflationary policies, but rising food prices could continue to be a problem through much of 1973. And, as the economy is brought close to its potential next year, inflationary pressures are likely to become more generalised, raising the question of how reasonable price stability can be combined with a high-employment economy in the future. The current external account has remained weak but, assuming demand and inflation are kept under control at home, it should improve from now on, influenced by the effects of the currency realignments....

II ECONOMIC POLICY

The strong economic performance in recent quarters has been fostered by the stimulative policies followed since 1970. The Administration's new economic programme, initiated in August 1971, played a particularly important role in quickening the progress towards reducing inflation and unemployment. Stimulus from the new programme resulted primarily from cuts in excise taxes on automobiles, an acceleration of previously legislated tax cuts, and an investment tax credit. Better price performance was promoted initially through a 3-month price/wage freeze and then by less rigid controls in the November 1971-January 1973 period. Since January, the system has been primarily one of self-administered adherence to guidelines, with governmental review and intervention, but also including continued mandatory controls in some sectors.

Budgetary developments

Federal fiscal policy has been progressively eased from early 1970 to the end of 1972. Total Federal expenditures (NIA basis) increased at an 8 per cent rate in calendar years 1970 and 1971 and about 12 per cent last year. The rise in tax receipts has been moderated in the past years by various tax reductions. Of these, the most significant were contained in the Tax Reform Act of 1969 and the Revenue Act of 1971. The tax changes have provided a partial offset to the rise in revenues which resulted from a rapid economic advance. Nevertheless, tax receipts in 1972 turned out to be some $12½ billion higher than anticipated, largely due to substantial overwithholding of personal income tax. Revenues have continued to increase faster than was projected in the January budget, thus reducing the FY 1973 and FY 1974 deficits and exerting an automatic stabilizing effect on the economy.

Since mid-1972, the Administration has attempted to slow down the growth in Federal expenditures. Thus, the Administration requested Congress in June 1972 to impose a statutory spending ceiling of $246 billion on unified budget outlays, and the request was repeated in September of that year on the basis of a $250 billion ceiling. However, Congressional approval was not obtained, and restraint was instead exercised unilaterally by the Administration impounding funds already appropriated by Congress. In January 1973, Congress was again asked to establish a ceiling on spending, limiting total FY 1974 outlays to the $268.7 billion (unified basis) recommended in the new budget.

Prior to the presentation of the FY 1974 budget, it was widely believed that the Administration would find it difficult to adhere to its self-imposed $250 billion expenditure ceiling for FY 1973 and that the FY 1974 budget would continue to run a substantial, albeit reduced, high-employment deficit in the absence of a tax increase. The Administration has, however, engaged in a considerable amount of budget-cutting in a number of areas; in all, some 113 separate programmes are affected by the current budget pruning process. There are also proposals in the FY 1974 budget to reduce direct Federal involvement in the areas of education, law enforcement, manpower training and urban community development through replacing a large number of categorical grant programmes by special revenue sharing plans under which state and local governments would be free to decide on their own priorities rather than being tied by the earlier criteria attached to the spending of Federal funds.

Under the new and more tightly controlled Federal spending plans, and as a consequence of an unanticipated rise in revenues, the budget deficit in FY 1974 is expected by the Administration to be substantially reduced to $3 billion on a unified basis. The high-employment deficit is expected to be reduced by about $7 billion from FY 1973 to FY 1974. And, the plan of the Administration is to have the high-employment budget in a surplus position in FY 1974. However, Congress will undoubtedly attempt to salvage some of the programmes to be ended or reduced in size, and the Administration may find it difficult to effect the additional cuts necessary to maintain the planned fiscal position as new unbudgeted expenditure needs appear.

Monetary policy

Monetary policy became progressively more expansionary from 1969 to 1972. During 1970 the money stock (M1) increased by 6.0 per cent, followed by a 6.6 per cent growth in 1971 and an 8.3 per cent rise last year. Money plus net time deposits (M2) increased 10.8 per cent in 1972, or slightly below the 1971 rate, but above increases in 1970 and 1969.

The growth of the monetary aggregates in 1972 appears generally to have exceeded the desired targets of the Federal Reserve System. The behaviour of the money stock became particularly erratic late last year and in early 1973. Thus, while the Federal Open Market Committee at both its September and October meetings had agreed to seek "more moderate growth in monetary aggregates over the months ahead," there was in fact a sharp acceleration in the money supply late in the year on both the narrow (M1) and broad (M2) definitions followed by a deceleration in early 1973. The late 1972 acceleration may have been partly due to distortions caused by changes in Federal Reserve regulations D and J. And there may have been a reluctance on the part of the Federal Reserve to see short-term interest rates move up sharply as they might have done in view of the very strong demand for loanable funds. The official discount rate was maintained at a level of 4½ per cent throughout 1972, while the Federal Funds rate moved up to exceed 5 per cent later in the year. As a consequence, borrowing at the discount window increased sharply in the course of the second half of 1972. Although the Federal Reserve Board approved a one-half point increase in the discount rate in mid-January followed by further increases to 5½ per cent in late February, to 5¾ per cent in April, 6 per cent in May and 6½ per cent in early June, the continued spread between the Federal Funds and discount rate provided an incentive for bank borrowing from the Federal Reserve System. In May, the interest rate ceiling on large certificates of deposit (CD's) with maturities of 90 days and over was suspended. At the same time, the reserve ratio for CD's was raised, a reserve requirement was imposed on bank-related commercial paper, and the reserve requirement on Eurodollar borrowings by banks was lowered. On balance, the changes represented a slight tightening of monetary policy.

The demand for loanable funds has been very strong in the past two years, with private sector borrowing rising sharply since the fourth quarter of 1970. Relative to spending, borrowing was in fact unusually high throughout 1972. Total funds raised in the credit markets by non-financial borrowers increased from $102 billion in 1970 to $156 billion in 1971 and some $168 billion last year. Consumer credit growth has been remarkably rapid and total bank loans increased sharply since mid-1971, with some acceleration in the later part of 1972.

The strong demand for funds in recent quarters has put considerable upward pressure on interest rates. It will be recalled that interest levels dropped fairly sharply after the announcement of the new economic programme in August 1971. This decline continued into early 1972, bringing short-term rates back down to their early 1971 level. However, since the first quarter of 1972, rates have generally been on an uptrend at the shorter end of the maturity spectrum whereas long-term rates have remained relatively stable until recently. In fact, long term rates declined on balance in 1972, making for a divergent trend in long and short-term rates. Such a situation is unusual except for very short periods, since rates across the maturity spectrum generally tend to move in the same direction. The divergence in movement in 1972 can be explained on the basis of a downward revision of inflationary expectations and a moderate demand for short-term securities; one aspect of the latter phenomenon was the slower pace at which foreign central banks acquired short-term Treasury securities.

Several factors will be influencing the behaviour of interest rates in 1973 and early 1974. A continued strong demand for funds, perhaps in combination with an attempt by the Federal Reserve to maintain a moderate rate of monetary expansion, will continue to put upward pressure on rates. At the same time, inflationary expectations may have been reduced as a result of a relatively favourable price performance, apart from food prices, since August 1971 and by the end of direct US military involvement in Vietnam. The demand for long-term funds may also moderate somewhat as revenue sharing is implemented and large savings flows are generated by the expanding economy. The net result of these diverse influences on interest rates may be a continuation of the upward trend in short-term rates with long-term rates following more slowly. However, any new outbreak of inflationary pressures would tend to accelerate the increase in long term rates.

The extensive system of mandatory price and wage controls imposed in 1971 under the authority of the Economic Stabilisation Act was modified on 11th January, 1973, except for the food, health-care and construction industries which remain subject to Phase II procedures. A number of detailed measures were also taken to restrain future increases in food prices, and administrative actions of the Department of Agriculture affecting food supplies and prices were made subject to review by the Cost of Living Council. To limit the rise in food prices, the Administration announced at the end of March the establishment of a ceiling on the price of meat at the processing, wholesale and retail levels.

The previous system of tight and complex controls was replaced by a generally self-administered programme under which only the largest firms need report their major price and wage decisions. Companies with 5,000 or more workers must report wage changes to the Cost of Living Council and those with at least 1,000 employees must keep records of wage changes and produce these upon request. On the price side, companies with sales of $250 million or more, of which there are about 800, are obliged to file quarterly reports on prices, costs and profits, while companies with sales of more than $50 million (about 3,500 firms) must keep records of price and profit margin changes, and produce these upon request. In early May, a limited form of prenotification was reimposed on companies with annual sales exceeding $250 million. Such companies that intend to raise their average weighted price level more than 1.5 per cent above the authorized 10th January levels must now notify the Cost of Living Council thirty days before they intend to put such increases into effect. The Council could intervene to stop or defer these increases. Rents are free of any standards.

The price standard under the new programme is essentially the same as that of Phase II, but the rules on profits have been eased somewhat. Thus, companies may raise prices in proportion to increases in costs, provided their profit margin ceilings are not exceeded; the Cost of Living Council has extended the base period for the calculation of such ceilings to permit inclusion of any fiscal year that has been concluded since 15th August, 1971. An alternative method gives companies the possibility of making cost-justified price increases averaging 1½ per cent over a year, even when this may widen their profit margins beyond the fiscal-year formula. Raising prices may also be considered justified when this leads to a more efficient allocation of resources or appears necessary in order to maintain adequate levels of supply. On the side of wages, the general standard of 5.5 per cent plus 0.7 per cent in fringe benefits annually has been carried over from Phase II, and the philosophy of the new programme appears to continue to be generally opposed to applying a single guidepost to all contract settlements.

With respect to organization, the former Pay Board and Price Commission have been abolished and the new programme is now run by an expanded Cost of Living Council. A new committee with business and labour representatives has been established to review the operation of the present wage standard and to seek agreement on any modification of it. The Administration has retained the power to intervene in individual cases of price and wage setting, forestalling excessive increases or rolling back such increases if they have already taken place, and the Federal government has the authority to re-establish mandatory controls in situations where wage and price developments are clearly out of line. Generally, it appears that the new system provides the tools necessary to curb any serious tendencies to cost-push inflation, since the Administration has considerable statutory power under the extended Economic Stabilisation Act as compared with, for example, the guideposts of the early 1960's which lacked any legal authority for direct enforcement. The crucial question, of course, is the extent to which the Administration will continue to be prepared to use these powers and make its presence felt in important decisions of price and wage formation....

IV ECONOMIC OUTLOOK

Substantial policy ease since 1970 yielded strong growth in real demand and output last year, and present monetary and fiscal policies point to a continuation of the expansion albeit at decelerating rates into 1974. Although there may be some possibility of actual expansion falling short of the projections presented here, the more likely danger seems to be that the momentum will turn out to be too strong, entailing excessive demand pressures possibly followed by a downturn. The question thus arises whether the Administration will succeed in reducing the expansion gradually to the rate of growth of capacity, enhancing the likelihood of maintaining steadier activity growth than in the past. Another question relating to the speed with which the present GNP gap is closed is whether it will be possible to maintain a moderate rate of price increase.

The Administration expects an 11 per cent increase in nominal GNP between 1972 and 1973. The real increase is estimated at 7 per cent, with a slowdown towards the sustainable long run path in the second half. The implied increase in the GNP deflator is 4 per cent and the objective is to reduce the rise in the consumer price index to an annual rate of 2½ per cent by the end of the year. Many private forecasts expect a similar or a somewhat lower increase in the nominal GNP, with slightly slower real growth.

On a year to year basis, the OECD forecast for real GNP is not very different from that of the Administration, but the OECD forecast assumes a rather higher rate of increase in the second half of the year and into 1974. The very strong advance in new orders and other leading indicators in recent months points, in fact, to continued strong demand growth.

A large increase in Government purchases of goods and services is forecast for this year and the first half of 1974, with more of the rise coming from state and local governments and less from Federal purchases than was the case in 1972. The Federal fiscal outlook has already been discussed in some detail in Chapter II: in real terms Federal spending on goods and services is expected to remain almost stable over the forecasting period, following its earlier decline. With the introduction of revenue sharing adding to the large cash flows available from their own sources, the state and local governments are expected to contribute importantly to demand in 1973 and 1974. After years of deficits, these governments ran a surplus in 1972 even when their retirement schemes are excluded, and this financial situation is expected to continue into 1974.

Business fixed investment is expected to contribute substantially to demand growth both this year and in 1974. Continuing favourable financial conditions, rising profits, liberalised depreciation provisions, the restraint on dividend increases and the investment tax credit will all lend support to business investment plans, as already evident in the 1973 surveys. In line with earlier experience it has been assumed that investment plans will be raised upwards at the present stage of the business cycle. In spite of some continued overall slack in the economy, many sectors of manufacturing, such as rubber, autos and paper, are finding that their capacity is being strained and are, consequently, projecting a major expansion of their investment programmes. After three years of very poor performance, the outlook for non-residential construction thus seems buoyant. If these projections are realised, this would mean a real increase of about 13 per cent for total business fixed investment in 1973, with the strong advance continuing into next year.

Business inventory investment, which proceeded rather cautiously earlier in the upturn, has accelerated more recently. If sales increase as anticipated, stock building can be expected to expand strongly this year; this will be so even without much change in the present inventory/ sales ratio. Inventory investment is forecast to run at an annual rate of around $15 billion in current dollars by the end of 1973 and in the first part of 1974, with some subsequent tapering off.

Residential construction, which has been a major source of strength since 1970, is likely to play a far more modest role during the next few quarters. The expected slowdown will be due to rising interest rates and somewhat less favourable conditions in mortgage markets than previously. In addition, the high level of construction in the past two years has served to satisfy the backlog of demand which emerged in the late 1960s. But advance indicators, such as permits and starts, have remained relatively high and vacancies do not appear to be excessive. This year and next may, therefore, see the volume of residential construction declining only marginally.

Although a gradual slowdown from recent extraordinarily high rates of growth is expected in consumer spending, this expenditure component, supported by record income gains including the reimbursement of some $9 billion of overwithheld income tax—only partly offset by continued overwithholding—is likely to remain a strong element. Personal income growth from employment and pay gains will be supplemented by the increase in social security benefits that became effective in the last quarter of 1972; however, increased social security tax rates and a higher social security earnings base will have the opposite effect. Disposable income is expected to show a rise of 11½ per cent in 1973, boosted by the tax refunds. It is assumed, however, that a substantial part of the refunds will be saved and that the saving rate will rise during 1973.

The forecast of the current balance of payments is necessarily subject to a wide margin of error. Previous experience does not provide guidance for estimating the effects on imports and exports of the December 1971 and the February/May 1973 realignments of exchange rates. However, these changes entail a 17¼ per cent effective devaluation of the dollar against currencies of other industrially advanced countries and, on any reasonable assumptions about price behaviour and price elasticities, a marked improvement in the US current external account can be expected, although the full effects of the devaluation may take time to appear. With the US economy moving closer to its potential, import growth is likely to remain substantial in 1973 and into 1974, and rising energy needs will necessitate large increases in purchases of foreign oil and gas. But if the strong upturn in activity now under way in other Member countries continues, US exports should rise faster than imports.

If the present Secretariat forecasts are realised, the GNP gap would be reduced to 1 per cent of potential and the unemployment rate to the vicinity of 4½ per cent by mid-1974. Thus, the economy will clearly move into a critical zone in which it is faced with the threat of renewed demand pull inflation. A particularly heavy 1973 calendar of collective bargaining will increase the difficulty of holding wage increases (and consequent price increases) under control. Major wage contracts expiring this year cover some 4¾ million workers, as compared with 2.8 million in 1972. Thus the possibility of some cost push inflation being superimposed on renewed demand pull inflation cannot be excluded. In these circumstances, it must be uncertain whether the US authorities will be able to reduce the rate of consumer price increases to the ambitious objective of 2½ per cent by the end of the year. The Administration has indicated that it will watch the emerging price-wage situation carefully and will not hesitate to use "the club in the closet," i.e. the legal authority it has under the Economic Stabilisation Act. But, even if the Administration played a very active role enforcing the standards, rising expenses—including labour, fuel, raw materials costs and increased pollution abatement efforts—may justify price increases by business which, on balance, are incompatible with the 2½ per cent target.

V POLICY CONCLUSIONS

Over the past year, the recovery of economic activity has continued at a high rate and unemployment has been reduced. Price performance has been uneven, with an improvement in 1972, followed by a less satisfactory performance in recent months. The development of the balance of payments has been disappointing but, as noted earlier, a gradual improvement would now seem likely, influenced notably by the parity changes effected over the last two years.

Over the next 12 to 18 months economic policy will be put to a crucial test. As the recovery of activity is being completed and full employment conditions are being reached it is essential that the advance of aggregate demand should slow down to the rate of growth of potential, so that excess demand conditions can be avoided.

(a) Experience suggests that, as the margin of unused resources is disappearing, the maintenance of satisfactory price performance will become more difficult, and that it would become virtually impossible, even with restoration of stricter price and wage controls, if excessive demand pressures with widespread bottlenecks and shortages should develop.

(b) Overheating, accompanied by stronger inflation and spillover of domestic demand into imports, could jeopardize the improvement of the current foreign balance which is now in sight. The maintenance of non-inflationary conditions is clearly necessary if full advantage is to be taken of the devaluation of the dollar to improve the balance of payments and restore better international payments equilibrium.

On the basis of present trends and policies many forecasters, including the US authorities and the OECD Secretariat, expect the expansion to slow down in the second half of the present year and into 1974 to a rate closer to the growth of potential. Thus, judging from these forecasts, the possibility of avoiding excessive demand growth in the near future would seem good. But there are, of course, many uncertainties. As always, interpretation of leading indicators is difficult. Moreover, the Federal budget picture for fiscal year 1974 is not yet clear; despite Administration resistance there could well be expenditure increases going beyond what was proposed in the budget presented last January. What is clear in the present situation is that a strong expansionary momentum has developed and that the economy is moving into a more critical phase from the point of view of stabilisation policy.

Policy will, therefore, have to be adjusted to possible changes in the demand outlook. It is not clear, however, how quickly demand management policy can be changed in the United States. There is of course considerable flexibility as far as monetary policy is concerned, and a further tightening in this area may well be required to bring the pace of expansion down to the growth rate of potential output. A tightening of monetary policy would also be desirable from the point of view of strengthening the capital account of the balance of payments during the period before the full effects of the devaluation of the dollar have been felt. But it would probably be undesirable to let monetary policy carry the whole burden of policy adjustment, as in 1959, 1966/67 and 1968/69, entailing a distorted demand picture and the risk of a downturn in activity.

With regard to fiscal policy, however, it is less clear how quickly a tightening could be effected. In recent years the Administration has with considerable success relied on expenditure reductions to limit the fiscal stimulus imparted to the economy. But in view of the shift in the composition of Federal budget outlays in recent years away from spending on goods and services towards transfers and grants, further cuts in expenditure might be difficult, and probably undesirable on social considerations. Some form of tax action may therefore become necessary, particularly if Federal expenditures were to rise faster than suggested in the FY 1974 Federal budget presented last January.

Judging from past experience, the enactment of tax changes could take considerable time, and, thus, come too late from the point of view of good demand management. It would seem that more flexible fiscal arrangements are needed in the United States. In a modern economy prompt action is sometimes needed to keep the economy on an even keel, avoiding inflationary and deflationary tendencies from becoming cumulative. As noted in last year's OECD Survey on the United States, it is difficult to see how fiscal policy can be operated with sufficient flexibility under existing legislative arrangements; it is to be hoped that further consideration will be given to the possibility of granting the President limited stand-by authority, such as exists in a number of other countries, to vary tax rates and certain types of expenditures without prior legislative consent.

The problem of reconciling the movement to, and later preservation of, a state of high employment with satisfactory price performance is complicated by changes in the labour market situation over the past fifteen years. These changes, as discussed in Chapter III, have tended to raise the amount of unemployment and thus make it more difficult to achieve the employment targets which, in the past, were considered attainable without seriously compromising other policy objectives. The authorities are therefore faced with the dilemma that higher levels of employment tend to bring with them unacceptably high rates of inflation. In this new situation, general demand management, even if perfected with respect to degree and timing of policy response, is likely to prove inadequate so that it becomes necessary to search for ancillary approaches to achieve society's various economic goals simultaneously.

Policies on the supply side can make a contribution in this respect especially if given time. For example, to the extent that public sector employment programmes could be used to provide productive jobs and training for those unemployed whose low skills and other characteristics make them unemployable in the labour shortage areas, the expansion of such programmes could make a contribution to both economic and social values. At the same time, it is important that manpower programmes should not be too narrowly focussed on the problems of the disadvantaged and that they should not become essentially a social policy for redistributing income. Instead, while continuing a high level of assistance for the least skilled members of the labour force, such programmes should be expanded in design so as to train for and fill job vacancies at all skill levels. Thus, manpower programmes could make a contribution, not only in reducing unemployment in certain areas and groups, but also in reducing the likelihood of serious labour market bottlenecks in periods of strong economic peformance.

Some possibilities for exercising greater selectivity in demand management may also exist. In addition, the functioning of market forces could undoubtedly be improved in a number of ways; e.g. restrictive practices of business and labour might be reduced and government policies and regulations in a wide range of fields, such as quotas, price maintenance laws and agricultural policies, minimum wage laws, etc., should be continually reassessed with a view to enhancing the responsiveness of wages and prices to changes in the balance between supply and demand in product and factor markets. And, as argued in previous OECD surveys, government programmes and policies should be appraised with respect to their likely impact on prices. There may be areas where, for technological, structural, national security or other reasons, it may be difficult to improve market functioning. In such cases, it seems desirable for the authorities to continue monitoring and, where necessary, to intervene in important decisions of price and wage formation.

Contemplating such a more permanent system of price surveillance is distasteful in any society valuing the allocative efficiency of the free market. However, economic reality differs from the perfectly competitive market described in economic theory, and it may be desirable for the authorities to have some continuing means of intervention in those instances where imperfect competition or other conditions tend to insulate price decisions from competitive market forces. The retention of Phase II controls in the food, health-care and construction industries is a recognition of the need for government intervention in problem areas. As to the shift to a self-administered control programme, this move was largely unexpected in light of the apparent success of the earlier programme and the heavy calendar of collective bargaining this year. It remains to be seen whether this shift does not turn out to have been premature. However, as discussed in Chapter II, the Administration has retained considerable power to intervene in the market to prevent excessive price and wage increases and it has indicated that these powers will continue to be used to the extent necessary to maintain a satisfactory price performance.

DEBUT OF WHITE HOUSE TAPES

July 16, 1973

Existence of the famed White House tapes first came to light in surprise testimony before the Senate Select Committee on Presidential Campaign Activities. A former presidential aide disclosed July 16 that President Nixon's discussions with visitors at his offices In the White House and the Executive Office Building, and telephone conversations there and at a few other locations, had been taped beginning in the spring of 1971. Alexander P. Butterfield, administrator of the Federal Aviation Administration since March 1973, said the listening devices had been installed under Nixon's authority "for historical purposes." Butterfield's testimony, confirmed by the White House, raised hopes that the tapes would make it possible to settle conflicting claims as to the extent of the President's knowledge of the Watergate cover-up.

Some members of Congress, on the other hand, expressed indignation that conversations presumed to be private had been secretly recorded. House Speaker Carl Albert (D Okla.) called the recording practice "an outrage, almost beyond belief." Other voices on Capitol Hill were less bitter. "I wouldn't have minded if they told me," said Senate Democratic Leader Mike Mansfield (D Mont.). Sen. Barry Goldwater did not think it was "inappropriate to record for historical purposes." But the immediate concern of the Watergate investigating committee was to gain access to tapes of Nixon's conversations with persons who had given key testimony before the committee. The chief interest was in the President's talks with John W. Dean III, the former White House counsel who had put his word against Nixon's by linking the President directly to the Watergate cover-up.

The existence of the tapes was confirmed in a letter dated July 16 from special presidential counsel J. Fred Buzhardt Jr. Buzhardt asserted that "this system, which is still in use, is similar to that employed by the last administration and which had been discontinued from 1969 until the spring of 1971." The President said at a news conference Aug. 22 (see p. 739) that "this capability (to tape presidential conversations) not only existed during the Johnson administration, it also existed in the Kennedy administration...because they felt that they had some obligation particularly in the field of foreign policy and some domestic areas to have a record that would be accurate."

Butterfield's testimony led reporters to query the Secret Service for more details on how and to what extent the taping had been carried out. However, Nixon invoked executive privilege and ordered the Secret Service to withhold all information about the recordings. The Senate committee then asked the President for his "cooperation in making available to the committee records and tapes which are relevant" to its investigation. Sen. Howard H. Baker Jr. (R Tenn.), ranking minority member, said that access to the tapes was "a matter of monumental importance" to the committee.

When Nixon refused its request, the committee voted unanimously to subpoena the sought-after material. Special Watergate prosecutor Archibald Cox, who had also been refused access to the recordings, likewise announced his intention to subpoena certain tapes. The White House having failed to meet the deadline of July 26 set for compliance with the Cox subpoena, the prosecutor at once took his case to the courts. Judge John J. Sirica of the U.S. District Court for the District of Columbia ruled in Cox's favor on Aug. 29 and ordered President Nixon to release the tapes. After Sirica's decision was upheld by the U.S. Court of Appeals on Oct. 12, the administration decided not to appeal to the Supreme Court. Ultimately, the refusal of Cox to accept a compromise worked out by the White House—for surrender of summaries of the tapes rather than the tapes themselves—provoked Nixon to fire the special prosecutor. (See p. 859.)

Only three days later, on Oct. 23, Charles Alan Wright, special White House counsel, appeared before Judge Sirica and, to everyone's surprise, announced that the President would "comply in all respects" with Sirica's order of Aug. 29. Meanwhile, the Senate committee's independent attempt to gain possession of the tapes had come to naught when Sirica ruled, Oct. 17, that his court, for jurisdictional reasons, had no alternative but to dismiss the action brought by the committee.

> Excerpts from the transcript of an exchange, at a hearing July 16, between Fred D. Thompson, minority counsel of the Senate Watergate committee, and Alexander P. Butterfield, former deputy assistant to President Nixon. Thomp-

son was questioning Butterfield about the taping of presidential conversations:

Thompson: Mr. Butterfield, are you aware of the installation of any listening devices in the oval office of the President?

Butterfield: I was aware of listening devices, yes, sir.

Thompson: When were those devices placed in the oval office?

Butterfield: Approximately the summer of 1970. I cannot begin to recall the precise date. My guess, Mr. Thompson, is that the installation was made between—and this is a very rough guess—April or May of 1970 and perhaps the end of the summer or early fall 1970.

Thompson: Are you aware of any devices that were installed in the Executive Office Building office of the President?

Butterfield: ....They were installed at the same time.

Thompson: Would you tell us a little bit about how those devices worked, how they were activated, for example?

Butterfield: I don't have the technical knowledge, but I will tell you what I know about how those devices were triggered. They were installed, of course, for historical purposes, to record the President's business, and they were installed in his two offices, the oval office and the EOB (Executive Office Building) office....

Butterfield: ....In that the oval office and the Executive Office Building office were indicated on this locator box, the installation was installed in such a way that when the light was on "oval office," the taping device was at least triggered. It was not operating, but it was triggered—it was spring-loaded, if you will, then it was voice-actuated.

So when the light was on "oval office," in the oval office and in the oval office only, the taping device was spring-loaded to a voice-actuating situation. When the President went to the EOB office, the EOB light was on. In the EOB office, there was the same arrangement.

Thompson: ...What about the cabinet room? Was there a taping device in the cabinet room?

Butterfield: Yes, sir, there was.

Thompson: Was it activated in the same way?

Butterfield: No, sir, it was not, and my guess is, and it is only my guess, is because there was no cabinet room location per se on the locator box.

To ensure the recording of business conversations in the cabinet room, a manual installation was made....

Thompson: There were buttons on the desk in the cabinet room there that activated that device?

Butterfield: There were two buttons.... There was an off-on button, one said "Haldeman" and one that said "Butterfield" that was on and off respectively, and one on my telephone.

Thompson: So far as the oval office and the EOB office is concerned, would it be your testimony that the device would pick up any and all conversations no matter where the conversations took place in the room and no matter how soft the conversations might have been?

Butterfield: Yes, sir....

Thompson: Was it a little more difficult to pick up in the cabinet room?

Butterfield: Yes, sir, it was a great deal more difficult to pick up in the cabinet room.

Thompson: All right. We talked about the rooms now, and if we could move on to telephones, are you aware of the installation of any devices on any of the telephones, first of all, the oval office?

Butterfield: Yes, sir.

Thompson: What about the Executive Office Building office of the President?

Butterfield: Yes, sir. The President's business telephone at his desk in the Executive Office Building.

Thompson: What about the Lincoln Room?

Butterfield: Yes, sir, the telephone in the Lincoln sitting room in the residence.

Thompson: What about Aspen cabin at Camp David?

Butterfield: Only in, on the telephone at the President's desk in his study in the Aspen cabin, his personal cabin.

Thompson: It is my understanding this cabin was sometimes used by foreign dignitaries. Was the device still present during those periods of time?

Butterfield: No, sir, the device was removed prior to occupancy by chiefs of state, heads of government and other foreign dignitaries.

Thompson: All right. Would you state who installed these devices, all of these devices, so far as you know?

Butterfield: ....The Secret Service. The technical security division of the Secret Service.

Thompson: Would you state why, as far as your understanding is concerned, these devices were installed in these rooms?

Butterfield: There was no doubt in my mind they were installed to record things for posterity, for the Nixon library. The President was very conscious of that kind of thing. We had quite an elaborate setup at the White House for the collection and preservation of documents, and of things which transpired in the way of business of state.

Thompson: On whose authority were they installed, Mr. Butterfield?

Butterfield: On the President's authority by way of Mr. Haldeman and Mr. Higby. (H.R. Haldeman, then White House chief of staff, and Lawrence M. Higby, deputy assistant to the President)....

Thompson: Where were the tapes of those conversations kept, maintained?

Butterfield: I cannot say where. I am quite sure in the Executive Office Building in some closets or cupboards or files which are maintained by the technical security division of the U.S. Secret Service.

Thompson: Were these tapes checked periodically?

Butterfield: Yes, they were checked at least daily...I think some were used more frequently than others. The Secret Service knew this; they made sure that they were checked periodically and sufficiently....

Thompson: Were any of these tapes ever transcribed, reduced to writing or typewritten paper, so far as you knew?

Butterfield: To my recollection, no.

Thompson: Mr. Butterfield, as far as you know from your own personal knowledge, from 1970 then until the present time all of the President's conversations in the offices mentioned...were recorded as far as you know?

Butterfield: That is correct, until I left. Someone could have taken the equipment out, but until the day I left I am sure I would have been notified.

Thompson: And as far as you know, those tapes are still available?

Butterfield: As far as I know, but I have been away for four months, sir....

PHASE IV CONTROLS

July 18, 1973

President Nixon on July 18 turned his New Economic Policy back to a point similar to, but more restrictive than, Phase II, which had been abandoned in January. (See p. 43.) In still another attempt to cure the country's inflation-ridden economy, the President lifted a month-old freeze as it applied to meat and other food product prices and projected plans for a complex Phase IV economic control program to take effect in different sectors between July 18 and Sept. 12. The price freeze, announced June 13 (see p. 577) as a stopgap measure to shore up Phase III's largely unsuccessful program of voluntary economic guidelines, was to remain in effect until Aug. 12 for the industrial and service sectors.

Urging "a policy of patience," the President reiterated his desire for an end to all controls. But a move to lift all controls immediately, he said, "would most likely turn into a detour, back into a swamp of even more lasting controls." Instead, the Phase IV proposals were designed to take the economy out of the freeze on a sector-by-sector basis, starting with food. During that process, the administration would rely on a strengthened version of Phase II controls to spread out an expected post-freeze price bulge with minimal disruption of economic production.

The most complicated system of controls devised for peacetime uses, Phase IV was aimed at moderating inflation while fiscal and monetary restraints eased the need for any controls at all. Tailored to conditions in varying sectors, the new proposals went beyond Phase

703

II in limiting the businessman's right to translate rising costs into higher consumer prices. Moreover, the mandatory system was backed up by civil penalties. Treasury Secretary George P. Shultz told newsmen July 18 that the government would hire an additional 1,200 employees for the Cost of Living Council and Internal Revenue Service to administer the controls. In moving to end the price freeze by Aug. 12, the administration acknowledged that consumers would have to pay more for their purchases in Phase IV as the price of encouraging the stepped-up production needed to head off or overcome supply shortages that would intensify inflationary pressures.

Emphasizing the selective nature of the new controls, the administration announced that the lumber industry, public utilities, long-term coal contracts, security and commodity brokerage fees and rents would be decontrolled after Aug. 12. Meat and most other food prices were immediately exempted from the freeze, but as a part of this initial step, the President also set up a two-stage program for controlling food prices. The freeze on prices of a single food item, beef, limited since March 29 (see p. 427), was continued until Sept. 12. Raw agricultural products remained exempt from price controls. To add greater flexibility to the new economic initiatives, the Cost of Living Council retained authority under Phase IV to grant exemptions from controls if inflationary pressures were relieved, if inequities developed or if supply shortages were threatened. At its discretion, the Council could reimpose controls if necessary.

As announced by the Cost of Living Council July 19, the Phase IV regulations for industrial and service enterprises were considerably more stringent than similar Phase II rules. Cost increases could be passed through into price increases only on a dollar-for-dollar basis, with no profit margin markup. Corporations with annual sales of more than $100-million were required to give the Council a 30-day advance notice before increasing prices. Prices in effect during the last quarter of 1972 were to be the base prices against which new increases would be judged. That regulation forced companies to absorb cost increases incurred before that quarter but not yet reflected in price increases.

The Cost of Living Council proposed separate Phase IV ceilings on producers' and retailers' prices for gasoline and other petroleum products. At the production end, the regulations placed a ceiling on domestic crude oil prices at May 15 levels. At the wholesale and retail end, the prices on gasoline, diesel fuel and home heating oil were limited to the cost of the product to the dealer plus the same percentage markup he applied as of Jan. 10, 1973. Gasoline stations were required to post ceiling prices and octane ratings on their pumps.

704

Wholesale and retail merchandising firms were placed under still another set of regulations by the Phase IV proposals. They were allowed to increase prices on categories of goods in order to pass through increases in the cost of acquiring the goods, plus the same percentage markup used during the firm's last fiscal year ending before Feb. 5, 1973. Other complicated criteria were used by insurance companies that increased premiums above Aug. 12 levels. Health and property-liability companies with annual premium levels above a specified point were required to give 30-day prenotification of rate increases. Phase IV rules affecting labor remained essentially the same as under the looser Phase II and III standards, which allowed wage and benefit increases of 5.5 per cent and 0.7 per cent, respectively.

When Phase IV became effective on Aug. 12, President Nixon had moved the U.S. economy full circle—through a Phase I wage-price freeze, mandatory Phase II wage-price controls, voluntary Phase III controls, a second price freeze, and on to a still tougher set of price controls—all in the two years since he announced his New Economic Policy on Aug. 15, 1971. The President had overruled his closest economic advisers when, on June 13, 1973, he imposed the 60-day price freeze that was lifted by Phase IV. But the second freeze had created nearly as many economic problems as it had been expected to solve. Finally, the President admitted that "the freeze is holding down production and creating shortages which threaten to get worse, and cause still higher prices...."

After June 13, at least 87 food industry plants were reported to have closed. Some farmers drowned baby chicks, others sent pregnant sows to market. Treasury Secretary Shultz explained such actions by saying that "cost was greater than price, and that's something you can't make up in surplus." Producers of processed goods had been caught in a squeeze. Prices for raw materials had been allowed to rise under the freeze, but prices of processed goods were frozen. The result: middlemen had to absorb the higher prices of materials with a loss of profits. Some processors finally decided it was cheaper not to produce. Across the board, sellers of every variety found themselves hemmed in by this new phase of Phase III. Economic analysts both in and out of the Nixon administration criticized the midsummer freeze. The controlled price level had bought time, they conceded, but it did little to ease the overheated consumer demand for goods, the root of inflation.

Text of President Nixon's July 18 announcement of Phase IV controls, followed by text of Executive Order lifting price freeze on food products and health services:

The American people now face a profoundly important decision. We have a freeze on prices which is holding back a surge of inflation that would break out if the controls were removed. At the same time the freeze is holding down production and creating shortages which threaten to get worse, and cause still higher prices, as the freeze and controls continue.

In this situation we are offered two extreme kinds of advice.

One suggestion is that we should accept price and wage controls as a permanent feature of the American economy. We are told to forget the idea of regaining a free economy and set about developing the regulations and bureacracy for a permanent system of controls.

The other suggestion is to make the move for freedom now, abolishing all controls immediately.

While these suggestions are well meant, and in many cases reflect deep conviction, neither can be accepted. Our wise course today is not to choose one of these extremes but to seek the best possible reconciliation of our interests in slowing down the rate of inflation on the one hand, and preserving American production and efficiency on the other.

The main elements in the policy we need are these:

First, the control system must be *tough*. It has to hold back and phase in gradually a large part of the built-in pressure for higher prices which already exists in the economy.

Second, the system must be *selective*. It must permit relaxation of those restraints which interfere most with production, and it must not waste effort on sectors of the economy where stability of prices exists. The control system should also be designed to accommodate the special problems of various sectors of the economy under the strains of high use of capacity.

Third, the system must contain sufficient assurance of its *termination* at an appropriate time to preserve incentives for investment and production and guard against tendencies for controls to be perpetuated.

Fourth, the control system must be backed up by firm steps to *balance the budget*, so that excess demand does not regenerate inflationary pressures which make it difficult either to live with the controls or to live without them.

We have had in 1973 an extraordinary combination of circumstances making for rapid inflation. There was a decline of domestic food supplies. The domestic economy boomed at an exceptional pace, generating powerful demand for goods and services. The boom in other countries and the devaluation of the dollar, while desirable from most points of view, raised the prices of things we export or import.

These forces caused a sharp rise of prices in early 1973. The index of consumer prices rose at an annual rate of about 8 percent from December 1972 to May 1973. The freeze imposed on June 13 put a halt to this rapid rise of prices. But many of the cost increases and demand pressures working to raise prices in the early part of the year had not yet resulted in higher prices by the time the freeze was imposed. Thus a certain built-in pressure for a bulge of price increases awaits the end of the freeze. Moreover, aside from this undigested bulge left over by the freeze, the circumstances causing the sharp price increase in early 1973 will still be present although not on so large a scale. The demand for goods and services will be rising less rapidly than in the first half of the year. The supply of food will be rising, although not fast enough. Our position in international trade is improving and this will lend strength to the dollar.

All in all, the tendency for prices to rise in the remainder of 1973, a tendency which will either come out in higher prices or be repressed by controls, will be less than in the first half of the year but greater than anyone would like. Particularly, there is no way, with or without controls to prevent a substantial rise of food prices. However, by 1974, we should be able to achieve a much more moderate rate of inflation. By that time, the good feed crops in prospect for this year should have produced a much larger supply of food, and total demand should be rising less rapidly than in 1973.

This more satisfactory situation on the inflation front will be reached if three conditions are met:

First, we do not allow the temporary inflationary forces now confronting us to generate a new wage-price spiral which will continue to run after these temporary forces have passed. To do this we must hold down the expression of those forces in prices and wages.

Second, we do not allow the present controls to damp down 1974 production excessively, a problem that is most obvious in the case of meats and poultry.

Third, we do not permit a continuation or revival of excess demand that will generate new inflationary forces. That is why control of the Federal budget is an essential part of the whole effort.

The steps I am announcing or recommending today are designed to create these conditions.

The Phase IV Controls Program

Our decisions about the new control program have been reached after consulting with all sectors of the American society in over 30 meetings and after studying hundreds of written communications. The advice we received was most helpful, and I want to thank all those who provided it.

The Cost of Living Council will describe the Phase IV controls program in detail in statements and regulations. These will take effect at various times between now and September 12. They will include special regulations dealing with the petroleum industry, published for comment. Here I will only review the general features of the program, to indicate its basic firmness and the efforts that have been made to assure that production continues and shortages are avoided.

The controls will be mandatory. The success of the program, however, will depend upon a high degree of voluntary compliance. We have had that in the past. Study of the reports on business behavior during Phase III shows that voluntary compliance was almost universal. Nevertheless, the rules we are now proposing are stricter, and it is only fair to those who will comply voluntarily to assure that there is compulsion for the others.

Except for foods, the freeze on prices will remain in effect until August 12. However, modifications of the freeze rules will be made to relieve its most serious inequities.

The fundamental pricing rule of Phase IV is that prices are permitted to rise as much as costs rise, in dollars per unit of output, without any profit margin on the additional costs. Cost increases will be counted from the end of 1972; cost increases which occurred earlier but had not been reflected in prices may not be passed on. In addition to the cost rule, there remains the previous limitation on profit margins.

Large firms, those with annual sales in excess of $100,000,000, will be required to notify the Cost of Living Council of intended price increases and may not put them into effect for 30 days. During that period, the Council may deny or suspend the proposed increase.

The wage standards of Phase II and Phase III will remain in force. Notification of wage increases will continue to be required for large employment units.

These are, we recognize, tough rules, in some respects tougher than during Phase II. But the situation is also in many ways more difficult than during Phase II. So long as the system is regarded as temporary, however, we believe that business can continue to prosper, industrial peace can be maintained, and production continue to expand under these rules. Machinery will be established in the Cost of Living Council to consider the need for exceptions from these rules where they may be causing serious injury to the economy. And we will be prepared to consider modification of the rules themselves when that seems necessary or possible.

The Special Case of Food

Nowhere have the dilemmas of price control been clearer than in the case of food. In the early part of this year, rising food prices were the largest part of the inflation problem, statistically and psychologically. If price restraint was needed anywhere, it was needed for food. But since the ceilings were placed on meat prices on March 29, and especially since the freeze was imposed on June 13, food has given the clearest evidence of the harm that controls do to supplies. We have seen baby chicks drowned, pregnant sows and cows, bearing next year's food, slaughtered, and packing plants closed down. This dilemma is no coincidence. It is because food prices were rising most rapidly that the freeze held prices most below their natural level and therefore had the worst effect on supplies.

We must pick our way carefully between a food price policy so rigid as to cut production sharply and to make shortages inevitable within a few months and a food price policy so loose as to give us an unnecessary and intolerable bulge. On this basis we have decided on the following special rules for food:

1. Effective immediately processors and distributors of food, except beef, may increase their prices, on a cents-per-unit basis, to the extent of the increase of costs of raw agricultural products since the freeze base period (June 1-8).

2. Beef prices remain under present ceilings.

3. The foregoing special rules expire on September 12, after which time the same rules that apply to other products will apply to foods.

4. Raw agricultural products remain exempt from price control.

To relieve the extreme high prices of feeds, which have an important effect on prices of meat, poultry, eggs, and dairy products, we have placed limitations on the export of soybeans and related products until the new crop comes into the market. These limitations will remain in effect for that period. But permanent control of exports is not the policy of this Government, and we do not intend at this time to broaden the controls beyond those now in force. To a considerable degree, export controls are self-defeating as an anti-inflation measure. Limiting our exports reduces our foreign earnings, depresses the value of the dollar, and increases the cost of things we import, which also enter into the cost of living of the American family. Moreover, limiting our agricultural exports runs counter to our basic policy of building up our agricultural markets abroad. Unless present crop expectations are seriously disappointed, or foreign demands are extremely large, export controls will not be needed. However, reports of export orders for agricultural commodities will continue to be required. Our policy must always be guided by the fundamental importance of maintaining adequate supplies of food at home.

The stability of the American economy in the months and years ahead demands maximum farm output. I call upon the American farmer to produce as much as he can. There have been reports that farmers have been reluctant to raise livestock because they are uncertain whether Government regulations will permit them a fair return on their investment, and perhaps also because they resent the imposition of ceilings on food prices. I hope that these reports are untrue. In the past year *real* net income per farm increased 14 percent, a truly remarkable rise. I can assure the American farmer that there is no intention of the Government to discriminate against him. The rules we are setting forth today should give the farmer confidence that the

Government will not keep him from earning a fair return on his investment in providing food.

The Secretary of Agriculture will be offering more specific advice on increasing food production and will be taking several steps to assist; in particular he has decided that there will be no Government set-aside of land in 1974 for feed grains, wheat, and cotton.

I am today initiating steps to increase the import of dried skim milk.

When I announced the freeze, I said that special attention would be given, in the post-freeze period, to stabilizing the price of food. That remains a primary objective. But stabilizing the price of food would not be accomplished by low price ceilings and empty shelves, even if the ceilings could be enforced when the shelves are empty. Neither can stabilization be concerned only with a week or a month. The evidence is becoming overwhelming that only if a rise of food prices is permitted now can we avoid shortages and still higher prices later. I hope that the American people will understand this and not be deluded by the idea that we can produce low-priced food out of acts of Congress or Executive orders. The American people will continue to be well-fed, at prices which are reasonable relative to their incomes. But they cannot now escape a period in which food prices are higher relative to incomes than we have been accustomed to.

The Process of Decontrol

There is no need for me to reiterate my desire to end controls and return to the free market. I believe that a large proportion of the American people, when faced with a rounded picture of the options, share that desire. Our experience with the freeze has dramatized the essential difficulties of a controlled system—its interference with production, its inequities, its distortions, its evasions, and the obstacles it places in the way of good international relations.

And yet, I must urge a policy of patience. The move to freedom now would most likely turn into a detour, back into a swamp of even more lasting controls. I am impressed by the unanimous recommendation of the leaders of labor and business who constitute the Labor-Management Advisory Committee that the controls should be terminated by the end of 1973. I hope it will be possible to do so, and I will do everything in my power to achieve that goal. However, I do not consider it wise to commit ourselves to a specific date for ending all controls at this time.

We shall have to work our way and feel our way out of controls. That is, we shall have to create conditions in which the controls can be terminated without disrupting the economy, and we shall have to move in successive stages to withdraw the controls in parts of the economy where that can be safely done or where the controls are most harmful.

To work our way out of controls means basically to eliminate the excessive growth of total demand which pulls prices up faster and faster. The main lesson of that is to control the budget, and I shall return to that critical subject below.

But while we are working our way to that ultimate condition in which controls are no longer useful, we must be alert to identify those parts of the economy that can be safely decontrolled. Removing the controls in those sectors will not only be a step towards efficiency and freedom there; it will also reduce the burden of administration, permit administrative resources to be concentrated where most needed, and provide an incentive for other firms and industries to reach a similar condition.

During Phase II firms with 60 employees or fewer were exempt from controls. That exemption is now repeated. We are today exempting most regulated public utilities, the lumber industry (where prices are falling), and the price of coal sold under long-term contract. The Cost of Living Council will be studying other sectors for possible decontrol. It will also receive applications from firms or industries that can give assurance of reasonably noninflationary behavior without controls. In all cases, of course, the Cost of Living Council will retain authority to reimpose controls.

Balancing the Budget

The key to success of our anti-inflation effort is the budget. If Federal spending soars and the deficit mounts, the control system will not be able to resist the pressure of demand. The most common cause of the breakdown of control systems has been failure to keep fiscal and monetary policy under restraint. We must not let that happen to us.

I am assured that the Federal Reserve will cooperate in the anti-inflation effort by slowing down the expansion of money and credit. But monetary policy should not, and cannot, be expected to exercise the needed restraint alone. A further contribution from the budget is needed.

I propose that we should now take a balanced budget as our goal for the present fiscal year. In the past I have suggested as a standard for the federal budget that expenditures should not exceed the revenues that would be collected at full employment. We are meeting that standard. But in today's circumstances, that is only a minimum standard of fiscal prudence. When inflationary pressure is strong, when we are forced to emergency controls to resist that pressure, when confidence in our management of our fiscal affairs is low, at home and abroad, we cannot afford to live by that minimum standard. We must take as our goal the more ambitious one of balancing the actual budget.

Achieving that goal will be difficult, more difficult than it seems at first. My original expenditure budget for fiscal 1974 was $268.7

billion. Since that budget was submitted economic expansion, inflation, and other factors have raised the estimated revenues to about the level of the original expenditure estimate. However, while that was happening the probable expenditures have also been rising as a result of higher interest rates, new legislation enacted, failure of Congress to act on some of my recommendations, and Congressional action already far advanced but not completed.

It is clear that several billion dollars will have to be cut from the expenditures that are already probable if we are to balance the budget. That will be hard, because my original budget was tight. However, I regard it as essential and pledge myself to work for it.

We should remember that a little over a year ago I set as a goal for fiscal year 1973 to hold expenditures within a total of $250 billion. There was much skepticism about that at the time, and suggestions that the number was for political consumption only, to be forgotten after the election. But I meant it, the people endorsed it, and the Congress cooperated. I am able to report today that the goal was achieved, and total expenditures for fiscal year 1973 were below $249 billion.

I will take those steps that I can take administratively to reach the goal of a balanced budget for fiscal year 1974. I shall start by ordering that the number of Federal civilian personnel at the end of fiscal year 1974 total below the number now budgeted. The Office of Management and Budget will work with the agencies on this and other reductions. I urge the Congress to assist in this effort. Without its cooperation achievement of the goal cannot be realistically expected.

Despite the difficult conditions and choices we now confront, the American economy is strong. Total production is about 6 1/2 percent above a year ago, employment has risen by 3 million, real incomes are higher than ever. There is every prospect for further increases of output, employment, and incomes. Even in the field of inflation our performance is better than in most of the world. So we should not despair of our plight. But we have problems, and they are serious in part because we and the rest of the world expect the highest performance from the American economy. We can do better. And we will, with mutual understanding and the support of the American people.

Executive Order 11730, issued July 18, 1973, Further Providing for the Stabilization of the Economy:

On June 13, 1973, I ordered a freeze for a maximum period of 60 days on the prices of all commodities and services offered for sale except the prices charged for raw agricultural products. At that time, I stated that the freeze period would be usd to develop a new and more effective system of controls to follow the freeze. Planning for the Phase IV program has proceeded rapidly and I have, therefore, decided that the freeze on food, except for beef, should be removed and more flexible controls substituted in a two-stage process in the food industry. The first stage will be effective at 4:00 p.m., e.s.t., July 18, 1973. The freeze in other sectors of the economy will continue through August 12, 1973. I am also directing the Cost of Living Council to publish for comment now, proposed plans for Phase IV controls in other sectors of the economy. I have determined that this action is necessary to stabilize the economy, reduce inflation, minimize unemployment, improve the Nation's competitive position in world trade and protect the purchasing power of the dollar, all in the context of sound fiscal management and effective monetary policies.

Now, THEREFORE, by virtue of the authority vested in me by the Constitution and statutes of the United States, particularly the Economic Stabilization Act of 1970, as amended, it is hereby ordered as follows:

SECTION 1. Executive Order 11723 establishing a freeze on prices effective 9:00 p.m., e.s.t., June 13, 1973, for a maximum period of 60 days is hereby superseded except as hereinafter provided. Under the provisions of Executive Order 11695, the freeze regulations issued by the Cost of Living Council, pursuant to the authority of Executive Order 11723 remain in effect except as the Chairman of the Cost of Living Council may modify them. The price feeze established by Executive Order 11723 remains in effect until 11:59 p.m., e.s.t., August 12, 1973, except to the extent the Chairman of the Cost of Living Council may modify it.

SEC. 2. All orders, regulations, circulars, rulings, notices or other directives issued and all other actions taken by any agency pursuant to Executive Order 11723, and in effect on the date of this order are hereby confirmed and ratified, and shall remain in full force and effect unless or until altered, amended, or revoked by the Chairman of the Cost of Living Council.

SEC. 3. This order shall not operate to defeat any suit, action, prosecution, or administrative proceeding, whether heretofore or hereafter commenced, with respect to any right possessed, liability incurred, or offense committed prior to this date.

SEC. 4. Executive Order 11695 continues to remain in full force and effect.

RICHARD NIXON

The White House,
    July 18, 1973.

August

NEW U.S.-JAPANESE PARTNERSHIP

August 1, 1973

A new turn in Japanese-American relations occurred in the summer of 1973. During a brief two-day visit to this country by Japan's Prime Minister Kakuei Tanaka, all indications were that Japan had taken on new authority in its dealings with the United States. The first signal came during ceremonies welcoming Tanaka to the White House July 31. President Nixon praised Japan's rapid industrial growth and called its performance "one of the greatest epics of progress in the history of mankind." Then he said that in relations between the two countries, the United States could no longer be regarded as a "senior partner" or "big brother" to Japan. On the contrary, Nixon pledged the United States to accept Japan in "equal partnership" in world affairs.

Tanaka echoed the President's sentiments. Addressing the National Press Club Aug. 1, Japan's prime minister declared: "Not even the United States, with all its might, can unilaterally solve the problems that beset the world today. Nor should we expect it to do so. These challenges can be met only through the close collaboration of Japan, the U.S. and Europe." Of particular interest to Tanaka were the current problems of "world monetary instability and chronic inflation, natural resources and food supply, which are now new sources of tension." With Japan relying heavily on soybeans as a principal source of protein in the diet of its people, the prime minister termed the U.S. decision to cut back on exports of that product one of the "Nixon shocks." Watergate was another. It was this recent

*erratic U.S. behavior, Tanaka said, that had caused Japan to question
its postwar acceptance of the American word.*

*When formal talks between Nixon and Tanaka were concluded, the
two heads of government jointly issued an 18-point statement. The
communique called for the two countries to consider sharing oil supplies in time of emergency, for the United States to help in securing
Japan a permanent seat on the U.N. Security Council, for an exchange
of visits in the near future between Nixon and Japanese Emperor
Hirohito, for a Japanese donation of $10-million to American univer-
sities to promote Japanese studies, and for mutual efforts to improve
trade between the two nations.*

*The Tanaka visit was hailed as a general success from the American
viewpoint, and some believed it served to further deflect public attention from the omnipresent Watergate scandal. Some opposition to the
upcoming Nixon-Hirohito visits was voiced in Japan where the three
largest opposition parties were quick to voice criticism. No opposition
was apparent in this country.*

*Text of the 18-point joint statement issued Aug. 1, 1973,
by President Nixon and Japanese Prime Minister Kakuei
Tanaka:*

1. Prime Minister Tanaka and President Nixon met in Washington
July 31 and August 1 for comprehensive and fruitful explorations of a
wide variety of subjects of mutual interest.

2. The discussions of the two leaders, held in an atmosphere of
cordiality and trust, reflected in tone and content the breadth and
closeness of relations between Japan and the United States. The primary focus of this meeting was the many common goals which Japan
and the United States share and the common commitment of the
two nations to a new era in this friendly relationship. They emphasized
the high value they place on the important role that each plays in the
cause of world peace and prosperity and the strong desirability of
proceeding together toward that common objective by cooperative
efforts wherever possible around the globe.

3. The Prime Minister and the President confirmed the durable
character of the friendly and cooperative relations between Japan and
the United States, which are based on a common political philosophy
of individual liberties and open societies, and a sense of interdepen-
ence. They noted especially that the relationship between their two
countries has an increasingly important global aspect and makes a
significant contribution to the movement toward peaceful relations
throughout the world.

4. Expressing their satisfaction with the continuous dialogue which
has taken place at various levels on subjects of mutual interest since
their meeting in Hawaii in September 1972, the Prime Minister and

the President reviewed developments in the international situation. They discussed the global trend toward detente, as evidenced by the progress of the dialogue between the United States and the Union of Soviet Socialist Republics, the forthcoming negotiations on the mutual reduction of forces and armaments in Central Europe, the Conference on Security and Cooperation in Europe, the return of the People's Republic of China to the international community, and the signing of the Paris Agreements for a peace settlement in Indochina. They expressed the hope that this trend would lead to the peaceful settlement of disputes throughout the world.

5. The Prime Minister and the President agreed on the need to maintain continuous consultation on questions of mutual concern in the international political field. They expressed their satisfaction with progress made in the area of arms control and the avoidance of conflict, including the SALT agreements and the US-Soviet Agreement on the Prevention of Nuclear War.

6. The Prime Minister and the President noted with satisfaction the normalization of relations between Japan and the People's Republic of China and the movement toward more normal relations between the United States and the People's Republic of China. They expressed their strong hope for a stable and lasting peace in Indochina through scrupulous implementation of the Paris Agreements. They reaffirmed their resolve to assist the rehabilitation of Indochina. They welcomed the new developments in the Korean Peninsula, and expressed the readiness of their Governments to contribute to the furtherance of peace and stability in that area. They pledged to continue to facilitate regional cooperation in Asia as an important contributing factor in securing a lasting peace throughout that part of the world.

7. The President pointed out the desirability of a Declaration of Principles to guide future cooperation among the industrialized democracies. The Prime Minister expressed his positive interest therein. The Prime Minister and the President agreed that Japan and the United States would consult closely on the matter as preparations proceed toward a Declaration acceptable to all the countries concerned.

8. The Prime Minister and the President recognized that the existing framework of international relations had been the basis for the recent trend toward the relaxation of tensions in Asia and reaffirmed that continued close and cooperative relations between the two countries under the Treaty of Mutual Cooperation and Security are an important factor for the maintenance of stability in Asia. The President confirmed the intention of the United States to maintain an adequate level of deterrent forces in the region. The two leaders noted with satisfaction continuing efforts to ensure the smooth and effective implementation of the Treaty and concurred on the desirability of further

steps to realign and consolidate the facilities and areas of the United
States Forces in Japan.

9. Recognizing that the greatest transoceanic commerce between
two nations in the history of mankind greatly enriches the lives of
the peoples of Japan and the United States, the Prime Minister and
the President pledged to ensure that this trade continues to grow and
to contribute to the expansion and prosperity of the world economy as
a whole and to the over-all relationship between the two countries.
They reviewed with satisfaction the discussions at the July meeting in
Tokyo of the Japan-US Joint Committee on Trade and Economic
Affairs on the measures Japan has taken in the fields of trade and investment, for which the President again expressed the appreciation of
the United States; on the marked improvement in the trade imbalance between the two countries, and the intention of both Governments to pursue policies designed to maintain the momentum of
this improvement; on promoting investment between the two countries;
and on the United States intention to exert its best efforts to supply
essential materials including agricultural products to Japan, which
the President reaffirmed. The Prime Minister and the President confirmed the understanding reached in the above meeting that on
the basis of recent economic developments, Japan and the United
States could look forward to new perspectives in the development of
their economic relations.

10. The Prime Minister and the President reaffirmed the importance
which they attach to a successful conclusion of the multilateral negotiations in the trade and monetary fields. They endorsed the
objective of achieving an open and equitable world trade and investment, and a reformed international monetary system, responsive to
the needs of an increasingly interdependent world economy. They
expressed their mutual satisfaction that the Ministerial meeting to
launch the new round of multilateral trade negotiations would be held
in Tokyo in September. They emphasized the firm intention of their
Governments to work for as wide agreement as possible on the principles of monetary reform at the annual meeting of the International
Monetary Fund in Nairobi later in that month. In both of these undertakings, they pledged their cooperative efforts to assure early and constructive results in concert with other countries of the world.

Importance of U.S.-Japan Cooperation

11. The Prime Minister and the President agreed to continue to
coordinate efforts to ensure a stable supply of energy resources to
meet the rapidly growing requirements of their peoples. In this
connection, they expressed their common intention to pursue just and
harmonious relationships with the oil producing states; to examine
the possibility of developing within the framework of the OECD, an

arrangement on sharing oil in times of emergency; and greatly to expand the scope of cooperation for exploring and exploiting energy resources and for research and development of new energy sources.

12. The Prime Minister and the President affirmed the importance of close cooperation between the two Governments in securing a stable supply of enriched uranium, including cooperation in the necessary research and development. They agreed that the two Governments should exert their best efforts for the satisfactory realization of a Japan-US joint venture to that end. In this connection, the President announced that the United States Government had authorized a group of American companies to enter into a contract with a private Japanese party to conduct a joint study of the economic, legal, and technical factors involved in the construction of a uranium enrichment plant in the United States in which Japan might participate.

13. The Prime Minister and the President recognized that expanded programs for improved communication and understanding are vital to strengthening the relationship between the two countries. Noting the warm reception in the Unites States to the activities of the Japan Foundation, the Prime Minister announced that the Government of Japan will grant, through the Foundation, funds in the amount of $10 million to several American universities for institutional support of Japanese studies, including the endowment of chairs for this purpose. The President stated his intention to expand support for those United States cultural and educational projects which had been so productive in the past, and to ask the Congress in the near future to appropriate the funds remaining in the GARIOA account to strengthen Japan-US cultural and educational exchanges.

14. The Prime Minister and the President expressed satisfaction with the growing cooperation between Japan and the United States in the field of environmental protection. They commended the cooperative programs now in progress which would enable the two countries to cope more effectively with air and water pollution and other environmental problems, including those connected with sewage disposal and photochemical air pollution. They confirmed that such cooperative programs would be instrumental in protecting the environment and devising antipollution measures in both countries.

15. The Prime Minister and the President noted with satisfaction the achievements of the medical, scientific and technological cooperative programs developed during the last decade between the two countries. They agreed to make an overall review of cooperative relationships in such fields in light of the broader requirements of the coming decade.

16. The Prime Minister and the President, recognizing that the United Nations is making an important contribution to the furtherance of international cooperation and is an effective forum for collective consultations, agreed that Japan and the United States should co-

operate fully in their efforts to help move the Organization in a constructive direction. The President expressed the belief that for the Security Council to fulfill its primary responsibility under the United Nations Charter for the maintenance of international peace and security, a way should be found to assure permanent representation in that Council for Japan, whose resources and influence are of major importance in world affairs. The Prime Minister expressed his appreciation for this statement.

17. The President reconfirmed the standing invitation to Their Majesties, the Emperor and Empress of Japan, to visit the United States and hoped that the visit would take place in the near future at a mutually convenient time. The Prime Minister expressed his deep appreciation for this invitation, and on his part conveyed an invitation from the Government of Japan to President and Mrs. Nixon to visit Japan. In accepting this invitation, the President voiced his sincere gratitude for the warm sentiments toward the United States symbolized by it. It is hoped that the President's visit to Japan, to be arranged through diplomatic channels, will take place at a mutually convenient time before the end of 1974.

18. The Prime Minister was accompanied by Foreign Minister Masayoshi Ohira, Takeshi Yasukawa, Japanese Ambassador to the United States, and Kiyohiko Tsurumi, Deputy Vice Minister of Foreign Affairs. Also taking part in the conversations on the American side were William P. Rogers, Secretary of State, Dr. Henry A. Kissinger, Assistant to the President for National Security Affairs, and Robert S. Ingersoll, American Ambassador to Japan.

▼▼▼

BLACKMUN ON WATERGATE

August 5, 1973

In a rare indulgence in political debate, Justice Harry A. Blackmun, a 1970 Nixon appointee to the Supreme Court, deplored the ethics of those government officials whose behavior led to the Watergate scandal. Addressing the American Bar Association's prayer breakfast during its convention in Washington early in August, Blackmun said: "The pall of Watergate with all its revelations and with its accusations and insinuations, pro and con, of misplaced loyalties, of strange measures of the ethical, of unusual doings in high places, and with involvement by lawyer after lawyer after lawyer, is upon us." Indeed, he continued, the "very glue of our governmental structure seems about to become unstuck."

The Justice recalled the many instances of "adversity" in the American past that had led to "other scandals, large and small...that have rocked every administration of recent times." Noting that various public officials had recently been implicated in crimes or improprieties, Blackmun observed "a laxness in public life that in earlier years, if indulged in, could not be politically surmounted."

He chose the Old Testament book of Nehemiah as the text for his prayer breakfast speech. From Chapter 12, describing the rebuilding of the walls around Jerusalem in the fifth century B.C., Blackmun quoted a reference to the "Water Gate." Likening the rebuilding of Jerusalem's walls to the reconstruction of American political ethics, the Justice noted that in Jerusalem the people gathered to dedicate the walls which had been rebuilt despite threats by hostile outsiders.

"One may say that our Jerusalem is in ruins," Blackmun commented. But he asked pointedly, "Will it be said that, despite the opposition of announced displeasure, accusation, ridicule, anger, confusion, infiltration, blandishment, threat, temptation, and those repeated invitations to come down to the Plain of Ono and to delay and compromise and rationalize, we held steady and built again?"

When Blackmun finished his speech, the audience gave him a standing ovation. Judges have traditionally avoided discussion of public controversies, preferring to be "above debate" on issues they might have to adjudicate. Blackmun's willingness to speak to the bar on the moral issues of Watergate surprised many members. Some bar leaders had been pressing for ethical reform, while others denied that inadequacies in the profession had led to the Watergate scandal. Blackmun had carefully avoided mentioning in his speech any particular individual involved in the Watergate affair. He appeared to put chief blame for the abuses of Watergate on "an environment of diffuse but broad taint and corruption in our public life."

> *Excerpts from speech by U.S. Supreme Court Justice Harry A. Blackmun at American Bar Association prayer breakfast, Washington, D.C., Aug. 5, 1973:*

...When the wall had been rebuilt and the doors had been set in place, Nehemiah appointed keepers for the gates and gave administration of the city to two men he trusted....

Finally, there came the dedication of the wall—the leaders at the top of the wall—the two great choirs, one making its way to the right as far as the Water Gate, the other to the left as far as the Watch Gate.

"...and the joy of Jerusalem could be heard from far away."

Such is the tale of Nehemiah. It is a simple story of accomplishment and of rebuilding the ruins amid constant and varied opposition....

The reference to the Water Gate, on the east side of Jerusalem's walls is, for our national consciousness today, coincidental. But the significance and the verbal relationship for our profession are inescapable.

A year ago, at last year's ABA Prayer Breakfast in San Francisco, Mr. Justice Powell directed his remarks to his concern about America, and to its seeming withdrawal from, or its abandonment of, its long-accepted basic values. He spoke of the humanizing authority of four factors: the home, the church, the school, the community. He mentioned how a child gains from each of these and acquires an inner strength. He was concerned that all this seems to be fading; that the old and established ethics and values are being threatened and eroded; that self-interest, independent of those four factors, is spreading; that the work ethic is scorned; that there is a suggestion that society is obligated to the individual; that materialism is rampant; that we are awash in unanchored individualism; that even the concept of honor is questioned; and that we are ignoring a proper perspective of history.

The Justice called attention to the fact that America's history is a proud and a decent one, deserving study and respect. We must look back and learn from it. Our history is inseparable from the traditional values of our people. The church, the home, the school, the community, and their respective influences are irreplaceable. There is a worthiness in religion. Honor, duty, loyalty, work, patriotism, are not to be scorned or shunted aside. The Justice then reaffirmed his belief in them and expressed confidence that their intrinsic merit will again be realized.

I once heard a president of a great university describe government in nautical terms. He said that an enlightened autocracy is like a great sailing ship. It is beautiful to observe as it rides before fair winds. Usually it runs its course and reaches the harbor that was its goal. But sometimes it encounters adversity and often, when it does, it sinks. A well-tuned democracy, on the other hand, is like a raft. It may not sink, but one's feet are *always* wet.

So it has been with this Nation in the temptations of the Revolutionary Period; in the manipulation and money-grabbing aspects of Civil War days; in the power hunger episodes of the Nation's westward expansion; in the plundering of our natural resources; in Teapot Dome; in the other scandals, large and small, some investigated, some not investigated, that have rocked every administration of recent times; and, today, in certain aspects of the Watergate.

These *are* perilous and parlous times. Perhaps every age is dangerous.

Yet, if we confine our view just to lawyers and judges and to government, and to the areas and things in which lawyers and judges and politicians are interested, what does one see of late? One sees a high ranking federal judge and former governor of a great State presently standing convicted of serious crime. One sees a former Senator, and a former Congressman, and a then active Congressman disgraced or under a cloud. One sees conceded lawbreaking of various kinds by lawyers. One senses a laxness in public life that in earlier years, if indulged in, could not be politically surmounted.

And the pall of the Watergate, with all its revelations and with its accusations and insinuations, pro and con, of misplaced loyalties, of strange measures of the ethical, of unusual doings in high places, and with involvement by lawyer after lawyer after lawyer, is upon us. It is something that necessarily touches us all, irrespective of political inclination. The very glue of our governmental structure seems about to become unstuck. There is a resultant fear of consequent grave damage to the democratic process of which we have been so proud, and in which we firmly have believed, and which we have proclaimed to the world. Seemingly, there is an environment of diffuse but broad taint and corruption in our public life.

In the midst of our restless energies, we may be seeing the worst in ourselves. The Twentieth Century, for which we had such high hopes, seems indeed a Twentieth Century Limited.

I have chosen the story of Nehemiah today because, in a way, as is so often the case, history seems ready to repeat itself. The times are not dissimilar. One may say that *our* Jerusalem is in ruins. One may question, as did Mr. Justice Powell a year ago, whether its foundations are eroding and whether the walls, after all, are only rubble. There is a sadness all about us. Many appear to accept this as inevitable and to be willing merely to endure, as though this were a necessary consequence of self-government.

Perhaps far off in another Persia, or nearby, within all of us, is, hopefully, a bit of the spirit of Nehemiah.

Will that new Nehemiah, or we, see that this Nation is "in great trouble," to use the phrase in chapter 4? Will we be able to invoke the spirit of his day and of his people when under his leadership they said "let us rebuild" and "let us start"? Will it be said of us that "with willing hands" we "set about the good work"? ...Will it be said of us that we "put [our] hearts into [our] work," and that we proceeded, when necessary, with a weapon in one hand and a builder's tool in the other? Will it be said that, *despite* the opposition of announced displeasure, accusation, ridicule, anger, confusion, infiltration, blandishment, threat, temptation, and those repeated invitations to come down to the Plain of Ono and to delay and compromise and rationalize, we held steady and built again?

Perhaps we need to make our own peace with our Maker, to make our own solitary inspection of the walls; to plan; to cooperate; to resolve that it is worth doing; to provide leadership; to engage, if necessary, in activity that simultaneously is both defensive and constructive; to rededicate—or should I say dedicate—ourselves to what this Bar Association and this Nation stand for.

Would we be able, at the end, to say, as Nehemiah was able to say, that "I am engaged in a great undertaking and I *will not* come down"? If we are able to do this, then and only then can we emulate the situation that existed in Jerusalem 2,400 years ago and gain the satisfaction that "the joy of Jerusalem could be heard from far away." Perhaps if the work is undertaken and is completed, this group will be able to ask, appropriately and not self-centeredly, in the words with which the Book of Nehemiah closes, "Remember me, O my God, for good."

The choice, as it usually is, is ours. Judge Nelson, for his New Testament reading, chose the Twelfth Chapter of Saint Paul's Letter to the Romans. Verse 2 says, "Do not model yourselves on the behavior of the world around you, but let your behavior change, modelled by your *new* mind." (The Jerusalem Bible.) And Mr. Justice Goldberg in his opening reading chose the great 30th chapter of Deuteronomy. Verse

14 states "the work is very nigh unto thee...that thou mayest do it." And verse 19, "I have set before thee life *and* death, the blessing *and* the curse; therefore choose life, that thou mayest live...."

That was Nehemiah's choice. Today's question is, is it our choice? Which will prevail—the "better angels of our nature," to use Mr. Lincoln's words, or something far, far less?

SECRET BOMBING OF CAMBODIA

August 20, 1973

The United States recognized Cambodia as a neutral in the Indo-china conflict prior to May 1970, when American combat troops were dispatched across that country's borders. More than three years later, it became public knowledge that the U.S. Air Force had started secret bombing of Cambodian territory adjacent to South Vietnam in March 1969. The story of that bombing began to unfold on July 16, 1973, when former Air Force Major Hal M. Knight testified before the Senate Armed Services Committee that he had directed such missions. Knight said he had "routinely destroyed" records of the raids to prevent Congress and the public from finding out about them. Instead, he filed reports indicating that the missions were flown over South Vietnam. The areas bombed in Cambodia, described as "sanctuaries" by U.S. military officials, were used by North Vietnamese troops to attack U.S. outposts in South Vietnam.

Disclosure of this hitherto unknown offshoot of American involvement in Vietnam brought an .immediate response from Defense Secretary James R. Schlesinger. In a letter to the committee, Schlesinger said the decision to undertake the bombing, for the purpose of protecting American troops in South Vietnam, was taken "after careful consideration" at the highest "military and civilian levels in Washington." He added that the falsification and destruction of records was the work of the military command in Saigon. However, the Pentagon later admitted that "the special security requirements and special reporting procedures were authorized and directed from Washington."

Gen. Earle G. Wheeler, retired chairman of the Joint Chiefs of Staff, and former Defense Secretary Melvin R. Laird at first disclaimed authorizing false reports of the secret bombing. But Gen. Wheeler told the Senate Armed Services Committee, July 30, that President Nixon had personally ordered that the raids be carried out under "the tightest security." The Joint Chiefs instituted the system of dual reporting, Wheeler said, after receiving the President's order.

Under the dual reporting system, the secret 1969 and early 1970 raids were reported as having taken place over South Vietnam. But Nixon was not responsible for "those particular procedures," Wheeler pointed out. They were "something that just grew up." Wheeler objected to the committee's use of the word "false" to describe the reports sent to Congress. Those who were supposed to receive information on the bombings did receive it, he said. Among present members of Congress, only Sen. John C. Stennis (D Miss.), chairman of the Senate Armed Services Committee, and Rep. Edward F. Hebert (D La.), chairman of the House Armed Services Committee, were said to have been previously informed.

Following the initial disclosures, information about other secret missions came to light. Former Air Force Chief of Staff Gen. John D. Ryan informed the Senate Armed Services Committee that the Air Force had also falsified reports of raids over Laos between February 1970 and April 1972. A former Air Force captain testified to filing false reports of tactical bombing raids deep inside Cambodia after the American invasion in May 1970. At that time, the official statements had said that U.S. bombing was restricted to border areas. Three former Green Berets (Army Special Forces) told of secret ground operations as far as 30 miles inside Cambodia and Laos as early as 1966.

But the question persisted as to who had approved the falsification of records of secret bombing missions. Army Chief of Staff Gen. Creighton W. Abrams, who commanded all military operations in Vietnam from 1968 until 1972, admitted Aug. 8 that the Joint Chiefs had authorized both the secret B-52 bombing of Cambodia in 1969-70 and the strikes on the Cambodian interior after May 1970. He also acknowledged that special reporting procedures had been used in both operations. But he denied authorizing falsification of the reports.

The next day, Aug. 9, a declassified top secret 1969 memorandum from the Pentagon was made public. It showed that the "special reporting system" had been approved by former Defense Secretary Laird, acting on the recommendation of his advisers. The memo approved by Laird was written by Gen. Wheeler and dated Nov. 20, 1969. Wheeler had recommended that the secret air strikes be reported as having been carried out in South Vietnam. Other raids could be made on "cover targets in South Vietnam and other targets in Laos," he had suggested. And "strikes on these latter targets will provide a resem-

blance to normal operations thereby providing a credible story for replies to press inquiries."

Reacting to press headlines that he had approved "falsification" of reports, Laird said at a news conference Aug. 10 that he had authorized a "separate reporting system," but he denied that he had sanctioned "the falsification of any Air Force, Navy or Defense Department records." Laird said the dual reporting system had resulted more from diplomatic than from military necessity. The State Department had requested the special reporting procedures because Prince Norodom Sihanouk, who then headed the Cambodian government, had told the United States that he would have to condemn the strikes if they were made public. The State Department later said it had no record of such a request.

President Nixon chose the 74th national convention of the Veterans of Foreign Wars as an appropriate place to counter the adverse publicity given the secret Cambodian raids. He told several thousand veterans at the convention, Aug. 20, that it was time to answer the critics of "the policies which helped to bring Americans peace with honor in Vietnam." The President said the "truth" of the accusations of a "secret bombing campaign against the defenseless and neutral country of Cambodia in 1969" was that North Vietnamese troops had overrun the Cambodian border along South Vietnam. These troops had driven the population out of the area and had set up supply lines and bases. Nixon said he had ordered bombing strikes "employed directly and continually against the enemy-occupied base areas from which Communist soldiers had been attacking and killing American soldiers." The targets were North Vietnamese soldiers, not Cambodian citizens. The strikes were made known to the appropriate Cambodian government officials and congressional leaders. Nixon added that Prince Sihanouk had not objected to the strikes and had, in fact, invited him to make a state visit to Cambodia.

> Excerpts from President Nixon's speech of Aug. 20 at
> the 74th national convention of the Veterans of Foreign
> Wars in New Orleans, La.:

...I have spoken to the Veterans of Foreign Wars on several occasions since I have been President, and I am proud that this is the first time I have spoken to you when the United States is at peace with every nation in the world. It is a good time—a good time.

It is also rather an ironic time for those who follow the Washington scene, as some of you must. We find that some of the politicians and some of the members of the press who enthusiastically supported the Administration which got us into Vietnam 10 years ago, or were silent when the decisions were made that got us in, now are criticizing what I did to get us out. Well, let me say getting us out of the war took a lot of doing, and I am proud of what we have done. I would like to

talk to you about that today as to how we accomplished that goal. Because you see, my friends, I think the time has come before this organization to answer those who criticize the policies which helped to
bring Americans peace with honor in Vietnam.

Now, specifically, as some of you know, the President of the United
States has been accused of a secret bombing campaign against the defenseless and neutral country of Cambodia in 1969. That was 2 months
after I became President. I want to tell you the facts about that, what
happened, and let you judge for yourself what kind of a decision you
would have made as Commander in Chief of the Armed Forces of the
United States at that time. I remember the meeting in which that decision was made. Mr. Laird, who was then Secretary of Defense,
remembers; he was there. Henry Kissinger, to whom you will give an
award tonight, remembers it; he was there. The chairman of the CIA
was there. The Secretary of State, Secretary Rogers, was there. And
we looked over what was, to us, a totally indefensible position. Here
is what we found when I came into office.

Three hundred Americans were being killed every week in Vietnam;
540,000 Americans were in Vietnam with no plan at all to bring any
of them home. Over 500 were prisoners of war under the most cruel and
barbarous conditions, and no plans and no hope for any of them to be
returned home. That was what we found. So we decided to do something about it.

Incidentally, in pointing out what we found, I am not criticizing
previous Presidents. I am not criticizing the decisions that they felt were
in the national interest that had to be made, they felt, in Vietnam. I
am simply saying this is what we found, and we had to find a way to
bring the war to a conclusion, but to bring it to a conclusion in a way
that the United States would still be respected in the world and that
meant rejecting the views of those who said just bug out. We could
have bugged out of Vetnam. If we bugged out of Vietnam, we would
not be worth talking to any place in the world today. We have got to
maintain the respect of America throughout the world.

North Vietnam's Occupation of Bombed Area

Now, we come to Cambodia. All of you, particularly the young
people here who study the maps of these areas, know this country is
right on the border of Vietnam. When I took office, again in 1969 at
this meeting that took place, we found that there was a strip of
land 10 to 15 miles wide in which there were no Cambodians whatever. It was totally occupied by the enemy, the North Vietnamese.
They had overrun the entire border area.

The native Cambodian population had been evacuated or driven
out and along a 10-mile strip on the Cambodian side of the border,
sometimes 15, a network of supply lines and training bases had been

established, and the bulk of some 40,000 troops were there. That is what the CIA reports show and that is what also the reports of our own military, as they examined the situation there, show.

And so, what we find is the situation that we are referring to back there in 1969, so long ago when this war was at its height, when we were trying to do something to bring it to an honorable end, was that it was not the United States, but the North Vietnamese Communists who violated the neutrality of Cambodia.

The suggestion that these staging areas for enemy troops, supplies, and artillery a few thousand yards from American troops were what we call neutral territory, exempt from counterattack or bombing, is simply ludicrous. The Communists had made a mockery of the neutrality of these border regions. The United States was under no moral obligation to respect the sham.

By January of 1969, these enemy-occupied sanctuaries were no more neutral territory than was northern France or Belgium in the late spring of 1944 when those territories were occupied by the Germans.

And so, it was in February of 1969 when the North Vietnamese responded to President Johnson's 3-month-old bombing halt and peace initiative with a countrywide offensive in the South in which hundreds of Americans were killed every week, and thousands every month.

After this meeting that I have just spoken to, I made the decision. I ordered American airpower employed directly and continually against the enemy-occupied base areas from which Communist soldiers had been attacking and killing American soldiers.

And so today, there is great anguish and loud protest from the usual critics, "Why did the United States make a secret attack on tiny Cambodia?" Of course, this is absurd. These strikes were not directed at the Cambodian army or the Cambodian people; they were directed at the North Vietnamese invaders who, at that time, had occupied this area within Cambodia and were killing Americans from this area.

This is the significant thing: The Cambodian Government did not object to the strikes.

In fact, while they were in progress in the spring of that year, Prince Sihanouk, then the leader of the Cambodian Government, personally invited me very warmly to make a state visit to the Cambodian capital. This is after the strikes had been going on for a long time. That is a pretty good indication of what he thought about what we were doing.

Reasons for Secrecy

Now, as for secrecy, as I have already indicated, the fact that the bombing was disclosed to appropriate Government leaders, the ones I just referred to, and to appropriate Congressional leaders, those in the Military Affairs Committee like Eddie Hebert; what is most important, and here is the bottom line, soon after this bombing started, early in this Administration, there began a steady decline finally in American casualties along the Cambodian border, and the enemy was provided with one more incentive to move to the conference table, which they began to do. The secrecy was necessary to accomplish these goals—secrecy from the standpoint of making a big public announcement about it, although there was no secrecy as far as Government leaders were concerned, who had any right to know or need to know.

Had we announced the air strikes, the Cambodian Government would have been compelled to protest, the bombing would have had to stop, and American soldiers would have paid the price for this disclosure and this announcement with their lives.

My comrades, let me just read you a letter. The President gets a lot of very moving letters during and after any period of war. This is from the father of a soldier who served along the Cambodian-Vietnamese border back in 1969.

He said, "Dear Mr. President: Back in early 1969,"—and I have his letter he wrote then, too—"I wrote you requesting that you allow the bombing of the supply routes in North Vietnam and Cambodia. I wrote to you because my son, Douglas, who was with the 4th Infantry Division near Kontum, complained to us in his letters about all the materials and men the North was shipping in from Cambodia.

"...When my son was killed on March 1, 1969, I felt you let him and the other troops down by not allowing these supply lines to be bombed.

"Today I read where...you did approve the bombing early in 1969... I now believe the Lord led you to make a proper decision in this matter, and I sincerely feel your action saved many lives and shortened that dreadful war."

Just let me add a postscript to that letter. If American soldiers in the field today were similarly threatened by an enemy and if the price of protecting those soldiers was to order air strikes to save American lives, I would make the same decision today that I made in February of 1969.

Of course, we have had other complaints, too, the postmortems on what happened.

You remember the huge outcry when I ordered the mining of Haiphong in May of 1972. It was going to bring on world war III. We did it. What it brought on was the negotiation that helped to finally end the war. And you remember that at Christmas of last year, this was a terribly difficult decision—December 18—when I ordered the use of B-52's against Hanoi, military targets only, those were the targets, and there was a great outcry then that this was a wrong decision on the part of the President, and I don't say that all the decisions are right, but just let me say this, when I wonder about those decisions and I wonder what was wrong and what was right, I recall a very young man—to me he seemed very young—who came through a receiving line in May at a reception we gave for 600 POW's after they had returned. The line moved rather fast and there was not much time to say much to any one of them. This one man said, "I would like to ask you a question, sir," and I said, "Go ahead." He said, "Why did you wait so long to order in the B-52's?"

All I can say is this: Whether it was that decision or any other one, the decisions were made in the interests of bringing this war to an honorable conclusion as quickly as possible using the force that was necessary and no more than was necessary. And I say further that no future American President should ever send Americans into battle with one hand tied behind their backs....

NEWS CONFERENCE ON WATERGATE

August 22, 1973

Following through on a midsummer pledge, President Nixon held a news conference Aug. 22 to answer, in person, questions raised by the Senate Watergate hearings, which had recessed Aug. 7. Held on the lawn of the Western White House at San Clemente, this was the first presidential news conference since March 15, and the first before television cameras in 14 months.

In an opening statement, the President announced that Secretary of State William P. Rogers was resigning, and that National Security Adviser Henry A. Kissinger had been appointed to replace him. Although such a statement would normally have generated numerous questions, reporters quickly zeroed in on the subject of Watergate. Of the 20 questions asked during the 50-minute session, 17 pertained directly or indirectly to Watergate. Two others were about Vice President Agnew (see p. 746 and 750) and one about Cambodia (see p. 751).

Nixon's responses emphasized several points regarding Watergate. He said that while his capacity to govern had been hampered by the scandal, he never had considered resigning and would not consider it. Watergate, he asserted, was "water under the bridge" and it was time to move forward with "the business of the people." He remained adamant in his refusal to hand over tape recordings of crucial White House conversations to the Senate investigating committee, to special prosecutor Archibald Cox, or even to an independent intermediary. He accepted all the blame for the "climate" at the White

House and at the Committee for the Re-election of the President that resulted in the "abuses" of Watergate. H.R. Haldeman and John D. Ehrlichman, his former top aides who were deeply implicated in the scandal, were still, in his opinion, "two of the finest public servants" he had ever known. When questioned about wiretapping and burglary for purposes of national security, he said that both had occurred in previous administrations. He asserted that there had been more wire-tapping when Robert F. Kennedy was Attorney General, from 1961 until 1964, than during his administration.

The President's meeting with reporters followed on the heels of his Aug. 15 television address on Watergate. It thus gave newsmen an opportunity to raise questions previously left unanswered. But in the end, reporters generally felt that few details had been added to earlier statements. Nixon's answers to questions put to him at San Clemente were in line with what Haldeman and Ehrlichman had told the Senate Select Committee on Presidential Campaign Activities. Of particular interest was the President's response to a question concerning former Attorney General John N. Mitchell's testimony before the Senate committee that he had never told Nixon what he knew about Watergate because the President never asked him, and about his own assertion that he "kept pressing" to get the story out. Nixon said only that he "would have expected Mr. Mitchell to tell me in the event that he was involved or that anybody else was," and he regretted that Mitchell had not done so.

Reaction to the long-awaited Nixon press conference was in general a mixture of disappointment and surprise. A New York Times edi-torial commented the following day that "the President conducted him-self with such self-confident and conciliatory good humor that it is hard to understand why he had postponed for more than five months a televised interrogation for which the American people have clearly been waiting." But there was criticism about many of the President's statements. The same editorial found fault that Nixon "once again fell back on the now familiar line of defense that the rubric of 'na-tional security' sanctions virtually limitless use of Presidential powers for purposes of secret surveillance in domestic affairs." It also pointed to "not trivial discrepancies" in Nixon's and Haldeman's recollections of how many tapes had been made available to Haldeman. Even though Haldeman had admitted to listening to two tapes and to having several others at his home, the President said at his news conference that "the only tape that...Mr. Haldeman has listened to, he listened to at my request.... That is all he listened to."

Excerpts from President Nixon's news conference at San Clemente, Calif., Aug. 22, 1973:

THE PRESIDENT. Ladies and gentlemen, I have an announcement before going to your questions.

It is with the deep sense of not only official regret, but personal regret, that I announce the resignation of Secretary of State William Rogers, effective September 3. A letter, which will be released to the press after this conference, will indicate my appraisal of his work as Secretary of State.

I will simply say at this time that he wanted to leave at the conclusion of the first 4 years. He agreed to stay on because we had some enormously important problems coming up, including the negotiations which resulted in the end of the war in Vietnam, the Soviet summit, the European Security Conference, as well as in other areas— Latin America and in Asia—where the Secretary of State, as you know, has been quite busy over the past 8 months....

As his successor, I shall nominate and send to the Senate for confirmation, the name of Dr. Henry Kissinger. Dr. Kissinger will become Secretary of State, assume the duties of the office after he is confirmed by the Senate. I trust the Senate will move expeditiously on the confirmation hearings because there are a number of matters of very great importance that are coming up....

Dr. Kissinger's qualifications for this post, I think, are well known by all of you ladies and gentlemen, as well as those looking to us and listening to us on television and radio.

He will retain the position, after he becomes Secretary of State, of Assistant to the President for National Security Affairs. In other words, he will have somewhat a parallel relationship to the White House which George Shultz has. George Shultz, as you know, is Secretary of the Treasury, but is also an Assistant to the President in the field of economic affairs.

The purpose of this arrangement is to have a closer coordination between the White House and the departments, and in this case, between the White House, the national security affairs, the NSC, and the State Department, which carries a major load in this area....

And now, we will go to the questions. I think AP, Miss Lewine, has the first question.

The Watergate Investigation

Q. Mr. President, on Watergate, you have said that disclosure of the tapes could jeopardize and cripple the functions of the Presidency. Question: If disclosure carries such a risk, why did you make the tapes in the first place, and what is your reaction to surveys that show three out of four Americans believe you were wrong to make the tapes?

THE PRESIDENT. Well, with regard to the questions as to why Americans feel we were wrong to make the tapes, that is not particularly surprising. I think that most Americans do not like the idea of taping of conversations, and frankly, it is not something that particularly appeals to me.

As a matter of fact, that is why, when I arrived in the White House and saw this rather complex situation set up where there was a taping capacity, not only in the President's office, the room outside of his office, but also in the Cabinet Room, and at Camp David, and in other areas that I had the entire system dismantled.

It was put into place again in June of 1970 (1971) because my advisers felt it was important in terms particularly of national security affairs to have a record for future years that would be an accurate one, but a record which would only be disclosed at the discretion of the President, or according to directives that he would set forth.

As you know, of course, this kind of capability not only existed during the Johnson Administration, it also existed in the Kennedy Administration, and I can see why both President Johnson and President Kennedy did have the capability because—not because they wanted to infringe upon the privacy of anybody, but because they felt that they had some obligation, particularly in the field of foreign policy and some domestic areas, to have a record that would be accurate.

As far as I am concerned, we now do not have that capability, and I am just as happy that we don't. As a matter of fact, I have a practice, whenever I am not too tired at night, of dictating my own recollections of the day. I think that perhaps will be the more accurate record of history in the end....

Q. Mr. President, on July 6, 1972, you were warned by Patrick Gray that you were being mortally wounded by some of your top aides. Can you explain why you did not ask who they were, why, what was going on?

THE PRESIDENT. Well, in the telephone conversation that you refer to that has been, of course, quite widely reported in the press, as well as on television, Mr. Gray said that he was concerned that as far as the investigation that he had responsibility for, that some of my top aides were not cooperating.

Whether the term was used as "mortally wounded" or not, I don't know. Some believe that it was, some believe that it was not, that is irrelevant. He could have said that.

The main point was, however, I asked him whether or not he had discussed this matter with General Walters because I knew that there had been meetings between General Walters, representing the CIA, to be sure that the CIA did not become involved in the investigation, and between the Director of the FBI.

He said that he had. He told me that General Walters agreed that the investigation should be pursued, and I told him to go forward with a full press on the investigation to which he has so testified.

It seemed to me that with that kind of a directive to Mr. Gray, that that was adequate for the purpose of carrying out the responsibilities.

As far as the individuals were concerned, I assume that the individuals that he was referring to involved this operation with the CIA. That is why I asked him the Walters question. When he cleared that up, he went forward with the investigation, and he must have thought it was a very good investigation because when I sent his name down to the Senate for confirmation the next year, I asked him about his investigation. He said he was very proud of it. He said it was the most thorough investigation that had ever taken place since the assassination of President Kennedy, that he could defend it with enthusiasm, and that under the circumstances, therefore, he had carried out the directive that I had given him on July 6.

So, there was no question about Mr. Gray having direct orders from the President to carry out an investigation that was thorough.

Mr. Jarriel.

Tapes and Confidentiality

Q. Mr. President, Assistant Attorney General Henry Petersen has testified that on April 15 of this year he met with you and warned you at that time there might be enough evidence to warrant indictments against three of your top aides, Messrs. Ehrlichman, Haldeman, and Dean. You accepted their resignations on April 30, calling Mr. Haldeman and Mr. Ehrlichman two of the finest public servants you had known. After that you permitted Mr. Haldeman, after he had left the White House, to hear confidential tapes of conversations you had had in your office with Mr. Dean. My question is, why did you permit a man who you knew might be indicted to hear those tapes which you now will not permit the American public or the Federal prosecutors handling the case to listen to?

THE PRESIDENT. The only tape that has been referred to, that Mr. Haldeman has listened to, he listened to at my request, and he listened to that tape—that was the one on September 15, Mr. Jarriel— because he had been present and was there. I asked him to listen to it in order to be sure that as far as any allegations that had been made by Mr. Dean with regard to that conversation is concerned, I wanted to be sure that we were absolutely correct in our response. That is all he listened to. He did not listen to any tapes in which only Mr. Dean and I participated. He listened only to the tape on September 15— this is after he left office—in which he had participated in the conversation throughout.

Q. Mr. President, one of the lingering doubts about your denial of any involvement is concerning your failure to make the tapes available either to the Senate committee or the Special Prosecutor. You have made it perfectly clear you don't intend to release those tapes.

THE PRESIDENT. Perfectly clear?

Q. Perfectly clear. But is there any way that you could have some group listen to [the] tapes and give a report so that that might satisfy the public mind?

THE PRESIDENT. I don't believe, first, it would satisfy the public mind, and it should not. The second point is that as Mr. Wright, who argued the case, I understand very well, before Judge Sirica this morning, has indicated, to have the tapes listened to—he indicated this also in his brief—either by a prosecutor or by a judge or *in camera*, or in any way, would violate the principle of confidentiality, and I believe he is correct. That is why we are standing firm on the proposition that we will not agree to the Senate committee's desire to have, for example, its chief investigator listen to the tapes, or the Special Prosecutor's desire to hear the tapes, and also why we will oppose, as Mr. Wright did in his argument this morning, any compromise of the principle of confidentiality.

Let me explain very carefully that the principle of confidentiality either exists or it does not exist. Once it is compromised, once it is known that a conversation that is held with the President can be subject to a subpoena by a Senate committee, by a grand jury, by a prosecutor, and be listened to by anyone, the principle of confidentiality is thereby irreparably damaged. Incidentally, let me say that now that tapes are no longer being made, I suppose it could be argued that, what difference does it make now, now that these tapes are also in the past. What is involved here is not only the tapes; what is involved, as you ladies and gentlemen well know, is the request on the part of the Senate committee and the Special Prosecutor, as well, that we turn over Presidential papers, in other words, the records of conversations with the President made by his associates. Those papers, and the tapes as well, cannot be turned over without breaching the principle of confidentiality. It was President Truman that made that argument very effectively in his letter to a Senate committee, or his response to a Congressional committee, a House committee it was, in 1953, when they asked him to turn over his papers. So whether it is a paper or whether it is a tape, what we have to bear in mind is that for a President to conduct the affairs of this office and conduct them effectively, he must be able to do so with the principle of confidentiality intact, Otherwise, the individuals who come to talk to him, whether it is his advisers, or whether it is a visitor in the domestic field, or whether it is someone in a foreign field, will always be speaking in a eunuch-like way, rather than laying it on the line as it has to be laid on the line if you are going to have the creative kind of discussion that we have often had, and it has been responsible for some of our successes in the foreign policy period, particularly in the past few years.

Q. Mr. President, could you tell us who you personally talked to in directing that investigations be made both in June of '72 shortly after the Watergate incident, and last March 21, when you got new evidence and ordered a more intensive investigation?

THE PRESIDENT. Certainly. In June, I, of course, talked to Mr. MacGregor first of all, who was the new chairman of the committee. He told me that he would conduct a thorough investigation as far as his entire committee staff was concerned. Apparently that investigation was very effective except for Mr. Magruder, who stayed on. But Mr. MacGregor does not have to assume reponsibility for that. I say not responsibility for it because basically what happened there was that he believed Mr. Magruder, and many others have believed him, too. He proved, however, to be wrong.

In the White House, the investigation's responsibility was given to Mr. Ehrlichman at the highest level, and in turn he delegated them to Mr. Dean, the White House Counsel, something of which I was aware, and of which I approved.

Mr. Dean, as White House Counsel, therefore sat in on the FBI interrogations of the members of the White House Staff because what I wanted to know was whether any member of the White House Staff was in any way involved. If he was involved, he would be fired. And when we met on September 15, and again throughout our discussions in the month of March, Mr. Dean insisted that there was not—and I use his words—"a scintilla of evidence" indicating that anyone on the White House Staff was involved in the planning of the Watergate break-in.

Now, in terms of after March 21, Mr. Dean first was given the responsibility to write his own report, but I did not rest it there. I also had a contact made with the Attorney General himself, Attorney General Kleindienst, told him—it was on the 27th of March—to report to me directly anything that he found in this particular area, and I gave the responsibility to Mr. Ehrlichman on the 29th day of March to continue the investigation that Mr. Dean was unable to conclude, having spent a week at Camp David and unable to finish the report.

Mitchell's Silence

Mr. Ehrlichman questioned a number of people in that period at my direction, including Mr. Mitchell, and I should also point out that as far as my own activities were concerned, I was not leaving it just to them. I met at great length with Mr. Ehrlichman, Mr. Haldeman, Mr. Dean and Mr. Mitchell on the 22d. I discussed the whole matter with them. I kept pressing for the view that I had had throughout, that we must get this story out, get the truth out, whatever and whoever it is going to hurt, and it was there that Mr. Mitchell suggested that all the individuals involved in the White House appear in an executive session before the Ervin committee. We never got that far, but at least that is an indication of the extent of my own investigation.

Q. Mr. President, you have said repeatedly that you tried to get all the facts, and just now you mentioned the March 22 meeting. Yet former Attorney General John Mitchell said that if you had ever asked him at any time about the Watergate matter, he would have told you the whole story, chapter and verse. Was Mr. Mitchell not speaking the truth when he said that before the committee?

THE PRESIDENT. Now, Mr. Lisagor, I am not going to question Mr. Mitchell's veracity, and I will only say that throughout I had confidence in Mr. Mitchell. Mr. Mitchell, in a telephone call that I had with him immediately after it occurred, expressed great chagrin that he had not run a tight enough shop, and that some of the boys, as he called them, got involved in this kind of activity, which he knew to be very, very embarrassing, apart from its illegality, to the campaign. Throughout I would have expected Mr. Mitchell to tell me in the event that he was involved or that anybody else was. He did not tell me. I don't blame him for not telling me. He has given his reasons for not telling me. I regret that he did not, because he is exactly right. Had he told me, I would have blown my stack, just as I did at Ziegler the other day. *(Laughter)*

Q. Mr. President, I wonder, sir, how much personal blame, to what degree of personal blame do you accept for the climate in the White House, and at the reelection committee, for the abuses of Watergate?

THE PRESIDENT. I accept it all.

Approach to Judge Byrne

Q. Mr. President, I want to state this question with due respect to your office, but also as directly as possible.

THE PRESIDENT. That would be unusual. *(Laughter)*

Q. I would like to think not. It concerns——

THE PRESIDENT. You are always respectful, Mr. Rather. You know that.

Q. Thank you, Mr. President, It concerns the events surrounding Mr. Ehrlichman's contact, and on one occasion your own contact with the judge in the Pentagon Papers case, Judge Byrne.

THE PRESIDENT. Yes.

Q. As I understand your own explanation of events and putting together your statement with Mr. Ehrlichman's testimony, and what Judge Byrne has said, what happened here is that sometime late in March, March 17, I believe you said, you first found out about the break-in at the psychiatrist's office of Mr. Ellsberg, that you asked to have that looked into, and that you later, I think in late April, instructed Attorney General Kleindienst to inform the judge.

Now, my question is this. If while the Pentagon Papers trial was going on, Mr. Ehrlichman secretly met once with the judge in that case, you secretly met another time with the judge with Mr. Ehrlichman.

Now, you are a lawyer, and given the state of the situation and what you knew, could you give us some reason why the American people should not believe that that was at least a subtle attempt to bribe the judge in that case, and it gave at least the appearance of a lack of moral leadership?

THE PRESIDENT. Well, I would say the only part of your statement that is perhaps accurate is that I am a lawyer. Now, beyond that, Mr. Rather, let me say that with regard to the secret meeting that we had with the judge, as he said, I met with the judge briefly—after all, I had appointed him to the position—I met him for perhaps one minute outside my door here in full view of the whole White House Staff, and everybody else who wanted to see. I asked him how he liked his job, we did not discuss the case, and he went on for his meeting with Mr. Ehrlichman.

Now, why did the meeting with Mr. Ehrlichman take place? Because we had determined that Mr. Gray could not be confirmed, as you will recall. We were on a search for a Director of the FBI. Mr. Kleindienst had been here, and I asked him what he would recommend with regard to a Director, and I laid down certain qualifications.

I said I wanted a man preferably with FBI experience, and preferably with prosecutor's experience, and preferably, if possible, a Democrat so that we would have no problem on confirmation. He said, "The man for the job is Byrne." He said, "He is the best man." I said, "Would you recommend him?" He said, "Yes."

Under those circumstances then, Mr. Ehrlichman called Mr. Byrne. He said: Under no circumstances will we talk to you—he, Ehrlichman, will talk to you—if he felt that it would in any way compromise his handling of the Ellsberg case.

Judge Byrne made the decision that he would talk to Mr. Ehrlichman, and he did talk to him privately, here. And on that occasion, he talked to him privately, the case was not discussed at all—only the question of whether or not, at the conclusion of this case, Mr. Byrne would like to be considered as Director of the FBI.

I understand, incidentally, that he told Mr. Ehrlichman that he would be interested. Of course, the way the things broke eventually, we found another name with somewhat the same qualifications, although, in this case, not a judge. In this case, a chief of police with former FBI experience.

Now, with regard to the Ellsberg break-in, let me explain that in terms of that, I discussed that on the telephone with Mr. Henry Petersen on the 18th of April. It was on the 18th of April that I learned that the grand jury was going away from some of its Watergate investigation and moving into national security areas.

I told Mr. Petersen at that time about my concern about the security areas, and particularly about the break-in as far as the Ellsberg case is concerned.

And then he asked me a very critical question, which you, as a non-lawyer will now understand, and lawyers probably will, too. He said, "Was any evidence developed out of this investigation, out of this break-in?" And I said, "No, it was a dry hole." He said, "Good."

Now, what he meant by that was that in view of the fact that no evidence was developed as a result of the break-in—which is, incidentally, illegal, unauthorized, as far as I was concerned, and completely deplorable—but since no evidence was developed, there was no requirement that it be presented to the jury that was hearing the case. That was why Mr. Petersen, a man of impeccable credentials in the law enforcement field, did not, at that time on the 18th, at a time that I told him what I had known about the Ellsberg break-in, say, "Let's present it then to the grand jury," because nothing had been obtained that would taint the case.

It was approximately 10 days later that Mr. Kleindienst came in and said that, after a review of the situation in the prosecutor's office in Washington, in which Mr. Petersen had also participated, that they believed that it was best that we bend over backwards in this case and send this record of the Ellsberg break-in, even though there was no evidence obtained from it that could have affected the jury one way or another, send it to the judge.

When they made that recommendation to me, I directed that it be done instantly. It was done. Incidentally, the prosecutor argued this case just the way that I have argued it to you, and whether or not it had an effect on the eventual outcome, I do not know.

At least, as far as we know, Mr. Ellsberg went free, this being one of the factors, but that is the explanation of what happened and, obviously, you, in your commentary tonight, can attach anything you want to it.

I hope you will be just as fair and objective as I try to be in giving you the answer.

Vice President Agnew

Q. Mr. President, what is the state of your confidence in your Vice President at this point in time?

THE PRESIDENT. I have noted some press speculation to the effect that I have not expressed confidence in the Vice President, and therefore, I welcome this question because I want to set the record straight. I had confidence in the integrity of the Vice President when I selected him as Vice President when very few knew him, as you may recall back in 1968—knew him nationally. My confidence in his integrity has not been shaken, and, in fact, it has been strengthened by his courageous conduct and his ability even though he is controversial at times, as I am, over the past 4 1/2 years. So I have confidence in the integrity of the

Vice President and particularly in the performance of the duties that he has had as Vice President and as a candidate for Vice President.

Now obviously the question arises as to charges that have been made about activities that occurred before he became Vice President. He would consider it improper—I would consider it improper—for me to comment on these charges, and I shall not do so. But I will make a comment on another subject that I think needs to be commented upon and that is the outrageous leak of information from either the grand jury, or the prosecutors, or the Department of Justice or all three, and, incidentally, I am not going to put the responsibility on all three until I learn from the Attorney General who at my request is making a full investigation of this at the present time—I am not going to put the responsibility, but the leak of information with regard to charges that have been made against the Vice President and leaking them all in the press.

Convicting an individual—not only trying him but convicting him—in the headlines, and on television before he has had a chance to present his case in court is completely contrary to the American tradition. Even a Vice President has a right to some, shall I say, consideration in this respect let alone the ordinary individual. And I will say this, and the Attorney General I know has taken note of this fact, any individual in the Justice Department or in the prosecutor's office who is in the employ of the United States who has leaked information in this case to the press or to anybody else will be summarily dismissed from government service. That is how strongly I feel about it, and I feel that way because I would make this ruling whether it was the Vice President or any individual.

We have to remember that a hearing before a grand jury and that determination in the American process is one that is supposed to be in confidence, is supposed to be in secret, because all kinds of charges are made which will not stand up in open court and it is only when the case gets to open court that the press and the TV have a right to cover it—well, they have a right to cover it, but I mean have a right it seems to me to give such broad coverage to the charges.

Further Watergate Questions

Q. Mr. President, at any time during the Watergate crisis did you ever consider resigning and would you consider resigning if you felt that your capacity to govern had been seriously weakened, and in that connection how much do you think your capacity to govern has been weakened?

THE PRESIDENT. The answer to the first two questions is no, the answer to the third question is that it is true that as far as the capacity to govern is concerned that to be under a constant barrage—12 to 15 minutes a night on each of the three major networks for 4 months—

tends to raise some questions in the people's minds with regard to the President, and it may raise some questions with regard to the capacity to govern. But I also know this. I was elected to do a job. Watergate is an episode that I deeply deplore, and had I been running the campaign rather than trying to run the country and particularly the foreign policy of this country at this time it would never have happened, but that is water under the bridge, it is gone now.

The point that I make now is that we are proceeding as best we know how to get all those guilty brought to justice in Watergate. But now we must move on from Watergate to the business of the people, and the business of the people is continuing with initiatives we began in the first Administration....

Q. As long as we are on the subject of the American tradition and following up Mr. Rather's question, what was authorized, even if the burglary of Dr. Fielding's office was not, what was authorized was the 1970 plan which by your own description permitted illegal acts, illegal breaking and entering, mail surveillance and the like.

Now under the Constitution you swore an oath to execute the laws of the United States faithfully. If you were serving in Congress, would you not be considering impeachment proceedings and discussing impeachment possibility against an elected public official who had violated his oath of office?

THE PRESIDENT. I would if I had violated the oath of office. I would also, however, refer you to the recent decision of the Supreme Court or at least an opinion that even last year which indicates inherent power in the Presidency to protect the national security in cases like this. I should also point out to you that in the 3 Kennedy years and the 3 Johnson years through 1966, when burglarizing of this type did take place, when it was authorized on a very large scale, there was no talk of impeachment and it was quite well known.

I shall also point out that when you ladies and gentlemen indicate your great interest in wiretaps, and I understand that, that the height of the wiretaps was when Robert Kennedy was Attorney General in 1963. I don't criticize it, however. He had over 250 in 1963, and of course the average in the Eisenhower Administration and the Nixon Administration is about 110. But if he had had ten more and as a result of wiretaps had been able to discover the Oswald plan, it would have been worth it.

So I will go to another question.

Q. Mr. President, do you still consider Haldeman and Ehrlichman two of the finest public servants you have ever known?

THE PRESIDENT. I certainly do. I look upon public servants as men who have got to be judged by their entire record, not by simply parts of it. Mr. Ehrlichman and Mr. Haldeman, for 4 1/2 years, have served with great distinction, with great dedication, and like everybody in this deplorable Watergate business, at great personal sacrifice and with no personal gain.

We admit the scandalous conduct. Thank God there has been no personal gain involved. That would be going much too far, I suppose.

But the point that I make with regard to Mr. Haldeman and Mr. Ehrlichman is that I think, too, that as all the facts come out, that—and when they have an opportunity to have their case heard in court and not simply to be tried before a committee, and tried in the press, and tried in television—they will be exonerated.

Mr. Horner.

Q. Mr. President, could you tell us your recollection of what you told John Dean on March 21 on the subject of raising funds for the Watergate defendants?

THE PRESIDENT. Certainly. Mr. Haldeman has testified to that, and his statement is accurate. Basically, what Mr. Dean was concerned about on March 21 was not so much the raising of money for the defendants, but the raising of money for the defendants for the purpose of keeping them still—in other words, so-called hush money. The one would be legal—in other words, raising a defense fund for any group, any individual, as you know, is perfectly legal and it is done all the time. But if you raise funds for the purpose of keeping an individual from talking, that is obstruction of justice.

Mr. Dean said also on March 21 that there was an attempt, as he put it, to blackmail the White House, to blackmail the White House by one of the defendants. Incidentally, that defendant has denied it, but at least this was what Mr. Dean had claimed, and that unless certain amounts of money were paid, I think it was $120,000 for attorneys' fees and other support, that this particular defendant would make a statement, not with regard to Watergate, but with regard to some national security matters in which Mr. Ehrlichman had particular responsibility.

My reaction, very briefly, was this: I said, as you look at this, I said, "Isn't it quite obvious, first, that if it is going to have any chance to succeed, that these individuals aren't going to sit there in jail for 4 years? They are going to have clemency; isn't that correct?"

He said, "Yes." I said, "We can't give clemency." He agreed. Then, I went to another point. I said, "The second point is that isn't it also quite obvious, as far as this is concerned, that while we could raise the money"—and he indicated in answer to my question, it would probably take a million dollars over 4 years to take care of this defendant, and others, on this kind of basis—the problem was, how do you get the money to them, and also, how do you get around the problem of clemency, because they are not going to stay in jail simply because their families are being taken care of. And, so, that was why I concluded, as Mr. Haldeman recalls perhaps, and did testify very effectively, one, when I said, "John, it is wrong, it won't work. We can't give clemency and we have got to get this story out. And therefore, I direct you, and I direct Haldeman, and I direct Ehrlichman, and I direct Mitchell to get together tomorrow and then meet with me as to how we get this story out."

The Vice President

Q. Mr. President, a follow-up question on the Agnew situation, you have said in the past that any White House official who was indicted would be suspended and that anyone convicted would be dismissed. Should Vice President Agnew be indicted, would you expect him to resign or somehow otherwise stand down temporarily until cleared?

THE PRESIDENT. Now, Mr. Theis, that is a perfectly natural question and one that any good newsman, as you are, would ask. But, as you know, it is one that it would be most inappropriate for me to comment upon. The Vice President has not been indicted, charges have been thrown out by innunendo and otherwise, which he has denied to me personally and which he has denied publicly. And to talk about indictment and to talk about resignation, even now—I am not questioning your right to ask the question, understand—but for me to talk about it would be totally inappropriate and I make no comment in answer to that question....

Wiretaps and Secret Service

Q. Mr. President, you recently suggested today that if the late Robert Kennedy had initiated ten more wiretaps he would have been able to discover the Oswald plan, as you described it, and thereby presumably prevent the assassination of President Kennedy.

THE PRESIDENT. Let me correct you, sir. I want to be sure that the assumption is correct. I said if ten more wiretaps could have found the conspiracy, if it was a conspiracy, or the individual, then it would have been worth it. As far as I am concerned, I am no more of an expert on that assassination than anybody else, but my point is that wiretaps in the national security area were very high in the Kennedy Administration for a very good reason; because there were many threats on the President's life, because there were national security problems, and that is why that in that period of 1961 to '63, there were wiretaps on news organizations, on news people, on civil rights leaders, and on other people. And I think they were perfectly justified, and I am sure that President Kennedy and his brother, Robert Kennedy, would never have authorized them, as I would never have authorized them, unless he thought they were in the national interest.

Q. Do you think then that threats to assassinate the President merit more national security wiretaps particulary?

THE PRESIDENT. No, No, as far as I am concerned, I was only suggesting that in terms of those times—of those times—to have the Oswald thing happen just seemed so unbelievable. With his record—with his record—that with everything that everybody had on him, that that fellow could have been where he was in a position to shoot the President of the United States, seems to me to have been a terrible breakdown in our protective security areas.

I would like to say, however, that as far as protection generally is concerned, I don't like it, and my family does not like it. Both of my daughters would prefer to have no Secret Service. I discussed it with the Secret Service. They say they have too many threats, and so they have to have it. My wife does not want to have Secret Service, and I would prefer, and I recommended this just 3 days ago, to cut my detail by one third, because I noticed there were criticisms of how much the Secret Service is spending.

Let me say that we always are going to have threats against the President, but I frankly think that one man probably is as good against a threat as a hundred. That is my view, but my view does not happen to be in a majority there, and it does not happen to agree with the Congress—so I will still have a great number of Secret Service around me, more than I want, more than my family wants....

U.S. Bombing of Cambodia

Q. Mr. President, in your Cambodian invasion speech of April 1970, you reported to the American people that the United States had been strictly observing the neutrality of Cambodia. I am wondering if you in light of what we now know, that there were 15 months of bombing of Cambodia previous to your statement, whether you owe an apology to the American people?

THE PRESIDENT. Certainly not, and certainly not to the Cambodian people, because as far as this area is concerned, the area of approximately 10 miles, which was bombed during this period, no Cambodians had been in it for years. It was totally occupied by the North Vietnamese Communists. They were using this area for the purpose of attacking and killing American Marines and soldiers by the thousands. The bombing took place against those North Vietnamese forces in enemy-occupied territory, and as far as the American people are concerned, I think the American people are very thankful that the President ordered what was necessary to save the lives of their men and shorten this war which he found when he got here, and which he ended.

HELEN THOMAS (UPI). Thank you, Mr. President.

WALDHEIM'S WORLD MESSAGE

August 23, 1973

United Nations Secretary General Kurt Waldheim called on U.N. member nations in late August to "take a hard look" at the organization and to reassess their attitudes toward it. In the introduction to his annual report to the members of the world organization, Waldheim conceded there was public disenchantment with the United Nations. He attributed the public disappointment in part to the fact that some member nations apparently wanted the organization to be little more than "a forum for the pursuit of national policies." Whether the member preferred "an organization which can play a useful and active role," was "the basic question facing the member states," he asserted. The Secretary General thus struck a note some observers considered unusually realistic, or even unusually pessimistic coming from the top U.N. official.

"There seems...to be no clear understanding among the member states as to which road the organization should take," Waldheim stated, "and it is sometimes hard to avoid the feeling that not all governments are fully prepared to accept the consequences of their membership in the United Nations or the need to orient their national policies in the ways required to make such an organization work." He expressed hope that the United Nations would play a more effective role in the future toward easing world tensions and settling international disputes. While conceding that the organization hardly could find solutions for all international difficulties, Waldheim maintained that it had kept and could continue to keep numerous problems from getting worse.

The Secretary General observed that the United Nations "would be a more effective organization if the majority of governments of member states were more interested in pursuing long-term international aims, and in providing leadership in the pursuit of those aims, than in using the United Nations to achieve narrow goals and to protect short-term national interests." Another means of increasing the effectiveness of the world organization, he said, would be to work toward strengthening the protection of human rights, "an area where the credibility of the United Nations is especially at stake." Major targets of criticism in this respect had been the Soviet Union, which had restricted the emigration of Jews; South Africa, which maintained a system of apartheid; Portugal, which had a record of violence in its African territories; and the Arab states and Israel, which accused one another of violating human rights.

Waldheim counseled "the use of multilateral preventive diplomacy" to help resolve international conflicts. As for world trade and international monetary policy, he urged "a comprehensive new look at the world [rich and poor nations] live in, at the resources they depend upon, and at the organization and machinery of international co-operation."

> *Excerpts from the "Introduction to the Report of the Secretary-General on the Work of the Organization":*

I

In recent years the United Nations has taken important steps toward universality of membership, and for the first time in history an organization representing the whole of humanity is within our reach. It will be very different from the organization which the founders had in mind at San Francisco, but, if its Members so desire, it could have a vitality, a variety and a potential unmatched by any human institution which has existed before.

The necessity for international—even global—co-operation on a wide range of human activities has never been so great or so urgent. Quite apart from the political and security-related challenges of our time, there is now a whole range of global problems which can probably only be dealt with effectively through institutionalized multilateral channels. This fact also fundamentally affects the future of international organization.

The growing involvement of the United Nations in the fields of environment, natural resources, population, outer space and the sea-bed is a testimony to the awareness of States of this necessity. But while this development is to be welcomed, we must not lose sight of the fact than an important aspect of public disillusionment and disenchantment with the United Nations lies in the fact that a world in need as never before of peaceful and legitimate order to ensure its survival appears to be still institutionally incapable of assuring it.

Inevitably it will require time for us to learn how best to use wisely such a unique instrument as a universal organization, for it will present great problems as well as great possibilities. Nor will it always be easy to adjust international instruments created more than a quarter of a century ago to the global challenges which we now face. But time is not on our side, and we need action as well as thought, innovation as well as criticism, determination as well as idealism, if mankind is not to be overtaken once again by the destructive side of human nature.

The main purpose of this introduction is to provide a basis for constructive debate on the present state of our Organization and on some of the problems of its future development as a universal instrument in a world of interdependent sovereign States.

II

The United Nations and its family of organizations were set up to deal with the problems of a world very different from the one we live in today. The past quarter of a century has seen an unprecedented degree of change in the political, military, economic, social and technological circumstances of our planet.

The fact that, after 28 years, the United Nations is very different from the organization envisaged at San Francisco has given rise in many countries—and especially among some of the founding Members of the Organization—to considerable disappointment with its performance and effectiveness. This disappointment sometimes has tended to overshadow the promise of the new directions and forms of United Nations activities which have been developing. Indeed, the flexibility of the United Nations and its adaptability to new problems and possibilities has been one of its major strengths. This promise, however, can only properly be fulfilled if there is a widespread willingness to make a realistic assessment of the Organization's capacity and potential, and to decide on constructive, contemporary and imaginative ways in which it can be used to meet the present and future problems which we face. In this process, many fundamental adjustments will inevitably be necessary.

...The cold war, the revolutionary development in weapons-systems of mass destruction, the change in the relative status of various major Powers, the rapid process of decolonization, and the increasing imbalance in economic resources between nations are only a few of the major post-war developments which have to some extent affected the machinery for maintaining international peace and security which was created at San Francisco. As a result the United Nations—and especially the Security Council—has often been frustrated and has developed various procedures and techniques in order to meet the challenges of the contemporary world. Such developments, though often less precise and decisive than the full range of activities provided for in the Charter, nevertheless demonstrate the vitality and resourcefulness of the world Organization.

On the economic and social side, many of our present world-wide problems were scarcely foreseen at all when the United Nations system of organizations was created. The pressing and global nature of such interrelated problems as development, trade, population, natural resources and environment requires an integrated response which is often hard to achieve through the international machinery set up for far more limited purposes over a quarter of a century ago. In fact in the economic and social fields the United Nations, far from being sidestepped, has become increasingly involved at so rapid a pace that institutions created in 1945 often no longer correspond to current needs.

It is in no spirit of defeatism that I have referred to some of the shortcomings of our international institutions in relation to the world of today. On the contrary, I believe that these institutions provide the indispensable and solid foundation for future activity. But I am convinced that, if the United Nations is to live up to the resounding aims of the Charter and is to engage the confidence and support of the peoples of the world, the Member States, the Secretary-General, the secretariats and all the organizations and individuals—including the mass media—that play an important part in international co-operation, must consider the realities of the situation frankly and with a full measure of critical appraisal. The United Nations will not develop through ritual public statements of approval and support which are not backed by inner conviction, realism and whole-hearted participation. If the United Nations is to become the organization which the Governments and peoples of the world require and which their problems demand, we have to make a continuous effort to assess the challenge of the radical changes in the world, to make the necessary adjustments and, where needed, to develop new machinery and methods.

Let there be no doubt about the importance and difficulty of this task. It does not require only that States should examine the United Nations with care and imagination; they must also ask themselves whether their own attitudes, their assumptions, their goals and their machinery are adequate or appropriate for our times. We need to take a hard look at matters as they are, and to compare our high ambitions with our actual performance, our bold claims with our actual achievements.

III

The original concept of the United Nations as an organization of which the primary function was to maintain, and if necessary impose, international peace and security has long been replaced by a more pragmatic approach. At the risk of oversimplification, the present efforts of Governments within the United Nations framework may be summarized under three forms of activity which proceed simultaneously.

There is the day-to-day effort to maintain peace and security, to deal with, and if possible prevent, conflict and to face immediate international problems in the political or other fields, as for example in emergency relief operations. There is the middle-term activity, which represents the vast proportion of the Organization's effort in terms of manpower and money. This deals with urgent problems requiring sustained efforts over a longer period, such as disarmament, development, trade, population, environment and natural resources, as well as preparing for the future in such questions as the sea-bed and outer space. Finally, there is the long-term goal for which these activities are the workshop, preparation and experimental ground. This is the process through which the present association of States in the United Nations may develop by practical experience into a more reliable instrument of world order and co-operation, accepted and respected by all Governments and capable of safeguarding the common interests of mankind in a crowded world of increasingly interdependent but sovereign States.

IV

It is the first of these categories of activity which attracts most public attention and gives rise to much of the doubt concerning the Organization's effectiveness. Here especially the actual development has been very far from what was foreseen at San Francisco, and this has given rise in some countries to a disillusionment which has tended to obscure what the United Nations has actually done or can do in matters affecting peace and security. One difficulty here is the widespread idea that international problems invariably can and should be solved by logical and reasonable means and through established institutional procedures. This popular illusion accounts for much of the criticism of the political organs of the United Nations, especially the Security Council. The reality of the kind of hard-core political problems which come to the United Nations is of course very different. The proceedings of the Security Council, the work of Governments of Member States on these problems within the framework of the United Nations, and the efforts of successive Secretaries-General and the Secretariat have, it seems to me, been far more useful than is widely supposed.

Past experience has shown that the United Nations cannot either successfully deal with disputes if the Governments concerned do not wish it to do so, or, against their opposition, impose the settlement of a dispute. But throughout its history the Security Council has played a vital role on many occasions in defusing and de-escalating the problems brought before it by great and small Powers alike.

A large part of the agenda of the United Nations is a list of the chronic ailments of the international community. The United Nations may not often be able to cure these ailments, but it can, and does, do a great deal to prevent them from getting worse and from spreading and infecting new areas. In fact the conflict situations, or potential conflict situtations, where the United Nations has been involved have tended to be far less violent and destructive than those where it has not been involved, even when the Organization has been unable to effect a settlement of the basic problems concerned.

The use of multilateral preventive diplomacy and good offices by one or other organ of the United Nations are activities which can certainly be further developed. Such efforts are not in competition with the normal bilateral dealings of Governments but are complementary to them. They reflect the fact that there are some problems which are not soluble either by bilateral negotiations or through the general improvement in the international climate or *detente* among the great Powers. Examples of such problems are the Middle East conflict, the burning problems of southern Africa, and the situation in Cyprus. In such situations—and one could give other examples—the multilateral approach of the United Nations is complementary to normal bilateral diplomacy. It is necessary to emphasize that there is no inevitable clash between bilateral and multilateral diplomacy. They are, or should be, mutually supporting, each having particular advantages in particular situations. There is no single road to peace—we have to try all roads.

The fact that the international climate has greatly improved—especially as regards the relations among the great Powers—is an encouraging development. Great-Power confrontation, with all its potentially disastrous consequences, has begun to give way to constructive negotiations which have already produced results in some important and particularly difficult problems. Recent personal meetings between leading statesmen are encouraging cases in point.

Obviously the relaxation of international tensions by any means contributes to the general search for peace in the world. Thus, for example, the opening session of the European Conference on Security and Co-operation at Helsinki in July of this year, whatever difficulties may lie ahead, is an important and promising event. A Europe living harmoniously within itself, responsive to the needs of others and aware of its great international responsibilities and potential, would be a positive element in the establishment of a durable peace in the world.

Another example of an important initiative by a group of States in the general search for peace is the annual meetings of non-aligned Governments, the latest of which is taking place in September of this year in Algiers. The non-aligned countries have constantly expressed their full support for the United Nations and play a vital role in the work of the General Assembly and other United Nations organs.

It is to be hoped that the effects of great-Power *detente* will have an important influence in areas of special United Nations concern, such as disarmament, although the achievement of political *detente* is no automatic guarantee of progress in this field. Quite apart from the peril which the continuing world-wide escalation of armaments presents to world peace, mankind will continue to be deprived of vast human and material resources urgently required for more constructive purposes unless real progress can be made in disarmament. It is self-evident that a major relaxation of international tensions is an essential prerequisite for any significant advance. Bilateral and regional negotiations are an important part of the effort to achieve the larger objective of a more general process of disarmament.

The Convention concerning bacteriological (biological) weapons is one example of real progress, and it is to be hoped that the international community will soon move towards an effective prohibition of chemical warfare. Over almost two decades the issue of nuclear testing has been under active negotiation. The conclusion of the partial nuclear test ban treaty 10 years ago was a significant first step in this process. The time has now surely come for a general agreement to stop all nuclear weapons testing...

V

The activities of our Organization on specific problems are reported on in full in other documents. In this introduction, therefore, I shall touch only briefly on some which have particular significance in the context of the effectiveness and future direction of the United Nations.

This year has seen a new effort by the Security Council—the first since 1967—to tackle the problem of the Middle East as a whole. In the past six years many efforts have been made, both within and outside the United Nations, to assist the parties to finding a just and lasting settlement to this infinitely complex problem. My predecessor and I have both worked with the Special Representative to this end, and we have been constantly on the alert for new possibilities and approaches which might offer some promise of success. But despite all of these efforts and the recent deliberations of the Security Council, a peace settlement in the Middle East remains elusive.

The intractable nature of this extremely complex problem lies not only in the deep emotions which it arouses in all the protagonists concerned, but also in the fundamental principles involved—the sanctity of the territorial integrity of States, the right of every State to be secure within its territorial boundaries, and the inalienable right of self-determination of peoples. These principles are of crucial importance in the formulation of any peace agreement.

Time is not on our side in this highly explosive situation. While much can be, and is, done through the United Nations to reduce tension and prevent escalation, the search for a settlement is crucial and must continue. In this search, the co-operation of the parties concerned is of decisive importance....[*Section VI, dealing with relief problems, not included here.*]

VII

Of course there is infinite room for improvement in the way the United Nations is used on immediate issues. It would be a far more effective Organization, for example, if Member States developed the habit of consistently responding to and respecting the decisions and findings of the main organs. It would be a more effective Organization if Member States were always prepared to put their influence behind the implementation of the decisions of its organs. It would be a more effective Organization if the majority of Governments of Member States were more interested in pursuing long-term national aims, and in providing leadership in the pursuit of those aims, than in using the United Nations to achieve narrow goals and to protect short-term national interests. It would be a more effective Organization if there was a general recognition, in deeds as well as in words, that the present conditions of life on our planet demand much more of international co-operation than only the protection of national interests, and that the ability to co-operate in the pursuit of common interests and common goals may well in the end be a matter of human survival....

The protection of human rights is an area where the credibility of the United Nations is especially at stake. Over the past years the international community has been faced with a number of matters affecting human rights, which have posed—sometimes in a very acute form—the difficulty of reconciling the sovereign jurisdiction of Member States with the principles laid down in the Universal Declaration of Human Rights. The United Nations has been active in attempting to improve fundamental human rights and freedoms in some areas but has proved unable to act in other cases. This has provoked considerable criticism. It has been possible for the Secretary-General to exercise his good offices in certain humanitarian situations, but it is clearly necessary that Member States continue to address themselves to the problem of developing more effective action by the Organization on problems of human rights wherever they occur. The twenty-fifth anniversary of the proclamation of the Universal Declaration of Human Rights, which will occur on 10 December this year, might be the occasion for renewed efforts in this field. Further steps to ratify the International Covenants on Human Rights would be one significant advance.

VIII

The second category of activities, which I called the middle-term activities, absorb by far the largest proportion of the United Nations effort in terms of money and manpower. Although the bulk of the work in this category is more or less within the economic and social field, much of it has political overtones and implications as well. The value of the Organization's effort in these fields is that it constitutes a continuous endeavour to formulate approaches to global problems from the point of view not of a few great Powers but of the international community as a whole. It is essential that United Nations activities be undertaken in this spirit. Such enterprises as the United Nations Conference on the Human Environment and the forthcoming World Population Conference, for example, are not undertakings imposed on Member States. They are approaches to global problems undertaken essentially in the interest of all mankind.

In the economic and social field it seems to me that the time has come for a concerted effort to use the international system to re-establish confidence. The prevailing mood of uncertainty is not confined to the developing world, but now besets even the basic system of commercial and monetary interchanges between great trading nations. It is becoming increasingly clear that rich countries as well as poor ones are in need of a comprehensive new look at the world they live in, at the resources they depend upon, and at the organization and machinery of international co-operation.

The review and appraisal undertaken this year of the International Development Strategy for the Second United Nations Development Decade makes it plain that we face a major task in breathing new life into the global development effort. The fact that the growth rates of many countries are below the average, that debt burdens are threatening to get out of hand, and that aid levels are gravely short of target expectations requires our immediate and critical attention. Obviously negotiations now under way on the future shape of the international monetary system and on the world-wide trading arrangement under the General Agreement on Tariffs and Trade will have a very important bearing upon the future of development and of the poorer countries.

The concept of collective economic security has recently been brought forward for renewed attention in the sessions of the Economic and Social Council....

Certainly the attempt to assure the economic security of all Member States through collective action is a highly ambitious undertaking, but it should not be beyond the capacity of the United Nations system to make substantial progress towards this goal if the Members really desire it....

The sustained efforts now under way to translate much of the consensus of the United Nations Conference on the Human Environment into programme terms demonstrate the international community's ability to act when the will to act exists. In another field of vital international concern, the oceans and the sea-bed, a large-scale effort is under way to combine such action with the safeguarding of a considerable diversity of national interests, an undertaking which involves adaptation of the law of the sea to meet new realities. The United Nations, as the centre for harmonizing the actions of States, has an essential interest in this process and will no doubt continue to play a major part in bringing this undertaking to a successful conclusion. Our new knowledge of the seas and oceans shows clearly the immense possible benefits and resources that should be used and husbanded for the good of all mankind....

The demographic evolution of the world also underlies the urgency of assuring the future of marine resources, for they will be needed desperately and needed soon. The outlook is still for the doubling of the world's population in 30 years. The World Population Conference, to be held at Bucharest in August 1974, should help us to see the demographic situation more clearly in all its many dimensions....

IX

The problems I have just mentioned call urgently for effective international action, but such action can only result from a general political will to solve them. Obviously legitimate national interests can never be ignored, but it is essential to increase our capacity for striking a balance between national interests and the international goal of the welfare of all mankind.

Another obstacle to be surmounted is the temptation to take on problems piecemeal and out of context and to look for swift and easy solutions to issues which are inherently complex and which together form a pattern of interrelationships where each part affects all the others. The increasing interdependence of nation States has been matched by the growing complexity of the network of economic, social, technological and political interrelationships in which these States must live. The United Nations system is poised at the apex of this pyramid of relationships which are in constant and precarious motion. The task of the United Nations system, and especially of the Economic and Social Council, is, or should be, to assist Member States to move toward agreed goals at a steady pace and rhythm under conditions of equilibrium. This immensely complex task requires continuous and patient negotiation and a clear vision both of the different parts of the puzzle and of the over-all conception of the world which the international community wishes to make a reality....

...The natural desire of different groups of Governments to give effect to their particular conception of the nature and goals of international co-operation has had an important impact on the way the system as a whole has developed. It is, I believe, vitally important that this natural tendency should be matched by a parallel effort to achieve the maximum degree of co-operation and thus to bridge the divergence of interests between major groups of countries.

X

The United Nations system is confronted with the problem of striking an effective balance between the decentralization of functional responsibility and the necessity for maintaining a co-ordinated and coherent approach to complex problems. I fully recognize the value of diversity, decentralization and freedom of initiative in the different parts of the United Nations system. Certainly nothing could be less useful than to try to impose the control of an all-embracing central bureaucracy on all of the parts of the system. On the other hand, many of the problems we face require an integrated, disciplined and highly co-ordinated approach if the United Nations system is to operate with maximum effectiveness and if it is to be capable of clearly identifying degrees of urgency and of setting priorities in full knowledge of what is involved—in fact, of formulating a general policy.... I feel very strongly that a determined effort must be made on all sides to exploit the advantages of interdependence rather than to succumb to the temptation to fragment and proliferate the system. This applies equally at the planning and operational end and at the administrative, financial and managerial level, where some degree of uniformity and common practice is essential if the United Nations system is to avoid becoming an increasingly disunited and undirected enterprise....

A most important development in the administrative field holding great promise for the achievement of higher levels of effectiveness in management has been the inauguration of programme budgeting and of a biennial budget cycle, replacing the annual budget presentations of past years. The adoption of programme budgeting is designed to give to Member States, when they consider the budgetary requirements of the United Nations at the General Assembly, a clearer insight into the actual programmes being planned or undertaken, the objectives towards which each programme or project is directed, what it is hoped or expected to achieve within the budget period as well as over the longer term, and what the programme or project is expected to cost....

XI

The Organization has continued to make every effort to solve its financial problems. As a result of a policy of austerity, accompanied by a temporary freeze on recruitment, adopted early in 1972, a further deterioration of the Organization's debt position was held in check for that year. In addition, a number of Member States have made their payments at earlier dates than in previous years, which has helped further in covering the financial requirements of the earlier months. Despite these actions, however, a further special effort will be required of Member States in order to meet our obligations during the latter part of 1973....

XII

In the preceding pages I have touched upon a number of trends and developments which I believe to be significant for the life and future of our Organization. As always, an institution works and develops only if there exists among its members the political will to make it work and develop. I hope that some of my comments may point to ways in which this political will might be usefully applied.

There can be little doubt that a world organization such as the United Nations is necessary and even essential. At present there seems, however, to be no clear understanding among the Member States as to which road the Organization should take, and it is sometimes hard to avoid the feeling that not all Governments are fully prepared to accept the consequences of their membership in the United Nations or the need to orient their national policies in the ways required to make such an organization work.

Two questions inevitably arise. What kind of world organization do we need? And what kind of world organization are Governments prepared in reality to accept? An analysis of the problems which we undoubtedly face should provide a logical response to the first question, but the second is more difficult to answer. Do the majority of Member States really want an organization which is more than a conference machinery and a forum for the pursuit of national policies? Do they really want an organization which can play a useful and active role in focusing international efforts on the solution of the most difficult and controversial problems and which in doing so will in certain situations develop an impetus of its own? This is the basic question facing Member States in formulating their policies in the United Nations and other international organizations.

As in most political institutions we see in the United Nations the clash between idealism and realism, between the code of international behaviour of the Charter and the interests and pressures which confront Governments. Earlier in this introduction I mentioned the very long-term goal, for which all our efforts are in a sense the preparation—the goal of a reliable instrument of world order and cooperation, accepted and respected by all Governments and capable of safeguarding the common interests of mankind. In spite of present shortcomings and disappointments, it is essential to keep that goal in mind and develop our capacity to co-operate in reaching it. Only by doing so can we hope to shape a universal Organization which will really serve the needs of future generations.

KURT WALDHEIM
Secretary-General

CHINA'S PARTY CONGRESS

August 24-28, 1973

The People's Republic of China disclosed Aug. 29 that the 10th congress of the Chinese Communist party had been held in Peking during
the last week of August. The annnouncement stated that the 1,249
delegates participating in the congress had adopted a revised party
constitution, formally expelled from the party the late Marshal Lin
Piao, selected a new Central Committee which in turn chose a new
politburo or presidium, and approved a report presented by Premier
Chou En-lai. In contrast to the 9th party congress, which was announced
when it convened on April 1, 1969, the latest meeting was kept secret
until the day after its conclusion. Even the site of the five-day session
was not immediately made known by the Chinese press agency Hsinhua.
Fear of hostile Soviet action of some kind was cited by observers as a
possible reason for keeping secret the meeting of most of China's top
political leaders.

The nine previous congresses in the 52-year history of the party had
been the instrumentality through which Chinese Communists adjusted
to changing political conditions. The 10th congress was believed to
have been convened to effect changes in party structure made
advisable by developments since 1969. Of particular concern was the
reported attempted assassination of Chairman Mao Tse-tung in 1971
by the late Lin Piao, Mao's designated successor.

According to the communique issued by the congress, that body
denounced Lin Piao "once and for all" and termed him a "bourgeois
careerist, conspirator, counter-revolutionary double-dealer, renegade

and traitor." Chou's report to the congress contained the first official statement that Lin had tried to have Mao assassinated in September 1971, as news sources in Hong Kong had reported. Chou also confirmed the story that Lin had been killed in an aircraft crash as he attempted to flee to Russia.

Although Mao was again "unanimously" elected chairman of the presidium and presided over the congress, a new hierarchy of Chinese leadership emerged from the meeting. In contrast to the 9th congress, which had named Lin vice chairman and successor to Mao, the 10th congress elected five deputy chairmen led by Chou En-lai. Next in line was the little-known 36-year-old Wang Hung-wen, a former Shanghai textile worker whose political star was obviously rising. The appointment of five deputy chairmen led some China specialists to speculate that a collective leadership would rule the country after Mao's death. Mao's wife, Chiang Ching, previously ranked third or fourth in the party, was not included in the group of deputy chairmen although she was listed as a member of the presidium.

The congress voted to expand the membership of both the Central Committee and the presidium, China's two major political organs through which the party runs the government. The new Central Committee, with 195 members and 124 alternate members, became the largest committee to hold office. Similarly, the congress expanded the ruling presidium from 13 to 21 full members.

Peking laid strong emphasis on the spirit of unity emanating from the congress. In its communique, the party described the meeting as a "congress of unity, a congress of victory, and a congress full of vigor." The communique instructed the "whole party, the army and the people" to "unite and don't split; be open and above board, and don't intrigue and conspire."

Criticism of U.S. and USSR

Chou En-lai's report to the congress dealt in part with China's reaction to the current global situation. Chou denounced both the United States and the Soviet Union for actions he interpreted as "contending for hegemony." Chou conceded that Chinese-American relations had "improved to some extent" and "American imperialism" was "increasingly on the decline." He reserved his strongest criticism for the "revisionist ruling clique" of the Soviet Union which had "made a socialist country degenerate into a social-imperialist country." The Soviets, he asserted, had "restored capitalism, enforced a fascist dictatorship and enslaved the people." Criticizing Russia because it "massed its troops along the Chinese border" and "sent troops into Mongolia," Chou declared that China would not be "deceived or cowed" into yielding northern lands to the Soviets.

Text of the English translation of the communique of the 10th national congress of the Chinese Communist party, as distributed Aug. 29 by Hsinhua, the official Chinese press agency; and excerpts from the report delivered to the congress by Premier Chou En-lai Aug. 24, and adopted by the congress Aug. 28:

The 10th national Congress of the Communist party of China was held solemnly in Peking from Aug. 24 to 28. It was a Congress of unity, a Congress of victory and a Congress full of vigor.

The great leader of our party, Comrade Mao Tse-tung presided over the Congress.

The agenda of the Congress were:

1. Comrade Chou En-lai delivered the political report on behalf of the Central Committee of the Communist party of China;

2. Comrade Wang Hung-wen delivered the report on the revision of the party constitution on behalf of the Central Committee of the Communist party of China and submitted to the Congress the "Draft of the Constitution of the Communist Party of China";

3. The 10th Central Committee of the Communist party of China was elected.

The Congress formerly opened on Aug. 24.

When Chairman Mao appeared on the rostrum, cheers resounded through the hall. The delegates excitedly greeted him with prolonged and hearty applause and cheered, "Long live our great leader Chairman Mao! A long, long life to Chairman Mao!" Chairman Mao warmly waved to the delegates.

The Congress elected a presidium composed of 148 delegates.

The Congress unanimously elected Chairman Mao Tse-tung chairman of the presidium, Comrades Chou En-lai, Wang Hung-wen, Kang Sheng, Yeh Chien-Ying and Li Teh-sheng vice chairmen of the presidium and comrade Chang Chun-chao secretary general of the presidium.

Also seated in the front row on the rostrum were: Comrades Liu Po-Cheng, Chiang Ching, Chu Teh, Hsu Shih-Yu, Chen Hsilien, Le Hsien-Nien, Yao Wen-Yuan, Tung Pi-Wu, Chi Teng-Kuei, Wang Tung-Hsing, Hua Kuo-Feng and Wu Teh.

'Lin Piao Clique Smashed'

The 10th national Congress of the Communist party of China convened at a time when the Lin Piao antiparty clique has been smashed, the line of the party's ninth national Congress has won great victories and the situation both at home and abroad is excellent.

The Central Committee of the Communist party of China and comrades throughout the party made full preparations for this historic Congress. A total of 1,249 delegates were elected to the Congress at the end of an extensive democratic process, which included repeated deliberations and consultations about the candidates and seeking the opinions of the masses both inside and outside the party in the areas or organizations to which the candidates belonged.

Prior to the formal opening of the Congress, all the delegates had seriously discussed the drafts of all the Congress documents. Inspired and joyful, the people of the whole country greeted the 10th Congress with concrete deeds.

On the day the Congress formally opened, the delegates from the four corners of our great socialist motherland entered the stately assembly hall by way of a spacious lobby with huge portraits of Marx, Engels, Lenin and Stalin on the wall.

Among the delegates were those from the party membership of the industrial workers and the poor and lower-middle peasants, those from the party membership in the Peoples Liberation Army, who came from frontier outposts where they vigilantly guarded our motherland, and those from the party membership of revolutionary cadres, revolutionary intellectuals and other working people.

Delegates from among the worker, peasant and soldier party members accounted for 67 per cent of the total number. Over 20 per cent of the delegates were women party members. Delegates of fraternal nationalities other than the Hans also constituted a certain proportion of the total. Delegates elected from party members in various places of our country, who were natives of Taiwan-Province, our motherland's sacred territory yet to be liberated, attended a national Congress of the party for the first time.

Bearing the mandate of the 28 million party members throughout the country and bringing with them the aspirations of hundreds of millions of people of all the nationalities, the delegates worked together with our great leader Chairman Mao in an atmosphere of unity, alertness, earnestness and liveliness.

Reports Are Adopted

On Aug. 28, after serious and lively political discussions, the Congress unanimously adopted the political report given by Comrade Chou En-lai, the report on the revision of the party constitution given by Comrade Wang Hung-wen and the constitution of the Communist party of China.

The delegates said with joy that these documents, guided by Marxism-Leninism-Mao Tse-tung Thought, analyze the excellent situation both at home and abroad, fully affirm the great victories won on all fronts under the guidance of the line of the ninth Congress, sum up the basic experience of the two-line struggle, especially that of the struggle to smash the Lin Piao anti-party clique and further define the orientation and tasks of continuing the revolution under the dictatorship of the proletariat, and that they constitute the fighting program for the whole party, army and people.

After repeated deliberation and discussion, the Congress elected the 10th Central Committee of the Communist party of China by secret ballot. When the results of the election were announced, thunderous and enthusiastic applause and cheers reverberated again through the hall.

The 195 members and 124 alternate members elected to the Central Committee embody the combination of the old, middle-aged and the young.

Some are proletarian revolutionaries of the older generations, who went through the first and second revolutionary civil wars in the early years of the party, some are leading cadres from various fronts, who stood the test of gunfire in the war of resistance against Japan, the war of liberation and the war to resist U.S. aggression and aid Korea, others are outstanding fighters in the three great revolutionary movements, i.e. class struggle, the struggle for production and scientific experiment, and in the struggle against imperialism, revisionism and reaction during the period of socialist revolution, and still others are young comrades who newly joined the party during the Great Proletarian Cultural Revolution.

Gathered together, the old, the middle-aged and the young studied side by side and encouraged each other. The delegates said gladly that the composition of the 10th Central Committee fully demonstrates that our party is flourishing and has no lack of successors and that it is firmly united on the basis of Marxism-Leninism-Mao Tse-tung Thought.

Party Expels Lin Piao

The Congress indignantly denounced the Lin Piao antiparty clique for its crimes. All the delegates firmly supported this resolution of the Central Committee of the Communist party of China: expel Lin Piao, the bourgeois careerist, conspirator, counterrevolutionary double-dealer, renegade and traitor from the party once and for all; expel Chen Po-ta, principal member of the Lin Piao anti-party clique, anti-Communist Kuomintang element, Troskyite, renegade, enemy agent and revisionist from the party once and for all, and dismiss him from all posts inside and outside the party. The delegates unanimously supported the decisions made and all the corresponding measures taken by the Central Committee of the Communist Party of China with regard to the other principal members of the Lin Piao antiparty clique.

The 10th National Congress of the Communist party of China called on the whole party, army and people to study its documents conscientiously and implement them thoroughly, persist in continuing the revolution under the dictatorship of the proletariat, adhere to the basic principles "Practice Marxism, and not revisionism; unite and don't split; be open and above-board, and don't intrigue and conspire," and unite to win still greater victories!

The Congress pointed out: at present we should continue to put the task of criticizing Lin Piao and rectifying style of work above all else. We should make full use of that teacher by negative example, the Lin Piao antiparty clique, to educate the whole party, army and people in class struggle and two-line struggle, and should study Marxism-Leninism-Mao Tse-tung thought and criticize revisionism and the bourgeois world outlook. We should continue to do well the work of struggle-criticism-transformation in the superstructure including all spheres of culture, work hard to grasp revolution and promote production, other work and preparedness against war and do our work better in all fields.

We should act in accordance with the political line defined by the 10th Congress and the new party constitution adopted by it, and build our party into an even stronger and more vigorous party, which will lead the people of all nationalities in the country and unite with all the forces than can be united to further consolidate the dictatorship of the proletariat.

'Disorder Is a Good Thing'

The Congress pointed out: the present international situation is characterized by great disorder on the earth. Such great disorder is a good thing, and not a bad thing, and it is further developing in a direction favorable to the people of all countries and unfavorable to imperialism, modern revisionists and all reaction.

We must uphold proletarian internationalism, adhere to the consistent policies of our party, strengthen our unity with the proletariat, the oppressed people and nations of the whole world, strengthen our unity with all the countries subjected to imperialist aggression, subversion, interference, control and bullying and form the broadest united front against imperialism, colonialism and neocolonialism and in particular against the hegemonism of the two superpowers—the U.S. and the U.S.S.R.

We must unite with all genuine Marxist-Leninist parties and organizations the world over and carry the struggle against modern revisionism through to the end.

The Congress called on the working class, the poor and lower-middle peasants, the commanders and fighters of the People's Liberation Army and the people of all nationalities in our country to strengthen without fail their preparations against wars of aggression, be on guard against the outbreak of an imperialist world war and particularly against surprise attacks by social-imperialism and be ready to wipe out resolutely, thoroughly, wholly and completely any enemy that dare invade us!

Long live the great, glorious and correct Communist party of China!

Long live the 10th National Congress of the party, a Congress of unity and victory!

Long live Marxism-Leninism-Mao Tse-tung thought!

Long live our great leader Chairman Mao! A long, long life to Chairman Mao!

Excerpts from Report to the Tenth National Congress of the Communist Party of China by Chou En-lai:

Comrades:

The Tenth National Congress of the Communist Party of China is convened at a time when the Lin Piao antiparty clique has been smashed, the line of the party's Ninth National Congress has won great victories and the situation both at home and abroad is excellent.

On behalf of the Central Committee, I am making this report to the Tenth National Congress. The main subjects are: On the line of the Ninth National Congress, on the victory of smashing the Lin Piao antiparty clique and on the situation and our tasks.

The party's Ninth Congress was held when great victories had been won in the Great Proletarian Cultural Revolution personally initiated and led by Chairman Mao.... As we all know, the political report to the Ninth Congress was drawn up under Chairman Mao's personal guidance. Prior to the congress, Lin Piao had produced a draft of a political report in collaboration with Chen Po-ta. They were opposed to continuing the revolution under the dictatorship of the proletariat, contending that the main task after the Ninth Congress was to develop production.

This was a refurbished version under new conditions of the same revisionist trash that Liu Shao-chi and Chen Po-ta had smuggled into the resolution of the Eighth Congress, which alleged that the major contradiction in our country was not the contradiction between the proletariat and the bourgeoisie, but that "between the advanced socialist system and the backward productive forces of society." Naturally, this draft by Lin Piao and Chen Po-ta was rejected by the Central Committee.... However, during and after the Ninth Congress, Lin Piao continued with his conspiracy and sabotage in spite of the admonishments, rebuffs and efforts to save him by Chairman Mao and the party's Central Committee. He went further to start a counterrevolutionary coup d'etat, which was aborted, at the second plenary session of the Ninth Central Committee in August 1970, then in March 1971 he drew up the plan for an armed counterrevolutionary coup d'etat entitled "Outline of Project '571'," and on September 8, he launched the coup in a wild attempt to assassinate our great leader Chairman Mao and set up a rival central committee. On September 13, after his conspiracy had collapsed, Lin Piao surreptitiously boarded a plane, fled as a defector to the Soviet revisionists in betrayal of the party and country and died in a crash at Undur Khan in the People's Republic of Mongolia.

Shattering of Lin Piao Clique

The shattering of the Lin Piao antiparty clique is our party's greatest victory since the Ninth Congress and a heavy blow dealt to enemies at home and abroad. After the September 13th incident, the whole party, the whole army and the hundreds of millions of people of all nationalities in our country seriously discussed the matter and expressed their intense proletarian indignation at the bourgeois careerist, conspirator, double-dealer, renegade and traitor Lin Piao and his sworn followers, and pledged resolute support for our great leader Chairman Mao and the party's Central Committee which he headed. A movement to criticize Lin Piao and rectify style of work has been launched throughout the country....

Spurred by the movement to criticize Lin Piao and rectify style of work, the people of our country overcame the sabotage by the Lin Piao antiparty clique, surmounted serious natural disasters and scored new victories in socialist construction. Our country's industry, agriculture, transportation, finance and trade are doing well. We have neither external nor internal debts. Prices are stable and the market is flourishing. There are many new achievements in culture, education, public health, science and technology.

In the international sphere, our party and government have firmly implemented the foreign policy laid down by the Ninth Congress. Our revolutionary friendship with fraternal socialist countries and with the genuine Marxist-Leninist parties and organizations of various countries and our cooperation with friendly countries have been further strengthened. Our country has established diplomatic relations with an increasing number of countries on the basis of the five principles of peaceful coexistence. The legitimate status of our country in the United Nations has been restored. The policy of isolating China has gone bankrupt; Sino-U.S. relations have been improved to some extent. China and Japan have normalized their relations. Friendly contacts between our people and the people of other countries are more extensive than ever; we assist and support each other, impelling the world situation to continue to develop in the direction favorable to the people of all countries.

Revolutionary practice since the Ninth Congress and chiefly the practice of the struggle against the Lin Piao antiparty clique have proved that the political and organizational lines of the Ninth Congress are both correct and that the leadership given by the party's Central Committee headed by Chairman Mao is correct....

Mao's Teaching

Chairman Mao teaches us that "THE CORRECTNESS OR INCORRECTNESS OF THE IDEOLOGICAL AND POLITICAL LINE DECIDES EVERYTHING." If one's line is incorrect, one's downfall is inevitable, even with the control of the central, local and army leadership. If one's line is correct, even if one has not a single soldier at first, there will be soldiers, and even if there is no political power, political power will be gained. This is borne out by the historical experience of our party and by that of the international communist movement since the time of Marx. Lin Piao wanted to "have everything under his command and everything at his disposal," but he ended up in having nothing under his command and nothing at his disposal. The crux of the matter is line. This is an irrefutable truth....

Chairman Mao calls on the whole party: "PRACTICE MARXISM, AND NOT REVISIONISM; UNITE, AND DON'T SPLIT; BE OPEN AND ABOVEBOARD, AND DON'T INTRIGUE AND CONSPIRE." He thus puts forward the criterion for distinguishing the correct line from the erroneous line, and gives the three basic principles every party member must observe. Every one of our comrades must keep these three principles firmly in mind, uphold them and energetically and correctly carry on the two-line struggle within the party....

Under the guidance of the correct line represented by Chairman Mao, the great, glorious and correct Communist Party of China has had prolonged trials of strength with the class enemies both inside and outside the party, at home and abroad, armed and unarmed, overt and covert. Our party has not been divided or crushed. On the contrary, Chairman Mao's Marxist-Leninist line has further developed and our party grown ever stronger....

International Disorder

...The present international situation is one characterized by great disorder on the earth. "The wind sweeping through the tower heralds a rising storm in the mountains." This aptly depicts how the basic world contradictions as analysed by Lenin show themselves today. Relaxation is a temporary and superficial phenomenon, and great disorder will continue. Such great disorder is a good thing for the people, not a bad thing. It throws the enemies into confusion and causes division among them, while it arouses and tempers the people, thus helping the international situation develop further in the direction favourable to the people and unfavourable to imperialism, modern revisionism and all reaction.

The awakening and growth of the Third World is a major event in contemporary international relations. The Third World has strengthened its unity in the struggle against hegemonism and power politics of the superpowers and is playing an ever more significant role in international affairs. The great victories won by the people of Vietnam, Laos and Cambodia in their war against U.S. aggression and for national salvation have strongly encouraged the people of the world in their revolutionary struggles against imperialism and colonialism. A new situation has emerged in the Korean people's struggle for the independent and peaceful reunification of their fatherland. The struggles of the Palestinian and other Arab peoples against aggression by Israeli Zionism, the African peoples' struggle against colonialism and racial discrimination and the Latin American peoples' struggles for maintaining 200-nautical-mile territorial waters or economic zones all continue to forge ahead....

Rivalry of U.S. and U.S.S.R.

Lenin said that "AN ESSENTIAL FEATURE OF IMPERIALISM IS THE RIVALRY BETWEEN SEVERAL GREAT POWERS IN THE STRIVING FOR HEGEMONY." Today, it is mainly the two nuclear superpowers—the U.S. and the USSR—that are contending for hegemony. While hawking disarmament, they are actually expanding their armaments every day. Their purpose is to contend for world hegemony. They contend as well as collude with each other. Their collusion serves the purpose of more intensified contention. Contention is absolute and protracted, whereas collusion is relative and temporary. The declaration of this year as the "year of Europe" and the convocation of the European security conference indicate that strategically the key point of their contention is Europe.

The West always wants to urge the Soviet revisionists eastward to divert the peril towards China, and it would be fine so long as all is quiet in the West. China is an attractive piece of meat coveted by all. But this piece of meat is very tough, and for years no one has been able to bite into it. It is even more difficult now that Lin Piao the "super-spy" has fallen. At present, the Soviet revisionists are "making a feint to the east while attacking in the west," and stepping up their contention in Europe and their expansion in the Mediterranean, the Indian Ocean and every place their hands can reach. The U.S.-Soviet contention for hegemony is the cause of world intranquility. It cannot be covered up by any false appearances they create and is already perceived by an increasing number of people and countries. It has met with strong resistance from the Third World and has caused resentment on the part of Japan and West European countries. Beset with troubles internally and externally, the two hegemonic powers—the U.S. and the USSR—find the going tougher and tougher. As the verse goes, "flowers fall off, do what one may," they are in a sorry plight indeed. This has been further proved by the U.S.-Soviet talks last June and the subsequent course of events.

Russia's Social Imperialism

"THE PEOPLE, AND THE PEOPLE ALONE, ARE THE MOTIVE FORCE IN THE MAKING OF WORLD HISTORY." The ambitions of the two hegemonic powers—the U.S. and the USSR—are one thing, but whether they can achieve them is quite another. They want to devour China, but find it too tough even to bite. Europe and Japan are also hard to bite, not to speak of the vast Third World. U.S. imperialism started to go downhill after its defeat in the war of aggression against

Korea. It has openly admitted that it is increasingly on the decline; it could not but pull out of Vietnam. Over the last two decades, the Soviet revisionist ruling clique, from Khrushchev to Brezhnev, has made a socialist country degenerate into a social-imperialist country. Internally, it has restored capitalism, enforced a fascist dictatorship and enslaved the people of all nationalities, thus deepening the political and economic contradictions as well as contradictions among nationalities. Externally, it has invaded and occupied Czechoslovakia, massed its troops along the Chinese border, sent troops into the People's Republic of Mongolia, supported the traitorous Lon Nol clique, suppressed the Polish workers' rebellion, intervened in Egypt, causing the expulsion of the Soviet experts, dismembered Pakistan and carried out subversive activities in many Asian and African countries. This series of facts has profoundly exposed its ugly features as the new czar and its reactionary nature, namely, "SOCIALISM IN WORDS, IMPERIALISM IN DEEDS." The more evil and foul things it does, the sooner the time when Soviet revisionism will be relegated to the historical museum by the people of the Soviet Union and the rest of the world.

Recently, the Brezhnev renegade clique have talked a lot of nonsense on Sino-Soviet relations. It alleges that China is against relaxation of world tension and unwilling to improve Sino-Soviet relations, etc.... If you are so anxious to relax world tension, why don't you show your good faith by doing a thing or two—for instance, withdraw your armed forces from Czechoslovakia or the People's Republic of Mongolia and return the four northern islands to Japan? China has not occupied any foreign countries' territory. Must China give away all the territory north of the Great Wall to the Soviet revisionists in order to show that we favour relaxation of world tension and are willing to improve Sino-Soviet relations? The Chinese people are not to be deceived or cowed. The Sino-Soviet controversy on matters of principle should not hinder the normalization of relations between the two states on the basis of the five principles of peaceful coexistence. The Sino-Soviet boundary question should be settled peacefully through negotiations free from any threat. "WE WILL NOT ATTACK UNLESS WE ARE ATTACKED; IF WE ARE ATTACKED, WE WILL CERTAINLY COUNTER-ATTACK" —this is our consistent principle. And we mean what we say....

What China Must Do

In the excellent situation now prevailing at home and abroad, it is most important for us to run China's affairs well. Therefore, on the international front, our party must uphold proletarian internationalism, uphold the party's consistent policies, strengthen our unity with the proletariat and the oppressed people and nations of the whole world and with all countries subjected to imperialist aggression, subversion, interference, control or bullying and form the broadest united front against imperialism, colonialism and neo-colonialism, and in particular, against the hegemonism of the two superpowers—the U.S. and the USSR. We must unite with all genuine Marxist-Leninist parties and organizations the world over, and carry the struggle against modern revisionism through to the end....

We must uphold Chairman Mao's teachings that we should "BE PREPARED AGAINST WAR, BE PREPARED AGAINST NATURAL DISASTERS, AND DO EVERYTHING FOR THE PEOPLE" and should "DIG TUNNELS DEEP, STORE GRAIN EVERYWHERE, AND NEVER SEEK HEGEMONY," maintain high vigilance and be fully prepared against any war of aggression that imperialism may launch and particularly against surprise attack on our country by Soviet revisionist social-imperialism. Our heroic People's Liberation Army and our vast militia must be prepared at all times to wipe out any enemy that may invade....

Economically ours is still a poor and developing country. We should thoroughly carry out the general line of GOING ALL OUT, AIMING HIGH AND ACHIEVING GREATER, FASTER, BETTER AND MORE ECONOMICAL RESULTS IN BUILDING SOCIALISM, grasp revolution and promote production. We should continue to implement the principle of "TAKING AGRICULTURE AS THE FOUNDATION AND INDUSTRY AS THE LEADING FACTOR" and the series of policies of walking on two legs, and build our country independently and with the initiative in our own hands, through self-reliance, hard struggle, diligence and frugality.... On this basis, planning and co-ordination must be strengthened, rational rules and regulations improved and both central and local initiative further brought into full play. Party organizations should pay close attention to questions of economic policy, concern themselves with the well-being of the masses, do a good job of investigation and study, and strive effectively to fulfill or over-fulfill the state plans for developing the national economy so that our socialist economy will make still greater progress....

Comrades: The Tenth National Congress of the party will have a far-reaching influence on the course of our party's development. We will soon convene the Fourth National People's Congress. Our people and the revolutionary people of all countries place great hopes on our party and our country. We are confident that our party, under the [leadership] of Chairman Mao, will uphold his proletarian revolutionary line, do our work well and live up to the expectations of our people and the people throughout the world!

THE FUTURE IS BRIGHT, THE ROAD IS TORTUOUS. Let our whole party unite, let our people of all nationalities unite. BE RESOLUTE, FEAR NO SACRIFICE AND SURMOUNT EVERY DIFFICULTY TO WIN VICTORY!

Long live the great, glorious and correct Communist Party of China!
Long live Marxism-Leninism-Mao Tse-tung Thought!
Long Live Chairman Mao! A long, long life to Chairman Mao!

September

STATUS OF U.S. SCIENCE

September 5, 1973

The National Science Board of the National Science Foundation submitted to Congress Sept. 5 its fifth annual report, explaining "the state of the science enterprise in the United States" through 1972. The 145-page analysis quantitatively expressed the factors that had caused concern among American scientists in recent years. Examining widely divergent subjects, ranging from the position of U.S. science in the international arena to the government and industrial resources available for research and development, the report detailed declines in funding for scientific endeavors, in the number of persons working or studying in science fields, and in overall U.S. scientific activity relative to that of other nations.

Among the conclusions reached were the following: the percentage of federal government expenditures allotted for scientific research and development (R & D) steadily declined after 1964; the number of scientists and engineers engaged in R & D dropped nearly 20 per cent between 1969 and 1972; basic research expenditures, after rising through the 1960s, turned down after 1968; the growth in graduate enrollment in science doctorate departments turned downward for the first time during 1969-1972; and federal expenditures to universities and colleges for support of R & D declined by 75 per cent between 1965 and 1971. According to H. E. Carter, chairman of the National Science Board, "the ultimate goal" of the report was "a set of indices which would reveal the strengths and weaknesses of U.S. science and technology, in terms of the capacity and performance of the enterprise in contributing to national objectives." What the indicators demonstrated about the

781

period up to and including 1972 bore out the professional concern about the state of American science.

The last two chapters of the annual report pulled together the results of the National Science Board's own survey of professional and public attitudes and opinions on the state of American science. Representatives from a wide cross section of the scientific and technological community identified pollution control, energy resources and industrial productivity as areas warranting greatest R & D efforts. The group found detrimental to continued R & D the frequent rapid changes of programs and the directions of the funding for those programs. They cited the lack of incentives and government policies as major impediments to technological innovation, and they urged broadening the training of engineers and scientists by integrating work and education and by reducing the extent of specialization. An overriding view of the professionals was that R&D was essential for alleviating many of the nation's problems, but that its full effectiveness was dependent on appropriate social, economic and political policies.

In the course of 1973, the American scientific community worried that the role of science in the councils of government was faltering. This concern, expressed in science journals and by leading scientists, had been reinforced by two decisions by President Nixon—his reshuffling of the White House science advisory staff and the emphasis placed on applied science in the federal budget he sent Congress for fiscal year 1974. The first decision was interpreted as a sign of science's diminishing influence in the administration and the second as a further sign of declining support for basic research.

By his first action, Reorganization Plan No. 1 of 1973, issued Jan. 26, Nixon ordered the Office of Science and Technology (OST) moved out of the White House and abolished the post of presidential science adviser. This reorganization also marked the end of the President's Science Advisory Committee, which had come into prominence and influence in 1957, soon after Russia sent the first earth satellite into orbit. The functions of the OST were transferred to the National Science Foundation (NSF). The reshuffling drew immediate criticism from the campuses and laboratories. From the point of view of the scientific community, the most controversial of Nixon's three maneuvers was his decision to transfer the functions of the OST from the White House to NSF. The Federation of American Scientists, a group of 4,500 scientists, issued the following statement Jan. 26 in response to the reorganization: "We view with dismay and alarm this further decline in the role of scientists in government.... As the issues of national science policy become more complicated, the voice of science becomes more necessary. We believe that disinterested expertise should be sought rather than suppressed. The policies being followed by the administration in down-grading science are leaving the scientific community with an ever greater feeling of frustration."

Nixon's proposed fiscal year 1974 budget did request additional funding for several areas of applied science, including increases funneled toward research on pollution, energy shortages, heart disease and cancer. (See budget story, p. 174.) *But in the midst of the scientific debate over applied science versus basic research, these proposals were taken as signals of a greater emphasis on short-term results at the expense of pure or basic research. By some calculations, only about 15 per cent of the spending on science was to be for basic research. Basic—in contrast to applied—research might not yield immediate benefits, but, scientists argued, it could well lay the foundation for future achievements.*

In recent years, the debate over the level of federal support for basic research had sharpened. Nixon, in sending the first presidential Message on Science and Technology to Congress, March 16, 1972, put strong emphasis on the advantages of applied research. "I have felt for some time," he said, "that we should also be doing more to apply our scientific and technological genius directly to domestic opportunities." In 1971, the Nixon administration had requested goal-oriented science policy from NSF, an organization traditionally concerned with supporting basic research. NSF then instituted the Research Applied to National Needs (RANN) program which immediately became controversial, especially in the academic community. Harvey Brooks, dean of engineering and applied physics at Harvard, wrote in the spring of 1971 that "some fear that second-rate research is being supported lavishly because it promises practical results, while first-rate pure science languishes.... Others argue, however, that RANN is encouraging a long overdue reorientation and restructuring of the academic science community, breaking down often artificial and obsolete barriers between disciplinary departments."

> *Excerpts from the first five chapters of the National Science Board's fifth annual report,* Indicators 1972, *made public Sept. 5, 1973:*

Introduction

The National Science Board is charged by the Congress with providing an annual report of the state of science in the United States. In its first four reports, the Board dealt with selected aspects of this subject, but with this, the fifth report, the Board begins the development of a system of indicators for describing the state of the entire scientific endeavor. These indicators, expanded and refined in the coming years, are intended to measure and monitor U.S. science—to identify strengths and weaknesses of the enterprise and to chart its changing state....

International Position of U.S. Science and Technology

The proportion of the gross national product (GNP) spent for research and development (R&D) between 1963-71 declined in the United States, France, and the United Kingdom but increased in the Union of Soviet Socialist Republics (U.S.S.R.), Japan, and West Germany. By 1971, U.S. expenditures for R&D were 2.6 percent of GNP, as compared with an estimated 3.0 percent for the U.S.S.R., approximately 2.0 percent for the United Kingdom and West Germany, and 1.8 percent for both Japan and France.

The number of scientists and engineers engaged in R&D per 10,000 population declined in the United States after 1969 but continued to increase in the U.S.S.R., Japan, West Germany, and France, with the result that by 1971 the number per 10,000 population for the U.S.S.R. was 37 as compared with 25 for the United States and Japan, 15 for West Germany, and 12 for France.

All countries included in the comparisons significantly reduced the proportion of their government R&D expenditures for national defense between 1961 and 1969, with such expenditures in the United States dropping from 65 to 49 percent of total government R&D spending. Increases in the United States and most other countries occurred in the areas of space, community services, and economic development.

In seven of eight scientific areas studied, the United States produces a larger share of the world's scientific and technical literature than any of the other major developed countries; the U.S. share remained essentially unchanged between 1965-71....

The United States had an increasingly favorable position in the sale of "technical know-how"—patents, techniques, formulas, franchises, and manufacturing rights—during 1960-71; Japan was the major purchaser of U.S. "know-how," surpassing all of Western Europe after 1967....

Resources for Research and Development

National expenditures for R&D increased throughout the 1961-72 period when expressed in current dollars; in terms of constant 1958 dollars, however, expenditures declined 6 percent between 1968 and 1971, but increased slightly in 1972 to a level equivalent to that of 1966-67.

Total R&D expenditures as a proportion of the gross national product declined to 2.5 percent in 1972 from a high of 3.0 in 1964; the decline was due to continued growth of the GNP coupled with the reduced growth of Federal R&D expenditures.

784

Federal Government expenditures for R&D in current dollars leveled off after 1968 and declined slightly thereafter—primarily as the result of reduced expenditures for space R&D—before rising in 1971 and 1972; the result in constant 1958 dollars was a reduction which continued through 1971 and amounted to a 12-percent decline.

The number of scientists and engineers engaged in R&D reached almost 560,000 in 1969 before declining each year thereafter for a total reduction of some 35,000 by 1972; almost all the decline occurred in the industrial sector.

Most affected by the funding reductions were development activities which leveled off in 1970 before rising again in 1971 and 1972; in constant 1958 dollars, however, expenditures for development declined after 1969 and remained at the lower level through 1972.

The fraction of total Federal outlays devoted to R&D fell from 12 to 7 percent between 1965-72. The decline was due in large part to the growth of Federal expenditures in areas which have small R&D outlays, such as income security, and to reductions in space R&D.

Some 73 percent of all Federal R&D expenditures in 1972 went for national defense and space exploration. National defense received 54 percent of total Federal R&D funds in 1972 and space exploration received some 19 percent of the total.

Federal expenditures for R&D in civilian areas (areas other than national defense and space) increased throughout the 1963-72 period, rising to 27 percent of the total in 1972, up from 14 percent in 1963. Areas receiving the bulk of funds in 1972 were health (8.7 percent), advancement of science and technology (4.4 percent), transportation (3.8 percent), environment (3.2 percent), and energy conversion and development (2.5 percent)....

Basic Research

Basic research expenditures, in current dollars, rose continually during the period 1960-72, although the rate of growth slowed after 1968; in constant 1958 dollars, basic research spending in 1972 was approximately equal to the 1967 level, and some 6 percent lower than the peak year of 1968.

The 1968-72 decline in constant 1958 dollar expenditures for basic research was least in universities and colleges (3 percent) and largest in industry (14 percent).

The share of total basic research expenditures used by the different sectors changed significantly between 1960-72; the universities' share increased from 43 to 57 percent, while industry's share fell from 28 to 16 percent.

The Federal Government provided 62 percent of the total 1972 funds for basic research in the United States, as compared with 52 percent in 1960; basic research funds provided by universities and colleges rose from some 16 percent of the total in the early and mid-1960's to approximately 20 percent in 1972.

Basic research funds (in current dollars) provided by the Federal Government increased rapidly between 1960-68 but slowed to small annual increments thereafter; in constant 1958 dollars, however, a 10-percent decline in funding occurred between 1968-72, which included a 16-percent reduction in basic research funds to industry, a 10-percent reduction to universities and colleges, and a 7-percent decline for nonprofit institutions....

Total funds for basic and applied research per scientist and engineer in Ph.D.-granting institutions declined 15 percent between 1968-72 in constant 1961 dollars, as a result of reduced Federal expenditures and continued growth of faculty; research funds per scientist and engineer decreased in all fields except the social sciences, with the largest declines occurring in physics (32 percent), clinical medicine (21 percent), and engineering (17 percent).

The proportion of Ph.D. scientists in universities and colleges engaged in basic research supported by the Federal Government declined from 69 percent in 1964 and 1966 to 57 percent in 1970.

Federal support for young investigators (those holding a Ph.D. less than seven years) in universities and colleges declined to a greater extent than support for senior investigators; the proportion of young investigators supported fell from 65 percent in 1964 to 50 percent in 1970, versus 73 percent to 63 percent for senior investigators.

Government expenditures for basic research in Federal laboratories declined by almost 20 percent in constant 1961 dollars between 1970-72, with the largest reductions occurring in laboratories funded by the National Aeronautics and Space Administration and the Department of Health, Education, and Welfare.

Current dollar expenditures for industry-funded basic research, which accounts for only a small fraction of all such research, increased until 1966 and remained at nearly that level until 1972 when they again increased; in 1958 constant dollars, however, expenditures declined by some 17 percent between 1966-72.

Basic research in industry is concentrated in the fields of chemistry and engineering, followed by physics and the life sciences. Recent declines in constant 1958 dollar expenditures for basic research were largest in the areas of physics and chemistry....

Science and Engineering Personnel

The total pool of active scientists and engineers in the United States grew by about 50 percent from 1960 to 1971, rising to some 1,750,000. The number with doctorates doubled during the period, reaching 10 percent of the total.

Scientists and engineers comprised an increasingly larger proportion of total civilian employment over the last two decades, although the extent of the increase in the 1960's (167 to 210 per 10,000 workers) was less than that during the 1950's (93 to 167 per 10,000 workers).

The proportion of natural scientists and engineers engaged in R&D increased to 37 percent between 1960-64, but declined steadily thereafter. This downward trend was more pronounced among academic than industrial scientists and engineers, and reflects the growth in faculty needed for teaching, as well as the leveling off of R&D funds.

Between 1968 and 1970 the number of natural scientists and engineers in industrial R&D declined to the 1967 level, the first such decline during the 1960's.

The distribution of scientists and engineers among major types of employers changed between 1960-70, with the proportion in industry declining from 74 to 66 percent and the fraction in universities and colleges rising from 11 to 18 percent.

Total enrollments in high school courses of social sciences, natural sciences, and mathematics grew faster than total secondary enrollments between 1960-70, with the largest increases occurring in psychology and economics and the smallest in physics, chemistry, and mathematics. Physics was the only field in which the proportional growth was less than the increase in total enrollments.

The number of undergraduate students at the junior-year level who declared majors in physics, engineering, and chemistry declined between 1970-71, whereas the number declaring majors in the applied social sciences and professional life sciences increased significantly.

Graduate enrollments (full-time and part-time combined) in science doctorate departments declined by almost 4 percent between 1969 and 1971, the first such absolute decrease in the 1960's. Such enrollments in science and engineering, as a percent of total graduate enrollments, declined steadily from 38 percent in 1963 to 31 percent in 1970.

The number of full-time graduate students in science and engineering receiving Federal support declined by 15 percent between 1969-71, while those depending on self-support increased by 19 percent from a lower base.

Annual awards of bachelor's level degrees in science and engineering increased by a factor of 2.2 over the 1959-71 period, with the largest gains in the social sciences (4.1 times) and the smallest in the physical sciences (1.3) and engineering (1.2). First degrees in science and engineering, as a fraction of all bachelor's level degrees, remained essentially constant at 30 percent, due in large part to the rapid growth of social science degrees.

Annual awards of master's degrees in science and engineering rose by a factor of 2.5 over the 1959-71 period, with the largest gains in mathematical sciences (3.8) and social sciences (3.1) and the smallest

787

in the physical sciences (1.9). Science and engineering master's degrees, as a fraction of all master's degrees, declined from a high of 30 percent to 22 percent in 1970-71, with the largest proportional declines occurring in engineering and the physical sciences.

Annual awards of Ph.D. degrees in science and engineering rose by a factor of 3.0 over the 1959-71 period, with the largest gains in engineering (4.6) and mathematical sciences (4.4) and the smallest in the physical sciences (2.4). Science and engineering Ph.D. degrees, as a fraction of all Ph.D. degrees, declined from 62 percent in the mid-1960's to 58 percent in 1970-71, with the largest proportional declines in the physical sciences.

During the last decade, awards of science and engineering doctorates, in terms of location of high school graduation, became more evenly distributed among geographic regions of the United States. The proportion, however, is almost 50 percent lower in the South Atlantic and East South Central regions than in other areas of the country.

Unemployment rates for scientists and engineers rose after 1969, reaching 2.6 and 2.9 percent, respectively, by early 1971. These rates—which were less than half those reported for all workers—declined to early 1970 levels by late 1972....

Institutional Capabilities

The number of academic institutions awarding degrees in science and engineering increased from some 1,100 in 1960-61 to almost 1,300 in 1969-70, with the largest increases occurring in institutions which awarded master's and Ph.D. degrees.

Doctoral-granting institutions employed almost 75 percent of all academic scientists and engineers in recent years, and awarded more than 80 percent of all master's degrees in science and engineering and more than 50 percent of the bachelor's degrees.

The 20 institutions awarding the most Ph.D. degrees in science and engineering accounted for a decreasing fraction of all such degrees awarded, down from one-half of the total awards in 1963 to two-fifths in 1971. Science and engineering graduate enrollments in these institutions declined proportionally over the period.

Private doctoral institutions awarded a decreasing proportion of all Ph.D. degrees in science and engineering, falling from 41 percent of the total awards in 1963 to 34 percent in 1971. Science and engineering graduate enrollments in these institutions peaked in 1969 and declined thereafter in contrast to the continued growth of such enrollments in public institutions.

New doctoral programs in existing doctoral departments increased at the net rate of 1 program per 26 departments during 1970-72; plans for 1972-74 indicate a reduction of the ratio of new additions to 1:66. The largest net increases were in the areas of computer sciences and psychology.

Expenditures for laboratory equipment provided through research grants from the National Science Foundation and major National Institutes of Health, declined between 1966-71. These expenditures as a fraction of total grant funds, fell from 12 percent to 6 percent during the period.

Federal obligations to universities and colleges for R&D plant and major equipment declined 75 percent between 1965 and 1971. As a proportion of all Federal obligations for academic science, funds for R&D plant dropped from 8 percent to 1 percent during the period....

LIMITS ON DETENTE
September 9, 1973

Late in the summer of 1973, Russia's principal engineer of the hydro-gen bomb, nuclear physicist Andrei D. Sakharov, warned the West that a desire to preserve its new-born detente with the Soviet Union should not foreclose efforts to exert pressure on Moscow to relax the rigid controls in Soviet society. Sakharov's comments set off a two-week Soviet press campaign to discredit him. As official denunciation of the scientist increased and his arrest appeared likely, Western critics responded strongly to what they considered unjustifiable infringement of individual rights in Russia.

On Sept. 9, the executive council of the National Academy of Sci-ences, a private American organization entrusted with official responsi-bility for scientific exchanges with the Soviet Union, sent a cablegram to the head of the Soviet Academy of Sciences expressing "deep con-cern" for Sakharov, who was a member of both the U.S. and the Soviet scientific academies. The American scientists warned that the arrest or further harassment of Sakharov might lead to curtailment of U.S. scientific cooperation with the Soviet Union. It was the first time the National Academy had spoken out on behalf of a foreign scientist.

The possible impact of this affair on Soviet-American trade relations was emphasized when Rep. Wilbur D. Mills (D Ark.) said, also on Sept. 9, that "I cannot see the United States expanding commercial markets with the Soviet Union if the price is to be paid in the martyrdom of men of genius like Solzhenitsyn and Andrei Sakharov." Mills, as chairman of the House Ways and Means Committee, was in position to obstruct the granting of most-favored-nation tariff treatment to imports from Russia in fulfillment of provisions of the trade agreement concluded with the Soviet Union on Oct. 18, 1972 (see Historic Documents, 1972, p. 845). Most nations trading with the United States already enjoy most-favored-nation status, but its extension to additional countries depends on approval by Congress. Implementation of the trade agreement awaited that action. Restrictions on emigration of Russian Jews, as well as Moscow's attitude toward dissident scientists, affected American opinion toward cooperation with the Soviets.

The criticism in the West triggered a rebuttal from Communist Party General Secretary Leonid I. Brezhnev. He gave notice that there should be no attempt to barter for concessions in moving toward a relaxation of world tension. On Sept. 19, he cautioned the United States not to attach conditions to new agreements with Moscow and said that the series of pacts achieved in the last few years should be adhered to consistently and honestly "without playing games or engaging in ambiguous maneuvers." In apparent reference to Sakharov's charges against the Soviet government, Brezhnev denounced "ill-conceived propaganda campaigns that are aimed at sowing mistrust in the policies of the U.S.S.R. and other socialist countries."

A position of noninterference in Soviet domestic affairs was supported by the Nixon administration. Henry A. Kissinger, at the start of Senate hearings on his confirmation as Secretary of State, said he sympathized with Sakharov, but believed that the United States should not let Soviet domestic policies impede strides toward accommodation with the Moscow government. On Oct. 8, at a conference in Washington sponsored by the Center for the Study of Democratic Institutions, Kissinger and Chairman J. W. Fulbright (D Ark.) of the Senate Foreign Relations Committee gave their views on the question.

More than a month after the U.S. National Academy of Sciences had warned the parallel body in Russia that harassment of Sakharov would endanger "successful fulfillment of American pledges" of cooperative research, the president of the Soviet Academy of Sciences directed an open letter to American scientists. "Let us say directly that we think your claims are groundless and it would be useless to continue the exchange of letters on this," the Russian wrote on Oct. 17. He insisted that members of the Soviet body, as scientists and as Soviet citizens, valued "the process of relaxation of international tension, reconstruction of international relations on the basis of the peaceful coexistence between states of different social systems and development of mutually advantageous relations between them." But he added: "Another important principle of international relations should, of course, be strictly observed—noninterference in internal affairs of each other." The Russian stressed that "Attempts to use these exchanges to influence the political positions of Soviet scientists are absolutely hopeless,

*not to mention the ethical side of the matter." His letter was given
wide advance circulation by Tass, the Soviet news agency, and played
a key part in a resumed press campaign against Sakharov.*

> *Text of the cablegram of Sept. 9 from the president of the
> U.S. National Academy of Sciences, Dr. Philip Handler,
> to Mstislav V. Keldysh, president of the Soviet Academy
> of Sciences; an unofficial translation of the return letter
> from Keldysh to Handler, Oct. 17; and excerpts from re-
> marks on Oct. 8 by Secretary of State-designate Henry A.
> Kissinger and Sen. J. W. Fulbright (D Ark.) pertaining to
> Soviet dissidence and Soviet-American trade:*

Dr. Handler's cable:

This will convey to the Academy of Sciences of the U.S.S.R. the deep
concern of the Council of the National Academy of Sciences of the
U.S.A. for the welfare of our foreign associate member, academician
Andrei Sakharov.

We have warmly supported the growing detente being established by
our respective governments. We have done so in the belief that such a
course would bring significant social and economic benefits to our
peoples and generate opportunity for alleviation of that division of
mankind which threatens its destruction by nuclear holocaust. We were
heartened by the fact that the various agreements signed by our political leaders in Moscow in 1972 and in Washington in 1973 gave so prominent a role to cooperation in scientific endeavors. We joyfully extended
those intergovernmental agreements by the signature, in 1972 and again
in 1973, of protocols pledging the mutual cooperation of our respective
academies in specific appropriate scientific areas.

Implicit in this prominence of scientific cooperation in our recent
binational agreements was: (1) The recognition that science, itself,
knows no national boundaries; (2) The awareness that the world scientific community shares a common ethic, a common value system and,
hence, is international; (3) Appreciation that mankind, the world over,
derives deep satisfaction from our ever more profound understanding
of the nature of man and the universe in which he finds himself. So true
and important are these relationships that the national scientific communities of the world also share heroes; witness the rosters of foreign
members of academies of science, including yours and ours.

But neither your country nor ours sustains its large scientific enterprise "for science's own sake." We also share a faith in the continuing
truth of the historically demonstrated fact that the wise, humane
application of scientific understanding constitutes the most powerful
means available to our societies to improve the condition of man.

Unhappily, as Sakharov and others have noted, application of scientific understanding has also generated the means for deliberate anni-

hilation of human beings on an unprecedented scale. The industrialization process made possible by science can, if unregulated, occasion unwitting damage to man and the flora and fauna with which we share the planet. Indeed, by reducing death rates more successfully than increasing agricultural productivity, application of science may even have created the possibility of malnutrition and famine on a huge scale.

If the benefits of science are to be realized, if the dangers now recognized are to be averted, and if the full life which can be made possible by science is to be worth living, then, in the words of academician Sakharov, "Intellectual freedom is essential to human society—freedom to obtain and distribute information, freedom for open minded and unfearing debate, and freedom from pressure by officialdom and prejudice." Scientists will recognize this description of a vital, functioning society as a restatement of the ethos of science itself. Violation of that ethos during the period of Lysenkoism deprived the Soviet Union and the world of the full potential of the scientific genius of the Russian people.

Accordingly, it is with great dismay that we have learned of the heightening campaign of condemnation of Sakharov for having expressed, in a spirit of free scholarly inquiry, social and political views which derive from his scientific understanding. Moreover, it was with consternation and a sense of shame that we learned of the expression of censure of Sakharov's contributions to the cause of continuing human progress that was signed by 40 members of your academy including five of our foreign associate members. This attack revives memories of the failure of our own scientific community to protect the late J. R. Oppenheimer from political attack. The case of Andrei Sakharov, however, is far more painful for the fact that some of our Soviet colleagues and fellow scientists are among the principal attackers when one of the scientific community courageously defends the application of the scientific ethos to human affairs.

Were Sakharov to be deprived of his opportunity to serve the Soviet people and humanity, it would be extremely difficult to imagine successful fulfillment of American pledges of binational scientific cooperation, the implementation of which is entirely dependent upon the voluntary effort and goodwill of our individual scientists and scientific institutions. It would be calamitous indeed if the spirit of detente were to be damaged by any further action taken against this gifted physicist who has contributed so much to the military security of the Soviet people and who now offers his wisdom and insights to that people and to the entire world in the interest of a better tomorrow for all mankind.

Response from Soviet Academy of Sciences president:

Having become acquainted with your letter relating, as you put it, to the fate of A. Sakharov, my colleagues and I cannot help but express resolute objection to its content and tone, which do not correspond either to the nature of the affair or to the spirit of relations between our two academies.

We do not think it necessary to speak at length about your letter, which contained general themes on the role of science in the contemporary world, on its global character, on the ethics of a scientist, on universal values, etc. Some of these theses are obvious and unquestionable; some are not acceptable to us. However, that is quite another matter.

In your letter, you picture the affair as if Soviet scientists condemn Sakharov for his "contribution to the cause of progress or humanity" or for his "spirit of free scientific inquiry." This is an apparent distortion of the genuine motives and position of Soviet scientists.

'Slander of Reality' Seen

Members of the Academy of Sciences of the Soviet Union criticize Sakharov because he, as a matter of fact, stood against a relaxation of tension and strengthening of positive shifts in international life, against normalization of relations between Western countries and the Soviet Union. More than that, he called upon the West to improve these relations only if the Soviet Union accepts a number of ultimatums affecting the sovereign rights of the Soviet people.

A. D. Sakharov slandered Soviet reality and the aims of our country in international relations, by having ascribed aggressive intentions to it. By such actions, academician A. D. Sakharov causes harm to the interests not only of the Soviet Union but also the peoples of other countries, which sincerely strive for relaxation of tension and international cooperation.

The degree of political blindness achieved by Sakharov was shown to the entire world recently when he called the terror unleashed by the Fascist junta in Chile 'an era of renaissance and consolidation.'

And after that you suggested that we, Soviet scientists, should not condemn the actions of Sakharov and, more than that, should protect him. Let us say directly that we think your claims are groundless and it would be useless to continue the exchange of letters on this.

The problem is not whether Sakharov enjoys intellectual freedom— there are no doubts about that—but how and with what purposes he uses it.

As is known, Sakharov was not subjected and is not subjected to any discrimination. Until now he has full opportunities for active scientific work. If recently he in fact left science, it happened not through someone's fault but at his own wish. The noisy campaign started in the West around Sakharov, to our convictions, is profitable only for those forces which would like to return the world to the sad days of the cold war.

Of course, we were not surprised that in the U.S.A. and some other countries, there are figures who were pleased by Sakharov's appeals

and they did not wait to take advantage of them. But we believe, Mr.
Handler, that American scientists, in any case their majority, will be
able to understand the difference between intellectual freedom and the
concrete actions of one or another person, in this case Sakharov,
directed against the interests not only of his own people but the interests of peace, of humanity as a whole.

Reference to Scientific Exchanges

We, Soviet scientists, fully aware of the great responsibility of the
people of science to the peoples of their countries, to all humanity,
highly value, as do all the Soviet people, the process of relaxation
of international tension, reconstruction of international relations on the
basis of the peaceful coexistence between states of different social
systems and development of mutually advantageous relations between
them. Another important principle of international relations should,
of course, be strictly observed—noninterference in internal affairs
of each other.

This refers also to the question raised in your letter about scientific
exchanges and scientific cooperation between our countries. Actively
developing such exchanges with American scientists and being ready
to carry on in the future, we always considered and now consider that
this is a strictly voluntary affair which represents identical interests
for both sides.

Attempts to use these exchanges to influence the political positions
of Soviet scientists are absolutely hopeless, not to mention the ethical
side of the matter. We stand for a broad development of scientific
cooperation under conditions of mutual observance of traditions and
rules existing in each country.

Excerpts from Kissinger's speech, Oct. 8:

...Foreign policy must begin with the understanding that it involves
relationships between sovereign countries. Sovereignty has been defined as a will uncontrolled by others; that is what gives foreign policy
its contingent and ever incomplete character.... A nation's values define
what is just; its strength determines what is possible; its domestic structure decides what policies can in fact be implemented and
sustained....

The policy maker, therefore, must strike a balance between what is
desirable and what is possible.... The pursuit of peace must therefore
begin with the pragmatic concept of coexistence—expecially in a
period of ideological conflict.

We must, of course, avoid becoming obsessed with stability. An excessively pragmatic policy will be empty of vision and humanity. It
will lack not only direction, but also roots and heart.... America
cannot be true to itself without moral purpose. This country has always
had a sense of mission. Americans have always held the view that
America stood for something above and beyond its material achieve-

ments. A purely pragmatic policy provides no criteria for other nations to assess our performance and no standards to which the American people can rally.

But when policy becomes excessively moralistic it may turn quixotic or dangerous. A presumed monopoly on truth obstructs negotiation and accommodation. Good results may be given up in the quest for ever elusive ideal solutions. Policy may fall prey to ineffectual posturing or adventuristic crusades....

The outsider demonstrates his morality by the precision of his perceptions and the loftiness of his ideals. The policy maker expresses his morality by implementing a sequence of imperfections and partial solutions in pursuit of *his* ideals.... What we need is the confidence to discuss issues without bitter strife, the wisdom to define together the nature of our world as well as the vision to chart together a more just future.

Detente with the Soviet Union

Nothing demonstrates this need more urgently than our relationship with the Soviet Union.

This Administration has never had any illusions about the Soviet system. We have always insisted that progress in technical fields, such as trade, had to follow—and reflect—progress toward more stable international relations. We have maintained a strong military balance and a flexible defense posture as a buttress to stability. We have insisted that disarmament had to be mutual. We have judged movement in our relations with the Soviet Union, not by atmospherics, but by how well concrete problems are resolved and by whether there is responsible international conduct....

Until recently the goals of detente were not an issue. The necessity of shifting from confrontation toward negotiation seemed so overwhelming that goals beyond the settlement of international disputes were never raised. But now progress has been made—and already taken for granted. We are engaged in an intense debate on whether we should make changes in Soviet society a precondition for further progress—or indeed for following through on commitments already made. The cutting edge of this problem is the Congressional effort to condition most-favored-nation [MFN] trade status for other countries on changes in their domestic systems.

This is a genuine moral dilemma. There are genuine moral concerns—on both sides of the argument. So let us not address this as a debate between those who are morally sensitive and those who are not, between those who care for justice and those who are oblivious to humane values. The attitude of the American people and government has been made emphatically clear on countless occasions, in ways that have produced effective results. The exit tax on emigration is not being collected and we have received assurances that it will not be reapplied; hardship cases submitted to the Soviet Government are being given specific attention; the rate of Jewish emigration has been in the tens of thousands where it was once a trickle. We will continue our vigorous efforts on these matters.

But the real debate goes far beyond this: Should we now tie demands which were never raised during negotiations to agreements that have already been concluded? Should we require as a formal condition internal changes that we heretofore sought to foster in an evolutionary manner?

Let us remember what the MFN question specifically involves. The very term "most favored nation" is misleading in its implication of preferential treatment. What we are talking about is whether to allow *normal* economic relations to develop—of the kind we now have with over 100 other countries and which the Soviet Union enjoyed until 1951. The issue is whether to abolish discriminatory trade restrictions that were imposed at the height of the Cold War. Indeed, at that time the Soviet Government discouraged commerce because it feared the domestic impact of normal trading relations with the West on its society.

The demand that Moscow modify its domestic policy as a precondition for MFN or detente was never made while we were negotiating; now it is inserted after both sides have carefully shaped an overall mosaic. Thus it raises questions about our entire bilateral relationship.

Finally the issue affects not only our relationship with the Soviet Union, but also with many other countries whose internal structures we find incompatible with our own. Conditions imposed on one country could inhibit expanding relations with others, such as the People's Republic of China.

We shall never condone the suppression of fundamental liberties. We shall urge humane principles and use our influence to promote justice. But the issue comes down to the limits of such efforts. How hard can we press without provoking the Soviet leadership into returning to practices in its foreign policy that increase international tensions? Are we ready to face the crises and increased defense budgets that a return to Cold War conditions would spawn? And will this encourage full emigration or enhance the well-being or nourish the hope for liberty of the peoples of Eastern Europe and the Soviet Union? Is it detente that has prompted repression—or is it detente that has generated the ferment and the demand for openness which we are now witnessing?

For half a century we have objected to communist efforts to alter the domestic structures of other countries. For a generation of Cold War we sought to ease the risks produced by competing ideologies. Are we now to come full circle and *insist* on domestic compatibility as a condition of progress?...

Our policy with respect to detente is clear: We shall resist aggressive foreign policies. Detente cannot survive irresponsibility in any area, including the Middle East. As for the internal policies of closed systems the United States will never forget that the antagonism between freedom and its enemies is part of the reality of the modern age. We are not neutral in that struggle. As long as we remain powerful we will use our influence to promote freedom, as we always have. But in the nuclear age we are obliged to recognize that the issue of war and peace also involves human lives and that the attainment of peace is a profound moral concern....

Excerpts from Fulbright's speech, Oct. 8:

Nonintervention in the internal affairs of other countries is one of the cardinal rules of international law and relations, and it is codified in the United Nations Charter. The essential purpose of the rule of nonintervention is to prevent larger countries from bullying smaller ones, and to prevent quarrels arising from gratuitous meddling. There are times when nonintervention seems harsh and immoral, as when an oppressive government is left free to mistreat its own people. At times an exception may be warranted, as when a society disintegrates into barbarism, or when an internal issue becomes a threat to international peace, as that is defined in the United Nations Charter. Much more often than not, however, nonintervention is more likely to advance justice than to detract from it. As we Americans discovered in Vietnam, outsiders are seldom wise enough, just enough, or disinterested enough to advance the morality or welfare of a society not their own. The Russian people have lived under dictatorship throughout their history; it is not for us, at this late date, to try to change that by external pressure, especially at a time when there is a better chance than ever to build a cooperative relationship between the Soviet Union and the United States....

While I sympathize with the plight of the dissidents and minorities in the Soviet Union, I cannot concur in the approach of Mr. Sakharov, the Soviet physicist, who says that there can be no detente without democracy, or the novelist Solzhenytsin, who says that "mankind's sole salvation lies in everyone making everything his business." This asks too much of human nature, assuming that involvement will always be benign rather than aggressive, moral rather than predatory. Were everyone to make everything his business, the result would be war not peace, imperialism not democracy. Men have capricious notions of what is and is not their business; that is why it is usually better for them to mind their own. I do believe that the world can be made better, and that man is capable of aiding its betterment, but I am equally a believer in selectivity of means. Important as it is to know what we hope to achieve, it is equally important to know what we are incapable of achieving; which is to say that humane aspiration must be tempered by realism.

799

Choosing from among alternatives is, of course, inevitable in politics, even on the part of those who would base detente upon sweeping standards of morality and justice. Why indeed are they so distressed by the denial of civil rights in the Soviet Union, when we have close and amicable relations with—and give material assistance to—a large number of non-Communist dictatorships who mistreat their citizens? Why do we suddenly require measures of democracy in the Soviet Union as the price of our trade? In Chile a freely elected but Marxist government has been overthrown by a book-burning military dictatorship. Do you suppose we will require a return to democracy before resuming trade and investment with the military junta there? If we wish to apply pressure for democracy and human rights, would it not make sense to start with Chile, Brazil or Greece, all of whom are vulnerable and should be responsive to American pressures, and none of whom are as essential partners for the maintenance of world peace as is the Soviet Union? Why start with the Soviet Union, a superpower which can, if it must, live without our trade and investment, and the one country whose cooperation is absolutely essential for building a structure of peace which I know we all desire?

The Soviet Government, it is true, has already yielded a great deal under our pressure: emigration to Israel, which was kept to only 1,000 three years ago, is now being permitted at a rate of over 30,000 a year. But we should not conclude that the Russians will continue indefinitely to yield to American pressure. The adoption of the Jackson amendment might induce the Russians to remove remaining restraints, or it might anger them into clamping the controls back on. If ever there is to be an authentic liberalization in the Soviet Union, it will come about as the result of internal pressures from increasingly assertive professional, managerial and intellectual classes within the Soviet Union....

I would judge that the most we can do to advance the cause of liberties within the Soviet Union is to help create an international atmosphere calculated to diminish rather than aggravate neurotic fears of Western ideas on the part of the Soviet leaders. In practice this would mean a continuation of measures of detente already begun, in trade, investment, cultural exchange, and above all arms control.

SPECIAL STATE OF UNION SPEECH

September 9, 1973

President Nixon appealed to the American people, Sept. 9, to work with him to maintain a strong national defense, to hold down government expenditures, and to recognize that "the American system requires both a strong Congress and a strong Executive." The President wound up a radio address on current legislative needs by declaring that "We... must not place limits on Presidential powers that would jeopardize the capacity of the President, in this and in future administrations, to carry out his responsibilities to the American people." Only a few months earlier, it had been Congress that feared encroachment by the President (see p. 3).

The radio speech and an accompanying message to Congress, referred to collectively as a special State of the Union message, followed a pattern established earlier in 1973. Nixon on Feb. 2 transmitted to Congress a written "overview" of the State of the Union and supplemented it later with five written messages on specific areas of domestic policy. And each of the five separate messages was preceded by a presidential radio speech (see p. 209 and p. 303). The additional State of the Union speech and message were intended to refocus attention, diverted by Watergate, to major legislative proposals still awaiting action by Congress.

In the 13,500-word written message delivered to Congress Sept. 10, Nixon reiterated much of what he had proposed earlier in the year. He put special emphasis on 50 pieces of legislation that he insisted should be approved before the end of the 1973 session. He told Congress that

he would veto any bill that substantially reduced the defense budget
or that sizably increased the cost of domestic programs. "Although my
military budget—measured in constant dollars—is down by almost
one-third since 1968," he said, "the Congress is now threatening
further defense cuts which could be the largest since 1949. To take such
unilateral action—without exacting similar concessions from our adversaries—could undermine chances for further mutual arms limitation or reductions." He added: "I will veto any bill that includes cuts
which would imperil our national security."

The President said he would "welcome a congressional renaissance,"
but he declared that he would "continue to oppose all efforts to strip
the Presidency of the powers it must have to be effective" and would
"strongly resist efforts by Congress to impose unreasonable demands
upon necessary foreign policy prerogatives of the executive branch."

Congress divided in general along party lines in its response to the
President's message. While one senior Republican representative, William B. Widnal (N.J.), said he liked the message because "the element
of give is in there, and hasn't been before," Democrats saw little to
be optimistic about. Senate Majority Leader Mike Mansfield (D Mont.)
said Senate Democrats would continue to try to cut the defense budget
despite Nixon's threats to veto bills that undermined the defense
posture. Mansfield maintained that some wasteful and spiraling defense
costs would be checked without weakening the country's defensive
capabilities.

> Text of President Nixon's radio address of Sept. 9, 1973, on
> "national legislative goals"—goals which were discussed in
> detail in a special message to Congress on Sept. 10:

Good afternoon.

Now that the Congress has returned from its August recess, it is important that we focus our attention on what the Congress and the Administration can do together to improve the well-being of all the American
people.

Tomorrow, I shall send to the Congress an extensive special message
highlighting more than 50 major legislative proposals which this
Administration has urged and which still await final Congressional
action. Each of these messages is a measure in which you have a stake
because the needs it addresses are your needs.

Today, I want to share with you some thoughts about these proposals
and about the way in which together we can best advance the business
of the people.

In these few minutes, I shall not run through all the details, or
even all the proposals. Those will be spelled out in tomorrow's message.
What I do want to do is to focus on some of the highlights, to explain

why I believe action is needed promptly, and to indicate how you can help get that action.

Together, the Congress and the Administration have a heavy legislative workload in these remaining months of 1973. We were elected less as Republicans or Democrats than as public officials charged with a public responsibility. The work to be done is your work, and every week's delay is a week of your time lost.

In considering the work before us here at home, there is a lesson in our achievements internationally.

We have ended America's longest and most difficult war. By working together, we now can build America's longest and best peace....

This year, for the first time in 12 years, Americans are not at war anywhere in the world, and our courageous prisoners of war have returned to their homes.

This year, for the first time in a generation, no American is being drafted into the Armed Forces.

In these past 4½ years, we have set the Nation on a new course internationally, and we have laid the foundation for a structure of peace that can last far into the future.

The particular lesson I would stress today is this: We were able to achieve this because we sought to turn the world away from those things that divide it and to build a new pattern of relationships on the basis of those things that can unite nations and peoples whatever their differences.

By the same token, the time has come to focus here at home on those great goals that can unite all Americans, that affect all Americans, and in which all Americans have a direct and personal stake.

Common Interest in Six Areas

Today, for example, we face urgent needs in six major areas that affect all of the people and in which the Congress has an opportunity to take actions that will help all the people.

We all share a common interest in establishing a stable prosperity without inflation.

We all share a common interest in ensuring that the Nation's energy needs are met.

We all share a common interest in building better and more livable communities.

We all share a common interest in making full use of our Nation's human resources and ensuring greater opportunity for all.

We all share a common interest in combating the scourge of crime and drugs.

We all share a common interest in maintaining a level of national defense that will enable us to maintain the peace.

In all of these six areas, as well as in the other areas of important common interest which I shall also stress in tomorrow's message, legislative proposals now before the Congress can have a significant impact on the life of each of you.

Of these six major areas, the one that affects all of us most urgently and most directly is the Nation's economy.

Our goal is to achieve what America has not enjoyed since the days of President Eisenhower—full prosperity, without inflation and without war.

We have already made substantial progress toward this goal, and because of this progress, the average American family today—despite inflation—has a higher level of real spendable income than ever before. For the first time in 16 years, unemployment in peacetime is below 5 percent.

However, we still face a major challenge. We must check the rise in prices.

We must move on four fronts at once if we are to win the battle against inflation. We must expand production. We must exercise monetary restraint. For as long as controls are necessary, we must make sure they are effective.

We are doing all these things. The tough new Phase IV controls come into full force this month. The Federal Reserve is checking the growth in the Nation's money supply. We have moved vigorously to expand production, especially food production, and so to reduce the pressure on food prices.

But we could succeed on these three fronts that I have mentioned and we still would lose the battle against inflation unless we prevail also on the fourth front and that is—we must hold the line on Federal spending.

We still face the prospect of strong new inflationary pressures as a result of overspending by the Federal Government.

Programs which the Congress either has already passed or is now considering would produce an additional deficit of $6 billion, and in addition, the Congress has not yet made nearly a billion and a half dollars of cuts that I have recommended. If these actions by the Congress stand, the result will be higher prices for every American family.

The Federal budget is your budget. It is your budget because you pay for it with your taxes; it is also your budget because it determines whether the prices of what you buy allow you to stay within your family budget.

The most important contribution the Congress can make toward holding down the cost of living is to hold down the cost of government. But we cannot expect the Congress to do this without your help— without your support in those difficult decisions every Member of Congress faces when confronted with a vote on a bill that would help some of the people, but that would raise the cost of living for all of the people.

The stable prosperity we seek depends also on our full participation in an increasingly prosperous world. A unique and historic opportunity now exists to negotiate an open and equitable world of trade. Most nations have declared their readiness to join in this endeavor. To give us the tools we need for this full participation in this effort, I urge the Congress to act promptly on the Trade Reform Act of 1973 which I proposed in April. This legislation will enable us, in the difficult negotiations which lie ahead, to assure jobs for American workers, markets for American investors, and lower prices for American consumers.

Proposals to Help Most Energy Needs

Assuring sufficient energy supplies, now and in the future, is another area of urgent national concern. We had a gasoline scare this summer. We could have serious shortages of heating oil this winter. Unless we take prompt and effective action, we can expect little relief from fuel scarcity in the years ahead.

We have taken important administrative actions already to relieve the situation, and we will take additional steps in the next few weeks. But the solution to the energy problem in the long run requires action by the Congress and action now.

There are seven important proposals now before the Congress, designed to help meet our energy needs, on which I am awaiting action. To avoid a major energy crisis in the years ahead, it is vitally important that the Congress act on these seven proposals before it recesses this year. These proposals include, among others, measures to expand the supply of natural gas by deregulating prices; to open the way for creation of the deep water ports needed for modern oil tankers; to improve our organization to meet energy needs; and, of particular importance, to give the go-ahead for building the Alaska pipeline, which already has been delayed too long and which is vital for making the enormous oil reserves of Alaska available to all of the American people.

I call upon all of you to join me in urging decisive action by the Congress on energy legislation, so that we will have enough heat for our homes, enough fuel for our transportation, enough energy to run the factories that produce our goods and provide our jobs.

Making our towns and cities more livable affects each of us individually, and all of us as a Nation—and so does the plain fact that the time has passed for the old, paternalistic, Washington-knows-best ways of doing things. We need new and better ways of meeting our social needs, ways that place the power and resources where the problems are, that enlist the energies of the people and the communities themselves, and that recognize that not all wisdom is in Washington.

Better Communities and Better Schools

This Administration has submitted to the Congress a landmark Better Communities Act, which would greatly enhance the ability of all of our communities to make effective use of Federal assistance and to shape their own future. Within the next 10 days, I shall send to the Congress new housing policy recommendations, based on an intensive 6-months study of the strengths and failures of the old legislation and of the changing pattern of the Nation's needs. Vital transportation legislation also awaits action—including a measure to keep the bankrupt railroads serving the Northeast and Midwest in operation without saddling an undue share of the burden on the taxpayer.

America's greatest resource is its people themselves—you, your family, your neighbors. In the area of human resources, among the measures awaiting action is a Better Schools Act which would help concentrate Federal education dollars where the needs are greatest, for example, on education for the disadvantaged, for the handicapped, and on vocational education—education to prepare people for jobs. Most important, what we need is a measure which would have the decisions affecting your child's education made by your State, by your local school board, rather than by social planners in Washington, D.C.

Also pending are important proposals in the areas of pension reform, job training, health and others that can go far toward expanding opportunity for millions of Americans, and thus make this a better Nation for all of us.

After nearly 20 years of continuous and sometimes shockingly dramatic increases in the rate of crime, the figures for 1972—released just last month—show that we have finally turned the tide in our battle for a safer America. For the first time in 17 years, serious crime in 1972 was down from the year before.

Much of the credit goes to the new crime legislation that has been enacted during the past 4 years. Much of the credit goes to local law enforcement officials, and much of the credit goes to a changed public attitude toward crime and criminals—away from the era of permissiveness, and toward a renewed respect for law, order, and justice.

We must now step up our efforts to ensure that this will be a decisive turning point and that we can continue to make our communities safer once again for law-abiding citizens. Three of the legislative measures on which I urge swift action are designed to do just that: a heroin trafficking bill to tighten enforcement against heroin pushers, a bill to restore the death penalty for certain of the most serious offenses, and a bill to modernize and reform the entire Federal Criminal Code.

National Defense

Finally, we come to an area of transcendent importance: that of national defense. In recent years, it has been fashionable to suggest that whatever we want in the way of extra programs at home could be painlessly financed by just lopping $5 or $10 or $20 billion out of the defense budget. This approach is worse than foolhardy, it is suicidal. Because we could have the finest array of domestic programs in the world and they would mean nothing if because of our weakness we lost our freedom or we were plunged into the abyss of nuclear war.

The world's hope for peace depends on America's strength. It depends absolutely on our never falling into the position of being the second strongest nation in the world.

For years now, we have been engaged in a long, painstaking process of negotiating mutual limits on strategic nuclear arms. Historic agreements have already been reached; others are in prospect. Talks are also going forward this year aimed at a mutual and balanced reduction of forces in Europe. But the point of all these negotiations is that, if peace is to be preserved, the limitations and the reductions of arms must be mutual. What one side is willing to give up for free, the other side will not bargain for.

If America's peace and America's freedom are worth preserving, they are worth the cost of whatever level of military strength it takes to preserve them, and we must not yield to the folly of breaching that level and so undermining our hopes and the world's hopes for peace now and in the future.

The questions at issue in achieving these various goals are not ones of partisanship—of Republicans versus Democrats. And neither, for the most part, are they ones of the President versus the Congress.

In some cases, there are real philosophical differences over how best to meet the needs that we face. The American tradition has always been that we argue these differences out—we compromise some, we settle others by a test of strength. But it is important that we act, that we decide, that we get on with the business of government—that we not let whatever may be our disagreements over the means of achieving these goals bar us from the achievement.

It is important, on all sides, that we approach this legislative season with a willingness to make those reasonable adjustments that are necessary to reach a common objective.

Three Basic Principles

Within that spirit, there are three basic principles which I feel are essential.

We must maintain a national defense sufficient to safeguard us from attack and to provide an incentive for mutual reductions in the burden of armanents for all the world.

We must hold down the total of our expenditures, so that new programs will not be bought at the cost of losing the war against higher prices and higher taxes.

We must recognize that the American system requires both a strong Congress and a strong Executive, and we, therefore, must not place limits on Presidential powers that would jeopardize the capacity of the President, in this and in future Administrations, to carry out his responsibilities to the American people.

There is still enough time to make 1973 a year in which we not only ended the longest war in America's history but in which we laid the foundation for turning the blessings of peace into a better life for all.

With the Congress, the Administration, and the people working together toward this goal, we can achieve it. It means using to the fullest the days and weeks remaining in this year 1973. It means a willingness on the part of both the Executive and the Congress to cooperate and to seek solutions that are in the common interest.

It also means holding the spotlight of public attention and public debate on those issues that directly and personally affect you and your lives. For it is your attention—your participation in the debate and discussion—that in the final analysis will determine whether and how well these goals are achieved.

It means that the Congress should join the Executive in making up for the precious time lost this year in failing to act on those measures which vitally affect every American by going into extra session, if necessary, to complete the people's business before the year ends.

It will take all of us together—the Congress, the Administration, and the public—but we can make this a year of achievement of which we can all be proud. I ask for your best efforts, and I pledge you mine.

Thank you and good afternoon.

KISSINGER, GROMYKO AT THE U.N.

September 24-25, 1973

The opening of the 28th annual General Assembly of the United Nations Sept. 18 occasioned the gathering of a host of foreign ministers and other dignitaries and provided the first official forum for newly installed Secretary of State Henry A. Kissinger, sworn in by the Chief Justice Sept. 22. The Nobel Prize-winning diplomat, who had carved out a reputation for his negotiating achievements in ending U.S. involvement in Vietnam, told the assembled members Sept. 24 that the United States was dedicated to solidifying the currently uneasy world peace and working with other nations to seek solutions to mutual problems. "Beyond recent bilateral diplomacy and pragmatic agreements," Kissinger said, "the United States envisages a comprehensive institutionalized peace encompassing all nations which the United Nations is uniquely situated to foster and to anchor in the hearts of men."

Elaborating on this theme, Kissinger said the United States would strive "for a peace whose stability rests not merely on a balance of forces, but on shared assumptions." Any world structure, he said, "which ignores humane values will prove cold and empty and unfulfilling to most of mankind."

Kissinger's speech was aimed at provoking serious thinking without providing any decisive details. He laid out several proposals, among them the development of effective U.N. peacekeeping machinery, a matter that has remained in deadlock for 28 years; a permanent seat for Japan on the U.N. Security Council; a world conference on food to look into the problems of hunger and malnutrition; assurance of

*membership in the United Nations for any nation that desires it;
and a plan to close the gap between the rich and the poor, a proposal
first suggested by Mexico. But Kissinger left his suggestions in skeletal
form. His aides said he had deliberately omitted details in an effort to
open a dialogue among other nations.*

*Kissinger was followed at the U.N. podium the next day by Soviet
Minister for Foreign Affairs Andrei A. Gromyko. Reviving a proposal he
had set forth in 1958, Gromyko suggested Sept. 25 that members of the
U.N. Security Council reduce their armaments budgets by 10 per cent
and turn over 10 per cent of the savings to developing countries. He
also reiterated Soviet warnings to the West to refrain from interfering
in the internal affairs of that country. Gromyko cited the most publicized example of Western concern: the emigration of Soviet Jews.
Earlier in the month, the U.S. National Academy of Sciences had issued
a warning to its Soviet counterpart, indicating that further harassment
of Soviet scientists could jeopardize joint U.S.-Soviet scientific efforts.
(See p. 793.)*

*Gromyko's plan to reroute national defense expenditures to develop-
ing countries was greeted with many doubts by Western diplomats.
Some questioned the viability of the proposal because the size of the
Soviet defense budget could not be determined. One British spokesman
noted that his country already allotted to development aid an amount
equal to at least 10 per cent of British defense expenditures. He claimed
also that the Soviet Union presently spent only a half of one per cent on
aid for the developing countries.*

> *Text of Secretary of State Henry A. Kissinger's speech to
> the United Nations General Assembly Sept. 24, and ex-
> cerpts from the text of Soviet Foreign Minister Andrei A.
> Gromyko's speech to the same body the following day,
> Sept. 25:*

Kissinger:

I come before you today—confirmed in office but two days ago—as
probably the world's most junior foreign minister. That President Nixon
should ask as my first official act to speak here for the United States
reaffirms the importance that my country attaches to the values and
ideals of the United Nations.

It would be idle to deny that the American people, like many others,
have sometimes been disappointed because this organization has not
been more successful in translating the hopes for universal peace of its
architects into concrete accomplishments.

But despite our disappointments, my country remains committed to
the goal of a world community. We will continue to work in this parliament of man to make it a reality.

Two centuries ago the philosopher Kant predicted that perpetual peace would come eventually—either as the creation of man's moral aspirations or as the consequence of physical necessity. What seemed utopian then looms as tomorrow's reality; soon there will be no alternative. Our only choice is whether the world envisaged in the Charter will come about as the result of our vision or of a catastrophe invited by our shortsightedness.

The United States has made its choice. My country seeks true peace, not simply an armistice. We strive for a world in which the rule of law governs and fundamental human rights are the birthright of all. Beyond the bilateral diplomacy, the pragmatic agreements and dramatic steps of recent years, we envisage a comprehensive, institutionalized peace encompassing all nations, large and small—a peace which this organization is uniquely situated to foster and to anchor in the hearts of men.

This will be the spirit of American foreign policy.

This attitude will guide our work in this organization.

Bedrock of Solid Progress

We start from a bedrock of solid progress. Many of the crises that haunted past General Assemblies have been put behind us. Agreement has been reached on Berlin; there is a cease-fire in the Middle East; the Vietnam war has been ended. The rigid confrontation that has dominated international life and weakened this organization for a quarter of a century has been softened.

The United States and the Soviet Union have perceived a commonality of interest in avoiding nuclear holocaust and in establishing a broad web of constructive relationships. Talks on strategic arms limitation have already produced historic accords aimed at slowing the arms race and insuring strategic stability; we have, today, resumed negotiations on this subject. The positive results we hope for will enhance the security of all mankind.

Two decades of estrangement between the United States and the People's Republic of China has given way to constructive dialogue and productive exchanges. President Nixon has met with the leaders of that nation; we have agreed to a historic communique that honestly sets forth both our differences and our common principles; and we have each opened a liaison office in the capital of the other.

Many other countries have seized the initiative and contributed—in substance and spirit—to the relaxation of tensions. The nations of Europe and North America are engaged in a conference to further security and cooperation. The two German states have taken their place in this Assembly. India, Pakistan and Bangladesh have begun to move toward a welcome reconciliation. North and South Korea are at last engaged in a dialogue, which we hope will lead to a new era of peace and security between them.

Yet these achievements, solid as they are, have only made less precarious the dangers and divisions inherited from the postwar era. We have ended many of the confrontations of the cold war; yet, even in this room, the vocabulary of suspicion persists. Relaxation of tensions is justified by some as merely a tactical interlude before renewed struggle. Others suspect the emergence of a two-power condominium. And as tension between the two original blocs has eased, a third grouping increasingly assumes the characteristics of a bloc of its own—the alignment of the nonaligned.

So the world is uneasily suspended between old slogans and new realities, between a view of peace as but a pause in an unending struggle and a vision of peace as a promise of global cooperation.

In 1946 James Byrnes, the first Secretary of State to address this Assembly, spoke of how the United Nations could help break down habits of thinking in national isolation and move toward "universal understanding and tolerance among all peoples."

The United States will never be satisfied with a world of uneasy truces, of offsetting blocs, of accommodations of convenience. We know that power can enforce a resigned passivity, but only a sense of justice can enlist consensus. We strive for a peace whose stability rests not merely on a balance of forces but on shared aspirations. We are convinced that a structure which ignores humane values will prove cold and empty and unfulfilling to most of mankind.

The United States deeply believes:

That justice cannot be confined by national frontiers.

That truth is universal, and not the peculiar possession of a single group of people or group or ideology.

That compassion and humanity must ennoble all our endeavors.

In this spirit we ask this Assembly to move with us from detente among the big powers to cooperation among all nations, from coexistence to community.

Our journey must begin with the world as it is and with the issues now before us. The United States will spare no effort to ease tensions further and to move toward greater stability.

We shall continue, in the spirit of the Shanghai communique, our search for a new relationship with the People's Republic of China.

We shall work to promote positive trends elsewhere in Asia. The uncertain peace in Indochina must be strengthened; the world community cannot afford, or permit, a relapse into war in that region.

We shall continue to pursue vigorously the building of constructive relations with the Soviet Union.

We shall strive to promote conciliation in Europe. In the negotiations beginning next month we shall seek a reduction of the military forces that have faced each other for so long across that divided continent.

We shall give new vigor to our policy of partnership in the Western Hemisphere.

We shall honor our pledge to promote self-determination, economic development and human dignity across the continent of Africa.

We shall press on with strategic arms limitation talks. We consider them crucial for security and stability in this period.

We shall search for solutions to the worldwide problem of conventional weapons, which drain our resources and fuel the fires of local conflict.

Fundamental Guiding Principles

In all these efforts the United States will be guided by fundamental principles:

We have no desire for domination. We will oppose—as we have consistently opposed throughout this century—any nation that chooses this path. We have not been asked to participate in a condominium; we would reject such an appeal if it were made.

We will never abandon our allies or our friends. The strengthening of our traditional ties is an essential foundation for the development of new relationships with old adversaries.

We will work for peace through the United Nations as well as through bilateral relationships.

We recognize our special obligation, as a permanent member of the Security Council, to assist in the search for just solutions in those parts of the world now torn by strife, such as the Middle East. While we cannot substitute for the efforts of those most directly involved, we are prepared to use our influence to generate a spirit of accommodation and to urge the parties toward practical progress.

But progress on the traditional agenda is not enough. The more we succeed in solving political problems the more other and perhaps deeper challenges emerge. As the world grows more stable we must confront the question of the ends of detente. As the threat of war recedes the problem of the quality of life takes on more urgent significance.

We are, in fact, members of a community drawn by modern science, technology, and new forms of communication into a proximity for which we are still politically unprepared. Technology daily outstrips the ability of our institutions to cope with its fruits. Our political imagination must catch up with our scientific vision. This is at the same time the greatest challenge and the greatest opportunity of this organization.

The pollution of the skies, the seas and the land is a global problem.

The increased consumption of cereals has reduced world food reserves to dangerously low levels.

The demand for energy is outrunning supply, and the need for technological innovation is urgent.

The growth of the world's economy is inhibited by restrictive trading blocs and an insufficiently flexible international monetary system.

The exploitation of the resources of the ocean beds, which is essential for the needs of burgeoning populations, requires global cooperation lest it degenerate into global contention.

Challenges of this magnitude cannot be solved by a world fragmented into self-contained nation-states or rigid blocs.

Requirements of a World Community

I do not intend, today, to cover the whole agenda of international cooperation. Rather, I shall speak briefly of some illustrative areas of common action. I pledge the readiness of the United States to solve these problems cooperatively and to submit proposals aimed at their resolution:

First, a world community requires the curbing of conflict.

The United Nations, in its 28-year history, has not always been idle in this sphere. In Indonesia, the Indian subcontinent, the Middle East, the Congo and in Cyprus, it has shown its ability for effective fact-finding, mediation and peace-keeping missions. This central aspect of the United Nations' work must be strengthened. On a small planet, so bound together by technology and so interdependent economically, we can no longer afford the constant eruption of conflict and the danger of its spread.

Yet, in recent years, we have found ourselves locked in fruitless debates about the inauguration of peace-keeping operations and over the degree of control the Security Council would exercise over peace-keeping machinery—an impasse which has insured only that permanent peace-keeping machinery would not come into being. Each peace-keeping unit we have formed has been an improvisation growing out of argument and controversy.

We should delay no longer. The time has come to agree on peace-keeping guidelines so that this organization can act swiftly, confidently and effectively in future crises. To break the deadlock, the United States is prepared to consider how the Security Council can play a more central role in the conduct of peace-keeping operations. If all countries concerned approach this problem with a desire to achieve a cooperative solution, the United Nations can achieve a major step forward during this session.

Second, a world community must have the widest possible membership.

The exclusion of any qualified state denies representation not only to governments but to peoples. Membership in this body should be a step toward reconciliation, not·a source of conflict. The time has come for North and South Korea to be offered their rightful places here, without prejudice to a future evolution toward unification.

In this spirit also we support the permanent membership of Japan in the Security Council.

Third, a world community must assure that all its people are fed.

The growing threat to the world's food supply deserves the urgent attention of this Assembly. Since 1969 global consumption of cereals has risen more rapidly than production; stocks are at the lowest levels in years. We now face the prospect that—even with bumper crops—the world may not rebuild its seriously depleted reserves in this decade.

No one country can cope with this problem. The United States therefore proposes:

That a world food conference be organized under United Nations auspices in 1974 to discuss ways to maintain adequate food supplies and to harness the efforts of all nations to meet the hunger and malnutrition resulting from natural disasters.

That nations in a position to do so offer technical assistance in the conservation of food. The United States is ready to join with others in providing such assistance.

Fourth, a world community cannot remain divided between the permanently rich and the permanently poor.

Let us therefore resolve that this Assembly, this year, initiate a search —drawing on the world's best minds—for new and imaginative solutions to the problems of development. Our search must be candid and realistic, but it must also be free of peremptory demands, antagonistic propositions, ideological confrontation or propagandistic rhetoric—or we will surely fail.

The United States is prepared to join in this new search, providing freely of the experience gained over two decades. We have learned not to exaggerate our capacity to transform nations—but we have also learned much about what progress is possible.

We will participate without preconditions, with a conciliatory attitude and a cooperative commitment. We ask only that others adopt the same approach.

In this spirit the United States is willing to examine seriously the proposal by the distinguished President of Mexico for a charter of the economic rights and duties of states. Such a document will make a significant and historic contribution if it reflects the true aspirations of all nations; it will accomplish nothing if it is turned into an indictment of one group of countries by another. To command general support—and to be implemented—the proposed rights and duties must be defined equitably and take into account the concerns of industrialized as well as of developing countries. The United States stands ready to define its responsibilities in a humane and cooperative spirit.

Fifth, finally, a world community must harness science and technology for the benefit of all.

We must begin to match our remarkable technological skills with our equally remarkable technological needs. We must find the means for the cooperative and judicious development of our energy resources. We must responsibly confront the problems of population growth, which are fast pushing humanity towards the limits of what our earth can sustain. We must embark on a new scientific revolution to increase agricultural productivity in all lands. No field of human endeavor is so dependent upon an open world for its advancement; no field is so in need of international cooperation to cope with its potential dangers.

Mr. President, fellow delegates:

Are we prepared to accept and infuse our labors with a new vision? Or shall we content ourselves with a temporary pause in the turmoil that has wracked our century? Shall we proceed with one-sided demands and sterile confrontations? Or shall we proceed in a spirit of compromise produced by a sense of common destiny? We are convinced that we must move from hesitant cooperation born of necessity to genuine collective effort based on common purpose.

It is a choice no country can make alone. We can repeat old slogans or strive for new hope. We can fill the record of our proceedings with acrimony or we can dedicate ourselves to dealing with man's deepest needs. The ideal of a world community may be decried as unrealistic —but great constructions have always been ideals before they can become realities. Let us dedicate ourselves to this noblest of all possible goals and achieve at last what has so long eluded us: true understanding and tolerance among mankind.

Gromyko:

Mr. President, distinguished delegates, the past year was rich in important international events. Some of them, even taken individually, constitute historic milestones. But the main feature characteristic of all of them in their totality is the development and consolidation of the turn from a long period of tension in the world towards detente and businesslike co-operation. From this standpoint the past year may in a sense be called a turning point.

An end has been put to the war in Vietnam. The flames of one of the most dangerous hotbeds of war have been extinguished. The just cause of the Vietnamese people has won a major victory.

In South Asia further steps are being taken to lessen tensions which in the past have repeatedly given rise to open conflicts. It is gratifying that all three States of the Subcontinent—India, Pakistan and Bangladesh—have joined in this process.

Even more discernible are the positive shifts in the European situation. The task of normalizing relations between the States of the East and the West of Europe is practically close to accomplishment. We express the hope that no one will create artificial obstacles in the way of completing this process. The convening of the all-European Conference has opened a new and extremely important stage in providing security and organizing peaceful co-operation on the scale of the whole continent.

The danger of a global confrontation between the two world social systems, which would inevitably result in a dreadful catastrophe for the whole of mankind, is diminishing. This is how the entire world assesses the Agreement between the USSR and the USA on the Prevention of Nuclear War concluded during the visit of the General Secretary of the Central Committee of the CPSU, Leonid Brezhnev, to the United States.

The principle of peaceful co-existence is now not only recognized as the only possible basis of relations between socialist and capitalist countries, it is ever increasingly being implemented and embodied in treaties and agreements. The process of detente is becoming broader and deeper, embracing an ever greater number of States and ever more important spheres of relations between them....

The changes for the better in international affairs are evoking special gratification in the Soviet Union. This is certainly not because other peoples are less interested in peace than the Soviet people. The fact that the trend towards detente and co-operation is gaining ground we also regard as a proof of the correctness of the consistent foreign policy line of the Soviet Union.

Motto of Soviet Foreign Policy

Peace and friendship among nations have always been the motto of Soviet foreign policy and its invariable goal.... Now it must be clear to any unprejudiced person that this is not a policy based on considerations of the moment but the long-term, permanent policy of the Soviet Union. It is determined by the very nature of our social system.

The turn taken by developments in the international arena over the past few years convincingly shows that the securing of durable peace on earth is not merely a noble, though remote, ideal but a feasible goal of practical policy.

No less obvious is another fact. The positive results achieved up to now did not emerge of their own accord....

There is probably no government that would not declare its desire for peace, durable peace and even eternal peace. But for these declarations not to remain mere dreams they should be buttressed by persistent day-to-day work.

This is what the Soviet Union and our allies are calling for. And they are not simply calling for it, but, closely coordinating their efforts and taking into account the evolution of the international situation, they are coming out with concrete initiatives.... [I]t is essential that all the States concerned should by joint effort consolidate the changes that have taken place in the international arena, consistently implement the agreements and treaties that have been concluded and steadily move forward to the main goal of ensuring durable peace.

It is no secret to anyone that detente has its adversaries whose resistance should not be underestimated. Certain inertia has to be overcome too. After all, what we are dealing with is the solution of problems that have been piling up for years, and in certain instances for decades.

But still greater is the number of those who support detente, and it is necessary that their activity increase and not subside....

In the conditions of detente possibilities are widening for nonaligned and neutral States to exert positive influence on the development of the international situation. No small number of useful initiatives, including some within the framework of the United Nations, were given a start thanks to the political weight of those countries....

Detente by its very nature cannot be confined to the improvement of relations between several States or to individual geographical regions. To acquire an irreversible character detente should be the concern of all States and ultimately become universal....

One sometimes hears it said that since the Soviet Union and the United States are improving their relations and coming to important agreements which promote the lessening of international tensions, the other States have nothing else to do but wait passively. Some go even further and try to spread groundless suspicions implying that this could be detrimental to the interests of third countries.

Quite apart from the fact that such allegations distort, wittingly or unwittingly, the true state of affairs, in practice they can only lead to curbing initiative and hindering detente....

It is important to chart political routes to a further detente. But it is no less important to translate them into real life. Efforts in this direction cannot be confined to government offices. They must be supplemented by broad and unremitting action in favour of peace on the part of various social forces....

Of course, the situation in the world has improved in the past year. It is immeasurably better than five or ten years ago. But does this mean that the international horizon has fully cleared? No, far from it.

Hotbeds of War Danger

There still exist hotbeds of war danger in several parts of the world....

The situation in Indochina still remains complicated. Hostilities are relatively limited there now. But full detente in the region requires the completion of a political settlement in accordance with the legitimate rights and interests of all the peoples of Indochina.

The key to this lies in strict observance by all parties of the Paris Agreement on Ending the War and Restoring Peace in Vietnam, in respect for the understandings reached in Laos and in permitting the people of Cambodia to settle their domestic affairs at their own discretion without foreign interference.

True to its convictions of internationalism, the Soviet Union will continue to render the necessary assistance and support to the Democratic Republic of Vietnam and to side with the patriotic forces of Indochina.

Again and again we have to go back to the situation in the Middle East—and it must be said outright that the situation there is dangerous due to the continuing aggression of Israel. Can the fact that today the hotbed of war is smouldering there rather than blazing give any reason for complacency? There is a risk of the flames of war breaking out at any moment. And who can foretell the consequences of that?

Before the eyes of the whole world the aggressor seized foreign territory and continues to hold it by force. This involves gross violations of the rules of international law. Suffice it to recall just the latest provocative actions in respect of the neighboring Arab countries, actions that were quite recently condemned once again by the Security Council. And this is not merely an act of recklessness or desperation by a group of individuals but the considered policy of the State of Israel.

No Arab can be persuaded that he should put up with the existing situation. The only wish of the Arab States who fell victim to imperialist aggression is to retrieve what was seized from them by force. And they are right.

As before, the Soviet Union is convinced that the Middle East problem is soluble. There is a basis for this, and it is constituted by the well-known decisions of the Security Council. They enjoy the support of the overwhelming majority of member States of our Organisation—a fact that was once again confirmed by the recent discussion of the Middle East problem in the United Nations. The refusal of the aggressor to accept a settlement is becoming ever more challenging.

Everything must be done to ensure that both in Israel and in those countries and circles which patronize its present policy it should finally be understood that a more sober approach is necessary and that they really take the path of solving the problem.

As to the Soviet Union, its position is clear: the situation in the Middle East should be settled on the basis of a complete, we repeat, a complete withdrawal of Israeli troops from the occupied Arab territories, on the basis of respect for the independence and the inalienable rights of the States and peoples of the region, including the Arab people of Palestine. Our principal decisive interest in the Middle East is to assist in reaching a just and durable peace. With all clarity the Soviet Union reiterates this from the rostrum of the United Nations....

The problem of problems is the continuing arms race. The development of the means of mass destruction and the stockpiling of weapons have long ago exceeded the level beyond which their use becomes absurd, for as V. I. Lenin foresaw as long as half a century ago, it leads to undermining the very conditions for the existence of human society. The perilousness of further increasing military arsenals should be clear to all. Yet only in recent years has it become possible to make the first steps towards curbing the arms race.

It would be wrong to underestimate the importance of the measures already taken. They put certain barriers in the way of an unrestricted proliferation of weapons and, in the first place, the most destructive types of weapons....

However, further efforts will be required which naturally cannot be confined to the two nuclear powers, even though the most powerful militarily. In particular, we would welcome the willingness of other States to adhere to the principles jointly formalized by the Soviet Union and the United States of renouncing the use of force and taking decisive measures to prevent the outbreak of nuclear war, which would be of paramount importance for ensuring universal and stable peace.

Today military needs still consume enormous resources. The development of military programmes is continuing....

No one can conceivably deny that the solution of the problems of disarmament involves great difficulties. But those international issues which have been successfully resolved by now also seemed to be insolvable at the beginning. Therefore, references to objective difficulties do not reveal the essence. The crux of the matter lies in policy. And responsibility for policy rests with people, primarily those who are entrusted with power, those who stand at the helm of government.... However, today we will have more experience in settling international issues than we had yesterday. And that experience shows that in the field of disarmament, too, real progress can be achieved in certain directions. What is needed is to observe in practice the truth that is likely to be universally recognized in theory: instead of advocating the thesis of "all or nothing at all" we should single out one by one those problems on which agreement can already be reached at this stage and solve them. Life has shown that such an approach is practicable even as regards the most sensitive security problems involving the main type of weapons, rocket-nuclear arms. Is not that the implication of the relevant Soviet-American agreements?

There is another aspect which does not raise any doubts either. These agreements would not have been possible if they had put either side at a disadvantage and if the principle of equal security had not been scrupulously observed.

But if two countries have found it possible to start limiting their arms on such a basis, then why cannot, say, five powers do likewise, provided, of course, that the security of neither of them is prejudiced? This being the case, what could impede the application of such a method in regard to a larger number of countries? The more States participate in the practical solution of the disarmament problem, the more tangible will be the benefit for the security of all peoples.

Furthermore, the successes scored in the process of detente make it possible, in our view, to allocate already now substantial additional means to assist the developing countries.

Soviet Proposal for Aiding Developing Countries

Proceeding from all this, the Soviet Union proposes that the following question be included in the agenda of the twenty-eighth session of the General Assembly of the United Nations as an important and urgent item: "Reduction of the military budgets of States permanent members of the UN Security Council by 10 per cent and the use of a part of the funds thus saved for providing assistance to developing countries...."

We consider it advisable to take as a starting point for the proposed reduction the level of military budgets for the current year of 1973. The part of the funds released as a result of the reduction to be used for rendering assistance to developing States could amount, for example, to 10 per cent.

Of course, this measure requires the participation of all States permanent members of the Security Council without exception. It is also desirable that other States possessing big economic and military potentials should reduce their military budgets, too.

We suggest that the funds allocated for purposes of economic assistance to developing countries should first of all be granted to those countries of Asia, Africa and Latin America which have experienced great difficulties this year because of grave natural disasters, drought or floods.

This distribution of the said funds should be carried out on an equitable basis. The amounts of funds to be granted to individual countries and the time-limits for granting them could be determined by an international committee established on a temporary basis and consisting of representatives of developing countries, States permanent members of the Security Council and the countries reducing their military budgets.

It is obvious that the States carrying out the reduction of military budgets would also benefit from the implementation of such measures. They would obtain a possibility to channel considerable resources for the peaceful needs of their peoples, for the improvement of their living standards....

The Soviet Union believes that the early implementation of the solemn declaration of the General Assembly on behalf of the States members of the United Nations concerning the renunciation by them of the use of force in international relations and the permanent prohibition of the use of nuclear weapons would be an effective means for making one of the principles of the UN Charter a law of international life. This requires the adoption by the Security Council of a resolute decision on this question.

For its part, the Soviet Union is ready to come to an agreement and duly formalize with all, and I stress, with all nuclear Powers mutual obligations on the non-use of force, including the simultaneous prohibition of the use of nuclear weapons....

Within a mere eighteen months or two years a great distance has been covered in relations between the Soviet Union and the United States of America. As a result of the Soviet-American summit talks during President R. Nixon's visit to Moscow in May 1972 and the visit of the General Secretary of the Central Committee of the CPSU, Leonid Brezhnev, to the United States this year a good foundation has been laid for such a development of relations between the two countries which is fully consistent with the principle of peaceful co-existence and which reveals the tremendous opportunities latent in it. A series of agreements have been concluded covering various fields. All these agreements have been made public and they speak for themselves. The accords do not remain on paper: a lot is being done to fill them with specific content.

It is of fundamental importance that the improvement in Soviet-American relations is being achieved with reciprocal regard for the opposite nature of the social systems and ideologies of the two States and on the understanding that the rapprochement between the USSR and the United States is not directed against anyone and is without prejudice to anyone's interests.

The Soviet Union is convinced that if both sides strictly fulfill all the obligations assumed, including the rigorous observance of the cardinal principle of international relations, non-interference in each other's internal affairs—and this is what we proceed from—Soviet-American relations will be a permanent positive factor of international peace—and that is of historic importance....

The Soviet Union is ready to expand relations of mutually advantageous cooperation with all countries of Europe and of other continents which for their part desire this—whether in seeking solutions to topical political international problems or in achieving large-scale economic agreements, uniting efforts to utilize the fruits of scientific and technological progress, or in conducting mutual exchanges of spiritual values.

The opening of the present session of the General Assembly coincided with the commencement of the second stage of the Conference on Security and Co-operation in Europe. This is a major endeavour which has no precedent. It is for the first time that all European States, and the USA and Canada, have gathered around the same table in order to jointly define measures which would contribute to assuring the peoples of Europe of a peaceful future for the historically foreseeable period.

The Soviet Union appraises the prospects for the work of the Conference with a considerable degree of optimism. Its participants have already to a certain extent found a common language, at least they do not differ in realizing that the Conference is faced with tasks of great importance which require a businesslike and constructive consideration. If such an approach prevails to the end, the participants in the Conference will be able with a feeling of satisfaction to put on the scales of history their contribution to the strengthening of universal peace. This will be to the benefit not only of the States directly concerned with European affairs but of all peoples.

There exists a possibility to score a good, and, in terms of its potential impact, even a historic success as a result of the Conference. To that end it is only necessary for all the participants to display a responsible and serious approach to the problems confronting them. No one should yield to the temptation of teaching others how to manage their internal affairs. It is no secret that there are some who would like to try to impose their own domestic practices upon others. But internal practices, internal laws constitute the line on the threshold of each State at which others must stop.

Objections to Interference in Internal Affairs

Were we to take the path of imposing our practices upon other countries, be it in the field of economic affairs or in the field of ideology, then those who are trying to persuade us to adopt alien laws, morals or customs would probably object. And this is understandable and justifiable. Were States and their representatives in the United Nations to attempt to act in such a manner, none of us here would ever move a step forward in solving serious problems, and people would try—not without reason—to draw an analogy between the activities of the United Nations and the biblical legend about Babel, when people ceased to understand one another and failed to complete what they wanted to build.

In the meantime, some in the West are not loath to launch noisy propaganda campaigns and even to resort to methods of blackmail in order to cover up their own attempts to interfere in the affairs of other countries. Sometimes things reach the point when attempts are made to arrogate the right to instruct others as to who should resolve matters of emigration from this or that country, and how, and in what capacity, and within what time-limit, and where specifically. In so doing, they do not scruple to heap praise on those who represent no one and who are—willingly or thoughtlessly—nothing more than blind instruments operated by the forces opposed to international detente.

The Soviet Union vigorously rejects that approach and condemns it. We shall allow nobody to interfere in our internal affairs....

The main thing today is not to let the poisoned atmosphere created around trumped-up matters overshadow the major, and really important tasks faced by States.

The Soviet Union considers it desirable to supplement political detente in Europe with a military detente. This purpose may be served by another major endeavor involving the participation of several States, namely the negotiations on the mutual reduction of forces and armaments in Central Europe due to begin on October 30, 1973.

In connection with the positive changes in the international situation prerequisites are increasing for considering in a new light the situation in Asia, too....

The Soviet Union is in favour of the equal participation of all Asian countries, without any exception, in the system of collective security. The intention to have collective security in Asia directed against any State is quite alien to us, regardless of all attempts to ascribe it to us....

We believe that the relaxation of international tensions is conducive to a situation where young States could, in peace, devote all their efforts and resources to economic and social progress and to the improvement of the living standards of their peoples and shape their future without fear of outside interference.

The healthier the general climate in the world, the more outdated look the surviving remnants of colonialism, reservations of apartheid and racial discrimination, the more wrathful condemnation they merit and the more vigorous struggle is necessary to bring about their complete elimination. The immediate duty of the United Nations is to contribute to an early and complete elimination of these shameful survivals of colonialism, wherever they still exist, be it Angola or Mozambique, Bissau or Southern Rhodesia, South or South-West Africa....

The peoples expect from the United Nations measures contributing to the further invigoration of the international situation. With favourable changes taking place in the world possibilities are expanding for the United Nations to make its important contribution to consolidating detente and to making it stable and irreversible.

For its part, the Soviet Union will spare no effort for the triumph of the cause of peace on earth. This is the essence of its peaceful policy and its Peace Programme advanced by the 24th Congress of the Communist Party of the Soviet Union. Every State, every political leader may rest assured that the Soviet Union will continue to be their reliable partner at any time and in any place where activities are conducted against the danger of war and for the benefit of peace.

▼▼▼

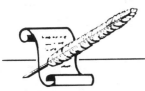

October

AGNEW RESIGNATION

October 10, 1973

Vice President Spiro T. Agnew resigned Oct. 10 in the face of charges that he had accepted payoffs from contractors while serving as executive of Baltimore County, as Governor of Maryland, and later as Vice President. Under investigation in Maryland for alleged violations of conspiracy, extortion, bribery and tax statutes, Agnew agreed to resign and plead "nolo contendere" (no contest) to a single charge of federal income tax evasion. The plea resulted from a month of White House-initiated plea bargaining between the Justice Department and Agnew's attorneys. Agnew said in a letter to Nixon Oct. 10 that because of the "long, divisive and debilitating struggle in the Congress and the courts" that would be necessary to conclude his case, he felt it was "in the best interests of the Nation" that he resign.

Only the second Vice President in history to resign (John C. Calhoun had done so in 1832), Agnew continued to profess his innocence even as he submitted his official resignation. He had informed President Nixon of his decision the evening of Oct. 9. On Oct. 12 President Nixon nominated House Minority Leader Gerald R. Ford (R Mich.) to fill the vacancy. (See p. 969.) The 25th Amendment, ratified in 1967, required the President to nominate a vice presidential successor to take office upon confirmation by both houses of Congress. In the interim, Speaker of the House Carl Albert (D Okla.) stood next in line for the presidency.

Minutes after the delivery of his letter of resignation, Agnew appeared in U.S. District Judge Walter E. Hoffman's Baltimore courtroom, pleaded no contest to charges of failing to report $29,500 in 1967 income, and was fined $10,000 and sentenced to three years of unsupervised probation. The fine and the probationary sentence on the tax charge were the product of a complicated plea bargaining process involving the Justice Department, Agnew's attorneys and White House counsel J. Fred Buzhardt Jr. After three weeks of bargaining over the amount of evidence against Agnew to be made public, the Justice Department agreed to request a lenient sentence in exchange for the Vice President's resignation and his acceptance of sentencing on the charge of tax evasion. An extensive 40-page document outlining other instances of alleged misconduct by Agnew was submitted to the court by the Justice Department without pressing charges.

Agnew's Fight Against Charges

On Aug. 1, 1973, U.S. Attorney for Maryland George Beall had informed Agnew's attorney, Judah Best, that the Vice President was under investigation for allegedly accepting kickbacks from private architectural and engineering firms that had been awarded state or federal contracts. During the next two months, Agnew made a three-pronged effort to curb the probe. Asserting that leaks to the press about the investigation jeopardized his civil rights, he requested Attorney General Elliot L. Richardson on Aug. 21 to investigate leaking of information from the Justice Department. On Sept. 25, citing precedents for a congressional investigation of alleged vice presidential misconduct, Agnew urged, in a letter to Speaker Carl Albert, that the House take over the probe into his earlier activities. In addition, Agnew's attorneys on Sept. 28 petitioned the special federal grand jury in Baltimore to halt the inquiry on the ground that a vice president could not be indicted while in office.

All of these moves failed. Albert's prompt rejection of the bid for a House investigation foreclosed possibilities that Congress would relieve the pressure of the imminent court proceedings. The Justice Department on Sept. 27 began presentation of evidence to the special federal grand jury in Baltimore. In arguments filed Oct. 5, the government contended that while a President could not be indicted while in office because such action would "incapacitate" the government, a vice president could be indicted because his functions were not "indispensable to the orderly operation of government." His options dwindling, Agnew appeared an isolated man.

In the middle of it all, refusing to take sides—and thus, in the view of many Agnew sympathizers, tacitly contributing to the Vice President's political destruction—was President Nixon. Although Agnew met periodically with Nixon throughout the two months prior to his resignation, conflicting reports emerged on the President's reaction to the *affair. Staving off attempts to link the Agnew probe to the Watergate investigation, the White House denied Aug. 14 that Nixon had asked the Vice President not to turn over his subpoenaed records to prosecutors lest an adverse precedent be established that might force Nixon to relinquish Watergate documents. Responding to news reports in mid-September, the White House denied there was "a disposition on the part of the White House or the people in the White House to force the Vice President to resign."*

With this supporting background, Agnew on Sept. 29 attempted to mobilize public opinion in his favor. In an emotional windup to a speech before 2,000 delegates to a convention of the National Federation of Republican Women in Los Angeles, he accused top Justice Department officials of attempting to destroy him with "malicious and outrageous" news leaks. Without mentioning him by name but clearly referring to Assistant Attorney General Henry E. Petersen, head of the criminal division, Agnew offered the theory that Petersen, and others in the department, were trying to recover reputations which he said had been lost through "ineptness and blunder" in the Watergate affair and other criminal investigations.

"I'm their big trophy," said Agnew. "Well, I'm not going to fall down and be his victim, thank you." Though he made it clear that he regarded his political career as beyond redemption, the Vice President said that he would not resign even if indicted. Richardson quickly came to the defense of Petersen by saying the Assistant Attorney General would not still be at his post if the government doubted his competence.

Final Bargaining, Resignation, Sentencing

By Oct. 1, events began to move quickly. That day, the White House confirmed reports that Buzhardt was involved in a "direct and indirect way" in negotiations between Agnew's lawyers and the Justice Department. In court, the Justice Department continued to hit hard at the arguments of the Agnew defense team, contesting the line that a vice president was immune from prosecution and attacking Agnew's claims of a calculated campaign of news leaks. Buzhardt and Judah Best, Agnew's attorney, conferring Oct. 5-6, reached agreement on the terms under which Agnew would resign and accept sentencing on the single charge of income tax evasion. According to Agnew's attorneys, two provisions were crucial to the final agreement: Agnew would be free to deny in court the information contained in the Justice Department's outline of other alleged misconduct and he would be able to review the evidence compiled against him.

On Oct. 10, Agnew formally submitted his resignation, pleaded no contest to the single tax charge, and was sentenced. Still professing innocence, he told newsmen upon leaving the courtroom that he planned to address the nation about his case. Five days later, on Oct. 15, via national television, he bade farewell to the American people and blamed news leaks for the legal troubles that led to his resignation. Although he said he did not want to bow out "in a paroxysm of bitterness," he unleashed an attack on those who "improperly and unconscionably" leaked details of the grand jury investigation and on the news media that published the "scurrilous and inaccurate" reports. He also repeated his earlier denials of wrongdoing. As for his court plea of no contest, which Judge Hoffman called the "full equivalent of a plea of guilty," Agnew said it was made "because it was the only quick way to resolve the situation," the only way "to still the raging storm."

Included below are the following documents: (1) text of letter from Vice President Spiro T. Agnew to U.S. Attorney George Beall, dated Aug. 14, 1973, making available Agnew's financial records to the Maryland prosecutors; (2) text of statement by President Nixon released after Nixon conferred with Agnew on Sept. 25; (3) text of statement by Attorney General Elliot L. Richardson, Sept. 25, announcing the Justice Department's intention to present evidence against Agnew to the federal grand jury in Baltimore; (4) text of Agnew's letter to Speaker Carl Albert, dated Sept. 25, requesting a House of Representatives investigation into charges of vice presidential misconduct; (5) excerpts from a 40-page document, submitted to the grand jury Oct. 10, listing payoffs the government said Agnew accepted; (6) text of Agnew's letter of resignation to Secretary of State Henry A. Kissinger; (7) text of Agnew's letter to Nixon confirming the Vice President's resignation; and (8) text of Nixon's response to Agnew's letter of resignation:

Vice President Agnew's letter to U.S. District Attorney George Beall, Aug. 14, 1973:

Dear Mr. Beall:

In your letter of August 1st you request that I make certain of my personal records available to you. I am prepared to do so immediately.

The records you request have been assembled and are at my offices. You and any of your assistants may inspect them there at any time you may desire. My staff have been instructed to give you the fullest cooperation. Should you wish, they will prepare copies for you of any of the records. And you may, of course, compare the copies with the originals to verify their accuracy.

You understand that, by making these records available to you I do not acknowledge that you or any grand jury have any right to records of the Vice President. Nor do I acknowledge the propriety of any grand jury investigation of possible wrongdoing on the part of the Vice President so long as he occupies that office. These are difficult constitutional questions which need not at this moment be confronted.

As I advised you many months ago, I wish in no way to impede your investigation. I have done nothing wrong. I have nothing to hide. And I have no desire save that justice be done speedily and efficiently. Accordingly, the records you request are now available to you.

My desire to cooperate in your investigation does not stop here. I am eager to be of any help I can. Specifically, should you wish, I shall be glad to meet with you and your colleagues for a personal interview so that I may answer any questions you may have.

Very Truly Yours,
/s/Spiro T. Agnew

President Nixon's Sept. 25 statement after meeting with Agnew:

I held a discussion with the Vice President this morning about the charges that have been made against him in the course of an investigation being conducted in Baltimore under the direction of the United States Attorney for Maryland.

This discussion followed an assessment of the situation which was presented to me by Attorney General Richardson and Assistant Attorney General Petersen.

During our discussion, the Vice President again—as he had done in our previous meetings—denied the charges that have been made against him. He also informed me that he intended to request that the House of Representatives undertake an inquiry into the matter.

I wish to emphasize my strong belief that during these proceedings the Vice President is entitled to the same presumption of innocence which is the right of any citizen, and which lies at the heart of our system of justice. During these past four and a half years, the Vice President has served his country with dedication and distinction. He has won the respect of millions of Americans for the candor and courage with which he has addressed the controversial issues of our time. As he moves through this difficult period, I urge all Americans to accord the Vice President the basic, decent consideration and presumption of innocence that are both his right and his due.

Attorney General Richardson's Sept. 25 statement:

Recently there has been widespread and highly varied public speculation regarding both the substance and the procedure related to the investigation of the Vice President. Although it would be improper to discuss the substance of the investigation at this stage, I feel it necessary to clarify certain procedural points in order to reduce unwarranted and potentially harmful speculation.

In the period of Sept. 12 to the present, meetings and discussions have taken place between myself, Assistant Attorney General Henry E. Petersen, and United States Attorney for the District of Maryland, George Beall, representing the Department of Justice, and Messrs. Jay H. Topkis, Martin London and Judah Best, counsel to the Vice President. The Department of Justice agreed to participate in these meetings in response to a request by the Vice President's counsel to discuss procedural aspects of the case and options available to the Vice President. The department did so with a view toward the possible prompt resolution of problems which might otherwise result in a constitutional dilemma of potentially serious consequence to the nation. These discussions took place with the approval of the President's counsel and the President.

The discussions have, however, failed to yield a satisfactory resolution. It has proved impossible, to this point, to reconcile the Vice President's interests, as represented by his counsel, with the Department of Justice's perception of its responsibility to assure that justice is pursued fully and fairly.

On Sept. 13, I authorized U.S. Attorney Beall to present evidence regarding the Vice President to the federal grand jury sitting in Baltimore. It is the intention of the Department of Justice to present such evidence to the grand jury when it reconvenes on Sept. 27.

The grand jury will be used, in accordance with well-established practice, as an investigative body. This is a traditional function of a federal grand jury, whose role, as representative of the community, is to ensure the fairness of the investigative process.

Agnew's letter of Sept. 25 to House Speaker Carl Albert:

The Honorable Carl Albert
Speaker of The House of Representatives
The House of Representatives
Washington, D.C. 20515

Dear Mr. Speaker:

I respectfully request that the House of Representatives undertake a full inquiry into the charges which have apparently been made against me in the course of an investigation by the United States Attorney for the District of Maryland.

This request is made in the dual interests of preserving the Constitutional stature of my Office and accomplishing my personal vindication.

After the most careful study, my counsel have advised me that the Constitution bars a criminal proceeding of any kind—federal or state, county or town—against a President or Vice President while he holds office.

Accordingly, I cannot acquiesce in any criminal proceeding being lodged against me in Maryland or elsewhere. And I cannot look to any such proceeding for vindication.

In these circumstances, I believe, it is the right and duty of the Vice President to turn to the House. A closely parallel precedent so suggests.

Almost a century and a half ago, Vice President Calhoun was beset with charges of improper participation in the profits of an Army contract made while he had been Secretary of War. On December 29, 1826, he addressed to your Body a communication whose eloquent language I can better quote than rival:

"An imperious sense of duty, and a sacred regard to the honor of the station which I occupy, compel me to approach your body in its high character of grand inquest of the nation.

"Charges have been made against me of the most serious nature, and which, if true ought to degrade me from the high station in which I have been placed by the choice of my fellow-citizens, and to consign my name to perpetual infamy.

"In claiming the investigation of the House, I am sensible that, under our free and happy institutions, the conduct of public servants is a fair subject of the closest scrutiny and the freest remarks, and that a firm and faithful discharge of duty affords, ordinarily, ample protection against political attacks; but, when such attacks assume the character of impeachable offences, and become, in some degree, official, by being placed among the public records, an officer thus assailed, however base the instrument used, if conscious of innocence, can look for refuge only to the Hall of the immediate Representatives of the People."

Vice President Calhoun concluded his communication with a "challenge" to "the freest investigation of the House, as the only means effectually to repel this premeditated attack." Your Body responded at once by establishing a select committee, which subpoenaed witnesses and documents, held exhaustive hearings, and submitted a Report on February 13, 1827. The Report, exonerating the Vice President of any wrongdoing, was laid on the table (together with minority views even more strongly in his favor) and the accusations were thereby put to rest.

Like my predecessor Calhoun, I am the subject of public attacks that may "assume the character of impeachable offences," and thus require urgent investigation by the House as the repository of "the sole Power of Impeachment" and the "grand inquest of the nation." No investigation in any other forum could either substitute for the investigation by the House contemplated by Article I, Section 2, Clause 5 of the Constitution or lay to rest in a timely and definitive manner the unfounded charges whose currency unavoidably jeopardizes the functions of my Office.

The wisdom of the Framers of the Constitution in making the House the only proper agency to investigate the conduct of a President or Vice President has been borne out by recent events. Since the Maryland investigation became a matter of public knowledge some seven weeks ago, there has been a constant and ever-broadening stream of rumors, accusations and speculations aimed at me. I regret to say that the source, in many instances, can have been only the prosecutors themselves.

The result has been so to foul the atmosphere that no grand or petit jury could fairly consider this matter on the merits.

I therefore respectfully call upon the House to discharge its Constitutional obligation.

I shall, of course, cooperate fully. As I have said before, I have nothing to hide. I have directed my counsel to deliver forthwith to the Clerk of the House all of my original records of which copies have previously been furnished to the United States Attorney. If there is any other way in which I can be of aid, I am wholly at the disposal of the House.

I am confident that, like Vice President Calhoun, I shall be vindicated by the House.

Respectfully yours,
Spiro T. Agnew

Excerpts from Justice Department document submitting evidence against Agnew to the grand jury, Oct. 10:

I. The Relationship of Mr. Agnew, I. H. Hammerman II and Jerome B. Wolff.

In the spring of 1967, shortly after Mr. Agnew had taken office as Governor of Maryland, he advised Hammerman that it was customary for engineers to make substantial cash payments in return for engineering contracts with the state of Maryland. Mr. Agnew instructed Hammerman to contact Wolff, then the new chairman-director of the Maryland State Roads Commission, to arrange for the establishment of an understanding pursuant to which Wolff would notify Hammerman as to which engineering firms were in line for state contracts so that Hammerman could solicit and obtain from those engineering firms cash payments in consideration therefor.

Hammerman, as instructed, discussed the matter with Wolff, who was receptive but who requested that the cash payments to be elicited from the engineers be split in three equal shares among Agnew, Hammerman and Wolff. Hammerman informed Mr. Agnew of Wolff's attitude; Mr. Agnew informed Hammerman that the split of the cash monies would be 50 per cent for Mr. Agnew, 25 per cent for Hammerman and 25 per cent for Wolff. Hammerman carried that message to Wolff, who agreed to that split.

The scheme outlined above was then put into operation. Over the course of the approximately 18 months of Mr. Agnew's remaining tenure as Governor of Maryland, Hammerman made contact with approximately eight engineering firms. Informed periodically by Wolff as to which engineering firms were in line to receive state contracts, Hammerman successfully elicited from seven engineering firms substantial cash payments pursuant to understandings between Hammerman and the various engineers to whom he was talking that the substantial cash payments were in return for the state work being awarded to those engineering firms. The monies collected in that manner by Hammerman were split (among Hammerman, Agnew and Wolff) in accordance with the understanding earlier reached....

Wolff, as chairman-director of the Maryland State Roads Commission, made initial tentative decisions with regard to which engineering firms should be awarded which state contracts. These tentative decisions would then be discussed by Wolff with Governor Agnew. Although Governor Agnew accorded Wolff's tentative decisions great weight, the Governor always exercised the final decision-making authority....

Hammerman also successfully solicited, at Governor Agnew's instruction, a substantial cash payment from a financial institution in return for that institution's being awarded a major role in the financing of a large issue of state bonds.

II. The Relationship between Mr. Agnew and Allen Green.

Shortly after Mr. Agnew's election in November 1966 as governor of Maryland, he complained to Allen Green, principal of a large engineering firm, about the financial burdens to be imposed upon Mr. Agnew by his role as Governor. Green responded by saying that his company had benefited from state work and had been able to generate some cash funds from which he would be willing to provide Mr. Agnew with some financial assistance. Mr. Agnew indicated that he would be grateful for such assistance.

Beginning shortly thereafter, Green delivered to Mr. Agnew six to nine times a year an envelope containing between $2,000 and $3,000 in cash. Green's purpose was to elicit from the Agnew administration as much state work for his engineering firm as possible. That purpose was clearly understood by Governor Agnew....

Green continued to make cash payments to Vice President Agnew three or four times a year up to and including December 1972. These payments were usually about $2,000 each. The payments were made both in Mr. Agnew's vice presidential office and at his residence in the Sheraton-Park Hotel, Washington, D.C. The payments were not discontinued until after the initiation of the Baltimore County investigation by the United States Attorney for the District of Maryland in January 1973.

III. The Relationship between Mr. Agnew and Lester Matz.

Lester Matz, a principal in another large engineering firm, began making corrupt payments while Mr. Agnew was County Executive of Baltimore County in the early 1960s. In those days, Matz paid 5 per cent of his fees from Baltimore County contracts in cash to Mr. Agnew through one of Mr. Agnew's close associates.

After Mr. Agnew became Governor of Maryland, Matz decided to make his payments directly to Governor Agnew. He made no payments until that summer of 1968 when he and his partner calculated that they owed Mr. Agnew approximately $20,000 in consideration for the work which their firm had already received from the Governor's administration. The $20,000 in cash was generated in an illegal manner and was given by Matz to Governor Agnew in a manila envelope in Governor Agnew's office on or about July 16, 1968....

Matz made no further corrupt payments to Mr. Agnew until shortly after Mr. Agnew became Vice President, at which time Matz calculated that he owed Mr. Agnew approximately $10,000 more from jobs and fees which the Matz firm had received from Governor Agnew's administration since July 1968. After generating $10,000 in cash in an illegal manner, Matz met with Mr. Agnew in the Vice President's office and gave him approximately $10,000 in cash in an envelope....

In or around April 1971, Matz made a cash payment to Vice President Agnew of $2,500 in return for the awarding by the General Services Administration of a contract to a small engineering firm in which Matz had a financial ownership interest. An intermediary was instrumental in the arrangement for that particular corrupt payment.

> *Agnew's letter of resignation, addressed to Secretary of State Kissinger:*

October 10, 1973

The Honorable Henry A. Kissinger
The Secretary of State
Washington, D.C. 20520

Dear Mr. Secretary:

I hereby resign the Office of Vice President of the United States, effective immediately.

Sincerely,

/s / Spiro T. Agnew

Agnew's letter to Nixon:

October 10, 1973

Dear Mr. President:

As you are aware, the accusations against me cannot be resolved without a long, divisive and debilitating struggle in the Congress and in the Courts. I have concluded that, painful as it is to me and to my family, it is in the best interests of the Nation that I relinquish the Vice Presidency.

Accordingly, I have today resigned the Office of Vice President of the United States. A copy of the instrument of resignation is enclosed.

It has been a privilege to serve with you. May I express to the American people, through you, my deep gratitude for their confidence in twice electing me to be Vice President.

Sincerely,

/s/ Spiro T. Agnew

The President
The White House
Washington, D.C.

Nixon's letter to Agnew in response to the Vice President's resignation:

October 10, 1973

Dear Ted:

The most difficult decisions are often those that are the most personal, and I know your decision to resign as Vice President has been as difficult as any facing a man in public life could be. Your departure from the Administration leaves me with a great sense of personal loss. You have been a valued associate throughout these nearly five years that we have served together. However, I respect your decision, and I also respect the concern for the national interest that led you to conclude that a resolution of the matter in this way, rather than through an extended battle in the Courts and the Congress, was advisable in order to prevent a protracted period of national division and uncertainty.

As Vice President, you have addressed the great issues of our times with courage and candor. Your strong patriotism, and your profound dedication to the welfare of the Nation, have been an inspiration to all who have served with you as well as to millions of others throughout the country.

I have been deeply saddened by this whole course of events, and I hope that you and your family will be sustained in the days ahead by a well-justified pride in all that you have contributed to the Nation by your years of service as Vice President.

Sincerely,

/s/ Richard Nixon

The Vice President
Executive Office Building
Washington, D.C.

COURTS ON WHITE HOUSE TAPES

October 12, 1973

In a precedent-setting decision handed down Oct. 12, the Circuit Court of Appeals for the District of Columbia ruled that claims of executive privilege and presidential immunity did not negate President Nixon's obligation to turn over White House tapes to the Watergate grand jury. The historic 5-2 ruling upheld in substance the Aug. 29 decision of U.S. District Judge John J. Sirica which had marked the first time a president of the United States had been ordered to provide evidence to a grand jury. Both Sirica and the appellate court ordered Nixon to make available nine subpoenaed tapes of White House conversations for in camera inspection and determination of the claim of executive privilege. The Court of Appeals gave Nixon until Oct. 19 to work out an alternative arrangement with special Watergate prosecutor Archibald Cox, appeal the decision to the Supreme Court or comply with its order.

Nixon apparently chose to seek an out-of-court settlement with prosecutor Cox. On Oct. 19, Nixon announced a "compromise plan" aimed at circumventing production of the original tapes and instead delivering an authenticated presidentially prepared summary to the court. Reportedly believing the summary to be an ample concession, President Nixon ordered Attorney General Elliot L. Richardson to direct Cox to cease further attempts to gain access to the presidential tapes through the judicial process. The refusal by Cox to carry out the compromise plan exploded Oct. 20 in the firing of Cox, and the resignations of Richardson and Deputy Attorney General William D. Ruckelshaus. (See p. 859.)

As a storm of public reaction gained strength across the nation and the possibility loomed larger that President Nixon would be held in contempt of court for not presenting the tapes to Judge Sirica, Nixon's lawyer Charles Alan Wright appeared in Sirica's courtroom Oct. 23 to announce quietly that the President would comply with Sirica's order, affirmed by the appeals court. In disclosing the totally unexpected reversal, Wright told the court that the President still maintained his previous position but said that even if the court upheld it, "there would have been those who would have said the President is defying the law." Wright added: "This President does not defy the law and he has authorized me to say he will comply in full with the orders of the court."

The surprise announcement of compliance did not end the tapes controversy. Rather, it only set the stage for another set of disquieting discoveries of coincidental absences of certain material. First it was disclosed that two of the subpoenaed tapes did not exist at all. Hearings were begun on the tapes, before Sirica, in an effort to trace their production, safekeeping, and the record of persons who had had access to them. During those sessions, there were still more surprises—chief among them the fact that significant "gaps" existed in the remaining subpoenaed tapes.

Background of Final Agreement

The final agreement to relinquish the White House tapes climaxed months of legal arguments over the grand jury's and the special prosecutor's rights to the taped conversations. In handing down the first decision on the White House tapes Aug. 29, Sirica directed Nixon to turn over the nine tapes subpoenaed by Cox. He ruled that the tapes be presented for in camera examination. Sirica also ruled that his court had jurisdiction on the issue of executive privilege in the case and authority to enforce the subpoena demanding production of the tapes. Rejecting Nixon's claim of presidential immunity, the judge said he had found "unpersuasive" the argument that the constitutional separation of powers shielded the President from compulsory court process. On the issue of executive privilege, Sirica admitted that his examination of the tapes might indeed "compromise" that right. But he said it would be an "extremely limited infraction and in this case an unavoidable one," because it was not for the President alone to decide whether the privilege was properly asserted.

Caution had been the signal characteristic of proceedings in Sirica's courtroom. Cognizant both of the historic nature of the confrontation mounted over the presidential tapes and of the judiciary's inability to enforce its orders, the judge sought a middle road, a compromise, instead of collision. Sirica stated clearly that he was attempting to "walk the middle ground between failure to decide the question of privilege at one extreme, and a wholesale delivery of the tapes to the grand jury at the other."

A statement issued Aug. 30 from the Western White House said that Nixon would appeal Sirica's order. Cox said Aug. 29 that he was "very pleased" and would seek to expedite the appeals proceedings. Sen. Sam J. Ervin Jr. (D N.C.), chairman of the Senate Select Committee on Presidential Campaign Activities, called the ruling "a great victory for the search for truth." Sen. Howard Baker (R Tenn.), vice chairman of that committee, said the decision provided "adequate safeguards on the national security and separation of powers issues" growing out of the dispute. Later, on Oct. 17, Sirica dismissed a separate suit for access to presidential tapes by Ervin's committee on the ground that a federal district court did not have the jurisdiction to settle a dispute between a Senate committee and the White House.

Both sides chose to appeal Sirica's ruling, the White House seeking a reversal and Cox seeking delivery of the tapes directly to the grand jury without judicial intervention. In appealing Sirica's decision Sept. 7, Cox first asked that the tapes be handed over directly to the grand jury without judicial intervention. But, should the court affirm in camera *inspection, he then asked that standards be laid down for that procedure. He went on to suggest that he be allowed to participate in examination of the tapes so that he would have an opportunity to point out to Sirica the relevance of information contained on the tapes as it might pertain to the grand jury investigation.*

The White House rested its appeal on the argument that disclosure of the subpoenaed tapes would be equivalent to "breaching the wall of confidentiality" of presidential conversations. Nixon's lawyers contended that the President's discussions with aides were in pursuit of Nixon's "constitutional duty to see that the laws are faithfully executed," and, because of their nature, were exempt from grand jury scrutiny. In oral arguments Sept. 11, Wright cautioned that to uphold Sirica's order would lay open the way for Watergate defendants to gain access to sensitive national security information. Wright conceded that tradition was "very strong that judges should have the last word" in citing the evidence to be brought forward, but he said that there were times "when that simply cannot be true."

On Sept. 13, the appeals court, in an unusual move, sent a memorandum to Nixon, Sirica and Cox, asking them to try to settle their dispute without further court action. The court suggested that Nixon, or his representative, Cox and Wright might review the tapes to determine what was privileged and what portions should go to the grand jury. On Sept. 20, the deadline for reaching an out-of-court settlement, Cox and Wright reported to the court that they had failed to reach an agreement. It was then up to the appeals court to decide the issue it had hoped to avoid.

"Sovereignty remains at all times with the people, and they do not forfeit through elections the right to have the law construed against and applied to every citizen," stated the appeals court Oct. 12. By a 5-2 vote, the court upheld Sirica's order directing President Nixon to turn over tapes sought by the original grand jury investigating the Watergate break-in and coverup. But the court modified Sirica's order by setting guidelines for handling of the tapes. Sirica was to receive custody of the original recordings and White House lawyers were to be given the opportunity to present the argument of executive privilege for segments of the taped conversations. Sirica was to decide on each of the claims before turning over any portions of the tapes to the grand jury. Joining in the unsigned (per curiam), 44-page majority opinion were Chief Judge David L. Bazelon and Judges J. Skelly Wright, Carl McGowan, Harold Leventhal and Spottswood W. Robinson III. All five were appointed by Democratic presidents. Two lengthy dissenting opinions, giving a view of executive privilege as absolute and exercised at the sole discretion of the President were written by Judges George E. MacKinnon and Malcolm R. Wilkey, both Nixon appointees.

The court found that the grand jury's need for the tapes had been clearly demonstrated. Because Nixon had allowed his present and former aides to testify before the Senate committee on the Watergate affair and because their testimony had indicated a strong possibility that a high-level conspiracy had existed, important evidence of which was contained in statements made during conversations of those aides with Nixon, there was a clear need for the taped records to clear up questions about exactly what was said during those conversations, the court stated. "The practice of judicial review would be rendered capricious—and very likely impotent—if jurisdiction vanished whenever the President personally denoted an executive action or omission as his own." Thus the court ruled that the President is not immune from such orders: "The Constitution makes no mention of special presidential immunities."

The appellate decision emphasized the role of the courts in determining the application of the privilege: "whenever a privilege is asserted... it is the courts that determine the validity of the assertion and the scope of the privilege." To recognize an absolute privilege, the court continued, could lead to a bottling up of information vital to the operations of other branches of government. "The Freedom of Information Act could become nothing more than a legislative statement of unenforceable rights. Support for this kind of mischief simply cannot be spun from incantation of the doctrine of separation of powers."

> Full text of Judge John J. Sirica's Aug. 29 order to President Nixon to turn over subpoenaed White House tapes; excerpts from Sirica's opinion on the tapes; excerpts from the U.S. Circuit Court of Appeals for the District of Columbia

decision Oct. 12 affirming and modifying Sirica's order; and excerpts from the dissenting opinions of Judges George E. MacKinnon and Malcolm R. Wilkey:

IN THE UNITED STATES DISTRICT COURT
FOR THE DISTRICT OF COLUMBIA

IN RE GRAND JURY SUBPOENA)
DUCES TECUM ISSUED TO)
RICHARD M. NIXON, OR ANY)
SUBORDINATE OFFICER, OF-)   Misc. No. 47-73
FICIAL, OR EMPLOYEE WITH)
CUSTODY OR CONTROL OF CERTAIN)
DOCUMENTS OR OBJECTS)

ORDER

This matter having come before the Court on motion of the Watergate Special Prosecutor made on behalf of the June, 1972 grand jury of this district for an order to show cause, and the Court being advised in the premises, it is by the Court this 29th day of August, 1973, for the reasons stated in the attached opinion,

ORDERED that respondent, President Richard M. Nixon, or any subordinate officer, official or employee with custody or control of the documents or objects listed in the grand jury subpoena *duces tecum* of July 23, 1973, served on respondent in this district, is hereby commanded to produce forthwith for the Court's examination *in camera*, the subpoenaed documents or objects which have not heretofore been produced to the grand jury; and it is

FURTHER ORDERED that the ruling herein be stayed for a period of five days in which time respondent may perfect an appeal from the ruling; and it is

FURTHER ORDERED that should respondent appeal from the ruling herein, the above stay will be extended indefinitely pending the completion of such appeal or appeals.

(signed) John J. Sirica
Chief Judge

Excerpts from District Court Chief Judge John J. Sirica's Aug. 29, 1973, opinion on the presidential tapes begin on the following page:

The Court has found it necessary to adjudicate but two questions for the present: (1) whether the Court has jurisdiction to decide the issue of privilege, and (2) whether the Court has authority to enforce the subpoena *duces tecum* by way of an order requiring production for inspection *in camera*. A third question, whether the materials are in fact privileged as against the grand jury, either in whole or in part, is left for subsequent adjudication. For the reasons outlined below, the Court concludes that both of the questions considered must be answered in the affirmative.

A search of the Constitution and the history of its creation reveals a general disfavor of government privileges, or at least uncontrolled privileges. Early in the Convention of 1787, the delegates cautioned each other concerning the dangers of lodging immoderate power in the executive department. This attitude persisted throughout the Convention, and executive powers became a major topic in the subsequent ratification debates. The Framers regarded the legislative department superior in power and importance to the other two and felt the necessity of investing it with some privileges and immunities, but even here an attitude of restraint, as expressed by James Madison, prevailed.... The upshot...regarding a definition of executive privileges was that none were deemed necessary, or at least that the Constitution need not record any.

...Are there, then, any rights or privileges consistent with, though not mentioned in, the Constitution which are necessary to the Executive? One answer may be found in the Supreme Court decision, *United States v. Reynolds,* 346 U.S. 1 (1953). The Court recognized an executive privilege, evidentiary in nature, for military secrets. *Reynolds* held that when a court finds the privilege is properly invoked under the appropriate circumstances, it will, in a civil case at least, suppress the evidence. Thus, it must be recognized that there can be executive privileges that will bar the production of evidence. The Court is willing here to recognize and give effect to an evidentiary privilege based on the need to protect Presidential privacy.

The Court, however, cannot agree with Respondent that it is the Executive that finally determines whether its privilege is properly invoked. The availability of evidence including the validity and scope of privileges, is a judicial decision.... In all the numerous litigations where claims of executive privilege have been interposed, the courts have not hesitated to pass judgment. Executive fiat is not the model of resolution....

The measures a court should adopt in ruling on claims of executive privilege are discussed under Part III herein.

If after judicial examination *in camera,* any portion of the tapes is ruled not subject to privilege, that portion will be forwarded to the grand jury at the appropriate time. To call for the tapes *in camera* is thus tantamount to fully enforcing the subpoena as to any unprivileged matter. Therefore, before the Court can call for production *in camera,* it must have concluded that it has authority to order a President to obey the command of a grand jury subpoena as it relates to unprivileged evidence in his possession. The Court has concluded that it possesses such authority.

Analysis of the question must begin on the well established premises that the grand jury has a right to every man's evidence and that for purposes of gathering evidence, process may issue to anyone.... The important factors are the relevance and materiality of the evidence.... The burden here then, is on the President to define exactly what it is about his office that court process commanding the production of evidence cannot reach there. To be accurate, court process in the form of a subpoena *duces tecum* has already issued to the President, and he acknowledges that...courts possess authority to direct such subpoenas to him. A distinction is drawn, however, between authority to issue a subpoena and authority to command obedience to it. It is this second compulsory process that the President contends may not reach him. The burden yet remains with the President, however, to explain why this must be so. What distinctive quality of the Presidency permits its incumbent to withhold evidence? To argue that the need for Presidential privacy justifies it, is not persuasive. On the occasions when such need justifies suppression, the courts will sustain a privilege. The fact that this is a judicial decision has already been discussed at length, but the opinion of Chief Justice Marshall *(United States v. Burr,* 25 Fed. Cas. 30, 1807) on the topic deserves notice here. When deciding that a subpoena should issue to the President, the Chief Justice made it clear that if certain portions should be excised, it being appropriate to sustain a privilege, the Court would make such a decision upon return of the subpoena....

To argue that it is the constitutional separation of powers that bars compulsory court process from the White House, is also unpersuasive. Such a contention overlooks history. Although courts generally, and this Court in particular, have avoided any interference with the discretionary acts of coordinate branches, they have not hesitated to rule on non-discretionary acts when necessary. Respondent points out that these and other precedents refer to officials other than the President, and that this distinction renders the precedents inapplicable. Such an argument tends to set the White House apart as a fourth branch of government....

The Special Prosecutor has correctly noted that the Framers' intention to lodge the powers of government in separate bodies also included a plan for interaction between departments. A "watertight" division of different functions was never their design. The legislative branch may organize the judiciary and dictate the procedures by which it transacts business. The judiciary may pass upon the constitutionality of legislative enactments—and in some instances define the bounds of Congressional investigations. The executive may veto legislative enactments, and the legislature may override the veto. The executive appoints judges and justices and may bind judicial decisions by lawful executive orders. The judiciary may pass on the constitutionality of executive acts....

That the Court has not the physical power to enforce its order to the President is immaterial to a resolution of the issues. Regardless of its physical power to enforce them, the Court has a duty to issue appropriate orders. The Court cannot say that the Executive's persistence in withholding the tape recordings would "tarnish its reputation," but must admit that it would tarnish the Court's reputation to fail to do what it could in pursuit of justice. In any case, the courts have always enjoyed the good faith of the Executive Branch, even in such dire circumstances as those presented by *Youngstown Sheet & Tube Co.* v. *Sawyer,* 343 U.S. 579 (1952), and there is no reason to suppose that the courts in this instance cannot again rely on that same good faith. Indeed, the President himself has publicly so stated.

It is important also to note here the role of the grand jury. Chief Justice Marshall, in considering whether a subpoena might issue to the President of the United States, observed:

> In the provisions of the constitution, and of the statute, which give to the accused a right to the compulsory process of the court, there is no exception whatever. *(United States* v. *Burr, 25 Fed. Cas. 20, 1807)*

Aaron Burr, it will be remembered, stood before the court accused though not yet indicted. The Chief Justice's statement regarding the accused is equally true with regard to a grand jury: "there is no exception whatever" in its right to the compulsory process of the courts. The Court, while in a position to lend its process in assistance to the grand jury, is thereby in a position to assist justice....

In all candor, the Court fails to perceive any reason for suspending the power of courts to get evidence and rule on questions of privilege in criminal matters simply because it is the President of the United States who holds the evidence. The Burr decision left for another occasion a ruling on whether compulsory process might issue to the President in situations such as this. In the words of counsel, this is "a new question," with little in the way of precedent to guide the Court. But Chief Justice Marshall clearly distinguished the amenability of the King to appear and give testimony under court process and that of this nation's chief magistrate. The conclusion reached here cannot be inconsistent with the view of that great Chief Justice nor with the spirit of the Constitution.

In deciding whether these tape recordings or portions thereof are properly the objects of a privilege, the Court must accommodate two competing policies. On the one hand, as has been noted earlier, is the need to disfavor privileges and narrow their application as far as possible. On the other hand, lies a need to favor the privacy of Presidential deliberations; to indulge a presumption in favor of the President. To the Court, respect for the President, the Presidency, and the duties of the office, gives the advantage to this second policy. This respect, however, does not decide the controversy....

The teaching of *Reynolds* is that a Court should attempt to satisfy itself whether or not a privilege is properly invoked without unnecessarily probing into the material claimed to be privileged. A decision on how far to go will be dictated in part by need for the evidence....

The grand jury's showing of need here is well documented and imposing. The Special Prosecutor has specifically identified by date, time and place each of the eight meetings and the one telephone call involved. Due to the unusual circumstances of having access to sworn public testimony of participants to these conversations, the Special Prosecutor has been able to provide the Court with the conflicting accounts of what transpired. He thus identifies the topics discussed in each instance, the areas of critical conflict in the testimony, and the resolution it is anticipated the tape recordings may render possible. The relative importance of the issues in doubt is revealed....

The point is raised that, as in *Reynolds*, the sworn statements of witnesses should suffice and remove the need for access to documents deemed privileged. Though this might often be the case, here, unfortunately, the witnesses differ, sometimes completely, on the precise matters likely to be of greatest moment to the grand jury. Ironically, need for the taped evidence derives in part from the fact that witnesses *have* testified regarding the subject matter, creating important issues of fact for the grand jury to resolve. It will be noted as well in contradistinction to *Reynolds*, that this is a criminal investigation. Rather than money damages at stake, we deal here in matters of reputation and liberty. Based on this indisputably forceful showing of necessity by the grand jury, the claim of privilege cannot be accepted lightly.

In his Brief in Support, the Special Prosecutor outlines the grand jury's view regarding the validity of the Respondent's claim of privilege. Its opinion is that the right of confidentiality is improperly asserted here. Principally, the Special Prosecutor cites a substantial possibility, based on the sworn testimony of participants, that the privilege is improperly invoked as a cloak for serious criminal wrongdoing....

If the interest served by a privilege is abused or subverted, the claim of privilege fails. Such a case is well described in *Clark* v. *United States*, 289 U.S. 1 (1933), a decision involving the privilege of secrecy enjoyed by jurors....

These principles are, of course, fully applicable throughout government. A court would expect that if the privacy of its deliberations, for example, were ever used to foster criminal conduct or to develop evidence of criminal wrongdoings, any privilege might be barred and privacy breached. So it is that evidentiary privilege asserted against the grand jury may be ruled inapplicable if the interest served by the privilege is subverted.

Nevertheless, without discrediting the strength of the grand jury's position, the Court cannot, as matters now stand, rule that the present claim of privilege is invalid. The President contends that the recorded conversations occurred pursuant to an exercise of his duty to "take care that the laws be faithfully executed." Although the Court is not bound by that conclusion, it is extremely reluctant to finally stand against a declaration of the President of the United States on any but the strongest possible evidence. Need for the evidence requires that a claim not be rejected lightly. The Court is simply unable to decide the question of privilege without inspecting the tapes....

It is true that if material produced is properly the subject of privilege, even an inspection *in camera* may constitute a compromise of privilege. Nevertheless, it would be an extremely limited infraction and in this case an unavoidable one. If privileged and unprivileged evidence are intermingled, privileged portions may be excised so that only unprivileged matter goes before the grand jury (which also meets in secret proceedings). If privileged and unprivileged evidence are so inextricably connected that separation becomes impossible, the whole must be privileged and no disclosure made to the grand jury....

> *Following are excerpts from the District of Columbia Circuit Court of Appeals decision Oct. 12 affirming Judge Sirica's Aug. 29 order and from the dissenting opinions of Judges George E. MacKinnon and Malcolm R. Wilkey:*

PER CURIAM. This controversy concerns an order of the District Court for the District of Columbia entered on August 29, 1973, by Chief Judge John J. Sirica as a means of enforcing a grand jury subpoena *duces tecum* issued to and served on President Richard M. Nixon. The order commands the President, or any subordinate official, to produce certain items identified in the subpoena so that the Court can determine, by *in camera* inspection, whether the items are exempted from disclosure by evidentiary privilege.

Both the President and Special Prosecutor Archibald Cox, acting on behalf of the grand jury empanelled by the District Court in June, 1972, challenge the legality of this order. All members of this Court agree that the District Court had, and this Court has, jurisidiction to consider the President's claim of privilege. The majority of the Court approves the District Court's order, as clarified and modified in part, and otherwise denies the relief requested....

We turn...to the merits of the President's petition. Counsel for the President contend on two grounds that Judge Sirica lacked jurisdiction to order submission of the tapes for inspection. Counsel argue, first, that, so long as he remains in office, the President is absolutely immune from the compulsory process of a court; and, second, that Executive privilege is absolute with respect to presidential communications, so that disclosure is at the sole discretion of the President. This immunity and this absolute privilege are said to arise from the doctrine of separation of powers and by implication from the Constitution itself. It is conceded that neither the immunity nor the privilege is express in the Constitution....

We must...determine whether the President is *legally bound to comply with an order enforcing a subpoena.*

We note first that courts have assumed that they have the power to enter mandatory orders to Executive officials to compel production of evidence.

The courts' assumption of legal power to compel production of evidence within the possession of the Executive surely stands on firm footing. *Youngstown Sheet & Tube* v. *Sawyer,* in which an injunction running against the Secretary of Commerce was affirmed, is only the most celebrated instance of the issuance of compulsory process against Executive officials.... If *Youngstown* still stands, it must stand for the case where the President has himself taken possession and control of the property unconstitutionally seized, and the injunction would be framed accordingly. The practice of judicial review would be rendered capricious—and very likely impotent—if jurisdiction vanished whenever the President personally denoted an Executive action or omission as his own. This is not to say that the President should lightly be named as a party defendant.... Here, unfortunately, the court's order must run directly to the President, because he has taken the unusual step of assuming personal custody of the Government property sought by the subpoena.

The President also attempts to distinguish *United States* v. *Burr,* in which Chief Justice Marshall squarely ruled that a subpoena may be directed to the President. It is true that *Burr* recognized a distinction between the issuance of a subpoena and the ordering of compliance with that subpoena, but the distinction did not concern judicial power or jurisdiction. A subpoena *duces tecum* is an order to produce documents or to show cause why they need not be produced. An order to comply does not make the subpoena more compulsory; it simply maintains its original force....

The clear implication is that the President's special interests may warrant a careful judicial screening of subpoenas after the President interposes an objection, but that some subpoenas will nevertheless be properly sustained by judicial orders of compliance....

The Constitution makes no mention of special presidential immunities. Indeed, the Executive Branch generally is afforded none. This silence cannot be ascribed to oversight. James Madison raised the question of Executive privileges during the Constitutional Convention, and Senators and Representatives enjoy an express, if limited, immunity from arrest, and an express privilege from inquiry concerning "Speech and Debate" on the floors of Congress. Lacking textual support, counsel for the President nonetheless would have us infer immunity from the President's political mandate, or from his vulnerability to impeachment, or from his broad discretionary powers. These are invitations to refashion the Constitution, and we reject them.

Though the President is elected by nationwide ballot, and is often said to represent all the people, he does not embody the nation's sovereignty. He is not above the law's commands: "With all its defects, delays and inconveniences men have discovered no technique for long preserving free government except that the Executive be under the law...." Sovereignty remains at all times with the people, and they do not forfeit through elections the right to have the law construed against and applied to every citizen.

Nor does the Impeachment Clause imply immunity from routine court process. While the President argues that the Clause means that impeachability precludes criminal prosecution of an incumbent, we see no need to explore this question except to note its irrelevance to the case before us.... By contemplating the possibility of post-impeachment trials for violations of law committed in office, the Impeachment Clause itself reveals that incumbency does not relieve the President of the routine legal obligations that confine all citizens....

We of course acknowledge, the longstanding judicial recognition of Executive privilege.... The Judiciary has been sensitive to the considerations upon which the President seems to rest his claim of absolute privilege: the candor of Executive aides and functionaries would be impaired if they were persistently worried that their advice and deliberations were later to be made public. However, counsel for the President can point to no case in which a court has accepted the Executive's mere assertion of privilege as sufficient to overcome the need of the party subpoenaing the documents. To the contrary, the courts have repeatedly asserted that the applicability of the privilege is in the end for them and not the Executive to decide....

To do otherwise would be effectively to ignore the clear words of *Marbury* v. *Madison,* that "[i]t is emphatically the province and duty of the judicial department to say what the law is."...Whenever a privilege is asserted, even one expressed in the Constitution, such as the Speech and Debate privilege, it is the courts that determine the validity of the assertion and the scope of the privilege. To leave the proper scope and application of Executive privilege to the President's sole discretion would represent a mixing, rather than a separation, of Executive and Judicial functions.... The Constitution mentions no Executive privileges, much less any absolute Executive privileges....

If the claim of absolute privilege was recognized, its mere invocation by the President or his surrogates could deny access to all documents in all the Executive departments to all citizens and their representatives, including Congress, the courts as well as grand juries, state governments, state officials and all state subdivisions. The Freedom of Information Act could become nothing more than a legislative statement of unenforceable rights. Support for this kind of mischief simply cannot be spun from incantation of the doctrine of separation of powers....

The President's privilege cannot, therefore, be deemed absolute. We think the *Burr* case makes clear that application of Executive privilege depends on a weighing of the public interest protected by the privilege against the public interests that would be served by disclosure in a particular case. We direct our attention, however, solely to the circumstances here. With the possible exception of material on one tape, the President does not assert that the subpoenaed items involve military or state secrets; nor is the asserted privilege directed to the particular kinds of information that the tapes contain. Instead, the President asserts that the tapes should be deemed privileged because of the great public interest in maintaining the confidentiality of conversations that take place in the President's performance of his official duties....

Our conclusion that the general confidentiality privilege must recede before the grand jury's showing of need, is established by the unique circumstances that made this showing possible. In his public statement of May 22, 1973, the President said: "Executive privilege will not be invoked as to any testimony concerning possible criminal conduct or discussions of possible criminal conduct, in the matters presently under investigation, including the Watergate affair and the alleged cover-up." We think that this statement and its consequences may properly be considered as at least one factor in striking the balance in this case. Indeed, it affects the weight we give to factors on both sides of the scale. On the one hand, the President's action presumably reflects a judgment by him that the interest in the confidentiality of White House discussions in general is outweighed by such matters as the public interest, stressed by the Special Prosecutor, in the integrity of the level of the Executive Branch closest to the President, and the public interest in the integrity of the electoral process...it supports our estimation of the great public interest that attaches to the effective functioning of the present grand jury....

At the same time, the public testimony given consequent to the President's decision substantially diminishes the interest in maintaining the confidentiality of conversations pertinent to Watergate.

The simple fact is that the conversations are no longer confidential... [w]e see no justification, on confidentiality grounds, for depriving the grand jury of the best evidence of the conversations available....

Nonetheless, we hold that the District Court may order disclosure of all portions of the tapes relevant to matters within the proper scope of the grand jury's investigations, unless the Court judges that the public interest served by nondisclosure of *particular* statements or information outweighs the need for that information demonstrated by the grand jury.

The question remains whether, in the circumstances of this case, the District Court was correct in ordering the tapes produced for *in camera* inspection, so that it could determine whether and to what extent the privilege was properly claimed.... It is our hope that our action in providing what has become an unavoidable constitutional ruling, and in approving, as modified, the order of the District Court, will be followed by maximum cooperation among the parties. Perhaps the President will find it possible to reach some agreement with the Special Prosecutor as to what portions of the subpoenaed evidence are necessary to the grand jury's task.

Should our hope prove unavailing, we think that *in camera* inspection is a necessary and appropriate method of protecting the grand jury's interest in securing relevant evidence. The exception that we have delineated to the President's confidentiality privilege depends entirely on the grand jury's showing that the evidence is directly relevant to its decisions. The residual problem of this case derives from the possibility that there are elements of the subpoenaed recordings that do not lie within the range of the exception that we have defined....

With the rejection of this all-embracing claim of prerogative, the President will have an opportunity to present more particular claims of privilege, if accompanied by an analysis in manageable segments....

1. In so far as the President makes a claim that certain material may not be disclosed because the subject matter relates to national defense or foreign relations, he may decline to transmit that portion of the material and ask the District Court to reconsider whether *in camera* inspection of the material is necessary. The Special Prosecutor is entitled to inspect the claim and showing and may be heard thereon, in chambers. If the judge sustains the privilege, the text of the government's statement will be preserved in the Court's record under seal.

2. The President will present to the District Court all other items covered by the order, with specification of which segments he believes may be disclosed and which not. This can be accomplished by itemizing and indexing the material, and correlating indexed items with particular claims of privilege. On request of either counsel, the District Court shall hold a hearing in chambers on the claims. Thereafter the Court shall itself inspect the disputed items.

Given the nature of the inquiry that this inspection involves, the District Court may give the Special Prosecutor access to the material for the limited purpose of aiding the Court in determining the relevance of the material to the grand jury's investigations.... And, here, any concern over confidentiality is minimized by the Attorney General's designation of a distinguished and reflective counsel as Special Prosecutor. If, however, the Court decides to allow access to the Special Prosecutor, it should, upon request, stay its action in order to allow sufficient time for application for a stay to this Court.

Following the *in camera* hearing and inspection, the District Court may determine as to any items (a) to allow the particular claim of privilege in full; (b) to order disclosure to the grand jury of all or a segment of the item or items; or, when segmentation is impossible, (c) to fashion a complete statement for the grand jury of those portions of an item that bear on possible criminality. The District Court shall provide a reasonable stay to allow the President an opportunity to appeal. In case of an appeal to this Court of an order either allowing or refusing disclosure, this Court will provide for sealed records and confidentiality in presentation.

We end, as we began, by emphasizing the extraordinary nature of this case. We have attempted to decide no more than the problem before us—a problem that takes its unique shape from the grand jury's compelling showing of need. The procedures we have provided require thorough deliberation by the District Court before even this need may be satisfied. Opportunity for appeals, on a sealed record, is assured.

We cannot, therefore, agree with the assertion of the President that the District Court's order threatens "the continued existence of the Presidency as a functioning institution." As we view the case, the order represents an unusual and limited requirement that the President produce material evidence. We think this required by law, and by the rule that even the Chief Executive is subject to the mandate of the law when he has no valid claim of privilege.

Dissenting Opinions

MacKINNON, *Circuit Judge....*

By recognizing an absolute privilege, my opinion places the presidential communications privilege on an equal footing with that recognized for military or state secrets.... Military or state secrets are never subject to disclosure regardless of the weight of countervailing interests.

The rationale underlying the absolute privilege for military or state secrets is the policy judgment that the nation's interest in keeping this information secret always outweighs any particularized need for disclosure. A similar policy judgment supports an absolute privilege for communications between a President and his advisers on matters of official concern.

The interest supporting an absolute privilege for presidential communications is the confidentiality essential to insure thorough and unfettered discussion between a President and his advisers....

To allow the courts to breach presidential confidentiality whenever one of 400 federal trial judges considers that the circumstances of the moment demonstrate a compelling need for disclosure would frustrate the privilege's underlying policy of encouraging frank and candid presidential deliberations....

The lessons of legal history teach that it will be impossible to contain this breach of presidential confidentiality if numerous federal judges may rummage through presidential papers to determine whether a President's or a litigant's contentions should prevail in a particular case. Furthermore, the decision in this case inevitably will be precedent for assaults on the presently asserted absolute privileges of Congress and the Judiciary....

...The greatest vice of the decision sought by the Special Prosecutor is that it would establish a precedent that would subject every presidential conference to the hazard of eventually being publicly exposed at the behest of some trial judge trying a civil or criminal case. It is this precedential effect which transforms this case from one solely related to the recordings sought here, to one which decides whether this President, and all future Presidents, shall continue to enjoy the independency of executive action contemplated by the Constitution and fully exercised by all their predecessors.

After the President has claimed the privilege, the court must satisfy itself that "the circumstances are appropriate for the claim of privilege." In determining whether the privilege is appropriate in a particular case, the only inquiry is whether there is a "reasonable danger" that disclosure of the evidence would expose matters which the privilege is designed to protect. Since the presidential communications privilege is an absolute rather than a qualified privilege, there is no occasion to balance the particularized need for the evidence against the governmental interest in confidentiality. The balance between these competing interests was examined and resolved when the absolute presidential communications privilege was formulated. Having concluded that the privilege is available, the only inquiry is whether the President's invocation of the privilege promotes the policy which the privilege was designed to protect....

Yet the court must make this determination without forcing disclosure of the very communication which the privilege protects. Thus an *in camera* inspection is proper only if the court cannot otherwise satisfy itself that the privilege should be sustained. In the present case, we are satisfied that appropriate circumstances do exist and, therefore, would hold that even *in camera* inspection is improper.

WILKEY, *Circuit Judge....*

I respectfully submit that the errors in the *Per Curiam's* analysis stem from a frequent source of confusion, the failure to recognize and separate the two origins of the Executive Branch privilege: on one hand, the common sense-common law privilege of confidentiality necessary in government administration, which has been partly codified in statutes such as the Freedom of Information Act; on the other hand, the origin of the privilege in the Constitutional principle of separation of powers....

In theory, if only the ancient customary Governmental confidentiality privilege is involved, whether the Chief Executive should disclose the information should be decided no differently from the case of any other Government official.... It would be permissible for the courts to talk in terms of balancing the public interest of those seeking disclosure versus the public interest of the President in retaining confidentiality....

As a practical matter, as history shows, the theory breaks down. Not only is the grist of the Presidential mill of a higher quality than that processed by the average bureaucrat, but the institutions or individuals daring to confront the Chief Executive directly have been of a character and power to invoke immediately the other source of the Chief Executive's privilege, the Constitutional doctrine of separation of powers.... If the Chief Executive can be "coerced" by the Judicial Branch into furnishing records hitherto throughout our history resting within the exclusive control of the Executive, then the Chief Executive is no longer "master in his own house."

This is not a matter of "coercing" the Executive to "obey the law"; there has never before in 184 years been any such law that the Executive could be compelled by the Judiciary to surrender Executive records to the Judiciary. This is an assertion of privilege by the Executive, not a refusal to obey a court's interpretation of the law. This the Executive has *always* done, even when the Executive's interpretation of the law was different.... But also, the Executive has *always* been the one who decided whether the Executive Branch privilege of confidentiality of its records should be asserted, and to what extent, when confronted with demand of another Branch for such records....

...[W]here the privilege of the Chief Executive is derived from the *Constitutional principle* of separation of powers, it is no more subject to weighing and balancing than any other Constitutional privilege can be weighed and balanced by extraneous third parties....

We all know that when a Constitutional privilege under the Fifth Amendment is asserted by the humblest individual, the court does not weigh and balance the public interest in having the individual's testimony. All the court can do is make a preliminary inquiry as to a *prima facie* justification for the assertion of the privilege.... If the Constitutional privilege has been asserted, then no court has the right to determine what the President will or will not produce....

Throughout this nation's 184-year Constitutional history, Congress and the Executive have succeeded in avoiding any near-fatal confrontation over attempts by Congress to procure documents in the Executive's possession. In recognition of the delicate balance created by the doctrine of separation of powers, the two Branches have generally succeeded in fashioning a *modus vivendi* through mutual deference and cooperation....

Congressional demands for Executive papers are as numerous as autumn leaves, and frequently fall due to a frost between the two ends of Pennsylvania Avenue. In contrast, Judicial demands for Executive documents can be summarized in the drama and legal intricacies of one *cause celebre,* the two trials of Aaron Burr in 1807, the major historical example of the issuance by a federal court of a subpoena *duces tecum* directing the President to produce documents. Although the United States Circuit Court for Virginia, per Chief Justice Marshall, issued the subpoena *duces tecum* to President Jefferson, the court never directly decided the question of the scope of the President's asserted privilege to withhold documents or portions thereof, nor did it determine who should decide the scope of the privilege....

If we go on *what was actually done*, the Burr Trials prove that the final "weighing of the public interest" is done by the Chief Executive. If we go on what was *said* by Marshall, the *Burr* trials leave the ultimate issue of Who finally decides the public interest completely undecided, for Marshall never faced up, even verbally, to a confrontation with the President himself with the issue drawn on the question of separation of powers.

These two great Constitutional and political antagonists—Marshall and Jefferson, Chief Justice and President—had circled each other warily, each maintaining his position, each, out of respect for the other and for the delicate fabric of the Constitution, not forcing the ultimate issue. Who *should decide* the scope and applicability of the Chief Executive's privilege? The portions of the letter determined by the President to be confidential remained confidential; the full letter was never produced to the court....

...[T]he real issue...is whether it is appropriate for the court to determine the legal validity of a claim of privilege by the President, or whether the Constitutional principle of separation of powers requires the court to yield to the President's judgment as to where the public interest lies. My answer would be the latter....

It was and is the President's right to make that decision initially, and it is the American people who will be the judge as to whether the President has made the right decision, *i.e.*, whether it is or is not in the public interest that the papers (tapes) in question be furnished or retained. If his decision is made on visibly sound grounds, the people will approve the action of the Executive as being in the public interest. If the decision is not visibly on sound grounds of national public interest, in political terms the decision may be ruinous for the President, but it is his to make. The grand design has worked; the separate, independent Branch remains in charge of and responsible for its own papers, processes and decisions, not to a second or third Branch, but it remains *responsible* to the American people....

The Founding Fathers were not looking for the most *efficient* government design. After all, they had been subject to and rebelled against one of the most efficient governments then existing. What the Founding Fathers designed was *not efficiency, but protection against oppression.* Leaving the three Branches in an equilibrium of tension was just one of their devices to guard against oppression.

This healthy equilibrium of tension will be destroyed if the result reached by the *Per Curiam* is allowed to stand. My colleagues cannot confine the effect of their decision to Richard M. Nixon.

The precedent set will inevitably have far-reaching implications on the vulnerability of any Chief Executive to judicial process, not merely at the behest of the Special Prosecutor in the extraordinary circumstances of Watergate, but at the behest of Congress. Congress may have equally plausible needs for similar information. The fact that Congress is usually or frequently locked in political battle with the Chief Executive cannot mean that Congress' need or right to information in the hands of the Chief Executive is any less than it otherwise would be....

To put the theoretical situation and possibilities in terms of "absolute" privilege sounds somewhat terrifying—*until one realizes that this is exactly the way matters have been for 184 years of our history,* and the Republic still stands. The practical capacity of the three independent Branches to adjust to each other, their sensitivity to the approval or disapproval of the American people, have been sufficient guides to responsible action, without imposing the authority of one co-equal Branch over another....

FIRING OF WATERGATE PROSECUTOR

October 20, 1973

Special Watergate Prosecutor Archibald Cox was fired, U.S. Attorney General Elliot L. Richardson resigned and Deputy Attorney General William D. Ruckelshaus was discharged Oct. 20 over Cox's refusal to accept a Nixon plan aimed at averting a showdown in the Supreme Court on the production of controversial White House tapes. The U.S. Court of Appeals Oct. 12, in affirming the decision of Federal District Judge John J. Sirica, had given President Nixon until the end of the working day Friday Oct. 19 to turn over the tapes to Sirica, appeal the decision, or find an alternative plan agreeable to Cox. (See p. 839.) Nixon let the deadline expire and several hours later made public a "compromise" plan whereby he would provide authenticated "summaries" of the tapes to the court but forbid Cox to use the judicial process to obtain additional presidential material.

Cox's refusal that night to accept the plan led to an order from Nixon to Richardson to fire Cox. Richardson and then Ruckelshaus refused to carry out the order; Richardson resigned, Ruckelshaus was fired. The Justice Department's third man in line, Solicitor General Robert H. Bork, finally dismissed Cox. The double firing and resignation was the most startling shake-up in the Nixon administration since the Watergate-related departure of Attorney General Kleindienst and three top White House aides in late April. (See p. 499.) With Cox's departure, the Watergate investigation was returned temporarily to the Justice Department, until Leon Jaworski was appointed Nov. 1 to fill the post vacated by Cox.

The events of what came to be known as "the Saturday night massacre" precipitated a wave of public reaction and the dropping of Nixon's popularity to an all-time low. Nearly a quarter of a million telegrams flowed into Washington in the ensuing three days, the "heaviest concentrated volume on record," Western Union reported. Members of Congress concurred that the messages were largely in favor of impeachment. In front of the White House, motorists raised a horn-honking din in response to protesters' signs that read: "Honk for Impeachment." Outrage was also voiced in Congress where eight impeachment resolutions were introduced in the House of Representatives Oct. 23 when that body reconvened following a brief recess.

The week preceding the firing had been one of mounting suspense as the deadline for appeal to the Supreme Court approached. During the week, Cox, Richardson and Nixon's legal consultant Charles Alan Wright attempted to reach agreement on a proposal put forth by Nixon on Monday, Oct. 15. That plan was not made public until Oct. 19. It would have had a verifier—disclosed Oct. 19 to have been Sen. John C. Stennis (D Miss.)—authenticate presidentially prepared summaries of the tapes by listening to the original recordings. The verified summaries would then have been turned over to Judge Sirica. A second and more controversial provision of the plan would have forbidden Cox to subpoena additional presidential papers or tapes concerning Watergate.

In a memorandum dated Oct. 17, Richardson set forth the plan to Cox who by the following day had raised 11 objections to it. Other parties, however, seemed agreeable to the plan. Stennis was reportedly in accord, although weeks later questions arose as to whether he had actually agreed to it. The chairman and vice chairman of the Senate select Watergate committee, Senators Sam J. Ervin Jr. (D N.C.) and Howard H. Baker Jr. (R Tenn.), also reportedly were in agreement on the plan although, like Stennis, they later disagreed on their interpretation of the plan's details. Cox, however, refused to accept the limitation on his future investigative efforts. By week's end, further exchanges between Cox and Wright had failed to bring the parties closer together. (See texts of letters and memos between Cox, Richardson and Wright, p. 864-869.)

On the evening of Oct. 19, with the deadline for appeal to the Supreme Court passed, Nixon announced a "compromise." He would not give Cox the tapes but would prepare summaries of their contents and permit Stennis to listen to the tapes to verify the presidential account. "So that the constitutional tensions of Watergate would not be continued," Nixon also announced that "there would be no further attempt by the special prosecutor to subpoena still more tapes or other presidential papers of a similar nature." Even though Cox had rejected this plan, Nixon said, he had decided to take "de-

cisive actions" in order to head off a "constitutional crisis." He said the plan had been drawn up by Richardson and agreed to by Stennis, Ervin and Baker. Carrying through on the announcement, Nixon sent a letter to Richardson Oct. 19 instructing him to forbid Cox to go to court to gain access to other presidential materials. (Text of Nixon's compromise and letter to Richardson, p. 869-872.)

Following the President's announcement, Cox issued a statement rejecting the plan and saying that acceptance of it would "defeat the fair administration of criminal justice." Because "the President is refusing to comply with the court decrees," Cox said, he would take his objections to court to argue for full disclosure. Nixon's instructions, Cox continued, "are in violation of the promises which the Attorney General made to the Senate when his [Richardson's] nomination was confirmed." Cox said he would have a more complete statement at a later time.

Cox held a nationally televised news conference at the National Press Club the following afternoon, Saturday Oct. 20, to reiterate his objections to the President's compromise plan. Cox said it was his "duty...to bring to the court's attention what seems to be noncompliance with the court's order." He cited four "insuperable difficulties" with the compromise. They were (1) that the real evidence had been and would be available to only two or three men operating in secrecy and to only one man who was not a presidential aide or associated with those under prosecution; (2) that the criteria for excluding information, even if limited to the single criterion of national security, would not be definitive in light of the national security reasons cited in the break-in at the office of Daniel Ellsberg's psychiatrist (see p. 537); (3) that the summary would probably be inadmissible in court as evidence and would therefore jeopardize prosecution; and (4) that the prosecution of other cases would be jeopardized, especially where defendants were claiming the tapes essential to their cases.

Cox also recounted the "frustration" of seeking to gain access to presidential papers. He said the papers of many presidential aides had been "taken out of the usual files and put in something special called presidential files." In seeking an inventory of files, logs of meetings, and other memoranda, Cox said: "The delays have been extraordinary." Of the week's negotiations with Wright, Cox said, "It was my impression that I was being confronted with things that were drawn in such a way that I could not accept them."

Richardson was in basic agreement with Cox. He later disclosed at a news conference Oct. 23 that he wrote the President Oct. 20 saying that while he considered the Stennis part of the proposal to be reasonable and constructive and hoped Judge Sirica would accept it, he could not accept the ban on any future attempts by Cox to obtain records from the White House. Instructions to curb Cox's activity, as contained in Nixon's letter, "intrude on the independence you promised me with regard to Watergate when you announced my appointment," Richardson wrote. (Text, p. 872.)

At 8:24 that Saturday evening, White House Press Secretary Ronald L. Ziegler announced that President Nixon had ordered Richardson to fire Cox, and that Richardson had refused to carry out the order and had resigned. Ruckelshaus had then been ordered to fire Cox, had refused and was fired—even as he wrote his resignation. Solicitor General Bork had then become Acting Attorney General and had dismissed Cox. Ziegler also announced that FBI agents had sealed off the offices of Cox, Richardson and Ruckelshaus to prevent the removal of papers.

Cox issued a one-sentence statement the night of his ouster: "Whether ours shall continue to be a government of laws and not of men is now for Congress and ultimately the American people [to decide]."

In the next few days, members of the administration sought to calm the public outrage. Counselor to the President Melvin R. Laird Oct. 21 defended Nixon's actions saying that no one under the President "should be in a position where they demand total surrender." Laird said Cox had won "a tremendous victory" in the tapes compromise plan. Bork announced Oct. 22 that the Watergate investigation had been returned to the jurisdiction of Henry E. Petersen, the assistant attorney general who had been in charge of the case for 16 months prior to the appointment of Cox, May 18, 1973. At a news conference Oct. 24, Bork stated his determination to fully investigate the Watergate case. "If the law entitles us to any item of evidence, I will go after it," he pledged. He said he would not be the person "who in any way compromised any investigation."

Richardson held a news conference Oct. 23 to explain his part in the fast-moving events of the weekend. He said he had found part of Nixon's compromise plan—the submission of verified summaries to the court—acceptable, provided Judge Sirica agreed. But Richardson said his pledge at his Senate confirmation hearings of total independence for the special prosecutor had made it impossible for him to curb Cox's investigative authority or to fire him. Richardson resigned therefore "because to continue would have forced me to refuse to carry out a direct order of the President." He added: "I did not agree with the decisions which brought about the necessity for the issuance of that order." Rather, he said, requests for additional information should have been dealt with as they arose. He praised Cox's handling of the Watergate cases, saying: "I would have done what he has done."

Richardson also said that the possibility of firing Cox had arisen earlier in the week during discussions he had with White House aides as "one way of mooting the [tapes] case, and thereby in effect resolving the constitutional impasse." Richardson said he rejected the suggestion as "totally unacceptable." But he said there had been "continuing concerns on the part of the President's counsel" about the wide range of the Cox investigation, and "continuing arguments" between the White House and Cox "over the issue of jurisdiction and access to particular notes, memoranda, documents and so on."

Four days after the deadline for compliance with the court's order to appeal to the Supreme Court or turn over the tapes, the cumulative effect of Nixon's actions continued to stir critical public reaction. In Congress, House members took first steps toward a serious consideration of impeachment. Speculation mounted that Judge Sirica was preparing to cite Nixon for contempt for his failure to comply with court orders. Against this backdrop, Nixon's legal consultant Charles Alan Wright appeared in Judge Sirica's courtroom Tuesday, Oct. 23, to announce that Nixon would relinquish the subpoenaed presidential tapes. (See p. 840.) "This President does not defy the law," Wright told the court, "and he has authorized me to say he will comply in full with the orders of the court."

Full texts of the following documents and statements will be found on the next pages: (1) an exchange of five letters between Attorney General Elliot L. Richardson, Special Watergate Prosecutor Archibald Cox and White House legal consultant Charles Alan Wright, dated Oct. 17-19, concerning a possible compromise on access to the White House tapes; (2) text of President Nixon's Oct. 19 statement announcing his decision not to appeal the Watergate tapes decision of the U.S. Circuit Court of Appeals and his compromise plan for revealing a summary of the tapes' contents; (3) text of Cox's statement Oct. 19 rejecting Nixon's compromise plan; (4) text of Nixon's letter to Richardson, dated Oct. 19, instructing Richardson to direct Cox to cease all attempts to obtain presidential documents or tapes by the judicial process; (5) text of Richardson's letter to Nixon, Oct. 20, saying that he could not carry out Nixon's order; (6) text of White House Press Secretary Ronald L. Ziegler's Oct. 20 announcement that Richardson had resigned, Deputy Attorney General William D. Ruckelshaus had been fired and that Solicitor General Robert H. Bork had fired Cox; (7) texts of three letters, Richardson's and Ruckelshaus's resignations and Nixon's subsequent letter to Richardson; (8) texts of Nixon's letter to Bork instructing him to fire Cox and Bork's letter to Cox informing him that he had been dismissed; and (9) text of opening statement read by Richardson at his news conference Oct. 23.

(1) Exchange of letters Oct. 17-19:

OCT. 17 RICHARDSON PROPOSAL

The Objective

The objective of this proposal is to provide a means of furnishing to the court and the grand jury a complete and accurate account of the content of the tapes subpoenaed by the special prosecutor insofar as the conversations recorded in those tapes in any way relate to the Watergate break-in and the cover-up of the break-in, to knowledge thereof on the part of anyone, and to perjury or the subornation of perjury with regard thereto.

The Means

The President would select an individual, the verifier, whose wide experience, strong character, and established reputation for veracity would provide a firm basis for the confidence that he would put above any other consideration his responsibility for the completeness and accuracy of the record.

Procedure

The subpoenaed tapes would be made available to the verifier for as long as he considered necessary. He would also be provided with a preliminary record consisting of a verbatim transcript of the tapes except (a) that it would omit continuous portions of substantial duration which clearly and in their entirety were not pertinent and (b) that it would be in the third person. Omissions would be indicated by a bracketed reference to their subject matter.

With the preliminary record in hand, the verifier would listen to the entire tapes, replay portions thereof, as often as necessary, and, as he saw fit, make additions to the preliminary record. The verifier would be empowered to paraphrase language whose use in its original form would in his judgment be embarrassing to the President and to paraphrase or omit references to national defense or foreign relations matters whose disclosure he believed would do real harm. The verifier would take pains in any case where paraphrased language was used to make sure that the paraphrase did not alter the sense or emphasis of the recorded conversation. Where, despite repeated replaying and adjustments of volume, the verifier could not understand the recording, he would so indicate.

Having by this process converted the preliminary record into his own verified record, the verifier would attach to it a certificate attesting to its completeness and accuracy and to his faithful observance of the procedure set forth above.

Court Approval

Court approval of the proposed procedure would be sought at two stages: (a) In general terms when or soon after the verifier began his task, but without identifying him by name, and (b) when the verified record was delivered to the court with the verifier's certificate. At the second stage, the special prosecutor and counsel for the President would join in urging the court to accept the verified record as a full and accurate record of all pertinent portions of the tapes for all purposes for which access to those tapes might thereafter be sought by or on behalf of any person having standing to obtain such access.

Assurance Against Tampering

Submission of the verified record to the court would be accompanied by such affidavits with respect to the care and custody of the tapes as would help to establish that the tapes listened to by the verifier had not at any time been altered or abbreviated.

OCT. 18 COX RESPONSE TO RICHARDSON MEMO

The essential idea of establishing impartial but non-judicial means for providing the special prosecutor and grand jury with an accurate record of the content of the tapes without his participation is not unacceptable. A courtroom "victory" has no value per se. There should be no avoidable confrontation with the President, and I have not the slightest desire to embarrass him. Consequently, I am glad to sit down with anyone in order to work out a solution along this line if we can.

I set forth below brief notes on a number of points that strike me as highly important.

1. The public cannot be fairly asked to confide so difficult and responsible a task to any one man operating in secrecy, consulting only with the White House. Nor should we be put in the position of accepting any choice made unilaterally.

2. Your idea of tying a solution into court machinery is a good one. I would carry it farther so that any persons entrusted with this responsibility were named "special masters" at the beginning. This would involve publicity but I do not see how the necessary public confidence can be achieved without open announcement of any agreement and of the names of the special masters.

3. The stated objective of the proposal is too narrow. It should include providing evidence that in any way relates to other possible criminal activity under the jurisdiction of this office.

4. I do not understand the implications of saying that the "verbatim transcript...would be in the third person." I do assume that the names of all speakers, of all persons addressed by name or tone,

and of all persons mentioned would be included. (The last is too broad. I mean to refer only to persons somehow under investigation.)

5. The three standards for omission probably have acceptable objectives, but they must be defined more narrowly and with greater particularity.

6. A "transcript" prepared in the manner projected might be enough for investigation by the special prosecutor and grand jury. If we accept such a "transcript" we would try to get it accepted by the courts (as you suggest). There must also be assurance, however, that if indictments are returned, if evidence concerning any of the nine conversations would, in our judgment, be important at the trial, and if the court will not accept our "transcript" then the evidence will be furnished to the prosecution in whatever form the trial court rules is necessary for admissibility (including as much of the original tape as the court requires). Similarly, if the court rules that a tape or any portion must be furnished a defendant or the case will be dismissed, then the tape must be supplied.

7. I am glad to see some provision for verifying the integrity of the tapes even though I reject all suggestions of tampering. Should we not go further to dispel cynicism and make provision for skilled electronic assistance in verifying the integrity of the tapes and to render intelligible, if at all possible, portions that appear inaudible or garbled?

8. We ought to have a chance to brief the special masters on our investigations, etc., so as to give them an adequate background. The special masters should be encouraged to ask the prosecutor for any relevant information. What about a request for reconsideration in the case of an evident mistake?

9. The narrow scope of the proposal is a grave defect, because it would not serve the function of a court decision in establishing the special prosecutor's entitlement to other evidence. We have long pending requests for many specific documents. The proposal also leaves half a lawsuit hanging (i.e., the subpoenaed papers). Some method of resolving these problems is required.

10. I am puzzled about the practical and political links between (a) our agreeing upon a proposal and (b) the demands of the Ervin committee.

11. The Watergate special prosecution force was established because of a widely felt need to create an independent office that would objectively and forthrightly pursue the prima facie showing of criminality by high Government officials. You appointed me, and I pledged that I would not be turned aside. Any solution I can accept must be such as to command conviction that I am adhering to that pledge.   A.C.

OCT. 18 LETTER FROM WRIGHT TO COX

Dear Mr. Cox:

This will confirm our telephone conversation of a few minutes ago.

The fundamental purpose of the very reasonable proposal that the Attorney General put to you, at the insistence of the President, was to provide a mechanism by which the President could voluntarily make available to you, in a form the integrity of which could not be challenged, the information that you have represented you needed to proceed with the grand jury in connection with nine specified meetings and telephone calls. This would have also put to rest any possible thought that the President might himself have been involved in the Watergate break-in or cover-up. The President was willing to permit this unprecedented intrusion into the confidentiality of his office in order that the country might be spared the anguish of further months of litigation and indecision about private Presidential papers and meetings.

We continue to believe that the proposal as put to you by the Attorney General is a reasonable one and that its acceptance in full would serve the national interest. Some of your comments go to matters of detail that we could talk about, but your comments, 1, 2, 6 and 9 in particular, depart so far from that proposal and the purpose for which it was made that we could not accede to them in any form.

If you think that there is any purpose in our talking further, my associates and I stand ready to do so. If not, we will have to follow the course of action that we think in the best interest of the country. I will call you at 10 A.M. to ascertain your views.

Sincerely,
Charles Alan Wright

OCT. 19 LETTER FROM COX TO WRIGHT

Dear Charlie:

Thank you for your letter confirming our telephone conversation last evening.

Your second paragraph referring to my comments 1, 2, 6, and 9 requires a little fleshing out although the meaning is clear in the light of our telephone conversation. You stated that there was no use in continuing conversations in an effort to reach a reasonable out-of-court accommodation unless I would agree categorically to four points.

Point One was that the tapes must be submitted to only one man operating in secrecy, and the President has already selected the only person in the country who would be acceptable to him.

Point Two was that the person named to provide an edited transcript of the tapes could not be named special master under a court order.

Point Three was that no portion of the tapes would be provided under any circumstances. This means that even if the edited transcript contained evidence of criminality important in convicting wrongdoers and even if the court were to rule that only the relevant portion of the original tapes would be admitted in evidence, still the portion would be withheld. It is also clear that, under your Point Three, the tapes would be withheld even if it meant dismissal of prosecutions against former Government officials who have betrayed the public trust.

Point Four was that I must categorically agree not to subpoena any other White House tape, paper, or document. This would mean that my ability to secure evidence bearing upon criminal wrongdoing by high White House officials would be left to the discretion of White House counsel. Judging from the difficulties we have had in the past receiving documents, memoranda, and other papers, we would have little hope of getting evidence in the future.

These points should be borne in mind in considering whether the proposal put before me is "very reasonable."

I have a strong desire to avoid any form of confrontation, but I could not conscientiously agree to your stipulations without unfaithfulness to the pledges which I gave the Senate prior to my appointment. It is enough to point out that the fourth stipulation would require me to forgo further legal challenge to claims of executive privilege. I categorically assured the Senate Judiciary Committee that I would challenge such claims so far as the law permitted. The Attorney General was confirmed on the strength of that assurance. I cannot break my promise now.

Sincerely,
Archibald Cox
Special Prosecutor

OCT. 19 LETTER FROM WRIGHT TO COX

Dear Archie:

This is in response to your letter of this date. It is my conclusion from that letter that further discussions between us seeking to resolve this matter by compromise would be futile, and that we will be forced to take the actions that the President deems appropriate in these circumstances. I do wish to clear up two points, however.

On what is referred to in your letter today as Point Three, that no portion of the tapes would be provided under any circumstances, the proposal of the Attorney General was simply silent. That would have been an issue for future negotiation when and if the occasion arose. Your comments of the 18th, however, would have required an advance commitment from us that we cannot make on an issue that we think would never arise.

In what you list as Point Four you describe my position as being that you "must categorically agree not to subpoena any other White House tape, paper, or document." When I indicated that the ninth of your comments of the 18th was unacceptable, I had in mind only what I referred to in my letter as "private Presidential papers and meetings," a category that I regard as much, much smaller than the great mass of White House documents with which the President has not personally been involved.

I note these points only in the interest of historical accuracy, in the unhappy event that our correspondence should see the light of day. As I read your comments of the 18th and your letter of the 19th, the differences between us remain so great that no purpose would be served by further discussion of what I continue to think was a "very reasonable"—indeed an unprecedentedly generous—proposal that the Attorney General put to you in an effort, in the national interest, to resolve our disputes by mutual agreement at a time when the country would be particularly well served by such agreement.

Sincerely,
Charles Alan Wright

(2) Nixon's compromise plan of Oct. 19:

For a number of months, there has been a strain imposed on the American people by the aftermath of Watergate, and the inquiries into and court suits arising out of that incident. Increasing apprehension over the possibility of a constitutional confrontation in the tapes cases has become especially damaging.

Our Government, like our Nation, must remain strong and effective. What matters most, in this critical hour, is our ability to act in a way that enables us to control events, not to be paralyzed and overwhelmed by them. At home, the Watergate issue has taken on overtones of a partisan political contest. Concurrently, there are those in the international community who may be tempted by our Watergate-related difficulties at home to misread America's unity and resolve in meeting the challenges we confront abroad.

I have concluded that it is necessary to take decisive actions that will avoid any possibility of a constitutional crisis and that lay the groundwork upon which we can assure unity of purpose at home and end the temptation abroad to test our resolve.

It is with this awareness that I have considered the decision of the Court of Appeals for the District of Columbia. I am confident that the dissenting opinions, which are in accord with what until now has always been regarded as the law, would be sustained upon review by the Supreme Court. I have concluded, however, that it is not in the national interest to leave this matter unresolved for the period that might be required for a review by the highest court.

Throughout this week, the Attorney General, Elliot Richardson at my instance, has been holding discussions with Special Prosecutor Archibald Cox, looking to the possibility of a compromise that would avoid the necessity of Supreme Court review. With the greatest reluctance, I have concluded that in this one instance I must permit a breach in the confidentiality that is so necessary to the conduct of the Presidency. Accordingly, the Attorney General made what he regarded as a reasonable proposal for compromise, and one that goes beyond what any President in history has offered. It was a proposal that would comply with the spirit of the decision of the Court of Appeals. It would have allowed justice to proceed undiverted, while maintaining the principle of an independent Executive Branch. It would have given the Special Prosecutor the information he claims he needs for use in the grand jury. It would also have resolved any lingering thought that the President himself might have been involved in a Watergate cover-up.

STENNIS CHOICE

The proposal was that, as quickly as the materials could be prepared, there would be submitted to Judge Sirica, through a statement prepared by me personally from the subpoenaed tapes, a full disclosure of everything contained in those tapes that has any bearing on Watergate. The authenticity of this summary would be assured by giving unlimited access to the tapes to a very distinguished man, highly respected by all elements in American life for his integrity, his fairness, and his patriotism, so that that man could satisfy himself that the statement prepared by me did indeed include fairly and accurately anything that might be regarded as related to Watergate. In return, so that the constitutional tensions of Watergate would not be continued, it would be understood that there would be no further attempt by the Special Prosecutor to subpoena still more tapes or other Presidential papers of a similar nature.

I am pleased to be able to say that Chairman Sam Ervin and Vice Chairman Howard Baker of the Senate Select Committee have agreed to this procedure and that at their request, and mine, Senator John Stennis has consented to listen to every requested tape and verify that the statement I am preparing is full and accurate. Some may ask why, if I am willing to let Senator Stennis hear the tapes for this purpose, I am not willing merely to submit them to the court for inspection in private. I do so out of no lack of respect for Judge Sirica, in whose discretion and integrity I have the utmost confidence, but because to allow the tapes to be heard by one judge would create a precedent that would be available to 400 district judges. Further, it would create a precedent that Presidents are required to submit to judicial demands that purport to override Presidential determinations on requirements for confidentiality.

SPECIAL PROSECUTOR

To my regret, the Special Prosecutor rejected this proposal. Nevertheless, it is my judgment that in the present circumstances and existing international environment, it is in the overriding national interest that a constitutional confrontation on this issue be avoided. I have, therefore, instructed White House counsel not to seek Supreme Court review from the decision of the Court of Appeals. At the same time, I will voluntarily make available to Judge Sirica—and also to the Senate Select Committee—a statement of the Watergate-related portions of the tapes, prepared and authenticated in the fashion I have described.

I want to repeat that I have taken this step with the greatest reluctance, only to bring the issue of Watergate tapes to an end and to assure our full attention to more pressing business affecting the very security of the nation. Accordingly, though I have not wished to intrude upon the independence of the Special Prosecutor, I have felt it necessary to direct him, as an employee of the Executive Branch, to make no further attempts by judicial process to obtain tapes, notes, or memoranda of Presidential conversations. I believe that with the statement that will be provided to the court, any legitimate need of the Special Prosecutor is fully satisfied and that he can proceed to obtain indictments against those who may have committed any crimes. And I believe that by these actions I have taken today America will be spared the anguish of further indecision and litigation about tapes.

Our constitutional history reflects not only the language and inferences of that great document, but also the choices of clash and accommodation made by responsible leaders at critical moments. Under the Constitution it is the duty of the President to see that the laws of the Nation are faithfully executed. My actions today are in accordance with that duty, and in that spirit of accommodation.

(3) Cox's rejection of compromise plan:

In my judgment, the President is refusing to comply with the court decrees. A summary of the context of the tapes lacks the evidentiary value of the tapes themselves. No steps are being taken to turn over the important notes, memoranda and other documents that the court orders require. I shall bring these points to the attention of the court and abide by its decision.

The President's directions to make no further attempts by the judicial process to obtain tapes, notes or memoranda of presidential conversations will apply to all such matters in the future.

These directions would apply not only to the so-called Watergate investigation but all matters within my jurisdiction.

The instructions are in violation of the promises which the Attorney General made to the Senate when his nomination was confirmed. For me to comply to those instructions would violate my solemn pledge to the Senate and the country to invoke judicial process to challenge exaggerated claims of executive privilege. I shall not violate my promise.

Acceptance of these directions would also defeat the fair administration of criminal justice. It would deprive prosecutors of admissible evidence in prosecuting wrongdoers who abused high government office. It would also enable defendants to go free, by withholding material a judge ruled necessary to a fair trial. The President's action already threatens this result in the New York prosecution of John Mitchell and Maurice Stans. I cannot be a party to such an arrangement.

I shall have a more complete statement in the near future.

(4) Nixon's letter instructing Richardson to curb Cox's attempts to gain presidential documents by judicial process:

October 19, 1973

Dear Elliot:

You are aware of the actions I am taking today to bring to an end the controversy over the so-called Watergate tapes and that I have reluctantly agreed to a limited breach of Presidential confidentiality in order that our country may be spared the agony of further indecision and litigation about those tapes at a time when we are confronted with other issues of much greater moment to the country and the world.

As a part of these actions, I am instructing you to direct special prosecutor Archibald Cox of the Watergate Special Prosecution Force that he is to make no further attempts by judicial process to obtain tapes, notes, or memoranda of Presidential conversations. I regret the necessity of intruding, to this very limited extent, on the independence that I promised you with regard to Watergate when I announced your appointment. This would not have been necessary if the Special Prosecutor had agreed to the very reasonable proposal you made to him this week.

Sincerely,

RICHARD NIXON

(5) Richardson's Oct. 20 refusal to carry out Nixon's order:

Dear Mr. President:

Thank you for your letter of October 19, 1973, instructing me to direct Mr. Cox that he is to make no further attempts by judicial process to obtain tapes, notes or memoranda of Presidential conversations.

As you point out, this instruction does intrude on the independence you promised me with regard to Watergate when you announced my appointment. And, of course, you have every right as President to withdraw or modify any understanding on which I hold office under you. The situation stands on a different footing, however, with respect to the role of the special prosecutor.

Acting on your instruction that if I should consider it appropriate, I would have the authority to name a special prosecutor, I announced a few days before my confirmation hearing began that I would, if confirmed, "appoint a special prosecutor and give him all the independence, authority, and staff support needed to carry out the tasks entrusted to him."

I added, "Although he will be in the Department of Justice and report to me—and only to me—he will be aware that his ultimate accountability is to the American people."

At many points throughout the nomination hearings, I reaffirmed my intention to assure the independence of the special prosecutor, and in my statement of his duties and responsibilities I specified that he would have "full authority" for "determining whether or not to contest the assertion of 'executive privilege' or any other testimonial privilege."

And while the special prosecutor can be removed from office for "extraordinary improprieties," his charter specifically states that "the Attorney General will not countermand or interfere with the special prosecutor's decisions or actions."

Quite obviously, therefore, the instruction contained in your letter of October 19 gives me serious difficulty. As you know, I regarded as reasonable and constructive the proposal to rely on Senator Stennis to prepare a verified record of the so-called Watergate tapes and I did my best to persuade Mr. Cox of the desirability of this solution of that issue.

I did not believe, however, that the price of access to the tapes in this manner should be the renunciation of any further attempt by him to resort to judicial process, and the proposal I submitted to him did not purport to deal with other tapes, notes, or memoranda of Presidential conversations.

In the circumstances I would hope that some further accommodation could be found along the following lines:

First, that an effort to be made to persuade Judge Sirica to accept for purposes of the grand jury the record of the Watergate tapes verified by Senator Stennis. In that event, Mr. Cox would, as he has, abide by Judge Sirica's decision.

Second, agreement should be sought with Mr. Cox not to press any outstanding subpoenas which are directed merely to notes or memoranda covering the same conversations that would have been furnished in full through the verified record.

Third, any future situation where Mr. Cox seeks judicial process to obtain the record of Presidential conversations would be approached on the basis of the precedent established with respect to the Watergate tapes. This would leave to be handled in this way only situations where a showing of compelling necessity comparable to that made with respect to the Watergate tapes had been made.

If you feel it would be useful to do so, I would welcome the opportunity to discuss this matter with you.

Respectfully,

ELLIOT L. RICHARDSON

(6) Ziegler's Oct. 20 announcement of the firing of Cox and resignations of Richardson and Ruckelshaus:

I know many of you are on deadline. I have a brief statement to give at this time, and following the reading of the statement we will have an exchange of a series of letters relating to action which President Nixon has taken tonight.

President Nixon has tonight discharged Archibald Cox, the Special Prosecutor in the Watergate case. The President took this action because of Mr. Cox's refusal to comply with instructions given Friday night through Attorney General Richardson that he was not to seek to involve the judicial process further to compel production of recordings, notes or memoranda regarding private Presidential conversations.

Further, the office of the Watergate special prosecution force has been abolished as of approximately 8:00 p.m. tonight. Its function to investigate and prosecute those involved in the Watergate matter will be transferred back into the institutional framework of the Department of Justice, where it will be carried out with thoroughness and vigor.

In his statement Friday night, and in his decision not to seek Supreme Court review of the Court of Appeals decision with regard to the Watergate tapes, the President sought to avoid a constitutional confrontation by an action that would give the Grand Jury what it needs to proceed with its work with the least possible intrusion of Presidential privacy. That action taken by the President in the spirit of accommodation that has marked American constitutional history was accepted by responsible leaders in Congress and the country. Mr. Cox's refusal to proceed in the same spirit of accommodation, complete with his announced intention to defy instructions from the President and press for further confrontation at a time of serious world crisis, made it necessary for the President to discharge Mr. Cox and to return to the Department of Justice the task of prosecuting those who broke the law in connection with Watergate.

Before taking this action, the President met this evening with Attorney General Richardson. He met with Attorney General Richardson at about 4:45 today for about thirty minutes.

The Attorney General, on hearing of the President's decision, felt obliged to resign, since he believed the discharge of Professor Cox to be inconsistent with the conditions of his confirmation by the Senate.

As Deputy Attorney General, Mr. William Ruckelshaus, refused to carry out the President's explicit directive to discharge Mr. Cox. He, like Mr. Cox, has been discharged of further duties effective immediately.

We have available for you now the exchange of letters between Attorney General Richardson and the President and the other correspondence.

(7) Text of letters exchanged in the resignations of Richardson and Ruckelshaus:

RICHARDSON RESIGNATION

October 20, 1973

The President
The White House

Dear Mr. President:

It is with deep regret that I have been obliged to conclude that circumstances leave me no alternative to the submission of my resignation as Attorney General of the United States.

At the time you appointed me, you gave me the authority to name a special prosecutor if I should consider it appropriate. A few days before my confirmation hearing began, I announced that I would, if confirmed, "appoint a special prosecutor and give him all the independence, authority, and staff support needed to carry out the tasks entrusted to him." I added, "Although he will be in the Department of Justice and report to me—and only to me—he will be aware that his ultimate accountability is to the American people."

At many points throughout the nomination hearings, I reaffirmed my intention to assure the independence of the special prosecutor, and in my statement of his duties and responsibilities, I specified that he would have "full authority" for "determining whether or not to contest the assertion of 'Executive Privilege' or any other testimonial privilege." And while the special prosecutor can be removed from office for "extraordinary improprieties," I also pledged that "The Attorney General will not countermand or interfere with the Special Prosecutor's decisions or actions."

While I fully respect the reasons that have led you to conclude that the Special Prosecutor must be discharged, I trust that you understand that I could not in the light of these firm and repeated commitments carry out your direction that this be done. In the circumstances, therefore, I feel that I have no choice but to resign.

In leaving your Administration, I take with me lasting gratitude for the opportunities you have given me to serve under your leadership in a number of important posts. It has been a privilege to share in your efforts to make the structure of world peace more stable and the structure of our own government more responsive. I believe profoundly in the rightness and importance of those efforts, and I trust that they will meet with increasing success in the remaining years of your Presidency.

Respectfully,

ELLIOT L. RICHARDSON

NIXON TO RICHARDSON

October 20, 1973

Dear Elliot:

It is with the deepest regret and with an understanding of the circumstances which brought you to your decision that I accept your resignation.

Sincerely,

RICHARD NIXON

Honorable Elliot L. Richardson
The Attorney General
Justice Department
Washington, D.C.

RUCKELSHAUS TO NIXON

Dear Mr. President,

It is with deep regret that I tender my resignation. During your Administration, you have honored me with four appointments—first in the Justice Department's Civil Division, then as administrator of the Environmental Protection Agency, next as acting director of the Federal Bureau of Investigation, and finally as Deputy Attorney General. I have found the challenge of working in the high levels of American Government an unforgettable and rewarding experience.

I shall always be grateful for your having given me the opportunity to serve the American people in this fashion.

I am, of course, sorry that my conscience will not permit me to carry out your instruction to discharge Archibald Cox. My disagreement with that action at this time is too fundamental to permit me to act otherwise.

I wish you every success during the remainder of your Administration.

Respectfully,

William D. Ruckelshaus

(8) *Nixon's letter to Bork instructing him to fire Cox and Bork's letter dismissing Cox:*

NIXON TO BORK

October 20, 1973

Dear Mr. Bork:

I have today accepted the resignations of Attorney General Richardson and Deputy Attorney General Ruckelshaus. In accordance with Title 28, Section 508(b) of the United States Code and of Title 28, Section 0.132(a) of the Code of Federal Regulations, it is now incumbent upon you to perform both the duties as Solicitor General, and duties of and act as Attorney General.

In his press conference today Special Prosecutor Archibald Cox made it apparent that he will not comply with the instruction I issued to him, through Attorney General Richardson, yesterday. Clearly the Government of the United States cannot function if employees of the Executive Branch are free to ignore in this fashion the instructions of the President. Accordingly, in your capacity of Acting Attorney General, I direct you to discharge Mr. Cox immediately and to take all steps necessary to return to the Department of Justice the functions now being performed by the Watergate Special Prosecution Force.

It is my expectation that the Department of Justice will continue with full vigor the investigations and prosecutions that had been entrusted to the Watergate Special Prosecution Force.

Sincerely,

RICHARD NIXON

Honorable Robert H. Bork
The Acting Attorney General
Justice Department
Washington, D.C.

BORK TO COX

October 20, 1973

Dear Mr. Cox:

As provided by Title 28, Section 508(b) of the United States Code and Title 28, Section 0.132(a) of the Code of Federal Regulations, I have today assumed the duties of Acting Attorney General.

In that capacity I am, as instructed by the President, discharging you, effective at once, from your position as Special Prosecutor, Watergate Special Prosecution Force.

Very truly yours,

ROBERT H. BORK
Acting Attorney General

Honorable Archibald Cox
Special Prosecutor
Watergate Special Prosecution Force
1425 K Street, N.W.
Washington, D.C.

(9) Richardson's opening statement at a nationally televised news conference Oct. 23:

There can be no greater privilege and there is no greater satisfaction than the opportunity to serve one's country. I shall always be grateful to President Nixon for giving me that opportunity in several demanding positions.

Although I strongly believe in the general purposes and priorities of his administration, I have been compelled to conclude that I could better serve my country by resigning from public office than by continuing in it. This is true for two reasons:

(1) Because to continue would have forced me to refuse to carry out a direct order of the President.

(2) Because I did not agree with the decisions which brought about the necessity for the issuance of that order.

In order to make clear how this dilemma came about, I wish to set forth as plainly as I can the facts of the unfolding drama which came to a climax last Saturday afternoon. To begin, I shall go back to Monday of last week. Two courts—the District Court and the Court of Appeals of the District of Columbia—had ruled that the privilege protecting presidential communications must give way to the criminal process, but only to the extent that a compelling necessity had been shown. The President had a right of further review in the Supreme Court of the United States; he had a right, in other words, to try to persuade the Supreme Court that the long-term public interest in maintaining the confidentiality of presidential communications is more important than the public interest in the prosecution of a particular criminal case, especially where other evidence is available. Had he insisted on exercising that right, however, the issue would have been subject to continuing litigation and controversy for a prolonged additional period, and this at a time of acute international crisis.

Against this background, the President decided on Monday afternoon to make a new effort to resolve the impasse. He would ask Sen. John

Stennis, a man of impeccable reputation for truthfulness and integrity, to listen to the tapes and verify the completeness and accuracy of a record of all pertinent portions. This record would then be available to the grand jury and for any other purpose for which it was needed. Believing, however, that only the issue of his own involvement justified any breach of the principle of confidentiality and wishing to avoid continuing litigation, he made it a condition of the offer to provide a verified record of the subpoenaed tapes that access to any other tapes or records would be barred.

I regarded the proposal to rely on Sen. Stennis for a verified record (for the sake of brevity I will call it "the Stennis proposal") as reasonable, but I did not think it should be tied to the foreclosure of the right of the special prosecutor to invoke judicial process in future cases. Accordingly, I outlined the Stennis proposal to Mr. Cox later on Monday afternoon and proposed that the question of other tapes and documents be deferred. Mr. Cox and I discussed the Stennis proposal again on Tuesday morning.

On Wednesday afternoon, responding to Mr. Cox's suggestion that he could deal more concretely with the proposal if he had something on paper, I sent him the document captioned "A Proposal," which he released in his Saturday press conference. On the afternoon of the next day he sent me his comments on the proposal, including the requirement that he have assured access to other tapes and documents. The President's lawyers regarded Mr. Cox's comments as amounting to a rejection of the Stennis proposal, and there followed the break-off of negotiations reflected in the correspondence with Charles Alan Wright released by Mr. Cox.

My position at that time was that Sen. Stennis' verified record of the tapes should nevertheless be presented to the district court for the court's determination of its adequacy to satisfy the subpoenas, still leaving other questions to be dealt with as they arose. That was still my view when at 8 p.m. Friday evening the President issued his statement directing Mr. Cox to make no further attempts by judicial process to obtain tapes, notes or memoranda of presidential conversations.

A half hour before this statement was issued, I received a letter from the President instructing me to give Mr. Cox this order. I did not act on the instruction, but instead, shortly after noon on Saturday, sent the President a letter restating my position. The President, however, decided to hold fast to the position announced the night before. When, therefore, Mr. Cox rejected that position and gave his objections to the Stennis proposal, as well as his reasons for insisting on assured access to other tapes and memoranda, the issue of presidential authority versus the independence and public accountability of the special prosecutor was squarely joined.

The President at that point thought he had no choice but to direct the attorney general to discharge Mr. Cox. And I, given my role in guaranteeing the independence of the special prosecutor, as well as my belief in the public interests embodied in that role, felt equally clear that I could not discharge him. And so I resigned.

At stake in the final analysis is the very integrity of the governmental processes I came to the Department of Justice to help restore. My own single most important commitment to this objective was my commitment to the independence of the special prosecutor. I could not be faithful to this commitment and also acquiesce in the curtailment of his authority. To say this, however, is not to charge the President with a failure to respect the claims of the investigative process: given the importance he attached to the principle of presidential confidentiality, he believed that his willingness to allow Sen. Stennis to verify the subpoenaed tapes fully met these claims.

The rest is for the American people to judge. On the fairness with which you do so may well rest the future well-being and security of our beloved country.

KISSINGER ON MIDDLE EAST

October 25, 1973

First official indications of the vulnerability of the Soviet-American detente turned up Oct. 25 in the wake of continued fighting in the Middle East regardless of the adoption of United Nations cease-fire resolutions on Oct. 22 and Oct. 23. Calling together newsmen at the State Department Oct. 25, Secretary of State Henry A. Kissinger sought to explain that the U.S. military alert initiated in the early hours that day, reportedly in response to the possibility of a unilateral Soviet movement of troops into the Mideast to supervise a military truce, had been "precautionary" and was "not in any sense irrevocable." Kissinger said U.S. forces had been alerted because of the "ambiguity" of the situation. Ringing clear in his deliberately chosen mild words was the recognition that any concrete threat to Soviet-American pledges of "peaceful coexistence" could indeed topple the entire interdependent detente—and thereby destroy President Nixon's policy of improved relations with the Soviet Union, fostered at the Moscow and Washingtom summits. (See Historic Documents 1972, p. 431; this volume, p. 587.) Kissinger also warned that events could not be allowed to race beyond the control of the two powers lest both countries find themselves in the position of having to choose between their allies and the newly gained detente.

At the root of the crisis was the danger that the Middle East war could draw the super powers into a direct confrontation. The issue of a peacekeeping force, which arose just at the Middle East truce appeared to be taking hold, threatened to produce such a collision. But the near confrontation was averted the afternoon of Oct. 25 when

Soviet Ambassador Yakov Malik told the United Nations that his country would accept the U.S.-backed proposal for a supervisory force without big-power participation. The U.N. Security Council approved that afternoon a resolution establishing the force and calling for the third time for a truce in the Mideast. Plans for the truce   had initially been drawn up in Moscow Oct. 20-21 during talks between Kissinger and Soviet Communist Party leader Leonid I. Brezhnev and had been accepted by Israel and Egypt. But following adoption of the first two U.N. truce resolutions, the Egyptian military position had steadily deteriorated. Israeli troops had crossed to the west bank of the Suez canal and isolated 20,000 Egyptians.

The sense of crisis over a possible U.S.-Soviet confrontation in the Mideast had been heightened mid-day Oct. 25 when Sen. Henry M. Jackson (D Wash.) stated that the Soviet Union had sent a "brutal" note to the United States warning that Russian forces would be sent unilaterally to the Mideast if the United States refused to join in a peacekeeping operation. At this press conference, Kissinger played down Jackson's remark, noting that the senator had not been party to the White House discussions. Kissinger also abruptly dismissed any suggestion that the crisis over the Middle East had been created by the Nixon administration as a smokescreen for its Watergate troubles. He called the suggestion a "symptom" of what had happened to the country. President Nixon said at his news conference Oct. 26 (see p. 905) that the Brezhnev note "was very firm and...left very little to the imagination as to what he intended." It was "the most difficult crisis we have faced since the Cuban confrontation of 1962," the President asserted. But Brezhnev took issue with Nixon the same day and accused the United States of the "artificial drumming up" of a crisis over the Middle East in order to justify the U.S. military alert. Brezhnev called "fantastic" any American assumption that the Soviet Union would take unilateral military action in the Mideast. A month later the Washington Post *carried a report of the contents of Brezhnev's message to Nixon. The* Post *Nov. 28 quoted the Soviet leader as having said during the crisis: "I will say it straight" that if the United States will not act "with us in this matter, we should be faced with the necessity urgently to consider the question of taking appropriate steps unilaterally."*

> *Text of Secretary of State Henry A. Kissinger's remarks to newsmen at a State Department news conference on the Middle East Oct. 25:*

Secretary Kissinger: Ladies and gentlemen, I thought the most useful introduction to your questions would be a summary of events between October 6 and today so that you can evaluate our actions, the situation in which we find ourselves, and our future course.

The crisis for us started at 6 a.m. on October 6, when I was awakened with the information that another Arab-Israeli war was in progress. I mention this personal detail because it answers the question that the United States intervention prevented Israel from taking preemptive action. The United States made no demarche to either side before October 6, because all the intelligence at our disposal and all the intelligence given to us by foreign countries suggested that there was no possibility of the outbreak of a war. We had no reason to give any advice to any of the participants, because we did not believe—nor, may I say, did the Israeli Government—that an attack was imminent.

In the three hours between 6 a.m. and 9 a.m., we made major efforts to prevent the outbreak of the war by acting as an intermediary between the parties, of assuring each of them that the other was—attempting to obtain the assurance of each side that the other one had no aggressive intention.

Before this process could be completed, however, war had broken out. And it started the process in which we are still engaged.

I do not think any useful purpose is served in reviewing every individual diplomatic move, but I thought it would be useful to indicate some of the basic principles we attempted to follow.

Throughout the crisis the President was convinced that we had two major problems: first, to end hostilities as quickly as possible—but, secondly, to end hostilities in a manner that would enable us to make a major contribution to removing the conditions that have produced four wars between Arabs and Israelis in the last 25 years.

We were aware that there were many interested parties. There were, of course, the participants in the conflict—Egypt and Syria on the Arab side, aided by many other Arab countries; Israel on the other. There was the Soviet Union. There were the other permanent members of the Security Council. And, of course, there was the United States.

It was our view that the United States could be most effective in both the tasks outlined by the President—that is, of ending hostilities, as well as of making a contribution to a permanent peace in the Middle East—if we conducted ourselves so that we could remain in permanent contact with all of these elements in the equation.

Throughout the first week, we attempted to crystallize a consensus in the Security Council which would bring about a cease-fire on terms that the world community could support. We stated our basic principles on October 8. We did not submit them to a formal vote, because we realized that no majority was available and we did not want sides to be chosen prematurely. On October 10 the Soviet Union began an airlift, which began fairly moderately but which by October 12 had achieved fairly substantial levels.

Let me say a word here about our relationship with the Soviet Union throughout this crisis and what we have attempted to achieve. The United States and the Soviet Union are, of course, ideological and, to some extent, political adversaries. But the United States and the Soviet Union also have a very special responsibility. We possess—each of us—nuclear arsenals capable of annihilating humanity. We—both of us—have a special duty to see to it that confrontations are kept within bounds that do not threaten civilized life. Both of us, sooner or later, will have to come to realize that the issues that divide the world today, and foreseeable issues, do not justify the unparalleled catastrophe that a nuclear war would represent. And therefore, in all our dealings with the Soviet Union, we have attempted to keep in mind and we have attempted to move them to a position in which this overriding interest that humanity shares with us is never lost sight of.

In a speech—Pacem in Terris—I pointed out that there are limits beyond which we cannot go. I stated that we will oppose the attempt by any other country to achieve a position of predominance, either globally or regionally; that we would resist any attempt to exploit a policy of detente to weaken our alliances; and that we would react if the relaxations of tensions were used as a cover to exacerbate conflicts in international trouble spots. We have followed these principles in the current situation.

It is easy to start confrontations, but in this age we have to know where we will be at the end and not only what pose to strike at the beginning.

Throughout the first week we attempted to bring about a moderation in the level of outside supplies that were introduced into the area and we attempted to work with the Soviet Union on a cease-fire resolution which would bring an end to the conflict.

This first attempt failed, on Saturday, October 13, for a variety of reasons—including, perhaps, a misassessment of the military situation by some of the participants. We were then faced with the inability to produce a Security Council resolution that would command a consensus, and the substantial introduction of arms by an outside power into the area. At this point, on Saturday, October 13, the President decided that the United States would have to start a resupply effort of its own. And the United States, from that time on, has engaged in maintaining the military balance in the Middle East in order to bring about a negotiated settlement that we had sought.

Concurrent with this, we informed the Soviet Union that our interest in working out an acceptable solution still remained very strong and that as part of this solution we were prepared to discuss a mutual limitation of arms supply into the area.

In the days that followed, the Soviet Union and we discussed various approaches to this question, the basic difficulty being how to reconcile the Arab insistence on an immediate commitment to a return to the 1967 borders with Israeli insistence on secure boundaries and a negotiated outcome.

As you all know, on October 16, Prime Minister Kosygin went to Cairo to work on this problem with the leaders of Egypt. He returned to the Soviet Union on October 19.

We began exploring a new formula for ending the war that evening, though it was still unacceptable to us. And while we were still considering that formula, General Secretary Brezhnev sent an urgent request to President Nixon that I be sent to Moscow to conduct the negotiations in order to speed an end to hostilities that might be difficult to contain were they to continue.

The President agreed to Mr. Brezhnev's request, and as all of you know, I left for Moscow in the early morning of October 20.

We spent two days of very intense negotiations, and we developed a formula which we believe was acceptable to all of the parties and which we continue to believe represented a just solution to this tragic conflict.

The Security Council resolution had, as you all know, three parts. It called for an immediate cease-fire-in-place. It called for the immediate implementation of Security Council Resolution 242, which was adopted in November 1967 and which states certain general principles on the basis of which peace should be achieved in the Middle East. And, thirdly, it called for negotiations between the parties concerned under appropriate auspices to bring about a just and durable peace in the Middle East.

This third point was the first international commitment to negotiations between the parties in the Middle East conflict. The United States and the Soviet Union were prepared to offer their auspices, if this proved to be acceptable to the parties, to bring about and then to speed the process of negotiations. The United States continues to be ready to carry out this understanding. This, then, was the situation when I returned from Moscow and Tel Aviv on Monday evening.

Since then, events have taken the following turn. On the first day— that is, Tuesday—of the implementation of the cease-fire, there was a breakdown of the cease-fire which led to certain Israeli territorial gains. The United States supported a resolution which called on the participants to observe the cease-fire, to return to the places from which the fighting started, and to invite United Nations observers to observe the implementation of the cease-fire. This seemed to us a fair resolution.

In the last two days, the discussion in the Security Council and the communications that have been associated with it have taken a turn that seemed to us worrisome. We were increasingly confronted with a cascade of charges which were difficult to verify in the absence of United Nations observers and a demand for action that it was not within our power to take. There was a proposal, for example, that joint U.S. and Soviet military forces be introduced into the Middle East to bring about an observance of the cease-fire.

I would like to state on behalf of the President the United States position on this matter very clearly. The United States does not favor and will not approve the sending of a joint Soviet-United States force into the Middle East. The United States believes that what is needed in the Middle East above all is a determination of the facts, a determination where the lines are, and a determination of who is doing the shooting, so that the Security Council can take appropriate action. It is inconceivable that the forces of the great powers should be introduced in the numbers that would be necessary to overpower both of the participants. It is inconceivable that we should transplant the great-power rivalry into the Middle East or, alternatively, that we should impose a military condominium by the United States and the Soviet Union. The United States is even more opposed to the unilateral introduction by any great power, especially by any nuclear power, of military forces into the Middle East in whatever guise those forces should be introduced. And it is the ambiguity of some of the actions and communications and certain readiness measures that were observed that caused the President at a special meeting of the National Security Council last night at 3 a.m., to order certain precautionary measures to be taken by the United States.

The United States position with respect to peace in the Middle East is as follows: The United States stands for a strict observance of the cease-fire as defined in the United Nations Security Council Resolution 338, adopted on October 22. The United States will support and give all assistance and is willing to supply some personnel to a United Nations observer force whose responsibility it is to report to the Security Council about the violations of the cease-fire and which would have the responsibility, in addition, of aiding the parties in taking care of humanitarian and other concerns that are produced by the fact that on the Egyptian-Israeli front a series of enclaves exist in which demarcation is extremely difficult.

If the Security Council wishes, the United States is prepared to agree to an international force, provided it does not include any participants from the permanent members of the Security Council, to be introduced into the area as an additional guarantee of the cease-fire.

The United States is prepared to make a major effort to help speed a political solution which is just to all sides.

The United States recognizes that the conditions that produced the war on October 6 cannot be permitted to continue, and the United States, both bilaterally and unilaterally, is prepared to lend its diplomatic weight to a serious effort in the negotiating process foreseen by paragraph 3 of Security Council Resolution 338.

We are therefore at a rather crucial point.

From many points of view, the chances for peace in the Middle East are quite promising.

Israel has experienced once more the trauma of war and has been given an opportunity for the negotiations it has sought for all of its existence, and it must be ready for the just and durable peace that the Security Council asks for.

The Arab nations have demonstrated their concern and have received international assurances that other countires will take an interest in these negotiations.

The Soviet Union is not threatened in any of its legitimate positions in the Middle East. The principles I mentioned earlier of the special responsibility of the great nuclear powers to strike a balance between their local interests and their global interest and their humane obligations remain.

And, seen in this perspective, none of the issues that are involved in the observance of the cease-fire would warrant unilateral action.

As for the United States, the President has stated repeatedly that this administration has no higher goal than to leave to its successors a world that is safer and more secure than the one we found. It is an obligation that any President, of whatever party, will have to discharge, and it is a responsibility which must be solved—if mankind is to survive—by the great nuclear countries at some point, before it is too late.

But we have always stated that it must be a peace, with justice. The terms that have been agreed to in the United Nations provide an opportunity for the peoples of the Middle East to determine their own fate in consultation and negotiation—for the first time in 25 years.

This is an opportunity we are prepared to foster. It is an opportunity which is essential for this ravaged area and which is equally essential for the peace of the world. And it is an opportunity that the great powers have no right to be permitted to miss.

Now I'll be glad to answer questions.

Q. Dr. Kissinger, could you go into a little more detail on the Soviet threat that caused the alerting of U.S. military elements last night? And also, if you could tell us if Ambassador Dobrynin [Anatoly F. Dobrynin, Soviet Ambassador to the United States] delivered you a brutal note, as described by Senator Jackson, on the Middle East situation?

Secretary Kissinger: Senator Jackson is a good friend of mine, but he does not participate in our deliberations.

I will not discuss the details of individual communications.

We became aware of the alerting of certain Soviet units, and we were puzzled by the behavior of some Soviet representatives in the discussions that took place.

We do not consider ourselves in a confrontation with the Soviet Union. We do not believe it is necessary, at this moment, to have a confrontation. In fact, we are prepared to work cooperatively toward the realization of the objectives which we have set ourselves.

But cooperative action precluded unilateral action, and the President decided that it was essential that we make clear our attitude toward unilateral steps.

Q. Mr. Secretary, when you were, early on, talking about the special responsibilty of the two nuclear superpowers to avoid anything which would eliminate or incinerate humanity, you went on to say that there are limits beyond which we can't go. And among those, you said we would resist any attempt to exploit the detente in a manner to weaken others or weaken our allies—I didn't get that exactly, but you will recall what you said.

And what I want to know—what I wanted to ask you is whether you believe that the action of the Russians so far, particularly in departing from what you thought was an agreement, has gone to the point where it threatens exploitation of the detente to an adverse extent.

Secretary Kissinger: We are not yet prepared to make this judgment. We have to realize, of course, as I pointed out in my remarks, that the Soviet Union and we are in a very unique relationship. We are at one and the same time adversaries and partners in the preservation of peace.

As adversaries, we often find ourselves drawn into potential confrontations and each of us has friends that let themselves pursue objectives that may not be sought fully by either of us.

When we took the precautionary steps of which you are all aware, we did so because we thought there might be a possibility that matters might go beyond the limits which I have described. But we are not yet prepared to say that they have gone beyond these limits, and we believe that the possibility of moving in the direction that the Security Council has established earlier this week is still very real. And if the Security Council today were to pass a resolution that permitted the introduction of United Nations forces except those of the permanent members, the United States would feel that we are back on the road that had been charted earlier this week.

Q. Mr. Secretary, could you tell us whether the United States received a specific warning from the Soviet Union that it would send its forces unilaterally into the Middle East? Do you have intelligence that the Russians are preparing for such an action? The reason I raise these questions—as you know, there has been some line of speculation this morning that the American alert might have been prompted as much perhaps by American domestic requirements as by the real requirements of diplomacy in the Middle East. And I wonder if you could provide some additional information on that.

Secretary Kissinger: Marvin [Marvin Kalb, CBS News], we are attempting to conduct the foreign policy of the United States with regard for what we owe not just to the electorate but to future generations. And it is a symptom of what is happening to our country that it could even be suggested that the United States would alert its forces for domestic reasons.

We do not think it is wise at this moment to go into the details of the diplomatic exchanges that prompted this decision. Upon the conclusion of the present diplomatic efforts, one way or the other, we will make the record available, and we will be able to go into greater detail. And I am absolutely confident that it will be seen that the President had no other choice as a responsible national leader.

Q: Dr. Kissinger, would you say, sir, why the United States feels that the permanent members of the Security Council should not send forces, although there is a chapter in the U.N. Charter, I believe, that calls upon all members of the U.N. to provide forces if called upon to do so.

Secretary Kissinger: We believe that the particular provision of the charter which you mentioned should be seen in the light of the particular circumstances. When you have a situation in which several of the permanent members may have conflicting interests, and when the presence of the forces of the permanent members may themselves contribute to the tension in the area, it seems to us the only possible course is to exclude the members—the forces of all permanent members.

It would be a disaster if the Middle East, already so torn by local rivalries, would now become, as a result of a U.N. decision, a legitimized theater for the competition of the military forces of the great nuclear powers.

And therefore it seemed to us that the political purposes would be best served if any international force that were introduced were composed of countries that have no possiblity of themselves being drawn into rivalry as a result of being—

Q. Dr. Kissinger, it may seem obvious, but I would just like to ask you—is the purpose of the alert which is now going on to tell the Soviet Union that if they send forces into the Middle East we will do the same?

Secretary Kissinger: I don't want to speculate about what the President may decide to do in circumstances which we fervently hope will not arise. It would seem to us that to threaten all that has been achieved in the search for peace by unilateral action would be a step of irresponsibility that we do not believe is likely. And therefore I do not want to speculate what the United States would do if it should appear that instead of beginning an era of cooperation we were thrown back to the confrontations which sooner or later will have to be surmounted—because humanity cannot stand the eternal conflict of those who have the capacity to destroy it.

Q. Mr. Secretary, Cairo Radio said that such an offer of Soviet troops for enforcing the cease-fire has been received from Moscow. Has such an offer been made, and if so, have the Soviet troops indeed been alerted and are they on the move?

Secretary Kissinger: We are not, of course, aware of the diplomatic exchanges that may go on between the Government of Eygpt and the Government of the Soviet Union. We are also not aware of any Soviet forces that may have been introduced into Eygpt. And we believe, and we will bend every effort in that direction, that any actions that are taken by any country in the Middle East will be within the framework of the Security Council and of United Nations decisions.

I want to repeat again: We do not now consider ourselves in a confrontation with the Soviet Union. We continue to be prepared, and we believe it is entirely possible to maintain the direction that has brought us to this point and on which the peace of the world depends.

Q. Mr. Secretary, do you believe that the Soviet Union has threatened unilateral action and pushed this circumstance to the brink of confrontation? Do you see it possible that they saw the events of last weekend as having so weakened the President—he was threatened with impeachment—that they saw a target of opportunity and decided to move?

Secretary Kissinger: Speculation about motives is always dangerous. But one cannot have crisis of authority in a society for a period of months without paying a price somewhere along the line.

Q. Dr. Kissinger, from a public standpoint, until this morning the public would have had the belief and the view that this crisis was in hand, that the cease-fire was taking hold. You have declined to discuss the diplomatic context of the specific communications. But was there prior to this latest sudden development any indication that this situation might go into such a direction?

Secretary Kissinger: No, there was not. Until yesterday afternoon we had every reason to believe that the basic direction that had been established, and to which all parties had agreed, would in fact be implemented. And I repeat: We still believe that it is possible to continue in this direction. Nobody can gain from introducing great power rivalry or from compounding—by compounding great-power rivalry. The overriding goal in the Middle East must be a just and durable peace between the Arab nations and Israel. That, the United States is prepared and, indeed, determined to promote. And that is the issue to which we should address ourselves.

Q. Dr. Kissinger, to follow that up, please, Senator Jackson, among others, has said that this government has been operating under what he called an illusion of detente from the very beginning.

Can you be a little more precise now under these circumstances about the status of the detente with the Soviet Union?

Secretary Kissinger: Mr. Lisagor [Peter Lisagor, Chicago Daily News], we have, from the beginning of this administration, recognized that there is a—that we are dealing with an ideological and political adversary. We have also believed that we had a historic obligation, precisely in these conditions of being in opposition, to attempt to remove the dangers of war. We have always made clear, and we have always practiced, that we would resist any foreign policy adventures through the many crises in the early parts of this administration.

Where we have differed with some of our critics, it was in our conviction that it was dangerous to attempt to interfere in the domestic affairs of a country with such a different domestic structure and such a different ideological orientation.

We have maintained the integrity of our allies and the security of the United States while reducing the danger of war.

As I said in my remarks, this is a historic task that somebody will have to solve and that it is in the interests of all Americans and all of mankind that it be solved as quickly as possible.

As for the status of the detente, I think we can make a better judgment when we know whether peace has taken hold. If the Soviet Union and we can work cooperatively, first toward establishing the cease-fire, and then toward promoting a durable settlement in the Middle East, then the detente will have proved itself. If this does not happen, then we have made an effort—for which we have paid no price—that had to be made. And then one has to wait for another moment when the task of insuring or of bringing peace to mankind can be attempted.

Q. Dr. Kissinger, the reports of this joint—the Soviet plan for a joint Soviet-U.S. force were rather widespread before you went to Moscow, especially in Eastern Europe. Did Mr. Brezhnev discuss this idea with you in any way? And if not, why do you think he kept quiet about it then only appear to activate it a few days later?

Secretary Kissinger: I don't know what plans were widespread in Eastern Europe. I can only deal with plans which reach us in some official manner. The plan for a joint U.S.-Soviet military force in the Middle East was never broached to us, either publicly or privately, until. yesterday. And we immediately made clear that we would not participate in such a force and also that we would oppose any unilateral moves.

Q. Dr. Kissinger, you have said that U.S.-Soviet auspices might be useful in moving this along diplomatically. Are you prepared personally to play a role in getting these talks started? And secondly, have all the parties accepted the necessity for direct Arab-Israeli talks?

Secretary Kissinger: We have not been in equally close contact with all of the parties. And we have reason to believe that a sufficient number of the parties have accepted these talks for them to start. And indeed, as late as yesterday afternoon, preliminary conversations took place between Ambassador Dobrynin and me about the site, the participation, ant the procedures for these talks.

Q. *Dr. Kissinger, earlier you referred to legitimate Soviet interests in the Middle East and indicated that we felt they were not threatened there. Have the Soviets indicated they agree with your assessment?*

Secretary Kissinger: On the basis of the conversations that I had with General Secretary Brezhnev as late as last Sunday and the communications that were exchanged afterward between the President and General Secretary Brezhnev, there was every reason to expect that while of course our interests were not congruent, and while of course there were differences in approach, that a certain parallelism could develop in the direction of producing a permanent peace. And therefore I would have to say that we had reason to believe, and we have no reason yet to alter our estimate, that the joint auspices of which the Security Council resolution speaks can yet be implemented.

Q. *Dr. Kissinger, between the two cease-fire resolutions in the United Nations, in that period the Israeli forces have made substantial military gains on the ground. Is the United States prepared to urge Israel to comply with the resolution which calls for all parties to withdraw to the lines at the time of the first cease-fire?*

Secretary Kissinger: The United States supported both resolutions and is today supporting another resolution containing similar provisions as well as a provision for an international force drawn from all member states of the United Nations—for which all member states of the United Nations would be eligible except the permanent members of the Security Council.

Q. *Dr. Kissinger, I notice that you said the President decided on the military alert and that you said the President had no other choice. Did you recommend this, or did the President initiate the military alert matter, and do you feel that it is a totally rational decision?*

Secretary Kissinger: Mr. Mollenhoff [Clark R. Mollenhoff, Des Moines Register and Tribune], I have a general rule not to provide a checklist of what advice I give to the President. But due to the particular implications of your remark, I may say that all of the President's senior advisers—all the members of the National Security Council—were unanimous in their recommendation, as a result of a deliberation in which the President did not himself participate, and which he joined only after they had formed their judgment, that the measures taken—that he in fact ordered—were in the essential national interest.

Q. *Dr. Kissinger, would you say what, in your judgment, changed from the period yesterday when you and Ambassador Dobrynin were talking about participation and site and so on for talks and the period*

last night which led the Soviets to take the action that they took?
What, in your estimation, changed?

Secretary Kissinger: I would like to make clear that as of now the
Soviet Union has not yet taken any irrevocable action. It is our
hope that such an action will not be taken.

I repeat again what I have said on many occasions in this press
conference. We are not seeking an opportunity to confront the Soviet
Union. We are not asking the Soviet Union to pull back from anything
that it has done.

The opportunity for pursuing the joint course in the Security Council
and in the diplomacy afterward is open. The measures we took and
which the President ordered were precautionary in nature. They
were not directed at any actions that had already been taken. And
therefore, there is no reason for any country to back off anything that it
has not yet done.

As to the motives, I think we should assess that after the current
situation is over.

Q. Dr. Kissinger—

Q. Mr. Secretary—

Secretary Kissinger: Well, let me get this question, and then you.

Q. Sir, in the reasons that prompted the President to make his de-
cision, did any of those reasons include a threat aimed against this
country as opposed to a threat in the Middle East?

Secretary Kissinger: I really do not think it is appropriate for me
to go into the details of the diplomatic exchanges. We are not talking
of threats that have been made against one another. We are not talking of a missile-crisis-type situation. We are talking of a situation where
72 hours ago we still introduced joint resolutions, where the
necessity for a joint movement toward peace is as real now as it was
then, where the participants in the Middle East have everything to
gain from a period of quiet and from at least watching or attempting to
see what an American diplomatic effort can produce. And therefore
we are talking about a precautionary situation and not an actual one.

Q. Mr. Secretary, it seems to me that you are asking the Ameri-
can people—you and the President—who are already badly shaken
by the events of the last week, to accept a very dramatic military
alert involving nuclear forces, on the basis of a kind of handful of
smoke without telling them or us exactly why. If I understood you
earlier, you said that we had discovered the alert of some Soviet
forces, and we were disturbed by the behavior apparently of some
people that American officials were dealing with. And that is all
we really have to justify this alert.

Now, this country is pretty badly shaken right now. And I wonder
if you can give us any more information that will help convince people
that there is some solid basis for the actions that have been taken.

Secretary Kissinger: We are attempting to preserve the peace in very difficult circumstances. It is up to you ladies and gentlemen to determine whether this is the moment to try to create a crisis of confidence in the field of foreign policy as well. We have tried to give you as much information as we decently and safely and properly can under these conditions. As soon as there is a clear outcome we will give you the full information. And after that you will be able to judge whether the decisions were taken hastily or improperly.

The alert that has been ordered is of a precautionary nature and is not of any major and irrevocable—it is not in any sense irrevocable. It is what seemed to be indicated by the situation.

We will be prepared, however, and I am certain within a week, to put the facts before you.

But there has to be a minimum of confidence that the senior officials of the American government are not playing with the lives of the American people.

Q. Dr. Kissinger, the chief problem in the Middle East at the moment seems to be the concern by the Egyptians for the safety of its 3d Army on the east bank of the canal. Are there any steps being taken to possibly ameliorate their situation? And secondly, could you give us some more details about the results of your conversations as to forthcoming talks? About 12 hours ago everybody was waiting for talks to begin. Can you tell us in which direction we can anticipate that will go?

Secretary Kissinger: We believe that the particular problems that are raised by a cease-fire in which the forces are deployed in such curious fashion—each army having units behind the lines of the other—that these conditions first of all produce, especially in the initial phases, many difficulties. We also are absolutely convinced that with the presence of observers, with good will on all sides, and with the active participation of the United States and the Soviet Union, that the difficulties can be substantially eased and eventually removed.

It is my understanding, for example, that some humanitarian supplies reached the 3d Army today.

And we would certainly be prepared to lend our good offices to an effort in which neither side gained a decisive advantage as a result of the deployment of their forces.

I therefore am convinced that the particular conditions of the cease-fire, difficult as they are, can be dealt with, and can be ameliorated with statemanship on all sides.

Q. Mr. Secretary, you have surely told Dobrynin and others what you have told us and perhaps even more. Can you give us any indication of what effect this had on these people?

Secretary Kissinger: We are at this moment in the Security Council debating the resolution that we are supporting. If that resolution is accepted and carried out, we believe that it will lead to an immediate easing of the situation and to a restoration of the conditions as we observed them at noon yesterday.

May I say also that this press conference was scheduled at a time before this latest event was known or suspected. And I went through with it in order to be able to put into perspective the evolution that brought us here and as much of the reasoning as I could, given the delicacy of the situation.

Q. You didn't answer the second half of my question, Dr. Kissinger—

Secretary Kissinger: What was the second half?

Q. About negotiations, where they were going to go.

Secretary Kissinger: We believe that negotiations can and should begin in a matter of a very few weeks.

Q. How?

Secretary Kissinger: How?

Q. Yes. You said we were discussing participation and forum. I wondered if you could give us more details.

Secretary Kissinger: I think we should wait until the parties are prepared to announce this.

Q. Mr. Secretary, have you any indication of how the Soviet Union will vote on the resolution today?

Secretary Kissinger: I think the debate is still in process. And once we know the result of that vote—

Q. Is there any indication of how they might vote?

Secretary Kissinger: We are hopeful that the Soviet Union will vote for the resolution.

Q. If the resolution is passed, Dr. Kissinger, do you expect the alert would be taken off?

Secretary Kissinger: The alert will not last one minute longer than we believe is necessary.

Q. Dr. Kissinger—

Secretary Kissinger: And it would be taken off as soon as any danger of unilateral action is removed.

Q. Dr. Kissinger, concerning the role that the United States may play in obtaining conditions for an enduring peace, several months ago you were reported as saying that you were supportive of an American policy that supports Israel but not Israeli conquests. What is your view on that now?

Secretary Kissinger: I think I was quoted to that effect four and a half years ago before I understood the special nomenclature that is attached to the various ground rules.

Our position is, as I have stated publicly, that the conditions that produced this war were clearly intolerable to the Arab nations and that in a process of negotiations it will be necessary to make substantial concessions.

The problem will be to relate the Arab concern for the sovereignty over territories to the Israeli concern for secure boundaries.

We believe that the process of negotiations between the parties is an essential component of this. And as the President has stated to the four Arab Foreign Ministers, and as we have stated repeatedly, we will make a major effort to bring about a solution that is considered just by all parties. But I think no purpose would be served by my trying to delimit the exact nature of all of these provisions.

The press: Mr. Secretary, thank you very much.

▼▼▼

NIXON'S ATTACKS ON NEWS MEDIA

October 26, 1973

President Nixon held a nationally televised news conference Oct. 26 to explain his reasons for firing special Watergate prosecutor Archibald Cox, accepting the resignations of U.S. Attorney General Elliot L. Richardson and Deputy Attorney General William D. Ruckelshaus and initiating the Oct. 25 world-wide U.S. military alert. (Story of firing and resignations, see p. 859; U.S. military alert, see p. 881.) But the President diverted the spotlight from those urgent matters by unleashing what some viewed as his strongest attack to date on the news media. Coming down hard on the television networks, he characterized their reporting of the Cox firing as "outrageous, vicious," "frantic" and "hysterical." Asked why he was so angry with television and other news reporters, Nixon retorted in a final crushing blow, "Don't get the impression that you arouse my anger.... You see, one can only be angry with those he respects."

From the outset of the news conference, Nixon sought to de-emphasize the departure of the Justice Department's two top men and the subsequent firing of Cox and instead to play up the greater importance of the Middle East crisis. He characterized himself as a strong, decisive leader in his efforts to help settle the Arab-Israeli war. "Even in this week, when many thought that the President was shell-shocked, unable to act, the President acted decisively in the interest of peace, in the interest of the country," he said, "and I can assure you that whatever shocks gentlemen of the press may have or others—political people— these shocks will not affect me in doing my job."

In an opening statement, Nixon outlined the chronology of negotiations between the United States and the Soviet Union for enforcing
the settlement of the Israeli-Arab war. A "very significant and potentially explosive crisis developed" on Oct. 24, Nixon said. "We obtained
information which led us to believe that the Soviet Union was planning
to send a very substantial force into the Mideast—a military force."
As a result, he said he had ordered a "precautionary" world-wide
military alert for American forces shortly after midnight to signal to
the Soviets that the United States "could not accept any unilateral
move on their part to move military forces into the Mideast." Shortly
thereafter, Nixon sent Soviet Communist Party Leader Leonid I.
Brezhnev "an urgent message" asking him not to send troops, and
urging instead that the Soviets join the United States in supporting a
United Nations resolution that would exclude major powers from
participating in a peacekeeping force. "We reached the conclusion
that we would jointly support the resolution, which was adopted in the
United Nations."

Concerning Watergate, Nixon defended his firing of Cox and announced that Acting Attorney General Robert H. Bork would appoint
a replacement. But Nixon added that the new special prosecutor would
not be given documents "involving a conversation with the President."
Nixon also endorsed the handling by his long-time friend, C. G. (Bebe)
Rebozo, of a $100,000 cash contribution from an emissary of billionaire
Howard Hughes. Nixon said Rebozo had exercised "very good judgment in doing what he did."

Turning away from the events of the previous weeks, which had
included court orders to turn over the taped White House conversations (see p. 839), the introduction in Congress of multiple resolutions
to impeach Nixon, and the resignation and subsequent sentencing of
Vice President Agnew (see p. 827), Nixon vented his outrage over the
conduct of the news media. He launched a fiery attack on the national
television and radio networks, saying that the electronic media had
changed the country's means of coping with "shocks." He argued that
"when people are pounded night after night with that kind of frantic,
hysterical reporting, it naturally shakes their confidence." He claimed
that in 27 years of public life, "I have never heard or seen such outrageous, vicious, distorted reporting." Columnist James Reston wrote
in The New York Times Oct. 27 that Nixon's statement that one was
angered only by those he respected was "about the most vicious remark any American President has made about his critics." Reston
interpreted Nixon's attack on the media as indication that "he was
still boiling mad and emotional underneath the calm, and this startled
his audience and raised again the central question of his judgment
and capacity to govern."

Nixon's political career had been marked with clashes with the press. Perhaps the most publicized encounter occurred in 1962 when he conceded his defeat in the race for governor of California. Nixon blasted the press at that time for its coverage of his campaign and concluded: "You won't have Nixon to kick around anymore, gentlemen, because this is my last press conference." Friction between Nixon and the media persisted when he assumed office in 1969. His administration came under fire from critics who accused it of attempting to influence newsmen and networks to give administration actions and views favorable treatment. For example, Vice President Agnew's blasts at the networks and certain newspapers drew criticism because, critics said, they were backed by implied threats of government reprisal through licensing and antitrust powers.

Other instances of administration-media conflict were the unsuccessful attempt to block publication of the classified Pentagon Papers (for outcome of subsequent trial, see p. 537), the Justice Department's argument that it did not adversely affect freedom of the press to require a reporter to appear before a grand jury, and White House Director of Telecommunications Policy Clay T. Whitehead's insistence that broadcast regulations be changed in order to "restore equilibrium to the broadcasting system." These events had fostered the view that the Nixon administration was generally hostile to the news media; but many newsmen characterized Nixon's remarks Oct. 26 as his strongest attack yet on the press.

Text of President Nixon's Oct. 26 news conference, dealing with the Middle East crisis and Watergate, in which he strongly criticized the news media:

OPENING STATEMENT: THE SITUATION IN THE MIDDLE EAST

THE PRESIDENT. Ladies and gentlemen, before going to your questions, I have a statement with regard to the Mideast which I think will anticipate some of the questions, because this will update the information which is breaking rather fast in that area, as you know, for the past 2 days.

The cease-fire is holding. There have been some violations, but generally speaking it can be said that it is holding at this time. As you know, as a result of the U.N. resolution which was agreed to yesterday by a vote of 14 to 0, a peacekeeping force will go to the Mideast, and this force, however, will not include any forces from the major powers, including, of course, the United States and the Soviet Union.

The question, however, has arisen as to whether observers from major powers could go to the Mideast. My up-to-the-minute report on that, and I just talked to Dr. Kissinger 5 minutes before coming down, is this: We will send observers to the Mideast if requested by the Secretary General of the United Nations, and we have reason to expect that we will receive such a request.

With regard to the peacekeeping force, I think it is important for all of you ladies and gentlemen, and particularly for those listening on radio and television, to know why the United States has insisted that major powers not be part of the peacekeeping force, and that major powers not introduce military forces into the Mideast. A very significant and potentially explosive crisis developed on Wednesday of this week. We obtained information which led us to believe that the Soviet Union was planning to send a very substantial force into the Mideast, a military force.

When I received that information, I ordered, shortly after midnight on Thursday morning, an alert for all American forces around the world. This was a precautionary alert. The purpose of that was to indicate to the Soviet Union that we could not accept any unilateral move on their part to move military forces into the Mideast. At the same time, in the early morning hours, I also proceeded on the diplomatic front. In a message to Mr. Brezhnev, an urgent message, I indicated to him our reasoning, and I urged that we not proceed along that course, and that, instead, that we join in the United Nations in supporting a resolution which would exclude any major powers from participating in a peacekeeping force.

As a result of that communication, and the return that I received from Mr. Brezhnev—we had several exchanges, I should say—we reached the conclusion that we would jointly support the resolution which was adopted in the United Nations.

We now come, of course, to the critical time in terms of the future of the Mideast. And here, the outlook is far more hopeful than what we have been through this past week. I think I could safely say that the chances for not just a cease-fire—which we presently have and which, of course, we have had in the Mideast for some time—but the outlook for a permanent peace is the best that it has been in 20 years.

The reason for this is that the two major powers, the Soviet Union and the United States, have agreed—this was one of the results of Dr. Kissinger's trip to Moscow—have agreed that we would participate in trying to expedite the talks between the parties involved. That does not mean that the two major powers will impose a settlement. It does mean, however, that we will use our influence with the nations in the area to expedite a settlement.

The reason we feel this is important is that first, from the standpoint of the nations in the Mideast, none of them, Israel, Egypt, Syria, none of them can or should go through the agony of another war.

The losses in this war on both sides have been very, very high. And the tragedy must not occur again. There have been four of these wars, as you ladies and gentlemen know, over the past 20 years. But beyond that, it is vitally important to the peace of the world that this potential troublespot, which is really one of the most potentially explosive areas in the world, that it not become an area in which the major powers come together in confrontation.

What the developments of this week should indicate to all of us is that the United States and the Soviet Union, who admittedly have very different objectives in the Mideast, have now agreed that it is not in their interest to have a confrontation there, a confrontation which might lead to a nuclear confrontation and neither of the two major powers wants that.

We have agreed, also, that if we are to avoid that, it is necessary for us to use our influence more than we have in the past, to get the negotiating track moving again, but this time, moving to a conclusion—not simply a temporary truce, but a permanent peace.

I do not mean to suggest that it is going to come quickly because the parties involved are still rather far apart. But I do say that now there are greater incentives within the area to find a peaceful solution, and there are enormous incentives as far as the United States is concerned, and the Soviet Union and other major powers, to find such a solution.

Turning now to the subject of our attempts to get a cease-fire on the home front, that is a bit more difficult.

PRESIDENTIAL TAPES

Today White House counsel contacted Judge Sirica—we tried yesterday, but he was in Boston, as you know—and arrangements were made to meet with Judge Sirica on Tuesday to work out the delivery of the tapes to Judge Sirica.

WATERGATE SPECIAL PROSECUTOR

Also, in consultations that we have had in the White House today, we have decided that next week the Acting Attorney General, Mr. Bork, will appoint a new special prosecutor for what is called the Watergate matter. The special prosecutor will have independence. He will have total cooperation from the executive branch, and he will have as a primary responsibility to bring this matter which has so long concerned the American people, bring it to an expeditious conclusion, because we have to remember that under our Constitution it has always been held that justice delayed is justice denied. It is time for those who are guilty to be prosecuted, and for those who are innocent to be cleared. And I can assure you ladies and gentlemen, and all of our listeners tonight, that I have no greater interest than to see that the new special prosecutor has the cooperation from the executive branch and the independence that he needs to bring about that conclusion.

And now I will go to Mr. Cormier [Frank Cormier, Associated Press].

901

QUESTIONS

THE SPECIAL PROSECUTOR

Q. Mr. President, would the new special prosecutor have your go-ahead to go to court if necessary to obtain evidence from your files that he felt were vital?

THE PRESIDENT. Well, Mr. Cormier, I would anticipate that that would not be necessary. I believe that as we look at the events which led to the dismissal of Mr. Cox, we find that these are matters that can be worked out and should be worked out in cooperation and not by having a suit filed by a special prosecutor within the executive branch against the President of the United States.

This, incidentally, is not a new attitude on the part of a President. Every President since George Washington has tried to protect the confidentiality of Presidential conversations, and you remember the famous case involving Thomas Jefferson where Chief Justice Marshall, then sitting as a trial judge, subpoenaed the letter which Jefferson had written which Marshall thought or felt was necessary evidence in the trial of Aaron Burr. Jefferson refused to do so but it did not result in a suit. What happened was, of course, a compromise in which a summary of the contents of the letter which was relevant to the trial was produced by Jefferson, and the Chief Justice of the United States, acting in his capacity as Chief Justice, accepted that.

That is exactly, of course, what we tried to do in this instant case....

The matter of the tapes has been one that has concerned me because of my feeling that I have a constitutional responsibility to defend the Office of the Presidency from any encroachments on confidentiality which might affect future Presidents in their abilities to conduct the kind of conversations and discussions they need to conduct to carry on the responsibilities of this Office. And, of course, the special prosecutor felt that he needed the tapes for the purpose of his prosecution.

That was why, working with the Attorney General, we worked out what we thought was an acceptable compromise, one in which Judge Stennis, now Senator Stennis, would hear the tapes and would provide a complete and full disclosure, not only to Judge Sirica, but also to the Senate Committee.

Attorney General Richardson approved of this proposition. Senator Baker, Senator Ervin approved of the proposition. Mr. Cox was the only one that rejected it.

Under the circumstances, when he rejected it and indicated that despite the approval of the Attorney General, of course, of the President, and of the two major Senators on the Ervin Committee, when he rejected the proposal, I had no choice but to dismiss him.

Under those circumstances, Mr. Richardson, Mr. Ruckelshaus felt that because of the nature of their confirmation that their commitment to Mr. Cox had to take precedence over any commitment they might have to carry out an order from the President.

Under those circumstances, I accepted with regret the resignations of two fine public servants.

Now we come to a new special prosecutor. We will cooperate with him, and I do not anticipate that we will come to the time when he would consider it necessary to take the President to court. I think our cooperation will be adequate.

Q. This is perhaps another way of asking Frank's question, but if the special prosecutor considers that information contained in Presidential documents is needed to prosecute the Watergate case, will you give him the documents, beyond the nine tapes which you have already given him?

THE PRESIDENT. I have answered that question before. We will not provide Presidential documents to a special prosecutor. We will provide, as we have in great numbers, all kinds of documents from the White House, but if it is a document involving a conversation with the President, I would have to stand on the principle of confidentiality. However, information that is needed from such documents would be provided. That is what we have been trying to do.

Q. Mr. President, you know in the Congress there is a great deal of suspicion over any arrangement which will permit the executive branch to investigate itself or which will establish a special prosecutor which you may fire again. And 53 Senators, a majority, have now cosponsored a resolution which would permit Judge Sirica to establish and name an independent prosecutor, separate and apart from the White House and the executive branch. Do you believe this arrangement would be constitutional, and would you go along with it?

THE PRESIDENT. Well, I would suggest that the action that we are going to take, appointing a special prosecutor, would be satisfactory to the Congress, and that they would not proceed with that particular matter.

Mr. Rather [Dan Rather, CBS News].

QUESTIONS OF IMPEACHMENT OR RESIGNATION

Q. Mr. President, I wonder if you could share with us your thoughts, tell us what goes through your mind when you hear people, people who love this country, and people who believe in you, say reluctantly that perhaps you should resign or be impeached.

THE PRESIDENT. Well, I am glad we don't take the vote of this room, let me say And I understand the feelings of people with regard to impeachment and resignation. As a matter of fact, Mr. Rather, you may remember that when I made the rather difficult decision—I thought the most difficult decision of my first term—on December 18, the bombing by B-52's of North Vietnam—that exactly the same words were used on the networks, I don't mean by you, but they were quoted on the networks—that were used now: tyrant, dictator, he has lost his senses, he should resign, he should be impeached.

But I stuck it out, and as a result of that, we not only got our prisoners of war home, as I have often said, on their feet rather than on their knees, but we brought peace to Vietnam, something we haven't had and didn't for over 12 years.

It was a hard decision, and it was one that many of my friends in the press who had consistently supported me on the war up to that time disagreed with. Now, in this instance I realize there are people who feel that the actions that I have taken with regard to the dismissal of Mr. Cox are grounds for impeachment.

I would respectfully suggest that even Mr. Cox and Mr. Richardson have agreed that the President had the right, constitutional right, to dismiss anybody in the Federal Government, and second, I should also point out that as far as the tapes are concerned, rather than being in defiance of the law, I am in compliance with the law.

As far as what goes through my mind, I would simply say that I intend to continue to carry out, to the best of my ability, the responsibilities I was elected to carry out last November. The events of this past week—I know, for example, in your head office in New York, some thought that it was simply a blown-up exercise; there wasn't a real crisis. I wish it had been that. It was a real crisis. It was the most difficult crisis we have had since the Cuban confrontation of 1962.

But because we had had our initiative with the Soviet Union, because I had a basis of communication with Mr. Brezhnev, we not only avoided a confrontation, but we moved a great step forward toward real peace in the Mideast.

Now, as long as I can carry out that kind of responsibility, I am going to continue to do this job....

THE NATION'S CONFIDENCE

Q. Mr. President, in 1968, before you were elected, you wrote that too many shocks can drain a nation of its energy and even cause a rebellion against creative change and progress. Do you think America is at that point now?

THE PRESIDENT. I think that many would speculate—I have noted a lot on the networks particularly and sometimes even in the newspapers. But this is a very strong country, and the American people, I think, can ride through the shocks that they have—.

The difference now from what it was in the days of shocks, even when Mr. Lisagor and I first met 25 years ago, is the electronic media. I have never heard or seen such outrageous, vicious, distorted reporting in 27 years of public life. I am not blaming anybody for that. Perhaps what happened is that what we did brought it about, and therefore, the media decided that they would have to take that particular line.

But when people are pounded night after night with that kind of frantic, hysterical reporting, it naturally shakes their confidence. And yet, I should point out that even in this week, when many thought that the President was shell-shocked, unable to act, the President acted decisively in the interests of peace, in the interests of the country, and I can assure you that whatever shocks gentlemen of the press may have, or others, political people, these shocks will not affect me in my doing my job....

OIL AND THE MIDDLE EAST

Q. Mr. President, a question from the electronic media related to the Middle East—

THE PRESIDENT. Radio.

Q. [Forrest J. Boyd, Mutual Broadcasting System] Radio. I have heard that there was a meeting at the State Department this afternoon of major oil company executives on the fuel shortage.

Whether or not you confirm that, has this confrontation in the Middle East caused a still more severe oil problem, and is there any thinking now of gasoline rationing?

THE PRESIDENT. Well, we have contingency plans for gasoline rationing and so forth which I hope never have to be put into place....

I can only say on that score that Europe which gets 80 percent of its oil from the Mideast would have frozen to death this winter unless there had been a settlement, and Japan, of course, is in that same position.

The United States, of course, gets only approximately 10 percent of its oil from the Mideast.

What I am simply suggesting is this: that with regard to the fuel shortage potentially in the United States and in the world, it is indispensable at this time that we avoid any further Mideast crisis so that the flow of oil to Europe, to Japan, and to the United States can continue.

EXCHANGES WITH GENERAL SECRETARY BREZHNEV

Q. Mr. President, against this background of detente, Mr. Brezhnev's note to you has been described as rough or perhaps brutal by one Senator. Can you characterize it for us and for history in any way?

THE PRESIDENT. ...Rather than saying, Mr. Theis, that his note to me was rough and brutal, I would say that it was very firm, and it left very little to the imagination as to what he intended.

And my response was also very firm and left little to the imagination of how we would react. And it is because he and I know each other and it is because we have had this personal contact, that notes exchanged in that way result in a settlement rather than a confrontation.

Q. Mr. President.

THE PRESIDENT. Mr. Deakin [James Deakin, St. Louis Post-Dispatch].

MR. REBOZO AND CAMPAIGN CONTRIBUTIONS

Q. Yes, Mr. Deakin. Is it credible, can the American people believe that your close friend, Mr. Rebozo, for 3 years, during which time you saw him weekly sometimes, kept from you the fact that he had $100,000 in cash from Mr. Howard Hughes? Is that credible? Is it credible that your personal attorney, Mr. Kalmbach, knew about this money for at least a year and never told you about it? And if this was a campaign contribution, as your press secretaries say, who authorized Mr. Rebozo to collect campaign contributions for your re-election or for the Republican Party? What campaign committee was he an official of?

THE PRESIDENT. Well, it is obviously not credible to you, and I suppose that it would sound incredible to many people who did not know how I operate. In terms of campaign contributions, I have had a rule, Mr. Deakin, which Mr. Stans and Mr. Kalmbach and Mr. Rebozo and every contributor will agree has been the rule—I have refused always to accept contributions myself. I have refused to have any discussion of contributions. As a matter of fact, my orders to Mr. Stans were that after the campaign was over, I would then send notes of appreciation to those that contributed, but before the election, I did not want to have any information from anybody with regard to campaign contributions.

Now, with regard to Mr. Rebozo, let me say that he showed, I think, very good judgment in doing what he did. He received a contribution. He was prepared to turn it over to the Finance Chairman when the Finance Chairman was appointed. But in that interlude, after he received the contribution, and before the Finance Chairman was appointed, the Hughes company, as you all know, had an internal fight of massive proportions, and he felt that such a contribution to the campaign might prove to be embarrassing.

At the conclusion of the campaign, he decided that it would be in the best interests of everybody concerned rather than to turn the money over then, to be used in the '74 campaigns, to return it intact. And I would say that any individual, and particularly a banker who would have a contribution of $100,000 and not touch it—because it was turned back in exactly the form it was received—I think that is a pretty good indication that he is a totally honest man, which he is.

PRESIDENTIAL TAPES

Q. Mr. President, after the tapes are presented to Judge Sirica and they are processed under the procedure outlined in the U.S. Court of Appeals, will you make those tapes public?

THE PRESIDENT. No, that is not the procedure that the court has ordered, and it would not be proper....

Q. Mr. President.

THE PRESIDENT. Mr. ter Horst [J. F. terHorst, Detroit News].

PRESIDENTIAL STRESS

Q. Mr. President, Harry Truman used to talk about the heat in the kitchen.

THE PRESIDENT. I know what he meant. [*Laughter*]

Q. —and a lot of people have been wondering how you are bearing up emotionally under the stress of recent events. Can you discuss that?

THE PRESIDENT. Well, those who saw me during the Middle East crisis thought I bore up rather well, and, Mr. terHorst, I have a quality which is—I guess I must have inherited it from my Midwestern mother and father—which is that the tougher it gets, the cooler I get. Of course, it isn't pleasant to get criticism. Some of it is justified, of course. It isn't pleasant to find your honesty questioned. It isn't pleasant to find, for example, that, speaking of my friend, Mr. Rebozo, that despite the fact that those who printed it, and those who said it, knew it was un-true—said that he had a million-dollar trust fund for me that he was handling—it was neverthless put on one of the networks, knowing it was untrue. It isn't pleasant, for example, to hear or read that a million dollars in campaign funds went into my San Clemente property, and even after we had a complete audit, to have it repeated.

Those are things which, of course, do tend to get under the skin of the man who holds this office. But as far as I am concerned, I have learned to expect it. It has been my lot throughout my political life, and I suppose because I have been through so much, that may be one of the reasons that when I have to face an international crisis, I have what it takes.

WATERGATE INFLUENCE ON MIDDLE EAST CRISIS

Q. Mr. President.... To what extent do you think your Watergate troubles influenced Soviet thinking about your ability to respond in the Mideast, and did your Watergate problems convince you that the U.S. needed a strong response in the Mideast to convince other nations that you have not been weakened?

THE PRESIDENT. Well, I have noted speculation to the effect that the Watergate problems may have led the Soviet Union to miscalculate. I tend to disagree with that, however.

I think Mr. Brezhnev probably can't quite understand how the President of the United States wouldn't be able to handle the Watergate problems. He would be able to handle it all right, if he had them. [*Laughter*] But I think what happens is that what Mr. Brezhnev does understand is the power of the United States. What he does know is the President of the United States.

What he also knows is that the President of the United States, when he was under unmerciful assault at the time of Cambodia, at the time of May 8, when I ordered the bombing and the mining of North Vietnam, at the time of December 18, still went ahead and did what he thought was right; the fact that Mr. Brezhnev knew that regardless of the pressures at home, regardless of what people see and hear on television night after night, he would do what was right. That is what made Mr. Brezhnev act as he did.

PRESIDENTIAL VIEWS ON TELEVISION COVERAGE

Q. Mr. President, you have lambasted the television networks pretty well. Could I ask you, at the risk of reopening an obvious wound, you say after you have put on a lot of heat that you don't blame anyone. I find that a little puzzling. What is it about the television coverage of you in these past weeks and months that has so aroused your anger?

THE PRESIDENT. Don't get the impression that you arouse my anger. [Laughter]

Q. [Robert C. Pierpoint, CBS News] I'm afraid, sir, that I have that impression. [Laughter]

THE PRESIDENT. You see, one can only be angry with those he respects.

REGAINING THE CONFIDENCE OF THE PEOPLE

Q. Mr. President, businessmen increasingly are saying that many chief executive officers of corporations do not get the latitude you have had, if they have the personnel problems that you have had, to stay in the job and correct them. You have said you are going to stay. Do you have any plan set out to regain confidence of people across the country, and these businessmen who are beginning to talk about this matter? Do you have any plans, besides the special prosecutor, which looks backward, do you have any plan that looks forward for regaining confidence of people?

THE PRESIDENT. I certainly have. First, to move forward in building a structure of peace in the world, in which we have made enormous progress in the past and which we are going to make more progress in in the future: our European initiative, our continued initiative with the Soviet Union, with the People's Republic of China. That will be the major legacy of this Administration.

Moving forward at home in our continuing battle against the high cost of living, in which we are now finally beginning to make some progress, and moving forward also on the matters that you referred to, it is true that what happened in Watergate, the campaign abuses, were deplorable. They have been very damaging to this Administration; they have been damaging certainly to the country as well.

Let me say, too, I didn't want to leave an impression with my good friend from CBS over here that I don't respect the reporters. What I was simply saying was this: that when a commentator takes a bit of news and then, with knowledge of what the facts are, distorts it, viciously, I have no respect for that individual.

Q. Mr. President.

THE PRESIDENT. You are so loud, I will have to take you.

Q. [Clark R. Mollenhoff, Des Moines Register and Tribune]. I have to be, because you happen to dodge my questions all of the time.

THE PRESIDENT. You had three last time.

EXECUTIVE PRIVILEGE

Q. Last May you went before the American people and you said executive privilege will not be invoked as to any testimony concerning possible criminal conduct or discussing of possible criminal conduct, including the Watergate affair and the alleged coverup.

If you have revised or modified this position, as you seem to have done, could you explain the rationale of a law-and-order Administration covering up evidence, prima facie evidence, of high crimes and misdemeanors?

THE PRESIDENT. Well, I should point out that perhaps all of the other reporters in the room are aware of the fact that we have waived executive privilege on all individuals within the Administration. It has been the greatest waiver of executive privilege in the whole history of this Nation.

And as far as any other matters are concerned, the matters of the tapes, the matters of Presidential conversations, those are matters in which the President has a responsibility to defend this office, which I shall continue to do.

MR. CORMIER. Thank you, Mr. President.

November

NIXON'S ENERGY SPEECH

November 7, 1973

President Nixon outlined for the public Nov. 7 a far-reaching program to curb the country's fuel consumption in the face of growing shortages. In a televised address to the nation, Nixon announced six steps that he would take immediately which did not require congressional approval. Beyond those, he proposed new emergency legislation, urged quick action on four long-range measures already pending in Congress and unveiled a crash program to achieve energy self-sufficiency in the United States by 1980. In remarks added at the conclusion of his address, the President declared that he had "no intention" of resigning from office.

Nixon said the Arab embargo on oil shipments to the United States "sharply altered" earlier expectations of "temporary shortages" for the winter of 1973-74. He estimated that the embargo would result in a reduction of two million barrels of oil daily by the end of November. "We must, therefore, face up to a very stark fact," he added. "We are heading toward the most acute shortages of energy since World War II." He predicted that fuel shortages would range between 10 and 17 per cent during the winter. The fuel shortages did not mean "we will freeze in our homes or offices," the President said. But the fuel crisis would require "some sacrifice" by everyone. The shortages were due to increased American affluence, Nixon explained. The United States, with six per cent of the world's population, used more than 30 per cent of world energy supplies, he said. The Nov. 7 statement was the fifth the President had made on the energy situation during the year. (See p. 465.)

President Nixon declared it was "imperative" that the emergency legislation "be on my desk for signature before Congress recesses in December." In an effort to reach that goal, the administration decided not to send its own legislation to Congress, but to work with a bill already introduced by Sen. Henry M. Jackson (D Wash.). Among the provisions of that emergency measure were a return to year-round daylight saving time, presidential authority to relax environmental regulations to balance "our environmental interests...with our energy requirements," restrictions on outdoor lighting and working hours for shopping centers and other commercial enterprises, and presidential authority to reduce speed limits on federal highways to 50 miles per hour.

Nixon also announced that he would take six steps which did not require congressional approval in order to curb fuel consumption. Efforts would be made, he said, to convert power plants that use oil to the use of coal; and those plants already utilizing coal would be prevented from converting to oil. Fuel allocation to commercial aircraft would be reduced, requiring a 10 per cent reduction in the number of flights. Fuel allocation to homes and offices would be reduced by about 15 per cent, an action which would be aided, Nixon said, by turning down home thermostats to 68 degrees and by lowering thermostats or curtailing working hours in offices. Temperatures in federal offices would be reduced and government vehicles would be limited to traveling no faster than 50 m.p.h. The Atomic Energy Commission would be asked to speed up the licensing of nuclear power plants. In the states, governors and mayors would be asked to take appropriate actions to conserve energy.

Congressional failure to act on long-term energy problems could seriously endanger the economy and weaken the ability of "America to continue to keep the peace that we have won at such great cost," Nixon asserted. He urged prompt action on energy legislation to which he had already given "urgent" priority. These measures included legislation to authorize construction of the trans-Alaskan pipeline, to increase production of "our vast quantities of natural gas," to set reasonable standards for the surface mining of coal, and to authorize the organizational structures to meet and administer energy programs. Nixon said he had stressed repeatedly the need to increase U.S. energy research and development efforts. He pointed out that he had announced a five-year, $10-billion program in June to "develop better ways of using energy and to explore and develop new energy sources."

Nixon also announced a "Project Independence" designed to free the United States from "foreign energy sources" by 1980. He compared it to the Manhattan Project which developed the atomic bomb in World War II and to Project Apollo which placed an American on the moon in

1969. Nixon said he already had committeed more funds to the goal of energy self-sufficiency than were spent on the Manhattan Project.

Later in the month, President Nixon again tightened energy measures and announced five steps his administration was taking to curb the consumption of scarce fuels. In a radio and television address to the American people Nov. 25, he said such actions would take care of about 10 per cent of a 17 per cent fuel shortage projected for the 1973-74 winter. The five measures were (1) a 15 per cent reduction in gasoline distributed to wholesalers and retailers, (2) a ban on gasoline sales from 9:00 p.m. Saturday to midnight Sunday, (3) a nationwide reduced speed limit of 50 m.p.h. for cars and 55 m.p.h. for trucks, (4) a curb on ornamental outdoor lighting for homes and the elimination of all commercial outdoor lighting except for identification of places of business, and (5) a further 15 per cent reduction in the consumption of jet fuels for commercial flights, bringing the total reduction in that area to 25 per cent.

By the time Congress adjourned for the year, Dec. 22, both the House and the Senate were still bogged down over a compromise on the emergency energy legislation, drafted by House-Senate conferees after passage of differing versions in the two chambers. In the Senate, a filibuster staged Dec. 21 by two senators from oil-producing states destroyed all chances for immediate passage of the compromise bill. But early action on the controversial provisions of the measure was expected when Congress reconvened Jan. 21, 1974.

Text of President Nixon's address to the nation, Nov. 7, outlining steps to deal with the energy emergency:

Good evening.

I want to talk to you tonight about a serious national problem, a problem we must all face together in the months and years ahead.

As America has grown and prospered in recent years, our energy demands have begun to exceed available supplies. In recent months, we have taken many actions to increase supplies and to reduce consumption. But even with our best efforts, we knew that a period of temporary shortages was inevitable.

Unfortunately, our expectations for this winter have now been sharply altered by the recent conflict in the Middle East. Because of that war, most of the Middle Eastern oil producers have reduced overall production and cut off their shipments of oil to the United States. By the end of this month, more than 2 million barrels a day of oil we expected to import into the United States will no longer be available.

We must, therefore, face up to a very stark fact: We are heading toward the most acute shortages of energy since World War II. Our supply of petroleum this winter will be at least 10 percent short of our anticipated demands, and it could fall short by as much as 17 percent.

Now, even before war broke out in the Middle East, these prospective shortages were the subject of intensive discussions among members of my Administration, leaders of the Congress, Governors, mayors, and other groups. From these discussions has emerged a broad agreement that we, as a Nation, must now set upon a new course.

In the short run, this course means that we must use less energy—that means less heat, less electricity, less gasoline. In the long run, it means that we must develop new sources of energy which will give us the capacity to meet our needs without relying on any foreign nation.

The immediate shortage will affect the lives of each and every one of us. In our factories, our cars, our homes, our offices, we will have to use less fuel than we are accustomed to using. Some school and factory schedules may be realigned, and some jet airplane flights will de canceled.

This does not mean that we are going to run out of gasoline or that air travel will stop or that we will freeze in our homes or offices anyplace in America. The fuel crisis need not mean genuine suffering for any American. But it will require some sacrifice by all Americans.

We must be sure that our most vital needs are met first—and that our least important activities are the first to be cut back. And we must be sure that while the fat from our economy is being trimmed, the muscle is not seriously damaged.

To help us carry out that responsibility, I am tonight announcing the following steps:

First, I am directing that industries and utilities which use coal— which is our most abundant resource—be prevented from converting from coal to oil. Efforts will also be made to convert powerplants from the use of oil to the use of coal.

Second, we are allocating reduced quantities of fuel for aircraft. Now, this is going to lead to a cutback of more than 10 percent of the number of flights and some rescheduling of arrival and departure times.

Third, there will be reductions of approximately 15 percent in the supply of heating oil for homes and offices and other establishments. To be sure that there is enough oil to go around for the entire winter, all over the country, it will be essential for all of us to live and work in lower temperatures. We must ask everyone to lower the thermostat in your home by at least 6 degrees, so that we can achieve a national daytime average of 68 degrees. Incidentally, my doctor tells me that in a temperature of 66 to 68 degrees, you are really more healthy than when it is 75 to 78, if that is any comfort. In offices, factories, and commercial establishments, we must ask that you achieve the equivalent of a 10-degree reduction by either lowering the thermostat or curtailing working hours.

Fourth, I am ordering additional reductions in the consumption of energy by the Federal Government. We have already taken steps to reduce the Government's consumption by 7 percent. The cuts must now go deeper and must be made by every agency and every department in the Government. I am directing that the daytime temperatures in Federal offices be reduced immediately to a level of between 65 and 68 degrees, and that means in this room, too, as well as in every other room in the White House. In addition, I am ordering that all vehicles owned by the Federal Government—and there are over a half-million of them —travel no faster than 50 miles per hour except in emergencies. This is a step which I have also asked Governors, mayors, and local officials to take immediately with regard to vehicles under their authority.

Fifth, I am asking the Atomic Energy Commission to speed up the licensing and construction of nuclear plants. We must seek to reduce the time required to bring nuclear plants on line—nuclear plants that can produce power—to bring them on line from 10 years to 6 years, reduce that time lag.

Sixth, I am asking that Governors and mayors reinforce these actions by taking appropriate steps at the State and local level. We have already learned, for example, from the State of Oregon, that considerable amounts of energy can be saved simply by curbing unnecessary lighting and slightly altering the school year. I am recommending that other communities follow this example and also seek ways to stagger working hours, to encourage greater use of mass transit and car pooling.

How many times have you gone along the highway or the freeway, wherever the case may be, and seen hundreds and hundreds of cars with only one individual in the car. This we must all cooperate to change.

Consistent with safety and economic considerations, I am also asking Governors to take steps to reduce highway speed limits to 50 miles per hour. This action alone, if it is adopted on a nationwide basis, could save over 200,000 barrels of oil a day—just reducing the speed limit to 50 miles per hour.

Now, all of these actions will result in substantial savings of energy. More than that, most of these are actions that we can take right now— without further delay.

The key to their success lies, however, not just here in Washington, but in every home, in every community across this country. If each of us joins in this effort, joins with the spirit and the determination that have always graced the American character, then half the battle will already be won.

But we should recognize that even these steps, as essential as they are, may not be enough. We must be prepared to take additional steps, and for that purpose, additional authorities must be provided by the Congress.

I have therefore directed my chief adviser for energy policy, Governor Love, and other Administration officials, to work closely with the Congress in developing an emergency energy act.

I met with the leaders of the Congress this morning, and I asked that they act on this legislation on a priority, urgent basis. It is imperative that this legislation be on my desk for signature before the Congress recesses this December.

Because of the hard work that has already been done on this bill by Senators Jackson and Fannin and others, I am confident that we can meet that goal and that I will have the bill on this desk and will be able to sign it.

This proposed legislation would enable the executive branch to meet the energy emergency in several important ways:

First, it would authorize an immediate return to Daylight Saving Time on a year-round basis.

Second, it would provide the necessary authority to relax environmental regulations on a temporary, case-by-case basis, thus permitting an appropriate balancing of our environmental interests, which all of us share, with our energy requirements, which, of course, are indispensable.

Third, it would grant authority to impose special energy conservation measures, such as restrictions on the working hours for shopping centers and other commercial establishments.

And fourth, it would approve and fund increased exploration, development, and production from our Naval Petroleum Reserves. Now, these reserves are rich sources of oil. From one of them alone—Elk Hills in California—we could produce more than 160,000 barrels of oil a day within 2 months.

Fifth, it would provide the Federal Government with authority to reduce highway speed limits throughout the Nation.

And finally, it would expand the power of the Government's regulatory agencies to adjust the schedules of planes, ships, and other carriers.

If shortages persist despite all of these actions and despite inevitable increases in the price of energy products, it may then become necessary—may become necessary—to take even stronger measures.

It is only prudent that we be ready to cut the consumption of oil products, such as gasoline, by rationing, or by a fair system of taxation, and consequently, I have directed that contingency plans, if this becomes necessary, be prepared for that purpose.

Now, some of you may wonder whether we are turning back the clock to another age. Gas rationing, oil shortages, reduced speed limits —they all sound like a way of life we left behind with Glenn Miller and the war of the forties. Well, in fact, part of our current problem also stems from war—the war in the Middle East. But our deeper energy problems come not from war, but from peace and from abundance. We are running out of energy today because our economy has grown enormously and because in prosperity what were once considered luxuries are now considered necessities.

How many of you can remember when it was very unusual to have a home air-conditioned? And yet, this is very common in almost all parts of the Nation.

As a result, the average American will consume as much energy in the next 7 days as most other people in the world will consume in an entire year. We have only 6 percent of the world's people in America, but we consume over 30 percent of all the energy in the world.

Now, our growing demands have bumped up against the limits of available supply, and until we provide new sources of energy for tomorrow, we must be prepared to tighten our belts today.

Let me turn now to our long-range plans.

While a resolution of the immediate crisis is our highest priority, we must also act now to prevent a recurrence of such a crisis in the future. This is a matter of bipartisan concern. It is going to require a bipartisan response.

Two years ago, in the first energy message any President has ever sent to the Congress, I called attention to our urgent energy problem. Last April, this year, I reaffirmed to the Congress the magnitude of that problem, and I called for action on seven major legislative initiatives. Again in June, I called for action. I have done so frequently since then.

But thus far, not one major energy bill that I have asked for has been enacted. I realize that the Congress has been distracted in this period by other matters. But the time has now come for the Congress to get on with this urgent business—providing the legislation that will meet not only the current crisis but also the long-range challenge that we face.

Our failure to act now on our long-term energy problems could seriously endanger the capacity of our farms and of our factories to employ Americans at record-breaking rates—nearly 86 million people are now at work in this country—and to provide the highest standard of living we, or any other nation, has ever known in history.

It could reduce the capacity of our farmers to provide the food we need. It could jeopardize our entire transportation system. It could seriously weaken the ability of America to continue to give the leadership which only we can provide to keep the peace that we have won at such great cost, for thousands of our finest young Americans.

That is why it is time to act now on vital energy legislation that will affect our daily lives, not just this year, but for years to come.

We must have the legislation now which will authorize construction of the Alaska pipeline—legislation which is not burdened with irrelevant and unnecessary provisions.

We must have legislative authority to encourage production of our vast quantitites of natural gas, one of the cleanest and best sources of energy.

We must have the legal ability to set reasonable standards for the surface mining of coal.

And we must have the organizational structures to meet and administer our energy programs.

And therefore, tonight, as I did this morning in meeting with the Congressional leaders, I again urge the Congress to give its attention to the initiatives I recommended 6 months ago to meet these needs that I have described.

Finally, I have stressed repeatedly the necessity of increasing our energy research and development efforts. Last June, I announced a 5-year, $10 billion program to develop better ways of using energy and to explore and develop new energy sources. Last month I announced plans for an immediate acceleration of that program.

We can take heart from the fact that we in the United States have half the world's known coal reserves. We have huge, untapped sources of natural gas. We have the most advanced nuclear technology known to man. We have oil in our continental shelves. We have oil shale out in the Western part of the United States, and we have some of the finest technical and scientific minds in the world. In short, we have all the resources we need to meet the great challenge before us. Now we must demonstrate the will to meet that challenge.

In World War II, America was faced with the necessity of rapidly developing an atomic capability. The circumstances were grave. Responding to that challenge, this Nation brought together its finest scientific skills and its finest administrative skills in what was known as the Manhattan Project. With all the needed resources at its command, with the highest priority assigned to its efforts, the Manhattan Project gave us the atomic capacity that helped to end the war in the Pacific and to bring peace to the world.

Twenty years later, responding to a different challenge, we focused our scientific and technological genius on the frontiers of space. We pledged to put a man on the moon before 1970, and on July 20, 1969, Neil Armstrong made that historic "giant leap for mankind" when he stepped on the moon.

The lessons of the Apollo project and of the earlier Manhattan Project are the same lessons that are taught by the whole of American history: Whenever the American people are faced with a clear goal and they are challenged to meet it, we can do extraordinary things.

Today the challenge is to regain the strength that we had earlier in this century, the strength of self-sufficiency. Our ability to meet our own energy needs is directly limited to our continued ability to act decisively and independently at home and abroad in the service of peace, not only for America, but for all nations in the world.

I have ordered funding of this effort to achieve self-sufficiency far in excess of the funds that were expended on the Manhattan Project. But money is only one of the ingredients essential to the success of such a project. We must also have a unified commitment to that goal. We must have unified direction of the effort to accomplish it.

Because of the urgent need for an organization that would provide focused leadership for this effort, I am asking the Congress to consider my proposal for an Energy Research and Development Administration separate from any other organizational initiatives, and to enact this legislation in the present session of the Congress.

Let us unite in committing the resources of this Nation to a major new endeavor, an endeavor that in this Bicentennial Era we can appropriately call "Project Independence."

Let us set as our national goal, in the spirit of Apollo, with the determination of the Manhattan Project, that by the end of this decade we will have developed the potential to meet our own energy needs without depending on any foreign energy sources.

Let us pledge that by 1980, under Project Independence, we shall be able to meet America's energy needs from America's own energy resources.

In speaking to you tonight in terms as direct as these, my concern has been to lay before you the full facts of the Nation's energy shortage. It is important that each of us understands what the situation is and how the efforts we together can take to help to meet it are essential to our total effort.

No people in the world perform more nobly than the American people when called upon to unite in the service of their country. I am supremely confident that while the days and weeks ahead may be a time of some hardship for many of us, they will also be a time of renewed commitment and concentration to the national interest.

We have an energy crisis, but there is no crisis of the American spirit. Let us go forward, then, doing what needs to be done, proud of what we have accomplished together in the past, and confident of what we can accomplish together in the future.

Let us find in this time of national necessity a renewed awareness of our capacities as a people, a deeper sense of our responsibilitites as a Nation, and an increased understanding that the measure and the meaning of America has always been determined by the devotion which each of us brings to our duty as citizens of America.

I should like to close with a personal note.

It was just one year ago that I was reelected as President of the United States of America. During this past year we have made great progress in achieving the goals that I set forth in my reelection campaign.

We have ended the longest war in America's history. All of our prisoners of war have been returned home. And for the first time in 25 years, no young Americans are being drafted into the Armed Services. We have made progress toward our goal of a real prosperity, a prosperity without war. The rate of unemployment is down to 4 1/4 percent, which is the lowest unemployment in peacetime that we have had in 16 years, and we are finally beginning to make progress in our fight against the rise in the cost of living.

These are substantial achievements in this year 1973. But I would be less than candid if I were not to admit that this has not been an easy year in some other respects, as all of you are quite aware.

As a result of the deplorable Watergate matter, great numbers of Americans have had doubts raised as to the integrity of the President of the United States. I have even noted that some publications have called on me to resign the Office of President of the United States.

Tonight I would like to give my answer to those who have suggested that I resign.

I have no intention whatever of walking away from the job I was elected to do. As long as I am physically able, I am going to continue to work 16 to 18 hours a day for the cause of a real peace abroad, and for the cause of prosperity without inflation and without war at home. And in the months ahead, I shall do everything that I can to see that any doubts as to the integrity of the man who occupies the highest office in this land—to remove those doubts where they exist.

And I am confident that in those months ahead, the American people will come to realize that I have not violated the trust that they placed in me when they elected me as President of the United States in the past, and I pledge to you tonight that I shall always do everything that I can to be worthy of that trust in the future.

WAR POWERS

November 7, 1973

Congress on Nov. 7 finally won a long struggle to restrict the right of the President to use his powers as Commander in Chief to inject armed forces of the United States into foreign wars or into situations abroad where hostilities seem inevitable. President Nixon had vetoed the war powers resolution on Oct. 24. Because eight previous vetoes in 1973 had been sustained, there was slight expectation that the ninth could be overridden. But the House and Senate succeeded in mustering the strength needed to enact H J Res 542 into law notwithstanding the President's objections.

Efforts by Congress to assert a voice in foreign-affairs decisions involving the use, or probable use, of the armed forces date back to the late 1960s when opposition to the widening Indochina conflict was mounting. That opposition led to the repeal in January 1971 of the Gulf of Tonkin resolution, which had been cited since its adoption by Congress in 1964 as legislative authorization for U.S. participation in the Vietnam War. Despite the Tonkin repeal, American soldiers continued to fight in Indochina. Resolutions providing at the least for presidential consultation with Congress in advance of troop commitments abroad were adopted periodically by Senate or House, but agreement of the two chambers on a resolution of that kind was not achieved until 1973.

The stated purpose of the joint resolution finally enacted over a presidential veto on Nov. 7 was to "insure that the collective judgment of both the Congress and the President will apply to the introduction of United States armed forces into hostilities, or into situations where imminent involvement in hostilities is clearly indicated by the cir- cumstances." To carry out that purpose, the resolution laid down rules requiring the President to consult with and report to the Congress un- der specified circumstances. And it limited the commitment of armed forces by the President in such situations to a period of 60, or at most 90, days unless in the meantime Congress had declared war or specif- ically authorized use of the forces in the particular situation. Further- more, if at any time the armed forced were engaged in hostilities out- side the United States in the absence of a declaration of war or specific statutory authorization, the Congress would have the right, by adopting a concurrent resolution (not requiring the President's signature), to order their removal.

Nixon's Objections and Passage Over Veto

President Nixon in his veto message described the war powers resolution as "both unconstitutional and dangerous to the best in- terests of our nation." The founding fathers, he asserted, had chosen "not to draw a precise and detailed line of demarcation between the foreign policy powers of the two branches" because they "understood the impossibility of foreseeing every contingency that might arise in this complex area." The resolution, he asserted, would "strictly limit" the President's constitutional authority and was therefore unconsti- tutional, for "the only way in which the constitutional powers of a branch of the government can be altered is by amending the Constitu- tion."

The President said that he was "also deeply disturbed by the prac- tical consequences of this resolution." He believed it would "seriously undermine this nation's ability to act decisively and convincingly in times of international crisis." He cited, among various examples, the Berlin crisis of 1961, the Cuban missile crisis of 1962 and, in addition, "our recent actions to bring about a peaceful settlement of the hostil- ities in the Middle East."

Congress, however, did not agree. The House of Representatives voted 284 to 135 (4 votes more than the required two-thirds) and the Senate 75 to 18 (13 votes more than necessary) to override the veto. This result could be attributed to various factors or combinations of factors. Accumulated frustration over the painful and protracted Vietnam experience was probably the most important.

Whether the war powers resolution would or could avert another experience comparable to the involvement in Vietnam, or actually increase the influence of Congress in such situations, only the future could tell. Congress all along has had the sole power to declare war, but it has never done so except in response to the President's recom-

*mendations. Beginning with the Spanish-American War in 1898, decla-
rations of war by Congress have taken the form not of an outright
declaration but of recognition of an existing state of war. Where there
were no declarations, as in the Korean and Vietnam wars, public
opinion, at least initially, swept Congress along in support of the executive action that led the country into war. Hence there was ground
to question whether even the detailed procedures set forth in the new
legislation would be sufficient to effect decisive change in a future
emergency.*

*Text of the war powers resolution enacted into law by
Congress, Nov. 7, 1973, over President Nixon's veto:*

SECTION 1. This joint resolution may be cited as the "War Powers
Resolution".

Purpose and Policy

SEC. 2. (a) It is the purpose of this joint resolution to fulfill the intent of the framers of the Constitution of the United States and insure
that the collective judgment of both the Congress and the President
will apply to the introduction of United States Armed Forces into
hostilities, or into situations where imminent involvement in hostilities
is clearly indicated by the circumstances, and to the continued use of
such forces in hostilities or in such situations.

(b) Under article I, section 8, of the Constitution, it is specifically
provided that the Congress shall have the power to make all laws
necessary and proper for carrying into execution, not only its own
powers but also all other powers vested by the Constitution in the
Government of the United States, or in any department or officer
thereof.

(c) The constitutional powers of the President as Commander-in-
Chief to introduce United States Armed Forces into hostilities, or into
situations where imminent involvement in hostilities is clearly indicated by the circumstances, are exercised only pursuant to (1) a declaration of war, (2) specific statutory authorization, or (3) a national
emergency created by attack upon the United States, its territories or
possessions, or its armed forces.

Consultation

SEC. 3. The President in every possible instance shall consult with
Congress before introducing United States Armed Forces into hostili-

ties or into situations where imminent involvement in hostilities is clearly indicated by the circumstances and after every such introduction shall consult regularly with the Congress until United States Armed Forces are no longer engaged in hostilities or have been removed from such situations.

Reporting

SEC. 4. (a) In the absence of a declaration of war, in any case in which United States Armed Forces are introduced—

(1) into hostilities or into situations where imminent involvement in hostilities is clearly indicated by the circumstances;

(2) into the territory, airspace or waters of a foreign nation, while equipped for combat, except for deployments which relate solely to supply, replacement, repair, or training of such forces; or

(3) in numbers which substantially enlarge United States Armed Forces equipped for combat already located in a foreign nation:

the President shall submit within 48 hours to the Speaker of the House of Representatives and to the President pro tempore of the Senate a report, in writing, setting forth—

(A) the circumstances necessitating the introduction of United States Armed Forces;

(B) the constitutional and legislative authority under which such introduction took place; and

(C) the estimated scope and duration of the hostilities or involvement.

(b) The President shall provide such other information as the Congress may request in the fulfillment of its constitutional responsibilities with respect to committing the Nation to war and to the use of United States Armed Forces abroad.

(c) Whenever United States Armed Forces are introduced into hostilities or into any situation described in subsection (a) of this section, the President shall, so long as such armed forces continue to be engaged in such hostilities or situation, report to the Congress periodically on the status of such hostilities or situation as well as on the scope and duration of such hostilities or situation, but in no event shall he report to the Congress less often than once every six months.

Congressional Action

SEC. 5. (a) Each report submitted pursuant to section 4(a)(1) shall be transmitted to the Speaker of the House of Representatives and to the President pro tempore of the Senate on the same calendar day. Each report so transmitted shall be referred to the Committee on Foreign Affairs of the House of Representatives and to the Committee on Foreign Relations of the Senate for appropriate action. If, when the report is transmitted, the Congress has adjourned sine die or has adjourned for any period in excess of three calendar days, the Speaker of the House of Representatives and the President pro tempore of the Senate, if they deem it advisable (or if petitioned by at least 30 percent of the membership of their respective Houses) shall jointly request the President to convene Congress in order that it may consider the report and take appropriate action pursuant to this section.

(b) Within sixty calendar days after a report is submitted or is required to be submitted pursuant to section 4(a)(1), whichever is earlier, the President shall terminate any use of United States Armed Forces with respect to which such report was submitted (or required to be submitted), unless the Congress (1) has declared war or has enacted a specific authorization for such use of United States Armed Forces, (2) has extended by law such sixty-day period, or (3) is physically unable to meet as a result of an armed attack upon the United States. Such sixty-day period shall be extended for not more than an additional thirty days if the President determines and certifies to the Congress in writing that unavoidable military necessity respecting the safety of United States Armed Forces requires the continued use of such armed forces in the course of bringing about a prompt removal of such forces.

(c) Notwithstanding subsection (b), at any time that United States Armed Forces are engaged in hostilities outside the territory of the United States, its possessions and territories without a declaration of war or specific statutory authorization, such forces shall be removed by the President if the Congress so directs by concurrent resolution.

Congressional Priority Procedures for
Joint Resolution or Bill

SEC. (a) Any joint resolution or bill introduced pursuant to section 5(b) at least thirty calendar days before the expiration of the sixty-day period specified in such section shall be referred to the Committee on Foreign Affairs of the House of Representatives or the Committee on Foreign Relations of the Senate, as the case may be, and such committee shall report one such joint resolution or bill, together with its recommendations, not later than twenty-four calendar days before the expiration of the sixty-day period specified in such section, unless such House shall otherwise determine by the yeas and nays.

(b) Any joint resolution or bill so reported shall become the pending business of the House in question (in the case of the Senate the time for debate shall be equally divided between the proponents and the opponents), and shall be voted on within three calendar days thereafter, unless such House shall otherwise determine by yeas and nays.

(c) Such a joint resolution or bill passed by one House shall be referred to the committee of the other House named in subsection (a) and shall be reported out not later than fourteen calendar days before the expiration of the sixty-day period specified in section 5(b). The joint resolution or bill so reported shall become the pending business of the House in question and shall be voted on within three calendar days after it has been reported, unless such House shall otherwise determine by yeas and nays.

(d) In the case of any disagreement between the two Houses of Congress with respect to a joint resolution or bill passed by both Houses, conferees shall be promptly appointed and the committee of conference shall make and file a report with respect to such resolution or bill not later than four calendar days before the expiration of the sixty-day period specified in section 5(b). In the event the conferees are unable to agree within 48 hours, they shall report back to their respective Houses in disagreement. Notwithstanding any rule in either House concerning the printing of conference reports in the Record or concerning any delay in the consideration of such reports, such report shall be acted on by both Houses not later than the expiration of such sixty-day period.

Congressional Priority Procedures for Concurrent Resolution

SEC. 7. (a) Any concurrent resolution introduced pursuant to section 5(c) shall be referred to the Committee on Foreign Affairs of the House of Representatives or the Committee on Foreign Relations of the Senate, as the case may be, and one such concurrent resolution shall be reported out by such committee together with its recommendations within fifteen calendar days, unless such House shall otherwise determine by the yeas and nays.

(b) Any concurrent resolution so reported shall become the pending business of the House in question (in the case of the Senate the time for debate shall be equally divided between the proponents and the opponents) and shall be voted on within three calendar days thereafter, unless such House shall otherwise determine by yeas and nays.

(c) Such a concurrent resolution passed by one House shall be referred to the committee of the other House named in subsection (a) and shall be reported out by such committee together with its recommendations within fifteen calendar days and shall thereupon become the pending business of such House and shall be voted upon within three calendar days, unless such House shall otherwise determine by yeas and nays.

(d) In the case of any disagreement between the two Houses of Congress with respect to a concurrent resolution passed by both Houses, conferees shall be promptly appointed and the committee of conference shall make and file a report with respect to such concurrent resolution within six calendar days after the legislation is referred to the committee of conference. Notwithstanding any rule in either House concerning the printing of conference reports in the Record or concerning any delay in the consideration of such reports, such report shall be acted on by both Houses not later than six calendar days after the conference report is filed. In the event the conferees are unable to agree within 48 hours, they shall report back to their respective Houses in disagreement.

Interpretation of Joint Resolution

SEC. 8. (a) Authority to introduce United States Armed Forces into hostilities or into situations where involvement in hostilities is clearly indicated by the circumstances shall not be inferred—

(1) from any provision of law (whether or not in effect before the date of the enactment of this joint resolution), including any provision contained in any appropriation Act, unless such provision specifically authorizes the introduction of United States Armed Forces into hostilities or into such situations and states that it is intended to constitute specific statutory authorization within the meaning of this resolution; or

(2) from any treaty heretofore or hereafter ratified unless such treaty is implemented by legislation specifically authorizing the introduction of United States Armed Forces into hostilities or into such situations and stating that it is intended to constitute specific statutory authorization within the meaning of this joint resolution.

(b) Nothing in this joint resolution shall be construed to require any further specific statutory authorization to permit members of United States Armed Forces to participate jointly with members of the armed forces of one or more foreign countries in the headquarters operations or high-level military commands which were established prior to the date of enactment of this joint resolution and pursuant to the United Nations Charter or any treaty ratified by the United States prior to such date.

(c) For purposes of this joint resolution, the term "introduction of United States Armed Forces" includes the assignment of members of such armed forces to command, coordinate, participate in the movement of, or accompany the regular or irregular military forces of any foreign country or government when such military forces are engaged, or there exists an imminent threat that such forces will become engaged, in hostilities.

929

(d) Nothing in this joint resolution—

(1) is intended to alter the constitutional authority of the Congress or of the President, or the provisions of existing treaties; or

(2) shall be construed as granting any authority to the President with respect to the introduction of United States Armed Forces into hostilities or into situations wherein involvement in hostilities is clearly indicated by the circumstances which authority he would not have had in the absence of this joint resolution.

Separability Clause

SEC. 9. If any provision of this joint resolution or the application thereof to any person or circumstance is held invalid, the remainder of the joint resolution and the application of such provision to any other person or circumstance shall not be affected thereby.

Effective Date

SEC. 10. This joint resolution shall take effect on the date of its enactment.

EGYPTIAN-ISRAELI TRUCE TERMS

November 9-12, 1973

Egypt and Israel signed a six-point agreement Nov. 11 aimed at shoring up the U.N. cease-fire resolutions adopted Oct. 22, 23 and 25 and at clearing up other matters relating to the recently concluded fighting in the Sinai and along the Suez Canal. The agreement was reached in Cairo Nov. 7 during talks between Secretary of State Henry A. Kissinger and Egyptian President Anwar Sadat. At that time, Kissinger and Sadat also "agreed in principle" to a resumption of diplomatic ties between their countries. Egypt had severed relations with the United States in 1967 in the first days of the six-day war because it thought that U.S. planes were assisting Israel. After the Kissinger-Sadat talks, U.S. Assistant Secretary of State Joseph J. Sisco conveyed the final provisions of the six-point plan to Israeli leaders in Tel Aviv. Official signing of the agreement, which had been made public by the United States Nov. 9, was postponed from Nov. 10 to Nov. 11 when Israel received assurances that Egypt would lift its unacknowledged blockade of the Strait of Bab el Mandeb. Israel also wanted clarification of provisions calling for the release of prisoners of war.

The final truce terms provided for (1) scrupulous observation of the U.N. cease-fire; (2) immediate discussions "to settle the question of the return to the Oct. 22 positions in the framework of agreement on the disengagement and separation of forces under the auspices of the United Nations"; (3) daily supplying of the Egyptian III Corps encircled on the east bank of the Suez Canal; (4) replacement of Israeli checkpoints along the Cairo-Suez road by U.N. forces; (5) unimpaired access to the east bank of the Suez Canal for nonmilitary supplies; and (6) ex-

change of prisoners of war immediately subsequent to the establishment
of the U.N. checkpoints. Absent from the provisions of the plan were
two frequently mentioned points: (1) an official truce between Israel
and Syria because, while observing it de facto, Syria had not signed
a cease-fire resolution with Israel; and (2) a formal peace conference
set to be held in Geneva starting Dec. 21, omitted because details had
yet to be worked out.

In the two weeks preceding the signing of the six-point plan, efforts
to resolve the continuing Mideast disputes had proceeded on three
fronts. First, in a flurry of diplomatic activity, Kissinger met repeatedly with Arab and Israeli leaders in Washington before embarking on a whirlwind tour of seven Arab states. On a second front, Arab
leaders conferred among themselves in an attempt to unite before
going to the conference table with Israel or before renewed fighting
broke out. Thirdly, the United Nations peacekeeping force, the United
Nations Emergency Force (UNEF), went into operation, patrolling
the Sinai territory and taking over checkpoints along the Cairo-Suez
road. Meanwhile, the Organization of Arab Petroleum Exporting Countries (OAPEC) announced Nov. 5 its decision to reduce oil production
to 75 per cent of the level of September—an effort aimed at penalizing
supporters of Israel.

At issue initially in Kissinger's diplomatic overtures was the relief
of Egyptian III Corps troops, encircled on the east bank of the Suez
Canal by Israeli troops who allegedly had completed their maneuvers
to trap the troops after the first U.N. cease-fire resolution was adopted
on Oct. 22. Kissinger and President Nixon Oct. 29-31 met with Egyptian
Foreign Minister Ismail Fahmy and then Soviet Ambassador Anatoly
Dobrynin seeking to work out an accommodation. By himself, Kissinger
intensified efforts, meeting Nov. 1-3 with Israeli Premier Golda Meir,
again with Fahmy, then Syrian Deputy Foreign Minister Mohammed F.
Ismail and then again with Meir and Fahmy. After the Washington-
based efforts to bring the disputing parties closer together, Kissinger
took off for the Middle East where he met with leaders of Morocco,
Tunisia, Egypt, Jordan, Saudi Arabia, Pakistan and Iran.

Seeking to strengthen their own position, leaders of the Arab states
conferred Nov. 1 with Egyptian President Anwar Sadat as he made a
one-day tour of the aligned states. That week, divergent Arab positions
had been declared with varir le toughness. Syrian President Hafez
al-Assad had said Oct. 29 that his country had accepted a cease-fire
with Israel because of Soviet "guarantees" that Israel would withdraw from Arab territories and would recognize the rights of the
Palestinians. Unless this occurred, Assad said, Syria would "resume
the armed struggle." After Sadat's day of talks, Libyan officials
denounced the cease-fire with Israel and said that their "battle

against Israel must continue because if it is halted it will be difficult to resume."

UNEF efforts to establish a buffer between Israeli and Egyptian troops in the Sinai were expanded Oct. 28-Nov. 2 with the addition of seven more nations to the four-nation patrol force. Canada joined Austria, Finland, Ireland and Sweden on Oct. 28; and on Nov. 2, a U.N. resolution adopted by the Security Council added Poland, Panama, Peru, Ghana, Indonesia and Nepal to the peacekeeping force. China took no part in the resolution; it accused the United States and the Soviet Union of attempting to promote their influence in the Mideast.

The need to shore up the U.N. cease-fire resolution was evident after weeks of sporadic fighting and charges of truce violations by both Israel and the Arab states. Snags in efforts to exchange prisoners of war also undermined observance of the truce. Another problem had been Israel's reluctance to meet Egypt's demands to withdraw its troops from along the Cairo-Suez road upon turning over their checkpoints there to U.N. forces. Fist fights had erupted between Israeli troops and Finnish troops of the UNEF when the Israelis reportedly ordered the UNEF to pull out.

> *Texts of a letter Nov. 9 from Secretary of State Henry A. Kissinger to U.N. Secretary General Kurt Waldheim setting forth the agreement carrying out the Middle East cease-fire, and of Kissinger's comments Nov. 12 to representatives of the three major American television networks during an interview on the Middle East held in Peking, China:*

Dear Mr. Secretary General:

I have the honor to transmit the following message to you from the Secretary of State of the United States of America:

Dear Mr. Secretary General:

I have the honor to inform you that the Governments of Egypt and Israel are prepared to accept the following agreement which implements Article I of the United Nations Security Council Resolution 338 and Article I of United Nations Security Council Resolution 339.

The text of this agreement is as follows:

A. Egypt and Israel agree to observe scrupulously the cease-fire called for by the United Nations Security Council.

B. Both sides agree that discussions between them will begin immediately to settle the question of the return to the Oct. 22 positions in the framework of agreement on the disengagement and separation of forces under the auspices of the United Nations.

C. The town of Suez will receive daily supplies of food, water and medicine. All wounded civilians in the town of Suez will be evacuated.

D. There shall be no impediment to the movement of nonmilitary supplies to the east bank.

E. The Israeli checkpoints on the Cairo-Suez road will be replaced by United Nations checkpoints. At the Suez end of the road, Israeli officers can participate with the United Nations to supervise the non-military nature of the cargo at the bank of the canal.

F. As soon as the United Nations checkpoints are established on the Cairo-Suez road, there will be an exchange of all prisoners of war, including wounded.

It has also been agreed by the two parties that they will hold a meeting under the auspices of the United Nations Commander at the usual place (kilometer 109 on the Suez-Cairo road) to sign this agreement and to provide for its implementation. I would be most grateful if you would take the appropriate steps to insure that a meeting is held on Saturday, Nov. 10, 1973, or at such other time as may be mutually convenient of representatives of the parties to take the appropriate steps.

We intend to make public this letter at noon, New York time (7:00 P.M., Cairo and Tel Aviv time) on Friday, Nov. 9, 1973.

Best regards

Henry A. Kissinger

Accept, Excellency, the assurances of my highest consideration.

John Scali

Text of Kissinger's interview Nov. 12 with representatives of the three major American television networks:

Q. Mr. Secretary, how much pressure is the United States willing to apply to get Israel to make the kind of concessions that will be necessary for a fair settlement?

A. First you are assuming something that will still remain to be revealed through the process of negotiation. Israel has always agreed that the final borders will not be the cease-fire lines either of 1967 or of 1973, and we have every hope that through the process of negotiation a mutually acceptable settlement will be achieved. The United States stated during the conflict and has stated since that it would make a major effort to bring the parties together. That will be our intention. We don't expect that it will require major pressure on either of the sides.

Q. Are you satisfied that the major powers in sponsoring this peace conference will not try to use it in the future to gain a major edge in the Middle East?

A. The temptation is always there to exploit a situation to the advantage of one or the other of the superpowers. However, if the superpowers understand their own interests and the world interests, they ought to realize that the other side can always match them in terms of military equipment. And that the attempt to turn this into a super-power confrontation must lead to a constantly increasing danger of war. The effort may be made. When it is made we will resist it as we have in the past. We hope, and that will certainly be our attitude, that the Soviet Union will approach these negotiations with the same spirit we shall—namely that a settlement just to all parties is in the interest of everybody. If they do not, then we will have to see what else can be done.

Q. Mr. Secretary, the Soviet Union has direct bilateral arrangements with Egypt, Syria, Iraq and a number of other Arab countries. Senator Fulbright in the past has called for the establishment of a bilateral treaty between the United States and Israel. Would the Administration support that?

A. It has been a constant American policy, supported in every Administration and carrying wide bipartisan support, that the existence of Israel will be supported by the United States. This has been our policy in the absence of any formal arrangement and it has never been challenged no matter which administration was in office. The question then is where are the borders and what are the security arrangements, and this is what is going to be negotiated in the next phase in accordance with Security Council Resolution 242. Whether the security guarantees should be expressed in some formal document or in some other way, I think we should wait until the negotiations are completed, but it is one of the ideas that is under consideration.

Q. Mr. Secretary, what have you been talking to the Chinese about?

A. Ever since we established contact with the Chinese we have been meeting at this level twice a year, and there is generally an exchange of views about the whole range of international problems and also a discussion of where Sino-U.S. relations should go over the next period and that has been the main subject of our conversation.

Q. Can you be more specific about what you have been discussing?

A. In general, you can assume we have discussed all outstanding international issues as well as Sino-U.S. relationships.

Q. On the Middle East, when and how will the peace conference proceed?

A. We have had from the beginning two objectives: One is to stabilize the cease-fire and then, once the cease-fire has stabilized, we move from there to a peace conference. As you know, Israel and Egypt yesterday signed the cease-fire stabilization arrangement that was worked out last week. They have to negotiate some of the implementation of modalities of this. When that is completed, which we hope will be soon, we will move into setting up the peace conference. Our expectation is that this should not be more than a matter of weeks.

Q. Mr. Secretary, isn't it inherently dangerous for the superpowers, the U.S. and Russia, to become committed to guaranteeing peace arrangements in the Middle East?

A. So far there has not been any precise discussion of guarantees. What we have done up to now is not to guarantee any particular settlement but try to be helpful to the parties in narrowing the difference between them. The Arab nations and Israel have been fighting each other for nearly a generation and many issues are fraught with tremendous emotion with them. Therefore, if we can strip away some of the emotion and present it in a way that is more acceptable to both sides, we can make some progress as was made last week.

We have not yet given any particular guarantees. However, I would assume that if the peace negotiations succeed there will be a very serious problem, especially for Israel, of how its security can be assured under conditions when the final borders will certainly be different from the cease-fire lines and when withdrawals are involved as Security Council Resolution 242 provides.

At this point the question of guarantees will arise and we have to then ask the question what sort of guarantees—unilateral, several countries and so forth. Second, moreoover, the great powers are already involved to some extent in the Middle East. What we have to do is to try to prevent every crisis from turning into a clash of the superpowers. In that respect I agree with you.

Oil and Israel

Q. In that connection, Mr. Secretary, given the oil situation, the number of people and territory involved, the new relationship with the Soviet Union, why is it in the American national interest to support Israel so strongly? I ask that within the context of guaranteeing the existence of Israel.

A. The United States in the postwar period has supported the concept that international conflicts should not be settled by force. It has, moreover, supported the concept that nations should not be eliminated simply by the superior numbers or in any manner of their neighbors.

The United States has supported Israel because of the emotional ties that have existed, because of the democratic tradition of Israel, and because of the fact that it is a going concern in this area and because, as I have said about our opposition to the domination of one nation by force to others.

The oil situation will continue for the indefinite future and while we are highly respectful of the views of the Arab world, it is not possible for us to be swayed in the major orientation of our policy by the monopoly position or the temporary monopoly position enjoyed by a few nations.

Q. Do you get no indication from King Faisal or others in your recent journey that the oil restrictions might be changed?

A. We had very extensive talks with King Faisal and with his advisers, and it is a problem that has many complexities both for us as well as for King Faisal, and I think that both sides are studying its adoption in the light of the developing situation.

Outlook on Arms Flow

Q. Mr. Secretary, as you get into the formal negotiations now, is it safe to assume that arms deliveries by the U.S. to Israel, the Soviet Union to the Arabs, will continue or do you have some kind of arrangement already with the Soviet Union that when you reach a point in the negotiations both of the superpowers will knock down the flow of arms.

A. No such arrangement exists as of now, but the United States has always held the view that it was prepared to discuss limitation of the flow of armaments into the Middle East in order to avoid the present situation of the piling up of armaments on both sides. If there is a limitation of the flow of armaments, it has, however, to include all those countries which might transfer their arms to one or more of the combatant and not just the parties in the last war.

Q. Mr. Secretary, there are some people that argue that detente was exposed as a myth during the Middle East crisis because the Russians threatened to use military force even though their own vital interests were not affected. How do you answer them?

A. There has been a misunderstanding in many respects about detente. There has been the idea that detente reflects the fact that the two sides agree with each other and that it reflects an era of good feeling or similar domestic structures. We have always believed that detente is necessary precisely because we have opposing interests in many parts of the world and totally different social systems. Detente is necessary because of the danger posed by the accumulation of nuclear weapons on both sides.

We are in favor of detente because we want to limit the risks of major nuclear conflict. That gives us an opportunity to communicate and to move rapidly if we want to. It does not eliminate the conflicting interests. It does not prevent occasional clashes. What it does make possible is a more rapid settlement and a certain amount of restraint when crises develop when both of these things occur, but there are limitations beyond which it cannot go.

Mr. Secretary, thank you for your time.

SKYLAB
November 16, 1973

The third crew to man America's first space station and laboratory workshop was sent into space Nov. 16 in the fourth and final phase of a $2.6-billion project to gain information about the sun, the earth and man's ability to cope with extended periods of life in space. The Skylab program was designed to allow for extensive experimentation as a prelude to manned exploration of the solar system. The launching Nov. 16 of the third crew followed the initial launch, May 14, 1973, of the $294-million, 100-ton unmanned space station, and the subsequent launchings of the first two crews who were aboard the craft May 25-June 22 and July 28-Sept. 25 respectively. The scheduled 84-day record flight of Skylab-4, the third crew, was to bring the 10-month, multiple crew mission to an end in early February 1974. Together with the 28-day flight of Skylab-2 and the 59-day flight of Skylab-3, Skylab-4 was aimed at bringing the total number of manned days in space to a record 171. The launching of the third crew was to be America's final manned mission until the joint flight with the Soviet Union in July 1975.

The Skylab project began May 14 with an uncertain start when a structural defect threatened to cut short, if not cancel, the manned missions. Sixty-three seconds after blast-off of the unmanned space station, the space laboratory's meteoroid shield slammed against the craft and eventually tore off. The resultant jamming of one solar panel used to generate electricity and the tearing off of the other panel endangered the capability of the workshop to produce its own electric power.

A further problem developed when temperatures climbed to above 100⁰ inside the vehicle in the absence of the protective shield.

Scientists working with the project scrambled to develop various "sunshades" that could be taken into orbit by the first Skylab crew and assembled there in order to cool the overheated space workshop. Not knowing exactly what the crew would find when they arrived at the disabled craft, the Skylab ground crew prepared three alternatives. The launch of the first crew was delayed 10 days as the new equipment was built and tested, and the astronauts were trained to deploy it. Finally sent into space on May 25, the crew May 26 deployed a parasol-type sunshade that by June 4 had brought Skylab's inside temperatures down to 75⁰. Later, the first team manually freed the jammed solar panel so that the craft could again generate a sufficient electrical supply.

Skylab's purpose was to enrich man's scientific knowledge of Earth, the sun, and man's adaptability to prolonged flights in space. William C. Schneider, director of the Skylab program at NASA (National Aeronautics and Space Administration), testified Feb. 28, 1973, before the House Appropriations Subcommittee on NASA about the nature of the first space laboratory project: "The Skylab program is predominantly utilitarian in nature, putting the space vehicles and operating knowhow developed by Apollo in the service of a wide range of scientific and technological disciplines while increasing enormously the opportunities for man to perform useful tasks in space." Of the aims of the project, Schneider said: "The scientific investigations...to be conducted on the Skylab mission embrace almost every discipline that can take advantage of the unique properties of the orbital environment—the broad view of Earth and the biosphere, the availability of the entire electromagnetic spectrum for celestial observation, and the virtual elimination of the effects of gravity." To enhance the missions's scientific capability, two solar scientists, Dr. Owen Kay Garriott and Edward George Gibson, were selected to go into space.

NASA released a preliminary report July 23 on the launch of the unmanned space station and the flight of the first crew and another report Nov. 2 on the second manned mission. The two reports demonstrated that the first two manned missions had yielded rich scientific results. A more extensive analysis of the entire 10-month project was scheduled for release in mid-1974.

Excerpts from the two reports published by the National Aeronautics and Space Administration on the first two manned Skylab missions:

SKYLAB STATUS: WHAT HAPPENED

[Launch of unmanned space station and arrival of first

Skylab crew, as described in NASA's report of

July 23, 1973]

The unmanned Skylab space station was launched on May 14. Approximately one minute after liftoff, at the time of highest aerodynamic pressure, the meteoroid shield around the outside of the workshop was torn off and apparently caused one of two solar panels used to generate electricity for the laboratory also to be torn away, and jammed the other in a way that prevented its full deployment.

The net result was that Skylab was in good orbit, but had only about half of its power-generating capability in operation and the spacecraft was overheating. The overheating occurred because the lost meteoroid shield also provided thermal balance. It was painted in a way to reflect enough sunlight so that the laboratory would stay cool....

The Skylab team responded quickly to the situation. The first task was to stabilize conditions. Temperatures were increasing rapidly. External skin temperatures were estimated to be as high as 325 degrees Fahrenheit. There was concern that the unrefrigerated on-board food, medicines, and film might spoil.

The flight control team tried to find an attitude or position of Skylab which would minimize the heating and at the same time cast sufficient sunlight on the remaining solar cells, those attached to the ATM [Apollo Telescope Mount], to generate the electricity required to operate the space station. Ground controllers oriented the orbiting space station from one attitude to another to control temperatures and still obtain enough sunlight for power generation.

After a great deal of calculation, analysis and some experimentation, inside temperatures were stabilized at approximately 125 degrees and power levels at about 2800 watts, which barely covered the unmanned housekeeping requirements. Although some food and medicines were assumed to have been spoiled, there remained sufficient unspoiled food on board for all three missions, and some of the medicines were replaced by the first crew to go aboard.

While the laboratory was being stabilized, it became very clear that a fix would be required. The laboratory was too hot for normal habitation and the temperature was too high to carry out the medical experiments.

The temporary pitched-up attitude of the laboratory was determined by the need to balance solar heating and power generation, and was therefore not fully appropriate for either the solar experiments (which require precise pointing at the Sun) or the Earth resources experiments (which require equally precise pointing at the Earth). The best way to fix the Skylab was to provide quickly a sunshade which would once again reflect away the proper amount of sunlight so that the laboratory would remain cool and regain its pointing flexibility.

By the third day after launch, a number of approaches to thermal control had been well enough defined to develop a firm design, development, manufacturing, test and training schedule. The aerospace industry and NASA [National Aeronautics and Space Administration] centers had responded fast and well to the call for help. The crew launch date was then reset for Friday, May 25, a delay of 10 days.

On the day before launch, three different sunshades were selected to go along with the crew because no one really knew what the astronauts would find when they rendezvoused with Skylab. Officials didn't know if the meteoroid shield was completely and cleanly severed or whether parts of it were obstructing areas where the sunshade might be installed. By carrying several different sunshades, the crew would at least have one suitable for the situation.

One sunshade...was a trapezoidal awning to go on ropes that would stretch from the base of the Skylab work shop to a hand rail on the apollo telescope mount.... [T]he 22-by-24-foot sail would be positioned over the workshop.

A different "twin-boom" sunshade was designed to be deployed.... With poles forming an inverted vee extending back over the workshop, a sheet of reflecting material would be hooked on the ropes and pulled, like a sail, to a position over the workshop where the meteoroid shield should have been.

Actually used by the first Skylab crew was the simpler parasol concept.... After docking and entering the Skylab, the crew extended a folded canopy through the scientific airlock on the Sun side of the workshop. Once outside the spacecraft, the nylon and aluminized Mylar material was deployed mechanically, like a parasol, to form a 22-by-24-foot rectangular thermal shield over the workshop's exposed area. This approach offered the least difficult means of quickly bringing the heating problem under control.

The astronauts had trained with all three concepts at the Johnson Space Center and in the zero-gravity simulator at the Marshall Space Flight Center.

Prior to launch, program officials approved...the undocked command module to remove any debris that covered the scientific airlock and to attempt, if feasible, to free the jammed solar array. The decision was made to carry bolt cutters, tin snips, and a bending tool to help with the tasks.

On launch day, Pete Conrad, Joe Kerwin and Paul Weitz went through launch and rendezvous, soft docked, prepared for standup EVA [Extravehicular Activity; operations outside spacecraft], undocked, and tackled the salvage problem....

The scientific airlock was clear of debris....

The next day, the astronauts followed procedures written just two days ealier and deployed the parasol. By the 11th mission day the inside temperatures had dropped to 75 degrees.

Immediately after parasol deployment the crew started operating experiments. They found that one, the S019 ultraviolet stellar astronomy experiment, had a mirror tilt gear drive mechanism that was jammed. They promptly disassemb'.d and assembled it again....

Then, as temperatures dropped and flight planners began to see daylight, Skylab encountered a new problem on day five.

During the first full EREP [Earth Resources Experiment Package] pass, the space station left solar orientation and went to "local vertical" as planned. This moves the solar arrays out of the sunlight and the batteries go to discharge. On that first pass, four battery systems which had gotten hot in the unmanned "pitch-up" attitude showed they were taking less than one-half charge, and one battery system dropped off the line completely. The loss was serious even though there are 18 such battery packs in the ATM power supply system.

However, the backup astronaut crew, plus a small sleepless group of specialists had been continuing to work on procedures to remove the strap that held the solar wing undeployed.

The procedures were radioed up on day 12, the crew practiced in space (inside the workshop) on day 13, and went [outside] on day 14. Kerwin and Conrad cut the strap, broke a restraining bolt, and erected the solar wing. Within hours the solar wing was supplying electricity. Skylab was in full working order to carry out its planned 270 scientific and technical investigations.

In addition, the crew performed a number of other actions that saved certain experiments which otherwise could not have functioned. And...they solved the problem of a malfunctioning ATM battery relay by banging on it with a hammer, a repair technique warmly endorsed by appliance owners and machinery operators everywhere....

SKYLAB 3 [Second Manned] MISSION ANALYSIS

[NASA report of Nov. 2, 1973]

The recovery of the space craft and crew off the coast of California, near San Diego, on September 25, 1973 signalled the conclusion of the Skylab 3 Mission, clearly the most productive demonstration so far that men can operate effectively for long periods in space and that there is important and valuable work for them to do there.

Early in the flight, a series of problems threatened to disrupt the mission, or at least to degrade it significantly. The crew suffered motion sickness, there were unexplained leaks of oxidizer in the Service Module reaction control system, the Airlock Module primary coolant system lost coolant pressure, and the attitude control rate gyros behaved erratically.

Despite these early difficulties, improvement in crew health and corrective actions and work-arounds allowed this mission to proceed well. The crew found they could work well ahead of the pre-mission flight plan. The flight control teams and the mission management operated smoothly and with a flexibility that made it possible to take advantage of the crew's efficiency such that unscheduled tests and experiments were added to Skylab 3 which helped to significantly increase experiment yield above premission planning.

MISSION EVENTS

Skylab 3 was launched from Kennedy Space Center, Florida, on time at 7:11 a.m. EDT, July 28, 1973.

Rendezvous with the Saturn Workshop was accomplished during the first five orbits and completed at 3:38 p.m. EDT over the Canarvon tracking station.

During the rendezvous maneuvers, a leak was detected in the Command Service Module Reaction Control System, quad B thruster. Subsequent analysis indicated an oxidizer valve was stuck in the open or partially opened position. Quad B was isolated and it was decided that all deorbit mission rules could be satisfied. During the fifth revolution, approximately 23 minutes of planned television coverage was conducted on rendezvous, fly-around, and docking. However, the camera color wheel did not operate properly and this resulted in a monochromic picture through one of the color wheels, and part of the field of view was obstructed by an opaque portion of the color wheel. Later investigation revealed the color wheel was jammed. The crew later cleared the problem and the camera worked satisfactorily throughout the remainder of Skylab 3.

Subsequent to docking the crew ate dinner in the Command Service Module, then at approximately 4:00 p.m. EDT they entered the Multiple Docking Adapter and started the workshop activation tasks. Activation was curtailed due to the crew's motion sickness. Reactivation of the systems and stowage of equipment transported in the Skylab 3 Command Service Module was completed on August 1 as the crew adjusted to the environment and began to overcome their sickness.

On August 2, another thruster leak was discovered in the service module thruster Quad D and actions were taken to prepare a rescue vehicle if needed. At the same time, ground personnel initiated studies of the thruster failures. The two leaks were found to be unrelated and not indicative of a general system breakdown. Computer studies and ground simulations showed that it was feasible and safe to reenter using the two remaining thruster quads if the need should arrive and the Skylab 3 crew was given permission to complete their scheduled mission.

EVA-1 was performed on August 6 after being rescheduled from the fourth and eighth days because of the crew's motion sickness and the Quad D thruster failure. Activities during the Extravehicular Activity included successful deployment of the twin-pole Sun shield, successful deployment of experiment S149 (Particle Collection); removal of experiment S055 (Ultraviolet Spectrometer) ramp latch; inspection of Airlock Module coolant loop for leaks; inspection of CSM RCS quads B and D for leaks; inspection of the Apollo Telescope Mount power transfer distributor for damage; and retrieval and installation of Apollo Telescope Mount film.

Astronauts Garriott and Bean began EVA-1 at 1:30 p.m. EDT. The twinpole Sun shield deployment lowered temperatures at the workshop forward and aft compartments before the EVA was completed. No external leaks were noted during inspection of either the Airlock Module coolant loop or the CSM Quads B and D. The hatch was closed and EVA-1 operations concluded with repressurization at 8:01 p.m. EDT. The elapsed times with a record space walk of 6:31 (hr:min).

EVA-2 was performed by Astronauts Garriott and Lousma and started at depressurization, 12:24 p.m. EDT on August 24. A 6-pack rate gyro installation proceeded without incident and was completed in 40 minutes. During the rate gyro installation, the vehicle drifted approximately nine degrees, but return to solar inertial attitude was accomplished without difficulty. Also during the EVA, a torque applied to the vehicle required using the Thruster Attitude Control System for attitude correction. The Johnson Space Center sail sample (deployed to test its durability) was installed on the structural Handrail. ATM film retrieval and replacement was completed without any problems. Performance of the stowage and retrieval of S149 and removal of S056 and S082A aperture door ramp latch were also successful operations. The airlock module was repressurized and EVA-2 operations concluded at 4:31 p.m. EDT. Elapsed time was 4:30.

EVA-3 was performed by Astronauts Bean and Garriott and started at 7:18 a.m. EDT on September 22. ATM film was retrieved and replaced, experiment S149 (Particle Collection), experiment S230 (Magnetospheric Particle Composition) and the parasol samples were retrieved. EVA-3 operations concluded at 9:59 a.m. EDT. Elapsed time was 2:41.

The 58th and 59th days were essentially concerned with transferring stowed return items to the Command Module, deactivating the workshop systems not required for unmanned Skylab 4 activities, and stowing workshop equipment to be retained for the follow-on Skylab 4 mission. Deactivation was completed as planned without anomalies.

Last day activities consisted of workshop closeout, suit donning and checkout, undocking, deorbit, and entry. Tunnel hatch installation was completed at 10:30 a.m. EDT on September 25 and undocking occurred at 3:34 p. EDT. Separation occurred at 3:50 p.m. EDT. There was no workshop flyaround maneuver following undocking. The Service Propulsion System engine deorbit maneuver was performed at 5:38 p.m. EDT and resulted in spacecraft splashdown approximately 250 miles southwest of San Diego, California, at 6:20 p.m. EDT. Following a stable II (apex down) landing, the spacecraft assumed a stable 1 attitude after flotation bag deployment. Recovery operations were completed approximately 43 minutes after splashdown.

The crew was returned to San Diego onboard the USS New Orleans, where detailed medical examinations were performed....

▼▼▼

NIXON TO MANAGING EDITORS

November 17, 1973

President Nixon vigorously asserted his innocence in the Water-gate and related matters during an hour-long televised question-and-answer session Nov. 17 with some of the nation's managing editors. Nixon told participants in the Associated Press Managing Editors Association convention at Walt Disney World near Orlando, Fla.: "People have got to know whether or not their President is a crook. Well, I'm not a crook." The remark came in response to a question about Nixon's personal finances and tax payments. Press reports in previous days had noted that Nixon paid only $1,670 in income taxes for 1970 and 1971 on an income of $400,000. In his answer, Nixon did not confirm or deny the figures, stating only that he paid "nominal amounts" in taxes for those years.

Nixon said his low tax payments resulted from the $500,000 worth of income deductions he claimed for donating his vice presidential papers to the government. This decision, he said, had been recommended to him by former President Lyndon B. Johnson, and had not been questioned by the Internal Revenue Service. Nixon then detailed some of his personal finances, saying that he left the office of vice president in 1961 with a $47,000 net worth, but during the next eight years earned between $100,000 and $250,000 annually from his law practice and from a book he wrote. "I make my mistakes," the President went on, "but in all my years of public life, I have never profited, never profited from public service—I have earned every cent.... People have got to know whether or not their President is a crook."

947

These were extraordinary remarks from a President, but they came at an extraordinary time, when allegations of impropriety and illegality against him were rampant. With Nixon's popularity at a record low, he sought to bring himself and his case before the public in November. "Operation Candor" the White House called it. Nixon made speeches and visits around the country and held private meetings with members of Congress to explain his actions and urge their support.

During the press conference with the managing editors, half of the 20 questions concerned Watergate and related events. Nixon repeated his innocence of any wrongdoing and promised to supply more evidence to prove his case. While conceding he had made a mistake in not more closely supervising his 1972 campaign, he refused to blame subordinates. Asked if he still considered former White House aides John D. Ehrlichman and H. R. Haldeman the "finest public servants" he had ever known, as he had characterized them when they quit under fire in April (see p. 499), Nixon replied that they were "dedicated, fine public servants" who eventually would be proved innocent of any wrongdoing.

The questioning turned to two of the nine tape recordings of White House conversations that were not turned over to the Watergate grand jury under a court order. Nixon reiterated the White House explanation of Oct. 31, namely, that the tapes had never existed. One conversation, he said, was held on a telephone that was not hooked up to the automatic recording device, and the other conversation took place after the recording machine in his office had run out of tape. Nixon said he was first informed on Sept. 29 or 30 that the tapes might not exist, but that this was not confirmed to him until about Oct. 27.

As additional explanation for the missing tapes, Nixon characterized the recording devices as unsophisticated. He called one "a little Sony" with "little lapel mikes" in his desk, and said the system cost about $2,500. This was a contradiction of testimony by Alexander P. Butterfield, a former White House aide, who told of an elaborate arrangement of tapes, microphones, and triggering devices in Nixon's offices and telephones. Butterfield, in startling testimony in July, had disclosed the existence of White House tape recordings. (See p. 697.)

None of Nixon's interrogators asked him about the controversial milk price supports case, so he brought it up himself. It had been alleged that in exchange for a $422,500 donation to the Nixon reelection campaign from the dairy industry, former Secretary of Agriculture Clifford Hardin reversed himself in March 1971 and ordered increased price supports for milk producers. The increase was estimated to add $500-million to $700-million in income for dairy *farmers. But, according to Nixon, nothing of the sort occurred. He related that he had accepted Hardin's original recommendation not to raise price supports, but that three weeks later, "Congress put a gun to our head." He agreed to an increase when his legislative advisers told him that members of Congress, mostly Democrats, he said, wanted the increase and could override his veto if he tried to prevent it.*

Nixon was questioned about reports that the Secret Service had tapped the telephone of his brother, F. Donald Nixon. He confirmed that the tap took place, but gave no details as to time or place. Nixon said the tap was put on Donald Nixon for "security reasons," not national security reasons, but did not explain what he meant by the former description. He said his brother was aware of the tap and approved it. "The surveillance involved not what he was doing. The surveillance involved what others who were trying to get him, perhaps to use improper influence and support, might be doing, and particularly anybody who might be in a foreign country," Nixon stated.

Excerpts from the text of the question-and-answer session between President Nixon and participants at the Associated Press Managing Editors Association's annual convention, in Orlando, Fla., Nov. 17:

Presidential Tapes

...Q. ...Would you please tell us, sir, when did you personally discover that two of the nine subpoenaed White House tapes did not exist, and why did you apparently delay for a matter of weeks disclosing this matter to the Federal court and to the public?

THE PRESIDENT. Well, the first time that the fact that there were no recordings of the two conversations to which you referred—that they did not exist—came to my attention on approximately September 29 or September 30.

At that time, I was informed only that they might not exist because a search was not made, because seven of the nine recordings requested did exist, and my secretary, listening to them for me and making notes for me, proceeded to go through those seven tapes.

I should point out, incidentally, that the two which did not exist, in which there were no tape recordings of the conversations, were not ones that were requested by the Senate committee, and consequently, we felt that we should go forward with the ones that were requested by both the Senate committee and the others.

When we finally determined that they could not be in existence, was on October 26 of this year. And we learned it then when I directed the White House Counsel, Mr. Buzhardt, to question the Secret Service operatives as to what had happened to make sure that there might not be a possibility, due to the fact that the mechanism was not operating properly, that we might find them in some other place.

He questioned them for 2 days, and reported on the 27th that he could not find them. He then, having had a date made—and he asked for the date sooner with Judge Sirica, he asked for a date on Thursday, you may recall I pointed that out in my press conference on the 26th—Judge Sirica saw him on Tuesday *in camera.* The White House Counsel reported to Judge Sirica that the two tapes did not exist and gave him the reasons for it.

The judge decided, and I think quite properly, that the reasons for the tape not existing should be made public and those involved with access to the tapes and those who operated the machines should be questioned so that there would be no question of the White House, somebody around the President, or even the President himself, having destroyed evidence that was important even though the Senate committee had not, as I have already pointed out, subpoenaed either of these two tapes. And since we are on this subject, and I do not want to be taking all of the time on it except that I know there is going to be enormous interest in it, not only among this audience here, but among our television viewers, let me point this out.

I have done everything that I possibly can to provide the evidence that would have existed had we found the tapes:

First, with regard to the tape of June 20, as you may recall, it was a 5-minute telephone conversation with the former Attorney General, John Mitchell, who had just left as campaign manager or was planning to leave as campaign manager at that time.

I have a practice of keeping a personal diary—I can assure you not every day. Sometimes you are too tired at the end of a day to either make notes or dictate it into a dictabelt.

On that particular day I happened to have dictated a dictabelt, and on the dictabelt for June 20, which I found, I found that I had referred to the conversation to John Mitchell, and I think it is fair to disclose to this audience what was there because it will be disclosed to the court. It has already been offered to the court and eventually I assume will be made public.

It said, first, that I called John Mitchell to cheer him up because I knew he was terribly disheartened by what had happened in the so-called Watergate matter. Second, he expressed chagrin to me that the organization over which he had control could have gotten out of hand in this way. That was what was on that tape.

Now, turning to the one on April 15, I thought I might have a dictabelt of that conversation as well.

Let me tell you first why the telephone conversation was not recorded, not because of any deliberate attempt to keep the recording from the public, but because the only telephones in the residence of the White House which are recorded—the only telephone, there is only one, is the one that is in the office, the little Lincoln Sitting Room right off the Lincoln Bedroom. The call I made to John Mitchell was made at the end of the day at about 6:30 just before going into dinner from the family quarters, and no telephones in the family quarters ever were recorded. That is why the recording did not exist.

Turning to April 15, the conversation referred to there was at the end of the process in which Mr. Dean came in to tell me what he had told the U.S. attorneys that day. He saw me at 9 o'clock at night, Sunday night. There should have been a recording. Everybody thought there probably was a recording. The reason there was not a recording is that the tape machines over the weekend only can carry 6 hours of conversation, and usually that is more than enough, because I do not use the EOB office, that is, the Executive Office Building office rather than the Oval Office, over the weekend to that extent.

But that weekend I was in the EOB for a long conversation with Dr. Kissinger on foreign policy matters. I was there for 2 other hours, or 2 or 3 other hours, and the tape ran out in the middle of a conversation with Mr. Kleindienst in the middle of the afternoon, Sunday afternoon.

And a later conversation I had, the rest of Kleindienst's conversation, a later conversation I had also with Mr. Petersen, and the conversation at 9 o'clock at night with Mr. Dean was not there.

So I tried to find whatever recording, whatever record that would help the prosecutor in this instance to reconstruct the evidence, because it was the evidence that he was after and not just the tape.

What I found was not a dictabelt. What I found was my handwritten notes made at the time of the conversation. I have turned those over to or have authorized my counsel to turn those notes over to the judge, so that he can have them checked for authenticity, and I understand there are ways that he can tell that they were written at that time. Those handwritten notes are available.

And then I did one other thing which I think will also be helpful. The next day I had a conversation with Mr. Dean in the morning at 10 o'clock. That conversation was recorded, and in that conversation there are repeated references to what was said the night before. and when compared with my handwritten notes it is clear that we are discussing the same subjects.

That entire tape, as well as the conversation, I had in the afternoon with Mr. Dean for about 20 minutes will be made available to the court even though the court has not subpoenaed them.

I would just simply say in conclusion you can be very sure that this kind of a subject is one that is a difficult one to explain. It appears that it is impossible that when we have an Apollo system that we could have two missing tapes when the White House is concerned. Let me explain for one moment what the system was. This is

no Apollo system. I found that it cost—I just learned this—$2,500.
I found that instead of having the kind of equipment that was there
when President Johnson was there, which was incidentally much better equipment, but I found and I am not saying that critically—
but I found that in this instance it was a Sony, a little Sony that
they had, and that what they had are these little lapel mikes in my
desks. And as a result the conversations in the Oval Office, the conversations in the Cabinet Room, and particularly those in the EOB,
those are three rooms, only those three rooms, where they recorded—for example, the Western White House had no recording
equipment, and my house in Key Biscayne had none—but as far as
those particular recordings are concerned, the reason that you have
heard that there are difficulties in hearing them is that the system
itself was not a sophisticated system.

I do not mean to suggest by that that the judge, by listening to them,
will not be able to get the facts, and I would simply conclude by saying this: I think I know what is on these tapes from having listened
to some, those before March 21, and also from having seen from
my secretary's notes the highlights of others. And I can assure you
that those tapes when they are presented to the judge and, I hope,
eventually to the grand jury, and I trust in some way we can find a
way at least to get the substance to the American people, they will
prove these things without question:

One, that I had no knowledge whatever of the Watergate break-
in before it occurred.

Two, that I never authorized the offer of clemency to anybody
and, as a matter of fact, turned it down whenever it was suggested. It
was not recommended by any member of my staff but it was, on occasion, suggested as a result of news reports that clemency might become a factor.

And third, as far as any knowledge with regard to the payment of
blackmail money, which, as you recall, was the charge that was made,
that Mr. Hunt's attorney had asked for $120,000 in money to be paid
to him or he would tell things about members of the White House
Staff, not about Watergate, that might be embarrassing.

Testimony had been given before the Senate committee that I was
told that before the 21st of March, actually told it on the 13th of
March. I know I heard it for the first time the 21st of March, and I
will reveal this much of the conversation—I am sure the judge
wouldn't mind.

I recall very well, Mr. Dean, after the conversation began, telling
me, "Mr. President, there are some things about this I haven't
told you. I think you should know them." And then he proceeded
then for the first time to tell me about that money.

Now, I realize that some will wonder about the truth of these
particular statements that I have made. I am going to hand out

later—I won't hand them out, but I will have one of your executives hand out my May 22 statement, my August 15 statement, and one with regard to these two tapes. You can believe them if you want—I can tell you it is the truth because I have listened to or have had knowledge of, from someone I have confidence in, as to what is in the tapes.

Q. ...Could you tell us your personal reaction and your political reaction—and within that word I mean your credibility with the American people—your reaction to the discovery that the Dean and Mitchell tapes did not exist?

THE PRESIDENT. Well, my personal reaction was one of very great disappointment, because I wanted the evidence out, and I knew that where there was any indication that something didn't exist, immediately there would be the impression that some way, either the President, or more likely, perhaps somebody on the President's staff, knew there was something on those tapes that it wouldn't be wise to get out. But let me point out again, while I was disappointed, let me say I would have been a lot more disappointed if the tapes that had been considered important by both Mr. Cox, the Special Prosecutor, and the Ervin committee, if any one of those had been missing, because I should point out the tape of September 15 when, as you recall, has been testified that I was first informed there was a coverup—that, of course, is there.

The tape of March 13, where it has been testified, as I pointed out in the answer to the Louisville Courier-Journal, where it has been testified that I was informed then of the demands for money for purposes of blackmail, that is available. And the tape of March 21, where we discussed this in great detail, as well as three other tapes in which Mr. Dean participated, three other conversations, are all available.

But as far as these two tapes are concerned, even though they were not considered by the Ervin committee to be an indispensable part of their investigation, the fact that they were not there was a great disappointment, and I just wish we had had a better system—I frankly wish we hadn't had a system at all, then I wouldn't have to answer this question.

The Ellsberg Case

Q. ...Did you tell Mr. Cox to stay out of the Ellsberg case, and if you did, why, and do you think that the new Special Prosecutor should be kept from investigating the Ellsberg case?

THE PRESIDENT. I have never spoken to Mr. Cox at all; as a matter of fact, however, I did talk to Mr. Petersen about it, before Mr. Cox took over.

I told Mr. Petersen that the job that he had—and I would have said the same thing to Mr. Cox—was to investigate the Watergate matter, that national security matters were not matters that should be investigated, because there were some very highly sensitive matters involved, not only in Ellsberg but also another matter so sensitive that even Senator Ervin and Senator Baker have decided that they should not delve further into them.

I don't mean by that that we are going to throw the cloak of national security over something because we are guilty of something. I am simply saying that where the national security would be disserved by having an investigation, the President has the responsibility to protect it, and I am going to do so.

Status of The Watergate Investigation

Q. ...Are you personally satisfied, sir, that the investigation of the Watergate matter is complete, to your satisfaction, and if so, could you tell us what your plans are to tell the American people about the facts of the case with regard, again, to your credibility on this matter?

THE PRESIDENT. First, with regard to whether the investigation is complete, as you know, there is now a new Special Prosecutor, Mr. Jaworski. He is a Democrat. He has always supported the Democratic ticket. He is a highly respected lawyer, former president of the ABA in the year 1971. I may have met him. I have never talked to him personally and certainly have never talked to him about this matter. I refuse to because I want him to be completely independent.

He cannot be removed unless there is a consensus of the top leadership of both the House and Senate, Democrat and Republican: the Speaker and the Majority and Minority Leaders of the House and the President pro tem, the Majority and Minority Leaders of the Senate and the ranking two members of the Judiciary Committees of both the House and Senate, which, incidentally, gives you, as you can see, a very substantial majority, as far as the Democrats are concerned.

The second point, and the point I am trying to make is, one he is qualified; two, he is independent, and will have cooperation; and three, he will not be removed unless the Congress, particularly the leaders of the Congress, and particularly the Democratic leaders who have a strong majority on this group that I have named, agree that he should be removed, and I do not expect that that time will come.

As to what I can tell the American people, this is one forum, and there may be others. As to what the situation is as to when it can be done, it is, of course, necessary to let the grand jury proceed as quickly as possible to a conclusion, and I should point out to you, as you may recall, Mr. Petersen testified before the Ervin committee that when he was removed from his position—you recall he was removed in April and a Special Prosecutor was put in—that the case was 90 per cent ready. For 6 months, under the Special Prosecutor who was then appointed, the case has not been brought to a conclusion.

And I think that now, after 6 months of delay, it is time that the case be brought to a conclusion. If it was 90 percent finished in April, they ought to be able to finish it now.

Those who are guilty, or presumed to be guilty, should be indicted. Those who are not guilty at least should get some evidence of being cleared because in the meantime, the reputations of men, some maybe who are not guilty, have been probably irreparably damaged by what has happened in the hearings that they have appeared before publicly. They have already been convicted and they may never recover. And that isn't our system of government.

The place to try a man or a woman for a crime is in the courts and not to convict them either in the newspapers or on television before he has a fair trial in the courts.

John Ehrlichman and H. R. Haldeman

Q. ...When Mr. Ehrlichman and Mr. Haldeman left your Administration, you said they were guiltless in the Watergate affair, and they were, quote, two of the finest public servants you had ever known, end quote. After what has transpired and been revealed, since then, do you still feel the same way about both men and both statements?

THE PRESIDENT. First, I hold that both men and others who have been charged are guilty until I have evidence that they are not guilty, and I know that every newspaper man and newspaper woman in this whole audience would agree with that statement. That is our American system. Second, Mr. Haldeman and Mr. Ehrlichman had been and were dedicated, fine public servants, and I believe, it is my belief based on what I know now, that when these proceedings are completed that they will come out all right.

On the other hand, they have appeared before the grand jury before, they will be appearing again, and as I pointed out in answer to an earlier question, it probably does not make any difference, unforunately, whether the grand jury indicts them or not, whether they are tried or not, because, unfortunately, they have already been convicted in the minds of millions of Americans by what happened before a Senate committee.

Further Questions on the Ellsberg Case

Q. ...At the time you gave Egil Krogh approval for the Dr. Ellsberg project, was there any discussion of surreptitious entry to any premises and was there any discussion of legality or illegality in that situation?

THE PRESIDENT. I think, sir, that you have made an assumption that Mr. Krogh and others have not testified to—I am not saying that critically, but I think I do remember what the evidence is. I don't think Mr. Krogh has said, or Mr. Ehrlichman or anybody else, that I specifically approved or ordered the entrance into Dr. Ellsberg's psychiatrist's office. As a matter of fact, on the other hand, I learned of that for the first time on the 17th of March, which I have stated in my August 15 statement, which will be available to the members of the press when this meeting is concluded.

Second, with regard to such activities, I personally thought it was a stupid thing to do, apart from being an illegal thing to do, and third, I should also point out that in this particular matter, the reason that Mr. Krogh and others were engaged in what we call the "plumbers operation" was because of our concern at that time about leaks out of our Government—the Pentagon Papers, which is, you recall, what Ellsberg was all about, as well as other leaks which were seriously damaging to the national security, including one that I have pointed out that was so serious that even Senator Ervin and Senator Baker agreed it should not be disclosed. That is what they were working on.

The President's Income Taxes

Q. ...The [Providence] Journal-Bulletin on October 3 reported that you paid $792 in Federal income tax in 1970, and $878 in 1971. Are these figures accurate, and would you tell us your views on whether elected officials should disclose their personal finances?

THE PRESIDENT. Well, the answer to the second question is I have disclosed my personal finances, and an audit of my personal finances will be made available at the end of this meeting, because obviously you are all so busy that when these things come across your desk, maybe you don't see them. I can simply point out that that audit I paid for—I have not gotten the bill yet but I know it is several thousands of dollars—and I think that that audit is one that is a pretty good one. That audit, however, deals with the acquisition of my property and knocks down some of the ideas that have been around. But since this question has been raised, let me, sir, try to respond to it as fully as I can.

I paid $79,000 in income tax in 1969. In the next 2 years, I paid nominal amounts. Whether those amounts are correct or not, I do not know, because I have not looked at my returns, and obviously the Providence Journal has got much better sources than I have to find such returns. And I congratulate you, sir, for having such a lively staff.

Now, why did I pay this amount? It was not because of the deductions for, shall we say, a cattle ranch or interest or, you know, all of these gimmicks that you have got where you can deduct from, which most of you know about, I am sure—if you don't, your publishers do. But the reason was this. Lyndon Johnson came in to see me shortly after I became President. He told me that he had given his Presidential papers, or at least most of them, to the Government. He told me that under the law, up until 1969, President or Vice Presidential papers given to the Government were a deduction, and should be taken, and could be taken as a deduction from the tax.

And he said, "You, Mr. President, ought to do the same thing." I said, "I don't have any Presidential papers." He said, "You have got your Vice Presidential papers."

I thought of that a moment and said, "All right, I will turn them over to the tax people." I turned them over. They appraised them at $500,000. I suppose some wonder how could the Vice President's papers be worth that. Well, I was, shall we say, a rather active Vice President. All of my personal notes, including matters that have not been covered in my book—which I don't advise other people to write, but in any event I wrote one and I will stand by it—all of my papers on the Hiss case, on the famous fund controversy in 1952, on President Eisenhower's heart attack, on President Eisenhower's stroke, on my visit to Caracas when I had a few problems in 1968 [1958], and on my visit with Khrushchev, all of those papers, all of my notes, were valued, many believe conservatively, at that amount.

And so, the tax people who prepared it, prepared the returns, and took that as a deduction. Now no question has been raised by the Internal Revenue about it, but if they do, let me tell you this: I will be glad to have the papers back and I will pay the tax because I think they are worth more than that.

I can only say that we did what we were told was the right thing to do and, of course, what President Johnson had done before and that doesn't prove, certainly, that it was wrong, because he had done exactly what the law required.

Since 1969, of course, I should point out Presidents can't do that. So, I am stuck with a lot of papers now that I have got to find a way to give away or otherwise my heirs will have a terrible time trying to pay the taxes on things that people aren't going to want to buy.

Correction of Earlier Statement

Q. ...[M]ay I suggest that you may have misspoke yourself when you said that you assumed Haldeman and Ehrlichman are considered guilty until proven not guilty.

THE PRESIDENT. Yes, I certainly did, if I said that—thank you for correcting me....

The President's Personal Finances

Let me just respond, if I could, sir, before going to your question—I will turn left and then come back to the right; I don't want to tilt either way at the moment, as you can be sure—[*laughter*] since the question was raised a moment ago about my tax payments, I noted in some editorials and perhaps in some commentaries on television, a very reasonable question.

They said, you know, "How is it that President Nixon could have a very heavy investment in a fine piece of property in San Clemente and a big investment in a piece of property in Florida," in which I have two houses, one which I primarily use as an office and the other as a residence and also an investment in what was my mother's home, not very much of a place but I do own it—those three pieces of property.

I want to say first, that is all I have. I am the first President since Harry Truman who hasn't owned any stock since ever I have been President. I am the first one who has not had a blind trust since Harry Truman. Now that doesn't prove that those who owned stocks or had blind trusts did anything wrong, but I felt that in the Presidency it was important to have no question about the President's personal finances, and I thought real estate was the best place to put it.

But, then the question was raised by good editorial writers—and I want to respond to it because some of you might be too polite to ask such an embarrassing question—they said, "Now, Mr. President, you earned $800,000 when you were President. Obviously, you paid at least half that much or could have paid half that much in taxes or a great deal of it—how could you possibly have had the money? Where did you get it?"

And then, of course, overriding all of that is the story to the effect that I have a million dollars in campaign funds which was broadly printed throughout this country with retractions not quite getting quite as much play as the printing of the first, and particularly not on television. The newspapers did much better than television in that respect, I should point out.

And second, they said, "How is it that as far as this money is concerned, how is it possible for you to have this kind of investment when all you earned was $800,000 as President?"

Well I should point out I wasn't a pauper when I became President. I wasn't very rich as Presidents go. But you see in the 8 years that I was out of office—first, just to put it all out and I will give you a paper on this, we will send it around to you, and these figures I would like you to have, not today, but I will have it in a few days—when I left office after 4 years as a Congressman, 2 years as a Senator, and 8 years at $45,000 a year as Vice President, and after stories had been written, particularly in the Washington Post to the effect that the [Vice] President had purchased a mansion in Wesley Heights and people wondered where the money came from, you know what my net worth was? Forty-seven thousand dollars total, after 14 years of Government service, and a 1958 Oldsmobile that needed an overhaul.

Now, I have no complaints. In the next 8 years, I made a lot of money. I made $250,000 from a book and the serial rights which many of you were good enough to purchase, also. In the practice of law—and I am not claiming I was worth it, but apparently former Vice Presidents or Presidents are worth a great deal to law firms—and I did work pretty hard.

But also in that period, I earned between $100,000 and $250,000 every year. So that when I, in 1968, decided to become a candidate for President, I decided to clean the decks and to put everything in real estate. I sold all my stock for $300,000—that is all I owned. I sold my apartment in New York for $300,000—I am using rough figures here. And I had $100,000 coming to me from the law firm.

And so, that is where the money came from. Let me just say this, and I want to say this to the television audience: I made my mistakes, but in all of my years of public life I have never profited, never profited from public service—I have earned every cent. And in all of my years of public life, I have never obstructed justice. And I think, too, that I could say that in my years of public life, that I welcome this kind of examination, because people have got to know whether or not their President is a crook. Well, I am not a crook. I have earned everything I have got.

Surveillance of the President's Brother

Q. ...[T]here have been reports that the Secret Service was asked, at your direction or authorization, to tap the telephone of your brother, Donald Nixon. Is this true, sir, and if so, why?

THE PRESIDENT. That, of course, is a question that has been commented upon before. It will not take long to respond to it.

The Secret Service did maintain a surveillance. They did so for security reasons, and I will not go beyond that. They were very good reasons, and my brother was aware of it.

And may I say, too, to my friend from the Washington Post, I like your sport page. [Laughter] And make sure [Shirley] Povich isn't paid too much for what I just said then.

Q. ...Was your brother aware before, or after, the fact of the surveillance?

THE PRESIDENT. Before or after the fact?

Q. Yes.

THE PRESIDENT. He was aware during the fact, because he asked about it, and he was told about it. And, he approved of it. He knew why it was done.

Q. Excuse me. Does it make any sense to conduct surveillance when somebody knows about it?

THE PRESIDENT. Does it make any sense? Certainly. The surveillance involved not what he was doing; the surveillance involved what others who were trying to get him, perhaps, to use improper influence, and so forth, might be doing, and particularly anybody who might be in a foreign country.

Communication of the Facts

Q. Is some of this a full story that you say you can't say now today because of national security? Have you told that to Congressmen or anyone else? Will this story come out in the next few weeks, as you present more of the facts?

THE PRESIDENT. Yes, as a matter of fact, I should tell all of the editors—and I don't want to leave any implication that you have not tried to publish as much as you could—you have just got so much room in your newspapers, but I do want you to know that—well, since you haven't raised some of these subjects, I will raise them myself— ITT; how did we raise the price of milk—I wish somebody would ask me that one; and who else wanted it raised? What about the situation with regard to the $1 million secret stock portfolio that you have; a few of those things. I think all of those things need to be answered, and answered effectively, and I think the best way to answer them—twofold:

One, obviously through the medium of a televised conference like this; but two, through sending to the editors of the Nation's newspapers, all 10,000 of them, the facts. I trust that you will use them. And if you don't believe them, I don't mean—what I mean, I am not suggesting that you wouldn't believe them—but if you feel you need more information, write to me and I will give it to you. I want the facts out, because the facts will prove that the President is telling the truth...

Executive Privilege

Q. Do you feel that the executive privilege is absolute?

THE PRESIDENT. I, of course, do not. I have waived executive privilege with regard to all of the members of my staff who have any knowledge of or who have had any charges made against them in the Watergate matter. I have, of course, voluntarily waived privilege with regard to turning over the tapes, and so forth.

Let me point out it was voluntary on my part, and deliberately so to avoid a precedent that might destroy the principle of confidentiality for future Presidents, which is terribly important.

If it had gone to the Supreme Court—and I know many of my friends argued, "Why not carry it to the Supreme Court and let them decide it?"—that would, first, have had a confrontation with the Supreme Court, between the Supreme Court and the President. And second, it would have established very possibly a precedent, a precedent breaking down constitutionality that would plague future Presidencies, not just President.

I could just say in that respect, too, that I have referred to what I called the Jefferson rule. It is the rule, I think, that we should generally follow—a President should follow—with the courts when they want information, and a President should also follow with committees of Congress, when they want information from his personal files. Jefferson, as you know, in that very, very famous case, had correspondence which it was felt might bear upon the guilt or innocence of Aaron Burr. Chief Justice Marshall, sitting as a trial judge, held that Jefferson, as President, had to turn over the correspondence. Jefferson refused.

What he did was to turn over a summary of the correspondence, all that he considered was proper to be turned over for the purposes of the trial.

And then Marshall, sitting as Chief Justice, ruled for the President.

Now, why did Jefferson do that? Jefferson didn't do that to protect Jefferson. He did that to protect the Presidency. And that is exactly what I will do in these cases. It isn't for the purpose of protecting the President; it is for the purpose of seeing that the Presidency, where great decisions have to be made—and great decisions cannot be made unless there is very free flow of conversation, and that means confidentiality—I have a responsibility to protect that Presidency.

At the same time, I will do everything I can to cooperate where there is a need for Presidential participation.

I will come to you next, sorry....

John Mitchell

Q. ...Back to Watergate. Former Attorney General John Mitchell has testified that the reason he did not give you details on the Watergate problems was that you did not ask him.

Now, I realize that you were very busy at that time, as you said, but there were reports in newspapers that linked people very high in your staff with Watergate problems.

Could you tell us, sir, why you did not ask Mr. Mitchell what he knew?

THE PRESIDENT. For the very simple reason that when I talked to Mr. Mitchell—and I saw him often in that period—that I had every reason to believe that if he were involved, if he had any information to convey, he would tell me. I thought that he would. As a matter of fact, when I called him on the telephone, what did he say—he expressed chagrin that anything like that could have happened in his organization.

Looking back, maybe I should have cross-examined him and said, "John, did you do it?" I probably should have asked him, but the reason I didn't is that I expected him to tell me, and he had every opportunity to, and decided he wouldn't apparently. At least—now, that doesn't mean to tell me that he was involved, because you understand that is still a matter that is open. The question is: Whether he could have told me about other people that might be involved where he had information where members of my staff did not have information.

Yes, sir....

Post-Retirement Plans

Q. ...[W]hen you do leave the White House, what do you plan to do?

THE PRESIDENT. I think that depends on when I leave. [*Laughter*]

No, seriously, I know that this group has asked very good questions and very appropriate ones. I was hoping you would ask me about the milk—would you mind asking me about the milk? [*Laughter*]

Q. I don't know anything about the milk.

THE PRESIDENT. I will answer this, and then I will go to the milk—in the back.

As far as retirement, at that time I understand I will be 63 years of age, and I am relatively healthy at the present time. I don't know how healthy I will be then.

Among the things I will not do, I will not practice law, I won't go on any board of directors. I will tell you, after being President, you never want to sit at any other end of the table, and being on a board of directors—it pays well, but it is rather boring. That is, at least, what I found when I was Vice President—not out of any conceit or anything, it is just the fact boards of directors are fine, but I don't think for former Presidents.

What I probably will do is to do a little writing. I will not do any speaking. I have made enough speeches in a year to last most people for a lifetime, particularly my audiences.

And so, under the circumstances, what I probably will do will be do some writing, and perhaps contribute to bettering the political process. Let me just say this: Neither party is without fault in the campaign of 1972—quite a bit of violence on the other side, I never spoke anyplace without getting a pretty good working over.

Neither party was without fault with regard to the financing. They raised $36 million, and some of that, like some of ours, came from corporate sources and was illegal because the law had been changed, and apparently people didn't know it.

And as far as Congressmen and Senators are concerned, they will tell you that with the new laws and so forth, there ought to be some changes.

I think that if we can't get the Congress to act on the proposal I gave to them 6 months ago to provide a commission to set up new rules for campaign contributions—limiting them—new rules for campaign procedures, then after I leave office, I am going to work for that, because I don't want to be remembered as the man who maybe brought peace for the first time in 12 years, who opened to China, who opened to Russia, maybe avoided a war in the Mideast, maybe if we can continue it, cut unemployment down for the first time in 18 years, for the first time in peacetime it is down to 4½ percent. It was never at that level, never below 5 percent in the sixties, any time in the sixties, neither the Kennedy nor the Johnson Administration except during the war years.

I want to be remembered, I would trust, as a President that did his best to bring peace, and also did his best to bring a degree of prosperity, perhaps a contribution in the energy field, in the environmental field, but also one who did his best, when his own campaign got out of hand, to do everything possible to see that other campaigns didn't get out of hand in the future.

Now we will go to the milk case.

The Milk Case

A. Mr. President, APME would like to ask you about the milk case, but our 60-minute commitment of time has run out. APME appreciates your appearance before us this evening and we thank——

THE PRESIDENT. I will take the time. Televisions, keep me on just a minute. [*Laughter*]

Q. Thank you.

THE PRESIDENT. It is a lousy movie anyway tonight. [*Laughter*]

The reason the milk case question—and this will be the one I will take—ought to be asked, as it is, is that just some awful nice people are getting a bad rap about it. And I am not referring about myself. I am referring about people in the Administration. They have had John Connally down. They have run him around the track. I guess they are going to have Cliff Hardin down, and Pete Peterson, and all the rest.

The whole charge is basically this: That this Administration, in 1971, raised the support price for milk as a quid pro quo for a promise by the milk producers that they would contribute substantial amounts, anywhere from $100,000 to $2 million to $10 million, to our campaign.

Now that is just not true. I will tell you how it happened—I was there. Cliff Hardin, in the spring of that year, came in and said, "The milk support prices are high enough." I said, "All right, Cliff, that is your recommendation, the Department of Agriculture?" He said, "Yes." Within 3 weeks after he had made that announcement, Congress put a gun to our head.

Let me tell you what it was. Republicans? Uh-uh. One hundred and two members of Congress signed a petition demanding not 85 percent of parity, but a 90 percent support price, and 28 members of the Senate, most of them Democrats, including Senator McGovern, signed a petition demanding—a petition, or signed a bill, which would have made the milk support price between 85 and 90 percent.

So I talked to my legislative leaders, and I said, "Look here, what I am concerned about—what I am concerned about—is what people pay for that milk, and I don't want to have that price jigged up here if we can keep it and get the supply with the present support price." You know what I was told. They said, "With the kind of heat that we are getting from the Congress, there is no way that you are not going to get on your desk a bill—and they will be able to override your veto— that will raise the support price probably to 90 percent." So, we said 85 percent.

And that is why it was done and that is the truth.

Well, thank you very much, gentlemen. I guess that is the end.

JFK REMEMBERED

November 22, 1973

On Nov. 22, 1963, an assassin's bullet fired in Dallas, Texas, cut short the life of the nation's 35th President, John F. Kennedy. It took the life of the youngest man and the first Roman Catholic to hold the nation's highest office. And it left in its trail a mourning people, shocked by the tragedy that struck down a popular, highly esteemed and active President. Ten years later, "Jack" Kennedy lived on in the fond memories of millions of Americans. Senate Majority Leader Mike Mansfield (D Mont.), who had eulogized President Kennedy in the Capitol Rotunda 10 years before, honored the anniversary of his assassination with a self-penned tribute: "John Fitzgerald Kennedy, a Remembrance."

Kennedy's eloquence and enthusiasm had uplifted the spirit of America. His inaugural address, delivered Jan. 20, 1961, became famous for its inspiring language that called on Americans "to bear the burden of a long twilight struggle, year in and year out...against the common enemies of man: tyranny, poverty, disease and war itself." In an immortalized phrase, he called on his "fellow Americans: ask not what your country can do for you—ask what you can do for your country." Kennedy followed through on his calls for sweeping reform and delivered a record number of messages to Congress proposing broad programs to promote rapid economic growth, reform tax legislation, provide better care for the aged, improve urban housing and development, and rehabilitate depressed areas. But most of these requests did not become law until the administration of his successor, Lyndon B. Johnson. Among the major crises and issues of the Kennedy years were the

Bay of Pigs incident in 1961, erection of the Berlin wall the same year, the Cuban missile crisis of 1962, the issue of nuclear testing which culminated in the signing of the U.S.-Soviet test ban treaty in 1963, initiation of the Alliance for Progress with Latin American countries, and revitalization of American relations with Europe.

Kennedy's assassination, the fourth of a President, came as he waved from his open convertible to the crowds that lined a parade route through Dallas. Suddenly, shots fired allegedly by Lee Harvey Oswald cut through the cheers and left the young President dead in the lap of his wife.

Text of Senate Majority Leader Mike Mansfield's poem in tribute to John F. Kennedy on the occasion of the 10th anniversary of his assassination, Nov. 22, 1973:

John Fitzgerald Kennedy, a Remembrance

What is 10 years remembered:
Is it shots of infamy in a Dallas street?
A clinical report of a murder,
Is it a dress dark-splotched with blood?
The swollen faces of grief.
Is it a rain-filled sky over Washington?
A silent throng under the Capitol's dome.
Is it two children and a child's single cry?
A riderless horse.
An intonation in a cathedral.
The flickering of a flame.

What is 10 years remembered:
How much rain beating on a gravesite?
How much snow falling and filtered sunlight?
How many mind-flashes of a man?
Of his humor and humanity.
Of his sense and sensitivity.

Ten years after, it is all remembered and more:
An assertion of human decency
A trust of freedom
A confidence in reason
A love of country
A kindled hope for the nation.
This was John Fitzgerald Kennedy.
This is John Fitzgerald Kennedy.
Ten years after.

December

VICE PRESIDENT FORD

December 6, 1973

With a pledge to do "the very best that I can for America," Gerald R. Ford of Michigan became the 40th vice president of the United States Dec. 6, an hour after the House of Representatives voted 387-35 to confirm him. The country had been without a vice president for eight weeks, since Spiro T. Agnew resigned Oct. 10 before being sentenced on a charge of federal income tax evasion (see p. 827). Ford, the 60-year-old Republican minority leader of the House, took the oath of office before a joint session of Congress, as President Nixon, his cabinet, the entire Supreme Court, members of the diplomatic corps and galleries packed with friends and visitors looked on. It was the first time a vice president had been sworn in separately from a president. Under provisions of the 25th Amendment to the Constitution, ratified in 1967, the President was required to nominate a vice presidential successor in the event of a vacancy. As stipulated, the nominee would take office upon confirmation by a majority vote in both houses of Congress. The Senate had approved Ford's nomination Nov. 27 by a 92-3 vote.

Ford's wife held the Bible as Chief Justice Warren E. Burger administered the oath in the chamber of the House, which Ford called his home for 25 years. A "man of Congress," like 30 of his 39 predecessors, Ford was first elected in 1948. He became House Minority Leader in 1965. He frequently said his life's ambition was to be speaker of the House. Following his nomination by Nixon Oct. 12, he said repeatedly he did not seek the presidency and did not intend to run in 1976. However, his confirmation heightened speculation that he might become president—that Nixon would resign or be impeached. Nixon accompanied Ford to the swearing-in but did not speak. In his speech, Ford pledged "dedication to the rule of law and equal justice for all Americans." The main arguments in opposition to Ford's nomination had been that he lacked the qualities of leadership needed in a president, that he was insensitive to the needs of the poor and the black and to the rule of law, and that no nomination should be considered at all until the question of impeaching President Nixon had been resolved.

Eric Sevareid, in a CBS News analysis Dec. 6, observed that: "In Ford, both the President and the Congress have chosen safety." The following evening Sevareid again discussed Ford's vice presidency: "Integrity is the bottom line in the social contract," he said, "not brilliance, eloquence or magnetism, and we've reached the bottom line. Candidness, simplicity, believability—these are the qualities the people want and need, which is why Gerald Ford, if he keeps his feet on the ground, can become a formidable figure for years ahead." Speculating on the results of Ford's potential position within the administration, Sevareid said: "In a real sense Ford stands midway between the President who chose him and a growing band of dissident congressional Republicans. He cannot, even in private, take an anti-Nixon stance. To do that would lay him open to the charge of coveting the Presidency. If he becomes the President's champion, and the President does, indeed, regain his own footing, then Ford's position will be unassailable. If he does that, and the President's position deteriorates further, then Ford's will deteriorate as well."

Transcript of the swearing-in ceremony for Vice President Gerald R. Ford in the House of Representatives Dec. 6, and the text of his brief address following that ceremony:

The Swearing-In

SPEAKER CARL ALBERT: The Senate, by a vote of 92 yeas to three nays on Nov. 27, 1973, having confirmed the nomination of Gerald R. Ford of the State of Michigan to be Vice President of the United States, and the House of Representatives by a vote of 387 yeas to 35 nays, on today having confirmed the nomination of Gerald R. Ford of the State of Michigan to be Vice President of the United States, the proceedings required by Section 2 of the 25th Amendment to the United States Constitution have been complied with.

The gentleman from Michigan, Mr. Gerald R. Ford, has advised the Chair that he has transmitted his letter of resignation as a Representative of the Fifth District of the State of Michigan to the Governor and the Secretary of the State of Michigan as required by the law of that state.

The chair now requests the Chief Justice of the United States to administer the oath of office to the Vice President.

CHIEF JUSTICE BURGER: Raise your right hand, Mr. Ford. Place your hand on the Bible; and repeat after me: I, Gerald R. Ford, do solemnly swear.

MR. FORD: I, Gerald R. Ford, do solemnly swear.

CHIEF JUSTICE: That I will support and defend the Constitution of the United States.

MR. FORD: That I will support and defend the Constitution of the United States.

CHIEF JUSTICE: Against all enemies, foreign and domestic.

MR. FORD: Against all enemies, foreign and domestic.

CHIEF JUSTICE: That I will bear true faith and allegiance to the same.

MR. FORD: That I will bear true faith and allegiance to the same.

CHIEF JUSTICE: That I take this obligation freely.

MR. FORD: That I take this obligation freely.

CHIEF JUSTICE: Without any mental reservation or purpose of evasion.

MR. FORD: Without any mental reservation or purpose of evasion.

CHIEF JUSTICE: And that I will well and faithfully discharge.

MR. FORD: That I will well and faithfully discharge.

CHIEF JUSTICE: The duties of the office.

MR. FORD: The duties of the office.

CHIEF JUSTICE: On which I am about to enter.

MR. FORD: Of the office on which I am about to enter.

CHIEF JUSTICE: So help me God.

MR. FORD: So help me God.

MR. ALBERT: Mr. President, members of the Congress and distinguished guests, I have the high personal honor of presenting to you a dear friend and former colleague, whom we shall all miss but whom we all congratulate, the Vice President of the United States.

Address by Ford

Mr. President, Mr. Speaker, Mr. Chief Justice, Mr. President pro tempore, distinguished guests, and friends: Together we have made history here today. For the first time we have carried out the commands of the 25th Amendment.

In exactly eight weeks we have demonstrated to the world that our great Republic stands solid, stands strong upon the bedrock of the Constitution.

I'm a Ford, not a Lincoln.

My addresses will never be as eloquent as Mr. Lincoln's. But I will do my very best to equal his brevity and his plain speaking.

I'm deeply grateful to you, Mr. President, for the trust and the confidence your nomination implied.

As I have throughout my public service under six Administrations, I will try to set a high example of respect for the crushing and lonely burdens which the nation lays upon the President of the United States.

Mr. President, you have my support and loyalty.

To the Congress assembled, my former colleagues who have elected me on behalf of our fellow countrymen, I express my heartfelt thanks.

As a man of Congress, let me reaffirm my conviction that the collective wisdom of our two great legislative bodies while not infallible will in the end serve the people faithfully and very, very well.

I will not forget the people of Michigan who sent me to this chamber, or the friends that I have found here.

Mr. Speaker, I understand that the United States Senate intends in a very few minutes to bind me by its rules. For their presiding officer, this amounts practically to a vow of silence.

Mr. Speaker, you know how difficult this is going to be for me. Before I go from this house, which has been my home for a quarter-century, I must say I am forever in its debt.

And particularly, Mr. Speaker, thank you, for your friendship which I certainly am not leaving. To you, Mr. Speaker, and to all of my friends here, however you voted an hour ago, I say a very fond good-bye. May God bless the House of Representatives and guide all of you in the days ahead.

Mr. Chief Justice, may I thank you personally for administering the oath.

And thank each of the honorable Justices for honoring me with your attendance.

I pledge to   ., as I did the day I was first admitted to the bar, my dedication to the rule of law and equal justice for all Americans.

For standing by my side, as she always has, there are no words to tell you, my dear wife and mother of our four wonderful children, how much their being here means to me.

As I look into the faces that fill this familiar room; and as I imagine those faces in other rooms across the land, I do not see members of the legislative branch, or the executive branch, or the judicial branch—though I am very much aware of the importance of keeping the separate but coequal branches of our Federal Government in balance—I do not see Senators or Representatives, nor do I see Republicans or Democrats, vital as the two-party system is to sustain freedom and responsible government.

At this moment of visible and living unity, I see only Americans. I see Americans who love their country. Americans who work and sacrifice for their country and their children. I see Americans who pray without ceasing for peace among all nations and for harmony at home.

I see new generations of concerned and courageous Americans—but the same kind of Americans: the children and grandchildren of those Americans who met the challenge of Dec. 7—just 32 years ago.

Mr. Speaker, I like what I see.

Mr. Speaker, I am not discouraged. I am indeed humble to be the 40th Vice President of the United States. But I am proud, very proud to be one of 200 million Americans.

I promise, my fellow citizens, only this: to uphold the Constitution, to do what is right as God gives me to see the right and within the limited powers and duties of the Vice-Presidency to do the very best that I can for America.

I will do these things with all the strength and good sense that I have and with your help and through your prayers.

Thank you.

INTERVIEW WITH REBOZO

December 19, 1973

One of Richard Nixon's closest friends since the 1950s has been Florida banker and businessman Charles G. "Bebe" Rebozo. Although the two men were termed "constant companions" after Nixon became President in 1969, Rebozo nonetheless remained relatively unknown to the public. But by the end of 1973, news accounts of his financial dealings with the President brought Rebozo publicity he sought to avoid. Although he had declined interviews previously, he consented to talk with CBS News commentator Walter Cronkite Dec. 19 in the board room of his Key Biscayne Bank and Trust Company. Rebozo's comments—on the controversial $100,000 campaign contribution from billionaire Howard Hughes, the President's reaction in April 1973 to fast-breaking Watergate charges, and the President's sense of humor—were aired in a three-part series by CBS News Dec. 19-21.

During 1973, as Nixon's personal finances came under increasing scrutiny by the press, Rebozo's name made increasing appearances in print. An audit of the financing of Nixon's homes in San Clemente, Calif., and Key Biscayne, Fla., released Aug. 27 by the White House disclosed for the first time that Rebozo had played a major part in the President's acquisition of the San Clemente estate. Reports of other Nixon-Rebozo ties heightened suspicion that Rebozo's friendship with Nixon had afforded the banker unusual administration favors. In June, former White House counsel John W. Dean III testified before the Senate committee on Watergate that he had received "instructions" that the author of a news story unfavorable to Rebozo "should have some problems."

The amount of influence Rebozo wielded in the Nixon administration was brought up again when, in July 1973, two directors of Rebozo's bank were granted a charter by the Federal Home Loan Bank Board for a savings and loan institution in Key Biscayne. Only a month earlier, the Comptroller of the Currency had rejected a similar request by another group and disregarded recommendations by regional federal bank examiners that competition with Rebozo's bank was "necessary."

Rebozo's return in September 1973 of a secret $100,000 cash campaign contribution, made in two installments in 1969 and 1970 by billionaire Howard Hughes, triggered an investigation by the Senate Watergate committee looking into campaign financing. Rebozo told Senate investigators that the money had been intended for Nixon's 1972 re-election campaign, but a Hughes associate asserted that it was earmarked for the 1970 congressional elections.

Watergate investigators sought to clarify the circumstances surrounding the donation. It was unclear why the money had not been spent during either the 1970 or the 1972 election campaigns but instead held by Rebozo in a Key Biscayne safe deposit box. Investigators were looking into reported allegations by former Hughes aide Robert A. Maheu that the money was intended to influence the outcome of two federal antitrust cases involving Hughes' business interests. Two such cases were decided in favor of Hughes during the three or four years that Rebozo held the money: in July 1969, the Civil Aeronautics Board approved Hughes' purchase of a small California commercial airline; and in the late summer of 1970 the Justice Department dropped an antitrust case that, if prosecuted successfully, would have forbidden Hughes to acquire additional gambling and hotel interests in Las Vegas.

In addition, committee investigators considered the possibility of a connection between the $100,000 and Nixon's payments on his San Clemente estate. Rebozo told the Watergate committee that he received the second of the two installments of the Hughes money on July 3, 1970, at San Clemente. In a related action, committee personnel also probed reports that the White House "plumbers" (a group of men who carried out the burglary of the office of Daniel Ellsberg's psychiatrist—see p. 537—and allegedly other clandestine operations) had planned a raid on the office of Las Vegas publisher Hank Greenspun in search of papers concerning the Hughes contribution.

Excerpts from Walter Cronkite's interview with Charles G. "Bebe" Rebozo, aired in three parts by CBS News Dec. 19-21:

Dec. 19, 1973

CBS News Anchorman Roger Mudd: Rebozo...told Cronkite about the controversial $100,000 Howard Hughes campaign contribution, which Rebozo says he held for three years and then returned.

CRONKITE: Why would they select you as the conduit for this?

REBOZO: Well, that—that has happened with a lot of people. You know, in political campaigns, sometimes the people are not sure that the money they contributed made its way to the source—to the proper one, and knowing of my close relationship with the President, I presume that—that that's the reason, because I'm not a campaign solicitor; I'm not a fund raiser. It—it's hard for me to—I've worked on the United Fund, and I've been connected with the Boys Clubs 25 years, and sometimes we have to raise money, but it's awful difficult for me to do it; it's just not my nature. But—but many people made contributions through me or would send me a check and say, "Put this in to help our friend," and so on. The monies were all accounted for. Everything else went through a regular checking account. The IRS has checked all that. GAO has checked it. The Watergate committee's checked it. The bank examiners have been through it all. And the IRS has completed 14 weeks of in-depth investigation of me, the bank, every partnership and corporate entity that I'm associated with, going for three years, and completed it and said that they found no wrongdoing.

CRONKITE: Now, about what the money was for, there seemed to be some conflict.... How do you resolve that conflict?

REBOZO: Well, I don't know what was in their minds, but they told me, when they gave me the first package, that it was the same money that they had tried to get me to take, the identical bills that had been in the vault all this time, had tried to get me to take two years before. And, in my mind, there was only one race, and that was the President's race. They didn't designate any campaigns that they would like me to favor them with, and, contrary to some published reports, they didn't ask any favors. There was no quid pro quo involved, whatsoever....

Dec. 20, 1973

CRONKITE: Through his close personal friendship with the President, Charles "Bebe" Rebozo has had the unique advantage of observing first-hand Mr. Nixon's reactions to the unfolding scandals of Watergate. In an interview with me yesterday at his Key Biscayne bank, Rebozo talked about the President and Watergate.

REBOZO: If he has a fault, this fault would lie in his loyalty to his people. When he's got somebody working for him, he'll stand up for 'em. If they make a mistake, that's—he'll take the blame for it. But he—he delegates the authority, and maybe he delegated too much sometimes.

CRONKITE: Did he never make reference to the fact that I don't know what the newspapers are talking about in all this stuff, or any recognition that he was reading it or absorbing anything about the charges?

REBOZO: No, he—he really—he really doesn't read anything but the sports section at the—but he gets his press briefings, and they're in there, but, if you remember, they were denying all this to him, and they're his people, his appointees.

CRONKITE: On that night of April 15th or 16th, when—when he heard from Petersen and others and was about to hear from Dean about Watergate, and you say you went on the boat and had dinner. Did he explode to you at that time and say anything?

REBOZO: Well, he was—he was obviously upset. He apparently had gotten the bulk of this news for the first time. I don't know whether he'd had some before or after, but it appeared to me that—that that was the first time he fully realized the impact—the problem that he was involved with. I don't necessarily fault the people that worked for him. I think maybe sometimes they're mistakes of—of the head, not of the heart. They thought that the President, with all his other problems, didn't want to bother him with it, or they thought it would be taken care of, or it would disappear, or whatever.

CRONKITE: Did he say anything about I've got to get to the bottom of this, or?

REBOZO: Well, he—he didn't say a lot. You know—of course I knew that—that he was upset, and he—and he indicated that apparently there were others involved that he didn't know were involved, and, without going into any detail, because, frankly, I—I've followed the practice of trying not to know too much about what's going on in there. I—I'm—I'm—I'm not interested in—in politics, myself. He's my friend, and my friend happens to be President.

CRONKITE: The accusation has been made that the Administration was monarchial of nature, was arrogant in its power, rode over the civil rights and the constitutional rights of the people in some aspects. How do you answer that question? Did you—did you feel any of that attitude in this Administration?

REBOZO: Well, when you speak of the Administration, naturally, the connotation is always the President, and, starting with that, I would have to say there's nothing monarchial about the President, and—he's anything but that. Now, I must confess that I have seen occasions that I did think that your observation is justified, but the President never saw them. Had he seen them, he'd have done something about it.

CRONKITE: Did you ever advise the President of your feeling that some of those around him maybe were displaying a—air of arrogance?

REBOZO: No, I—I—I think that on one occasion some time back I— I mentioned that I felt there might be, in some areas, insensitivity to people's sensitivities, but not beyond that. Again, it goes back—I know that people think because I see him a lot, and I'm up there a lot, that we're talking about affairs of state and such as that. Well, that's not true, and I don't think that that's my part to play. He asks my opinion about something, I'll—I'll—I'll give it to him free, and that's just about what it's worth.

CRONKITE: I think you were there—I think Julie said that you were there the time that they talked impeachment and resignation, and the explanation that came along a little later was that—was that it was a theoretical discussion, and that he wasn't suggesting he was going to do—

REBOZO: Yeah.

CRONKITE: —or be subject to either of these things. Did he bring up the subject, or did somebody else?

REBOZO: No, I—it was at Camp David. As I recall it, I think it was more of a devil's advocate type of question, you know, and—

CRONKITE: And that he brought up.

REBOZO: —and I think what—what—I think what he was probably doing—again, now, this is conjecture, which I shouldn't indulge in— what he was probably doing was asking the question would the nation be better off if I stepped down just to get 'em settled down? More as a devil's advocate question than as a thought of impeachment—No, I—

CRONKITE: Did any of the family say yes?

REBOZO: Oh, no. I—I have said from a personal position that I hate to see him continue to endure all this, but from a practical and sensible one, I don't think he can, and—and I don't think he ever will— convinced he won't, and I believe that, if they would just get off his back for awhile, they'll find the great President back in the saddle doing the great job that he can do....

Dec. 21, 1973

CRONKITE: Tonight in the third excerpt of my interview with Charles "Bebe" Rebozo, he talks about his close personal friendship with Richard Nixon, the man, not Richard Nixon, the President. The interview was conducted on Key Biscayne Wednesday:

Well, is the President ever with—out on—out on your boat, with his feet up there on the rail, and a fishing rod in his hand, ever say, "Darn it, Bebe, they're, you know, they're—look what they're doing to me on that milk-fund thing, and—

REBOZO: No...he doesn't cry. He—he's got this unique mind-over-matter powers, got this unique capacity for storing knowledge and for blocking out things that—that are trivial.

CRONKITE: What do you talk about on the boat?

REBOZO: Well,—hard to say. [Laughter]...Well, he's—he will sometimes—just sit for a long time saying nothing. He just—he's got a way of—of concentrating on whatever the problem of the moment is, and the minute he's got it solved, and it's tucked away, he can—it's there forever....

CRONKITE: Is he always thinking about a problem?

REBOZO: No—no—no, he relaxes. In fact, the—the two things that relax him is being on the water and being before a fireplace, and he does his best thinking, I believe, like that.

CRONKITE: And, does he think out loud, I mean, do you—...

REBOZO: No, he doesn't talk to himself. [Laughs]

CRONKITE: Well, excuse—excuse me, but where is the charm of being with him, I mean just sitting out there on the boat? Why, you might as well be out there alone.

REBOZO: He's got a great sense of humor, and a very unique sense of humor that people don't see, but it's so quick coming, and it comes with the occasion, and, if you try to repeat it, it doesn't have the zing that it has with him.

CRONKITE: Do you—do—does he tell jokes? Do you tell him jokes?

REBOZO: I tell him a few jokes.

CRONKITE: I hear that he's a practical joker....

REBOZO: Oh, very much so. I tell ya, he's pulled some on me, and we've pulled 'em on others, and—

CRONKITE: Like what? [Rebozo laughs] Give us an example of presidential practical joking.

REBOZO: I don't—I don't know if I can recall one right at—[Laughs] right at the moment. [Pause] He—

CRONKITE: Think of one.

REBOZO: [Laughs] [Pause] We had— [Pause] had one time—you know these—somebody gave me a couple of these ladies' legs—it looks like real leg— they're skin-colored and all—they're blown up. And so, Abplanalp was going to come over to visit us, so we decided to play a trick on him, and we borrowed a wig and a wig-stand from a neighbor, put it in a bed with the wig hanging over the thing and the legs sticking out from under—under the sheet, and I hid while the President was going to show Abplanalp through the house. [Clears throat] Bob came in, and, when he saw that, he—he was—he—he [laughs] didn't—he didn't know whether to act like he didn't see it, or leave, or what, but it was quite a riot. But I was hiding around the corner with a—with a flash camera and took a picture of Abplanalp hovering over this figure in bed. But it's—it's—we just—it's hard to recall incidents, because—but he—but he really has a rare and a quick sense of humor, very quick.

CRONKITE: How do you feel that the President is bearing up under these tremendous pressures today?

REBOZO: Beautifully. Beautifully.

CRONKITE: He seems to be turning grayer, though, I see—I notice....

REBOZO: We all are. [Laughs].... No—no—he is—he's—I don't know how, you know, he can continue to do his job, because he really doesn't vacation. When he comes down here, he's working all the time. He'll—he'll work part of the night and be up in the morning, and then maybe he'll knock off at four o'clock to take a swim or something like that, and it's Saturday and Sunday and Christmas and whatever it is. He just—if there's something to be done, or something that's—that's in his mind that's bothering him, he's not going to be comfortable until he gets it solved, and, once he solves it, and stores it away in that cubbyhole mind of his, it'll stay there forever....

CUMULATIVE INDEX, 1972-73

CUMULATIVE INDEX, 1972-73

X, Y, Z